MARY JANE MOSSMAN
Osgoode Hall Law School
York University

WILLIAM F. FLANAGAN
Faculty of Law
Queen's University

Property Law

Cases and Commentary

1998
EMOND MONTGOMERY PUBLICATIONS LIMITED
TORONTO, CANADA

Printed in Canada.

Edited, designed, and typeset by WordsWorth Communications, Toronto.

Canadian Cataloguing in Publication Data

Mossman, Mary Jane
    Property law : cases and commentary

ISBN 0-920722-81-4

1. Real property – Canada – Cases.   I. Flanagan, W. II. Title.

KE625.A7M68 1997   346.7104'3   C97-932427-2
KF569.M68 1997

Preface

This casebook provides an introduction to the principles of property law and critical commentary on them. It is a published version of course materials that were developed over several years of teaching property law to students in the first year of the LLB program. The original course materials had two primary objectives—to help students recognize, understand, and work with basic property principles; and, equally important, to enable students to become informed and imaginative critics of these principles and the ways in which they are used in differing societal contexts.

The original materials emphasized the importance of property in law and society; they were designed to examine how property concepts define entitlement and distinguish the rights of those who hold property interests from those who do not. The materials examined traditional property principles in terms of their coherence within the legal system and in relation to public policy goals, and also took into account their impact on issues of race, class, family status, sexual orientation, and gender. Over a number of years, the materials were organized in order to present critical perspectives in the context of traditional legal principles, an approach that aspired to integrating (rather than segregating) accepted property principles with ideas that challenge them. For example, the materials included treatment of a number of important issues about aboriginal property, introduced at relevant points throughout the casebook rather than being treated as a special topic separate from mainstream legal principles. In relation to aboriginal property issues as well as other topics, the materials presented an introduction to concepts and critiques concerning property, and provided a foundation for further examination of these issues by students in their upper year courses.

In addition to these objectives, the original materials were designed to achieve a number of other related goals. First, the organization of the materials reflected a sense of the continuity of legal principles concerning real and personal property. Instead of presenting materials about personal property (such as finders, bailment, and gifts) within one unit, the materials presented these topics concerning personal property in conjunction with issues affecting real property—concepts of possession in relation to both finders and possessory title to land; the division of title and possession in relation to both bailment of personal property and leases; and transfers of proprietary interests by gift and sale of both real and personal property. This approach permitted an examination of property principles in the context of chattels and land, and an assessment of the continuing validity of the law's traditional distinctions between them. Second, the original materials were designed to provide an introduction to fundamental property principles as a foundation for more advanced courses in upper LLB curriculum, such as real estate law, succession law, commercial law, family law, environmental law, aboriginal law, and others. In the published casebook, I have provided additional references, problems, and suggestions for further research that may be useful for instructors and students who want to pursue particular areas of interest. Third, the original materials deliberately provided some movement from introductory to more sophisticated analyses, with later chapters being somewhat more sophisticated than earlier ones, thereby giving students a sense of their own progression with respect to the development of their conceptual understanding and analytical skills within the first year program as a whole.

The origins and inspirations for this casebook reflect my experiences of teaching a first-year course in property law over a number of years in different law schools in Canada and Australia. In publishing this casebook, we have retained the original structure and organization of my course materials for the first-year property law course. I have benefited from the suggestions of Professor Flanagan, who has used my materials for his teaching for several years, and from a number of other property law teachers across Canada who have assisted me in "re-visioning" the materials that represent the core of this casebook. In deciding to publish these materials, I wanted to build on the organization and themes of the original materials, and to introduce additional notes and problems to assist student understanding of the principles in context. The exercises in chapter 3, for example, are based on questions that Professor Flanagan and I developed together for our teaching in order to make the legal principles—and informed critique of them—more accessible to students. In preparing the work for publication, I also wanted to provide interested students and teachers with ideas about other sources and approaches that could broaden and deepen ideas about property analysis from a critical perspective.

The preparation of my property materials for publication has been a rewarding, even joyful, research and writing task. I take responsibility for all of chapters 1, 2, 6, 7, and 8. Professor Flanagan prepared an early draft of chapter 5, but I take responsibility for this chapter in its published form. Although my original materials focused on property law in Ontario, I have been delighted to be able to include cases and references to property law in the Atlantic provinces, my place of origin. I have also tried to provide some references to property law in the western provinces, where the Torrens registration system is in place, and I hope that the casebook, perhaps with some supplementary materials, will be useful in these provinces as well. Thus, although this casebook has not been designed to be a national casebook on the law of property, I hope that it can be used successfully in many common law provinces.

As will be apparent, chapters 1, 2, 5, 6, 7, and 8 have been arranged to focus on a series of major cases or problems in the law of property, with a number of questions and comments relating to them. The original materials were designed for a full-year course with three hours of classroom time in each week for both semesters. However, the arrangement of the materials permits instructors to choose specific topics, and to focus on all or part of the commentary relating to the cases and problems. In chapter 1, for example, there are three interrelated case studies about the meaning of property—*Victoria Park*; *Harrison v. Carswell* and its subsequent development; and *Moore v. Regents of the University of California*. While the three case studies are designed to build on each other, they could be used individually to present particular principles of property law and to provide critical perspectives on them. In addition, while the overall organization of these materials reflects my objectives for a first-year property course, I hope that instructors with differing objectives can use the casebook successfully. The table of cases has been designed to assist those who may wish to use the casebook creatively for their own purposes.

No teaching materials are produced without relying on work that has gone before. I acknowledge gratefully the excellent efforts of other teachers and scholars of property law and the insights reflected in their teaching materials, law review articles, case commentaries, and monographs. In particular, I acknowledge with thanks the inspiration of texts and teaching materials in Canada, the United Kingdom, the United States, and Australia: Bruce Ziff, *Principles of Property Law*; W.B. Rayner and A.H. Oosterhof, *Anger and Honsberger Law of Real Property*; D. Mendes da Costa, R. Balfour, and E. Gillese, *Property Law: Cases, Text, and Materials*; A. Sinclair and M. McCallum, *Introduction to Real Property Law*; B. Laskin, *Cases and Materials on Property*; K. Gray and P. Symes, *Real Property and Real People: Principles of Land Law*; R. Chused, *Cases, Materials and Problems in Property*; and M. Neave, C. Rossiter, and M. Stone, *Sackville and Neave: Property Law, Cases and Materials*. I also warmly acknowledge the support and help of a number of property teachers and scholars in Canada and elsewhere: Brian Bucknall and Beverley Baines; Bruce Ziff, Kent McNeil, Chris Rossiter, Philip Girard, Ellen Zweibel, and Moe Litman; and all of those who have been involved in the (as yet unrealized) efforts to produce a national property casebook in Canada. I am grateful to my students in Australia and Canada whose questions spurred me to find ways to explain property principles in context, to a number of research assistants over several years whose help has been critical to the ongoing project, and to Tamara Barclay, Ned Djordjevic, and Naizam Kanji whose splendid research assistance is reflected in the published casebook. My chapters reflect the expert and often inspired assistance of librarians and staff of the Osgoode Hall law school library, the support of the law school in funding research assistance for this project, word-processing talent and extraordinary patience on the part of Hazel Pollack at Osgoode, and the cheerful and unflappable editorial and other support at Emond Montgomery Publications and WordsWorth Communications.

I welcome comments and suggestions.

M.J.M.

Among the various subjects raised in the study of property law, I find the historical complexity of property interests in land of particular interest and was pleased to prepare chapter 3 of these matierals. In this area, I have been inspired by F.H. Lawson and B. Rudden, *The Law of Property*. The authors examine and demystify the unique common law tradition of "splitting what may in a general way be called ownership into its component parts and making each of them an abstract entity." For students, one of the great challenges of property law is understanding the diverse ways in which property interests can be fragmented at common law, and the social, political, historical, and economic reasons for this fragmentation. Adopting the framework proposed by Lawson and Ruden, chapter 3 examines this long history of fragmented interests in land, tracing its historical evolution and exploring its contemporary relevance.

and Ruden, chapter 3 examines this long history of fragmented interests in land, tracing its historical evolution and exploring its contemporary relevance.

In preparing chapter 4, and contributing to chapter 5, I had the opportunity to explore areas of contemporary reform in property law. These include the dynamic relationship between property law, contract law, and equity, as illustrated in the termination remedies in leases, and in the creation and transfer of interests in property. The materials demonstrate the modern evolution of property law principles, as property law responds to a rapidly changing social and commercial context.

I would like to acknowledge my old property law professor, R.E. Scane of the University of Toronto, for his scholarly and lively introduction to the study of property law; P. Girard of Dalhousie University, for his passion for the historical richness of the common law property tradition; and the Faculty of Law at Queen's University for providing me with the resources and support to complete this project. Finally, I am grateful to Professor Mossman for inviting me to work with her on this new property law casebook, and for her generous assistance throughout.

W.F.F.

Acknowledgments

This book, like others of its nature, contains extracts from published materials. We have attempted to request permission from and to acknowledge in the text all sources of such material. We wish to make specific reference here to the authors, publishers, journals, and institutions that have been generous in giving their permission to reproduce works in this text. If we have inadvertently overlooked any acknowledgment, we offer our sincere apologies and undertake to rectify the omission in any further editions.

Alberta Law Review	J. McBean,"The Implications of Entrenching Property Rights in Section 7 of the Charter of Rights" (1988), 26 *Alberta Law Review* 548. Reprinted by permission.
American Journal of Comparative Law	Brian Slattery, "The Hidden Constitution: Aboriginal Rights in Canada" (1984), 32 *American Journal of Comparative Law* 361.
Harry Arthurs	Harry Arthurs, "Labour Law—Picketing on Shopping Centres" (1965), 43 *Canadian Bar Review* 357. Reprinted by permission.
Richard Bartlett	Richard Bartlett, "Indian Self-Government, the Equality of the Sexes, and the Application of Provincial Matrimonial Property Laws" (1986), 5 *Canadian Journal of Family Law* 188.
Brian Bucknall	Brian Bucknall, "Two Roads Diverged: Recent Decisions on Possessory Title" (1984), 22 *Osgoode Hall Law Journal* 375. Reprinted by permission.
Canadian Bar Association	Harry Arthurs, "Labour Law—Picketing on Shopping Centres" (1965), 43 *Canadian Bar Review* 357. Reprinted by permission.
Canadian Bar Association	A.J. McClean, "Severance of Joint Tenancies" (1979), 57 *Canadian Bar Review* 1. Reprinted by permission.

Canadian Journal of Family
Law

Richard Bartlett, "Indian Self-Government, the Equality
of the Sexes, and the Application of Provincial
Matrimonial Property Laws" (1986), 5 *Canadian
Journal of Family Law* 188. Reprinted by permission.

M.E. Turpel, "Home/Land" (1991), 10 *Canadian
Journal of Family Law* 17. Reprinted by permission.

Canadian Journal of Law and
Society/Revue canadienne
droit et société

Joan Gilmour, "'Our' Bodies: Property Rights in
Human Tissue" (1993), 8 *Canadian Journal of Law
and Society* 113. Reprinted by permission.

Canadian Journal of Women and
the Law

M. McCallum, "*Caratun v. Caratun*: It Seems That
We Are Not All Realists Yet" (1994), 7 *Canadian
Journal of Women and the Law* 197. Reprinted by
permission.

Canadian Native Law Reporter

M. Montour, "Iroquois Women's Rights with
Respect to Matrimonial Property of Indian Reserves"
(1987), 4 *Canadian Native Law Reporter* 1.
Reprinted by permission.

Clarendon Press

K. McNeil, *Common Law Aboriginal Title* (Oxford:
Clarendon Press, 1989).

Constitutional Forum

B. Ryder, "Aboriginal Rights and *Delgamuukw v.
The Queen*" (1994), 5 *Constitutional Forum* 43.
Reprinted by permission.

Georgia Law Review

Richard A. Epstein, "Possession as the Root of Title"
(1979), 13 *Georgia Law Review* 1221. Reprinted by
permission.

M.A. Glendon

M.A. Glendon, *The New Family and the New
Property* (Toronto: Butterworths, 1981).

Her Majesty's Stationery Office

United Kingdom, "Twenty-First Report—Final
Report on Limitation of Actions," Cmnd. 6923
(London: HMSO, 1977). Crown copyright is
reproduced with the permission of the Controller of Her
Majesty's Stationery Office. Reprinted by permission.

Journal of Legal Education

Jennifer Jaff, "Frame-Shifting: An Empowering
Methodology for Teaching and Learning Legal
Reasoning" (1986), 36 *Journal of Legal Education* 249.

Law and History Review

C. Backhouse, "Married Women's Property Law in Nineteenth-Century Canada" (1988), 6 *Law and History Review* 211. Reprinted by permission.

Manitoba Law Journal

J. Whyte, "Fundamental Justice: The Scope and Application of Section 7 of the Charter" (1983), 13 *Manitoba Law Journal* 455. Reprinted by permission.

A.J. McClean

A.J. McClean, "Severance of Joint Tenancies" (1979), 57 *Canadian Bar Review* 1. Reprinted by permission

Leroy Little Bear

Leroy Little Bear, "Aboriginal Rights and the Canadian 'Grundnorm,'" in J. Rick Ponting, ed., *Arduous Journey: Canadian Indians and Decolonization* (Toronto: McClelland & Stewart, 1986). Reprinted by permission.

M. McCallum

M. McCallum, "*Caratun v. Caratun*: It Seems That We Are Not All Realists Yet" (1994), 7 *Canadian Journal of Women and the Law* 197. Reprinted by permission.

M.J. Mossman

M.J. Mossman, "Toward 'New Property' and 'New Scholarship'" (1985), 23 *Osgoode Hall Law Journal* 633. Reprinted by permission.

New York University Law Review

John D. Johnston, Jr., "Sex and Property: The Common Law Tradition, the Law School Curriculum, and Developments Toward Equality" (1972), 47 *New York University Law Review* 1033. Reprinted by permission.

Osgoode Hall Law Journal

Brian Bucknall, "Two Roads Diverged: Recent Decisions on Possessory Title" (1984), 22 *Osgoode Hall Law Journal* 375. Reprinted by permission.

M.J. Mossman, "Toward 'New Property' and 'New Scholarship'" (1985), 23 *Osgoode Hall Law Journal* 633. Reprinted by permission.

Parkdale Community Legal Services

Parkdale Community Legal Services, "Homelessness and the Right to Shelter: A View from Parkdale" (1988), 4 *Journal of Law and Social Policy* 35. Reprinted by permission.

Queen's Printer for Ontario

Ontario Law Reform Commission, *Report on Covenants Affecting Freehold Land* (Toronto: Ministry of the Attorney General, 1989). © Queen's Printer for Ontario, 1989. Reproduced with permission.

Ontario Task Force on the Law Concerning Trespass to Publicly-Used Property as It Affects Youth and Minorities (Raj Anand, Chair). (Toronto: Ministry of the Attorney General, 1987). © Queen's Printer for Ontario, 1987. Reproduced with permission.

Ernie S. Lightman, *A Community of Interests*. The Report of the Commission of Inquiry Into Unregulated Residential Accommodation (1992).

M.E. Turpel

M.E. Turpel, "Home/Land" (1991), 10 *Canadian Journal of Family Law* 17.

University of British Columbia Law Review

M. Jackson, "The Articulation of Native Rights in Canadian Law" (1984), 18 *University of British Columbia Law Review* 225. Reprinted by permission.

University of Chicago Law Review

Carol Rose, "Possession as the Origin of Property" (1985), 52 *University of Chicago Law Review* 73. Reprinted by permission.

University of Toronto Faculty of Law Review

D. Johnston, "The Quest of the Six Nations Confederacy for Self-Determination" (1986), 44 *University of Toronto Faculty of Law Review* 1. Reprinted by permission.

University of Toronto Law Journal

J. Knetsch, "Some Economic Implications of Matrimonial Property Rules" (1984), 34 *University of Toronto Law Journal* 263.

University of Toronto Press

C.B. Macpherson, *Property: Mainstream and Critical Positions* (Toronto: University of Toronto Press, 1978). Reprinted by permission.

University of Western Ontario

C. Backhouse, "Married Women's Property Law in Nineteenth-Century Canada" (1988), 6 *Law and History Review* 211. Reprinted by permission.

John Whyte

J. Whyte, "Fundamental Justice: The Scope and Application of Section 7 of the Charter" (1983), 13 *Manitoba Law Journal* 455. Reprinted by permission.

Table of Contents

Preface iii
Acknowledgments vii
Table of Cases xxv

CHAPTER ONE CONCEPTS OF PROPERTY IN LAW 1

Introduction: Property as "Relationship"—Not "Thing" 1
  Property as Relationship: Implications 2
  Subjects and Objects of Property Relationships 2
  Property Relationships in Context 3
    Discussion Notes 4
      Differing Conceptions of Property 4
      Philosophical Perspectives About Property 4
An Introduction to Property Claims 5
  Victoria Park Racing and Recreation Grounds Co. Ltd. v. Taylor 5
    Discussion Notes 13
      Different Approaches to the Legal Category of "Nuisance" 13
      Private Property, Common Property, and State Property 14
      The Right to Privacy 17
      The Role of Precedent 17
      Frame Shifting: Explaining Different Approaches? 18
      International News Service v. Associated Press 21
The Right To Exclude Others 24
  Harrison v. Carswell 24
    Discussion Notes 36
      Facts and Precedents 36
      Shopping Centres: "Private" or "Public" Property? 36
      The Context of Shopping Centre Picketing 38
      The Charter and Protection for Property 39
      Litigation or Dispute Resolution? 40
  The Aftermath of *Harrison v. Carswell*: Shifting the Paradigm? 41
    Discussion Notes 42
      The Consequences of Legislative Difference 42
      RWDSU v. T. Eaton Company Limited 42

            Constitutional Guarantees: *The Queen v. Committee for the*
               Commonwealth of Canada   46
            Shopping Centres as "Common Property"   59
      New Challenges: Property and Body Parts   63
         Moore v. Regents of the University of California   63
         Joan Gilmour, " 'Our' Bodies: Property Rights in Human Tissue"   63
         Discussion Notes   70
            Property Concepts in Relation to Reproductive Technology   70
            Bill C-47: The Human Reproductive and Genetic Technologies Act   72
            Moore and Subsequent US Decisions   72
            Property, Human Will, and Psychological Theories of Ownership . .   74
            Humans Conceptualized as Objects of Property   75
            The Role for Courts and Legislatures   76
      Alternative Visions and Property Claims   77
         Aboriginal Concepts of Property   77
            Leroy Little Bear, "Aboriginal Rights and the Canadian
               'Grundnorm'"   78
            Discussion Notes   81
               Property as a Relationship Among Subjects and the Aboriginal
                  Conception of Property Interests   81
               An Introduction to *Mabo v. Queensland*   81
         Property, Power, Poverty   83
            Discussion Notes   84
               Local 1330, United Steel Workers v. US Steel Corp.   84
               Property and Economic Inequality   84
            Note: The Classification of Property Interests   85
            Problems   87

CHAPTER TWO   THE CONCEPT OF POSSESSION   91

The Concept of "First Possession"   91
   Carol Rose, "Possession as the Origin of Property"   92
   Discussion Notes   96
      Possessory Rights: Subject and Object Revisited   96
      Possession and First Nations   97
      The Problems of First Possession   97
      Possessory Interests and Common Law Decision Making   98
Possession and the Finders of "Lost" Objects   100
   Finders and First Possession   100
      Armory v. Delamirie   100
      Discussion Notes   101
         The Principle of First Possession in Context   101
         The Remedy of Trover   101
         Employer's Liability for Actions of Employees   101
      Parker v. British Airways Board   102

Discussion Notes 114
   Courts and the Evolution of Legal Principles 114
   Rights of Finders and Occupiers 115
   Possession, Policy Issues, and the Duties of Finders 116
   Interpreting Judicial Decisions and the Scope of Legal Advice 116
   Litigation and Negotiation as Processes for Problem Solving 117
Joint Finding: A Critical Perspective? 117
   Keron v. Cashman 118
   Edmonds v. Ronella 119
Discussion Note 119
   Shared Rights in Cases of Finding: A Different Voice? 119
The Issue of Intention 120
   Bird v. Fort Frances 121
Discussion Notes 125
   Formulating the Concept of Intention: *R v. Christie* 125
   Intention and Objects That Are "Lost" or "Abandoned":
     Moffatt v. Kazana 126
   AG of Canada v. Brock 129
   Legislative Reform of the Law of Finders 133
Extinguishing the Rights of the True Owner 133
   New Brunswick Regulation 86-76 Under the Police Act 134
Possession in Relation to Land 135
   Possession as a Proprietary Interest in Land 135
   Possessory Title 135
   Asher v. Whitlock 136
Discussion Notes 138
   The Concept of "Prior Possession" 138
   Historical Development of Principles of Possession and Seisin 138
   The *Jus Tertii* Issue: *Perry v. Clissold* 140
   Barring the Right of the "True Owner": Statutes of Limitation 141
   Property Arrangements in Families 141
   Remedies: The Self-Help Alternative 142
Possession and Aboriginal Title to Land 142
K. McNeil, Common Law Aboriginal Title 143
Discussion Note 148
Possessory Interests and the Operation of Statutes of Limitations 148
Statutes of Limitation: History and Purposes 148
Carol Rose, "Possession as the Origin of Property" 149
Discussion Notes 152
   Underlying Justifications for Statutes of Limitation 152
   The Context of Claims Based on Possession 152
Acts of Possession: Commencement of the Limitation Period 153
Re St. Clair Beach Estates Ltd. v. MacDonald 154
Discussion Notes 161
   The Test for Dispossession 161

Possessory Claims Among Co-Owners 162
Possessory Claims and the Tenancy at Will 163
MacLean v. Reid 163
    Commencement of Limitation Period in the Context of Legal
        Disability 167
    The Limitation Period and Leaseholds: *Fairweather v.*
        St. Marylebone Property Co. Ltd. 168
    The Quality of Possession Under Statutes of Limitation 169
The Element of Intention 170
Keefer v. Arillotta 170
Discussion Notes 177
    Intention and Possessory Title 177
Brian Bucknall, "Two Roads Diverged: Recent Decisions on
    Possessory Title" 177
        Treloar v. Nute 186
Inconsistent User, Intention, Mistakes, and "Land-Grabbing" 189
Giouroukos v. Cadillac Fairview Corp. Ltd. 189
Discussion Notes 205
    Commencement of the Limitation Period 205
    The Relevance of Intention 205
    Underlying Purpose in Statutes of Limitation 206
    Mutual Mistake: The Relevance of Intention? 207
Wood v. Gateway of Uxbridge Properties Inc. 207
    Intention and Possession Under Torrens Registration Systems 217
    "Quieting Titles" Legislation 217
    "Tacking" of Periods of Possession 218
Problems 218

CHAPTER THREE   FUNDAMENTAL PRINCIPLES GOVERNING
PROPERTY INTERESTS IN LAND 221

The Doctrine of Tenure 223
    Classification of Tenure 225
    Seisin 226
    Alienability of Interests in Land 227
    The Statute Quia Emptores (1290) 228
    Tenure and Reception of English Law in Canada 229
    Tenure and Native Title 231
        Brian Slattery, "The Hidden Constitution: Aboriginal Rights
            in Canada" 234
        M. Jackson, "The Articulation of Native Rights in Canadian Law" 237
        Discussion Notes 242
            Common Law Recognition of Native Title 242
            Establishing Native Title 243
            Native Title and Beneficial Ownership 243

Native Rights of Self-Government 243
Extinguishing Native Title 244
Reserve Lands 244
Tenure: A Need for Reform? 245
Feminist Challenges to the Doctrine of Tenure 245
The Doctrine of Estates 246
Freehold Estates: Life Estates, Fee Simple, and Fee Tail 247
Life Estate 247
Fee Simple 248
Fee Tail 249
Capacity To Hold Estates in Land 250
Freehold and Leasehold Estates 251
Creating Freehold Property Interests: *Inter Vivos* Transfer and Succession .. 251
Exercise 1: Creating Freehold Estates 254
Variations on the Fee Simple Estate 255
Determinable Fee Simple 256
Fee Simple Subject to a Condition Subsequent 256
Fee Simple Subject to a Condition Precedent 257
Remoteness 258
Void Conditions 258
The Effect of a Void Condition 260
*Re Essex (County) Roman Catholic Separate School Board
and Antaya* 260
Discussion Notes 264
In re Tuck's Settlement Trusts 264
Discussion Notes 269
Re Down 269
Discussion Notes 275
The Doctrine of Estates and Native Title 275
Exercise 2: Qualified Fee Simple Estates 276
Life Estates 278
Re Waters 279
Discussion Note 281
Re McColgan 282
Discussion Notes 290
Life Estates "*Pur Autre Vie*" 290
Life Estates and Successive Interests in Land 291
Exercise 3: Life Estates And Estates "*Pur Autre Vie*" 292
The Rule in *Shelley's Case* 294
Re Rynard 296
Discussion Notes 305
Exercise 4: Successive Interests and the Rule in *Shelley's Case* 305
Present and Future Interests 306
Exercise 5: Future Interests 308
Future Interests at Common Law 308

Vested and Contingent Remainders 309
   Exercise 6: Vested and Contingent Remainders 312
The Common Law Remainder Rules 313
   Rule One: No Remainders After a Fee Simple 314
   Rule Two: No Springing Freeholds 314
   Rule Three: Timely Vesting 315
   Rule Four: No Shifting Freeholds 316
Equitable Estates 317
   Exercise 7: Conveyances to Uses (Before the Statute of Uses (1535)) .. 322
The Statute of Uses 323
   Limits of the Statute of Uses 324
   The Statute of Uses and Legal Executory Interests 325
   The Rule in *Purefoy v. Rogers* 326
   Exercise 8: Conveyances to Uses (After the Statute of Uses (1535)) ... 327
      The Operation of the Statute of Uses (1535) 327
      Limits to the Statute of Uses (1535) 330
   The Statute of Uses (1535) and Testamentary Dispositions 330
   The Statute of Uses and Conveyancing 331
   Exhausting the Operation of the Statute of Uses 331
Future Interests Under Wills 334
   Exercise 9: The Modern Trust 335
The Modern Trust 336
The Rule Against Perpetuities 338
   "An Interest Must Vest" 340
   "If at All" 341
   "Within the Perpetuity Period" 342
   Statutory Reform 344
   Exercise 10: The Rule Against Perpetuties 345

**CHAPTER FOUR   BAILMENT, LICENCES, AND LEASES:
DIVIDING TITLE AND POSSESSION** 347

Bailment 348
   Heffron v. Imperial Parking Co. 350
   Discussion Notes 358
      Bata v. City Parking Canada Ltd. 358
      Minichiello v. Devonshire Hotel (1967) Ltd. 358
      Clauses Excluding Liability 359
      Length of Term of the Bailment 360
      Burden of Proof 361
      The Bailor's Duties 361
      Assignment and Sub-Bailment 361
      Bailment and the Employment Relationship 362
      Strict Liability of Common Carriers and Innkeepers 362
      Bailments and Third Parties 363

Title, Possession, and Leasehold Estates in Land 364
  Leases and Licences 365
  Long-Term Care Facilities: Leases or Licences? 367
    Ernie S. Lightman, *A Community of Interests* 368
    Discussion Notes 372
  Commercial Leases and Licences 374
    Re British American Oil Co. and DePass 374
    Discussion Notes 381
      Factors Suggesting a Lease 381
      Shell-Mex and BP Ltd. v. Manchester Garages Ltd. 381
    Metro-Matic Services Ltd. v. Hulmann 381
    Discussion Notes 387
      A Lease or a Licence? 387
      Pacific Wash-A-Matic Ltd. v. R.O. Booth Holdings Ltd. 388
    Re Canadian Pacific Hotels Ltd. and Hodges 388
    Discussion Notes 392
  Principles of Property and Contract in Leaseholds: Termination Remedies .. 392
  Termination of Leasehold Estates 393
  Commercial Leaseholds 394
  Highway Properties Ltd. v. Kelly, Douglas & Co. 394
  Discussion Notes 402
    Property Law Remedies for a Tenant's Repudiation of the Lease ... 402
    Contract Law Remedies for a Tenant's Repudiation of the Lease ... 402
    Lessor's Duty To Mitigate 402
    Pacific Centre Ltd. v. Micro Base Development Corp. 403
    Notice 404
    Privity of Contract 405
    Residential Tenancies and the Duty To Mitigate 405
    190 Lees Avenue Ltd. Partnership v. Dew, Tanguary and Whissell .. 406
    Bailment and Prospective Loss 406
  Residential Leaseholds 406
  Grounds for Early Termination of the Lease by the Lessor 408
  "No Pets" Clauses 410
  Kay v. Parkway Forest Developments 410
  Discussion Notes 413
    Grounds To Terminate the Tenancy 413
  M and N Properties (Cassandra Towers) v. Ryll 414
  Discussion Notes 420
    Substantial Interference 420
    Freedom of Contract and Leases 420
    Judicial Discretion 420
    Amendments to the Landlord and Tenant Act 420
    No-Pets Clauses and Non-Profit Housing Cooperatives 422
    No-Pets Clauses and Condominiums 423
    Animals and Bill 96 423

Judicial Discretion and the Termination of Residential Tenancies 424
Peel Non-Profit Housing Corporation v. McNamara and Cherry 425
Discussion Notes 430
Proposed Amendments in Bill 96 430
Problems 431

**CHAPTER FIVE   TRANSFERRING PROPERTY INTERESTS BY
GIFTS AND SALE: THE ROLE OF EQUITY** 433

The Legal Context 433
Transferring Property Interests by Gift 434
Gift Relationships 434
Requirements for a Valid Gift Inter Vivos 436
Delivery 436
Cochrane v. Moore 436
Discussion Notes 442
Historical Development of the Requirement of Delivery 442
Defining "Delivery" in Cochrane 443
Gifts and Trusts 443
Express Trusts 443
Resulting and Constructive Trusts 445
Deed of Gift 446
In re Cole 447
Discussion Notes 455
"Delivery" in the Context of Common Possession of the Donor
and Donee 455
Constructive (and Symbolic) Delivery 456
Delivery of a *Chose in Action* 457
Intention 457
Thomas v. Times Book Co. Ltd. 458
Discussion Notes 463
Evidence, Presumptions, and Onus 463
Capacity (Fraud, Undue Influence, and Duress): *Csada v. Csada* .. 464
Intention and Future Enjoyment: Inter Vivos and
Testamentary Gifts 470
Acceptance 471
Donatio Mortis Causa 471
Re Zachariuc; Chevrier v. Public Trustee 472
Discussion Notes 477
Delivery 477
Intention 478
The *Donatio Mortis Causa* and Land: *Sen v. Headley* 479
Transferring Interests in Land: Legal and Equitable Interests 481
Conveyances and Contracts for Sale 481
Conveying the Legal Estate: Requirements of the Statute of Frauds 482
Equitable Interests in Agreements for Purchase and Sale 483

Lysaght v. Edwards 483
Discussion Notes 485
  Equitable Interests and the Remedy of Specific Performance:
   Semelhago v. Paramadevan 485
  A Valid Contract 488
  The Statute of Frauds and Contracts for Sale 489
  The "Fusion" of Law and Equity: *Walsh v. Lonsdale* 490
Equity and Part Performance: Beyond the Statute of Frauds 493
Starlite Variety Stores Ltd. v. Cloverlawn Investments Ltd. 495
Discussion Notes 500
  The Principles of Part Performance 500
  Acts of Part Performance, the Contract, and the Payment of Money:
   Deglman v. Guaranty Trust Co. of Canada 501
  The Principles in Context: *Hollett v. Hollett* 501
  Part Performance, Specific Performance, and Damages in Lieu of
   Specific Performance 503
Equities: At the Boundaries of Gift, Trust, Contract, and Sale? 504
A Note on Unjust Enrichment, Trusts, and *Quantum Meruit* 506
Hussey v. Palmer 507
Discussion Notes 512
  Characterizing the Nature of a Family Arrangement 512
  Proprietary Estoppel: Estoppel by Acquiescence 513
Inwards v. Baker 514
Discussion Notes 516
  Characterizing the Arrangement 516
  "A Licence Coupled with an Equity" 517
Pascoe v. Turner 518
Discussion Notes 524
  Characterizing the Arrangement 524
  Proprietary Estoppel 524
A Note on Priorities and Registration 525
  Priorities at Common Law 526
  Registration 528
  Problems 530

**CHAPTER SIX NON-POSSESSORY INTERESTS IN LAND:
"PRIVATE" PLANNING AND THE USE OF LAND** 533

The *Profit à Prendre* 534
Discussion Notes 537
  R v. Sparrow: Sui Generis Aboriginal Rights 537
  Licence or *Profit à Prendre*? 537
Easements 537
  Characterizing Easements: *Gypsum Carrier Inc. v. The Queen* 537
  Discussion Notes 538
  The Four Requirements for Creating an Easement 539

Requirement of a Dominant and Servient Tenement 539
Requirement That the Easement Accommodate the Dominant Tenement 541
In re Ellenborough Park 542
Discussion Notes 543
    Defining the Nature of "Accommodation" 543
    Jengle v. Keetch 545
The Dominant and Servient Tenements Cannot Be Owned or Occupied
    by the Same Persons 545
The Easement Must Be Capable of Forming the Subject Matter
    of a Grant 545
Shelf Holdings Ltd. v. Husky Oil Operations Ltd. 546
Discussion Notes 553
    "Exclusive" Possession and Intention 553
    The *"Jus Spatiandi"*: Sufficiently Definite? 554
The Creation of Easements: General Principles 555
Express Grant or Reservation: *Hill v. Attorney General of
    Nova Scotia* 555
Implied Grant or Reservation: Necessity, Common Intention, and
    Non-Derogation: *Hirtle v. Ernst* 556
Discussion Notes 558
    Judicial or Legislative Evolution of Easements of Necessity 558
    Intention: *Wong v. Beaumont* 559
    The Principle of *Wheeldon v. Burrows*: Its Application in
        Baton v. Raine 560
    The Scope of Easements 563
Easements by Prescription 564
Discussion Notes 565
Negative Easements: The Relationship Between Easements
    and Covenants 565
Phipps v. Pears 565
Discussion Notes 568
    Negative Easements: The Policy Context 568
    The Issue of Prescriptive Rights to Light and Air 569
Covenants and the Use of Land 570
General Principles: Privity of Contract and Estate 573
Ontario Law Reform Commission, *Report on Covenants Affecting
    Freehold Land* 573
Discussion Notes 574
    Covenants and Priority of Contract 574
    Terminology of Covenants: "Benefit" and "Burden" 575
Leasehold Covenants: An Overview 576
Discussion Notes 577
    Leasehold Covenants: *Tichborne v. Weir* 577
Freehold Covenants: Enforcement at Law 577
The Benefit of the Covenant 578

The Burden of the Covenant 579
Discussion Notes 579
   Applying the Principle: *Parkinson v. Reid* 579
   Austerberry v. Corporation of Oldham 580
Overcoming the Common Law Principle About the Burden of Covenants ... 582
Discussion Notes 584
   Applying the Principles: *Re Metropolitan Toronto Condominium*
     Corp. No. 979 584
   The Principle of *Halsall v. Brizell*: *Tito v. Waddell* 584
Freehold Covenants: Enforcement in Equity 586
The Burden of the Covenant 586
Tulk v. Moxhay 587
Discussion Notes 588
   Covenants and the Creation of Property Interests 588
   Policy Rationales for Enforcing Covenants 588
   The Requirement of Notice 589
   The Requirement That the Covenant Be Negative 590
   The Requirement That the Covenantee Retain Land Benefited by
     the Covenant 591
   The Need to Reassess Developments After *Tulk v. Moxhay* 593
The Benefit of the Covenant 594
A Case Study: Restrictive Covenants and Business Competition 595
Canada Safeway Ltd. v. Thompson (City) 595
Discussion Notes 606
   "Non-Competition" Covenants and the "Touch and Concern"
     Requirement 606
Covenants and Discrimination 607
Re Drummond Wren 608
Noble and Wolf v. Alley 614
Discussion Notes 618
   The Litigation Context 618
   Approaches to Interpreting Racially Restrictive Covenants 620
   Restrictive Covenants and Restraints on Alienation 621
   Restrictive Covenants: Beyond Racial Restrictions 622
A Note on Breach of Covenant, Extinguishment, and Discharge 623
Discussion Note 624
Reforming the Law of Covenants 624
Non-Possessory Interests: "Private" Planning, "Public" Planning, and
Conservation 625
Problems 628

**CHAPTER SEVEN CONCURRENT INTERESTS AND "FAMILY"
PROPERTY** 631

The Concept of Concurrent Interests 631

Traditional Concurrent Interests 633
    Joint Tenancies and Tenancies in Common 633
        McEwen v. Ewers and Ferguson 634
        Consequential Differences: The Right of Survivorship 636
        Discussion Notes 636
            Joint Tenancy or Tenancy in Common 636
            Joint Tenancies: Family Property Arrangements 637
            Simultaneous Death of Joint Tenants 638
            Joint Tenancies: Corporations 638
            Severance of Joint Tenancy 638
        Conceptual Distinctions: The Four Unities 639
        Discussion Notes 639
            Unities of Possession, Interest, Title, and Time 639
            Mutual Rights and Responsibilities Among Co-Owners 640
        Language: Identifying Forms of Concurrent Interests 640
        Discussion Notes 641
            Statutory Presumption in Favour of Tenancies in Common ... 641
            The Interpretation of Section 13 641
    A Note on Tenancies by the Entireties and Co-Parcenary 642
        Tenancy by the Entireties 642
        Co-Parcenary 643
        Discussion Note 643
    Severance of a Joint Tenancy 644
        General Principles of Severance 644
        A.J. McClean, "Severance of Joint Tenancies" 644
        Discussion Notes 646
            Severance of Joint Tenancies: Intention, Negotiation, and
                Completed Acts 646
            Severance of a Joint Tenancy by Murder 647
            Unintentional Severance of a Joint Tenancy 648
            Severance and Conveyance by One or More Joint Tenants 648
        Severance in a "Family" Context 649
        Knowlton v. Bartlett 649
        Discussion Notes 652
            Severance: Principles of Interpretation and Notice 652
            Severance and Family Property Statutes 653
    Rights and Obligations of Co-Owners: General Principles 654
    Termination of Concurrent Interests by Partition and Sale 656
        Cook v. Johnston 656
        Knowlton v. Bartlett 658
"Family" Property: A Study in Legislative and Judicial Reforms 660
    The Historical Background 661
        Dower and Curtesy: Common Law Entitlements 663
        Equitable Settlements and Statutory Reforms 664
        Property and the Impact of Divorce Reforms 668

Legislating "Family" Property Reform for Married Spouses After 1968 670
    Caratun v. Caratun 672
    Discussion Notes 676
        Property and Professional Degrees 676
Critical Perspectives on Property and Professional Degrees 677
    J. Knetsch, "Some Economic Implications of Matrimonial Property
        Rules" 678
        The Context of Claims to Property in Degrees 683
Equity and "Family" Property Reform for Cohabitees 684
    Pettkus v. Becker 684
    Discussion Notes 690
        Defining Contribution: Household Work 690
        Subsequent Refinements of the Constructive Trust 691
        Same-Sex Cohabitees and Constructive Trusts 692
        Problems of Enforcement in *Pettkus v. Becker* 692
The Limits of "Family" Property Reform: First Nations Communities 693
M.E. Turpel, "Home/Land" 693
    Discussion Notes 703
        Indian Self-Government and Family Property 703
    Problems 706

CHAPTER EIGHT   CURRENT CHALLENGES IN PROPERTY LAW:
THE "PUBLIC" NATURE OF PRIVATE PROPERTY 709

Property Claims and First Nations 710
    B. Ryder, "Aboriginal Rights and *Delgamuukw v. The Queen*" 711
    Discussion Notes 715
        Aboriginal Title to Land and the Charter 715
        The Context of Land Claims and Self-Government 716
        Aboriginal Land Rights: *Mabo v. Queensland* 721
"Old" Property, "New" Property: Constitutional Protection? 725
Property and the Charter of Rights and Freedoms 725
    J. McBean, "The Implications of Entrenching Property Rights in
        Section 7 of the Charter of Rights" 725
    J. Whyte, "Fundamental Justice: The Scope and Application of
        Section 7 of the Charter" 733
    Discussion Notes 736
        Property and the Charter 736
        Economic Rights and Section 7 737
        Manitoba Fisheries Ltd. v. The Queen 738
        Property Rights and Liberty 739
        Wartime Confiscation of Property: The Need for Charter
            Protection? 739
        International Protection for Property 740
"New Property" Challenges 741

M.A. Glendon, *The New Family and the New Property*   741
Discussion Notes   744
    "New" Property in Welfare Benefits and Jobs?   744
    Protection of "New" Property Interests in Intangible Objects   747
    "New" Property, "New" Poverty, and Homelessness   749
The Need for Reform of Property Law?   758
    M.J. Mossman, "Toward 'New Property' and 'New Scholarship' "   758
    Discussion Notes   769
    Problems   770

Table of Cases

A page number in bold-face type indicates that the text of the case or a portion thereof is reproduced. A page number in light-face type indicates that the case is merely quoted briefly, referred to, or mentioned.

190 Lees Avenue Ltd. Partnership v. Dew, Tanguary and Whissell 406
Abel v. Village of Woodbridge 564
Ackroyd v. Smith 539, 540
Allcard v. Skinner **464**
Almad Investments Ltd. v. Mister Leonard Holdings Ltd. 403
Alvi v. Lal 501
Anderson v. Luoma 692
Armory v. Delamirie **100**
Arora, US v., 73
Asher v. Whitlock **136**, 138, 141
Austerberry v. Corporation of Oldham **580**

Ballard's Conveyance, Re, 593
Barton v. Raine **560**
Bata v. City Parking Canada Ltd. 358
Beaney, Re, 470
Bedford, The Duke of, v. The Trustees of the British Museum 589
Bird v. Fort Frances **121**
Blackburn v. McCallum 259
Bollinger, J., v. Costa Brava Wines Co. Ltd. 17
Britain v. Rossiter 500
British American Oil Co. and DePass, Re, **374**
British United Automobiles Ltd. and Volvo Canada Ltd. 591
Brock, AG of Canada v., **129**
Brown v. Rotenberg 464
Bruce and Bruce v. Dixon 629
Burnett v. The Queen in Right of Canada 748

Cadillac Fairview Corp. Ltd., Re, and RWDSU 45
Calder v. British Columbia 242
Campbell v. Sovereign Securities and Holdings Co. Ltd. 642, 643
Canada Safeway Ltd. v. Thompson (City) **595**
Canadian AIDS Society v. Ontario 739
Canadian Construction Co. v. Beaver (Alberta) Lumber Ltd. 592
Canadian Pacific Hotels Ltd. and Hodges, Re, **388**, 392
Caratun v. Caratun **672**, 682
Chaulk v. Fairview Construction Ltd. 487
Chevrier v. Public Trustee see Zachariuc, Re; Chevrier v. Public Trustee
Christie, R. v, 125
Clarke v. Clarke 682
Cochrane v. Moore **436**, 442, 443, 457
Cole, In re, **447**, 455, 456, 505
Committee for the Commonwealth of Canada, The Queen v., 46, **47**, 55
Connelly v. 904 Water Street Ontario Ltd. 490
Cook v. Johnson **656**
Copeland v. Greenhalf 553
Corles v. Corles 671
Cornish v. Brook Green Laundry 493
Csada v. Csada 464

Daly and City of Vancouver, Re, 592
D'Arundel's Case 252
Dassios v. Budai 422
Davis v. Davis 73, 739

Davis v. Town Properties Investment
  Corporation Ltd. 577
Deglman v. Guaranty Trust Co. of
  Canada 494, 495, 501, 505, 506
Delgamuukw et al. v. British Columbia 243,
  244, 716
Deloitte and Touche Inc. v. 1035839 Ontario
  Inc. 87
Dennis v. Dennis 642
Derrickson v. Derrickson 693
Desny v. Wilder 17
Dillwyn v. Llewelyn 513
Dobson v. Tulloch 556
Dodsworth v. Dodsworth 517, 524
Dor-O-Matic of Canada Inc., Re, 86
Down, Re, **269**
Drulard v. Welsh 230
Drummond Wren, Re, **608**, 620, 621
Dukart v. District of Surrey 554

Edmonds v. Ronella **119**
Ellenborough Park, In re, 541, **542**, 546
Elwes v. Brigg Gas Co. 133
Essex (County) Roman Catholic Separate
  School Board and Antaya, Re, 258, **260**
Euclid, Village of, v. Ambler Realty Co. 40

Fairweather v. St. Marylebone Property Co.
  Ltd. 168
Fire v. Longtin 529
Fitchett v. Mellow 557
Flemming v. Nestor 224
Fontainebleau Hotel Corp. v. Forty-Five
  Twenty-Five, Inc. 569

Galbraith v. The Madawaska Club Ltd. 591, 594
Georg v. Hassanali 690
Giecewicz v. Alexander 563
Giouroukos v. Cadillac Fairview Corp.
  Ltd. **189**, 205
Goldberg v. Kelly 744
Gottstein v. Hedges 471
Gruen, Michael, v. Kemija Gruen 434
Guerin v. The Queen 338, 715
Gypsum Carrier Inc. v. The Queen 537, 538, 539

Harrison v. Carswell **24**, 36, 38, 40, 41, 45,
  83
Harvey v. Burger 404, 405

Haywood v. The Brunswick Permanent Benefit
  Building Society 590
Hecht v. Superior Court (Kane) 72
Heffron v. Imperial Parking Co. **350**, 359
Henderson v. Eason 655
Higginson v. Treasury 15
Highway Properties Ltd. v. Kelly, Douglas &
  Co. **394**, 402, 403, 404, 405
Hill v. Attorney General of Nova Scotia 555
Hill v. C.A. Parsons Ltd. 505
Hillebrant v. Brewer 443
Hirtle v. Ernst **557**
Hodgson v. Marks 527
Hoegy v. General Accident Assurance Co. of
  Canada 86
Hollett v. Hollett 501
Horne v. Horne Estate 653
Hubbs v. Black 541
Hussey v. Palmer 505, **507**, 512

INS v. AP see International News Service v.
  Associated Press
International News Service v. Associated
  Press **21**
Inwards v. Baker 505, 513, **514**, 517
Irons v. Smallpiece 442

Janzen v. Platy Enterprises 101
Jengle v. Keetch 545
Johnson v. McIntosh 97
Jordan & Geisel Management Ltd. v.
  Napham 422

K.A. Reed Services Pty. Ltd., Government
  Insurance Office v., 585
Kay v. Parkway Forest Developments **410**,
  414
Keast v. Keast 671
Keefer v. Arillotta **170**, 177
Keneric Tractor Sales Ltd. v. Langille 402
Keppell v. Bailey 579, 590
Keron v. Cashman **118**
Knowlton v. Bartlett 649, 652, 657, **658**
Kreadar Enterprises Ltd. v. Duny Machine
  Ltd. 216

Laing v. Allied Innkeepers Ltd. 362
Lands Protection Act (PEI), Reference
  re, 737

Langer v. McTavish Brothers Ltd. 456
Layton, The Queen v., 45
Linton v. Linton 672
Local 1330, United Steel Workers v. US Steel
  Corp. 84
London County Council v. Allen 591
Lubben v. Veltri & Sons Corp. 486
Lucas v. Hamn 339
Lugosi v. Universal Pictures 770
Luta v. Kawa 217
Lysaght v. Edwards **483**

M and N Properties (Cassandra Towers) v.
  Ryll **414**, 421
Mabo v. Queensland 81, 242, 721, 722
MacLean v. Reid **163**
Maddison v. Alderson 494
Manitoba Fisheries Ltd. v. The Queen 738
Mason v. Clarke 534
McBride v. Sandland 494
McColgan, Re, **282**
McColl v. McColl 655
McDonald's Restaurants of Canada Limited v.
  West Edmonton Mall Ltd. 624
McEwen v. Ewers and Ferguson **634**, 638,
  640, 642
McKellar, Re, 311
McPhail v. Persons Unknown 142
Metro-Matic Services Ltd. v. Hulman 381,
  387
Metropolitan Toronto Condominium
  Corporation No. 949 v. Irvine 423
Metropolitan Toronto Condominium Corp.
  No. 979, Re, 584
Miles, Inc. v. Scripps Clinic and Research
  Foundation 73
Miller v. Herzfeld 471
Millirrpum v. Nablaco Pty. Ltd. and the
  Commonwealth of Australia 82
Milroy v. Lord 524
Minichiello v. Devonshire Hotel (1967)
  Ltd. 358, 360, 363
Mitchell v. Arblaster 641
Moffatt v. Kazana 126, **127**, 129
Monaghan v. Moore 565
Moore v. Regents of the University of
  California **63**, 83
Morgan v. Davis 646
Morgan v. Morgan 677

Murdoch v. Barry 647
Murdoch v. Murdoch 668, 670

Naylor v. Naylor 480
Newell v. National Bank of Norwich 478
Nisbet and Potts' Contract, Re, 589
Noble and Wolf v. Alley **614**, 618, 619, 620,
  621
North Bay TV & Audio Ltd. v. Nova
  Electronics Ltd. 404

One Twenty-Five Varsity Road Ltd. v.
  Township of York 591
Ontario Sawridge Band v. Canada 715
O'Reilly (No. 2), Re, 162, 631
Osachuk v. Osachuk 655

Pacific Centre Ltd. v. Micro Base
  Development Corp. 403, 404
Pacific Wash-A-Matic Ltd. v. R.O. Booth
  Holdings Ltd. 388
Pakenham's Case 579
Pamajewon, R v. 715
Paradise Beach and Transportation Co. Ltd.
  v. Price-Robinson 162
Parker v. British Airways Board **102**, 116,
  117
Parkinson v. Reid 579
Pascoe v. Turner 517, **518**, 525
Peel Non-Profit Housing Corporation v.
  McNamara and Cherry **425**
Perry v. Clissold 135, 140, 141
Peter v. Beblow 691
Peters, R v., 36
Pettkus v. Becker 446, **684**, 690, 692
Phipps v. Pears **565**, 568, 571, 575, 629
Pierson v. Post 96, 97
Piper v. Stevenson 154
Pruneyard Shopping Center v. Robins 58
Punch v. Savoy's Jewellers Ltd. 361
Purefoy v. Rogers 326, 327

RWDSU v. T. Eaton Company Limited 42, **43**
Rathwell v. Rathwell 670, 690
Regent Oil Co. v. J.A. Gregory (Hatch End)
  Ltd. 576
Robertson v. Fraser 642
Robichaud v. Watson 646
Robson, Re, 334

Rosenberger v. Volz 479
Rynard, Re, **296**

St. Catherines Milling and Lumber Co. v. The
  Queen 230
St. Clair Beach Estates Ltd., Re, v.
  MacDonald **154**
Schilthuis v. Arnold 447
Schobelt v. Barber 648
Sekretov and City of Toronto, Re, 594
Semelhago v. Paramadevan 485, 486
Sen v. Headley 479
Shack, State v., **56**
Shelf Holdings Ltd. v. Husky Oil Operations
  Ltd. 546
Shell-Mex and BP Ltd. v. Manchester Garages
  Ltd. 381
Shelley v. Kraemer 622
Shelley's Case see Wolfe v. Shelley
Shepherd Homes Ltd. v. Sandham 623
Silva v. Silva 660
Smith and Snipes Hall Farm Ltd. v. River
  Douglas Catchment Board 578
Sorochan v. Sorochan 691
South Shore Venture Capital Ltd. v. Haas 503
Sparrow, R v., 232, 276, **535**, 537, 715
Speck, Re, 640
Speelman v. Pascal 471
Spencer's Case 576
Stanish v. Parasz 691
Starlite Variety Stores Ltd. v. Cloverlawn
  Investments Ltd. **495**, 500, 503, 504
Stewart, R v., 748
Street v. Mountford 366
Strong v. Bird 445

Taylor v. Rawana 494, 495, 500
Teis v. Corp. of Town of Ancaster 217
Tellier v. Dujardin 455
Tener, R in Right of British Columbia v., 535
Thomas v. Times Book Co. Ltd. **458**

Tichborne v. Weir 577
Tito v. Waddell (Ocean Island) 584
Tiverton Estates Ltd. v. Wearwell Ltd. 489
Toronto Housing Co. Ltd. v. Postal
  Promotions Ltd. 403
Treloar v. Nute 186
Tuck's Settlement Trusts, In re, 259, **264**
Tulk v. Moxhay **587**, 589, 590

Van Dorp and Van Dorp, Re, 654
Vannini v. Public Utilities Commission of
  Sault Ste. Marie 541
Ventura Park Housing Co-operative Inc. v.
  Conway 422
Victoria Park Racing and Recreation Grounds
  Co. Ltd. v. Taylor **5**, 13, 14, 15, 16, 17, 83

Walsh v. Lonsdale 488, **490**, 493, 503
Ward v. Turner 472
Ward Locke & Co. (Ltd.) v. Operative
  Printers' Assistants' Society 17
Watters, Re, **279**
Weibe v. Lepp 362
Wheeldon v. Burrows 560
The Wik Peoples v. Queensland 725
Wildwood Mall Ltd. v. Stevens 42
Wing Lee Holdings Ltd. v. Coleman 405
Wishart Estate, Re, 74
Wolfe v. Shelley 295, 296
Wong v. Beaumont 559
Wood v. Gateway of Uxbridge Properties
  Inc. **207**
Woodworth v. Woodworth 676
Wright v. Gibbons 636, 643
Wrotham Park Estate Co. Ltd. v. Parkside
  Homes Ltd. 593, 623
Wyld v. Silver 631
Wynn v. Wynn 703

Zachariuc, Re; Chevrier v. Public
  Trustee **472**

CHAPTER ONE

Concepts of Property in Law

INTRODUCTION: PROPERTY AS "RELATIONSHIP"—NOT "THING"

Most people, including lawyers, define property as something that is owned by someone—a book, a car, a house, a block of land, etc. Although this definition is acceptable
in day-to-day social interactions, it needs to be recharacterized for the purposes of
examining property in law. By contrast with day-to-day usage, the legal concept of
property concerns

> the network of legal relationships prevailing between individuals in respect of
> things ... . Seen in this way, "property" comprises bundles of mutual rights and
> obligations between "subjects" in respect of certain "objects," and the study of the law
> of property becomes an inquiry into a variety of socially defined relationships and
> morally conditioned obligations.

(K.J. Gray and P.D. Symes, *Real Property and Real People* (London: Butterworths,
1981) (hereafter Gray and Symes), at 8-9.)

This idea of property as relationship is well illustrated in Jeremy Waldron's description of Susan and her motor car, a Porsche. (See Jeremy Waldron, *The Right to Private
Property* (Oxford: Clarendon Press, 1988), at 26ff.) As Waldron explains, our day-to-day
description is that "Susan owns that Porsche." However, this description must be
recharacterized for legal purposes so as to define the relationship between Susan and
other people (the *subjects* of the legal relationship) and the Porsche (the *object* of the
legal relationship) (at 27):

> With regard to Susan's Porsche, there are all sorts of legal relations between Susan and
> other people ... . Susan has a legal liberty to use it in certain ways [but] she is not at
> liberty ... to drive it at all without a licence from the authorities ... . She has what
> Hohfeld called a "claim-right" against everyone else (her neighbours, her friends, the
> local car thief, everyone in the community) that they should not use her Porsche without
> her permission. But Susan also owes certain duties to other people in relation to her
> vehicle ... . She is liable to pay damages if it rolls into her neighbour's fence. These
> rights, liberties and duties are the basic stuff of ownership.

As Waldron further explains, Susan may alter these legal relationships by her dealings with the Porsche—by selling it, giving it away, bequeathing it in her will at the time

of her death, or lending it to a friend for the day. If she fails to pay debts, it is possible that the car may be seized in satisfaction of her debts. As a result, the legal definition of Susan's relationship to the Porsche is that she has a "bundle of rights" that constitute a proprietary interest *in* the Porsche. (W.N. Hohfeld's analysis, referred to by Waldron, is more fully explained in his article "Some Fundamental Legal Conceptions as Applied in Judicial Reasoning" (1913), 23 *Yale Law Journal* 16.)

Property as Relationship: Implications

The concept of property as a relationship among people in respect of things is both complex and dynamic. It is complex because there are many different ways to assemble the "bundle of rights" in different contexts, especially where the *objects* of property differ. For example, Waldron has asserted (at 31) that ownership of a Porsche is quite different from ownership of a piece of agricultural land, and different again from owner-ship of intangible ideas, like copyright. In this context, assertions that "X owns the car," "Y owns the land," and "Z owns the copyright" are not helpful legal statements because they cannot convey "any common content for these quite different bundles."

In addition to being complex, the concept of property as a relationship among people in respect of things is dynamic. C.B. Macpherson, for example, has explained the dynamic quality of property as follows:

> The meaning of property is not constant. The actual institution, and the way people see it, and hence the meaning they give to the word, all change over time ... . The changes are related to changes in the purposes which society or the dominant classes in society expect the institution of property to serve.

(C.B. Macpherson, "The Meaning of Property," in C.B. Macpherson, ed., *Property: Mainstream and Critical Positions* (Toronto: University of Toronto Press, 1978) (here-after Macpherson), at 1.) Macpherson has also described (at 7) how the concept of property as relationship was well recognized in day-to-day language until the late 17th century. As the economy changed from feudalism to capitalism, the idea of property also changed because "as rights in land became more absolute, and parcels of land became more freely marketable commodities, it became natural to think of the land itself as the property." According to Macpherson, current legal arrangements about property in the late 20th century confirm that it is once again regarded as a "right," not a "thing," an approach that is consistent with the basic notion of property as a *relationship among people in respect of objects*.

Subjects and Objects of Property Relationships

The dynamic nature of both subjects and objects of property interests is explored by Gray and Symes. They note that some persons in the past, including serfs and married women, were excluded by law from holding—that is, being *subjects* of—property inter-ests, and that children under the age of 18 continue to be precluded from holding property interests. In this context, they assert (at 10) that the definition of who can be the "subject" of property interests has "an important political significance precisely because the delineation of potential right-holders fundamentally affects both the balance of power and the distribution of goods within a society." In the late 20th century, few classes of people are *explicitly* precluded from holding interests in property. Yet, the legal right to become the "subject" of a property interest has not resulted in equality among all persons in relation to property interests. In this way, there is an important relationship between property law and issues of social and economic inequality. For an examination of these issues in another historical period, see Jennifer Nedelsky, "Law, Boundaries and the Bounded Self," in Richard Chused, ed., *A Property Anthology* (Cincinnati: Anderson Publishing, 1993), 28.

In addition to changing subjects of property, there is a dynamic quality about the objects of proprietary interests. For example, both slaves and married women were once considered objects of property relationships, but such arrangements are no longer legally acceptable. By contrast, land has always been regarded as an object of property, although it may have less value now than in some former times. In the late 20th century, there are also forms of "new property" that are often claimed as objects of property— professional licences, pensions, and even the right to a job or to security of housing. As Gray and Symes point out (at 11):

> The things which are today of real value to the man [sic] in the street are assets like his job, his pension, and the right to undisturbed possession of his home. On the fringes of these new categories of property lie certain less well defined rights such as the right to education, the right to health and the right to a wholesome environment.

A classic formulation of these "new property" interests is found in Charles Reich, "The New Property" (1964), 73 *Yale Law Journal* 733. See also Mary Ann Glendon, *The New Family and the New Property* (Toronto: Butterworths, 1981). These issues are more fully explored later in this and subsequent chapters.

Property Relationships in Context

The idea of property is controversial. Philosophers and political economists have debated its merits and its justifications for a long time, as is evident in the differing points of view in the essays collected in Macpherson, and in the work of Carol Rose, *Property and Persuasion: Essays on the History, Theory, and Rhetoric of Ownership* (Boulder, CO: Westview Press, 1994) (hereafter Rose).

The law of property is also controversial, especially in the context of "new property" claims that reflect desires to overcome insecurity or dependency in the lives of many people in the late 20th century. Perhaps surprising, the law of property is also "old" law, much of it reflecting principles developed centuries ago in very different contexts. In this way, property law provides a dual challenge—students must understand traditional property law principles in order to work with them effectively and, at the same time, they must assess traditional property law principles critically in the modern context. As Gray and Symes state succinctly (at 9): "To confine property law to its mechanical aspects and to ignore the inevitable infusion of extra-legal factors, is to impoverish legal study by forcing it into a moral and social vacuum." In considering these materials, you need to become proficient in using the principles of property law and, at the same time, to understand how these principles work in their broader social, economic, and political context.

Discussion Notes

Differing Conceptions of Property

In considering the broader social, economic, and political context in relation to property law, it is important to note that there are differing conceptions of property and the meaning of "ownership." For some groups—aboriginal peoples; blacks, whose racial history meant that they were excluded from being subjects of property relationships; and women—some of these differing conceptions have been identified. Aboriginal peoples developed a unique set of laws and customs concerning property interests; African Canadians have sometimes been prohibited from holding property interests; and women sometimes "lost" their property rights on marriage. These issues are considered in this and other chapters. For an introduction to these issues, see Leroy Little Bear, "Aboriginal Rights and the Canadian 'Grundnorm,'" in J. Rick Ponting, *Arduous Journey: Canadian Indians and Decolonization* (Toronto: McClelland and Stewart, 1986), at 243; Patricia Williams, "On Being an Object of Property," in Williams, *The Alchemy of Race and Rights* (Cambridge, MA: Harvard University Press, 1991), at 216; and Floyd Rudmin, "Gender Differences in the Semantics of Ownership: A Quantitative Phenomenological Survey Study" (1994), 15:3 *Journal of Economic Psychology* 487. These issues are more fully explored later in this book.

Philosophical Perspectives About Property

The law of property often reflects philosophical perspectives about the nature or purposes of property. In her introduction to *Property and Persuasion*, at 1-7, Carol Rose briefly described differing philosophical perspectives. For Rose, a need to reconceptualize ideas of property led to a focus on "norms and narratives" and the links between them. As she explained (at 5-6):

> Community norms—the common beliefs, understandings, and culture that hold property regimes together—raise the issue of persuasion. Where do people get those understandings about property anyway, and what gets them over that peculiar gap between property-as-thing and property-as-relationship? Just as important, what persuades people to ease up on self-interest or convinces them to pay attention to the norms that let them manage property regimes as a whole, and in so doing become more prosperous? How do people *change* norms to accommodate different property arrangements that might enhance their well-being?

Rose's reflections emphasize the idea of property as a social concept, and these and other ideas about property are explored in this book. For an overview of different philosophical approaches to property, see also Bruce Ziff, *Principles of Property Law*, 2d ed. (Scarborough, ON: Carswell, 1996) (hereafter Ziff), chapter 1; and the overview in Macpherson's essay, reproduced in chapter 8.

AN INTRODUCTION TO PROPERTY CLAIMS

Victoria Park Racing and Recreation Grounds Co. Ltd. v. Taylor
(1937), 58 CLR 479

[In "Property in Thin Air" (1991), 50 *Cambridge Law Journal* 252, at 264, Kevin Gray described *Victoria Park* as "pivotal" for understanding property law:

> The case embodies one of the last great problems of property law and reverberates with a significance which has outlived its particular facts. With justification it may be said that the concept of property cannot be entirely satisfactorily explained without accounting, in some way or other, for the ruling in *Victoria Park Racing*.

The case concerned a suit for an injunction by the plaintiff who owned the Victoria Park racecourse in Australia. The plaintiff sought the injunction against three defendants: Mr. Taylor, who owned land adjoining the racecourse and who had built a raised wooden platform so that one could see the racecourse and the notice boards with information (including starting prices) about the races; Mr. Angles, who stood on the platform and commented on the races by telephone, announcing the winner of each race; and the Commonwealth Broadcasting Corporation, which broadcast the commentaries of Mr. Angles. Gray described (at 265) the impact of the defendants' activities on the plaintiff's business as follows:

> The instant popularity of these transmissions stimulated an illicit off-course betting industry in Sydney, and there was unchallenged evidence that punters who would otherwise have attended the race meetings in person now preferred to follow those proceedings either from the comfort of their own homes or, even better, from their local hostelry. The plaintiff, perturbed by the catastrophic loss of business, sued for an injunction.

In the Supreme Court of New South Wales, Nicholas J refused the plaintiff's request for an injunction and this decision was then appealed to the High Court of Australia. Three justices (Latham CJ, and Dixon and McTiernan JJ) dismissed the appeal, while two others (Rich and Evatt JJ) dissented.

The excerpts from the judgments illustrate differing approaches to the analysis of proprietary interests and differing views about the roles of courts and legislatures in responding to new property claims.]

LATHAM CJ: ... The plaintiff's case is put as an action upon the case for nuisance affecting the use and enjoyment of the plaintiff's land. It is also contended that there is an unnatural user of Taylor's land by Angles to which the Broadcasting Co. is a party and of which it takes advantage. The unnatural user is, I understand, alleged to consist in the erection of the wooden structure on Taylor's land which Angles uses and the use of the land for broadcasting purposes. It is contended that, there being this unnatural user of the land, the defendant is liable for all the damage which may happen to any person, including the plaintiff, as a result of such user.

The first contention is that the plaintiff's land has been made suitable for a race-course, that by reason of the action of the defendants it has been deprived of at least some measure of that suitability, and that therefore this is a case of nuisance—an unlawful interference with the use and enjoyment of land. No analogous case has been cited to the court. I agree that the category of nuisance is not closed and that if some new method of interfering with the comfort of persons in the use of land emerges the law may provide a remedy. For example, the increasing use of electricity, with the possibility of the escape of electricity into an adjoining property, has provided a new possible source of interference with the use of land and the law provides a remedy in such a case.

In this case, however, in my opinion, the defendants have not interfered in any way with the use and enjoyment of the plaintiff's land. The effect of their actions is to make the business carried on by the plaintiff less profitable, and they do so by providing a competitive entertainment. It is unnecessary to cite authorities for the proposition that mere competition (certainly if without any motive of injuring the plaintiff) is not a cause of action. The facts are that the racecourse is as suitable as ever it was for use as a racecourse. What the defendants do does not interfere with the races, nor does it interfere with the comfort or enjoyment of any person who is on the racecourse. The alleged nuisance cannot be detected by any person upon the land as operating or producing any effect upon the plaintiff's land. It is consistent with the evidence that none of the persons on that land may, at any given moment, be aware of the fact that a broadcast is being made. The only alleged effect of the broadcast is an effect in relation to people who are not upon the land, that is, the people who listen in or have the opportunity of listening in and who therefore stay away from the land. In my opinion the defendants have not in any way interfered with the plaintiff's land or the enjoyment thereof. ...

I am unable to see that any right of the plaintiff has been violated or any wrong done to him. Any person is entitled to look over the plaintiff's fences and to see what goes on in the plaintiff's land. If the plaintiff desires to prevent this, the plaintiff can erect a higher fence. Further, if the plaintiff desires to prevent its notice boards being seen by people from outside the enclosure, it can place them in such a position that they are not visible to such people. At sports grounds and other places of entertainment it is the lawful, natural and common practice to put up fences and other structures to prevent people who are not prepared to pay for admission from getting the benefit of the entertainment. In my opinion, the law cannot by an injunction in effect erect fences which the plaintiff is not prepared to provide. The defendant does no wrong to the plaintiff by looking at what takes place on the plaintiff's land. Further, he does no wrong to the plaintiff by describing to other persons, to as wide an audience as he can obtain, what takes place on the plaintiff's ground. The court has not been referred to any principle of law which prevents any man from describing anything which he sees anywhere if he does not make defamatory statements, infringe the law as to offensive language, & c., break a contract, or wrongfully reveal confidential information. The defendants did not infringe the law in any of these respects.

The plaintiff further contended that there was an unnatural user of land by the defendant Taylor and that all the defendants were liable for resulting damage to the plaintiff's land or to the plaintiff's business. In my opinion, this contention cannot be supported. "Prima facie, it is lawful to erect what one pleases on one's own land"

(*Rogers v. Rajendro Dutt*). It is not suggested that Taylor has broken any building regulation. If he had done so the remedy would be the same in all material particulars if Taylor had a two-storey house from the upper storey of which Angles made his broadcast. In my opinion it would be impossible to contend that there was an unnatural user of the land and house because they were used for that purpose. If Taylor complies with any relevant provision under the Federal *Post and Telegraph Act* or the *Wireless Telegraphy Act*, he is entitled to have a telephone and to use his premises as an originating point for broadcasting. So also the Commonwealth Broadcasting Co. is entitled to broadcast under the licence granted in pursuance of the Federal regulations. I am not prepared to assent to what I regard as the surprising argument that the use of land for broadcasting is an unnatural user of land within the principle of *Rylands v. Fletcher*. Broadcasting of races could doubtless be prevented, either altogether or without the consent of the persons who undertake the trouble and expense of organizing race meetings, by a regulation dealing with the conditions of broadcasting licences; but no such regulation has yet been made.

In reality there is no particular connection between the use of the defendant Taylor's land as land and the wrong which the plaintiff alleges that it suffers. The position in all material particulars would be exactly the same if the broadcasting were done from a motor car on a road from which the racecourse could be seen or by a man standing on high land of which he was not the owner or the occupier. Reference to Taylor's land in the argument is introduced only for the purpose of relying upon an alleged unnatural user of that land. As I have already said, in my opinion, there is no such user.

The claim under the head of nuisance has also been supported by an argument that the law recognizes a right of privacy which has been infringed by the defendant. However desirable some limitation upon invasions of privacy might be, no authority was cited which shows that any general right of privacy exists. The contention is answered, in my opinion, by the case of *Chandler v. Thompson*; see also *Turner v. Spooner*: "With regard to the question of privacy, no doubt the owner of a house would prefer that a neighbour should not have the right of looking into his windows or yard, but neither this court nor a court of law will interfere on the mere ground of invasion of privacy; and a party has a right even to open new windows, although he is thereby enabled to overlook his neighbour's premises, and so interfering, perhaps, with his comfort"; see also *Tapling v. Jones*.

It has been argued that by the expenditure of money the plaintiff has created a spectacle and that it therefore has what is described as a quasi-property in the spectacle which the law will protect. The vagueness of this proposition is apparent upon its face. What it really means is that there is some principle (apart from contract or confidential relationship) which prevents people in some circumstances from opening their eyes and seeing something and then describing what they see. The court has not been referred to any authority in English law which supports the general contention that if a person chooses to organize an entertainment or to do anything else which other persons are able to see he has a right to obtain from a court an order that they shall not describe to anybody what they see. If the claim depends upon interference with a proprietary right it is difficult to see how it can be material to consider whether the interference is large or small—whether the description is communicated to many persons by broadcasting or by a newspaper report, or only to a few persons in conversation or correspondence. Further, as I have already said, the mere fact that damage results to a plaintiff from such a description cannot be relied upon as a cause of action.

I find difficulty in attaching any precise meaning to the phrase "property in a spectacle." A "spectacle" cannot be "owned" in any ordinary sense of that word. Even if there were any legal principle which prevented one person from gaining an advantage for himself or causing damage to another by describing a spectacle produced by that other person, the rights of the latter person could be described as property only in a metaphorical sense. Any appropriateness in the metaphor would depend upon the existence of the legal principle. The principle cannot itself be based upon such a metaphor.

Even if, on the other hand, a spectacle could be said to exist as a subject matter of property, it would still be necessary, in order to provide the plaintiff in this case with a remedy, to show that the description of such property is wrongful or that such description is wrongful when it is widely disseminated. No authority has been cited to support such a proposition. ...

RICH J: ... The question to be solved is, "How far can one person restrain another from invading the privacy of land which he occupies, when such invasion does not involve actual entry on the land?" (Professor Winfield, *Law Quarterly Review*, vol. 47, p. 24). The defendants contended that the law provides no remedy as their action did not fall within any classification of torts and that the plaintiff's remedy lay either in self-defence, e.g., raising the height of the fences round the course, or in an application to the legislature. It does not follow that because no precedent can be found a principle does not exist to support the plaintiff's right. Nuisance covers so wide a field that no general definition of nuisance has been attempted but only a classification of the various kinds of nuisance. Courts have always refrained from fettering themselves by definitions. "Courts of equity constantly decline to lay down any rule, which shall limit their power and discretion as to the particular cases in which such injunctions shall be granted or withheld. And there is wisdom in this course; for it is impossible to foresee all the exigencies of society which may require their aid and assistance to protect rights, or redress wrongs. The jurisdiction of these courts, thus operating by way of special injunction, is manifestly indispensable for the purposes of social justice in a great variety of cases, and therefore should be fostered and upheld by a steady confidence." ...

An action on the case in the nature of nuisance was one of the flexible remedies capable of adaptation to new circumstances falling within recognized principles. This case presents the peculiar features that by means of broadcasting—a thing novel both in fact and law—the knowledge obtained by overlooking the plaintiff's racecourse from the defendants' tower is turned to account in a manner which impairs the value of the plaintiff's occupation of the land and diverts a legitimate source of profit from its business into the pockets of the defendants. It appears to me that the true issue is whether a non-natural use of a neighbour's land made by him for the purpose of obtaining the means of appropriating in this way part of the profitable enjoyment of the plaintiff's land to his own commercial ends—a thing made possible only by radio—falls within the reason of the principles which give rise to the action on the case in the nature of nuisance. There is no absolute standard as to what constitutes a nuisance in law. But all the surrounding circumstances must be taken into consideration in each case. As regards neighbouring properties their interdependence is important in arriving at a decision in a given case. An improper or non-natural use or a use in excess of a man's right which curtails or impairs his neighbour's legitimate enjoyment of his property is "tortious and hurtful" and constitutes a nuisance. A man has no absolute right "within the ambit of his own land" to act as he pleases. His right is qualified and such of his acts as invade his neighbour's property are lawful only in so far as they are reasonable having regard to his own circumstances and those of his neighbour (*Law Quarterly Review*, vol. 52, p. 460; vol. 53, p. 3). The plaintiff's case must, I am prepared to concede, rest on what is called nuisance. But it must not be overlooked that this means no more than that he must complain of some impairment of the rights flowing from occupation and ownership of land. One of the prime purposes of occupation of land is the pursuit of profitable enterprises for which the exclusion of others is necessary either totally or except upon conditions which may include payment. In the present case in virtue of its occupation and ownership the plaintiff carries on the business of admitting to the land for payment patrons of racing. There it entertains them by a spectacle, by a competition in the comparative merits of racehorses, and it attempts by all reasonable means to give to those whom it admits the exclusive right of witnessing the spectacle, the competition and of using the collated information in betting while that is possible on its various events. This use of its rights as occupier is usual, reasonable and profitable. So much no one can dispute. If it be true that an adjacent owner has an unqualified and absolute right to overlook an occupier whatever may be the enterprise he is carrying on and to make any profitable use to which what he sees can be put, whether in his capacity of adjacent owner or otherwise, then to that extent the right of the occupier carrying on the enterprise must be modified and treated in law as less extensive and ample than perhaps is usually understood. But can the adjacent owner by virtue of his occupation and ownership use his land in such an unusual way as the erection of a platform involves, bring mechanical appliances into connection with that use, i.e., the microphone and land line to the studio, and then by combining regularity of observation with dissemination for gain of the information so obtained give the potential patrons a mental picture of the spectacle, an account of the competition between the horses and of the collated information needed for betting, for all of which they would otherwise have recourse to the racecourse and pay? To admit that the adjacent owner may overlook does not answer this question affirmatively. ...

There can be no right to extend the normal use of his land by the adjoining owner indefinitely. He may within limits make fires, create smoke and use vibratory machinery. He may consume all the water he finds on his land, but he has no absolute right to dirty it. Defendants' rights are related to plaintiff's rights and each owner's rights may be limited by the rights of the other. *Sic utere tuo* is not the premise in a syllogism but does indicate the fact that *damnum* may spring from injuria even though the defendant can say: "I am an owner." All the nuisance cases, including in that category *Rylands v. Fletcher*, are mere illustrations of a very general principle "that law grows and ... though the principles of law remain unchanged, yet (and it is one of the advantages of the common law) their application is to be changed with the changing circumstances of the times. Some persons may call this retrogression, I call it progression of human opinion" (*R v. Ramsay and Foote*). I adapt Lord Macmillan's words and say: "The categories of 'nuisance' are not closed" (*Donoghue v. Stevenson*). Nuisance is not trespass on the case and physical or material interference is not necessary. The "vibration" cases and the "besetting and eavesdropping" cases are certainly against such a contention. What appears to me to be the real point in this case is that the right of view or observation from adjacent land has never been held to be an absolute and complete right of property incident to the occupation of that land and exercisable at all hazards notwithstanding its destructive effect upon the enjoyment of the land overlooked. In the absence of any authority to the contrary I hold that there is a limit to this right of overlooking and that the limit must be found in an attempt to reconcile the right of free prospect from one piece of land with the right of profitable enjoyment of another. ...

DIXON J: The foundation of the plaintiff company's case is no doubt the fact that persons who otherwise would attend race meetings stay away because they listen to the broadcast made by the defendant Angles from the tower overlooking the course. Beginning with the damage thus suffered and with the repetition that may be expected, the plaintiff company says that, unless a justification for causing it exists, the defendants or some of them must be liable, inasmuch as it is their unauthorized acts that inflict the loss. It is said that to look for a definite category or form of action into which to fit the plaintiff's complaint is to reverse the proper order of thought in the present stage of the law's development. In such a case it is for the defendants to point to the ground upon which the law allows them so to interfere with the normal course of the plaintiff's business as to cause damage.

There is, in my opinion, little to be gained by inquiring whether in English law the foundation of a delictual liability is unjustifiable damage or breach of specific duty. The law of tort has fallen into great confusion, but, in the main, what acts and omissions result in responsibility and what do not are matters defined by long-established rules of law from which judges ought not wittingly to depart and no light is shed upon a given case by large generalizations about them. We know that, if upon such facts as the present the plaintiff could recover at common law, his cause of action must have its source in an action upon the case and that in such an action, speaking generally, damage was the gist of the action. There is, perhaps, nothing wrong either historically or analytically in regarding an action for damage suffered by words, by deceit or by negligence as founded upon the damage and treating the unjustifiable conduct of the defendant who caused it as matter of inducement. But, whether his conduct be so described or be called more simply a wrongful act or omission, it remains true that it must answer a known description, or, in other words, respond to the tests or criteria laid down by established principle. ...

So far as freedom from view or inspection is a natural or acquired physical characteristic of the site, giving it value for the purpose of the business or pursuit which the plaintiff conducts, it is a characteristic which is not a legally protected interest. It is not a natural right for breach of which a legal remedy is given, either by an action in the nature of nuisance or otherwise. The fact is that the substance of the plaintiff's complaint goes to interference, not with its enjoyment of the land, but with the profitable conduct of its business. If English law had followed the course of development that has recently taken place in the United States, the "broadcasting rights" in respect of the races might have been protected as part of the quasi-property created by the enterprise, organization and labour of the plaintiff in establishing and equipping a racecourse and doing all that is necessary to conduct race meetings. But courts of equity have not in British jurisdictions thrown the protection of an injunction around all the intangible elements of value, that is, value in exchange, which may flow from the exercise by an individual of his powers or resources whether in the organization of a business or undertaking or the use of ingenuity, knowledge, skill or labour. This is sufficiently evidenced by the history of the law of copyright and by the fact that the exclusive right to invention, trade marks, designs, trade name and reputation are dealt with in English law as special heads of protected interests and not under a wide generalization.

In dissenting from a judgment of the Supreme Court of the United States by which the organized collection of news by a news service was held to give it in equity a quasi-property protected against appropriation by rival news agencies, Brandeis J gave reasons which substantially represent the English view and he supported his opinion by a citation of much English authority (*International News Service v. Associated Press*). His judgment appears to me to contain an adequate answer both upon principle and authority to the suggestion that the defendants are misappropriating or abstracting something which the plaintiff has created and alone is entitled to turn to value. Briefly, the answer is that it is not because the individual has by his efforts put himself in a position to obtain value for what he can give that his right to give it becomes protected by law and so assumes the exclusiveness of property, but because the intangible or incorporeal right he claims falls within a recognized category to which legal or equitable protection attaches. ...

In my opinion, the right to exclude the defendants from broadcasting a description of the occurrences they can see upon the plaintiff's land is not given by law. It is not an interest falling within any category which is protected at law or in equity. I have had the advantage of reading the judgment of Rich J, but I am unable to regard the considerations which are there set out as justifying what I consider amounts not simply to a new application of settled principle but to the introduction into the law of new doctrine. ...

EVATT J: ... In the present case, the plaintiff relies upon all the surrounding circumstances. Its use and occupation of land is interfered with, its business profits are lessened, and the value of the land is diminished or jeopardized by the conduct of the defendants. The defendants' operations are conducted to the plaintiff's detriment, not casually but systematically, not temporarily but indefinitely; they use a suburban bungalow in an unreasonable and grotesque manner, and do so in the course of a gainful pursuit which strikes at the plaintiff's profitable use of its land, precisely at the point where the profit must be earned, viz., the entrance gates. Many analogies to the defendants' operations have been suggested, but few of them are applicable. The newspaper which is published a considerable time after a race has been run competes only with other newspapers, and can have little or no effect upon the profitable employment of the plaintiff's land. A photographer overlooking the course and subsequently publishing a photograph in a newspaper or elsewhere does not injure the plaintiff. Individuals who observe the racing from their own homes or those of their friends could not interfere with the plaintiff's beneficial use of its course. On the other hand, the defendants' operations are fairly comparable with those who, by the employment of moving picture films, television and broadcasting would convey to the public generally (i) from a point of vantage specially constructed, (ii) simultaneously with the actual running of the races, (iii) visual, verbal or audible representations of each and every portion of the races. If such a plan of campaign were pursued, it would result in what has been proved here, viz., actual pecuniary loss to the occupier of the racecourse and a depreciation in the value of his land, at least so long as the conduct is continued. In principle, such a plan may be regarded as equivalent to the erection by a landowner of a special stand outside a cricket ground for the sole purpose of enabling the public to witness the cricket match at an admission price which is lower than that charged to the public bodies who own the ground, and, at great expense, organize the game.

In concluding that, in such cases, no actionable nuisance would be created, the defendants insist that the law of England does not recognize any general right of privacy. That is true, but it carries the defendants no further, because it is not merely an interference with privacy which is here relied upon, and it is not the law that every interference with privacy must be lawful. The defendants also say that the law of England does not forbid one person to overlook the property of another. That also is true in the sense that the fact that one individual possesses the means of watching, and sometimes watches what goes on on his neighbour's land, does not make the former's action unlawful. But it is equally erroneous to assume that under no circumstances can systematic watching amount to a civil wrong, for an analysis of the cases of *J. Lyons & Sons v. Wilkins* and *Ward Locke & Co. (Ltd.) v. Operative Printers' Assistants' Society* indicates that, under some circumstances, the common law regards "watching and besetting" as a private nuisance, although no trespass to land has been committed. ...

The fact that there is no previous English decision which is comparable to the present does not tell against the plaintiff because not only is simultaneous broadcasting or television quite new, but, so far as I know, no one has, as yet, constructed high grandstands outside recognized sports grounds for the purpose of viewing the sports and of enriching themselves at the expense of the occupier. ...

McTIERNAN J: ... It is not shown that the broadcasting interferes with the use and enjoyment of the land or the conduct of the race meetings or the comfort or enjoyment of any of the plaintiff's patrons. Indeed, it appears quite impossible that any such result would be caused by the action of Angles in standing on this platform aloof from the racecourse, observing the races and talking into a microphone or telephone. The principle upon which liability for acts in the nature of nuisance is founded is not to be restrained by the instances in which that liability has been found to exist. The list of acts which may give rise to an action on the case in the nature of nuisance is not closed against broadcasting. But to broadcast a lawful description of what is happening on premises cannot be an actionable nuisance at least unless it causes substantial interference with the use and enjoyment of the premises. It is conceivable that broadcasting may be made an adjunct to conduct constituting the actionable nuisance of watching and besetting premises, the nature of which is discussed in *J. Lyons & Sons v. Wilkins*. But no facts are proved to bring the broadcasting of which the plaintiff complains within the scope of the principle which was applied in that case.

Appeal Dismissed

Discussion Notes

Different Approaches to the Legal Category of "Nuisance"

As *Victoria Park* illustrates, a plaintiff's claim fall must usually fall within a defined legal category in order for the plaintiff to obtain a legal remedy. In *Victoria Park*, the plaintiff tried to show that the actions of the defendants constituted the tort of nuisance, affecting "the use and enjoyment" of the plaintiff's land. Examine the approach of Latham CJ to this issue. Compare his approach to that of Rich J. How do they differ? Why do their differing approaches lead to different outcomes? To what extent does the "novel" context affect their choices?

In reflecting on these questions, consider the following comment made by Jerome Frank in *Law and the Modern Mind* (New York: Anchor Books, 1963), at 160-61:

> The decision of a judge after trying a case is the product of a unique experience ... . The function of juristic logic and the principles which it employs seem to be like that of language, to describe the event which has already transpired ... . The rules a judge announces when publishing his [sic] decision are, therefore, intelligible only if one can relive the judge's unique experience while he was trying the case—which, of course, cannot be done.

To what extent do the decisions of Latham CJ and Rich J appear to "describe the event which has already transpired"? For another view of judicial decision making, see Martha Minow, "Judging Inside Out" (1990), 61 *Colorado Law Review* 795.

A number of legal scholars have suggested that common law principles may be applied by judges in ways that reflect prevailing political and economic ideas. In relation to the law of nuisance in the United States, for example, Morton Horowitz examined two interpretations of 18th century legal principles concerning the use of property. He described one as "an explicitly antidevelopmental theory" that limited property owners to what courts regarded as the "natural" (mainly agricultural) use of land, a principle reflected in the maxim "*sic utere tuo*" in nuisance law referred to in *Victoria Park*. In addition, courts also developed a theory of property rights based on "priority of development"—that is, that someone with a prior developmental right (who had "developed" the land for industrial purposes) could arrest a future conflicting use on the part of an adjoining owner. By the 19th century, the potential for conflict between these principles began to surface and, in general, priority of development became "the dominant doctrine of property law in the early stages of American growth." Rejecting a Machiavellian explanation for this choice, however, Horowitz suggested that the judges were

> simply guided by the conception of efficiency prevailing at the moment. Practical men, they may never have stopped to reflect on the changes they were bringing about, nor on the vast differences between their own assumptions and those of their predecessors.

(Morton Horowitz, *The Transformation of American Law, 1780-1860* (Cambridge, MA: Harvard University Press, 1977), at 34.)

To what extent can a case-by-case approach to decision making take account of the need to develop broader principles applicable to a wide range of facts? Is it possible to distinguish in advance those cases that have broader implications? Should such cases be decided using different processes, different kinds of evidence?

Private Property, Common Property, and State Property

In *Victoria Park*, the plaintiff also claimed that by the expenditure of money he had created a spectacle that constituted "quasi-property." Latham CJ did not accept this argument. Examine his reasoning using the analysis of property as a relationship among persons (subjects) in respect of things (objects). Using this analysis, is it possible to find that there is property in a spectacle? Why or why not? How important was it that the "property" in question was intangible rather than tangible? Are there intangible forms of property? Should the expenditure of money lead to a conclusion that the interest was one of property? Does this mean that, in some circumstances, something that has value may not be considered property and fall outside the law's protection? What was the practical impact of the court's conclusion that the plaintiff's actions in this case did not create "property"?

According to Gray, *Victoria Park* offers "a rare opportunity to learn something of the tacit rules which govern the propertisation of resources." As he explains, if something is not an object of private property, then it must be "common property," and thus available to all. By contrast, if something is private property, the "owner" may exclude others from its enjoyment. By concluding that the plaintiff's spectacle was not his private property, the court in *Victoria Park* left the plaintiff without legal protection—in this way, the racecourse appeared to become common property. See Gray, "Property in Thin Air" (1991), 50 *Cambridge Law Journal* 252, at 268ff.

C.B. Macpherson described the distinction between private property and common property. According to him, private property means that there is an individual (or a corporate entity) that is the subject of the property relationship. By contrast, the concept of common property creates an entitlement for individuals, enforced by the state, so that all individuals are subjects of the property interest and no one is excluded. For Macpherson, common property could be enjoyed only by natural persons, not by corporations or the state. Does this description accord with the plaintiff's racecourse in *Victoria Park*? See C.B. Macpherson, "The Meaning of Property," in Macpherson, 1, at 4ff.

Using Macpherson's categories, how should we characterize the east coast fishery in Canada, a public park at the edge of Georgian Bay, or the rail lines abandoned by VIA Rail? In thinking about these issues, consider the following comments made about the fishery some years ago by Wallace Clement in *Class, Power and Property: Essays on Canadian Society* (Toronto: Methuen, 1983), at 215:

> As far as rights of access to fish, the sea has been transformed from common to private
> property for the most part. The state excludes some from the use or benefit of the
> products of the sea, not simply regulating its use (as can be the case with common

property). The licences themselves, which are "tickets" to the amount of fish which may be gathered, the species, time and location, take on a value of their own. They become private property—the state grants the rights, individuals (or corporations) have the rights, and in the case of some fishing rights, these can be sold as private property. An important illustration of the state creating private property out of common property occurred in the initial stages of colonization in North America when the bulk of the land was alienated from the native people and turned into private property, often given over to corporations such as the Hudson's Bay Company.

Is Clement's analysis the same as that of C.B. Macpherson? What aspects of "private" property became "common" property in *Victoria Park*? See also A. Bartholomew and S. Boyd, "Toward a Political Economy of Law," in W. Clement and G. Williams, eds., *The New Canadian Political Economy* (Kingston, ON: McGill-Queen's University Press, 1989), at 212. For an account of the history of the "commons" in England, see J. Neeson, *Commoners: Common Right, Enclosure, and Social Change in England 1700-1820* (New York: Cambridge University Press, 1993).

For another analysis of ideas about common property, see Carol Rose, "The Comedy of the Commons: Custom, Commerce, and Inherently Public Property," in Rose, 105; responding to Garrett Hardin, "The Tragedy of the Commons" (1968), 162 *Science* 1243. Rose examined (at 106) the classic economic argument that "the whole world of valuable things is best managed when divided among private property owners." In the absence of such a private property regime, the economic result is "the tragedy of the commons":

> When things are left open to the public, it is said, they are wasted, either by overuse or under investment. No one wishes to care for things that may be taken away tomorrow, and no one knows whom to approach to make exchanges. All resort to snatching up what is available for "capture" today, leaving behind a wasteland—thus the tragedy. From this perspective, "public property" is an oxymoron: things left open to the public are not property at all but rather its antithesis.

By contrast with this analysis, Rose examined the ways in which public access to common property—for example, roads and waterways—increased its value economically by fostering commerce. She also noted how common property in recreational parks was promoted in the 19th century by Frederick Law Olmsted as "a socializing influence and an education in democratic values." In *Higginson v. Treasury*, 99 NE 523 (MA Sup. Jud. Ct. 1912), the court asserted that parks are a public good because they "civilize" people living in urban congestion. (A good account of the history of Olmsted's views is found in Geoffrey Blodgett, "Frederick Law Olmsted: Landscape Architecture as Conservative Reform" (1976), 62 *Journal of American History* 869.) In the 20th century, parks are often owned by the government, so that they represent a third category of property: state property. According to C.B. Macpherson, state property is similar to private property because the state may grant or withhold access to it. How then does "state property" differ from "common property"?

According to Rose (at 110-12) (footnotes omitted), there are categories of private property rights and property held (and managed) by government. In addition, she asserted that both English and American law historically recognized "public property." This category included government-held property and, in addition, "property collectively 'owned' by society at large, with claims independent of and indeed superior to the claims of any purported governmental manager."

Thus it appears that older public property doctrine vested some form of property rights in the *un*organized public. But what could it mean for the unorganized public to have "rights" in any property at all? How could its members possibly assert their rights except through a governmental body? And even if they could do so, how could the unorganized public be thought the best property manager, or even a manager at all? Property in such a public would amount to an unlimited commons, which seems not to be property at all but at best only a mass of passive "things" awaiting reduction to private property through the rule of capture—and this, of course, is the situation that leads not to good management of resources but rather to their squandering, in the dreaded tragedy of the commons. Nevertheless, strange though it seems, precisely this unorganized version of the "public" is strongly suggested in some of the earlier public property doctrine—as it is in some modern law as well. ...

In America the chief doctrinal support for public property came in the form of "public trust" in waterways and "prescription" for roadways. I will call these the "strong" doctrines, since they were so much more prevalent than a third, "weak" doctrine of custom. Still, this weak doctrine of custom turns out to be singularly informative. Although custom only appeared from time to time in the older cases, and then very tentatively, it nevertheless provides some powerful insights into the questions of just who the public was thought to be, and in the reasons why some property seemed to be thought public by its very nature.

As will appear below, commercial travel was a central factor behind the presumption that certain property—notably roadways and waterways—were to be open to the public. When used for commerce, these properties had qualities akin to infinite returns to scale, because commerce becomes ever more valuable as it expands to larger numbers of persons. Thus here, the commons was not tragic at all but comedic, in the classical sense of a story with a happy outcome—the more people engaged, the better off we all become. What is more interesting, however, is the point that customary doctrines also suggest something else about commerce: that it might be thought a "comedy of the commons" not only by its infinite capacity to expand our wealth but also by its propensity, at least in part, to make us more sociable and better attuned to each other's needs and interests. ...

[In] the twentieth century there may be other versions of the comedy of the commons and other practices, aside from commerce, that have the power to enhance our sociability. We might even think that properties devoted to such noncommercial uses as recreation or speech could have these qualities and thus might reach their highest value where they are accessible to the public at large—that is, where we envision the commons not as wasteful tragedy but as happy and productive comedy.

Do these arguments explain the majority view in *Victoria Park*—that is, that making the racecourse "common property" would "enhance ... sociability [by being] accessible to the public at large"? What action would you expect the plaintiff to take after the court's decision? Is the racecourse different from roadways or waterways?

The Right to Privacy

Another argument presented unsuccessfully by the plaintiff in *Victoria Park* was that the defendants' actions had interfered with a right of privacy on the part of the plaintiff. In his dissenting judgment, Evatt J pointed to cases that had decided that "systematic watching" on the part of trade union activists who were picketing an employer (without trespassing on the employer's property) constituted nuisance (*Ward Locke & Co. (Ltd.) v. Operative Printers' Assistants' Society* (1906), 22 TLR 327 (CA)). He then concluded that it was "erroneous to assume that under no circumstances can systematic watching amount to a civil wrong." Evatt J was a well-known labour lawyer in Australia prior to his appointment to the High Court. What is the significance of his use of these precedents in this case?

For a classic argument about the need for a tort of invasion of privacy in the American common law, see Warren and Brandeis, "The Right to Privacy" (1890), 4 *Harvard Law Review* 193. Arguably, such a right has also received some qualified recognition in England: see *Duchess of Argyll v. Duke of Argyll*, [1967] Ch. 302 (Ch.D). There are also cases where issues of the tort of "passing off" or breach of copyright have been raised— for example, see *J Bollinger v. Costa Brava Wines Co Ltd*, [1960] Ch. 262 (Ch.D) (concerning a claim for an injunction on the part of wine producers from the Champagne district in France to prevent Spanish wine producers from marketing their product as "champagne" or "Spanish champagne"). Similarly, in *Desny v. Wilder*, 299 P2d 257 (Calif. Sup. Ct. 1956), the plaintiff alleged an interference with property rights in relation to a plot synopsis used by a director, Billy Wilder, for a film. Should the plaintiff recover?

The Role of Precedent

All of these arguments—the principles of nuisance, whether or not the spectacle was property, and the right to privacy—were considered by the justices in *Victoria Park* in relation to the common law doctrine of precedent. The role of precedent is fundamental to judicial reasoning in the common law and is the subject of much debate in practice, even though the principle is relatively straightforward—like cases should be treated alike in subsequent decisions. As is evident in *Victoria Park*, however, there is little agreement about what approach to take when there is no precedent because the issue has not been considered before.

At several points in his judgment, Latham CJ stated that there was no precedent applicable to the facts in *Victoria Park*: "No analogous case has been cited to the court"; "The court has not been referred to any principle of law which prevents any man from describing anything which he sees"; or "No authority has been cited to support such a proposition." As is evident from his conclusion, the absence of precedent precluded a finding in favour of the plaintiff's claim. By contrast, Rich J stated clearly: "It does not follow that because no precedent can be found a principle does not exist to support the plaintiff's right," and proceeded to provide a remedy to the plaintiff.

These two approaches demonstrate clearly diametrically opposite approaches to judicial decision making. When there is no applicable precedent, some judges conclude that there is no legal remedy available while others decide that the case must be decided on the basis of general principles, such as fairness or equity. Similarly, while judges are required to apply previous decisions as precedents, they may distinguish them (for a variety of reasons) and "make new law." An Australian academic commentator has explained these differing approaches in this way:

> The work of English courts from the medieval period onwards represents a great achievement in legislation by reference to the changing facts of social life as seen in the actual behaviour of associations of men [sic] for the time being. And this proceeds not by means of, but rather in spite of, the apparent reliance on existing legal conceptions and propositions and on deductions from them ... . [The use of precedents] helps to keep alive such important legal ideals as certainty, stability, uniformity and order ... . [These two aspects of law] should leave us not with the cynical jibe that the law *speaks one way and acts another*, but with the conundrum how the law can *simultaneously act in two such mutually inconsistent ways*.

(Julius Stone, *Legal System and Lawyers' Reasonings* (Stanford, CA: Stanford University Press, 1964), at 231.) See also Julius Stone, *Precedent and Law: Dynamics of Common Law Growth* (Sydney: Butterworths, 1985).

These issues have been considered by many other legal scholars. In the United States, for example, Margaret Jane Radin has considered similar arguments about precedent in relation to "facts," concluding that there is great flexibility in the process of deciding what are "the facts" of a case:

> Many beginning law students assume that there is a world of hard facts out there waiting to be observed. Especially for the naive legal positivist, hard facts are needed to plug into the formalist equation: Rules + Facts = Decision. In the formalist equation, both rules and facts must be found objects, not malleable creations dependent upon who is observing them and the process of observation. ...
>
> Lawyers need to know [by contrast] that perception is an active process, always dependent upon the person doing the perceiving and the social construction of the context in which she [sic] perceives. Perception depends upon [pre]conception. We tend to see what will make sense to us in light of our conceptions and in light of what we expect to see. Perception can also depend upon educational and class background, one's job or profession, and much else.

(Margaret Jane Radin, " 'After the Final No There Comes a Yes': A Law Teacher's Report" (1990), 2 *Yale Journal of Law and the Humanities* 252, at 259.) See also Peter Gabel, "Reification in Legal Reasoning," in James Boyle, ed., *Critical Legal Studies* (New York: New York University Press, 1994).

Frame Shifting: Explaining Different Approaches?

Some scholars have approached these issues about judicial decision making to suggest a need for reform. For example, Jennifer Jaff started from the perspective of first year law students who have begun to notice that "when two judges write a majority and a dissent in a case, although both have looked at the same factual situation and the same progression of inquiry or line of precedent, each has reached a different conclusion" [like the justices in *Victoria Park*]. See Jennifer Jaff, "Frame-Shifting: An Empowering Methodology for Teaching and Learning Legal Reasoning" (1986), 36 *Journal of Legal Education* 249, at 251.

According to Jaff, this result occurs because judges shift their frame of reference from broad to narrow, or from narrow to broad, to construct rationales that justify differing results. Thus, for example, in a criminal law context, one judge may determine the issue of voluntariness of a confession by focusing on the state of mind of the accused at the moment in question, while another will assess the issue of voluntariness by looking at the broader context of the accused's sociological condition, and the extent to which it may affect the accused's ability to take action voluntarily. According to Jaff (at 262), this frame shifting is an important part of legal reasoning, and one that can empower students:

> Frame-shifting is an attempt to systematize the thought-processes that lawyers and judges use almost unconsciously. It is a product of self-conscious thinking about thinking that requires a precise identification of the goal we have in mind, the knowledge we seek to gain and to convey, as well as an identification of the starting point of our inquiries and of all of the steps in between our first questions and our conclusions. As such, it shows students how to think for themselves. Thus frame-shifting is an empowering pedagogy, for it not only provides students with knowledge; it also provides them with a method, a way to gain access to knowledge for themselves.

In addition to these benefits, Jaff recommended (at 263) frame shifting for students as a way of coming to terms with the legal process as one that embodies the aspirations and desires of different kinds of people:

> I want students to see this process as more than a game of logic: they must come to see it as a way of articulating the needs and desires of real people. To do this, they must be shown the legitimacy, even the relevance, of their own personal concerns and those of litigants.

In considering these goals, Jaff focused (at 265) (footnotes omitted) on Carol Gilligan's research on complementary "male" and female" perspectives on ethics in human development, and particularly on the disparate approaches of Amy and Jake, two 11-year-olds:

> Gilligan asked two children in the same sixth-grade class at school, Amy and Jake, to resolve a classic moral dilemma: "[A] man named Heinz considers whether or not to steal a drug which he cannot afford to buy in order to save the life of his wife." Jake "discerns the logical priority of life and uses that logic to justify his choice" that Heinz should steal the drug:
>
> > For one thing, a human life is worth more than money, and if the druggist only makes $1,000, he is still going to live, but if Heinz doesn't steal the drug, his wife is going to die. ... [T]he druggist can get a thousand dollars later from rich people with cancer, but Heinz can't get his wife again.

Jake's reasoning sounds not unlike the weighing of interests that courts engage in to determine the nature and extent of procedural due process. Both analyses involve a balancing of the values of property and life.

Amy, on the other hand, in deciding that Heinz should not steal the drug, "considers neither property nor law but rather the effect that theft could have on the relationship between Heinz and his wife":

> If he stole the drug, he might save his wife then, but if he did, he might have to go to jail, and then his wife might get sicker again, and he couldn't get more of the drug, and it might not be good. So, they should really just talk it out and find some other way to make the money.

Amy sees "a world comprised of relationships rather than of people standing alone, a world that coheres through human connection rather than through systems of rules." It remains, then, to translate this focus into legal analysis. ...

Law teachers must begin to recognize that such a position is not necessarily naive or irrelevant. It involves a choice, a voluntary decision to favor the personal over the institutional. It may, therefore, be inefficient in economic terms, or impractical in organizational terms; however, it may reflect an educated and conscious choice to subordinate those terms to something that is judged more important: how people feel.

It is also important that the teacher take care to ensure that frame-shifting does not itself lead to domination, albeit of a different form than that inherent in the Socratic method. Teaching students how to do legal reasoning may facilitate their ability to dominate their clients. A truly empowering methodology would teach not only empowerment of students, but also empowerment of all persons, including clients. To this end, the teacher must sensitize the student to the necessity of being as explicit with clients as the teacher is with students. If students as lawyers understand and appreciate the client's need to know how we get from point A to point B through frame-shifting, they will be more explicit with their clients, thus empowering them.

A truly empowering pedagogy would do more than be explicit; it would also integrate a personal, relational perspective into traditional legal analysis. Frame-shifting "in a different voice" helps to teach legal reasoning in a truly productive—that is, empowering—way. An integrated and explicit pedagogy is necessary for producing integrated and empowered lawyers and people.

See also Carol Gilligan, *In a Different Voice: Psychological Theory and Women's Development* (Cambridge, MA: Harvard University Press, 1982). Gilligan's work has been influential in legal literature about legal dispute resolution generally—for example, see Carrie Menkel-Meadow, "Portia in a Different Voice: Speculations on a Woman's Lawyering Process" (1985), 1 *Berkeley Women's Law Journal* 39. For another approach to women's status in legal bargaining, see Carol Rose, "Women and Property: Gaining and Losing Ground" (1992), 78:2 *Virginia Law Review* 421. For an argument applying Gilligan's analysis to claims of property in relation to the "information highway," see Shelley Wright, "Property, Information and the Ethics of Communication" (1994), 9 *Intellectual Property Journal* 47.

To what extent do Jaff's comments help to explain the differences between the majority and dissenting judgments in *Victoria Park*? Is there a difference in the extent to which "connections" between the parties are taken into account? What are the implications of Gilligan's work for legal processes?

International News Service v. Associated Press

In the *Victoria Park* case, decided in Australia in 1937, Dixon J referred to a decision of the US Supreme Court in 1918 that raised similar issues. (Such a case is considered "persuasive," but not "binding" in terms of precedent because it is from another jurisdiction.) In *International News Service v. Associated Press*, 248 US 215 (1918), the plaintiff Associated Press (AP) sought an injunction to restrain certain activities on the part of its competitor in the news-gathering business, International News Service (INS). The case was complicated and controversial in the context of news reports during World War I, especially since people relied on newspapers almost exclusively for information in the absence of radio and television. The owner of Associated Press, Melville Stone, wished to try to establish the concept of "property in news," and sued in part to prevent International News Service's practice of "copying" news from early editions of AP newspapers on the eastern seaboard of the United States and then selling it to customers of International News Service on the west coast (taking advantage of the difference in time zones, of course).

In general, the Supreme Court agreed to enjoin International News Service to some extent in relation to its practices, although there was no agreement that there was "property in the news," even though labour and money had been expended to create it. Brandeis J dissented (and his decision was relied on by Dixon in *Victoria Park*). His comments (at 250) about the nature of property, as well as the role of courts in defining new kinds of property interests, remain relevant:

> An essential element of individual property is the legal right to exclude others from enjoying it. If the property is private, the right of exclusion may be absolute; if the property is affected with a public interest, the right of exclusion is qualified. But the fact that a product of the mind has cost its producer money and labor, and has a value for which others are willing to pay, is not sufficient to ensure to it this legal attribute of property. The general rule of law is, that the noblest of human productions—knowledge, truths ascertained, conceptions, and ideas—become, after voluntary communication to others, free as the air to common use. Upon these incorporeal productions the attribute of property is continued after such communication only in certain classes of cases where public policy has seemed to demand it. These exceptions are confined to productions which, in some degree, involve creation, invention, or discovery. But by no means all such are endowed with this attribute of property. The creations which are recognized as property by the common law are literary, dramatic, musical, and other artistic creations; and these have also protection under the copyright statutes. The inventions and discoveries upon which this attribute of property is conferred only by statute, are the few comprised within the patent law. There are also many other cases in which courts interfere to prevent curtailment of plaintiff's enjoyment of incorporeal productions; and in which the right to relief is often called a property right, but is such only in a special sense. In those cases, the plaintiff has no absolute right to the protection of his production; he has merely the qualified right to be protected as against the defendant's acts, because of the special relation in which the latter stands or the wrongful method or

means employed in acquiring the knowledge or the manner in which it is used. Protection of this character is afforded where the suit is based upon breach of contract or of trust or upon unfair competition.

The knowledge for which protection is sought in the case at bar is not of a kind upon which the law has heretofore conferred the attributes of property; nor is the manner of its acquisition or use nor the purpose to which it is applied, such as has heretofore been recognized as entitling a plaintiff to relief. ...

The great development of agencies now furnishing country-wide distribution of news, the vastness of our territory, and improvements in the means of transmitting intelligence, have made it possible for a news agency or newspapers to obtain, without paying compensation, the fruit of another's efforts and to use news so obtained gainfully in competition with the original collector. The injustice of such action is obvious. But to give relief against it would involve more than the application of existing rules of law to new facts. It would require the making of a new rule in analogy to existing ones. The unwritten law possesses capacity for growth; and has often satisfied new demands for justice by invoking analogies or by expanding a rule or principle. This process has been in the main wisely applied and should not be discontinued. Where the problem is relatively simple, as it is apt to be when private interests only are involved, it generally proves adequate. But with the increasing complexity of society, the public interest tends to become omnipresent; and the problems presented by new demands for justice cease to be simple. Then the creation or recognition by courts of a new private right may work serious injury to the general public, unless the boundaries of the right are definitely established and wisely guarded. In order to reconcile the new private right with the public interest, it may be necessary to prescribe limitations and rules for its enjoyment; and also to provide administrative machinery for enforcing the rules. It is largely for this reason that, in the effort to meet the many new demands for justice incident to a rapidly changing civilization, resort to legislation has latterly been had with increasing frequency.

The rule for which the plaintiff contends would effect an important extension of property rights and a corresponding curtailment of the free use of knowledge and of ideas; and the facts of this case admonish us of the danger involved in recognizing such a property right in news, without imposing upon news-gatherers corresponding obligations. A large majority of the newspapers and perhaps half the newspaper readers of the United States are dependent for their news of general interest upon agencies other than the Associated Press. The channel through which about 400 of these papers received, as the plaintiff alleges, "a large amount of news relating to the European war of the greatest importance and of intense interest to the newspaper reading public" was suddenly closed. The closing to the International News Service of these channels for foreign news (if they were closed) was due not to unwillingness on its part to pay the cost of collecting the news, but to the prohibitions imposed by foreign governments upon its securing news from their respective countries and from using cable or telegraph lines running therefrom. For aught that appears, this prohibition may have been wholly undeserved; and at all events the 400 papers and their readers may be assumed to have been innocent. For aught that appears, the International News Service may have sought then to secure temporarily by arrangement with the Associated Press the latter's foreign news service. For aught that appears, all of the 400 subscribers of the International News Service would gladly have then become members of the Associated Press, if they could have secured election thereto. It is possible, also, that a large part of the readers of these papers were so situated that they could not secure prompt access to papers served by the Associated Press. The prohibition of the foreign governments might as well have been extended to the channels through which news was supplied to the more than a thousand other daily papers in the United States not served by the Associated Press; and a large part of their readers may also be so located that they can not procure prompt access to papers served by the Associated Press.

A Legislature, urged to enact a law by which one news agency or newspaper may prevent appropriation of the fruits of its labors by another, would consider such facts and possibilities and others which appropriate enquiry might disclose. Legislators might conclude that it was impossible to put an end to the obvious injustice involved in such appropriation of news, without opening the door to other evils, greater than that sought to be remedied. Such appears to have been the opinion of our Senate which reported unfavorably a bill to give news a few hours' protection; and which ratified, on February 15, 1911, the convention adopted at the Fourth International American Conference; and such was evidently the view also of the signatories to the International Copyright Union of November 13, 1908; as both these conventions expressly exclude news from copyright protection.

Or legislators dealing with the subject might conclude, that the right to news values should be protected to the extent of permitting recovery of damages for any unauthorized use, but that protection by injunction should be denied, just as courts of equity ordinarily refuse (perhaps in the interest of free speech) to restrain actionable libels, and for other reasons decline to protect by injunction mere political rights; and as Congress has prohibited courts from enjoining the illegal assessment or collection of federal taxes. If a legislature concluded to recognize property in published news to the extent of permitting recovery at law, it might, with a view to making the remedy more certain and adequate, provide a fixed measure of damages, as in the case of copyright infringement.

Or again, a legislature might conclude that it was unwise to recognize even so limited a property right in published news as that above indicated; but that a news agency should, on some conditions, be given full protection of its business; and to that end a remedy by injunction as well as one for damages should be granted, where news collected by it is gainfully used without permission. If a legislature concluded, (as at least one court has held, *New York & Chicago Grain & Stock Exchange v. Board of Trade*, 127 Illinois, 153) that under certain circumstances news-gathering is a business affected with a public interest, it might declare that, in such cases, news should be protected against appropriation, only if the gatherer assumed the obligation of supplying it, at reasonable rates and without discrimination, to all papers which applied therefor. If legislators reached that conclusion, they would probably go further, and prescribe the conditions under which and the extent to which the protection should be afforded; and they might also provide the administrative machinery necessary for ensuring to the public, the press, and the news agencies, full enjoyment of the rights so conferred.

Courts are ill-equipped to make the investigations which should precede a determination of the limitations which should be set upon any property right in news or of the circumstances under which news gathered by a private agency should be deemed affected with a public interest. Courts would be powerless to prescribe the detailed regulations essential to full enjoyment of the rights conferred or to introduce the machinery required for enforcement of such regulations. Considerations such as these should lead us to decline to establish a new rule of law in the effort to redress a newly-disclosed wrong, although the propriety of some remedy appears to be clear.

Do you agree with Brandeis J that it is more appropriate for legislatures to create new property, and that judges are not well-placed to consider such claims? What are the factors that were taken into account by Brandeis J in reaching his conclusion? Are there other relevant factors that should be considered by judges in such cases? How should courts balance the need for stability and certainty on the one hand with the need to do justice in appropriate cases on the other?

Broadcasting is a matter that is now generally regulated in both Australia and Canada by legislation. In Australia, see Broadcasting and Television Act, 1942 (Cth); in Canada, see Canadian Radio-Television and Telecommunications Commission Act RSC 1985, c. C-22. Does the existence of legislation show that Dixon and Brandeis were right to conclude that the courts should not provide a remedy in *Victoria Park* and in *International News Service v. Associated Press*? As a practical matter, if a litigant applies to a court for a remedy for which there is no existing precedent and is successful, who should pay the costs of the application?

For an excellent analysis of the historical context of *International News Service v. Associated Press*, see Richard Chused, *Cases, Materials and Problems in Property* (New York: Matthew Bender, 1988), at 2ff. An interesting philosophical comparison of *Victoria Park* and *International News Service* is found in S. Coval, J.C. Smith, and Simon Coval, "The Foundations of Property and Property Law" (1986), 45 *Cambridge Law Journal* 457. A classic discussion of the nature of private property is found in S. Felix Cohen, "Dialogue on Private Property" (1954), 9:2 *Rutgers Law Review* 357. More generally, for an overview of philosophical approaches to property, see Ziff, chapter 1, and the collection of essays in C.B. Macpherson.

THE RIGHT TO EXCLUDE OTHERS

Harrison v. Carswell
[1976] 2 SCR 200

[The idea of private property involves the right to exclude others, as was evident in the competing arguments presented in *Victoria Park*. By contrast, common property is property to which all individuals have access. The post-war development of shopping malls in Canada has resulted in an ongoing legal debate about whether these malls are private property since they are "owned" by private corporations, or whether they are the modern equivalent of the "market place"—common property to which all should have access. These issues have been particularly controversial in relation to the actions of picketers, often in conjunction with labour union activity, demonstrating against the employers of individual shops in a mall. In these cases, the issue is the extent to which the owner of the shopping mall can exclude or control picketing and other labour union activity, having regard to legislation such as Ontario's Labour Relations Act, 1995, SO 1995, c. 1.

These issues were addressed in *Harrison v. Carswell*, which follows. In the Supreme Court of Canada, the judges' decisions also considered the relevance of an earlier case, *R v. Peters* (1971), 17 DLR (3d) 128, in relation to the doctrine of precedent. Examine the differing approaches to ideas about private and common property in this case, by contrast with *Victoria Park*.]

Appeal by the prosecutor from the decision of the Court of Appeal for Manitoba 17 CCC (2d) 521, 48 DLR (3d) 137, [1974] 4 WWR 394, setting aside the accused's conviction under the *Petty Trespasses Act* (Man.).

DICKSON J: The respondent, Sophie Carswell, was charged under the *Petty Trespasses Act*, RSM 1970, c. P-50, with four offences (one on each of four days) of unlawfully trespassing upon the premises of the Fairview Corporation Limited, trading under the firm name and style of Polo Park Shopping Centre, located in the City of Winnipeg, after having been requested by the owner not to enter on or come upon the premises. The appellant, Peter Harrison, manager of Polo Park Shopping Centre, swore the information. The charges were dismissed by the Provincial Judge, but on a trial *de novo* in the County Court, Mrs. Carswell was convicted and fined $10 on each of the charges. The convictions were set aside by the Manitoba Court of Appeal (Freedman CJM and Matas JA, with Guy JA, dissenting) [(1974), 17 CCC (2d) 521; 48 DLR (3d) 137; 4 WWR 394] and the present appeal followed, by leave of this Court.

With great respect, I am unable to agree with the majority reasons, delivered in the Court of Appeal by Chief Justice Freedman, for I find it difficult, indeed impossible, to make any well-founded distinction between this case and *R v. Peters* (1971), 17 DLR (3d) 128, decided by this Court four years ago in a unanimous decision of the full Bench. The constitutional issue raised in *Peters* no longer concerns us; the only other issue was whether the owner of a shopping plaza had sufficient control or possession of the common areas, having regard to the unrestricted invitation to the public to enter upon the premises, as to enable it to invoke the remedy of trespass. The Court decided it did. That case and the present case came to us on much the same facts, picketing within a shopping centre in connection with a labour dispute. In *Peters*, the picketing was carried out by the president of the Brampton Labour Council and seven other persons, carrying placards and distributing leaflets in front of a Safeway store, seeking a boycott of Safeway for selling California grapes. In the present case, the picketing was carried out by Mrs. Carswell and 11 other persons, carrying placards and distributing leaflets, in front of the premises of their employer, Dominion Stores. In both instances the picketing was peaceful. Although the question posed in *Peters* did not recite the facts upon which the case rested, the question was worded thus:

Did the learned Judges in appeal err in law in determining that *the* owner of *the* property had sufficient possession of *the* shopping plaza sidewalk to be capable of availing itself of the remedy for trespass under the Petty Trespass Act, RSO 1960, Chapter 294, Section 1(1)?

(italics are my own) and in my view is so expressed, with repeated use of the definite article, as to relate the question to the circumstances in respect of which the Judges made their determination.

The judgment of the Ontario Court of Appeal in *R v. Peters* (1970), 2 CCC (2d) 336, 16 DLR (3d) 143, [1971] 1 OR 597, was delivered by Chief Justice Gale who said, at p. 338 CCC, p. 146 DLR:

> With respect to the first ground of appeal, it is our opinion that an owner who has granted a right of entry to a particular class of the public has not thereby relinquished his or its right to withdraw its invitation to the general public or any particular member thereof, and that if a member of the public whose invitation to enter has been withdrawn refuses to leave, he thereby becomes a trespasser and may be prosecuted under the *Petty Trespass Act*. Here, the invitation extended by the owner was of a general nature and included tenants, employees, agents and all persons having or seeking business relations with the tenants. However, notwithstanding the general nature of the invitation, the owner did not thereby lose its right to withdraw the invitation from the general public or any particular member thereof. In addition, it is also our view with respect to trespass that possession does not cease to be exclusive so long as there is the right to control entry of the general public, and here the owner had not relinquished that right of control.

The brief judgment in this Court, answering in the negative the question asked, neither adopted nor repudiated the reasons delivered in the Court of Appeal, but it should not be overlooked that when the *Peters* case was before the Ontario Court of Appeal, counsel for Peters relied upon the decision of the Court of Appeal for Saskatchewan in *Grosvenor Park Shopping Centre Ltd. v. Waloshin et al.* (1964), 46 DLR (2d) 750, 49 WWR 237. That case arose out of injunction proceedings during a strike of employees of Loblaw Groceries Co. Ltd., in Saskatoon, who were picketing with placards on the sidewalk adjacent to store premises located in a shopping centre. The pertinent part of the judgment of the Saskatchewan Court of Appeal reads [at p. 755]:

> Learned counsel for the appellant argued that the respondent did not have that degree of possession essential to an action in trespass.
>
>   The area upon which it is alleged the appellants have trespassed is part of what is well known as a shopping centre. While legal title to the area is in the respondent, it admits in its pleadings that it has granted easements to the many tenants. The evidence also establishes that the respondent has extended an unrestricted invitation to the public to enter upon the premises. The very nature of the operation is one in which the respondent, both in its own interests and in the interests of its tenants, could not do otherwise. Under the circumstances, it cannot be said that the respondent is in actual possession. The most that can be said is that the respondent exercises control over the premises but does not exercise that control to the exclusion of other persons. For that reason, therefore, the respondent cannot maintain an action in trespass against the appellants: *vide* 38 Hals., 3d ed., p. 743, para. 1212. Support, too, for this view may be found in *Zeller's (Western) Ltd. v. Retail Food & Drug Clerks Union, Local 1518* (1963), 42 DLR (2d) 582, 45 WWR 337.

Chief Justice Gale, in *Peters*, offered this observation with respect to *Grosvenor Park* [(1970), at 338-39 CCC; 146 DLR]:

> The solicitor for the appellant relied very heavily upon a decision of the Court of Appeal for Saskatchewan in *Grosvenor Park Shopping Centre Ltd. v. Waloshin et al.* (1964), 46 DLR (2d) 750, 49 WWR 237. If our view in this appeal does not harmonize with the reasoning of the Court in the *Grosvenor Park* case, we must respectfully disagree with that reasoning.

So when the *Peters* case came to this Court for consideration, the Court had before it the reasoning of the Court of Appeal for Ontario in that case and the reasoning, difficult to reconcile, of the Court of Appeal for Saskatchewan in *Grosvenor Park*; the reasoning of the Ontario Court prevailed. There has been no suggestion that *Peters* was wrongly decided; therefore, I would think it must be regarded as controlling unless it can properly be distinguished from the case at bar. No distinction can be made on the ground of contract; there is a copy of the lease from Fairview to Dominion Stores, among the papers, but it would not appear, nor has it been argued, that any distinction can rest on that document. As to a possible statutory distinction, the petty trespass acts of Manitoba and Ontario do not differ in any material respect and indeed s. 24 of the *Labour Relations Act*, 1972 (Man.), c. 75 (continuing consolidation, c. L10), specifically preserves rights against trespassers. Therefore it would seem the appeal must succeed unless a valid distinction can be drawn on the ground that the president of the Brampton Labour Council, in *Peters*, was a mere member of the general public from whom permission to remain on the premises could be withdrawn at will, whereas Mrs. Carswell was an employee of one of the tenants of the shopping centre on strike in support of a current labour dispute, from whom permission to remain on the premises could not, as a matter of law, be withdrawn. I find myself unable to accept that any ground in law supports such a distinction.

The evidence discloses that distribution of pamphlets or leaflets in the mall of Polo Park Shopping Centre or on the parking lot, has never been permitted by the management of the centre and that this prohibition has extended to tenants of the centre. The centre as a matter of policy has not permitted any person to walk in the mall carrying placards. There is nothing in the evidence supporting the view that in the present case the owner of the centre was acting out of caprice or whimsy or *mala fides*. In a comment entitled *Labour Law—Picketing in Shopping Centres*, 43 *Can. Bar Rev.* 357 at p. 362 (1965), H.W. Arthurs referred to the following as one of the legitimate concerns of the landlord of a shopping centre:

> … while public authorities may, on behalf of the community, strike a reasonable balance between traffic and picketing on public sidewalks and streets, the shopping centre owner can hardly be expected to make such a choice: he has no authority to speak for the community; to grant picketing or parading privileges to all would invite chaos, while to do so selectively would invite commercial reprisals. He is thus driven to adopt a highly restrictive approach to granting permission to groups who wish to parade or picket in the shopping centre.

It is urged on behalf of Mrs. Carswell that the right of a person to picket peacefully in support of a lawful strike is of greater social significance than the proprietary rights of an owner of a shopping centre, and that the rights of the owner must yield to those of the picketer. The American example has been cited, but I cannot say that I find the American cases to which we have been referred of great help. The facts in *Schwartz-Torrance Investment Corp. v. Bakery and Confectionery Workers' Union, Local 31* (1964), 394 P2d 921, decided by the Supreme Court of California are almost identical with those in *Grosvenor Park*, but I think it not unimportant to note that in *Schwartz-Torrance*, Justice Tobriner, early in his judgment, drew attention to the fact that the Legislature of the State of California had expressly declared that the public policy of the State favoured concerted activities of employees for the purpose of collective bargaining and had enacted the policy into an exception to the criminal trespass law. Construing that exception, the California Supreme Court in a case antedating *Schwartz-Torrance* had concluded that the Legislature, in dealing with trespasses, had specifically subordinated the rights of the property owner to those of persons engaged in lawful labour activities. *Schwartz-Torrance* is, therefore, of small aid in this case and indeed can be said to support, in a negative sense, a position inimical to that of Mrs. Carswell. And one need only read *Amalgamated Food Employees' Union, Local 590 v. Logan Valley Plaza Inc.* (1968), 391 US 308, and then read *Lloyd Corp. Ltd. v. Tanner* (1972), 407 US 551, to apprehend the uncertainties and very real difficulties which emerge when a Court essays to legislate as to what is and what is not a permissible activity within a shopping centre.

The submission that this Court should weigh and determine the respective values to society of the right to property and the right to picket raises important and difficult political and socio-economic issues, the resolution of which must, by their very nature, be arbitrary and embody personal economic and social beliefs. It raises also fundamental questions as to the role of this Court under the Canadian Constitution. The duty of the Court, as I envisage it, is to proceed in the discharge of its adjudicative function in a reasoned way from principled decision and established concepts. I do not for a moment doubt the power of the Court to act creatively—it has done so on countless occasions; but manifestly one must ask—what are the limits of the judicial function? There are many and varied answers to this question. Holmes J said in *Southern Pacific Co. v. Jensen* (1917), 244 US 205 at p. 221: "I recognize without hesitation that judges do and must legislate, but they can do it only interstitially; they are confined from molar to molecular actions." Cardozo, *The Nature of the Judicial Process* (1921), p. 141, recognized that the freedom of the Judge is not absolute in this expression of his view:

> This judge, even when he is free, is still not wholly free. He is not to innovate at pleasure. He is not a knight-errant, roaming at will in pursuit of his own ideal of beauty or of goodness. He is to draw his inspiration from consecrated principles.

The former Chief Justice of the Australian High Court, Sir Owen Dixon, in an address delivered at Yale University in September, 1955, "Concerning Judicial Method," had this to say:

> But in our Australian High Court we have had as yet no deliberate innovators bent on express change of acknowledged doctrine. It is one thing for a court to seek to extend

the application of accepted principles to new cases or to reason from the more fundamental of settled legal principles to new conclusions or to decide that a category is not closed against unforeseen instances which in reason might be subsumed thereunder. It is an entirely different thing for a judge, who is discontented with a result held to flow from a long accepted legal principle, deliberately to abandon the principle in the name of justice or of social necessity or of social convenience. The former accords with the technique of the common law and amounts to no more than an enlightened application of modes of reasoning traditionally respected in the courts. It is a process by the repeated use of which the law is developed, is adapted to new conditions, and is improved in content. The latter means an abrupt and almost arbitrary change.

See also: Jaffe, *English and American Judges as Lawmakers* (1969); McWhinney, *Canadian Jurisprudence* (1958) pp. 1-23; Friedmann, *Law in a Changing Society*, 2d ed. (1972), pp. 49-90; and Allen, *Law in the Making*, 7th ed. (1964), pp. 302-11.

Society has long since acknowledged that a public interest is served by permitting union members to bring economic pressure to bear upon their respective employers through peaceful picketing, but the right has been exercisable in some locations and not in others and to the extent that picketing has been permitted on private property the right hitherto has been accorded by statute. For example, s. 87 [since rep. & sub. 1975, c. 33, s. 21] of the *Labour Code of British Columbia Act*, 1973 (BC) (2d Sess.), c. 122, provides that no action lies in respect of picketing permitted under the Act for trespass to real property to which a member of the public ordinarily has access.

Anglo-Canadian jurisprudence has [traditionally] recognized, as a fundamental freedom, the right of the individual to the enjoyment of property and the right not to be deprived thereof, or any interest therein, save by due process of law. The Legislature of Manitoba has declared in the *Petty Trespasses Act* that any person who trespasses upon land, the property of another, upon or through which he has been requested by the owner not to enter, is guilty of an offence. If there is to be any change in this statute law, if A is to be given the right to enter and remain on the land of B against the will of B, it would seem to me that such a change must be made by the enacting institution, the Legislature, which is representative of the people and designed to manifest the political will, and not by this Court.

I would allow the appeal, set aside the judgment of the Court of Appeal for Manitoba and restore the judgment of the County Court Judge.

LASKIN CJC (dissenting): I would be content to adopt the reasons of Freedman CJM and, accordingly, to dismiss this appeal without more if I did not feel compelled, in view of the course of argument, to add some observations bearing on the decision of this Court in *R v. Peters* (1971), 17 DLR (3d) 128, dismissing an appeal from the judgment of the Ontario Court of Appeal (1970), 2 CCC (2d) 336, 16 DLR (3d) 143, [1971] 1 OR 597. The observations I am about to make about the *Peters* case carry into two areas of concern respecting the role of this Court as the final Court in this country in both civil and criminal causes. Those areas are, first, whether this Court must pay mechanical deference to *stare decisis* and, second, whether this Court has a balancing role to play, without yielding place to the Legislature, where an ancient doctrine, in this case trespass, is invoked in a new setting to suppress a lawful activity supported both by legislation and by a well-understood legislative policy.

The factual setting for these issues in the present case needs no great elaboration. The locale is a shopping centre, in which a large number of tenants carry on a wide variety of businesses. The shopping centre has the usual public amenities, such as access roads, parking lots and sidewalks, which are open for use by members of the public who may or may not be buyers at the time they come to the shopping centre. There can be no doubt that at least where a shopping centre is freely accessible to the public, as is the one involved in the present case, the private owner has invested members of the public with a right of entry during the business hours of his tenants and with a right to remain there subject to lawful behaviour. Counsel for the appellant owner in this case stated that members of the public entered and remained in the shopping centre at the owner's whim, under what may be called a revocable licence, and were subject to liability for trespass if they did not leave when requested, regardless of how proper their conduct was at the time. This is an extravagant position. It is a sufficient demonstration of its hollowness to point out that a member of the public who came to the shopping centre at the express invitation of a tenant for business reasons could not lawfully be excluded by the private owner. I need not pursue the extreme of the appellant's submission, but put it to one side to deal with the specific trespass claim that arose here.

An employee of a tenant in the shopping centre participated in a lawful strike and then proceeded to picket peacefully on the sidewalk in front of the tenant's premises. The struck employer took no action to prohibit the picketing and, on the record, an action by the employer would probably have been unsuccessful. The owner of the shopping centre introduced himself into the situation and told the picketer, the respondent in this appeal, that picketing was not permitted in any area of the shopping centre, and if she did not leave she would be charged with trespass. He advised her to move to a public sidewalk which was some distance away. She continued to picket on the shopping centre sidewalk and charges against her under the *Petty Trespasses Act*, RSM 1970, c. P-50 followed.

The *Peters* case also involved picketing in a shopping centre. However, the picketing there arose not out of a labour dispute with an employer tenant of premises in the shopping centre, but was by way of a boycott appeal against the selling of California grapes. The oral reasons of Gale CJO, for the Ontario Court of Appeal, were undoubtedly geared to the specific facts before him, and it is therefore unfair, in my view, to read, without that context, his general statement [at 338 CCC; 146 DLR] that:

> ... an owner who has granted a right of entry to a particular class of the public has not thereby relinquished his or its right to withdraw its invitation to the general public or any particular member thereof, and that if a member of the public whose invitation to enter has been withdrawn refuses to leave, he thereby becomes a trespasser and may be prosecuted under the *Petty Trespass Act*.

Be that as it may, the case came to the Supreme Court of Canada not at large but on two specific questions of law, the second of which concerned the constitutional validity of the provincial *Petty Trespasses Act*, a matter which did not become an issue here. That was made clear to the sole intervenant in the present case, the Attorney-General for Saskatchewan, who appeared to defend the validity of such legislation.

The first question put to this Court in the *Peters* case was framed as follows:

Did the learned Judges in appeal err in law in determining that the owner of the property had sufficient possession of the shopping plaza sidewalk to be capable of availing itself of the remedy for trespass under the Petty Trespass Act, RSO 1960, Chapter 294, section 1(1)?

This question, a strictly legal one without any context of fact, was answered unanimously in the negative by the full Court of which I was a member. The Court gave the briefest of oral reasons (see 17 DLR (3d) 128), and I regarded the answer as a response to a narrow question of whether a shopping centre owner can have sufficient possession of a sidewalk therein to support a charge of trespass under the provincial Act. The question, to me, was whether the owner had divested itself of possession so as to make the shopping centre sidewalk a public way upon which there could be no trespass as against such owner in any circumstances.

It is, of course, open to others to read this Court's disposition of the *Peters* case differently, but I can say for myself that the brief reasons would not have sufficed had the question that was asked been put in a factual frame as is often done when questions are formulated for the consideration of this Court. For me, it follows that the *Peters* case is neither in law, nor in fact a controlling authority for the present case which came to this Court not upon specific questions of fact, but at large so as to enable this Court to consider both law and fact as they bear on the position *inter se* of the shopping centre owner and of the lawful picketer in a legal strike.

My brother, Spence, who also sat as a member of this Court in the *Peters* case, associates himself with me in the view of it that I have put forward, and I would think that this should give pause to any suggestion that the *Peters* case has concluded the issue now before us, an issue arising on different facts and on a broader question of law than that to which an answer was sought and given in the *Peters* case.

This Court, above all others in this country, cannot be simply mechanistic about previous decisions, whatever be the respect it would pay to such decisions. What we would be doing here, if we were to say that the *Peters* case, because it was so recently decided, has concluded the present case for us, would be to take merely one side of a debatable issue and say that it concludes the debate without the need to hear the other side.

I do not have to call upon pronouncements of members of this Court that we are free to depart from previous decisions in order to support the pressing need to examine the present case on its merits. Pressing, because there are probably many hundreds of shopping centres in this country where similar issues have arisen and will arise. The Saskatchewan Court of Appeal has dealt with a picketing situation in a shopping centre in a different way than did the Ontario Court of Appeal in the *Peters* case, albeit on different facts and in respect of civil action rather than in a penal proceeding: see *Grosvenor Park Shopping Centre Ltd. v. Waloshin et al.* (1964), 46 DLR (2d) 750, 49 WWR 237. There are judgments in related cases, that were cited to us in argument, that need to be taken into consideration in order to enable this Court to begin to draw lines which Courts are habitually called upon to do. There should be, at least, some indication that the Court has addressed itself to the difficult issues that reside in the competing contentions that were made in this case and to which I will refer later on in these reasons. But, above all, this Court has not shown itself to be timorous in tackling important issues where it could be said, with some justification, that an important consideration was absent from an earlier judgment, even a recent one, upon which reliance was placed to foreclose examination of a similar issue in a subsequent case.

I refer to the judgment of this Court in *Brant Dairy Co. Ltd. et al. v. Milk Com'n of Ontario et al.* (1972), 30 DLR (3d) 559, [1973] SCR 131, as evidence of the approach which I think is compelled in the present case. Of course, it was a different case and turns on the neglect of this Court to consider earlier conflicting decisions when deciding the case that was pressed as an authority to conclude the decision in the *Brant Dairy* case itself. What is important, however, is not whether we have a previous decision involving a "brown horse" by which to judge a pending appeal involving a "brown horse," but rather what were the principles, and indeed the facts, upon which the previous case, now urged as conclusive, was decided. I need only add that there can be no doubt on the question whether the present case provides a developed set of facts that raise the important issues of law that require decision here. It certainly does.

I come then to those issues, and they can only be understood if we look at the present case not only from the position asserted by the shopping centre owner, but as well from the position asserted by the lawful picketer. An ancient legal concept, trespass, is urged here in all its pristine force by a shopping centre owner in respect of areas of the shopping centre which have been opened by him to public use, and necessarily so because of the commercial character of the enterprise based on tenancies by operators of a variety of businesses. To say in such circumstances that the shopping centre owner may, at his whim, order any member of the public out of the shopping centre on penalty or liability for trespass if he refuses to leave, does not make sense if there is no proper reason in that member's conduct or activity to justify the order to leave.

Trespass in its civil law sense, and in its penal sense too, connotes unjustified invasion of another's possession. Where a dwelling-house is concerned, the privacy associated with that kind of land-holding makes any unjustified or unprivileged entry a trespass, technically so even if no damage occurs. A Court, however, would be likely to award only nominal damages for mere unprivileged entry upon another's private premises where no injury occurs, and it is probable that the plaintiff would be ordered to pay costs for seeking empty vindication. If the trespasser refuses to leave when ordered, he could be forcibly removed, but, more likely, the police would be called and the issue would be resolved at that point, or a basis for an action, or for a penal charge would arise. In short, apart from privileged entry, a matter to which I will return in these reasons, there is a significant element of protection of privacy in resort to trespass to exclude or remove persons from private dwellings.

The considerations which underlie the protection of private residences cannot apply to the same degree to a shopping centre in respect of its parking areas, roads and sidewalks. Those amenities are closer in character to public roads and sidewalks than to a private dwelling. All that can be urged from a theoretical point of view to assimilate them to private dwellings is to urge that if property is privately owned, no matter the use to which it is put, trespass is as appropriate in the one case as in the other and it does not matter that possession, the invasion of which is basic to trespass, is recognizable in the one case but not in the other. There is here, on this assimilation, a legal injury albeit no actual injury. This is a use of theory which does not square with economic or social fact under the circumstances of the present case.

What does a shopping centre owner protect, for what invaded interest of his does he seek vindication in ousting members of the public from sidewalks and roadways and parking areas in the shopping centre? There is no challenge to his title and none to his possession nor to his privacy when members of the public use those amenities. Should he be allowed to choose what members of the public come into those areas when they have been opened to all without discrimination? Human rights legislation would prevent him from discriminating on account of race, colour or creed or national origin, but counsel for the appellant would have it that members of the public can otherwise be excluded or ordered to leave by mere whim. It is contended that it is unnecessary that there be a reason that can stand rational assessment. Disapproval of the owner, in assertion of a remote control over the "public" areas of the shopping centre, whether it be disapproval of picketing or disapproval of the wearing of hats or anything equally innocent, may be converted (so it is argued) into a basis of ouster of members of the public. Can the common law be so devoid of reason as to tolerate this kind of whimsy where public areas of a shopping centre are concerned?

If it was necessary to categorize the legal situation which, in my view, arises upon the opening of a shopping centre, with public areas of the kind I have mentioned (at least where the opening is not accompanied by an announced limitation on the classes of public entrants), I would say that the members of the public are privileged visitors whose privilege is revocable only upon misbehaviour (and I need not spell out here what this embraces) or by reason of unlawful activity. Such a view reconciles both the interests of the shopping centre owner and [those] of the members of the public, doing violence to neither and recognizing the mutual or reciprocal commercial interests of [the] shopping centre owner, business tenants and members of the public upon which the shopping centre is based.

The respondent picketer in the present case is entitled to the privilege of entry and to remain in the public areas to carry on as she did (without obstruction of the sidewalk or incommoding of others) as being not only a member of the public but being as well, in relation to her peaceful picketing, an employee involved in a labour dispute with a tenant of the shopping centre, and hence having an interest, sanctioned by the law, in pursuing legitimate claims against her employer through the peaceful picketing in furtherance of a lawful strike.

The civil law doctrine of abusive exercise of rights provides, in my opinion, an apt analogue for the present case. I do not press it as having precise application, but in so far as it embraces a balancing of rights, a consideration of the relativity of rights involving advertence to social purpose as well as to personal advantage, it is the peaceful picketer who has cause for complaint against interference with her, rather than the shopping centre owner having a legally cognizable complaint: see, generally, Gutteridge, "Abuse of Rights" 5 Camb. LJ 22 (1933-35); Castel, *The Civil Law System of the Province of Quebec* (1962), pp. 409*ff.* The shopping centre owner has no overriding or even coequal interest to serve in intervening in the labour dispute, and, if anything, is acting as surrogate of the struck tenant in a situation where the latter has not and probably could not claim redress or relief.

It seems to me that the present case involves a search for an appropriate legal framework for new social facts which show up the inaptness of an old doctrine developed upon a completely different social foundation. The history of trespass indicates that its introduction as a private means of redress was directed to breaches of the peace or to acts likely to provoke such breaches. Its subsequent enlargement beyond these concerns does not mean that it must be taken as incapable of further adaptation, but must be applied on what I can only characterize as a level of abstraction which ignores the facts. Neither logic nor experience (to borrow from Holmes' opening sentence in his classic *The Common Law*) supports such a conclusion.

Recognition of the need for balancing the interests of the shopping centre owner with competing interests of members of the public when in or on the public areas of the shopping centre, engaged Courts in the United States a little earlier than it did the Courts in this country. Making every allowance for any constitutional basis upon which Courts there grappled with this problem, their analyses are helpful because they arise out of the same economic and social setting in which the problem arises here. Thus, there is emphasis on unrestricted access to shopping centres from public streets, and on the fact that access by the public is the very reason for the existence of shopping centres; there is the comparison drawn between the public markets of long ago and the shopping centre as a modern market place; there is the appreciation that in the light of the interests involved there can be no solution to their reconciliation by posting a flat all or nothing approach. The cases in the United States, and I cite a few of them here without further elaboration, appear to me to reject the appellant's proposition that (as his counsel put it) "the issue is trespass, not picketing" because that, in my opinion, involves a predetermination without regard to the issues of fact: see *Schwartz-Torrance Investment Corp. v. Bakery & Confectionery Workers' Union, Local 31* (1964), 394 P2d 921 (Calif.); *Amalgamated Clothing Workers of America v. Wonderland Shopping Center, Inc.* (1963), 122 NW 2d 785 (Mich.); *Amalgamated Food Employees' Union, Local 590 v. Logan Valley Plaza Inc.* (1968), 391 US 308; *Lloyd Corp. Ltd. v. Tanner* (1972), 407 US 551.

A more appropriate approach, to which I adverted earlier, is to recognize a continuing privilege in using the areas of the shopping centre provided for public passage subject to limitations arising out of the nature of the activity thereon and to the object pursued thereby, and subject as well to a limitation against material damage. There is analogy in existing conceptions of privilege as an answer to intentional torts, such as trespasses. The principle is expressed in Prosser, *Handbook of the Law of Torts*, 4th ed. (1971), at pp. 98-9 as follows:

> "Privilege" is the modern term applied to those considerations which avoid liability where it might otherwise follow. In its broader sense, it is applied to any immunity which prevents the existence of a tort; but in its more common usage, it signifies that the defendant has acted to further an interest of such social importance that it is entitled to protection, even at the expense of damage to the plaintiff. He is allowed freedom of action because his own interests, or those of the public require it, and social policy will best be served by permitting it. The boundaries of the privilege are marked out by current ideas of what will most effectively promote the general welfare.

The question of "privilege" arises almost exclusively in connection with intentional torts. Much the same considerations have weight in negligence cases, in determining whether the defendant's conduct is reasonable under the circumstances. Negligence, however, is a matter of risk and probability of harm; and where the likelihood of injury to the plaintiff is relatively slight, the defendant will necessarily be allowed greater latitude than where the harm is intended, or substantially certain to follow.

As the defendant's interest gains weight in the scale of social values, his privilege becomes greater. It may be absolute, in the sense that there is immunity from all liability, regardless of the motive or purpose for which he acts. The acts of judicial officers, done under authority of law, for example, are absolutely privileged, even though malicious or corrupt. It may be conditioned upon a proper motive and reasonable behavior, as in the case of the privilege of self-defense. It may be limited, in the sense that the defendant may not be restrained in advance from acting, and is not liable for any mere technical tort, but is still liable for any substantial damage that he may cause. The sliding scale by which the law balances the interests of the parties to accomplish a social purpose is nowhere better illustrated than in the field of privilege.

See also, Bohlen, "*Incomplete Privilege to Inflict Intentional Invasions of Interests of Property and Personality,*" 39 *Har. L Rev.* 307 (1926), where it is said, at pp. 319-20:

The liability for a harmless invasion of either an interest of personality or property is either punitive or compensatory. In so far as it is punitive, there is no reason why, if the good likely to result from an act is greater than the harm it is intended to cause, the actor should be punished either criminally by fine or imprisonment, or by damages, whether labelled punitive or not, imposed in a civil action. And clearly there is no more reason for imposing either punishment because the harm intended and done is a harmless invasion of a dignitary interest of personality rather than a harmless invasion of a similar interest of property.

Illustrations were given during the course of argument of situations which might put the respondent's activity in a different light relative to the place of picketing and to the object of picketing and which, correlatively, might provide some redeeming interest of the shopping centre owner in exercising control over the public areas. The character of a shopping centre, such as the one involved here, is one thing, and the nature and place of activities carried on there are something else. I would agree that it does not follow that because unrestricted access is given to members of the public to certain areas of the shopping centre during business hours, those areas are available at all times during those hours and in all circumstances to any kind of peaceful activity by members of the public, regardless of the interest being prompted by that activity and regardless of the numbers of members of the public who are involved. The Court will draw lines here as it does in other branches of the law as may be appropriate in the light of the legal principle and particular facts. In the present case it is the respondent who has been injured rather than the shopping centre owner.

I would dismiss the appeal.

Martland, Judson and Ritchie JJ concur with Dickson J.

Spence J concurs with Laskin CJC.
Pigeon J concurs with Dickson J.
Beetz J concurs with Laskin CJC.
De Grandpre J concurs with Dickson J.

Appeal allowed; conviction restored.

Discussion Notes

Facts and Precedents

The reasons of Dickson J and Laskin CJC illustrate differing approaches to the issue of whether the court's previous decision in *R v. Peters* (1971), 17 DLR (3d) 128 (SCC) constituted a precedent for this case. In reflecting on these differing approaches, consider the underlying assumptions that they demonstrate about whether a shopping centre should be characterized as fundamentally "private" property or "common" property. Note that Dickson J concluded that it was not a relevant distinction that the picketer in *Peters* was "a mere member of the general public" while the picketer in *Harrison* was a striking employee of one of the tenants of the shopping centre. What factors supported this conclusion? What arguments were rejected?

Laskin CJC concluded that the *Peters* case was not a precedent for *Harrison*, and that even if it was a precedent, the Supreme Court should not be "mechanistic." Instead, he stated that the court should decide cases on the merits, even if that required the court to reconsider its own precedent. Do you agree with Laskin's suggestion that this case is not a case about a "brown horse," assuming that *Peters* was a case about a "brown horse"? Why, or why not? What kinds of factors should be considered "relevant" in the process of applying or distinguishing precedents? Should the existence of decisions of a number of provincial appellate courts that are not consistent be a relevant factor in such a context? Why is consistency in the treatment of picketers in shopping centres across the country a matter of importance that should be addressed by the Supreme Court of Canada? In considering these issues, re-examine the critiques outlined above in relation to *Victoria Park*, under the headings "The Role of Precedent" and "Frame Shifting: Explaining Different Approaches?" The issue of whether an appellate court like the Supreme Court of Canada should follow its own precedents, and what factors should be considered before a court decides to depart from one of its own precedents, was reviewed by G. Bale in "Casting Off the Mooring Ropes of Binding Precedent" (1980), 58 *Canadian Bar Review* 255.

Shopping Centres: "Private" or "Public" Property?

Is there a difference in the characterization of the shopping centre in the two judgments? Note that Laskin CJC identified different parts of the shopping centre, concluding that certain parts of the shopping centre were more "public" than "private." How does such a characterization assist in supporting his conclusion? What is the impact of his characterization on the potential effectiveness of striking picketers in a shopping centre? By contrast, if the shopping centre as an entire entity is characterized as "private" property, what will be the impact on the potential effectiveness of striking picketers?

Does *Harrison* establish that the owner of private property has an absolute right to exclude? If the right is not an absolute one, what limits are recognized in *Harrison*? Some political theorists have argued that the concept of private property should be reconceptualized in terms of "a right not to be excluded." For example, see C.B. Macpherson, "Liberal-Democracy and Property," in Macpherson, 199, at 201:

> I shall argue that we have all been misled by accepting an unnecessarily narrow concept of property, a concept within which it is impossible to resolve the difficulties of any liberal theory. We have treated as the very paradigm of property what is really only a special case. It is time for a new paradigm, within which we may hope to resolve difficulties that could not be resolved within the old.
>
> As I have already shown, property, although it must always be an individual right, need not be confined, as liberal theory has confined it, to a right to exclude others from the use or benefit of some thing, but may equally be an individual right not to be excluded by others from the use or benefit of some thing. When property is so understood, the problem of liberal-democratic theory is no longer a problem of putting limits on the property right, but of supplementing the individual right to exclude others by the individual right not to be excluded by others. The latter right may be held to be the one that is most required by the liberal-democratic ethic, and most implied in a liberal concept of the human essence. The right not to be excluded by others may provisionally be stated as the individual right to equal access to the means of labour and/or the means of life.

Recall the categories of property identified above in relation to *Victoria Park*, under the heading "Private Property, Common Property, and State Property." How would you characterize Macpherson's concept of the "right not to be excluded" in relation to these categories? For another analysis, see A. Reeve, "The Theory of Property: Beyond 'Private" Versus 'Common Property,'" in D. Held, ed., *Political Theory Today* (Stanford, CA: Stanford University Press, 1991), 91.

Macpherson's concept of property as the right not to be excluded is revealed, for example, in an analysis of the employment relationship by R.M. Fischl in "Some Realism about Critical Legal Studies" (1987), 41 *University of Miami Law Review* 505, at 527. Fischl described a typical employee making widgets in a company setting. At the end of the day, having built four widgets, the employee "tenders to her boss an amount in cash equal to the cost of the necessary materials and their procurement, the reasonable rental value of her workspace and tools, and the apportioned cost of other managerial expenses. She then leaves the shop and takes the widgets with her, planning to sell them and keep the profit." Fischl described how such an analysis is perplexing to most people who hear it because they think that the employee is guilty of theft. The author then suggests that, on the same basis, an employer may commit theft when the employer pays an employee a reasonable "rent" for her labour, "keeps the widgets for himself and sells them for his own profit." In response to the suggestion that the employer's actions do not amount to theft, by contrast with those of the employee, because "the law says that [the widgets] are his property," Fischl concluded (at 527) that this result demonstrates how the law reflects the interests of capitalism:

The law reflects and enforces a core assumption about the relationship between employer and employee in a market economy: the employee's legally protected interest in the job is limited to his wage, while the employer is accorded the exclusive right to both the widgets and the profits to be earned from their sale.

Using this approach, consider the reasoning in *Harrison v. Carswell*. Is this case an example of law reflecting the interests of capitalism? In thinking about this issue, reconsider the analysis presented by Stone (above in relation to *Victoria Park*, under the heading "The Role of Precedent") that the law may "simultaneously act in two ... mutually inconsistent ways." How should we explain the differing approaches of the majority and the dissent in *Harrison*? For a critique of Fischl's analysis, suggesting that the employment relationship is justified in terms of arguments of economic efficiency, see R.A. Black, R.S. Kreider, and M. Sullivan, "Critical Legal Studies, Economic Realism, and the Theory of the Firm" (1988), 43 *University of Miami Law Review* 343.

The Context of Shopping Centre Picketing

In *Harrison*, the shopping centre's owner argued that it had established a policy, universally applied, prohibiting the distribution of pamphlets by anyone, including tenants of the shopping centre. How is this corporate policy relevant to the arguments in *Harrison*? Should such a policy override rights in provincial legislation that permit peaceful picketing by striking workers? If striking workers are permitted to picket on the grounds of shopping centres, should they also be permitted to do so on university campuses? Are there any differences in the "private" character of a shopping centre and a university campus?

In his reasons, Dickson J referred to an academic article that outlined the "legitimate concerns of the landlord of a shopping centre." The author, a respected labour law academic, published this article as a commentary on the conflicting decisions across Canada in relation to picketing and shopping centres, reviewing US as well as Canadian decisions and assessing the competing interests of shopping centre owners and striking workers. In fact, as the following excerpt makes clear, the author reached a conclusion opposite to that excerpted in the reasons of Dickson J. See H. Arthurs, "Note" (1965), 43 *Canadian Bar Review* 357, at 362 (footnotes omitted):

> There remains, then, the task of weighing up the competing interests of the labour union and the picketed tenant or landowner in the special context of shopping centre picketing. In the ordinary industrial dispute, of course, public policy acknowledges the union's interest in peacefully advertising the existence of a labour dispute through picketing. Such picketing is lawful even though it interferes with the use and enjoyment of the picketed property. To this extent, shopping centre picketing presents no special problem. Likewise, minor, casual, impediments to pedestrian and vehicular traffic may accompany both ordinary and shopping centre picketing, and are not wrongful where they are not deliberate. Even the risk of accidentally (but not purposely) causing inconvenience to adjacent shopowners is common to both situations, and can be handled by requiring the pickets to confine their activities to the immediate vicinity of the dispute.
>
> The special factor in shopping centre picketing is the landlord, a neutral in the labour dispute. First, he is responsible for the maintenance of orderly traffic movement in the

public areas of the shopping centre. Whereas the expenditure of tax funds on public roads and sidewalks may justify a little interference with traffic flow to serve the greater public good of publicizing labour controversies, no such justification exists in the shopping centre. The landlord spends his own money on the public areas of the shopping centre, and does so for the sole purpose of making a profit. Second, while public authorities may, on behalf of the community, strike a reasonable balance between traffic and picketing on public sidewalks and streets, the shopping centre owner can hardly be expected to make such a choice: he has no authority to speak for the community; to grant picketing or parading privileges to all would invite chaos, while to do so selectively would invite commercial reprisals. He is thus driven to adopt a highly restrictive approach to granting permission to groups who wish to parade or picket in the shopping centre.

Set against these two legitimate concerns of the landlord is the union's contention that unless picketing is allowed on the public areas of the shopping centre, it cannot take place at all. The theoretical alternative, of course, is picketing on the adjacent public highways. To such picketing there are both legal and practical obstacles. Legally, the risk is that picketing on the perimeter of the shopping centre will be construed as illegal pressure against all of its tenants, no matter how explicit the picket signs. Practically, the difficulty is that many more pickets are required to patrol the perimeter of the entire shopping centre than the immediate vicinity of the tenant's store.

Weighing these considerations in the scales of public policy, it is hard to say that peaceful informational picketing should be forbidden in shopping centres. The flow of traffic may be protected by requiring that the pickets remain few in number, well-behaved, and in a confined area; both the landlord and the union are better served by the legal rationale adopted in California, which does not depend on the owner's permission or invitation to picket; the union is not exposed to the legal and practical disadvantages of perimeter picketing. Happily the appellate courts of Saskatchewan and British Columbia appear to have struck this balance, whether consciously or otherwise.

In the context of the policy considerations identified in Arthurs's commentary, examine the two judgments in *Harrison v. Carswell* in relation to their focus on policy concerns. What kinds of sources were used by Laskin CJC to support his conclusion? How would you characterize his view about the role of the court? Note that Dickson J specifically noted the "power of the court to act creatively," while also identifying the "limits of the judicial function." Does this case reflect differing views on the part of the two justices about the role of the courts as well as about policy concerns and the effects of precedent? Which of these concerns is most significant in terms of the outcome of the case?

The Charter and Protection for Property

In the penultimate paragraph of his reasons, Dickson J stated:

Anglo-Canadian jurisprudence has [traditionally] recognized, as a fundamental freedom, the right of the individual to the enjoyment of property and the right not to be deprived thereof, or any interest therein, save by due process of law.

This language reflects the 14th amendment of the US Constitution, a provision that has often been used to restrain governmental action to regulate land ownership. See, for example, *Village of Euclid v. Ambler Realty Co.*, 272 US 365 (1926) where the court upheld the general validity of state zoning laws so long as they were "reasonable." This constitutional protection for property in the United States means that all statutes and judicial decisions must conform to the constitutional requirement. For an interesting historical analysis of "takings" law in the United States, see Joseph F. DiMento, "Mining the Archives of *Pennsylvania Coal*: Heaps of Constitutional Mischief" (1990), 11 *Journal of Legal History* 396.

At the time when *Harrison* was decided, there was no comparable constitutional guarantee in Canadian law. Moreover, when Canada's Charter of Rights and Freedoms was adopted in 1982, property rights were not explicitly protected. To what extent does Dickson J's statement that "Anglo-Canadian jurisprudence has [recognized a right] to the enjoyment of property" conflict with his assertion about the limits of the courts' "power to act creatively"? See Canadian Charter of Rights and Freedoms, part I of the Constitution Act, 1982, being schedule B of the Canada Act, 1982 (UK), 1982, c. 11; reprinted RSC 1985, app. II, no. 44 (hereafter the Charter). For an excellent assessment of strategies for "progressive lawyers," especially in the context of corporate enterprises and workers' rights, see Harry Glasbeek, "Some Strategies for an Unlikely Task: The Progressive Use of Law" (1989), 21 *Ottawa Law Review* 387, especially at 406-9. For an analysis of *Harrison v. Carswell* in relation to the Charter's guarantee of freedom of expression, see M.M. Litman, "Freedom of Speech and Private Property: The Case of the Mall Owner," in D. Schneiderman, ed., *Freedom of Expression and the Charter* (Scarborough, ON: Thomson, 1991), at 361, and the discussion of this issue later in this chapter.

Litigation or Dispute Resolution?

Sophie Carswell was charged with four counts of trespass under the Petty Trespass Act of Manitoba. The charges were initially dismissed by the provincial judge, but she was convicted on a trial *de novo* (a form of appeal that requires a new trial) in the County Court and she was fined $10 on each of the four charges. Her total fine was therefore $40. On appeal to the Manitoba Court of Appeal, the convictions were set aside, leading to this further appeal with leave of the Supreme Court of Canada. Why did Sophie Carswell's case, involving a monetary issue of $40, proceed to the Supreme Court of Canada? Were there important interests at stake for the parties? Were there important interests at stake for others who were not parties to this action?

Although the judgment does not address the issue of costs, it is likely that "costs followed the event." The unsuccessful party bears the costs of the successful party, a considerable amount in this case, with four levels of courts involved. Was this a case where the parties should have tried to settle their dispute without resorting to litigation? What factors might have constrained such action? If there were important public issues at stake in this case, should the normal rules about costs apply? In relation to a similar case about picketing in a shopping centre in the United States—for example, *Hudgens v. National Labor Relations Board*, 424 US 507 (1976)—Chused commented on the impact of the protracted proceedings in these cases, and the general usefulness of litigation:

> The incredibly convoluted history of this litigation re-emphasizes several themes ... .
> The legal system may be a disastrous place to take a dispute. The cost and length of

some litigation is enormous. Perhaps that is why so many of the cases ... [are] either grudge matches or, like *Hudgens*, test cases. Who, other than a "grudge" or a tester with outside financial support, would possibly pursue litigation far beyond the point justified by monetary loss or gain?

(R. Chused, *Cases, Materials and Problems in Property* (New York: Matthew Bender: 1989), at 344-45.) Do these comments appear applicaable in *Harrison v. Carswell*?

The Aftermath of Harrison v. Carswell: Shifting the Paradigm?

Since *Harrison v. Carswell* was decided in 1975, the issue of the shopping centre owner's "right to exclude" has arisen in a number of other cases. In many of these cases, *Harrison v. Carswell* has been distinguished. As a result, the definition of the shopping centre owner's private property interest must now take account of the reasoning not only in *Harrison v. Carswell*, but also in several subsequent cases. These cases demonstrate the dynamic quality of common law decision making—a process that illustrates how subsequent decisions may alter the legal status of an earlier landmark decision.

This process of ongoing refinement in the common law bears some similarity to Alfred Kuhn's theory of "paradigm shifts" in science. Kuhn's explanation for changes in scientific understandings has been described by Janice Moulton in "A Paradigm of Philosophy: The Adversary Method," in S. Harding and M.B. Hintikka, eds., *Discovering Reality: Feminist Perspectives on Epistemology, Metaphysics, Methodology and Philosophy of Science* (Boston: D. Reidel, 1983), 149, at 152:

> Kuhn ... argued that even the reasoning used in science is not value free or certain. Science involves more than a set of independent generalizations about the world waiting to be falsified by a single counter-instance. It involves a system, or "paradigm," of not only generalizations and concepts, but beliefs about the methodology and evaluation of research: about what are good questions to ask, what are proper developments of the theory, what are acceptable research methods. One theory replaces another, not because it functions successfully as a major premise in a greater number of deductions, but because it answers some questions that the other theory does not—even though it may not answer some questions the other theory does. Theory changes occur because one theory is more *satisfying* than the other, because the questions it answers are considered more *important*. Research under a paradigm is not done to falsify the theory, but to fill in and develop the knowledge that the paradigm provides a framework for. The reasoning involved in developing or replacing a paradigm is not simply deductive, and there is probably no adequate single characterization of how it proceeds. This does not mean that it is irrational or not worth studying, but that there is no simple universal characterization of good scientific reasoning.

In the legal context as well, the process of common law decision making permits change to occur. Whether the decisions after *Harrison v. Carswell* have added enough distinctions to the original decision so that we can say that a paradigm shift has occurred may be open to debate. Clearly, however, it is impossible to assert that the law is the same now as in 1975, and this result has occurred through both judicial decision making and some statutory reform. As you examine the notes and cases that follow, try to assess whether there has been a paradigm shift in the content of private property rights for shopping centre owners. More pragmatically, suppose that you are legal counsel for a shopping centre and must advise your client about the issues in *Harrison v. Carswell*. What advice would be legally appropriate?

Discussion Notes

The Consequences of Legislative Difference

In *Wildwood Mall Ltd. v. Stevens*, [1980] 2 WWR 638 (Sask. QB), the facts were similar to those in *Harrison v. Carswell*. However, the court distinguished *Harrison* on the ground that there was no legislation in Saskatchewan analogous to the Petty Trespasses Act in Manitoba, pursuant to which Sophie Carswell was charged. Why should this legislative difference be determinative?

RWDSU v. T. Eaton Company Limited

Harrison v. Carswell was also considered in *RWDSU v. T. Eaton Company Limited* (1986), 10 Can. LRBR (NS) 289 (OLRB). The union initiated a complaint before the Ontario Labour Relations Board (OLRB), alleging that Cadillac Fairview and the Eaton's store at the Toronto Eaton Centre had violated the rights of employees at the Eaton's store to belong to a union.

Cadillac Fairview managed and controlled the Toronto Eaton Centre shopping mall on a day-to-day basis, and it had adopted a "no solicitation" policy for the mall. When representatives of the Eaton's store notified Cadillac Fairview that union organizers were handing out informational material and leaflets on Eaton's premises, Cadillac Fairview informed the union organizers that the distribution of leaflets, etc., on mall property was prohibited. Due to the physical location of the Eaton's store within the Toronto Eaton Centre shopping centre, no public entrances were available to union organizers except those on the shopping mall's premises. Thus, the union commenced its action before the OLRB, asserting that both Cadillac Fairview and Eaton's were in violation of the Ontario Labour Relations Act. (See now RSO 1990, c. L.2 as amended; some of these amendments are discussed later in this chapter.)

Specifically, the union asserted that Cadillac Fairview was in breach of s. 64 (now s. 65) of the Act, a section that provides that

> [n]o employer ... and no person acting on behalf of an employer ... shall participate in or interfere with the formation, selection or administration of a trade union.

In finding Cadillac Fairview in breach of s. 64 (now s. 65—the "unfair labour practices" section of the Act), the board specifically noted that this section "was not ... before the Court in *Harrison v. Carswell*, and we do not think that anyone would argue that the Court, by its decision, was granting to mall-owners a blanket exemption for unfair labour practices."

The board's decision then focused on evidentiary issues about the relationship between Cadillac Fairview and Eaton's to determine whether Cadillac Fairview was "a person acting on behalf of an employer," pursuant to the section (at paras. 71-73):

The two respondents [Cadillac Fairview and Eaton's] are, to begin with, obviously not "strangers" to one another with respect to the shopping-centre here in question. Quite apart from Eaton's 20 per cent holding in the head leasing company, and its seats on the Board of Directors, Cadillac Fairview and Eaton's operate in the shopping centre in the daily commercial relationship of landlord and tenant. Clearly this relationship alone is insufficient to establish that any act of Cadillac Fairview which has the effect of benefitting Eaton's is an act done "on behalf of" Eaton's, and the approach of the majority of the Court in *Harrison v. Carswell* would seem to underscore this. The Board takes it as established in *Harrison* that the owner/landlord of a shopping mall has an identifiable commercial interest of his own in ensuring generally that traffic in the mall is not disrupted nor customers distracted, even by peaceful and orderly forms of activity, and where activity occurs which poses a tangible threat to such interest, the landlord may well be viewed as acting on his own in taking steps to stop it. Where, however, neither interference, nor, indeed, contact with the shopping public can be shown to exist at all, it becomes more difficult for the landlord to argue that it is acting pursuant to any interest other than that of satisfying the wishes of its tenant (and in this case, its prime tenant in the shopping-centre which bears the tenant's name) in restricting, to the extent that it has, the efforts of those seeking to organize the employees of that tenant.

We have not forgotten that the respondent Cadillac Fairview asserts that it maintains a *broad, non-discriminatory* solicitation policy as a means of maintaining necessary control over the activities which take place in this popular centre of pedestrian traffic. Nor have we any doubt that such controls are needed. The problem is, as with the case of employers, that a broad solicitation policy does not stand on the same legal footing *vis-a-vis* activities which are specifically protected by statute, and those which are not. This was recognized in the United States, for example, at least as early as the *Republic Aviation*, 324 US 793 (1944), where the Circuit Court of Appeals concluded its judgment by stating:

> In the *Republic Aviation* case, petitioner urges that irrespective of the validity of the rule against solicitation, its application in this instance did not violate s. 8(3) [prohibiting discrimination] because the rule was not discriminatorily applied against union solicitation but was impartially enforced against all solicitors. It seems clear, however, that if a rule against solicitation is invalid as to union solicitation on the employer's premises during the employee's own time, a discharge because of violation of that rule discriminates within the meaning of s. 8(3) in that it discourages membership in a labor organization.

Or as more broadly put by the National Labour Relations Board in *Marshall Field*, 98 NLRB 88 at 91 (1952):

> The Respondent asserts that union organizers and employees acting in that capacity are not given treatment disparate from that accorded other solicitors. The record supports the contention that the Respondent attempts to exclude all soliciting for whatever purposes from the public areas of the store. It is thus true that union organizers are not discriminated against in comparison to other groups. That fact, however, does not render the Respondent's prohibition of union solicitation in non-selling public areas lawful. The right of employees to engage in concerted activity,

of which solicitation on behalf of a union is an inherent part, is guaranteed by the Act, unlike solicitation for such purposes as insurance, boat rides, or newspaper subscriptions. The lack of any discrimination, therefore, between the treatment accorded union solicitors and other solicitors cannot excuse the denial of the statutory right protecting the former.

And more recently by the Canada Labour Relations Board in its *Canadian Imperial Bank of Commerce* case, *supra*, at p. 22:

In dealing first with the question of the Bank's policy regarding solicitation, the Board wishes initially to indicate that one must distinguish between the Bank's right to prohibit solicitation by organizations such as the United Appeal or Canada's Wonderland from the right of the Bank to prohibit solicitation by a trade union. The former is completely within the purview of the Bank to allow or not. The latter is not.

It seems to us that Cadillac Fairview is in the same position. If it is found to be a person acting "on behalf of" the employer Eaton's, neither a record of non-discrimination nor a "floodgates" kind of argument is available to it as a justification for conduct which patently interferes with the statutory organizing rights of Eaton's employees. Cadillac Fairview's "defence" in this case, therefore, must rest on the risk of *actual* interference to its commercial interest in the mall. But [how] is its commercial interest affected when organizers of the complainant seek to carry on their statutorily-endorsed activities by attending in the area of the mall at "two below" immediately outside Eaton's doors, at a time well before store opening when, to all intents and purposes, the only persons traversing that Mall area are employees of Eaton's, or to a much lesser extent suppliers, and the only persons raising any detectible complaint about the activity are the management personnel of Eaton's, or other employees of Eaton's equally unenthusiastic about the prospect of Union organization? Such persons in either of those categories are, of course, wholly entitled to hold the views that they do. But neither of them in the circumstances under consideration can show any interference with their own legitimate activities, such as would offset the importance of access to that mall area at that hour of the day to the exercise of statutory organizing rights.

Nor can Cadillac Fairview. In light of its commercial relationship with Eaton's, the Board does not find it persuasive that Cadillac Fairview has from time to time tightened or loosened its policy of control with respect to the activities of the complainant's organizers in the Mall, or that its security officers decided, notwithstanding requests from Eaton's supervisors, to curtail the organizers' activities only to the extent that they exceeded the limits of that policy in effect at a given time. Rather, the Board finds that the respondent, Cadillac Fairview, in both the broad no-solicitation policy that it did enforce, and its letter of September 28, 1984, pursued an *overall* policy of control which was clearly in line with the desires of Eaton's. Where that policy lacked a sustainable business justification of its own, we find it to have been an unlawful interference with the organizing rights of the Eaton's employees, carried out on behalf of its prime tenant Eaton's. More specifically, we find no sustainable business justification has been made out for Cadillac Fairview having sought to prohibit organizers for the complainant from standing as they did outside the Eaton's doors at "two below" in an area of the mall *otherwise open to the public*, at a time when no other members of the public at large were in any way interfered with, for the purpose of handing out literature to employees entering the Eaton's store, without obstructing that entry, or of being available to engage in conversation with any employees who so chose. In the absence of such business justification, we find the action of Cadillac Fairview to have been simply an unfair labour practice, in violation of [now s. 65] of the *Labour Relations Act*.

Harrison v. Carswell involved an action instituted by the shopping centre owner under the Manitoba Petty Trespasses Act, RSM 1970, c. P-50, while the above case concerned an action instituted by the union claiming that a shopping centre owner had engaged in unfair labour practices under the Ontario Labour Relations Act, RSO 1980, c. 228. What reasoning was adopted by the board to distinguish *Harrison v. Carswell*? Is the difference in the nature of the actions in the two cases a relevant distinction? What about the differences in the legislative framework or the forum for decision? An application to quash this decision of the Ontario Labour Relations Board was denied: *Re Cadillac Fairview Corp. Ltd. and RWDSU* (1988), 62 OR (2d) 337 (Div. Ct.), and this decision was affirmed by the Ontario Court of Appeal: (1988), 71 OR (2d) 206. In a related action, Jack Layton, a municipal councillor, was arrested after refusing to leave the premises where he was leafletting Eaton's employees during a union organizing drive. Layton was charged under Ontario's Trespass to Property Act, 1980, (now RSO 1990, c. T.21) and he was convicted. He appealed his conviction, arguing that his actions were protected within the guarantee of freedom of expression under the Charter. On appeal, Judge Scott held that the method of distribution was an important factor for determining whether the actions were protected by the Charter guarantee. Concluding that Layton was offering literature to employees in a "peaceful and friendly manner," she overturned the conviction. Judge Scott expressly rejected the respondent's argument that allowing the accused's appeal would result in "a state of peril" for property rights in Canada. See *The Queen v. Layton* (1986), 38 CCC (3d) 550 (Prov. Ct. Crim. Div.). Is this decision consistent with *Harrison v. Carswell*? Why, or why not? This question also requires an examination of the Charter's guarantees, an issue addressed more explicitly in *The Queen v. Committee for the Commonwealth of Canada*, [1991] 1 SCR 139, which follows. For a similar decision, see *Russo v. Ontario Jockey Club* (1987), 62 OR (2d) 731 (HC).

As Dickson J noted, legislation in British Columbia at the time of the decision in *Harrison* provided that, in relation to picketing, no trespass occurred in respect of real property "to which a member of the public ordinarily has access." In 1992, Ontario's legislation was similarly amended. The Labour Relations and Employment Statute Law Amendment Act, 1992, SO 1992, c. 21 added s. 11.1 to the Ontario Labour Relations Act. The new amendment provided as follows:

11.1(1) This section applies with respect to premises to which the public normally has access and from which a person occupying the premises would have a right to remove individuals.

(2) Employees and persons acting on behalf of a trade union have the right to be present on premises described in subsection (1) for the purpose of attempting to persuade employees to join a trade union. Attempts to persuade the employees may be made only at or near but outside the entrances and exits to the employees' workplace. ...

(8) In the event of a conflict between a right described in subsection (2) [and others] … and other rights established at common law or under the *Trespass to Property Act*, the right described in those subsections prevails.

This legislation was repealed later and replaced by the Labour Relations and Statute Law Amendment Act, 1995 SO 1995, c. 1 and now forms part of the Labour Relations Act, 1995. Consider the impact of the decision in *Harrison v. Carswell* between 1992 and 1995, and after 1995, in Ontario. To what extent would it have been affected by this provincial legislation? Consider the impact of *Harrison v. Carswell* in provinces without such explicit legislative provisions: see, for example, Nova Scotia's Trade Union Act, RSNS 1989, c. 475, s. 53; and New Brunswick's Industrial Relations Act, RSNB 1973, c. I-4, s. 3.

Constitutional Guarantees: The Queen v. Committee for the Commonwealth of Canada

The issues in *Harrison v. Carswell* must now be considered in the context of entrenched constitutional guarantees in the Canadian Charter of Rights and Freedoms. In *The Queen v. Committee for the Commonwealth of Canada*, [1991] 1 SCR 139, plaintiffs-respondents were members of an organization called the Committee for the Commonwealth of Canada. They had wished to distribute pamphlets about their organization at the Montreal airport at Dorval. They had been prevented from doing so by airport officials, who were relying on government regulations that prohibited any advertising or solicitation in the airport: the Government Airport Concession Operations Regulations, SOR/70-373.

Plaintiffs initiated an action in the Federal Court—Trial Division requesting a declaration that the airport officials had failed to respect their Charter-guaranteed right to freedom of expression (s. 2(b)). They also requested a declaration that the airport property constituted a "public forum" where such freedoms could be exercised. They succeeded with both claims, but on appeal, the Federal Court of Appeal approved the first declaration, but declined to rule on the second. On a further appeal to the Supreme Court of Canada, the appeal was dismissed.

Section 2(b) of the Canadian Charter of Rights and Freedoms provides constitutionally entrenched protection for freedom of expression. Any law that violates this entrenched guarantee is void unless the violation can be justified by s. 1 of the Charter. To assist in understanding the judgment of the Supreme Court of Canada, the text of ss. 1 and 2(b) follows:

1. The Canadian Charter of Rights and Freedoms guarantees the rights and freedoms set out in it subject only to such reasonable limits prescribed by law as can be demonstrably justified in a free and democratic society.
2. Everyone has the following fundamental freedoms: …
    (b) freedom of thought, belief, opinion and expression, including freedom of the press and other media of communication.

In the Supreme Court of Canada, different approaches to the issues were evident in the multiple reasons released for the court's decision. In relation to *Harrison v. Carswell*, L'Heureux-Dubé J stated (at 187):

There is no doubt that if the purpose of the regulation here in question is not to restrict political expression, then the effect most certainly is. Therefore, s. 2(b) of the Charter has been breached. The provision categorically excludes advertising and solicitation, and is applied to all such activity except, we are told, veterans selling poppies in November. Hence, aside from that exception, the regulation is invoked uniformly; it reflects an invariable practice of prohibiting all means of expression, and thus constitutes a restriction of the guaranteed freedom according to the criteria enunciated above.

However, this case also raises an additional element in the equation. The events in question here occurred on government property. How does this affect the right of freedom of expression and prospective limitations with respect to that right? The government has argued that its proprietary rights are no different from private property rights generally, and thus it should be allowed to control all activity and exclude others as it sees fit. The respondents have argued that because certain types of government property have a public function and character—streets, squares, and parks are notable examples—the properties should therefore be completely open to public manifestations of free expression.

The judge noted that the concept of "public forum" had originated in US jurisprudence. She also noted that the attorney general of Ontario, an intervenor, had recommended the term "public arena" so as to avoid confusion with the US concept. She concluded that the action in question on the part of the defendant-appellant constituted a breach of s. 2(b) of the Charter and then considered whether the regulations could nonetheless be upheld as "a reasonable limit prescribed by law, demonstrably justified in a free and democratic society" pursuant to s. 1 of the Charter. In considering this question, L'Heureux-Dubé J considered the issue of property rights:

The appellant takes a hard line in urging this court to allow the appeal, submitting that as owner of property, the government has the right to exclude whomever it wants, and to impose conditions on invitees to its property without limitation by the Charter (translation):

It is therefore accurate, in our view, to state that the *Charter* did not have the effect of reducing in any way the government's rights and prerogatives as an owner.

Taken to their extreme, the consequences of such a determination would undermine the crucial function of government and the responsibility it bears to its constituents. If the government had complete discretion to treat its property as would a private citizen, it could differentiate on the basis of content, or choose between particular viewpoints, and grant access to sidewalks, streets, parks, the courthouse lawn, and even Parliament Hill only to those whose message accorded with the government's preferences. Such a standard would be antithetical to the spirit of the Charter, and would stultify the true import of freedom of expression.

When calibrating the s. 1 barometer, the political quality of the stifled expression must be weighed against whatever governmental arguments are raised in opposition. Unlike the American system whereby delineated tests are required for the various "types" of expression, our s. 1 is flexible enough to accommodate all these types, the result depending on what objectives are put forward by the government, and what means are selected to advance these objectives. This enables us to construct a contextual rather than a categorical approach, focusing not only on the scope of the right, but also on the setting in which the freedom of expression claim is made. As Wilson J explained in *Edmonton Journal v. Alberta, supra*, at pp. 583-4:

> One virtue of the contextual approach, it seems to me, is that it recognizes that a particular right or freedom may have a different value depending on the context. It may be, for example, that freedom of expression has greater value in a political context than it does in the context of disclosure of the details of a matrimonial dispute. The contextual approach attempts to bring into sharp relief the aspect of the right or freedom which is truly at stake in the case as well as the relevant aspects of any values in competition with it. It seems to be more sensitive to the reality of the dilemma posed by the particular facts and therefore more conducive to finding a fair and just compromise between the two competing values under s. 1.

The specific context of this claim is that the respondents are asserting a right to use inexpensive means of communication—leafletting and solicitation—in a government venue that by its nature concentrates a significant number of persons in one place at one time. Furthermore, many of those persons have time to kill and little to do, and so might be more receptive to information and ideas than they would be in other contexts.

The crux of the government's attempt to defend the provision at issue relates to its property interest in the airport. It relied heavily on the dissent of Pratte J at the Federal Court of Appeal, who held at p. 507 that:

> Dorval airport belongs to the federal government. The government has the same rights as any owner with respect to its property. Its ownership right, therefore, is exclusive like that of any individual. The only qualification to this rule arises from the fact that the property owned by the government is frequently intended for use by the public, which then has a right to use it for the purposes for which the government intends it.

Hence, the s. 1 analysis in this case must be sensitive to the unique relationship between government and its property. This will be instrumental as well in establishing criteria for what constitutes a "public" place, and what effect that has on the rationalization of freedom of expression limitations.

Freedom of expression and its relationship to public property

This court has long recognized that freedom of expression could be affected by governmental regulation of public property. In *Saumur v. City of Quebec, supra*, a municipal by-law forbidding the distribution of pamphlets in city streets without the permission of the chief of police was struck down as (in the opinion of three justices) *ultra vires* the province. Rand J stated at pp. 672-3, with respect to the arbitrary discretion of municipal officers and the need to use public property to disseminate ideas:

> What is proposed before us is that a newspaper, just as a religious, political or other tract or handbill, for the purposes of sale or distribution through use of streets, can be placed under the uncontrolled discretion of a municipal officer; that is, that the

province, while permitting all others, could forbid a newspaper or any other writing of a particular colour from being so disposed of. That public ways, in some circumstances the only practical means available for any appeal to the community generally, have from the most ancient times been the avenues for such communications, is demonstrated by the Bible itself: in the 6th verse of Chapter XI of Jeremiah these words appear: "Proclaim all these words in the cities of Judah, and in the streets of Jerusalem"; and a more objectionable interference, short of complete suppression, with that dissemination which is the "breath of life" of the political institutions of this country than that made possible by the by-laws can scarcely be imagined.

Kellock J stressed that a by-law prohibiting all distribution in the streets would raise "entirely different considerations," but this one was objectionable because it allowed the chief of police to decide between viewpoints.

An example of how public property is to be contrasted with private property can be found in arts. 399 and 400 of the *Civil Code of Lower Canada*:

399. Property belongs either to the Crown, or to municipalities or other corporations, or to individuals.

That of the first kind is governed by public or administrative law.

That of the second is subject, in certain respects as to its administration, its acquisition and its alienation, to certain rules and formalities which are peculiar to it.

As to individuals, they have the free disposal of the things belonging to them, under the modifications established by law.

400. Roads and public ways maintained by the state, navigable and floatable rivers and streams and their banks, the sea-shore, lands reclaimed from the sea, ports, harbours and roadsteads and generally all those portions of territory which do not constitute private property, are considered as being dependencies of the Crown domain.

The same rule applies to all lakes and to all non-navigable and non-floatable rivers and streams and their banks, bordering on lands alienated by the Crown after the 9th of February 1918.

The combined effect of arts. 399 and 400 of the *Civil Code of Lower Canada* is that all lands belong to someone. If property rights alone can be invoked to limit, restrain, or abridge a fundamental freedom on any given place of public property, the Charter's guarantees lose all meaning—only those holding the property-owner's permission could express themselves.

The obvious negative implications of such a standard have motivated the United States Supreme Court to hold that in some extreme circumstances, such as a company town, even technically private ownership may be tantamount to public ownership for the purposes of expression and debate:

Ownership does not always mean absolute dominion. The more an owner, for his advantage, opens up his property for use by the public in general, the more do his rights become circumscribed by the statutory and constitutional rights of those who use it.

Marsh v. Alabama, 326 US 501 (1946), at p. 506.

But in *Harrison v. Carswell* (1975), 62 DLR (3d) 68, 25 CCC (2d) 186, [1976] 2 SCR 200, a pre-Charter decision, the majority of this court held that an employee of a tenant in a shopping centre had no right to picket on the shopping centre sidewalk. The centre, as a matter of policy, had never permitted the distribution of pamphlets or leaflets, or the carrying of placards, within the mall. As Dickson J wrote for the majority at p. 83:

> Anglo-Canadian jurisprudence has traditionally recognized, as a fundamental freedom, the right of the individual to the enjoyment of property and the right not to be deprived thereof, or any interest therein, save by due process of law. The Legislature of Manitoba has declared in the *Petty Trespasses Act* that any person who trespasses upon land, the property of another, upon or through which he has been requested by the owner not to enter, is guilty of an offence. If there is to be any change in this statute law, if A is to be given the right to enter and remain on the land of B against the will of B, it would seem to me that such a change must be made by the enacting institution, the Legislature, which is representative of the people and designed to manifest the political will, and not by the Court.

Chief Justice Laskin dissented, holding at p. 73 that:

> The considerations which underlie the protection of private residences cannot apply to the same degree to a shopping centre in respect of its parking areas, roads and sidewalks. Those amenities are closer in character to public roads and sidewalks than to a private dwelling. All that can be urged from a theoretical point of view to assimilate them to private dwellings is to urge that if property is privately owned, no matter the use to which it is put, trespass is as appropriate in the one case as in the other, and it does not matter that possession, the invasion of which is basic to trespass, is recognizable in the one case but not in the other. There is here, on this assimilation, a legal injury albeit no actual injury. This is a use of theory which does not square with economic or social fact under the circumstances of the present case.

In *Pruneyard Shopping Center v. Robins*, 447 US 74 (1980), the appellant was a private shopping center which had a policy of not permitting visitors to "engage in any publicly expressive activity" while on the premises. The respondents were soliciting signatures for a political cause. The case was essentially about the right of the appellant to control the use of its property and its right to exclude others, versus the right of the respondents to engage in expressive activity on the shopping mall property. The court upheld the decision of the California Supreme Court, which interpreted the *State* Constitution as protecting "speech and petitioning, reasonably exercised, in shopping centers even when the centers are privately owned." The United States Supreme Court held, at p. 87, that:

> Most important, the shopping center by choice of its owner is not limited to the personal use of appellants. It is instead a business establishment that is open to the public to come and go as they please. The views expressed by members of the

public in passing out pamphlets or seeking signatures for a petition thus will not likely be identified with those of the owner. Second, no specific message is dictated by the State to be displayed on appellants' property. There consequently is no danger of governmental discrimination for or against a particular message. Finally, as far as appears here appellants can expressly disavow any connection with the message by simply posting signs in the area where the speakers or handbillers stand. Such signs, for example, could disclaim any sponsorship of the message and could explain that the persons are communicating their own messages by virtue of state law.

However, this distinction is not at issue in this appeal. For our present purposes it is only necessary to consider the Charter's impact on the distribution of leaflets on *government* property.

L'Heureux-Dubé J expressly refused to decide the Charter's effect on leafletting on *private* property since that issue was not squarely before the Court. She continued:

If members of the public had no right whatsoever to distribute leaflets or engage in other expressive activity on government-owned property (except with permission), then there would be little if any opportunity to exercise their rights of freedom of expression. Only those with enough wealth to own land, or mass media facilities (whose ownership is largely concentrated), would be able to engage in free expression. This would subvert achievement of the Charter's basic purpose as identified by this court, i.e., the free exchange of ideas, open debate of public affairs, the effective working of democratic institutions and the pursuit of knowledge and truth. These eminent goals would be frustrated if, for practical purposes, only the favoured few have any avenue to communicate with the public.

On the other hand, the Charter's framers did not intend internal government offices, air traffic control towers, prison cells and judges' chambers to be made available for leafletting or demonstrations. It is evident that the right to freedom of expression under s. 2(b) of the Charter does not provide a right of access to all property whether public or private. Such a wholesale transformation of all government property is not necessary to fulfil the Charter's purposes, or to avoid a stifling of free expression. As this court held in *R v. Big M Drug Mart, supra*, at p. 380, while the Charter should be given a broad and generous interpretation, "it is important not to overshoot the actual purpose of the right or freedom in question."

The logical compromise then is to recognize that some, but not all, government-owned property is constitutionally open to the public for engaging in expressive activity. Restrictions on expression in particular places will be harder to defend than in others. In some places the justifiability of the restrictions is immediately apparent. As Chief Justice Dickson explained in *R v. Oakes* (1986), 26 DLR (4th) 200 at p. 227, 24 CCC (3d) 321, [1986] 1 SCR 103: "I should add, however, that there may be cases where certain elements of the s. 1 analysis are obvious or self-evident."

Certain criteria, while not themselves dispositive, can assist in determining what locations are appropriately open for public expression, and bear the earmarks of "public arenas." The status of airports can then be determined in light of these standards.

"Public forums," "public arenas," and airports

In *A-G Can. v. Dupond* (1978), 84 DLR (3d) 420, [1978] 2 SCR 770, 5 MPLR 4, *sub nom. Dupond v. City of Montreal*, Beetz J for the majority expressed the opinion [at p. 439] that "[f]ar from being the object of a right, the holding of a public meeting on a street or in a park may constitute a trespass against the urban authority in whom the ownership of the street is vested," and that freedom of expression could not be relied upon to strike down a by-law prohibiting all demonstrations for one month. However, this was before the Charter, and the case is evidence of, if nothing else, an understanding that the law of trespass may act as a legal limit on freedom of expression.

But the distinctive nature of government property whittles away at the application of trespass law. As the United States Supreme Court held in *Hague v. Committee for Industrial Organization*, 307 US 496 (1939), at pp. 515-6:

> Wherever the title of streets and parks may rest, they have immemorially been held in trust for the use of the public and, time out of mind, have been used for purposes of assembly, communicating thoughts between citizens, and discussing public questions. Such use of the streets and public places has, from ancient times, been a part of the privileges, immunities, rights, and liberties of citizens. The privilege of a citizen of the United States to use the streets and parks for communication of views on national questions may be regulated in the interest of all; it is not absolute, but relative, and must be exercised in subordination to the general comfort and convenience, and in consonance with peace and good order; but it must not, in the guise of regulation, be abridged or denied.

And as Harry Kalven, Jr. stated in: "The Concept of the Public Forum: *Cox v. Louisiana*," [1965] Sup. Ct. Rev. 1, at pp. 11-12:

> ... in an open democratic society the streets, the parks, and other public places are an important facility for public discussion and political process. They are in brief a public forum that the citizen can commandeer; the generosity and empathy with which such facilities are made available is an index of freedom.

However, even the right of political self-expression is not completely unfettered, and as the US Supreme Court explained in *Cox v. Louisiana*, 379 US 536 (1965), at p. 554:

> The rights of free speech and assembly, while fundamental in our democratic society, still do not mean that everyone with opinions or beliefs to express may address a group at any public place and at any time. *The constitutional guarantee of liberty implies the existence of an organized society maintaining public order, without which liberty itself would be lost in the excesses of anarchy.*

(Emphasis added.)

Following discussion and rejection of the American "public forum" doctrine, L'Heureux-Dubé J continued:

> The Federal Court of Appeal refused to recognize the American "public forum" approach. Applying such a broad prohibition here would virtually deny the government

any power to regulate expressive activities at airports, and go beyond the jurisprudence of the US Supreme Court to date. Furthermore, too broad a holding might have far-reaching consequences for regulation of expressive activities on public property generally.

With this in mind, when designing "made in Canada" criteria for determining what places are to be considered public, I am of the view that we should selectively draw upon some of the American specifications, without importing them wholesale. As stated, the AGO has suggested that we employ the term "public arena" to avoid confusion with the American terminology, and has also offered certain factors to be considered when inquiring as to whether a given place qualifies. The proposed determinants include:

1. The traditional openness of such property for expressive activity.
    This criterion is not a *sine qua non* as in the US. Absence of tradition would not preclude the declaration of a public arena, as the other factors may very well yield the same conclusion.
2. Whether the public is ordinarily admitted to the property as of right.
3. The compatibility of the property's purpose with such expressive activities.
    If the activity interfered with the property's purpose, it would be less likely to be justified. Properties with multiple purposes would be problematic under this criterion.
4. The impact of the availability of such property for expressive activity on the achievement of s. 2(b)'s purposes.
5. The symbolic significance of the property for the message being communicated.
    This is a contextual criterion, linking the property with the purpose or cause of the demonstration.
6. The availability of other public arenas in the vicinity for expressive activities.
    A property would be more open to activities if no other property was available.

I find these criteria very valuable. While they are not meant to be dispositive in any given case, they do provide useful guidelines. It was submitted that it should be up to the claimant, as part of demonstrating a case of infringement, to show that the property is a "public arena." If so, then the onus would shift to the government to justify the limitation under s. 1. I disagree for the reasons discussed above. As stated, whether a location qualifies as a "public arena" is simply the "place" component when considering the constitutionality of time, place, and manner regulations generally. Therefore, such place's classification for constitutional purposes should be evaluated under s. 1.

Balancing the interests at stake

While the United States Supreme Court has declined to pronounce on whether the "public forum" label should attach to airports, lower courts have held that an airport is a public forum: *Chicago Area Military Project v. City of Chicago*, 508 F2d 1243 (9th Cir. 1981); *US Southwest Africa/Namibia Trade & Cultural Council v. United States*, 708 F2d 760 (DC Cir. 1983). The logic of these cases is that airports have become "contemporary crossroads"; they are functionally equivalent to other public thoroughfares, and should therefore be on the same constitutional footing as streets and parks.

Lehman v. City of Shaker Heights, 418 US 298 (1974), involved a challenge by a candidate for political office against an ordinance prohibiting political placards on all buses and streetcars. The court upheld the regulation. As Douglas J, concurring, expressed at pp. 306-7:

> [I]f we are to turn a bus or streetcar into either a newspaper or a park, we take great liberties with people who because of necessity become commuters and at the same time captive viewers or listeners.
>
> In asking us to force the system to accept his message as a vindication of his constitutional rights, the petitioner overlooks the constitutional rights of the commuters. While the petitioner clearly has a right to express his views to those who wish to listen, he has no right to force his message upon an audience incapable of declining to receive it. In my view the right of the commuters to be free from forced intrusions on their privacy precludes the city from transforming its vehicles of public transportation into forums for the dissemination of ideas upon this captive audience.

Similarly airplanes, even if publicly owned, could not be characterized as a public forum. People who find certain political expression unpleasant or disquieting in a park or on a street can easily move elsewhere. On planes the costs of premature exit are too high. However, bus stations and airports have much more in common with streets and parks than they do with the buses or airplanes which they service. These locations are "contemporary crossroads" or "modern thoroughfares," and thus should be accessible to those seeking to communicate with the passing crowds.

In order to assess whether airport terminals are properly considered public arenas, we must explore their function in contemporary society. Airport terminals are freely accessible to all members of the public. However, the terminals themselves can be divided broadly into security zones—such as Customs, check-in counters, metal detector surveillance areas, and baggage inspection—and non-security zones—such as lounges, waiting areas, restaurants, gift and cigar shops, news-stands, and the connecting halls and foyers. Certain expressive activity is clearly more compatible within the latter areas than within the former.

Airports also draw a tremendous number of travellers over the course of a day. The Dorval operations manager testified that about 20,000 passengers use the airport daily, often accompanied by other persons. Few locations can parallel this reliable concentration of people. Bus, train and airport terminals are indeed modern boulevards, extensions of Main Street. The list of sites traditionally associated with public expression is not static. As means of locomotion progress, people shall begin to gather in areas heretofore unknown. Hence the "traditional" component of the public arena analysis must appreciate the "type" of place historically associated with public discussion, and should not be restricted to the actual places themselves.

This same reasoning applies when assessing the symbolic significance of the property. While the symbolism of a courthouse lawn or Parliament Hill is self-evident, streets and parks have also acquired special significance as places where one can have access to and address his or her fellow citizens on any number of matters. This distinctive attribute does not accrue to a street or a park merely because of its designation. A park has no intrinsic value as a public arena, it only obtains this characteristic because the public chooses to frequent parks. Whether a tree falling in an uninhabited park makes a sound is not a constitutional question. To what extent impediments may be placed upon a person addressing passers-by in a park is.

The same holds true for airport terminals. Respondents did not select the airport in order to convey their message to planes, but rather chose the airport for the people who would be present within it. While airport terminals do not have a monopoly on high concentrations of passers-by, few locations offer similar opportunities to encounter such a wide cross-section of the community. For the aforementioned reasons, and upon consideration of the above factors, the non-security zones within airport terminals, in my view, are properly regarded as public arenas. Therefore, the government cannot simply assert property rights, or claim that expression is unrelated to an airport's function, in order to justify the restriction.

Is this decision consistent with the decision in *Harrison v. Carswell*? What factors are relevant to this question? Is an airport owned by a government less "private" property than a shopping centre owned by a corporation? Would the Committee for the Commonwealth of Canada be permitted to leaflet in a shopping centre? Why, or why not? The constitutional issues are complex, and you may want to reconsider this case again after examining the materials later in this book. For a good overview of the issues, see J. Cameron, "A Bumpy Landing: The Supreme Court of Canada and Access to Public Airports Under Section 2(b) of the Charter" (1991), 2 *Media & Communications Law Review* 91.

Consider the comments of C.B. Macpherson about property owned by the government—"state property":

> [State property] consists of rights which the state has not only created but has kept for itself or has taken over from private individuals or corporations ... . Various enterprises, e.g., railways and airlines, are in many countries owned by the state. The rights which the state holds and exercises in respect of these things, the rights which comprise the state's property in these things, are akin to private property rights, for they consist of the right to the use and benefit, and the right to exclude others from the use and benefit, of something. In effect, the state itself is taking and exercising the powers of a corporation: it is acting as an artificial person ... . State property, then, is not common property as we have defined it: state property is not an individual right not to be excluded. It is a corporate right to exclude. As a corporate right to exclude others it fits the definition of (corporate) private property.

(C.B. Macpherson, "The Meaning of Property," in Macpherson, 1, at 5.)

Do you agree that "state property" is more like "private property" than "common property"? On what basis? Is this analysis consistent with the decision of the SCC?

In *Committee for the Commonwealth of Canada*, L'Heureux-Dubé J identified different parts of the airport that might be more or less "public" parts of the property, in much the same way that Laskin CJC identified different parts of the shopping centre as more or less "public." Is it possible to regard parts of these properties as "private" or "state" property, while other parts are "common property"? Would such a resolution be more likely to be achieved by negotiation or by litigation? Why? These issues were considered in a different context in relation to the regulation of taxis at the airport in Toronto: see *R v. Trabulsey* (1995), 22 OR (3d) 314 (CA).

In the United States, the constitutionality of trespass statutes was considered in *State v. Shack*, 277 A2d 369 (NJ Sup. Ct. 1971). In that case, the defendants were two employees of agencies funded by the Office of Economic Opportunity. One was a field worker with responsibilities for health services for migrant workers, and the other was a staff attorney with an agency that provided legal advice and assistance to migrant workers. The defendants had entered the plaintiff's land to meet with migrant workers (one of whom was injured) who lived in housing provided by their employer, the plaintiff. The plaintiff refused to permit the defendants to see the migrant workers except in the presence of the plaintiff, and when the defendants did not agree to this arrangement and refused to leave the plaintiff's land, the plaintiff charged them with trespass. They were convicted at trial. On appeal to the New Jersey Supreme Court, however, the defendants successfully challenged the constitutionality of the trespass statute. In assessing the following comments in the appellate court's decision, note especially the court's efforts to define the boundaries of the "right to exclude." Would this approach be preferable in the context of a case like *Harrison v. Carswell*?

Property rights serve human values. They are recognized to that end, and are limited by it. Title to real property cannot include dominion over the destiny of persons the owner permits to come upon the premises. Their well-being must remain the paramount concern of a system of law. Indeed the needs of the occupants may be so imperative and their strength so weak, that the law will deny the occupants the power to contract away what is deemed essential to their health, welfare, or dignity.

Here we are concerned with a highly disadvantaged segment of our society. We are told that every year farm workers and their families numbering more than one million leave their home areas to fill the seasonal demand for farm labor in the United States. ...

The migrant farmworkers are a community within but apart from the local scene. They are rootless and isolated. Although the need for their labors is evident, they are unorganized and without economic or political power. It is their plight alone that summoned government to their aid. In response, Congress provided under Title III-B of the Economic Opportunity Act of 1964 (42 US CA § 2701 et seq.) for "assistance for migrant and other seasonally employed farmworkers and their families." Section 2861 states "the purpose of this part is to assist migrant and seasonal farmworkers and their families to improve their living conditions and develop skills necessary for a productive and self-sufficient life in an increasingly complex and technological society." Section 2862(b)(1) provides for funding of programs "to meet the immediate needs of migrant and seasonal farmworkers and their families, such as day care for children, education, health services, improved housing and sanitation (including the provision and maintenance of emergency and temporary housing and sanitation facilities), legal advice and representation, and consumer training and counseling." As we have said, SCOPE is engaged in a program funded under this section, and CRLS also pursues the objectives of this section although, we gather, it is funded under § 2809(a)(3), which is not limited in its concern to the migrant and other seasonally employed farmworkers and seeks "to further the cause of justice among persons living in poverty by mobilizing the assistance of lawyers and legal institutions and by providing legal advice, legal representation, counseling, education, and other appropriate services."

These ends would not be gained if the intended beneficiaries could be insulated from efforts to reach them. It is in this framework that we must decide whether the camp operator's rights in his lands may stand between the migrant workers and those who would aid them. The key to that aid is communication. Since the migrant workers are outside the mainstream of the communities in which they are housed and are unaware of their rights and opportunities and of the services available to them, they can be reached only by positive efforts tailored to that end. *The Report of the Governor's Task Force on Migrant Farm Labor* (1968) noted that "One of the major problems related to seasonal farm labor is the lack of adequate direct information with regard to the availability of public services," and that "there is a dire need to provide the workers with basic educational and informational material in a language and style that can be readily understood by the migrant" (pp. 101-102). The report stressed the problem of access and deplored the notion that property rights may stand as a barrier, saying, "In our judgment, 'no trespass' signs represent the last dying remnants of paternalistic behavior" (p. 63).

A man's right in his real property of course is not absolute. It was a maxim of the common law that one should so use his property as not to injure the rights of others. Broom, Legal Maxims (10th ed. Kersley 1939), p. 238; 39 Words and Phrases, "Sic Utere Tuo ut Alienum Non Laedas," p. 335. Although hardly a precise solvent of actual controversies, the maxim does express the inevitable proposition that rights are relative and there must be an accommodation when they meet. ...

Thus approaching the case, we find it unthinkable that the farmer-employer can assert a right to isolate the migrant worker in any respect significant for the worker's well-being. The farmer, of course, is entitled to pursue his farming activities without interference, and this defendants readily concede. But we see no legitimate need for a right in the farmer to deny the worker the opportunity for aid available from federal, State, or local services, or from recognized charitable groups seeking to assist him. Hence representatives of these agencies and organizations may enter upon the premises to seek out the worker at his living quarters. So, too, the migrant worker must be allowed to receive visitors there of his own choice, so long as there is no behavior hurtful to others, and members of the press may not be denied reasonable access to workers who do not object to seeing them.

It is not our purpose to open the employer's premises to the general public if in fact the employer himself has not done so. We do not say, for example, that solicitors or peddlers of all kinds may enter on their own; we may assume for the present that the employer may regulate their entry or bar them, at least if the employer's purpose is not to gain a commercial advantage for himself or if the regulation does not deprive the migrant worker of practical access to things he needs.

And we are mindful of the employer's interest in his own and in his employees' security. Hence he may reasonably require a visitor to identify himself, and also to state his general purpose if the migrant worker has not already informed him that the visitor is expected. But the employer may not deny the worker his privacy or interfere with his opportunity to live with dignity and to enjoy associations customary among our citizens. These rights are too fundamental to be denied on the basis of an interest in real property

and too fragile to be left to the unequal bargaining strength of the parties. See
Henningsen v. Bloomfield Motors, Inc., 32 NJ 358, 403-404, 161 A2d 69 (1960);
Ellsworth Dobbs, Inc. v. Johnson, 50 NJ 528, 555, 236 A2d 843 (1967).

It follows that defendants here invaded no possessory right of the farmer-employer.
Their conduct was therefore beyond the reach of the trespass statute. The judgments are
accordingly reversed and the matters remanded to the County Court with directions to
enter judgments of acquittal.

The issue of migrant workers' rights to security and the decision in *State v. Shack* were
considered again in *Vasquez v. Glassboro Service Association Inc.*, 415 A2d 1156
(NJ Sup. Ct. 1980).

In an assessment of the continuing usefulness of *Harrison v. Carswell* after the
Charter, M. Litman concluded that there were several reasons for being optimistic "that
Harrison v. Carswell will be reconsidered and reversed":

> The majority view in that case seems to have been based on the supposition that
> property is inherently absolute and that the dramatic step of depriving its owner, even to
> a limited extent, of its unbridled power is a matter for legislative policy. This
> supposition ... as a matter of historical record, is not entirely accurate. Proprietary rights
> of exclusion, like other private rights, have been modified or subordinated to
> accommodate a variety of interests since the early days of the common law, and
> continue today to yield to such interests ... . There is no reason in principle why free
> speech should not be part of the constellation of considerations which affect the
> determination of whether property rights exist and, if so, whether those rights are
> tempered by the public interest.

(M.M. Litman, "Freedom of Speech and Private Property: The Case of the Mall Owner,"
in D. Schneiderman, ed., *Freedom of Expression and the Charter* (Scarborough, ON:
Thomson, 1991), 361, at 407.) See also two cases concerning municipal bylaws limiting
portable signs in relation to s. 2(b) of the Charter: *Canadian Mobile Sign Assn. v.
Burlington (City)* (1977), 34 OR (3d) 134 (CA), and *Stoney Creek (City) v. Advantage
Signs Ltd.* (1997), 34 OR (3d) 65 (CA).

Some US courts have held that a shopping centre may not prohibit the exercise of
freedom of expression. In *Pruneyard Shopping Center v. Robins*, 447 US 74 (1980), the
US Supreme Court reviewed a decision of the California Supreme Court that held that
the state constitution protected persons soliciting petition signatures in a private shopping centre. The Supreme Court considered whether this decision constituted an unconstitutional "taking" by government of the mall owner's property rights, and held that it
did not, concluding (at 83) that there was no basis for finding that "this sort of activity
will unreasonably impair the value or use of their property as a shopping center." For
interesting comments on the nature of the public/private distinction in the property
context, see M. Horwitz, "The History of the Public/Private Distinction" (1982), 130
University of Pennsylvania Law Review 1423 and D. Kennedy, "The Stages of the
Decline of the Public/Private Distinction" (1982), 130 *University of Pennsylvania Law
Review* 1349.

Shopping Centres as "Common Property"

There have also been some policy developments that suggest a concept of shopping centres as "common property." Ontario's Trespass to Property Act, RSO 1990, c. T.21 defines the offence of trespass as follows:

> 2.(1) Every person who is not acting under a right or authority conferred by law and who,
>
> > (a) without the express permission of the occupier, the proof of which rests on the defendant,
> >
> > > (i) enters on premises when entry is prohibited under this Act, or
> > >
> > > (ii) engages in an activity on premises when the activity is prohibited under this Act; or
> >
> > (b) does not leave the premises immediately after he is directed to do so by the occupier of the premises or a person authorized by the occupier,
>
> is guilty of an offence and on conviction is liable to a fine of not more than $1,000.
>
> (2) It is a defence to a charge under subsection (1) in respect of premises that is land that the person charged reasonably believed that he had title to or an interest in the land that entitled him to do the act complained of. ...
>
> 9.(1) A police officer, or the occupier of premises, or a person authorized by the occupier may arrest without warrant any person he believes on reasonable and probable grounds to be on the premises in contravention of section 2.
>
> (2) Where the person who makes an arrest under subsection (1) is not a police officer, he shall promptly call for the assistance of a police officer and give the person arrested into the custody of the police officer.

This legislation is similar to statutes elsewhere: see Protection of Property Act, SNS 1982, c. 13 and Trespass Act, SNB 1983, c. T-11.2. Consider the language of the Ontario statute in the light of the facts of *Harrison v. Carswell*. Would it have been decided in the same way pursuant to the Ontario legislation? Why, or why not?

The Ontario legislation was subjected to criticism by a task force report in 1987 that considered the law of trespass in relation to the experience of youth and minorities in shopping malls. In reading the following excerpt from the task force's report, consider how its recommendations might be reflected in the language of the Trespass to Property Act. To what extent is there a need for a different conception of property interests? Are the task force arguments the same or different from those asserted by Laskin CJC in dissent in *Harrison v. Carswell*? See Ontario, Task Force on the Law Concerning Trespass to Publicly-Used Property as It Affects Youth and Minorities (Raj Anand, Chair) (Toronto: Ontario Ministry of the Attorney General, 1987), at ii-x (footnotes omitted):

The Trespass to Property Act, 1980

The traditional common law of trespass to property was predicated upon absolute notions of private property and its attributes, such as the right to exclude others. The last two centuries of industrialization and other social change have seen an accelerating process of limitation of private property rights where public and private interests in the use of such property have diverged. As late as the mid-1970's, the Supreme Court of Canada enunciated a "duty of common humanity" on property owners toward trespassers who suffered injury.

Viewed in its common law context, the *TPA* was unfortunate in certain respects. It took no account of the developing trends in balancing the competing social interests in publicly-used property. It instead crystallized the absolutist common law position in Ontario, and thereby foreclosed further development. The *TPA*, like its predecessors, makes no distinction between different types of property and the degree of public use. Under the *Act*, a shopping mall is no different than a private home, in that it carries with it a general right of exclusion of any visitor, and the exercise of this right is legally subject to the owner's whim.

Potential for abuse

On its face, the *TPA* creates the potential for unduly restrictive or discriminatory enforcement against minorities and youth. An occupier or manager of publicly-used property or a security guard can require any member of the public to leave the property at any time, for any reason, or for no reason at all. This can be accomplished either orally or by written notice. If the person does not leave immediately, he or she commits an offence punishable by a fine of up to $1,000 and may be arrested by the official and delivered into the custody of a police officer. Failure to pay can result in a jail term under the *Provincial Offences Act*.

Moreover, there is no necessary time limit on the prohibition against entry. Thus, unless the occupier voluntarily limits the duration of the "ban," the visitor who leaves when directed to do so cannot re-enter the property later the same day, or the next day, or indeed the next year.

Wide "prosecutorial" discretion is vested in the occupier of publicly-used property to choose when, how and for how long to exclude any individual person among the multitudes who avail themselves of the general invitation to enter such property. The *TPA* is unusual in that it places private citizens—those who own publicly-used property—in the central role of policing this *Act*. Implementation of society's prohibition against unacceptable conduct is left largely in hands of persons who have no necessary accountability or indeed training for the role. Furthermore, there is no requirement in the *TPA* of an overt act or misconduct by an unwanted visitor other than sheer presence on the premises. It is the occupier's right to exclude for the simple reason that "this is private property." This virtually absolute discretion is seriously out of step with the role and social significance of publicly-used property, particularly shopping centres, in contemporary Ontario society.

Public perceptions

The widespread public perception is that shopping centres are "public property" or "public places," in the sense that persons have the right to enter freely, walk around, converse with others and remain within the common areas as long as they wish, much as they would conduct themselves in a city square. This public perception was asserted by most individuals and representatives of youth and minorities (the "user groups") and was acknowledged by most of the owners and enforcers of the *Act* (the "owner groups"). The inconsistency between the legal position and the common understanding was cited by the police forces, security officers and the Ontario Human Rights Commission as a central problem which resulted in strained communications between enforcement officials and the public, and frequent resentment by minority groups and young people.

Social importance and social responsibility

Academic research confirms the evidence received by this Task Force: that there is a lack of suitable community facilities for people—particularly young people—to simply meet, converse, "see and be seen"; that these needs are vital ones, and providing them is a principal function of urban and town planning; and that shopping malls have willingly and for good commercial reasons accepted this role. The central role of shopping centres as a location for community interaction is reflected in the fact that in terms of time spent by the average citizen, shopping centres rank third, after (1) home and (2) work or school.

"Hanging out" is not a problem in itself. It is a healthy and indeed necessary pastime in a contemporary world which is increasingly dominated by the concerns of family and work. In earlier Ontario society and in many of the countries of origin of recent immigrants "hanging around" on street corners and squares has been indispensable to effective social participation. In Ontario, suburban areas frequently grew up without much planning for public spaces and social facilities, and malls became the accidental capitals of suburbia. In downtown areas, shopping malls literally displaced and enclosed city streets, street corners and plazas. Into the mall and onto its closed streets, have been added most of the amenities associated with community life; moreover, essential services are often found in shopping plazas and nowhere else in the neighbourhood.

Shopping centre representatives stressed the role of these facilities as community centres with community responsibilities to the towns which they serve. It was important for such places to become an integral part of the community around them, and to provide more than a selection of materials and goods. There has, however, been an insufficient recognition by owners of publicly-used property of the need to provide for the uses by the public which may not contribute, directly or indirectly, to the principal goal of profitability. The privatization of the town square must carry with it a corresponding obligation to provide for "non-productive uses." This obligation must be implemented through legal recognition in the *TPA* of the public use of such private property and by addressing design issues in the construction of publicly-used spaces.

As this task force report noted, suburban development in Canada and elsewhere has often resulted in the separation of housing from commercial and other amenities. As a result, residents of suburban housing developments may require transport to do daily errands or engage in social or other activities. Such an arrangement may create difficulties for teenagers without access to cars, with the result that they "hang out" at the local shopping mall. In urban centres, the development of shopping malls may take the place of "open space," including "street space," where malls are created by enclosing parts of city streets. In these malls, teenagers may congregate as if they were on street corners. However, these activities may cause difficulty in both suburban and urban shopping malls because the mall is private property. What options are available to mall owners in these circumstances? What are the mall owner's legal rights pursuant to Ontario's Trespass to Property Act, for example? Are there other considerations that need to be taken into account, such as business or human rights considerations? Are the teenagers exercising freedom of expression in "hanging out" at the mall, just as the Committee for the Commonwealth of Canada was exercising this right at the Montreal airport?

The task force report was created as a result of complaints from Toronto's Black community that they were being unfairly banned from shopping centres, including the Eaton Centre and the shopping malls in the Jane-Finch area of North York. As a result of the report, the provincial government introduced a bill to amend the Trespass to Property Act, but it died on the order paper before the end of the legislative session.

In 1993, a task force to stop racism at Scarborough Town Centre was created by community members in response to the incidence of "trespass bans" against young Filipino Canadians. The task force alleged that security guards at the mall were evicting young Filipino Canadians and charging them pursuant to the Trespass to Property Act, although the young people were not engaged in suspicious behaviour. In recommending changes to the mall's policies with respect to these actions, the task force relied on Ontario's Human Rights Code, RSO 1990, c. H.19, s. 1, which guarantees the right to equal treatment "with respect to services, goods and facilities" without discrimination "because of race, ancestry, place of origin, colour, ethnic origin, citizenship, creed, sex, sexual orientation, age, marital status, family status or handicap." The Scarborough Town Centre task force asserted that the banning and harassment of Filipino Canadian youth constituted a clear violation of the Code (see (1993), 4 *Law Times* October 25-31, at 5), and noted that the Human Rights Code prevails over the Trespass to Property Act. Taking account of the requirements of both these statutes, consider what elements would need to be included in a mall's policy with respect to its security arrangements? What kinds of instructions should be given to security guards?

A different approach was adopted by the Dufferin Mall in Toronto, where there had been serious problems relating to drugs, youth alienation, women's safety, and loneliness among the elderly. Among other community projects, the mall decided to operate a special "mall school" for students who work in the mall, as well as a re-entry program for high school dropouts. In 1994, the manager of the mall declared (as reported in the *Toronto Star*, April 16, 1994, at B4):

> We had two choices: to adopt a fortress mentality, erecting metaphorical walls to keep all undesirable elements at bay or, conversely, to remove all walls and actively deal with the problems.

The same newspaper report stated that "traffic increased to 8.5 million people in 1993, despite the recession, and the kids still hang out there." In another report the next year, the mall manager also suggested that "business is shortsighted if it fails to recognize that the better the quality of life in a neighbourhood, the better the business environment." (*Toronto Star*, February 19, 1995, at A12.) How would a lawyer draft this mall's policy regarding "hanging out"? What kinds of instructions would be drafted for security guards? To what extent can a lawyer "shape" such a policy in the drafting process?

NEW CHALLENGES: PROPERTY AND BODY PARTS

Moore v. Regents of the University of California
51 Cal 3d 120, 793 P2d 479 (Calif. Sup. Ct. 1990)

[As part of a process of treatment for a rare form of leukaemia, John Moore had his spleen removed in 1976. Dr. Golde, Moore's physician at the University of California in Los Angeles (UCLA), used tissue samples from this spleen, and made two findings that aided in his own research on the aetiology of this form of leukaemia. Dr. Golde's assistant, Shirley Quan, found that they were able to develop a cell line (a sample of cells grown in an artificial medium) from Moore's cells and, further, that Moore's cells were unusually rich in certain commercially valuable immune system chemicals. Thus, the cell line was worth preserving and developing.

From 1976 to 1983, Dr. Golde obtained further samples of Moore's blood and bodily substances. These were also used in Dr. Golde's research. In 1984, Golde and Quan were awarded a patent on the cell line and a number of products were derived from it. They assigned the patent to UCLA and entered into contracts with two companies to collaborate on the commercial exploitation of the cell line and products derived from it. Six months after they received the patent, John Moore sued Golde and Quan. Among other issues was the question whether the actions of Golde and Quan constituted the tort of conversion, an action dependent on a finding that Moore had some proprietary interest in his bodily tissues. In reading Joan Gilmour's critique of the *Moore* case, consider the similarities and differences in the approaches of the judges in this case, by contrast with *Victoria Park* and *Harrison v. Carswell*.]

Joan Gilmour, " 'Our' Bodies: Property Rights in Human Tissue"
(1993), 8:2 *Canadian Journal of Law and Society* 113, at 120-23 and 128-36
(footnotes omitted)

Moore finally became suspicious of the need for continuing visits to the UCLA in September 1983, when he was pressured by Dr. Golde to sign a second consent form that included a "voluntary" grant to the University of California of any and all rights he might have in any cell line or any other potential product which might be developed from the blood and bone marrow obtained from him. He refused. In September 1984, Moore commenced an action against Golde, Quan, UCLA, Genetics Institute, Sandoz Inc., and others. Moore alleged that pursuant to contractual arrangements among the defendants, Genetics gave Golde 75,000 shares of its stock at a nominal price, and that Sandoz and Genetics paid the UCLA and Golde $440,000 over three years. He alleged further that by the time he commenced the lawsuit, Golde's stock was worth $3,000,000, and that the products developed from the Mo cell line had a potential market value many times that amount. The statement of claim set out thirteen causes of action, which can be broken down into two categories—first, those that flowed from Moore's assertion of ownership or proprietary right in his cells and the Mo cell line and derivative products, and second, those associated with the allegations of failure to obtain Moore's informed consent to the removal of his tissue. The defendants responded with demurrers—that is, preliminary objections that the plaintiff had failed to state any reasonable cause of action. The defendants were successful in their attack on Moore's claim of conversion (and hence, on all the other property-dependent claims) in the first instance before the Superior Court, Los Angeles County. On appeal, the California Court of Appeal reversed, holding that Moore had adequately stated a cause of action for conversion. The Supreme Court of California granted review and held that Moore did not have a cause of action for conversion, although he could proceed with the action insofar as it was based on lack of informed consent and breach of fiduciary duty. The United States Supreme Court denied *certiorari*.

The California Court of Appeal and the Supreme Court of California reached diametrically opposed conclusions on Moore's proprietary claims to the cells and the cell line (although not without strong dissents at each level). The end result is foretold in each court's initial phrasing of the pre-existing analytical framework by which it saw itself constrained. The Court of Appeal started from the premise that there was "no legal authority, no public policy and no universally known facts of biological science that would *compel a conclusion*" that the plaintiff could not have "sufficient legal interest in his own body tissues amounting to personal property." In other words, no existing law or jurisprudence would force the court to close the door on a finding of property rights in one's own tissue. By way of contrast, when the Supreme Court of California turned to consider whether Moore could maintain an action for conversion, it noted that "no court ... has ever in a reported decision imposed conversion liability for the use of human cells in medical research." To the Supreme Court, quite clearly, the door Moore would have to open—the onus he would have to discharge—to convince it to recognize his claim to property rights in his own tissue was a very heavy one indeed. That is probably because, as is quickly apparent from a reading of the Supreme Court's judgment, the majority saw such a finding less as opening a door than as opening the lid on a Pandora's box and letting loose a host of undesirable consequences.

Both levels of court worked within traditional legal concepts in order to determine, first, what is entailed in having a property interest in something, and second, how to decide who holds that interest. Relative to the first issue—what it means to have a property interest—the analysis invokes the now familiar idea of property as a bundle of rights, with the precise content of the bundle varying depending on the nature of the property, the situation of the owner, and the context. Even though the content of that bundle may have a contingent and contested quality in any particular instance, the ability to control use of and access to "the property" is one of the elements that is commonly thought of as constitutive of whether a property right in the material exists or *can* exist, and in whom it lies. Consequently, the scope of and limits on Moore's control of the material taken from his body were, not surprisingly, a crucial enquiry for both levels of court.

The Court of Appeal characterized a property interest as the "right and interest or domination rightfully obtained over an object." The conclusion that the cells, which had been part of a human *subject*, Moore, were transformed on excision into an *object* and could be treated like any other object of property on their removal from him is implicit but remains unspoken in the judgment. Since Moore enjoyed the unrestricted right to the use, control, and disposition of his spleen, the Court of Appeal concluded that "[t]hese rights and interests are so akin to property interests that it would be subterfuge to call them something else." It regarded the various statutory regimes to which human tissue is subject in California as simply confirming that individuals are indeed able to determine what is done with parts of their own bodies, subject to limitations arising from public health concerns.

On appeal, the Supreme Court of California differed. It took the position that California statute law so drastically circumscribed a patient's right of control over excised cells as to leave nothing to call "property" in terms of rights a patient could assert over the cells. Effectively, said the court, once the cells have been excised from a patient's body, he loses control over them and hence, loses any proprietary interest he may have had in them. Although the Supreme Court disclaimed any suggestion that its holding meant excised cells could never be property for any purpose whatsoever, its rejection of the various bases on which a property right was asserted by the human source was so thorough and wide ranging that its claim to still leave the possibility of property analysis open in some unspecified instance seems no more than an empty rhetorical flourish, included only out of an abundance of caution.

Additionally, the majority inappropriately mixed patent requirements with ownership requirements in considering whether Moore could have a property interest in his cells, going to considerable lengths to make the point that Moore's cells were not unique—he just had more of one particular type than most people. The question of the cells' uniqueness had nothing to do with whether they could be Moore's property. Uniqueness is entirely irrelevant to a proprietary claim; there are many objects that are unquestionably not unique, but are equally unquestionably owned—books, telephones, cars, and so on. The element of uniqueness is only relevant to the award of a patent, not to a property interest. Moore's claim was that whether or not the cells taken from his body were unique, they were *his* from the beginning (before any patent was granted or even sought), and that he therefore had a claim to some share in the cell line grown from them. By inaccurately interchanging property and patent requirements, the majority avoided having to grapple fully with this portion of Moore's argument.

[The author reviewed the courts' handling of the second issue—who could exercise property rights to the material—and their differing conclusions. According to the Court of Appeal, Moore necessarily retained a continuing property right in the tissue removed; by contrast, the Supreme Court dismissed the possibility of the human source's owning the cells both because of a lack of the requisite degree of control and because the cells were not unique. Thus, the Supreme Court concluded that only the researchers had a proprietary interest through their "labours" which created the cell line. In doing so, the court relied on the "labour-added" theory of property of John Locke and the need to protect the legitimate economic expectations of researchers (echoing the work of Jeremy Bentham, another 19th century philosopher).]

Although Moore's claims were dismissed to the extent that they depended on establishing a property interest, he was allowed to proceed with his claims of breach of fiduciary duty and failure to obtain his informed consent before removing his tissue, based on the failure to disclose either his physician's research or his economic interest in the cells. Proving entitlement to any significant recovery pursuant to these theories of liability could, however, prove substantially more difficult than had he been able to rely on conversion. The test Moore would have to meet, the measure of damages that would be applied, and the extension of liability to defendants other than Moore's treating physician all present greater hurdles than would establishing conversion, which is essentially a strict liability tort.

The extent of Moore's recovery will await a trial on the merits; what is apparent at this point is that the California Supreme Court has blocked Moore's straightest path to a share in the profits from products developed from the cell line grown from his tissue. To many, that seems intuitively "not right." As Edith Deleury has observed: "Certes il peut apparaître choquant que ces substances, objet d'une cession à titre gratuit, puissent être génératrices de profits pour des tiers." The researchers and drug companies can own the cell line and control what others do with it and Moore cannot; they can even own the cells of his body and control what others can do with them and he cannot. Somehow, this does not sit well.

Property Rights in Human Tissue?

So then one asks, what if the property rights analysis that found favor with the Court of Appeal had prevailed? Would it prove a better vehicle to protect human dignity and privacy and to ensure that physicians and other third parties are not enriched (unjustly or otherwise) quite literally off the backs of patients? At first glance, the solution is appealing. In the United States, a number of writers have argued forcefully that there is a necessary interconnection between property and personhood—that an individual needs some control over resources in the external environment in order to achieve proper self-development, and that the necessary assurances of control take the form of property rights. Margaret Radin has been one proponent of that school of thought. In connection with that thesis, she has suggested that "[i]f property in one's body is not too close to personhood to be considered property at all, then it is the clearest case of property for personhood." The Court of Appeal's decision in *Moore* can itself be regarded as an example of this type of thinking, with its emphasis on property rights in one's body being protective of and instrumental in promoting privacy and human dignity. It is interesting that both levels of court seemed to proceed from the premise that if Moore retained a sufficient degree of control over the cells, then he had a proprietary interest in them. That raises questions as to why the presence or absence of an ability to exercise some degree of control over an object is automatically translated into a property right, with all the other implications that term carries with it, and how the characterization of the cells as an object quickly became a self-evident truth, when they were (at least originally) indisputably a part of a human subject, John Moore. Why is it that neither court in *Moore* stopped for even a minute in its legal analysis at some halfway house—for instance, recognizing the continuation of certain rights of control over excised tissue without having to make the stronger claim for the control being equivalent to or a manifestation of "property rights"?

This tendency to automatically equate control with property rights is marked when we think of individuals and their own bodies. It is interesting and perhaps more than coincidental that the language we use with respect to body parts—"my hand," "your foot," and so on—is interchangeable with the language of possession and, indeed, of ownership. Whether or not it is borne out in practice (and there are often major departures from the ideal), a property right is commonly considered one of the strongest claims that can be asserted to be able to exclude others and assert our own dominion. Perhaps the tendency to think in property terms relative to body parts arises because part and parcel of a property right is the implicit posting of the biggest, most unequivocal "Keep Out" sign that we know of, and that is precisely the message we want to give about our bodies. In this context, then, a property claim is valued for its supposed unequivocal support for boundary-drawing. The ready resort to the language of property is related strongly to a generalized belief in its inviolability—the belief that property rights are somehow more secure than other rights, despite historic examples to the contrary, and despite knowing that property rights exist only so long as and as far as the state is prepared to enforce them. The generalized belief, then, is in part wishful thinking; its specific application to individuals and their own bodies would likely be as well. The tendency to think in terms of property rights may be in part a response as well. As the factual background in *Moore* makes evident, others clearly already regard parts and products of the human body as property, giving rise to a felt need for the strong power of a property claim in the human source to withstand those incursions.

Recognizing property rights in human tissue, though, can be a two-edged sword. Doing so would represent a clear, strong acknowledgement of a continuing right of control over one's "self," at least the corporeal aspect. Given current high levels of approval of ideals of autonomy, bodily integrity, and self-determination in our society (now even enshrined in the *Canadian Charter of Rights and Freedoms*), that is consistent with widely accepted societal norms. At the same time, it can be a short step from being property of and for oneself to being property of and for someone else, as the sale of kidneys and other types of human tissue in countries where such practices are legal or tolerated makes graphically evident. It should be borne in mind that it is most often the dispossessed who are left with few options other than to sell their remaining "possessions"—parts of their bodies. The choice of legal categories in this area cannot be made absent an appreciation of the influence of factors of wealth and class and the pressures they will exert on those least well-off and least powerful in society. Recognizing property rights in one's own person will do little to enhance human dignity and autonomy if it results in selling bits and pieces of one's self in order to secure the means of existence.

An additional factor to consider is one also suggested by Margaret Radin. She notes that with property, as in so many other areas, the rhetoric used shapes and is shaped by reality. If one resorts to the language of property, then that tends to bring with it other concepts that we associate with a property regime in addition to the right to exercise control over the material owned. In particular, "property" imports with it market concepts—an economic orientation. Radin points out some risks of this—the inherent distortion, as easily monetizable matters occupy the center of the map and personal and community matters move to the (distorted) edges of the discourse, and the tendency to conceive of everything—even personal characteristics—as alienable objects rather than personal attributes. This tendency is exemplified by the claim of the defendant Sandoz Inc. in *Moore* that the plaintiff's cells could be the subject of the exercise of UCLA's powers of eminent domain. Sandoz argued that if Moore had a proprietary interest in his cells, he had lost it through UCLA's exercise of that right—in other words, Sandoz asserted that as an institution of higher learning, UCLA had the right to expropriate property it needed, and it had done so to Moore's cells. It is unclear whether Sandoz seriously relied on this argument, or whether it was put forward to graphically illustrate the parade of horribles that would follow if the source of human tissue were recognized as having continuing property rights in it. In any event, the Supreme Court found it unnecessary to deal with this argument.

Categorizing something as "property" does not stop with or signify only the right to control; it also carries with it expectations of a market model and market behaviour as the norm. The property, whatever it may be, becomes something it is thought appropriate to buy and sell through a market. Once one adopts the language of property in order to obtain its strong protection for the right of control, one cannot necessarily control all the associations that the institution of property will bring with it—expectations of economic exchange value, rights of alienability, and so on. Even though legislation can limit the rights generally ascribed to an owner of property (and this is typical in many contexts— property rights are not absolute), there is often a sense that in doing so, one is *taking away* something that is rightfully the owner's—diminishing the owner's entitlements, somehow—rather than enhancing or refining the ability to achieve the policy goals intended in recognizing a property interest in the first place.

How do these general propositions about the expectations inherent in a property claim fit with the situation of John Moore and the response I adverted to earlier that the result in that case strikes many as somehow "not right"? Frequently, the reaction on the part of those reading the Supreme Court decision or simply hearing of the case is that Moore was unjustly "done out of" something. That sense does not grow exclusively out of a conviction that Moore ought to have had or at least have been offered the chance to exercise a continuing right of control over the tissue taken from his body because it was part of his autonomous self. It is also very much a sense that he was deprived of his fair share of the economic rewards to be garnered from the products developed from his cells. The loss to Moore that audiences identify is not just (and perhaps not even primarily) the loss of control, but the loss of a market share—the economic loss. The unfairness typically identi- fied is that nobody else—no other player in the scenario—was precluded from asserting a property claim in all its commonly understood aspects, including economic. Justice Arabian in his concurring Supreme Court judgment in *Moore* argued that denying the human source any continuing proprietary interest in excised tissue would preserve human dignity and serve to keep the sacred apart from the profane. It is certainly true that human beings are regarded as having such status and entitled to that level of respect. However, it has been suggested that with advances in technological capabilities and possibilities over the last few decades, it is not so much the legal status of the human person that is at issue as it is the status of the body and body parts. The two are not necessarily the same. In any event, Justice Arabian's argument seems a faint hope when it is quite clear that the marketplace— the economic regime—can and does govern in this area for everyone else. There is now an economic value to at least some corporeal personal attributes, in addition to their noneconomic value. Refusing to adopt a particular discourse (property rights for the source of human tissue) may affect who shares in that economic value, but it will not alter that reality. *Moore* does not change the existence of that market; it simply excludes the human source of the tissue from sharing in it as a co-owner or originator.

It may be that the economic factor assumes such significance in *Moore* not only because of the large amounts of money potentially involved, but also because in the circumstances, there is no direct, one-to-one "gift of life," as with blood donations or *inter vivos* or even cadaveric organ donations. The transfer is mediated by profit-making others, "the biotechnology companies and researchers," making it more normatively acceptable for the human source to profit from what his or her tissue has become as well. Biotechnology companies may not be far wrong in asserting that cell lines and their derivatives are products, no longer in any way part of a person. It is perhaps because the material has lost its "personified spirit," its association as a part of one's self, that the source can think of profiting from it—can think of selling it. The distancing both from the source and the ultimate human recipient occasioned by the structure and process of biotechnological research, product development, and marketing plays a large role in changing conceptions of the subject matter of this lawsuit from part of a person (subject) to a commodity (object).

These observations must lead one to question whether the debate about property rights in human tissue has been overtaken by events. While it would seem that, for the reasons identified earlier, property may not be the wisest choice of discourse in this area, we live in a world already made. That world may have irretrievably and irreversibly shaped the discourse in this area. This is a field where mere possibilities become practice very quickly, leaving legal theorists far behind. The biotechnology industry makes extensive and ever-increasing use of human tissue in its products. To refer back to what are often put forward as three of the constitutive elements of property, biotechnology companies and scientists assert and are accepted as having rights to *use* human tissue, to *exclude* others from its use, and to *transfer* it to others. As we saw in *Moore*, it is possible to obtain a patent on a cell line developed from human cells (although the situation may be somewhat different in Canada). The reality is that human tissue is already treated as property. Because biotechnology organized along private enterprise and private property lines is widely accepted as having had and continuing to have significant beneficial results, there is unlikely to be a willingness or ability to entirely turn back the clock on that development.

At an instrumental or reactive level, the argument really is over whether the human source of tissue will have any claim to a continuing interest in it, particularly to a share in its economic value, and if so, how best to structure that participation. More fundamentally, the specific issue raises a multitude of questions about how the use of material of human origin ought to be regulated, to what ends, and with what effects. It is easy to lose sight of the larger concerns in responding to the particular fact situation. Those larger concerns are too important to be subsumed in the concrete example that fell to be decided in *Moore*. The factors referenced above may seem to make a property analysis at some level inevitable, but recognizing the forces at work is not necessarily synonymous with accepting present directions in their entirety, far less institutionalizing them. The tensions and risks need to be understood and addressed.

Neither legislation governing patents nor that regulating donations of human tissue addresses this issue. Nor can we look to the common law for an adequate response. Courts are adept at applying traditional legal doctrines and categories and at developing them within limits to meet new situations, but the world of biotechnology does not fit particularly well into existing categories. As the California Supreme Court noted in *Moore*, conversion as a theory of liability arose in and is generally used to resolve "traditional, two-party ownership disputes ... [such as] whether the loser or finder of a horse had better title." In disputes such as these, there is at least general agreement that the subject matter of the dispute can be owned. Biotechnological developments based on human tissue present very different concerns and raise an array of new moral, ethical, and philosophical questions. Without legislation, courts are unlikely to be able to move beyond traditional, partial, and inadequate analyses and justifications, such as are evident in *Moore*. In recognition of these limits, various regulatory regimes have been proposed. These have included a licensing system with fixed profit-sharing for the source of the tissue, incomplete commodification to allow the source of the tissue, but no one else, to receive compensation for certain body parts, permitting donation of tissue but no other form of alienation, allowing *inter vivos* sales of organs in limited circumstances, with compensation being paid by the health insurance system, and requiring biotechnology enterprises to return a share of their profits to the community, specifically to research. Writers have also canvassed the possibility of establishing a new legal category—"chose humaine et à la finalité humaine"—to reflect a new understanding and appreciation of the nature of materials of human origin and the implications of their use and regulation, as well as a needs-based approach to entitlement to body parts, and recognizing a common heritage of humankind, specifically in our "collective gene pool," importing public trust concepts and a need to exercise stewardship in the management of this resource.

[In conclusion, Gilmour argued that there is a need for different rules relating to persons and objects. There is a need for a non-property regulatory system that will release one from the needs to classify material of human origin as "object" and to justify departures from the abstract ideal of what is meant by classifying something as property.]

Discussion Notes

Property Concepts in Relation to Reproductive Technology

Gilmour identified a number of factors that have contributed to a sense of urgency about the need for legal regulation concerning human body parts—the pace of technological advances, the potential for economic gain, and the international nature of biotechnology enterprises. Concern about these issues in Canada resulted in the creation of the federal Royal Commission on New Reproductive Technologies. Its report *Proceed With Care* (Ottawa: the commission, 1993) adopted a broad ethical orientation, the "ethic of care," and eight guiding principles—individual autonomy, equality, respect for human life and dignity, protection of the vulnerable, non-commercialization of reproduction, appropriate use of resources, accountability, and balancing individual and collective interests.

Significantly, the commission did not adopt a proprietary analysis. In relation to reproductive materials and services, for example, the report stated (at 55-56):

> [I]t is fundamentally wrong for decisions about human reproduction to be determined by a profit motive—introducing a profit motive to the sphere of reproduction is contrary to basic values and disregards the importance of the role of reproduction and its significance in our lives as human beings. Commodifying human beings and their bodies for commercial gain is unacceptable because this instrumentalization is injurious to human dignity and ultimately dehumanizing. We therefore consider commercialization for reproductive materials and reproductive services to be inappropriate.

For a detailed review of property concepts in relation to reproductive technology, see the background paper prepared for the commission by M.M. Litman and G.B. Robertson, "Reproductive Technology: Is a Property Law Regime Appropriate?" in *Royal Commission on New Reproductive Technologies: Overview of Legal Issues in New Reproductive Technologies* (Ottawa: Supply and Services Canada, 1993), 233. The authors expressed concern about the extent to which some reform proposals may reject the label of property law, but nonetheless embrace proprietary principles. They also suggested that there is great potential for misunderstanding of property law principles in the context of new reproductive technologies, and concluded (at 267-68):

> Thus, for symbolic (as well as political) reasons, it may be advisable to refrain from applying the term "property" to reproductive materials. Moreover, using the term "property" to describe reproductive materials to a certain extent may create inappropriate preconceptions about the judicial nature of these unique materials. Accordingly, it is our recommendation that any legislative scheme should characterize reproductive material as *sui generis* .... A legislative scheme that characterizes reproductive material as *sui generis*, but that does not reject property principles, affords courts this latitude without evoking an unwarranted and unnecessary emotional debate.

In the light of the issues in *Moore*, do the commission's principles offer a solution? To what extent does the *sui generis* approach suggested by Litman and Robertson offer a different kind of solution? Why might it be desirable to characterize bodily tissues as property? Would such a characterization necessarily enhance personal control over one's body or body tissues? Are proprietary claims about reproductive materials different from the claims in *Victoria Park* and *Harrison v. Carswell*? For a review of the commission's recommendations, see Diana Majury, "Is Care Enough?" (1994), *Dalhousie Law Journal* 279. For an analysis of *Moore* in the context of first year property, see John Martinez, "A Cognitive Science Approach to Teaching Property Rights in Body Parts" (1992), 42 *Journal of Legal Education* 290. See also B. Dickens, "Living Tissue and Organ Donors and Property Law: More on *Moore*" (1992), 8 *Journal of Contemporary Health Law and Policy* 73 and B. Knoppers, T. Caulfield, and D. Kinsella, eds., *Legal Rights and Human Genetic Material* (Toronto: Emond Montgomery, 1996) (hereafter Knoppers, Caulfield, and Kinsella).

In the United Kingdom, the Nuffield Council on Bioethics issued a report in 1995 recommending that human tissue, including blood, eggs, and sperm, should not be bought and sold for profit, and that hospitals should not be permitted to make money by selling such material: *Human Tissue: Ethical and Legal Issues* (London: Nuffield Council on Bioethics, 1995). According to a newspaper report (*The Guardian*, April 21, 1995), Professor Ian Kennedy, a member of the working party responsible for the Nuffield Council's report and a professor of law and medical ethics, explained the legal problem and his view that human tissue should not be regarded as property:

> There is uncertainty about the status of tissue once it is removed. Is it property? Is it amenable to being owned and traded? We are having to use Victorian precedents about body stealing to try to fashion an understanding of the law at the end of the 20th century.

In Ontario, the Human Tissue Gift Act, RSO 1990, c. H.20 governs *inter vivos* gifts for transplant of human tissue and post-mortem gifts for transplant and other uses. This system is based on the consent of a living donor or family of a deceased individual. There are statutory prohibitions on sales of human tissues, but these may fail to regulate the commercial exploitation of products derived from human tissue. For other provincial legislation, see Human Tissue Gift Act, SNS 1973, c. 9 and Human Tissue Act, RSNB 1973, c. H-12. See also B.M. Dickens, "The Control of Living Body Materials" (1977), 27 *University of Toronto Law Journal* 142.

Bill C-47: The Human Reproductive and Genetic Technologies Act

Following the royal commission's report, legislation was introduced by the federal Parliament—Bill C-47: The Human Reproductive and Genetic Technologies Act. The Bill received first reading on June 14, 1996 and second reading on November 5, 1996, but it remained unenacted when Parliament dissolved in April 1997. The Bill's preamble acknowledged "the health and ethical dangers inherent in the commercialization of human reproduction, including the sale of reproductive materials," and identified among its objectives "the appropriate treatment of human reproductive materials outside the body in recognition of their potential to form human life" (s. 3(2)). Sections 4 to 7 prohibited a large number of activities, and sections 8 to 12 provided for both fines and imprisonment upon conviction for engaging in a prohibited activity. For example, s. 6(1) provided:

> 6(1) No person shall sell, purchase, barter or exchange, or offer to sell, purchase, barter or exchange, any ovum, sperm, zygote, embryo or foetus, or any part thereof.

Does this provision preclude a proprietary interest in ova or sperm? How do these provisions envisage "property" in relation to body substances? For other approaches, see B. Knoppers, "Reproductive Technology and International Mechanisms of Protection of the Human Person" (1987), 32 *McGill Law Journal* 32 and Knoppers, Caulfield, and Kinsella.

Moore and Subsequent US Decisions

The *Moore* case has been considered in a number of subsequent decisions in the United States. In *Hecht v. Superior Court (Kane)*, 20 Cal. Rptr. 2d 275 (Calif. Sup. Ct. 1993), the court considered *Moore* in relation to the question of "ownership" of frozen sperm vials after the sperm donor's death. The court concluded (at 281) that the deceased's interest in his frozen sperm vials, even if not governed by the general law of property, occupied "an interim category that entitles [the frozen sperm vials] to special respect because of their potential for human life." In support of its conclusion, the court cited *Davis v. Davis*, 842 SW 2d 588 (TN Sup. Ct. 1992), at 597, a case concerning entitlement to "pre-embryos" at divorce. In Hecht, the court held that the deceased's directives in his will governed disposition of the frozen sperm vials. See also *Del Zio v. Presbyterian Hospital*, unreported 1978, cited in M.M. Litman and G.B. Robertson, above, under the heading "Property Concepts in Relation to Reproductive Technology," at 255, and *York v. Jones*, 717 F Supp. 421 (US Dist. Ct. 1989).

In *Miles, Inc. v. Scripps Clinic and Research Foundation*, 810 F Supp. 1091 (US Dist. Ct., Cal. SD 1993), the court held that the plaintiff had a property interest in the right to commercialization of a cell line. The plaintiff pharmaceutical company sought damages for conversion against the defendant, a research foundation and joint venturer in the research project. However, in spite of the property interest in the right to commercialization, the plaintiff's claim based on conversion failed; the court indicated that the essence of the claim was in breach of contract or patent law.

In *US v. Arora*, 810 F Supp 1091 (Md. D 1994), the court reviewed these decisions in relation to another conversion action when the defendant, Dr. Arora, destroyed materials relating to a new cell line. In this context, the court distinguished *Moore* and *Miles*, stating (at 1099):

> The fact is that the United States Supreme Court has recognized that a living cell line is a property interest capable of protection [citing *Diamond v. Chakrabarty*, 447 US 303 (1980) and *Pasteur v. United States*, 814 F2d 624 (1987)]. The Court thus sees no reason why a cell line should not be considered a chattel capable of being converted. Indeed, if such a cause of action is not recognized, it is hard to conceive what civil remedy would ever lie to recover a cell line that might be stolen or destroyed, including one with immense potential commercial value, as this one apparently had and has [citing M. Valerio Barrad, "Genetic Information and Property Theory" (1993), 87 *Northwestern University Law Review* 1037]. The Court is satisfied, therefore, ... that the Alpha 1-4 cell line was capable of being converted and that in fact Dr. Arora converted it.

Are these US decisions consistent? What overall legal principle can you devise in relation to them? Does your analysis suggest that there is any property interest in bodily substances? How important to your analysis are doctrinal principles of property law, policy concerns, or ethical issues? For additional comment, see M.A. Pieper, "Frozen Embryos—Persons or Property? *Davis v. Davis*" (1990), 23 *Creighton Law Review* 807; J. Lavoie, "Ownership of Human Tissue: Life after *Moore v. Regents of the University of California*" (1989), 75 *Virginia Law Review* 1363; and B.M. Dickens, "Comparative Judicial Embryology: Judges' Approaches to Unborn Human Life" (1990), 9 *Canadian Journal of Family Law* 180.

Suppose that a testator died, leaving a will requesting that all the testator's horses should be destroyed after his death. Is this direction legally enforceable? In other words, if the horses formed part of the testator's estate at the time of his death, should the testator's instructions in his will be determinative with respect to his horses? Is your analysis different in relation to horses that may form part of the testator's estate, by contrast with sperm or other body substances? Is this a matter of doctrine, of policy, or of ethics? For an interesting analysis of the problem in relation to a testator's will concerning his horses, see *Re Wishart Estate* (1992), 46 *Estates and Trusts Reports* 311 (NB QB). The court held that a testator's direction cannot be performed where to do so would be contrary to public policy.

Property, Human Will, and Psychological Theories of Ownership

As Gilmour suggested, issues about bodily integrity are related to ideas of property as the object of human will. The philosopher G. Hegel asserted that human beings become fully liberated through the projection of their wills on objects, and this approach resulted in Hegel's belief in humans having an absolute right of appropriation. Similarly, in *Moore*, the plaintiff's loss of control over his bodily tissues seemed to impair his freedom and integrity. For an interesting debate about these issues more generally, see Margaret Jane Radin, *Reinterpreting Property* (Chicago: University of Chicago Press, 1993). See also Radin, "Property and Personhood" (1982), 34 *Stanford Law Review* 957; a response by S. Schnably, "Property and Pragmatism: A Critique of Radin's Theory of Property and Personhood" (1993), 45 *Stanford Law Review* 347; and Radin's response in the same volume, at 409. See also Radin, "Market-Inalienability" (1987), 100 *Harvard Law Review* 1849, where Radin developed a theory about market alienability "based on a conception of personhood or human flourishing that differs from that of traditional liberalism or economics" (at 1852), and applied these principles to issues about the commodification of sexuality and reproductive capacity—prostitution, baby-selling, and surrogacy. For other views, see J.R.S. Pritchard, "A Market for Babies?" (1984), 34 *University of Toronto Law Journal* 341 and Wanda Wiegers, "Economic Analysis of Law and 'Private Ordering': A Feminist Critique" (1992), 42 *University of Toronto Law Journal* 170.

In the context of psychological ideas about property, an empirical study of ideas about ownership undertaken by F. Rudmin among three groups of men and women suggested that "conventional definitions of ownership do not encompass the full psychological domain of the concept." This conclusion was evident in the responses of both men and women in the study, but Rudmin also identified some differences in their views of ownership. According to Rudmin (at 504-5), the responses showed that

> ownership tends to be more directly and positively related to the self for women than it is for men ... . [After referring to the work of Margaret Radin, Rudmin continued his report on the study.] The data of this study show that women more frequently relate property to explicit terms of self and of pride. The emerging image of women's sense of ownership includes a self unconstrained by property boundary definitions, ready to shade boundaries or to erase them, depending on social contexts. Property boundaries adjust to interpersonal boundaries, not vice versa. Men, however, tend to define self by negation and derivation, in a way very dependent on the property boundary. The image is of an insecure self set in contrast to hostile others restrained by regimes of rights and by sharp rule-bound relationships. At the extreme, property boundaries define the interpersonal relationships.

(Floyd Rudmin, "Gender Differences in the Semantics of Ownership: A Quantitative Phenomenological Survey Study" (1994), 15:3 *Journal of Economic Psychology* 457, at 502ff.)

What is the significance of a theory of property based on the idea of human will and personhood? What conclusions should we draw from possible gender differences in ideas about property and personhood? For other views, see R. Hirschon, ed., *Women and Property—Women as Property* (New York: St. Martin's Press, 1984); M. Ferber and J. Nelson, eds., *Beyond Economic Man: Feminist Theory and Economics* (Chicago: University of Chicago Press, 1993); and Judith Roof, "The Ideology of Fair Use: Xeroxing and Reproductive Rights" (1992), 7:2 *Hypatia* 63. The latter is discussed in detail by M.L. McCall in her MA thesis, "Copyright Law and the Procreative Autonomy of Women" (Ottawa: Carleton University, 1993). For some interesting critiques of the law's perspectives on the body, see P. Cheah, D. Fraser, and J. Grbich, eds., *Thinking Through the Body of the Law* (New York: New York University Press, 1996) and J. Schroeder, "Virgin Territory: Margaret Radin's Imagery of Personal Property as the Inviolate Feminine Body" (1994), 79 *Minnesota Law Review* 55.

Humans Conceptualized as Objects of Property

Ideas about property and personhood must also take account of the impact on human beings who are conceptualized as objects, rather than subjects, of property interests. Consider, for example, an advertisement (original on display at the Art Gallery of Ontario, 1993) that was published in a Toronto newspaper on February 10, 1806 by Peter Russell, a member of the Executive Council of Upper Canada:

To Be Sold

A black woman, named Peggy, aged about forty years; and a Black Boy her son named Jupiter, aged about fifteen years, both of them the property of the Subscriber [that is Peter Russell].

The woman is a tolerable Cook and washer woman and perfectly understands making soap and candles. ...

They are each of them servants for life. The Price for the Woman is one hundred and fifty dollars—for the Boy two hundred dollars, payable in three years with Interest from the day of Sale and to be properly secured by Bond, etc. But one fourth less will be taken in ready money.

This advertisement in Upper Canada occurred after the passage in 1793 of An Act To Prevent the Further Introduction of Slaves. This legislation provided that no one would be enslaved after 1793, but those already slaves in that year were to continue as slaves until death. This compromise seems to have resulted because a number of members of the Assembly and of the Legislative Council of Upper Canada were themselves slave-owners, including Peter Russell who placed the above advertisement. Slavery was eventually abolished in the British colonies by an Act of the Imperial Parliament as of 1834, although it had diminished somewhat as a result of judicial decisions before that date. According to Robin Winks, *The Blacks in Canada* (Montreal: McGill-Queen's University Press, 1971), at 110:

While slavery remained legal in all British North American colonies until 1834, the combination of legislative and judicial action had so severely limited its growth, applicability, and confidence as virtually to end the practice by the 1820's throughout the provinces. The last known private advertisements for slaves appeared in Halifax in 1820, in Quebec in 1821; occasional wills of a later date attest to slaves as property, and local legends throughout eastern and central Canada credit various Negroes with having been the "last slave" to die.

Although slavery was prohibited after 1834, blacks in Canada have often experienced difficulties in relation to land-holding, a subject discussed in more detail in chapter 6. In addition, some black communities have also experienced "relocation" of the whole population, such as that of the Africville community in Halifax between 1964 and 1967, an action that resulted in dislocation and loss for many of the former residents of Africville: see Africville Exhibition Committee, *Africville: A Spirit That Lives On* (Halifax: Art Gallery, Mount Saint Vincent University, 1989). For an account of the historically important decision of Lord Mansfield in England in 1772, freeing James Sommersett, a slave from Virginia who deserted his master, see E. Fiddes, "Lord Mansfield and the Sommersett Case" (1934), 50 *Law Quarterly Review* 499. For a personal account of the impact of slavery in American Law, see Patricia Williams, *The Alchemy of Race and Rights* (Cambridge, MA: Harvard University Press, 1991). For another analysis, see M.I. Finley, *Ancient Slavery and Modern Ideology* (New York: Viking Press, 1980).

How would you characterize the relationship between property and personhood in the context of the slavery of blacks in Canada? Significantly, the Royal Commission on Reproductive Technologies drew an analogy to slavery in relation to commercial surrogacy arrangements—that is, where a woman gestates a foetus and gives birth to a child for others, in return for payment. According to the commission:

> We do not allow people to give up their freedom and become slaves, even if they make a choice to do so, because of our collective conviction that this would negate the value we attach to human dignity and the inalienability of the person. Similarly, assigning a commercial value to the human function of reproduction would result eventually in a new and, in our view, undesirable social understanding of the value and dignity of women, their reproductive capacity, and their bodily integrity.

(Royal Commission on Reproductive Technologies, *Proceed With Care* (Ottawa: the commission, 1993), at 684.)

The Role for Courts and Legislatures

Reconsider the arguments in *Victoria Park* and in *INS v. AP* about the respective roles of courts and legislatures. Are your views about the merits of these arguments different in relation to issues about bodily integrity?

In reflecting on this question, consider the views of Janice Moulton in "A Paradigm of Philosophy: The Adversary Method," in S. Harding and M. Hintikka, eds., *Discovering Reality: Feminist Perspectives on Epistemology, Metaphysics, Methodology and*

Philosophy of Science (Boston: D. Reidel, 1983), 149, at 159. According to Moulton, the idea that the adversary method is the best way of determining the objective validity of arguments is flawed:

> The Adversary Paradigm accepts only the kind of reasoning whose goal is to convince an opponent, and ignores reasoning that might be used in other circumstances: to figure something out for oneself, to discuss something with like-minded thinkers, to convince the indifferent or the uncommitted. The relations of ideas used to arrive at a conclusion might very well be different from the relations of ideas needed to defend [that conclusion] to an adversary. And it is not just less reasoning, or fewer steps in the argument that distinguishes the relations of ideas, but that they must be, in some cases, quite different lines of thought.

Does this critique of the adversary method in philosophical inquiries apply to the process of presenting arguments to courts? If so, does this suggest that legislation may be a preferable means of making law than judicial decision making? Why or why not? Is the adversary method used at all in the legislative context? Does this critique assist in explaining the problem experienced by the plaintiff in *Moore*? Did Moore have a choice about using the courts or the legislature?

ALTERNATIVE VISIONS AND PROPERTY CLAIMS

As the analysis of the cases in this chapter demonstrates, the concept of property is complex, revealing both doctrinal principles and policy concerns with respect to subjects and objects in proprietary relationships. At the same time, this concept of property in the western common law tradition is just one of many different ideas about property. For example, the former communist regimes in eastern Europe created a property regime quite different from common law arrangements, and recent political changes in eastern Europe have again affected concepts about property. For some analysis of these issues, see George Ginsburgs, ed., *The Revival of Private Law in Central and Eastern Europe* (The Hague, The Netherlands: Kluwer Law Int'l, 1996) and essays in David L. Weimer, ed., *The Political Economy of Property Rights* (Cambridge: Cambridge University Press, 1997).

Aboriginal Concepts of Property

In the North American context, it is also critical to take account of aboriginal concepts of property, particularly because they are fundamental to an understanding of land claims litigation. One of the clearest assertions of aboriginal relationships with land is found in the recorded testimony of Chief Seattle at the ceremony to sign a treaty with Europeans in 1854:

> Every part of this earth is sacred to my people.
> Every shining pine needle,
> every tender shore,
> every vapor in the dark woods,

every clearing, and
every humming insect
are holy
in the memory and experience of my people.

The earth does not belong to the white man,
the white man belongs to the earth.
This we know.
All things are connected
like the blood
which unites our family.

(Ted Perry, inspired by Chief Seattle, "how can one sell the air?," in Eli Gifford and R. Michael Cook, eds., *How Can One Sell the Air? Chief Seattle's Vision* (Summertown, TN: The Book Publishing Co., 1992), at 31 and 46. "Seattle" is more correctly spelled "Seathl," although literary references are to "Seattle." These passages are from a speech given by Chief Seattle in Lushotseed, Seattle's native tongue, and then translated by Dr. Henry B. Smith.) Some of these ideas are more fully analyzed in the following extract. To what extent can you identify similarities and differences between aboriginal and common law concepts of property?

Leroy Little Bear, "Aboriginal Rights and the Canadian 'Grundnorm'"
in J. Rick Ponting, ed., *Arduous Journey: Canadian Indians and Decolonization*
(Toronto: McClelland and Stewart, 1986), at 244-47 (footnotes omitted)

The Aboriginal Peoples' Standard

In contrast to the Western (occidental) way of relating to the world—namely, a linear and singular conception—the aboriginal philosophy views the world in cyclical terms. A good example of linear thinking is the occidental conception of time. Time is conceptualized as a straight line. If we attempt to picture "time" in our mind, we would see something like a river flowing toward and past us. What is behind is the past. What is immediately around us is the present. The future is upstream, but we cannot see very far upstream because of a waterfall, a barrier to knowing the future. This line of time is conceptualized as quantity, especially as lengths made of units. A length of time is envisaged as a row of similar units. A logical and inherent characteristic of this concept of time is that once a unit of the river of time flows past, that particular unit never returns—it is gone forever. This characteristic lends itself to other concepts such as "wasting time," "making up time," "buying time," and "being on time," which are unique to occidental society.

Another characteristic of this linear concept of time is that each unit of time is totally different and independent of similar units. Consequently, each day is considered a different unit, and thus a different day. Every day is a new day, every year is a new year. From this we can readily understand why there is a felt need in Western culture to have names for days and months, and numbers for years. In general, Western philosophy is a straight line. One goes from A to B to C to D to E, where B is the foundation for C, and C is the foundation for D, and on down the line.

Native people think in terms of cyclicity. Time is not a straight line. It is a circle. Every day is not a new day, but the same day repeating itself. There is no need to give each day a different name. Only one name is needed: "day." This philosophy is a result of a direct relationship to the macrocosm. The sun is round; the moon is round; a day is a cycle (daylight followed by night); the seasons follow the same cycle year after year. A characteristic of cyclic thinking is that it is holistic, in the same way that a circle is whole. A cyclical philosophy does not lend itself readily to dichotomies or categorization, nor to fragmentation or polarizations; conversely, linear thinking lends itself to all of these, and to singularity. For example, in linear thinking there is only one "great spirit," only one "true rule," only one "true answer." These philosophical ramifications of Western habitual thought result in misunderstanding holistic concepts, as Westerners relate themselves to only one aspect of the whole at a time.

The linear and singular philosophy of Western cultures and the cyclical and holistic philosophy of most native peoples can be seen readily in the property concepts in each society. Indian ownership of property, like Indians' way of relating to the world, is holistic. Land is communally owned; ownership rests not in any one individual, but rather belongs to the tribe as a whole, as an entity. The members of a tribe have an undivided interest in the land; everybody, as a whole, owns the whole. Furthermore, the land belongs not only to people presently living, but also to past generations and future generations, who are considered to be as much a part of the tribal entity as the present generation. In addition, the land belongs not only to human beings, but also to other living things (the plants and animals and sometimes even the rocks); they, too, have an interest.

Although the native conception of title to land is distinct from the British concept in important ways, the two do have some points of overlap. The native concept of title is somewhat like a combination of different British concepts ... . To Natives it is as though the Creator, the original one to grant the land to the Indians, put a condition on it whereby the land remains Indian land "so long as there are Indians," "so long as it is not alienated," "on the condition that it is used only by Indians," etc. In other words, the Indians' concept of title is not equivalent to what today is called "fee simple title" ... ; it is actually somewhat less than unencumbered ownership because of the various parties (plants, animals, and members of the tribe) that have an interest in it and because of the above-noted conditions attached to the ownership. Finally, a point raised above must be emphasized: that is, the source of Indians' title to their land can be traced back to the Creator, who gave it not only to human beings, but to all living creatures. In other words, deer have the same type of interest in the land as does any human being.

This concept of sharing with fellow animals and plants is one that is quite alien to Western society's conception of land. To Western society, only human beings have a right to land, and everything else is for the convenience of humans. Yet, the concept of Indians sharing the land ownership with fellow living things is not entirely unrelated to the concept of social contract that has been put forward by such occidental philosophers as Rousseau and Locke. However, whereas Rousseau's and Locke's social contract encompasses human beings only, the Indian social contract embraces all other living things.

The question inevitably arises as to just what the Indians surrendered when they signed treaties with European nations. First, the Indian concept of land ownership is certainly not inconsistent with the idea of sharing with an alien people. Once the Indians recognized them as human beings, they gladly shared with them. They shared with Europeans in the same way they shared with the animals and other people. However, sharing here cannot be interpreted as meaning that Europeans got the same rights as any other native person, because the Europeans were not descendants of the original grant-ees, or they were not parties to the original social contract. Also, sharing certainly cannot be interpreted as meaning that one is giving up his rights for all eternity.

Second, the Indians could not have given unconditional ("fee simple") ownership to Europeans in any land transactions in which they may have engaged because they did not themselves have fee simple ownership. They were never given such unconditional ownership by their grantor (the Creator), and it is well known in British property law that one cannot give an interest greater than he or she has.

Third, Indians could not have given an interest even equal to what they were origi-nally granted, because to do so would be to break the condition under which the land was granted by the Creator. Furthermore, they are not the sole owners under the original grant from the Creator; the land belongs to past generations, to the yet-to-be-born, and to the plants and animals. Has the Crown ever received a surrender of title from these others?

Fourth, the only kind of interest the native people have given or transferred must be an interest lesser than they had, for one can always give an interest smaller than one has. Thus, from all of the above we can readily conclude that, from their perspective, the Indians did not surrender very much, if they surrendered anything at all.

Thomas Berger, in a recent study of the Alaska Native Land Claim Settlement Act, summarizes the viewpoint of the native people of Alaska. His remarks can be applied readily to other native people. Writes Berger:

> The European discoveries, their descendants, and the nations they founded, including the United States, imposed their overlordship on the peoples of the New World. The Europeans came, and they claimed the land. No one has ever advanced a sound legal theory to justify the taking of native land from the Natives of the New World, whether by the Spanish, the Portuguese, the French, the Dutch, the Americans, or—in Alaska—by the Russians.
>
> Certain European powers claimed, by virtue of discovery, the exclusive right to purchase land from its original inhabitants. [However,] the rule of discovery depends upon the concept of native sovereignty: only if the original inhabitants had the right to sell their land could the discoverer exercise his right to purchase it. ...
>
> Before and after contact native peoples of the New World governed themselves according to a variety of political institutions; they were acknowledged to be sovereign as distinct peoples.

In summary, the standard or norm of the aboriginal peoples' law is that land is not transferable and therefore is inalienable. Land and benefits therefrom may be shared with others, and when Indian nations entered into treaties with European nations, the subject of the treaty, from the Indians' viewpoint, was not the alienation of the land but the sharing of the land.

Discussion Notes

Property as a Relationship Among Subjects and the Aboriginal Conception of Property Interests

Reconsider the idea of property as a relationship among subjects with respect to the objects of proprietary interests. How would an aboriginal conception of property interests "redefine" this relationship? In thinking about these issues, consider the comments of R. Ross in *Dancing with a Ghost: Exploring Indian Reality* (Markham: Octopus Book, 1992), xxiii-iv:

> [W]e have not approached Native people with the expectation of difference which is essential for communication and understanding to commence. Not having perceived that a gulf divides us, we have never truly tried to bridge it. Unless we do, it is my fear that we are doomed to increasing mutual frustration and … overt hostilities.

Helen Stone suggested that lawyers who make claims on behalf of aboriginal persons may often try to show the "congruence" between ideas about time and history among aboriginal people on the one hand and among the dominant members of Canadian society on the other, even though (as Little Bear explained) there are major distinctions between them. See Helen Stone, "Living in Time Immemorial—Concepts of 'Time' and 'Time Immemorial': Why Aboriginal Rights Theory Is Problematic in the Courts and Around the Negotiating Table" (Carleton University, MA thesis, 1993). For differing perspectives, see J. Cruikshank, "Legend and Landscape: Convergence of Oral and Scientific Traditions in the Yukon Territory" (1981), 18:2 *Arctic Anthropology* 67 and J. Webber, "Relations of Force and Relations of Justice: The Emergence of Normative Community Between Colonists and Aboriginal Peoples" (1995), 33 *Osgoode Hall Law Journal* 623. These issues will be examined in more detail in subsequent chapters in relation to particular aspects of aboriginal conceptions of property.

For an overview of issues, see K. Hazlehurst, *Legal Pluralism and the Colonial Legacy: Indigenous Experiences of Justice in Canada, Australia and New Zealand* (Aldershot, UK: Avebury, 1995). For details of legal issues, see B. Morse, ed., *Aboriginal Peoples and the Law: Indian, Métis and Inuit Rights in Canada* (Ottawa: Carleton University Press, 1991) and *Report of the Royal Commission on Aboriginal Peoples* (Ottawa: the commission, 1996).

An Introduction to Mabo v. Queensland

One of the most significant common law decisions about aboriginal property issues is *Mabo v. Queensland* (1992), 107 Aust. LR 1 (HC). In that case, the High Court of Australia considered a claim on the part of the Meriam people to the land of the Murray Islands in the Torres Strait. The Meriam people had been in occupation of the Islands for generations before the first European contact and the present inhabitants were descendants of the original inhabitants. There were a number of property issues discussed in the case, and it is significant for its conclusion that the Meriam people had a proprietary interest in the land of the Murray Islands. Although these issues will be explored in more detail in subsequent chapters, it is useful at this point to examine how the court characterized the basic proprietary interest and the idea of the Meriam people's right to exclude others (at 36):

> BRENNAN J: Whether or not land is owned by individual members of a community, a community which asserts and asserts effectively that none but its members has any right to occupy or use the land has an interest in the land that must be proprietary in nature: there is no other proprietor. It would be wrong, in my opinion, to point to the inalienability of land by that community and, by importing definitions of "property" which require alienability under the municipal laws of our society, to deny that the indigenous people owned their land. The ownership of land within a territory in the exclusive occupation of a people must be vested in that people: land is susceptible of ownership, and there are no other owners. True it is that land in exclusive possession of an indigenous people is not, in any private law sense, alienable property for the laws and customs of an indigenous people do not generally contemplate the alienation of the people's traditional land. But the common law has asserted that, if the Crown should acquire sovereignty over that land, the new sovereign may extinguish the indigenous people's interest in the land and create proprietary rights in its place and it would be curious if, in place of interests that were classified as non-proprietary, proprietary rights could be created. Where a proprietary title capable of recognition by the common law is found to have been possessed by a community in occupation of a territory, there is no reason why that title should not be recognised as a burden on the Crown's radical title when the Crown acquires sovereignty over that territory. The fact that individual members of the community, like the individual plaintiff Aboriginals in *Millirrpum*, enjoy only usufructuary rights that are not proprietary in nature is no impediment to the recognition of a proprietary community title. Indeed, it is not possible to admit traditional usufructuary rights without admitting a traditional proprietary community title. There may be difficulties of proof of boundaries or of membership of the community or of representatives of the community which was in exclusive possession, but those difficulties afford no reason for denying the existence of a proprietary community title capable of recognition by the common law. That being so, there is no impediment to the recognition of individual non-proprietary rights that are derived from the community's laws and customs and are dependent on the community title. A fortiori, there can be no impediment to the recognition of individual proprietary rights.

For official commentary on the *Mabo* decision, see "Mabo, the High Court Decision on Native Title" (Canberra: Australian Government Publishing Service, 1993). A number of recent cases in Canada have focused on aboriginal property rights and the extent to which they were extinguished by treaties or otherwise. For example, see B. Ryder, "Aboriginal Rights and *Delgamuuku v. The Queen*" (1994), 5:2 *Constitutional Forum* 43 and *Chippewas of Kettle & Stony Point v. Canada (Attorney-General)* (1996), 31 OR (3d) 97 (CA). The earlier Australian decision referred to in *Mabo—Millirrpum v. Nabalco Pty Ltd and the Commonwealth of Australia* (1971), 17 FLR 141 (Sup. Ct. NT)—held that aboriginal claims were not proprietary in nature, mainly because they did not correspond to common law concepts of property. What is the difference in approach between *Millirrpum* and *Mabo*? These issues are explored more fully in subsequent chapters, especially chapter 8.

Property, Power, Poverty

Dependence is the flip side of the property coin. The absence of property leads to dependence and therefore any analysis of property can, by extension, reveal as much about dependence as it does about power. Both are aspects of the same picture, a picture which shows the unequal distribution of that which is valued in any society and obviously can be analysed according to groups or class.

(P. Symes, "Property, Power and Dependence: Critical Family Law" (1987), 14 *Journal of Law and Society* 199, at 200.)

Symes' comments suggest a need to examine the way in which the concept of property serves not only to confer entitlements to some people but also to deny rights to others. For the plaintiffs in *Victoria Park* and *Moore*, and for Sophie Carswell, the courts' analyses of property interests meant that they were unable to enforce rights that were significant to them. In this way, they were without power, by contrast with the other parties in the litigation. Beyond the obvious economic power at issue in the cases, moreover, Symes suggested (at 201) that the idea of property also involves "a kind of personal power, power to effect change, power to exercise choice, to be a self-determining individual: [to have] independence." Since individual autonomy and independence are important values in current western society, those who are dependent and without property are often powerless and poor. Comparisons of those who have property with those who do not thus reveal some of the important elements of ideas about property. For example, see J. Waldron, "Homelessness and the Issue of Freedom" (1991), 39 *University of California Law Review* 295. The issue of whether there is a right to property as a fundamental human right remains controversial in international law. For an overview in relation to the European community, see James Kingston, "Rich People Have Rights Too? The Status of Property as a Fundamental Human Right," in L. Heffernan, ed., *Human Rights: A European Perspective* (Dublin and Portland, OR: Round Hall Press in association with Irish Centre for European Law, 1994).

As noted in relation to the discussion of *Harrison v. Carswell*, ideas about property in relation to inequality represented an important part of the work of C.B. Macpherson. Macpherson suggested that liberal theory should reconceptualize property—instead of focusing on property as the "right to exclude," it should redefine property as including the "right not to be excluded from" the use or benefit of some thing:

When property is so understood, the problem of liberal-democratic theory is no longer a problem of putting limits on the property right, but of supplementing the individual right to exclude others by the individual right not to be excluded by others. The latter right may be held to be the one that is most required by the liberal-democratic ethic, and most implied in a liberal concept of the human essence. The right not to be excluded by others may provisionally be stated as the individual right to equal access to the means of labour and/or the means of life.

(C.B. Macpherson, "Liberal-Democracy and Property," in Macpherson, at 201.) You may want to examine these ideas more fully in the context of constitutional protection, presented in chapter 8.

Discussion Notes

Local 1330, United Steel Workers v. US Steel Corp.

Consider Macpherson's ideas in relation to *Local 1330, United Steel Workers v. US Steel Corp.*, 631 F2d 1264 (US Ct. of Appeals 1980): In 1980, the US Court of Appeals reviewed a lower court decision concerning an application by a union to keep steel plants operating in Ohio, or sell the facilities to the union. One plant had been in operation since 1901, the other since 1918. Together, the two plants employed 3,500 workers. US Steel wanted to demolish the plants because they had become obsolete, and the costs of modernization were greater than the costs of demolition. As the Court of Appeals subsequently noted (at 1265), the company's decision:

> will ... mean a devastating blow to [the workers and their families], to the business community and to the City of Youngstown itself ... . [This is] an economic tragedy of major proportion to Youngstown and Ohio's Mahoning Valley.

The union eventually initiated legal action, claiming a right on the part of the workers to purchase the plant. In the initial hearing, the trial judge made some comments about the possibility of a property interest arising out of the long relationship between the company and the employees. However, he subsequently concluded that there was no precedent for such a property right. The Court of Appeals agreed.

In "The Reliance Interest in Property" (1988), 40 *Stanford Law Review* 614, J.W. Singer argued (at 621) that there was scope in this case for recognition of the workers' property rights arising out of their relationship with US Steel: "Such a new legally protected interest would place obligations on the company toward the workers and the community to alleviate the social costs of its decision to close the plant. Protection of this reliance interest could take a variety of forms."

What kinds of property analyses could be used to establish this entitlement? What forms would it take? In formulating your arguments, consider the importance of property as a "social" relationship as well as the connections between property, power, and poverty. Singer suggested (at 662-63), for example:

> The social relations approach asks us to be sensitive to the power inequalities within those relationships; some members of the common enterprise are more vulnerable than others. These inequalities are not natural; they are the direct result of the allocation of power determined by the assignment of legal entitlements. We should focus on the various ways in which vulnerable persons rely on relationships of mutual dependence. This perspective will give us a deeper understanding of how the legal system regulates economic life.

Property and Economic Inequality

According to Ziff, a portrait of emergency shelters on a given day in 1987 revealed 10,000 emergency residents in Canada. Over 60 percent were adult men, while 27.5 percent were women and 11.5 percent were children under 15 years of age. Other studies have not only revealed great disparities of wealth, but stark gender inequalities as well.

As Ziff stated, at 76: "This situation is troubling, especially given the levels of opulence enjoyed in so many households." See also I. Bakker, "The Political Economy of Gender," in W. Clement and G. Williams, eds., *The New Canadian Political Economy* (Kingston: McGill-Queen's University Press, 1989), 99.

Can you think of arguments about the nature of property that might be employed to challenge this economic inequality? In reflecting on this challenge, consider the following comments by C. Rose, "Seeing Property," in Rose, 267, at 297:

> There is an old adage, told of plain people and plain things: what you see is what you get. Property seems plain in this way too: what you see is what you get. But things are more complicated than that. With property, the nature of "things" imposes their own quite fascinating constraints. Yet even with those, *what you see* in property is what you and others have talked yourselves into about those "things"; and given some imagination, you may always talk yourselves into seeing something else—with all the effects on understanding and action that a new "envisioning" may bring.

NOTE: THE CLASSIFICATION OF PROPERTY INTERESTS

Historically, the classification of property interests was critical to defining what rights and remedies were available to protect them. By contrast, in the late 20th century, many of these historical distinctions have been abolished so that the principles of property apply more uniformly. Nonetheless, because statutes, judges, and lawyers continue to use traditional classifications, it is important to be able to recognize them and to understand their former significance.

The basic classification in property law was that relating to "real" property and "personal" property. This distinction derived from two different remedies available in medieval legal procedures for the return of property. In some cases, the plaintiff was entitled, by way of remedy, to the return of the object itself or (in Latin) the "*res*." In this case, the plaintiff's action was called an action "*in rem*" or a "real" action, and property that could be recovered in such an action was called "real" property. Land, which was regarded as unique in the medieval period, was recoverable by a plaintiff using an action "*in rem*" so it became classified as "real property."

By contrast with land, other forms of property were not recoverable "*in specie*." Instead, the plaintiff was entitled to the value of the property, as damages for wrongful interference with it on the part of the defendant. This action was "*in personam*"—that is, it was an action against the defendant personally. Property for which the plaintiff could recover damages alone became known as "personal property." Since land was "real property," other forms of property became "personal property." Because an action *in rem* permitted recovery of the proprietary object, such an action was regarded as enforceable against the whole world. By contrast, since an action *in personam* resulted in damages only, it was regarded as enforceable merely between the parties to the dispute. Some of these ideas continue to be important in the principles concerning legal remedies.

These distinctions reflect, at least to some extent, the concepts of movable and immovable property recognized in civil law systems. However, the common law's focus on procedure as the basis for classification resulted in an anomaly in relation to leaseholds. In the medieval period, a tenant did not have a proprietary interest in leased land, but merely a contractual relationship with the landlord. Hence, leaseholds were classified as personal property, and personal property was subdivided further into "chattels real" (leaseholds) and "chattels personal" (other personal property). In turn, "chattels personal" were subdivided into two groups—"*choses* in possession" (tangible property) and "*choses* in action" (intangible property), such as promissory notes and bonds, and also including trademarks, patents, and copyright. Real property also has two further subdivisions—corporeal hereditaments (interests capable of being held in possession) and incorporeal heraditaments (non-possessory interests such as a right of way that enables someone to walk across a neighbour's land, but does not permit this person to have possession of the neighbouring land). For good overviews of the classification of real and personal property, see Ziff, at 69ff., and D. Jackson, *Principles of Property Law* (Sydney: The Law Book Co., 1967), at 24ff. For an historical assessment, see A.H. Chaytor and W.J. Whittaker, eds., *F.W. Maitland, The Forms of Action at Common Law: A Course of Lectures* (Cambridge, UK: University Press, 1965).

As the language demonstrates, this classification of property interests reflects the historical origins of the law of property. Moreover, the classification system really focuses on the *object* of proprietary interests, not on proprietary interests themselves, so that the classification may seem less useful to modern property analyses which focus on relationships among subjects with respect to proprietary objects. In addition, earlier distinctions between real and personal property sometimes have been changed by statute, and courts also have declared "*sui generis*" property interests, especially (but not only) in relation to aboriginal property claims.

Notwithstanding these developments, the distinction between real and personal property continues to be significant in some situations. Consider the following examples:

1. Two farmers successfully sued H, who had contracted to spray their flax crops to control weeds and, in doing so, destroyed the crops. In turn, H attempted to recover under his policy of insurance. The insurance policy provided coverage to H in relation to "all sums which the Insured shall become obligated to pay by reason of the liability imposed upon him by law for damages because of injury to or destruction of property caused by accident." However, the insurance policy excluded from coverage "any personal property."

Can H recover under the policy of insurance? How should growing crops be characterized—as personal property or as real property? In *Hoegy v. General Accident Assurance Co of Canada* (1977), 75 DLR (3d) 44 (Ont. Co. Ct.), Carter J concluded that the flax did not constitute personal property and that H was therefore entitled to recover the sum claimed under the insurance policy. In reaching this conclusion, the court expressly applied the principle that ambiguity in an insurance policy is to be resolved in favour of the insured. Assuming that the insurance company wished to exclude such claims in future, how should the policy be drafted? In considering what language is necessary to achieve this objective, can you identify reasons why the policy's original exclusion clause simply referred to "personal property"? What are the advantages and disadvantages of using this language in an insurance contract?

For other examples of situations in which the distinction between real and personal property has been considered, see *Re Dor-O-Matic of Canada Inc.* (1996), 28 OR (3d)

125 (Gen. Div.), and *Deloitte and Touche Inc. v. 1035839 Ontario Inc.* (1996), 28 OR (3d) 139 (Gen. Div.).

2. A owns a mobile home situated in a mobile home subdivision. If A wants to take out a mortgage in relation to his home, it will be necessary to decide whether the mobile home is personal property or real property. How should a mobile home be characterized?

According to Ziff, at 101, the mobile home is "a structurally and teleologically equivocal dwelling" so that the cases sometimes classify these homes as chattels, while at other times they are regarded as "fixtures" annexed to land and thus real property. Through the doctrine of "fixtures," property that is personal property may be transformed into real property. As Ziff explained (at 100), the test as to whether personal property has become a "fixture" depends on an objective test of intention, having regard to the extent of annexation and the purpose of annexation. For a review of the cases, see Ziff, at 101, footnote 95.

What problems are created for property law when there is uncertainty as to whether objects are "fixtures"—that is, whether they are chattels or have become affixed to land so as to become real property?

In this book, principles of real and personal property are examined together, wherever possible. Thus, the next chapter explores the concept of possession in relation to personal property in the "finders' cases" and in relation to land in the concept of "possessory title." Chapter 4 similarly examines the relationship between property law and contract law in the context of bailment of personal property and leaseholds, and chapter 5 explores the concept of transferring proprietary interests in relation to gifts of real and personal property and the sale of land. One purpose of this arrangement is to permit a critical assessment of the continued usefulness of the historical classification of proprietary interests, although you must also be attentive to important distinctions.

PROBLEMS

1. John Adams is the owner of a 100-acre parcel of land north of Toronto. Some years ago, he decided to discontinue his general farming operation on this parcel and instead to create a wildlife reserve. This decision was consistent with Adams' lifelong fascination with wild animals and birds in North America. He was delighted to find that he could satisfy his own interests in wildlife and make a living at the same time, by charging admission to visitors to the wildlife reserve. For the past decade, the wildlife reserve has provided him with a very satisfactory livelihood.

Two months ago, Adams became aware of an intrusion to his wildlife reserve. For a six-week period, his neighbour on the adjoining property, Fred Bloggs, permitted a film crew to set up their equipment. On inquiry, Adams learned that Bloggs had agreed, in return for an undisclosed sum of money, to permit the film crew to use Bloggs' land as a base from which to film the background sequences for a documentary production about Canadian wildlife. The film crew, using special cameras and photographic techniques for filming at a distance, were able to simulate "life in the wild" by filming the birds and animals on Adams' wildlife reserve, although no one ever set foot on his land. For the film company, such an arrangement was both more efficient and much less costly than filming "in the wild."

John Adams wants to know whether the actions of the film company or of his neighbour Fred Bloggs are legally permissible, and what remedies may be available.

2. Ford-Fair is the corporate owner of a small shopping mall just outside the town of Vineyards, Ontario. As a result of recent extensive renovations, the mall is now a major commercial complex, with professional offices and services, as well as a department store and small shops.

Animal Heaven, a pet clinic providing vet services and overnight lodging for cats and dogs, is a relatively new tenant in the mall. The pet clinic is located beside Klik Kliks, a hairdressing shop for men and women, which has been located in the mall for more than a decade. Joe Bright, who is the owner of Klik Kliks and well-known for his fastidious ways, has been dismayed to see the usually serene ambiance of his hairdressing shop reduced, indeed almost destroyed according to him, by the animal sounds next door. He has complained to the mall owner without success. As a result, he has recently been considering whether he could take independent action against his neighbour in the mall, Animal Heaven.

In addition to his problem with the neighbouring pet clinic, Joe Bright has also decided to ask Ford-Fair to help him to get rid of some demonstrators who have begun to picket in front of his shop, handing out leaflets decrying Klik Kliks' wig business. The demonstrators are critical of his shop's use of "real hair" for wigs, claiming that it contributes to the oppression of poor women who must sell their hair at cut rates to provide for their families. Although the demonstrators have been quite peaceful for the past few days, Joe Bright has noticed a drop-off in business since they started to demonstrate in front of his shop. He wants to ask Ford-Fair to eject the demonstrators from the mall.

Can Joe Bright compel Animal Heaven to carry on its business in a way that does not interfere with the serenity of Klik Kliks? (You may assume that there are no special issues related to the fact that these neighbouring shops are run by *tenants* in the mall.) Can Klik Kliks request the mall owner to evict the "real hair" demonstrators?

3. In her article about frame shifting, Jennifer Jaff stated:

[D]ecision makers shift their frame of reference from broad to narrow, narrow to broad, to construct rationales that justify differing results … . By using different frames of reference, two judges can arrive at two competing yet equally "legally sound" decisions in a single case.

Explain what Jaff means by frame shifting, and show how it might be applied to explain the majority and dissenting judgments in *Victoria Park Racing v. Taylor* and *International News Service v. Associated Press*. Explain whether "frame shifting" helps to explain the problems of recognition (or non-recognition) of aboriginal property concepts in Canadian law.

4. Is property law an appropriate regulatory device for determining legal issues generated by new reproductive technologies? In particular, are reproductive materials

such as gametes (ovum or sperm) and the products of conceptions (zygotes, embryos, and fetuses) susceptible of "ownership" and if so, who are the owners?

The recent Royal Commission on New Reproductive Technologies (1993) concluded that property law and the market should have no significant role in the regulation of new reproductive technologies. Instead, the commission recommended the establishment of a National Reproductive Technologies Commission, with broad powers to regulate and license the development of reproductive technologies.

Define the extent to which we currently "own" our bodies (including our gametes)? How might the regulation of reproductive materials as property enhance human dignity? How might it diminish human dignity?

The commission adopts the "ethic of care" as its guiding principle. How is this principle different from other approaches to the question of reproductive materials as property, and how does it inform the commission's conclusions? According to the commission, the ethic of care provides a range of "more creative solutions that can remove or reduce conflict, rather than simply subordinating one person's interests to another." Do you agree?

CHAPTER TWO

The Concept of Possession

THE CONCEPT OF "FIRST POSSESSION"

"Possession is nine-tenths of the law." This old adage reflects the traditional importance of the concept of possession in the law of property, but possession continues to be an important concept in some modern property disputes as well. This chapter explores the concept of possession in relation to proprietary interests in chattels and in land.

At the outset, it is important to identify three related matters concerning possession. First, as was evident in the examination of the concept of "property," the everyday meaning of the word "possession" often differs from the legal concept of possession. Courts and statutes frequently make important distinctions in defining possession—for example, as "actual possession," "constructive possession," a "right to possession," or "pedal possession." In the cases and examples in this chapter, take careful note of these different formulations of the concept of possession and how they affect the interpretation of proprietary interests.

Second, the concept of possession demonstrates the basic common law principle that property interests are always relative, never absolute. Thus, even though someone may have "title" to a chattel or to land, a person who holds a possessory interest may nonetheless have a superior claim over someone who subsequently interferes with that possession (by theft, for example). This principle is often referred to as the principle of the "relativity of title": the plaintiff who can establish a right based on possession that is prior in time to the defendant's claim can succeed in an action against the defendant, even if there is a "true owner"—a person with a better title than the plaintiff's. Usually, the defendant cannot rely on the fact that someone else—a person not party to the suit—has a claim prior to or better than the plaintiff's claim. (The third party is sometimes referred to as the *jus tertii*.) Thus, it is always necessary to observe how a possible claim by a "true owner" does, or does not, affect litigation between a plaintiff and the defendant.

Finally, as is clear from this discussion of the "relativity of title" in property law, a person's possession of a chattel or land may, *by itself*, create a proprietary interest. This principle is sometimes expressed in terms of "possession as a root of title" or "possessory title." Although the common law historically recognized possession as creating proprietary claims in this way, the normative question why possession should continue to justify such legal claims remains a vexing one. This chapter begins with an excerpt from Carol Rose's inquiry about the concept of possession as a basis for original claims to property.

91

Carol Rose, "Possession as the Origin of Property"
(1985), 52 *University of Chicago Law Review* 73, at 73-77 and 82-88
(footnotes omitted)

How do things come to be owned? This is a fundamental puzzle for anyone who thinks about property. One buys things from other owners, to be sure, but how did the other owners get those things? Any chain of ownership or title must have a first link. Someone had to do something to anchor that link. The law tells us what steps we must follow to obtain ownership of things, but we need a theory that tells us why these steps should do the job.

John Locke's view, once described as "the standard bourgeois theory," is probably the one most familiar to American students. Locke argued that an original owner is one who mixes his or her labor with a thing and, by commingling that labor with the thing, establishes ownership of it. This labor theory is appealing because it appears to rest on "desert," but it has some problems. First, without a prior theory of ownership, it is not self-evident that one owns even the labor that is mixed with something else. Second, even if one does own the labor that one performs, the labor theory provides no guidance in determining the scope of the right that one establishes by mixing one's labor with something else. Robert Nozick illustrates this problem with a clever hypothetical. Suppose I pour a can of tomato juice into the ocean: do I now own the seas?

A number of thinkers more or less contemporary to Locke proposed another theory of the basis of ownership. According to this theory, the original owner got title through the consent of the rest of humanity (who were, taken together, the first recipients from God, the genuine original owner). Locke himself identified the problems with this theory; they involve what modern law-and-economics writers would call "administrative costs." How does everyone get together to consent to the division of things among individuals?

The common law has a third approach, which shares some characteristics with the labor and consent theories but is distinct enough to warrant a different label. For the common law, *possession* or "occupancy" is the origin of property. This notion runs through a number of fascinating old cases with which teachers of property law love to challenge their students. Such inquiries into the acquisition of title to wild animals and abandoned treasure may seem purely academic; how often, after all, do we expect to get into disputes about the ownership of wild pigs or long-buried pieces of eight? These cases are not entirely silly, though. People still do find treasure-laden vessels, and statesmen do have to consider whether someone's acts might support a claim to own the moon, for example, or the mineral nodes at the bottom of the sea. Moreover, analogies to the capture of wild animals show up time and again when courts have to deal on a nonstatutory basis with some "fugitive" resource that is being reduced to property for the first time, such as oil, gas, ground water, or space on the spectrum of radio frequencies.

With these more serious claims in mind, then, I turn to the maxim of the common law: first possession is the root of title. Merely to state the proposition is to raise two critical questions: what counts as possession, and why is it the basis for a claim to title? In exploring the quaint old cases' answers to these questions, we hit on some fundamental views about the nature and purposes of a property regime.

Consider *Pierson v. Post*, a classic wild-animal case from the early nineteenth century. Post was hunting a fox one day on an abandoned beach and almost had the beast in his gun sight when an interloper appeared, killed the fox, and ran off with the carcass. The indignant Post sued the interloper for the value of the fox on the theory that his pursuit of the fox had established his property right to it.

The court disagreed. It cited a long list of learned authorities to the effect that "occupancy" or "possession" went to the one who killed the animal, or who at least wounded it mortally or caught it in a net. These acts brought the animal within the "certain control" that gives rise to possession and hence a claim to ownership.

Possession thus means a clear act, whereby all the world understands that the pursuer has "an unequivocal intention of appropriating the animal to his individual use." A clear rule of this sort should be applied, said the court, because it prevents confusion and quarrelling among hunters (and coincidentally makes the judges' task easier when hunters do get into quarrels).

The dissenting judge commented that the best way to handle this matter would be to leave it to a panel of sportsmen, who presumably would have ruled against the inter-loper. In any event, he noted that the majority's rule would discourage the useful activity of fox hunting: who would bother to go to all the trouble of keeping dogs and chasing foxes if the reward were up for grabs to any "saucy intruder"? If we really want to see that foxes don't overrun the countryside, we will allocate a property right—and thus the ultimate reward—to the hunter at an earlier moment, so that he will undertake the useful investment in keeping hounds and the useful labor in flushing the fox.

The problem with assigning "possession" prior to the kill is, of course, that we need a principle to tell us when to assign it. Shall we assign it when the hunt begins? When the hunter assembles his dogs for the hunt? When the hunter buys his dogs?

Pierson thus presents two great principles, seemingly at odds, for defining posses-sion: (1) notice to the world through a clear act and (2) reward to useful labor. The latter principle, of course, suggests a labor theory of property. The owner gets the prize when he "mixes in his labor" by hunting. On the other hand, the former principle suggests at least a weak form of the consent theory: the community requires clear acts so that it has the opportunity to dispute claims, but may be thought to acquiesce in individual owner-ship where the claim is clear and no objection is made.

On closer examination, however, the two positions do not seem so far apart. In *Pierson*, each side acknowledged the importance of the other's principle. Although the majority decided in favor of a clear rule, it tacitly conceded the value of rewarding useful labor. Its rule for possession would in fact reward the original hunter most of the time, unless we suppose that the woods are thick with "saucy intruders." On the other side, the dissenting judge also wanted some definiteness in the rule of possession. He was simply insisting that the acts that sufficed to give notice should be prescribed by the relevant community, namely hunters or "sportsmen." Perhaps, then, there is some way to reconcile the clear-act and reward-to-labor principles. ...

[It] turns out that the common law of first possession, in rewarding the one who communicates a claim, *does* reward useful labor; the useful labor is the very act of speaking clearly and distinctly about one's claims to property. Naturally, this must be in a language that is understood, and the acts of "possession" that communicate a claim will vary according to the audience. Thus, returning to *Pierson v. Post*, the dissenting judge may well have thought that fox hunters were the only relevant audience for a claim to the fox; they are the only ones who have regular contact with the subject matter. By the same token, the mid-nineteenth-century California courts gave much deference to the mining-camp customs in adjudicating various Gold Rush claims; the Forty-Niners themselves, as those most closely involved with the subject, could best communicate and interpret the signs of property claims and would be particularly well served by a stable system of symbols that would enable them to avoid disputes.

The point, then, is that "acts of possession" are, in the now fashionable term, a "text," and that the common law rewards the author of that text. But, as students of hermeneutics know, the clearest text may have ambiguous subtexts. In connection with the text of first possession, there are several subtexts that are especially worthy of note. One is the implication that the text will be "read" by the relevant audience at the appropriate time. It is not always easy to establish a symbolic structure in which the text of first possession can be "published" at such a time as to be useful to anyone. Once again, *Pierson v. Post* illustrates the problem that occurs when a clear sign (killing the fox) comes only relatively late in the game, after the relevant parties may have already expended overlapping efforts and embroiled themselves in a dispute. Very similar problems occurred in the whaling industry in the nineteenth century: the courts expended a considerable amount of mental energy in finding signs of "possession" that were comprehensible to whalers from their own customs and that at the same time came early enough in the chase to allow the parties to avoid wasted efforts and the ensuing mutual recriminations.

Some objects of property claims do seem inherently incapable of clear demarcation—ideas, for example. In order to establish ownership of such disembodied items we find it necessary to translate the property claims into sets of secondary symbols that our culture understands. In patent and copyright law, for example, one establishes an entitlement to the expression of an idea by translating it into a written document and going through a registration process—though the unending litigation over ownership of these expressions, and over which expressions can even be subject to patent or copyright, might lead us to conclude that these particular secondary symbolic systems do not always yield widely understood "markings." We also make up secondary symbols for physical objects that would seem to be much easier to mark out than ideas; even property claims in land, that most tangible of things, are now at their most authoritative in the form of written records.

It is expensive to establish and maintain these elaborate structures of secondary symbols, as indeed it may be expensive to establish a structure of primary symbols of possession. The economists have once again performed a useful service in pointing out that there are costs entailed in establishing *any* property system. These costs might prevent the development of any system at all for some objects, where our need for secure investment and trade is not as great as the cost of creating the necessary symbols of possession.

There is a second and perhaps even more important subtext to the "text" of first possession: the tacit supposition that there is such a thing as a "clear act," unequivocally proclaiming to the universe one's appropriation—that there are in fact unequivocal acts of possession, which any relevant audience will naturally and easily interpret as property claims. Literary theorists have recently written a great deal about the relativity of texts. They have written too much for us to accept uncritically the idea that a "text" about property has a natural meaning independent of some audience constituting an "interpretive community" or independent of a range of other "texts" and cultural artifacts that together form a symbolic system in which a given text must be read. It is not enough, then, for the property claimant to say simply, "It's mine" through some act or gesture; in order for the "statement" to have any force, some relevant world must understand the claim it makes and take that claim seriously.

Thus, in defining the acts of possession that make up a claim to property, the law not only rewards the author of the "text"; it also puts an imprimatur on a particular symbolic system and on the audience that uses this system. Audiences that do not understand or accept the symbols are out of luck. For *Pierson*'s dissenting judge, who would have made the definition of first possession depend on a decision of hunters, the rule of first possession would have put the force of law behind the mores of a particular subgroup. The majority's "clear act" rule undoubtedly referred to a wider audience and a more widely shared set of symbols. But even under the majority's rule, the definition of first possession depended on a particular audience and its chosen symbolic context; some audiences win, others lose.

In the history of American territorial expansion, a pointed example of the choice among audiences made by the common law occurred when one group did not play the approved language game and refused to get into the business of publishing or reading the accepted texts about property. The result was one of the most arresting decisions of the early American republic: *Johnson v. McIntosh*, a John Marshall opinion concerning the validity of opposing claims to land in what is now a large part of Illinois and Indiana. The plaintiffs in this case claimed through Indian tribes, on the basis of deeds made out in the 1770's; the defendants claimed under titles that came from the United States. The Court found for the defendants, holding that the claims through the Indians were invalid, for reasons derived largely from international law rather than from the law of first possession. But tucked away in the case was a first-possession argument that Marshall passed over. The Indians, according to an argument of the claimants from the United States, could not have passed title to the opposing side's predecessors because, "[b]y the law of nature," the Indians themselves had never done acts on the land sufficient to establish property in it. That is to say, the Indians had never really undertaken those acts of possession that give rise to a property right.

Although Marshall based his decision on other grounds, there was indeed something to the argument from the point of view of the common law of first possession. Insofar as the Indian tribes moved from place to place, they left few traces to indicate that they claimed the land (if indeed they did make such claims). From an eighteenth-century political economist's point of view, the results were horrifying. What seemed to be the absence of distinct claims to land among the Indians merely invited disputes, which in turn meant constant disruption of productive activity and dissipation of energy in warfare. Uncertainty as to claims also meant that no one would make any productive use of the land because there is little incentive to plant when there is no reasonable assurance that one will be in possession of the land at harvest time. From this classical economic perspective, the Indians' alleged indifference to well-defined property lines in land was part and parcel of what seemed to be their relatively unproductive use of the earth.

Now it may well be that North American Indian tribes were not so indifferent to marking out landed property as eighteenth-century European commentators supposed. Or it may be that at least some tribes found landed property less important to their security than other forms of property and thus felt no need to assert claims to property in land. But however anachronistic the *Johnson* parties' (ultimately mooted) argument may now seem, it is a particularly striking example of the relativity of the "text" of possession to the interpretative community for that text. It is doubtful whether the claims of any nomadic population could ever meet the common law requirements for establishing property in land. Thus, the audience presupposed by the common law of first possession is an agrarian or a commercial people—a people whose activities with respect to the objects around them require an unequivocal delineation of lasting control so that those objects can be managed and traded.

But perhaps the deepest aspect of the common law text of possession lies in the attitude that this text strikes with respect to the relationship between human beings and nature. At least some Indians professed bewilderment at the concept of owning the land. Indeed they prided themselves on not marking the land but rather on moving lightly through it, living with the land and with its creatures as members of the same family rather than as strangers who visited only to conquer the objects of nature. The doctrine of first possession, quite to the contrary, reflects the attitude that human beings are outsiders to nature. It gives the earth and its creatures over to those who mark them so clearly as to transform them, so that no one else will mistake them for unsubdued nature.

We may admire nature and enjoy wildness, but those sentiments find little resonance in the doctrine of first possession. Its texts are those of cultivation, manufacture, and development. We cannot have our fish both loose and fast, as Melville might have said, and the common law of first possession makes a choice. The common law gives preference to those who convince the world that they have caught the fish and hold it fast. This may be a reward to useful labor, but it is more precisely the articulation of a specific vocabulary within a structure of symbols approved and understood by a commercial people. It is this commonly understood and shared set of symbols that gives significance and form to what might seem the quintessentially individualistic act: the claim that one has, by "possession," separated for oneself property from the great commons of unowned things.

Discussion Notes

Possessory Rights: Subject and Object Revisited

As Carol Rose explained, the judgments in *Pierson v. Post*, 3 Cai. R 175 (NY SC 1805) illustrate legal reasoning about possession, and the philosophical limits of the labour theory and the consent theory in the context of claims based on first possession. Consider these arguments in relation to some of the theories in chapter 1 that were used to justify property entitlement. Is the concept of first possession consistent with Macpherson's proposed formulation of a concept of property as the right not to be excluded? In thinking about how to conceptualize possessory rights from the perspective of those who have limited opportunities to acquire things by possession, consider the following story told by Patricia Williams about *Pierson v. Post*, as reinterpreted by a child, from the perspective of the fox. In reflecting on the story, Williams linked the perspective of the fox and the perspective of her great-great-grandmother who was a slave in the United States and the personal property of her slave-owner, Austin Miller:

> In reviewing those powerfully impersonal documents [the documents of her ancestor's sale as a slave to Austin Miller], I realized that both she and the fox shared a common lot, were either owned or unowned, never the owner. And whether owned or unowned, rights over them never filtered down to them; rights to their persons were never vested in them. When owned, issues of physical, mental, and emotional abuse or cruelty were assigned by the law to the private tolerance, whimsy, or insanity of an external master. And when unowned—free, freed, or escaped—again their situation was controllably precarious, for as objects *to be* owned, they and the game of their conquest were seen only as potential enhancements to some other self. (In *Pierson*, for example, the dissent described the contest as between the "gentleman" in pursuit and the "saucy intruder." The majority acknowledged that Pierson's behaviour was "uncourteous" and "unkind" but decided the case according to broader principles of "peace and order" in sportsmanship.) They were fair game from the perspective of those who had rights; but from their own point of view, they were objects of a murderous hunt.

(Patricia Williams, "The Pain of Word Bondage," in *The Alchemy of Race and Rights* (Cambridge, MA: Harvard University Press, 1991), at 156ff.)

This analysis of those who are "owners" in the context of a principle of first possession reflects the distinction between subjects and objects of property interests, addressed earlier in chapter 1. Can the problems identified by Williams be solved by making "objects" into "subjects" of property interests, or is the problem more fundamental?

Possession and First Nations

As Rose suggested, *Johnson v. McIntosh*, 21 US (8 Wheat.) 543 (1823) was significant for its definition of what constituted "possession" in the context of native land claims. According to Richard Chused (at 106-7) "*Johnson v. McIntosh* is the root case for almost all of modern tribal law" in the United States (*Cases, Materials and Problems in Property* (New York: Matthew Bender, 1988). The decision was also influential in cases about native title in Canada in the 19th and early 20th centuries. For a different perspective on the concept of possession and First Nations in Canada, see the excerpt from Kent McNeil, *Common Law Aboriginal Title* (Oxford: Clarendon Press, 1989), reproduced later in this chapter.

The Problems of First Possession

The case of *Pierson v. Post* is one example, among a number of others, of the concept of first possession as a basis for establishing a proprietary interest. While *Pierson* involved fox hunting, there have been other cases concerning "first possession" of fish in Lake

Erie (*Ohio v. Shaw*, 65 NE 875 (OH SC 1902)), seals on the east coast of Canada (*MV Polar Star v. Arsenault* (1964), 43 DLR (2d) 354 (PEI SC)), whales (*Swift v. Gifford*, 2 Lowell 110 (1872)), and bees (see the Bees Act, RSO 1990, c. B.6, and C.A. Wright, "The Right to Pursue Bees" (1939), 17 *Canadian Bar Review* 130). A US property casebook (Casner and Leach, *Cases and Text on Property*, 2d ed. (Boston: Little, Brown, 1969), at 25) has suggested (facetiously) that the concept of first possession has even been used to deal with the problem of beached whales on Cape Cod:

> The whaling industry has long since disappeared from Cape Cod, but not the whales. They are periodically washed up on the beach where they first attract and later repel the tourist trade. The disposal problem is traditionally solved by waiting until a curious New Yorker approaches near enough to the whale to be charged with possession, and hence title, thereof; then requiring the New Yorker as owner to give the whale decent burial under the public health laws.

For another charming example of the problems of first possession in the context of ice-fishing holes, see Ted Russell, "Stealin' the Holes," in *Tales from Pigeon Inlet* (St. John's: Breakwater Books, 1977), at 107. The author presents a fictitious account of a court case about a dispute that arose when Uncle Sol took advantage of holes cut in the ice for herring fishing by Skipper Rige Bartle. Part of Uncle Sol's (unsuccessful) defence was that "possession was nine pints (sic) of the law."

Possessory Interests and Common Law Decision Making

The philosophical justifications for the concept of first possession as a root of title were also explored in Richard Epstein's article, "Possession as the Root of Title" (1978-79), 13 *Georgia Law Review* 1221. Epstein concluded (at 1241) that the concept of first possession is justified in part because it has been "the organizing principle of most social institutions, and the heavy burden of persuasion lies upon those who wish to displace it." In reaching this conclusion, however, he suggested that it was not necessary to adopt the first possession principle with respect to things as yet unexploited by individuals or nations, such as the ocean bed or the Antarctic regions. In these cases, he asserted (at 1242) that we have the possibility of adopting "alternative systems of property rights that depart significantly from the first possession principle."

In considering the merits of his approach, Epstein also commented on the relative merits of using common law processes to design and develop the concept of first possession. In assessing his comments (at 1222ff.) (footnotes omitted), consider what kinds of administrative arrangements would be appropriate for resolving property disputes if a different principle were adopted for unexploited things such as the ocean bed.

> In dealing with the rule of first possession, it is vital to keep to the fore several institutional features that bind all common law (here used in the loose sense of case law, comprising both common law and equity) judges. The first of these points is that common law judges have—and traditionally have had—at their disposal only limited remedies to apply to redress a violation of a substantive right. The common law courts could award damages or demand the return of land or of a specific chattel; the courts of equity could enter decrees for specific performance (as in land sale contracts) or

injunctions (as in nuisances). In both cases the judges have nothing like the vast administrative powers available to the officials in the modern bureaucratic state.

Now the question of remedy seems at first blush posterior to the more basic matter of right, and as a logical matter it is. As a historical and institutional matter, however, the two questions are very much intertwined. A court with modest remedial powers is not apt to choose, or even stumble upon, property doctrines whose enforcement requires elaborate administrative machinery. The definition of rights is therefore apt to be made along certain "natural lines"; there will be broad general propositions that can apply to all against all, and there will be no reference to the numbers or formulas (you may build only thirty feet from the street, and you must leave ten percent of your land vacant on either side of your lot) that can be generated by direct administrative controls, such as zoning. The rule that possession lies at the root of title is one that a court can understand and apply; absent a better alternative it becomes therefore an attractive starting point for resolving particular disputes over the ownership of particular things.

Second, the common law court cannot order the docket of cases that come before it. It grows and develops with the society in which it emerges. The question, how does any person obtain rights against the world in any thing, may be first in the philosophical theory of property rights; yet there is no guarantee that this question will be first on the judicial agenda. Should the first case before the court concern the transfer of land by deed, then that is the question that must first be addressed, even if there is no explanation of why *A* has property rights in the land that he wishes to transfer to *B*. The intellectual process takes its toll upon the substantive results. A court will first make rules about the transfer, descent, and protection of property interests even for cases where the original claim of title rests upon first possession. How then can it escape the consequence of its decisions when called upon to adjudicate the force of the original title? The intellectual process forces common law courts to commit themselves on a succession of little points, which in turn denies them the freedom to switch ground when the large issues are formally presented for adjudication.

The judicial concern with its own docket influences the common law treatment of property rights in yet a third fashion. Although property rights are defined as against the entire world, they are fashioned in legal disputes between two (or at least very few) parties. The dispute may be between the plaintiff who found the shell and the defendant who took it from him. Third persons may as a matter of abstract theory have entitlements in the property in question; yet the very form of adjudication tends to postpone their claims until they themselves assert them. The point is of especial importance for possible ownership claims by the state, as actions between two private parties will never throw matters of public ownership into high relief. Although it is possible, and indeed correct, to argue that no adjudication between private parties can preclude the claims of the state, the steady stream of private litigation can set up the type of expectations that makes it very difficult for the state to assert its own ownership claims at some later date.

Does Epstein's analysis lead to a conclusion that "new" property or possessory rights should preferably be created by legislatures rather than courts? Is his view consistent with your assessment of this issue in relation to *Moore v. Regents of the University of California*, 51 Cal. 3d 120 (1990), 793 P2d 479, presented in chapter 1?

POSSESSION AND THE FINDERS OF "LOST" OBJECTS

In 1988, a Toronto newspaper reported that a lawyer who had recently purchased a 103-year-old house in the city experienced great surprise when the contractor whom she had hired to do renovations began tearing out the old plaster. According to the newspaper account, paper money started raining down on the renovation workers, eventually totalling between $46,000 and $50,000. The money was turned over to the police and was then held in trust pending a determination about who was entitled to it. Claims were made by the lawyer who owned the house, by the contractor whose workers found the money, and by the daughter of former owners of the house.

Assuming that none of these claimants was the "true owner" of the money, how does the concept of possession as a root of title assist in solving a dispute in the context of finding "lost" objects? What arguments support assertions of first possession on the part of each of these three claimants? (Remember that "possession" may be defined in differing ways.) What definition of first possession is most appropriate—that is, who has the relatively better claim in this situation?

This case was settled, and the exact nature of the settlement has never been disclosed. In examining the materials that follow, try to assess the strength of each claim. What settlement is appropriate in the light of the principles of possession?

Finders and First Possession

Armory v. Delamirie
(1722), 1 Strange 505; 93 ER 664 (KB)

PRATT CJ: The plaintiff being a chimney-sweeper's boy found a jewel and carried it to the defendant's shop (who was a goldsmith) to know what it was, and delivered it into the hands of the apprentice, who under pretence of weighing it, took out the stones, and calling to the master to let him know it came to three halfpence, the master offered the boy the money, who refused to take it, and insisted to have the thing again; whereupon the apprentice delivered him back the socket without the stones. And now <u>in trover</u> against the master these points were ruled:

1. That the finder of a jewel, though he does not by such finding acquire an absolute property or ownership, yet he has such a property as will enable him to keep it against all but the rightful owner, and consequently may maintain trover.
2. That the action well lay against the master, who gives a credit to his apprentice, and is answerable for his neglect.
3. As to the value of the jewel several of the trade were examined to prove what a jewel of the finest water that would fit the socket would be worth; and the Chief Justice directed the jury, that unless the defendant did produce the jewel, and shew it not to be of the finest water, they should presume the strongest against him, and make the value of the best jewels the measure of their damages: which they accordingly did.

Discussion Notes

The Principle of First Possession in Context

The first principle stated by the judge represents one formulation of the first possession principle. In considering it, think about the parties involved in the dispute in *Armory v. Delamirie*. Were there others who might have had competing claims who were not parties to this suit? Consider the problem noted above where the claimants included the lawyer-owner, her contractor, the workers doing the renovation, and the daughter of the previous owners of the house. Does the principle of first possession permit an assessment of all of these cliams? To what extent?

The Remedy of Trover

In this case, the plaintiff sued in trover, a common law action available to remedy an interference with chattels:

> "Trover" is derived from Old French and means "to find." The law initially adopted the fiction that the wrongdoer had found the property—to distinguish this action from detinue or trespass to chattels. Nineteenth century legislation removed that pretense from legal pleadings. The name "trover" is no longer appropriate ... . [The remedy now is "conversion."] Conversion provides a remedy where property is destroyed, or wrongfully "converted" to the use of another.

(Law Reform Commission of British Columbia, *Report on Wrongful Interference with Goods* (Vancouver: Ministry of the Attorney-General, 1992), at 4 and footnote 15.) There are a number of different actions in tort for interference with property, including detinue, trespass, conversion, and others. The Law Reform Commission Report, above (at 55), recommended that they be replaced by a single statutory tort, devised to deal with any wrongful interference with property. For a similar analysis and recommendations, see Ralph Simmonds and George Stewart, *Study Paper on Wrongful Interference with Goods* (Toronto: Ontario Law Reform Commission, 1989).

According to the judge in *Armory v. Delamirie*, what was the measure of damages in an action in trover, if the chattel itself were not returned? For further discussion of remedies, see the reports of the Law Reform Commission, above.

Employer's Liability for Actions of Employees

This case also confirmed an employer's liability for actions of an employee or apprentice. This early example of an employer's liability for employees' (wrongful) acts is now recognized in other kinds of situations. For example, in *Janzen v. Platy Enterprises*, [1989] 1 SCR 1252, the Supreme Court of Canada held an employer liable for sexual harassment when one employee harassed another. See also *Robichaud v. Canada (Treasury Board)*, [1987] 2 SCR 84.

Parker v. British Airways Board
[1982] 2 WLR 503 (CA)

DONALDSON LJ: On November 15, 1978, the plaintiff, Alan George Parker, had a date with fate—and perhaps with legal immortality. He found himself in the international executive lounge at terminal one, Heathrow Airport. And that was not all that he found. He also found a gold bracelet lying on the floor.

We know very little about the plaintiff, and it would be nice to know more. He was lawfully in the lounge and, as events showed, he was an honest man. Clearly he had not forgotten the schoolboy maxim "Finders keepers." But, equally clearly, he was well aware of the adult qualification "unless the true owner claims the article." He had to clear customs and security to reach the lounge. He was almost certainly an outgoing passenger because the defendants, British Airways Board, as lessees of the lounge from the British Airports Authority and its occupiers, limit its use to passengers who hold first class tickets or boarding passes or who are members of their Executive Club, which is a passengers' "club." Perhaps the plaintiff's flight had just been called and he was pressed for time. Perhaps the only officials in sight were employees of the defendants. Whatever the reason, he gave the bracelet to an anonymous official of the defendants instead of to the police. He also gave the official a note of his name and address and asked for the bracelet to be returned to him if it was not claimed by the owner. The official handed the bracelet to the lost property department of the defendants.

Thus far the story is unremarkable. The plaintiff, the defendants' official and the defendants themselves had all acted as one would have hoped and expected them to act. Thereafter the matter took what, to the plaintiff, was an unexpected turn. Although the owner never claimed the bracelet, the defendants did not return it to the plaintiff. Instead they sold it and kept the proceeds which amounted to £850. The plaintiff discovered what had happened and was more than a little annoyed. I can understand his annoyance. He sued the defendants in the Brentford County Court and was awarded £850 as damages and £50 as interest. The defendants now appeal.

It is astonishing that there should be any doubt as to who is right. But there is. Indeed, it seems that the academics have been debating this problem for years. In 1971 the Law Reform Committee reported that it was by no means clear who had the better claim to lost property when the protagonists were the finder and the occupier of the premises where the property was found. Whatever else may be in doubt, the committee was abundantly right in this conclusion. The committee recommended legislative action but, as is not uncommon, nothing has been done. The rights of the parties thus depend upon the common law.

As a matter of legal theory, the common law has a ready made solution for every problem and it is only for the judges, as legal technicians, to find it. The reality is somewhat different. Take the present case. The conflicting rights of finder and occupier have indeed been considered by various courts in the past. But under the rules of English jurisprudence, none of their decisions binds this court. We therefore have both the right and the duty to extend and adapt the common law in the light of established principles and the current needs of the community. This is not to say that we start with a clean sheet. In doing so, we should draw from the experience of the past as revealed by the previous decisions of the courts. In this connection we have been greatly assisted both by the arguments of counsel, and in particular those of Mr. Desch upon whom the main burden fell, and by the admirable judgment of the deputy judge in the county court.

Neither the plaintiff nor the defendants lay any claim to the bracelet either as owner of it or as one who derives title from that owner. The plaintiff's claim is founded upon the ancient common law rule that the act of finding a chattel which has been lost and taking control of it gives the finder rights with respect to that chattel. The defendants' claim has a different basis. They cannot and do not claim to have found the bracelet when it was handed to them by the plaintiff. At that stage it was no longer lost and they received and accepted the bracelet from the plaintiff on terms that it would be returned to him if the owner could not be found. They must and do claim on the basis that they had rights in relation to the bracelet immediately *before* the plaintiff found it and that these rights are superior to the plaintiff's. The defendants' claim is based upon the proposition that at common law an occupier of land has such rights over all lost chattels which are on that land, whether or not the occupier knows of their existence.

The common law right asserted by Mr. Parker has been recognised for centuries. In its simplest form it was asserted by the chimney-sweep's boy who, in 1722, found a jewel and offered it to a jeweller for sale. The jeweller refused either to pay a price acceptable to the boy or to return it and the boy sued the jeweller for its value: *Armory v. Delamirie* (1722) 1 Stra. 505. Pratt CJ ruled:

> That the finder of a jewel, though he does not by such finding acquire an absolute property or ownership, yet he has such a property as will enable him to keep it against all but the rightful owner, and consequently may maintain trover.

In that case the jeweller clearly had no rights in relation to the jewel immediately before the boy found it and any rights which he acquired when he received it from the boy stemmed from the boy himself. The jeweller could only have succeeded if the fact of finding and taking control of the jewel conferred no rights upon the boy. The court would then have been faced with two claimants, neither of which had any legal right, but one had de facto possession. The rule as stated by Pratt CJ must be right as a general proposition, for otherwise lost property would be subject to a free-for-all in which the physically weakest would go to the wall.

Pratt CJ's ruling is, however, only a general proposition which requires definition. Thus one who "finds" a lost chattel in the sense of becoming aware of its presence, but who does no more, is not a "finder" for this purpose and does not, as such, acquire any rights.

Some qualification has also to be made in the case of the trespassing finder. The person vis à vis whom he is a trespasser has a better title. The fundamental basis of this is clearly public policy. Wrongdoers should not benefit from their wrongdoing. This requirement would be met if the trespassing finder acquired no rights. That would, however, produce the free-for-all situation to which I have already referred, in that anyone could take the article from the trespassing finder. Accordingly, the common law has been obliged to give rights to someone else, the owner ex hypothesi being unknown. The obvious candidate is the occupier of the property upon which the finder was trespassing.

Curiously enough, it is difficult to find any case in which the rule is stated in this simple form, but I have no doubt that this is the law. It is reflected in the judgment of

Chitty J in *Elwes v. Brigg Gas Co.* (1886), 33 Ch.D 562, 568, although the chattel concerned was beneath the surface of the soil and so subject to different considerations. It is also reflected in the judgment of Lord Goddard CJ in *Hibbert v. McKiernan*, [1948] 2 KB 142, 149. That was a criminal case concerning the theft of "lost" golf balls on the private land of a club. The only issue was whether for the purposes of the criminal law property in the golf balls could be laid in someone other than the alleged thief. The indictment named the members of the club, who were occupiers of the land, as having property in the balls, and it is clear that at the time when the balls were taken the members were very clearly asserting such a right, even to the extent of mounting a police patrol to warn off trespassers seeking to harvest lost balls.

It was in this context that we were also referred to the opinion of the Judicial Committee in *Glenwood Lumber Co. Ltd. v. Phillips*, [1904] AC 405 and in particular to remarks by Lord Davey, at p. 410. However, there the occupier knew of the presence of the logs on the land and had a claim to them as owner as well as occupier. Furthermore, it was not a finding case, for the logs were never lost.

One might have expected there to be decisions clearly qualifying the general rule where the circumstances are that someone finds a chattel and thereupon forms the dishonest intention of keeping it regardless of the rights of the true owner or of anyone else. But that is not the case. There could be a number of reasons. Dishonest finders will often be trespassers. They are unlikely to risk invoking the law, particularly against another subsequent dishonest taker, and a subsequent honest taker is likely to have a superior title: see, for example, *Buckley v. Gross* (1863), 3 B & S 566. However, he probably has some title, albeit a frail one, because of the need to avoid a free-for-all. This seems to be the law in Ontario, Canada: *Bird v. Fort Frances*, [1949] 2 DLR 791.

In the interests of clearing the ground and identifying the problem, let me now turn to another situation in respect of which the law is reasonably clear. This is that of chattels which are attached to realty (land or buildings) when they are found. If the finder is not a wrongdoer, he may have some rights, but the occupier of the land or building will have a better title. The rationale of this rule is probably either that the chattel is to be treated as an integral part of the realty as against all but the true owner and so incapable of being lost or that the "finder" has to do something to the realty in order to get at or detach the chattel and, if he is not thereby to become a trespasser, will have to justify his actions by reference to some form of licence from the occupier. In all likely circumstances that licence will give the occupier a superior right to that of the finder.

Authority for this view of the law is to be found in *South Staffordshire Water Co. v. Sharman*, [1896] 2 QB 44 where the defendant was employed by the occupier of land to remove mud from the bottom of a pond. He found two gold rings embedded in the mud. The plaintiff occupier was held to be entitled to the rings. Dicta of Lord Russell of Killowen CJ, with whom Wills J agreed, not only support the law as I have stated it, but go further and may support the defendants' contention that an occupier of a building has a claim to articles found *in* that building as opposed to being found attached to or forming part of it. However, it is more convenient to consider these dicta hereafter. *Elwes v. Brigg Gas Co.*, 33 Ch.D 562, to which we were also referred in this context, concerned a prehistoric boat embedded in land. But I think that, when analysed, the issue really turned upon rival claims by the plaintiff to be the true owner in the sense of being the tenant for life of the realty, of the minerals in the land and of the boat if it was a chattel and by the defendants as lessees rather than as finders.

Again, in the interest of clearing the ground, I should like to dispose briefly of some of the other cases to which we were quite rightly referred and to do so upon the grounds that, when analysed, they do not really bear upon the instant problem. Thus, *In re Cohen, decd.; National Provincial Bank Ltd. v. Katz*, [1953] Ch. 88 concerned money hidden in a flat formerly occupied by a husband and wife who had died. The issue was whether the money belonged to the estate of the husband or to that of the wife. The money had been hidden and not lost and this was not a finding case at all. In *Johnson v. Pickering*, [1907] 2 KB 437 the issue was whether the sheriff on behalf of a judgment creditor had a claim to money which the judgment debtor took to his house at a time when the sheriff had taken walking possession of that house, albeit the sheriff had been unaware of the arrival of the money. This again is not a finding case. In *Moffatt v. Kazana*, [1969] 2 QB 152 the claimant established a title derived from that of the true owner. This does not help. Finally, there is *Hannah v. Peel*, [1945] KB 509. This was indeed a finding case, but the claimant was the non-occupying owner of the house in which the brooch was found. The occupier was the Crown, which made no claim either as occupier or as employer of the finder. It was held that the non-occupying owner had no right to the brooch and that therefore the finder's claim prevailed. What the position would have been if the Crown had made a claim was not considered.

[handwritten margin note: *cases distinguished*]

I must now return to the respective claims of the plaintiff and the defendants. Mr. Brown, for the plaintiff, relies heavily upon the decision of Patteson J and Wightman J, sitting in banc in *Bridges v. Hawkesworth* (1851), 21 LJ QB 75; 15 Jur. 1079. It was an appeal from the county court by case stated. The relevant facts, as found, were as follows. Mr. Bridges was a commercial traveller and in the course of his business he called upon the defendant at his shop. As he was leaving the shop, he picked up a small parcel which was lying on the floor, showed it to the shopman and, upon opening it in his presence, found that it contained £65 in notes. Mr. Hawkesworth was called and Mr. Bridges asked him to keep the notes until the owner claimed them. Mr. Hawkesworth advertised for the true owner, but no claimant came forward. Three years later Mr. Bridges asked for the money and offered to indemnify Mr. Hawkesworth in respect of the expenses which he had incurred in advertising for the owner. Mr. Hawkesworth refused to pay over the money and Mr. Bridges sued for it. The county court judge dismissed his claim and he appealed.

Patteson J gave the judgment of the court. The decision is sufficiently important, and the judgment sufficiently short and difficult to find, for me to feel justified in reproducing it in full. In so doing, I take the text of the report in the *Jurist*, 15 Jur. 1079, 1082 but refer to the *Law Journal* version, 21 LJ QB 75, 77-78, in square brackets where they differ. It reads:

> The notes which are the subject of this action were incidentally ["evidently"] dropped by mere accident, in the shop of the defendant, by the owner of them. The facts do not warrant the supposition that they had been deposited there intentionally, nor has the case been put at all upon that ground. The plaintiff found them on the floor, they being manifestly lost by some one. The general right of the finder to any article which has

been lost, as against all the world, except the true owner, was established in ... *Armory v. Delamirie*, 1 Stra. 505, which has never been disputed. This right would clearly have accrued to the plaintiff had the notes been picked up by him outside the shop of the defendant; and if he once had the right, the case finds that he did not intend, by delivering the notes to the defendant, to waive the title (if any) which he had to them, but they were handed to the defendant merely for the purpose of delivering them to the owner, should he appear. Nothing that was done afterwards has altered the state of things; the advertisements inserted ["indeed"] in the newspaper, referring to the defendant, had the same object; the plaintiff has tendered the expense of those advertisements to the defendant, and offered him an indemnity against any claim to be made by the real owner, and has demanded the notes. The case, therefore, resolves itself into the single point on which it appears that the learned judge decided it, namely, whether the circumstance of the notes being found inside [word emphasised in *Law Journal*] the defendant's shop gives him, the defendant, the right to have them as against the plaintiff, who found them. There is no authority in our law to be found directly in point. Perhaps the nearest case is that of *Merry v. Green* (1841), 7 M & W 623, but it differs in many respects from the present. We were referred, in the course of the argument, to the learned work of Von Savigny, edited by Perry CJ; but even this work, full as it is of subtle distinctions and nice reasonings, does not afford a solution of the present question. It was well asked, on the argument, if the defendant has the right, *when* did it accrue to him? If at all, it must have been antecedent to the finding by the plaintiff, for that finding could not give the defendant any right. If the notes had been accidentally kicked into the shop ["the street" in *Law Journal*, which must be right], and there found by someone passing by, could it be contended that the defendant was entitled to them from the mere fact of their being originally dropped in his shop? If the discovery had never ["not"] been communicated to the defendant, could the real owner have had any cause of action against him because they were found in his house? Certainly not. The notes never were in the custody of the defendant, nor within the protection of his house, before they were found, as they would have been had they been intentionally deposited there; and the defendant has come under no responsibility, except from the communication made to him by the plaintiff, the finder, and the steps taken by way of advertisement. These steps were really taken by the defendant as the agent of the plaintiff, and he has been offered an indemnity, the sufficiency of which is not disputed. We find, therefore, no circumstances in this case to take it out of the general rule of law, that the finder of a lost article is entitled to it as against all persons except the real owner, and we think that the rule must prevail, and that the learned judge was mistaken in holding that the place in which they were found makes any legal difference. Our judgment, therefore, is that the plaintiff is entitled to these notes as against the defendant; that the judgment of the court below must be reversed, and judgment given for the plaintiff for £50.

The ratio of this decision seems to me to be solely that the unknown presence of the notes on the premises occupied by Mr. Hawkesworth could not without more, give him any rights or impose any duty upon him in relation to the notes.

Mr. Desch, for the defendants, submits that *Bridges v. Hawkesworth*, 15 Jur. 1079 can be distinguished and he referred us to the judgment of Lord Russell of Killowen CJ,

Bridges v. Hawkesworth: RATIO

with which Wills J agreed, in *South Staffordshire Water Co. v. Sharman*, [1896] 2 QB 44. *Sharman's* case itself is readily distinguishable, either upon the ground that the rings were in the mud and thus part of the realty or upon the ground that the finders were employed by the plaintiff to remove the mud and had a clear right to direct how the mud and anything in it should be disposed of, or upon both grounds. However, Lord Russell of Killowen CJ in distinguishing *Bridges v. Hawkesworth* expressed views which, in Mr. Desch's submission, point to the defendants having a superior claim to that of the plaintiff on the facts of the instant case. Lord Russell of Killowen CJ said, at p. 46:

> The principle on which this case must be decided, and the distinction which must be drawn between this case and that of *Bridges v. Hawkesworth*, is to be found in a passage in *Pollock and Wright, Possession in the Common Law*, p. 41: "The possession of land carries with it in general, by our law, possession of everything which is attached to or under that land, and, in the absence of a better title elsewhere, the right to possess it also. And it makes no difference that the possessor is not aware of the thing's existence. ... It is free to anyone who requires a specific intention as part of a de facto possession to treat this as a positive rule of law. But it seems preferable to say that the legal possession rests on a real de facto possession, constituted by the occupier's general power and intent to exclude unauthorised interference." That is the ground on which I prefer to base my judgment. There is a broad distinction between this case and those cited from *Blackstone's Commentaries*. Those were cases in which a thing was cast into a public place or into the sea—into a place, in fact, of which it could not be said that anyone had a real de facto possession, or a general power and intent to exclude unauthorised interference ... . *Bridges v. Hawkesworth* stands by itself, and on special grounds; and on those grounds it seems to me that the decision in that case was right. Someone had accidentally dropped a bundle of banknotes in a public shop. The shopkeeper did not know they had been dropped, and did not in any sense exercise control over them. The shop was open to the public, and they were invited to come there. A customer picked up the notes and gave them to the shopkeeper in order that he might advertise them. The owner of the notes was not found, and the finder then sought to recover them from the shopkeeper. It was held that he was entitled to do so, the ground of the decision being, as was pointed out by Patteson J, that the notes, being dropped in the public part of the shop, were never in the custody of the shopkeeper, or "within the protection of his house." It is somewhat strange that there is no more direct authority on the question; but the general principle seems to me to be that where a person has possession of house or land, with a manifest intention to exercise control over it and the things which may be upon or in it, then, if something is found on that land, whether by an employee of the owner or by a stranger, the presumption is that the possession of that thing is in the owner of the *locus in quo*.

For my part, I can find no trace in the report of *Bridges v. Hawkesworth*, 21 LJ QB 75, of any reliance by Patteson J upon the fact that the notes were found in what may be described as the public part of the shop. He could, and I think would, have said that if the notes had been accidentally dropped in the *private* part unbeknownst to Mr. Hawkesworth and had later been accidentally kicked into the street, Mr. Hawkesworth would have had no duty to the true owner and no rights superior to that of the finder.

However, I would accept Lord Russell of Killowen CJ's statement of the general principle in *South Staffordshire Water Co. v. Sharman*, [1896] 2 QB 44, 46-47, provided that the occupier's intention to exercise control over anything which might be on the premises was manifest. But it is impossible to go further and to hold that the mere right of an occupier to exercise such control is sufficient to give him rights in relation to lost property on his premises without overruling *Bridges v. Hawkesworth*, 21 LJ QB 75. Mr. Hawkesworth undoubtedly had a right to exercise such control, but his defence failed.

South Staffordshire Water Co. v. Sharman was followed and applied by McNair J in *City of London Corporation v. Appleyard*, [1963] 1 WLR 982. There workmen demolishing a building found money in a safe which was recessed in one of the walls. The lease from the corporation to the building owners preserved the corporation's right to any article of value found upon any remains of former buildings and the workmen were employed by contractors working for the building owners. McNair J upheld the corporation's claim. The workmen claimed as finders, but it is clear law that a servant or agent who finds in the course of his employment or agency is obliged to account to his employer or principal. The contractor similarly was bound to account to the building owner and the building owner, who was the occupier, was contractually bound to account to the corporation. The principal interest of the decision lies in the comment of McNair J, at p. 987, that he did not understand Lord Russell of Killowen CJ as intending to qualify or extend the principle stated in *Pollock and Wright, Possession in the Common Law* (1888), p. 41, that possession of land carries with it possession of everything which is *attached to or under* that land when the Chief Justice restated the principle, [1896] 2 QB 44, 47:

> ... where a person has possession of house or land, with a manifest intention to exercise control over it and the things which may be *upon or in* it, then, if something is found *on* that land, whether by an employee of the owner or by a stranger, the presumption is that the possession of that thing is in the *owner* of the locus in quo. (My emphasis.)

We were also referred to two Canadian authorities. In *Grafstein v. Holme and Freeman* (1958), 12 DLR (2d) 727, the Ontario Court of Appeal considered the competing claims of Mr. Grafstein, the owner-occupier of a dry goods store, and Mr. Holme and Mr. Freeman, his employees. Mr. Holme found a locked box in premises which Mr. Grafstein had acquired as an extension to his store. He showed it unopened to Mr. Grafstein and was told to put it on a shelf and leave it there. Two years later Mr. Holme and Mr. Freeman decided to open the box and found that it contained Canadian $38,000 in notes. The court treated the moment of finding the money as that at which the box was opened, rather than when the box was found. It held that Mr. Grafstein had a superior claim because he took possession and control of the box and of its unknown contents when its existence was first brought to his attention. LeBel JA took a different view of Lord Russell of Killowen CJ's judgment in *South Staffordshire Water Co. v. Sharman*, [1896] 2 QB 44 from that of McNair J in *City of London Corporation v. Appleyard*, [1963] 1 WLR 982. He considered that Lord Russell of Killowen CJ intended to extend the statement of principle in *Pollock and Wright, Possession in the Common Law* to include things upon land or in a house. He commented, 12 DLR (2d) 727, 734:

> ... I do not think that anyone could seriously quarrel with the principle as extended by Lord Russell in that way so long as it is established in evidence as a basis for the

presumption that the occupier has in fact the "possession of house or land, with a manifest intention to exercise control over it [i.e., the land or the house] and the things which may be upon or in it. ..." I say this because I think there must be a natural presumption of possession in favour of the person in occupation—a presumption which hardly needs a legal decision for its authority.

The court did not decide the issues upon the basis that Messrs. Holme and Freeman were the employees of Mr. Grafstein acting within the scope of their employment, and LeBel JA indicated that in his view a claim by Mr. Grafstein based upon that relationship might well have failed.

The second Canadian decision is that of the Manitoba Court of Appeal in *Kowal v. Ellis* (1977), 76 DLR (3d) 546. The plaintiff was driving across the defendant's land when he saw an abandoned pump on that land. Some question arose as to whether he was a trespasser, but the court held that at the time when he took possession of the pump he had the defendant's permission to go on the land. The judgment of the court was delivered by O'Sullivan JA and, so far as is material, was in the following terms, at pp. 548-549:

> The plaintiff, when he took possession of the pump, acquired a special property in it arising out of his relationship to the unknown owner. The relationship was one of bailment and, like any other bailee, the plaintiff has become entitled to sue in trover or, as here, in detinue anyone who has interfered with his right of possession, save only the true owner or someone claiming through or on behalf of the true owner. This is in accord with what was decided by Patteson J, in *Bridges v. Hawkesworth*, 21 LJ QB 75, 78: "We find, therefore, no circumstances in this case to take it out of the general rule of law, that the finder of a lost article is entitled to it as against all parties except the real owner, and we think that that rule must prevail. ..." *Bridges v. Hawkesworth* was followed by Birkett J in *Hannah v. Peel*, [1945] KB 509. It follows that the plaintiff is entitled to possession of the pump, unless the defendant asserts and proves a title to the pump superior to that of the plaintiff. Such a superior title may arise independently of the original owner of the pump if the original owner has dealt with it in such a way as to enable the landowner to assert a claim as owner of the chattel, or it may arise by reason of the landowner having himself already become the bailee of the chattel on behalf of the true owner. In *Elwes v. Brigg Gas Co.*, 33 Ch.D 562, the landowner succeeded against the finder of a boat because the landowner proved that it was the owner of the boat, which had become embedded in the soil. In that case, Chitty J said, at p. 568: "The first question which does actually arise in this case is whether the boat belonged to the plaintiff [landowner] ... I hold that it did. ..." Naturally, a bailee by finding must surrender possession to the true owner of the chattel and, once it was held that the landowner owned the boat, the case was closed. A similar result was effected in *Hibbert v. McKiernan*, [1948] 2 KB 142. Once there was a finding that the golf balls belonged to the members of the golf course, it followed that the finder had no right of possession as against the true owners of the balls. One can imagine cases where a chattel is abandoned by its first owner and may then become the property of someone else, perhaps a landowner who exercises control and dominion over it. In such a case, the landowner would assert a claim against the finder, not by virtue of his right as owner of land, but by virtue of his right as owner of the chattel. In the case before us, however, the

defendant asserts no such right of ownership. The pump in question appears to have been cached rather than abandoned. So this is a case where the defendant does not even assert that he is the owner of the chattel in question; that being so, the defendant can succeed only by showing that he himself was in possession of the pump at the time of the finding in such a way that he, the defendant, had already constituted himself a bailee for the true owner. I know there have been weighty opinions expressed in favour of the proposition that the possessor of land possesses all that is on the land, and there is a sense in which that may be so, but to oust the claim of a bailee by finding it is not enough to establish some kind of metaphysical possession. What must be shown is that the landowner claimant, who has not acquired ownership of a chattel, is a prior bailee of the chattel with all the rights, but also with all the obligations, of a bailee. I am sure that no one would be more surprised than the defendant if, prior to the finding by the plaintiff, the true owner had come along and asserted that the defendant landowner owed him any duty either to take care of the pump or to seek out the owner of it. The reality is that the defendant, not even being aware of the existence of the pump, owed no duty with respect to it to its true owner. He was not a bailee of the pump and consequently has no claim to possession which can prevail over the special property which the plaintiff has by virtue of his having become a bailee by finding.

One of the great merits of the common law is that it is usually sufficiently flexible to take account of the changing needs of a continually changing society. Accordingly, Mr. Desch rightly directed our attention to the need to have common law rules which will facilitate rather than hinder the ascertainment of the true owner of a lost chattel and a reunion between the two. In his submission the law should confer rights upon the occupier of the land where a lost chattel was found which were superior to those of the finder, since the loser is more likely to make inquiries at the place of loss. I see the force of this submission. However, I think that it is also true that if this were the rule and finders had no prospect of any reward, they would be tempted to pass by without taking any action or to become concealed keepers of articles which they found. Furthermore, if a finder is under a duty to take reasonable steps to reunite the true owner with his lost property, this will usually involve an obligation to inform the occupier of the land of the fact that the article has been found and where it is to be kept.

In a dispute of this nature there are two quite separate problems. The first is to determine the general principles or rules of law which are applicable. The second, which is often the more troublesome, is to apply those principles or rules to the factual situation. I propose to confront those two problems separately.

Rights and Obligations of the Finder

1. The finder of a chattel acquires no rights over it unless (a) it has been abandoned or lost and (b) he takes it into his care and control.
2. The finder of a chattel acquires very limited rights over it if he takes it into his care and control with dishonest intent or in the course of trespassing.
3. Subject to the foregoing and to point 4 below, a finder of a chattel, whilst not acquiring any absolute property or ownership in the chattel, acquires a right to keep it against all but the true owner or those in a position to claim through the true owner or

one who can assert a prior right to keep the chattel which was subsisting at the time when the finder took the chattel into his care and control.

4. Unless otherwise agreed, any servant or agent who finds a chattel in the course of his employment or agency and not wholly incidentally or collaterally thereto and who takes it into his care and control does so on behalf of his employer or principal who acquires a finder's rights to the exclusion of those of the actual finder.

5. A person having a finder's rights has an obligation to take such measures as in all the circumstances are reasonable to acquaint the true owner of the finding and present whereabouts of the chattel and to care for it meanwhile.

Rights and Liabilities of an Occupier

1. An occupier of land has rights superior to those of a finder over chattels in or attached to that land and an occupier of a building has similar rights in respect of chattels attached to that building, whether in either case the occupier is aware of the presence of the chattel.

2. An occupier of a building has rights superior to those of a finder over chattels upon or in, but not attached to, that building if, but only if, before the chattel is found, he has manifested an intention to exercise control over the building and the things which may be upon it or in it.

3. An occupier who manifests an intention to exercise control over a building and the things which may be upon or in it so as to acquire rights superior to those of a finder is under an obligation to take such measures as in all the circumstances are reasonable to ensure that lost chattels are found and, upon their being found, whether by him or by a third party, to acquaint the true owner of the finding and to care for the chattels meanwhile. The manifestation of intention may be express or implied from the circumstances including, in particular, the circumstance that the occupier manifestly accepts or is obliged by law to accept liability for chattels lost upon his "premises," e.g. an innkeeper or carrier's liability.

4. An "occupier" of a chattel, e.g. a ship, motor car, caravan or aircraft, is to be treated as if he were the occupier of a building for the purposes of the foregoing rules.

Application to the Instant Case

The plaintiff was not a trespasser in the executive lounge and, in taking the bracelet into his care and control, he was acting with obvious honesty. Prima facie, therefore, he had a full finder's rights and obligations. He in fact discharged those obligations by handing the bracelet to an official of the defendants' although he could equally have done so by handing the bracelet to the police or in other ways such as informing the police of the find and himself caring for the bracelet.

The plaintiff's prima facie entitlement to a finder's rights was not displaced in favour of an employer or principal. There is no evidence that he was in the executive lounge in the course of any employment or agency and, if he was, the finding of the bracelet was quite clearly collateral thereto. The position would have been otherwise in the case of most or perhaps all the defendants' employees.

The defendants, for their part, cannot assert any title to the bracelet based upon the rights of an occupier over chattels attached to a building. The bracelet was lying loose on the floor. Their claim must, on my view of the law, be based upon a manifest intention to exercise control over the lounge and all things which might be in it. The evidence is that they claimed the right to decide who should and who should not be permitted to enter and use the lounge, but their control was in general exercised upon the basis of classes or categories of user and the availability of the lounge in the light of the need to clean and maintain it. I do not doubt that they also claimed the right to exclude individual undesirables, such as drunks, and specific types of chattels such as guns and bombs. But this control has no real relevance to a manifest intention to assert custody and control over lost articles. There was no evidence that they searched for such articles regularly or at all.

Evidence was given of staff instructions which govern the action to be taken by employees of the defendants if they found lost articles or lost chattels were handed to them. But these instructions were not published to users of the lounge and in any event I think that they were intended to do no more than instruct the staff on how they were to act in the course of their employment.

It was suggested in argument that in some circumstances the intention of the occupier to assert control over articles lost on his premises speaks for itself. I think that this is right. If a bank manager saw fit to show me round a vault containing safe deposits and I found a gold bracelet on the floor, I should have no doubt that the bank had a better title than I, and the reason is the manifest intention to exercise a very high degree of control. At the other extreme is the park to which the public has unrestricted access during daylight hours. During those hours there is no manifest intention to exercise any such control. In between these extremes are the forecourts of petrol filling stations, unfenced front gardens of private houses, the public parts of shops and supermarkets as part of an almost infinite variety of land, premises and circumstances.

This lounge is in the middle band and in my judgment, on the evidence available, there was no sufficient manifestation of any intention to exercise control over lost property before it was found such as would give the defendants a right superior to that of the plaintiff or indeed any right over the bracelet. As the true owner has never come forward, it is a case of "finders keepers."

I would therefore dismiss the appeal.

EVELEIGH LJ: It is accepted on both sides that for the defendants to succeed it must be shown that they had possession of the bracelet at the time when the plaintiff found it and took it into his possession. Whatever the difficulties which surround the concept of possession in English law, the two elements of control and animus possidendi must co-exist. Each of these elements varies greatly in the circumstances of each case. We are concerned to consider them in relation to a bracelet, obviously lost by its owner, found on the floor of the executive lounge at London Airport. Against all but the true owner a person in possession has the right to possess. It should follow therefore that an innocent handler of property who intends to take it for the purpose of discovering the owner and returning it to him should not be in danger of infringing any right in a third party. This makes it essential that the elements of possession should be apparent.

In *South Staffordshire Water Co. v. Sharman*, [1896] 2 QB 44, 47, Lord Russell of Killowen CJ said:

> It is somewhat strange that there is no more direct authority on the question; but the general principle seems to me to be that where a person has possession of house or land, with a manifest intention to exercise control over it and the things which may be upon or in it, then, if something is found on that land, whether by an employee of the owner or by a stranger, the presumption is that the possession of that thing is in the owner of the locus in quo.

In relation to the facts of the present case, I respectfully agree with Donaldson LJ when he says that he would accept Lord Russell of Killowen CJ's statement of the general principle, provided that the occupier's intention to exercise control over anything which might be on the premises was manifest. Indeed, I regard Lord Russell of Killowen CJ as saying that it is necessary for the occupier to prove that his intention was obvious. A person permitted upon the property of another must respect the lawful claims of the occupier as the terms upon which he is allowed to enter, but it is only right that those claims or terms should be made clear. What is necessary to do this must depend on the circumstances. Take the householder. He has the key to the front door. People do not enter at will. They come by very special invitation. They are not members of a large public group, even a restricted group of the public, as users of the executive lounge may be. I would be inclined to say that the occupier of a house will almost invariably possess any lost article on the premises. He may not have taken any positive steps to demonstrate his animus possidendi, but so firm is his control that the animus can be seen to attach to it. It is rather like the strong room of a bank, where I think it would be difficult indeed to suggest that a bracelet lying on the floor was not in the possession of the bank. The firmer the control, the less will be the need to demonstrate independently the animus possidendi.

The absence of both elements in *Bridges v. Hawkesworth*, 21 LJ QB 75, was emphasised by Lord Russell of Killowen CJ in *South Staffordshire Water Co. v. Sharman*, [1896] 2 QB 44, 47, when he said:

> The shopkeeper did not know they had been dropped, and did not in any sense exercise control over them. The shop was open to the public, and they were invited to come there.

I do not myself support the criticism that has been levelled against Lord Russell of Killowen CJ's words by those who state broadly that the place makes no difference and call in support the words of Patteson J in *Bridges v. Hawkesworth*, 21 LJQB 75, 78: "... the learned judge was mistaken in holding that the place in which they were found makes any legal difference." He was not saying that the place is an irrelevant consideration. He was saying that there was nothing in the place where the notes were found to rebut the principle of "finders keepers." There was nothing special about it. It was open to the public. One could not infer any special conditions of entry. Earlier, however, he said, at p. 78: "The notes never were in the custody of the defendant, nor within the protection of his house before they were found. ..." I see in those words a recognition of the fact that other considerations might apply in the case of a private house. In the present case I have come to the conclusion that there is nothing so special in the place and no other evidence to indicate that the defendants, on whom is the burden of proof, in any way demonstrated that they possessed the intention to exercise exclusive control over lost property or that the permission to enter as a member of the travelling public, albeit having purchased the special privilege of the executive lounge, was upon the terms that the commonly understood maxim "finders keepers" would not apply. I therefore would dismiss this appeal.

SIR DAVID CAIRNS: I agree that this appeal should be dismissed. While there is no authority which is binding on this court, it seems to me that *Bridges v. Hawkesworth*, 21 LJQB 75 is the closest case on its facts to the present case. Though *Bridges v. Hawkesworth* has been the subject of much academic discussion, it has been either applied or distinguished in all the reported cases of disputes between finders and occupiers for 130 years and I consider that it should be followed on this occasion unless it can properly be distinguished.

The only possible distinction is that in *Bridges v. Hawkesworth* the notes were apparently found in the part of the shop to which the public had, in practice, unrestricted access, whereas in the instant case there was some degree of control of access to the lounge where the bracelet was found.

In my judgment, that is not a sufficient ground for deciding this dispute in favour of the occupier rather than the finder. There could be no logical reason for according more favourable treatment to an airways board which admits only a fraction of the public to a particular lounge (but a fraction which includes all first class passengers and some others) and a shopkeeper who imposes no restriction on entry to his shop while it is open (but who would be entitled to refuse entry to anybody if he thought fit).

I agree with both Donaldson LJ and Eveleigh LJ that, in a situation at all similar to that which we are considering, the occupier has a better claim than the finder only if he had possession of the article immediately before it was found and that this is only so (in the case of an article not *in* or *attached to* the land but only *on* it) when the occupier's intention to exercise control is manifest. I also agree that such an intention would probably be manifest in a private house or in a room to which access is very strictly controlled. Where the borderline should be drawn would be difficult to specify, but I am satisfied that this case falls on the wrong side of the borderline from the defendants' point of view.

I am in full agreement with the analysis of the authorities which Donaldson LJ has made in his judgment in relation to the facts in this case. As to thieves and trespassers (in the sense of trespassers to the place where the thing was found) I express no concluded opinion, since the plaintiff was not in either of those categories.

Appeal dismissed with costs.

Discussion Notes

Courts and the Evolution of Legal Principles

The *Parker* case is an example of a common law court consciously contributing to the "evolution" of legal principles about the concept of possession. What factors were identified by Donaldson LJ as reasons for the court's action in this case? Do you agree that the absence of legislative action always warrants such judicial activism? What competing arguments might lead to the opposite conclusion? In considering these issues in relation to *Parker*, you may want to reassess the relationship between courts and legislatures explored in chapter 1. Would the role of a Canadian court in a factual case similar to *Parker* be the same as its role in a case involving a Charter claim? Why?

Rights of Finders and Occupiers

As is evident in the reasoning of Donaldson LJ, some of the previous cases about finding lost objects were difficult to reconcile in terms of their doctrinal principles. On the one hand, there were cases that seemed to follow the basic principle of *Armory v. Delamirie*—"finders keepers"—such as *Bridges v. Hawkesworth* (1851) 21 LJQB 75; *Hannah v. Peel*, [1945] KB 509 (TD); and *Kowal v. Ellis* (1977), 76 DLR (3d) 546 (Man. CA). On the other hand, some cases seemed to favour the occupier or owner of land where the lost object was found—for example, *South Staffordshire Water Co. v. Sharman*, [1896] 2 QB 44 (AD); *Elwes v. Brigg Gas Co.* (1886), 33 Ch.D 562 (Ch.D); *Grafstein v. Holme and Freeman* (1958), 12 DLR (2d) 727) (Ont. CA); *Hibbert v. McKiernan*, [1948] 2 KB 142 (CA); and *City of London Corporation v. Appleyard*, [1963] 1 WLR 982 (QBD).

Examine the reasoning of Donaldson LJ closely in relation to these cases. To what extent do his conclusions depend on identifying differences "on the facts" in relation to the cases? Note, for example, the significance of the finder's right to be in the place where the lost object is found. Does this factor satisfactorily explain the difference in the outcome of litigation in *Bridges v. Hawkesworth* by contrast with *Hibbert v. McKiernan*? Was the chimney-sweep in *Armory v. Delamirie* in a "public" or "private" place when he found the jewel?

Consider also the importance of an employer–employee relationship as a factor in reconciling the cases, including *Grafstein v. Holme and Freeman* or *City of London Corporation v. Appleyard*. What principle of possession justifies the conclusion that an employer is entitled to a lost object found on the premises by an employee? For another decision confirming an employer's entitlement to chattels found by an employee in the course of employment, see *White v. Alton-Lewis Ltd.* (1975), 49 DLR (3d) 189 (Ont. Cty. Ct).

In thinking about these issues, consider the reasoning of Donaldson LJ in relation to the principle that an occupier has a relatively better claim than a finder when the object has become "attached to" the land or building. Is this principle in *Parker* consistent with Lord Russell's statement in *South Staffordshire Water Co. v. Sharman* that possession of land carries with it possession of all chattels "in or upon" the land? Consider the following assessment of this aspect of the *Parker* case:

> One is inevitably led to the conclusion that the distinction propounded by Donaldson LJ in *Parker* is one based upon the most tenuous authority, and that it is merely intended to rid the law of the earlier confusion. ...
>
> But a more serious difficulty with the distinction is that it is irrational. It seems absurd that the conflicting rights of finder and occupier to a lost chattel should be made

to depend on such a fortuitous occurrence as the circumstances in which it was lost and subsequent events. For example, suppose that a chattel is lost in a field, and that at the time of losing it is lying on the land surface. The conflicting rights of finder and occupier may then depend upon whether someone unwittingly later tramples upon it so that it becomes embedded in the soil. If it does become so embedded, the occupier will automatically have the superior title, if not, the finder or the occupier may have the superior title depending on whether the occupier had manifested an intention to possess the chattel prior to the finding.

(T.J. Follows, "*Parker v. British Airways Board* and the Law of Finding Chattels" (1982), 12 *Kingston Law Review* 1 (hereafter Follows).) The author offers a detailed critique of the decision in *Parker*.)

Possession, Policy Issues, and the Duties of Finders

Can the outcomes in *Parker* and in the previous cases be reconciled more satisfactorily on the basis of underlying legal policy? What is the legal policy promoting the finder's entitlement in *Armory v. Delamirie*? What is the legal policy promoting the finder's entitlement in *Parker v. British Airways Board*? What other policies might promote the entitlement of finders to claim title to lost chattels? Do the principles enunciated in *Parker* concerning the duties of finders tend to achieve these goals? For an excellent overview of doctrinal and policy issues (written prior to the *Parker* case), see D.R. Harris, "The Concept of Possession in English Law," in A.G. Guest, ed., *Oxford Essays in Jurisprudence* (Oxford: Oxford University Press, 1961), at 69.

In *Parker*, Donaldson LJ defined the duties of finders of lost objects. He also defined, apparently for the first time, the duties of occupiers who may discover lost objects on their property. How can these duties be enforced in practice?

Interpreting Judicial Decisions and the Scope of Legal Advice

The principles in *Parker* establish rights to a lost object for an occupier of a building where the object is "upon or in, but not attached to" the building, but only if "before the object is found, [the occupier] has manifested an intention to exercise control over the building and the things which may be upon it or in it." What actions had been taken by British Airways in the *Parker* case—actions that were regarded as insufficient to demonstrate the airline's intention to exercise control over lost objects? What arrangements would have satisfied Donaldson LJ that the airline had manifested such an intent? What arrangements would have satisfied Eveleigh LJ, in terms of his stated requirements of "control and *animus possidendi*"? Is the principle of "manifest intent" in the *Parker* case consistent with ideas about property and human will, as presented in chapter 1? Is the idea of intent, in practice, the same for the finder and the airline in *Parker*? In a recent decision in Alberta, for example, the Court of Queen's Bench held that the finders of a cache of Canadian bills ($75,960 in total) on land that was a well-site were entitled because the lessee-occupier of the land had failed to manifest an intent to exercise control over it (*Trachuk v. Olinek*, [1996] 4 WWR 137 (Alta. QB)).

The *Parker* case is a good example of how a judicial decision results in a need for expert legal advice about exactly how a corporation can organize its affairs to meet legal requirements and avoid (further) litigation. After the decision in *Parker*, corporations such as British Airways probably requested advice from their lawyers in exactly this way. Reconsider your suggestions about arrangements that the airline should make to satisfy the test in *Parker*, taking account of additional issues of cost and practical effectiveness for a corporation such as British Airways. Is the legal principle in *Parker* sufficiently clear for you to provide the airline with a definite legal opinion? Why does Donaldson LJ identify how the airline's actions were insufficient rather than defining exactly how the airline could act to meet the legal test? Why doesn't Sir David Cairns identify more precisely "where the line should be drawn"? As a member of the legal department of an airline like British Airways, how would you draft instructions to employees that satisfy the test in *Parker*?

Litigation and Negotiation as Processes for Problem Solving

The *Parker* case also raises an interesting question about why British Airways decided to pursue an appeal to the English Court of Appeal. In the light of the costs of such an appeal, it seems clear that the value of the bracelet was not the reason for doing so. Why then was this appeal worthwhile for the airline? Is this a case where all of the costs of the case should have been borne by the unsuccessful appellant? Are there societal interests that benefitted from the airline's decision to litigate here? (In thinking about this question, you may want to imagine the task faced by law students and lawyers prior to *Parker* in resolving issues of finders' rights.)

This case also raises questions about whether Mr. Parker and the airline attempted to negotiate a settlement of this claim prior to commencing litigation. How might such a process have occurred? What role do lawyers play in encouraging or discouraging out-of-court settlements? Do the legal principles set out in *Parker* encourage or discourage settlement of such claims? In thinking about the prospects for negotiating a solution here, you may want to reconsider the differing approaches of Amy and Jake in Carol Gilligan's analysis in chapter 1. While Jake's approach appears similar to typical legal reasoning in the law of finders, it may be more difficult to contemplate how Amy's approach would work in practice. According to her approach, the parties should talk to each other instead of to a third party, and they should find a solution that preserves relationships and connections important in the context of the dispute. How do these concerns apply to the dispute between Mr. Parker and the airline? Is there a creative legal solution here that meets the needs of both parties, one that goes beyond being "just a compromise"? How would a lawyer using an "ethic of care," and approaching this problem from the perspective of both Jake and Amy, provide advice in a case such as *Parker*?

Joint Finding: A Critical Perspective?

The issue of entitlement to an object when more than one person is involved in the process of discovery presents a different challenge for judicial decision making. It is perhaps significant that some of these cases have been resolved by permitting all members of the group to share the bounty discovered. In the examples that follow, try to identify the definition of possession that resulted in group entitlement. Is this idea of possession similar to the concept used in *Parker*? How is the issue of intention defined? Is it the same as the definition of intention in *Parker*?

Keron v. Cashman
33 A 1055 (NJ Ct. Ch. 1896)

FACTS

[Five boys who were walking home from church along a railway track in the city of Elizabeth found $775 in bills when an old stocking they were playing with broke open. The youngest boy, Crawford, stated that he found the stocking, which the oldest boy, Cashman, snatched from him. However the other boys declared Crawford threw the stocking down the embankment and then all the boys began playing with the stocking.

Since the police were unable to locate the true owner, Crawford claimed all the money, but the other boys claimed an equal division of the money.]

EMERY VC: Upon consideration of the evidence in this case, I reach the conclusion that the lost money which is the subject of the present controversy must be treated as legally found while in the common possession of all the defendants. This common possession arises from the fact that the old stocking which contained the money and other articles was, at the time the stocking burst open, in actual use by all the defendants as a plaything, and for the purpose of play only. The stocking itself, in the condition in which it was found, was not, in my view of the evidence, treated either by the boy who first picked it up or by any of the others as an article over which any ownership or possession was intended to be asserted for the purpose of examining or appropriating its contents. The evidence is conflicting as to whether the boy who first picked up the stocking threw it away again, or whether it was snatched from him by one of the older boys. The weight of evidence is that it was thrown away by him, and was then picked up again by Cashman. There is no sufficient evidence to establish that Crawford retained or desired to retain the stocking for the purpose of examining [it], or that it was taken from him for that purpose by the older [boy], Cashman. When Cashman first got the stocking, whether by picking it up or by snatching, he did not proceed to examine it, but commenced the play with it; and the only intention or state of mind in any of the boys in relation to the stocking and its contents, as found, established by the evidence, in my view, is that the stocking was treated by all of them only as a plaything, to be used as such, in the condition it was when found. In the course of the play with it, after it had passed from one hand to another, and while one boy was beating another with it, the stocking burst open, and it was then disclosed to all of the boys that the stocking contained money. This money within the stocking was therefore the lost property, and as to this money the first intention, idea, or "state of mind," as it is called in some of the authorities, arose on this discovery. As a plaything, the stocking with its contents was in the common possession of all the boys; and inasmuch as the discovery of the money resulted from the use of the stocking as a plaything, and in the course of the play, the money must be considered as being found by all of them in common. Had the stocking been like a pocketbook, an article generally used for containing money, or had the evidence established that Crawford, the boy who first picked up the stocking, retained it, or tried to retain it, for the purpose of examining its contents, or that it had been snatched from him by Cashman, another boy, for the purpose of opening or appropriating the contents himself, and preventing Crawford's examining, I think the original possession or retention of the stocking by Crawford, its original finder, for such purpose of examination, might perhaps be considered as the legal "finding" of the money inclosed, with other articles, in the stocking. But, inasmuch as none of the boys treated the stocking when it was found as anything but a plaything or abandoned article, I am of the opinion that the money within the stocking must be treated as lost property, which was not "found," in a legal sense, until the stocking was broken open during the play. At that time, and when so found, it was in the possession of all, and all the boys are therefore equally finders of the money, and it must be equally divided between them.

Edmonds v. Ronella
342 NY Supp. 2d 408 (SC 1973)

While rummaging through trash in a supermarket parking lot on their way home from church, two boys aged 9 and 12 found a bag with a manila envelope containing $12,300 cash. Antoinette Ronella aged 15 was among the friends who came to the boys' assistance. She picked up the bag and the boys accompanied her to her house where her parents called the police who gave her a receipt as the "sole" finder of the money. At trial, the boys denied her testimony that they had disclaimed any interest in the money. Hammer J stated:

> A finder has been defined as the person who first takes possession of lost property but to be a legal finder, an essential element is an intention or state of mind with reference to the lost property.

> On the basis of the principles of equity and the testimony given at trial, the court determined that the lost property was not found, in a legal sense, until the plaintiffs and defendant had removed it from the parking lot. Since possession was jointly obtained, the joint finders were entitled to an equal share of the money, a one-third share each.

Discussion Note

Shared Rights in Cases of Finding: A Different Voice?

If the concept of possession is sufficiently flexible to permit "joint" finders to share the value of their discovered chattel, could the same principle be used in disputes between a finder and an occupier? Such a recommendation was made, for example, in relation to the issue in *Parker* by Follows:

> A far more preferable rule, in the writer's view, would be one of equal division of the proceeds of sale of the lost chattel between occupier and finder, the sale being ordered by the court. The primary merit of such a rule would be its clarity. Such equality of

treatment of finder and occupier would moreover accurately reflect the ethics of the situation, that unless the finder is dishonest or a trespasser, neither party has the morally superior claim. Admittedly the law must accord possession of the lost chattel to *someone* in order to avoid a "free-for-all situation" but it by no means follows that it must accord possession to one party to the exclusion of the other.

If this principle of sharing by a finder and an occupier were adopted, the result in *Parker* would be different. Should the principle be applicable to all such claims? Consider, for example, a finder's claim to a gold bracelet found in an apartment occupied by her friend? Were the claims of all the parties in these "joint" finding cases of equal weight? What do these cases suggest about the institutional potential and limits of judicial decision making?

Are the "joint" finding cases examples of "a different voice" in legal principles about possession and the law of finders? In Carol Gilligan's example of two children resolving their differing choices about whether to play "next-door neighbours" (the four-year-old girl's choice) or "pirates" (the four-year-old boy's choice), the little girl resolved the dilemma by suggesting a game called "the pirate who lives next door." According to Gilligan:

> She has reached what I would call *an inclusive solution* rather than *a fair solution*—the fair solution would be to take turns and play each game for an equal period. "First we will play pirates for ten minutes and then we will play neighbors for ten minutes." Each child would enter the other's imaginative world. The girl would learn about the world of pirates and the boy would learn about the world of neighbors. It is a kind of tourism on a four-year-old's level. Really, it's simple. But the interesting thing is that neither game would change—the pirate game would stay the pirate game, and the neighbor game would stay the neighbor game. ...
>
> Now look what happens in the other solution, what I would call *the inclusive solution*. By bringing a pirate into the neighborhood, both the pirate game and the neighbor game change. In addition, the pirate–neighbor game, the combined game, is a game that *neither* child had separately imagined. In other words, a new game arises through the relationship.
>
> That is basically my point: [t]he inclusion of two voices in moral discourse, in thinking about conflicts, and in making choices, transforms the discourse ... . We are at the beginning of a process of inquiry, in which the methods themselves will have to be re-examined because the old methods are from the old game.

(Carol Gilligan, in the 1984 James McCormick Mitchell Lecture, "Feminist Discourse, Moral Values, and the Law: A Conversation," (1985), 34 *Buffalo Law Review* 11, at 45.) Are the "joint" finding cases examples of an inclusive legal approach, or do they represent only a compromise?

The Issue of Intention

The issue of intention is relevant in a number of different ways in defining possessory interests in the law of finders. As has been shown, the principle entitling an occupier of a building to claim possession of a lost chattel is whether the occupier has "manifested an intention to exercise control" over the building and chattels found within it, a test not met by British Airways in *Parker*. As well, the finders' intentions were relevant to determining their claims to possession in the "joint" finding cases. In addition to these examples, the issue of intention in defining rights to possession is relevant to disputes between a finder and someone who subsequently interferes with the finder's possession of a chattel. In the case that follows, note again how the concept of possession is defined in terms of competing claims to a lost object. Can you identify someone who is not a party to this action and whose claim might be relatively better than the claims of either the plaintiff or the defendant?

Bird v. Fort Frances
[1949] 2 DLR 791 (Ont. HC)

McRUER CJHC: This is an action brought to recover the sum of $1,430 from the defendant, the amount of a sum of money taken from the plaintiff by Chief Constable Gaston Louis Camerand, and subsequently handed over to the treasurer of the defendant municipality, and now held by him on deposit in a savings account in the local branch of the Dominion Bank.

In the month of May, 1946, the plaintiff, who was at that time about 12 years of age, was playing with a number of other boys in the rear of a pool-room built on private property in the Town of Fort Frances. As part of the game he attempted to crawl under the building and while doing so observed a can on a sill forming part of the understructure. On investigation he found this can to contain a large sum of money in bills. He took possession of it and after some incident in a coal bin, which was not clearly developed at the trial and is immaterial to this action, during which some of the money was lost, he took between fourteen and fifteen hundred dollars home, the substantial part of which he handed over to his mother, who hid it under the cushion of a chair. Some days later, as a result of the plaintiff's generous spending, the Chief Constable questioned him. The plaintiff gave a true account of the facts and disclosed that he had $60 on his person and where the balance of the money was. The Chief Constable went to the plaintiff's home, without a search warrant, and asked Mrs. Bird for the money, which she handed over without objection. The Chief Constable said in evidence that his purpose in securing the money was to return it to the rightful owner if he should be found. He says that he kept it for some time and, finding no owner, turned it over to the town treasurer. The town treasurer says that when he received the package of money from the Chief Constable the latter told him that it was money found and asked him to keep it in safe-keeping. It was eventually deposited, on December 23, 1946, in a special savings account to the credit of the Town of Fort Frances marked "Funds for Court disposal." The balance shown in the account on September 27, 1948 was $1,460.61.

The defendant in its statement of defence alleges that the moneys were found on premises owned by the late John Sandul and were rightfully retained by it as trustee for the true owner. Paragraph 2 reads as follows:

> The Defendant submits that it has retained these moneys in good faith as trustee for the true owner and asks the direction of the Court with respect to the disbursement thereof,

bearing in mind that the executor of the estate of the late John Sandul has already made a demand upon the Defendant for the return of the monies to him.

There was no evidence given at the trial of any demand made by the executor of the estate of the late John Sandul, and my understanding of what counsel said is that no such claim is made to the money. During the course of the trial counsel said that the executor wished to make a statement to the Court. I intimated that unless the executor was making a claim to the money, and would formally do so at the consequent risk of costs, I would not hear him. With that the matter was dropped. Whatever the rights of the estate of John Sandul may be, they cannot be considered or disposed of in this action as framed.

The facts are simple, but the law applicable has been a subject of absorbing interest to legal philosophers, jurists and textbook writers throughout the evolution of our jurisprudence, and in some aspects the British law cannot yet be said to be settled.

It is convenient first to consider the case in the following aspects: the rights of the plaintiff as the finder of the money; whether the removal of the money from the property of another was a felonious act; if so, how far his right to recover against this defendant is affected thereby; and whether the plaintiff's possession was subsisting at the time the money was handed over to the Chief Constable or had been so interrupted as to deprive him of a right to maintain this action.

The plaintiff's right of action, if any, depends on a finding that he was wrongfully deprived of possession of the money by the Chief Constable, and that the defendant continues to interfere wrongfully with his possession. I know of no better preface to a consideration of the law applicable than the chapter on "Possession" in Holmes, Common Law, 1948, from which I adopt the language of the learned author at p. 239 to express a cardinal principle of great antiquity: "The facts constituting possession generate rights as truly as do the facts which constitute ownership, although the rights of a mere possessor are less extensive than those of an owner."

Since *Armory v. Delamirie* (1722), 1 Str. 505, 93 ER 664, by the law of England the finder of a chattel, though he does not acquire absolute property or ownership, yet has such property as will enable him to keep it against all but the rightful owner (or at least one superior in title), and consequently may maintain trover. In that case a chimney-sweep found a jewel and carried it to the defendant's shop to know what it was. One of the defendant's employees, after a pretence of weighing it, refused to return the stone. Judgment was given in favour of the plaintiff.

Where the contest is between the finder and the owner of the premises on which a chattel is found the law still remains in an unsettled state, and I refer to it only as far as it throws some indirect light on the subject I have to consider, and not for the purpose of entering the lists of the legal debate that still continues on this subject.

In *Bridges v. Hawkesworth* (1851), 21 LJQB 75, the plaintiff found a parcel of bank-notes which had been dropped on the floor in the part of a shop frequented by customers. He handed them to the shopkeeper to hold pending inquiry by the true owner. The true owner was not found and the plaintiff sued the shopkeeper to recover the notes. Judgment was given in his favour.

This case, together with all other relevant cases on the subject, has been the subject of consideration in two recent judgments in the English Courts. In *Hannah v. Peel*, [1945] KB

509, the defendant was the owner of a house which he himself had never occupied. While the house was under requisition for war purposes the plaintiff, a soldier, found in a bedroom used as a sick bay, loose in a crevice on top of a window frame, a brooch, the owner of which was unknown. There was no evidence that the defendant had any knowledge of the existence of the brooch before it was found, but the police, to whom the plaintiff handed it for the purpose of ascertaining its owner, delivered it to the defendant, who claimed it as being found on the premises of which he was the owner. After a full discussion of the somewhat conflicting authorities, including *Elwes v. Brigg Gas Co.* (1886), 33 Ch.D 562, and *South Staffordshire Water Co. v. Sharman*, [1896] 2 QB 44, Birkett J followed the decision in *Bridges v. Hawkesworth, supra*, and gave judgment for the plaintiff.

In *Hibbert v. McKiernan*, [1948] 1 All ER 860, Lord Goddard CJ was required to consider the subject in a different aspect. McKiernan had been charged with the theft of eight golf balls, which had been lost and abandoned by their original owners and picked up and carried away by him while trespassing on the course. The Justices found that the balls had been abandoned by their original owners and only one was capable of being identified. They were of the opinion that the appellant took the balls for the purpose of selling them and that by taking the balls the appellant meant to steal them and did steal them, but stated a case on the questions of law which they considered arose, in the main whether the appellant, by finding them, acquired title to the balls which, as they had been abandoned by their original owners, would prevail against the owners of the land on which they were found.

After referring to *Bridges v. Hawkesworth, Elwes v. Brigg Gas Co.* and *South Staffordshire Water Co. v. Sharman*, the Lord Chief Justice said [at 861]: "These cases have long been the delight of professors and text writers, whose task it often is to attempt to reconcile the irreconcilable." He pointed out that "the Corpus Professor of Jurisprudence at Oxford and the Professor Emeritus of English Law at Cambridge have expressed the opinion that *Bridges v. Hawkesworth* was wrongly decided." He referred to the decision of Birkett J in *Hannah v. Peel* as having reinvigorated that "much-battered case" and leaves it to wiser heads than his to end the controversy "which will, no doubt, continue to form an appropriate subject for moots till the House of Lords lays it to rest for all time."

This discussion bears only on the case I have to decide in considering whether the plaintiff was a "true finder" as the term is used in the cases, or whether the owner of the land on which the money was found had an interest in it; and if he had whether the plaintiff was a mere wrongful taker or in law guilty of a felonious act. If the taking in this case amounted to a felony then for the first time in British law, as far as I can determine, the question must be expressly decided whether a thief can maintain an action for trover or conversion against one who has wrongfully deprived him of possession of the thing stolen. If the taking was "wrongful taking" with no felonious intent, the course to be followed is much more clearly defined.

[The court reviewed a number of texts and cases, and concluded:]

In applying the law I have discussed to the facts of the case before me I am convinced that the plaintiff was not a "true finder" within the meaning of the term as used by jurists and writers. The money was not found in a public highway or public conveyance or in any place to which the public had access by leave or licence, nor was there anything to lead one to believe that it had been lost in the true sense. It had been carefully put in the container for the purpose of hiding it in the place in which it was discovered. It may well be that it was hidden by a thief, or it may be that it was abandoned, but it was not lost in the sense that a wallet is lost if dropped in the street or that the bank-notes in *Bridges v. Hawkesworth, supra,* or the jewel in *Armory v. Delamirie, supra,* or the brooch in *Hannah v. Peel, supra,* were lost. The person who put the money where it was found put it there deliberately.

The plaintiff had no right to remove it from the property of another, and undoubtedly was a wrongful taker. The more difficult question to decide is whether he had a felonious intent and the taking was felonious; and if so, whether he would have the same rights as a wrongful taker who took under circumstances that it did not amount to a felony. The case is to be distinguished from *Bridges v. Hawkesworth* and *Hannah v. Peel* on the ground that in both those cases the plaintiff made immediate disclosure, on the one hand to the shopkeeper, and on the other hand to the police, which disproved any *animus furandi,* while in the present case every effort was made to conceal the fact that the plaintiff had taken possession of the money and removed it from the place where it was found.

A very comprehensive discussion of the law both ancient and modern on this aspect of the case is to be found in Pollock & Wright, *op. cit.,* pp. 171-87. The conclusion I have come to is that it is not necessary for me to decide whether the taking was with felonious intent or not, as I think in this case the same result flows. In my view the authorities with which I have dealt justify the conclusion that where A enters upon the land of B and takes possession of and removes chattels to which B asserts no legal rights, and A is wrongfully dispossessed of those chattels, he may bring an action to recover the same.

The next question to consider is whether the plaintiff had parted with possession of the money to his mother under such circumstances as to deprive him of his right of action. The mere fact that the plaintiff's possession may have been interrupted does not necessarily deprive him of the right to maintain an action against someone who wrongfully dispossesses his successor in possession. While it is not an authoritative statement of the law, I adopt the reasoning in Holmes, *op. cit.,* pp. 236-7:

> But it no more follows, from the single circumstance that certain facts must concur in order to create the rights incident to possession, that they must continue in order to keep those rights alive, than it does, from the necessity of a consideration and a promise to create a right *ex contractu,* that the consideration and promise must continue moving between the parties until the moment of performance. When certain facts have once been made manifest which confer a right, there is no general ground on which the law need hold the right at an end except the manifestation of some fact inconsistent with its continuance, although the reasons for conferring the particular right may have great weight in determining what facts shall be deemed to be so. Cessation of the original physical relations to the object might be treated as such a fact; but it never has been, unless in times of more ungoverned violence than the present. ... Accordingly, it has

been expressly decided, where a man found logs afloat and moored them, but they again broke loose and floated away, and were found by another, that the first finder retained the rights which sprung from his having taken possession, and that he could maintain trover against the second finder, who refused to give them up.

In order to sue for the recovery of goods, the finder or wrongful taker must actually have taken possession, but when possession is once acquired it is not necessary, in order to retain it, that the effective control which must be used to gain possession originally should continue to be actively exercised. Possession will not be lost so long as the power of resuming effective control remains: Williams, *op. cit.*, p. 53. Any difficulty that might arise out of the contention that the plaintiff had voluntarily parted with possession of the money to his mother could be overcome by adding Mrs. Bird as a party in her personal capacity. This contention was not set up in the pleadings and I think it may be dismissed from further consideration.

There remains the question whether the police took possession of the money by due process of law. ...

I can find no authority for the police officer taking possession of the money as he did in this case as of right. That being so, the proper construction to be put on the transaction between him and the plaintiff's mother is that the police officer, believing that the true owner could be found, requested that the money be handed over to him to be held by him as the bailee of the plaintiff pending the search for the true owner. When he was unable to ascertain who the true owner was, in the absence of any other claim, he ought to have returned the money to the custody from which it came. The defendant can have no higher right than the police officer would have had, had he not handed the money over to the defendant and it is therefore liable for the amount of the money at the suit of the plaintiff.

Even, in the circumstances, if the money had been seized under a search warrant the constable would have been obliged to return it to the custody from which it was taken upon there being no conviction and no true owner found.

There will be judgment for the plaintiff for $1,430 together with the interest accrued in the bank account. The money will be paid into Court to the credit of the infant and paid out when he reaches the age of 21 years. Costs will follow the event.

Judgment for plaintiff.

Discussion Notes

Formulating the Concept of Intention: R v. Christie

How did the court formulate the concept of intention on the part of the plaintiff in *Bird*? By contrast, consider the court's approach to the issue of intention in *R v. Christie* (1978), 41 CCC (2d) 282 (NB SC AD). In *Christie*, the police found marijuana in the trunk of the accused's car after an automobile accident. The accused told police that she had discovered the marijuana in the trunk and panicked, fearing that her children were involved with drugs. She had then driven around in a panic state looking for friends. At trial, she was acquitted on a charge of possession of narcotics for the purposes of trafficking contrary to the provisions of the Narcotic Control Act (Can.) [now RSC 1985, c. N-1]. On appeal, the Crown argued that the trial judge erred in failing to convict the accused of possession. Hughes CJNB dismissed the appeal, commenting as follows on the requisite intention for an accused in relation to a charge of possession under the Criminal Code:

> This Court must ask itself whether on the whole of the evidence any rational hypothesis of innocence exists. Any such hypothesis must rest in the explanation given by the accused, and that amounted to this that she had no intent to exercise control over the marijuana which she had found in the trunk of her car, and that at the time of the accident she had been driving about the city for about an hour looking for friends from whom she might obtain advice as to what she should do with it. The learned trial Judge did not think the defendant had consented to possession of the drug, and I infer that it was on this ground he acquitted her.
>
> In my opinion, there can be circumstances which do not constitute possession even where there is a right of control with knowledge of the presence and character of the thing alleged to be possessed, where guilt should not be inferred, as where it appears there is no intent to exercise control over it. An example of this situation is where a person finds a package on his doorstep and upon opening it discovers it contains narcotics. Assuming he does nothing further to indicate an intention to exercise control over it, he had not, in my opinion, the possession contemplated by the *Criminal Code*. Nor do I think such a person who manually handles it for the sole purpose of destroying or reporting it to the police has committed the offence of possession. In the instant case the accused contended, under oath, that she was panic stricken and did not know what she should do when she found the narcotic in the trunk of her car, and that she drove around the city for about an hour before the accident in an attempt to find some of her friends from whom she might obtain advice as to what she should do with it. While the evidence is extremely suspicious I cannot say that the learned trial Judge erred in failing to convict the accused if he had a reasonable doubt as to whether she intended to exercise dominion or control over the narcotic.
>
> For the foregoing reasons I would dismiss the appeal.

Are the tests of intention in relation to possession the same in *Bird* and in *Christie*. Why? For a case similar to *Christie* where the accused was convicted of theft, see *R v. Pace*, [1965] 3 CCC 55 (NS SC). On what basis could a court reach the conclusion to convict the accused of theft?

Intention and Objects That Are "Lost" or "Abandoned": Moffatt v. Kazana

The issue of intention is also relevant to claims of possession in the law of finders in defining whether a chattel has been "lost" or "abandoned." In some cases, courts have denied a finder's claim on the basis that the chattel "discovered" was never really lost. Such reasoning suggests a continuing intention (perhaps implicit) on the part of a "true owner" to assert possessory title to the chattel. Compare the reasoning in relation to this issue in *Bird* with that in *Moffatt v. Kazana*, [1969] 2 QB 152 (HC). In *Moffatt*, the defendant Kazana purchased a bungalow from Mr. and Mrs. Russell in 1961. Three years after the purchase, workers dislodged a biscuit tin from the main chimney, and discovered that the tin contained £1,987 in £1 notes. The money was turned over to the police, and in due course the police turned it over to the defendant Kazana. The Russells, however, claimed the biscuit tin and its contents. Examine how Wrangham J defined "possession" in this case:

> Mrs. Russell testified that in 1951 when she and her husband drove their last load of furniture to their bungalow, No. 19 Northcliffe Avenue, which they had purchased in 1950, the biscuit tin was on the seat between them. Upon their arrival, her husband, carrying the biscuit tin, climbed into the false roof while she held the ladder. Then a few years later, Mr. Russell offered their son-in-law a loan for a car. The son-in-law remembered watching Mr. Russell climb into the false roof and reappear a few minutes later with £98 in £1 notes.
>
> Mr. Russell died during the proceedings so his executors continued the action to determine whether the contents of the biscuit tin belonged to the plaintiffs or the defendant.

In discussing the issue of possession, Wrangham J stated, with respect to the quantity of notes:

> It is not in dispute that, if it belongs to the plaintiffs, the plaintiffs are entitled to judgment for that amount. Of course, it is not disputed that if it belongs to the defendant the plaintiffs are not entitled to judgment for anything. It was first submitted to me on the part of the defendant that the evidence was not satisfactory enough to enable me to draw the inference that the money in the biscuit tin ever belonged to Mr. Russell at all. Of course, it is very odd that, if the money did belong to Mr. Russell, Mr. Russell did not think of it at the time when he sold the house to the defendant. One can only assume that he must have forgotten all about it. I have been given no evidence as to the mental or physical condition of Mr. Russell at the time of the sale or later; but he must then have been capable of doing business, otherwise he could not have sold the house. All I know is that he was within a few years of the end of his life. I know no more than that.
>
> In those circumstances, the fact that this bungalow was sold to the defendant in 1961 without any reference to this biscuit tin, which according to the evidence of Mrs. Russell had been deposited there in 1951, does raise some doubt whether the evidence proffered on behalf of the plaintiffs is correct and accurate or not; but I have come to the conclusion that the evidence for the plaintiffs which seemed perfectly straightforward, is susceptible of only one reasonable inference, namely, that there was £1,987 or thereabouts in the biscuit tin belonging to Mr. Russell which was deposited by him in the false flue of No. 19 Northcliffe Avenue when he moved into that bungalow.
>
> If one starts from that point, it is argued on behalf of the plaintiffs that Mr. Russell was the true owner of the money in the tin box in 1951 when he deposited it in the flue and that, as he had never done anything to divest himself of the property in that money, he remained the true owner of the money from beginning to end.
>
> There are a certain number of cases in which the ownership or possession of articles which apparently had been lost and had been found has been considered. The first one which was cited to me was the case of *Merry v. Green* (1841), 7 M & W 623. The facts in

that case were that a bureau was bought at a public auction and subsequently the buyer discovered a secret drawer in it which contained a purse and money. As a result of that there was litigation, the precise form of which is not relevant to my inquiry; but Baron Parke delivering the judgment of the Court of Exchequer said at p. 631:

> But it seems to us, that though there was a delivery of the secretary—an early 19th century phrase for "bureau"—and a lawful property in it thereby vested in the plaintiff, there was no delivery so as to give a lawful possession of the purse and money. The vendor had no intention to deliver it, nor the vendee to receive it; both were ignorant of its existence.

The facts of that case were, of course, not quite the same as the facts of this case, because in this case Mr. Russell who sold the bungalow had at one time known about the biscuit tin in the flue; but it seems to me to be only reasonable to draw the inference that at the time when he entered into the conveyance, and subsequently, he had so completely forgotten the existence of the tin in the flue that he was in precisely the same position as if he had never known anything about it at all.

So the position was that, in selling the bungalow, the seller had wholly forgotten the existence of the tin and the buyer had never known anything about it at all. There are, of course, a number of cases in which disputes have arisen between the finder of property and the occupier of land upon which that property was found. A typical example is the case of *City of London Corporation v. Appleyard*, [1963] 1 WLR 982. There two workmen in the course of their employment on a building operation found in the cellar of a demolished building a safe built into the wall and inside the safe a wooden box with bank notes to the value of £5,700. The question arose who was entitled to those bank notes, the competitors being the occupiers of the land and the finders. It was held that the occupiers of the land had a better title than the finders. The other matters that are disposed of in that case I need not deal with.

What is of importance is that McNair J in considering this problem expressed himself in this way, towards the foot of p. 987:

> In my judgment, the notes having been found within the safe which itself formed part of the demised premises, the party in possession of the premises, whether it be Venture or Yorkwin, had, in the absence of any evidence as to the true ownership of the notes, a better title thereto than the finders.

The clear implication from that judgment, which is consistent with other older authorities upon the point, is that the true owners had they been discoverable would have had a better title than either the finders or the occupiers of the land. Much the same position is to be found in such authorities as *In re Cohen, decd., National Provincial Bank Ltd. v. Katz*, [1953] Ch. 88, where quantities of bank notes and coin were discovered after the death of a husband and wife who had lived in a flat, in various places in the flat. It is sufficient for me to say that Vaisey J held that in the absence of any trustworthy evidence of ownership recourse must be had to the legal presumption that the owner of land is, prima facie, the owner of chattels found on the land.

It is clear therefore that in the existing authorities there is an implication at least from the language in which the judgments are expressed that the true owner of a chattel found on land has a title superior to that of anybody else. Accordingly, having disposed of the authorities in that way, Mr. Appleby on behalf of the plaintiffs was able to say that the plaintiffs are, as representatives of Mr. Russell, the true owners of this money and they must be held to remain the true owners of the money unless they or Mr. Russell had divested himself or themselves of the ownership by one of the recognised methods, abandonment, gift or sale.

In *Moffatt*, the court held that the "true owner's" claim was relatively stronger than the finder's claim, concluding that there had been no gift or sale of the biscuit tin by the Russells. The court also concluded that Mr. Russell had never abandoned the biscuit tin and notes, even though he seemed to have forgotten about them. By contrast with the court's conclusion, the defendant had argued that the court should conclude that the sale of the house should include a sale of "lost" property in it, so as to avoid the absurd result that the plaintiff would have no right to trespass to claim the chattel. The court declined to rule on this problem.

The problem of entering the land of another to recover a chattel, without the assistance of the legal process, is called "recaption." The right to recaption, at least in some cases, seems to permit a technical trespass to the land of another, so long as no damage is done to the land as a result. For a good overview of recaption, see Ralph Simmonds and George Stewart, *Study Paper on Wrongful Interference with Goods* (Toronto: Ontario Law Reform Commission, 1989), chapters 8-10.

AG of Canada v. Brock

The issues of an accused's intention and the proper characterization of objects as "lost" or "abandoned" were canvassed in Canada in *AG of Canada v. Brock* (1991), 67 CCC (3d) 131 (BC SC). Compare the approaches to these issues in the decisions at trial and on appeal. Which decision better reflects the legal principles? To what extent are the principles shaped by policy objectives?

A police officer stopped a car because of a minor traffic violation, and then arrested the driver because of discrepancies in the vehicle ownership and the driver's licence. When the car was searched, a bag containing nearly $300,000 in uncirculated US $100 and $50 bills was discovered. When questioned by the police, the driver denied any knowledge of the money. The next day, however, in the company of a lawyer, the driver made a claim to the sum of money "on behalf of offshore investors." A few weeks later, the driver was found dead as a result of cocaine overdose. The RCMP did not lay any further charges. Both the driver's estate and the municipality claimed the money.

At trial, MacDonell J held that the estate of the driver was entitled to the money. After reviewing numerous cases and particularly *Parker v. British Airways*, MacDonell J held (at 140), referring to 35 Hals., 4th ed., para. 1122:

> *Possession prima facie title.* The presumption of law is that the person who had *de facto* possession also has the property, and accordingly such possession is protected, whatever its origin, against all who cannot prove a superior title. This rule applies equally in criminal and civil matters. Thus, as against a stranger or a wrongdoer, a person in actual or apparent possession, but without the right to

possession, has all the rights and remedies of a person entitled to and able to prove a present right to possession.

In my opinion, an application of this principle to the facts of the case at bar results in a finding that Brock was in possession of the money at the moment he was pulled over. If he was aware of the hidden money, as I believe he was, in the absence of evidence to the contrary, the presumption is that he is the owner of that money. If he was unaware of its existence, the fact that it was concealed in a car lawfully owned by him would indicate that he was in *de facto* control and possession of the money and his right to title was superior to that of anyone other than the true owner.

The next issue to be addressed is: did Brock abandon the money when he responded to Det. Beatty that it was not his?

Abandonment is generally defined as the voluntary relinquishment by its owner or holder, with the intention of terminating his ownership, possession and control and without vesting ownership in any other person. More particularly, it is a renunciation of a right or of property or the giving up of something to which one has an entitlement.

American jurisprudence has found that it is the relinquishment of a right by the owner thereof without any regard to future possession by himself or any other person and with the intention to desert the right. However, the case-law would indicate that the intention must be absolute. A necessary element of abandonment is an intention to relinquish the property or right and not to reclaim it or resume its possession at any future time. The requisite intention may be manifested by express declaration or by acts or conduct or may be inferred from the circumstances.

Personal property upon being abandoned ceases to be the property of any person until it is appropriated by another with the intent to acquire ownership of it.

Such property may be appropriated by anyone if it has not been reclaimed by the former owner: *Fidelity-Philadelphia Trust Co. v. Lehigh Valley Coal Co.*, 143 A 474, 294 Pa. 47 (1928). If, however, one other than the former owner first appropriates the abandoned property, he will obtain a right superior to that of the former owner.

The onus of proving abandonment rests on the one who asserts or relies on it and he is required to establish that the property or right has been relinquished by its owner or holder with no intention of reclaiming: *Simpson v. Gowers* (1981), 121 DLR (3d) 709, 32 OR (2d) 385 (CA).

It is my opinion that Brock did not abandon the money at the moment he denied ownership. Upon his being pulled over, he unsuccessfully attempted to bluff the police officer so he could be on his way. It was only after he was told that Cst. Almas had discovered the money that he took matters seriously and shortly thereafter refused to answer any more questions.

Brock did not want to be associated with those funds for whatever reasons, legitimate or otherwise. In an attempt to divorce himself from further problems, he initially disclaimed ownership of the money.

However, he attempted to reclaim the money the following day. In order to hold that Brock was too late to reclaim the money, it must be found that another party, West Vancouver, had since acquired a right to it. The case-law would appear to indicate that mere possession of the subject matter is insufficient; the money must have been appropriated by West Vancouver with the intention of acquiring ownership of it. There is no evidence to suggest that this was the case. The date following its discovery, it was forwarded to the RCMP for the purpose of investigating the money as being proceeds of crime. ...

In conclusion, the case before the court is not one which involves the law of finding because, on the facts, I do not believe the money was ever lost. The evidence indicates that, whether it was Brock who owned the money or whether he was merely holding it for others, it was Brock who hid the money and clearly had possession over it.

On appeal to the BC Court of Appeal, (1993), 83 CCC (3d) 200 (BC CA), Hinkson JA concluded that there was no (credible) evidence that the driver of the car was the owner of the money. Rather, the court held that the presumption of ownership relied on by MacDonell J was a rebuttable presumption and that it had been rebutted. The court stated (at 207):

> On this appeal the respondents did not contend that Brock was the owner of the money.
>
> Rather, the respondents relied upon the alternative conclusion reached by the chambers judge, namely, that Brock was in *de facto* possession of the money and hence his right to it was superior to that of the appellant.
>
> The learned chambers judge said [at 142]:
>
> > In conclusion, the case before the court is not one which involves the law of finding because, on the facts, I do not believe the money was ever lost. The evidence indicates that, whether it was Brock who owned the money or whether he was merely holding it for others, it was Brock who hid the money and clearly had possession over it. The day following his release and without prompting, he was able to identify the quantity of money discovered and the manner in which it was packaged in two separate sums.
>
> If Brock was not the owner of the money, as I have concluded, then it is necessary to consider the respondents' claim that he had possession of the money at the time when the appellant found it and took it into its possession. Counsel referred to the leading cases in this field of the law, including *Bridges v. Hawkesworth* (1851), 21 LJQB 75, [1843-60] All ER 122 (QB); *South Staffordshire Water Co. v. Sharman*, [1896] 2 QB 44 (QB); *Corporation of London v. Appleyard*, [1963] 2 All ER 834 (QB); *Hannah v. Peel*, [1945] 2 All ER 288 (KB); *Bird v. Fort Frances*, [1949] 2 DLR 791, [1949] OR 292, [1949] OWN 223 (HJC); *Grafstein v. Holme & Freeman* (1958), 12 DLR (2d) 727, [1958] OR 296, [1958] OWN 161 (CA); *Kowal v. Ellis* (1977), 76 DLR (3d) 546, [1977] 2 WWR 761 (Man. CA); *Parker v. British Airways Board*, [1982] 1 All ER 834 (CA).
>
> All of these decisions cannot be easily reconciled. Each turns on its own facts and each involves land rather than a chattel.
>
> In the present case the learned chambers judge relied upon the fact that Brock had possession of his vehicle on January 18, 1990, and relying upon the land cases, concluded that he had possession of the contents of the vehicle whether or not he was aware of the contents.
>
> He went further and found that it was Brock who hid the money in the vehicle. The evidence does not support that conclusion. Rather the evidence indicates Brock did not

know of the presence of the money in his vehicle on that day. In my opinion, Brock did not have possession of the vehicle in a way that would entitle him to the money. Brock informed Detective Beatty that from time to time he loaned his vehicle to a buddy and that the last time was a couple of days before January 18, 1990. Thus, Brock was not exercising exclusive possession of the vehicle. He and others each used it independently.

In *Grafstein v. Holme & Freeman, supra*, LeBel JA said at p. 738:

> Thus, the acquisition of a chattel does not necessarily import the acquisition of its contents. Whether it does, or does not, appears to be a question of fact. And that is the conclusion reached by Salmond. He says at p. 381: "Whether the possession of one thing will bring with it the possession of another that is thus connected with it depends upon the circumstances of the particular case."

Here the evidence supports the conclusion that while Brock on the day in question had possession of the vehicle he did not have possession of the money contained in the vehicle.

In *Parker v. British Airways Board, supra*, Donaldson LJ discussed the respective rights and obligations of the finder and an occupier. Dealing with the rights and liabilities of an occupier, he said at p. 843:

> 4. An "occupier" of a chattel, e.g. a ship, motor car, caravan or aircraft, is to be treated as if he were the occupier of a building for the purposes of the foregoing rules.

After quoting that statement, the learned chambers judge continued [at 139]:

> In *Parker*, it was found that the airline had not manifested its intention to exercise control over the lounge and all things in it. The bracelet had been found in a passenger lounge. The airline was unaware of its existence.
>
> The *obiter dicta* of Donaldson LJ would suggest that a similar finding would have resulted had the bracelet been found in a vehicle such as a taxicab. Where the occupier of the vehicle is unaware of its existence and exercises no control over it, he will not displace the right of entitlement of the finder.

In *Parker v. British Airways Board, supra*, Eveleigh LJ, who agreed with Donaldson LJ, said at p. 844:

> It is accepted on both sides that for the defendants to succeed it must be shown that they had possession of the bracelet at the time when the plaintiff found it and took it into his possession. Whatever the difficulties which surround the concept of possession in English law, the two elements of control and *animus possidendi* must co-exist. Each of these elements varies greatly in the circumstances of each case.

On the facts of the present case these two elements are missing. On January 18, 1990, Brock did not purport to control the money in the vehicle nor did he in any way indicate an intention to possess it. In the absence of these two elements it cannot be concluded that Brock possessed the money in the vehicle on that day.

The BC Court of Appeal therefore allowed the appeal, and ordered the funds transferred to the Corporation of the District of West Vancouver, noting that the Corporation must be accountable should the "true owner" come forward and establish ownership. Is the court's conclusion about Brock's absence of intention to exercise control in this case consistent with that concerning Mr. Russell in *Moffatt v. Kazana*?

Legislative Reform of the Law of Finders

In relation to some kinds of chattels, especially those of historical significance, the intention of the finder may be rendered irrelevant. For example, anyone who takes possession of a wreck must deliver it to the government receiver of wrecks pursuant to the Canada Shipping Act, RSC 1985, c. S-9. There is also legislation concerning the log salvage industry in British Columbia: see The Forest Act, RSBC 1979, c. 140 [now RSBC 1996, c. C.157]. The finding of treasure trove (cached gold and silver in coin, bullion, or manufactured form) may also be subject to a claim by the Crown: see N.E. Palmer, "Treasure Trove and the Protection of Antiquities" (1981), 44 *Modern Law Review* 178. As was explained by Michael Nash in "Are Finders Keepers? One Hundred Years Since *Elwes v. Brigg Gas Co.*" (1987), 137 *New Law Journal* 118, the use of metal detectors in the field of archeology and of sonar equipment in marine archaeology has created an urgent need for legislative regulation.

In reviewing the issues, Nash also commented on the *Elwes* case (1886), 33 Ch.D 562 (Ch.D), a case decided using principles similar to those discussed in *Parker*. The case concerned the discovery in 1885 of a prehistoric boat, embedded in the clay, by the lessee gas company in the course of its routine excavations. Both the lessee gas company and the landowner claimed a proprietary interest. The court considered many of the cases referred to in *Parker*, concluding that the lessor (the lord of the manor of Britt) had constructive possession of chattels, including the long-buried boat. According to the court, Elwes' awareness of the boat's existence was not necessary, and it was not part of the leasehold transferred to the gas company. For some years thereafter, Elwes exhibited the boat to the public in a specially constructed building and then later presented it to a museum in Hull. In 1943, it was destroyed in an air raid on the museum. For another comment on this case and the general problem of finders of such chattels, see O'Keefe and Prott, *Law and the Cultural Heritage* (Abingdon, UK: Professional Books, 1984).

Extinguishing the Rights of the True Owner

Extinguishment of an owner's rights to a chattel may occur where the owner has abandoned the chattel. In such a case, the finder's possessory interest (one which is good against all the world except the true owner) appears to be correspondingly more significant. For a case addressing the issue of when abandonment occurs, see *Simpson v. Gowers* (1981), 32 OR (2d) 385 (CA). In addition to abandonment, provincial legislation, generically referred to as statutes of limitation, establish time limits for bringing lawsuits. Thus, for example, the Limitations Act, RSO 1990, c. L.15, provides that an action for trespass to goods (for example, a finder with possession of a chattel belonging to a true owner) must be commenced within six years after the cause of action arose. (See also Limitation of Actions Act, RSNS 1989, c. 258; Limitation of Actions Act, RSNB 1973, c. L-8; and Statute of Limitations, RSPEI 1988, c. S-7.) The question of exactly when a cause of action arises may be difficult to determine in practice, an issue which is addressed in more detail in the next section concerning possession of land. For an overview and recommendations for legislative reform, see "Discussion Draft on Proposed Limitations Act (1977)" (Toronto: Ministry of the Attorney General, 1977).

In practice, the more usual problem is how to dispose of "lost property." In the following example, consider how and to what extent the principles of possession in the law of finders have been augmented by these regulations under the Police Act, SNB 1977, c. P-9.2.

New Brunswick Regulation 86-76 Under the Police Act
(OC 86-322) Filed April 30, 1986

Under section 38 of the *Police Act*, the Lieutenant-Governor in Council makes the following Regulation:

1. This Regulation may be cited as the *Found Personal Property Regulation— Police Act.*

2.(1) Where

(a) personal property is found by a person other than a police officer and is delivered to and received by a police officer,

(b) personal property that has been found comes into the possession of a police officer by any other means than that referred to in paragraph (a), or

(c) personal property is found by a police officer,

the police officer or any other employee of the police force of which the police officer is a member shall prepare a report containing a detailed description of the personal property and shall attempt to locate the owner of the personal property.

2.(2) Where

(a) found personal property has no apparent commercial value,

(b) reasonable efforts have been made to locate the owner of the found personal property with no results,

(c) the finder of the personal property has relinquished, in writing, any interest in the property, and

(d) the found personal property is not or will not be required as evidence in any proceeding

the chief of the police force which is in possession of the found personal property may cause the property to be destroyed.

2.(3) Subject to subsection (5), where

(a) found personal property has some commercial value,

(b) efforts have been made to locate the owner of the found personal property with no results,

(c) three months have passed since a police officer came into the possession of the found personal property,

(d) the finder of the personal property is not a police officer, and

(e) the found personal property is not or will not be required as evidence in any proceeding, the chief of the police force which is in possession of the found personal property shall cause a notice to be sent by mail to the finder of the personal property notifying him of the right to procure the found personal property and shall return the property to the finder upon his signing a document acknowledging receipt of the personal property. ...

2.(5) Where

(a) the conditions described in paragraphs (3)(a), (b), (c) and (d) have been met and the finder of the personal property

(i) is a police officer, or

(ii) is a person who cannot be located, or

(b) the finder of the personal property has not procured or caused the property to be returned to him at his expense within thirty days of the receipt of the notice referred to in subsection (3),

the chief of the police force which is in possession of the found personal property shall cause the property to be disposed of through public sale and shall forward the proceeds, in the case of a municipal police force, to the treasurer of the municipality in which the property was found, and, in the case of the New Brunswick Highway Patrol, to the Minister of Finance.

3. Where found personal property is destroyed in accordance with this Regulation, a certificate of destruction shall be

(a) completed by a police officer of the police force which is in possession of the property,

(b) witnessed by an employee of the police force which is in possession of the property, and

(c) filed with the chief of the police force which is in possession of the property.

4. This Regulation comes into force on July 1, 1986.

An example of the operation of such regulations in practice was reported by the *Toronto Star* in 1983. A 16-year-old orphan in Florida found a bag of jewels alongside a railway track while playing hooky from school. He assumed they were costume jewellry and showed them off to other students and teachers at school until his aunt persuaded him to turn them over to police. The relevant regulations provided that a person was entitled to claim found chattels if the owner had not appeared within 180 days. Thus, 183 days after finding the jewels, the young orphan received the jewellry which was worth $1.3 million. The newspaper article declared "Honesty Does Pay" (*Toronto Star*, September 21, 1983, A19).

POSSESSION IN RELATION TO LAND

Possession as a Proprietary Interest in Land

Possessory Title

In 1907, a case was presented to the Judicial Committee of the Privy Council (JCPC) on appeal from the High Court of Australia. At issue was whether the plaintiffs, as trustees of the will of Frederick Clissold, could establish a *prima facie* case for compensation. The claim for compensation related to land resumed by the state government for a public school site in 1891. At that time, the land was in the possession of Frederick Clissold who had enclosed and fenced it in 1881, and who had been exclusively in possession of the land from that date until his death, which occured just after the land was resumed by the state government. Clissold had leased the land to various tenants and, according to the official records of the municipalities, he had regularly paid rates and taxes.

Assuming that the legislation provided for compensation to be paid to a claimant in respect of an interest in land, should this claim on behalf of Frederick Clissold have succeeded? On what basis? What is the legal principle applicable? In thinking about these facts, what is the relevance of the "true owner" to your analysis of Clissold's entitlement?

In *Perry v. Clissold*, [1907] AC 73 (PC), the state government argued in the Privy Council that Clissold was "a mere trespasser, without any estate or interest in the land." The members of the JCPC disagreed, stating (at 79):

> It cannot be disputed that a person in possession of land in the assumed character of owner and exercising peaceably the ordinary rights of ownership has a perfectly good title against all the world but the rightful owner.

In the context of claims relating to land, Clissold had possessory title. In reaching its conclusion, the JCPC referred to an earlier decision, *Asher v. Whitlock*. In reading the judgment that follows, consider the relationship between a claim to possessory title and the claim of the "true owner." Who was the "true owner" in *Asher v. Whitlock*?

Asher v. Whitlock
[1865] LR 1 (QB)

Ejectment for a cottage, garden, and premises, situate at Keysoe Row, in the parish of Keysoe, in the county of Bedford; the writ stated that the female plaintiff claimed possession as heir-at-law of Mary Ann Williamson, an infant deceased.

The defendant defended for the whole.

At the trial before Cockburn CJ, at the last Bedfordshire Spring Assizes, the following facts appeared in evidence. About Michaelmas, in the year 1842, Thomas Williamson inclosed from the waste of a manor a piece of land by the side of the highway; and in 1850, he inclosed more land adjoining, and built a cottage; the whole being the land as described and claimed in the writ. He occupied the whole till his death in 1860. By his will he devised the whole property, describing it as "a cottage and garden, in Keysoe Row, in which I now dwell," to his wife Lucy Williamson, for and during so much only of her natural life as she might remain his widow and unmarried; and from and after her decease, or second marriage, whichever event might first happen, to his only child Mary Ann Williamson, in fee. After the death of Thomas Williamson, his widow remained in possession with the daughter, and in April, 1861, married the defendant; and from that time they all three resided on the property till the death of the daughter, aged eighteen years, in February, 1863. On her death, the defendant and his wife, the widow of the testator, continued to reside on the premises; the widow died in May, 1863, and the defendant still continued to occupy.

The female plaintiff is the heir-at-law of the testator's daughter Mary Ann Williamson. The writ was issued 11th of April, 1865.

FACTS

These facts being undisputed, the Chief Justice directed a verdict for the plaintiff for the whole of the property claimed; with leave to move to enter the verdict for the defendant, on the ground that the testator had no devisable interest in any part of the property.

A rule *nisi* was afterwards obtained to enter the verdict for the defendant, on the ground that no title in the plaintiffs was shewn to either portion of the land enclosed.

COCKBURN CJ: I am of opinion that this rule should be discharged. The defendant, on the facts, is in this dilemma; either his possession was adverse, or it was not. If it was not adverse to the devisee of the person who inclosed the land, and it may be treated as a continuance of the possession which the widow had and ought to have given up, on her marriage with the defendant, then, as she and the defendant came in under the will, both would be estopped from denying the title of the devisee and her heir-at-law. But assuming the defendant's possession to have been adverse, we have then to consider how far it operated to destroy the right of the devisee and her heir-at-law. Mr. Merewether was obliged to contend that possession acquired, as this was, against a rightful owner, would not be sufficient to keep out every other person but the rightful owner. But I take it as clearly established, that possession is good against all the world except the person who can shew a good title; and it would be mischievous to change this established doctrine. In *Doe v. Dyeball* one year's possession by the plaintiff was held good against a person who came and turned him out; and there are other authorities to the same effect. Suppose the person who originally inclosed the land had been expelled by the defendant, or the defendant had obtained possession without force, by simply walking in at the open door in the absence of the then possessor, and were to say to him, "You have no more title than I have, my possession is as good as yours," surely ejectment could have been maintained by the original possessor against the defendant. All the old law on the doctrine of disseisin was found on the principle that the disseisor's title was good against all but the disseisee. It is too clear to admit of doubt, that if the devisor had been turned out of possession he could have maintained ejectment. What is the position of the devisee? There can be no doubt that a man has a right to devise that estate, which the law gives him against all the world but the true owner. Here the widow was a prior devisee, but *durante viduitate* only, and as soon as the testator died, the estate became vested in the widow; and immediately on the widow's marriage the daughter had a right to possession; the defendant however anticipates her, and with the widow takes possession. But just as he had no right to interfere with the testator, so he had no right against the daughter, and had she lived she could have brought ejectment; although she died without asserting her right, the same right belongs to her heir. Therefore I think the action can be maintained, inasmuch as the defendant had not acquired any title by length of possession. The devisor might have brought ejectment, his right of possession being passed by will to his daughter, she could have maintained ejectment, and so therefore can her heir, the female plaintiff. We know to what extent encroachments on waste lands have taken place; and if the lord has acquiesced and does not interfere, can it be at the mere will of any stranger to disturb the person in possession? I do not know what equity may say to the rights of different claimants who have come in at different times without title; but at law, I think the right of the original possessor is clear. On the simple ground that possession is good title against all but the true owner, I think the plaintiffs entitled to succeed, and that the rule should be discharged.

MELLOR J: I am of the same opinion. It is necessary to distinguish between the case of the true owner and that of a person having no title. The fact of possession is *prima facie* evidence of seisin in fee. The law gives credit to possession unless explained; and Mr. Merewether, in order to succeed, ought to have gone on and shewn the testator's title to be bad, as that he was only tenant at will, but this he did not do. In *Doe v. Dyeball* possession for a year only was held sufficient against a person having no title. In *Doe v. Barnard* the plaintiff did not rely on her own possession merely, but shewed a prior possession in her husband, with whom she was unconnected in point of title. Here the first possessor is connected in title with the plaintiffs; for there can be no doubt that the testator's interest was devisable. In the common case of proving a claim to landed estate under a will, proof of the will and of possession or receipt of rents by the testator is always *prima facie* sufficient, without going on to shew possession for more than twenty years. I agree with the Lord Chief Justice in the importance of maintaining, that possession is good against all but the rightful owner.

    Lush J concurred.

Rule discharged.

Discussion Notes

The Concept of "Prior Possession"

Why did the plaintiff in *Asher v. Whitlock*, who had never been in possession of the premises, have a better claim than the defendant? How would you formulate the concept of "prior possession" in the light of this case? Note also the principle that periods of possession by different persons in succession may now be added together to create a "chain" of possessory title, an important basis for creating a statutory limitation period (as described more fully in the next section).

Historical Development of Principles of Possession and Seisin

There is a subtle difference between the reasoning of Cockburn CJ and Mellor J, even though they are in agreement as to the outcome in *Asher v. Whitlock*. Basically, the judgment of Cockburn CJ formulated the principle in the context of a possessory claim to land in the same way that the principle was stated in relation to finders of "lost objects"—that is, possession is good title against all but the true owner or someone claiming prior possession. By contrast, Mellor J stated that "the fact of possession is *prima facie* evidence of seisin in fee," a statement that seems to suggest that possession is merely *evidence* of "seisin," and that seisin is the basis for the plaintiff's entitlement to succeed in *Asher v. Whitlock*. This formulation was regarded as more accurate by Professor Hargreaves in "Terminology and Title in Ejectment" (1940), 56 *Law Quarterly Review* 376, although it has also been suggested that "there seems to be little point in retaining terminology that derives from forms of action discarded long ago ... . The general principle stated by Cockburn CJ is readily intelligible and simple enough to apply" (R. Sackville and M.A. Neave, *Property Law: Cases and Materials*, 2d ed. (Sydney: Butterworths, 1975), at 97).

To understand the difference in the approaches of Cockburn CJ and Mellor J, the historical development of principles about possession needs to be explained. First of all, the concept of "seisin" in early land law—that is, from about the 15th century—described the special nature of the possessory entitlement of an "owner" to land or real property. Not all persons "in possession" of land had seisin, the easiest example being the lease-holder or tenant who (according to historical principles) had possession but not seisin. Entitlement to seisin was important in a context where procedural rights to recover land after being dispossessed depended on whether or not a claimant could show seisin prior to dispossession. Moreover, a transfer of an interest in land required a transfer of seisin, accomplished in medieval times by the ceremony of "livery of seisin," in which the grantor and the grantee stood together on the land to be conveyed. In the presence of witnesses, the grantor symbolically delivered seisin to the grantee by handing him a twig or handful of sod, while at the same time expressing appropriate words of transfer.

According to K. Gray and P. Symes, *Real Property and Real People* (London: Butterworths, 1981), at 48-49:

> Seisin thus expressed the organic element in the relationship between man [sic] and land and as such provided presumptive evidence of ownership within the medieval framework of rights in land. Furthermore it was only the person seised of the land who could avail himself of an owner's rights in respect of the land.

Gray and Symes have suggested that the concept of seisin has markedly influenced the development of common law property principles, particularly the emphasis on rights flowing from factual possession by contrast with abstract title. In a similar way, Alice Tay has argued that the concept of seisin has promoted ideas about privacy and indi-vidual freedom in the common law: see Tay, "Law, the Citizen and the State," in E. Kamenka, R. Brown, and A.E.S. Tay, eds., *Law and Society: The Crisis in Legal Ideals* (London: E. Arnold, 1978), at 11ff.:

> The common law, then, begins with and long maintains a bias in favour of the factual situation—the citizen's actual behaviour and powers *against* the claims of privilege and authority as such ... . The role of the underlying seisin-possession concept in the common law is to recognize and protect those still important areas in which men [sic] live, work and plan as user-owners ... to give them an area of privacy in which they have a right to be free of state and community interference.

The historical concept of seisin will be further explored in chapter 3. For a detailed analysis of the nature and development of the concept of seisin in English common law, see the classic studies by F.W. Maitland: "The Mystery of Seisin" (1886), 2 *Law Quarterly*

Review 481; "The Beatitude of Seisin. I" (1888), 4 *Law Quarterly Review* 24; and "The Beatitude of Seisin. II" (1888), 4 *Law Quarterly Review* 286.

In addition to the concept of seisin, it is important to understand how the procedural arrangements for recovering land after dispossession influenced common law principles relating to possession of land. Briefly, the early common law was characterized by highly technical "forms of action," and claims could be brought *only* in accordance with these technical, formalized processes. Inevitably, since the facts of individual claims differed widely from the formal actions available, the processes were often characterized by "fictions" as well. In this context, the forms of action for recovering land where a claimant had seisin prior to dispossession were different from those available to a claimant (such as a leaseholder) who had held possession but not seisin prior to being dispossessed. Interestingly, the forms of action available to the claimant who had held seisin were also more complex and difficult to use in practice, and they were ultimately superseded by the action available to leaseholders for recovering land after being dispossessed—the action of ejectment. Note that the court in *Asher v. Whitlock* is dealing with a claim for ejectment. For more details about the forms of action at common law in this context, see J.H. Baker, *An Introduction to English Legal History*, 3d ed. (London: Butterworths, 1990).

The Jus Tertii Issue: Perry v. Clissold

In *Perry v. Clissold*, [1907] AC 73 (PC), the Privy Council also addressed the *jus tertii* issue—that is, the issue whether the existence of a better claim by someone other than the plaintiff would defeat the plaintiff's claim against the defendant. The Privy Council rejected this argument, relying (at 79) on the decision in *Asher v. Whitlock*:

> On behalf of the Minister reliance was placed on the case of *Doe v. Barnard*, which seems to lay down this proposition, that if a person having only a possessory title to land be supplanted in the possession by another who has himself no better title, and afterwards brings an action to recover the land, he must fail in case he shews in the course of the proceedings that the title on which he seeks to recover was merely possessory. It is, however, difficult, if not impossible, to reconcile this case with the later case of *Asher v. Whitlock*, in which *Doe v. Barnard* was cited. The judgment of Cockburn CJ is clear on the point. The rest of the Court concurred, and it may be observed that one of the members of the Court in *Asher v. Whitlock* (Lush J) had been of counsel for the successful party in *Doe v. Barnard*. The conclusion at which the Court arrived in *Doe v. Barnard* is hardly consistent with the views of such eminent authorities on real property law as Mr. Preston and Mr. Joshua Williams. It is opposed to the opinions of modern text-writers of such weight and authority as Professor Maitland and Holmes J of the Supreme Court of the United States.
>
> Their Lordships are of opinion that it is impossible to say that no prima facie case for compensation has been disclosed.
>
> They do not think that a case for compensation is necessarily excluded by the circumstance that under the provisions of the Act of 1900 the Minister acquired not merely the title of the person in possession as owner, but also the title, whatever it may

have been, of the rightful owner out of possession, who never came forward to claim the land or the compensation payable in respect of it, and who is, as the Chief Justice says, "unknown to this day."

The Act throughout from the very preamble has it apparently in contemplation that compensation would be payable to every person deprived of the land resumed for public purposes. It could hardly have been intended or contemplated that the Act should have the effect of shaking titles which but for the Act would have been secure, and would in process of time have become absolute and indisputable, or that the Governor, or responsible Ministers acting under his instructions, should take advantage of the infirmity of anybody's title in order to acquire his land for nothing. Even where the true owner, after diligent inquiry, cannot be found the Act contemplates payment of the compensation into Court to be dealt with by a Court of Equity.

Although the court's analysis of the *jus tertii* plea was criticized by S.A. Wiren in "The Plea of *Jus Tertii* in Ejectment" (1925), 41 *Law Quarterly Review* 139, the accepted view now seems to be that the principle adopted in *Perry v. Clissold* is the better view. (See Hargreaves, "Terminology and Title in Ejectment" (1940), 56 *Law Quarterly Review* 376.

Barring the Right of the "True Owner": Statutes of Limitation

The decision in *Perry v. Clissold* referred briefly to a related issue concerning claims based on possession—that is, whether the "true owner's" right to recover possession from Frederick Clissold might have become barred by the effluxion of time. This issue concerns the interpretation of legislation—for example, Ontario's Limitations Act, RSO 1990, c. L.15—and is sometimes referred to as the problem of adverse possession. As the Privy Council stated in *Perry v. Clissold* (at 79):

> It cannot be disputed that a person in possession of land in the assumed character of owner and exercising peaceably the ordinary rights of ownership has a perfectly good title against all the world but the rightful owner. And if the rightful owner does not come forward and assert his title by process of law within the period prescribed by the provisions of the Statute of Limitations applicable to the case, his [sic] right is forever extinguished, and the possessory owner acquires an absolute title.

Examine this statement closely. Can you define the rationale for the decision? Obviously, in circumstances where the "true owner's" interest is subsequently barred as a result of the passing of the limitation period, the *jus tertii* argument will be unavailable. The operation of statutes of limitation will be more fully explored later in the chapter.

Property Arrangements in Families

Although *Asher v. Whitlock*'s main importance is its reasoning, subsequently approved by the Privy Council in *Perry v. Clissold*, the case also shows the important connections between familial relationships and property arrangements. It is of course possible that there is an appropriate explanation for the deaths of Thomas Williamson and his wife and daughter, all within three years, and also for the widow Williamson's remarriage to the defendant only one year after her husband's death. At the same time, it is possible to imagine a less benign explanation for the defendant's actions during these years. For example, think about family and property connections in the plays of William Shakespeare or the novels of Jane Austen and Charles Dickens. Some issues about property and families are considered in chapters 3, 5, and 7.

Remedies: The Self-Help Alternative

In *Asher v. Whitlock*, the plaintiff initiated legal action in ejectment as a means of recovering possession. At common law, however, the plaintiff also had the alternative option of self-help—that is, a physical retaking of possession. In *McPhail v. Persons Unknown*, [1973] 3 All ER 393 (CA), the UK Court of Appeal considered whether the court had discretion to suspend the enforcement of a court order for possession. One factor considered by the court was a plaintiff's right to exercise the remedy of self-help immediately. It was suggested that the court should not disadvantage a plaintiff seeking an order for possession from the court by granting a period of delay in executing the order. The case is equally important, however, because of its analysis of the role of the courts in the context of a claim for possession against homeless persons ("squatters") who had taken possession of vacant office buildings. Referring to an earlier decision of the Court of Appeal (*Southwark London Borough Council v. Williams*, [1971] Ch. 734 (CA), at 744), Lord Denning MR reiterated the relevant principles:

> If homelessness were once admitted as a defence to trespass, no one's house could be safe … . So the courts must, for the sake of law and order, take a firm stand. They must refuse to admit the plea of necessity to the hungry and homeless and trust that their distress will be relieved by the charitable and the good.

After considering the arguments in detail, Lord Denning MR held (in *McPhail*, at 399) that the court had no discretion to suspend enforcement of the order, suggesting however that

> whilst this is the law, I trust that owners will act with consideration and kindness in the enforcing of it—remembering the plight which the homeless are in.

Why didn't the squatters' claim to possession succeed in this case? What does this case suggest about the limits of claims based on possession of land? Consider again whether the principle of prior possession is consistent with C.B. Macpherson's conception of property as "the right not to be excluded."

Possession and Aboriginal Title to Land

The idea of possession of land as the basis for a legally recognized claim is especially significant for aboriginal land claims in North America. In the following excerpt, Kent McNeil examines common law principles of possession in relation to First Nations in Canada. McNeil examines the reasons why traditional principles of possession were not made applicable to lands occupied by indigenous peoples. You may wish to examine this argument again in relation to issues addressed in chapter 3.

K. McNeil, Common Law Aboriginal Title
(Oxford: Clarendon Press, 1989), at 298-306 (footnotes omitted)

The doctrine of common law aboriginal title is based on the presumptions arising in English law from occupation of land. A person in factual occupation is first of all presumed to have possession. From this conclusion of law other consequences follow, for seisin is presumed from possession, and the person seised is presumed to have a fee simple estate. Moreover, possession not shown to be wrongful is presumed to be rightful. An occupier of land is therefore presumed to have not only a fee simple estate, but a valid title as well.

Every one of these presumptions can be rebutted in appropriate circumstances. An occupier does not have possession if, for example, he is acting on behalf of another, or is an intruder on Crown land. Possession is not seisin if the possessor is a leaseholder. Nor does a person who is seised necessarily have an estate in fee simple, for (at common law at least) he may have a fee tail or life estate. Finally, the presumptive title of a possessor can be rebutted by showing that someone else has a better title.

In the absence of proof of a customary system of land tenure in a colony acquired by the Crown by settlement, these presumptions would be applicable to indigenous people as well as to settlers, as part of the general body of English law which flowed into such colonies the moment they were acquired. Where indigenous people were in occupation of lands at the time, they would be presumed to have possession, and therefore to be seised for estates in fee simple. They would also be presumed to have title. This presumptive title, which would cover the subsurface (excluding precious metals) as well as the surface, is what is meant in this book by common law aboriginal title.

The question, then, is whether any of the above presumptions could be rebutted where indigenous occupation was concerned. Customary law apart, we can no doubt dismiss the possibility of the occupiers being shown to have estates other than fees simple, as in the circumstances there would be no means by which other estates could have been created. But could either the presumption of possession or the presumption of title be rebutted in this context?

If it could be established that the occupiers were in fact acting on behalf of other indigenous people, those people would be accorded possession by English law, and would thus have the benefit of the presumptions arising therefrom. Alternatively, if it were shown that other indigenous people had title by customary law, that would rebut the presumptive title of the occupiers. In either case, however, the occupiers would still be entitled to retain the lands as against anyone other than the indigenous people in question, or someone claiming under them. Proof of the *jus tertii* would prevail against those in occupation when the colony was acquired only in the second case, and then only if they had lost the lands and were trying to recover them without proof of ouster or title by limitation.

Claims by other indigenous people aside, the other potential contenders for title to the occupied lands would be the settlers and the Crown. Any claim by settlers should be readily dismissed, since apart from statute, adverse possession, or Crown grant (or possibly purchase from indigenous people), they could not acquire title to lands for themselves. However, the question of whether there would be a valid basis for a claim by the Crown demands careful consideration.

The Crown acquired territorial sovereignty over a settlement by occupancy of the territory as a unit. This took place at the international level, where the Crown has extensive prerogative power. Rightly or wrongly, the Crown apparently could ignore the presence of indigenous people for this purpose, treating them as devoid of sovereignty and the territorial unit as *res nullius.* However, title to territory is one thing, title to land quite another. At the international level the Crown might be able to deny that indigenous people had sovereignty, but at the municipal level it could not ignore their physical occupation of lands. It might be able to treat the *territory* as *res nullius*, but it could not pretend that *occupied lands* were such, any more than an occupant of a manor could pretend that lands occupied by freehold tenants were part of the manor's demesne. If the Crown wanted to acquire title to occupied lands along with sovereignty, it would have had to seize those lands into its own hands by act of state before annexing the territory to its dominions. After that, the indigenous people would be British subjects, and the Crown would be bound by English law.

It has sometimes been assumed, however, that English law itself, by virtue of the doctrine of tenures, would give the Crown title to all lands in a settlement irrespective of indigenous occupation. This assumption misconstrues the effect of the doctrine, which is primarily concerned with feudal relations, especially the relationship between the Crown as lord paramount and landholding subjects as tenants. In order to assure the Crown of this paramount lordship in England, legal ingenuity invented the fiction that the Crown originally owned all the lands, and that subjects' titles were all derived from Crown grants. But in reality, of course, perfectly good titles can and do exist independently of grant, as in the case of title by limitation, or (formerly) title by occupancy of a vacant *pur autre vie* estate. Likewise, indigenous people would not need Crown grants to have title to lands occupied by them at the time a settlement was acquired. The effect of the doctrine of tenures in that context would be to create a tenurial relationship between the Crown as lord and the indigenous occupiers as tenants. Escheat apart, the doctrine would not operate to defeat the presumptive title which the occupiers would have. Where the Crown claims lands from subjects who are in occupation, as a general rule it must prove its title like anyone else.

But, it may be asked, if all this is so, and if indigenous people not shown to have customary law title would have acquired this common law aboriginal title to lands occupied by them in settled colonies, why is there no direct authority to this effect? *A-G for British Honduras v. Bristowe* and the example of Pitcairn Island are precedents of sorts, but of course neither involved indigenous people. American and Canadian decisions acknowledge that Indians and Inuit have (or had) some kind of title by virtue of their occupation, but not to fee simple estates. Even Hall J, when he said in *Calder v. A-G of BC* that "ownership" can be presumed from indigenous possession, does not seem to have meant ownership in an English law sense.

A possible explanation for this lack of direct authority is that the arguments presented in this book may never have been made in this context before. Upon reflection, this is not as surprising as it may sound. The general European attitude to indigenous people during the colonial period was notoriously ethnocentric. The proposition that in English law indigenous people of North America and Australia had the same rights to lands occupied by them as fee simple tenants with valid titles had to their cottages and gardens in England was probably beyond contemplation. Moreover, it was obviously not in the interest of the colonizers to formulate arguments that would tend to make acquisition of lands costlier and more difficult. Nor were the indigenous people themselves in a position to articulate claims on the basis of English law principles. The matter was simply not thought out in this way by any of the persons concerned.

When questions involving indigenous land rights began to come before the courts, the tendency was to look for answers outside English law. Chief Justice Marshall's early American decisions in particular ignored common law principles and constructed a vague theory of Indian title on the basis of doubtful premises drawn to some extent from his own perceptions of international law. In effect, what Marshall did was invent a body of law which was virtually without precedent. But, one may ask, what if the Chief Justice and others after him did make new law when the question of aboriginal land rights came before them—is that so unusual? Are not judges obliged to be creative when faced with an issue of first impression, and fashion new rules if necessary to deal with the novel situation? Did not the collision of cultures and interests resulting from the arrival of European settlers among people whose livelihood depended largely on hunting and gathering demand just this sort of judicial ingenuity? Finally, are not the approaches which have been worked out by the courts fair attempts to strike an even-handed balance between conflicting values and claims in cases involving questions for which there are no readily available answers?

Admittedly, judges can and do make new law when confronted with novel situations: indeed, it is by this very process that the common law has developed. But if the law is to be reasonably certain and consistent, new rules generally should not be invented when existing law contains adequate solutions. Exceptional circumstances may occasionally arise, however, which are so different from those for which the old rules were made that it would be inappropriate to apply those rules, even though possible to do so. Arguably, the Crown's acquisition of territories inhabited by indigenous people presented just this sort of exceptional situation. To apply English real property law to people who may not have had even a concept of ownership of land would be illogical, on this view, and would have anomalous consequences. The relationship of hunters and gatherers to land clearly does not correspond with that of English people, whose legal system contains intricate rules governing proprietary interests in land. To apply those rules to indigenous people who ranged over vast areas, and thereby accord them fee simple title, as we have argued should be done, is simply inappropriate.

In response to this, it may first be noted that English land law has been thought to be applicable where the supposed effect has been to *deny* land rights to indigenous people. Blackburn J's decision in *Milirrpum v. Nabalco Pty.* is a prime example of this. So if it can be shown that the reception of English law had the effect of *establishing* aboriginal land rights, those who have relied on that law to deny the existence of such rights would undermine its legitimacy and authority were they to turn round and contend that it does not apply. Moreover, it must be remembered that at the time a territory was made British by settlement, the other principal claimant to lands occupied by indigenous people would be the Crown. Act of state apart, the Crown's claim could be based only on English law. Surely one cannot seriously argue that English law would apply to give title to the Crown, while at the same time denying the benefit of that law to the people who were actually on the land, using and occupying it as their ancestors had done for generations. Any suggestion that English law should be applied in such a selective and unequal manner deserves to be rejected as a transparent attempt to manipulate the law in favour of the colonizers.

Customary law aside, it would therefore seem that as a matter of principle one should either apply English law to all concerned in these circumstances and accept the consequences, or look for a new solution altogether. In the United States and Canada judges generally seem to have preferred the latter approach. They have purported to accord land rights of some sort to indigenous people, but have not felt constrained to equate the interest held by them with any precise English law interest. Unfortunately, however, judges have been extremely vague when it has come to specifying just what rights and interests indigenous people have.

In the United States Indian title remained virtually undefined until 1955 when the Supreme Court finally concluded that it confers no proprietary interest at all—that the holders of this "title" are merely permissive occupiers of government-owned land. This can hardly be described as a fair attempt to strike an even-handed balance between the competing claims of Indians and Europeans. Rather than using the novel circumstances arising from the colonization of America to come up with an equitable solution, the Supreme Court has responded to the challenge by practically denying that the Indians had any legal rights to lands after the European powers annexed the territories inhabited by them. No wonder many indigenous people are wary of relying on judges to fabricate just doctrine where their aboriginal land rights are concerned.

In Canada, the land rights issue is still unresolved. As we have seen, the Supreme Court's most recent remarks [see *R v. Guerin*, [1984] 2 SCR 335, discussed in chapter 3] on the matter described the Indians' interest in lands traditionally occupied by them as *sui generis*: a unique interest which, strictly speaking, is neither beneficial nor personal and usufructuary in nature. The members of the court who dealt with this issue said the Indian interest is best characterized by its general inalienability, coupled with the fact that surrender of the interest to the Crown creates a fiduciary obligation on the part of the Crown to deal with the lands for the Indians' benefit. That is as close as the Canadian judiciary has come to explaining aboriginal title, even though the courts have had ample opportunity over the past century to display substantial creativity in this area. Rather than seize the chance to develop a coherent body of law relating to aboriginal land rights, judges have studiously avoided the issue whenever possible, cautiously confining themselves to vague general statements. As a result, this area is probably one of the most uncertain in Canadian law.

It is thus apparent that the judiciaries of the three common law jurisdictions dealt with here have so far failed to come up with a satisfactory solution to what one author has called "the riddle of aboriginal title." Not only have courts in the United States, Canada, and Australia approached the matter in different ways, but within each of these jurisdictions there has been—and still is—much perplexity and a great deal of controversy over just what land rights indigenous people have. So even if one admits that this is an area where the exercise of judicial initiative is appropriate, the fact is that judges have not fulfilled the law-making function which on this view should be assumed by them. This book proposes a return to fundamental common law principles as a way out of this muddle. If applied in this context, these principles are capable of providing a comprehensive legal solution to what has long been an intractable problem.

From a policy perspective, some may be concerned about the consequences of concluding that at common law indigenous people would have fee simple title to any lands occupied by them in settled territories at the time the Crown acquired sovereignty. Where occupied lands which were neither purchased by treaty (or otherwise) nor confiscated by valid legislation are involved, this could mean that any taking of those lands from the indigenous occupiers would have been unlawful. That this may be so, however, is certainly not a sufficient reason in law for rejecting the conclusion that the occupiers had title. On the contrary, if the conclusions reached in this book are correct, and by English law a right to fee simple estates did vest in indigenous occupiers, then (statutory bars aside) no one can contend that it is too late to declare the law, and enforce the right. Moreover, if indigenous people have been dealt with unfairly in the past, from an ethical point of view that may be all the more reason for justice to be done by enforcing their rights today.

It is possible, however, that present-day holders of lands which may have been unlawfully taken would be protected by statutes of limitation and registry or land titles Acts. If so, what is at stake here is not so much lands which have already passed into private hands, as lands which have been regarded as part of the public domain, but which in many areas have never been developed and are often still occupied by indigenous people. In some instances, these "public" lands have remained untouched because aboriginal land claims have not yet been settled. More often, however, these lands have not been developed because they are unsuitable for agriculture and, until recently, could not profitably be exploited for natural resources. The main issue, then, is who should control the development of, and reap the benefit from, any resources these lands are capable of producing. Should it be the people who have lived there for generations, and who rely on the land for their livelihood and the maintenance of their culture? Or should it be the public at large, as represented by government? In an age when undeveloped lands and societies which depend on such lands for their survival are disappearing at an ever-increasing rate, it may not be unreasonable to leave the fate of at least some of these lands in the hands of those whose lives are intimately connected with them.

Policy issues of this kind obviously cannot be resolved by the sort of legal analysis presented in this book. In fact, any strictly legal approach to the problem of aboriginal land rights may be regarded as inadequate, since legal analysis is incapable of taking sufficient account of many of the economic, sociological, and other factors which deserve to be considered. Ultimately, just solutions to aboriginal land claims can best be achieved through compromise, by balancing the various interests involved in any particular claim and trying to arrive at a result which is fair to all. As a rule, compromise is a product of negotiation. Unfortunately, however, indigenous people who lack sound legal arguments to support their claims are at a definite disadvantage at the bargaining table. All too often these people have been unfairly dealt with in the past because it was thought that their claims did not have a legal basis. A major aim of this book has been to dispel this false impression by showing that even by the colonizers' own rules indigenous people did—and in some cases no doubt still do—have title to lands occupied by them. With this kind of legal argument behind them, indigenous people should be in a position to negotiate from strength. One can only hope that the result will be a just resolution of claims which have been ignored or denied for far too long.

Discussion Note

Some of the arguments raised by McNeil are addressed more fully in chapter 3. At this point, however, it is important to understand the claims in terms of theories about possession, as one strand in legal arguments about land claims by First Nations people in Canada. What exactly is the argument that McNeil makes for the recognition of possessory title claims by First Nations in Canada? Do you agree with his suggestions as to why these arguments were not presented in earlier times? Do you think the absence of these arguments in 19th-century cases reflects a lack of legal understanding or legal imagination? This issue is also important in relation to current issues about aboriginal land claims, discussed in chapter 8. How can we overcome the impact of dominant cultural values in the presentation or recognition of legal claims? For a comparative analysis of aboriginal land claims in Canada, Australia, and New Zealand, see K. Hazlehurst, ed., *Legal Pluralism and the Colonial Legacy* (Aldershot, UK: Avebury, 1995).

Possessory Interests and the Operation of Statutes of Limitations

Statutes of Limitation: History and Purposes

Statutes of limitation define the relationship between a person with an interest based on possession and the person who is the "true owner" (the person with "paper title"). The common law's historical emphasis on physical possession rather than "abstract title" and its insistence on the idea of relativity of title rather than absolute ownership meant that a person with a possession-based interest was accorded the benefit of some legal protection vis-à-vis the person with paper title. Statutes of limitation "built upon" this common law foundation of possessory title by providing that the right of the paper title holder to bring an action to recover possession (against someone claiming entitlement by possession) did not last forever. At present, this right of the paper title holder is time-limited to the period defined in the statutes of limitation in each province. Thus, for example, a paper title holder (the "true owner") in Ontario must bring an action to recover possession of land within 10 years after the possessory interest was established—for example, by a squatter. According to s. 15 of the Limitations Act, RSO 1990, c. L.15:

> 15. At the determination of the period limited by this Act to any person for making an entry or distress or bringing any action, the right and title of such person to the land or rent, for the recovery whereof such entry, distress or action, respectively, might have been made or brought within such period, is extinguished.

For comparable provisions, see Limitation of Actions Act, RSNS 1989, c. 258, s. 22; Limitation of Actions Act, RSNB 1973, c. L-8, s. 60; Statute of Limitations Act, RSPEI 1988, c. S-7, s. 46; and Limitation of Realty Actions Act, RSN 1990, c. L-16, s. 26.

Section 15 provides for the extinguishment of the paper title holder's right to bring an action to recover possession. It does *not* transfer the paper title holder's title to the possessor.

In the context of the common law's concept of relativity of title, however, it means that the possessor's interest may be less vulnerable because the "true owner's" interest is no longer enforceable. Yet the strength of the possessor's title, in relation to other claims, still depends on the nature of the possessory claim. In this way, the statutes of limitation simply add to the common law principles by defining time limits within which the paper title holder must take action in order to preserve the relative priority of his or her claim.

The common law's historical focus on physical possession—recall the ceremony of livery of seisin, for example—may provide an explanation for statutes of limitation and their limiting of rights of "true owners." In earlier centuries when records about interests in land were often non-existent or unreliable, the common law's protection of a person in actual possession may have been perfectly sensible. In the late 20th century, however, when sophisticated land registry systems exist, it is sometimes more difficult to explain why legal principles should continue to protect squatters' rights at the expense of the interests of the paper title holder. Indeed, this issue raises numerous questions about the modern relationship between "owners" of land and resources and the rights of "users" of land. Should the law protect the rights of someone who owns land and who makes no use of it, especially when others have been using it for productive purposes—or wish to do so?

Because these are important questions, there have been numerous efforts to justify the underlying principles of statutes of limitation and the barring of the rights of action of "true owners." Charles Callaghan, in *Adverse Possession* (Columbus OH: State University Press, 1961), at 87ff., examined three such justifications. The first is that the law is punishing the owner for neglect in relation to the land, a theory rejected by Callaghan because punishment is the business of criminal law and should have no place in the context of statutes of limitations. The second possible rationale is that these statutes serve to encourage the use of land by "rewarding" the active use of the possessor (rather than punishing the paper title holder). In Callaghan's view, this justification begs the question whether we need to encourage the use of land and, even if one agrees with this view, whether statutes of limitation represent an effective means of accomplishing this purpose. Rejecting these two justifications, Callaghan conceded some validity to a third justification, the "clearing of title to land," a purpose identified in the opening words of the first Statute of Limitations in 1623—"For quieting of men's estates." As Callaghan admitted, a public registry of interests in land may not always be exactly in accord with what has occurred "on the ground." There may be a need for some legal means of "curing" titles so that registered descriptions of parcels of land are congruent with the location of boundary fences.

In thinking about these justifications and their current validity, consider another excerpt from Carol Rose's article "Possession as the Origin of Property." In this excerpt, Rose examines the relationship between theories of possessory rights and the operation of statutes of limitation, focusing on the case of *Brumagim v. Bradshaw*, 39 Cal. 24 (1870).

Carol Rose, "Possession as the Origin of Property"
(1985), 52 *University of Chicago Law Review* 73, at 77-82 (footnotes omitted)

Brumagim v. Bradshaw involved two claimants to a considerable amount of land that had become, by the time the litigation was brought, the residential and commercial

Potrero district of San Francisco. Each party claimed ownership of the land through a title extending back to an original "possessor" of the land, and the issue was whether the first of these purported possessors, one George Treat, had really "possessed" the land at all. If he had not, his successors in interest could not claim ownership through him, and title would go to those claiming through a later "first possessor."

Those who claimed through Treat put a number of facts before the jury to establish his original possession. They noted particularly that Treat had repaired a fence across the neck of the Potrero peninsula—to which the other side rejoined that outsiders could still land in boats, and that, in any event, there was a gap in the fence. The Treat claimants also alleged that Treat had made use of the land by pasturing livestock on it—though the other side argued that the land had not been suitable for cattle even then, because San Francisco was expanding in that direction. The court ruled that the jury should decide whether Treat's acts gave sufficient notice to the public that he had appropriated the property. If so, he had "possessed" it and could pass it on as an owner.

This instruction would seem to come down clearly on the side of the "clear act" theory of possession. Yet that theory seems to leave out some elements of the evidence. The fence question, to be sure, bore on whether Treat's acts informed the public of his claim. But the parties' arguments over whether Treat's use was "suitable" seemed to reflect concern over an aim of rewarding useful labor. If suitable use were a relevant issue, why did the court's jury instruction ignore the value of rewarding labor?

The answer to this question may well be that suitable use is also a form of notice. If outsiders would think that a large area near a growing city was abandoned because it was vacant except for a few cows, they might enter on the land and claim some prime waterfront footage for themselves. In other words, if the use that Treat made was unsuitable, his use would not give notice of his claim to others. Thus, to ask whether Treat used the land suitably is just another way of asking whether he informed others of his claim, particularly those others who might have been interested in buying the land from Treat or settling it for themselves. Society is worst off in a world of vague claims; if no one knows whether he can safely use the land, or from whom he should buy it if it is already claimed, the land may end up being used by too many people or by none at all.

Possession now begins to look even more like something that requires a kind of communication, and the original claim to the property looks like a kind of speech, with the audience composed of all others who might be interested in claiming the object in question. Moreover, some venerable statutory law obligates the acquiring party to *keep on* speaking, lest he lose his title by "adverse possession."

Adverse possession is a common law interpretation of statutes of limitation for actions to recover real property. Suppose I own a lot in the mountains, and some stranger to me, without my permission, builds a house on it, clears the woods, and farms the lot continuously for a given period, say twenty years. During that time, I am entitled to go to court to force him off the lot. But if I have not done so at the end of twenty years, or some other period fixed by statute, not only can I not sue him for recovery of what was my land, but the law recognizes him as the title owner. The doctrine of adverse possession thus operates to transfer property to one who is initially a trespasser if the trespasser's presence is open to everyone, lasts continuously for a given period of time, and if the title owner takes no action to get rid of him during that time.

Here again we seem to have an example of a reward to the useful laborer at the expense of the sluggard. But the doctrine is susceptible to another interpretation as well; it might be designed, not to reward the useful laborer, but to require the owner to assert her right publicly. It requires her to make it clear that she, and not the trespasser, is the person to deal with if anyone should wish to buy the property or use some portion of it.

Courts have devoted much attention to the elements of a successful claim of adverse possession. Is grazing livestock a continuous use, so as to entitle the livestock owner to claim full ownership of the pasture as an adverse possessor? How about farming (where intensive use may be merely seasonal) or taking care of a lawn? Is a cave that encroaches deep under my land something that is obvious to me, so that I should be required to kick out the trespasser who operates it as a commercial attraction? No matter how much the doctrine of adverse possession seems to reward the one who performs useful labor on land at the expense of the lazy owner who does nothing, the crucial element in all these situations is, once again, communication. "Possession" means acts that "apprise the community[,] ... arrest attention, and put others claiming title upon inquiry."

In Illinois, for example, an adverse possessor may establish his claim merely by paying taxes on the property, at least against an owner who is familiar with real estate practice and records. Why is this? Naturally the community likes to have taxes paid and is favorably disposed toward one who pays them. But more important, payment of taxes is a matter of public record, and the owner whose taxes are paid by someone else should be aware that something peculiar is happening. Just as important, the *public* is very likely to view the taxpayer as the owner. If someone is paying taxes on my vacant lot or empty house, any third person who wants to buy the house is very likely to think that the taxpayer is the owner because people do not ordinarily pay taxes on land they do not own. If I want to keep my land, the burden is upon me to correct the misimpression. The possibility of transferring titles through adverse possession once again serves to ensure that members of the public can rely upon their own reasonable perceptions, and an owner who fails to correct misleading appearances may find his title lost to one who speaks loudly and clearly, though erroneously.

Possession as the basis of property ownership, then, seems to amount to something like yelling loudly enough to all who may be interested. The first to say, "This is mine," in a way that the public understands, gets the prize, and the law will help him keep it against someone else who says, "No, it is *mine*." But if the original communicator dallies too long and allows the public to believe the interloper, he will find the interloper has stepped into his shoes and has become the owner.

Similar ideas of the importance of communication, or as it is more commonly called, "notice," are implicit in our recording statutes and in a variety of other devices that force a property claimant to make a public record of her claims on pain of losing them altogether. Indeed, notice plays a part in the most mundane property-like claims to things that the law does not even recognize as capable of being reduced to ownership. "Would you please save my place?" one says to one's neighbor in the movie line, in order to ensure that others in line know that one is coming back and not relinquishing one's claim. In my home town of Chicago, one may choose to shovel the snow from a parking place on the street, but in order to establish a claim to it one must put a chair or some other object in the cleared space. The useful act of shovelling snow does not speak as unambiguously as the presence of an object that blocks entry.

Why, then, is it so important that property owners make and keep their communications clear? Economists have an answer: clear titles facilitate trade and minimize resource-wasting conflict. If I am careless about who comes on to a corner of my property, I invite others to make mistakes and to waste their labor on improvements to what I have allowed them to think is theirs. I thus invite a free-for-all over my ambiguously held claims, and I encourage contention, insecurity, and litigation—all of which waste everyone's time and energy and may result in overuse or under use of resources. But if I keep my property claims clear, others will know that they should deal with me directly if they want to use my property. We can bargain rather than fight; through trade, all items will come to rest in the hands of those who value them most. If property lines are clear, then, anyone who can make better use of my property than I can will buy or rent it from me and turn the property to his better use. In short, we will all be richer when property claims are unequivocal, because that unequivocal status enables property to be traded and used at its highest value.

Discussion Notes

Underlying Justifications for Statutes of Limitation

Do you agree with the justifications for statutes of limitation offered by Callaghan and by Rose? What are the underlying concerns being addressed by the justifications proposed? Are they consistent with possessory claims that occur innocently, negligently, or intentionally? Do they "justify" the possessory claims of trespassers who assert "squatters' rights" as well as those who are just mistaken about their boundaries? These issues are important because judicial interpretation of the plain words in statutes of limitations appears to have added an element of intention, and these judicial developments are sometimes explained by commentators in terms of underlying policies and purposes—for example, see Thomas Merrill, "Property Rules, Liability Rules, and Adverse Possession" (1985), 79 *Northwestern University Law Review* 1122. Indeed, the expression "adverse possession" is often used to describe a "possessor" with an intention "adverse" to that of the true owner, an approach that represents a further development in common law principles of possession. In this way, this area of property law requires an understanding of common law principles of possession, the impact of statutory reform, and subsequent interpretation of the statutes by judges. The complex relationships among these principles may be better understood in the context of underlying justifications, as proposed by Callaghan and Rose. Thus, you should keep their suggestions in mind in considering the cases in this section.

The Context of Claims Based on Possession

The justifications proposed by Callaghan and Rose provide an explanation for the operation of statutes of limitation in relation to interests in land in the eastern provinces of Canada and in parts of Ontario. By contrast, the process of barring the rights of title holders has been abolished by statute in some jurisdictions where the Torrens system of land registration has been adopted and by the Land Titles Act, RSO 1990, c. L.5, which applies to some Ontario land. For example, s. 51 of the Land Titles Act provides:

> 51.(1) Despite any provision of this Act, the *Limitations Act* or any other Act, no title to and no right or interest in land registered under this Act that is adverse to or in derogation of the title of the registered owner shall be acquired hereafter or be deemed to have been acquired heretofore by any length of possession or by prescription.

For a similar provision in Manitoba, see the Real Property Act, RSM 1988, c. R30, s. 61(2). See also *Report for Discussion: Limitations* (Edmonton: Alberta Institute of Law Research and Reforms, 1986).

The cases that follow address a number of different aspects of "adverse possession." For example, it is important to define when the limitation period starts to run (the commencement of the limitation period), the quality of possession required for the running of the limitation period, and the relevance of intention on the part of the possessor and also on the part of the paper title holder. Although these issues are examined separately, pay close attention to the ways that they overlap in the cases.

Acts of Possession: Commencement of the Limitation Period

The statutes of limitation define the required time period within which an action to recover possession must be initiated by the paper title holder. They also define when the time period commences—that is, when time begins to run against the paper title holder. For example, the Ontario Limitations Act, RSO 1990, c. L.15, ss. 4 and 5(1) provide:

> 4. *No person shall* make an entry or distress, or *bring an action to recover any land* or rent, *but within ten years next after the time at which the right* to make such entry or distress, or *to bring such action*, first accrued to some person through whom the person making or bringing it claims, or if the right did not accrue to any person through whom that person claims, then within ten years next after the time at which the right to make such entry or distress, or to bring such action, *first accrued to the person* making or bringing it.

> 5.(1) *Where the person claiming such land* or rent, or some person through whom that person claims, *has, in respect of the estate or interest claimed, been in possession* or in receipt of the profits of the land, or in receipt of the rent, *and has, while entitled thereto, been dispossessed, or has discontinued such possession* or receipt, *the right to* make an entry or distress or *bring an action to recover the land* or rent *shall be deemed to have first accrued at the time of the dispossession or discontinuance of possession*, or at the last time at which any such profits or rent were so received.

(Emphasis added.) The language of the statute is difficult, reflecting its historical origins, but by reading the emphasized words, it is possible to summarize the statutory principles, as follows:

s. 4 The paper title holder shall bring an action to recover land within 10 years after the right to bring such an action accrued to the person bringing it.

s. 5(1) Where the person claiming an interest in land was formerly in possession and was dispossessed *or* has discontinued possession, the right to bring an action to recover the land shall be deemed to have accrued at the time of the dispossession *or* discontinuance of possession.

Taking this formulation as a starting point, it is clear that it is necessary to define exactly what acts constitute "dispossession or discontinuance of possession" in order to define the moment when the limitation period begins to run. There may also be an issue about what acts are sufficient to qualify as "dispossession or discontinuance" of possession.

In thinking about these requirements, consider the following fact situation. In September 1901, Ms Piper arranged for the fencing of six lots of land that she had purchased. In constructing the fence, it seems that she enclosed (apparently by mistake) not only these six lots but also two adjoining lots to which her neighbour claimed title. The eight lots enclosed by Ms Piper formed a block and were completely enclosed by her fences from September 1901 until her neighbour brought an action for trespass against her in June 1912. In the intervening years, Ms Piper had ensured that the eight lots were ploughed as one block, fertilized by manure, and sown and harvested. In 1905 and 1906, buildings were erected and Ms Piper moved in, continually residing there to the time the suit commenced in 1912. Assuming that Ms Piper did not have title to the two extra lots, did her actions constitute "dispossession" pursuant to the Limitations Act? Which of her actions is determinative? Would it have been sufficient just to fence in the two extra lots? Was her farming activity necessary also? Was it necessary for her to erect buildings and live there?

In *Piper v. Stevenson* (1913), 28 OR 379 (AD), the trial judge concluded (at 382) that "until 1906 everything was done upon the land that an owner could do in reaping the full benefit of it; and since the spring of that year, everything was done that an owner in actual, constant occupation would do," thereby holding that Ms Piper had dispossessed her neighbour in 1901. Her actions constituted "dispossession" according to s. 5(1) and the limitation period had thus commenced in September 1901, expiring 10 years later and prior to her neighbour's law suit in June 1912. The appeal was also dismissed, Clute J commenting on the arguments presented against Ms Piper's entitlement and concluding (at 383) that "[she had] fenced them in, in September 1901; and her possession of them and of the land in question was continuous and exclusive from the date of fencing." In thinking about the judicial interpretation of ss. 4 and 5(1) of Ontario's Limitations Act, consider the similarities and differences between *Piper v. Stevenson* and *Re St. Clair Beach Estates Ltd. v. MacDonald*, which follows. Is the judicial formulation of the test in Ontario's Limitations Act the same in both cases?

Re St. Clair Beach Estates Ltd. v. MacDonald
(1974), 5 OR (2d) 482 (HCJ Div. Ct.)

PENNELL J: In this appeal the appellants (objectors), Donald M. MacDonald and Rita L. MacDonald, seek to reverse the order of His Honour Judge Zalev who dismissed an appeal by way of trial *de novo* pursuant to s. 29(1) of the *Land Titles Act*, RSO 1970, c. 234, from the order of the Deputy Director of Titles that the application of the respondent (applicant), St. Clair Beach Estates Limited, for first registration under the

Land Titles Act of certain land forming part of the Gore Lot, West of Pike Creek, in the Village of St. Clair Beach, in the County of Essex, be accepted.

The question to be determined is whether the appellants have established their claim to a possessory title of the land in question. Possession is a matter of fact depending on all the particular circumstances of the case. Therefore, I start from the facts as to which there is no dispute. Those facts, compendiously stated, are as follows:

1. The application for first registration by the respondent covered a large parcel of land in the Village of St. Clair Beach formerly known as the Grant Farm.

2. The Grant Farm was an irregularly shaped parcel some 3,100 ft. in depth lying between the south side of Riverside Dr. and the north side of St. Gregory Rd. The parcel has a width of approximately 900 ft. The Grant Farm excluded certain small residential parcels fronting on Riverside Dr.

[The following figure is the author's—it is not part of the original case:]

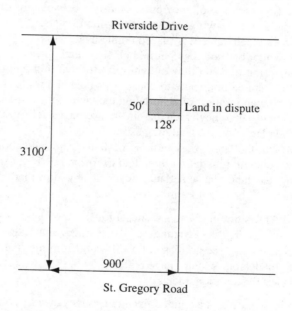

Riverside Drive

50′ — Land in dispute
128′

3100′

900′

St. Gregory Road

3. The respondent is the absolute owner in fee simple in possession of the Grant Farm subject to certain encumbrances which are not relevant to these proceedings. They purchased from the Grant estate in 1969.

4. The appellants purchased one of the residential parcels fronting on Riverside Dr. in August, 1961. Their title also comes from the Grant estate via a certain John Gazo and Mary Gazo. The appellants took possession of their parcel in August, 1961, and have occupied it to the present time.

5. The land in dispute abuts the southerly limit of the parcel of the appellants by the full width of the parcel and extends southerly to the northerly edge of a soybean field running in an irregular east–west line across the Grant Farm.

6. In August, 1961, the land in dispute was partly grass but generally was overgrown in weeds, trees and rubble. It is a rectangular piece of land 128.79 ft. wide running southerly from the southerly limit of the appellants' parcel for a distance of 50 ft. The area to the south was ploughed ground.

7. The house on the appellants' land was constructed in 1954. It has a septic tank for sewage and the weeping tiles for this tank are located on the lands in dispute. This weeping tile was installed when the system was built in 1954 and was in place when the appellants purchased the property.

8. The appellants' use of the land in dispute was the normal domestic and recreational use which an owner would make of his own backyard. By way of illustration I refer to the following acts:

(a) In the fall of 1961 they removed trees, brush and rubble.

(b) In February, 1962, they bought a dog and set up a dog run of some 50 ft. in the south–west corner of the lands.

(c) In 1962 they seeded the land with grass, fertilized it and cut it.

(d) In the summer of 1962 they put a sand-box between the cherry trees on the land in question, installed swings and planted some flowers.

(e) In 1963 a picnic table was placed on the land.

(f) In the winter of 1964 they put in their first skating rink.

(g) In the spring of 1965 they bought a 22-ft. boat hull and over the next two years they used the area in dispute to construct a boat and trailer for transporting it. Thereafter the boat and trailer were stored on the land in the fall and winter months.

(h) In or about 1965 they erected a bird-house on a steel [post and] placed it on a temporary foundation on the land in question.

(i) In 1967, at the latest, they built a dog-house and pole about 15 ft. high and embedded in a concrete foundation three feet deep and one foot across.

9. In so using the land the appellants never at any time had the permission or consent of the owners of the Grant Farm.

So much for the facts not in dispute. Counsel for the appellants contended that there was no evidence to support other findings of the learned trial Judge. I have carefully examined the evidence and I see no reason for differing from his findings. I adopt them as the basis of the conclusions which I have reached.

The following are the additional facts:

10. The land in dispute was excluded from the conveyance by John Gazo and Mary Gazo to the appellants and this limitation on the actual extent of the conveyance was known to the appellants.

11. There were a few cherry trees on the land in dispute and the Grants picked cherries from time to time from these trees.

12. The predecessors in title to the respondent, Mrs. Annie Grant and her family, were never out of possession of the property in question, but continued to carry on farming operations on so much of the land as was arable having regard to its nature and characteristics. The reason the ploughing was limited was threefold. First, a hydro pole interfered with the equipment. Secondly, the cherry trees proved an obstacle, and thirdly, the sandy soil made it difficult to get on the land with farm equipment.

13. Substantially speaking, the Grants and the appellants were on a friendly basis. The use of the land in question was in the nature of a neighbourly acquiescence by the Grants.

Two more findings of fact should be particularly set out.

14. The title of the Grant family to the land in dispute was acknowledged by the appellants. On two occasions they attempted to purchase the property in question. They made an offer to purchase to Mrs. Annie Grant shortly before her death on May 14, 1966. In 1969 they renewed the offer to her estate at a price of $1,000. On the second occasion, the appellants deposited a certified cheque in that amount with their solicitor for completion of the transaction, but nothing came of it.

15. In 1969 the respondent purchased the Grant Farm and caused a line of surveyor's stakes to be put in which clearly demarked the south boundary of the parcel owned by the appellants. At all times the appellants were aware of the presence of these stakes but did not deal with them except in silence until May, 1972. At that time the appellants became concerned about the location of the weeping tile of the septic system and then they tried to acquire part of the land in question from the respondent.

Those are the facts on which the learned trial Judge came to the conclusion that the respondent was entitled to an order for first registration. The contention between the parties depends far more on the inferences which are to be drawn from the facts of the case than in any different view as to the existence of the facts themselves.

The short basis of the case made for the appellants was that the learned trial Judge erred on three counts: (a) that he erred in failing to find that the appellants had acquired title to the land in question by adverse possession over the relevant statutory period within the meaning of the *Limitations Act*, RSO 1970, c. 246; (b) that he erred in finding that the appellants required an *animus possidendi* with the intention to exclude the title holders from the property to acquire title by adverse possession; and (c) that he erred in finding that the acts of the Grants in picking cherries constituted actual possession on their part or, alternatively, that the evidence would not support a finding that the Grants picked cherries during the relevant period.

To understand what the law on the matter is, I must refer to the *Limitations Act*.

[Pennell J referred to ss. 4 and 5, and continued:]

It is plain on its face that the *Limitations Act* is a defence.

The Courts have been generous in elucidating the nature of the burden upon a party seeking to establish title by possession. From a long stream of cases I select, first, that of *Pflug and Pflug v. Collins*, [1952] OR 519, [1952] 3 DLR 681; affirmed [1953] OWN 140, [1953] 1 DLR 841. In that case, at p. 527 OR, p. 689 DLR, Wells J (as he then was) made it clear that to succeed the appellants must show:

(1) [a]ctual possession for the statutory period by themselves and those through whom they claim;

(2) that such possession was with the intention of excluding from possession the owners or persons entitled to possession; and

(3) discontinuance of possession for the statutory period by the owners and all others, if any, entitled to possession.

If they fail in any one of these respects, their claim must be dismissed.

As regards the "discontinuance" aspect which I have mentioned, a question arose at trial whether the Grants had discontinued their possession of the land north of the plough-line throughout the relevant period. In reaching a decision one must have regard to the particular circumstances of the case and the nature of the land in question (*Leigh v. Jack* (1879), 5 Ex.D 264).

The learned trial Judge answered the question in these words:

> The Grant Farm (including the disputed land) was agricultural land prior to 1961, and was used solely for agricultural purposes at least to 1966. During that time, the Grants made such use of the disputed land as might reasonably be expected of an owner in possession, namely, ploughing as far north as the hydro pole, trees, and nature of the soil would permit. The area north of the plough-line was used for the only agricultural purpose possible, namely, picking cherries off the trees. The deedholders have constructive possession of the lands described in their deed, and it is not necessary for them (as contrasted with trespassers) to show that they have pedal possession. I find that the Grants were never out of possession prior to 1966. As to the lands south of the plough-line, actual possession was maintained by ploughing, and as to the lands north of the plough-line, actual possession was maintained by the simple act of picking cherries. There is no dispossession of the owner or discontinuance of possession by the owner within the meaning of s. 5 of the *Limitations Act*, RSO 1970, c. 246, until there are acts by the claimants which interfere with the purpose to which the owner devoted the land. The smallest act by the owner would be sufficient to show that there was no discontinuance of his possession: *per* Bramwell LJ, in *Leigh v. Jack* (1879), 5 Ex.D 264 at p. 272. Where the land in dispute is unenclosed then the only safe rule to follow is to confine the trespasser to the actual area from which he has by visible occupation excluded the title holder, but occasional use of the disputed land by the title holder in a manner consistent with the uses to which such land may be put is sufficient to deprive the claimants of exclusive possession: *Walker et al. v. Russell et al.*, [1966] 1 OR 197, 53 DLR (2d) 509.

One of the questions on this appeal is whether there was evidence on which the learned County Court Judge could so find. The inference drawn by him from the evidence of the picking of cherries was impeached. In my view, the evidence on which the learned County Court Judge acted was sufficient evidence on which he could properly find that the respondent was never out of possession of the land north of the plough-line prior to 1966. In some cases possession cannot in the nature of things be continuous from day to day and possession may continue to subsist notwithstanding that there are sometimes long intervals between the acts of user. The owner of a farm cannot be said to be out of possession of a piece of land merely because he does not perform positive acts of ownership all the time.

The evidence led the learned trial Judge to the conclusion that at best the appellants had joint possession with the Grants. It is a small point but, for myself, I am doubtful that for the purposes of possession under the *Limitations Act* it is strictly correct legal parlance to speak of concurrent possession. In this connection it seems to me possession is single and exclusive. No doubt the appellants occupied the land. With every respect to the opinion of the learned trial Judge, I think that the land should be regarded as in the possession of one or the other of the two parties concerned. On that footing it follows from the judgment of the learned trial Judge that the respondent, having picked cherries, remained at that period in possession of the land.

If this conclusion be right, it is enough to decide the case in the respondent's favour. I note, however, that a point much agitated before this Court was whether the learned trial Judge erred in law in finding that the appellants required an intention to defeat or exclude the true owners from the land. I think I ought to deal with this point, though the careful judgment of the trial Judge, with which I agree, absolves me from attending to the matter in great detail.

It is, I think, beyond the reach of controversy that the appellants never had any intention, nor claimed any intention of excluding the Grants. The dominant feature in the case is the fact that as late as 1969 the appellants offered to purchase the land from the Grant estate for the sum of $1,000. Counsel for the appellants, however, contended that the concept of adverse possession does not involve an intention on the part of the person in possession to acquire a right against a particular person. He founded himself on a passage in the judgment of Osler J, in *Smaglinski et al. v. Daly et al.*, [1970] 2 OR 275, 10 DLR (3d) 507; affirmed [1971] 3 OR 238, 20 DLR (3d) 65. On p. 272 OR, p. 514 DLR, Osler J uses this language:

> ... I think it can be said that a person who remains in exclusive possession, even though uncertain of his right to do so, can nevertheless acquire a possessory title. In the present case Joseph Norlock, though uncertain of and quite probably unconcerned about the precise legal nature of his occupancy, did act in a manner entirely consistent with ownership in clearing and sowing the land and there is no evidence whatever that his right to do so was questioned at any time by Philip Norlock, owner of the paper title.

I do not read the language of my learned friend, Mr. Justice Osler, as I gather that counsel for the appellants does. I am myself unable to accept the suggestion that Justice Osler was saying that an intention to defeat the true owner was unnecessary. Moreover, there is nothing to show that the minds of the trial Judge or the members of the Court of Appeal were directed to the point.

The question, however, is not a new one. It was raised before the Court of Appeal in *A-G Can. v. Krause*, [1956] OR 675, 3 DLR (2d) 400, and (to my mind) there deliberately answered. There the subject of controversy was a claim of title by possession. The judgment was delivered by Roach JA, who stated at p. 691 OR, p. 408 DLR:

> The occupation, the holding or enjoying contemplated by The Nullum Tempus Act and which would bar the Crown, is such as would constitute a civil possession against a subject owner: see the reasons of Duff J, as he then was, in *Hamilton et al. v. The King* (1917), 54 SCR 331 at 371, 35 DLR 226. This means that throughout the statutory period as against the Crown, there must have been, if the defendant is to succeed, (1) exclusive occupation in the physical sense, i.e., detention, and (2) the *animus possidendi*.

As to the meaning of *animus possidendi*, the observation of Lord Lindley MR, in *Littledale v. Liverpool College*, [1900] 1 Ch. 19 at p. 23, is most instructive. The particular passage to which I refer reads as follows:

> They could not be dispossessed unless the plaintiffs obtained possession themselves; and possession by the plaintiffs involves an *animus possidendi*—i.e., occupation with the intention of excluding the owner as well as other people.

Confirmation for what has been said as to the meaning of *animus possidendi* by Lord Lindley is to be found in Black's Law Dictionary, 4th ed. (1951), p. 114, as follows: "*Animus Possidendi*. The intention of possessing."

New strength, I think, is given to definitions such as these when one passes to the decision of the Court of Appeal in *Krause v. Happy*, [1960] OR 385, 24 DLR (2d) 310. McGillivray JA, in delivering the judgment of the Court, quoted with approval the language of Roach JA, in the passage which I just cited from *A-G Can. v. Krause*. At p. 394 OR, p. 314 DLR, he goes on to discuss the evidence in these terms:

> That the evidence did not indicate *animus possidendi* of the plaintiffs' part is indicated by the testimony of Wm. Krause Sr. Referring to the property he said, "I wouldn't steal it from him" and "I didn't expect to get the land for nothing."

This observation, I think, suggests on its face that the Court was concerned with the question of intention in considering the burden upon the one seeking to establish title by possession.

I agree, therefore, with the trial Judge that the question whether there was an intention on the part of the appellants to dispossess the owner was a matter to be considered.

I have mentioned the fact that the weeping bed of the appellants' septic tank system was located in 1954 on the land in dispute. I can dispose in brief terms of a subsidiary point that emerged out of that fact. The point was neither in the pleadings nor argued in the Court below. In this Court, counsel for the appellants very faintly adumbrated the suggestion that by now (1974) there was here something which is [in] the nature of a proprietary interest. Counsel did not pursue the matter further. I assume without deciding that he was referring to something in the nature of an easement—a right to pass the septic tank overflow under the respondent's land; a right in respect of which the respondent's land had become (so to speak) a servient tenement. As I have said, the Court was not invited (for obvious reasons) to consider the matter and I express no view on it.

It remains for me to notice a second subsidiary point. It was argued by counsel for the appellants that an action shall not be deemed to have been brought within the meaning of the *Limitations Act* until notice of the application for first registration has been served on the appellants. The application for first registration was filed on or about March 8, 1972. Notice of the application was not served on the appellants until December 18, 1972. It was argued that at the latest there was adverse possession on the part of the appellants from the spring of 1962 onward and the action was not brought until December 18, 1972. Accordingly (it was said), the right of action had accrued at a date more than 10 years before the proceedings and therefore the respondent could not avail itself of the defence afforded by the *Limitations Act*.

An action is defined in s. 1(a) of the *Limitations Act* as follows:

> (a) "action" includes an information on behalf of the Crown and any civil proceedings;

It will at once be observed that the definition just quoted is an inclusive, rather than an exclusive, definition. If by virtue of filing an application for first registration a party becomes entitled to invoke the jurisdiction of the master of title in a matter relating to the title of land, then it seems *prima facie*, though I express no final view on the matter because it is unnecessary that an "action" within the meaning of the *Limitations Act* would cover an application for first registration. That, however, is unnecessary to decide because I am not prepared to differ from the judgment of the learned Judge in the Court below. I adopt and repeat here the final passage from that judgment:

> The conduct of the MacDonalds alleged to amount to possession was a series of acts over a number of years. Even if we assume that Annie Grant was not in possession, when did she have a right of action for recovery of her land as opposed to a right of action for trespass? I do not think that it can be said beyond a balance of probabilities that such a cause of action would have accrued to her or her successors more than 10 years before the filing of the application for first registration herein. Indeed, the evidence before me indicates that such a cause of action could not possibly have been maintained before the planting of the lawn in the spring of 1962. The exact date of such planting was not established by the MacDonalds, but it is unlikely that it would have been done as early as March. It seems to me that the cumulative effect of the acts of the MacDonalds would have given Annie Grant a right of action for recovery of the disputed lands sometime in 1965 when the bird-house was erected, and the hull and trailer parked on the disputed property. This is far short of the 10 years required under the statute.

For these reasons I would dismiss the appeal.

Appeal dismissed.

Discussion Notes

The Test for Dispossession

Identify the test used in this case to decide whether the appellants had established "dispossession" according to the Limitations Act. What is the effect of using the test of "dispossession *and* discontinuance" in the judgment as opposed to "dispossession *or* discontinuance," which is found in s. 5(1) of the Act? What element of the test has been added by this decision? How would you describe the difference in the intent of the appellants here from that of Ms Piper in *Piper v. Stevenson*? Is this difference critical to the reasoning or the outcome? Is this difference consistent with the common law principles regarding possessory interests or with the underlying purposes of "adverse" possession principles proposed by Callaghan and Rose?

Possessory Claims Among Co-Owners

The issue of the commencement of the limitation period arises in a variety of circumstances. In two kinds of cases, for example, family "arrangements" may lead to such
claims. First, where a number of persons are jointly entitled to property but only a few
of them have actual possession, those in possession may claim that the running of the
limitation period has extinguished the rights of those out of possession to recover possession. This fact pattern occurs typically when a parent dies, leaving a will designating
joint interests to the children, and then some children remain at home while others leave.
What is the appropriate test for determining whether those out of possession "discontinued" possession or were "dispossessed" by those remaining at home? Is mere possession
sufficient, or do those in possession have to act so as to clearly show an intent to
dispossess those not in actual possession. For a case that held that the limitation period
started to run when two sisters remained in possession of the family farm after their
father died, having left the farm to them and to other siblings jointly, and the other
siblings remained out of possession, see *Paradise Beach and Transportation Co. Ltd. v.
Price-Robinson*, a decision of the Privy Council on appeal from the Bahamas, [1968]
AC 1072 (PC). Lord Upjohn very clearly rejected the idea that the statute required
anything more than mere possession to start the limitation period, and stated that there
was no requirement of "adversity" (an adverse intent?), stating at 1084:

> It seems to their Lordships clear from the language of the Act and the authorities already
> referred to that subject to the qualification mentioned below where the right of entry has
> accrued more than 20 years before action brought the co-tenants are barred and their
> title is extinguished whatever the nature of the co-tenants' possession. That right of
> entry ... accrued in 1913 [the date of the father's death].

For relevant statutory definitions regarding joint possession and the commencement of
the limitation period, see Limitations Act, RSO 1990, c. L.15, s. 11; Limitation of Actions Act, RSNS 1989, c. 258, s. 15; Limitation of Actions Act, RSNB 1973, c. L-8,
s. 32; Statute of Limitations, RSPEI 1988, c. S-7, s. 33; Limitation of Realty Actions
Act, RSN 1990, c. L-16, s. 13.

In Ontario, the issue of possessory claims among co-owners was considered in *Re
O'Reilly (No.2)* (1980), 28 OR (2d) 481 (HCJ), aff'd. (1981), 33 OR (2d) 352 (CA). In
that case, the Ontario Court of Appeal applied the equitable principle of "laches" to bar
the claim of beneficiaries "who had allowed their siblings to run a farm, with all its
obligations for 33 years." For a good overview of the relationship between the equitable
principle of laches and statutes of limitation, see G. Creighton, "Equitable Limitations,"
in *Limitation of Actions* (Toronto: Canadian Bar Association—Ontario, 1985). According to Creighton (at 4), these equitable principles are not strictly limitations: "In no case
is a certain period prescribed, following which no proceeding may be brought. Rather,
on general principle it may become unconscionable to allow enforcement of a right in
equity after an effluxion of time." Thus, since the basis for such a principle is unconscionability, there will be more flexibility (and less certainty) about when such a claim
may be sustained. By contrast, the statutes of limitation provide greater certainty in
defining the length of time after which claims by a true owner are extinguished. Is it

accurate to say that there is no flexibility in the application of the statutes of limitation? Is there a continuing need for the equitable principle? In what circumstances?

Possessory Claims and the Tenancy at Will

A second example concerning the commencement of the limitation period occurs in family "arrangements" to occupy land or premises with permission of the paper title holder. Such permission may create a tenancy at will, and statutes of limitation generally provide that the limitation period commences one year after the tenancy at will was created. For example, s. 5(7) of the Ontario Limitations Act, RSO 1990, c. L.15 provides:

> 5(7) Where a person is in possession or in receipt of the profits of any land, or in receipt of any rent, as tenant at will, the right of the person entitled subject thereto, or of the person through whom that person claims, to make an entry or distress, or to bring an action to recover the land or rent, shall be deemed to have first accrued either at the determination of the tenancy, or at the expiration of one year after the commencement of the tenancy, at which time the tenancy shall be deemed to have determined.

Consider the operation of similar provisions in the Nova Scotia case that follows, noting in particular the extent to which the court's test includes an element of intention:

MacLean v. Reid
(1978), 94 DLR (3d) 118 (NS SC AD)

MacDONALD JA: At issue in this appeal is in effect the title to, ownership of, or possession of a farm property comprising approximately 50 acres located at Dean's Settlement, Upper Mosquodoboit, Halifax County.

The respondent, David Reid, is now about 68 years of age and has resided on the property his entire life (it being the Reid homestead property) with the exception of a six-month period in the 1960's and another period around 1950 when he was working in Pictou County. On the latter occasion he returned to the homestead on week-ends.

The property was conveyed to the father of the respondent in 1915. By deed dated June 10, 1935, and registered on January 15, 1936, the parents of the respondent conveyed the lands to the latter's brother, Clarence Reid. Clarence Reid and his wife in turn deeded the property to the appellants Edward and Leona MacLean by conveyance dated November 8, 1971, and registered on July 31, 1972.

The appellants brought action against the respondent asking for an order requiring the latter to vacate the lands; an injunction restraining him from entering the lands and damages. The respondent raised as his principal defence that he had acquired title to the property by adverse possession. In other words, that Clarence Reid's title to the property was extinguished by virtue of the *Statute of Limitations*, RSNS 1967, c. 168, because the respondent had been in possession of the property as a tenant at will of Clarence Reid for a period in excess of 21 years. The respondent counterclaimed against the appellants for relief similar to that claimed against him by them.

The respondent testified that his brother Clarence told him in 1936 that "I could stay there [on the property] as long as I liked." The trial Judge, the Honourable Mr. Justice A.M. MacIntosh, found that the appellants were not *bona fide* purchasers for value without notice of the respondent's interest in the lands and held that the latter had an interest therein equivalent to a life tenancy. From such decision, the appellants appeal and the respondent cross-appeals.

In this reserved decision the learned trial Judge said in part:

The plaintiff testified as to the movements of Clarence Reid vis-à-vis the Reid farm from the time he received the deed, i.e. 1935, until their purchase of same in 1971. Where there is any conflict of evidence, I accept the defendant's version as to the brother's whereabouts and his own dealings with the homestead.

The defendant stated that he has spent all his life to the present time on this family farm. From 1935 until 1968 he farmed the property, raising cattle, sheep, poultry, grain and vegetable crops. He bought and paid for all the farm machinery. He kept the cattle in a lean-to he built onto the barn. He also purchased a horse stable and moved it onto the property. From 1935 onwards he paid the municipal taxes.

From 1935 to 1940 the defendant's brother, Clarence Reid, worked as a woodsman, returning to the farm on week-ends. He never farmed the property. In 1940 he joined the Canadian Army and proceeded overseas. At the conclusion of hostilities he returned home for a short while, leaving to reside permanently in Ireland some time during 1946. Nothing was done by him relative to the farm until 1971 when he conveyed whatever interest he possessed to the plaintiffs.

The defendant stated that he was told by his brother that he, the defendant, could remain on the farm all his lifetime. He never knew that his brother had title by deed.

• • •

In pursuance of his agreement with his brother, the defendant stayed on the farm property, operating, maintaining and improving same, and while they were living, provided a home for his mother and sister. This period of time commenced in 1935. In 1971 the brother conveyed whatever interest he had in the property to the plaintiff.

The learned trial Judge made no mention in his decision of the respondent's claim that he had acquired title to the lands by adverse possession. That issue is therefore at large before us and, in my opinion, for reasons I shall give, is decisive of this appeal. The pertinent sections of the *Statute of Limitations* are ss. 9 and 10(f) which provide:

9. No person shall make an entry or distress, or bring an action to recover any land or rent, but within twenty years next after the time at which the right to make such entry or distress or to bring such action first accrued to some person through whom he claims, or if such right did not accrue to any person through whom he claims, then within twenty years next after the time at which the right to make such entry or distress, or to bring such action, first accrued to the person making or bringing the same.

10. In the construction of this Act the right to make an entry or distress, or bring an action to recover any land or rent, shall be deemed to have first accrued at such time as hereinafter as mentioned, that is to say:

• • •

(f) where any person is in possession or in receipt of the profits of any land, or in recept of any rent as tenant at will, the right of the person entitled subject thereto, or the person through whom he claims, to make any entry, or distress, or bring an action to recover such land or rent, shall be deemed to have first accrued either at the determination of such tenancy, or at the expiration of one year next after the commencement of such tenancy, at which time such tenancy shall be deemed to have determined.

At the time of the conveyance to Clarence Reid his father was not living on or farming the lands. After receiving the deed to the property Clarence Reid did not farm the lands but did live there on week-ends.

At the time of the conveyance of the lands to Clarence Reid the respondent was occupying and working them. Upon being told by Clarence that he could stay on the lands as long as he liked the respondent did so. The learned trial Judge has accurately detailed the nature of the respondent's occupation of the lands and the activities he carried on. ...

[MacDonald JA referred to a number of other authorities concerning tenancies at will and the operation of statutes of limitation and then continued:]

Returning to the present case the facts indicate:

1. *That* when Clarence Reid received the deed to the property in question the respondent was then in occupation of it as he had been all his life.

2. *That* in 1936 Clarence Reid told the respondent that he could live on the property as long as he liked.

3. *That* the respondent paid the real property taxes on the property from 1935-36 to approximately 1966 and made certain improvements and did the other things alluded to by the trial judge.

4. *That* the respondent did not pay rent to his brother Clarence nor was any demanded of him.

5. The respondent testified that about two years or "a little better than that" before the trial (January 21, 1977) he received a letter from his brother Clarence that he was planning on selling the land.

6. The appellant Edward MacLean testified that he purchased one piece of property from Clarence Reid in 1966 and that with respect to the property here involved Clarence wrote him in 1970 and "wanted to sell it to me."

7. Attached to the deed from Fred Reid and his wife to Clarence Reid, dated June 10, 1935, is a note dated May 17, 1971, written by either Clarence Reid or his wife. This note states:

To Whome [sic] it may concern

I, Clarence Reid, have sold the property in this will to:

Edward McLean
RR No. 1, Upper Musquodoboit,
Halifax Co.,
Nova Scotia
Canada

Signed

Clarence Reid
Ballyduff
Thurles
Co. Tipperary
Ireland

Obviously Clarence Reid thought he could convey the property to Mr. MacLean by attaching the foregoing note to the original deed to himself. Mr. MacLean advised him that the transfer could not be affected in such manner and had the deed of November 8, 1971, prepared and executed by Clarence Reid and his wife.

8. The appellant Edward MacLean had lived in the Dean Settlement area since the 1920s and was well acquainted with David Reid. Mr. MacLean testified that in 1935 Fred Reid, the father of David and Clarence lived across the road from the lands in question and in fact never occupied them thereafter.

9. The appellant Edward MacLean testified that he knew that the respondent David Reid lived on the lands in question from at least 1935 to the time of trial.

10. The appellant Edward MacLean said in evidence that he has been paying taxes on the property since 1966.

Section 12 of the *Statute of Limitations* of this Province provides:

> 12. No person shall be deemed to have been in possession of any land, within the meaning of this Act merely by reason of having made an entry thereon.

I refer to this section because there is evidence that Clarence Reid spent week-ends at the property during the years 1935 to 1940 and certainly made an entry on it upon his return from overseas in 1945. There is absolutely no evidence that the permission given by Clarence to David that the latter could stay on the lands as long as he liked was ever revoked or rescinded by Clarence unless the letter referred to earlier wherein he advised David that he was planning to sell the property could be construed as a determination of the tenancy.

In *McCowan et al. v. Armstrong* (1902), 3 OLR 100, Meredith CJCP said at pp. 104-6:

> The defendant has continued in possession of the farm ever since he entered on it, occupying it for his own benefit, and having the exclusive enjoyment of the profits of it. His possession, occupation, and enjoyment of it differed in no respect, as far as was apparent to others, from those of an owner in possession; he paid no rent and rendered no service or other return for it, and gave no acknowledgement of his father's title.
>
> While he has been in possession he has made valuable permanent improvements in clearing, draining, fencing, and otherwise improving the farm, as well as in the erection of buildings upon it; these improvements represent at least half the present value of the farm, though they cost more than that; and they have all been made at the expense of the defendant, except that in the first year or two of his possession the father gave him some timber which was required for a building which the defendant was then erecting.
>
> On the state of facts, I am of opinion that the right and title of the testator to the lands in question had, long before his death, by force of the Real Property Limitation Act (RSO 1897 c. 133), become extinguished.

The defendant became, upon his entry with the permission of his father, a tenant at will, and the father's right of entry is to be deemed to have first accrued either at the determination of that tenancy or at the expiration of one year next after the commencement of it (which ever first happened): sec. 5, sub-sec. 7; and as it does not appear thus far that the tenancy was ever in fact determined, the father's right of entry was barred at the expiration of eleven years from the commencement of the tenancy, and his right and title to the lands was then extinguished. . . .

The facts to which I have alluded, considered in light of the authorities cited, lead me to the conclusion that the respondent David Reid became a tenant at will of his brother Clarence in 1936 and that such tenancy by operation of s. 10(f) of the *Statute of Limitations* was determined one year later. If I am in error as to the time of determination of such tenancy because Clarence Reid made a re-entry onto the lands and possibly took possession of them in 1945 then, in my opinion, at that time a new tenancy at will was created which was determined by statute no later than 1947.

I would now refer to s. 21 of the *Statute of Limitations* which provides:

21. At the determination of the period limited by this Act to any person for making an entry, or distress, or bringing any action, the right and title of such person to the land or rent, for the recovery whereof such entry, distress, or action respectively might have been made or brought within such period, shall be extinguished.

In my opinion the respondent David Reid was a tenant at will of Clarence Reid from no later than 1946. That tenancy expired by operation of s. 10(f) of the *Statute of Limitations* a year later in 1947. From that time on the respondent had, to the knowledge of the appellants, actual, exclusive, continuous, open, visible and notorious possession of the lands in question. This possession extinguished the right and title thereto of the registered owner, Clarence Reid, and consequently of the appellants, no later than 1968. The result is that the respondent is entitled to possession of the lands in question with a title resting on the absence of the right of others to eject him.

For other similar fact situations where courts have applied statutes of limitation in the context of family "arrangements," see *Hoyt v. Hoyt* (1990), 101 NBR (2d) 436(QB TD); *Casey v. Canada Trust Co.* (1960), 25 DLR (2d) 764 (Ont. HCJ); and *Train v. Metzger* (1974), 51 DLR (3d) 24 (HCJ). For other provincial statutory provisions concerning limitation periods and tenancies at will, see Limitation of Actions Act, RSNS 1989, c. 258, s. 11(f); Limitation of Actions Act, RSNB 1973, c. L-8, s. 43(1); Statute of Limitations Act, RSPEI 1988, c. S-7, s. 30(1); and Limitation of Realty Actions Act, RSN 1990, c. L-16, s. 8(1).

Commencement of Limitation Period in the Context of Legal Disability

There are numerous statutory provisions concerning the commencement of the limitation period when a person in possession is under a legal disability—for example, because of mental infirmity or because the person is a minor (a status that may differ among provinces based on the applicable legislation). For one example, see Limitations Act, RSO 1990, c. L.15, ss.36-39.

The Limitation Period and Leaseholds: Fairweather v. St. Marylebone Property Co. Ltd.

A different kind of issue concerning the running of limitation periods and tenancies occurred in *Fairweather v. St. Marylebone Property Co. Ltd.*, [1963] AC 510 (HL). In that case, the paper title holder in 1893 leased a plot of land to a tenant for 99 years (a common arrangement in the United Kingdom), and then M in 1920 possessed a shed partly on the tenant's plot and partly on the adjoining plot owned by M. The limitation period was 12 years, and there was general agreement that the tenant's right to recover possession had been extinguished therefore by 1932. As a result, M claimed a right to use the shed until 1992, the year when the 99-year-lease would come to an end. However, the tenant surrendered the lease to the lessor in 1959, thereby terminating the leasehold arrangement. As Lord Denning MR stated, the statute declared that the tenant's "title" had been extinguished in 1932, but it was unclear exactly what that meant. After examining several alternatives, he decided that the effect of the statute of limitations in this situation was that the tenant's right was extinguished as against M, but that time would not start to run against the lessor's interest until the expiry of the lease, in 1992 rather than 1932. Because the tenant in this case had surrendered the lease to the lessor, however, the tenancy had ended prematurely in 1959. As Lord Denning MR explained at 547:

> If the lessee surrenders his term, the freeholder is at once entitled to evict the trespasser for the simple reason that, on the surrender, the lease is determined, and there is no bar whatever to the freeholder recovering possession: see *Ecclesiastical Commissioners of England and Wales v. Rowe*. And I see no reason why the same reasoning should not apply even though, at the date of the surrender, the trespasser is a squatter who has been there more than 12 years. For, as against the freeholder, he is still a trespasser. The freeholder's right to possession does not arise until the lease is determined by the surrender. It then comes into being and time begins to run against him under section 6(1) of the Limitation Act, 1939.
>
> The only reason, it seems to me, which can be urged against this conclusion is that it means that a squatter's title can be destroyed by the leaseholder and freeholder putting their heads together. It is said that they can by a surrender—or by a surrender and regrant—destroy the squatter's title completely and get rid of him. So be it. There is no way of preventing it. But I would point out that, if we were to deny the two of them this right, they could achieve the same result in another way. They could easily do it by the leaseholder submitting to a forfeiture. If the leaseholder chooses not to pay the rent, the freeholder can determine the lease under the proviso for re-entry. The squatter cannot stop him. He cannot pay the rent without the authority of the leaseholder. He cannot apply for relief against forfeiture. The squatter's title can thus be defeated by a forfeiture—or by a forfeiture and regrant—just as it can by a surrender—or by a surrender and regrant. So there is nothing in the point.
>
> My Lords, so far as these questions under the Limitation Acts are concerned, I must say that I see no difference between a surrender or merger or a forfeiture. On each of those events the lease is determined and the freeholder is entitled to evict the squatter, even though the squatter has been on the land during the lease for more than 12 years: and on the determination of the lease, time then begins to run against the freeholder.

If the tenant's "title" to the shed was extinguished in 1932, what "rights" were available to be surrendered to the lessor in 1959? Is this a case where there is tension between principles of possession on the one hand and policy concerns about trespassers and squatters? Does the element of intention play a role in Lord Denning's decision? In exploring these questions, consider the following excerpt from the report of the UK Law Reform Committee that examined the *Fairweather* case in 1977.

> We also invited comments on the decision of the House of Lords in *St. Marylebone Property Co. Ltd. v. Fairweather*, where it was held that a lessee whose own title had been extinguished by adverse possession could nevertheless, by surrendering the lease, enable his lessor to evict the squatter. The evidence we received revealed a considerable difference of opinion among those who commented on this decision. Those who disapproved of it argued that, as a matter of logic, the lessee could, once his title was extinguished, have nothing left to surrender and that, therefore, no action on his part should be allowed to prejudice the squatter. They accordingly suggested that the squatter ought to be entitled to remain in possession for the remainder of the term. Those who supported the decision thought that the law should not assist squatters and that the rule declared by the House of Lords could not cause any injustice, because the squatter would not, at the time of taking adverse possession, have any knowledge of the duration or conditions of the lease and would, therefore, have no expectation of remaining in possession for any particular time.
>
> We have not been able to reach a decided view on this difficult issue and we are about equally divided on it. Some of us feel that an amendment of the law under which the lessor obtained no greater rights by virtue of a surrender of the lease than he would by virtue of an assignment would produce a more logical situation. The contrary view is that, although the law is not entirely satisfactory, ... no alternative is likely to be more satisfactory. Further, since the situation arises but rarely and since a carefully drawn covenant would anyhow circumvent a statutory reversal of the *St. Marylebone* decision, there is not sufficient justification for a change in the law. In view of the disagreement, we make no recommendation on the point.

(United Kingdom, "Twenty-First Report–Final Report on Limitation of Actions," Cmnd. 6923 (London: HMSO, 1977), at 43-44 (footnotes omitted).) Do the purposes identified by Callaghan and Rose for this area of property law point to any solution in this context?

The Quality of Possession Under Statutes of Limitation

There are many examples of cases where the issue was whether the acts of a possessor were sufficient to trigger the commencement of a limitation period. As well, there are cases about whether the possessor's actions were sufficiently continuous during the limitation period, and whether the possessor's actions related to all or only part of the land held by the paper title holder. These issues are generally considered in terms of the nature of the land and its appropriate use (including seasonal use, for example), as was demonstrated by *Re St. Clair Beach Estates Ltd. v. MacDonald* (1974), 5 OR (2d) 482 (HCJ Div. Ct.). For other examples, see *Walker v. Russell* (1966), 53 DLR (2d) 509 (Ont. HCJ) and

Georgia-Pacific Resins Inc. v. Blair (1991), 121 NBR (2d) 349 (QB TD). There is also a helpful list of cases in Mendes da Costa, Balfour, and Gillese, *Property Law: Cases, Text, and Materials*, 2d ed. (Toronto: Emond Montgomery, 1990), at 12:34-35. In *Leichner v. Canada* (1997), 31 OR (3d) 700 (CA), the Ontario Court of Appeal allowed an appeal by the federal Crown, denying the plaintiff's claim to possession in relation to a strip of land along the Rideau Canal, part of the Federal Crown Reserve. In part, the decision was based on the absence of acts by the plaintiff sufficient to show actual possession and an intention to exclude the true owner. Even though the plaintiff's predecessors in title had fenced the property, Rosenberg JA held (at 709) that "line fencing to protect pasture or keep in cattle and not done for the purpose of taking possession is not sufficient to establish possessory title." In this case, the fencing was not along the shoreline and did not prevent members of the public from gaining access to the Canal for swimming. Can you distinguish this case from *Piper v. Stevenson*? How?

The Element of Intention

The issue of intention on the part of the paper title holder was significant in *Keefer v. Arillotta* (1976), 13 OR (2d) 680 (CA). In examining the majority and dissenting views in the Ontario Court of Appeal on this issue, reflect again on the tension between principles about possession at common law and the underlying purposes of statutes of limitation. How does the test of "inconsistent user" adopted in *Keefer* resolve this tension?

Keefer v. Arillotta
(1976), 13 OR (2d) 680 (CA)

WILSON JA: This is an appeal from an order of His Honour Judge Nicholls holding that the respondents had acquired a possessory title to a portion of the appellants' land subject to an easement remaining in the appellants.

The facts are more fully set out in the reasons for judgment of the learned trial Judge but the more significant ones for purposes of this appeal may be summarized under the following headings:

1. The nature and location of the land in issue;
2. The chain of title;
3. The conduct of the owners.

The Nature and Location of the Land in Issue

It is unnecessary to describe the land by its metes and bounds description. Suffice it to say that it is a narrow strip of land 8 ft. wide by 105 ft. deep running between the residential property of the respondents to the south and the business premises of the appellants to the north. The most easterly 41 ft. of the strip running back from the street line is a stone driveway. Extending westward from the driveway is a grassy area running up to a frame garage owned by the respondents and located at the rear of the strip. A concrete walk-way adjacent to the appellants' store runs up the side of the store alongside the stone driveway to a set of steps which lead up to a concrete landing giving access to an apartment located over the store. To the west of the steps and concrete landing is an entrance door to an addition which was built on to the rear of the store in 1949 by the appellants' predecessors in title.

[The following figure is the author's—it is not part of the original case:]

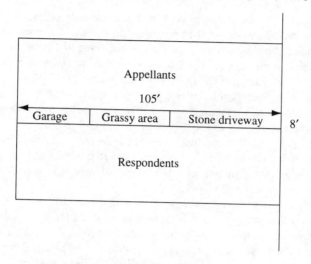

The Chain of Title

The appellants' and the respondents' properties were initially owned by one Martin Cloy. In 1918 Mr. Cloy conveyed the property now owned by the respondents to one Elzear Lynch together with a right of way of ingress and egress over a portion of his own property, the strip of land in issue on this appeal. In each subsequent conveyance of that property, including the conveyance made in July of 1957 to the respondents, the right of way over the appellants' land was granted.

When Mr. Cloy died in July of 1921, the land he had retained, now owned by the appellants, passed to his widow Maude Cloy who was also his executrix. As executrix she conveyed it to herself as devisee under the will but inadvertently included in the conveyance the lands already conveyed by her husband to Mr. Lynch. To rectify this error Mrs. Cloy made a new deed to Mrs. Lynch, who had acquired the land on her husband's death, and this deed made in April of 1926, included the grant of right of way over the strip of Mrs. Cloy's land. In November of 1952, Mrs. Cloy transferred her land to her son Douglas Cloy and again through inadvertence omitted to make that conveyance subject to the right of way in favour of Mrs. Lynch. Douglas Cloy remedied this in March of 1958 by a quitclaim deed in favour of the respondents who by that time had become the owners of the adjoining land. In August of 1972, when Douglas Cloy sold his property to the appellants' predecessors in title, he made the grant subject to the respondents' right of way and, when they in turn sold it to the appellants in February, 1973, they likewise made their grant subject to the respondents' right of way. ...

The Conduct of the Owners

The learned trial Judge made a number of important findings with respect to the use of the strip of land made over the years by the owners of the two adjoining properties.

(a) The Respondents and Their Predecessors in Title

Since the respondents' property has always been used as a dwelling-house, the main use of the strip made by the owners of that property has been as a driveway. Up until about 1956, the respondents' car was kept in the garage but since that time the garage has been used as a storage shed and the car has been left on the driveway at night. Although the respondent Mr. Keefer uses the car to go back and forth to work, it is also sometimes parked in the driveway during the day and so occasionally are the cars belonging to the respondents' friends when they come to visit. The trial Judge found that in the 1960s a disabled car was left at the rear of the driveway for some four years.

The trial Judge found also that the Keefers on several occasions had put gravel on the driveway at their own expense. They also kept it free of snow in the winter-time. This may not be significant since they have a right of way over it and the Cloys closed down the store every winter and went to Florida.

As far as the grassy area to the west of the stone driveway is concerned, the evidence disclosed that the grass had for many years been tended by the owners of the respondents' property, including the respondents themselves, and that the respondents occasionally held barbecues and picnics on it with no objection from the Cloys. The evidence that the Keefers made a skating-rink of part of the grassy area on three winters does not appear to be significant since it was when the Cloys were wintering in Florida. The evidence, however, that no objection was made by Mr. Cloy when in 1952 Mr. Keefer moved the garage located at the rear of his property over onto the rear of the strip in order to line it up with the driveway is clearly significant.

(b) The Appellants and Their Predecessors in Title

The appellants' premises have always been used for business purposes, first in Martin Cloy's time as a grocery store and later by Douglas Cloy as a marine supply store for vessels plying up and down the Welland Canal. Since 1972, when Douglas Cloy sold the property to the respondents' predecessors in title, it has been used as a general variety store. Douglas Cloy was assisting his father in the business prior to the conveyance to Elzear Lynch and gave evidence on behalf of the appellants as to the use made by his parents and himself of the property from 1918 to 1972. The Cloys never lived on this property.

The strip of land was used by the Cloys in the early days to give access to an ice-house at the rear of the store. The ice-house was filled in the winter with blocks of ice cut from the Welland Canal. Deliveries were made from it originally by means of a horse and wagon and later by truck. In 1949 the ice-house was removed and a one-storey addition was built on to the rear of the store. The addition was used partly as an office and partly for the storage of soft drinks. Access to the addition was through a door to the west of the stone steps and landing which provided access to the apartment over the store. Soft drinks were delivered by truck to the storeroom. If there was a car parked in the driveway, the soft drinks would be taken by a small hand-cart; if the driveway was clear, the truck would drive up to the entrance door to make its deliveries.

Mr. Cloy testified that he never parked his car in the driveway but that trucks parked there occasionally when unloading supplies if the driveway was clear. Mr. Cloy's customers also sometimes parked in the driveway for short periods of time when making purchases.

The tenants of the apartment above the store entered from the street by the concrete walk-way running alongside the driveway, but the one tenant who owned a car did not leave his car in the driveway. Moving trucks used the driveway and, when tenants were moving in or out, the Keefers always moved their car if it happened to be in the driveway at the time. The owners used the walk-way to visit the apartment. They also used a portion of the grassy area to get to and from the side entrance to the storage and office premises built on to the rear of the store in 1949.

Mr. Cloy testified that both he and his father had put gravel on the driveway over the years, but he acknowledged that the last time he had put gravel on was probably in 1956. Because of the store's being closed in the winters from December to March every year when he and his family went to Florida, no trucks or customers' cars would be parked in the driveway during the winter months. His evidence was that they had been wintering in Florida for the past 18 years.

The Issue

His Honour Judge Nicholls, after reviewing the evidence of user by both owners over the years, stated:

> The possession [of the plaintiffs and their predecessors in title] was not consistent with the rights accruing from the specific grant of right of way but far exceeded them.
> Counsel for the plaintiff expressed the opinion that the grant of right of way matured into a possessory title.

He also stated:

> The possession of the plaintiffs and their predecessors in title was open, visible and continuous for far more than the requisite number of years, but the question arises as to whether there was exclusive possession.

With all due respect to the learned trial Judge, I believe that the crucial question in this case is whether the respondents' possession challenged in any way the right of the legal owner to make the use of the property he wished to make of it. This is not a case where the Keefers could be viewed as trespassers on their neighbours' property so that any act of theirs on the property was a challenge to the constructive possession of the owners. Possession is not adverse to the extent it is referable to a lawful title: *Thomas v. Thomas* (1855), 2 K & J 79 at p. 83, 69 ER 701, *per* Sir William Page Wood VC. The Keefers were on their neighbours' property pursuant to their grant of right of way and, even if they exceeded the rights they had by virtue of the right of way, this would not necessarily mean that their right of way matured into a possessory title.

The use an owner wants to make of his property may be a limited use and an intermittent or sporadic use. A possessory title cannot, however, be acquired against him by depriving him of uses of his property that he never intended or desired to make of it. The *animus possidendi* which a person claiming a possessory title must have is an intention to exclude the owner from such uses as the owner wants to make of his property.

Viewed in this light the evidence that the Cloys never parked their car or truck on the strip of land, far from being helpful to the respondents' case, is harmful to it. It shows that the Cloys never intended or wanted to use the strip for parking. Indeed, this is clear from the fact that they gave the owner of the adjoining property a right of ingress and egress over it. Similarly, the fact that the respondents created a skating-rink on the grassy area in the winter-time when the appellants were in Florida has in my view no real significance in terms of the ouster of the true owner. The true owner was probably quite content to give the Keefers full rein on the property while the store was not in operation. The trial Judge was obviously correct in his finding that, even when the appellants were operating the store, the respondents were using the strip for more than just a means of ingress and egress to their property. I do not believe, however, that this is the test for the acquisition of a possessory title. The test is not whether the respondents exceeded their rights under the right of way but whether they precluded the owner from making the use of the property that he wanted to make of it: *Re St. Clair Beach Estates Ltd. v. MacDonald et al.* (1974), 5 OR (2d) 482, 50 DLR (3d) 650. Acts relied on as dispossessing the true owner must be inconsistent with the form of enjoyment of the property intended by the true owner. This has been held to be the test for adverse possession since the leading case of *Leigh v. Jack* (1879), 5 Ex.D 264.

The onus of establishing title by possession is on the claimant and it is harder for a claimant to discharge this onus when he is on the property pursuant to a grant from the owner. It was held in *Littledale v. Liverpool College*, [1900] 1 Ch. 19 that acts done on another's land may be attributed to the exercise of an easement, even an excessive exercise of an easement, rather than to adverse possession of the fee.

In *Pflug and Pflug v. Collins*, [1952] OR 519 at p. 527, [1952] 3 DLR 681 at p. 689 [affirmed [1953] OWN 140; [1953] 1 DLR 841], Mr. Justice Wells (as he then was) made it clear that a person claiming a possessory title must establish (1) actual possession for the statutory period by themselves and those through whom they claim; (2) that such possession was with the intention of excluding from possession the owner or persons entitled to possession; and (3) discontinuance of possession for the statutory period by the owner and all others, if any, entitled to possession. If he fails in any one of these respects, his claim fails.

In my view the respondents fail in both (2) and (3) above. I do not believe that while the Cloys owned the strip of property in issue the Keefers ever intended to oust them from the limited use they wanted to make of it. The evidence discloses that the relationship between the Cloys and the Keefers was excellent and that there never was any trouble with the respondents when delivery trucks occasionally used the driveway for unloading supplies, when customers parked for short periods on the driveway when making purchases at the store, when tenants were moved in and out of the upstairs apartment and when they came and went to the apartment. Nor did Douglas Cloy take any exception to the Keefers parking their car in the driveway. Why would he, even if it were an excessive use of the right of way, if it did not impede him in the use he wanted to make of the property? His whole posture appears to have been that of an accommodating neighbour anxious to avoid any trouble. This is clear from the one contentious incident disclosed by the evidence, i.e., the incident when one of Mr. Cloy's tenants in the upstairs apartment left his car in the driveway and had a "run-in" with Mr. Keefer. When his tenant reported this to him, Mr. Cloy told him to park somewhere else because "I do not want to fight with my neighbours."

The evidence of Mr. Keefer was "I never had any problems with Doug (Mr. Cloy) as far as the drive-way was concerned." He testified that on one occasion Mr. Cloy left his car in the driveway overnight so that he was unable to get his car out in the morning. He therefore pushed Mr. Cloy's car out onto the road and Mr. Cloy apparently made no objection to his having done that. I cannot attach great significance to this as evidencing an assertion of possessory title by the Keefers since the Cloys, having given the Keefers a right of ingress and egress, had no right to block Mr. Keefer's egress. Mr. Keefer was perfectly entitled to do what he did. I cannot find on the evidence that the Keefers' possession was with the intention of excluding the Cloys from the limited use they wanted to make of the property. I think that the issue of a possessory title is something that has arisen since the Cloy's property changed hands and the hitherto amicable relations between the adjoining owners disintegrated.

As far as proof of the discontinuance of possession by the owner is concerned, I do not believe that the Cloys did discontinue their possession of any part of the strip of land other than the portion at the rear occupied by the respondents' garage. I think that with respect to that portion the constructive possession of the owners was displaced by the actual possession of the Keefers for more than the statutory period. However, as far as the balance of the strip is concerned, I think the owners made such use of it as they wanted. It was used as an access to the apartment above the store and to the entrance to the addition at the rear of the store. It is true that the Cloys may not have used the full width of the strip for this purpose, but the authorities make it clear that the constructive possession which a legal owner has of the whole of his property is not ousted simply because he is not in actual possession of the whole. Possession of part is possession of the whole if the possessor is the legal owner: *Great Western R Co. v. Lutz* (1881), 32 UCCP 166. I find, therefore, that the respondents have not discharged the onus of proving discontinuance of possession of the strip (other than the portion occupied by their garage) by the owners for the statutory period.

I would allow the appeal and hold the respondents entitled to a declaration that the appellants' title has been extinguished only with respect to that part of the land occupied by the respondents' garage.

The appellants should have their costs of the appeal.

MacKINNON JA (dissenting): The plaintiffs asked for a declaration that they are the owners of an eight-foot strip of land lying between their residence, known municipally as 57 Chapel St. S in the Town of Thorold, and the lands of the defendants immediately to the north, known municipally as 53 Chapel St. S. The defendants counterclaimed for a declaration that they are entitled to absolute possession and ownership of the strip of land, and for an injunction restraining the plaintiffs from using the said strip except as a right of way.

The plaintiffs were granted the requested declaration based on a title acquired by prescription and the counterclaim was dismissed. The defendants now appeal.

The issue as to whether a prescriptive right has been acquired is a question of fact and an appellate tribunal must be careful not to re-try such an issue on appeal: *Johnston et al. v. O'Neill et al.*, [1911] AC 552; *Godson Contracting Co. v. Grand Trunk RW Co.* (1917), 13 OWN 241. In the instant case the learned trial Judge heard some 11 witnesses, seven of whom gave evidence on behalf of the plaintiffs. After thoroughly canvassing the evidence, and accepting the evidence given on behalf of the plaintiffs, he made his finding of fact. There is no suggestion that he misunderstood the evidence and unless it is clear that he misunderstood or misapplied the relevant law, this Court should not interfere with his finding. ...

The plaintiffs have shown the necessary *animus possidendi* to support their claim, having the clear intention from the evidence of excluding the owner as well as all others. In the course of his reasons for judgment the learned trial Judge stated that the plaintiffs, with regard to the right of way, "treated it and used it as their own, notwithstanding the grant of right of way in their favour." Clear findings of fact as found by the learned trial Judge with evidence to support them, ought not to be disturbed or varied by this Court on appeal except for the most cogent of reasons. Accordingly, upon a finding of possession and the requisite *animus*, in order to stop the time from running there has to be some act by the holder of the paper title made *animo possidendi*. The intermittent and desultory acts of the owner, through having soft drinks delivered by hand carrier from time to time, without more, were not such, under the circumstances found by the trial Judge, as to stop the time from running.

In my view, the learned trial Judge was correct in holding that the title of the servient owners had been extinguished and that the plaintiffs have gained title by the fact of uninterrupted possession. There is none now who has the right to eject them. The possession here clearly was not equivocal or for a temporary purpose. By 1956 the plaintiffs had abandoned the use of the lands in issue as a right of way and the owner was under an obligation to assert his title to the land to prevent the time running against him, or to ask for a declaration that, because of the abandonment of the use as a right of way, the land had now reverted to him as owner free from any such use. The use made by the plaintiff was no longer referable to a lawful title but rather was totally inconsistent with it: *Thomas v. Thomas* (1855), 2 K & J 79, 69 ER 701. ...

Counsel for the plaintiffs agreed it would make more sense to extend due east to the street line the line running from the north wall of the frame garage to the south face of the precast concrete landing and steps. Such a line would be the north boundary of the land acquired by prescription.

Subject to this variation, I would dismiss the appeal with costs.

Appeal allowed.

Discussion Notes

Intention and Possessory Title

The majority judgment in *Keefer* suggests that where the paper title holder has no immediate wish to use land, a possessor's use will never be inconsistent with such (absence of)
intention. Such a principle means that land held "for future development" can never be
the subject of "dispossession" under statutes of limitation. Does this interpretation accord
with the purposes of these statutes as identified by Callaghan and Rose? What about the
possessor's intention? Does it matter that the plaintiffs knew that they were using their
neighbour's land? Would it have made any difference to the application of the inconsistent user test by Wilson J if the plaintiffs had been innocently mistaken as to the boundary
of their lot? In thinking about these questions, consider the following article criticizing
the use of intention in cases about possession and statutes of limitation.

Brian Bucknall, "Two Roads Diverged: Recent Decisions on Possessory Title"
(1984), 22 *Osgoode Hall Law Journal* 375 (footnotes omitted)

I. Introduction

Let *Piper v. Stevenson* serve as a starting point. In 1901, Miss Piper purchased six lots
from Mr. Whaley with the intention of setting up a farm. For some reason, Miss Piper
fenced in eight rather than six lots and began to farm them. She lived on another farm
during this period and went on the property only for the purposes of cultivating and
harvesting. In 1905 and 1906 she had buildings constructed and moved to her new farm.
In 1911, the holder of paper title to the two erroneously enclosed lots sold them to Mr.
Stevenson. Mr. Stevenson knocked down Miss Piper's fences and himself fenced off the
lands which Miss Piper thought she owned and Miss Piper sued successfully for a
declaration that she had acquired a possessory title.

Compare that result to the decision over sixty years later in *Masidon Investments
Ltd. v. Ham* [(1982), 39 OR (2d) 534 (HCJ), (1984), 45 OR 563 (CA)]. In 1958, Mr.
Ham, a lawyer in Oakville, rented a 100 acre parcel of land with the intention of using it
as his residence. The landlord apparently considered that the land was a long-term
speculation in real estate and had little concern for the actual use made by Mr. Ham. Mr.
Ham was a flying enthusiast and laid out a grassy airstrip suitable for use by light
planes. It was a fair weather field, with no electric light, radar or radio assistance. The
field did, however, become popular with other flyers and from time to time as many as
twelve planes would be parked there. Around 1967, Mr. Ham's landlord defaulted on his
mortgage on the property and an order of foreclosure was registered against the entire
100 acres. After some shuffling of papers, Mr. Ham's landlord re-acquired title to a fifty
acre parcel at the west end of the farm, which was the parcel on which Mr. Ham lived,
while Masidon Investments Ltd. held title to the fifty acre parcel at the east end of the
farm, which was the parcel on which Mr. Ham had established his airstrip. From 1968
on, Mr. Ham continued to occupy the entire 100 acres. He continued to fly planes from
the east half of the parcel, to use the buildings on that side of the parcel, to have the land

cultivated by neighbouring farmers, to maintain fences and to make minor improvements to his airstrip. In 1979, the owners of the east half of the parcel realized what had
been going on and brought action against Mr. Ham for a declaration that they owned the
lands and sued for punitive damages for his trespasses. Masidon was successful in its
suit for declaratory relief and it was held that Mr. Ham had not acquired possessory title.

The two cases provide some striking similarities. In both, vacant land was in question and the holders of paper title appeared to be indifferent to the steps taken by the
persons in possession. The legislation governing the claims brought in each case, the
Limitations Act, remained substantially the same over the entire period separating the
two decisions. On the bare facts, none of the "distinctions" so beloved of lawyers will
explain the contrast in results. One can only conclude that: *Piper v. Stevenson* was
wrongly decided, or *Masidon v. Ham* was wrongly decided, or the law has changed.

The hallmark of the decision in *Masidon* is the reliance which Mr. Justice
Carruthers, at the trial level, and Mr. Justice Blair on appeal, place on the doctrine of
adversity. He concluded that whatever action Mr. Ham took could not be inconsistent
with Masidon's intention to sell the land at a future date for development. Insofar as
Ham did not and, indeed, could not, do anything inconsistent with Masidon's intentions—because Masidon had no intention—Masidon's rights were inviolable. This
analysis, which on the face of it would appear to have been equally available in *Piper v.
Stevenson*, was not even mentioned in the earlier case.

Before one can conclude that the law has changed in the decades following *Piper v.
Stevenson*, one further decision should be considered. *Beaudoin v. Aubin* concerned a
dispute over a strip of land along the edge of a residential lot. Mr. Beaudoin and his wife
rented the home adjacent to the disputed strip of property in 1951. In 1966, they purchased the home. From 1951 on, however, they had occupied the subsequently disputed
strip on the assumption that it was their own. They learned at the time of their purchase
that the strip had actually been registered in the name of the adjoining property owners
but continued thereafter to use the lands as they had used them before. In 1979, the
adjoining owners, by this time the Aubin family, became aware of paper title and disputed Mr. Beaudoin's rights. The parties brought the matter to court for declaratory
relief. Mr. Justice Anderson specifically reviewed the Aubins' contention that, since the
occupation of the land had arisen as the result of a mistake as to the boundary line
between the parcels, no rights whatever could accrue. That is to say, in the absence of
knowledge of the true state of title to the property, there could be no adversity and no
intention to possess adversely. Mr. Justice Anderson rejected the intention test entirely
and considered at length the question of whether the intention and adversity tests were,
in fact, appropriate elements of the law in Ontario. He concluded that they were not and
granted a declaration as to title to Mr. Beaudoin.

The decision in *Beaudoin v. Aubin* preceded the decision in *Masidon v. Ham* by over
a year. Curiously enough, *Beaudoin* was not even discussed by Mr. Justice Carruthers in
Masidon even though it had been relied upon by counsel for Mr. Ham. The divergence
in approach is almost as striking as the divergence in result between *Piper v. Stevenson*
and *Masidon v. Ham*. Nor are the two recent decisions uncharacteristic of the law in this
area. Contrary to what might be professional expectations, the number of cases dealing
with questions of possessory title does not seem to diminish year by year, nor does the

jurisprudence used in those cases become more stable and consistent. It seems that the time has come for a reconsideration of some of the underlying doctrines.

II. *Masidon Investments Ltd. v. Ham: New Applications of the Adversity Test*

Mr. Justice Carruthers: The Trial Decision

The judgment in *Masidon v. Ham* is disturbing for a number of reasons. ... [T]here are suggestions throughout the decision that some of the basic doctrines with regard to possessory titles have been misunderstood. Mr. Justice Carruthers concluded, at one point, that Mr. Ham had, by perhaps improper means, "fashioned a design to acquire possessory title to the lands in dispute." Later, while considering the onus which a person claiming possessory title must bear, he pointed out that "the relevant provisions of the *Limitations Act* did not come into being in order to promote the obtaining of possessory title." In the traditional analysis, the *Limitations Act* had no relationship whatever to the "acquisition" or "obtaining" of possessory title. Possession was, in its nature, a species of title assertible against the entire world other than the true owner. A stranger to Masidon as well as to Mr. Ham could not have asserted any rights to the lands while Mr. Ham was in possession on the basis that Masidon, in fact, had a better title than Mr. Ham. From the beginning of the common law period, Mr. Ham's possession in those circumstances would have been defended and the raising of the *jus tertii* would have been rejected. By this analysis Mr. Ham, Miss Piper and Mr. Beaudoin had obtained possessory title to the lands which they claimed at the time that they respectively went into possession. The *Limitations Act* did not create that title. The Act simply established situations in which such title became indefeasible through the lapse of time. Section 15 of the Act reflects the situation precisely. When a limitations period had elapsed against a person who has established a possessory title, the former title is *extinguished*. Nothing is said about the creation of a new title or a transfer of title from the former owner to the new owner.

This misinterpretation of the principles underlying possessory doctrines is reflected in a plethora of findings of fact and statements of law which may or may not bear on the issues at hand. Mr. Justice Carruthers found, for example, that the holder of an interest in the disputed lands had not been put on notice that Mr. Ham was making use of them, even though in 1974 they received a property appraisal which made reference to the "private airstrip for small aircraft." The implication is clearly that the degree of knowledge which the holder of paper title has with regard to the use of the disputed lands is important. The absence of such knowledge somehow improves the position of the holder of paper title. The point is not explored, nor is acknowledgement given to the fact that the *Limitations Act* specifically makes reference to knowledge of use by another party in only one instance: where the lands are in a "state of nature." The fact that, by statute, knowledge becomes a question in that instance would suggest that it is not an issue in other instances and, indeed, the cases have so held.

As mentioned previously, the heart of the matter appears to have been that the use which Mr. Ham made of the property was not appropriate for the running of a limitations period. In this respect, Mr. Justice Carruthers relied heavily on the decisions of Madame Justice Wilson, then of the Ontario Court of Appeal, in *Keefer v. Arillotta* and in *Fletcher v. Storoschuk*. One extract which Mr. Justice Carruthers took from the *Keefer* decision conveys the essence of the argument:

> The use an owner wants to make of his property may be a limited use and an intermittent or sporadic use. A possessory title cannot, however, be acquired against him by depriving him of uses of his property that he never intended or desired to make of it. The *animus possidendi* which a person claiming a possessory title must have is an intention to exclude the owner from such uses as the owner wants to make of his property.

Both Madame Justice Wilson and Mr. Justice Carruthers relied on the old English case of *Leigh v. Jack* for this proposition.

Madame Justice Wilson's words create the implication that possessory title is "acquired" by some ongoing process. Implicitly, the old doctrine that an estate in possession will either exist or not exist at any given instant in time, and will become indefeasible through the provisions of the statute, is ignored. Secondly, the quotation identifies not one but two tests of intention where a possessory interest is to be claimed. There is, first, the intention of the person in possession, which must be to "exclude the owner from such uses as the owner wants to make," and second, the intention of the owner, which may be to make some use, or no use, of the lands. To phrase the principle positively, a person in possession of lands which he does not own can "acquire" title only if he knows that he does not own the lands, knows who does own the lands, knows the intentions which the true owner has with regard to the use of the lands, and acts in a manner inconsistent with those intentions.

The phrasing of the principle in a positive form does, of course, display its weaknesses. Proof of any intention is difficult, especially over a ten year period. Certainly there would be few owners who would confess to having any immediate and consistent intention to use lands which they have not tried to occupy for over a decade. Mr. Justice Carruthers himself confessed that his approach to the doctrine may well mean that possessory title cannot be obtained against "development land which is in the holding stage." Further, the formulation is almost impossible to apply in what is the most common instance, situations where both the paper title holder and the possessor are simply mistaken about the nature and extent of their respective rights and cannot therefore establish an intention consistent with the proposed legal test. ...

Mr. Justice Blair: The Decision on Appeal

Mr. Ham appealed the decision of Mr. Justice Carruthers and took the matter before Justices Zuber, Blair and Goodman of the Court of Appeal. Mr. Justice Blair wrote on behalf of the bench .... Again, the decisions of Madame Justice Wilson on this topic, and particularly the decision in *Keefer v. Arillotta*, were central to the analysis. Mr. Justice Blair summarized the principles applicable to possessory title as follows:

> It is clear that the claimant with possessory title throughout the statutory period must have:
>
> (1) had actual possession;
> (2) had the intention of excluding the true owner from possession;

(3) effectively excluded the true owner from possession.

Mr. Justice Blair noted that "the claim will fail unless the claimant meets each of these three tests and time will begin to run against the owner only from the last date when all of them are satisfied."

Mr. Ham was found to have failed to meet the tests. It is not clear, however, whether he failed on one branch, two branches or all three branches of the analysis. The major issue appears to be whether he "effectively excluded the possession of the true owner." The concept of "effective exclusion" is, in Mr. Justice Blair's treatment, the obverse of the coin of "adversity." A holder of paper title who has no interest in coming on the land cannot be "excluded" by the person in possession. To put the matter another way, a person in possession cannot hold adversely to the interest of someone who does not care what is happening to the land. ...

In Mr. Justice Blair's view (and it is a view echoed by Mr. Justice Robins in the recent Court of Appeal decision in *Giouroukos v. Cadillac Fairview*) there is something of a moral standard to be resorted to in the application of the doctrines of possessory title. Mr. Justice Blair adopted Mr. Justice Carruthers' observation that perhaps possessory title cannot be obtained in circumstances where land is being held for development purposes:

> This result, however, is not surprising. There is no policy reason for concern about the rights of the appellant in this case or, indeed, any trespassers seeking to acquire possessory title to land held for development. The appellant deliberately embarked on a course of conduct which ultimately led to an intention to dispossess the respondents of their property. In my opinion, Justice Carruthers was correct in concluding that the purpose of the Limitations Act was not "to promote the obtaining of possessory title" by a person in the position of the appellant.

This new test seems to cut in all directions: a person in possession of land without intending to harm the true owner's right will acquire nothing, a person in possession of land with the intention of acquiring the true owner's right will not have the assistance of the court.

III. Beaudoin v. Aubin: The Adversity Test Denied

The facts in *Beaudoin v. Aubin*, as outlined above, are difficult to analyse with reference to some test which makes the intentions of the possessor and of the holder of paper title paramount. The parties there proceeded on the basis of a mutual mistake with regard to their common boundary and their respective rights over the disputed land. The holder of paper title could form no intention with regard to lands which he did not know he owned nor could the possessor be expected to demonstrate that he was acting adversely to the true owner's interests since all he hoped to do was use the property which he thought he owned. Mr. Justice Anderson was called upon to consider the entire body of doctrine with regard to possessory title and, in a thorough and scholarly decision, he concluded that Mr. Beaudoin in fact, established an indefeasible title even though he had not acted with that intention. Mr. Justice Anderson began with a close analysis of the history of the *Limitations Act*. He pointed out that, prior to the passage of the *Real Property*

Limitation Act, 1833 in England, the common law for both Canada and England had employed the concept of "adversity" in a very technical sense when testing the question of whether or not a possessory title had been established. With the passage of the Act in 1833, the focus shifted to the question of whether or not an action against the possessor should have been brought by the true owner. The Act, after the manner of limitations acts generally, was simply procedural in its nature, not substantive.

Mr. Justice Anderson quoted Mr. Justice Smily in *McGugan v. Turner* to the effect that in the applicable section of the *Limitations Act*:

> [N]o exception is made ... of ignorance or mistake as to true ownership. In fact it has been held that a common error by the owners in regard to the true line of division between the properties does not prevent the statute running where the statute does not require it to be shown that possession was adverse and not with acquiescence or permission.

Justice Anderson pointed out that the change in the legislation led early commentators in Ontario to state that, for the purposes of this province, the concept of "adverse possession" in its original form had been abolished and the phrase had continued to be used only as a matter of convenience.

For at least fifteen years Mr. Beaudoin occupied land that he thought was his by right. Mr. Justice Anderson had to address directly the question of whether it was necessary to show that any particular intention was associated with his acts. He distinguished several cases, in which intention had been found to be an important element, by showing that they focused on factual situations in which the acts of possession were equivocal. He concluded that the possession of the lands by Mr. Beaudoin was certain and unequivocal and the *animus possidendi* could therefore be presumed. He ended his analysis with a condemnation of the doctrines requiring demonstration of some subjective intention:

> The application of judicial statements, without due regard for the facts of the case in which the statement is made, is a pregnant and perennial source of error. Upon such statements the defence has propounded the argument that, before a party can successfully rely upon sections 4 and 15 of the statute, he must establish a subjective intention, with knowledge of the rights of the plaintiff present in his mind, to occupy in defiance or denial of those rights. No case which I have considered, when one looks to the facts, supports that proposition and it is utterly inconsistent with the decisions in *Martin v. Weld, Babbitt v. Clarke, Nourse v. Clark*, and *McGugan v. Turner*.

IV. Possession, Intention, Adversity: A Reconsideration

While *Beaudoin v. Aubin* has, arguably, restated some important principles with regard to possessory title and *Masidon v. Ham* has, similarly, confused the matter once more, it must not be suggested that the tests which Mr. Justice Carruthers and Mr. Justice Blair adopted in *Masidon* are wholly inapplicable. Rather, the analysis which was applied in the *Masidon* case is required by the nature of the legal principles applicable to possessory titles. The objection is that the analysis was wrongly conducted.

The doctrines of possessory title are, as suggested earlier, something of a hybrid in our law. The essential analysis goes back to medieval questions of who is seised of an interest and under what circumstances that person's seisin can be challenged. Onto this medieval root had been grafted a branch of statutory law limiting the time within which a challenge to the estate of the person in possession can be brought. Perhaps it would be useful to separate the two parts of the doctrine in order to see where the various tests of possessory usage arise and where they can be helpful.

The possessory estate, which the common law would have protected against all persons other than the true owner, was an estate established by the possessor acting as if he had an interest of indefinite duration (which was, therefore, a freehold interest and, furthermore, a seised estate) which was his as of right. A mere trespass across a piece of land, or a series of trespasses, would not give rise to the same sort of right. Hence, the requirement that possession be continuous. A person who asserted rights based on a stealthy or secretive use of a piece of property would, of course, face an evidentiary problem but was also thought not to be using the lands in a manner consistent with the assertion of a seised interest; thus the requirement that possession be open and obvious. Similarly, a person whose sole claim to property was that he was physically and violently keeping the true owner away was not seen to be enjoying any estate of his own in the lands. Finally, the common law recognized that a person who was in possession of property with the permission of the true owner was simply exercising the true owner's rights and not enjoying an independent estate of his own. The medieval shorthand for these doctrines was that the possession of land which was defensible as an estate in the land was possession "*nec calme, nec vie, nec precaria*" (without stealth, without violence and without permission).

While we have, in many cases, lost sight of the foundation for the tests which we now use, the principles remain the same. The tests for the running of a limitations period have been reformulated for modern application. The calls for "open, obvious and continuous" usage, "peaceful, open and obvious usage" and "usage as of right" are, however, all ways in which the court seeks to establish whether or not the claimant to a possessory title has in fact been enjoying the type of estate which the common law protected.

The problem is, of course, that the usages which can and should be made of lands are as varied as the lands themselves. Can someone, such as the farmer in *Piper v. Stevenson*, who simply visits property at seed and harvest time, be said to be in possession at all, let alone continuous possession? Can someone, such as Miss Carson in *Carson v. Musialo*, who walks upon a stream bank and picks flowers there from time to time, be said to be threatening the interest of the true owner of the land who did not have any other use for the property?

When it is remembered that the common law looked for a usage of land analogous to that which would be made by a person claiming an estate as of right, the decisions (that Miss Piper did establish a possessory interest and Miss Carson did not) become at least explicable, if not obvious. The requirement that usage be "open" should be treated as being a means of ascertaining that the claimant to possessory title has acted in a manner consistent with the holding of an estate in land. It should not be confused with any expectation on the part of the court that a paper title holder must be given a warning that his interests might be endangered. (The test of possessory title grew up before limitations acts in their present form were available and these tests were, in fact, in place at a time when a true owner's interests could not, at law, have been endangered by any length of possession by another party.)

Openness of possession was one of the indicia of the existence of a possessory estate. Similarly, an intention to possess can also be an indicium of a possessory estate in circumstances where the facts of possession are themselves ambiguous. Where the land is in such condition that a true owner would not be expected to constantly make use of it, a person who is making such use as a true owner would make may have his position advanced somewhat by showing that he had, in fact, intended to use the property as his own. The intention in such a case is an intention with regard to the use of an estate in land, not an intention with regard to the acquisition of an estate of land. The older law would not have recognized the idea that a person actually in possession had anything more to acquire. An intention test is, therefore, not wholly inappropriate in circumstances of ambiguity. It must not, however, be allowed to ripen into a threshold test for the assertion of a possessory interest. In the vast majority of instances, possessory interests arise through mistakes innocently made to which no intention whatever can be attached.

The statutory branch of the analysis is in many respects parallel to the common law doctrine. Just as the common law would focus on the question of whether an estate had been brought into existence, the statute focuses on the question of whether or not "an entry or distress ... or action to recover any land" can be brought. Just as a series of trespasses would not establish an estate at common law for which an "action for recovery" would be the appropriate remedy, a series of trespasses will not provide the foundation for such an action under the statute. (Trespasses to land are dealt with as "personal actions" under section 45(1)(g) of the Ontario *Limitations Act* and have their own separate limitations periods.) The tests used to establish whether or not a possessory estate exists are, therefore, appropriate as well to the question of whether or not the right to bring an action to recover land has existed. Again, open, obvious and continuous occupation are important considerations, as might be, in ambiguous situations, the establishment of an intention to use land as a true owner would use it.

The question of the true owner's intention with regard to the land is not definitive under either the common law or the statutory branch of the doctrine. As Mr. Justice Anderson pointed out in *Beaudoin v. Aubin*, the intention of the true owner is, in fact, a test peculiar to the jurisprudence of England.

If the analysis which I have been discussing is helpful, the law dealing with possessory interests might be set out under the following principles:

a) The common law doctrine that a person in peaceful possession of land will himself have a species of seised estate from the commencement of such possession remains the foundation of our possessory doctrine.

b) The peaceful possession of land which is to be treated as amounting to a possessory estate is the type of possession which a true owner would himself wish to make. Note, however, that this principle is subject to the qualification that property which is not in its nature susceptible to some degree of open and continuous ownership will remain the estate of the paper title holder unless the claimant to a possessory estate takes unusual measures to establish the existence of his interests.

c) The establishment of a possessory estate can be demonstrated through a variety of indicia, none of which is either sufficient in its own right to establish the estate or necessary to establish the estate. Among these indicia are the enclosure of the lands in question, continuous possession, formal repudiation of claims by the true owner and a demonstrated intention to possess the lands as if the claimant were the true owner.

d) Where the facts with regard to open, obvious and continuous possession are well established an "intention to possess" (*animus possidendi*) will be presumed. Indeed, in such circumstances intention is not an issue. Where the facts with regard to possession are equivocal, and especially where the lands in question would not in normal circumstances be in continuous use, the subjective intention of the possessor may be a relevant factor in establishing the existence of a possessory estate.

e) The analysis which can be employed for the purpose of establishing whether or not a possessory estate would exist at common law is useful for the parallel purpose of establishing whether or not a suit to recover the land could (and therefore should) have been brought under the *Limitations Act*.

f) At common law a person in possession of land with the permission of the true owner did not run a possessory period. Similarly, except for the specific instances of tenancies and tenancies-at-will set out in the *Limitations Act*, the fact that a person is in possession without the authorization of the paper title holder is a necessary element in the establishment of a right to bring an action to recover the land and, therefore, a necessary element in the running of a limitations period. For the purposes of the law of Ontario, this is the entire extent of the "adversity" doctrine insofar as the rights and interests of the holder of paper title are concerned.

V. Conclusion

As was indicated at the outset, cases dealing with possessory title arise with surprising frequency. What is even more surprising is that they have in recent years become more, rather than less, confusing in their approaches to the problem. These inconsistencies appear to have arisen through insufficient attention to the historical foundations of the doctrine of possessory estates and the manner in which the *Limitations Act* is intended to affect that doctrine. Some of the more recent decisions create a danger that the overall purpose of the *Limitations Act*, which is to reduce areas in which disputes can be prosecuted, may be thwarted by the adoption of a set of rules which will promote, rather than diminish, litigation. It is in the light of these considerations that the decision in *Beaudoin v. Aubin* has provided a welcome restatement of some long established doctrines and the decision in *Masidon v. Ham* has, rather disappointingly, created new complications.

Do you agree that *Masidon v. Ham* should be decided using the same principles of possession that were applied in *Beaudoin v. Aubin*? Why did the judges in these cases reach different conclusions? Are these differing outcomes consistent with common law principles of possession, the language of statutes of limitation, or the underlying purposes identified by Callaghan and Rose?

Treloar v. Nute

As is evident in the judgment of Wilson JA in *Keefer v. Arillotta*, the origin of the "inconsistent user" test was a series of cases in the United Kingdom, including *Leigh v. Jack* (1879), 5 Ex. D 264 (Ex. Ct.), *Williams Brothers Direct Supply Stores Ltd. v. Raftery*, [1958] 1 QB 159 (CA), and *Wallis's Cayton Bay Holiday Camp Ltd v. Shell-Mex and BP Ltd.*, [1975] QB 94 (CA). These cases (referred to as a "special type of case") were reviewed by the English Court of Appeal in *Treloar v. Nute*, [1976] 1 WLR 1295 (CA). In that case, the trial judge had confirmed entitlement on the part of the paper title holder to a small disputed parcel of land, although the adverse possessor had taken possession of the parcel for purposes of grazing animals and for dumping excess soil. According to the trial judge, these actions did not inconvenience the paper title holder. On appeal, the court reviewed this approach and rejected it (at 1302) as follows:

> We return to the present case. The judge found, as we read his judgment, that the defendant's father took possession of the disputed land outside the limitation period but that this possession was not adverse by reason that it caused no inconvenience to the plaintiff. In our judgment the second part of this finding is contrary to the plain terms of section 10 of the Act of 1939 which in effect defines adverse possession as possession of some person in whose favour the period of limitation can run. It is not permissible to import into this definition a requirement that the owner must be inconvenienced or otherwise affected by that possession. Apart from the cases relating to special purpose no authority has been cited to us which would support the requirement of inconvenience to the owner and we are not ourselves aware of any such authority. On the contrary, so far as our own experience goes, the typical instance in which a possessory title is treated as having been acquired is that in which a squatter establishes himself upon a piece of land for which the owner has no use. Indeed, if inconvenience to the owner had to be established it would be difficult indeed ever to acquire a possessory title since the owner if inconvenienced would be likely to take proceedings.
>
> We conclude that, once it is accepted that the judge found, and could properly find, that the defendant's father took possession of the disputed land before the commencement of the limitation period, and in the absence of any evidence of special purpose on the part of the plaintiff, time began to run from such taking of possession, irrespective of whether the plaintiff suffered inconvenience from the possession, and that the defendant must be treated as having acquired a possessory title before the commencement of this action.

Subsequently, the UK Law Reform Committee issued its *Twenty-First Report— Final Report on Limitation of Actions*, Cmnd. 6923 (London: HMSO, 1977), which confirmed the main principles enunciated in the appeal in *Treloar v. Nute* and recommended the restriction of the "special type of case":

> The nature of the difficulty may be simply stated. When considering the initial step towards acquiring a title by 12 years adverse possession, namely the taking of

possession, the courts—in our view rightly—have never been astute to find that possession has in fact been taken. This approach has been particularly marked in relation to small pieces of land which cannot immediately be economically exploited—for example, a narrow strip of land ultimately intended as an access road—and for which the true owner had no immediate use. None of us would wish to detract from the necessity of jealous scrutiny of acts alleged to have resulted in possession being taken of such a parcel of land. Thus what have happily been called "trivial" acts of trespass, even if repeated over many years, have never been equated with the acquisition of possession.

However, as the result of the cases we have referred to, there has now apparently been established a quite general doctrine of an implied licence from the true owner to the would-be adverse possessor permitting him to commit the acts of possession upon which he seeks to rely, without any specific factual basis for such an implication. The effect of implying such a licence is to prevent time running in favour of the adverse possessor, since time does not run in favour of a licensee. If this doctrine extends as far as it appears to have been extended by the most recent decision of the Court of Appeal, it amounts in effect, to a judicial repeal of the statute. The philosophy behind this approach has been expressed by the Master of the Rolls, Lord Denning, as follows:

> The reason behind the decisions is because it does not lie in that other person's mouth to assert that he used the land of his own wrong as a trespasser. Rather his user is to be ascribed to the licence or permission of the true owner.

We, however, prefer the more traditional approach recently restated by Sir John Pennycuick, delivering the judgment of the Court of Appeal in *Treloar v. Nute*, in which he said:

> ... if a squatter takes possession of land belonging to another and remains in possession for 12 years to the exclusion of the owner, that represents adverse possession and accordingly at the end of the 12 years the title of the owner is extinguished. That is the plain meaning of the statutory provisions. ...

It is clear that these two approaches cannot be reconciled, except on the basis that the "implied licence" theory is an attempted rationalisation of the "trivial acts of trespass" approach. This might have been possible with the decision in the earlier of the two cases already cited (*Wallis*): it is not possible with the decision of the latter case (*Gray v. Wykeham-Martin*). It is also impossible to reconcile the approaches of the Court of Appeal in those cases and in *Treloar v. Nute*.

We consider that the law should be restored to the law as stated in *Treloar v. Nute*. There can, in our view, be no justification for implying a licence, or other similar position, in any case in which there is no factual basis for such an implication. The precise formula for such a restoration is not easy, since the present law is that if the land is in the possession of some person in whose favour the period of limitation can run, then such possession is "adverse" (Limitation Act 1939 section 10(1)) and this appears to be quite plain. We do not consider that the suggestion of the Institute—that there should be a presumption that possession is adverse—would really add anything to this existing provision. Accordingly, we think that it may be necessary for amending legislation expressly to provide that for the purposes of the Limitation Act "possession" is to bear its ordinary meaning in law, so that it is not to be artificially stripped of its character of being adverse by the application of any implication or presumption not grounded upon the actual circumstances of the case. Such a formula, whilst leaving full scope for the application of the "trivial acts of trespass" approach, would effectively reverse the recent unsatisfactory line of cases.

The Limitation Act 1980, 1980, c. 58, s. 8 was enacted in the UK Parliament to implement these principles:

> 8(4) For the purpose of determining whether a person occupying any land is in adverse possession of the land it shall not be assumed by implication of law that his occupation is by permission of the person entitled to the land merely by virtue of the fact that his occupation is not inconsistent with the latter's present or future enjoyment of the land.
>
> This provision shall not be taken as prejudicing a finding to the effect that a person's occupation of any land is by implied permission of the person entitled to the land in any case where such a finding is justified on the actual facts of the case.

For a case that interprets the new legislation, see *Bucks County Council v. Moran* (1989), 139 New Law Journal 257 (CA). In that case, a municipal council acquired a plot of land with a view to carrying out a road diversion some time in the future. For the statutory period, the possessor (an adjoining home-owner) maintained the plot as a garden, enclosing it fully so that the only access to the plot was through the occupier's garden. The court concluded (at 258) that title had been acquired by possession.

> In the present case, the defendant was well aware that the council had acquired the plot in order to construct a road on it at some time in the future and meantime had no present use for the land. This factor, which Mr. Douglas naturally stressed in the course of his argument, should make the court the more cautious before holding that the defendant had had both a factual possession and *animus possidendi* sufficient to confer on him a possessory title.
>
> Nevertheless, every *Leigh v. Jack* type of case such as this must involve questions of fact and degree. I would, for my part, reject the submission that since the 1980 Act there remains any special rule which requires the words "possessed" and "dispossessed" or similar words to be given anything other than their natural and ordinary meaning in the *Leigh v. Jack* type of case.
>
> Thus far, therefore, I conclude that (1) if by October 28, 1973 the defendant had taken possession of the plot, his possession must have been adverse to the council; (2) the question whether or not the defendant had taken possession of the plot by October 28, 1973 falls to be decided by reference to conventional concepts of possession and dispossession and not by departing from the ordinary and natural meaning of the relevant statutory provisions merely because this is a *Leigh v. Jack* type of case.
>
> Nevertheless, I agree with the judge that "what is required for this purpose is not an intention to own or even an intention to acquire ownership but an intention to possess"—that is to say, an intention *for the time being* to possess the land to the exclusion of all other persons, including the owner with the paper title. No authorities cited to us establish the contrary proposition. ...

In the light of the line of authorities to which we have been referred, beginning with *Leigh v. Jack*, I have already accepted that the court should be slow to make a finding of adverse possession in a case such as the present. However, as the judge pointed out, in none of those earlier cases where the owner with the paper title successfully defended his title, was there present the significant feature of complete enclosure of the land in question by the trespasser. On the evidence in the present case he was, in judgment, right in concluding that the defendant had acquired adverse possession of it ever since. There is no evidence that any representative of the council has even set foot on the plot since that date.

Are the decisions in Ontario such as *Keefer v. Arillotta, Masidon v. Ham*, and *Beaudoin v. Aubin* consistent with UK decisions such as *Treloar v. Nute* and *Bucks County Council v. Moran*? Are there factual differences that explain the differing outcomes? Is it relevant, for example, that part of the land in dispute in *Keefer* was a right of way? If legislative reform is needed to make these cases more consistent, what policy objectives should a revised statute seek to accomplish?

Inconsistent User, Intention, Mistakes, and "Land-Grabbing"

The legislative reform that has occurred in the United Kingdom has not been replicated in Ontario. Proposed reforms were suggested in the *Discussion Paper on Proposed Limitations Act* (Ontario: Ministry of the Attorney-General, 1977), including the following provision:

> 3.(2) The following actions shall not be brought after the expiration of ten years after the date on which the right to do so arose.
>
> • • •
>
> (g) an action for possession of land where the person entitled to possession of the land has been dispossessed in circumstances amounting to trespass.

What would be accomplished by such a provision?

In spite of such proposals for reform, the inconsistent user test has continued to be influential. A good example is the following decision of the Ontario Court of Appeal.

Giouroukos v. Cadillac Fairview Corp. Ltd.
(1983), 3 DLR (4th) 595 (Ont. CA)

ROBINS JA: This is an appeal by the defendants, the Cadillac Fairview Corporation Limited and Garden Centre Developments Ltd., from a judgment of Madam Justice Van Camp declaring that the plaintiff, Soturos Giouroukos, has acquired a possessory title to certain lands in the City of London and that the defendants' right to recover possession of those lands and their title thereto has been extinguished.

The Facts

The plaintiff is the registered owner of a rectangular parcel of land at the south–east corner of Richmond St. and Fanshawe Park Rd. in the City of London, approximately

185 ft. by 90 ft. in size ("the plaintiff's land"). The defendants are the registered owners of a larger irregularly-shaped parcel lying immediately to the south of the plaintiff's land and fronting on Richmond St. ("the defendants' land"). In dispute is a part of the defendants' land consisting of an area of about 185 ft. by 60 ft. which abuts the plaintiff's land ("the disputed land"). The plaintiff claims title to the disputed land through adverse possession on the part of himself and his predecessors for a period in excess of the ten-year limitation period prescribed by the *Limitations Act*, RSO 1980, c. 240. ...

[The following figure is the author's—it is not part of the original case:]

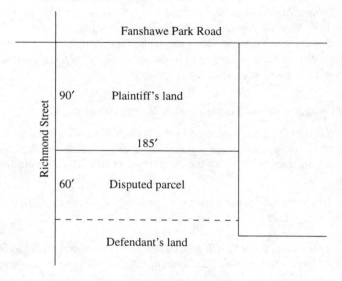

By way of background, it appears that at one time the plaintiff's and the defendants' lands were owned by Nora Smith and together constituted "the Smith farm." In 1945, Mrs. Smith severed the farm by selling the plaintiff's lands to Fred Nelson. He built a drive-in restaurant on the site, called "The Knotty Pine Inn," and that restaurant has been in operation there ever since. In 1950, the land was conveyed to Stanley Nelson ("Nelson") who ran the business, alone and in partnership, until 1968; in referring hereafter to "Nelson," I include his various partners. On June 3, 1968, Nelson and his then partner, Peter Brown, sold the property to the plaintiff. He operated the restaurant personally until 1975 when he leased the land and premises to Malibu Restaurant Limited. That company has continued to operate the business to the present time. Since 1957, the disputed land has been used as an additional parking area for the restaurant.

On February 23, 1956, Nora Smith sold the remainder of her farm (that is, the defendants' land) to Isabel Rodgers who took title only as nominee for the beneficial owner, Loblaws Groceterias Co. Ltd. ("Loblaws"). On February 9, 1972, a deed in favour of Loblaws was registered. Loblaws purchased the property with the intention of holding it for future development as a supermarket or as a shopping centre or other type of commercial complex in which Loblaws would be present. In the meantime, Loblaws did nothing with the property other than lease the entire parcel, including the dwelling-house located on it, for residential purposes. Throughout the period from July, 1956 until January, 1971, the defendants' land was continuously in the possession of successive tenants of Loblaws under the terms of written leases. In 1971, the dwelling was demolished and the land thereafter remained vacant until August 11, 1978, when Loblaws sold it to the defendants.

Following their acquisition, the defendants applied for a rezoning to extend the permissible land uses, and, it appears, a by-law has now been approved which permits the land to be developed as a shopping centre and used for other commercial and high-density residential purposes. On June 7, 1979, the defendants' solicitors informed the plaintiff of their clients' intended development of the disputed land and advised that he could continue to use the parking area pending construction provided he agree to discontinue such use on 30 days' notice and acknowledge the defendants' title. In response, on July 6, 1979, the plaintiff instituted this action claiming a possessory title to the disputed land, and the defendants counterclaimed for possession of the land. As already indicated, the action succeeded at trial and the counterclaim was dismissed. The defendants now appeal from that judgment.

This brings me more specifically to the land in dispute. Until 1954, this section of the Smith farm was surrounded by an old wire fence and used by Nora Smith as a horse pasture. After it was abandoned as a pasture, the land became overgrown with burdock and high grass, and the fence on its northern limit, that is, on the dividing line between the plaintiff's and defendants' land, fell into disrepair. In 1956, shortly after Loblaws became the owner of the defendants' land, Nelson, who then owned and operated The Knotty Pine restaurant, decided to use the disputed land as an additional parking-lot for his restaurant. He proceeded to tear down the fence, clear the area, and spread gravel over it to furnish a base for parking; and, in the spring of following years he added more gravel. In doing this, Nelson was not under any misapprehension or mistaken notion as to his legal position. He knew full well that he had no right, legal or moral, to enter forcibly and use the disputed land, but for the purposes of his own business interests he decided to "take a chance."

The trial judge expressly found that while Nelson's use of the disputed lands as a parking-lot began in 1957 and that such use was continued by him and his successors until the trial of this action, it was not until 1960, when parking was restricted to customers of the restaurant and signs were erected to that effect, that he "went beyond trespass or mere user of the land" and "asserted actual and complete possession to the exclusion of all others" [37 OR (2d) 364, at 368, 135 DLR (3d) 249, at 253, 24 RPR 226]. The trial judge, therefore, set 1960 as the date of commencement of the statutory period prescribed by the *Limitations Act*. In her view, Nelson's possession in that year became adverse to Loblaws and hence Loblaws' right of action against Nelson accrued and time began to run under the *Limitations Act*.

The fact is that Loblaws had leased the defendants' land, through and in the name of a local real estate agent, continuously from 1956 to 1971. In 1960, the land was in the possession of Mrs. Mary Miller, or perhaps Mrs. Miller and her husband, pursuant to a lease, executed by Mrs. Miller alone, which took effect on July 1, 1959. It is not clear from the evidence whether Mr. Miller was also a tenant under that lease, nor is it clear whether, following his death in 1962, his estate continued as a tenant with Mrs. Miller under a second lease which took effect on January 1, 1962, to which I shall come in a moment. In any event, Mrs. Miller continued to be a tenant throughout the period of these leases and, for the purposes of this appeal, it is not important whether her husband or his estate was also a tenant. For simplicity, I shall refer to Mrs. Miller as the tenant. Her lease was preceded by one to Albert Noyes which created a monthly tenancy that began on June 1, 1956, and terminated immediately before the Miller lease. Mrs. Miller remained in actual occupation of the defendants' lands from July 1, 1959 to April, 1970, when Noyes again became a monthly tenant under a written lease. Noyes' tenancy lasted only until January 2, 1971, when the dwelling was demolished.

Mrs. Miller's tenancy is crucial to the defendants' appeal. As already indicated, she held possession during her 11-year tenure under the terms of two leases. The first lease is dated June 30, 1959, and under it she was granted possession of the defendants' lands (described therein as the "Smith property") as a tenant from month to month at a rental of $30 per month. The second lease is dated November 21, 1961, and was executed by Mrs. Miller and her husband, who died in 1962. This lease was for a two-year term commencing January 1, 1962, at a rental of $40 per month terminable on 60 days' notice in the event of a *bona fide* sale of the property and provides for a monthly tenancy on the same terms if occupancy is continued after the expiration of the term. Mrs. Miller was in actual possession of the defendants' land when the plaintiff's predecessors first asserted adverse possession in 1960 or, to put the matter in another way, when they first manifested the *animus possidendi* necessary for the acquisition of a possessory title. Her possession under her leasehold arrangements with Loblaws continued uninterrupted until April, 1970.

Mrs. Miller gave evidence at the trial. It is clear from her testimony that the entire parcel constituting the defendants' land was leased to her. She understood from her discussions with Loblaws' rental agent that the gravelled area used for restaurant parking belonged, as she put it, to "our place" and formed part of the lands and premises demised to her. She knew, in short, that she was entitled to the use and enjoyment of the disputed land. However, as she explained, she had no need for this land; she did not have a car and her visitors used the driveway to the south of her house and, moreover, she had enough other land upon which to grow potatoes and other vegetables and upon which her guests could picnic and children visiting her could play. Consequently, she chose not to exercise her right as tenant to occupy the disputed land during her tenancy and, further, chose not to raise any objection to the neighbouring restaurant's use of this land which would otherwise have remained vacant and served no useful purpose.

Loblaws was unaware throughout that the disputed land was being used by the plaintiff and his predecessors as a parking-lot and, of course, registered no objection to such use. The company's local agent saw that the cars were being parked on the property but, as the trial judge found, "showed no disturbance" at such use and did not object. It appears that having expressly advised the tenant that her lease included this land, he treated its use as a matter for the tenant.

This brings me to 1968, when the plaintiff became the owner and operator of the restaurant. He was cognizant of the fact that the disputed land was not included in his purchase. No mention was made of it in the agreement of purchase and sale or in any of the legal documents transferred on closing, and no part of the purchase price was attributable to it. The plaintiff acknowledged at trial that Nelson told him he did not own this land and that Nelson made no representations with respect to it other than that he had "use[d] it for many, many years and nobody told him to get out." Clearly, the plaintiff knew that municipal taxes were being paid by the owner (as they had been throughout) and, knowing that, made no effort to make these payments himself or to notify the owner or the municipal authorities of the ownership which he now says he then had. He did nothing more than spread additional gravel over the land from time to time, place new signs restricting parking to restaurant customers, and take steps to ensure that others did not park there. The defendants think it revealing that, following his purchase of the restaurant, the plaintiff put a new asphalt surface on the parking area within the boundaries of his own lands but made no such improvement to the area in dispute. The plaintiff says that paving this area was unnecessary and would have been too expensive, and his not having done so was unrelated to the question of ownership.

In 1969, the plaintiff proposed an exchange of land with Loblaws. It appears that after ascertaining that Mrs. Miller was only a tenant of the defendants' land, the plaintiff retained a real estate agent to approach the owner in Toronto. According to the plaintiff, in order to extend his parking area, the agent was instructed to offer to trade a house owned by the plaintiff on a lot having a frontage of about 50 ft. on Richmond St. and a depth of 298 ft. situate to the south of the defendants' land in exchange for the house leased to Mrs. Miller and the part of the defendants' land on which the house was located having a frontage of 40 ft. on Richmond St. by a depth of 185 ft. lying immediately to the south of the disputed land. The agent ascertained Loblaws' ownership of the property and, in the autumn of 1969, met with the vice-president and general counsel of the company. His proposal on the plaintiff's behalf is stipulated in a letter dated October 23, 1969, attached to which is a plot plan clearly outlining the two parcels proposed to be traded. The agent said that the plaintiff was willing to "trade even and pay $2,000.00 difference to take care of any legal costs" and, adverting to the contemplated future development of the defendants' lands, indicated that the trade "might well eliminate any objection to the zoning of the property." Loblaws responded that it was not interested in the proposed exchange.

The point of this is that the disputed land, according to the plot plan, was clearly to be included in the trade. It shows a frontage of 100 ft. on Richmond St. abutting the Knotty Pine lands with a uniform depth of 184 ft. The plaintiff testified at trial that, notwithstanding his agent's plot plan, the proposal was intended to relate only to the house and was not to include the disputed land; in his contention he already owned those lands and had no need to effect a trade to acquire them. But the proposal actually submitted to Loblaws was not limited in this way and on its face appears expressly to acknowledge Loblaws' ownership of the disputed land.

Counsel for the defendants argues that the facts relating to this proposal, particularly the agent's correspondence and plot plan, establish that the plaintiff sought to purchase the disputed land in 1969, and the offer should be construed as demonstrating that the plaintiff's possession was not adverse. Further, it is argued, the offer constitutes a written acknowledgement within the meaning of s. 13 of the *Limitations Act* so as to prevent time from running prior to the date of the acknowledgement. The trial judge, however, accepted the plaintiff's evidence and refused to hold that he authorized the disputed lands to be included in the proposed trade or that the letter, which, of course, was not signed by him, could amount to an acknowledgement of the defendants' title under s. 13 and have the effect of starting time running afresh. The argument can conveniently be disposed of at this stage. Accepting the contention that the plaintiff's evidence on this point is self-serving and flimsy at best, the matter is one for the trial judge; she was entitled to reach the conclusion she did on the evidence before her and, in my view, there is no basis upon which this Court is entitled to disturb her finding in this respect. However, it might be added that the proposal as framed would assuredly not raise any suspicion on the part of the true owner that the neighbouring restaurant was claiming a possessory title to the disputed land. Whereas, if, as the plaintiff says, the proposal related to only 40 ft. of house frontage and had so indicated, a suspicion would indeed have been raised.

There is one other factual matter which I also think convenient to deal with now. Counsel for the defendants challenges the trial judge's finding that the vice-president of Loblaws testified "that the use of these lands [the disputed lands] by the plaintiff and his predecessors as a parking lot would interfere with the use that Loblaws intended to make of the property" [at 367 OR, 252 DLR] and submits that that statement is not in accord with the evidence. The matter is of some importance in that the trial judge drew support from her understanding of this witness's testimony in reaching her conclusion that the possession of the plaintiff and his predecessors was adverse to Loblaws' ownership interests even though Loblaws had only an intention to develop the land in the future and had no present use for it.

As I read the record, the learned judge appears to have misapprehended the purport of this witness's evidence, no doubt as a result of the number of objections taken during the course of it. He did not testify that the gravelling and use of the disputed lands for parking purposes would interfere with Loblaws' ability to develop the lands or have any impact on the company's long-range interests. The point he sought to make was that the company intended to develop the lands they owned and "to have less than those lands would interfere with our proposed development. That is what I was trying to say ... I think there would be less use and less ownership if we had less lands." That evidence can hardly be a source of argument. Whether possession of the kind involved in this case can be considered "adverse," as that term is understood in this area of the law, remains a matter to be determined on the facts and circumstances of the case. But, contrary to the view expressed below, the evidence of this witness cannot serve to support the conclusion that the possession was in fact adverse, nor can it be taken as advancing the plaintiff's position in this regard.

The Issues

The arguments advanced on behalf of the defendants resolve themselves into two main issues: First, having regard to the fact that the disputed land was leased from 1956 to 1971, when did time begin to run against the owner of the land? And second, having regard to the owner's intended use of the land, were the acts of possession of the plaintiff and his predecessors sufficient to constitute adverse possession against the owner?

When Time Begins To Run

Section 4 of the *Limitations Act* provides that:

> 4. No person shall ... bring an action to recover any land ... but within ten years next after the time at which the right to ... bring such action, first accrued to the person ... bringing it.

That provision is founded in the traditional notion that it is more important that long and undisturbed possession of land be protected, even if initially wrongful, than that the law should lend its aid to the enforcement of stale claims. Thus, in Ontario, a person who is wrongfully dispossessed of land has ten years within which to bring an action to recover the land. At the end of that period not only is his action statute-barred, his right of ownership is extinguished and the wrongful dispossessor obtains title by adverse possession: s. 15 of the *Limitations Act*; and see, generally, Williams, *Limitation of Actions in Canada*, 2d ed. (1980), c. 7; Megarry and Wade, *The Law of Real Property*, 4th ed. (1975), c. 16; *Cheshire's Modern Law of Real Property*, 12th ed. (1976), p. 883 *et seq.*

In this case, if the use of the disputed land by the plaintiff and his predecessors constituted "adverse possession" and if such possession were adverse to Loblaws, the owner throughout the relevant time, there is no doubt that the statutory period would long since have run its course against Loblaws and, it follows, against the defendants. The period was held to have commenced in 1960 and continued unbroken to 1979. The trial judge made a finding of fact that in 1960 the plaintiff's predecessors "asserted actual and complete possession to the exclusion of all others" [at 368 OR, 253 DLR] and concluded that from then until December, 1975, "the plaintiff and his predecessors in title had actual, exclusive, continuous, visible and notorious occupation of the premises and that from December, 1975, to June, 1979, the plaintiff had such occupation through his tenants" [at 367 OR, 252 DLR].

In the submission of the defendants, however, if the possession was adverse, it was not adverse to the owner and, as against the owner, time could not have begun to run from 1960. The critical fact in this submission is that the actual possession of the disputed land was held continuously by tenants of Loblaws under the terms of written leases until January, 1971. Accordingly, the defendants argue, the plaintiff's possession and that of his predecessors was adverse to the tenants' possessory rights but was not adverse to Loblaws. Loblaws' interest was then non-possessory and, vis-à-vis it, the statutory period could not have begun before 1971 when it resumed possession. Because ten years had not elapsed when the defendants asserted their claim in this action, the plaintiff is not entitled to invoke the *Limitations Act* to defeat their right to recover possession of their land or to impugn their title.

That submission was rejected in the court below. In the view of the trial judge the leases in question did not operate to prevent time from running against Loblaws during this pendency. Since those leases were in the main monthly leases and Loblaws was in a position "to regain possession and take action against the plaintiff," the learned judge considered the English precedents upon which the defendants relied distinguishable, and computed the limitation period as though no leases were ever in existence. Loblaws was treated as being in actual possession of the disputed land from 1960 when the adverse possession upon which the plaintiff relies was first asserted.

I, respectfully, do not agree that the leases can be disregarded on that basis, nor do I agree that Loblaws was in possession of the disputed land in 1960 when the statutory period was found to have commenced.

A party seeking to acquire a possessory title to leasehold land must prove adverse possession for the requisite period of time against both the tenant and the landlord. The tenant's leasehold interest and the landlord's freehold interest must each be extinguished before an absolute possessory title can be successfully established. While there is no authority in this province or elsewhere in Canada on the point, under English law, if an intruder enters upon and adversely possesses a part or the whole of leasehold land, time begins to run in his favour against the tenant from the date the tenant is dispossessed, and the right of the tenant to that part of the leasehold land will be statute-barred at the end of the applicable period. So long, however, as the tenancy continues, the landlord's freehold interest remains unaffected; time does not run against him until the tenancy determines. It is only then that the landlord becomes entitled to possession and, accordingly, it is only then that his right of action arises.

Authority for that proposition may be found in a number of decisions, only three of which I need refer to. In *Tichborne v. Weir* (1892), 67 LT 735 (CA), it was decided that an adverse possessor who holds adversely to a tenant cannot be treated as an assignee of the tenant so as to be rendered liable on the covenants of the lease. In the course of his judgment, Bowen LJ, recognizing the separate and distinct interests of the landlord and tenant vis-à-vis the adverse possessor, made the following observation (at p. 737) which has since been generally quoted and applied:

> From 1802 to the present time nothing has been done to bar any right of the original lessor. Giraud [the adverse possessor] never acquired the fee simple, it was only as against Baxter [the tenant] that he acquired anything. *The most that can be said is, that he acquired an absolute title to the land as against everybody but the landlord.* (Emphasis added.)

In *Taylor v. Twinberrow*, [1930] All ER 342 (KB), a tenant had allowed his brother-in-law to occupy his leasehold premises without paying rent. The brother-in-law occupied the premises as a subtenant at will for the requisite statutory period and as a consequence claimed to be entitled to remain in possession. The tenant in this case had purchased the landlord's freehold interest and brought the action as owner of the fee simple and not as tenant. Scrutton and Lawrence LJJ, sitting as judges of the King's Bench Division, found that while the brother-in-law's possession successfully excluded the tenant, it did not exclude the landlord. Thus, distinguishing the two interests which must be extinguished before an absolute possessory title to leasehold land can be acquired, the plaintiff in his capacity as holder of the fee simple was able to oust his overholding brother-in-law, a result he would not have been able to achieve in his capacity as tenant. Scrutton LJ, in his judgment, quoted the above passage of Bowen LJ in *Tichborne v. Weir* in support of his conclusion that the landlord's freehold interest was not affected by the adverse possession as against the tenant, and at p. 344 said:

> It would not destroy the right of the freeholder, if Taylor's [the tenant's] tenancy was determined, to eject the sub-tenant [the adverse possessor]. The freeholder would not be

in any way bound by the legal relations between tenant and sub-tenant [adverse possessor] after the expiry of the tenant's tenancy.

More recently, in *Fairweather v. St. Marylebone Property Co., Ltd.*, [1962] 2 All ER 288, the House of Lords dealt with a situation in which, in simplified form, a house and garden containing a shed were leased for 99 years. The shed was occupied adversely to the tenant by a neighbour for a period in excess of the statutory period. While the lease was still running, the tenant surrendered it to the landlord. The question was whether the landlord, *qua* freeholder, could resume possession immediately or whether he had no such right until the lease determined by effluxion of time. The majority of the House of Lords held that by surrendering the lease the tenant had abandoned the right to possession with the result that his tenancy had merged in the freehold and had disappeared. The landlord, therefore, was entitled to recover possession of the shed on the strength of his own right to immediate possession of the freehold. All of the law lords were in agreement that the possessory estate acquired by a squatter against a tenant's leasehold interest does not affect the landlord's freehold interest.

Lord Radcliffe made it clear that a squatter's possession defeats only the rights of those to whom it has been adverse. "No one," he emphasized at p. 292, "supposes that adverse possession against a lessee during his term is itself adverse possession against his landlord"; and at p. 295 he observed, "nor can it matter whether the interest defeated by adverse possession is a fixed term of years or a tenancy from year to year." His conclusion is summarized at p. 292 as follows:

> In my opinion both for the purposes of s. 2 of the Real Property Limitation Act, 1874, and for the purposes of s. 6(1) of the Limitation Act, 1939, which has taken the place of the relevant portion of that section, an owner in fee simple subject to a term of years has an estate or interest in reversion or remainder and, consequently, his right of action against a squatter on the demised land is to be deemed to have accrued at the date when the preceding estate or interest represented by the term determines in such manner that his estate or interest falls into possession.

Lord Denning regarded the proposition as equally plain, saying at pp. 296-7:

> The first suggestion is that the title of the leaseholder to the shed is extinguished completely, not only against the squatter, but also against the freeholder. So that the leasehold interest disappears altogether, and the freeholder becomes entitled to the land. I reject this suggestion completely ... . *The correct view is that the freehold is an estate in reversion within s. 6(1) of the Limitation Act, 1939, and time does not run against the freeholder until the determination of the lease.* ... [Emphasis added.]
>
> • • •
>
> The fourth suggestion is that the title of the leaseholder to the shed is extinguished *as against the squatter*, but remains good *as against the freeholder*. This seems to me the only acceptable suggestion. If it is adopted, it means that time does not run against the freeholder until the lease is determined—which is only just.

Lord Morris, while dissenting on the main issue, agreed that no right of action accrues in favour of a landlord against a squatter until the end of the lease. He noted at p. 302:

After a lessor has granted a lease to a lessee for a term of years the right to possession for the duration of the term is the substance of the lessee's title and if anything is gained in this case by speaking separately of his estate or interest—of his estate or interest as well. If a third person trespasses on the land the lessee has a right of action to eject him but at the expiration of the period prescribed by Parliament for the bringing of an action to recover possession the title of the lessee "to the land" is extinguished (see the Limitation Act, 1939, s. 16 …). There is then no one who can eject the adverse possessor and he has the best right to bring an action against anyone who in turn intrudes on his possession. *There is no one with a better title to possession until the time arrives when, at the end of the period of the lease, the lessor is entitled to possession.* (Emphasis added.)

The *rationale* of those decisions can be applied with equal force to the circumstances of the present case and, in my opinion, should be. As I view this matter, it makes no difference whether the leasehold interest is created by means of a tenancy for a term certain or a periodic tenancy of no stated duration from year to year or month to month; nor do I attach any significance to the fact that the tenancy is terminable on short notice. So long as the lease continues in effect, possession is vested in the tenant who, as a normal consequence of the landlord-tenant relationship, has control over and the power to exclude others from the leased property. The landlord's interest is non-possessory and remains so until the lease is terminated and possession reverts to him. Until then the possessory rights of the tenant continue intact, and the possession of a squatter initiated during the term of the lease, while adverse to the tenant, cannot be adverse to the landlord. It follows, that until the landlord's interest becomes possessory, his right of action does not accrue and the statutory period does not run against him. This conclusion accords with s. 5(1) of the Act which makes clear that a right of action does not accrue unless a party entitled to possession has been dispossessed while so entitled. See also s-ss. 5(11) and (12) of the Act.

In this case, when Nelson first asserted adverse possession in 1960, Mrs. Miller was possessed of the disputed land, and remained so until 1970. It is true that during most of that period Loblaws could have regained possession by exercising its right to terminate her leasehold interest on 30 days' notice. But, contrary to the view expressed in the judgment appealed from, I do not agree that that fact of itself transforms Loblaws' non-possessory future interest into a possessory present interest. An unexercised power of termination is not tantamount to immediate possession. Only when the power is enforced does the owner become entitled to possession—and only then does the owner's right of action accrue. Here, of course, Loblaws did not exercise its power to terminate. Accordingly, the statutory period could not be computed from 1960 or, indeed (subject to the issue arising by successive leases, to which I shall come in a moment), from any date prior to the date on which Mrs. Miller vacated the premises and possession was returned to Loblaws.

As a practical matter, I see no reason why Loblaws should be required to avail itself of its power of termination and [to] destroy the existing landlord-tenant relationship or, failing that, suffer the consequence of having time run against it from 1960 when adverse possession was initiated. Loblaws' interest in the land was then, and in fact

remained, non-possessory. This is not a case of an impermissible change or improvement being made to the physical condition of leased property to the knowledge of the
owner. This owner's inactivity can in no sense be regarded as a representation that the
wrongful possession will not be disturbed, and the doctrine of equitable estoppel is
inapplicable here.

Mrs. Miller chose, for whatever reason, not to assert her right to possession and
prohibit the restaurant owners from placing gravel and parking cars on the vacant leasehold land under her occupation and control. But the tenant's failure to oust a squatter
should not prejudice the landlord's right of action when the tenancy determines. And
particularly so in the present circumstances where it is manifest that the condition of the
land was not altered in any significant way by the acts of the plaintiff or his predecessors, nor was Loblaws' intended use interfered with or its reversionary interest affected
by those acts. This, it should perhaps be added, is not, as counsel for the plaintiff
suggests, a case falling within the line of authority in which leasehold premises are
permanently damaged and the present economic value of the landlord's reversionary
interest diminished, so that even though the landlord is not in possession, an immediate
cause of action is held to accrue: *Woodfall's Law of Landlord and Tenant*, 28th ed.
(1978), pp. 737-9. The landlord's complaint here is based on wrongful possession and
not on any injury to or loss of value of the land. That cause of action arises after the
landlord resumes possession.

When then did time begin to run against Loblaws? Clearly, as the defendants concede, the statutory period had begun as of January 2, 1971, when the Noyes' lease
concluded and actual possession was delivered up to Loblaws. If this is the proper
starting date, the defendants' claim is not barred. This action was instituted in July,
1979, and, for the plaintiff to succeed, the statutory period must have commenced prior
to July, 1969. The Noyes' lease came into effect only in April, 1970, and obviously
cannot affect the result. Consequently, I think it unnecessary to consider the submission
that, if the statutory period began when Mrs. Miller relinquished possession, the Noyes'
lease stopped time from running for the term of the Noyes' tenancy. I propose, therefore,
to treat the statutory period as having begun by April, 1970, at the latest, and I proceed
on that basis.

The question then is, did the statutory period begin any earlier than April, 1970?
The answer to that question depends on the Miller tenancy. Indeed, the defendants'
claim stands or falls on whether time began to run against Loblaws during or after the
Miller tenancy.

Clearly, Loblaws was not possessed of the disputed land in 1960 when the plaintiff's predecessors initiated their adverse possession. If Mrs. Miller had continued in
possession from 1960 to 1970 pursuant to the terms of the periodic tenancy created by
her 1959 lease, for the reasons already stated, time would not have begun to run before
April, 1970, when Loblaws actually regained possession. Accepting that conclusion, the
argument put against the defendants is that when the second Miller lease commenced on
January 1, 1962, the first lease was surrendered by operation of law immediately prior to
the second lease coming into effect. The surrender was necessary to enable Loblaws to
grant possession under the second lease. Accordingly, the argument proceeds, there was
an instant in time between the two leases when possession reverted to Loblaws, and in

that instant a right of action accrued in favour of Loblaws against the adverse possessor. Thus, the argument concludes, even if the trial judge erred in computing the statutory period from 1960, time began to run against Loblaws in 1962 when Mrs. Miller's monthly lease was surrendered and her two-year lease commenced, and the defendants are none the less statute-barred.

The plaintiff finds support for the argument in the decision of the House of Lords in *Ecclesiastical Com'rs of England & Wales v. Rowe* (1880), 5 App. Cas. 736. That case is taken as standing for the proposition that if a lease is surrendered and a new lease granted contemporaneously to the lessee, the reversion must be considered as falling into possession at the time the new lease is granted and, as against an adverse possessor of the demised premises whose adverse possession began during the currency of the old lease, a right of action accrues to the reversioner at the date of the new lease and time runs against him from that date: 28 Hals., 4th ed., pp. 332-3, para. 737.

On its facts, *Rowe* concerned church lands first owned by the dean of the local parish and later by the ecclesiastical commissioners. In 1812, the dean granted a lease to Morris for 21 years from August, 1809. In 1820, the lease was assigned to Jones and in consideration of the surrender of the original lease, a new lease was granted to Jones. This lease was renewed in 1828, 1834, 1842 and finally in 1848, each renewal being granted in consideration of the surrender of the former lease. In 1859, the commissioners purchased the existing lease and became entitled to possession of all of the lands and premises demised by the lease. In 1821, Sarah Moulton had purchased a part of the leasehold lands and premises from the original tenant. She and the defendant Rowe, who derived his title from her, remained in undisturbed possession until 1877. However, as the original tenant had no right to convey the lands, Sarah Moulton and Rowe were held to have been in adverse possession. In 1877, the commissioners brought the action to eject Rowe.

Although the case was decided on the issue as to whether a 20 or 60-year limitation period applied to the right of action accruing to the commissioners, the date on which the right of action first accrued would be the same whether the limitation period were 20 years or 60 years. The House of Lords held that a right of action accrued at the date of the first lease renewal during which Sarah Moulton was in possession of part of the leased premises. The Lord Chancellor, Lord Selborne, in the course of his speech, stated at pp. 741-2:

> If no right of action had accrued to the dean before 1854, when Dean Luxmoore died, the Appellants ought to succeed, for the lease which was current in 1854 was not surrendered till 1859, and the action was brought within twenty years from that time. But I am of opinion that a right of action did, before 1854, accrue to the dean, and that this right accrued not later than the earliest grant of a lease by way of renewal which was made by the dean after the commencement of the possession of Sarah Moulton.
>
> • • •
>
> If so, her possession commenced during the currency of the lease granted by the dean to Hugh Jones on the 2d of May, 1820, which lease continued to subsist until the 18th of June, 1828, when it was surrendered contemporaneously with and in consideration of the grant of the new lease of that date. On that surrender, a right of

action to recover the premises of which Sarah Moulton was then in possession accrued to the dean, and all the new leasehold interests then and on each subsequent renewal created were, in my opinion, derived from and out of the estate in possession, which then became vested in the dean. That surrender, although not effected by a separate instrument, must, in my opinion, be deemed to have preceded the new grant; and I cannot assent to the argument addressed to your Lordships by the Appellant's counsel, that the effect of a renewal contemporaneous with a surrender, is, to prevent the accruer of a right of action to the lessor by the surrender of the former lease against a *disseisor* or trespasser; an argument which seems to me inconsistent with the provisions as to reversionary estates contained in the 3d and 5th sections of the *Statute of Limitations*, and which if well founded, would prevent that statute from ever running in favour of any length of possession whatever against a title to church leaseholds renewed from time to time in the manner which was formerly customary, and of which an example is found in this case.

Lord Blackburn dissented on the 60-year limitation point but expressly agreed with the Lord Chancellor as to when the right of action to recover the land first accrued.

In reaching its conclusion, the House of Lords found it necessary to distinguish a decision of the Court of Appeal, *President & Scholars of Corpus Christi College, Oxford v. Rogers* (1879), 49 LJ Ex. 4 (CA), upon which counsel for the ecclesiastical commissioners had relied. In that case, the plaintiff college had for centuries leased certain property which included a cottage and garden. In 1818, the tenant let the cottage and garden to the defendant Rogers (or rather, her father, from whom she derived title) who paid rent until 1853. Thereafter she continued in possession without payment of any rental until 1878 when the college brought the action to recover possession of the cottage and garden. In 1851, the college had renewed the then existing lease by granting the tenant a new 20-year lease. In 1857, however, that lease was superseded by a second lease granted by the college to the tenant for 20 years from October, 1857. It appears that the college resumed possession after the expiry of the second lease in 1877. The action to recover possession was commenced in 1878 and was defended on the ground that it was then statute-barred.

On appeal, counsel for the defendant (whose position was that of an adverse possessor) contended that the 20-year limitation period began to run against the owner of the property in 1857 when the second lease was granted. When that lease was granted the earlier 1851 lease was thereupon surrendered by operation of law and the college acquired an estate in possession in the premises. There was, as he put it, "a moment of time" in which the right to possession vested in the owner. The granting of a new lease is the act of an owner in possession. Once an owner has gained an estate in possession time begins to run against him. To hold otherwise, it was contended, would allow recovery after any length of time and any number of renewals, and afford opportunity for the existence of the evils against which the statute was intended to provide.

The court had little difficulty in rejecting that contention. Lord Coleridge CJ at p. 5 said:

I think there is no ground for the appellant's contention. It is admitted that the only point in the case is whether, when the lease granted to [the tenant] in 1851 by the college, was surrendered by operation of law in 1857, the college could have done anything in the way of entering upon the premises, or asserting their right to them. In my opinion they could not. There was no mode in which the college could exercise any such right, and to construe the Act in the way suggested for the appellants would be to legalise spoliation.

Supposing the college, just before 1857, had known that this defendant had no title to the premises, and was paying no rent to [the tenant], then, according to the view presented to us, because the tenant does not pay his immediate landlord the superior landlord is to lose his property. [Council] contends for a similar proposition, because he says that where there is a surrender of a lease by the act and operation of law, on a new lease being granted, then there is some invisible moment of time in which the superior landlord loses his right.

• • •

I am of opinion that there is no point of time at which the superior landlord could enter upon or assert his right to the premises. ...

Bramwell LJ agreed adding that to bar the right to recover there must be "an appreciable moment of time between the grant and the surrender" [at 6]. Brett LJ contented himself with describing the contention as "ridiculous."

Corpus Christi was not overruled by the House of Lords in *Rowe* but was distinguished, mainly on the ground that the "facts of that case ... were altogether different from the present" [at 742]. I am frank to say that I have difficulty discerning factual distinctions between the two cases of sufficient significance to produce conflicting conclusions on the question central to both: when does time begin to run against the landlord? According to *Rowe*, time begins to run at the instant the existing lease is surrendered and the same tenant's new lease commences. According to *Corpus Christi*, the mere surrender of an existing lease, by act or operation of law, and the contemporaneous grant of a new lease to the same tenant does not set time running.

Neither of these judgments has been considered by a Canadian court and it appears that the point in issue has not previously been the subject of adjudication here. I, of course, recognize *Rowe* as the more authoritative decision and, although the issue appears rarely to have arisen, as the decision which has been followed in England. None the less, without attempting to draw factual distinctions between the obviously different background and circumstances of that case and this, I am, with all due deference, of the opinion that it ought not to be followed in this case.

As I view the matter, in cases where the tenant remains in actual possession, more than a theoretical entitlement to possession is required before a "right of action" can be said to "accrue" to the landlord, and time begins to run under the provisions of the *Limitations Act*. To my mind it would be unfair to compute the limitation on the owner's remedy from a time when, on any practical or realistic view, he is clearly not in possession and the possibility of his bringing action to recover a part of his leased land is non-existent or, at best, highly improbable. The gravamen of the action is the usurpation of the right to possession, and in the circumstances under discussion, the long and the short of the matter is that there is no such usurpation. Until the tenant vacates and the owner regains possession, the owner's rights have not been interfered with, he suffers no harm, and he has no cause to bring suit. The fact that the tenancy was continued by successive leases, in my opinion, is not an appropriate criterion for determining when time starts to run against the owner's remedy.

The conclusion that a landlord returns to possession when he grants a new lease to an existing tenant already in possession is founded on a legal fiction. If the tenant vacates the leased premises, clearly the landlord falls back into possession. But if the tenant remains in possession, how is the landlord also in possession? Only by employing the fiction is it possible to conclude that possession of leased premises has been surrendered to the landlord when in fact the tenant is in actual possession. The fiction, while appropriate to landlord-and-tenant law, ought not to constitute a starting point for the limitation period in adverse possession cases.

The doctrine of surrender by operation of law was developed to enable a landlord to grant a valid lease in cases where he is not in possession. The early cases employing the doctrine show that it was intended to provide landlords with a power they otherwise would not have. For instance, in *Ive's Case* (1597), 5 Co. Rep. 11a, 77 ER 64, a new lease was granted to a tenant who was currently holding under a prior lease from the same landlord. The Court of Common Pleas held, at p. 11b:

> That by the acceptance of a future lease to begin divers years after, the said lease of the wood for 62 years was presently surrendered, *because the lessee by acceptance thereof had affirmed the lessor to have ability to make the new lease*, which he had not, if the first lease shall stand. ... (Emphasis added.)

The doctrine is said to rest upon the principle of estoppel. The tenant is estopped from denying the landlord's power to grant a new lease, and the landlord is afforded a power which he would not have without the doctrine. This is illustrated in the leading case of *Lyon v. Reed et al.* (1844), 13 M & W 285, 153 ER 118, where, at pp. 305-6, the following passage appears:

> This term [surrender by operation of law] is applied to cases where the owner of a particular estate has been a party to some act, the validity of which he is by law afterwards estopped from disputing, *and which would not be valid if his particular estate had continued to exist ...* . Thus, if [a] lessee for years accept a new lease for his lessor, he is estopped from saying that his lessor had not power to make the new lease; *and, as the lessor could not do this until the prior lease had been surrendered*, the law says that the acceptance of such new lease is of itself a surrender of the former. (Emphasis added.)

See, generally, *Cheshire*, pp. 461-2; 27 Hals., 4th ed., pp. 352-4, paras. 446-7; and Megarry and Wade, pp. 667-8.

In this case, there is, of course, no issue as to whether Loblaws had the power to grant a second lease to Mrs. Miller. As between them, Loblaws may be deemed by operation of law to have returned to possession for the invisible moment needed to grant possession under the 1962 lease. But that fictional concept ought not to be employed to set time running under the *Limitations Act*. In a contest between a true owner of land and an adverse possessor, the issues should be determined on the real facts and circumstances pertinent to the actual possessory interests involved and not on an artificial basis. And particularly so when the fiction sought to be invoked was developed for purposes bearing no relationship to the law relating to possessory titles. It would be ironic in the extreme to employ a doctrine designed to assist landlords against them by diminishing the protection the reversionary rights to leasehold land would otherwise receive against adverse possessors. The reality of the tenant's actual possession, in my opinion, cannot be ignored in determining when the statutory period is to begin. In short, I would not use the fictional instant when, for other purposes, possession is said to revert to the landlord as a bench-mark for the accrual of claims in adverse possession cases. Accordingly, I am of the opinion that possession of the disputed land, for the purposes of the *Limitations Act*, did not revert to Loblaws until the Miller tenancy terminated in April, 1970, and Loblaws' right of action did not accrue before that date.

Finally, I might add that I can find no policy considerations militating in favour of the plaintiff in the circumstances of this case. He can claim no hardship resulting from the length of time that elapsed before the owner took action against him. He paid nothing for the disputed land; he knew it was not owned by his predecessors or conveyed to him; he made no improvements to it; he paid no taxes on it; he expended no money other than to spread some gravel over it, and, in renting his restaurant in 1975, he did not include this land as part of the demised premises and did not then, or at any other time, prejudicially change his position in reliance on an alleged possessory title. Further, unlike the situation manifested in the early English cases where under inadequate conveyancing and registration systems the doctrine of title by adverse possession became necessary as a protection to just titles, the state of this title was clear and beyond question. There was no confusion as to the ownership or boundaries of the plaintiff's or defendants' lands.

When all is said and done, this is a case of a businessman seeking to expand significantly the size of his commercial land holdings by grabbing a valuable piece of his neighbour's vacant property. The words of Mr. Justice Middleton used in denying the claim of an adverse possessor to enclosed land in *Campeau v. May* (1911), 19 OWR 751 at p. 752, are apposite:

> It may be said that this makes it very hard to acquire a possessory title. I think the rule would be quite different if the statute was being invoked in aid of a defective title, but I can see nothing in the policy of the law, which demands that it should be made easy to steal land or any hardship which requires an exception to the general rule that the way of the transgressor is hard.

Conclusion

In light of the conclusion I have reached on the defendants' first submission, I think it inappropriate to consider the second submission, namely, whether, having regard to the defendants' intended use of the land, the acts of possession of the plaintiff and his predecessors were sufficient to constitute adverse possession against the owner. That question is better left for another day but, in the meantime, I do not wish to be understood as necessarily agreeing with the conclusion reached by the trial judge on this point.

In the result, the defendants' claim to recover possession of their land is not barred by the *Limitations Act*. Accordingly I would allow the appeal, set aside the judgment at trial, and order that the plaintiff's action be dismissed. Judgment will go in favour of the defendants on their counterclaim ordering that the plaintiff forthwith deliver up possession of the disputed land. The defendants are entitled to the costs of the appeal and the trial.

Discussion Notes

Commencement of the Limitation Period

On appeal to the Supreme Court of Canada, the court issued a brief decision dismissing the appeal and confirming "complete agreement with the reasons of Robins JA." The court also declined (at 708) to address "the question whether the appellant had otherwise met the requirements of extinguishing the respondents' title pursuant to ss. 4 and 15 of the Limitations Act." See [1986] 2 SCR 707. In the light of this decision of the Supreme Court of Canada, how should we formulate the test for the commencement of the limitation period in statutes of limitation?

The Relevance of Intention

The decision of Robins JA in the Ontario Court of Appeal reversed the outcome in the decision at trial. In the trial judgment, Van Camp J held that since the lessor could have terminated the leases to tenants at any time on 30 days' notice, the lessor's interest (and not just that of the tenants) was at risk throughout the relevant period. Although he disagreed with Van Camp J on this analysis, Brian Bucknall agreed with her analysis of the issue of the relevance of intention. In "Case Comment: *Giouroukos v. Cadillac-Fairview Corp.*" (1982), 24 RPR 307, at 310, he suggested:

> On the second issue, Madame Justice Van Camp's decision is a welcome reassertion of what had been the standard Ontario position with regard to the quality of possession necessary to run a possessory period.
>
> The Ontario Limitations Act refers only to the question of whether an action at law is available to the holder of paper title. The problem of whether or not the holder of paper title might wish to bring such an action or might feel that the use being made of his land was of any concern to him is not addressed. Recent Ontario decisions have, however, emphasized an aspect of the English doctrine with respect to possessory titles which is not found in the Ontario legislation. These cases, beginning, to my mind, with *Keefer v. Arillotta* and following through with *Raab v. Caranci*, *Kosman v. Lapointe* and *Bea v. Robinson*, are sometimes cited for the principle that in order for a possessory period to run, the possession in question must be "adverse" to the interests of the true owner. In this case, the owners throughout the period in dispute had no present use for the land and only a future intention to redevelop. The simple clearing and stabilizing of the surface of the property could have very little impact on the long term interests of the owners. (It should be noted, however, that a vice president of the defendant was called to give evidence and stated "that the use of these lands by the plaintiff and his predecessors as a parking lot would interfere with the use that Loblaws intended to make of the property." What induced him to make so damaging, and apparently unnecessary, a statement is a mystery.) The situation in which the defendant found itself is almost directly analogous to the situation in *Williams Bros. Direct Supply Stores v. Raftery*, an English case in which some tenants established and maintained a "Victory Garden" during the Second World War on some vacant land to the rear of their apartment building. The garden continued to flourish when hostilities ceased and some

years later it was alleged that, in fact, a possessory interest had been established. The English Court held that since the owners of the vacant land were only waiting for the appropriate time for redevelopment, and since the garden did not impede in any way that redevelopment, no period could run. This case was relied on in *Keefer v. Arillotta*.

Madame Justice Van Camp does not use the *Williams v. Raftery* approach. Instead, she correctly distinguishes the recent decisions in *Fletcher v. Storoschuk* and *John Austin & Sons Ltd. v. Smith* (though these cases are best treated as situations in which there is no evidence of continuing possession of the disputed interests rather than situations where possession has occurred but has not been "adverse") and holds that the fact that the defendants and their predecessors had no immediate use for the lands while the plaintiffs and their predecessors possessed them was of no consequence. Her decision accords well with the recent decision of Mr. Justice Anderson in *Beaudoin v. Aubin*, a case in which the "intention" and "adversity" tests were thoroughly reviewed and rejected. Madame Justice Van Camp's decision stands for what I believe to be the preferable principle that once an action (in trespass or ejectment or for a writ of possession) lies, it should be brought regardless of the long range intentions of the holders of paper title.

Do you agree with Bucknall that *Giouroukos* should be decided in a way consistent with *Beaudoin v. Aubin*, a position which makes "long-range intentions" irrelevant? To what extent is the approach of Robins JA in *Giouroukos* consistent with the language of the statutes of limitation?

Underlying Purpose in Statutes of Limitation

The judgment of Robins JA is significant because it addresses expressly the issue of underlying purpose in statutes of limitation. Consider his comments in the context of the justifications offered by Callaghan and Rose that were examined earlier in this section. How does the assertion of a policy against "land-grabbing" accord with the underlying purpose of statutes of limitation as identified by Callaghan and Rose? In this context consider the following comment by T.W. Merrill in (1985), 79 *Northwestern University Law Review* 1122, at 1152-53:

> I suggested that courts manipulate the common law doctrine of adverse possession in order to punish or deter those who intentionally dispossess others of their property. A less dramatic means of achieving a similar end would be to apply a liability rule in cases of bad faith possession. A rule of limited indemnification would in effect impose a fine on bad faith dispossessors equal to the value of the property at the time of original entry. Squatters and thieves would know that, even if they could obtain title to property after the passage of the statute of limitations ... they would have to pay for their gain ... . If courts knew that the bad faith possessor would be faced with an action for indemnification, they might not feel compelled to manipulate the traditional common law doctrine in order to "punish" those who acquired the property in bad faith, and "reward" those who acquired it innocently.

Do you think this suggestion would have resulted in a better solution in *Giouroukos*? Is it appropriate, as Merrill suggests, to separate the issue of entitlement (and the application of traditional principles of possession) from the issue of remedy?

Would this solution have been more satisfactory than the approach adopted by Robins JA?

Mutual Mistake: The Relevance of Intention?

In the context of statutes of limitation, is there a way of distinguishing the possession of someone who is innocent or mistaken by contrast with that of a trespassing "land-grabber"? In examining the case that follows, consider whether the reasoning about legal principles in relation to the facts clarifies the principles regarding intention.

Wood v. Gateway of Uxbridge Properties Inc.
[1990] 75 OR (2d) 769 (Gen. Div.)

MOLDAVER J: ...

Brief Summary of Case

For almost 18 years, the applicants, Mr. and Mrs. Wood, have enjoyed the exclusive use of a two-acre parcel of land, abutting upon a large tract of land which they purchased in 1972. Until 1989, they honestly believed that the two acres belonged to them.

For almost 17 years, their neighbours to the south had no idea that they were the rightful owners of the two-acre parcel. They too honestly believed that it belonged to the applicants.

As it turns out, everyone was mistaken. This became apparent in 1989, when the respondent, a company known as The Gateway of Uxbridge Property Inc. (Gateway), purchased the land immediately south of the property owned by the applicants. At that time, a new survey was prepared. It established beyond doubt that Gateway held paper title to the two acres.

Nature of This Action

The applicants seek a declaration against the respondents extinguishing all of their rights and title to the two-acre parcel. The respondent Gateway opposes this. The other named respondents are mortgagees of the Gateway lands. They do not oppose the application.

In order to succeed, the applicants must establish that Gateway's right to recover possession of the two acres has been extinguished by operation of ss. 4 and 15 of the *Limitations Act*, RSO 1980, c. 240 ... . To do this, the applicants must show that for an uninterrupted period of ten years, they were in actual possession of the two-acre parcel; they intended to exclude the true owners from possession; and the true owners were in fact effectively excluded from possession. These are the tests set out in *Masidon Investments Ltd. v. Ham* (1984), 45 OR (2d) 563, 2 OAC 147, 31 RPR 200 (CA). In that case, after listing the three tests, Mr. Justice Blair stated, at p. 567 OR, p. 206 RPR:

> The claim will fail unless the claimant meets each of these three tests and time will begin to run against the owner only from the last date when all of them are satisfied.

In this case, the respondent Gateway conceded that the first test had been met. It was admitted that the applicants had been in actual possession of the two-acre parcel from 1972 to the present. However, the respondent submitted that the applicants had failed to satisfy the remaining tests.

The Issues

1. When mutual mistake exists, is it legally possible for the party seeking possessory title to establish the requisite intent to exclude the true owners from possession?

2. When mutual mistake exists, is it legally possible for the party seeking possessory title to establish effective exclusion of the true owners from possession?

3. Have the applicants, in fact, established the effective exclusion of the true owners during the requisite time frame?

The Facts

... Description of the Two-Acre Parcel

The two-acre parcel is found at the northwest corner of the lands purchased by the respondent Gateway. It is long and narrow and takes the form of a wedge. The parcel has been marked as Part 2 on the plan of survey prepared by H.F. Gander Company Limited, found at Appendix B.

[The following figure is the author's—it is not part of the original case:]

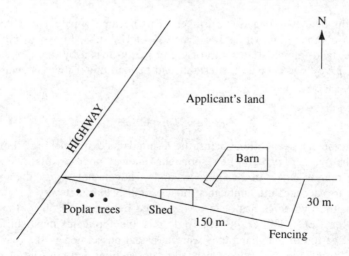

It will be seen that the northern boundary of the two-acre parcel borders, in part, on the southern boundary of the large parcel of land which the applicants purchased in 1972. At the east end of the northern boundary is a post and wire fence which extends in a southerly direction for about 30 metres. This fence then proceeds along the southern boundary of the two-acre parcel in a north-westerly direction for approximately 150 metres. Where the fence stops, a row of poplar trees forming a natural boundary continues north-westerly to the western end of the parcel, forming the point of the wedge.

Applicants' Belief

In 1972, the applicants purchased the large tract of land immediately north of the two-acre parcel. However, at the time of purchase, they believed that the two-acre wedge formed part of their land. They had good cause for this belief because this is what they were told. Mr. Rhodes, the prior owner, testified that he believed that the two acres formed part of the land that he was selling. He so advised the applicants. Mr. Rhodes had treated the two-acre parcel as his from the time that he purchased the north parcel in 1968.

In addition, a gravel driveway existed entirely within the two-acre parcel. It commenced at the point of the wedge, that is, the western extremity, and extended easterly for a distance of several hundred metres. This driveway was located immediately north of the poplar trees. It provided access to a house and barn located, for the most part, just north of the two-acre parcel. (The survey prepared by the respondent Gateway in 1989 showed that the southern extremities of both the house and barn encroached slightly upon the north edge of the two-acre parcel.) In addition, a third building, referred to as a frame shed, was located entirely within the two-acre wedge. The gravel driveway also provided access to this building.

Activities of the Applicants on the Two-Acre Parcel

From 1972 until the present, the applicants have lived in the house which encroaches slightly on the two-acre parcel. The applicants have used the gravel driveway on a daily basis as a means of ingress and egress to and from the property.

For approximately 15 years, the applicants farmed the east half of the two-acre parcel. As part of this, they used the barn which also encroaches slightly on the two-acre parcel. As well, they housed farm employees in the frame shed located entirely within the two acres.

Sometime around 1987, the applicants ceased farming and commenced a lumber business on the property. Since that time, the eastern portion of the two-acre parcel has been used as a lumber yard. The barn has been used to store lumber and supplies. The frame shed has been rented out commercially to tenants.

During the 18-year period, the applicants have maintained the gravel driveway and all of the buildings. As well, they have mended the post and wire fence which encloses the entire eastern boundary and a significant portion of the southern boundary of the two-acre parcel.

In summary, for the past 18 years, the applicants have openly and continuously enjoyed the use of the disputed land. They have at all times maintained the buildings, two of which encroach upon and one of which rests exclusively within the two-acre parcel. They have actively and continuously conducted significant commercial operations on this property for the same period of time. They have also maintained and repaired the fence which encloses almost half of the property. They have left standing the row of poplar trees immediately south of the driveway which forms a natural southern boundary on the west half of the two acres.

History of the Property Purchased by the Respondent Gateway

The evidence indicates that the large parcel of land known as the south lot was purchased by Mrs. Hester in 1973. She and her husband initially intended to build a home on this property. However, in April of 1974, these plans changed and the Hesters decided to keep the land for long term investment. At no time during their ownership did the Hesters make any use of their lot.

However, in 1977, they leased the "vacant portions" of their property to the applicants. The agreement, contained in a letter dated May 12, 1977, provided for no rent during 1977 and 1978 and payment of $13.50 per acre for the successive three years. This arrangement was advantageous to the Hesters since the applicants would farm their property and thereby relieve the Hesters from maintaining it.

The evidence is clear that the Hesters at all times believed that the two-acre parcel belonged to the applicants. They had complete knowledge of the activities carried out by the applicants and understandably, registered no complaint. When they leased the "vacant lands" to the applicants, they did not intend for the agreement to cover the two-acre parcel.

The Hesters sold the south lot to Mr. Garro in May of 1987. Mr. and Mrs. Garro purchased the land with the intention of building a house but they too abandoned these plans. The Garros made no use of the property except to build a small chicken barn at the south-east corner of their lot. The Garros were holding the property as an investment when the respondent Gateway purchased it in 1989.

Throughout their tenure, the Garros honestly believed that the applicants were the true owners of the two-acre parcel. They too had full knowledge of the activities carried out by the applicants and again, understandably, made no complaint.

Discovery of the Problem

In 1989, before purchasing the south lot from Mr. and Mrs. Garro, the respondent Gateway had a survey prepared. The survey clearly revealed that the two-acre parcel was in fact part of the south lot.

Throughout the course of each of the prior transactions regarding the north and south lots, all of the parties had available to them a survey which had been prepared in 1967. This survey was accurate as far as it went. However, it failed to demarcate the buildings, fences, poplar trees, driveway and the like, and therefore, no one knew how these related to the actual boundary lines. ...

[The court then examined the first issue—that is, whether it is ever possible for a person seeking possession, in a case of mutual mistake, to establish the requisite intent to exclude the true owners from possession. Citing Anderson J in *Beaudoin v. Aubin* (among other cases), the judge concluded:]

Evidence of mutual mistake may justify an inference that the party seeking possessory title did in fact intend to exclude all others, including the true owners. This is an inference which may be drawn. It is not a presumption which must be drawn.

The trier of fact must look to the whole of the evidence to determine whether the claimant did, in fact, have the requisite intent to dispossess the true owners. However, in the absence of any evidence to the contrary, evidence of mutual mistake could alone justify such a finding.

For these reasons, I am satisfied that in cases of mutual mistake, it is legally possible for the party seeking possessory title to establish the requisite intent to dispossess the true owners. Issue one must therefore be answered "Yes."

Issue Two—The Law

When mutual mistake exists, is it legally possible for the party seeking possessory title to establish effective exclusion of the true owners from possession?

In *Masidon, supra*, Mr. Justice Blair held that a person seeking possessory title must establish the effective exclusion of the true owners from possession. To decide this, the court posed the following question at p. 568 OR, p. 207 RPR:

> Was the use of the land made by the appellant inconsistent with that of the respondents? The question [is one] of "adverse possession."

In the next major paragraph, Mr. Justice Blair made the following observation [at 568 OR, 207 RPR]:

> As a consequence of the reforming statutes of the 1830s, adverse possession is established where the claimant's use of the land is inconsistent with the owner's "enjoyment of the soil for the purposes for which he intended to use it": *Leigh v. Jack* (1879), 5 Ex.D 264 at p. 273, *per* Bramwell LJ, and see Megarry and Wade, *The Law of Real Property*, 4th ed. (1975), p. 1013.

His Lordship then continued p. 568 OR, pp. 207-08 RPR:

> Recent decisions in this Court have established that not every use of land will amount to adverse possession excluding that of the owner. Madam Justice Wilson summarized the effect of these decisions in *Fletcher v. Storoschuk et al., supra*, at p. 724 as follows:

> > ... [A]cts relied on to constitute adverse possession must be considered relative to the nature of the land and in particular the use and enjoyment of it intended to be made by the owner: see *Lord Advocate v. Lord Lovat* (1880), 5 App. Cas. 273 at 288; *Kirby v. Cowderoy*, [1912] AC 599 at 603. The mere fact that the defendants did various things on the ... land is not enough to show adverse possession. The things they did must be inconsistent with the form of use and enjoyment the plaintiff intended to make of it: see *Leigh v. Jack* (1879), 5 Ex.D 264; *St. Clair Beach Estates Limited v. MacDonald et al.* (1974), 5 OR (2d) 482, 50 DLR (3d) 650; *Keefer v. Arillotta* (1976), 13 OR (2d) 680, 72 DLR (3d) 182. Only then can such acts be relied upon as evidencing the necessary "*animus possidendi*" vis-à-vis the owner.

I must confess some difficulty applying this "test" to the case at bar. I say this because the true owners did not know that they were the rightful owners of the two-acre parcel during the requisite time frame. How then is it possible to determine what use they intended for the property when they at no time even contemplated its use? And if they had no intended use for the property, how can one compare the use of the applicants to find consistency or lack thereof with a non-existent intended use?

The respondent Gateway argued that the onus was upon the applicants to establish that the activities carried out by the applicants were inconsistent with the intended use of the property by the respondent or its predecessors. But since the respondent and its predecessors had no intended use for the property, the respondent submitted that the application must of necessity fail due to legal impossibility.

I cannot accept this proposition. If accurate, it would mean that in cases involving mutual mistake, no action could ever lie for a declaration of possessory title. And yet, there are numerous examples, already cited, where possessory title has been awarded in cases involving mutual mistake. These include: *Clarke v. Babbitt; Nourse v. Clarke; McGugan v. Turner; Laing v. Moran; Beaudoin v. Aubin*; and *Keil v. 762098 Ontario Inc.*, all *supra*. None of these cases even referred to the "inconsistency" test.

In *Masidon, supra*, it will be recalled that the court distinguished the facts in that case from a situation involving colour of right or mutual mistake. The extract bears repetition [at 575 OR, 215 RPR]:

> The appellant's occupancy of the land was not justified by any suggestion of colour of right or mistake as to title or boundaries. Occupation under colour of right or mistake might justify an inference that the trespasser occupied the lands with the intention of excluding all others which would, of course, include the true owners.

I do not read this to mean that in cases of mutual mistake, an application for possessory title must of necessity fail. Surely the Court of Appeal would have said so had this been the case. They did not because that simply is not the law.

The "Inconsistency Test"

As previously indicated, no mention of the "inconsistency" test is found in cases involving mutual mistake. In my opinion, this is so because the relevance of the "test," if it is a "test" at all, is restricted to situations where a trespasser seeks possessory title. Here, I refer to a trespasser as a person who uses land knowing that it belongs to someone else. This is a far different situation from a person who uses land under an honest, albeit mistaken, belief as to rightful ownership.

In cases of trespass, the law has placed a very high onus on those who would seek to dispossess the rightful owner. The reason for this is simple. It is a rather shocking proposition that a trespasser should be able to make use of property, knowing full well that it belongs to someone else, and then rely upon acts of illegitimate user to dispossess the true owner.

In *Masidon, supra*, this policy was clearly spelled out by Mr. Justice Blair at p. 574 OR, pp. 214-15 RPR:

The policy underlying the *Limitations Act* was stated by Burton JA in *Harris v. Mudie* (1883), 7 OAR 414, as follows at p. 421:

> The rule, as I understand it, has always been to construe the Statutes of Limitations in the very strictest manner where it is shewn that the person invoking their aid is a mere trespasser ... and such a construction commends itself to one's sense of right. They were never in fact intended as a means of acquiring title, or as an encouragement to dishonest people to enter on the land of others with a view to deprive them of it.

Robins JA speaking for this Court in the *Giouroukos* case, *supra*, reiterated this policy when he said at pp. 187-8:

> When all is said and done, this is a case of a businessman seeking to expand significantly the size of his commercial land holdings by grabbing a valuable piece of his neighbour's vacant property. The words of Mr. Justice Middleton used in denying the claim of an adverse possessor to enclosed land in *Campeau v. May* (1911), 19 OWR 751 at p. 752, are apposite:
>
> > It may be said that this makes it very hard to acquire a possessory title. I think the rule would be quite different if the statute was being invoked in aid of a defective title, but I can see nothing in the policy of the law, which demands that it should be made easy to steal land or any hardship which requires an exception to the general rule that the way of the transgressor is hard.

In my opinion, the "inconsistency" test arose in order to avoid apparent injustice to rightful owners and to prevent the unjust enrichment of wanton trespassers.

The test appears to have originated in the case of *Leigh v. Jack* (1879), 5 Ex.D 264, 49 LJQB 220, 28 WR 452 (CA), where the plaintiff retained a strip of land adjacent to the land conveyed to the defendant, intending that it be used at some future time as a street. For more than 20 years, the defendant used the strip as a refuse dump for his foundry. On these facts, the English Court of Appeal held that the defendant had not obtained possessory title. Bramwell LJ stated at p. 273 Ex.D:

> I do not think that there was any dispossession of the plaintiff by the acts of the defendant: acts of user are not enough to take the soil out of the plaintiff and her predecessors in title and to vest it in the defendant; *in order to defeat a title by dispossessing the former owner, acts must be done which are inconsistent with his enjoyment of the soil for the purposes for which he intended to use it*: that is not the case here, where the intention of the plaintiff and her predecessors in title was not either to build upon or to cultivate the land, but to devote it at some future time to public purposes. The plaintiff has not been dispossessed, nor has she discontinued possession, her title has not been taken away, and she is entitled to our judgment. (Emphasis added.)

There is a divergence in the jurisprudence as to the rationale for such a test. Some authorities related it to the quality of possession; others to the requisite intent to dispossess.

The "quality of possession" rationale was explained in *Wallis's Cayton Bay Holiday Camp Ltd. v. Shell-Mex & BP Ltd.*, [1975] QB 94, [1974] 3 All ER 575, [1974] 3 WLR 387 (CA), where Lord Denning MR said at p. 103 QB:

> The reason behind the decisions is because it does not lie in that other person's mouth to assert that he used the land of his own wrong as a trespasser. Rather his user is to be ascribed to the licence or permission of the true owner. By using the land, knowing that it does not belong to him, he impliedly assumes that the owner will permit it: and the owner, by not turning him off, impliedly gives permission. And it has been held many times in this court that acts done under licence or permitted by the owner do not give a licensee a title under the *Limitation Act 1939*. They do not amount to adverse possession: see *Cobb v. Lane*, [1952] 1 TLR 1037; *British Railways Board v. GJ Holdings Ltd.*, March 25, 1974; Bar Library Transcript No. 81 of 1974 in this court.

In my opinion, the approach taken by the Court of Appeal in *Masidon, supra*, reflected this rationale. Mr. Justice Blair related the "inconsistency" test to the question of the effective exclusion of the true owners, an important factor in assessing the overall quality of possession.

The "requisite intent" rationale was explained in *Keefer v. Arillotta* (1976), 13 OR (2d) 680, 72 DLR (3d) 182 (CA), where Madam Justice Wilson said:

> The use an owner wants to make of his property may be a limited use and an intermittent or sporadic use. A possessory title cannot, however, be acquired against him by depriving him of uses of his property that he never intended or desired to make of it. The *animus possidendi* which a person claiming a possessory title must have *is an intention to exclude the owner from such uses as the owner wants to make of his property*. (Emphasis added.)

This proposition was referred to again in *Fletcher v. Storoschuk* (1981), 35 OR (2d) 722, 128 DLR (3d) 59, 22 RPR 75 (CA), where Madam Justice Wilson said at p. 724 OR:

> ... [A]cts relied on to constitute adverse possession must be considered relative to the nature of the land and in particular the use and enjoyment of it intended to be made by the owner: see *Lord Advocate v. Lord Lovat* (1880), 5 App. Cas. 273 at 288; *Kirby v. Cowderoy*, [1912] AC 599 at 603. The mere fact that the defendants did various things on the ... land is not enough to show adverse possession. The things they did must be inconsistent with the form of use and enjoyment the plaintiff intended to make of it: see *Leigh v. Jack* (1879), 5 Ex.D 264; *St. Clair Beach Estates Limited v. MacDonald et al.* (1974), 5 OR (2d) 482, 50 DLR (3d) 650; *Keefer v. Arillotta* (1976), 13 OR (2d) 680, 72 DLR (3d) 182. *Only then can such acts be relied upon as evidencing the necessary "animus possidendi" vis-à-vis the owner.* (Emphasis added.)

Both of these cases involved trespassers as I have defined them.

To summarize, it would seem that acts of user carried out by trespassers which could not be said to be inconsistent with the rightful owner's intended use of the land would not suffice to establish possessory title because they either (1) carried with them the implied permission of the true owner, or (2) they negatived a finding of the requisite intent to dispossess.

It is of interest to note that although the "inconsistency" test originated in England as a result of cases such as *Leigh v. Jack, supra*, it has been the focus of a great deal of controversy in that country for many years. The nature and extent of this controversy is fully explored in Derek Mendes da Costa and Richard J. Balfour, *Property Law: Cases, Text and Materials* (Emond Montgomery, 1982), at pp. 614-19. Suffice it to say that as a result of the twenty-first Report of the Law Reform Committee (1977), the English *Limitations Act, 1939* (UK, 2 & 3 Geo. 6), c. 21, was amended as follows:

> For the purposes of determining whether a person occupying any land is in adverse possession of the land it shall not be assumed by implication of law that his occupation is by permission of the person entitled to the land merely by virtue of the fact that his occupation is not inconsistent with the latter's present or future enjoyment of the land.
>
> This provision shall not be taken as prejudicing a finding to the effect that a person's occupation of any land is by implied permission of the person entitled to the land in any case where such a finding is justified on the actual facts of the case.

See s. 8(4) of Part I of Schedule I to the *Limitation Act, 1980* (UK), c. 58.

For the purpose of this case, it need not be decided whether the "inconsistency" test is relevant to the quality of possession or the issue of intent or both. Furthermore, it need not be decided whether it creates a legal presumption against a trespasser seeking possessory title or whether it should simply be a factor to be considered, along with all of the other evidence, in assessing either the quality of possession or the issue of intent. Whatever the case may be, in my opinion, it has no application in cases involving mutual mistake as to title.

For these reasons, I am satisfied that in cases of mutual mistake, it is legally possible for the party claiming possessory title to establish effective exclusion of the true owners from possession. Issue two must therefore be answered "Yes."

Issue Three

Have the applicants in fact established the effective exclusion of the true owners during the requisite time frame?

This issue arises from the evidence of Mr. Hester, who testified that he and his wife leased their vacant land to the applicants from 1977 to 1981. It will be remembered that the Hesters purchased the south lot in 1973. They sold the property to Mr. and Mrs. Garro in 1987.

The respondent submitted that [the] lease included the two-acre parcel. Thus, for a period of five years, the applicants used the two-acre parcel with the express permission of the rightful owners. The applicants were therefore precluded from establishing that they had, in fact, effectively excluded the true owners for a continuous and uninterrupted period of ten years.

In my opinion, this argument must fail for two reasons. First, the lease related to "vacant land." Minimally, the two-acre parcel contained a shed which the applicants initially used to house farm employees and later as a source of rental income. Second and of greater significance, the Hesters did not intend for the two-acre parcel to form a part of the leased property. Nor could they have. They honestly believed that it belonged to the applicants.

For these and other reasons which follow, issue three must also be answered "Yes."

Conclusion

Applying the three tests in *Masidon, supra*, to the case at bar, I am satisfied beyond any doubt that the applicants have established possessory title by way of adverse possession. Simply put, the possession of the applicants of the two-acre parcel has been open, notorious, constant, continuous, peaceful and exclusive of the rights of the true owners for almost 18 years. The applicants not only intended to exclude the true owners for this period of time; they in fact did so.

For 18 years the applicants carried out significant commercial activities on the property. They maintained and repaired the post and wire fence which encloses the entire east half of the two-acre parcel. They maintained the driveway on the western portion of the parcel and used it on a daily basis for ingress and egress to their house and barn, both of which encroach slightly on the two-acre parcel. Furthermore, the applicants have at all times used the shed located squarely within the boundaries of the parcel, first as a residence for farm employees, and more recently as a source of rental income.

Tracking the words of Mr. Justice Roach in *Laing v. Moran, supra*, the applicants for 18 years have asserted a claim to the soil. Within the statutory period, the true owners did not awake from their own inaction. It was only as a result of a new survey prepared for the respondent Gateway in 1989 that the problem came to light. By then, in my opinion, it was too late. The rights of the true owners to this land had been barred by statute.

In result, there will be an order as against the respondents extinguishing all of their rights and title to the two-acre parcel, more particularly defined as Part 2 in the plan of survey attached as Appendix B.

Further, there will be a declaration that the applicants are entitled as against the respondents to ownership of the said property in fee simple.

If counsel cannot agree, I may be spoken to as to the costs of this application.

Order accordingly

Note that the *Gateway* decision purports to apply the principles of *Masidon v. Ham*. Reconsider the cases in which possessors have successfully established their claims (*Gateway v. Aubin, Piper v. Stevenson*) by contrast with the cases where the possessor's claim was defeated (*Re St. Clair Beach, Masidon v. Ham, Giouroukos*). Can the differences in outcome be explained in terms of legal principles of possession, in accordance with the statutes of limitation? To what extent have the statutes been revised by judicial interpretation? In assessing these issues, consider the following comments of O'Connor J in *Kreadar Enterprises Ltd. v. Duny Machine Ltd.* (1995), 42 RPR (2d) 274 (Ont. Gen. Div.). In *Kreadar*, the defendant had used land to which the plaintiff held paper title for about 20 years, and had made various minor improvements to it. In deciding that the defendant had not established the requisite criteria for a possessory claim, O'Connor J stated:

The issue is whether the concept of acquiring title through adverse possession still exists in Ontario. If so, what are the modern criteria for successfully obtaining title to another's land by such methods? ... There would appear to be very limited circumstances, if they exist at all in Ontario, when a knowing trespasser, who has enjoyed the use of property over an extended period of time without payment of rent or taxes and who has made minimal improvements to it, would gain title to such property. In my view, that is how it should be.

To what extent are these judicial approaches to issues of possessory title consistent with the language of statutes of limitation, the underlying purposes of recognizing claims based on possession, and the balance between owners' and users' interests in the late 20th century? For another example involving a claim to possession against (in part) the Crown, see *Moran v. Pappas* (1997), 34 OR (3d) 251 (Gen. Div.). The Ontario Court of Appeal approved the decision in *Wood v. Gateway* in *Teis v. Corp. of Town of Ancaster*, [1997] OJ no. 3512 (at 17). The court held that "the test [of inconsistent user] does not apply to cases of mutual mistake." To what extent is the doctrine of inconsistent user, and the exception concerning mutual mistake, consistent with the basic concepts of possessory title and the purposes of limitation statutes?

Intention and Possession Under Torrens Registration Systems

Intention was carefully examined in the context of a Torrens registration statute in Alberta in *Lutz v. Kawa* (1980), 112 DLR (3d) 271 (Alta. CA). Although Torrens registration systems often preclude any claims based on possession since Torrens registration depends on the "register" as the sole basis for determining title, the Alberta Land Titles Act had permitted the continuation of such claims. In the circumstances, the court concluded on this issue that the remedy should be provided by the legislature. What are the problems or limits of legislative reform in this area?

"Quieting Titles" Legislation

In cases where a person can show a title based on possession, an application may be made to register such an interest under legislation traditionally known as "quieting titles" legislation. In Ontario such an application is made pursuant to the Courts of Justice Act, 1984, c. 11, s. 208. In other provinces, such legislation continues to be known as quieting title statutes: see Quieting Title Act, RSNS 1989, c. 382; Quieting of Titles Act, RSNB 1973, c. Q-4; Quieting of Titles Act, RSN 1990, c. Q-3; and Quieting Title Act, RSPEI 1988, c. Q-2.

Where a registered deed fails to describe a parcel accurately, it is possible to make a claim for rectification of the deed. For a recent case allowing such a claim for rectification, see *Brisebois v. Chamberland* (1990), 1 OR (3d) 417 (CA). In another case where the defendant mistakenly constructed a cottage partly on land owned by the plaintiff, the court invoked section 37(1) of the Conveyancing and Law of Property Act to permit the defendant to make an appropriate payment to the plaintiff: see *Noel v. Page* (1995), 47 RPR (2d) 116 (Ont. Gen. Div.). There may also be connections between claims based on possession and statutes concerning property taxes—for example, see *Zeitel v. Ellscheid* (1991), 5 OR (3d) 449 (CA), appeal to the SCC denied at (1994), 17 OR (3d) 782.

"Tacking" of Periods of Possession

As several of the previous cases have suggested, periods of possession by a continuous succession of persons may be added together to create the statutory period of possession, a process often referred to as "tacking." For a critical reflection on the appropriate theoretical rationale for permitting "tacking" on the part of those asserting possessory claims, see Margaret Jane Radin, "Time, Possession, and Alienation" (1986), 64 *Washington University Law Quarterly* 739.

PROBLEMS

1. Amy Andrews has worked as a shop assistant in a children's clothing store in the local shopping centre for about 10 years. A few weeks ago, all the employees including Amy (all of whom are members of a registered trade union) decided to take strike action to protest their employer's decision to import clothing from third-world countries rather than to continue selling only "made in Canada" items in the store.

As a result of the decision to strike, none of the employees has reported for work for several days, and most of them, including Amy, have been involved in picketing the store in the shopping centre during working hours. The rules of the shopping centre expressly prohibit picketing on shopping centre property, and Amy and the other employees have been warned that they will be sued under the Trespass to Property Act if they continue their action. To date, however, no one has been sued by the shopping centre.

On Friday, October 22, Amy Andrews reported for picket duty at 8:30 a.m. and picketed quietly for two hours. At that point, leaving her sign with another striking employee, Amy went to the food hall in the shopping centre for a coffee. While there, her friend Barb Branscan, who was just doing a bit of shopping, joined Amy at her table for coffee. The two friends chatted happily. Amy reached down for her handbag to show Barb some recent family photos. She then became aware of a small parcel at her feet and asked Barb whether she had dropped anything. Barb looked under the table, but thought that the parcel was just garbage. Intrigued, Amy picked it up, laid it on the table, and asked Barb to help her open it. To the great surprise of the two friends, the parcel contained $10,000 in $1,000 notes.

Amy and Barb have told no one about their discovery. They want to do whatever is right in the circumstances and they seek your immediate advice.

What legal principles need to be considered to provide the advice requested? What action should Amy and Barb take to protect their rights in this situation? What other information do you need in order to resolve this problem? You may want to consider issues examined in this chapter as well as chapter 1 in providing advice.

2. In 1988, the new owners of a block of land in London, Ontario wanted to use it to build a house, but they were informed that the adjoining-lot neighbours were claiming a portion of the lot by way of adverse possession, having used this portion as a gravel driveway since 1962. There was no fence, but the predecessors of the new owners never crossed the boundary of the neighbours' driveway. The new owners argued that they had intended to retain the land in its current form until eventual development as a residential parcel.

Can the neighbours successfully argue that they acquired possessory title to the portion of the lot used as a driveway? What arguments would you make on behalf of the new owners, and on behalf of their neighbours? How should a judge decide this dispute? To what extent are policy concerns as well as legal principles of possession relevant to your conclusions? See *Keil v. 762098 Ont. Inc.* (1992), 91 DLR (4th) 752 (Ont. CA).

3. Anne Abbott is the owner-director of a well-known wilderness camp for boys and girls several hours' drive north of Toronto. The camp is based on 2,000 acres of property bordering the edge of a large lake. While there are comfortable cabins and other amenities at the camp headquarters beside the lake, some other parts of the camp acreage are quite wild with rocky outcrops and few trees. One of the great attractions of the camp is the challenge of two- or three-day hiking expeditions away from the camp headquarters, with the necessity of carrying food and other provisions in order to be self-sufficient in nature.

Ms Abbott is currently seeking legal advice about an unusual discovery made by a group of campers a few months ago. In late August, a group of eight campers set off for a three-day hike with one of the camp leaders, Barb Bartoli. On the second day, the group stopped for the night beside a small river in a grove of pine trees. As they set up their tents, one of the campers, Jan Jung, felt a small depression in the earth, which she then discovered was a shallow cavity covered with a piece of birchbark over which moss had grown. Pulling up the birchbark covering, she discovered an old, discoloured, leather bag concealed in the cavity. Suddenly nervous, she called to her friend Petra for help. Petra immediately called their leader, Barb. Surrounded by the other campers, Barb Bartoli opened the bag to discover 18th-century French coins. The campers were astonished. They returned to camp headquarters the next day to report their find to Anne Abbott. On further inquiry with the local museum, Anne discovered that the location of the campsite where the cache was found was probably on the route of French fur traders, and that the coins are now worth a great deal of money. Ms Abbott wants to know who is entitled to the value of the coins found by the campers.

Matters have become further complicated as a result of the publicity surrounding the unusual discovery. The 2,000 acres used by the camp are leased from the Great Northern Development Company, an investment company that owns large tracts of land in the area. Because of the discovery, there has been great interest in identifying the location where the cache of coins was found, especially on the part of those interested in old fur-trading routes. As a result, Anne Abbott has learned that the cache was found on land owned by the Great Northern Development Company. However, instead of being part of the 2,000 acres leased to her for the camp, the cache was actually located on adjoining land, currently unoccupied, and, of course, unfenced. Because of the recent publicity, Ms Abbott has now learned that the river beside which the campers had pitched their tents is not the boundary of her 2,000 acres—the boundary of her leased parcel is, in fact, 100 feet to the east.

Nonetheless, Ms Abbott has asserted a right to the land where the cache was found. She can demonstrate that campers have used the land continuously since 1963—the year the camp was established—assuming that the boundary of their 2,000 acres was the river. In 1963, the Great Northern Development Company created a 40-year lease of the camp land. In 1960, it had leased the adjoining land to a logging company for 20 years, but very little logging activity had taken place. In 1980, when the 20-year lease expired, Great Northern immediately entered into a two-year lease with a second logging company. It has continued to create two-year leases with a succession of tenants, some of whom have engaged in intermittent logging activity. However, Ms Abbott has claimed that, because there was no obvious sign of any logging near the river, she had no idea that the boundary of the land leased to the camp did not extend to the river. Thus, she is now claiming title to this land as well as to the cache of coins found on it. She is also asserting that neither the campers nor their leader, Barb Bartoli, are entitled to the cache because her rights as occupier of the land are superior to anyone else's.

Is Ms Abbott's claim to the parcel of land near the river valid? Assuming that she is the occupier of the land near the river where the coins were discovered, is her claim to the coins valid?

4a. A took possession of Blackacre, but B subsequently ousted A. Can A now recover possession? Why?

Suppose that B claims to derive title from X, the person whom A ousted when A took possession? Can A now maintain his claim to possession? Why?

b. K took possession of vacant land. Five years later, K died and his estate was inherited by Q. If Z ousts Q, can Q maintain a claim to possession? Why?

Suppose that K had left his estate to Q by will and Q remains in possession for six years. What is the position of the owner of the vacant land? Why?

c. L held paper title to Redacre and leased it to T for four years in 1975. P took possession of Redacre in 1976. In 1979, when the lease ended, L leased it to T for a second four-year period, ending in 1983. In 1983, L leased the same land again to T for a further four-year period, ending in 1987. What is L's position in 1990? Why?

Assume the same fact situation, except that in 1979, L leased to M (a tenant unrelated to T); and in 1983, L leased to K (also unrelated to T or M). What is L's position as of 1990?

CHAPTER THREE

Fundamental Principles Governing Property Interests in Land

Property law is rooted in history. Property interests in land, known generally as real property, can only be understood with some background into the historical evolution of the law of real property. The basic principles were established by the Norman conquest of England in 1066, modified in later centuries, and eventually adopted in common law colonial jurisdictions, such as Canada. These principles evolved in a haphazard manner largely in response to the social, economic, and political forces prevalent at various times in history. This chapter examines this evolution within this historical context. It begins with the introduction of feudalism in England and then examines the gradual decline of the feudal state in England, the introduction of common law property into colonial jurisdictions and its interaction with pre-existing native title, and the further evolution of these principles in modern day Canada.

There is a basic distinction in the common law between real property and personal property, a distinction derived not from the character of the property but from the forms of action that governed civil procedure in medieval England. In disputes over most rights to land, parties could bring a "real" action to recover possession of the property (known as the *res*, which is Latin for "the thing"). In other disputes over property, parties could bring only an action to recover monetary damages. If successful, there would be an order *in personam* made against the defendant personally. This second type of property interest came to be known as personal property (sometimes called "chattel") because these property interests were enforced only by an order *in personam*. By contrast, disputes over real property were enforced by recovery of the *res* itself. Leasehold interests, although interests in land, were not originally enforced by real actions. Instead, a leasehold gave rise only to an order for damages and was therefore technically classified as personal property. Later, when it became possible to recover possession of the property itself under a leasehold agreement, the leasehold came to be known as a "chattel real."

This chapter examines the fundamental principles governing interests in real property. Although the study of real property law may seem distinct from other areas of property law, certain similarities remain. As considered in the previous chapters, much of the study of property law (either personal property or real property) examines how property interests can be fractured and held by several individuals either concurrently or successively. Property law attempts to regulate and balance these competing interests. For example, chapter 2 examines the competing claims between finders of lost chattel and the occupiers of the land on which the chattel was found. Chapter 2 also considers the competing claims between the "true owners" of real property and those who had established a possessory claim through adverse possession. In both cases, property law recognizes the occasionally conflicting property interests of the various claimants to the property, and the law attempts to resolve disputes that may arise between the parties.

Similarly, the study of real property is greatly concerned with the myriad ways in which the law permits and facilitates the division of interests in land. This area of the law addresses the question how these interests may be divided, and how the relationship is regulated between those who hold these various interests. There are at least five ways in which interests in land can be fractured:

- doctrine of tenure (now largely obsolete, except in relation to the Crown),
- doctrine of estates,
- legal and equitable interests in land (the trust),
- co-ownership, and
- leases and licences.

Of the various ways to fracture interests in land, the most common are co-ownership and leases. Co-ownership, examined in chapter 7, arises whenever two or more persons hold an undivided interest in a piece of land. Similarly, as discussed in chapter 4, where land is subject to a lease, both the lessee and the lessor hold a concurrent interest in the land. Property law generally applies to the relationship between co-owners, or lessors and lessees.

The subjects of this chapter—the doctrine of tenure, estates, and equitable interests in land—are somewhat more difficult to grasp than co-ownership or leases. Tenure, now effectively obsolete in Canada, requires an understanding of the ancient laws that governed feudal England. Feudalism was a complex legal and political system that permitted large numbers of persons, from the smallest farmer to the sovereign, to hold *concurrent* interests in the same piece of land. The doctrine of estates was, and remains, the legal system that governs *successive* interests in land. Finally, the split between legal and equitable interests in land raises entirely different types of concurrent interests in land—one interest recognized by the courts of common law, and another enforced by the courts of equity.

Although the historical roots of this area of law arose in England, the English have in large measure abandoned much of the more technical and archaic aspects of this law, starting with reforms in the late 19th and early 20th centuries. For better or worse, these reforms have not been generally adopted in most of the common law provinces, with the somewhat ironic result that property law in most of Canada, including Ontario, remains more antiquated than in England.

This chapter is a general introduction to real property law. The following Canadian and English texts were helpful in preparing this chapter and are recommended for further references in this area:

A.H. Oosterhoff and W.B. Rayner, *Anger and Honsberger Real Property* (Aurora, ON: Canada Law Book, 1985), at 14-570 (hereafter Oosterhoff and Rayner);

B. Ziff, *Principles of Property Law*, 2d ed. (Scarborough, ON: Carswell, 1996), at 49-74 and 147-202 (hereafter Ziff);

A.M. Sinclair and M.E. McCallum, *Introduction to Real Property Law*, 4th ed. (Toronto: Butterworths, 1997), at 1-30 and 63-102 (hereafter Sinclair and McCallum);

R. Megarry and H.W.R. Wade, *The Law of Real Property*, 5th ed. (London: Stevens & Sons, 1984), at 12-140 and 231-310 (hereafter Megarry and Wade);

A.W.B. Simpson, *A History of the Land Law*, 2d ed. (Oxford: Oxford University Press, 1986);

E.H. Burn, *Cheshire and Burn's Modern Law of Real Property*, 14th ed. (London: Butterworths, 1988), at 1-342; and

K. Gray and P. Symes, *Real Property and Real People* (London: Butterworths, 1981).

THE DOCTRINE OF TENURE

On October 14, 1066, William the Conqueror was successful at the battle he fought at Hastings. With his conquest, he brought to England a system of landholding common in continental Europe—feudalism. Although prior to his conquest land was held in England in a manner somewhat similar to feudalism, William introduced a more consistent and well-developed model. At this time, land was the primary source of economic and political power. To secure his claim to the English throne, William needed to secure control over all the land in England. Immediately after the conquest, William not only established himself as king, but also purported to seize ownership of all of the land in England in the name of the Crown. He then proceeded to parcel out most of this land to his trusted supporters, thereby replacing the previous English aristocracy. The feudal system he put in place provided that his supporters would hold their interest in the land only if they remained loyal to him and provided him with various services, such as the provision of knights. As a result, whatever interest they held in the land, they held "of the Crown," because the Crown in theory retained "ownership" of the land. This concept became known as "tenure" from the Latin term, *"tenere,"* meaning "to hold."

William was thereby able to establish and maintain an aristocracy loyal to him. This aristocracy, known as "tenants-in-chief" or lords, held huge parcels of land. They in turn entered into agreements with others, known as "tenants." These tenants would be granted an interest in a particular section of the land on condition that they rendered certain services and remained loyal to the lord, much as the lord held his interest in the land "of the Crown." In this way, all interests in land in England could eventually be traced to the Crown. All of these interests were ultimately held "of the Crown," and the system depended on the provision of tenurial services to the lord and the Crown. No person held absolute ownership of the land they occupied, as the ownership of the land rested in all cases in the Crown and was never transferred from the Crown. As a result, in England, unlike civil law jurisdictions, there never developed a concept of "allodial" or absolute title. Instead, interests in land were held according to this feudal pyramid, with the sovereign at its apex. Thus arose the phrase *nulle terre sans seigneur* (no land without a lord).

For any parcel of land in England, there could be a large number of people with a concurrent property interest in the land. First, the Crown claimed ownership. Second, the person who held immediately of the Crown, the tenant-in-chief, had an interest in the land. The tenant-in-chief would render certain services to the Crown, and in turn he would parcel out most of his land to various persons, generally known as "mesne lords" (intermediate lords) who held the land in return for services to the tenant-in-chief. Finally, the actual occupant of the land, usually a farmer known as the "tenant in demesne," would retain an interest in the land as long as he rendered service to the mesne lord. It was not uncommon for four or more persons to hold property interests in the exact same piece of land. However, none of these persons, with the exception of the sovereign, actually "owned" the land in question. Although called "tenants," the conditions and terms under which they held the land had nothing to do with the more modern leasehold estate, a matter further explored below. Finally, men and women had separate and unequal places in feudal society. As is examined in chapter 7, married women were rarely permitted to hold interests in land. As a result, most lords and tenants were men, and the use of masculine nouns and pronouns when describing the rights of landholders is a historical reminder of this inequality.

The feudal system of landholding effectively created the social, political, and constitutional order of feudal society. As M.H. Ogilvie stated:

> To think of one's social identity in terms of promising loyalty to a benefactor who will in exchange protect one's interests is alien to twentieth century thinking which defines identity and social relationships in terms of belonging to a socio-economic class, a profession, a trade union or a neighbourhood ... . The personal bond as an organizing social principle had deep roots; indeed, the chaos and disintegration in Western Europe from the fifth to the tenth centuries intensified the need for a personal concept of society for sheer survival.

(M.H. Ogilvie, *Historical Introduction to Legal Studies* (Scarborough, ON: Carswell, 1982), at 29.)

Others disagree that the concept of the "personal bond" as an organizing social principle is really so alien to contemporary thought. Charles Reich has argued, for example, that the relationships of personal entitlement to government benefits in the 20th century are similar to the relationships between the tenant-in-chief and the tenant in demesne in the feudal pyramid. Citing *Flemming v. Nestor*, 363 US 603 (1960), in which the US Supreme Court upheld a law that retroactively made membership in the Communist Party cause for deportation and the termination of old-age benefits under the Social Security Act, Reich argued:

> The philosophy of *Flemming v. Nestor* ... resembles the philosophy of feudal tenure. Wealth is not "owned" or "vested" in the holders. Instead, it is held conditionally, the conditions being ones which seek to ensure the fulfillment of obligations imposed by the state. Just as the feudal system linked lord and vassal through a system of mutual dependence, obligation, and loyalty, so government largess binds man to the state.

(Charles Reich, "The New Property" (1964), 73 *Yale Law Journal* 733, at 764.)

The provision of feudal services was an integral part of this personal bond, forming a crucial part of the political and constitutional order of feudal society. Much like taxation today, feudal services provided the Crown and the feudal aristocracy with the resources it needed to operate. As with taxation, the aristocracy and the courts jealously guarded these essential sources of revenue. The evolution of property law was greatly influenced by the ongoing struggle between landholders seeking to enforce these services and others seeking to evade them. The nature of these services varied. Over time they became standardized and were generally identified by the type of service required. The different methods of holding land were knows as "tenure," and the type of tenure indicated the terms under which the tenant held his interest in the land.

Classification of Tenure

Tenures were divided into "free" or "unfree" tenures. Common labourers generally held their land by an unfree tenure, and it was the most onerous form of tenure. The types of services due to the lord were not predetermined and were subject to the lord's discretion. The unfree tenant was at the mercy of the lord, required to do his bidding at any time. Failure to comply would result in the loss of his tenure. Unfree tenures, in a much-changed form known as copyhold tenure, continued to exist in England until the turn of the century. See Megarry and Wade, at 22-32. This form of tenure was never introduced in Canada.

Free tenures were distinguished from unfree tenures because the services required under a free tenure were specified in advance and were "certain." Providing the tenant complied with these specific services, he was entitled to retain his interest. The lord could not arbitrarily increase or alter the terms of the tenure, or terminate the tenure without cause. Generally speaking, the free tenure was the tenure of landed proprietors and independent farmers, while the unfree tenure was the tenure of the common labourers. The kinds of services provided by those with a free tenure included the provision of knights for the sovereign's army (the tenure of "knight's service") or the performance of some other personal service to the sovereign, such as serving some office in the royal court (the tenure of "grand sergeanty"). These two types of tenure, known as "tenures in chivalry," were most frequently held by tenants-in-chief. Other types of tenure included "spiritual tenures," called "frankalmoign," whereby church lands were held in return for spiritual services (such as prayers for the lord). The most common form of tenure was "tenure in socage" whereby the tenant rendered agricultural services to the lord. Most tenants in demesne held their land in socage tenure.

In addition to tenurial services, there were other obligations known as "incidents of tenure." These incidents applied primarily to the tenures in chivalry, although some of these incidents also applied to socage tenure. These incidents provided the lord with a valuable source of revenue, and they exercised a crucial influence on the evolution of interests in property. Among the various incidents, the most important were *wardship and marriage*, *relief*, *aids*, and *escheat*.

Wardship and marriage. These incidents affected infant heirs to the land. Wardship was the lord's right to manage for his own profit the lands of a tenant who left as his heir a male under 21 or a female under 14 (or 16, if not married before the land descended to her). In this way, the lord was compensated for his underage tenant's incapacity for service. Marriage was the lord's right to select a spouse for any tenant in wardship and to fine the tenant for declining a suitable spouse or for marrying under age without the lord's licence. Marriage and wardship were often of great value to the lord, and could be bought, sold, and bequeathed by the lord to third parties, and eventually came to be classified as chattels real.

Relief. Death duties in the amount of one year's income from the land, known as relief, were payable on descent of the land to an heir.

Aids. The lord had the right to call for financial contributions, known as aids, in certain circumstances, such as when the lord was imprisoned and required a ransom.

Escheat. Unlike the other incidents of tenure, escheat has retained its importance over the centuries and it is the only incident of tenure that likely remains in existence today. Whenever a tenancy came to an end, the land escheated back to the lord. Two types of escheat were common. The land escheated to the lord if and when the tenant died without heirs, and this is the form of escheat that has survived to this day. Second, the land also escheated to the lord if the tenant were convicted of a very serious crime, such as murder, suicide, or robbery.

Eventually, tenurial services became increasingly obsolete. For example, the Crown eventually found it desirable to maintain a permanent army loyal to the Crown, rather than rely on various lords to provide knights of less certain loyalty. Over time, most tenurial services were commuted to a fixed money payment that with inflation, greatly decreased in value. As a result, as the tenurial services declined in value, the remaining incidents of tenure became a very important source of revenue for the feudal system.

Seisin

The feudal system was greatly concerned with the enforcement of the incidents and services associated with tenure. The feudal social and political order relied heavily on these incidents and services. Thus arose the concept of seisin. The person "seised" of the land was the person against whom feudal services could be enforced. For example, a tenant in demesne might hold an interest in a parcel of land known as "Blackacre." The tenant in demesne was said to be seised of Blackacre because he owed duties to the mesne lord. The mesne lord was also seised of Blackacre because he was entitled to the benefits of these incidents of tenure, what was called his seignory. It was always essential to know who was seised of the land at any given time, as this determined the distribution of the burdens and benefits of the feudal system. The common law thus abhorred what was called an "abeyance of seisin"—that is, any period of time during which it might be unclear who was seised of the land. As will be seen, this abhorrence of an abeyance of seisin played a crucial role in the evolution of interests in real property.

It is sometimes said that seisin is the closest the common law has ever come to recognizing an ownership interest in property, because the person seised of the land effectively "owns" the land. However, under the feudal system any number of persons could be seised of the land at any given time. In the above example, all those on the feudal pyramid who held an interest in Blackacre were seised of the land. In feudal times, rather than speaking of "ownership" of the land, which in theory simply rested with the Crown, the overriding concern was instead to determine who was seised of the land.

From the concept of seisin also arose the practice of "livery of seisin." This was the formal ceremony whereby a person seised of the land, the "feoffor," could convey it to another, the "feoffee." The feoffor entered on the land and, in the presence of witnesses, delivered seisin to the feoffee either by some symbolic act, such as handing him a twig or sod of earth, or by uttering some words such as "Enter into this land and God give you joy." At a time when written records and literacy were uncommon, this pubic ceremony was the only means to transfer an interest in real property. It was vital that the ceremony be witnessed so that there could be no dispute as to who was seised of the land. For further discussion of seisin, see chapter 2.

Alienability of Interests in Land

Originally, the relationship between the lord and the tenant was a personal one involving the provision of services, and was in some ways similar to the modern contract of employment. Because of the personal nature of the obligation, the tenant was not permitted to alienate his interest in the land without the consent of the lord. Similarly, on the death of the tenant, the relationship was terminated. This enabled the lord to determine at all times who would assume the duties associated with the tenure. For example, the lord generally accepted the eldest son of a deceased tenant in his father's place, as primogeniture required. However, the son had to pay the lord a sum known as "relief" or the lord would not consent to the transfer. If the tenant died with no possible heirs, the lord would then reclaim the entire property by escheat. Thus, although the tenant occupied the land, and enjoyed the rights of possession to the land, the tenant did not enjoy an unrestricted right to alienate the land or make a will disposing of the land. In effect, the occupier of the land did not hold both the right of possession and alienation of the land.

There were two types of alienation available to tenants—alienation by *substitution* or alienation by *subinfeudation*. A grant by substitution would occur if B, who held A's land, conveyed his entire interest to C. Thereafter, C would occupy the land and be solely responsible for all of the incidents of tenure owed to A. B would have no further role and, not being seised of the land, B would no longer be responsible for any of the incidents of tenure. As noted above, alienation by substitution originally required the consent of the lord, due to the personal nature of the tenurial services. However, it appears to have become the general rule by the 13th century that tenants could alienate by substitution without their lord's consent.

Alternatively, B could also decide, in effect, to become a lord himself. B could alienate his interest to C in exchange for which C would assume tenurial duties toward B. B would continue to render duties to A, and C would render duties to B. This was called alienation by subinfeudation, and it had the effect of lengthening the feudal pyramid. On the whole, the lords disliked subinfeudation because it could interfere with their incidents of tenure. For example, B might die without heirs in which case all his land escheated to A. However, given that B had subinfeudated his land to C, B's only remaining interest in the land was certain services from C. Upon B's death without heirs, A would acquire the right to these services only and not the land itself. The effect of subinfeudation in this case was to deprive A of a very valuable incident of tenure—his right to reclaim the land in escheat. Similarly, B could simply disappear after subinfeudating his land to C. A would not know if B died without heirs, and B's interest had escheated to A. B's disappearance would make it impossible for A to benefit from any of the incidents of tenure, and A would essentially lose all revenue from the land.

The Statute Quia Emptores (1290)

Because subinfeudation was obnoxious to the more influential lords, the practice was eventually abolished by the statute Quia Emptores (1290), 18 Edw. 1, cc. 1-3. Quia Emptores, which means "those who are purchasers," did two things. First, it confirmed the right to alienate any interest in land without the consent of the lord. The law thereby took a very important step in the direction of the free alienability of property, disregarding the once intensely personal relationship between lord and tenant. Second, Quia Emptores provided that all alienation of land was to be done by substitution only, and prohibited any further subinfeudation of the land. As a result, no new tenures could be created (except by the Crown, which was not bound by the statute). Both these provisions remain a fundamental part of the law of real property in Canada. Whenever land is sold, it is done pursuant to Quia Emptores, which ensures that all alienation is by substitution only.

Because no new tenures could be created, the feudal pyramid began to flatten. It was no longer possible to establish oneself as a lord and alienate land by subinfeudation. For example, when land escheated back to the lord, he could no longer subinfeudate the land to another tenant. He could alienate this land only by substitution, and the purchaser would hold the land on the same terms *as* the lord—not *of* the lord. The result was that, over a long period of time, most of the land of England came to be held directly of the Crown. The mesne lords largely disappeared. However, the feudal system remained. The Crown, as the sole remaining feudal lord, retained an active interest in continuing to profit from the incidents of tenure. These incidents provided the Crown with substantial revenue independent of any control of Parliament. This led to conflict between the Crown and landholders, who objected to these unevenly applied, haphazard, and costly incidents of tenure. As examined below, in an effort to avoid these incidents, the law of trusts was created.

In exchange for other sources of tax revenue (on beer for example), the Crown was finally forced to relinquish its claim to incidents of tenure in the Tenures Abolition Act, 1660, 12 Car. 2, c. 24. This legislation effectively converted all remaining tenures into "free and common socage" tenure. This type of tenure was "free" of any tenurial services, and "common" in that it was not subject to any special incidents of tenure. This was the only type of tenure that was ever introduced in Canada, and all land in Canada today remains held of the Crown in free and common socage. Although in theory the Crown remains even today the feudal lord, the relationship no longer has any particular consequence because it is no longer associated with any services or incidents of tenure, with the one exception of escheat.

Escheat is the sole remaining incident of tenure that still has some modern significance. When a person dies intestate (without a will), and there are no statutory successors (relatives of the deceased, designated by statute, who are entitled to the deceased's estate if there is no will), then the estate escheats to the Crown in the right of the province: see *The Attorney General of Ontario v. Mercer* (1883), 8 App. Cas. 767 (PC). This doctrine relies on the fact that the Crown remains, even today, the feudal lord of all land. Most of the common law provinces now provide for the statutory succession of real and personal property on intestacy to the Crown, and no longer rely solely on this ancient feudal incident. For example, s. 47(7) of the Succession Law Reform Act, RSO 1990, c. S.26 provides:

> 47(7) Where a person dies intestate in respect of property and there is no surviving spouse, issue, parent, brother, sister, nephew, niece or next of kin, the property becomes the property of the crown, and the *Escheats Act* applies.

The Escheats Act, RSO 1990, c. E.20, s. 1 provides that once the intestate's property has become the property of the Crown, pursuant to s. 47(7) of the Succession Law Reform Act, the public trustee may bring an action to recover this property on behalf of the province.

Tenure and Reception of English Law in Canada

All the common law jurisdictions in Canada today reflect their origins in English land law. Both the manner and the timing of the reception of English law differ among the common law jurisdictions, so that there are often technical questions about the applicability of some English statutes in different common law provinces. However, the process by which English property law was introduced into Ontario is a typical example. See, generally, Oosterhoff and Rayner, at 52-76.

At the time of the English conquest of New France (including most of early Canada) in the battle on the Plains of Abraham in 1759, there were two pre-existing claims to these lands—claims of the French settlers and those of the native occupants. In incorporating a new legal system into this territory, the British had to resolve the question whether and to what extent they would recognize and enforce these pre-existing claims to the land. In both cases, the British determined that they would recognize them to some extent. The French settlers' occupation of the land was undisturbed by the conquest. By contrast, British law adopted a different approach to the native occupants, accepting recognition of some form of pre-existing native claims to the land, but in a manner quite different from the recognition of the pre-existing claims of French settlers. It is helpful to examine first the incorporation of English law in New France and later Ontario, and then consider the effect this had on pre-existing native claims to the land.

Shortly after the English conquest of New France in 1759, France agreed to cede the territory of New France to the British Crown in the Treaty of Paris in 1763. According to s. 4 of this treaty, the king of France ceded in "the most ample manner" Canada, with all its dependencies, to the British Crown. In 1763, this territory extended from Hudson Bay to the Gulf of Mexico. New France was ceded in its entirety as far west as the Mississippi, with the exception of the two islands of St. Pierre and Miquelon. According to one historian, these islands remained "the sole remnants of the French empire in America north of the West Indies, and their retention did help ensure that fishermen were still available to man the Atlantic squadrons of the French navy." See W.L. Morton, *The Kingdom of Canada* (Toronto: McClelland and Stewart, 1963), at 148.

In New France, all ungranted land had been vested in the French king, and accordingly this ungranted land was deemed to have vested in the British Crown pursuant to the Treaty of Paris. In *St. Catherines Milling and Lumber Co. v. The Queen* (1887), 13 SCR 577, at 645 (appeal to the Privy Council dismissed (1888), 14 AC 46), Taschereau J stated:

> Now when by the treaty of 1763, France ceded to Great Britain all her rights of sovereignty, property and possession over Canada, and its islands, lands, places and coasts, including, as admitted at the argument, the lands now in controversy, it is unquestionable that the full title to the territory ceded became vested in the new sovereign, and that he thereafter owned it in allodium as part of the crown domain, in as full and ample a manner as the King of France had previously owned it.

Any lands that were ungranted or unoccupied at the time of conquest thus vested in the British Crown, and the Crown asserted not only sovereignty over all the territory as a result of the Treaty of Paris, but ownership over all the ungranted lands. This principle has also been held to apply to territory acquired not by conquest, but by settlement or "discovery," where the settlement of the territory gave to the Crown not only sovereignty, but also title in the unoccupied lands. See *The Attorney-General v. Brown* (1847), 2 SCR (NSW), appendix 30.

Although claiming title in unoccupied or ungranted lands, the British Crown recognized the pre-existing claims of French settlers. The Treaty of Paris provided that the British Crown would preserve the inhabitants' possessions. This obligation was later expressly included in the Quebec Act, 1774, 14 Geo. 3, c. 83 (Imp.), which specified that the French settlers remained secure in the holding and enjoyment of any property previously held under the French Crown. In some cases, notably *Drulard v. Welsh* (1907), 14 OLR 54 (CA), it was difficult to establish the nature and extent of the pre-existing title of the French settlers. In *Drulard*, the plaintiff sought a declaration as to the boundary of his land, claiming title to the land based on the pre-existing rights of certain French settlers. The land in question was located in Windsor, Ontario, an area that prior to the conquest had been "occupied by a settlement of *habitants*, kindred to the French population occupying the region of the St. Lawrence in old Quebec." The court noted that these pre-existing rights were protected under the Quebec Act, 1774. However, on the facts of that particular case, it was difficult to determine whether the plaintiff held a valid claim to the land that could be traced to the early French settlement. After an examination of the historical landholding system that had been used by the French settlement, the court determined that the plaintiff had failed to establish his claim to the land.

Although the Treaty of Paris required the British Crown to preserve the property held by French settlers, the treaty did not require that the British Crown preserve the laws of New France, among which was the civil code. Accordingly, by royal proclamation, the English common law system was introduced in the ceded territory immediately after the conquest. The inhabitants of French Canada were naturally dissatisfied with this foreign system of laws. In response, 11 years after the Treaty of Paris, the Quebec Act, 1774, reintroduced the civil code in Canada (including what is now Ontario), but maintained the English criminal law system (including trial by jury, a process unknown in French law).

Thereafter, Canada (including what is now Ontario) continued to be governed by the civil code. As the English minority grew in Canada, pressure mounted to divide the territory into two provinces—Upper Canada and Lower Canada. The Imperial Constitutional Act, 1791, 31 Geo. 3, c. 31 (Imp.) accordingly divided the territory, and further provided in s. 43 that in the territory of Upper Canada (now Ontario) all land was to be granted in free and common socage only:

> 43. [A]ll lands which shall be hereafter granted within the said province of *Upper Canada* shall be granted in free and common socage, in like manner as lands are now held in free and common socage, in that part of *Great Britain* called *England*; and that in every case where lands shall be hereafter granted within the said province of *Lower Canada*, and where the grantee thereof shall desire the same to be granted in free and common socage, the same shall be so granted; but subject nevertheless to such alterations, with respect to the nature and consequences of such tenure of free and common socage, as may be established by any law or laws which may be made by his Majesty, his heirs or successors, by and with the advice and consent of the legislative council and assembly of the province.

One of the very first acts of the new predominately English legislature of Upper Canada was, of course, to eliminate the application of the civil code in the new province and incorporate instead the laws of England. This was accomplished in the Property and Civil Rights Act, 1792, SUC 1792, c. 1; see now RSO 1990, c. P.29:

> 1. In all matters of controversy relative to property and civil rights, resort shall be had to the laws of England as they stood on the 15th day of October, 1792, as the rule for the decision of the same, and all matters relative to testimony and legal proof in the investigation of fact and the forms thereof in the courts of Ontario shall be regulated by the rules of evidence established in England, as they existed on that day, except so far as such laws and rules have been since repealed, altered, varied, modified or affected by any Act of the Imperial Parliament, still having the force of law in Ontario, or by any Act of the late Province of Upper Canada, or of the Province of Canada, or of the Province of Ontario, still having the force of law in Ontario.

As a result of these two statutes, the doctrine of tenure was introduced into Ontario law. The tenurial relationship was thus established, with the theory that the Crown remained a feudal lord. However, lands were to be granted in free and common socage only, that is, without any of the services or special incidents of tenure. The incorporation of the laws of England as of October 15, 1792, included, among other things, the statute Quia Emptores (1290), prohibiting the subinfeudation of land, and the Tenures Abolition Act (1660).

Although the history of incorporation of the laws of England varies for each common law province, the outcome was largely the same. Only free and common socage tenure was introduced in all of these provinces. See Oosterhoff and Rayner, at 80.

Tenure and Native Title

Native title to lands is not tenurial because it does not originate from a Crown grant. Instead, it arises by operation of law from a pre-existing right based on the historical occupation and possession of the lands in question. See *Guerin v. The Queen*, [1984] 2 SCR 335, at 376 and *Calder v. British Columbia (AG)*, [1973] SCR 313.

As a starting point, it is useful to distinguish the concept of native title from the concept of native sovereignty. On arrival, the Europeans generally regarded North America as lacking in sovereignty. According to arriving Europeans, the mere "discovery" of North America was sufficient to assert sovereignty, at least as against other European nations. Whether and to what extent the native occupants had sovereignty over the lands, and how that was affected by the arrival of the Europeans, is a matter that drew little attention. At the time, the Crown made frequent reference to "Nations or Tribes of Indians," as in the Royal Proclamation below, and the Crown further entered into "treaties" with these nations. Nonetheless, it is clear that from the time of the Royal Proclamation, the Crown asserted sovereignty over native lands in Canada. In *R v. Sparrow*, [1990] 1 SCR 1075, at 1103, the Supreme Court held:

> It is worth recalling that while British policy towards the native population was based on respect for their right to occupy their traditional lands, a proposition to which the Royal Proclamation of 1763 bears witness, there was from the outset never any doubt that sovereignty and legislative power, and indeed the underlying title, to such lands vested in the Crown.

The question of sovereignty is, moreover, generally considered to be a question of international law, and not a matter over which domestic or municipal courts can assert jurisdiction. See *Mabo v. Queensland* (1992), 66 ALJR 408 (High Ct.) and *Sobhuza II v. Miller*, [1926] AC 518, at 525.

Although claims of native sovereignty are not recognized in Canadian law, the concept of native title has been frequently considered and upheld. It is clear that although the British Crown asserted sovereignty, the Crown nonetheless acknowledged that the native occupants of Canada had a pre-existing and legally recognized interest in their lands, much as the British Crown also recognized the pre-existing interests of the French settlers. For example, at the time of the conquest, the British Crown was well aware of the political, economic, and military importance of the various native tribes in Canada. Recognizing that native support might be crucial in any further struggle with France, the British Crown attempted to address native concerns about encroaching European settlement. Shortly after the Treaty of Paris in 1763, the British Crown thus made the following Royal Proclamation on October 7, 1763 (The Royal Proclamation, RSC 1985, App. II, no. 1):

> And whereas it is just and reasonable, and essential to our Interest, and the Security of our Colonies, that the several Nations or Tribes of Indians with whom We are connected, and who live under our Protection, should not be molested or disturbed in the Possession of such Parts of Our Dominions and Territories as, not having been ceded to or purchased by Us, are reserved to them, or any of them, as their Hunting Grounds. We do therefore, with the Advice of our Privy Council, declare it to be our Royal Will and Pleasure, that no Governor or Commander in Chief in any of our Colonies of Quebec, East Florida, or West Florida, do presume, upon any Pretence whatever, to grant Warrants of Survey, or pass any Patents for Lands beyond the Bounds of their respective Governments, as described in their Commissions; as also that no Governor or

Commander in Chief in any of our other Colonies or Plantations in America do presume for the present, and until our further Pleasure be known, to grant Warrants of Survey, or pass Patents for any Lands beyond the Heads or Sources of any of the Rivers which fall into the Atlantic Ocean from the West and North West, or upon any Lands whatever, which, not having been ceded to or purchased by Us as aforesaid, are reserved to the said Indians, or any of them.

And We do further declare it to be Our Royal Will and Pleasure, for the present as aforesaid, to reserve under our Sovereignty, Protection, and Dominion, for the use of the said Indians, all the Lands and Territories not included within the Limits of Our said Three new Governments, or within the Limits of the Territory granted to the Hudson's Bay Company, as also all the Lands and Territories lying to the Westward of the Sources of the Rivers which fall into the Sea from the West and North West as aforesaid.

And We do hereby strictly forbid, on Pain of our Displeasure, all our loving Subjects from making any Purchases or Settlements whatever, or taking Possession of any of the Lands above reserved, without our especial leave and Licence for that Purpose first obtained.

And, We do further strictly enjoin and require all Persons whatever who have either wilfully or inadvertently seated themselves upon any Lands within the Countries above described, or upon any other Lands which, not having been ceded to or purchased by Us, are still reserved to the said Indians as aforesaid, forthwith to remove themselves from such Settlements.

And whereas great Frauds and Abuses have been committed in purchasing Lands of the Indians, to the great Prejudice of Our Interests, and to the great Dissatisfaction of the said Indians; In order, therefore, to prevent such Irregularities for the future, and to the end that the Indians may be convinced of our Justice and determined Resolution to remove all reasonable Cause of Discontent, We do, with the Advice of our Privy Council strictly enjoin and require, that no private Person do presume to make any purchase from the said Indians of any Lands reserved to the said Indians, within those parts of our Colonies where, We have thought proper to allow Settlement; but that, if at any Time any of the Said Indians should be inclined to dispose of the said Lands, the same shall be Purchased only for Us, in our Name, at some public Meeting or Assembly of the said Indians, to be held for that Purpose by the Governor or Commander in Chief of our Colony respectively within which they shall lie; and in case they shall lie within the limits of any Proprietary Government, conformable to such Directions and Instructions as We or they shall think proper to give for that Purpose; And we do, by the Advice of our Privy Council, declare and enjoin, that the Trade with the said Indians shall be free and open to all our Subjects whatever, provided that every Person who may incline to Trade with the said Indians do take out a Licence for carrying on such Trade from the Governor or Commander in Chief of any of our Colonies respectively where such Person shall reside, and also give Security to observe such Regulations as We shall at any Time think fit, by ourselves or by our Commissaries to be appointed for this Purpose, to direct and appoint for the Benefit of the said Trade.

The Royal Proclamation established the fundamental principle that no native lands in America were to be taken by British subjects without consent. But aboriginal title is not contingent on the Proclamation (*St. Catherines Milling & Lumber Co. v. The Queen*,

(1888), 14 App. Cas. 46 (PC)). Instead, it is a pre-existing inherent right, recognized under the common law and simply reflected in the Proclamation. It is founded on the historic occupation and use of native lands.

The principle outlined in the Proclamation led to negotiation with native peoples as European settlement continued. The Crown entered into treaties with the various native peoples, whereby their rights would be extinguished only by voluntary cession in exchange for rights to specified territories, known as "reserves," and other benefits. The following two excerpts provide a more detailed analysis of the affect of the Royal Proclamation and a critique of the history of the negotiation and enforcement of treaties in Canada.

Brian Slattery, "The Hidden Constitution: Aboriginal Rights in Canada"
(1984), 32 *American Journal of Comparative* Law 361, at 368-72 (footnotes omitted)

The Royal Proclamation of 1763

By 1763, Great Britain's long struggle with France for American empire was over. At the Peace of Paris, France ceded all its remaining territories in Canada to the British Crown, as well as its territories east of the Mississippi River. Britain also obtained Florida from the Spanish Crown, thus completing its claims to the eastern and northern sectors of America. Only one area was left to another European power, namely the lands west of the Mississippi that France had relinquished to Spain the previous year.

These treaties temporarily sorted out the claims of the three main European rivals among themselves. But the French Crown could not give Great Britain what it did not possess itself, namely authority over the native groups inhabiting the ceded territories. These nations were, in many cases, trading partners of the French and sometime military allies. If they were not prepared to accept direct French authority, neither were they willing to accept that France might deposit them in the pocket of the English King.

As the Chippewa leader, Minivavana, told an English trader:

> Englishman, although you have conquered the French, you have not yet conquered us. We are not your slaves. These lakes, these woods and mountains, were left to us by our ancestors. They are our inheritance; and we will part with them to none.

A similar viewpoint was expressed by certain Wabash River Indians:

> You tell us, that when you Conquered the French, they gave you this Country. That no difference may happen hereafter, we tell you now the French never conquered, neither did they purchase a foot of our Country, nor have [they a right] to give it to you[.] [W]e gave them liberty to settle for which they always rewarded us and treated us with great Civility.

Britain was well aware in 1763 of the precarious nature of its relations with the old Indian allies of France, and the growing dissatisfaction of its own native allies and trading partners. Since mid-century, the British government had been increasingly occupied with Indian affairs, and the war with France had emphasized the importance of native friendship and support. For some time, a plan had been afoot to assure the Indians

of the Crown's good intentions by removing a principal cause of Indian discontent—
white intrusion on Indian lands. This plan culminated in the publication of a Royal
Proclamation on 7 October 1763. The interest of the document is not purely historical,
for its main terms have never been generally repealed in Canada. Although it must be
read in the light of later developments, it still forms a principal basis for aboriginal land
claims in many areas.

The Proclamation is one of those legal instruments that does simple things in complicated ways. The central idea of its Indian provisions is very simple: to ensure that no
Indian lands in America are taken by British subjects without native consent. This
objective is secured by three main measures: colonial governments are forbidden to
grant any unceded Indian lands, British subjects to settle on them, and private individuals to purchase them, with a system of public purchases adopted as the official mode of
extinguishing Indian title. The British government was particularly concerned at the
prospect of white settlement spreading indiscriminately into the American interior, and
so the Proclamation temporarily seals off much of that area to settlers, designating it an
exclusive Indian territory. But the document's main measures are not confined to the
Indian Territory; they apply throughout British North America.

The Indian provisions of the Proclamation begin with a preamble, where the King
explains his basic aims:

> And whereas it is just and reasonable, and essential to our Interest and the Security of
> Our Colonies, that the several Nations or Tribes of Indians, with whom We are connected,
> and who live under Our Protection, should not be molested or disturbed in the Possession
> of such Parts of Our Dominions and Territories as, not having been ceded to, or
> purchased by Us, are reserved to them, or any of them, as their Hunting Grounds[.]

While the King asserts ultimate sovereignty over the Indians, he also acknowledges
their semi-autonomous status, describing them as Nations or Tribes "with whom We are
connected, and who live under Our Protection." He recognizes that the Indians are
entitled to undisturbed possession of the lands reserved to them, and, in an important
formula repeated later in the text, defines these reserves as any Indian lands that have
not been ceded to or purchased by the Crown. The King claims these lands as part of his
dominions, but at the same time recognizes the existence of an Indian interest requiring
extinguishment by cession or purchase. In technical terms, the Indian interest constitutes
a legal burden on the Crown's ultimate title until surrendered.

In 1763, most of the American territories claimed by Britain were unceded lands
held by native peoples. Under the Proclamation, such lands were automatically deemed
Indian reserves. Their boundaries were determined negatively by past Indian cessions
and positively by current Indian possessions. Much of the unorganized American interior was still, of course, unceded. But other unceded lands lay within the undisputed
boundaries of existing colonies, including the northern colonies of Rupert's Land, Quebec, Newfoundland, and Nova Scotia, now forming part of Canada.

It is sometimes argued that the Proclamation recognized aboriginal land rights only
in the exclusive Indian Territory created in the American hinterland. On this supposition,
Indian title was not recognized in areas specifically excluded from the Territory, such as
the coastal belt east of the Appalachian Mountains, and the colonies of Quebec and

Rupert's Land. But the text does not support this view. After describing the boundaries of the territory, the Proclamation orders the removal of all persons who have settled either within the territory "or upon *any other Lands*, which, not having been ceded to, or purchased by Us, are still reserved to the said Indians as aforesaid" (emphasis added). This provision clearly assumes that unceded Indian lands located outside the Indian Territory are reserved for Indian use. The King also forbids colonial Governors to make grants of "any Lands whatever, which, not having been ceded to, or purchased by Us as aforesaid, are reserved to the said Indians, or any of them." The ban applies to unceded Indian lands generally, wherever they happen to be located. Finally, the Proclamation provides that no private person shall make any purchases from the Indians "of any Lands reserved to the said Indians, within those Parts of Our Colonies where We have thought proper to allow Settlement," and specifies that if the Indians are ever inclined to dispose of such lands, they shall be purchased for the Crown in a public assembly. Since the provision only applies in areas where settlement was permitted, and the Indian Territory was, for the time being, expressly closed to "any Purchases or Settlements whatever," it could only refer to unceded Indian lands found outside the Territory, in eastern and northern colonies where settlement was still allowed.

In brief, the Proclamation recognized that lands possessed by Indians throughout British territories in America were reserved for their exclusive use, unless previously ceded to the Crown. Prior to a public cession of such lands, they could not be granted away or settled. These provisions applied not only to the Indian Territory, but to the full range of British colonies in North America, no matter how humble or peripheral. In this respect, Rupert's Land, Quebec, Nova Scotia, Newfoundland, the Thirteen Colonies, and the Floridas were brought under a uniform legal regime. The Indian Territory was placed in a special position. Whereas in other areas Indian lands might still be purchased by public authorities, in the territory such purchases were forbidden altogether for the time being. The idea was to divert the flow of white settlement from the American interior to the northern and southern colonies, which were still relatively sparsely settled. However, the Crown envisaged that in due course parts of the Territory might be opened up, in which case the standard regime governing purchase of Indian lands would take effect.

There has been some controversy whether the Proclamation applied to the far western reaches of the American continent, notably modern British Columbia and the Yukon Territory. The question has usually been treated as depending on how much territory Great Britain claimed in 1763. Here, the historical evidence indicates that British claims extended indefinitely westward to the Pacific Ocean in latitudes now occupied by Canada. But a better basis exists for resolving the issue. Many of the Proclamation's provisions are framed in general terms, referring broadly to "Our Dominions and Territories" and "Our Colonies or Plantations in America." Imperial enactments using such terms were normally given a prospective application, so as to apply not only to colonies and territories held when the legislation was enacted but also to those acquired subsequently, unless this result was clearly excluded. The purpose of the Proclamation was to supply a uniform set of rules governing Indian lands throughout British territories in North America. There is no reason to think that Indian lands located in territories acquired after 1763 needed less protection than those acquired earlier. It is natural to infer that the Proclamation applied to both.

The Proclamation of 1763 has a profound significance for modern Canada. Under its terms, aboriginal peoples held continuing rights to their lands except where these rights have been extinguished by voluntary cession. Treaties of cession have been signed for large parts of Canada, notably in Ontario and the Prairie Provinces. But no such treaties exist for the Atlantic Provinces, and parts of Quebec, British Columbia, the Yukon, and the Northwest Territories, as well [as] for pockets of land elsewhere. Moreover, there is doubt whether Canadian legislatures were competent to override the Proclamation's terms prior to 1931, when the Statute of Westminster was enacted. So native peoples may today hold subsisting aboriginal rights to large tracts of Canadian land.

M. Jackson, "The Articulation of Native Rights in Canadian Law"
(1984), 18 *University of British Columbia Law Review* 225, at 261-69
(footnotes omitted)

B. The Treaty-Making Process in the Nineteenth Century: The Dissonance Between the Indian and Euro-Canadian Legal Traditions

It is the procedure formalized by the Royal Proclamation of 1763 which has provided the constitutional basis for the hundreds of land cession treaties which have since been negotiated with the Indian nations across much of Canada. Up until 1850, the treaties covered relatively small areas and the terms of the treaty were limited in scope. In the period after 1850, as settlement moved westward, there was a dramatic increase in geographical scale. Moreover, post-1850 treaties contain provisions relating to the establishment of Indian reserves, Indian education and medical services, the payment of annuities and the supply of agricultural and farm implements as well as ammunition and twine for use in hunting and fishing. The treaties also guarantee to the Indians their continuing right to hunt, fish and trap.

Recent research undertaken by the Indian nations themselves, with the help of social scientists, has revealed some of the continuities between the treaty negotiations involving the Indian nations of western Canada in the late nineteenth century and the negotiations involving the Iroquois Confederacy in the previous century in the eastern colonies. As with the treaties negotiated in the eighteenth century with the Iroquois, the post-confederation treaties negotiated by the Indian nations of western Canada were viewed by them as establishing compacts to deal with the issues of territorial and political integrity within the framework of a protectorate relationship with the Crown. However, what had changed in the intervening century was the balance of power between the Indian nations and the colonial authorities, and the condition of the Indians as the result of the encroachment of European civilization. More specifically, the Indians were facing increasing white settlement, devastating epidemics, the influx of whisky traders and the disappearance of the buffalo, the staple of the tribes' economy. The protectorate role embodied in the treaties was accordingly not confined, in the Indians' eyes, to preserving their territorial and political integrity within the lands which they were not prepared to cede, but also extended to the protection of the traditional Indian economy and assistance in the development of new forms of Indian economic self-sufficiency.

The Canadian Government had a different view of what the treaties were intended to accomplish. They did not regard them as anything like a social contract in which different ways of life were to be accommodated within mutually acceptable limits. The government regarded the treaties primarily as the surrender of Indian rights to their land so that settlement and development could proceed. The payment of annuities, the provision of agricultural implements, the offers of medical and educational services and the establishment of reserves were conceived of in part as compensation but primarily as the means of change. The government's expectation was that backward people would, in time, abandon their seminomadic ways and, with the benefit of the white man's religion, education and agriculture, take their place in the mainstream of the economic and political life of Canada.

As the result of the recent research conducted by Indian nations it has now become clear that the dissonance between the Indian understanding of the treaties and the government's understanding, as that is reflected in the text of the treaties, is directly related to the different legal conceptions about how agreements are negotiated, recorded and interpreted. For the Indian negotiators, who brought to the negotiations an oral tradition, the promises and discussions during the negotiations formed the centrepiece of the agreements. For the negotiators on the Canadian Government's side, it was the written text of the treaty which determined its scope and meaning.

It has also become clear from the Indian nations' research that basic Indian values relating to the sharing of resources and distinctive concepts about the nature of land informed their view of the treaty negotiations. According to the text of Treaty #6, which was negotiated in 1876, the Indians, in the language of the treaty, "hereby cede, release, surrender and yield up to the Government of the Dominion of Canada for Her Majesty the Queen and her successors forever, all their rights, titles and privileges whatsoever, to the lands included within the following limits." A more comprehensive surrender of rights would be difficult to draft. Compare this wording in the text of the treaty with the statement made by Chief Crowfoot during the treaty negotiations:

> Our land is more valuable than your money. It will last forever. It will not perish as long as the sun shines and the waters flow, and through all the years it will give life to men and beasts.
>
> We cannot sell the lives of men and animals and therefore, we cannot sell the land. It was put here by the Great Spirit and we cannot sell it, because it does not really belong to us. You can count your money and burn it with the nod of a buffalo's head, but only the Great Spirit can count the grains of sand and the blades of grass on these plains. As a present to you, we will give you anything we have that you can take with you, but the land we cannot give.

The divergence between the text of the treaty and the Indians' understanding of the negotiations is illustrated in other areas. The treaty commissioners negotiated with the chiefs of the tribes. The terms of the treaties provide for annual payments to each member of the tribe, with larger payments for the chiefs. The chiefs also were provided with medals. To the Indians, in the context of negotiations in which their tribal governments negotiated with the Government of the Queen, these provisions affirmed the authority of their tribal governments and provided a diplomatic protocol for the annual review of the treaty agreements. The text of the treaty provides that each tribe shall be provided with a specific number of agricultural resources such as ploughs, scythes, oxen, cows and other farming animals. To the Indian negotiators, this was understood in terms of the protectorate relationship as a clause of economic aid, a prototype for the treaties of economic assistance which are now regularly entered into by the richer western countries with their allies in the Third World. The Indian negotiators understood these clauses to be a sharing by the white man of his forms of economic development to assist the Indian nations as they experienced increasing hardship in maintaining their traditional economies in the face of increased settlement.

In one area the divergence between the text of the treaty and the oral negotiations has been specifically acknowledged by the treaty commissioners who negotiated on behalf of the Canadian Government. The Indian nations were insistent throughout the treaty negotiations that their traditional economy based upon hunting, fishing and trapping be protected. Recent research has shown that some of the treaty negotiations would have broken down had not the government negotiators given guarantees that hunting, fishing and trapping rights would not be curtailed. However, the actual text of the treaties in relation to these rights is qualified. In Treaty #8, for example, the clause reads,

> And Her Majesty the Queen hereby agrees with the said Indians that they shall have the right to pursue their usual vocations of hunting, trapping and fishing throughout the tract surrendered ... *subject to such regulations as may from time to time be made by the Government of the country, ... and saving and excepting such tracts as may be required or taken up from time to time for settlement, mining, lumbering, trading or other purposes.* (Emphasis added.)

The treaty commissioners, in their report to the Government of Canada, make specific reference to the oral negotiations regarding the hunting, fishing and trapping rights clause:

> Our chief difficulty was the apprehension that the hunting and fishing privileges were to be curtailed. The provision in the treaty under which ammunition and twine is to be furnished went far in the direction of quieting the fears of the Indians ... but over and above the provision, *we had to solemnly assure them that only such laws as to hunting and fishing as were in the interest of the Indians and were found necessary in order to protect the fish and furbearing animals would be made, and that they would be as free to hunt and fish after the treaty as they would be if they never entered into it ... . We assured them that any treaty would not lead to any forced interference with their mode of life ... .* The Indians were generally adverse to being placed on reserves—it would have been impossible to have made a treaty if we had not assured them that there was no intention of confining them to reserves.

In the eighteenth century, in the context of English and French colonial rivalry and Indian military strength, the Indian nations in the eastern parts of North America had the power to compel the colonial governments with whom they negotiated treaties to respect their understanding of these treaty negotiations. The Indians in the west of Canada, one hundred years later, lacked this power to compel. Government Indian policy proceeded along lines which breached the Indians' understanding of their treaties: the role of traditional Indian governments was replaced by the authority of Indian agents, traditional religious ceremonies were prohibited and punished as offences, the traditional Indian economics were undermined by the encroachment of agriculture development and game laws, and the promised agricultural economic assistance was not forthcoming. In the years since the signing of these treaties, when Indian nations have gone to the courts to enforce their rights under the treaties, the Canadian courts have, with rare exceptions, looked to the literal text of the treaties and have disregarded the oral promises or the Indians' understanding of the negotiations.

The process of judicial revision of treaty rights as they were understood by native peoples is well illustrated by cases interpreting the relationship between federal and provincial game laws and Indian hunting. Notwithstanding the solemn assurances given by the treaty commissioners that Indian hunting would not be interfered with, the Canadian Government, in the years following the signing of Treaty #8, passed legislation restricting native hunting and trapping. In 1917, closed seasons were established in the Northwest Territories and Alberta on moose, caribou and other animals essential to the economy of the Dene. In 1918, the Migratory Birds Convention Act further restricted their hunting. The violation of the treaty promises by this legislation has been recognized by Canadian courts which, contrary to the Indians' conception of the binding character of the treaties, have consistently held that treaty promises may, as a matter of Canadian law, be abrogated by federal legislation without prior Indian consent. Canadian courts have thus sanctioned the federal government's unilateral alteration of treaty promises.

C. Native Rights as Articulated by the Canadian Courts: The Process of Judicial Revision

The Canadian courts have not only failed to adequately reflect the Indians' understanding of the treaties but have also engaged in a process of judicial revision of the original principles of native rights. Those principles developed in the treaty relationships entered into in the seventeenth and eighteenth centuries received their first judicial interpretation in decisions of the United States Supreme Court in a series of judgments in the 1820s and 1830s, culminating in the landmark decision of Chief Justice Marshall in *Worcester v. Georgia* (1832). This case reviewed the colonial law antecedents of native rights in North America and affirmed that the Indian tribes had legal rights to their lands which could only be acquired in the name of the Crown by consensual cession by the Indians. Paralleling this principle of consent to the cession of lands was the recognition that the Indians retained their rights to self-government as nations, notwithstanding their assumption of a protectorate relationship with the colonial governments in North America.

Canadian courts, while purporting to rely upon the Marshall decision, have departed from these principles in significant ways. The Canadian courts have given no recognition to the principle of Indian self-government as a part of native rights. On the issue of native rights to lands and resources traditionally used and occupied by them, the Canadian courts have rejected the principle of consent as the basis for the acquisition of these lands and resources.

In the leading case of *St. Catherine Milling and Lumber Company v. The Queen* (1889), the Privy Council, while affirming the existence of the concept of aboriginal or native title to the land based on the Royal Proclamation of 1763, stated that "the tenure of the Indians was a personal and usufructory right, dependent upon the goodwill of the sovereign." According to the interpretation which has been given to this passage in subsequent cases, native rights to lands and resources are not in fact rights but rather privileges which exist at the sufferance of the Crown. It is important to note that the *St. Catherine Milling* case, which until 1973 provided the judicial centrepiece for the Canadian concept of native rights, involved a dispute between federal and provincial governments arising from the ownership of lands which had been ceded by the Salteaux Indians in a treaty; there was, however, no Indian representation before the courts.

Subsequent to the *St. Catherine Milling* decision, in the wake of government policy designed to assimilate the Indians, the Canadian law of native rights went into an almost total eclipse. For example, in the Province of British Columbia, where with a few exceptions no treaties have ever been negotiated, the Indian nations found themselves faced with land policies of the Provincial Government which denied any entitlement of the Indians to their traditional lands, the policy of the Federal Government which denied them the right to maintain their traditional forms of government, and the policies of missionaries which, assisted by penal legislation enacted by the Federal Government, denied the Indians the right to maintain their most important religious ceremony, the Potlatch. The Potlatch, which is regarded by anthropologists as the hallmark of Northwest Coast Indian distinctiveness, combining elements of religious, economic and social organization, became an outlawed institution for the participation in which (for example, by dancing at the ceremony) Indian people were imprisoned in the 1920s. As part of this government policy of suppression and repression of the Indians' way of life, legislation was introduced in 1926, following a Federal Parliamentary Committee Report which found that the Indians of British Columbia had no rights to their land, *which made it a criminal offence to raise funds for the purpose of pressing any Indian claims*.

Even in the face of such draconian legislation Indian leaders never gave up their struggle to have their rights recognized. But from the 1920s until the early 1970s the issue of native rights ceased to be of major concern to Canadian politicians and ceased to exist in the minds of the legal profession. As late as 1969 a Federal Government policy paper on the issue of aboriginal rights' claims stated, "These are so general and undefined that it is not realistic to think of them as specific claims capable of remedy." Indeed, in that same year the Prime Minister of Canada, Mr. Trudeau, a lawyer and former professor of law, stated in a speech in Vancouver:

> Aboriginal rights, this really means saying "We were here before you. You came and you took the land from us and perhaps you cheated us by giving us some worthless things in return for vast expanses of land and we want to reopen this question. We want you to preserve our aboriginal rights and to restore them to us." And our answer—it may not be the right one and may not be one which is accepted—our answer is "No."

In the same year as the Prime Minister so categorically denied the legal viability of aboriginal rights, a case was initiated by the Nishga Indian Nation in British Columbia (the *Calder* case) [*Calder v. British Columbia*, [1973] SCR 313] which was to cause the federal government to acknowledge the historical and legal reality of aboriginal rights to land. The Nishgas, who had never signed a treaty of cession with either the colonial or

Canadian governments, sought a declaration that their aboriginal title to the Nass Valley, their homeland, had never been extinguished. The *Calder* case went to the Supreme Court of Canada which, in 1973, split on this issue. Three judges held that the aboriginal title of the Nishgas had been extinguished by colonial land legislation. Three other judges held that the Nishga rights had not been extinguished. A seventh judge held against the Nishgas on the purely procedural point that they needed the fiat or permission of the government to bring their case. While the *Calder* case is viewed as a major victory for native people in restoring to the legal and political lexicon the concept of aboriginal rights—all six judges who ruled on the merits acknowledged that such a concept existed in law—it is important to understand the limitations of the case from the perspective of the original principle of consent. The three judges who ruled that the Nishga aboriginal title had not been extinguished did so on the basis that an aboriginal title to land, once proven to exist by evidence of exclusive use and occupation by an Indian nation, could only be extinguished by specific legislation which showed a clear and plain intention to end the Indian rights. In the opinion of these judges there was no such legislation in British Columbia. Those judges who ruled in favour of the Nishgas did not, however, affirm the principle that Nishga lands could only be taken with their consent. The judgment in favour of the Nishgas conceives of their claims in this way:

> They claim the right to remain in possession themselves and to enjoy the fruits of that possession. They do not deny the right of the Crown to dispossess them but say the Crown has not done so.

This statement is of great importance. It is quite clear that the Nishga Nation, as a matter of fact, does dispute the right of Canadian federal or provincial governments to dispossess them of their homeland. They have always asserted, and continue to assert, that their consent is a prerequisite to any changes in their territorial rights within their traditional homeland. As a matter of law, asserting their claims in court within the context of the Canadian jurisprudence on native rights, they felt compelled to acknowledge that their rights could be taken without their consent. The dissonance between the Indians' understanding of their treaty rights and the courts' interpretation of those rights is thus closely paralleled by the dissonance in the non-treaty areas between native and judicial articulation of aboriginal rights.

Discussion Notes

Common Law Recognition of Native Title

In *Calder v. British Columbia*, [1973] SCR 313, the Supreme Court accepted that aboriginal or native title is recognized at common law and was not extinguished merely by the acquisition of Crown sovereignty. This native title existed where the native peoples were organized in societies and occupied the land when settlers arrived. A similar conclusion was also reached in a decision of the Australian High Court in *Mabo v. Queensland* (1992), 66 ALJR 408. In *Mabo*, the court noted that international law recognized three ways for a nation to acquire sovereignty over another territory—by conquest, by cession, or by occupation of land that was *terra nullius* (unoccupied). In Australia, the concept of *terra nullius* had been extended to include occupied lands if the native occupants were considered by the colonizers to be uncivilized. Under this concept, the mere acquisition of sovereignty by the British Crown over Australia effectively eliminated any pre-existing possessory rights of the native occupants, and native title was not recognized. In *Mabo*, the court rejected this concept as unjust discrimination based on prejudicial and false assumptions, finding that aboriginal peoples were entitled at common law to claim rights to the land they had occupied prior to European contact. For a further analysis of *Mabo*, see chapter 8.

Establishing Native Title

Establishing native title can be an onerous process. Native title does not refer to an individual's claim to ownership of a particular parcel of land. Instead, native title refers to the traditional custom that governed a tribe's collective use of particular territory. To establish this title, native peoples must establish that they are the descendants of the people who had collectively occupied the territory in question at the time of the assertion by England of sovereignty: see *The Baker Lake (Hamlet) v. Canada et al.*, [1980] 1 FC 518 (TD). The nature, extent, or degree of the occupation of the claimed land is determined by a subjective test. Claimants need not establish that their ancestors occupied the land in European ways, with clearings, fences, settlements, and so on. Rather, claimants need only establish ancestral land use that was consistent with the social and economic needs of aboriginal peoples.

Native Title and Beneficial Ownership

The Supreme Court of Canada has held that native title does not amount to beneficial ownership (or "fee simple") in the land: *Guerin v. The Queen*, [1984] 2 SCR 335. Instead, aboriginal rights to the land have been identified as *sui generis*, unique at law. Aboriginal rights give rise only to a right to occupy and exploit the land in a manner consistent with traditional practices: *R v. Sparrow*, [1990] 1 SCR 1075. Aboriginal rights can only be alienated to the Crown, as contemplated in the Royal Proclamation of 1763. These rights cannot be alienated to any other party. By contrast, the most common type of beneficial ownership rights in land, known as an "estate in fee simple," gives rise to much broader rights of alienation and exploitation. The subject of estates in land is examined in detail below.

Native Rights of Self-Government

The courts have also considered the question whether native title gives rise to certain rights of self-government, in addition to the right to occupy and exploit the land in a manner consistent with traditional practices. In *Delgamuukw et al. v. British Columbia* (1993), 5 WWR 97 (BC CA) (currently under appeal to the Supreme Court of Canada), the Court of Appeal considered whether a native right of self-government survived the assertion of sovereignty by the British Crown. The majority of the court (at 152) held that "a continuing aboriginal legislative power is inconsistent with the division of powers found in the Constitution Act, 1867 and introduced into British Columbia in 1871." The majority thus held that when the Crown imposed English law on all the inhabitants of the colony, the aboriginal peoples became subject to the legislative authorities in Canada, thereby losing any inherent right of self-government or any claim to sovereignty. By contrast, the dissenting judges held that a measure of self-government and self-regulation was an inherent aspect of aboriginal title and it survived the imposition of Crown sovereignty.

Extinguishing Native Title

Native title can be extinguished if the aboriginal peoples surrender their land rights in a treaty. Native title can also be extinguished by Crown action that shows a clear and plain intention to extinguish native title, such as the passing of legislation that expressly extinguishes native title. In *Delgamuukw et al. v. British Columbia*, above, the court considered whether various pre-confederation colonial legislation had extinguished native title in British Columbia. This legislation provided for the transfer of Crown lands to private owners and for reserves to be set aside for Indians, but did not specifically extinguish native title. The court held that this legislation was insufficient to extinguish native title because it did not foreclose the possibility of treaties or the possibility of the co-existence of native interests and Crown interests.

The state's ability to extinguish aboriginal title is now subject to constitutional constraints. Section 35 of the Constitution Act, 1982, RSC 1985, App. II, no. 44, provides that "existing Aboriginal and treaty rights of the Aboriginal peoples of Canada are hereby recognized and affirmed." Section 35 does not confer complete legislative immunity on Aboriginal entitlement; however, if a law interferes with an aboriginal right, then the state now bears the burden of justifying the violation and establishing that there has been appropriate compensation: *R v. Sparrow*, above.

Reserve Lands

The surrender of native title creates a fiduciary relationship between the Crown and the native people giving up their land rights. Much of Canada, particularly Ontario and the prairie west, was settled following the negotiation of treaties in which native peoples surrendered rights to land in exchange for specified "reserve" lands and the provision of health care, education, and other benefits. By contrast, in other parts of Canada—in particular, British Columbia, northern Quebec, and the Atlantic provinces—treaties have never been negotiated. Much of this land may still be subject to native title, giving rise to substantial contemporary native land claims. With regard to the reserve lands, under the Constitution Act, 1867, the federal government has jurisdiction over "Indians and lands reserved for Indians." Where reserves have been established, the federal Crown owns the land for the benefit of the native peoples entitled to occupy the land. Pursuant to s. 20 of the Indian Act, RSC 1985, c. I-5, individual natives cannot claim ownership rights in the lands, since the Crown retains title. Individual natives can, however, acquire a "certificate of possession" entitling them to possession of a particular piece of reserve land. These certificates are granted by the band council and are transferable only with the consent of the council and the responsible federal official. For a further discussion of certificates of possession in the context of family property on native reserves, see chapter 7.

Tenure: A Need for Reform?

In jurisdictions that have adopted the civil code, such as continental Europe, there is no concept of tenure. Instead, land is held in absolute ownership, or "allodial" title. For a discussion of allodial title, see *Matter of People (Melrose Avenue)*, 234 NY 48, 136 NE 235 (CA 1922). One might question whether the concept of tenure is now so obsolete that it should be eliminated from property law. The concept of tenure represents the survival of a legal concept through centuries and in geographical territories far removed from today. Perhaps it is inevitable that the history of tenure is presented as one of inexorable logic. Is there now a need for reform? Does the doctrine of tenure serve any useful function? If not, what kind of reform would be appropriate?

Feminist Challenges to the Doctrine of Tenure

Aspects of the doctrine of tenure have also long been subject to criticism. In the past, there were important challenges to the doctrine of tenure and its preference for male holders of proprietary interests. For an example of one successful challenge, see Sue Sheridan Walker, "Widowhood and Ward: The Feudal Law of Child Custody in Medieval England," in Susan Mosher Stuard, ed., *Women in Medieval Society* (Philadelphia: University of Pennsylvania Press, 1976), at 159. Recent historical scholarship (especially by feminist historians) has also begun to challenge the dominant view of land law in late feudal England. For example, A.L. Erickson, *Women and Property in Early Modern England* (London, UK: Routledge, 1993) argues that it is important to investigate the "normal conditions of property transmission" among ordinary men and women to understand how legal principles worked in practice. Her research indicates that many women were able to work around practices and laws that heavily restricted their right to enjoy property. Her research also suggests that feudal arrangements were surprisingly complex and fluid, thereby presenting a challenge to the modern tendency to regard feudal laws and practices as straightforward and inflexible (at 19-20):

> Widows commonly enjoyed much more property from the marital estate than the law entitled them to. But while ecclesiastical courts and dying husbands entrusted their wives with far more property and financial responsibility than the law required, at the same time a man very rarely went so far as to allow his widow complete discretion upon his death. The intent was to give her an ample maintenance, not to make her independently wealthy, and certainly did not extend to any principle of gender equality. The wealthier a man was, the smaller the proportion of his estate left to his widow, and also to his daughters.
>
> Widows and women who never married had different ideas about property from men. These women gave preference to their female relatives in dividing their property, they enabled their daughters or nieces or female cousins to live independently in cottages and smallholdings, and they gave bequests to the poor, tacitly recognizing women's susceptibility to poverty. If widows remarried, they took greater care to protect

their property than they had on their first "venture," on behalf of both their children and themselves. Although "venture" was used of either spouse throughout the seventeenth century, it was particularly appropriate in reference to a husband as "an undertaking without assurance of success," since women's economic security from the day of marriage depended so heavily upon their husbands' good will.

Despite the fact that women exercised considerably more power over property than has previously been allowed, both the legal system and individual men still kept women firmly subordinate. Women's dependence on their men's good will increased over the period, as the limited ecclesiastical protections of their property were eliminated by statute. The reality of women's receiving large amounts of property and exerting power over it in a distinctive way does not change the fact of oppression, but it does highlight the disjuncture between theory and practice. It also exhibits the ingenuity of many ordinary women in working within a massively restrictive system. Individually, they registered their collective disagreement with the principles of inheritance and marital property laws.

THE DOCTRINE OF ESTATES

Much as the doctrine of tenure permitted the division of interests in land along the feudal pyramid, the doctrine of estates in land is another method by which interests in land can be divided among a variety of people. Like tenure, the doctrine of estates is unique to English common law and unknown in the civil law system. It reflects once again that the concept of "ownership" vesting in one person, the root of the civil law system and allodial title, is not particularly helpful in understanding common law property. Tenure fragmented property interests along the lines of exploitation and alienation. The occupant (tenant) exploited or developed the land; the lord shared in this exploitation via tenurial services. Initially, both the tenant and the lord jointly held the right of alienation. The question of who "owned" the land was not helpful. Only the Crown could claim "ownership," even though the Crown's interest in the land was largely limited to tenurial services and did not generally include either possession or alienation of the land.

As tenure fragmented interests along the lines of exploitation and alienation, the doctrine of estates was the method developed to fragment interests in land over *time*. As with tenure, the doctrine of estates permits any number of people to hold interests in the same piece of land. However, in the case of estates, the holders of these estates in land will enjoy *possession* of the land in succession. The tenure by which one holds land determines the *quality* of the property interest—that is, by what terms or tenurial services and incidents the land is held (in the modern era, by free and common socage only). The doctrine of estates determines the *quantity* of the interest—that is, the period of time during which a particular holder of the interest will be entitled to possession of the land.

The doctrine of estates provides great flexibility to meet changing societal needs for increasingly complex arrangements for holding interests in land. It permits one person to be in possession of land, while another may have an estate in land that will entitle him or her to possession at some point in the future. There may be many people holding different estates in the same parcel of land, several of whom have no present rights to possession. All of these estates in land can be transferred by sale or gift.

Lawyers frequently use the doctrine of estates. For example, a lawyer may be asked to draft a will so that the testator's spouse can enjoy a property interest during the spouse's lifetime, and thereafter the interest will pass to the couple's children. This is typically accomplished by the creation of an "estate for life" for the surviving spouse as well as a "remainder in fee simple" that will entitle the children to possession after the spouse's death. In this example, the spouse will be entitled to possession at the death of the testator, while the children will not be entitled to possession until after the spouse's death. Although their possession is deferred until some time in the future, the children nonetheless have what is known as a *present estate* in the land because this estate can be transferred by sale or gift at any time, even before their right to possession arises.

Freehold Estates: Life Estates, Fee Simple, and Fee Tail

Life Estate

Two principle types of estates in land have survived to this day—the *fee simple* and the *life estate*. The simplest example of how estates in land operate is the case where the grantor (X) of an interest in land grants a life estate to A, and upon A's death, to B. A thus acquires an interest in the land that will last as long as she lives, and after her death, possession will pass to B. Such a grant of land can be illustrated as follows:

X to A for life, and then to B.

A, known as the *life tenant*, acquires a life estate, and B acquires what is called the *remainder* interest. In the days when most property owners were men, B was known as the *remainderman*. Today, B is known as the *remainderperson*. B's interest is that which remains after the grant to A. X, having alienated the land by substitution, retains nothing.

The grantor may also make a grant of a life estate to A, without specifying a remainderperson:

X to A for life.

In this case, the grantor has conveyed only a life estate to A, and the grantor retains the remaining interest in the land. The land will therefore revert back to the grantor, X, on A's death. In this case, the grantor is said to retain a *reversionary* interest in the land and is known as the *reversioner*. The reversion interest reverts back to the grantor, whereas a remainder interest is transferred to another grantee and "remains away" from the grantor.

The historical origin of the life estate is somewhat murky. In the feudal period, when the tenurial relationship was an intensely personal one, interests (or estates) in land generally terminated on the death of the tenant. Thus arose the concept of the life estate—an interest in the land that would last only as long as the tenant lived. The practice gradually evolved whereby the lord would permit the tenant's heir (the lineal descendant only) to take the land upon the tenant's death, providing *relief* was paid to the lord. It thus became accepted that entitlement to the land could continue, but only if the tenant had a child or grandchild who could take the land upon the tenant's death. This crucial development gave rise to an estate in land that could last longer than the life estate, that is, an estate in land that would last as long as there were surviving heirs. If there were no heir, the land would *escheat* to the lord. Because the only persons able to inherit the land were the lineal descendents, if the holder of land had no children or grandchildren, the estate would terminate upon his death and escheat to the lord. (As is discussed in greater detail below, prior to the Statute of Wills (1540), 31 Hen. 8, c. 1, landowners had no power to designate any other heir by will.) This longer estate in land, that could last as long as there were heirs, came to be known as a *fee simple*. The term "fee" indicates an estate of inheritance, distinguishing it from the life estate that terminates on the death of the life tenant.

In the above example, both A and B acquire what is known as a *present* estate. Both have a property interest in the same piece of land. Although B's right of possession is postponed until A's death, B nonetheless acquires a present interest in the land at the time of the grant. B can convey his remainder interest to a third party at any time prior to A's death, even though B is not in possession of the property. The purchaser will acquire B's remainder interest and will take possession of the land on A's death. Having a present estate, B's interest can be sold or otherwise alienated at any time. If B predeceases A, B's remainder interest will pass to his heirs, who will take possession of the land on A's death.

Fee Simple

Originally, the fee simple estate was created by a grant of land to A "and his heirs." This estate continued as long as A had lineal descendants (children or grandchildren). If A sold his interest to B, the estate B acquired continued as long as A had lineal descendants. B's estate would terminate and escheat back to the lord if A or one of his descendants died without heirs. Such a result was understandably inconvenient for B and other purchasers, because their purchased estate could suddenly terminate at any time according to the seemingly unrelated survival of A's line of descendants. By 1306, the principle was established that when a tenant (A) alienated his interest "to B and his heirs," B's estate continued as long as there were lineal descendants of B (not A). See Megarry and Wade, at 39. B essentially stepped into A's shoes, and acquired exactly the same estate held by A. Like the statute Quia Emptores (1290) (which permitted alienation by substitution without the lord's consent, and prohibited subinfeudation), this development was crucial in the law's ongoing project to permit and promote the free alienation of land.

After this point, the estate in fee simple became virtually unending and was subject to escheat only if the tenant died without heirs. The term "heirs" was originally interpreted narrowly, to include lineal descendants only. This interpretation was in the interest of the lords, because the smaller the possible class of heirs, the more likely the land might escheat back to the lord. However, early in the development of the law, "heirs" was broadened to include other relations such as collaterals (those who are not of the direct line of the deceased, but from a collateral line—that is, siblings, uncles, aunts, nephews, nieces, and cousins). With the passage of the Statute of Wills (1540), 32 Hen. 8, c. 1, tenants acquired for the first time the right to make testamentary dispositions of their property to anyone, simply by executing a will and designating a person as their heir. Thereafter, escheat became rare, and the fee simple, in essence, eternal.

The fee simple estate is thus the largest estate known in common law; it can potentially last longer than any other estate. The *fee simple estate in free and common socage* is today the most common way to hold an interest in land. The interest will endure as long as there are heirs (broadly defined to include any of the possible heirs on intestate succession, or by testamentary disposition), and it is not subject to any of the services or special incidents of tenure. It is this interest that most closely approaches the concept of "ownership" or allodial title so central to civil law. It is the largest bundle of rights that one person can hold in land under common law. It is not, strictly speaking, the equivalent of "ownership," because there remains a slim tenurial relationship with the Crown. The Crown retains "ownership," and the land is merely "held of the Crown." There also remains the slim possibility that the tenant will die without heirs, either intestate or testamentary, in which case the land will still, even today, escheat to the Crown pursuant to the statutory instruments explained earlier. Finally, although the fee simple estate is the largest interest known at common law, and includes broad rights of alienation and exploitation of the land, these rights are not unlimited. The use of land is subject to any number of statutory restraints regarding land use, environmental protection, and planning laws. There are also a variety of other restraints ranging from the rule against perpetuities (discussed below) to the law of nuisance (a branch of tort law, considered in chapter 1, that restricts the use of property in a manner that unreasonably interferes with a neighbour's interests).

Fee Tail

In addition to the life estate and fee simple, there was also the *fee tail* estate, now in effect obsolete in all provinces with the exception of Manitoba. See Oosterhoff and Rayner, at 146. The fee tail estate was created by a grant "to A and the heirs of his body." It lasted only so long as there were lineal descendants of A. As with the fee simple, the term "fee" denotes an estate of inheritance (distinguishing it from the life estate). The term "tail" indicated that only a certain class of heirs could take the land (lineal descendants). By contrast, in a fee simple estate, the term "simple" indicates that the interest can descend to "heirs general," including both lineal and collateral descendants. As noted above, with the Statute of Wills (1540), the class of heirs general also came to include heirs by testamentary disposition.

Unlike a fee simple estate, the grantee (A) of a fee tail acquired only a life estate interest. This was the crucial feature of a fee tail estate. Upon A's death, the estate passed to his lineal descendent, or if he had none, it escheated. Upon a conveyance of his interest to B, A could convey only his life interest. Upon A's death, B's interest would terminate, and A's lineal descendant would take the land. The fee tail estate was obviously of interest to wealthy families who wanted to ensure that an estate would remain forever in the family. Whoever held the estate at any given time held only a life interest and could not convey a fee simple to any purchaser. The great disadvantage of such an estate was that the land was effectively inalienable, as most purchasers were uninterested in acquiring only a life estate that could terminate unexpectedly at any time. As a result, land subject to a fee tail was frequently undervalued and underdeveloped, leading to its inefficient use. After some remarkably creative and complex legal manoeuvres, by the late

15th century a legal process was developed through which a fee tail could be "barred"—that is, enlarged into a fee simple estate. The land could then be developed and sold like any estate in fee simple. The fee tail estate was not very common in Canada, and has since been abolished in most Canadian provinces. As examined below, any attempt to create a fee tail estate today in Ontario is simply deemed by legislation to create a fee simple estate.

Capacity To Hold Estates in Land

The category of "legal persons" includes both natural persons (individuals) and corporations. Individuals may hold estates in land. Corporations, as legal persons, may also hold estates in land. Historically, the common law placed a variety of restrictions on certain individuals and corporations to hold and convey estates in land. Married women suffered severe restrictions in their ability to hold and convey estates in land, a matter discussed in greater detail in chapter 7. These restrictions have been removed by statute, and married women in Canada are now accorded the same legal capacity as unmarried people. See, for example, the Family Law Act, RSO 1990, c. F.3, s. 64.

At common law, minors had the power to hold an estate in land, subject to a restricted power of disposition. Statutory reform now generally grants courts wide powers to order the sale or disposition of a minor's interest in property where it is necessary or proper for the maintenance or education of the minor. See, for example, the Children's Law Reform Act, RSO 1990, c. C.12, s. 59. At common law, mental incompetents also had the capacity to hold estates but with stringent restrictions on the power of disposition. In Ontario, this matter is now governed by legislation dealing with substitute decision making, which generally provides for the management and disposition of such property under the supervision of the public trustee or a designated power of attorney. See, for example, the Substitute Decisions Act, 1992, SO 1992, c. 30.

At common law, foreign citizens (aliens) were incapable of passing land by descent and on death their estate vested in the Crown. By statute, aliens may now acquire, hold, dispose of, and inherit real property in the same manner as Canadian citizens. See Citizenship Act, RSC 1985, c. C-29, ss. 34-38 and Aliens Real Property Act, RSO 1990, c. A.18, s. 1. These acts cannot, however, be invoked to give aliens or non-residents any immunity from provincial laws that may otherwise restrict the rights of aliens or non-residents to hold interests in property: see *Morgan v. AG PEI* (1975), 55 DLR (3d) 527; [1976] 2 SCR 349.

Because a corporation can exist indefinitely, land held by corporations was effectively immune from many of the incidents of tenure, including relief and escheat. This state of affairs frustrated the lords who relied upon these incidents, and land held by corporations (including religious institutions) was described as falling into "mortmain," a word derived from the Norman French term for "dead hand." For this reason, many statutes were once enacted with the object of limiting the ability of corporations to acquire estates in land. Modern legislation now expressly provides that corporations have the capacity and rights of natural persons, giving to corporations the right to hold and dispose of land: Canada Business Corporations Act, RSC 1985, c. C-44, s. 15(1) and Business Corporations Act, RSO 1990, c. B.16, s. 15.

Freehold and Leasehold Estates

It is important to understand the distinction drawn between *freehold* and *leasehold* estates. The key feature of the freehold estate is that its duration is *uncertain*, as is the case with life estates, fee simple estates, and fee tail estates. Because it is always unknown when the death of a person will occur, the life estate is necessarily of uncertain duration. Similarly, because it is always unknown when a tenant may die without the required heirs, the fee simple and fee tail estates are also of uncertain duration. In feudal history, the freehold estates were regarded as the "higher" estates, because the freeholder was seised of the land and subject to any applicable tenurial services or incidents.

By contrast, the leasehold estate was and is known as a *non-freehold estate*. The major distinction between the freehold and leasehold estates is that the leasehold estate is of a maximum duration, fixed in time. A leasehold estate is either for a fixed term—for example, 1 year or 99 years—or, if not for a fixed term, it can be terminated on sufficient notice at any time. In this way, the leasehold estate, unlike the freehold estate that is of uncertain duration, is regarded as an estate of fixed duration.

The creation of a leasehold estate is a common method to divide interests in land over time. Leasehold estates are familiar—a leasehold estate arises whenever land is leased to a tenant for an agreed amount of time. The lessor, who holds a fee simple estate in the land, conveys possession of the land for a period of time to the tenant. The lessor retains the right to possession of the property at the expiration of the lease, a right known as the *reversion*. Unlike the remainder interest, above, this interest *reverts back* to its original grantor and does not pass to a third party. As is the case with the doctrine of tenure, the concept of "ownership" does not neatly apply to a leasehold estate, because neither the lessor nor the tenant enjoys sole and exclusive rights of ownership. Both the tenant and the lessor have interests (or estates) in the same piece of land. The tenant has a possessory interest (or an estate in possession) for the duration of the leasehold estate, and the lessor retains a reversion.

A leasehold was not always regarded as an estate in land. Historically, a lease was regarded exclusively as a contractual arrangement and, for this reason, the tenant was not regarded as being *seised* of the land. Rather, seisin remained with the lessor notwithstanding the leasehold agreement, and the lessor remained responsible for any of the services or incidents of tenure associated with being seised of the land in question. As a result, if A (the owner of an estate in fee simple) granted a lease to B for 10 years, B had possession for the duration of the leasehold estate, but A remained seised of the land. Because the leaseholder was not seised of the land, the leasehold estate remains known as a *non-freehold* estate in land. In feudal times, leasehold estates were deemed to be "estates less than freehold" and in theory inferior to freehold estates. Leasehold estates are further explored in chapter 4.

Creating Freehold Property Interests: Inter Vivos Transfer and Succession

The common law developed very strict rules regarding the precise words required to create an estate, and these rules have now been modified by statute. For historical reasons, the common law favoured the creation of life estates rather than estates in fee simple, perhaps as a relic of ancient times when grants of a freehold estate were for the life of the tenant only. To create an estate in land longer than the life estate, the use of certain, precise words were essential. Failure to use this precise wording resulted in the creation of a life estate only, regardless of the intention of the parties.

At common law, a freehold estate of inheritance could be created in an *inter vivos* conveyance (a transfer of land between living persons) only by a phrase that included the word "heirs." A grant of land to "X and his heirs" thus conveyed a fee simple estate. In contrast, a grant "to X," "to X forever," "to X in fee simple," or "to X and his issue" did not convey a fee simple, but only a life estate. (The common law took a similar approach with the creation of the fee tail, also requiring the use of the term "heirs.")

A different approach was adopted with respect to testamentary dispositions, where the courts developed a somewhat more generous policy. Perhaps recognizing that wills were frequently drawn up without professional assistance (unlike *inter vivos* transactions), the courts were more willing to give effect to a testator's manifest intention, even if the testator had failed to use the precise words required at common law to convey a fee simple estate. Testamentary dispositions "to X forever" or "to X and his issue" were sufficient to convey a fee simple estate to X. However, absent some other evidence of an intention to convey a fee simple, the words "to X" in a will would still convey only a life estate to X.

As determined in *D'Arundel's Case* (1225), Brac. NB 1054, the term "and his heirs" gives no actual estate in the land to these heirs. These words are known as "words of limitation" and not "words of purchase." Words of limitation define or delimit the *size* of the estate conveyed to the grantee—that is, whether it is a life estate or a fee simple estate. By contrast, words of purchase indicate to *whom* an interest is being conveyed. For example, at the time of the grant, the grantor (X) may have designated an heir (Y) by will. Y does not acquire any estate in the land until X's death, the time at which the testamentary gift will take effect. X, holding a fee simple interest, may at any time prior to his death convey this fee simple estate to a third party. If X does so, there simply will be nothing left for Y to take upon X's death. Y has no say in the matter. The term "and his heirs" (these words of limitation) thus merely determines that X has acquired a fee simple estate. This term does not convey any actual estate to X's heirs. As a result, in the grant "to X and his heirs," "to X" is an example of the words of purchase, because they indicate to whom the estate is being given. The words of limitation, "and his heirs," determine the size of estate granted to X (a fee simple).

Legislation has changed these strict common law requirements, effectively reversing the old presumption in favour of the life estate:

Conveyancing and Law of Property Act, RSO 1990, c. C.34

5.(1) In a conveyance, it is not necessary, in the limitation of an estate in fee simple, to use the word "heirs."

(2) For the purpose of such limitation, it is sufficient in a conveyance to use the words "in fee simple" or any other words sufficiently indicating the limitation intended.

(3) Where no words of limitation are used, the conveyance passes all the estate, right, title, interest, claim and demand that the conveying parties have in, to, or on the

property conveyed, or expressed or intended so to be, or that they have power in, to, or on the same.

(4) Subsection (3) applies only if and as far as a contrary intention does not appear from the conveyance, and has effect subject to the terms of the conveyance and to the provisions therein contained.

(5) This section applies only to conveyances made after the 1st day of July, 1886.

Section 10(2) of the Nova Scotia Conveyancing Act, RSNS 1989, c. 97 simply provides as follows: "A conveyance does not require a habendum or any special form of words, terms of art or words of limitation."

Pursuant to this legislative reform, the words "to X" in a conveyance after July 1, 1886 conveys to X all that the grantor holds, subject to any contrary intention expressed by the grantor. If the grantor holds a fee simple, X will acquire a fee simple. It is no longer necessary for the grantor to specify "to X and his heirs" in order for X to acquire a fee simple. By contrast, if the grantor intends to grant only a life estate, the grantor must expressly specify this limitation by using words such as "to X for life." Absent such words of limitation, the grantee will acquire the whole of the grantor's interest. Regarding a conveyance prior to July 1, 1886, the old common law rules continue to apply.

Similarly, the law governing testamentary dispositions has been changed by the Ontario Succession Law Reform Act, RSO 1990, c. S.26, s. 26:

26. Except when a contrary intention appears by the will, where real property is devised to a person without words of limitation, the devise passes the fee simple or the whole of any other estate or interest that the testator had power to dispose of by will in the property.

Because courts were somewhat more generous with testamentary dispositions, they attempted to give effect to a testator's intention, even if the testator had failed to use the precise words required by the common law to create a fee simple. However, there had to be at least some evidence that the testator intended to grant a fee simple, and absent this evidence, a life estate was presumed. The statutory provision above reverses this presumption. Unless there is evidence to the contrary, the law now presumes an intention to convey a fee simple (or the whole interest held by the testator, if less than a fee simple) and not a life estate. A testamentary disposition "to X" thus will convey to X the entire interest held by the testator. If the testator held a fee simple, X will acquire a fee simple estate.

Similar reform has taken place with respect to the fee tail estate, as seen in the Ontario Conveyancing and Law of Property Act, RSO 1990, c. C.34, s. 4

4. A limitation in a conveyance or will that before the 27th day of May, 1956, would have created an estate tail shall be construed as an estate in fee simple or the greatest estate that the grantor or testator had in the land.

The provision applies to both testamentary dispositions and *inter vivos* transactions. As a result, any attempt to create a fee tail estate today, by the use of the words "to X and the heirs of his body," will be construed as conveying to X the greatest estate held by the grantor. If this is a fee simple, X acquires a fee simple estate. The amendment does not apply to estate tails created before May 27, 1956, and some may have survived to this day.

See also Property Act, RSNB 1952, c. 177, s. 18; Real Property Act, RSNS 1954, c. 244, s. 5; and Real Property Act, RSPEI 1951, c. 138, ss. 15-16.

Exercise 1: Creating Freehold Estates

The exercises in this casebook are designed to illustrate how estates and future interests in land are created. The exercises include various *grants* or *devises*. You are required to analyze the grant or the devise, and determine what legal effect, if any, the purported grant or devise will have. For the purposes of these exercises, the jurisdiction is Ontario. In all cases of grants, assume that the grantor held a fee simple absolute, and in the case of devises, assume that the testator held a fee simple and is now dead. It is only upon the death of a testator that a testamentary disposition can have any effect.

In completing these exercises, you will become familiar with the doctrine of estates and the myriad ways in which the law permits property interests to be divided over time. At the end of these exercises, you will be able to analyze fairly sophisticated and complex grants and devises, and you will acquire the knowledge necessary to draft grants and devises that will achieve the desired legal effect.

The doctrine of estates and the law of future interests is complex. Although frustrating at times, it is important to note that this law, in all its archaic and complex glory, remains good law in most of common law Canada. It contains substantial pitfalls waiting to catch the unwary. With proper precautions, such as the use of equitable estates, these traps can usually be avoided; however, the student of law will be unable to identify these pitfalls, and advise the necessary precautions, without some understanding of the doctrine of estates and the law of future interests in its entirety.

Examine the effect of each of the grants or devises below. In particular, consider precisely what estate the grantee or devisee acquires. Is it an estate in fee simple, or simply a life estate?

1. Refer to the Conveyancing and Law of Property Act, RSO 1990, c. C.34, s. 5, effective on July 1, 1886. What was the effect of each grant at common law? What was the effect after July 1, 1886—that is, after the statutory amendments contained in the Conveyancing and Law of Property Act took effect?

Grant	Common law	After July 1, 1886
1. X to A and her heirs.		
2. X to A in fee simple.		
3. X to A forever.		
4. X to A.		

2. The following example is a devise. Recall that the common law governing the creation of estates in fee simple and life estates by testamentary disposition was different from that governing *inter vivos* transactions. These common law provisions were amended by statute in Ontario in the mid-19th century. See now the Succession Law Reform Act, RSO 1990, c. S.26, s. 26. Consider the effect of this devise, first at common law, and then pursuant to the current statutory regime.

Devise	Common law	SLRA, s. 26
X to A		

3. The following example deals with the fee tail estate. Review the statutory amendments affecting any attempts to create a fee tail estate in Ontario on or after May 27, 1956, pursuant to the Conveyancing and Law of Property Act, RSO 1990, c. C.34, s. 4. Note that this legislation applies to both grants and devises. Consider the effect of each of these grants or devises at common law, and today pursuant to these statutory amendments.

Grant or devise	Common law	After May 27, 1956
1. X to A and the heirs of his body.		
2. X to A in fee tail.		

Variations on the Fee Simple Estate

Estates in fee simple may be either *absolute* estates or *qualified* estates. It is possible to qualify a fee simple estate and create a freehold interest that is less than an absolute fee simple estate. Qualified fee simple estates can terminate not only on the death of the tenant without an heir (as is the case with all estates in fee simple), but also at an earlier date in certain circumstances. Qualified estates arise when the grantor or testator wishes to grant a fee simple estate that will terminate on the happening of some event, such as when the land is no longer used as a farm, or no longer used for charitable purposes. At this point, the grantor or the testator's estate may recover the land from the grantee. By contrast, an absolute estate in fee simple (known as a *fee simple absolute*) will terminate only if the holder of the estate dies without heirs, at which point the estate ends and the land escheats.

The qualified fee simple permits the grantor or testator to retain some ongoing control over the use of the land. The law has never been overly sympathetic to a landholder's desire to retain this control because, over time, such provisions tend to restrict the alienability of the land. Qualified estates are of less value than absolute estates because qualified estates may terminate if the condition on which the land is held is violated. If this occurs, the occupant of the land will be dispossessed. In many cases, particularly for the long-term occupant, this can work a harsh result. As a result, the law may at some point limit the "long arm" of the testator, reaching from the grave. The law attempts to balance the competing interests of the original landholder, who seeks ongoing control, and the current occupant, who may be dispossessed. Consequently, the law permits the creation and enforcement of only some types of qualified fee simples.

There are two types of qualified fee simple estates—the *determinable fee simple*, and the *fee simple subject to a condition subsequent*. The distinction between the determinable fee simple and the fee simple subject to a condition subsequent can be difficult to discern.

Determinable Fee Simple

The determinable fee simple will *automatically* "determine" on the occurrence of some specified event, which may never occur. The grantor's interest is called a *possibility of reverter*— that is, a possibility that the estate will revert back to the grantor upon the determining event. If the occurrence of the determining event becomes impossible, the determinable fee simple becomes absolute. The following is an example of a determinable fee simple:

X to A in fee simple until B marries.

In this case, A acquires a determinable fee simple and X retains the possibility of reverter. The fee simple will automatically determine if and when B marries. Upon B's marriage, the estate will automatically revert back to X. If B dies without marrying, the contemplated event has now become impossible. As a result, A acquires a fee simple absolute at the time of B's death. X no longer retains the possibility of reverter, and has no further interest in the land.

The critical feature of a determinable fee simple is that the determining event itself sets the limit for the estate granted. Words such as "so long as," "during," "while," and "until" typically create a determinable fee simple:

X to A so long as the land is used for school purposes.
X to A while the CN Tower stands.
X to A until the lands are no longer used for railway purposes.

Fee Simple Subject to a Condition Subsequent

Although similar on its face, the fee simple subject to a condition subsequent is created by the *addition* of a condition to a grant in fee simple, which may terminate the estate at the instance of the grantor. Unlike a determinable fee, where the determining event itself sets the limit for the estate, the condition subsequent is an independent clause *added* to a fee simple absolute. The following is an example of a condition subsequent:

X to A in fee simple on condition that A does not marry Y.

The condition has been added to a grant in fee simple absolute. As a result, words such as "on condition that," "provided that," and "but if" tend to create a fee subject to a condition subsequent.

In a fee simple subject to a condition subsequent, the grantor retains a *right of entry* (also known as a right of entry for condition broken). In contrast to a determinable fee, a fee upon a condition subsequent does not determine automatically. The grantor must re-enter in order to bring the estate to an end. If the grantor fails to do so, the estate continues and A will eventually acquire a fee simple absolute once the applicable limita-tion period in which to bring an action to recover the land has expired. By contrast, a determinable fee simple will determine automatically; the grantor of a determinable fee does not need to reclaim the fee simple. The purpose of a fee simple subject to a condition subsequent is to compel compliance with the condition, on the pain of forfei-ture. On the other hand, the determinable fee is intended only to give the land for a stated use, and when this use has ended, the land automatically returns to the grantor.

Although the distinction is a fine one, frequently referred to "as little short of disgraceful to our jurisprudence" (*Re King's Trust* (1892), 29 LR Ir. 401), the distinction remains important. Qualified estates may have entirely different results depending on whether the interest in question is characterized as a determinable fee simple or a fee simple subject to a condition subsequent. This is particularly evident as regards the application of the rule against perpetuities and the application of rules respecting uncer-tain or void conditions. Both matters are illustrated in the cases that follow.

Fee Simple Subject to a Condition Precedent

The estate upon a condition subsequent must be distinguished from an estate subject to a condition precedent, where the grantee will receive nothing unless the condition is satis-fied. A condition subsequent may defeat an estate that has already been granted and is thus a condition of *retention*, whereas a condition precedent is a condition of *acquisition*:

X to A on the condition that she marry B.

In the above grant, A will take no interest unless the condition is fulfilled. Her marriage is a condition of acquisition. If she is married to B, she will take a fee simple absolute.

It is sometimes difficult to determine if a particular grant or devise creates a fee subject to a condition precedent, a fee subject to a condition subsequent, or a determina-ble fee. The *characterization* of the grant or devise is often crucial to the basic question whether the grant will take effect. For example, the following devise was considered in *Re Down* (1968), 68 DLR (2d) (Ont. CA), reproduced below. This devise might be construed as a condition precedent, or a condition subsequent:

X to A when he reaches 30 provided that he stays on the farm.

It is clear that A must attain 30 before the devise can take effect, and this is a condition precedent. However, it is less clear whether A must simply *be* on the farm at the time he attains 30, thus satisfying a second condition precedent, or whether A must *continue* to stay on the farm as a condition subsequent—that is, a condition of retention. The question is obviously of great interest to A. If the devise only involves condition precedents, and both have been satisfied, A will take a fee simple absolute. If, however, the devise includes a condition subsequent, A will only take a fee simple subject to the condition subsequent, and the estate may be liable to forfeiture if he ever ceases to "stay" on the farm.

Remoteness

The rule against perpetuities, discussed in greater detail below, deals with the creation of interests in land that may arise in the future—for example, the right of entry, or the possibility of reverter. On the whole, the law dislikes interests that might arise at a very remote point in time. Such interests tend to cloud the title of land and restrict alienation and development. There may be an indefinite period of time during which the occupant's title is unstable because it remains subject to an outstanding possibility of reverter or a right of entry for condition broken. Because the common law has long favoured policies permitting the free alienation of land, it developed a complex system of rules to limit the extent to which such interests could arise in the future. This system is called the *rule against perpetuities*.

At this point, it is important simply to note that at common law the rule against perpetuities applied to the right of entry. If a right of entry might arise at a point too distant in the future, the common law rule against perpetuities would strike it down, and the fee simple subject to a condition subsequent became a fee simple absolute. A right of entry was thus eliminated if it could arise at a time too remote in the future, completely removing this cloud on the title. However, a determinable limitation, setting the *automatic* termination of the estate, could not last beyond the limiting event, no matter how far in the future the event might lie. Consequently, at common law the rule against perpetuities did not apply to the possibility of reverter, and such a possibility could forever cloud title to the land. At one time, this was a crucial distinction because many rights of entry would run afoul of the rule against perpetuities, much to the relief of the current occupant. However, the unfortunate occupant under a determinable fee would remain forever subject to the possibility of reverter. This inconvenient result has now been changed by statute, and all common law provinces now provide that the possibility of reverter is subject to the rule against perpetuities. (In Ontario, see the Perpetuities Act, RSO 1990, c. P.9, s. 15, which provides that the rule against perpetuities will apply to the possibility of reverter created in any instruments on or after September 6, 1966.)

In *Re Essex (County) Roman Catholic Separate School Board* (1977), 17 OR (2d) 307; 80 DLR (3d) 405 (HC), reproduced below, this distinction between a right of entry and a possibility of reverter was still important. In this case, the qualified estate in question was contained in a 1925 deed. If this 1925 qualified estate were characterized as a determinable fee simple, the possibility of reverter would continue to cloud the title indefinitely, because the rule against perpetuities applies only to a possibility of reverter in instruments executed after September 5, 1966. On the other hand, if the qualified estate is only a fee simple subject to a condition subsequent, and if the condition is void for some reason, the cloud will be removed and the occupant will obtain a fee simple absolute.

Void Conditions

Conditions may be invalid for a number of reasons. A condition may be "repugnant" to the interest granted, if the grantor has attached a condition inconsistent with the freedom of enjoyment, disposition, and management of the estate, such as an absolute prohibition of the sale of the land. A condition may be contrary to public policy, such as a complete prohibition of marriage. Finally, a condition may be too uncertain to enforce, such as a requirement to continue to reside in an area, "reside" being capable of various interpretations.

The most common type of condition that may be repugnant to the interest granted is a restraint on alienation. Common law, ever in favour of the free alienation of land, has long held that the power of alienation is an inseparable incident of ownership of a freehold estate in land, whether it be a fee simple or life estate. Although any restriction that *substantially* takes away the power of alienation is likely to be found void, partial restraints may be upheld. The nature of these prohibited restrictions include a total prohibition on the sale or mortgage of the land to anyone (*Re Corbit* (1905), 5 OWR 239), a provision that the land can be sold to one person only (*Attwater v. Attwater* (1853), 52 ER 131), a provision that the land must be held for the heirs of the grantee (*Re Casner* (1883), 6 OR 282 (HCJ)), or a provision that the land cannot be alienated without the consent of another person (*McRae v. McRae* (1898), 30 OR 54 (HCJ)). All of these restrictions have been held to constitute substantial interference with the power of alienation and thus have been held to be void. Total restraints, even for a limited period of time, such as for the life of the holder, or a substantial number of years after the testator's death, have also been held to be void: *Re Carr* (1914), 20 DLR 74 (BC SC).

On the other hand, a partial restraint on alienation may be upheld, such as a restraint prohibiting alienation to a particular person, or to a particular class of persons providing that the class is not so broad as to amount to a general restraint. See *Blackburn v. McCallum* (1903), 33 SCR 65, where the court held that a restraint on alienation except to children or grandchildren of the testator was valid because that left a sufficiently large class.

Conditions may also be contrary to public policy if the state has an interest in the non-performance of the condition. Conditions that incite the donee to commit a crime or other illegal act are an obvious example. Conditions that encourage the future separation of married parties are void (*Hindley v. Marquis of Westmeath* (1827), 108 ER 427); however, if the parties are already separated, and provision has been made for one party during the period of separation, the condition is valid. Conditions that interfere with parental obligations are void, such as a requirement that a child is not to reside with a particular parent: *Re Thorne* (1922), 22 OWN 28 (HC). A condition may forbid a change of religion for an adult or may prohibit conversion to another faith: *Wainwright v. Miller*, [1897] 2 Ch. 255. Although total restraints on marriage are generally void, partial restraints against marrying a certain person or a certain class of persons based on the religion of the person are valid, as in *Re Tuck's Settlement Trusts*, [1978] Ch. 49, reproduced later in this section.

Discriminatory restraints on alienation—for example, based on race or religion—are void as a matter of public policy. This public policy is reflected in the various provincial and federal human rights legislation. The Ontario Human Rights Code, RSO 1990, c. H.19, s. 3 provides that all persons have a "right to contract on equal terms without discrimination because of race, ancestry, place of origin, colour, ethnic origin citizenship, creed, sex, sexual orientation, age, marital status, family status or handicap." The right to contract, including the right to purchase land, falls within the scope of s. 3. A discriminatory restraint on alienation is inconsistent with this public policy and hence void. Moreover, a court might also find that such a restraint on alienation is over-broad and substantially and unduly interferes with the power of alienation.

Finally, conditions may also be void if they are too uncertain. One example is found in *Re Tuck's Settlement Trusts*, reproduced below, where the court considers whether a particular condition is too uncertain to enforce.

The Effect of a Void Condition

With respect to void conditions, there is a crucial distinction between condition precedents, condition subsequents, and determinable fees. If a condition precedent is void for some reason, the condition cannot be satisfied and the entire grant or devise will fail. This is unfortunate for the potential grantee, because the grant can never take effect. The common law generally favours an interpretation of a grant or devise that will permit the grant or devise to take effect or vest, known as a "vesting construction." As a result, courts are generally reluctant to find that a condition precedent is void and will strain to uphold such conditions. For example, even if the condition appears uncertain on its face, providing the donee can satisfy the court that whatever the condition might mean, it has at least been satisfied in the particular case, the grant may be valid. This test is sometimes known as "evidential uncertainty"; it is dealt with below in *Re Tuck's Settlement Trust*.

By contrast, if a condition subsequent is void, only the condition will fail, thus transforming the qualified estate into an absolute estate. Again, because the common law favours a vesting construction, the courts tend to take a different approach to conditions subsequent. A condition subsequent gives rise to a right of forfeiture on the part of the grantor, and the courts will construe it strictly. Particularly as regards potentially uncertain conditions subsequent, the courts will willingly find them void. The courts apply a stricter test, sometimes known as "conceptual uncertainty," to such conditions. Unless it can be seen from the moment of its creation, precisely and distinctly, what events will cause forfeiture, the courts will strike down the condition.

Finally, a determinable fee simple operates somewhat like a condition precedent. If the condition is void, the entire grant fails because the determining event is void: *Eisenhauer v. Eisenhauer*, [1943] 1 DLR 411 (NS SC). Again, this is unfortunate for the current occupant who will be dispossessed of the land, whether the condition has been breached or not. The courts will sometimes attempt to construe such a grant as a condition subsequent, rather than a determinable fee, in order to avoid this result. If the grant is construed as a condition subsequent, and the condition is void, the current occupant will simply acquire a fee simple absolute rather than be dispossessed of the land.

The following cases illustrate the various rules governing qualified estates. In all cases, the *characterization* of the grant or devise is crucial—that is, whether it is a condition precedent, condition subsequent, or determinable estate. As we have seen above, depending on how the court characterizes the grant or devise, dramatically different results are possible.

Re Essex (County) Roman Catholic Separate School Board and Antaya
(1977), 17 OR (2d) 307; 80 DLR (3d) 405 (HC)

[In *Re Essex (County)*, the court considered the question whether the grant in question was a determinable fee simple, or a fee subject to a condition subsequent. When reviewing the case, focus carefully on how the court characterized this grant. Why does the characterization matter? Depending on how the court resolved this question, how would the outcome differ? The facts of the case follow.

The respondent's father granted certain property to the applicant. The deed contained a covenant that the property was "to be used for school purposes only" and continued with the following words:

The said grantor reserves to himself and his heirs the preference to buy the said property at the current price should the same cease to be used for the purposes intended.

The applicant successfully brought a motion under the provisions of s. 167 of the Education Act, 1974 (Ont.), c. 109. This legislation permits a court to remove any restriction in a deed that limits the use of property for school purposes, if the property has been vested in a school board for at least 50 years.]

KREVER J: Before turning to the characterization of the nature of the limitation or restriction created by the deed, I should indicate why it matters whether one is concerned with a fee simple determinable or a fee simple subject to a condition subsequent. The short reason is that the former, on the basis of authority in Ontario, is not subject to the rule against perpetuities because the possibility of reverter immediately vests in the grantor, whereas the latter is subject to the rule because the right of entry for condition broken may not arise within the perpetuity period. See Morris and Leach, *The Rule Against Perpetuities*, 2d ed. (1962), pp. 210-11; *Re St. Patrick's Market* (1909), 14 OWR 794, 1 OWN 92; *Matheson v. Town of Mitchell* (1919), 46 OLR 546, 51 DLR 477; *Re McKellar*, [1973] 3 OR 178, 36 DLR (3d) 202; affirming [1972] 3 OR 16, 27 DLR (3d) 289; *Re Tilbury West Public School Board and Hastie, supra*. It is of passing interest to note that the rule against perpetuities, as modified by the *Perpetuities Act*, RSO 1970, c. 343, is, by s. 15 of that Act, made applicable to a possibility of reverter on the determination of a determinable fee simple just as it is to a right of entry for breach of a condition subsequent but that provision does not affect this case since, by virtue of s. 19, it applies only to instruments that take effect on or after September 6, 1966.

Did, then, the 1925 deed create a fee simple determinable with its attendant possibility of reverter which is not subject to the rule against perpetuities, as Miss Panchenko submitted it did? To begin with, if the hallmark of a fee simple determinable is the creation of a possibility of reverter, it is to be observed that the language of the covenant, with which I am concerned, does not give the grantor or his heirs, immediately upon the cessation of use of the lands for school purposes, anything more than a "preference to buy the said property at the current price." Beyond that it is instructive to examine the cases to find a test for the two different interests. It will, I think, be sufficient if the examination is limited to two cases.

Re Tilbury West Public School Board and Hastie, supra, contains a scholarly analysis of the authorities by Grant J, who was concerned with a motion for payment out of Court of money paid in as compensation for expropriation and for an order removing a certain restriction on the land in question and vesting the land in the applicant school board free from the restriction. The deed to the school trustees granted the property "for so long as it shall be used and needed for school purposes and no longer." The *habendum* clause mentioned the same restriction and went on to provide that "when the said piece or parcel of land is no longer used for school purposes it shall be returned to the owner of the said south half of lot number One North Range Middle Road Tilbury

West." To the usual covenant for quiet possession were added the words, "so long as used for school purposes and no longer" and to the usual release clause the words, "except when no longer used or needed for school purposes" were added. Grant J came to the conclusion that what was conveyed by the deed was a fee simple determinable. He did so after the following review of the tests that have been used (at pp. 23-24 OR, pp. 410-11 DLR):

> It must be determined first if the grant in question was a determinable fee simple subject to a right of reverter or a fee simple subject to a condition subsequent, because the cases and authors are not in agreement as to whether the rule applies equally to both such forms of limitations. It is difficult to define the difference between a determinable fee and a fee simple defeasible by condition subsequent and often each cannot be readily put in its proper classification. The essential distinction appears to be that the determining event in a determinable fee itself sets the limit for the estate first granted. A condition subsequent, on the other hand, is an independent clause added to a complete fee simple absolute which operates so as to defeat it: Megarry and Wade, p. 76. At p. 77 it is stated:
>
> > Words such as "while," "during," "as long as," "until" and so on are apt for the creation of a determinable fee, whereas words which form a separate clause of defeasance, such as "provided that," "on condition that," "but if," or "if it happen that," operate as a condition subsequent.
>
> In Cheshire at p. 280, the words "until," "so long as," and "whilst," are stated to be expressions creating determinable interests while phrases such as "on condition," "provided that," "if," "but if it happen," raise interests subject to condition subsequent. Cheshire at p. 281, points out the difference in the following words:
>
> > In short, if the terminating event is an integral and necessary part of the formula from which the size of the interest is to be ascertained, the result is the creation of a determinable interest; but if the terminating event is external to the limitation, if it is a divided clause from the grant, the interest granted is an interest upon condition.
>
> Both authors refer to *Challis's Real Property* where examples of determinable fees are set out at p. 255 of the 3d edition. At p. 256, examples 5 to 8 use the words "as long as," 9 uses "so long as," 10 to 18 use "till" or "until." The author states at p. 261 that:
>
> > where an estate is limited in fee simple, and the limitation contains no qualification, but, externally to the limitation, though in the same deed, or in another deed delivered at the same time, is contained a condition by a breach of which the fee simple is liable to be defeated; a breach does not *ipso facto* avoid the estate, but only makes it liable to be avoided by the entry of the person entitled to the possibility of reverter. No estate of freehold can be made to cease, without entry, upon the breach of a condition.
>
> Different consequences arise if the limitation is considered a determinable fee as opposed to a condition subsequent. A determinable fee automatically determines when the specified event occurs and the land reverts to the grantor or if dead to the heirs of the grantor. A fee simple subject to a condition subsequent merely gives the grantor (or whoever is entitled to his interest if dead) a right of re-entry to determine the estate.

Unless and until the entry is made a fee simple continues: Megarry and Wade, p. 77 and cases therein cited.

Thus a devise to a school in fee simple "until it ceased to publish its accounts" creates a determinable fee, whereas a devise to the school in fee simple "on condition that the accounts are published annually" creates a fee simple defeasible by condition subsequent: *Re Da Costa; Clark v. Church of England Collegiate School of St. Peter,* [1912] 1 Ch. 337.

Goodeve and Potter's Modern Law of Real Property (1929), states at p. 124:

> With a fee simple determinable the estate determines *ipso facto* by the happening of the event but where there is a condition, external to the limitation, the estate is not determined until entry by the person entitled to take advantage of the condition.

In *Re North Gower Township Public School Board and Todd, supra,* the Court of Appeal allowed an appeal from a judgment holding that a purchaser's objection to title was valid. In doing so it held that the restriction to which I shall refer offended the rule against perpetuities and as it was therefore invalid, it was not necessary for the vendor school board to apply to the Court to have it removed under the predecessor of s. 167(2) of the *Education Act, 1974.* The conveyance which gave rise to the problem granted the property, in 1896, "in fee simple. Subject however to terms and conditions hereinafter stated." The deed went on to say:

> that should the said parcel or tract of land at any time hereafter cease to be used for the purposes for which it is hereby granted the said lands ... shall revert to the said party of the first part, his heirs, executors, administrators or assigns and payment therefor of the said considerations or purchase price of Seventy-five dollars.

The *habendum* clause concluded with the words, "and subject also as aforesaid." At p. 66 OR, p. 424 DLR, Laskin JA said:

> Admittedly, the construction of a limitation upon a fee simple as being a condition subsequent or as giving rise to a possibility of reverter upon a determinable interest is often difficult unless a name is put to the interest in the document creating it, or unless the consequences which flow from the one interest or the other are spelled out. Certain words of limitation have come to be *indicia* of a fee simple upon condition subsequent and of a fee simple determinable, and I may refer to a recent discussion thereof by Grant J in *Re Tilbury West Public School Board and Hastie,* [1966] 2 OR 20, 55 DLR (2d) 407. But these formulae are not compelling, as is evident from a consideration of the reasoning and conclusion in *Hopper v. Liverpool Corp.* (1943), 88 Sol. Jo. 213. Without canvassing the host of cases, English and Canadian, which will be found in the judgment of Grant J, aforesaid, I am satisfied that the limitation before this Court is a fee simple upon condition subsequent. It is distinguishable from the wording of the limitation which Grant J found to be a fee simple determinable. The restriction in the present case is a superadded condition upon a grant of a fee simple rather than an integral part of the very limitation of the estate created in the School Board.

A consideration of the language used in the 1925 deed, and of these cases, persuade me that the deed did not create a fee simple determinable in the grantee with a possibility of reverter in the grantor and his heirs. In the words of Laskin JA, the handwritten "covenant" quoted earlier in these reasons was a "superadded condition upon a grant of fee simple rather than an integral part of the very limitation of the estate created in the School Board."

A decision that the deed did not give rise to a fee simple determinable is less difficult to make than a determination whether what I am faced with is a fee simple subject to a condition subsequent. Because of the presence of the words, "the said grantor reserved to himself and his heirs the preference to buy the said property at the current price," a case may be made for the creation of an option to purchase or a right of first refusal. I shall deal with these possibilities in the alternative because it is my opinion that the interest that was created was indeed a fee simple subject to a condition subsequent. The obligation on the part of the grantor or his heirs to pay for the property in the event that it should cease to be used for school purposes does not take the case out of the category of a condition subsequent. In the *North Gower* case the Court of Appeal held that the deed created a fee simple subject to a condition subsequent which was void as offending the rule against perpetuities and in that case the language which the deed used purported to provide that the parcel would revert on payment of the purchase price of $75. Perhaps more important is the test employed by Laskin JA, at p. 66 OR, p. 424 DLR of the report which, to repeat, was as follows:

> The restriction in the present case is a superadded condition upon a grant of a fee simple rather than an integral part of the very limitation of the estate created in the School Board.

The application of that test to the language of the deed before me results, in my view, in the same conclusion as that reached by Laskin JA in the *North Gower* case, that is, that the limitation with which I am dealing is a fee simple upon condition subsequent. The condition, the cessation of use for school purpose, is one which might not, and in the event, did not, occur within the perpetuity period, and, if the applicant were applying to the Court otherwise than under the *Education Act, 1974*, it would be entitled to a declaration that it holds an absolute fee simple.

Discussion Notes

Why might the court favour a conclusion that the grant in question was a condition subsequent, rather than a determinable fee? Are there underlying policy concerns, in addition to the stated reasons, that favour this result?

In the following case, consider whether the grant in question is a condition precedent, a condition subsequent, or a determinable fee. Why does it matter?

In re Tuck's Settlement Trusts
[1978] Ch. 49 (CA)

LORD DENNING MR: In 1910 Sir Adolph Tucker was made a baronet. He was rightly proud of this dignity. It was hereditary and on his death would pass to his successors in the male line of descent. Being a Jew himself, he was anxious to ensure that his successors to the title should all be of Jewish blood and Jewish faith. To do this he wanted his son to marry a wife who was Jewish; and his grandson likewise to marry a Jewish wife: and so on. So in 1912 he made a settlement by which he sought to ensure that each baronet in succession should marry an "approved wife." He put money in trust for "the Baronet for the time being if and when and so long as he shall be of the Jewish faith and be married to an approved wife." In the settlement, this was the definition of "an approved wife":

> "An approved wife" means a wife of Jewish blood by one or both of her parents and who has been brought up in and has never departed from and at the date of her marriage continues to worship according to Jewish faith.

Then he added this significant clause:

> As to which facts in case of dispute or doubt, the decision of the Chief Rabbi in London of either the Portuguese or Anglo German Community (known respectively as the Sephardim and the Ashkenasim Communities) shall be conclusive.

Sir Adolph himself died on July 3, 1926, leaving two sons and three daughters. He was succeeded by his eldest son, Sir William Tuck. He married an approved wife and had a son and daughter. Sir William died on May 12, 1954, and was succeeded by his son, Sir Bruce Tuck. Sir Bruce married first an approved wife and had two sons. But in 1964 there was a divorce. In 1968 he married a lady who was not an approved wife.

Now a question arises whether the settlement is valid or not. If it is valid, the fund will go to Sir Bruce Tuck and his two sons. If it is invalid, it will go to Sir Adolph's estate.

Mr. Dillon submitted that the definition of "approved wife" was so uncertain as to be void for uncertainty: that this uncertainty could not be cured by referring the matter to the Chief Rabbi: and that in consequence all the provisions in the settlement referring to an "approved wife" must be disregarded.

If this argument is correct, it means that the intentions of the settlor, Sir Adolph, have been completely defeated by the ingenuity of the lawyers: first, in discovering the uncertainty; and, secondly, in refusing to allow it to be cured by reference to the Chief Rabbi. I will deal with these two points in order.

The Issue of Uncertainty

In making his submissions, Mr. Dillon used two phrases which have begun to fascinate Chancery lawyers. They are "conceptual uncertainty" and "evidential uncertainty." After a little probing, I began to understand a little about them. "Conceptual uncertainty" arises where a testator or settlor makes a bequest or gift upon a condition in which he has not expressed himself clearly enough. He has used words which are too vague and indistinct for a court to apply. They are not sufficiently precise. So the court discards the condition as meaningless. It makes it of no effect, at any rate when it is a condition subsequent.

"Evidential uncertainty" arises where the testator or settlor, in making the condition, has expressed himself clearly enough. The words are sufficiently precise. But the court has difficulty in applying them in any given situation because of the uncertainty of the facts. It has to resort to extrinsic evidence to discover the facts, for instance, to ascertain those whom the testator or settlor intended to benefit and those whom he did not.

Evidential uncertainty never renders the condition meaningless. The court never discards it on that account. It applies the condition as best it can on the evidence available.

This dichotomy between "conceptual" and "evidential" uncertainty was adumbrated by Jenkins J in *In re Coxen*, [1948] Ch. 747, 761-762. It is implicit in Lord Upjohn's speech in *In re Gulbenkian's Settlements*, [1970] AC 508, 525 and accepted by Lord Wilberforce in *In re Baden's Deed Trusts*, [1971] AC 424, 457. I must confess that I find the dichotomy most unfortunate. It has led the courts to discordant decisions. I will give some relevant instances. On the one hand, a condition that a person shall "not be of Jewish parentage" has been held by the House of Lords to be void for conceptual uncertainty, at any rate in a condition subsequent: see *Clayton v. Ramsden*, [1943] AC 320: and a condition that a person shall be "of the Jewish race" was held by Danckwerts J to be void for conceptual uncertainty, even in a condition precedent: see *In re Tarnpolsk, decd.*, [1958] 1 WLR 1157. The reason in each case being that the testator had given no information or clue as to what percentage or proportion of Jewish blood would satisfy the requirement. Is it to be 100 per cent or will 75 per cent or 50 per cent be sufficient? The words do not enable any definite answer to be given.

On this reasoning the condition in the Tuck settlement that an "approved wife" should be "of Jewish blood" would seem to be afflicted with conceptual uncertainty.

On the other hand, a condition that a person shall be "of the Jewish faith" has produced diverse views. Four out of five Law Lords thought that it was void for conceptual uncertainty, at any rate in a condition subsequent: see *Clayton v. Ramsden*, [1943] AC 320, 329, 334-335: but Lord Wright thought it was sufficiently clear and distinct to be able to be applied: see *Clayton v. Ramsden*, at p. 331. Lord Cross of Chelsea afterwards agreed with him: see *Blathwayt v. Baron Cawley*, [1976] AC 397, 429. So also did Buckley J, at any rate in a condition precedent: see *In re Selby's Will Trusts*, [1966] 1 WLR 43. I should range myself with Lord Wright. His view is supported by reference to the cases on other religions. Thus a condition that a person should be or not be "of the Roman Catholic faith" is not open to objection on the ground of uncertainty, either in a condition precedent or a condition subsequent: see *Blathwayt v. Baron Cawley*, [1976] AC 397, 424-425 by Lord Wilberforce: nor a condition that he shall or shall not be an "adherent of the doctrine of the Church of England," at any rate in a condition precedent: see *In re Allen, decd.*, [1953] Ch. 810, 821: nor a condition that he shall be "of the Lutheran religion": see *Patton (WR) v. Toronto General Trusts Corporation*, [1930] AC 629. The reason being in each case that evidence can be given of the tenets of that religion or faith so as to see if the person is or is not an adherent of it.

On this reasoning the condition in the Tuck settlement about "Jewish faith" would seem to be valid and not avoided for conceptual uncertainty.

In addition to those troubles, there is another distinction to be found in the cases. It is between condition precedent and condition subsequent. Conceptual uncertainty may avoid a condition subsequent, but not a condition precedent. I fail to see the logic of this distinction. Treating the problem as one of construction of words, there is no sense in it. If the words are conceptually uncertain—so as to avoid a condition subsequent—they are just as conceptually uncertain in a condition precedent—and should avoid it also. But it is a distinction authorised by this court in *In re Allen, decd.*, [1953] Ch. 810, and acknowledged by Lord Wilberforce in *Blathwayt v. Baron Cawley*, [1976] AC 397, 424-425.

I deplore both these dichotomies, for a simple reason and a good reason. They serve in every case to defeat the intention of the testator or settlor. The courts say: "We are not going to give effect to his intentions—because he has not expressed himself with sufficient distinctness or clearness." That assertion gives rise to argument without end as to whether his words were sufficiently clear and distinct: and whether the condition in which they occur was a condition precedent or a condition subsequent.

The Chief Rabbi's Clause

How is any testator or settlor to overcome these legal difficulties? And all the costs, expense and time expended in resolving them? Sir Adolph Tuck in this settlement said: "Let any dispute or doubt be decided by the Chief Rabbi." That seemed to him a good solution, and it seems to me a good solution. The Chief Rabbi should be able to decide—better than anyone else—whether a wife was "of Jewish blood" and had been brought up "according to the Jewish faith." But Mr. Dillon said that that was not an admissible solution. He submitted that, in a case where there was conceptual uncertainty (where the words were not clear enough for the court) it followed inexorably that they were not clear enough for a rabbi either. He based this on the words of Jenkins J in *In re Coxen*, [1948] Ch. 747, 761 and on *In re Jones, decd.*, [1953] Ch. 125. Alternatively he said that, by entrusting the decision to a rabbi instead of to the court, the settlor was ousting the jurisdiction of the court. He based this on *In re Raven*, [1915] 1 Ch. 673 and *In re Wynn, decd.*, [1952] Ch. 271.

I cannot accept either of these submissions. Nor can I accept the decisions on which Mr. Dillon relies. All the cases on this subject need to be reconsidered in the light of *Dundee General Hospitals Board of Management v. Walker*, [1952] 1 All ER 896. A testator there gave money to a hospital provided that at his death it should not have been taken over by the state. He gave his trustees "sole and absolute discretion" to decide whether it had been taken over by the state. The House held that this entrusting to his trustees was perfectly valid: and their decision was to be upheld. It was a decision of the House of Lords in a Scottish case. It may not be binding on the English courts in an English case. But it is of the highest persuasive value. *Donoghue v. Stevenson*, [1932] AC 562 was a Scottish appeal. But it transformed the law of England. I venture to suggest that, on questions of principle, it is most desirable that the laws of England and Scotland should be uniform: and, accordingly, that a decision of the House of Lords—when founded on principle and not on authority—should be regarded as applicable to both countries: unless the House itself says otherwise. Why otherwise should we have Scottish Law Lords sitting on English cases or English Law Lords sitting on Scottish cases? The very constitution of the House shows that each system of law has much to learn from the other: and that a decision on a point of principle should reflect the best of both.

I see no reason why a testator or settlor should not provide that any dispute or doubt should be resolved by his executors or trustees, or even by a third person. To prove this, I will first state the law in regard to contracts. Here the general principle is that whenever persons agree together to refer a matter to a third person for decision, and further agree that his decision is to be final and binding upon them, then, so long as he arrives at his decision honestly and in good faith, the two parties are bound by it. They cannot reopen it for mistakes or errors on his part, either in fact or of law, or for any reason other than fraud or collusion. I collected the cases together in *Arenson v. Arenson*, [1973] Ch. 346, 363-364, especially in regard to awards by arbitrators, certificates of architects and engineers, and valuations by experts, and this was followed in *Campbell v. Edwards*, [1976] 1 WLR 403. Even if his decision involves points of law as well as of fact, his decision is binding on the two parties. This is especially the case where his decision involves the interpretation of words used in the business in which he is expert. Such an agreement (to abide by the decision of a third person) does not oust the jurisdiction of the courts. It only offends when the parties go further and seek by their agreement to take the law out of the hands of the courts and put it into the hands of a private tribunal without any recourse to the courts in case of error of law: see *Czarnikow v. Roth, Schmidt & Co.*, [1922] 2 KB 478 and *Lee v. Showmen's Guild of Great Britian*, [1952] 2 QB 329, 342.

If two contracting parties can by agreement leave a doubt or difficulty to be decided by a third person, I see no reason why a testator or settlor should not leave the decision to his trustees or to a third party. He does not thereby oust the jurisdiction of the court. If the appointed person should find difficulty in the actual wording of the will or settlement, the executors or trustees can always apply to the court for directions so as to assist in the interpretation of it. But if the appointed person is ready and willing to resolve the doubt or difficulty, I see no reason why he should not do so. So long as he does not misconduct himself or come to a decision which is wholly unreasonable, I think his decision should stand. After all, that was plainly the intention of the testator or settlor. He or his advisers knew that only too often in the past a testator's intentions have been defeated by various rules of construction adopted by the courts: and that the solution of them has in any case been attended by much delay and expense in having them decided by the courts. In modern times the courts have been much more sensible. Ever since *Perrin v. Morgan*, [1943] AC 399 and *In re Jebb, decd.*, [1966] Ch. 666. But still the testator may even today think that the courts of law are not really the most suitable means of deciding the dispute or doubt. He would be quite right. As this very case shows, the courts may get bogged down in distinctions between conceptual uncertainty and evidential uncertainty: and between conditions subsequent and conditions precedent. The testator may want to cut out all that cackle, and let someone decide it who really will understand what the testator is talking about: and thus save an expensive journey to the lawyers and the courts. For my part, I would not blame him. I would give effect to his intentions. Take this very case. Who better to decide these questions of "Jewish blood" and "Jewish faith" than a Chief Rabbi? The settlor mentions two Chief Rabbis. It is not necessary to ask both of them. Either one will suffice. I venture to suggest that his decision would be much more acceptable to all concerned than the decision of a court of law. I would let him decide it.

Conclusion

So it comes to this: if there is any conceptual uncertainty in the provisions of this settlement, it is cured by the Chief Rabbi clause. That was the view of Whitford J and I agree with it. If the Chief Rabbi clause is inoperative, then I would so construe the settlement as to hold that there is no conceptual uncertainty. This is the view of Lord Russell of Killowen, whose judgment in a moment will be read. And I agree with it, too.

In either case I would hold that the settlement is valid in all its provisions. I would, therefore, dismiss the appeal.

[Lord Russell of Killowen and Lord Eveleigh agreed, for different reasons, that the appeal should be dismissed.]

Discussion Notes

1. The court seems to assume that the grant in question is only a condition precedent. Could it also be construed as a condition subsequent or a determinable fee? If so, how would the outcome of the case change?

2. Should the law permit the grantor in this case to require that each baronet marry an "approved wife"? Should such a condition be void as a matter of public policy? If the court had held that this condition precedent were void, what would have been the outcome? Would the baronet get the property free of the condition, or would the entire grant fail?

3. Lord Denning states that he fails to see "the logic of the distinction" between conceptual uncertainty (that may void a condition subsequent) and evidential uncertainty (that may be used to uphold a condition precedent, even if it otherwise appears uncertain). He deplores the dichotomy, and he finds that the chief rabbi's clause is sufficient to resolve any uncertainty and cut out all the "cackle." Would the court have likely achieved the same result if the grant were a condition subsequent, rather than a condition precedent? Recall that a condition subsequent is a condition of forfeiture. Would the court have been as sympathetic if, on the facts of the case, a baronet was being threatened with forfeiture because he had failed to marry an "approved wife" according to the judgment of the chief rabbi? In such a case, would it be more likely that a court would apply the "conceptual uncertainty" test to the condition subsequent, and strike the condition down, leaving the baronet with an absolute estate, rather than dispossessed?

4. The reasons of the other judges are not reproduced above. In their view, it was evident that the condition precedent might be on its face uncertain. However, they also determined that it was possible to decide in most cases whether the condition had been satisfied. For example, if the baronet married the devout daughter of the chief rabbi, he would no doubt have satisfied the condition precedent, even if on its face the condition could be construed as "conceptually" uncertain. The majority preferred a construction of the grant that would permit it to take effect, if possible. Remember that if the court had found the condition precedent to be uncertain and thus void, the entire grant would have failed, even if the baronet had obviously satisfied the otherwise uncertain condition precedent. Would this be a reasonable result?

Re Down
(1968), 68 DLR (2d) 30 (Ont. CA)

[In the following case, the court further explores the judicial preference for a "vesting construction." What is the significance of this preference, and how does it influence the court when it is characterizing a grant or devise?]

LASKIN JA: An application for the construction of the will of the late David George Stanley Down came before Richardson J on December 1, 1967. Five questions were set out in the application, of which the first, if it was properly included, begs the issues that arise under the other four. It is the second question that, in its various parts, poses the problems of construction that lie at the base of the application; the succeeding questions are merely consequential upon the answers to the alternatives specified in question two. The first question asks whether the applicant, Harold Russell Down, a son of the testator, has an interest under the will, and, particularly, under para. 5 thereof. The second question is as follows:

2. If the answer to question 1 is that Harold Russell Down has an interest in the testator's estate, what qualification is placed on this interest by the use of the words in paragraph 5, "provided he stays on the farm"—

(a) do the said words import a precatory trust only?
(b) if the said words do not import a precatory trust only, do they import a condition upon the gift?
(c) if the said words import a condition on the gift, is the condition a condition precedent or a condition subsequent?
(d) if the said words import a condition, is the condition void for uncertainty?

Richardson J gave very short reasons for judgment on December 6, 1967; they are in one paragraph which I quote in full:

Having reviewed the material before me and considered the cases referred to by counsel for the parties, I think the answer to the first question in the application must be in the negative. It is my opinion that the devise to the application under para. 5 is conditional upon him staying on the farm and I think the words, "provided he stays on the farm" are clear, particularly when read along with paras. 3 and 4 of the will.

He thereupon directed issue of an order "declaring that the applicant has no interest in the farm under paragraph 5 of the Will." As is evident from the terms of the will set out below, the matter in dispute is not whether the applicant has an interest in a farm but rather whether he has an interest in the testator's real and personal estate.

The testator died on or about November 15, 1954, survived by two sons, the applicant and an older brother Stanley Linton Down, and by a sister Mary Elizabeth Down. The latter two, along with a nephew (not otherwise included in the will) were named executors. The applicant was 13 years of age when his father died. By reason of the terms of the will, it was important for him to know, he having attained his majority and, indeed, having passed his 26th birthday at the time of the application in this matter, what his position was if he should reach 30 years of age. The scheme of the will, as an aid to its construction, can best be shown by setting out its nine dispositive clauses and the concluding residuary clause, which are in these words:

I Give, Devise and Bequeath all my Real and Personal Estate of which I may die possessed in the manner following that is to say:

1. I give and bequeath unto my sister, Mary Elizabeth Down the use and occupation of our home place where we now reside on the South half of Lot Nine in the Fifth

Concession of the Township of Ekfrid for and during the term of her natural life together with the use of all the furniture and household goods of every kind now in the said home and together with a small plot of ground used for garden and free right-of-way over and upon the property for all purposes as she now has.

2. It is my desire that my son, Stanley Linton Down, shall have the use of all my farm property consisting of two hundred and twenty-five acres of land in the Township of Ekfrid subject to the payment to my said sister, Mary Elizabeth Down of the sum of Three Hundred dollars per year for and during the term of her natural life and subject also to the payment of Two Hundred dollars per year to my son, Harold Russell Down, until he arrives at the age of twenty-one years.

3. My said son, Harold Russell Down, is to have a home with my said sister, Mary Elizabeth Down, and my said son Stanley Linton Down, shall supply to my said son Harold Russell Down and my said sister, Mary Elizabeth Down, butter, eggs and milk and any meat he slaughters on the farm, sufficient for their requirements.

4. When my said son, Harold Russell Down, arrives at the age of twenty-one years and is desirous of farming, he may do so on the said farm but my said son, Stanley Linton Down, must pay him wages which are the going rate in that section of the country.

5. When my said son, Harold Russell Down, arrives at the age of thirty years, providing he stays on the farm, then I give, devise and bequeath all of my estate both real and personal of every nature and kind whatsoever and wherever situate unto my said sons Stanley Linton Down and Harold Russell Down to be divided between them equally share and share alike.

6. In the event of my said sister, Mary Elizabeth Down, dying any time before my said son Harold Russell Down arrives at the age of thirty years then all nursing, medical attendance and burial expenses shall be paid out of her estate and any deficiency shall be made up by my said son Stanley Linton Down. If my said son, Harold Russell Down, is beyond thirty years of age then any deficiency must be shared equally by my said sons Stanley Linton Down and Harold Russell Down.

7. My said farm of two hundred and twenty-five acres shall not be sold or encumbered in any way for and during the term of the natural life of my said sister and in no event until Harold Russell Down arrives at the age of thirty years.

8. I hereby instruct and authorize my said son, Stanley Linton Down to pay for Hydro, Telephone, Insurance and Taxes on the Home Place where my said Sister resides and to provide my said son, Harold Russell Down with medical, hospital and nursing care until he arrives at the age of twenty-one years.

9. I give and bequeath unto my said son, Harold Russell Down, my piano for his own absolute use forever.

All the residue of my Estate not hereinbefore disposed of I give, devise and bequeath unto my said son Stanley Linton Down, including my truck and my automobile.

Before turning to the matters raised by Q. 2, I can deal shortly with a contention advanced by the appellant applicant outside of the ambit of that question. The contention was that the qualification of age 30 did not in itself prevent an immediate vesting of whatever interest the younger son was given under para. 5; or, at least, did not prevent a vesting on attaining his majority, subject to a divestiture on dying before reaching age 30. There is no substance to this submission. Attainment of age 30 is, apart from other considerations, clearly spelled out as a qualifying circumstance if the applicant is to take at all.

The substantial issue is the force of the contingency represented by the words "providing he stays on the farm." There is the question whether this phrase introduces a condition precedent or a condition subsequent, and the question whether, in either event, it is void for uncertainty or is so void only if it is properly construed as a condition subsequent. Over and above these issues is the question whether the quoted words are merely precatory, expressive of a wish or hope but without limiting force in law. In support of a precatory construction, counsel for the applicant urged the reasoning in *Re Brace*, [1954] 2 All ER 354.

The material before the Court discloses that the testator's sister is still alive and lives (pursuant to the terms of the will) in what was the testator's home on the farm forming part of his estate. The older son, who is the respondent to the application and in the appeal in his personal capacity as a beneficiary, lives with his wife and children in another house on the farm. Although affidavit evidence is before us respecting the goings and comings of the applicant after he reached 17 or 18 years of age (involving, *inter alia*, his leaving the farm to work elsewhere and his returning thereto daily, and later on weekends), it is unnecessary to dilate upon it to resolve the legal issues in this case.

It is advisable to consider first whether the words "providing he stays on the farm" are precatory; because, if they are, nothing will stand in the way of the applicant's right to a half interest in the estate save attainment of age 30. Certainly, they are not ex facie precatory, and there is nothing in any other part of the will to put a precatory gloss upon them. Paragraph 4 does not do so since it makes the applicant's desire and not that of the testator a prerequisite of benefit: see *Moloney v. Moloney and Conden*, [1938] OR 73, [1938] 1 DLR 654. Indeed, I think that the precatory argument, based on such a construction in *Re Brace*, *supra*, is misconceived here. It is one thing to say that precatory words may or may not create a trust, obliging a beneficiary to apply certain property in a particular way; it is a different thing to say that words, couched in terms of a condition of a person taking or enjoying an interest, do not have that effect at all but should be construed as entitling him to take or enjoy without meeting its terms. I would note, further, that the contested words in *Re Brace*, "on condition that she will always provide a home for my daughter," concern an alleged benefit to a third person out of property given to another; and there is not, as here, a question whether the intended beneficiary qualifies. This is apart from the fact, which was material in *Re Brace*, that there was no gift over.

A precatory construction being rejected, I address myself to the question whether the words "providing he stays on the farm" introduce a condition precedent or a condition subsequent. The main contention of the appellant is that the words prescribe a condition subsequent which is void for uncertainty. The respondent's position is that they introduced a condition precedent which, if void for uncertainty, results in defeating the gift to the parties under para. 5; and, if certain, defeats the gift on the facts disclosed in the affidavits. The respondent submitted in this connection that the condition was operative only until the applicant reached age 30, basing himself principally on the provision in para. 7 of the will forbidding sale of the farm until the applicant reached age 30.

If the required period on the farm ends at age 30, when does it begin? Paragraph 2 of the will gives the use of the farm to the respondent, subject to certain payments to the testator's sister and to the applicant until he reaches his majority. By para. 4, the applicant, if at that time "desirous of farming," may do so on the farm, and his older brother comes under an obligation to pay him at current rates. Then comes para. 5 stating that when the applicant reaches age 30, "providing he stays on the farm," he and his brother shall share equally in the whole estate. It is an arguable conclusion from this that the testator put it up to his younger son to come to a decision on reaching his majority whether he wished to farm; and if he so determined and "stays on" the farm to age 30, he would share in the estate equally with his brother. The fact that the particular verb with which we are concerned is in the present tense must, on this argument, be viewed in the context of all the relevant clauses touching the farm; and there is the supporting submission that significance must be given to the phrase "stays on" (as contrasted with "stays at") as reflecting a continuation of a way of life chosen at age 21.

If this is the construction of the contingency, being therefore a condition precedent operative until age 30, then on the facts (unless it be the case that the respondent was at fault in the matter), the applicant has no claim under para. 5. I take this to be the conclusion of the Judge of first instance.

Two other constructions suggest themselves. There is the view that the proviso is correlated in time with the attainment of age 30, and should be read as requiring the applicant to come at that time or within a reasonable period thereafter to stay on the farm; and having done so he has satisfied the contingency. There is also the view that the contingency begins to operate from the attainment of age 30, and requires the applicant to stay on the farm thereafter (at the most, for his lifetime) to avoid a divestiture. Both of these views look upon the proviso as a condition subsequent. One problem which these views (and especially the second one) raise is whether the divesting on breach of condition subsequent would affect the interests of both the applicant and the respondent under para. 5 or only that of the applicant.

The answer to this question is bound up with the preliminary issue whether the proviso should be construed as a condition subsequent; and this, in my view, is influenced by whether the will provides for a gift over on failure to meet the terms of the proviso: see *Re Ross* (1904), 7 OLR 493. The relevant consideration here is the relation of the residuary clause (following para. 9 of the will) to para. 5.

In a sense both are residuary clauses; but the contingencies in para. 5 make it reasonable to read them together, and to view the later clause as taking effect (with respect to the estate not otherwise specifically disposed of) upon the failure of the applicant to meet the contingencies. I have already expressed the view that attainment of age 30 is a prerequisite to any taking by the applicant under para. 5. The fact that the proviso as to staying on the farm follows the age prescription (as well as being couched in the present tense) is an indication that it is susceptible of being a condition of retention rather than another condition of acquisition. Paragraph 7 is also consistent with this view in its prohibition of a sale of the farm during the sister's lifetime and "in no event until Harold Russell Down arrives at the age of thirty years." This paragraph does not relate retention of the farm as an asset of the estate to any desire of the applicant to work thereon, but only to his attainment of an age at which he will qualify for a half interest in the whole estate "providing he stays on the farm." It is as reasonable to read para. 7 in support of a condition subsequent construction as in support of a condition precedent construction of the proviso in para. 5.

There is also the consideration that difficulties of construction such as are posed by the will in this case should be resolved in favour of all the objects of the testator's bounty, especially where they are two sons, rather than be allowed to produce a result unfair to one of them, unless the language leaves no reasonable alternative. In the present case, I do not think that any more violence is done by reading the proviso as a condition subsequent than would be done by reading it as a condition precedent. I am fully aware of the preference for a vesting construction that the case law exhibits; and this fortifies me in concluding that the condition in question should be read as one of defeasance.

The remaining issue is that of certainty. I do not find this difficult of resolution, having regard to the well-known principles reflected in *Clavering v. Ellison* (1859), 7 HLC 707, 11 ER 282, and *Re Sifton*, [1938] OR 529, [1938] 3 DLR 577, [1938] AC 656, with which I agree. I would refer particularly to the following passage in *Clavering v. Ellison*, at p. 725:

> where a vested estate is to be defeated by a condition on a contingency that is to happen afterwards, that condition must be such that the Court can see from the beginning, precisely and distinctly, upon the happening of what event it was that the preceding vested estate was to determine.

The various meanings of "stay" as a verb, including "to remain," "to reside," "to sojourn," "to dwell upon," found in the standard dictionaries, manifest the uncertainty of what is demanded of the applicant; and even if a context is provided by the earlier reference, in para. 4 of the will, to "farming," there is still a question of the degree or extent, having regard especially to the division of the estate between the two brothers. Moreover, no period or duration is indicated (contrast, in this respect, *Oliver v. Davidson* (1882), 11 SCR 166), unless it be taken as a life commitment. I need not, however, rest my decision on this element but point out that the present case differs in this respect from *Re Sifton* which was concerned not with a capital gift made once and for all subject to a defeasance provision but with periodic payments which were subject to an abrogating condition.

I hold that the proviso as a condition subsequent is void for uncertainty and does not therefore trammel the applicant's interest under para. 5 once he qualifies for it by attaining age 30.

The appeal must therefore be allowed, the order below set aside, and in its place there will be an order declaring that the answer to Q. 1 is that the applicant has a half interest in the estate, pursuant to para. 5, contingent upon his attaining age 30; and that the answer to Q. 2 is that the words in dispute constitute a condition subsequent which is void for uncertainty. It is unnecessary to answer the other questions. As to costs, I think this is a case in which both parties should have their costs of the application and of the appeal out of the estate. I would fix the costs of each on the application at $250, and allow each their costs of the appeal.

Appeal allowed.

Discussion Notes

1. What would have been the result if the court had held that the devise in question was a condition precedent only, and not a condition subsequent? The court found that the condition to "stay" on the farm was uncertain and thus void. If the devise created a condition precedent and the condition were void, the entire gift would fail, even if the devisee reached 30 years old and never once left the farm. Would this be a reasonable result? If this had been only a condition precedent, would the court have likely found that the condition was uncertain?

2. As a result of the court's decision, what interest does the devisee acquire upon attaining 30 years old?

The Doctrine of Estates and Native Title

Native writer Leroy Little Bear provides a critique of the doctrine of estates, excerpts of which are reproduced below (Leroy Little Bear, "A Concept of Native Title" (1976), 17:2 *Canadian Association in Support of the Native People's Bulletin* 58). He notes that the native concept of ownership is in some respects similar to the common law system, because interests in land are fractured under the common law system and allodial title is unknown. He also notes the various qualified estates that can exist at common law, including the fee simple subject to a condition subsequent and the determinable fee simple. He contrasts this system to the native concept of ownership of land:

> Indian ownership of property, and in this case, land, is wholistic [sic]. Land is communally owned. Indian property ownership is somewhat akin to a joint tenancy: the members of a tribe have an undivided interest in the land; everybody, as a whole, owns the whole. In regards to title, to use the language of the estate system, the Native concept of title is somewhat like a[n] FSD [fee simple determinable], or a[n] FSSCS [fee simple subject to a condition subsequent], or a[n] FT [fee tail], or a combination of all three. It is as though the original grantor of the land to the Indians put a condition on it ... "so long as there are Indians"; "so long as it is not alienated"; "on the condition that it is used only by Indians" etc. In other words, the Indians' concept of title is not equivalent to a fee simple, but is somewhat less than a fee simple. This is not to say that they were not capable of conceiving a fee simple concept. If one attempts to trace the Indians' source of title, one will quickly find the original source is the Creator. The Creator, in granting land, did not give the land to human beings only but gave it to all living beings. This includes plants, sometimes rocks, and all animals. In other words, deer have the same type of estate or interest as any human being. ...
>
> An observation about the Indians' concept of land title includes a reference back to the basic philosophy. Indian property concepts are wholistic [sic]. Ownership does not rest in any one individual, but belongs to the tribe as a whole, as an entity. The land belongs not only to people presently living, but it belongs to past generations and to future generations. Past and future generations are as much a part of the tribal entity as the living generation. Not only that, but the land belongs not only to human beings, but also to other living things; they, too, have an interest.

Leroy Little Bear points out that the native concept of ownership stands in opposition to claims made by the Canadian state to ownership and sovereignty over native lands. He notes that the native concept of ownership is consistent with the practice of sharing the lands with an alien people, and sharing the land cannot be interpreted as waiving any claim to the land. He also argues that because native peoples have never held a fee simple absolute in the land, the land cannot be conveyed or claimed by Canada in fee simple absolute. Finally, he argues that the native peoples could not even convey an interest equal to what they were originally granted, as this would be inconsistent with the conditions on which the land was granted—that it remain held by natives. Leroy Little Bear thus concludes that the Canadian state has little grounds to claim title or sovereignty over native lands.

Contrast his position to the one taken by the Supreme Court of Canada in *R v. Sparrow*, [1990] 1 SCR 1075, at 1103. In this case, the court held that although the Crown recognized the right of native peoples to occupy their traditional lands, there was "never any doubt" that on the introduction of English law, the Crown acquired sovereignty, legislative power, and underlying title to these lands.

Exercise 2: Qualified Fee Simple Estates

For each of the grants or devises below, consider the type of interest that is created. Does the grant or devise create a determinable fee simple, a fee simple subject to a condition subsequent, or a fee simple subject to a condition precedent? What interest, if any, does X, the grantor or testator, retain? Consider as well whether the condition in question may be void for any reason. If so, what would be the outcome?

Grant or devise	Analysis
1. X grants to A and his heirs so long as A lives on the farm.	
2. X devises to A and her heirs on condition that she lives on the farm.	
3. X grants to A and his heirs for so long as [the land] is used and needed for a school and no longer. See *Re Tilbury West v. Hastie*, [1966] 2 OR 20; 55 DLR (2d) 407, as considered in *Re Essex (County) Roman Catholic Separate School Board* (1977), 80 DLR (3d) 405 (Ont. HC).	

Grant or devise	Analysis
4. X grants to A and her heirs in fee simple and subject to the condition noted below; [in a subsequent clause] if the use ceases then there shall be a reversion to the grantor on payment of $75. See *Re North Gower (Township) Public School Board v. Todd*, [1968] 1 OR 63; 65 DLR (2d) 421 (CA), as considered in *Re Essex County*.	
5. In 1892, X grants to the Canadian National Railways and its heirs so long as the land continues to be used for railway purposes; and subject to an understanding that if the land ceases to be used for such purposes, the fee simple shall revert to the grantor and he shall be entitled to enter thereon. See *Re McKellar* (1972), 27 DLR (2d) 70, aff'd. 36 DLR (3d) 202 (Ont. CA).	
6. X devises to A certain property, and adds "with regard to this property, as it has been in the family of my late mother for seven generations, it shall not be sold, mortgaged or exchanged, or conveyed in any way, ... forever." See *Re Collier* (1966), 60 DLR (2d) 70 (Nfld. SC).	
7. X devises to A, if and when she shall attain the age of twenty-one years, provided that upon the attainment of such age she shall then be resident in one of the countries of the British Commonwealth of Nations. See *Kotsar v. Shattock*, [1981] VR 13. Compare this devise to that in *Re Tuck's Settlement Trusts*.	

Grant or devise	Analysis
8. X grants to A and his heirs on condition that he remain a bachelor.	
9. X devises to A and her heirs on condition that she remain unmarried until the age of 35.	
10. X grants to A and his heirs on condition that he marries within the Catholic faith.	
11. X devises to my sister Mary Maconochie during such time as she may live apart from her husband the sum of $ per week for her maintenance while so living apart from her husband. See *Re Moore* (1888), 39 Ch.D 116.	
12. X grants to A and his heirs on condition that the land not be sold to Jews or to persons of objectionable nationality. See *Re Drummond Wren*, [1945] 4 DLR 674 (Ont HC), discussed more fully in chapter 6.	
13. X devises to A and his heirs if he has obtained a law degree.	
14. X devises to A if she lives on the farm.	

Life Estates

Like an estate in fee simple, a life estate can also be qualified. A life estate can be subject to a condition precedent or a condition subsequent, or be a determinable life estate. For example:

X to my widow for life so long as she remains unmarried.

In this case, the widow acquires a determinable life estate with two natural termination points—her death or her remarriage, whichever comes first. The grantor's estate retains both a possibility of reverter and a reversion in fee simple. If the widow remarries, her interest in the land determines and immediately reverts to the grantor's estate. If she never remarries, the estate reverts to the grantor's estate upon her death. By contrast, the following devise creates a life estate subject to condition subsequent:

X to my widow for life provided that she does not remarry.

The natural termination point of this life estate is the widow's death. However, if she remarries, this estate can be cut short by the executor of the grantor's estate if the executor exercises the right of entry.

A variety of problems can arise with such qualified life estates. First, as illustrated in *Re Waters* (1978), 21, OR (2d) 124, 89 DLR (3d) 742 (HC), reproduced below, it is occasionally unclear whether the testator or grantor intended to create a qualified life estate, or merely a personal *licence* to occupy the lands for a period of time. Chapter 4 discusses in greater detail the distinction between an estate in land and a licence. For the moment, it is important to note that a licence is merely a contractual right, granted by the owner, permitting another to enter onto the land usually for a specified purpose (such as entering into a movie theatre to sell popcorn). Given it is only a contract, and thus governed by the doctrine of privity of contract, a licence does not create an estate in land that will bind subsequent purchasers of the land in question. The rights enjoyed by the licencee under the licence cannot generally be conveyed to a third party. In other words, a licence is a less substantial interest in the land than is an estate in the land. An estate, such as a life estate or a fee simple, is enforceable against the world, and can be freely alienated. Consequently, it is a matter of considerable importance to determine whether a given grant or devise creates a qualified life estate or merely a licence.

Given that a life estate can be qualified in the same manner as a fee simple estate, similar problems also arise with respect to the characterization of the grant or devise, as examined in *Re McColgan*, [1969] 2 OR 152, 4 DLR (3d) 742 (HC), below. For example, if the condition in question is uncertain, the entire grant or devise will fail if it is characterized as either a condition precedent or a determinable life estate. On the other hand, if the grant or devise is characterized as a life estate subject to a condition subsequent, the condition will simply be struck down, converting the estate into an absolute life estate.

When reviewing the following two cases, examine how the court characterizes the grant or devise in question. Is it a personal licence, a determinable life estate, a life estate subject to a condition precedent, or a life estate subject to a condition subsequent? Why does it matter?

Re Waters
(1978), 21 OR (2d) 124; 89 DLR (3d) 742 (HC)

PENNELL J (orally): This is an application by way of an originating notice of motion for the advice and direction of the Court in construing the last will and testament of

Archibald George Waters, deceased. The testator died on June 12, 1975, leaving a will dated May 29, 1974, probate of which was granted to his son William George Waters and Roy Miller, the persons named as executors.

By cl. 6 of the will, the testator made the following devise:

> 6. I give the use of 48 Walker Avenue, in the City of Toronto, to Mrs. Ellen Jones for as long as she lives, or until she re-marries, or gives to my executors and trustees a written notice that she no longer needs and desires the use of the property. Taxes, insurance, repairs and other upkeep expenses shall be paid by Mrs. Ellen Jones. Upon the death, remarriage, or notice being given by Mrs. Jones that she no longer needs or desires the property, it shall become part of the residue of my estate.

Several questions arise as to the nature of the interest given to Mrs. Ellen Jones under cl. 6 of the will. It is the contention of counsel for the residuary beneficiaries that it was the intention of the testator that there was to be given to Mrs. Ellen Jones not a life interest, but merely a licence or personal right to occupy such property and, accordingly, she has no right to rent the premises and collect rental income.

I take it to be a cardinal rule of construction that the Judge must endeavour to place himself in the position of the testator at the time the will was made, and try to ascertain the intention of the testator, having regard to the language used, the context in which the language is used and the circumstances under which the will in question was made. This is the Geiger counter that must be passed over the whole of the will in order to ascertain what is the meaning of a part of it.

As regard to circumstances at the time the will was made, I notice that the testator states that the will was "made in contemplation of my marriage to Ellen Jones" and he then goes on to direct that the provisions of "... this my will shall be applicable whether or not a marriage shall be solemnized by me with Mrs. Ellen Jones."

As I read the will before me, there is a clear interest given to Mrs. Ellen Jones for life in the words, "I give the use of 48 Walker Avenue ... for as long as she lives." If the clause had ended there it would give a life estate. Is there anything in the will sufficient to prevent these words having their ordinary meaning or effect? It is to be observed that there is no gift over except if Mrs. Ellen Jones remarries or gives to the executors written notice that she no longer needs and desires the use of the property. If the testator had wished to introduce another proviso or exception, let us say that of personal occupation, he might easily have expressed it. He has expressed carefully what the provisos are on which the benefit is to cease. In my reading of the will as a whole, I see no condition annexed to her requiring personal occupation.

I am fortified in this view by the words of para. 7. In that clause the testator gives Mrs. Jones all the furniture and other household effects which are in 48 Walker Ave. and this bequest is entirely consistent with the devise of a life estate of the real property, and I would answer Q. 1 as follows: (1) Mrs. Ellen Jones was given a life estate under para. 6 subject to be determined by the proviso set out in the said paragraph.

It remains to consider another problem. A work order dated August 12, 1976, has been issued against 48 Walker Ave. by the Development Department of the City of Toronto requiring certain repairs, in order to place the property in conformity with the requirements of the housing by-laws. The executors have requested Mrs. Ellen Jones to make the said repairs, but she apparently has refused or neglected to do so. It appears that the City of Toronto has taken conviction proceedings against Mrs. Ellen Jones and against the executors for failure to make the repairs set out in the work order.

This circumstance then gives rise to the second question submitted to the Court and it is expressed in these terms:

> 2.(a) Under paragraph 6 of the Will, is Mrs. Ellen Jones responsible for the cost of remedying all the items set forth in a work order dated August 12, 1976.

The question comes down to this—What is the meaning of the word "repair"? The key to the sense in which the word is used in this clause, is to be found in the words immediately following, namely, "and other upkeep expenses." To repeat the material words of the sentence, "Taxes, insurance, repairs and other upkeep expenses shall be paid by Mrs. Ellen Jones."

To my mind, it was intended that Mrs. Ellen Jones should do such ordinary and necessary repairs, having regard to the age, character and locality of the property as a reasonably minded tenant would do to keep them reasonably fit for occupation. It seems to me the law is clear that where a person accepts a benefit under a will on a condition that she will discharge a certain liability, she takes the benefit encumbered by the burden: see *Jay et al. v. Jay et al.*, [1924] 1 KB 826; *Re Field; Sanderson v. Young*, [1925] Ch. 636.

The work order in question was issued pursuant to s. 6(1) of the *City of Toronto Act*, 1967 (Ont.), c. 131, as amended. The material parts of s. 6(1)(g) and (h) read as follows:

> (g) "repair" includes taking the necessary action to bring any dwelling to the standards;
> (h) "standards" means the standards for the maintenance and improvement of the physical condition and for the fitness for occupancy prescribed by a by-law under this section.

Prima facie, the repairs to be effected under the work order would seem to be of such a character of repairs required to keep the house in a reasonably fit condition for occupation, and presumably would involve no more than renewal or replacement of defective parts of a subsisting portion of the premises. It follows, in my view, that Mrs. Ellen Jones is responsible for these repairs. I would add this: I think Mrs. Ellen Jones would not be responsible for renewal or replacement of such a substantial character as to amount to a rebuilding of the building or any substantial part thereof. If there is any dispute as to the character of any one of the items of repair set out in the work order, then the matter may be spoken to.

Order accordingly.

Discussion Note

If the devise created only a personal licence, why would the devisee have "no right to rent the premises and collect a rental income"?

Re McColgan
(1969), 4 DLR (3d) 572 (Ont. HC)

KEITH J: The Guaranty Trust Company of Canada, as the executors of the last will and testament and trustees of the estate of the late Dr. James W. McColgan, seek the advice and direction of the Court on eight questions arising out of the language used by the testator in one paragraph of his will.

The circumstances which gave rise to the present application are related in the affidavits of the respondent Mary Kovalchick and of David Ernest Morrow, a trust officer in the employ of the applicant. The respondent Mary Kovalchick states that she first became acquainted with the late Dr. McColgan as his patient in the year 1928 at which time she was 18 years of age and Dr. McColgan was the only medical practitioner in the Town of Sagamore, Pennsylvania. The respondent and the testator became, in her words, "great and good friends which relationship lasted up to the date of his death." The respondent says, however, that between the years 1928 and 1958 when Dr. McColgan retired and moved to Toronto permanently, "We were frequently in each other's company and the question of marriage was discussed between us on many occasions but because of religious differences no ceremony was ever performed." She continues in her affidavit sworn on November 22, 1968:

> 4. In 1958, Dr. McColgan retired from the practice of medicine and came to Canada for his retirement alone at which time he occupied his residence at 39 Arjay Crescent, Willowdale, which he had purchased in 1956 or 1957 and in which he resided up to the time of his death.
>
> • • •
>
> 6. When the doctor retired to Ontario from Sagamore, Pennsylvania, he left me a power of attorney for the purposes of collecting his outstanding accounts and otherwise winding up his medical practice and, after the said medical practice was wound up, I visited with the late Dr. McColgan from 1959 to 1967 approximately three or four times each year at which time I would live with the doctor at 39 Arjay Crescent for several weeks at a time.
>
> 7. While I lived with the doctor in Toronto, I devoted myself completely to his comfort, well-being and needs and managed his home by supervising the housekeeper, day workers and repairmen, including the hiring and firing of such workers, attended to marketing and nursed the doctor and cooked his meals for him.
>
> 8. In 1965, the late Dr. McColgan insisted that I come to Ontario to stay with him permanently as he was alone and very sick and he had been informed that he had cancer.
>
> 9. My state of health at that time would not permit me to leave Sagamore, Pennsylvania for any protracted period in excess of two or three months and I was unable to accede to the doctor's request to come to Ontario to live with him permanently.
>
> 10. Throughout the period that I kept company with the late Dr. McColgan, he was at all times aware of my financial position and my state of health.
>
> 11. At the present time, I am suffering from a nervous condition which precludes the doing of heavy or extensive housework and my assets consist of the sum of

approximately $14,000.00 cash, being the balance of insurance monies made payable to me directly upon the doctor's death and provided by the late doctor, and a pension of $380.00 per month from [the] US Government.

12. The premises at 39 Arjay Crescent consist of nine rooms and large grounds and I am unable to carry out the normal duties required to maintain housekeeping of the premises without a housekeeper.

Dr. McColgan died at Toronto on June 26, 1967. His will was executed on May 13, 1965, a year that is specially mentioned in para. 8 of the respondent's affidavit, above-quoted.

All the questions propounded to the Court related to the provisions of para. III(f) of the will which reads as follows:

III I Give, Devise and Bequeath all property of every kind and description wherever situate of which I may die possessed or over which I may have any power of appointment unto my Trustee upon the following trusts: ...

(f) To hold my property at 39 Arjay Crescent, Willowdale as a home for Mary Kovalchick, of Sagamore, Pennsylvania until her death or until she is not residing therein personally, whichever shall first occur and thereafter to hold such property as a home for Carrie Leftdahl, of Plumville, Pennsylvania, until her death or until she is no longer residing therein personally, whichever shall first occur, when the said property shall fall into and form part of the residue of my estate; while such property is held for either of the aforesaid, all taxes, insurance, repairs and any other charges necessary for the general upkeep of the property shall be paid from a fund sufficient in the opinion of my Trustee to cover the same, which I direct it shall set aside upon my death and the balance of such fund shall fall into and form part of the residue of my estate as soon as the said property is no longer being held for either of the aforesaid.

Subparagraph (g) of said para. III contains the provisions with respect to the residue by way of remainder upon the termination of whatever the interests are of Mary Kovalchick and Carrie Leftdahl, as contained in subpara. (f).

The reference to 69 Arjay Cres. is a typographical error in the will, the correct street address being 39.

I was informed by counsel that the value of Dr. McColgan's estate was approximately $231,000 of which $52,000 was accounted for by 39 Arjay Cres. There were also substantial insurance payments made out of this jurisdiction and which are not included in the above valuation.

On this application it was ordered that the Official Guardian represent the infant remainderman John Allen Leftdahl and all unborn and unascertained potential interests in the remainder with respect to the residue.

No one appeared for Carrie Leftdahl, a potential beneficiary in the above-quoted subpara. (f) although she had been duly served with notice of this application.

Mary Kovalchick was residing with Dr. McColgan at the time of his death and had been so residing for some time prior thereto, really nursing him in his last illness. She continued to occupy 39 Arjay Cres. until about November 30, 1967, when she returned to Sagamore, Pennsylvania. On the same date she wrote to the solicitors for the applicant advising them that, due to illness, it was necessary to be under the care of a Dr. Wright in Sagamore for an indefinite period. She further said "however, I am not surrendering my rights to make my home at 39 Arjay Crescent." She returned to the said house on May 18, 1968, and has remained there ever since.

Questions have arisen between the executors and Miss Kovalchick as to the responsibility for various items of expense in connection with upkeep, heating and protection of the property and other incidental matters and as a result this application is now brought to settle these questions and to provide a comprehensive guide to the executors and others interested, for the administration of the property.

The questions propounded to the Court are as follows:

1. What estate or interest, if any, in 39 Arjay Crescent (hereinafter called the premises) passed to the said Mary Kovalchick under the provisions of the Will?

2. Has the estate or interest, in the premises, if any, which passed to the said Mary Kovalchick then terminated by reason of the facts adduced in evidence in support of this application, specifically her absence from the premises referred to in the affidavit of David Ernest Morrow?

3. Should this Honourable Court hold that the said Mary Kovalchick still has an estate or interest in the aforesaid premises, what conduct of the said Mary Kovalchick respecting the said premises would cause her estate or interest, if any, in the said premises, to become forfeited or to terminate?

4. Specifically, should this Honourable Court hold that the said Mary Kovalchick has an estate or interest in the premises, is it an incident of this estate or interest, as the case may be, that it carries with it not only the right of the said Mary Kovalchick to reside in the premises personally but also the right to whatever rents or profits may arise from the said premises during the period of her estate or interest? Specifically does she have the right to lease the said premises for her benefit to another person?

5. During the currency of the estate or interest of the said Mary Kovalchick in the said premises, if any, on whom does the responsibility (as between the estate and the said Mary Kovalchick) rest respecting the surveillance and safety of the premises having regard to the possibility of fire, damage and theft?

6. Specifically, is the duty or responsibility of the said Mary Kovalchick respecting the surveillance and safety of the premises, should she be so held to be responsible, terminated or affected in any way by her absence from the premises?

7. Should the said Mary Kovalchick fail in her duty or responsibility to maintain a surveillance of the premises is the trustee entitled to perform the said duty and charge her for the cost thereof?

8. Is the estate obliged to furnish, at its expense, a permanent, or any, house-keeper for the said premises and is it obliged to maintain and pay for telephone service for the premises during the currency of her estate or interest?

The answer to Q. 1 will, of course, seriously affect the resolution of the remaining questions.

Question 1 itself raises four issues, as follows:

(a) is the interest of Miss Kovalchick and *a fortiori* the subsequent interest of Carrie Leftdahl upon the termination of the interest of Miss Kovalchick, a mere personal licence to use and occupy and enjoy the premises, 39 Arjay Cres.;

(b) if the interest is more than a mere personal licence, does the language of the will create a determinable life estate or a life estate subject to a condition subsequent;

(c) if what is intended to be created is a determinable life estate, is the language determining such life estate clear and unambiguous, or is it the converse rendering the gift void for uncertainty and,

(d) if what is created on the other hand is a life estate subject to a condition subsequent, is the condition void for uncertainty thus leaving the life estate free of any condition.

In *Perrin v. Morgan*, [1943] AC 399, Viscount Simon LC, said at p. 406:

My Lords, the fundamental rule in construing the language of a will is to put on the words used the meaning which, having regard to the terms of the will, the testator intended. The question is not, of course, what the testator meant to do when he made his will, but what the written words he uses mean in the particular case—what are the "expressed intentions" of the testator.

And at p. 408:

I now turn to some of the reported cases, premising only that it seems to me a little unfortunate that so many of such cases should find their way into the books, for in most instances, the duty of a judge who is called on to interpret a will containing ordinary English words is not to regard previous decisions as constituting a sort of legal dictionary to be consulted and remorselessly applied whatever the testator may have intended, but to construe the particular document so as to arrive at the testator's real meaning according to its actual language and circumstances … . In *Abbott v. Middleton* (1858), 7 HLC 68, 119, a decision of this House in which Lord Chelmsford LC, Lord Cranworth, Lord St. Leonards, and Lord Wensleydale all took occasion to expound the governing rule as to the interpretation of wills, Lord Wensleydale observed: "A great many cases were cited at the bar, as they always are, when the question is on the construction of wills. Generally speaking, these citations are of little use. We are no doubt bound by decided cases, but when the decision is not upon some rule or principle of law, but upon the meaning of words in instruments which differ so much from each other by the context, and the peculiar circumstance of each case, it seldom happens that the words of one instrument are a safe guide in the construction of another.

By way of illustration of the difficulties involved in construing the language of a testator in matters of this sort, one may well consider the case of *Moore et al. v. Royal Trust Co. et al.*, [1956] SCR 880, 5 DLR (2d) 152.

In that case one of the paragraphs of the will that was before the Court for construction was as follows [at 881 SCR; 156 DLR]:

6. I Direct my Trustees to permit my son George Moore Junior and his wife Frances as long as either of them shall occupy the same to have the use and enjoyment

of my property known [words describing it] free of any duty rent or taxes and I Direct
that my Trustees shall out of my Trust Fund pay the cost of maintaining any building
thereon and the insurance of the same against damage by fire.

In the Court of first instance [[1954] 3 DLR 407; 13 WWR (NS) 113] it was held
that these words intended to create a determinable life estate but since the language was
ambiguous and uncertain as to the event that would terminate the estate, the whole gift
failed for uncertainty.

In the Court of Appeal [[1955] 4 DLR 313; 16 WWR 204] (BC) it was unanimously
held that these words did indeed create a determinable life interest and not a life estate
subject to a condition subsequent but that there was no ambiguity or uncertainty in the
words and therefore the gift was valid.

In the Supreme Court of Canada, however, it was equally unanimously held that all the
Judges below were wrong and that what was created was not an estate or interest in the
lands but a mere personal licence for the use, enjoyment and occupation of the property.

A similar situation arose in the Courts of New Brunswick in the case of *Re McLean*,
[1940] 3 DLR 307, 14 MPR 475, where Baxter CJ held that the words of a gift in a will
requiring trustees to hold property to allow the testator's daughter "to occupy and enjoy
for her life, or for such shorter period as she wishes the above-named premises" gave
her a mere licence to occupy the property. On appeal ([1941] 1 DLR 722, 15 MPR 338
sub nom. Re McLean and Royal Trust Co.) the majority of the Court held that what was
conveyed to the daughter under the terms of the will was a life estate.

I have made reference to this case only to illustrate the difficulties mentioned by
Viscount Simon and pointing out how essential it is to recall that the language in each
will that requires consideration must be viewed in the context of the particular circumstances of the testator, beneficiaries and the estate itself.

Turning then to the first issue raised by Q. 1, it seems to me that the language of the
will goes far beyond what one would deem appropriate to the creation of a mere personal licence. The obligations placed on the trustees "to hold my property at (sic) 39
Arjay Crescent, Willowdale, as a home for Mary Kovalchick of Sagamore, Pennsylvania, until her death" and to set aside a fund sufficient to cover the charges referred to in
the will are much more consistent in the circumstances peculiar to this will and the
persons involved with the intention to create an interest in the property rather than a
mere licence. This property is to be held as a "home" not held subject to a mere
permission to occupy. The interest created is a life interest.

In view of my opinion on the first issue let us now consider whether or not the interest
created is a determinable life estate or a life estate subject to a condition subsequent.

In *Re Tilbury West Public School Board and Hastie*, [1966] 2 OR 20 at p. 21, 55
DLR (2d) 407 at p. 408, Grant J was dealing with a deed in which the granting clause
was as follows:

Doth Grant unto the said parties of the Third Part and their ... Successors as Trustees for
so long as it shall be used and needed for school purposes and no longer.

The *habendum* was consistent with the granting clause but contained in addition
language to identify the owner of the reversionary interest.

At p. 23 OR, p. 410 DLR, Grant J stated:

It must be determined first if the grant in question was a determinable fee simple subject to a right of reverter or a fee simple subject to a condition subsequent .... It is difficult to define the difference between a determinable fee and a fee simple defeasible by condition subsequent and often each cannot be readily put in its proper classification. The essential distinction appears to be that the determining event in a determinable fee itself sets the limit for the estate first granted. A condition subsequent, on the other hand, is an independent clause added to a complete fee simple absolute which operates so as to defeat it.

Grant J held that the words quoted created a determinable fee simple.

The author of Cheshire's *The Modern Law of Real Property*, 9th ed., puts the importance of the distinction for the purposes of this case as follows at p. 284:

A condition subsequent which is void under the rules stated below or which becomes impossible of fulfilment by operation of law, is disregarded, and the gift takes effect as if the condition had not been imposed. On the other hand, a determinable interest fails entirely if the terminating event is void under the rules in question, for to treat it as absolute would be to alter its quantum as fixed by the limitation.

At p. 281, the same learned author defines the distinction in these words:

In short, if the terminating event is an integral and necessary part of the formula from which the size of the interest is to be ascertained, the result is the creation of a determinable interest; but if the terminating event is external to the limitation, if it is a divided clause from the grant, the interest granted is an interest upon condition.

The authors of Megarry and Wade, *The Law of Real Property*, 3d ed., pp. 77-8, put it this way:

It will be seen that the difference is really one of words; the determining event may be worked into the limitation in such a way as to create either a determinable fee, or a fee simple defeasible by condition subsequent, whichever the grantor wishes. The question is whether the words limit the utmost time of continuance of the estate, or whether they mark an event which, if it takes place in the course of that time, will defeat an estate already granted; in the first case the words take effect as a limitation, in the second as a condition. A limitation marks the bounds or compass of the estate, a condition defeats the estate before it attains its boundary.

As already stated, I have come to the conclusion that the interest granted to Miss Kovalchick was a life interest since the words "until her death" are merely another way of expressing the intention that the estate created was to endure for the term of her natural life. The subsequent words in the will "or until she is not residing therein personally, whichever shall first occur" are to my mind "external to the limitation"—"a divided clause from the grant" thus creating an interest upon condition, to adapt the words quoted from Cheshire; and "they mark an event which, if it takes place ... will defeat an estate already granted," thus taking effect as a condition as the authors of Megarry and Wade put it.

It now remains to be considered whether or not the condition attached to the life estate is valid or void itself for uncertainty.

In the old case of *Fillingham v. Bromley* (1823), Turn. & R 530, 37 ER 1204, Lord Eldon LC had to deal with a condition that the beneficiary live and reside on the property. In effect, he held that these words were a condition subsequent void for uncertainty and in so doing, at p. 536 said:

> Then comes the question what is living and residing: occupation is not living and residing: there are many purposes, for which the word inhabitant has been taken to include persons, as inhabitants of places in which they never were. The question comes to this, what it was the testator meant, and whether, unless a clear meaning can be put upon the will, the Court is to take upon itself to say that there has been a forfeiture.

In *Clavering v. Ellison* (1859), 7 HLC 707, 11 ER 282, Lord Cranworth said at pp. 725-6:

> And I consider that, from the earliest times, one of the cardinal rules on the subject has been this: that where a vested estate is to be defeated by a condition on a contingency that is to happen afterwards, that condition must be such that the Court can see from the beginning, precisely and distinctly, upon the happening of what event it was that the preceding vested estate was to determine.
>
> In my opinion, if there was no direct authority for it, I should still have arrived at the same conclusion; but I have looked at the authorities, especially that of Lord Eldon in the case of *Fillingham v. Bromley* (Turner and Russ 530). I think that, looking at the language here used, it is far too indefinite and uncertain to enable the Court to say what it was that the testator meant should be the event on which the estate was to determine. It was to go over in case one or more of such children should be educated abroad. What does that mean? No two minds would agree upon the question when education begins. Suppose the child was born abroad, and he was brought over to England before he could speak, of course you could not say that he had been educated abroad, though it is said that more ideas are taken in during the first two years of life than in all the years afterwards of the very longest life. If that would not have been a breach of the condition, would it be a breach if the child came back at the age of seven, or if he came back at the age of ten? If he remained abroad all his minority, you would certainly say in that case that he was educated abroad. But the question is, not whether in the particular case he was educated abroad, but whether you can predicate on reading the will, what it was that was to defeat the vested estate? I concur in Lord Eldon's observations about an estate being defeated by a person not living and residing in a particular house, which he thought too remote; and I think that this is far more remote than that.

This language was expressly adopted in *Re Sifton*, [1938] OR 529 at p. 535, [1938] 3 DLR 577 at pp. 583-4, [1938] AC 656 *sub nom. Sifton v. Sifton*, and again in *Re Down*, [1968] 2 OR 16 at p. 22, 68 DLR (2d) 30 at p. 36 (CA).

The facts already quoted with reference to Miss Kovalchick going to Sagamore in November, 1967, and returning to Toronto in May, 1968, are sufficient in themselves to demonstrate how uncertain and ambiguous the condition "until she is not residing therein personally" is. There is no problem in deciding when the condition is being complied with; it is another matter certainly to attempt to determine when it has been breached. It cannot be envisioned, for instance, that the testator meant that this respondent should forfeit her rights if she took an extended holiday or was required to enter hospital for treatment although one could certainly say that in those circumstances she was not residing at the house personally. The condition, therefore, fails completely in meeting the test put by Lord Cranworth, i.e., that the "condition must be such that the Court can see from the beginning, precisely and distinctly, upon the happening of what event it was that the preceding vested estate was to determine."

In the result, therefore, Q. 1 must be answered as follows: a life estate in 39 Arjay Cres. passed to Mary Kovalchick free and clear of any condition, the purported condition subsequent being void for uncertainty.

It follows that Q. 2 must be answered in the negative; that the answer to Q. 3 is simply that her life estate is not subject to disfeasance by any conduct of hers and that Q. 4 must be answered "Yes."

The answers to Qq. 5 to 8 inclusive, depend on what the testator must be taken to have intended by his use of the words "to hold ... as a home for" coupled with the words of the last part of the gift made by para. III(f), namely,

> while such property is held for either of the aforesaid, all taxes, insurance, repairs and any other charges necessary for the general upkeep of the property shall be paid from a fund sufficient in the opinion of my Trustee to cover the same, which I direct it shall set aside upon my death and the balance of such fund shall fall into and form part of the residue of my estate as soon as the said property is no longer being held for either of the aforesaid;

As has already been noted, the relationship between the testator and Miss Kovalchick was obviously an intimate one. He was familiar with the state of her health and her finances. The house is a large expensive nine-room house in an exclusive residential district and the income from his estate was ample to permit him in his lifetime to pay all the charges incidental to the enjoyment of the home without supplementing such income by working at his profession. In fact he had done so from retirement in 1958 until his death in 1967.

In the context of this will it is my opinion that he intended the enjoyment of the property as a home to be in no way dependent on the beneficiaries' own monetary resources.

If a housekeeper was required, or a gardener, or snow removal services, or the services of cleaning women, the fund to be set up was intended to defray the cost.

If circumstances arose as a result of which Miss Kovalchick considered it necessary or desirable that she lease the premises, or any part of them, then she must be entitled to the rents and profits free and clear of any charge against them. Obviously the estate would not be charged with the cost of a housekeeper for example for a tenant but the expenses of the upkeep of the property so that it would at all times be in a suitable condition for her to occupy as a home, must be met by the estate.

For these reasons I would answer Q. 5 as follows: The responsibility is that of the executors and trustees.

Questions 6 and 7 do not require further answers.

Question 8 should be answered "Yes."

I reserve the disposition of costs of this application until counsel have had the opportunity of addressing me on the subject for which purpose I shall be pleased to arrange an early appointment.

Order accordingly.

Discussion Notes

1. In the above case, the court found that the devise in question created a life estate subject to a condition subsequent, rather than a determinable life estate, notwithstanding the use of the term "until" in the devise. Given that the court found that the condition was uncertain and hence void, what would have been the outcome if the court had found that it was a determinable life estate?

2. The court also considered, and rejected, the argument that the devise gave only a personal licence. What would have been the outcome of the case had the court found a personal licence only?

Life Estates "Pur Autre Vie"

As with any estate in land, the life estate can be alienated to third parties. For example, in the following grant, A may alienate her life estate to B:

X to A for life and then to C.
A to B.

The life tenant (A) can only alienate the interest she has and no more. Consequently, the purchaser of the life estate (B) acquires a life estate that will last only so long as A lives, thereby creating a life estate that will last for the life not of the recipient (B), but of another person (A). When a life estate is created to last for the life of the recipient, it is known as an estate *pur sa vie* (for his or her life). By contrast, a life estate created to last for the life of another person is known as an estate *pur autre vie* (for another life). The person designated as the measuring life (A) is known as the *cestui que vie* (he who lives) and need not have any particular connection with the holder of the life estate (B). The remainderperson (C) will take possession of the land upon A's death. If B predeceases A, B's interest may pass to his heir, creating a rather unusual exception to the general rule that a life estate is not an estate of inheritance (see s. 2(a) of the Succession Law Reform Act, RSO 1990 c. S.26). Finally, the remainderperson (C) retains a keen interest in knowing the time of A's death, as at this point B's estate will come to an end. Occasionally, A might disappear after conveying her interest to B, making it difficult for the remainderperson to determine when B's estate ends. The law, ever vigilant, provides for this very possibility. In such cases, A is deemed to be dead if A has been absent for seven years and it cannot be ascertained if A is dead or alive (see the Conveyancing and Law of Property Act, RSO 1990, c. C.34, ss. 46-52).

Life Estates and Successive Interests in Land

The life estate gives rise to successive interests in the land. The life tenant will hold the land for life. After the death of the life tenant, the land will either revert to the grantor or pass to the remainderperson. Much in the way a lessor and tenant have shared interests in the land, and a shared interest in the maintenance and management of the leased premises, the life tenant and the remainderperson also have a shared interest in the land. Disputes can arise between the two parties regarding the management and maintenance of the land, and the law attempts to govern such disputes and allocate rights and responsibilities between them.

The life tenant of a life estate *pur sa vie* will enjoy the estate as long as she lives. She may exclude the remainderperson or reversioner, as the case may be, from physical access to the property. The remainderperson or reversioner will take possession of the estate only on her death. When land was the primary source of economic wealth, this type of arrangement, known as a "settled estate" or a "settlement," was a common means for the landed classes to provide security for family members in succession. The use of this arrangement is less common today. In many cases it has been replaced by trust law, where the property in question (personal or real property) is held in trust, and the trustee freely manages the property and provides an income to various beneficiaries in succession. Trust law successfully avoids most of the complexities associated with such arrangements. Nonetheless, the law still permits the creation of such successive interests in land.

Conflicts can arise between the life tenant and the remainderperson (or reversioner) regarding the maintenance, use, and development of the land in which they share an interest. The life tenant's interest is to enjoy to the maximum the property during his or her life estate, whereas the remainderperson's or reversioner's interest is to preserve the property for the future. For example, the life tenant may wish to add an addition to the house, which the remainderperson regards as undesirable and liable to reduce the long-term value of the property. On the other hand, the life tenant may wish to mortgage the property so that the house can be repaired, and the remainderperson objects to assuming this long-term debt. The law attempts to allocate the rights and responsibilities between these parties. The law's chief concern is to prevent the property from falling into disuse and disrepair. Accordingly, the more recent statutory amendments to the common law tend to grant to the life tenant fairly broad powers of management of the land (similar in some respects to that enjoyed by a trustee under a trust settlement).

The doctrine of waste governs what the life tenant can do to alter physically the real property. The tenant will be liable to the remainderperson or reversioner only for certain types of waste. The categories of waste can be divided as follows:

- *ameliorating waste*—acts that enhance the value of the land;
- *permissive waste*—damage resulting from the failure to preserve or repair the property;
- *voluntary waste*—conduct that diminishes the value of the freehold; and
- *equitable waste*—severe and malicious destruction.

On the whole, courts are reluctant to impose liability for ameliorating waste, as in most cases such waste simply increases the value of the remainderperson's or reversioner's interest: see *Doherty v. Allaman* (1878), 3 App. Cas. 709, 26 WR 513 (HL). Responsibility for permissive waste is also not automatic. Unless the instrument under which the estate was created expressly imposes liability on the life tenant for permissive waste, the life tenant is not required to maintain the property in good repair: *Patterson v. Central Canada Loan & Savings Co.* (1898), 29 OR 134 (Div. Ct.).

Liability for voluntary waste imposes the greatest obligations on the life tenant, and the tenant may be liable for the overcultivation of timber estates, the destruction of buildings, the opening of new mines, and other conduct that may diminish the long-term value of the property. However, in the instrument creating the settled estate, the donor may render the life tenant "unimpeachable" (free from liability) for waste, in which case the life tenant is not liable for any type of waste, with the exception of equitable waste. The life tenant remains liable for equitable waste in all cases, even if the donor has provided that the life tenant is unimpeachable for waste.

As regards other disputes that might arise between the life tenant and the remainderperson (or reversioner), the life tenant is responsible for all current expenses, including property taxes and any *interest* due on a mortgage debt. The remainderperson is responsible for any payment on the *principle* of the mortgage: *Macklem v. Cumings* (1859), 7 Gr. 318 (Ch.D). The life tenant is not required to insure the premises, nor can the life tenant maintain a claim against the remainderperson or reversioner for any improvements or repairs undertaken unilaterally.

On the whole, the common law governing disputes between life tenants and remainderpersons (or reversioners) was unsatisfactory. The life tenant's ability to exploit and develop the land was restricted by the law of waste, and the life tenant was unable to convey fee simple or mortgage the property without the consent of the remainderperson or reversioner. The life tenant was also unable to require the remainderperson or reversioner to contribute to the costs of repairing the property. As a result, land subject to such arrangements increasingly fell into disrepair. In England, where such arrangements—known as "settled estates"—were common, legislative reform gradually increased the management powers of the life tenant, including wide powers to lease, mortgage, and sell the property (Settled Land Act, 1882, 45 & 46 Vict. c. 38). Moneys received for the sale of the land would be held in trust for the benefit of the life tenant and the remainderperson or reversioner. Several Canadian provinces followed suit and enacted legislation giving similar powers to the life tenant (Settled Estates Act, RSO 1990, c. S.7; Land (Settled Estate) Act, RSBC 1979, c. 215; and Trustees Act, RSNB 1973, c. T-15).

Exercise 3: Life Estates And Estates "Pur Autre Vie"

Consider each of the following grants or devises. Does the instrument create a life estate subject to a condition subsequent, a life estate subject to a condition precedent, a determinable life estate, or a life estate *per autre vie*? What interest, if any, is retained by the grantor or testator, X? What happens to the estate after A's death? Consider whether the condition may be void for any reason. If so, what is the outcome?

Grant or devise	Analysis
1. X grants to A for life so long as the property is used as a farm.	
2. X grants to A for life on the condition that the property is used as a farm.	
3. X devises to A, the use of 48 Walker Ave., for as long as she lives, or until she remarries, or gives a written notice abandoning the property. See *Re Waters* (1978), 89 DLR (3d) (Ont. HC).	
4. X devises to my son and his wife as long as they occupy the property. See *Moore v. Royal Trust*, [1956] SCR 880; 5 DLR (2d) 152, as considered in *Re McColgan* (1969), 4 DLR (3d) 572 (Ont. HC).	
5. X devises to A to occupy for life, or a shorter period in her discretion. See *Re McLean*, [1940] 3 DLR 307, as considered in *Re McColgan* (1969), 4 DLR (3d) 572 (Ont. HC).	
6. X devises to A until her death or until she no longer lives there personally, whichever happens first. See *Re McColgan*, *supra*, devise 5.	
7. X grants to A for life.	

Grant or devise	Analysis
8. X grants to A for the life of B.	
9. X grants to A while B is alive.	
10. Consider the following sequence of grants and events. What is the effect of each grant or event? X grants to A for life (by way of a grant dated January 1, 1994). A grants to B (by way of a grant dated January 1, 1995). January 1, 1996: B dies. January 1, 1997: A dies.	

The Rule in Shelley's Case

The rule in *Shelley's Case* is an anachronism, but unfortunately one that continues to lie in wait, ready to catch the unwary legal drafter. Like much of common law property, the rationale for the rule is incomprehensible without an understanding of the historical feudal roots of the common law. A number of various theories have emerged to explain its origin. According to the most common of these theories, the rule arose as a way to prevent the evasion of certain incidents of tenure, including relief. As already discussed, the enforcement of the incidents of tenure was at one time a central project of common law property. It was always essential that someone be seised of the land, and this person was required to comply with all the tenurial duties and incidents associated with being seised of the estate in question. One of the more lucrative incidents of tenure was *relief*, which operated much like an inheritance tax, whereby the lord could require a payment of up to one year's income on the land from the heir of the deceased tenant. To inherit the land, the heir was required to pay relief.

Naturally, heirs to estates disliked paying relief to the lord, and some clever feudal lawyers devised a scheme to evade this form of inheritance tax. The law had developed such that relief could be required only when the heir took the land by *inheritance*. If the heir instead took the land by an *inter vivos* transaction (typically a gift), and not inheritance, the lord was not able to require the payment of relief. Seizing on this particular rule, landowners invented the following grant:

X to A for life, remainder to the heirs of A in fee simple.

On the face of this grant, it would appear that A is acquiring a life estate only. According to the practice of primogeniture in effect at this time, A's heir would be his eldest living son (B) at the time of A's death. B would take his interest in fee simple at the time of A's death. The crucial feature of this grant is that B's interest arises from the original grant, and B takes this interest as an *inter vivos* transaction, or gift, from X at the time of the original grant. B will not take his interest as an *inheritance* from A, as would be the case if A held a fee simple absolute rather than merely a life estate. Accordingly, when B took possession of the land upon A's death, the lord could not require B to pay relief, because B's interest was derived from an *inter vivos* transaction rather than inheritance.

Naturally, the lords were annoyed about this evasion of feudal incidents, and the law gradually developed so that this practice was no longer a successful way to evade relief. The rule can be traced to *Shelley's Case, Wolfe v. Shelley* (1581), 1 Co. Rep. 93b; 76 ER 206 (although the rule long predated this case), and can be stated as follows:

> If a freehold estate is granted or devised to a person and, by the same instrument, an estate is limited by way of remainder to his heirs or the heirs of his body, whether the reminder immediately follows his estate or follows an intermediate remainder, the word "heirs" is construed as a word of limitation and not purchase.

(Oosterhoff and Rayner, at 405.)

This rule provides that, in such a grant, the term "heirs" can only be construed as a word of limitation. As a result, the term "heirs" simply indicates the size of the estate given to the grantee, in this case a fee simple. Because the term "heirs" in such a grant is not construed as words of purchase, the heirs themselves (B in the above example) take no interest in the grant. Accordingly, although the above example appears on its face to give only a life estate to A, in fact it gives to A a fee simple absolute. A's heir, when he takes the land on A's death, will acquire the interest only by inheritance and only upon paying relief to the lord.

The rule in *Shelley's Case* was triggered only if the grantor used the words "heirs" as referring to the whole line of inheritable issue over the generations and not just those heirs alive at the time of A's death. In other words, if the evidence established that the grantor had a *specific* heir in mind who was to take the land on A's death, such as A's eldest child, this child would acquire the fee simple in remainder at the time of the grant, and A would acquire a life estate only. In this case, the rule did not apply to convert A's interest into a fee simple.

The rule in *Shelley's Case* is a "rule of law" and not a "rule of construction." In other words, the rule applies regardless of the manifest intent of the grantor. It is not a rule to aid merely in the construction or interpretation of a grant, such as a presumption that the grant will be interpreted in a certain way in the absence of any evidence to the contrary. Instead, it is a rule of law that applies even if it is obvious that the grantor intended a different result. As in the above example, the grantor expressly intended to grant only a life estate to A and thereby evade relief. However, the rule in *Shelley's Case*, as a rule of law, requires that the grant be interpreted as giving to A a fee simple absolute regardless of the grantor's intention. As a mere rule of construction, the rule in *Shelley's Case* would not have been successful in preventing the evasion of feudal incidents.

The rule also applied even if there was an intermediate remainder in the grant:

X to A for life, then to B for life, remainder to A's heirs.

In this case, the rule in *Shelley's Case* provides that A has two estates. He acquires not only a life estate for his life, but also an ultimate estate of inheritance in remainder following B's intermediate life estate. Again, A's heirs acquire nothing under the grant itself because the term "heirs" is interpreted as a word of limitation only. A can alienate both his life estate and his estate of inheritance in remainder. Where there is no intermediate estate—for example, "to A for life, remainder to A's heirs"—A will acquire an immediate fee simple absolute, by the combined operation of the rule in *Shelley's Case* and the "doctrine of merger." This doctrine provides that if the owner of a life estate acquires a remainder in fee simple, the lesser estate (the life estate) is said to merge into the greater (the remainder in fee simple), giving that person an immediate fee simple.

Later in this chapter, the distinction between legal and equitable interests in land will be explored in detail. At this point, it is important to note that the rule in *Shelley's Case* did not apply if the life estate and the remainder interest were not of the same kind. The rule applied only if these were both legal or both equitable interests: *Re Romanes and Smith* (1880), 8 PR (Ont); *Re Fanning*, [1934] OWN 397 (CA).

The rule in *Shelley's Case* has been much criticized as a historical anachronism. Remarkably, the rule has also been litigated in recent times, as indicated in *Re Rynard* (1980), 118 DLR (3d) 530 (Ont. CA), reproduced below. As noted by B. Ziff and M. Litman in "Shelley's Rule in a Modern Context: Clearing the 'Heir' " (1984), 34 *University of Toronto Law Journal* 170, the results of a survey conducted of lawyers specializing in estates revealed that even many specialists do not routinely recognize the impact of this rule. As the authors point out, the rule is subject to ridicule and derision, and "quickly forgotten after the writing of final examinations." They recommend either legislative reform or judicial activism to repeal this rule. Such an opportunity arose in the following case, but the Ontario Court of Appeal passed up this chance to repeal the rule. Instead, the court determined that the rule was still in effect in Ontario, but found other grounds to conclude that it did not apply in the given case. Consider how the court avoided the application of the rule in this case. What options were available to the court to find that the rule had been repealed in Ontario? Why was the court reluctant to find that the rule had been repealed?

Re Rynard
(1980), 31 OR (2d) 257; 118 DLR (3d) 530 (CA)

WILSON JA: This appeal reminds us that the roots of some of our law are deeply embedded indeed. It concerns the application of the rule in *Shelley's Case* (1581), 1 Co. Rep. 93b; 76 ER 206 to a will made in 1933. The matter came before us by way of appeal from an order of Mr. Justice Walsh answering certain questions on a motion for construction of the will of the late Margaret Rynard of the Village of Cannington, in Ontario.

The testatrix, Margaret Rynard, died on January 8, 1934, and was survived by her husband Philip Rynard and her two sons Bernard and Kennedy. These three are the sole beneficiaries of her estate, which was apparently modest, the main asset being a farm in Scott Township which she inherited from her father in circumstances which will be referred to later. It is submitted by the respondents that these circumstances have a bearing on the issues in this appeal.

The testatrix's husband, who was the residuary legatee under her will, died on April 23, 1960. Her two sons are the present executors of her will which is very short. After revoking all former wills and appointing her executors, she gives all her property to her executors upon the following trusts:

1. To carry on and conduct my Estate for three years after my death in the same manner as prior to my death.

2. To pay my just debts, funeral and testamentary expenses as soon after my death as possible.

3. From and after three years after my death my beloved son Kennedy Rynard shall have the use of my farm being the east half of lot no. twenty-seven in the sixth concession of the Township of Scott in the County of Ontario, until the death of his father, Philip H. Rynard, and shall pay to his father annually for such use the sum of One Hundred and sixty dollars of lawful money of Canada, and out of such annuity my beloved husband shall pay to my sister, Mrs. Jessie McKnight, the annuity of fifty dollars if she is entitled to it.

4. And after my beloved husband's death my son Kennedy shall continue to have the use of said lands until his death, subject to the annuity, if any, payable to Mrs. Jessie McKnight, and after my son Kennedy's death, my son Dr. Bernard Rynard shall be paid the sum of fifteen hundred dollars out of the said lands and the balance shall go to the heirs of my son Kennedy.

5. The provisions in this clause shall prevail notwithstanding anything to the contrary contained in this Will.

My son Kennedy Rynard shall not have the right to sell or Mortgage his interest in the said lands or dispose of it in anyway and my Executors shall have full discretion to grant or withhold his life estate in the said lands, and should any creditor attempt to seize, attach or sell his life estate, then his said life estate shall cease and be determined and shall be null and void and his said life estate shall become possessed by my son Dr. Bernard Rynard and his heirs, executors, administrators and assigns absolutely forever.

My desire and intention is that my son Kennedy shall have a means of livlihood [sic] but his said life estate shall not be anticipated, seized, attached or be taken under execution by any creditor of the said Kennedy Rynard.

6. All the Residue of my Estate shall be conveyed, assigned and assured to my beloved husband, Philip H. Rynard, absolutely forever.

It is immediately apparent that the major part of the will is given over to the specific devise of the farm contained in cls. 3, 4 and 5. It is on the language of these clauses that the appellant's counsel, Mr. Sheard, submits that the rule in *Shelley's Case* applies to vest the farm absolutely in his client, Kennedy Rynard.

The rule provides that where the ancestor by any gift or conveyance takes an estate of freehold, and in the same gift or conveyance an estate is limited, either mediately or immediately, to his heirs in fee or in tail, in such cases the words "to his heirs" are words of limitation of the estate and not words of purchase. While this language was perfectly intelligible to conveyancers in the days of Edward II when the rule first made its appearance in the Year Books, it requires some explanation today.

The rule had its origins in an even more ancient rule of law that whenever an ancestor received an estate for life, his heir could not under the same conveyance receive an estate "by purchase" but only "by descent." The reason for this was that in feudal times the lord of the manor received the fruits of his seigniory only when there was a descent of land upon the heir. If this descent were avoided by a purported direct gift to the heir on the death of the life tenant, the lord was viewed as having, in effect, been defrauded. Accordingly, the rule in *Shelley's Case* denied the effect of a remainder gift to the heirs of A and treated the gift of a life estate to A with remainder to his heirs on his death as a gift to A absolutely, his heirs taking only by descent on his death. Thus were the incidents of feudal tenure preserved to the lord of the manor and the invidious intent of the conveyancer frustrated.

Mr. Sheard submits that the rule applies to cl. 4 of the testatrix's will. He says that, in effect, the farm is devised to Kennedy Rynard for life (subject to the payment of certain annuities) with the remainder "to the heirs of my son" on his death. This, says Mr. Sheard, is the classic language for the application of the rule. Mr. Gardner, for the respondents, the next of kin of Kennedy Rynard, says that it is very clear from cls. 3, 4 and 5 of the will that Kennedy Rynard's interest in the farm was very carefully circum-scribed by the testatrix. He was to have "the use" of the farm until the death of his father. After that he was to "continue to have the use" of the farm until his own death. He was not to be able to sell or mortgage "his interest in the said lands" and, indeed, his interest was to be the subject of a protective trust for his benefit. How then, Mr. Gardner asks, can the rule apply in the face of such a clear expression of testamentary intention so as to give the farm absolutely to Kennedy? The testatrix, he submits, must have intended his heirs (next of kin) to take the remainder interest beneficially. The words "to the heirs of my son Kennedy" must be words of purchase and not words of limitation. Mr. Beatty, representing infant, unborn and unascertained members of the class of Kennedy Rynard's next of kin, takes the same position.

Much of the argument on this appeal dealt with the relevance of the testatrix's intention in determining whether or not the Rule applies. Mr. Sheard says it has no relevance. The rule is a rule of law, he submits, and not a rule of construction. It may, and frequently does, fly in the face of the testator's intention. Mr. Gardner and Mr. Beatty agree that it is a rule of law but they submit that there is a threshold question of construction which must be dealt with first, namely, when the testatrix used the word "heirs," did she mean the whole inheritable issue of her son down through the line of succession or did she merely mean her son's next of kin, those who would take under the *Devolution of Estates Act*, RSO 1970, c. 129, in force at the time of his death as if he had died intestate?

All counsel relied in their factums on Lord Davey's analysis of the rule in *Van Grutten v. Foxwell et al.*, [1897] AC 658. I quote what I consider to be the relevant part of his analysis at pp. 684-5:

> In my opinion the rule in *Shelley's Case* is a rule of law and not a mere rule of construction—i.e., one laid down for the purpose of giving effect to the testator's

expressed or presumed intention. The rule is this: that wherever an estate for life is given to the ancestor or propositus, and a subsequent gift is made to take effect after his death, in such terms as to embrace, according to the ordinary principles of construction, the whole series of his heirs, or heirs of his body, or heirs male of his body, or whole inheritable issue taking in a course of succession, the law requires that the heirs, or heirs male of the body, or issue shall take by descent, and will not permit them to take by purchase, notwithstanding any expression of intention to the contrary. Wherever, therefore, the Court comes to the conclusion that the gift over includes the whole line of heirs, general or special, the rule at once applies, and an estate of inheritance is executed in the ancestor or tenant for life, even though the testator has expressly declared that the ancestor shall take for life and no longer, or has endeavoured to graft upon the words of gift to the heirs, or heirs of the body, additions, conditions, or limitations which are repugnant to an estate of inheritance, and such as the law cannot give effect to. The rule, I repeat, is not one of construction, and, indeed, usually overrides and defeats the expressed intention of the testator; *but the question always remains, whether the language of the gift after the life estate properly construed is such as to embrace the whole line of heirs or heirs of the body or issue, and that question must be determined apart from the rule, according to the ordinary principles of construction, including those which I have already referred to.*

The testator may conceivably shew by the context that he has used the words "heirs," or "heirs of the body," or "issue" in some limited or restricted sense of his own which is not the legal meaning of the words—e.g., he may have used the words in the sense of children, or as designating some individual person who would be heir of the body at the time of the death of the tenant for life, or at some other particular time. *If the Court is judicially satisfied that the words are so used, I conceive that the premises for the application of the rule in* Shelley's Case *are wanting, and the rule is foreign to the case. But I repeat, that in every case the words are to be interpreted in their legal sense as words of limitation, unless it be made plain to the mind of the Court that they are not so used, and in what sense they are used by the testator.*

(Emphasis added.)

It seems to me that what Lord Davey is saying is that, while the rule is a rule of law, and *when applicable*, may well defeat the testator's intention, nevertheless it first has to be determined whether it *is* applicable and this involves a preliminary question of construction. The rule can only be applied if the words "to his heirs" are words of limitation and not words of purchase. This in turn hinges upon whether the testator in using these words was thinking of the whole line of inheritable issue of the tenant for life. If he was, then the tenant for life will take absolutely. But if the testator when he used the word "heirs" meant simply the children or issue or next of kin of the tenant for life then the tenant for life is confined to his life estate and his children or his issue or his next of kin take beneficially a remainder interest in the property. They are, in other words, "purchasers."

So, following the course charted by Lord Davey, the Court is required to determine through the application of ordinary principles of construction what the testatrix had in mind when she devised the farm to her son Kennedy for life (subject to the payment of the annuities) with remainder "to the heirs of my son" on his death.

Mr. Justice Walsh concluded that, if the devise to the heirs of Kennedy Rynard was a devise of real estate, he could not construe the word "heirs" in cl. 4 of the testatrix's will as meaning the whole line of Kennedy's inheritable issue because the *Wills Act*, RSO 1927, c. 149, in force at the time she made her will contained a directive as to how the word "heirs" was to be construed in such a devise. Section 31 provided:

> 31. Where any real estate is devised by any testator, dying on or after the 5th day of March, 1880, to the heir or heirs of such testator, or of any other person, and no contrary or other intention is signified by the will, the words "heir" or "heirs" shall be construed to mean the person or persons to whom the real estate of the testator, or of such other person as the case may be, would descend under the law of Ontario in case of an intestacy.

The learned Judge concluded therefore that the rule in *Shelley's Case* could not be applied to the testatrix's will. The statute, in effect, compelled a construction of "heirs" which made the words "to the heirs of my son" words of purchase and not words of limitation.

With respect, I think Mr. Justice Walsh was in error in giving to s. 31 of the *Wills Act* the effect of an implied repeal of the rule in *Shelley's Case*. I do not think the Legislature intended to repeal the rule by this section. I think it intended merely to negate the principle of primogeniture.

At common law "heir" had a very technical meaning. It referred to the eldest son who, upon an intestacy, alone could inherit his ancestor's real property. When used in the plural, as in the phrase "to A and his heirs," the heirs encompassed the eldest son of each successive generation of lineal descendants of A. Accordingly, a devise of real property "to A and his heirs" was absolute. The principle of primogeniture was, however, abolished in Upper Canada in 1852 by the Act of 14-15 Victoria, c. 6; (CSUC, c. 82) commonly known as the *Act Abolishing Primogeniture*. Initially there was some confusion as to whether that Act applied only to determine who the heirs were upon an intestacy or whether it applied also to determine who the heirs were in the case of a testamentary devise to "heirs": see *Tylee v. Deal* (1873), 19 Gr. 601. This issue was resolved by the passage of the Act of 1880 (43 Vict., c. 14), which made it clear that the principle of primogeniture was abolished with respect to testamentary devises also. "Heirs" as used by the testator in his will no longer had reference to the eldest son but to his brothers and sisters as well: see *Baldwin v. Kingstone* (1890), 18 OAR 63.

However, in none of the case-law dealing with the effect of these legislative provisions is it suggested that the Act of 1880 was intended to have a more far-reaching effect, namely, to require the words "to his heirs" when used in a testamentary devise of real estate to be construed always as words of purchase. There is no suggestion that one of the purposes of the Act of 1880 was to repeal, either expressly or impliedly, the rule in *Shelley's Case* by precluding the use of the words "to his heirs" as words of limitation. Rather, it seems to have been assumed that all the section was intended to accomplish was that the word "heirs" when used as a word of purchase would not be confined to the common law heir or eldest son. The weight of the early authority following the enactment of the 1880 legislation seems to indicate that the rule in *Shelley's Case* was still very much a part of our law: see *Sparks v. Wolff* (1898), 25 OAR 326; affirmed 29 SCR 585. Quoting from the judgment of Maclennan JA in the Ontario Court of Appeal at pp. 335-6:

[T]he word "heirs" may still be used technically, to limit or define an estate in fee simple or in fee tail as formerly, either in a deed or in a will. But here the word is not used as a word of limitation at all. It is a word of purchase. It is intended, not to limit or define the extent of the estate which is being devised, but to designate the person or class of persons to whom the estate is given.

Maclennan JA first resolved the preliminary question of construction as to whether the word "heirs" was used as a word of limitation or a word of purchase and then, having concluded that it was a word of purchase, he proceeded to apply the statutory definition.

I am confirmed in the view that s. 31 of the *Wills Act* was not intended to effect a repeal of the rule in *Shelley's Case* by two considerations, firstly, the fact that the Legislature in England, despite the existence of a comparable section, found it necessary to abolish the rule expressly by the *Law of Property Act*, 1925 (UK), c. 20; and secondly, the fact that our Courts continued to treat it as part of our law long after the enactment of the statutory definition of "heirs": see *Re Casner* (1884), 6 OR 282 (Ch.D); *Re Cleator* (1885), 10 OR 326 (CA); *Re Thomas* (1901), 2 OLR 660. Indeed, in *Re Gracey* (1931), 4 OWN 1, Masten JA was reluctantly forced to the conclusion that the rule in *Shelley's Case* applied even although it probably defeated the testator's intention. He drew attention to the fact that the Legislature in England had abolished the rule in 1925 and expressed the hope that some day it would meet a similar fate in Ontario. This has not yet happened.

Given then that the rule in *Shelley's Case* is still part of the law of Ontario and that s. 31 of the *Wills Act* applies only when it has first been determined that the words "to the heirs of my son" are words of purchase and not words of limitation, the preliminary problem of construction must be resolved. And it must be approached, as Lord Davey pointed out, on the basis that "the words are to be interpreted in their legal sense as words of limitation, unless it be made plain to the mind of the Court that they are not so used, and in what sense they are used by the testator." Has it been made plain to the Court that the testatrix did not mean the whole line of inheritable issue of her son Kennedy? And if so, has the testatrix made plain to the Court in what sense she did use the word "heirs"?

I think the testatrix has made it plain that she was not referring in cl. 4 to the whole line of inheritable issue of Kennedy, but rather to his next of kin living at his death. This is the only conclusion that can be drawn from a consideration of cl. 5 of her will and, in particular, the opening words of that clause. In my view, these opening words distinguish this case from those in which subsequent clauses inconsistent with an earlier devise have been disregarded as repugnant. In this will the testatrix states in cl. 5: "The provisions in this clause shall prevail notwithstanding anything to the contrary contained in this Will." She then goes on to make it clear that not only does she not intend her son Kennedy to take the farm outright under cl. 4 but even his life estate is to be determinable in certain circumstances.

Mr. Sheard submits that, despite the opening words of cl. 5, we should disregard the clause on the repugnancy principle. I do not think we can. The doctrine of repugnancy is premised on the fact that certain interests in property must, of their very nature, confer upon anyone to whom they belong the right to do certain things. Accordingly, if a testator gives a person such an interest in property and, at the same time, by imposing a condition on the gift attempts to deprive him of a right which the law considers to be an essential characteristic of that interest, the condition is void as repugnant to the interest given. The principle, however, has no application to determinable interests. It does not prevent a testator from giving an interest the duration of which will be determined by certain events. I think this is what the testatrix has done here by giving cl. 5 paramountcy over cl. 4. This case is, in my view, clearly distinguishable from *Re Armstrong*, [1943] OWN 43, in which Kelly J found that the subsequent clause was merely an expression of desire on the part of the testator and not intended by him to limit the inheritance expressed in the earlier clause.

The relevance of the determinable nature of Kennedy Rynard's life estate to the applicability of the rule in *Shelley's Case* is by no means clear-cut but it seems to me that an estate of inheritance cannot be executed in Kennedy under the rule when it will not be known until the death of Kennedy whether or not his life estate will be determined under cl. 5. I say that because of the underlying premise of the rule that, as soon as the ancestor is seized of his life estate, the inheritance limited to his heirs has the effect of turning his life estate into a fee simple absolute with all the incidents that adhere in law to such an interest. This interpretation of cl. 4 is totally inconsistent with cl. 5 to which the testatrix has in clear and unequivocal language given paramountcy. I appreciate that the rule, when applicable, may defeat the intention of the testatrix but, as Lord Davey pointed out, the first question to be determined is whether it applies at all and this must be ascertained by applying the ordinary principles of construction.

I do not believe that the testatrix, when she used the word "heirs" in cl. 4, could have intended to refer to the whole line of inheritable issue of Kennedy when in the next clause she went on to specify the circumstances in which he would be deprived of his life estate and it would pass to his brother. There is no doubt about the fact that she intended her son Kennedy's life estate to be determinable. She makes this perfectly clear in the concluding sentence of cl. 5. And, in my view, by giving cl. 5 paramountcy over cl. 4, she succeeded in doing so. The Court cannot, as Mr. Sheard suggests, discard cl. 5. We must look to it to discern the nature and extent of Kennedy's interest.

In *Re Woods*, [1946] OR 290, [1946] 3 DLR 394, the testator gave each of his daughters a share of his estate for life but with a restraint on alienation during coverture. The daughters were also given general powers of appointment over their shares and, in default of exercise of their powers, each daughter's share was to go to "her right heirs." Chief Justice McRuer held that the restraint on alienation during coverture made the rule in *Shelley's Case* inapplicable because the daughters did not have "complete life interests." He said at p. 294 OR, pp. 398-9 DLR:

> The premises for the application of the rule in *Shelley's Case* would require that there exist in the daughters a complete equitable life interest and in those who would in the due course of law take by descent in default of appointment a complete equitable interest in remainder.
>
> In such a case there would be a coalescence or merger of interest, so as to vest in each daughter an absolute equitable vested interest. However, I have been unable to find, in the legion of decided cases dealing with the rule in *Shelley's Case* in the English

courts, authority for the proposition that where on a careful reading of the whole will there appears to be in the ancestor something less than a complete life interest, coalescence or merger can take place so as to vest in the ancestor an absolute interest.

And, again, at p. 295 OR, p. 399 DLR he says:

> In this case, the testator did not, by his will, vest in the daughters a complete life interest in the shares in question. The shares were given to the trustees and the income only was payable to the daughters, without power of alienation during coverture. They were restricted by the very terms of the gift from full enjoyment of an absolute life interest during coverture. Had the subject of the gift been real property, beyond question the daughters could not have disposed of their life estate during coverture. That being true, I cannot see how the rule in *Shelley's Case* can be applied to defeat the express terms of the trust imposed upon the trustees.

It seems to me that Kennedy Rynard has something less than a complete life interest in this case. He has, in fact, a determinable life interest and it cannot on the basis of cls. 4 and 5 be said that Kennedy and his "heirs" together have the entirety. Accordingly, apart altogether from the question whether or not the testator intended when she used the word "heirs" to refer to the whole inheritable issue of Kennedy, the rule would be inapplicable on this ground. The two grounds are, however, in my view interrelated because cls. 4 and 5 have to be read together in order to determine the precise nature of the interest conferred on Kennedy and his heirs. In effect, the testatrix has made cl. 4 subject to cl. 5.

In *Fetherston v. Fetherston* (1834), 3 Cl. & Fin. 67, 6 ER 1363, referred to in *Van Grutten v. Foxwell et al.*, *supra*, Lord Brougham discussed when words which appear *prima facie* to be words of limitation will, in the larger context of the will, be construed as words of purchase. He said at p. 1366:

> I take the principle of construction as consonant to reason, and established by authority, to be this, that where by plain words, in themselves liable to no doubt, an estate tail is given, you are not to allow such estate to be altered and cut down to a life estate unless there are other words which plainly show the testator to have used the former as words of purchase, contrary to their natural and ordinary sense, *or unless in the rest of the provisions there be some plain indication of a general intent inconsistent with an estate tail being given by the words in question*, and which general intent can only be fulfilled by sacrificing the particular provisions, and regarding the expressions as words of purchase ... . *So again, if a limitation is made afterwards, and is clearly the main object of the will—which never can take effect unless an estate for life be given instead of an estate tail—here again the first words become qualified, and bend to the general intent of the testator, and are no longer regarded as words of limitation, which, if standing by themselves, they would have been.*

(Emphasis added.)

To sum up, the key issue facing the Court on this appeal is whether, as Mr. Sheard suggests, the Court must discard cl. 5 on the basis that the rule applies to cl. 4 and cl. 5 is therefore repugnant to Kennedy's absolute interest under the rule in *Shelley's Case*, or whether the Court must look to cls. 4 and 5 together to discern the nature and extent of Kennedy's interest and then conclude that the combined effect of these two clauses renders the rule inapplicable. I have found no case on point but the approach taken by Kelly J in the *Armstrong* case commends itself to me and compels me to the conclusion, applying ordinary principles of construction, that the testatrix has effectively limited Kennedy Rynard's interest to a determinable life estate. This being so, it is not open to the Court to apply the rule in *Shelley's Case* so as to convert his determinable life estate into a fee simple absolute.

I made reference earlier to the circumstances in which the testatrix herself came to acquire the farm. In fact, she acquired it pursuant to the following provision in her father's will:

> I give and devise to my daughter Maggie Rynard for her use and benefit during the term of her natural life, and after the decease of my said daughter Maggie Rynard to the heir or heirs of her body her surviving and failing such heir or heirs to my heirs surviving my said daughter Maggie Rynard.

There was no question on that language that the rule in *Shelley's Case* applied and accordingly it was necessary for the testatrix to execute a disentailing deed and have the lands reconveyed to her in order that she become the absolute owner. It would appear reasonable to conclude that in light of this experience the testatrix might be a little gun-shy of the rule in *Shelley's Case*. While I think the circumstances in which the testatrix herself acquired the farm are a legitimate and admissible guide to her intention as expressed in her own will, I would not attach as much weight to them as counsel for the respondents suggested.

Having concluded on the preliminary question of construction that the rule does not apply to Mrs. Rynard's will, it is not necessary for me to deal at length with the alternative grounds on which Mr. Justice Walsh supported his conclusion that it did not apply. His primary basis for rejecting its application was s. 31 of the *Wills Act*. In this I think he was in error for the reasons already given.

His second basis was that the remainder interest bequeathed to Kennedy Rynard's heirs was not a bequest of realty but a bequest of personality to which the rule does not apply. The learned Judge pointed out that the bequest to them was of "the balance" after a lump-sum payment had been made to his brother. The use of the word "balance," he felt, disclosed an intention on the part of the testatrix that the farm be sold on Kennedy's death. I am not persuaded that the language of cl. 4 is strong enough to give rise to a direction or trust for conversion of the real estate so as to preclude the application of the rule if the other conditions for its application are present.

In *McDonell v. McDonell et al.* (1894), 24 OR 468, Street J held that the direction of the testator to "pay" to each child his or her share of the residue on the life tenant's death, the residue consisting of realty, was not enough to require a conversion of the realty into personalty. Street J stated the rule at p. 471 as follows:

> The rule is that in order to work a conversion of realty into personalty an imperative trust or direction to sell must be gathered from the terms of the will, not necessarily express, but at all events to be necessarily implied from its terms: *Hyett v. Mekin*, 25

Ch.D 735. I have gone carefully through the cases cited to me upon this question and many more, and I can find no case in which a mere power of sale has been construed as a trust for conversion unless the duties imposed upon the trustee were inconsistent with the presumption that the real estate should continue to retain that character.

Nor can I accept the learned Judge's third ground for rejecting the application of the rule, namely, that the interests of Kennedy and his heirs are not of the same kind or quality. I would have thought that they were both equitable being part and parcel of the trusts to which the entire estate is made subject in the hands of the trustees.

For the reasons given I would dismiss the appeal and direct the costs of all parties except the respondent executor (who, having regard to his status as an appellant in his personal capacity, has taken no position on this appeal *qua* executor) to be paid out of the estate.

Appeal dismissed.

Discussion Notes

It has been held that the rule in *Shelley's Case* does not apply in Alberta: *Re Simpson*, 23 Alta. LR 374; [1927] DLR 817 (CA), affirmed on other grounds [1928] SCR 374; 3 DLR 773. The rule has also been abolished in England: Imperial Law of Property Act, 1925, 15 Geo. 5, c. 20, s. 131.

Exercise 4: Successive Interests and the Rule in Shelley's Case

Examine the grants and devises below. They illustrate the operation of successive interests in land, and the operation of the rule in *Shelley's Case*. Consider the types of interests created. Note that a variety of successive interests in land can be created; remainder interests can also be qualified.

Grant or devise	Analysis
1. X grants to A for life, remainder to B in fee simple.	
2. X grants to A for life, remainder to B for life, remainder to C in fee simple.	
3. X grants to A for life, remainder to B in fee simple so long as the property remains as a farm.	

Grant or devise	Analysis
4. X devises to A for life, remainder to the heirs of A in fee simple.	
5. X grants to A for life, remainder to the heirs of A's body.	
6. X devises to A for life, and after her death to his children.	
7. X devises, "after my husband's death, to Kennedy until his death, subject to the payment of an annuity to JM, and after Kennedy's death $1,500 to be paid to Bernard and the remainder to the heirs of Kennedy." See *Re Rynard* (1980), 118 DLR (3d) 530 (Ont. CA).	

Present and Future Interests

A future interest is an interest in property in which the right to possession and enjoyment of the property is postponed until sometime in the future. The owner of a fee simple absolute can divide his or her estate into lesser estates—life estates, leasehold estates, determinable estates, or those subject to a condition subsequent. The grantor can also create estates that will follow one another:

X to A for life, remainder to B in fee simple.

B's estate is a *future interest* because B will not be entitled to possession and enjoyment of the estate until A's death. Nevertheless, B also has a *present interest* in the property that B can convey to third parties, even prior to A's death. B, as remainderperson, also has the right to restrain A from committing certain types of waste on the property. Because the grant gives to B a present interest in the property, B is said to have an estate that is *vested in interest* at the time of the grant. B's estate will only *vest in possession* at the time of A's death. B's estate is called a *remainder* because it remains away from the grantor. (B's estate, vested in interest, is one kind of future interest. A second kind, where the interest has not yet vested in interest or possession, is known as *contingent remainders*, and is discussed below.)

An estate that is less than a fee simple is called a *particular estate*, because it is only a particle of the whole estate. In the example above, A obtains a particular estate because it is less than a fee simple estate. Estates can also precede one another in succession:

X to A for life, remainder to B for life, and then remainder to C in fee simple.

In this example, A acquires a life estate that is vested in interest and possession at the time of the grant. B acquires a life estate that is vested in interest at the time of grant and will vest in possession on A's death. Likewise, C acquires a remainder in fee simple that is vested in interest at the time of the grant and will vest in possession after A's and B's death. Both B and C acquire future interests because their right to possession and enjoyment of the property is postponed until a future time. Estates that precede one another in a series are called *prior particular estates*. In the above example, A has a life estate that precedes B's life estate; thus A's estate is known as a prior particular estate. Finally, the enjoyment of a future interest is not always guaranteed. In the above example, if B dies before A, B will never enjoy his life estate in possession, even though B acquired an estate vested in interest at the time of the grant. By contrast, if C predeceases B or A, C's remainder in fee simple will simply pass to C's heirs who will take possession of the estate after the death of both A and B.

If the grantor does not create a remainder after a prior particular estate, the property reverts back to the grantor at the termination of the prior particular estate:

X to A for life.

In this example, A acquires a life estate vested in interest and possession. The grantor has not created a remainder, so the estate will revert back to the grantor in fee simple upon A's death. If the grantor is deceased, the estate will simply revert to the grantor's heir. The grantor's retained interest is called a *reversion*, because the property will revert back to the grantor. Reversions are not created by express grant but arise by implication. A reversion is always implied whenever there is a grant of an estate less than fee simple.

The grant of an estate subject to a condition subsequent or a determinable estate will also create future interests. In a grant, "to A in fee simple provided that she does not marry Y," A acquires a fee simple subject to a condition subsequent and the grantor retains a right of entry for condition broken. In a grant, "to A in fee simple so long as she remains married to Y," A acquires a determinable fee simple and the grantor retains a possibility of reverter. Both the right of entry and the possibility of reverter are future interests in property because the right to possession and enjoyment of the property is postponed. There is no guarantee that these particular future interests will ever vest in possession because the conditions in question may never be breached. A right of entry will vest in possession only if the condition subsequent is broken and the grantor exercises the right of entry. Likewise, the possibility of reverter will vest in possession only if the condition in question is violated, thus causing the automatic determination of the estate.

The purpose of future interests is to enable the present holder of an estate to determine when and upon what conditions the next generation may enjoy possession of the land. For example, a testator may wish to provide for his spouse and children after his death. He can execute a devise that will give his wife a life estate, with the remainder in fee simple divided equally among his children. In other cases, the testator may not be confident that an unreliable or incapacitated child will wisely use an inheritance in fee simple absolute. He might fear that after his death the child may sell the property, squander the money, and leave nothing for other family members. In this case, the testator might prefer to devise only a life estate to this child, with a remainder in fee simple to other family members. In this way, the child is provided with some security, but it is assured that the child will never be able to squander the entire value of the property to the detriment of other family members.

Holders of estates do not have an unlimited discretion to determine how and when future generations may enjoy the property. The law has long tended to favour the free alienation of property and to disfavour undue and enduring restraints upon the power of alienation. As a result, there are a number of complex rules prohibiting the creation of a wide variety of future interests. Making matters even more complex, the courts of common law and the courts of equity developed very different sets of rules. The courts of common law permitted far fewer types of future interests than did the courts of equity. The following discussion will first consider the restrictive set of rules originally developed by the courts of common law, rules that remain in effect to this day.

Exercise 5: Future Interests

The following exercise provides a quick review of future interests. A future interest is an interest in property in which the right to possession and enjoyment of the property is postponed until sometime in the future. Identify the estates created below, including any future interests. Is the future interest a reversion or a remainder? Is the remainder qualified in some way? If so, what interest is retained by the grantor?

Grant or devise	Analysis
1. X to A for life.	
2. X to A for life, remainder to B in fee simple.	
3. X to A for life, remainder to B in fee simple so long as she continues to practise law.	

Future Interests at Common Law

The creation of future interests was severely restricted at common law. As noted at the beginning of this chapter, the feudal system was greatly concerned with the enforcement of the incidents and services associated with tenure. The person *seised* of the land was responsible for these feudal incidents and services, and the lord could seek a variety of legal remedies to enforce these duties. It was always of utmost importance to know who was seised of the land, so that the lord could easily enforce these obligations. The common law courts thus abhorred any situation where the identity of the person seised of the land might become uncertain:

> X grants to A when she turns 21. (A is 15 years old at the time of the grant.)

Because A is only 15 years old, A has not satisfied the condition precedent of this grant. For the common law courts, a grant of this nature created an "abeyance of seisin" because it was not clear who would be seised of the land for the six years prior to A's 21st birthday. Would the grantor remain liable for the tenurial incidents and services until A turned 21, or would this obligation immediately pass to A at the time of the grant even though she had not yet satisfied the condition precedent? This was a matter of grave concern to the lord. In response, the common law courts developed a complex set of rules, known as the *common law remainder rules*. These rules generally prohibit the creation of future interests that can give rise to an abeyance of seisin, such as the future interest in the above grant. According to these rules, A will take nothing in the above grant, even when she turns 21. The entire grant fails at the outset because it creates the possibility of an abeyance of seisin.

Today, the enforcement of the incidents of tenure is no longer of any relevance, because all land is now granted only in free and common socage. Nonetheless, these common law remainder rules remain in effect in most common law jurisdictions, including common law Canada.

Vested and Contingent Remainders

To understand the common law remainder rules, it is first essential to comprehend the distinction between vested and contingent remainders. The term "vested" has two possible meanings. An estate may "vest in possession" or "vest in interest." An estate vests in possession when the holder of the estate is entitled to immediate possession of the property. An estate can also vest in interest prior to vesting in possession, if the entitlement to possession arises only at the determination of a prior particular estate:

> X to A for life and then the remainder to B in fee simple.

As noted above, A, the life tenant, acquires immediate possession of the estate for her lifetime, an estate vested in possession and interest at the same time. A's estate is also known as a prior particular estate, because it is an estate less than fee simple and precedes B's estate. B acquires a fee simple in remainder vested *in interest* at the time of the grant. It is a present interest in land and can be conveyed to third parties, even though B is not entitled to possession of the property until A's death. B's estate will only vest *in possession* at the time of A's death.

> X to A for life and then the remainder to B in fee simple when he turns 21. (B is 15 at the time of the grant.)

In this example, A acquires the same interest as above. B's interest, however, is subject to a condition precedent because it is contingent on B turning 21 years old. B's interest is called a *contingent remainder* as distinguished from a *vested remainder*, because his remainder has not yet vested in interest. B will not acquire any interest in the land until he turns 21 years old, at which time his estate will vest in interest. B's estate will then vest in possession upon A's death.

X to A for life and then the remainder to A's widow for life.

In this case, the identity of A's widow, the remainderperson, will be unknown until A dies. It may or may not be A's current spouse. Because the identity of the remainderperson will remain unknown until A dies, the remainder cannot vest in interest until the moment of A's death. At this time, when the identity of the remainderperson is finally ascertained, the remainderperson's interest will vest in interest and possession simultaneously. This remainder interest is a contingent remainder because the vesting of the remainder interest is contingent upon determining the identity of the remainderperson.

A *vested* remainder can be defined as follows. It is (1) limited to a person who is in existence, (2) limited to a person who is ascertained, and (3) not subject to a condition precedent. See Oosterhoff and Rayner, at 350. If all three criteria do not apply, the interest is a *contingent* remainder rather than a *vested* remainder.

• *in existence*—the remainderperson must be in existence. For example, in a grant "to A for life and then the remainder in fee simple to A's first born child," if A has no children, the remainderperson is not yet in existence. The remainder interest is a contingent remainder because the remainder interest will not vest in interest until the birth of A's first child. (Recall that the rule in *Shelley's Case* does not apply to this grant because the remainder is to a specific person, not to the whole line of heirs.) If A has no children, the remainder interest will never vest. In this case, the fee simple will simply revert back to the grantor (or if deceased, the grantor's heirs) at the time of A's death, thus creating a possibility of a reversion. The reversion will arise if the remainder does not vest in interest.

• *ascertained*—the remainderperson must also be ascertained. In the grant "to A for life and then the remainder to A's widow for life," the identity of A's widow will remain unascertained until the moment of A's death. This remainder interest is a contingent remainder because it will not vest in interest until this time. Likewise, in a grant "to A for life and then the remainder in fee simple to A's surviving children," the identity of the children surviving A will only be known at the moment of A's death. Because these children remain unascertained until A's death, this grant creates a contingent remainder. If no children survive A, the estate will revert back to the grantor in fee simple.

• *no condition precedent*—finally, the remainder interest cannot be subject to a condition precedent. In a grant "to A for life and then the remainder to B in fee simple upon graduating from law school," the remainder interest is subject to a condition precedent. It is a contingent remainder because it will not vest in interest until B's graduation. Conditions may be something that the grantee can do, such as reach the age of 21 or get married. On the other hand, conditions may be something over which the grantee has no control, such as in a grant "to A for life and then the remainder in fee simple to B if A has no children" (or "remainder to B if A is unmarried"). If the condition precedent is never satisfied, the property will revert back to the grantor in fee simple upon A's death.

A contingent remainder can also contain more than one of the above uncertainties. In a grant "to A for life and then the remainder in fee simple to A's first born child upon reaching the age of 21," the child may not yet be in existence, and the remainder interest is also subject to a condition precedent. Once the child is born, there will be an ascertained person in existence, but the remainder interest will remain subject to the condition precedent and will not vest in interest until the child reaches 21.

A contingent interest also arises when there is a fee simple subject to a condition subsequent in which the grantor (or testator's estate, as the case may be) has retained the right of entry for condition broken. This right of entry is a contingent interest because it is subject to a condition precedent and will only arise and vest in interest if the condition in question is breached.

It is a curious feature of Canadian law that a possibility of reverter is not regarded as a contingent interest. The possibility of reverter is the interest that remains in a grantor who has conveyed a determinable fee simple (or the interest that remains in the testator's estate, if there is a devise of a determinable fee simple). It would appear that, like a right of entry, a possibility of reverter could only vest in interest if the terms on which the estate is held are breached. However, as was held in *Re McKellar* (1972), 27 DLR (2d) 70, aff'd. 36 DLR (3d) 202 (Ont. CA), a possibility of reverter is a vested interest (and thus not subject to the common law rule against perpetuities, a matter considered in greater detail below). Because the determining event is regarded as marking the natural limitation of the determinable estate, the possibility of reverter is regarded as vested in interest at the time of the grant or devise. See Ziff, at 207. By contrast, at least one English precedent has held that the possibility of reverter is subject to the common law rule against perpetuities, suggesting that the possibility of reverter is a contingent and not a vested interest: *Hopper v. Corp. of Liverpool* (1944), 88 Sol. Jo. 213.

In summary, a *vested* interest arises only if the remainderperson is in existence, is ascertained, and the interest is not subject to a condition precedent. In a grant "to A for life and then the remainder to B in fee simple," B is in existence, ascertained, and the interest is not subject to a condition precedent. As a result, B's remainder will vest in interest immediately at the time of the grant. Because this vesting is not contingent on any future event and vests immediately at the time of the grant, the interest is thus known as a *vested remainder*.

The distinction between vested and contingent remainders is crucial for a number of reasons. In particular, the common law courts developed a series of rules that greatly restricted the creation of contingent remainders. For the common law courts, many contingent remainders presented an intolerable possibility of an abeyance of seisin, and, for a long time, all contingent remainders were regarded as void at common law. For example, in the grant "to A for life and then the remainder to B in fee simple upon attaining 21," there was a possibility that B might not reach 21 until after A's death. During the time between A's death and B turning 21, it might be unclear who, if anyone, was seised of the land. For this reason, the common law favoured vested remainders over contingent remainders. With a vested remainder, there was never any doubt who would become seised of the land immediately upon the determination of the prior particular estate.

Exercise 6: Vested and Contingent Remainders

The following exercise requires you to identify vested and contingent remainders. Recall the distinction between interests that are vested in possession and those that are vested in interest. Those vested in possession give rise to a present property interest with immediate entitlement to possession. Those vested in interest give rise to a present property interest, but entitlement to possession will only vest at the determination of the prior particular estate. Because the right to possession is postponed until some point in the future, these are future interests.

In the examples below, identify which estates are vested in possession. Also identify the remainder interests and determine whether they are vested or contingent remainders. Recall that a contingent remainder arises if the remainderperson is not yet in existence (not born), is not yet ascertained (his or her identity is unknown), or if the remainder interest is subject to a condition precedent. On the other hand, a vested remainder arises only if the remainderperson is in existence, an ascertained person, and the remainder is not subject to a condition precedent.

Grant or devise	Analysis
1. X to A for life, remainder to B in fee simple provided that B is married.	
2. X to A for life, remainder to A's widow in fee simple.	
3. X to A for life, remainder to B if he survives A.	
4. X to A for life, remainder to B after A's death. Hint: Does this grant impose a condition precedent, that B must survive A? See *Re Leckie* (1921), 20 OWN 478 (HC).	
5. X to A and B for their joint lives, remainder to the survivor. See *Whitby v. Von Luedecke*, [1906] 1 Ch. 783.	

The Common Law Remainder Rules

There are four commonly identified remainder rules. Some of the rules apply only to contingent remainders, others to all remainders. The remainder rules apply only to interests created and enforced by the courts of common law. For historical reasons, the remainder rules were not applied by the courts of equity, and do not apply to equitable interests in property. Interests created at common law are known as *legal interests* in property, thereby distinguishing them from *equitable interests* and *legal executory interests.*

The courts of equity developed an entirely different set of rules governing interests in property, a development that eventually gave rise to equitable interests and legal executory interests. For the moment, it is important simply to point out that the remainder rules apply only to legal interests in property, not to equitable interests or legal executory interests. The significance of this will become clear when equitable interests and legal executory interests are examined below.

Because the common law courts were concerned with preventing any possible abeyance of seisin, they permitted the creation of only a small number of future interests. Originally, only the following four future interests were permitted:

- the reversion,
- the vested remainder,
- the possibility of reverter, and
- the right of entry for condition broken.

As discussed above, the reversion is the interest retained by the grantor after having conveyed a particular estate less than that held by the grantor. The remainder is the interest that remains out of the grantor on the termination of a particular estate created by the same instrument. The reversion and the vested remainder were permitted at common law because neither future interest raised the possibility of an abeyance of seisin. On the termination of the prior particular estate, seisin would pass immediately to the vested remainder or revert back to the grantor.

On the other hand, as noted above, the contingent remainder presented some concern regarding the smooth and predictable passage of seisin. For this reason, the common law courts initially refused to permit any contingent remainders. However, by the middle of the 15th century, contingent remainders were allowed to take effect if they in fact vested in interest during the continuation of the preceding estate (Megarry and Wade, at 1176). Interests that purported to spring up in the future—that is, interests that were not supported by a preceding vested estate—were not permitted. For example, a grant "to A when he attains 21" (A is 15) was not permitted because seisin would be in abeyance until A became 21.

Finally, as regards the possibility of reverter and the right of entry, the common law would not permit a vested interest to be defeated in favour of anyone other than the grantor or the grantor's heirs. As a result, these two future interests could not be conveyed or granted to a stranger. These various rules developed by the common law courts are summarized under the common law remainder rules below.

In property texts, the common law remainder rules are not always presented in the same order, however it is agreed that there are four basic rules.

Rule One: No Remainders After a Fee Simple

Once a grantor has disposed of a fee simple, the grantor has disposed of all his or her interest and has nothing further to grant. Where property is granted "to A and his heirs, remainder to B and his heirs," the remainder is thus void and B acquires nothing: *Duke of Norfolk's Case* (1681), 3 Ch. Ca. 1, at 31. Likewise, in a case where property was conveyed "to A in fee simple, with remainder to B if A should die without leaving children," the court held that the remainder after the fee simple was void, giving to A a fee simple absolute: *Re Chauvin* (1920), 18 OWN 178 (HC).

This rule also applies to qualified fees, making it impossible for a grantor to convey to a stranger the possibility of reverter or right of entry. As noted above, because the common law did not permit a vested interest to be defeated in favour of anyone other than the grantor or the grantor's heirs, the possibility of reverter or right of entry for condition broken could not be conveyed or granted to a stranger:

X to A in fee simple so long as the CN Tower stands, and if and when it falls down, to B in fee simple.

This grant gives to A a determinable fee simple. Although it purports to give to B the possibility of reverter, this remainder interest is void because it is a remainder after a fee simple. Likewise, a grant "to A in fee simple on condition that he use the land solely for residential purposes and if he ceases to do so, to B in fee," gives to A a fee simple subject to a condition subsequent. The remainder interest to B is void because it is a remainder after a fee simple.

Rule Two: No Springing Freeholds

A remainder must be supported by a prior particular estate of freehold created by the same instrument. This rule prohibits the creation of a freehold estate that springs up in the future by itself:

X to A's first born child. (A has no children.)
X to A upon A's marriage. (A is unmarried.)
X to A at the age of 21. (A is 15.)

These grants transfer nothing to A because the common law requires an immediate transfer of seisin at the time of the grant. There can be no abeyance of seisin prior to the grant taking effect. In the first grant, there can be no immediate transfer because the first born child is not yet in existence. Likewise, in the second and third examples, there can be no immediate transfer of seisin because the conditions have not yet been fulfilled. These purported interests, known as *springing freeholds* because they purport to "spring up" at some point in the future unsupported by a prior particular estate, are prohibited at common law.

If the grantor wishes to provide for A's first child upon birth, the grantor must support this future interest with a prior particular estate. For example, in the grant "to A for life and then the remainder to A's first born child," the contingent remainder is now supported by a prior particular estate of freehold (A's life estate). Seisin is transferred immediately to A for life, and upon his death, to his first born child. If A does not have any children during his life, the contingent remainder interest will never take effect and the estate will revert back to the grantor in fee simple (see rule three below).

Particular rules applied to leasehold estates. As discussed earlier, a leasehold estate is not an estate in freehold because it is not an estate of uncertain duration. Likewise, the tenant of a leasehold estate is not seised of the land because seisin remains with the freeholder (the landlord). Accordingly, a grant "to A for two years and then to B and her heirs upon attaining 21" (B is 20 years old), does not create a valid contingent remainder to B. The two-year lease to A is valid, but seisin (as well as the fee simple in reversion) remains with the grantor's estate. B takes nothing under the grant because a prior particular estate of *freehold* (a leasehold estate not being an estate of freehold) does not support B's contingent remainder interest. On the other hand, if B is 21 years old at the time of the grant, B's interest is no longer contingent, and B will take seisin immediately at the time of the grant. B will take a fee simple subject to a two-year lease in favour of A: *Boraston's Case* (1587), 76 ER 668. Because seisin passes immediately, this grant does not contemplate a freehold springing up in the future and is thus valid. Finally, a grant "to A for ten years when A attains 21" (A is not yet 21) does not offend this rule because seisin remains with the lessor at all times. A springing freehold is not contemplated, nor is there any abeyance of seisin, because a leasehold estate is not an estate in freehold and the lessor will never be seised of the land.

Rule Three: Timely Vesting

A contingent remainder is void unless it vests in interest by the end of the prior particular estate: *Cunliffe v. Brancker* (1876), 3 Ch.D 393 (CA). This rule derived from the common law's concern about any possible abeyance of seisin. The common law would not tolerate any gap in seisin between the prior particular estate and the next successive estate:

X to A for life and the remainder to B in fee simple upon attaining 21.

According to this rule, B's contingent remainder must vest in interest by the end of A's life estate. In other words, B must turn 21-years old before A dies or B's interest will never take effect. If B's interest fails to vest in time, there will be a reversion in fee simple to the grantor at the time of A's death, and B will never take any interest under the grant. This rule avoids any gap in seisin that would otherwise arise if B has not yet turned 21-years old at the time of A's death. The common law does not permit any such gap and thus developed the common law remainder rule that the contingent remainder must vest in interest by the end of the prior particular estate.

In most cases, the common law adopts a "wait and see" attitude to determine if the contingent remainder will vest in time. Providing B turns 21 while A is alive, B's remainder is valid. However, some grants on their face require a gap in seisin:

X to A for life and one year after A's death, remainder to B in fee simple.

This grant expressly requires a gap in seisin. Because such a gap violates the common law remainder rules, this contingent remainder is void *ab initio* (from the outset). B will never take any interest under this grant, and the estate will revert back to the grantor in fee simple upon A's death.

There is no gap in seisin if the contingent remainder vests at the moment of the termination of the prior particular estate. In the grant, "to A and B for life, remainder in fee to the survivor," the survivor will be unknown until the time when the first of either A or B dies. This contingent remainder will vest in interest and possession at this time. There is no gap in seisin and the remainder does not violate the common law remainder rules.

If the remainder is to a class of persons, such as in a grant "to A for life, remainder to such of his children as attain the age of 21," the remainder will be good only for those children who attain 21 during A's life: *Festing v. Allen* (1843), 152 ER 1204. Children who turn 21 after A's death will not take any interest because their contingent remainder did not vest during the prior particular estate. According to this "class closing rule," the class of persons who can take will close upon the termination of the prior particular estate.

Rule Four: No Shifting Freeholds

A remainder is void if it operates so as to defeat the prior particular estate of freehold. A remainder is required to vest in possession only upon the *natural* determination of the prior particular estate. This rule applies in one case only—where there is a life estate subject to a condition subsequent, with a remainder to a stranger:

X to A for life, but if A goes bankrupt, then the remainder to B in fee simple.

The grantor has attempted to create a life estate subject to a condition subsequent and convey to B (a stranger) the right of entry for condition broken. The common law does not permit the grantor to convey a right of entry to a stranger, as illustrated by remainder rule one (no remainders after a fee simple). Because the remainder in this example purports to defeat the prior particular estate in favour of B (a stranger) if A goes bankrupt, the gift to B violates this rule and is voidable. If A goes bankrupt, only the grantor may exercise the right of entry for condition broken, because at common law this right belongs solely to the grantor and his heirs. If the grantor exercises this right, the estate will revert back to the grantor in fee simple and B's remainder interest is void. On the other hand, if the grantor chooses not to exercise this right, A's life estate will continue and upon the *natural* termination of A's life estate (A's death), B's remainder will take effect: Oosterhoff and Rayner, at 394. If A's estate naturally terminates, B's remainder interest is not operating to *defeat* prematurely the prior particular estate, and B's remainder does not violate the fourth remainder rule.

This rule does not apply to determinable limitations. A determinable limitation sets the time at which the estate will *naturally* determine and revert back to the grantor. In a grant "to A and her heirs until the CN Tower falls," A's estate will naturally terminate and revert back to the grantor if the CN Tower falls. The limitation contained in a determinable estate is *part* of the definition of its duration and determines the natural termination of the estate, whereas with estates subject to a condition subsequent, the limitation is something *added* to the grant that can defeat the estate if the condition is violated.

X to A for life or until the CN Tower falls, and if the CN Tower falls, then the remainder to B in fee simple.

A's life estate will terminate naturally upon A's death or when the CN Tower falls, whatever comes first. B acquires a valid remainder that will vest in possession either upon A's death or when the CN Tower falls. In this case, B's remainder interest is not operating to defeat prematurely the prior particular estate and thus does not violate the fourth remainder rule. Instead, B's remainder interest is simply taking effect upon the natural termination of the prior particular estate, whether that be upon A's death or when the CN Tower falls.

In summary, the four common law remainder rules generally prohibit the creation of what are known as "springing interests" and "shifting interests." Springing interests are so described because they are not supported by a prior particular estate of freehold (rule two) or do not vest in interest during the prior particular estate (rule three). Instead of a smooth and predictable flow of seisin from one estate to the next, a springing interest simply purports to "pop up" at some point in the future. Shifting interests are interests that purport to shift abruptly from one person to another upon the happening of some event. This will arise if a grantor has attempted to grant a remainder after a determinable fee simple, conveying the possibility of a reverter to a stranger. The interest purports to "shift" from the holder of the determinable fee simple to the stranger upon the termination of the determinable fee, and this is prohibited under the common law remainder rule (rule one). A shifting interest also arises when a remainder operates to defeat a prior particular estate, as may arise where there is a life estate subject to a condition subsequent, and this is similarly prohibited (rule four).

Equitable Estates

The common law remainder rules applied only to legal estates. For a variety of historical reasons, the courts of equity developed a distinct set of interests in property that permitted a much wider range of future interests than was the case at common law. This development began with the *doctrine of uses*, first employed by religious institutions in England. For a very long time, the Statutes of Mortmain prevented corporations (including religious institutions) from holding interests in land without a licence from the Crown. Because corporations can exist indefinitely, land held by a corporation effectively evaded most of the incidents of tenure, including relief, wardship, and escheat. Corporations do not have children and do not die, so these various incidents would never arise once a corporation acquired land. The Statutes of Mortmain were designed to prevent land from falling into "dead hands" where the lord would no longer be able to profit from most of the incidents of tenure.

In an effort to evade the Statutes of Mortmain, religious corporate bodies developed a novel device—a grantor would grant his land to X with the direction that X was to permit the religious institution to have occupation and use of the land. X acquired the fee simple in the land, was seised of the land, and was liable for any of the incidents of tenure. The religious institution acquired no legal interest in the land. X's legal title was, however, intended to be purely nominal and was not intended to include any right to occupy and use the land. X was expected to hold the land for the use of the religious body, thus the device was called a *use*. The threat of spiritual punishment was the only way in which the religious institution could enforce X's obligation, because the institution held no interest in the land recognized by the common law courts. Such a conveyance was known as a "conveyance to uses," thus distinguishing it from a simple "common law conveyance" that did not employ a use. Although this particular evasion by religious corporate bodies was eventually prohibited by statute in 1391 (15 Ric. 2, c. 5), the use survived and prospered.

The use remained popular because it could be employed for a variety of other purposes. Most important, the use made it possible to make testamentary dispositions of land and evade many of the costly incidents of tenure. For a long period of time, property owners had very limited power to designate who would take their property on their death. Prior to the Statute of Wills (1540), 31 Hen. 8, c. 1, property owners did not have the right to designate their heir. The use provided a method to evade this restriction. Legal title was conveyed by livery of seisin to a trusted person (known as the "feoffee to uses"). The feoffee to uses promised to hold the property for the benefit of the grantor (known as the *cestui que use*, from the old French "*cestui a qui oes le feffment fut fait*"). The feoffee to uses also agreed to hold the property for whomever the grantor designated to take the property upon his death. In this way, the grantor retained possession of the land and acquired the power to designate his heir. The feoffee remained seised of the land at all times. There was one further advantage of this arrangement. The grantor's designated heir, not being seised of the land, did not have to pay relief to the lord to take possession of the land upon the grantor's death.

The use was also employed as a means to evade various other incidents of tenure. For example, knights who left for the Crusades frequently conveyed legal title in their lands to a trusted friend. If the knight died before his son was old enough to take over, the feoffee to uses continued to hold legal title to the estate, preventing the lord from profiting from wardship while the son was not yet of age.

For these reasons, the use became a very popular conveyancing device. By the end of the 14th century, much of the land of England came to be held in this fashion. In some cases, however, a feoffee to uses reneged on his responsibility to hold the land for the *cestui que use*. The courts of common law, concerned only with seisin, regarded the feoffee to uses as the only person seised of the land and the only person legally entitled to possession of the land. The *cestui que use* was not seised of the land, enjoyed no property interest recognized by the common law courts, and was unable to enforce the feoffee's obligation before the courts of common law: *Chudleigh's Case* (1595), 1 Co. Rep. 113b. As was the practice at the time, *cestui que uses* who had been deprived of their use and possession of the land petitioned the Crown for justice. Today such a grievance might be dealt with by legislative reform, but in the 14th century, Parliament in its present form had yet to evolve. Instead, the Crown was regarded as the "Fountain of Justice" and "keeper of the King's conscience." Where justice could not be found before the courts of common law, persons petitioned the Crown for relief, and such relief was granted on a case-by-case basis as the Crown determined. As such petitions became more common, the Crown delegated the petitions to the lord chancellor, a powerful statesman and eminent ecclesiastic. Gradually, relief came to be granted under the authority of the lord chancellor rather than the Crown. The lord chancellor eventually appointed various officials to assist in hearing these petitions, and the office came to be known as the court of chancery (or the court of equity) and the officials as judges in equity. This marked the beginning of equity as a distinct area of law.

Uses were peculiarly a matter of good faith and trust, and were therefore compelling subjects for the chancellor's equitable jurisdiction. By early in the 15th century, equitable relief was granted to protect the interests of the *cestui que use*. The chancellor could not directly interfere in legal matters between subjects, and had no power to amend or alter the common law. Nonetheless, the chancellor had jurisdiction over the body and mind of the subject, derived from the Crown's power as sovereign. He had the power to issue orders (known today as "injunctions") requiring individuals to act in accordance with the dictates of good conscience, thus the phrase "equity acts *in personam*" ("on the person"). The chancellor's ultimate sanction was to imprison for contempt anyone who disobeyed his decree. If a feoffee to uses was disregarding his solemn promise to hold the land for the use of another, the feoffee was acting in bad faith. The courts of equity would either direct the feoffee to comply with his promise, or order him to convey his legal interest in the land to the *cestui que use*. Originally, the *cestui que use* was not regarded as having an interest in the land itself and the feoffee's obligation was enforced as a matter similar to privity of contract. Later, the use was treated as creating an *equitable estate* in land, thus giving rise to the great cleavage between legal and equitable estates in property: *Brent's Case* (1583), 74 ER 319.

With the recognition of the equitable estate in property, it became possible to create an entirely new and different range of interests in property. This new range of interests in property persisted until there was a comparatively short-lived attempt to eliminate them in the Statute of Uses (1535), 27 Hen. 8, c. 10. Before examining the importance of this statute, and its continuing impact today, it is necessary first to understand what these equitable interests were and how they were created.

As discussed above, the legal fee simple can be divided into a number of lesser estates—such as life estates, leasehold estates, determinable estates, or estates subject to a condition subsequent. With the introduction of equitable estates, it also became possible to separate the legal from the equitable estate:

X to A and his heirs to the use of B and her heirs (prior to the Statute of Uses (1535)).

In this grant, A, the feoffee to uses, acquired the legal fee simple, recognized and enforced by the courts of common law, and was seised of the land. B acquired an equitable fee simple, recognized and enforced by the courts of equity, giving to B the use and possession of the property even though B was not seised of the land. The feoffee to uses (A) was the legal owner of the fee simple, and the *cestui que use* (B) was the beneficial or equitable owner in fee simple. Both the legal and the equitable estates could also be divided into lesser estates:

X to A and his heirs to the use of B for life and then the remainder to the use of C and her heirs (prior to the Statute of Uses (1535)).

As above, A acquired the legal fee simple. The equitable estates have, however, been divided into estates less than fee simple. In this grant, B acquired an equitable life estate and C acquired an equitable remainder in fee simple.

The courts of equity also took an entirely different approach to future interests in property. The common law, primarily concerned about seisin, developed the common law remainder rules that severely restricted the types of future interests that could be created, prohibiting both springing and shifting interests in property. The courts of equity had no similar concern regarding seisin. The feoffee to uses remained seised of the land and liable for any incidents of tenure. The *cestui que use* was never seised of the land and was not liable for these incidents, so seisin never had any particular relevance before the courts of equity. Accordingly, the courts of equity did not apply the common law remainder rules to equitable future interests:

> X to A and his heirs to the use of B when he turns 21 (prior to the Statute of Uses (1535)). B is 15 years old.

In this grant, A acquired a legal fee simple and remained seised of the land at all times. B's interest was intended to "spring up" when B reached 21-years old. Under the common law remainder rules (rule two), springing interests were prohibited. Under a simple common law grant "to B at 21," B takes nothing because he is not yet 21. However, if B's estate were created as an *equitable* springing interest, B's interest was permitted to take effect because the courts of equity did not apply the common law remainder rules. In the above grant, the courts of equity would require A to hold the land for B until B reached 21-years old. A remained seised of the land in fee simple, retaining legal title at all times, but A was required to hold the land for B if and when B reached 21. Until such time as B attained 21, the courts of equity imposed a *resulting use* in favour of the grantor (X). Whenever the beneficial entitlement to the land was unclear, the courts of equity determined that beneficial ownership would "result back" to the grantor. In this case, the grantor received an equitable fee simple, defeasible on B attaining 21.

The courts of equity also took a similar approach to the issue of timely vesting (rule three). According to the common law remainder rules, a contingent remainder must vest by the end of the prior particular estate. Thus, in a grant "to B for life and the remainder to B's children who attain 21," these children must attain 21 during B's life or their contingent remainder is void. In other words, according to this class-closing rule, the class of persons who can take as remainderpersons is closed upon the termination of the prior particular estate. This outcome could be avoided if the future interest was created in equity:

> X to A and his heirs to the use of B for life, remainder to the use of B's children who attain 21.

Before the courts of equity, the class of remainderpersons remained open until there was no possibility of other grantees meeting the condition. The class remained open, even after B's death, and any children who attained 21 before or after his death shared equally in the remainder interest. The interests of those children who had already turned 21 remained subject to partial divestment as other children reached 21 and claimed a share.

The courts of equity also permitted the creation of shifting interests in property:

> X to A and his heirs to the use of B in fee simple so long as the London Bridge stands, and if and when it falls, to C in fee simple (prior to the Statute of Uses (1535)).

In this grant, A acquired a legal fee simple. B acquired an equitable determinable fee simple. The remainder interest to C would be void at common law, because there cannot be a remainder after a determinable fee simple (rule one). At common law, the grantor cannot convey a possibility of reverter to a stranger. The interest cannot "shift" to C if London Bridge falls. However, the courts of equity enforced equitable shifting interests. As a result, C acquired what came to be known as a "gift over" of an equitable shifting interest to C if and when London Bridge falls: Sinclair and McCallum, at 83-84.

In summary, with the introduction of equitable interests in land, it became possible for the first time to create springing and shifting interests in property. This new class of future interests came to be known as "executory interests" because they have yet to be executed or carried into effect. They will only vest, if at all, at some point in the future. As noted above, equitable interests in land also made it possible to evade most incidents of tenure. Feudal incidents fell only upon the person or persons seised of the land. If legal title were conferred on several feoffees, as joint tenants, the events that would trigger feudal incidents could be postponed indefinitely. As discussed in chapter 7, on the death of a joint tenant, the interest of that tenant does not descend to an heir. Instead, it merges with the title of the surviving joint tenants. These survivors can simply appoint more joint tenants as others die. In this way, the land never passes by inheritance and is never held by an underage minor. Both wardship and relief could thus be avoided by keeping the land vested in two or more joint feoffees to uses of full age.

There was one further advantage associated with equitable estates. It became possible to convey equitable estates without the inconvenience and publicity of livery of seisin. Holders of equitable estates were not seised of the land, so conveyance of an equitable interest did not require livery of seisen. This particular feature proved immensely useful. Typically, parties would enter into a contract (known as a deed) prior to livery of seisin. In this contract, the purchaser would agree to pay a certain amount for the land, and the vendor of the legal fee simple would agree to convey his estate to the purchaser by livery of seisin at some point in the future, usually once payment had been made. If the vendor reneged on his contract, the purchaser could bring an action to recover monetary damages for breach of contract, but the purchaser could not bring a real action to recover the property because he was not yet seised of the land. Recognizing the unique value of land, and the fact that monetary damages might not be sufficient to satisfy the purchaser's claim, the courts of equity came to regard this contract as giving to the purchaser an equitable interest in the land. The courts of equity required the vendor to complete in good faith his promise of livery of seisin to the purchaser, and thereby convey to the purchaser the legal fee simple. The courts of equity thus ordered "specific performance" of the contract for sale. By the end of the 15th century, this contract for the sale of land came to replace the ancient and inconvenient practice of livery of seisin. The contract itself, known as a "bargain and sale," was sufficient to convey equitable title to the land. Because the courts of equity carefully protected equitable interests, it mattered little to the purchaser that the vendor retained legal title. See, generally, Sinclair and McCallum, at 79-80.

The security of an equitable estate was similar to that of a legal estate, with one major exception. The courts of equity would not use their jurisdiction to the disadvantage of the *bona fide* purchaser for value without notice." The courts of equity, keepers of the king's conscience, exercised their powers primarily to prevent unconscionable behaviour and acts of bad faith, such as was the case when a feoffee to uses acted in disregard of his solemn promise to hold the land for another. A difficult question arose if the feoffee to uses conveyed his legal title by livery of seisin to a good faith (*bona fide*) purchaser who had paid market value for the land, unaware that the conveyance was in breach of the feoffee's obligation to hold the land for another. In this case, the purchaser acted in good faith and paid fair value for the property without notice of any outstanding equitable interest in the land. There were no equitable grounds to require this innocent purchaser to hold the land for the *cestui que use*. As a result, the *cestui que use* had only a personal remedy in the courts of equity against the feoffee to uses, who had wrongfully deprived the *cestui que use* of his equitable estate, and no equitable remedy against the *bona fide* purchaser for value without notice. Such a purchaser took the land free of any equitable obligation.

By contrast, however, if the purchaser of the land was aware that the land was subject to an equitable interest—that is, the purchaser had *actual notice* of this interest—the purchaser was bound by the obligation. The courts of equity also developed the doctrine of *constructive notice*. If the purchaser failed to make all the usual and proper inquiries to determine if there were any outstanding equitable obligation, the courts of equity imposed this equitable obligation on the careless purchaser. Likewise, if the purchaser took the land by gift or inheritance, and was not a purchaser for *value*, the purchaser was also bound by the equitable obligation, even in the absence of actual or constructive notice.

Exercise 7: Conveyances to Uses (Before the Statute of Uses (1535))

Before the Statute of Uses, in a grant "to A and his heirs to the use of B and his heirs," A was the feoffee to uses and B was the *cestui que use*. A had the legal estate, recognized by the courts of common law. B had the equitable (or beneficial) estate, recognized and protected by the lord chancellor and then later by the courts of equity. The following exercise requires you to identify the legal and equitable interests created. Assume that these grants predate the Statute of Uses. Recall that the courts of equity did not adopt the common law remainder rules, and it was therefore possible to create equitable springing and shifting interests below, known as *executory interests*. Remember as well that there will be a resulting use implied back in favour of the grantor whenever beneficial entitlement to the land is unclear.

Grant or devise	Analysis
1. X to A and his heirs to the use of B for life, remainder to the use of C and her heirs.	
2. X to A and his heirs to the use of B for life, but if B marries C, then to the use of D and his heirs.	

Grant or devise	Analysis
3. X to A and his heirs to the use of B in fee simple at 21. (B is 15.)	
4. X to A and her heirs to the use of B for life, remainder to the use of C and his heirs five years after B's death.	

The Statute of Uses

The use had a highly detrimental effect on the collection of feudal incidents, much to the despair of those relying on this particular form of feudal taxation. After the statute Quia Emptores (1290), which prohibited any further subinfeudation, most of the land in England came to be held directly of the Crown. By the 16th century, this process was largely complete. The Crown, as the only major remaining feudal lord, had a keen interest in enforcing the very lucrative incidents of tenure. However, the widespread employment of uses had seriously depleted this source of royal revenue. The king at the time, Henry VIII, was determined to restore this royal revenue and eliminate the use as a means to evade feudal incidents. The landowners, well represented in Parliament, resisted this feudal tax grab, but eventually Henry VIII had his way with the passage of the Statute of Uses (1535), 27 Hen. 8, c. 10.

The Statute of Uses sought to reunite the legal and equitable title by removing the legal title from the feoffee to uses and placing it in the hands of the *cestui que use*, thereby "executing" the use. The Statute of Uses was part of the received law in the Canadian common law provinces and remains a key part of Canadian land law today. The operative section of the Statute of Uses, as reproduced in the statutes of Ontario (RSO 1980, appendix A), provides:

Where any person stands or *is seized of* and in *lands*, tenements, rents, services, reversions, remainders, or other hereditaments, *to the use, confidence or trust, of any other person, or of any body politic*, by reason of any bargain, sale, feoffment, covenant, contract, agreement, will, or otherwise, by any means whatsoever it be, *in every such case such person and body politic that shall have any such use, confidence or trust*, in fee simple, fee tail, for term of life, or for years, or otherwise, or any use, confidence or trust, in remainder or reversion, *shall from henceforth* stand and *be seized*, deemed *and adjudged in lawful seizin, estate and possession of and in the same lands*, tenements, rents, services, reversions, remainders, and hereditaments, with their appurtenances, to all intents, constructions and purposes in the law, *of and in such like estates as they had, or shall have, in use, trust or confidence*, of or in the same. *And the estate*, right, title and possession, *that was in such person that was, or shall be hereafter seized, of any lands*, tenements, or hereditaments, *to the use, confidence or trust, of any such person, or of any body politic, shall be from henceforth deemed and adjudged to be in him that hath such use, confidence or trust,* after such quality, manner, form and condition, *as he had before* in or to the use, confidence or trust, that was in him. [Emphasis added.]

The language is dense. The emphasized words indicate the essence of the section. The Statute of Uses provides that where one person (A) is seised to the use of another person or body politic (B or B Incorporated), the legal interest held by A will be "executed," and that interest will be transferred to B. Thereafter, B shall be seised of the land, making B liable for all the incidents of tenure that B had previously evaded. In all respects, B holds the same entitlement as B previously held under the use as originally granted. B's entitlement will simply be converted into a *legal* interest rather than an *equitable* interest.

X to A and his heirs to the use of B and his heirs.

Because of the Statute of Uses, A's interest is transferred to B, and B becomes seised of the land. B holds the same entitlement as he did before. Before the Statute, B held an equitable fee simple. After the Statute, B's entitlement becomes a legal rather than an equitable estate. B thus acquires a legal fee simple.

X to A and his heirs to the use of B for life and then the remainder to the use of C and her heirs.

Pursuant to the Statute, the use is executed and B acquires a legal life estate, and C acquires a legal vested remainder. B is seised of the land. Because C has a vested remainder, C's estate vests in interest at the time of the grant and will vest in possession upon B's death, at which time C will become seised of the land and liable for any incidents of tenure.

By this means, the Statute was able to "execute" the use and, for the moment, seal off the tax loophole that had permitted the evasion of the incidents of tenure. However, the tenacious use eventually survived this attempt at elimination, to reappear in an altered form known today as the *trust*.

Limits of the Statute of Uses

Before examining the evolution of the trust, it is necessary to consider in greater detail the impact of the Statute of Uses. The Statute did not eliminate all uses, and those that survived came in due course to be called trusts. First, the Statute only applies when one person (A) is *seised* to the use of another (B). If A is not seised of the land, but instead holds a leasehold estate, the use is not executed. A grant "to A for 999 years to the use of B for 999 years" is untouched by the Statute, and A will hold the land for the use of B for 999 years: Sinclair and McCallum, at 79.

Second, the Statute applies when any "person" (the feoffee to uses) is seised to the use of "any other person, or of any body politic." The term "body politic" refers to corporations, legally distinguishing them from individuals. In describing the feoffee to uses, the Statute does not include the term "body politic." Consequently, the Statute does not apply and the use is not executed where the feoffee to uses is a corporation. A grant "to A corporation for the use of B in fee simple" is thus unaffected by the Statute. The corporation remains seised of the land and retains the legal title in fee simple, holding the land to the use of B. B acquires an equitable estate in fee simple. By contrast, where a corporation is the *cestui que use* and seisin is in an individual, the use is executed.

The Statute can also be avoided if the feoffee to uses is given active duties to perform in the grant. Judicial interpretation limited the Statute to "bare uses" only, where the feoffees to uses had no obligations other than to hold seisin: *Romanes v. Smith* (1880), 8 PR 323 (Ch.D). Bare uses were likely regarded as merely a sham to evade the incidents of tenure and an appropriate target for the Statute. By contrast, if the feoffee has to manage the property and pay profits to the *cestui que use*, the separation of legal and equitable title is untouched by the Statute. Without legal title, feoffees to uses would be unable to fulfill their responsibilities. This exception remains important to this day. Modern trust documents often employ language that might seem to invite the application of the Statute, such as "to my trustees, to hold on trust for A, B, and C." Typically, such trust documents require the trustees to maintain or manage the property in some respect. These active duties prevent such trusts from being executed by the Statute: Ziff, at 185.

Finally, the Statute does not apply to personal property, including stocks, bonds, money, and other commercial instruments. The reforms of 1535 relate to interests in land only, and the Statute does not execute trusts relating to personal property. This exception remains relevant in contemporary times. In a capitalist economy, personal property has largely replaced real property as the primary source of economic security and power, and as such it is frequently the subject matter of modern trusts.

The Statute of Uses and Legal Executory Interests

Before the Statute of Uses, property owners were able to create equitable executory interests in land—that is, equitable shifting and springing interests—by employing a single use in a conveyance to uses. On the other hand, in a common law conveyance, shifting and springing interests were prohibited by the common law remainder rules. Following the Statute of Uses, the courts of common law had to decide what to do with the equitable executory interests that had been created before the Statute in a conveyance to uses:

X to A and his heirs to the use of B at 21. (B is 19.)

Before the Statute of Uses, A acquired a legal fee simple and was seised of the land. B acquired an equitable executory springing interest that would vest in interest and possession when B turned 21, at which time B would acquire an equitable fee simple. The grantor retained a resulting use in the form of an equitable fee simple defeasible upon B attaining 21. After the Statute of Uses, the use is now executed. Seisin passes from A to B, and according to the words of the Statute, B is seised of the same interest in the same "quality, manner, form and condition, as he had before." As a result, the Statute forced the common law courts to recognize that B holds the same interest that he held before (an executory interest), even if that type of interest was otherwise not permitted in a simple common law conveyance. B thus acquires a *legal* executory interest that will spring up on attaining 21. X retains a *legal* fee simple defeasible upon B attaining 21.

Of course, it is not possible in a simple common law conveyance to create an interest that will spring up in the future. However, if there is a single conveyance to uses that is executed by the Statute, the previously equitable executory interest held by B is converted into a legal interest (reluctantly) recognized by the common law courts. Following the Statute of Uses, it became possible for the first time to create executory interests in land recognized and enforced by the common law courts:

> X to A and his heirs to the use of B and his heirs, but if B marries C, then to the use of D and his heirs.

Before the Statute of Uses, A was seised of the land and held a legal fee simple. B held an equitable fee simple with a gift over of an equitable shifting executory interest to C, contingent on B marrying C. In equity, B's interest can also be described as a equitable fee simple "with a gift over" to D if B married C. After the Statute of Uses, A's interest is now executed. B acquires a *legal* fee simple subject to a *legal* shifting executory interest in fee simple (a gift over) to D if B marries C.

The Rule in Purefoy v. Rogers

Unfortunately, the legal remainder rules were not completely ousted by employing a conveyance to uses that was executed by the Statute. There remained one critical and knotty exception, known as the rule in *Purefoy v. Rogers* (1671), 85 ER 1181. The rule applied to contingent remainders contained in a conveyance to uses:

> X to A and his heirs to the use of B for life and then to B's first child to attain 21 years of age. (B has no children.)

Because of the Statute, A's interest is executed, and B acquires a legal life estate. The remainder interest is contingent because the remainderperson is unascertained (not yet born) and the remainder is also subject to a condition precedent (not yet 21). This contingent remainder will vest in interest when the first child attains 21, and vest in possession upon B's death. Of course, this contingent remainder may not vest in interest during the prior particular estate, if this first child does not turn 21 during B's life. In a common law conveyance, a contingent remainder that fails to vest during the prior particular estate (a springing interest) is void. If this interest fails to vest in time, the first child's interest can only take effect, if at all, as an executory springing interest when the child turns 21 after B's death.

As a result of the operation of the Statute, the common law courts were required to permit and enforce a broad range of legal executory interests. However, the common law courts took a more restrictive view when it came to contingent remainders. According to the rule in *Purefoy v. Rogers*, if a legal executory interest can comply with the common law remainder rules, it must. In other words, a legal executory interest will be void if it can comply with the common law remainder rules, but fails to do so. As a result, in the above grant, the first child's interest must vest in interest during B's life— that is, this child must turn 21 while B is still alive. If the child fails to do so, this interest *cannot* take effect as a legal executory interest, because this is an executory interest that *could have* complied with the common law remainder rules, but failed to do so. Where an executory interest could not comply with the remainder rules, the common law courts would permit it to take effect as a legal executory interest. In a grant, "to A and his heirs to the use of B at 21" (B is 15), the grant to B cannot comply with the remainder rules. It can only take effect as an executory springing interest, and the common law courts would permit it to do so because the Statute of Uses required that B would hold the same entitlement as before the Statute. But if a contingent remainder could comply with the common law remainder rules, the common law courts required that it do so in order to take effect.

In short, according to the rule in *Purefoy v. Rogers*, in a grant "to A and his heirs to the use of B for life and then to B's first child to attain 21 years of age," the first child's contingent remainder must vest in interest during B's life, or the interest will be void. Notwithstanding the fact that this grant is included in a conveyance to uses, the first child's interest can never take effect as a legal executory interest springing up after B's death.

To avoid the application of this troublesome rule, the grantor needs only to include the following italicized words:

X to A and his heirs to the use of B for life, and then to the use of B's first child to attain 21 *either before or after B's death.*

In this case, this grant may not comply with the remainder rules. This grant expressly contemplates that there may be a gap between the termination of the prior particular estate (B's life estate) and the vesting in interest of the contingent remainder. Contained in a common law conveyance, the contingent remainder interest would fail if it does not vest in interest during B's life. The common law adopted a "wait and see" attitude. If the contingent remainder vests in time, it is valid. However, if it does not, the interest fails because there can be no abeyance of seisin in a common law conveyance. Accordingly, the rule in *Purefoy v. Rogers* does not apply to this grant because this grant contemplates an executory springing interest that *cannot* comply with the remainder rules: *Re Lechmere and Lloyd* (1881), 18 Ch.D 524. If necessary, the child's interest can take effect as a legal executory interest. If B dies before the child turns 21, the child's interest will take effect as a legal executory interest springing up upon attaining 21. On the other hand, if the child turns 21 during B's life, the child's interest will vest in interest, and this legal vested remainder will vest in possession upon B's death.

Exercise 8: Conveyances to Uses (After the Statute of Uses (1535))

The Operation of the Statute of Uses (1535)

Where one person (A) is seised to the use of another person or body politic (B), the Statute of Uses provides that the legal interest held by A is executed, A's legal interest is given to B, B is seised of the land, and B holds the same entitlement that B held previously. Common law conveyances (conveyances that do not employ a use) are unaffected by the Statute and remain subject to the common law remainder rules that prohibit shifting and springing interest. Note that in a conveyance to uses, once the use is executed, B will hold the same entitlement that B held previously. If, before the use is executed, B held an equitable executory interest (a springing or shifting interest) under the conveyance to uses, B will continue to hold that same interest once the use has been executed. Although executory interests cannot be created in a simple common law conveyance (because of the common law remainder rules), executory interests recognized and enforced at common law (*legal* executory interests) can be created where a conveyance to uses has been executed by the Statute. As a result, once the use is executed, B's equitable executory interest will simply be converted into a *legal* executory interest. There is, however, one exception contained in the rule in *Purefoy v. Rogers*, dealing with contingent remainders—if the legal executory interest *can* comply with the common law remainder rules, it *must*.

Identify the interests created in each grant below before the Statute of Uses. Then consider the effect that the Statute has on the grant. In particular, identify any legal executory interests that are created by the operation of the Statute, as well as any interest that might be retained by the grantor.

Grant or devise	Analysis
1. X to B and his heirs: Pre-1535	
Post-1535	
2. X to A and his heirs to the use of B and his heirs: Pre-1535	
Post-1535	
3. X to B and his heirs when B is 21 (B is 19 at the time of the grant): Pre-1535	
Post-1535	

Grant or devise	Analysis
4. X to A and his heirs to the use of B and his heirs when B is 21 (B is 19 years old at the time of the grant): Pre-1535	
Post-1535	
5. X to B and his heirs, but if B marries C, then to D and his heirs: Pre-1535	
Post-1535	
6. X to A and his heirs to the use of B and his heirs, but if B marries C, then to the use of D and his heirs: Pre-1535	
Post-1535	
7. X to A and his heirs to the use of B for life and then the remainder to B's first child to marry. Hint: consider what happens if this first child does not marry during B's life. Pre-1535	
Post-1535	

Limits to the Statute of Uses (1535)

Recall that the Statute did not execute a use when (1) the feoffee to uses held only a leasehold estate, (2) the feoffee to uses is a corporation, and (3) when the feoffee to uses has active duties to perform with respect to the property. In these cases, the split between the legal and equitable interest, known today as a trust, remained unaffected by the Statute. Examine the following grants. What interests are created? Does the Statute execute the use in question? If not, why not?

Grant or devise	Analysis
1. X to B corporation to the use of A and his heirs.	
2. X to A and his heirs to the use of B corporation.	
3. X to A for 10 years to the use of B and his heirs.	
4. X to A to collect rents and income from the property to the use of B.	

The Statute of Uses (1535) and Testamentary Dispositions

Before the Statute of Uses, a conveyance to uses was the only way to make a testamentary disposition of land, as landowners had no general right to designate their heir upon death. As described earlier, the grantor simply conveyed his land to the use of the feoffee to uses, and the feoffee agreed to hold the land for the grantor and whomever the grantor designated to take the land upon his death. This was the only way that a landowner could make a testamentary disposition, making the use such a popular legal device. The Statute of Uses was generally regarded as having eliminated this power to make testamentary dispositions, leading to widespread protest by landowners. As a result, five years after the enactment of the Statute of Uses, Henry VIII agreed to the passage of the Statute of Wills (1540), 32 Hen. 8, c. 1, giving landowners for the first time the power to devise their lands at their "free will and pleasure." As noted earlier, the common law courts tended to interpret broadly this new testamentary power of disposition, finding that it was not necessary to use the magic words "and heirs" to devise a fee simple estate.

Similarly, the courts of common law determined that devises do not need to comply with the common law remainder rules, thus permitting the creation of legal executory interests in a devise: *Pells v. Brown* (1620), 79 ER 504. For example, in a devise "to A at 21," if A is 15 at the time of the testator's death, A's interest simply takes effect as a springing executory devise that will spring up when A turns 21. The testator's estate retains a legal fee simple defeasible to A if and when A turns 21. In short, the common law rules that prohibit springing interests do not apply to devises. Similarly, in a devise "to A, but if B marries, then to B," A acquires a legal fee simple subject to a legal shifting executory interest in fee simple (a gift over) to B if and when B marries. The common law rules that prohibit shifting interests do not apply to devises.

There remains some question about whether the rule in *Purefoy v. Rogers* applies to testamentary gifts. English case law suggests that it does not (*Re Robson*, [1916] 1 Ch. 116); however, a 1984 Ontario case suggests otherwise: *Re Crow* (1984), 48 OR (2d) 36, 12 DLR (4th) 415 (HC). See Ziff, at 233-34. The fact that devises now pass as equitable interests, as discussed below, may render this point moot.

It is critical to distinguish a devise from a simple common law conveyance. A devise does not need to comply with the common law remainder rules, so it is possible to create shifting and springing interests in a devise without employing a use. On the other hand, it is not possible to create shifting or springing interests in a simple common law conveyance that does not employ a use.

The Statute of Uses and Conveyancing

The Statute of Uses fundamentally altered conveyancing practices. Before 1535, legal title to a freehold estate in possession was conveyed by the ancient practice of livery of seisin. The Statute allowed landowners to evade this requirement. By a method known as "bargain and sale," the vendor would agree to transfer property to B for a stated price. Upon payment, an equity in favour of the purchaser was raised, and the Statute would operate, taking legal title from the vendor and passing it to the purchaser. Legal title was thereby transferred without any public livery of seisin. As examined in chapter 5, the modern deed of land as the mode of conveying title to land can be traced to this development.

Exhausting the Operation of the Statute of Uses

As discussed above, the Statute of Uses did not apply to all conveyances to uses. For example, a grant "to A corporation to the use of B" was unaffected by the Statute. The corporation acquired legal fee simple and B acquired an equitable fee simple. It was thereby possible to continue to create equitable interests in property, and avoid the common law remainder rules, even after the passage of the Statute.

About 150 years after the passage of the Statute, other means were developed to avoid its operation, making it possible once again to create equitable interests in property without difficulty, merely by the inclusion of a few words in any grant. In the early years after the passage of the Statute, neither the common law courts nor the chancellor would enforce what was known as a "use upon a use."

X to A and his heirs to the use of B and her heirs to the use of C and his heirs.

The legal interest held by A was executed by the Statute, and B acquired legal fee simple as well as the equitable interest B already held. C took nothing, as there was nothing left for C: *Tyrrel's Case* (1557), 73 ER 336. However, after the passage of the Tenures Abolition Act (1660), which converted all tenures into free and common socage, the Crown lost its claim to the various incidents of tenure. The Statute of Uses had been enacted originally to prevent the evasion of the incidents of tenure, and this rationale no longer applied. Accordingly, the courts of equity began to interpret the above grant as giving a legal fee simple to B and moving the equitable fee simple to C.

This practice began in the mid-1600s and was firmly established by 1700: *Symsom v. Turner* (1700), 1 Eq. Cas. Abr. 383. The Statute executed the first use, passing legal title to B. The operation of the Statute was thereby "exhausted" and the Statute did not execute the second use of the fee simple to C (the "use upon a use"). C thus acquired an equitable interest in fee simple, and this interest came to be known as a trust. Simply describing C's interest as a trust, however, is not sufficient to evade the Statute. In a grant "to B in trust for C," the trust is still executed because the Statute applies to any "use, confidence or trust." In law, there is no difference between a use and a trust; however, in practice "use" is reserved for uses executed by the Statute, and "trust" is used for interests that remain equitable.

It is also important not to confuse the distinction between a use *upon* a use, and a use *after* a use. The Statute is only exhausted by a use upon a use. A use *after* a use arises in a grant "to A and her heirs to the use of B for life and then to the use of C and his heirs." In this grant, the use is executed, B acquires a legal life estate and C acquires a legal vested remainder. It is described as a use *after* a use because the use in favour of B is followed by a remainder use in favour of C. A use *upon* a use only arises when there is a use of a *fee simple* on a use of a *fee simple*—"to A and her heirs, to the use of B and his heirs, in trust for C and her heirs." In this grant, the use upon a use (A's use upon B's use) exhausts the Statute, giving to C an equitable estate. In short, the Statute is only exhausted by successive uses of a fee simple.

This development was further refined by the invention of a compressed version of the following:

X unto B and his heirs to the use of B and his heirs in trust for C and her heirs.

In this case, B is seised to his own use, and the Statute does not apply where a person is seised to his own use. The words of the Statute require that one person be seised to the use of *another*, not himself. Accordingly, the first use is not executed and B retains legal title in the above grant. The trust given to C is also not executed by the Statute, because according to the practice described above, the courts of equity determined that the Statute does not execute a use upon a use. The language was then compressed as follows:

X unto and to the use of B in trust for C.

The simple addition of the phrase "unto and to the use of" had the effect of evading the Statute, making it once again possible to create equitable interests in property, much as had been the case before the Statute. This phrase can be further truncated "to the use of B in trust for C," giving B legal fee simple and C an equitable fee simple. However, the simple grant "to B in trust for C" does not successfully create separate legal and equitable estates, as the Statute will apply in this case, executing the use and giving to C legal fee simple.

This critical development laid the groundwork for the modern trust. Although the historical rationale for the Statute of Uses has long since become an anachronism, the Statute, as part of the received law in the common law provinces of Canada, continues in effect and remains fundamental to an understanding of how a trust can be created. Without an understanding of the Statute, it is impossible to understand why a grant "to A for 99 years in trust for C" will create a trust, but a grant "to A in trust for B" will not. Similarly, it is impossible to understand why a grant "to the use of A in trust for B" will create a trust, but a grant "to A to the use of B" will not. The distinctions are difficult to understand and frustrating for the novice. But they remain basic to any understanding of common law property in Canada, ready to catch the unwary drafter of legal documents.

The Statute of Uses was abolished in England in 1925 as part of a package of property law reforms: Law of Property Act, 1925 (UK), 15 & 16 Geo. 5, c. 20, Sched. 7. These reforms essentially prohibit the creation of legal future estates. See, generally, Megarry and Wade, at 123-40. In brilliant simplicity, the legislation provides that, after 1925, only two kinds of legal estates can exist in England—the fee simple absolute in possession, and the lease. All other interests, including any future interests, can only be created as equitable interests, and this can be done simply by appointing a trustee who will hold the legal fee simple in trust for various beneficiaries. Because there can be no legal future interests, the common law remainder rules are no longer relevant in England. Moreover, because there can be no legal executory interests, annoying exceptions like the rule in *Purefoy v. Rogers* are now only a historical curiosity. The only future interests that can be created are *equitable* future interests, and because equity has always freely permitted the creation of springing and shifting interests, all the problems associated with legal future interests, and the ancient and obsolete concern with seisin, were rendered irrelevant in one clean sweep. Finally, with the repeal of the Statute of Uses, the complexities regarding the precise words necessary to create a trust, and the necessity to avoid an inadvertent application of this ancient statute, are no longer of contemporary concern in England. The words "to A in fee simple in trust for B in fee simple" are all that is required to create a trust in England today. There is no need to use the ancient convention "unto and to the use of A in fee simple in trust for B in fee simple." See Megarry and Wade, at 1175. By contrast, such words as "to A in trust for B" in most of the common law provinces of Canada will still evoke the Statute of Uses, executing the use and conveying legal title to B.

Similar reform has taken place in Manitoba where legal future interests have also been abolished: Perpetuities and Accumulations Act, SM 1982-83, c. 43. It is regrettable that no similar reform has taken place in the other common law provinces in Canada. There may be little incentive for reform, because the complexities associated with legal future interests can be easily avoided. Grantors need only employ a trust, thereby creating equitable future interests that are immune from the ancient rules relating to legal future interests. Nonetheless, the law relating to legal future interests in land remains relevant. It is still possible in most of common law Canada to create legal future interests.

As long as that is the case, these ancient rules will continue to haunt Canadian property law, imposing an onerous obligation on law students and lawyers to remain familiar with these ancient feudal rules.

Future Interests Under Wills

As discussed above, after landowners first acquired the power to devise land pursuant to the Statute of Wills (1540), 31 Hen. 8, c. 1, the common law courts determined that devises did not need to comply with the common law remainder rules. It was therefore possible to create executory interests in a devise without employing a use or a trust, and such devises came to be known as springing and shifting devises. Modern devolution of estates legislation also creates a statutory trust in favour of the beneficiaries by specifying that the personal representative holds the estate's property in trust for the beneficiaries. For example, section 2(1) of the Ontario Estates Administration Act, RSO 1990, c. E.22 provides:

> 2.(1) All real and personal property that is vested in a person without a right in any other person to take by survivorship, on the person's death, whether testate or intestate and despite any testamentary disposition, devolves to and becomes vested in his or her personal representative from time to time as trustee for the persons by law beneficially entitled thereto, and, subject to the payment of the person's debts and so far as such property is not disposed of by deed, will, contract or other effectual disposition, it shall be administered, dealt with and distributed as if it were personal property not so disposed of.

The comparable section in English law has been held to have the effect of converting any and all legal interests in a will into equitable interests, thus protecting these interests from any of the rules relating to legal future interests, including the common law remainder rules and the rule in *Purefoy v. Rogers*: *Re Robson*, [1916] 1 Ch. 116. Moreover, *Re Robson* also held that interests in a will do not become subject to destruction when the personal representative conveys the interests to the beneficiaries, at which time these interests become legal rather than equitable. Although *Re Robson* has not been expressly adopted by a Canadian court, it is likely that it would be found persuasive. Nonetheless, there is one Canadian case where the court did not apparently consider *Re Robson* and appears to take an approach inconsistent with it: *Re Crow* (1984), 48 OR (2d) 36, 12 DLR (4th) 415 (HC). *Re Robson* has also been rendered academic in jurisdictions, such as England, that have abolished legal future interests.

Devises must, therefore, be distinguished from common law conveyances. Executory interests can be created in a devise, even without employing a use or a trust. A devise "to B at 21" (B is 15) will take effect as a springing devise for at least two reasons. First, the common law remainder rules do not apply to devises, and second, pursuant to devolution of estates legislation, the personal representative holds the estate in trust for B, which likely has the effect of transforming B's interest into an equitable executory springing interest. By contrast, a simple common law conveyance "to B at 21" (B is 15) is void and will never take because it is a future interest that is not supported by a prior particular estate of freehold.

Exercise 9: The Modern Trust

Notwithstanding the Statute of Uses (1535), by the mid-17th century, it became possible once again to create equitable interests in property without difficulty, by the simple inclusion of a few additional words in the grant. In a critical development, the courts of equity determined that the Statute of Uses did not execute a "use upon a use." Accordingly, in a grant "to A and his heirs to the use of B and his heirs in trust for C and her heirs," legal title passed from A to B pursuant to the Statute, but the use upon a use to C survived the Statute, giving to C an equitable fee simple. This grant was further simplified "to B and his heirs to the use of B and his heirs in trust for C and her heirs," and then contracted "unto and to the use of B in trust for C" or "to the use of B in trust for C." The Statute does not execute the first use to B, because the Statute only executes a use to another person, not a use to the same person. The second use to C is also not executed, because the Statute does not execute a use upon a use. Accordingly, B acquires legal fee simple and C acquires an equitable fee simple. The simple inclusion of "unto and to the use of B," or more simply, "to the use of B," is sufficient to evade the operation of the Statute of Uses, permitting the easy creation of equitable interests in property, much as was the case before the Statute of Uses. Moreover, the common law remainder rules do not, of course, apply to equitable interests in property, making it possible to create shifting and springing (executory) interests in equity.

The following examples illustrate how trusts are created today. Recall that the Statute of Uses did not execute all uses, and the effect of the Statute can also be evaded by employing a use upon a use. Examine the grants or devises below. Is there a split between legal and equitable interests? Why? Does the grant or devise create springing or shifting interests? If so, are they valid? Recall as well the crucial distinction between grants and devises. Executory interests can be created in a devise, even without employing a trust or a use. Early on, the common law courts determined that the common law remainder rules do not apply to devises. In more modern times, all devises also likely take effect as equitable interests because of the application of devolution of estates legislation, such as s. 2 of the Ontario Estates Administration Act, RSO 1990, c. E.22. Accordingly, the rules governing legal future interests do not apply to devises, thus permitting springing or shifting devises.

Grant or devise	Analysis
1. X unto and to the use of A in fee simple in trust for B in fee simple.	
2. X to Guaranty Trust Inc. in fee simple in trust for A in fee simple.	
3. X to A in fee simple to collect the rents and profits for the benefit of B in fee simple.	

Grant or devise	Analysis
4. X to the use of my trustees in trust for my wife for life and after her death for the benefit of my child Janice on her graduation from law school.	
5. X unto and to the use of my trustee in trust for my son James but if he becomes a lawyer then in trust for my nephew Mark.	
6. X to the Royal Trust Inc. in trust for my daughter Diana for life, but if she is not married by age 30, then in trust for my niece Hilda in fee simple.	
7. X devises to Anne when she is 25-years old. (Anne is 10-years old at the time of the testator's death.)	
8. X devises to John in fee simple, but if he renounces his Canadian citizenship, then to Hannah.	
9. X devises to Mary for life, and the remainder to Mary's children who attain 21 years of age. (At the time of X's death, Mary has two children, 22- and 19-years old respectively.)	

The Modern Trust

Equitable estates in property continue to flourish in Canadian law, with some changes in terminology. The ancient "feoffee to uses" is now generally referred to as the trustee, and the *cestui que use* is now referred to as the beneficiary of the trust. As noted above, although in law there is no difference between a use and a trust, in practice "use" is now generally reserved for uses executed by the Statute, and "trust" is used for interests that remain equitable. Just as in feudal times, the trust continues to be used to provide for children or dependent adults, shield property from taxation, and create executory interests that are not valid at common law.

Trusts are usually created expressly by a grant or devise, and there is a great deal of law on the question of the required formalities; the correct constitution of the trust; and the rights, responsibilities, and powers of the trustees. Trustees are also fiduciaries at law, imposing on them an obligation to act in good faith and in the best interests of the beneficiary of the trust. A fiduciary obligation is generally imposed in equity whenever one person reposes confidence in another person with the expectation that this person will act for his or her benefit. Fiduciary relationships can arise even in the absence of any express trust agreement, such as between a solicitor and his or her client, and a principal and his or her agent. The law governing trusts is generally considered beyond the scope of the study of property law and is instead covered in texts and courses dealing specifically with trust law.

Trusts may also arise in the absence of any express intention, as is the case with the *resulting trust* and the *constructive trust*. As described above, a resulting trust arises whenever the beneficial interest under a trust has not been fully disposed of, in which case there will be a resulting trust in favour of the grantor or, if deceased, the grantor's estate. A resulting trust may also arise in some cases where there has been a gratuitous transfer of property from the transferor to the transferee. If there is insufficient evidence that the transferor intended to make a gift of the property, the law will impose a resulting trust on the transferee in favour of the transferor, requiring the transferee to hold that property in trust for the transferor. The law has a general presumption against a finding of gift and assumes that the transferor, as a rationale economic being, did not intend to give beneficial ownership to the transferee unless there is sufficient evidence to the contrary. These issues are examined in greater detail in chapter 5.

A constructive trust may be imposed in equity where there is no intention to create an express trust, and no presumption of a resulting trust because there has generally been no transfer of property. Instead, the trust is imposed on the parties as a broad and flexible means to prevent unjust enrichment. Equity may impose a constructive trust where (1) a non-titled party has contributed money or labour to the acquisition or maintenance of property held by the titled party; (2) a non-titled party has thereby enriched the titled party; (3) this enrichment has resulted in a corresponding deprivation to the non-titled party; and (4) there is no juristic reason for this enrichment. See, generally, *Pettkus v. Becker*, [1980] SCR 834; 117 DLR (3d) 257; *Sorochan v. Sorochan*, [1986] 2 SCR 38; 29 DLR (4th) 1; and *Peter v. Beblow*, [1993] 1 SCR 980. These facts most commonly arise in family settings, and the constructive trust has been extensively employed in property disputes between unmarried cohabitants. A further discussion of constructive trusts is found in chapter 7.

The question of trust law also arises in the context of native lands. In particular, there has been considerable legal debate about whether native reserves are held in an express trust by the federal Crown as trustee on behalf of the native occupants. As discussed at the beginning of this chapter, through the negotiation of treaties, a native band might agree to surrender to the federal Crown its claim to native title in exchange for certain reserve lands and other various benefits. The Crown then holds the reserve lands for the native band, raising the question of the nature and extent of the Crown's powers and obligations with respect to native reserves. Before the decision in *Guerin v. The Queen*, [1984] 2 SCR 335, it was unclear whether the Crown held this land in an express trust for the native community, with the native community holding an equitable interest in the reserve land. The precise nature of the interest retained by the native community had not yet been determined.

In *Guerin*, the trial judge concluded that the Crown held the land as trustee, and further found that the Crown had breached its obligation as trustee when it entered into a lease of certain reserve lands on terms less favourable than had been approved by the band. On appeal, the Federal Court of Appeal held that the Crown was not a trustee of reserve lands, there being an absence of a clear intention to create a trust or impose an equitable obligation on the Crown. Instead, the Court of Appeal held that the federal Crown had only a "governmental" or political responsibility to the native band. On further appeal, the Supreme Court agreed that the federal Crown was not a trustee of the native reserve, finding that there was insufficient evidence of any intention to create an express trust. The court also suggested that the nature of the natives' interest in the property, whatever it might be, was insufficient to form the property interests of a trust. Nonetheless, the Supreme Court held that the Crown was under an equitable obligation to deal with the land for the benefit of the natives, arising from the Crown's fiduciary duty, and not merely a "governmental" responsibility. This fiduciary duty was imposed on the ground that the Crown had an equitable obligation to act in good faith and in the best interests of the native occupants. Finding that the Crown was in breach of its fiduciary duty when it entered into the disputed lease, the Supreme Court restored the trial judge's award of damages.

The decision in *Guerin* reflects the ongoing debate in Canadian law regarding the nature of native title, both on and off reserve lands. Frequently described by the courts as *sui generis* (of its own kind or class), the courts generally do not characterize native title as the equivalent of common law or equitable interests in land. *Guerin* indicates the Supreme Court's reluctance to characterize the native interest in reserve land as an equitable interest with the Crown as trustee. Instead, the court imposed an equitable obligation on the Crown through other means, by imposing a fiduciary duty on the Crown. See R. Bartlett, "The Fiduciary Obligation of the Crown to the Indians" (1989), 53 *Saskatchewan Law Review* 303 for a critique of the Supreme Court's decision in *Guerin*.

The Rule Against Perpetuities

Future interests enable property owners to determine who may enjoy property at some point in the future and on what conditions. This power gives to property owners the right to control the use and ownership of property long into the future, enabling the "far-reaching hand of the testator" to enforce his or her will on future distant generations. Although permitting property owners considerable power to create future interests, the law has long taken the view that such future interests should at some point be cut off. Future interests restrict the alienability of land, potentially tying up the land for many generations and reducing its value by making it effectively inalienable. It is difficult to sell land subject to potential future interests, and the owners of such land are unlikely to invest much in its maintenance or development. Having a depressed market value, such land can fall into disuse and disrepair. The law has long attempted to strike a balance between the interests of current property owners, who seek to control future entitlement to the land, and future property owners, who will need sufficient powers of alienation over the land, to ensure that it will not fall into disuse or disrepair.

The rule against perpetuities is designed to strike this balance, permitting a wide variety of future interests, yet at some point determining that further future interests will not be permitted. The common law remainder rules already set some limits on the period of time during which future interests can arise in a common law conveyance, particularly the rule regarding timely vesting. Because a contingent remainder in a common law conveyance must vest during the prior particular estate, these remainders generally vest, if at all, at a point not too distant in the future. However, the combined effect of the Statute of Uses (1535) and the Statute of Wills (1540) was to bring into existence a whole new range of executory interests immune from the time restrictions in the common law remainder rules. These executory interests could arise at very distant points in the future:

> X devises to B for life and then to B's grandchildren who marry before or after B's death.

Because this is a devise, the common law remainder rules do not apply. In a simple common law conveyance, B's grandchildren would have to marry during B's life to take any remainder interest, thus solving any problem about future interests that are unreasonably remote. However, in a devise, the remainder interest can take effect as an executory interest springing up after B's death. It is possible that this executory interest could arise well over a century after B's death. X may die when B is an infant. B may live 70 years and have a 20-year-old child when he dies. This child may marry 30 years later, producing a child (B's grandchild) who in turn marries 50 years later. Without any rule limiting future interests, this land could remain, for 150 years or more, subject to this executory interest that might spring up at any time, significantly reducing the market value and utility of the land during this entire period.

With the introduction of executory interests, pressure mounted to develop some common law rules that would prohibit future interests that arise at points too remote in time. Thus developed the rule against perpetuities, more or less finally settled in place by the end of the 17th century (the rule is usually traced to the *Duke of Norfolk's Case* (1685), 3 Ch. Ca. 1). The rationale behind the rule against perpetuities—the efficient and productive use of land—is easy to grasp. The operation of the rule itself is notoriously complex. The basic common law rule can be stated as follows:

> An interest must vest in interest, if at all, within the perpetuity period. This period is calculated by taking the lives in being at the date that the instrument takes effect, plus 21 years.

(Ziff, at 235.)

Although it can be succinctly stated, the rule's apparent simplicity is deceptive. In the famous case, *Lucas v. Hamn*, 364 P 2d 685 (Cal. SC 1961), an attorney's failure to understand the impact of this rule upon a testamentary instrument he had drafted was determined not to be below the standard of conduct of the ordinary practitioner. As a result, the attorney was able to avoid civil liability for his error. Whether an ordinary practitioner under Canadian law could so easily evade liability is an open question. Rather than test this point, Canadian practitioners are well advised to remain familiar with the rule of perpetuities and its subtle traps for the incautious.

The basic common law rule has also been modified in most common law jurisdictions by statutory intervention. However, most of the current statutory provisions continue to use the common law process for determining the length of the perpetuity period that will apply to any given contingent interest. For this reason, it is essential to understand the common law rule before considering how it has been modified by statute.

"An Interest Must Vest"

The rule against perpetuities applies to almost all *contingent interests* in property, real or personal, legal or equitable. The distinction between "vesting in interest" and "vesting in possession" has already been discussed, as well as the distinction between contingent and vested remainders. Contingent interests are future interests that have not yet vested in interest, and include contingent remainders and executory interests. A future interest is contingent if the person entitled to take the interest has not yet been ascertained (A's widow while A is still alive); is not yet in existence (A's first born child when no child has yet been born); or if this interest is subject to a condition precedent (to B if A should divorce). By contrast, future interests are vested in interest if the remainderperson is ascertained, in existence, and the remainder interest is not subject to a condition precedent. Such interests are not subject to the rule against perpetuities because, being already vested in interest, they will not vest in interest at some remote time in the future. Contingent interests are the focus of the rule against perpetuities, because these interests, particularly executory interests, can arise at very remote points in the future, placing an enduring cloud over title to land.

The rule against perpetuities applied to most, but not all, contingent interests. In particular, at common law, the rule did not apply to a possibility of reverter, as illustrated earlier in *Re Tilbury West Public School Board and Hastie*, [1966] 2 OR 20; 55 DLR (2d) 407 (HCJ). As discussed earlier, the possibility of reverter was regarded as a vested interest and not, therefore, subject to the rule against perpetuities. The rule did, however, apply to the right of entry for condition broken. The distinction appears anomalous because both interests can arise at remote future dates. In the grant of a determinable fee simple, "to A as long as the land is used for agricultural purposes," the possibility of reverter may not arise for centuries. Nonetheless, at common law it was immune from the rule against perpetuities. This has now been changed in all common law provinces. Possibilities of reverter are now subject to the rule against perpetuities as modified by statute. See Oosterhoff and Rayner, at 548. For example, in Ontario, the Perpetuities Act, RSO 1990, c. P.9, s. 15 provides:

> 15(1) In the case of,
>> (a) a possibility of reverter on the determination of a determinable fee simple;
> or

(b) a possibility of a resulting trust on the determination of any determinable
interest in property,

the rule against perpetuities as modified by this Act applies in relation to the provision
causing the interest to be determinable as it would apply if that provision were
expressed in the form of a condition subsequent giving rise on its breach to a right of re-
entry or an equivalent right in the case of personal property, and, where the event that
determines the determinable interest does not occur within the perpetuity period, the
provision shall be treated as void for remoteness and the determinable interest becomes
an absolute interest.

(2) In the case of a possibility of reverter on the determination of a determinable
fee simple, or in the case of a possibility of a resulting trust on the determination of any
determinable interest in any property, or in the case of a right of re-entry following on a
condition subsequent, or in the case of an equivalent right in personal property, the
perpetuity period shall be measured as if the event determining the prior interest were a
condition to the vesting of the subsequent interest, and failing any life in being at the
time the interests were created that limits or is a relevant factor that limits in some way
the period within which that event may take place, the perpetuity period is twenty-one
years from the time when the interests were created.

(3) Even though some life or lives in being may be relevant in determining the
perpetuity period under subsection (2), the perpetuity period for the purposes of this
section shall not exceed a period of forty years from the time when the interests were
created and shall be the lesser of a period of forty years and a period composed of the
relevant life or lives in being and twenty-one years.

"If at All"

Some contingent future interests will never vest in interest. If B never has children, a
contingent interest to B's first born will never vest in interest or possession. However, if
the interest ever does vest, it must comply with the rule against perpetuities. This qualification reflects the cardinal doctrine of the rule against perpetuities at common law. The
rule is concerned with what *may* happen, not what *does* happen. For example, under the
common law remainder rules, a "wait and see" principle is applied to the rule regarding
timely vesting. Although the contingent remainder may vest in interest after the termination of the prior particular estate and thus be void, the "wait and see" principle provides
that the common law court will wait and see if the contingent remainder vests in time. If
it does, it will be valid. If it does not, the remainder interest will never take effect.

In their dislike of remote future interests, the common law courts displayed no such
patience when the rule against perpetuities was developed. Instead, the common law
courts examined the *inter vivos* grant at the time at which it was executed, or the devise
at the moment of the testator's death. If at this moment there was *any* possibility, no
matter how unlikely or ludicrous, that the contingent interest might vest outside the
relevant perpetuity period, the contingent interest would be void *ab initio*. Even if the
contingent interest did, on the facts of a particular case, actually vest well within the
perpetuity period, the interest would still never take effect. The no "wait and see" rule
had the virtue of certainty because from the moment the gift took effect, it was possible

to determine whether the contingent interest violated the rule against perpetuities and was void *ab initio*. If void, this contingent interest would be struck down immediately and would not operate as a cloud over the title during any "wait and see" period. However, this rule also had the unfortunate effect of invalidating many contingent interests that would, as it turned out, vest well within the perpetuity period. As examined below, this harsh feature of the common law rule against perpetuities has in most common law jurisdictions now been changed by statute by incorporating a "wait and see" principle in the law governing perpetuities.

"Within the Perpetuity Period"

According to the common law rule against perpetuities, contingent interests must vest within the perpetuity period, and if there is any possibility that a contingent interest might vest outside this period, the interest was void *ab initio* at common law. Thus far, the rule against perpetuities is fairly straightforward. The real difficulties arise when trying to determine the exact perpetuity period that applies to any specific gift. This period is calculated according to a formula that consists of the duration of all "lives in being" plus a period of 21 years. This particular time period was likely chosen because a typical family settlement would provide that interests given to grandchildren would only vest when they had reached the age of majority, which was 21 at that time. The perpetuity period does not have a fixed length but varies from one conveyance to another, depending on the relevant "lives in being" for any given conveyance. If there are no lives in being specified or implied in the gift, the perpetuity period is 21 years.

Any living person or persons may be used as lives in being. However, only those persons mentioned in the gift either *expressly* or by *implication* are taken into consideration when determining the applicable perpetuity period.

> X devises to my grandchildren who marry during the life of A or within 21 years of A's death.

Devises only take effect on the death of the testator. As a result, when analyzing the legal effect of any devise, one can always assume that the testator is deceased and is not a relevant life in being. However, in the above devise A is a life in being because A is alive and expressly mentioned in the grant. According to the terms of the devise, the contingent springing executory interest given to the grandchildren will arise only if the grandchildren marry during A's life plus 21 years. Because the contingent interest will vest, if at all, during the life of a "life in being" (A) plus 21 years, the contingent interest does not violate the rule against perpetuities. It does not matter that A takes nothing under the grant or is not related in any way to the beneficiaries under the devise.

Although less frequent, a life in being can also arise by implication.

> X devises to my grandchildren who attain 21.

Because X is deceased, X can have no further children. The lives of X's children alive at the time of the devise can help to confine the period of time during which this contingent interest to the grandchildren can vest. Their contingent interest will necessarily vest within 21 years of the death of any of X's children, for no grandchild can take longer than 21 years from its parent's death to reach the age of 21. Although not expressly mentioned, X's children are lives in being that are implied by this devise and can be used to determine the relevant perpetuity period. Because the contingent interests will necessarily vest during one of the lives of X's children plus 21 years, the contingent interests are good.

In an *inter vivos* trust, X could also grant his grandchildren an executory interest springing up at 21. However, in this case, because X is not deceased, the grandchildren's executory interest can now conceivably violate the perpetuity period:

> X to the use of my trustee in trust for my grandchildren who attain 21.

X may have another child (A) after the trust has been established and then, more than 21 years after the death of all those alive at the time of the grant, this child may have a child (B). In this case, B's contingent interest will not vest during the life of a "life in being" plus 21 years. At common law, if there were no grandchildren who were 21 at the time when the trust was created, the entire contingent interest would fail because it was possible, even if unlikely, that the contingent interest could violate the rule against perpetuities. Even if various grandchildren under 21 were alive at the time of the grant, and therefore certain to attain 21 years within their lifetime (if at all), their contingent remainder would still fail: *Boreham v. Bignall* (1850), 8 Hare 131. This example reflects the inflexibility of the common law rule. The common law did not apply any "wait and see" principle to this contingent interest. If at the outset it was possible to conceive of a series of events whereby the contingent interest might vest outside the perpetuity period, the entire contingent interest was void *ab initio*. Moreover, it did not matter how unlikely it was that the contingent interest might vest outside the perpetuity period. For example, it did not matter if X in the above trust was a widow well beyond childbearing years and therefore unlikely to have any more children.

Some common law rules of interpretation were developed to mitigate the harshness of the rule against perpetuities, particularly the "class closing" rules as reflected in *Andrews v. Partington* (1791), 29 ER 610. A gift might be saved from the rule against perpetuities if it is possible to close the class at a moment when it is certain that the interests of those members of the class who are included must vest in time. For example, in the above grant, if at the time of the execution of the trust, there is one grandchild who has attained 21, the class of potential takers is closed, pursuant to *Andrews*, above. This class includes this one grandchild as well as all grandchildren alive when the trust was executed. All such persons are lives in being, and their interest will vest, if at all, during their own lifetime. Any grandchildren born after the trust is executed will not take any interest.

Because the common law was only concerned with possibilities rather than probabilities, there were a number of common traps for the unwary. In the above example, although X might be an 80-year-old widow, the common law would still presume that she might give birth to more children after the trust was executed, a trap known as the "fertile octogenarian." Another example was the "unborn widow." This trap can arise when a testator wishes to make successive provision for a child, this surviving child's spouse, and then their children.

> X devises to my son for life, then to his widow for life, and then the remainder to their surviving children.

The contingent remainder to the surviving children can possibly vest outside the perpetuity period and thus at common law was void *ab initio*. The identity of the widow will be unknown until the moment of the son's death. It is possible, even if unlikely, that it will be a person who was not alive at the time of the devise (thus the "unborn" widow). Likewise, one or more of the surviving children may not have been alive at the time of the devise. In this case, the only life in being that can support this grant is the son, and the contingent remainder to the surviving children could vest more than 21 years after his death, if his widow survives him by more than 21 years. Accordingly, at common law the contingent remainder was void and the surviving children took nothing. On the other hand, the interest to the widow is good, because it will vest, if at all, at the moment of the son's death and is thus within the perpetuity period.

Statutory Reform

The common law rule against perpetuities had the unfortunate effect of destroying many contingent interests, frustrating the expressed intentions of grantors and testators. Many contingent interests, even those likely to vest within a short period of time, were declared void *ab initio* if there was even the slightest possibility that it might vest outside the perpetuity period. This has been colourfully described as the "slaughter of the innocents." See W.B. Leach, "Perpetuities: Staying the Slaughter of the Innocents" (1952), 68 *Law Quarterly Review* 35. Some jurisdictions, such as Manitoba, have simply abolished the rule, thereby presumably permitting endless future interests: The Perpetuities and Accumulations Act, 1983, SM 1982-83-84, c. 43. In this case, the common law restrictions on undue restraints on alienation may replace the role of the rule against perpetuities, striking down remote future interests. See Ziff, at 243-44. Other jurisdictions have replaced the common law perpetuity period with a fixed period, usually 80 years. See, for example, the Perpetuities Act, RSBC 1979, c. 321 and the Perpetuities and Accumulations Act, c. 55 (1964 UK). Elsewhere, such as Alberta (Perpetuities Act, RSA 1980, c. P-4) and Ontario (Perpetuities Act, RSO 1990, c. P.9), reform efforts have simply added a "wait and see" rule to the common law rule against perpetuities, thus retaining most of the common law rule but with some modification. Under these latter reforms, three options are possible.

In reviewing a gift, it is first necessary to determine if there is any potential perpetuity problem. If the gift complies with the old common law rule because there is no contingent interest that might vest outside the perpetuity period, the gift is valid. Second, if there is a potential perpetuity problem, the statutes provide for specific remedies with somewhat more realistic assumptions for certain problems that frequently arose at common law. For example, to address the problem of the "fertile octogenarian," statutes such as s. 7(1) of the Ontario Perpetuities Act rather curiously provide that a male is able to have a child at the age of 14 or over, and a female is able to have a child at the age of 12 until the age of 55.

Finally, and most important, the statutes also provide for a "wait and see" period. First, the legislation provides that a contingent interest in real or personal property shall not be treated as void for perpetuity merely because the interest may possibly vest beyond the perpetuity period, thus reversing the common law on this point. See, for example, s. 3 of the Ontario Perpetuities Act. Second, the statutes provide that a contingent interest that is capable of vesting within or beyond the perpetuity period is presumptively valid until actual events establish either that it is incapable of vesting within the period, in which case it is void, or that it is incapable of vesting beyond the period, in which case it is valid. See, for example, s. 4(1) of the Ontario Perpetuities Act.

The wait and see process will render many grants valid that would otherwise be void at common law. This process allows actual events to determine whether the contingent interest is valid.

X devises to the first of A's daughters to marry. (A has no children when the testator dies.)

At common law, the devise was void because A is the only life in being, and one of A's daughters may be born after the testator's death and may marry more than 21 years after A's death. Under the statutory wait and see principle the gift will be valid if one of A's daughter's marries within 21 years of A's death.

The rule against perpetuities and the various statutory reforms are complex and are covered here only briefly. Difficult questions can arise, for example, when trying to identify the precise lives in being under the statutory reforms. For a more detailed review, see Oosterhoff and Rayner, at 435-570 and Megarry and Wade, at 231-310.

Exercise 10: The Rule Against Perpetuties

The common law rule against perpetuities provides that an interest must vest in interest, if at all, within the perpetuity period. This period is calculated by taking the lives in being at the date that the instrument takes effect, plus 21 years. Remember that the rule applies only to contingent interests in property. If there is no contingent interest in the grant, the rule has no application. To determine the perpetuity period, it is necessary to identity the "lives in being" relevant to the gift. Only living persons who are mentioned in the gift *expressly* or by *implication* qualify as "lives in being." In Ontario, the common law rule has been modified by statute, which now provides for a "wait and see" period: ss. 3-4, Perpetuities Act, RSO 1990, c. P.9. Pursuant to these reforms, a contingent interest that potentially violates the rule against perpetuities is no longer considered void *ab initio*. Instead, the law now applies a wait and see period. If, as events turn out, the contingent interest does vest within the perpetuity period, the gift is valid.

In the grants or devises below, first consider whether the gift involves a contingent interest that might vest in interest outside the relevant perpetuity period. If so, then consider the impact that the statutory reforms may have on the gift.

Grant or devise	Analysis
1. X devises to Queen's University so long as the land is used for university purposes. Hint: Review s. 15 of the Ontario Perpetuities Act.	

Grant or devise	Analysis
2. X devises to my daughter for life, then to her surviving spouse for life, and then the remainder to their surviving children. Hint: Recall the potential problem of the "unborn widow."	
3. X grants to A for life, and then the remainder in fee simple to A's children upon marriage. Hint: Do the common law remainder rules apply here?	
4. X devises to A's grandchildren when they marry.	

CHAPTER FOUR

Bailment, Licences, and Leases: Dividing Title and Possession

Property law governs the relationship between those who have competing claims to resources of value. Chapter 2, for example, examines the competing claims between finders of lost chattel and occupiers of land on which the chattels were found. Chapter 2 also considers the competing claims between the true owners of real property and those who had established a possessory claim, known as adverse possession. Chapter 3 examines how the fundamental legal principles governing real property evolved to permit a wide number of individuals to hold simultaneous (in the case of the doctrine of tenure) or successive (in the case of the doctrine of estates) interests in land. The law of real property governs these competing, simultaneous, and/or successive interests in land. It is commonly assumed that property law concerns itself with *exclusive* and *individual* interests in resources of value (often referred to as "ownership"). However, much of property law also deals with *inclusive* and *collective* interests, and the relationship between those who simultaneously or successively share interests in the disputed resource of value.

This chapter considers other ways in which property law can be used to create simultaneous interests in personal or real property—bailment, licences, and leases. Because many of these relationships are also contracts, the law of contracts plays an important role in understanding and shaping these relationships. In the case of bailment, licences, and leases, there is a division between "ownership," or title to the property, and lawful possession, or use of the property. One person will have "title" to a particular resource, while another enjoys lawful possession or use of it. Property law, occasionally supplemented by contract and/or tort law, governs the relationship between these parties, as illustrated in the following examples:

- a bailment arises when the owner of a car lends his or her car to a friend. The owner of the car is the *bailor*, and the borrower the *bailee*. Although the owner retains title, he or she no longer has possession of the car; instead the bailee is in lawful possession of the car;
- a licence arises when the owner of real property, the *licensor* (for example, an owner of a movie theatre) agrees to permit another, the *licensee* (the moviegoer) to enter onto the property; and
- a leasehold estate arises when the owner of real property, the *lessor* (or *landlord*), agrees to lease his or her property for a period of time to another, the *tenant* (or *lessee*).

The principles of property law, contracts, and torts may apply to the various situations above. These principles may supplement one another, or they may be in conflict. Where, for example, there has been no exchange of consideration between the bailor and the bailee—that is, the loan of the car is gratuitous—there is no contract between the parties and contract law does not apply. However, property and tort law may nonetheless impose some kind of obligation on the bailee to return the property in reasonable condition. Similarly, a licence may be granted without consideration (when one person invites another into his or her home, he or she has granted a gratuitous licence to the invitee), or with consideration (as in the case of the moviegoer, above). If there is consideration, contract law will generally apply to the terms and enforcement of the licence. Because a lease is usually accompanied by consideration, it is also a contract. Both property law and contract law principles apply to the interpretation and enforcement of leases, and in some cases there may be conflict between these principles.

Unlike the areas of property law examined in chapters 2 and 3, where *property* law generally governs the relationships in question, this chapter examinines areas of law where property, contract, and tort law intersect.

BAILMENT

Bailment is a common transaction in daily life, arising any time an owner parts with possession of a chattel—for example, a car, a book, or luggage—for a specified purpose—for example, repair, storage, loan, or transport. See generally N.E. Palmer, *Bailment* (Sydney: Law Book Co. Ltd., 1979) (hereafter Palmer). A bailment may be contractual—for example, in the case of a car rental—or gratuitous—for example, borrowing a book from a friend. The relationship is typically consensual, although it may arise where there is no consent or agreement between the bailor and bailee—for example, as discussed in *Kowal v. Ellis* (1977), 76 DLR (3d) 546 (Man. CA) (considered in *Parker v. British Airways Board*, [1982] 2 WLR 503, chapter 2), the finder of lost property might be considered in law to be the bailee of the lost property. In such cases, the finder is sometimes referred to as a quasi bailee. See B. Ziff, *Principles of Property Law*, 2d ed. (Scarborough, ON: Carswell, 1996) (hereafter Ziff), at 277. A bailment might also arise where one person is in possession of another person's goods, mistakenly thinking they are his or her own. In both cases, although there is no express agreement between the bailee and the bailor, the law might impose a relationship of bailment between the parties.

Bailment imposes certain obligations on the bailee with respect to the chattel in question. Originally, the bailee was held strictly liable for the loss or damage of the bailor's property, however caused: *Southcote's Case* (1601), 4 Co. Rep. 83b; 76 ER 1061 (KB). This onerous standard was later replaced as the law of negligence developed: *Coggs v. Bernard* (1703), 2 Ld. Raym. 909; 92 ER 107 (KB). From this point on, bailees were generally held liable only on the basis of fault, and a different level of care was imposed depending on the nature of the bailment:

1. In the case of bailments for the sole benefit of the bailor—for example, a gratuitous deposit for safekeeping that benefits the bailor only—the bailee assumes a low duty

of care and is liable for gross negligence only. See, for example, *Remme v. Wall* (1978), 29 NSR (2d) 39; 45 APR 39 (TD) and *Campbell v. Pickard* (1961), 30 DLR (2d) 152 (Man. CA).

2. In the case of bailments for the sole benefit of the bailee—for example, a gratuitous loan of a car for the sole benefit of the bailee—the bailee assumes a much higher duty of care, and is liable for slight negligence. See, for example, *Jenkins v. Smith* (1969), 6 DLR (3d) 309; (1965-69), 1 NSR 728 (TD).

3. In the case of bailments for mutual benefit (where there is an exchange of consideration and a contract exists), a duty of ordinary diligence applies, unless otherwise altered by the terms of the contract.

More recently, case law suggests that these various standards of care have been replaced with a general standard of negligence that is determined by bearing in mind which of the parties was intended to benefit by the arrangement. See, for example, *Houghland v. R.R. Low (Luxury Coaches) Ltd.*, [1962] 1 QB 694; [1962] 2 All ER 159; 106 Sol. Jo. 243 (CA) and *MacNaughton v. Farell* (1982), 54 NSR (2d) 361; 112 APR 361 (TD).

This duty of care might otherwise be altered in either of the following situations. First, what might appear to give rise to a bailment may in fact only give rise to a licence. Most commonly, this can arise where the owner of a car parks the car in a commercial parking lot. In some cases, the lot may be supervised and the owner of the car may be required to hand over the keys of the car to the parking lot attendant. This may give rise to a bailment, where control and possession of the car has been effectively transferred to the attendant. On the other hand, where a sufficient degree of control of the car has not been transferred, the owner of the car is merely purchasing a licence to enter onto the parking lot to park his or her car for a period of time. A mere licence to enter onto the property, a contractual agreement between the parties, will not generally impose any particular obligations on the parking lot to safeguard the chattel, unless the contract provides otherwise. As there is no bailment, the duty of care imposed by the law of bailment does not apply. The *characterization* of the arrangement is thus crucial. If there is only a licence, the parking lot will likely not be held liable for any damage done to the car while it is parked on the lot. However, if there is bailment, the parking lot owner may be liable for negligence.

Second, the duty of care might also be altered even if a bailment can be established between the parties. A bailment for the mutual benefit of the parties is also a contract, and the terms of the contract may include a clause designed to limit the liability of the parties in the event of a breach of that contract. Such clauses are commonly included in standard form parking lot tickets. The duty of care otherwise imposed by bailment might thus be altered. The extent to which the courts will recognize and enforce the clause limiting liability is a matter of contract law, not the law of bailment.

The following case examines these two issues. When reviewing the case, consider whether the court finds that the relationship in question gives rise to a licence or a bailment with its corresponding higher duty of care. Does the court accept that this duty of care can be altered by a clause excluding liability? If so, on what grounds does the court make this finding? Is the court's finding consistent with contemporary contract law on the question of clauses excluding liability?

Heffron v. Imperial Parking Co.
(1974), 46 DLR (3d) 642 (Ont. CA)

ESTEY JA [by whom the judgment of the court was delivered]: This is an appeal from a judgment pronounced by His Honour Judge Shortt in the County Court of the Judicial District of York on March 29, 1973, wherein the plaintiff was awarded $1,251.92 as damages for the loss of an automobile left by the respondent with the appellants, the operators of a parking lot, together with costs.

The respondent on October 10, 1970, parked his motor vehicle in the parking lot of the appellants in downtown Toronto paying the evening flat rate charge and receiving in return a ticket whereon there was printed:

No. 49801
PARKING CONDITIONS

we are not responsible for theft or damage of car or contents, however caused

IMPERIAL PARKING CO.
237 Victoria Street—364-4611
Corner Bond & Dundas Sts.
Open 8:00 am—12.00 pm

At the request of the appellants' attendant the respondent left the keys in the automobile. The lot was marked with three signs on which the same message was set out as appeared on the ticket. The learned trial Judge came to the conclusion "that the defendants took reasonable steps under the circumstances to draw the conditions of parking to the plaintiff's attention even though, as he admitted, he had not read the parking ticket but merely slipped it into his pocket." In addition to these signs there was a sign announcing the hours in which the parking lot was open and which were the same as set out on the ticket described above. I can find no reason to disturb the learned trial Judge's conclusion that the appellant had taken all reasonable measures to communicate to the respondent the parking conditions including the hours of operation.

The respondent returned to the parking lot about one hour after it had closed and was unable to locate his car. Three days later it was discovered abandoned in a damaged condition. The evidence is that when the car was left with the appellants by the respondent it contained some personal property of the respondent including clothing, a tape player and an electric razor; there is no evidence to indicate that the tape player was affixed to or formed part of the car. These items of personal property were not in the car when it was recovered.

There was evidence indicating that the appellants operated a parking garage across the street from the parking lot in question and that it was a normal practice for the attendant when leaving the lot at midnight to take the keys of any cars remaining on the lot to the office of the parking garage across the street which was operated by the appellant. The keys to the respondent's car were not found in either the kiosk on the parking lot or in the office of the parking garage.

The appellants called no evidence to describe or explain any of the events which occurred. The attendant on duty at the parking lot was not called to give evidence and the only evidence presented by the defence was that of the manager of the appellants who testified to some of the normal practices followed in the operation of the appellants' parking lots. This witness was asked on this point:

Q. What was the procedure with regard to keys left for cars with respect to cars that hadn't been picked up at the time the attendant left the lot? A. The procedure now?

Q. No. Then. A. The keys were taken out of the car and taken—we have a parking garage across the street directly next to the Imperial Theatre and the cars are—we ask the people to pick up their keys at the parking garage. We have a man posted there until 2:00 am.

Q. Were any keys ever left in the cars or in the kiosk at that time? A. Sometimes the—if the attendant would go out for coffee or something.

Q. No. I mean when he closed the lot. A. I honestly can't say.

BY THE COURT: Q. Just a moment. I am not clear. How would the customer know if he came back at one o'clock? A. There is a note left on the car, sir.

Q. That he should go across to the parking lot? A. "Please pick up your keys at the parking garage. ..."

Q. You mentioned that you have a lot in the immediate vicinity that is open until two o'clock? A. Yes. We have a man posted until 2:00 am.

Q. So you retain custody of the car and the keys by taking the keys over to the other lot, is that right? A. If the keys are left in the cars. If there are any cars on the parking lot left with keys, we try to do that.

The learned trial Judge in granting judgment in favour of the respondent stated:

The mere disappearance of the car does not of necessity import theft nor am I convinced that the admitted damage was done before the car left the parking lot. It would be going too far in view of "the magic words" to say that the defendant must negative negligence. It is, however, in my opinion, clearly necessary for the bailee to lead evidence to negative a fundamental breach or deviation from the contract of bailment which would render inoperative the exculpatory words: see *Williams & Wilson Ltd. v. OK Parking Ltd.*, [1971] 2 OR 151, 17 DLR (3d) 243.

The appellant relies upon the decision of this Court in *Samuel Smith & Sons Ltd. v. Silverman*, [1961] OR 648, 29 DLR (2d) 98, in support of its submission that the exculpatory condition in the ticket together with the same message in the signs posted on the parking lot are sufficiently broad in their terms to exonerate the appellant even when the damage occurred through negligence of the appellant, its servants or a third party. The appellant also submits that it is under no onus or obligation to advance any explanation for the non-delivery of the respondent's automobile and since the respondent was unable to show that its loss was occasioned by a fundamental breach of the contract by the appellant, the respondent's action should be dismissed. The appellant alternatively submits that the respondent in parking his automobile on the appellant's premises is a mere licensee and consequently, no bailment arose and therefore no duty in the appellants to explain the loss.

In the *Samuel Smith* case the parties conceded and the Court proceeded on the basis that at least where the parking lot operator has asked the motorist to leave the keys in the car so that it may be moved around the parking lot for convenience of the operator "that this is a true case of bailment." In that case and the one before this Court the principal argument made was that the terms of the contract excluded liability in the parking lot operator. Neither in the *Samuel Smith* case nor in this case was evidence led by the parking lot operator to explain the disappearance of the automobile. Much of the discussion in the *Samuel Smith* case dealt with the communication of the ticket conditions to the car owner and the only direct reference in the judgment to the effect of the limiting conditions on the ticket is found in the concluding portion of the judgment at p. 652 OR, p. 102 DLR:

> The words printed on the ticket and the signs in question are not susceptible of this criticism. The clear declaration that the defendant was not to be responsible for theft or damage of car or contents *however caused*, is sufficiently broad in its terms to extend to a case where the damage occurred through the negligence either of the defendant or his servants, or the negligence or carelessness of a third party whether lawfully on the premises or not.

The Court thereupon concluded that the exclusionary clause applied to the claim of the plaintiff. The applicability of the doctrine of fundamental breach was apparently not advanced and in any case was not dealt with by the Court.

In another line of cases a relationship different from bailment was found to arise between the parties to such a transaction as parking a car in a parking lot. In *Ashby v. Tolhurst*, [1973] 2 All ER 837, Lord Greene MR found that a somewhat similar transaction resulted in the establishment of a licence relationship and not a bailment relationship. This Court followed and applied the *Ashby* judgment in *Palmer v. Toronto Medical Arts Building Ltd.*, [1960] OR 60, 21 DLR (2d) 181. The trial Judge had found that the plaintiff was a mere licensee and that there was no bailment of his automobile. In any case he found that any bailment which may have arisen was gratuitous bailment and without gross negligence no liability arose in the parking lot owner. As in *Ashby v. Tolhurst*, the Court found in the circumstances of the case the car had not been delivered to the defendants for safe custody but only for "parking" and nothing more. A circumstance of significance mentioned by Schroeder JA, speaking for the Court in the *Palmer* case at p. 69 OR, pp. 187-8 DLR, was the lack of a ticket system:

> The fact that there was no system of giving a card or parking ticket to the persons using this parking lot has vital significance and should have suggested to the plaintiff the absence of any arrangement for supervision or control over the cars left on the lot, since no person was required to surrender a ticket or produce any other form of identification when removing his car.

In that case the surrender of keys to an attendant was an unusual occurrence brought about by a heavy snowfall that morning which made the usual practice of car parking by its owner impossible. The attendant made it clear to the plaintiff that he could, if he wished, retain control over his car or he could remove it to some other parking lot or accept the attendant's offer extended as a voluntary courtesy to park the car for him when space became available. Sir Wilfrid Greene MR, in the *Ashby* case, *supra*, at p. 840, mentions a further circumstance which indicates the relationship which arises in law between the parties to such a transaction:

> The first thing to do is to examine the nature of the relationship between the parties, a matter upon which the character of the ground is, I think, not without importance, but the most important element is the document itself. It describes the place in which the car is to be left as a "car park," and the document is described as a "car park ticket." I myself regard those words as being in one sense, in a real sense, I think, the most important part of the document, because they indicate the nature of the rights which the proprietor of the car is going to get. "Car park ticket": you take a ticket in order to park you [*sic*] car, and parking your cars means, I should have thought, leaving your car in a place. If you park your car in the street, you are liable to get into trouble with the police. On the other hand, you are entitled to park your car in places indicated by the police or the appropriate authorities for the purpose. Parking a car is leaving a car and, I should have thought, nothing else. The right, therefore, which this document starts off by giving on its face is a right to park the car.

In that case the plaintiff locked his car and did not leave the keys with the attendant.

The respective characteristics of the bailment and the licence relationships are guides to the application of the appropriate relationship to the case at hand. Bailment has been defined as "a delivery of personal chattels in trust, on a contract, express or implied, that the trust shall be duly executed, and the chattels redelivered in either their original or an altered form, as soon as the time or use for, or condition on which they were bailed, shall have elapsed or been performed": *Bacon's Abridgement*, adopted in *Re S. Davis & Co., Ltd.*, [1945] Ch. 402 at p. 405. A licence on the other hand is simply the grant of such authority to another to enter upon land for an agreed purpose as to justify that which otherwise would be a trespass and its only legal effect is that the licensor until the licence is revoked is precluded from bringing an action for trespass. Romer LJ, speaking at p. 844 in the *Ashby* case, *supra*, distinguished a bailment from all other relationships when he stated: "... in order that there shall be a bailment there must be a delivery by the bailor, that is to say, he must part with his possession of the chattel in question."

While no single fact may be of controlling importance in the isolation and categorization of the relationship between the parties to this appeal, the combination of the following factors favour the relationship of bailor–bailee, rather than licensor–licensee:

(a) the owner of the car delivered the keys and therefore the control over the movement of his automobile to the attendant at the attendant's request;

(b) the parking ticket had a serial number which would indicate that the surrender of the specific ticket would be necessary in order to obtain delivery from the attendant of the automobile;

(c) the provision of the attendant raises a reasonable inference that he is supplied by the owner of the business for more than the mere function of receiving money upon the parking of the car;

(d) the parking lot closed, according to the conditions announced on the ticket and signs, at midnight and no conditions were imposed concerning the removal of cars prior thereto;

(e) the notice of a closing hour reasonably infers an active operation of the parking lot rather than a passive allotment of parking stations from which the car owner could at any time, day or night, unilaterally withdraw his parked vehicle; and

(f) the practice of the parking lot owner (although unknown to the owner of the car) was to place the keys left in automobiles at the end of the day in the office of the appellants' car parking garage across the road.

In my view, the special circumstances of this case, which I have summarized above, indicate that there was no mutual intention of a mere parking of the car by the respondent owner on the appellants' lot without any action required by the appellants beyond the collection of the fee. The appellants did not hold out a single identified unit of parking space for the exclusive use of the respondent nor did the appellants represent to the respondent that there would be identified a small rectangular island of land somewhere in the appellants' parking lot on which either the respondent or the appellants would place the respondent's vehicle as an alternative to leaving it at the side of the street. The ticket system, the hours of operation, the operating habits of the appellants, including the disposition of car keys at the close of business, and the stipulation that the keys be left in the car so as to enable the appellants to place and move the car at their convenience anywhere within the appellants' parking facility, all indicate a relationship quite different from that of a licence passively granted by the appellant as licensor to the respondent. In the *Ashby* case, *supra*, the car was placed by its owner in a designated spot and locked and the keys were left by the owner with the parking lot supervisor. Here the respondent surrendered and the appellant accepted (indeed required) control of this valuable and highly mobile item of property. I therefore conclude that there was a delivery of possession by the respondent to the appellants of the automobile under a contract of bailment.

The exculpatory clause I have set out above and observe that it is in words identical with those appearing on the ticket which came before this Court in *Mitchell v. Silverman*, [1952] OWN 130, where Robertson CJO, in an oral judgment found that the contract between the parties excluded any liability in the parking lot operator and placed no burden on that operator to account for the missing automobile. The appellant has submitted that should it be found that it was a bailee the exculpatory terms of the contract relieve it from any liability including negligence of the appellant's servants. The respondent in turn has argued that by reason of the fundamental breach of the contract of bailment by the appellant the contract has been terminated including the exculpatory term and the appellant is therefore liable to the respondent for damages thereby occasioned.

Linked inextricably with the answer to the question of applicability of the exempting clause in any such transaction, is the determination of what onus, if any, lies upon the bailee once the bailor proves non-delivery. Lord Denning in *J. Spurling Ltd. v. Bradshaw*, [1956] 1 WLR 461 at p. 466, stated:

> A bailor, by pleading and presenting his case properly, can always put on the bailee the burden of proof. In the case of non-delivery, for instance, all he need plead is the contract and a failure to deliver on demand. That puts on the bailee the burden of proving either loss without his fault (which, of course, would be a complete answer at

common law) or, if it was due to his fault, it was a fault from which he is excused by the exempting clause. ...

Vide also *Woolmer v. Delmer Price Ltd.*, [1955] 1 QB 291 at p. 294. The onus in the case of a licence relationship is of course quite different and the licensor is not ordinarily called upon to discharge any burden or onus other than to demonstrate that he has honoured the existence of the licence.

We are left, therefore, with the unexplained disappearance of the respondent's automobile and the last question remaining to be answered is whether the exculpatory clause exonerates the appellants notwithstanding the appellants' complete failure to explain the cause of disappearance, or whether the clause ceased to operate upon the happening of the unexplained loss of the automobile by reason of a breach of a fundamental term of the contract. At one time it was clear that loss by the bailee of the subject of the bailment without any demonstration of the cause was a fundamental breach going to the root of the contract: *Karsales (Harrow), Ltd. v. Wallis*, [1956] 2 All ER 866 at p. 868.

The doctrine of fundamental breach came under review in the House of Lords judgments in *Suisse Atlantique Société d'Armement Maritime SA v. NV Rottersdamsche Kolen Centrale*, [1967] 1 AC 361. Lord Reid, Viscount Dilhorne and Lord Upjohn found no rule in the common law prohibiting the contracting out of liability for breach of a fundamental term of the contract. Lord Hodson concluded that as a matter of construction an exculpatory clause would be normally construed as not applicable to escape liability for a breach of a fundamental term going to the root of a contract.

Lord Wilberforce found the law to be that when the contractual intention of the parties is ascertained and did not embrace the events amounting to a breach of a fundamental term, the events must be outside the exculpatory clause which would therefore not apply. His Lordship added that in those circumstances for a Court to apply the exculpatory clause to exonerate the guilty party would be to convert the basic covenants of the contract into a "mere declaration of intention." Shortly thereafter Lord Denning MR, speaking in *Mendelssohn v. Normand, Ltd.*, [1969] 2 All ER 1215 at p. 1218, said of the *Suisse Atlantique* judgments: "It was there said to be all a matter of construction," and that the earlier contract doctrine restricting the operation of the exculpatory clauses to the performance of the contract in the stipulated manner and not extending to the violation of the terms thereof in a fundamental sense, is "in no way diminished by authority by Suisse Atlantique. ..."

This Court applied the substance of the doctrine of fundamental breach in a not dissimilar manner in *R.G. McLean Ltd. v. Canadian Vickers Ltd. et al.*, [1971] 1 OR 207, 15 DLR (3d) 15, where a contract clause purporting to limit a vendor's liability to the replacement of parts and to the repair of a printing machine and to exclude any liability for direct or indirect loss, was found to be inapplicable in the circumstances where the machine failed entirely to perform in the manner contemplated by the parties. Whether this result is obtained by applying the doctrine of fundamental breach as a matter of contract construction or as an independent principle of law, it is clear that the phenomenon is alive and prospering in the law of this Province.

On the facts now before this Court the question is whether the parties to this car parking transaction contemplated that upon the delivery of the complete possession and control over the car, the operator of the parking lot would be free to maintain silence and escape any liability upon his failure to deliver the car to the respondent on surrender of the appropriate serial parking ticket? To answer the question in the affirmative one must find that the owner, on surrendering his car to the lot operator upon payment of the requested fee for this service, thereupon accepted the implied condition that the operator could, when closing or at the end of the day, leave the car and its keys unprotected and available to any thief or joyrider who might happen upon the lot. Such an assumption would make meaningless the purpose of parking a car off the highway on a lot super-vised by an attendant and equipped with a kiosk from which the lot and the properties placed thereon could be supervised. Furthermore, the issue of a serially numbered ticket upon delivery of possession of the car would either be a meaningless ritual or, worse still, a practice intended to induce a false sense of security. Such an interpretation is denied by the strongest inference by the appellant itself whose president in evidence partially excerpted above detailed the steps followed at the end of the day for safeguard-ing the keys of automobiles still on the parking lot. It should be emphasized that the basic transaction here was on quite a different basis than the transaction in *Ashby v. Tolhurst*, [1937] 2 All ER 837, and *Palmer v. Toronto Medical Arts Building Ltd.*, [1960] OR 60, 21 DLR (2d) 181. In neither of these cases was the owner of the car required as a term of the transaction to leave the keys in the car for the convenience and presumably the greater profit of the operator. In the former case the keys were not left in the car and in the latter case the keys were taken by the attendant as a gratuitous courtesy offered to the owner to park his car when the lot had been cleared of snow.

In a recent decision of this Court, *Bata v. City Parking Canada Ltd.* (1973), 2 OR (2d) 446, 43 DLR (3d) 190, Schroeder JA, sitting alone on an appeal from the Small Claims Court, applied the *Ashby* and *Palmer* cases rather than the *Samuel Smith & Sons Ltd. v. Silverman*, [1961] OR 648, 29 DLR (2d) 98 line of reasoning by reason of the peculiar wording of the ticket given by the operator to the owner of the automobile. The ticket emphasized the charges were for "parking space only" and similar wording ap-peared on signs on the premises. The actual wording in all instances was "charges are for use of parking space only." For that reason the Court found the relationship to be that of licence rather than bailment and, in my view, is clearly distinguishable from the facts now before us.

But there is a further circumstance in this case which requires examination to com-pletely dispose of this transaction and the rights and obligations of the parties therein. As stated earlier, both the signs on the lot and the ticket referred to the closing of the lot at 12:00 pm, which the parties agreed in this instance means midnight. When the appellants asked the respondent to leave the keys in the car there arose the clearest implied duty in the appellants to take reasonable steps at the close of business to retain custody of the keys in a manner appropriate to the need of the respondent to recover his car and the necessity of protecting the keys and the car from loss. The appellants are unable to explain what became of the keys. They were never located in either the kiosk on the lot or in the appellants' parking garage across the road. Thus, the keys were either stolen during the day or after the lot closed. In either case the appellants must fail, in the first instance as bailee of the keys and the car for the reasons I have outlined earlier, and in the second instance for breach of duty to exercise reasonable care to safeguard the keys after the closing of the lot. This latter understanding and the duty arising therefrom are entirely unrelated to the exculpatory term set out in the parking ticket. It could not be otherwise as the law would then be unable to imply a duty to exercise reasonable care in the second stage of the custodial arrangement. I adopt the words of Devlin J, in *Firestone Tyre & Rubber Co. Ltd. v. Vokins & Co. Ltd.*, [1951] 1 Ll. Rep. 32 at p. 39: "It is illusory to say: 'We promise to do a thing, but we are not liable if we do not do it.' " Alternatively, if the exculpatory clause were to apply throughout the transaction breach of the primary, albeit an applied term, of the arrangement is as fundamental to the parties as failure to redeliver to the owner the subject of the bailment during the term of the bailment. In any case, the term of the bailment may expire but the consequential duty to make reasonable provision for the return of the keys to the owner continues. The appellants upon the unexplained failure to deliver are, therefore, faced with a fundamental breach of the contract of bailment during the term thereof or breach of duty with respect to the disposition of the keys to the automobile after the term of the bailment. The appellants have not, and presumably cannot, relate the non-delivery to either time period and I know of no principle of law requiring the respondent to do so as plaintiff in order to recover his damages.

There was some evidence that the ignition of the car was faulty prior to the disappearance of the car from the appellants' lot but in any event there is no evidence to dispel the ordinary explanation that the keys were used to improperly remove the automobile.

Finally, we turn to the question of the contents of the automobile which, when the car was subsequently recovered in a damaged condition, were not in the car. This personal property consisted of some tools, clothing, and a radio and tape player for which the respondent claimed in all $308.10, calculated on the basis of the value of the goods at the time of loss. These goods were generally of a type which one might reasonably be expected to carry in an automobile. The evidence does not indicate whether these articles were located in the trunk or the body of the car. However, once the keys fall into the hands of a person intent upon stealing the automobile it makes no difference whether the personal property mentioned above is located in the trunk or inside the car.

Laidlaw JA, in dealing with a similar claim in *Brown v. Toronto Auto Parks Ltd.*, [1955] OWN 456, [1955] 2 DLR 525, found neither actual nor constructive knowledge in the bailee of the presence of a quantity of books in the car and, hence, the contract of bailment did not extend to cover the books in the car. On the facts in the case before this Court the goods are not of such an unusual nature that would not reasonably be expected to be regularly found in an automobile and it, therefore, is not unreasonable for a parking lot operator to assume that a great many of the cars left in his custody will contain this kind of personal property in reasonable quantity. On this basis I conclude that the items mentioned above were constructively included in the bailment arrangement and were property included in the claims made by the respondent.

For these reasons I would dismiss the appeal with costs but in so doing wish to add that the Court was greatly assisted in the disposition of this matter by the thorough and detailed analysis of the authorities presented by both counsel.

Appeal dismissed.

Discussion Notes

Bata v. City Parking Canada Ltd.

In *Bata v. City Parking Canada Ltd.* (1973), 43 DLR (3d) 190 (Ont. CA), the plaintiff parked his car in a parking lot, and left his keys in the car on the request of the attendant. The car was stolen, and the plaintiff brought an action against the parking lot. The plaintiff was unsuccessful, as the court (at p. 194) determined that the relationship was a licence rather than a bailment:

> The words on the two signs and the words which appear on the parking ticket given the customer indicate in a very real sense the nature of the rights which the proprietor of a car may expect to enjoy under the arrangement into which he is entering. The words "charges are for use of parking space only," exclude at once any notion that the arrangement entered into is one of bailment, and if there is any doubt on that score the words "[t]his company assumes no responsibility whatever for loss or damage due to fire, theft, collision or otherwise to the vehicle or its contents, however caused" should effectively remove any doubt in the matter.

In *Heffron*, the court distinguished *Bata* on its facts. Can the cases be so easily distinguished? The major distinction appears to be the express inclusion of the words "charges are for use of parking space only" in the parking ticket in *Bata*. As a matter of fairness, is this a reasonable ground to allow the plaintiff in *Heffron* to recover damages, but not the plaintiff in *Bata*? As a matter of fairness, why should the plaintiff in either case be entitled to damages?

Minichiello v. Devonshire Hotel (1967) Ltd.

Generally, when a bailment exists, there will be constructive bailment of other items that might reasonably be expected to be in, or part of, the principle chattel. For this reason, the plaintiff in *Heffron* was able to recover the value of his personal property contained in the car, including some tools, clothing, a radio, and a tape player. In *Minichiello v. Devonshire Hotel (1967) Ltd.* (1978), 87 DLR (3d) 439 (BC CA), the plaintiff left his car (and his car keys) with the parking attendant. He paid 40 cents to park the car. He also informed the attendant that there were "valuables" in the car. In the car's trunk, there was a briefcase with over $16,000 worth of jewels. The briefcase disappeared, and the plaintiff was able to recover this amount on the grounds that the plaintiff's statement to the attendant was sufficient to enable the court to conclude that one could reasonably anticipate that property of such value might be in the car.

Is it reasonable to conclude that for a payment of 40 cents, the defendant parking lot should be held liable for the entire value of the lost jewels? What kind of legal advice would you offer to the defendant parking lot following this decision? Should the parking lot attendant be instructed to refuse to accept any cars, if informed that they contain "valuables"? Is this a feasible alternative? Should the parking lot ticket be amended to exclude liability for any damage or loss sustained while parked on the premises? Will this clause be effective in restricting the parking lot's liability?

Clauses Excluding Liability

Once the court in *Heffron* determined that a bailment existed, it then had to consider whether the clause limiting liability was effective in altering the duty of care otherwise owed to the plaintiff under the law of bailment. Had the court determined that there was only a licence and no bailment, the clause excluding liability would not have been particularly relevant, since no general duty of care would have been imposed on the car lot owner under the licence. However, having found a bailment and a corresponding duty of care, the question arose as to whether the parties had successfully modified this duty of care by the exculpatory clause. This is a question primarily of contract law, and it is covered in some detail in the study of contract law.

There is much discussion in *Heffron* about whether the "doctrine of fundamental breach" applies to this particular clause as a matter of "construction" or of "law." The court appears to leave the question open, and concludes that the doctrine of fundamental breach is "alive and prospering" in Ontario, whether it is a "matter of contract construction" or "an independent principle of law." In either case, the court seems to conclude that the exculpatory clause in question is unenforceable. However, it is difficult to see how the exculpatory clause in *Heffron* could be interpreted, as a matter of "construction," as failing to exclude liability for fundamental breach. The clause is very broadly worded and expressly excludes liability for theft. In other words, the clause is so broad that it appears to exclude liability even for fundamental breach and cannot easily be interpreted otherwise. How does the court in *Heffron* address this problem?

Since *Heffron*, the law has undergone considerable development. It is now clear that as a matter of Canadian law the doctrine of fundamental breach is merely a rule of construction and *not* a rule of law. See, for example, *Syncrude Canada Ltd. v. Hunter Engineering Co.*, [1989] 2 SCR 426; 57 DLR (4th) 321. The distinction is crucial. Previous case law had suggested that the doctrine of fundamental breach was rule of law. In the event of a "fundamental breach" of the contract, or a breach going to the "root" of the contract, the clause excluding liability would not be enforced, even if the clause itself expressly and clearly excluded such liability. The rationale was that parties should not as a matter of law be entitled to protect themselves from liability for breaching the most fundamental or basic terms of the contract. As the court suggested in *Heffron*, it seems ridiculous that a party can promise to do a specific thing, yet at the same time maintain that it will not be liable if it fails to do it.

However, subsequent case law has recognized that the parties to a contract can freely and knowingly negotiate a clause excluding liability even for fundamental performance under the contract. Providing that there is an equality of bargaining power between the parties, there is little reason not to enforce such clauses, and, consistent with the importance attached to freedom of contract, there may be every reason to enforce such clauses. For example, the consideration negotiated by the parties can expressly and reasonably rely on the fact that one party has extensively limited its liability under the contract. The parties can also purchase or decline to purchase insurance relying on this clause. There is no reason not to protect this reasonable reliance. As a result, subsequent case law has instead characterized the doctrine of fundamental breach as a rule of construction, rather than law. As a rule of construction, the courts have determined that the exculpatory clause will not be interpreted, or "constructed," as excluding liability for fundamental breach unless the clause does so in a clear and unambiguous fashion. By contrast, as a rule of law, even if the clause expressly excluded liability for fundamental breach, it would still be unenforceable.

As a result, it is now possible to contract out of liability for fundamental breach in Canada, providing that the parties do so in a clear and unambiguous manner. However, even if the parties have done so, the clause might still be found unenforceable if it is deemed unconscionable. The courts are sympathetic to finding such unconscionability where there is an inequality of bargaining power between the parties, particularly in the context of a standard form contract. In such cases, the court will consider whether any of the terms of the contract were subject to negotiation and whether the attention of the plaintiff was drawn to the exculpatory clause: see *Davidson v. Three Spruces Realty Ltd.*, [1977] 6 WWR 460, 79 DLR (3d) 481 (BC SC).

Given the evolution of the law, how would a court today likely resolve the question of the exculpatory clause in *Heffron*? How would this differ from the approach adopted in *Heffron*? Consider the result in *Minichiello v. Devonshire Hotel*, above, where the plaintiff paid only 40 cents to park the car, but was able to recover over $16,000 in damages for lost jewels. Assuming that there was an exculpatory clause in that case, could the parking lot owner argue that he had reasonably relied on the exclusionary clause when setting the very low fee to park the car, and when securing a low level of insurance coverage for his business? On the other hand, could the plaintiff successfully argue that the clause excluding liability is unconscionable? Given the parking lot owner's reasonable reliance on this clause, is it fair that a court might find it unenforceable? If the clause is unenforceable, what legal advice would you offer to the parking lot owner? Should the owner secure additional insurance, notwithstanding the apparent exclusion of liability?

Exculpatory clauses are also commonly included in cloakrooms, where a sign will be posted stating something like, "Not responsible for lost goods." A similar statement may be printed on the cloakroom ticket. Courts frequently strain to ignore or restrict such clauses. For example, the clause will apply only if the bailor has accepted it. The bailor must have either actual or constructive notice of the clause at the time he or she entered into the bailment. Thus the placement of the exculpatory clause is critical. If the clause is not prominently and obviously displayed, it may not apply. See Ziff, at 286. Similarly, if the agreement is tainted by unconscionability, as might be the case with standard form contracts, the clause may be ineffective. See *Davidson v. Three Spruces Realty Ltd.*

Length of Term of the Bailment

Bailments may be for a fixed term—for example, the long-term lease of machinery—or at will—for example, a gratuitous loan. Where there is a contract providing for a fixed term, the owner's right of possession is postponed until the term has expired, unless the bailee is in such serious breach of the contract that the bailor is permitted to retake possession. A bailment at will can be determined at any time by the bailor, giving the bailor an immediate right to repossess the article. See Ziff, at 279.

Burden of Proof

In most civil actions, the burden of proof rests on the plaintiff to establish all elements of liability, including the duty of care and the breach of this duty. By contrast, in bailment cases a presumption of negligence may arise, thereby shifting the burden of proof to the bailee. See Ziff, at 284-85. This presumption may arise if the plaintiff–bailor can establish that the act complained of—for example, the disappearance or damage of an article—occurred during the course of the bailment. Presumably, the bailee is in the better position to know the reason for the putative negligence. For this reason, the bailee bears the onus of proof to rebut the presumption of negligence. To evade liability, the bailee does not need to establish exactly what happened to the article. The bailee need only show that the system in place to safeguard the bailed goods was sufficient to meet legal requirements. See *United Refrigerator Parts Co. v. Consolidated Fastfrate Ltd.*, [1974] 5 WWR 166; 62 DLR (3d) 190 (Man. CA).

The Bailor's Duties

The bailor may also owe a duty of care to the bailee. If the chattel is defective, the bailor may be liable to the bailee, much as the vendor of defective goods may be liable to the purchaser. A bailor for reward—for example, a car rental company—must ensure that the chattels are reasonably fit and suitable for the purposes of the hirer and is liable for any defects that are known, or ought to have been known, by the bailor. On the other hand, a gratuitous bailor is likely only required to inform the bailee of known defects. See Ziff, at 285.

Assignment and Sub-Bailment

A bailee may assign or "sub-bail" his or her interest, providing that the terms of the original bailment expressly or impliedly permit it. Where the bailor has an immediate right to terminate the principal bailment—for example, when the goods have been lost—the bailor has a direct right of action against the sub-bailee: *Scott Maritimes Pulp Ltd. v. B.F. Goodrich Canada Ltd.* (1977), 72 DLR (3d) 680; 19 NSR (2d) 181 (CA). For example, A may give a ring to B for repair, and B may assign the work to C. If the ring is lost while in C's possession, A may bring an action against B (in contract) and C (in tort, given that there is no contractual relationship between A and C). If the sub-bailment between B and C contains an exculpatory clause relieving C of liability for the loss of the goods, difficult problems can arise. The basis of C's liability should in theory rest on the terms of the sub-bailment; however, in *Punch v. Savoy's Jewellers Ltd.* (1986), 54 OR (2d) 383; 26 DLR (4th) 546 (CA), the court held that C could rely on the exculpatory clause only if A expressly or impliedly consented to a sub-bailment containing such a clause. On the facts of the case, A was held not to have done so, and thus C could not rely on the exculpatory clause.

Is this result fair to C, particularly given the fact that C may have reasonably relied on this clause when negotiating the sub-bailment with B? Is it reasonable that A should not be bound by the clause excluding liability, given that A had failed to include any provision restricting B's power to enter into a sub-bailment? On the other hand, is it fair that A should be effectively bound by an exculpatory clause contained in a contract to which A is not a party?

Bailment and the Employment Relationship

An employee is not a bailee of the employer's property. For example, in *Weibe v. Lepp* (1974), 46 DLR (3d) 441 (Man. CA), the court found that an employee driving one of his employer's trucks was not a bailee of it. An employee is not in *possession* of the employer's property; the employee is only in *custody* of the employer's goods. See Palmer, at 235. The distinction between possession and custody is a fine one. A person merely in custody of another's goods may not be liable in bailment for negligence. For example, when a clerk permits a customer to handle goods in a store, there is no intention to hand over control and possession of the goods to the customer. Instead, the customer has only custody of the goods, and the owner of the goods retains the right of dominion over them. A similar analysis is applied to the relationship between employer and employee, where the employee is determined simply to be in custody of the employer's goods, and not in possession of them.

This rule has been criticized; it has been traced to the incapacity of slaves to own or possess property independently of their masters. See Palmer, at 235. Should employees be held to a higher standard of care with regard to the employer's property?

Strict Liability of Common Carriers and Innkeepers

As noted above, the law of negligence gradually replaced the historical standard of strict liability of the bailee. There are, however, two exceptions to this general rule. Common carriers and innkeepers remain strictly liable for damage to the property of persons for whom they provide their services. A common carrier contracts with other parties for the transportation of goods. Unless the common carrier's liability is altered by statute or the terms of the contract, the common carrier will be held strictly liable for any damage to the goods being transported: *Brookins v. Canadian National Railway Co.* (1974), 43 DLR (3d) 280 (PEI SC).

At common law, innkeepers were also held to a strict liability standard, likely to protect the interests of medieval travellers, who faced considerable risks. Today, this liability is typically altered by statute, as is the case in Ontario, the Innkeepers Act, RSO 1990, c. I.7. Section 4 provides that the innkeeper's liability for loss or injury to the guest's property is generally limited to $40, except where the goods have been stolen, lost, or injured "through the wilful act, default, or neglect of the innkeeper or the innkeeper's employee," or the goods "have been deposited expressly for safe custody with the innkeeper." Section 6 provides that the limited liability outlined in s. 4 will not be available to the innkeeper unless the innkeeper "conspicuously" posts a copy of s. 4 in the "office and public rooms and in every bedroom in the inn." This requirement was strictly enforced in *Laing v. Allied Innkeepers Ltd.* (1969), 8 DLR (3d) 708 (Ont. HC), where $400 was stolen from the plaintiff's hotel room. Although a proper notice had been posted in the plaintiff's room, the hotel was nonetheless found liable because it was unable to establish that the proper notice had been posted in all the other locations required by s. 6.

Bailments and Third Parties

Questions arise when a chattel is bailed and, through misuse or defect, causes injury or damage to a party other than the bailee. For example, A may bail a bookcase to B, and C, a customer in B's bookshop, may be injured because B has negligently assembled the bookcase. A is not liable to C for this injury because the alleged act of negligence was committed by B: *Oklahoma Publishing Co. v. Autry*, 463 P2d 334 (1969). Nonetheless, the owner of the chattel may be liable to a third party in at least three cases. See Palmer, at 962. First, if the bailee is acting simultaneously as the bailor's agent, the bailor may be liable for the negligent acts of the agent. Second, the bailor may be guilty of some personal negligence. For example, if the bailor provides careless instructions regarding the use of the chattel, leading to injury to the third party, the bailor may be liable in tort to the third party. Finally, the bailor may bail complicated machinery, along with an operator, to the bailee, in which case the bailor will remain liable for the operator's negligence. Typically, the third party is most likely to succeed when the injuries are related to a defect in the chattel itself. The bailor's liability in negligence can then be easily established, consistent with the tort of negligence outlined in *Donoghue v. Stevenson*, [1932] AC 562 (HL). In such cases, the bailor will be liable in negligence if it can be shown that the defect was in existence when the chattel was bailed, and the bailor knew or ought to have known about the defect.

Although a bailee is merely in lawful possession of the bailor's property, he or she may nonetheless maintain a right of action against a third party who has damaged or wrongfully deprived the bailee of the bailed property: *The "Winkfield,"* [1902] P 42 (Eng. CA). This follows from the fact that the bailee is in possession of the bailed goods and may recover possession from any wrongdoer, a point further explored in *Armory v. Delamirie* (1722), 93 ER 664 (KB), chapter 2. Questions can arise when it appears that the bailee is no longer in possession of the bailed goods. In *Minichiello v. Devonshire Motel (1967) Ltd. (No. 2)* (1978), 79 DLR (3d) 656 (BC SC), the plaintiff–jeweller had a case of jewellry stolen from his car while it was parked on the defendant's parking lot. The case included two rings owned by clients and left with the jeweller for repairs. The defendant argued that the plaintiff could not recover the value of these two rings, because the plaintiff, as bailee of the jewels, was no longer in actual possession of the bailed jewels during the time that the car was parked on the defendant's lot. Recall that in *Minichiello*, above, the court found that the defendant parking lot was liable for the value of the goods in the car, on the grounds that there had been a "constructive bailment" of these goods to the defendant. If the goods, including the car and the jewellry, had been bailed to the defendant, how could they remain in the jeweller's possession? The court managed to get around this difficulty by finding that the plaintiff was only required to show that he had the right to possession of the jewels, not actual possession, in order to maintain his action. Is this a convincing rationale?

Although not in possession of the bailed property, the bailor may nonetheless bring an action against a third party for any wrongdoing with respect to it, on the grounds that the bailor is entitled to recover his or her property interest in the bailed property: *Chapman v. Robinson* (1970), 71 WWR 515 (Alta. Dis. Ct.). However, in some cases, the bailor's right of action may be less extensive than the bailee's. The bailor may only be able to recover damages for "permanent" injury to the bailed property, suggesting that less serious injury may be recoverable only by the bailee: *Mears v. London and South Western Railway Col.* (1862), 11 CBNS 850; 142 ER 1029 (CP), and see Palmer, at 153-54.

TITLE, POSSESSION, AND LEASEHOLD ESTATES IN LAND

Much as a bailment for the mutual benefit of the parties constitutes a contract, a lease for consideration also creates a contract between the parties. As examined above, the principles of contract law may apply to a bailment for the mutual benefit of the parties, and an exculpatory clause in the bailment agreement may effectively alter the duty of care otherwise owed under the law of bailment. Similarly, the principles of contract law may apply to a lease.

As considered in chapter 3, a lease was historically regarded exclusively as a contract, and the law did not recognize that a lease gave rise to any estate in land. Leases were primarily entered into as a means to avoid objections to usury laws, which prohibited lenders from charging interest on loans. See E.H. Burn, *Cheshire and Burn's Modern Law of Real Property*, 14th ed. (London: Butterworths, 1988), at 34-35. To repay a debt, the debtor would lease lands at a nominal rent to the creditor, enabling the creditor to obtain interest at an agreed rate from the profits of the land. The actual interest charged was thus hidden in the agreement. Because the lease was regarded as a contractual arrangement only, if the lessor (debtor) were in breach of the lease agreement and wrongfully evicted the tenant (creditor), the tenant was not regarded as having any interest in the land that might give rise to an action to recover the land itself. Instead, the tenant was limited to recovering a monetary award of expectation damages in contract law, effectively recovering the debt due and no more. For this reason, leases have always been classified as personal property, not real property, because historically the lease did not give rise to an action to recover the land (the *res*) itself.

As the lease became a more popular legal device, this lack of security of tenure for the tenant, particularly the agrarian leaseholder, became increasingly problematic. Over time, the courts gradually permitted the tenant to bring an action in *ejectment*, which permitted the tenant to recover the land itself when wrongfully evicted from the leasehold premises. As a result, the tenant gradually began to acquire an enforceable interest in the land itself, and not merely a right to recover monetary damages for wrongful eviction. The leasehold interest thus began to resemble an estate in land. For this reason, the leasehold came to be known as a "chattel real"—that is, personal property, which nonetheless gave rise to a right to recover the property itself, when the tenant was wrongfully evicted. At this point, the leasehold estate was developed; it effectively resembled an estate in land and, on the whole, was regarded as a proprietary interest in land, governed primarily by the principles of property law (not contract law).

In contemporary law, this trend has been reversed. The principles of contract law have been increasingly applied to the leasehold estate, particularly in the context of remedies for breach of the leasehold agreement. The remedies developed by property law, which in effect relieved the lessor of any duty to mitigate in the face of the tenant's breach, have inefficient and undesirable results. Consequently, as illustrated in *Highway Properties Ltd. v. Kelly, Douglas, and Co.*, [1971] SCR 562, examined below, the courts have increasingly incorporated contract law remedies, and obligations, in the event of the tenant's breach. As a result, the leasehold estate (rather like bailment) is now situated at the crossroads of property law and contract law, and is subject to both bodies of law.

The lease, an unusual hybrid of property and contract law, must be contrasted with the licence, largely an exclusive creation of contract law. Occasionally, it is difficult to determine whether a particular agreement gives rise to a lease or a licence. The characterization of the agreement is crucial and can result in a variety of different outcomes for the parties.

Leases and Licences

A lease is a grant of exclusive possession giving rise to an estate in land, whereas a licence is merely a contractual right to enter onto the land of another for a specified purpose and constitutes little more than a defence to an action in trespass: A.H. Oosterhoff and W.B. Rayner, *Anger and Honsberger Law of Real Property* (Aurora, ON: Canada Law Book, 1985), at 918. The essence of a lease is that the tenant has a right to the exclusive possession of the leased premises, and the right to exclude all other persons including the lessor. A licence does not give rise to a right of exclusive possession, but merely permits the licensee to enter onto the premises.

The distinction between the two is crucial, as the following examples illustrate:

1. A lease creates an estate in land that, subject to the specific requirements of the relevant land recordation acts, is generally binding on the world. By contrast, a licence is merely an agreement between the contracting parties. As a result of the doctrine of privity of contract, a licence, like most contracts, is not generally binding on third parties. Because a lease is an estate in land, if the lessor sells his or her reversionary interest to a third party, this third party generally takes the reversion subject to the outstanding leasehold estate: *Metro-Matic Services Ltd. v. Hulmann* (1973), 48 DLR (3d) 326 (Ont. CA). On the other hand, if a licensor sells his or her interest in the land to a third party, generally the third party will take the land free of any obligation to the licensee, even if the third party had actual notice of the outstanding licence: *Re Toscano and Dorion*, [1965] 2 OR 514; 51 DLR (2d) 298 (CA). Nonetheless, under the principles of estoppel and unjust enrichment, a licence may in some cases bind subsequent purchasers of the land in question. This can arise if the owner of the land requests or allows the licensee to spend money on the land under a reasonable expectation, created by the owner of the land, that the licensee will be permitted to stay on the land: *Inwards v. Baker*, [1965] 2 QB 29; [1965] 1 All ER 336. Estoppel and unjust enrichment are further discussed in chapter 5.

2. If a tenant is wrongfully evicted from the leasehold estate, he or she may bring an action to recover the leasehold estate, and might be further protected by the remedies available under applicable landlord and tenant legislation, such as the Ontario Landlord

and Tenant Act, RSO 1990, c. L.7. Similarly, if the tenant is in breach of the leasehold agreement, the lessor may be able to employ the summary proceedings available under landlord and tenant legislation: *British American Oil Co. v. DePass* (1959), 21 DLR (2d) 110 (Ont. CA). By contrast, if a licensor is in breach of the licence, the licensee will generally be able to recover only monetary damages under contract law and is not protected by the various statutory protections available to residential tenants. Moreover, in the event of a breach by the licensee, the licensor will not be able to employ the summary proceedings under landlord and tenant legislation: *Re Canadian Pacific Hotels Ltd. and Hodges* (1978), 23 OR (2d) 577 (Co. Ct.).

In short, there is considerable disparity in the remedies available to tenants as opposed to licensees, and this disparity can lead to litigation. For example, in England, various lessors tried for some time to evade legal protections available to tenants, including English rent control legislation and landlord/tenant legislation, by attempting to construe their lease agreements as "licences": *Street v. Mountford*, [1985] AC 809; [1985] 2 All ER 289 (HL). To do so, some lessors drafted agreements that provided that the owner could enter the premises at any time without the "licensee's" permission, and further provided that the owner reserved the right to assign additional lodgers in the premises. Either provision is, on its face, inconsistent with the right of exclusive possession enjoyed by a tenant. The inclusion of such provisions was specifically designed to ensure that a court would construe the agreement as a licence rather than a leasehold estate. In practice, the lessors seldom if ever exercised such extraordinary rights, and the occupants effectively enjoyed exclusive possession of the premises. However, these same occupants, technically licensees, were denied any of the protections available in applicable rent control legislation or landlord and tenant legislation.

After much litigation, the House of Lords resolved the question largely in favour of the occupants in *Street v. Mountford*. The court found that notwithstanding the terms of the agreement, which seemed inconsistent with a grant of exclusive possession (such as the reservation of the right to assign additional lodgers), if the occupant in fact enjoys exclusive possession, and was meant to do so, then a tenancy will be found. The House of Lords was willing to recognize that such provisions were "shams" and not meant to reflect the reality of the situation. Accordingly, the ability of lessors in England to evade rent control laws, and landlord and tenant legislation, has been restricted. Nonetheless, there is evidence that some English lessors have continued to issue such "licences" in the hope that the occupants will remain unaware that they are in fact tenants who are entitled to all the legal protections available to residential tenants. For a further analysis of this problem, see Peter Vincent-Jones, "Exclusive Possession and Exclusive Control of Private Rented Housing" (1987), 14 *Journal of Law and Society* 445 and Charles Harpum, "Leases, Licences, Sharing and Shams" (1989), 48 *Cambridge Law Journal* 19.

There is no specific counterpart in Canadian law for the struggle between lessors and tenants in England. This may be due to the fact that some of the residential landlord and tenant legislation in Canada is broad enough to include such licence-like arrangements. For example, the Ontario Landlord and Tenant Act, RSO 1990, c. L.7, s. 1(a) includes within its definition of "residential premises," "accommodation in a boarding house, rooming house or lodging house." On the other hand, other provincial legislation, such as that in New Brunswick, expressly excludes accommodation in a "boarding house or lodging house" under the definition of "premises" covered by the residential tenancy legislation: the Residential Tenancies Act, SNB 1975, c. R-10.2, as am. SNB 1983, c. 82, s. 1(1)(e). In other provinces, boarding houses are not specifically included or excluded. In some cases the definition of the premises covered under the relevant landlord and tenant legislation may be broad enough to include boarding houses. See, for example, the Alberta Residential Tenancies Act, RSA 1980, c. R-15.3, s. 1(e), and the Nova Scotia Residential Tenancies Act, RSNS 1989, c. 401, s. 2(h), both of which define residential premises as any "place ... occupied by an individual as a residence."

Where boarding houses are expressly, or perhaps implicitly, covered under the relevant landlord and tenant legislation, the occupants in boarding houses are entitled to the benefits of the residential tenancy legislation. Accordingly, at least in those jurisdictions where boarding houses are expressly included, there may be less incentive to construct leases as licences, as any such attempt would not likely avoid the application of the relevant landlord and tenant legislation. Is it reasonable or fair that boarding houses should be treated differently from other forms of residential accommodation? Is there anything distinct about boarding houses that would justify differential treatment?

Long-Term Care Facilities: Leases or Licences?

Although Ontario landlord and tenant legislation covers residents in boarding houses, until recently this same legislation did not expressly cover residents in long-term care facilities, such as rest and retirement homes. These facilities provide some kind of supportive care for the residents and have typically enjoyed considerable power over who is admitted as a resident and under what conditions the resident may remain. For example, if the facility can no longer care for the resident, the resident may no longer be eligible to remain in the facility. For this reason, among others, the residential landlord and tenant legislation that extended greater security of tenure to the tenant was not regarded as appropriate for this setting. This view came under re-examination, particularly in the light of cases where residents in such facilities were abused. In 1992, the issue was the subject of an Ontario commission of inquiry, whose report led to legislative amendments in 1994.

In its report, the commission of inquiry documented the lack of suitably regulated accommodation in Ontario for persons with psychiatric histories, adults with developmental disabilities, and frail elderly persons. Noting the closure of many large psychiatric hospitals in the last 35 years, the commission described the circumstances faced by Ontarians with psychiatric histories, "living six or more to a room, sleeping in bunk beds or on floors, with few protections from exploitation, abuse, and capricious behaviour by landlords, staff, and sometimes complete strangers." Similarly, the commission described the plight of many frail elderly persons who are required to enter retirement homes where unscrupulous operators might victimize them. According to the commission, many of these vulnerable persons lived in accommodation that is "uninspected and outside the protection of rent control, the *Landlord and Tenant Act*, and other regulatory legislation." In the executive summary reproduced below, the commission outlined its recommendations for law reform.

Ernie S. Lightman, A Community of Interests
The Report of the Commission of Inquiry Into Unregulated
Residential Accommodation (1992)

Executive Summary

This Commission was created following the death of Joseph Kendall, a resident of Cedar Glen, an unregulated boarding home near Orillia, Ontario. The coroner's inquest into Mr. Kendall's death was the longest in Canadian history and produced more than eighty recommendations: key among these was that a Commission be appointed to inquire into unregulated residential accommodation in which vulnerable adults reside.

This Commission was appointed two days after the coroner's report was filed, in November 1990, and began its work on January 1, 1991, under the *Public Inquiries Act*. The Commission produced a widely circulated Discussion Paper in March 1991, which defined certain parameters for the Inquiry and raised several central questions for examination. The Commission consulted extensively, traveled to several communities across Ontario, visited a great variety of boarding, rest, and retirement homes, and met with residents, members of the public, and interest groups. We received some 230 written submissions.

Many vulnerable adults in Ontario live in unregulated settings, from luxury retirement homes to boarding/lodging/rest homes in which residents' only source of income may be social assistance [Family Benefits/(GAINS(D)) or General Welfare Assistance (GWA)], or Old Age Security (and its supplements). The accommodation is "unregulated" because there are no provincial licensing, standards or inspection; nor are there other viable protections for the lives and well-being of residents.

All premises within the scope of this Inquiry offer residents housing and limited care services (assistance with the activities of daily living); often some or all meals are provided. Virtually all are operated on a commercial or for-profit basis. Some are very small; one facility has 450 beds. Research conducted for the Commission uses census data to estimate there are 47,500 vulnerable adults living in unregulated accommodation in Ontario.

Some of the settings visited by the Commission appear to be exemplary: residents seem well cared for and content. Other premises revealed inadequate physical environments and unacceptable low-quality care: abuse of residents—physical, emotional, financial, and sexual—may occur with great regularity.

It is our general view that any setting in which both accommodation and care are supplied by operators creates a power imbalance between sellers and buyers, and the potential for abuse of this power.

The principal aim of this Inquiry has been to redress these structural imbalances, to empower vulnerable adults who live in unregulated settings, and to assist them to assume control of their lives to the maximum extent possible. Such control includes making decisions about where, how, and with whom to live. An allied goal of the Inquiry is to offer protection to those residents of rest homes who wish it.

The Commission considered two broad approaches:

1. Comprehensive regulation by the government of Ontario, on the nursing-home model, or by municipalities through municipal by-laws.

This approach would involve mandatory minimum standards set by government (provincial or municipal); government inspection; and, possibly, government funding to ensure these standards can be met. The rest home would be viewed as an institution, part of a continuum of institutional care—in effect, a low-level, care-providing commercial nursing home.

2. An empowerment approach, in which residents are given rights and the means to ensure that these rights are respected, combined with limited regulation to attain minimum standards in areas where a rights-based approach is unlikely to be effective.

This approach considers the rest home to be a permanent community residence rather than a place of temporary sojourn or a first-stage, low-level nursing home.

The Commission rejects the first alternative. The protections promised by comprehensive regulation are uncertain, the empowerment of residents modest or non-existent. This approach would also be costly to deliver and enforce; experience in other areas—particularly the nursing-home sector—also suggests there are many technical and operational obstacles to effective regulation.

The Commission recommends the second alternative, which should better achieve empowerment and protection, at lower overall cost.

To view the rest home as a form of permanent community housing is compatible with recent government directions: the development of new care-giving institutions is not being contemplated today. Instead, the goal is community care: to serve care needs in the community whenever possible; to lower the rate of institutionalization; and to limit institutional beds to those whose care needs are so high that they cannot be met in the community. As well, recent initiatives favour delinking (or separating) accommodation from the provision of care. The former would be provided by landlords and the latter delivered by non-profit community-based agencies to people in their own homes. Those for whom rest homes are home would then be fully eligible for all in-home services now available or developed in future under the long-term-care initiative.

We define "rest homes," whether retirement or boarding homes, as residences in which owners/operators provide or are paid to provide care services, or cause others to understand that they provide care.

We call for mandatory registration of all rest homes with the municipality. Registration merely makes rest-home operators known to municipal authorities: it is not dependent on meeting particular standards: and registrations, unlike nursing home licences, cannot be bought or sold. Registration will end the current practice by which rest homes may operate totally unknown to any level of government.

The Commission recommends a multi-faceted approach to empowerment while offering protection to rest-home residents. Specific elements include the following:

1. A Rest Home Residents' Bill of Rights, which contains protections and entitlements regarding the physical accommodation and the quality of care.

2. A Rest Homes Tribunal (RHT), through which residents, with assistance as desired, will seek enforcement of the protections and entitlements set out in the bill of rights; the RHT is premised on adequate advocacy supports, both informal—by relatives and friends—and those to be created under Bill 74, the proposed *Advocacy Act, 1991.*

3. Mandatory reporting of abuse in rest homes.

4. A police check of operators through the Canadian Police Information Centre to determine any criminal record, prior to registration.

5. Clarification of minimum safety standards regarding health, fire, and the physical environment, including the Building Code and municipal occupancy by-laws. (In considering minimum standards, the Commission has been particularly concerned to avoid the loss of low-income housing that might follow from standards—and costs—that are too high.)

The Commission also proposes to increase the accountability of local inspectors to residents for non-response or delayed/inadequate response to residents' complaints. No inspection visit should be announced in advance.

6. Mandatory minimum staff-to-resident ratios in all rest homes at all hours. These ratios will be premised on a safety function, i.e., in case of emergency, staff will be expected to obtain appropriate assistance expeditiously. The ratio is not premised on staff providing ongoing care to residents.

7. A minimum "competence" standard for all staff who assist with medications. Operators should not be required to assist residents with medications; however, should they choose to do so, staff must be adults, able to read and follow prescribed directions, and able to identify and communicate with each resident. They will not be required to have any medical training.

Following directly from our view of the rest home as permanent residential accommodation, the Commission also recommends:

1. coverage of all rest homes under part IV of the *Landlord and Tenant Act (LTA)*; and

2. coverage of all rest homes under the proposed *Rent Control Act (RCA)*.

These coverages should address many of residents' most commonly expressed problems, including capricious temporary or permanent eviction; failure to respect residents' privacy; denial of access to visitors; and sudden steep rises in costs.

We have also recommended criteria for *LTA* coverage for group homes, supportive housing, and rehabilitative and therapeutic residences.

Amendments to the *LTA* and proposed *RCA* are necessary to accommodate the special nature of rest homes. For example, eviction of a tenant can be time-consuming and difficult under the *LTA*; yet in some cases, particularly where accommodation is shared and living is communal, rapid departure is essential. Residents' care needs may suddenly exceed those that can be met in a rest home (either with operator- or community-supplied services); the result may be severe disruption of the residence and even physical danger to operators and other residents.

The Commission is satisfied there are sufficient grounds for eviction under the *LTA*, but timeliness is a problem. We recommend a new "fast-track" procedure under *LTA* through which operators will be able to obtain interim orders to temporarily remove residents from the premises when the behaviour of those residents likely meets existing grounds for eviction, and when delay is likely to cause serious harm to the person or property of operators or other residents.

Our approach to rent control differs from that of the February 1991 Ministry of Housing Green Paper on Rent Control. That document would have required operators to "debundle" (i.e., sell separately) accommodation and care services: all care would be sold as optional extras. We recommend that operators be permitted to sell a mandatory package including accommodation, meals, and care services. However, whatever is sold on a mandatory basis must be fully subject to rent control. The prices of optional care services will not be controlled; however, the timing of increases will be restricted, access to alternative providers must be available, and residents must have the opportunity to move out when prices of optional services rise.

With respect to retirement homes, whose residents have relatively high incomes, government's primary interest is to ensure that the market works as it should: operators must provide full pricing information to all potential residents, including a posted "rate sheet" and history of recent price increases. (They must also describe, in writing, any emergency-response system, including details of any commitment to a particular response; any staffing levels above legal requirements; and any internal complaint procedures.)

The Commission recommends that domiciliary hostels—rest homes in which residents are funded through GWA—be phased out as rapidly as possible. Currently, private operators may be paid a per diem (up to $1,015 per month) to provide accommodation, meals, and care services for each of about 4,500 vulnerable adults, most of whom have psychiatric and/or developmental disabilities. Accountability of operators is often limited or non-existent. In our view, operators of hostels should not be funded through a per diem to assess and meet care needs of residents; as quickly as possible, they should come to approximate traditional landlords.

We recommend that hostel residents who so desire should be assisted in leaving the hostels and reassigned to an appropriate category of social assistance. This will usually involve a shift from municipally administered GWA to provincially administered Family Benefits, potentially saving a municipality as much as $203 per resident per month.

The difference between current funding to operators and social assistance should be made available for the development and delivery of community-based care services. Residents should have a primary role in identifying, arranging, and, when possible, delivering these care services. Additional funding of about $1,000 per resident per year should be provided to approximate the cost of comparable community services currently provided to similar populations.

As interim measures, we recommend that all hostel contracts under GWA be limited to one-year renewable terms; and that the province set a maximum total-bed capacity for each domiciliary hostel. We also believe that operators should be prohibited from involvement in the distribution of the personal-needs allowance (PNA) to hostel residents.

The Commission also recommends:

1. that coverage of rest homes under the *Workers' Compensation Act* and *Hospital Labour Disputes Arbitration Act (HLDAA)* be consistent with the definition of rest homes as residential settings, not institutions;

2. that the *Planning Act* be amended to make accessory apartments and rooming, boarding, and lodging houses an as-of-right use in all zones where residential uses are permitted;

3. that a pilot project be considered, as resources permit, to implement full community-based services in one or more communities; and that Windsor be considered for inclusion in such a pilot project;

4. that the Residential Services Branch develop a precise legal definition of a nursing home, and that rest homes that offer high levels of care and serve, in effect, as "bootleg" nursing homes without nursing-home licences, cease offering nursing-home levels of care; [and]

5. that the Ministry of Health investigate the quality of medical care delivered to residents in rest homes, and the billing practices of doctors (including "house doctors") who regularly claim for multiple and sequential home visits in rest homes.

In an Appendix to the Report, the Commission also suggests that the announced intention of the government of Ontario to eliminate the funding differential between nursing homes and homes for the aged be deferred pending clear evidence of effective accountability to residents in nursing homes.

Much of this Report focuses on residents' day-to-day problems and quality of life. We argue that the protections promised by comprehensive regulation would not be effective. Instead, a variety of remedies and avenues for redress should be available to residents; we believe that, overall, such measures will be more powerful and more accountable:

1. violations of the residents' bill of rights may be pursued through the Rest Homes Tribunal, which will have available a wide array of remedies from mild reprimands, through orders to do or cease doing something, to permanent closure of premises and banning of individual operators from the industry;

2. the *LTA* and/or rent control may offer remedies for violations of the terms of the lease (mandatory package), including permanent or temporary abatement of rent and termination of lease; and

3. violations with respect to commercial contracts for optional services may be pursued through the courts.

In summary, this Report has placed before the people and government of Ontario a number of responses to the many problems identified in rest homes. To do nothing is unacceptable: abuses continue to be identified, and the quality of residents' lives in too many cases is frankly appalling. To regulate comprehensively, creating, in effect, a new set of care-giving institutions would be costly, and the outcome very uncertain.

An approach based on empowerment, which we endorse, has the potential to do more, and at less cost. However, the empowerment must be practical and operational, not merely theoretical—and this, ultimately, is the greatest challenge Ontarians face.

Discussion Notes

Professor Lightman's report resulted in amending legislation in 1994, the Residents' Rights Act, SO 1994, c. 2. The definition of residential premises covered under the Ontario Landlord and Tenant Act, RSO 1990, c. L.7, s. 1 was amended to include "any premises occupied or intended to be occupied by a person for the purpose of receiving care services, whether or not receiving the services is the primary purpose of the occupancy." The definition of the rental units covered under the Ontario Rent Control Act, SO 1992, c. 11 was also amended to include "care homes," defined under s. 1 as "a residential complex that is occupied or intended to be occupied by persons for the purpose of receiving care services, whether or not receiving the services is the primary purpose of the occupancy." Similarly, the Rental Housing Protection Act, RSO 1990, c. R.24, which provides certain restrictions on the demolition of rental property, was amended to include "care homes," defined above (see s. 1). As a result of these amendments, persons living in such "care homes" in Ontario have increased security of tenure, including security from rent increases prohibited under the Rent Control Act.

Consider whether these amendments will cover all rest and retirement homes, particularly in the light of the fact that some rest and retirement homes make care services available only at an extra cost to the tenant. If the care services are available only for an additional fee, are these premises "occupied by a person for the purposes of receiving care services"? What are the consequences if such premises are not included in the definition of care home?

The law governing care homes is about to undergo significant change in Ontario. Under Bill 96, the Tenant Protection Act, 1996, 1st Sess., 36th Leg. Ont., 1997, Ontario landlord and tenant law will be substantially amended. Bill 96 retains the same definition of "care homes" under the definition of residential units covered under the Bill (s. 1(1)), so the provisions of Bill 96 generally apply to care homes. However, Part IV of Bill 96 also provides for a variety of provisions specifically dealing with care homes. Section 86(1) provides that tenancy agreements in care homes shall be in writing, including any agreement with respect to "care services and meals and the charges for them." Under s. 95, the landlord may not increase any charges for care service or meals without first giving the tenant at least 90 days written notice. The written tenancy agreement must include a clause informing the tenant that the tenant has the right to consult a third party with respect to the agreement and cancel the agreement within five days after the agreement has been entered into (s. 88). Under ss. 19-21, a landlord's right to enter a leased premise is limited generally to emergencies and other specified circumstances. However, s. 89(1) permits landlords to enter a rental unit in a care home at regular intervals to check the tenant's condition if the tenancy agreement requires the landlord to do so. Section 89(2) permits a tenant to revoke unilaterally any prior agreement to permit the landlord to do so.

Under Bill 96, landlord and tenant disputes will be taken out of the hands of the civil courts and placed under the control of an administrative tribunal established under the Act, the Ontario Rental Housing Tribunal. Under s. 93(1), a landlord may apply to this tribunal for an order transferring a tenant out of a care home and evicting the tenant if the tenant no longer requires the level of care provided by the landlord, or the tenant requires a level of care that the landlord is not able to provide. Under s. 93(2), the tribunal may issue such an order only if it is satisfied that appropriate alternative accommodation is available for the tenant and the tenant's care needs cannot be met by community-based services provided in the care home in question. Bill 96, ss. 206-7, will also repeal the Ontario Rent Control Act, SO 1992, c. 11 and the Rental Housing Protection Act, RSO 1990, c. R.24, reducing the level of protection available to all tenants, including those in care homes, with respect to rent increases and the demolition of rental premises.

Examine the effect of Bill 96 on the residents of care homes. Does the bill enhance or diminish the protections available to the residents of care homes? Is Bill 96 responsive to the concerns expressed in the commission's report? Should lessors have the extraordinary power to apply to evict the residents of care homes if the tenant requires a level of care that the lessor is not able to provide?

Commercial Leases and Licences

The distinction between leases and licences remains important in Canadian law. In a commercial context, questions frequently arise regarding the characterization of various agreements as either leases or licences. These disputes tend to focus on (1) the question whether the owner or the occupant may avail itself of the provisions of the applicable landlord and tenant legislation, or (2) whether, on the sale of the land, the occupant's interest will bind the subsequent purchaser. In both cases, the characterization of the agreement is crucial in resolving this dispute. For example, in the case that follows, the lessor was seeking to employ the summary proceedings under the relevant landlord and tenant legislation to evict a commercial tenant. The tenant, in defence, argued that he was a licensee under the "lease" agreement, and not a tenant, because the agreement did not accord the occupant exclusive possession. Because he was not a "tenant," he argued that the court had no jurisdiction to evict him under the Landlord and Tenant Act. In terms of strategy, why might the occupant take the position that he was not a tenant? How might this position further his interest?

Re British American Oil Co. and DePass
(1959), 21 DLR (2d) 110 (Ont. CA)

SCHROEDER JA: On September 3, 1959, the appellant, the British American Oil Co. Ltd., as landlord, made application to His Honour Judge Macdonell in the County Court in the County of York for an order for a writ of possession directed to the Sheriff of the County of York, directing that official forthwith to place the applicant in possession of the service station premises located at 120 Fleet St. in the City of Toronto, which said premises were more particularly described in a lease entered into between the applicant as landlord and Jack Halpert as tenant on February 6, 1959. On the same date a similar application was made for an order for a writ of possession with respect to service station premises located at 929 Queen St. East in the City of Toronto, and more particularly described in a certain lease entered into between the applicant as landlord and the respondent, Richard DePass, as tenant, on February 6, 1959. The grounds of the said applications were that the leases entered into between the parties had been validly determined as of August 24, 1959, by service of a notice to quit dated July 25, 1959, given by the landlord pursuant to the terms of the said leases. It was alleged that the tenants, having wrongfully refused to go out of possession, were overholding tenants without permission of the landlord or right to possession or occupancy, and that they wrongfully held possession against the landlord. Each of the said applications was dismissed with costs. From these two orders British American Oil Co. now appeals.

The reasons for judgment of His Honour Judge Macdonell do not indicate the precise ground on which the applications were dismissed. He referred, without denominating them, to certain cases which had been cited which, in his view, were indistinguishable on the facts. One of those cases, we are now informed, was *Reliance Petroleum Ltd. v. Rosenblood*, [1953] OWN 115, decided by His Honour Judge Latchford in the County Court of the County of Wentworth in which a similar application under Part III of the *Landlord and Tenant Act*, RSO 1950, c. 199 was dismissed on the ground that the service station lease and the retail dealer sales agreement entered into between Reliance Petroleum Ltd. and Rosenblood, a service station operator, was to be construed not as creating the relationship of landlord and tenant, but the relationship of licensor and licensee. The County Court Judge decided in that case that the documents constituted "a mere device to secure the sale of McManus Petroleum Limited's products," [at 116] and further, that the service station operator had not been given the right to exclusive possession of the premises, but only a right to use them for the purpose of selling those products. We are informed that there were also certain unreported decisions of other County Court Judges cited to the County Court Judge in which the same reasoning was applied.

It is evident, therefore, that the reason for dismissal of the applications under review was that in the learned County Court Judge's opinion the true relationship between the parties was that of licensor and licensee and that he did not possess jurisdiction to hear the applications made by the landlord on the footing that the relationship was that of landlord and tenant.

On February 6, 1959, the parties signed a document described as a service station lease, and on the same date they signed a separate agreement described as an "equipment loan and retail dealer sales agreement." Both respondents are described in the former instrument as "tenant." It was provided in the leases that in consideration of the rents, covenants and agreements thereinafter reserved on the part of the tenant to be paid, kept, observed and performed, the British American Oil Co. did demise and lease unto the tenant the lands and premises therein described, followed by a *habendum* clause in the terms following: "To have and to hold the said premises for the term of one month to commence on the 1st January, 1959, and end on the 31st January, 1959, subject to earlier termination as herein provided." It was further stipulated that the leases should "automatically renew" themselves on the same terms and conditions (including this particular provision for automatic renewal) unless written notice of termination was given by either party to the other at least 30 days prior to the expiration of the term or any renewal thereof, or unless the lease or any renewal thereof had been terminated by the British American Oil Co. as thereinafter provided. The Retail Dealer Sales Agreement made on the same date obligated the lessee to sell only the products of the British American Oil Co. on the terms and conditions therein set forth, and also contained a list of the equipment furnished by the company to the tenants on loan upon the terms and conditions fully set forth in that contract.

The problem in this appeal is to decide what, upon the facts, is the true legal relationship between the parties. The County Court Judge thought that it was that of licensor and licensee and accordingly held that the summary procedure for which provision was made in Part III of the *Landlord and Tenant Act* could not be invoked by the appellant.

Counsel for the tenants submitted to this Court that the true legal relationship was that of licensor and licensee. He contended that on a proper construction of the formal documents and on an accurate appraisal of the proper inferences to be drawn from the surrounding circumstances and the conduct of the parties, the respondents should be held to have been given possession of the premises for the "limited purpose of selling the products of the appellants and for no other purpose"; that they had no effective control over the use of the premises, and if they attempted to use them for any purpose other than the sale of the appellant's products, their right of occupancy could be terminated forthwith; and that while the first mentioned document is in terms described as a lease and contains terms and conditions normally found in leases, that is not a decisive factor.

In support of his argument counsel referred to the several restrictive terms and conditions of the leases and retail dealers' agreements as hereinafter set out:

(a) The provisions in the leases that the tenant "will not use the demised premises for the storage or parking of motor vehicles nor will he permit the same, unless herein otherwise expressly authorized; he will indicate by signs, notices and such other methods as are satisfactory to BA that he is the sole proprietor of the business carried on in the demised premises; he will not erect any building or other structure on the said lands, and will not make any additions to or changes in the present buildings or equipment without the consent of BA in writing. ..."

(b) A covenant by the tenant "to execute BA's Retail Dealer Sales Agreement and further to observe and perform all the terms and conditions thereof. A breach of the terms of the Retail Dealer Sales Agreement aforesaid shall constitute a breach of the terms of this lease."

(c) A clause entitling the Oil Company "to erect and maintain such advertising signs on the demised premises as it deems advisable and a covenant that the Tenant will not erect or permit to be erected or to remain on the said premises any other signs or advertising except with the written consent of BA."

Counsel for the tenants also laid stress on certain provisions of the Retail Dealer Sales Agreements by which the company agreed to supply the dealer's entire requirements of gasoline, motor oil, greases and other petroleum products and anti-freeze compounds wanted for resale through the tenant's retail business. Reference was also made to cls. 4, 6, 7, 11 and 12 of the said Agreement which are reproduced hereunder:

4. The dealer covenants and agrees that during the term of this agreement he will, continuously and exclusively, by himself or his agents or tenants, purchase, sell, advertise, trade and deal in the particular kinds, grades, and brands of product marketed by the Company to the Retail Dealer Trade generally, at the time and point of delivery, and further covenants and agrees that during the term of this agreement no petroleum products other than those of the Company will be used, stored, sold or otherwise dealt in, on or about the above named premises or any other premises leased, owned or controlled by the Dealer within one mile of the said premises, said covenant being one of the main considerations for the Company entering into this agreement. The covenants set forth in this paragraph are to run with the lands comprising the above named premises.

6. The dealer agrees to provide and maintain without cost to the Company on the above named premises equipment and facilities for the storage, display, sale and delivery of the petroleum products hereinbefore mentioned and agrees that the said equipment and facilities during the term of this agreement will be used exclusively for the handling of products purchased from the Company.

7. The dealer covenants and agrees to use the BA Record Keeper for keeping proper accounting records and the salesman of the Company shall have the right of access to these records at any time. At the Company's discretion provision may be made for the garage operators to use their own accounting books of record in place of the BA Record Keeper.

11. This agreement supersedes all retail dealer sales agreements heretofore made between the parties.

12. This agreement shall remain in force for ten (10) years from the 1st day of January, 1957; and shall renew itself automatically from year to year thereafter unless written notice of termination is given by either party to the other at least ninety (90) days prior to the expiration of the said term or of any renewal period.

It was contended by counsel for the tenants that these restrictive provisions were so completely inconsistent with a tenant's free use and enjoyment of property demised under a tenancy agreement as to constitute an effective derogation from that right of exclusive possession to which a tenant is by law entitled; that consequently the tenants had been granted no higher right than a mere right of occupancy as licensees for the purposes mentioned in the material documents.

Wherever the relationship of landlord and tenant exists there is present the element of permission or consent on the part of the landlord, and subordination to the landlord's title and rights on the part of the tenant. There must be a reversion in the landlord, the creation of an estate in the tenant, and a transfer of possession and control of the premises to the tenant. The reservation of rent to the landlord is usual but not in all cases essential, and whether the rent reserved is payable in money or through some other medium has no particular significance. It will be observed, therefore, that the transmission of an estate to the tenant is an essential characteristic of the relationship of landlord and tenant. No estate in the land passes to a licensee and this, on the authorities, is the principal distinguishing trait between the two relationships. An agreement which confers exclusive possession of the premises as against all the world, including the owner, is a lease, while if it merely confers a privilege to occupy under the owner, it is a licence. It is often difficult to determine whether a particular agreement is to be regarded as a lease or a licence. Broadly speaking, however, the general concept of a licence is that it is a mere permission to occupy the land of another for some particular purpose.

In *Thomas v. Sorrell* (1673), Vaugh. 330 at p. 351, 124 ER 1098, Vaughan CJ defined a licence in these words: "A dispensation or licence properly passeth no interest, nor alters or transfers property in any thing, but only makes an action lawful, which without it had been unlawful."

In *Errington v. Errington*, [1952] 1 KB 290, Denning LJ stated at pp. 296-7 that in distinguishing between these two relationships a crucial test had sometimes been supposed to be whether the occupier had exclusive possession or not; that if he was let into exclusive possession he was said to be a tenant, albeit only a tenant at will, whereas if he had not exclusive possession he was only a licensee. After referring to *Doe d. Tomes v. Chamberlaine* (1839), 4 M & W 14 at p. 16, 151 ER 7; *Lynes v. Snaith*, [1899] 1 QB 486; *Peakin v. Peakin*, [1895] 2 IR 359; and *Howard v. Shaw* (1841), 8 M & W 118, 151 ER 973, Denning LJ stated: "The test of exclusive possession is by no means decisive."

The question was again considered by the Court of Appeal in England in *Addiscombe Garden Estates Ltd. v. Crabbe*, [1958] 1 QB 513. In that case the trustees of a members' lawn tennis club entered into an agreement with the owners of tennis courts and a club house, whereby the owners purported to "license and authorize" the trustees to use and enjoy the premises for 2 years from May 1, 1954 in consideration of monthly payments of "court fees." The agreement contained a number of clauses providing for repair and maintenance by the tennis club's trustees; for permitting the grantors to enter and inspect the condition of the premises, and for all other reasonable purposes. The owners also covenanted for quiet enjoyment, and the agreement provided that the grantors might "re-enter and determine the licence in the event of non-payment of any of the said payments of court fees ... or on any breach of ... the grantees' stipulations." The trustees continued to occupy the property after the expiration of the agreement, asserting that the agreement had granted them a tenancy which was protected by Part II of the *Landlord and Tenant Act* of 1954 which afforded security of tenure to any tenancy "where the property comprised in the tenancy is or includes premises which are occupied by the tenant and are so occupied for the purposes of a business carried on by him." It was held that the agreement taken as a whole, although described as a licence, on its true construction created the relationship of landlord and tenant and not that of licensor and licensee; that the true relationship was to be determined by the law and not by the label which the parties chose to put on it. At p. 528, Jenkins LJ referred to the statement of Denning LJ in *Errington v. Errington*, (*supra*) that: "The test of exclusive possession is by no means decisive." In commenting upon that statement, Jenkins LJ stated: "I think that wide statement must be treated as qualified by his [Denning LJ's] observations in *Facchini v. Bryson*, [1952] 1 TLR 1386 at 1389, and it seems to me that, save in exceptional cases of the kind mentioned by Denning LJ in that case [*Errington v. Errington*], the law remains that the fact of exclusive possession, if not decisive against the view that there is a mere licence, as distinct from a tenancy, is at all events a consideration of the first importance. In the present case there is not only the indication afforded by the provision which shows that exclusive occupation was intended, but there are all the various other matters which I have mentioned, which appear to me to show that the actual interest taken by the grantees under the document was the interest of tenants, and not the interest of mere licensees."

I am unable to accept the submission of counsel for the respondent that the nature of the reservations or restrictions contained in the documents under review is such as to prevent the service station leases, as modified or qualified by the accompanying agreements, from being in law demises of the land. An answer to this contention is afforded by the proposition laid down in *Glenwood Lumber Co. v. Phillips*, [1904] AC 405. In that case the Government of Newfoundland had granted a licence to the respondent giving him an exclusive right of occupation of the land, though subject to reservations and to a restriction as to its user. Before the granting of this licence the appellants, who expected that they themselves would obtain the licence, commenced cutting timber on the land comprised therein and continued to do so until 3 days after its grant, notwithstanding the receipt of a formal notice from the respondent, and thereafter they removed the logs which had been cut. It was held that the lessee had lawful possession of the logs so cut which established a good title against the appellants with the right to consequent relief, namely, to recover the value of the logs removed. At p. 408, Lord Davey, who wrote the opinion of the Board, disposed of the appellant's contention that the instrument was only a licence which did not carry with it an interest in the land itself in these words: "The appellants contended that this instrument conferred only a licence to cut timber and carry it away, and did not give the respondent any right of occupation or interest in the land itself. Having regard to the provisions of the Act under the powers of which it was executed and to the language of the document itself, their Lordships cannot adopt this view of the construction or effect of it. In the so-called licence itself it is called indifferently a licence and a demise, but in the Act it is spoken of as a lease, and the holder of it is described as the lessee. It is not, however, a question of words but of substance. If the effect of the instrument is to give to the holder an exclusive right of occupation of the land, *though subject to certain reservations or to a restriction of the purposes for which it may be used*, it is in law a demise of the land itself."

I can perceive no analogy between the present case and such cases as *Edwardes v. Barrington* (1901), 85 LT 650 (HL); *Frank Warr & Co. v. London County Council*, [1904] 1 KB 713 and *Clore v. Theatrical Properties Ltd. & Westby & Co.*, [1936] 3 All ER 483, which involved agreements for what are frequently described as "the front of the house rights," under which the owner or lessee of a theatre grants to the licensee the use of refreshments rooms in the theatre for the purpose of supplying refreshments to and for the accommodation of visitors to the theatre during specified periods of the day. In those cases it was held that the contracts did not confer an interest in land, and that the documents creating the rights were not leases, but licences only, which created a purely personal right. Other instances of agreements which were held to create licences are stated in 23 Hals., 3d ed., p. 429, para. 1025. In those cases the persons granted the right to use the premises were held not to have become entitled to the exclusive possession thereof, and the circumstances and conduct of the parties indicated that all that was intended was that the grantee should be granted a personal privilege with no interest in the land itself.

In *Wells v. Mayor, etc. of Kingston-upon-Hull* (1875), LR 10 CP 402, the defendants, a municipal corporation, owned a dock of which they allowed the use to ships requiring repairs. The regulations governing the use of the dock provided that it should be "let" to parties requiring the same for the repair of vessels at rates to be fixed by the council of the borough. The regulations contained provisions that the defendants should be entitled to detain the vessel in the dock until the dockage was paid, that the corporation foreman should open and shut the dock gates, and various other provisions tending to show that the defendants intended to retain possession of and control over the dock while in use by vessels. The plaintiffs complained that the defendants did not admit their vessel into the dock in her turn, and it was held in an action for breach of contract by the plaintiff that the contract was not for an interest in land within s. 4 of the *Statute of Frauds* and therefore was not required to be in writing, nor was it required to be under the seal of the corporation. In deciding this question the Court had to consider whether the parties intended to create, or the terms of the contract did in fact create the relation of landlord and tenant, or give an exclusive right to the occupation of the dock, or any other such right as would amount to an interest in land. It was held that what was granted to the plaintiff was no more than a personal licence to use the dock notwithstanding the use of the word "let" in the regulations.

To determine whether an agreement creates the relationship of landlord and tenant or merely that of licensor and licensee, the intention of the parties must be ascertained. In the present case the whole of the documents signed by the parties must be carefully scrutinized and considered. The first document, known as the service station lease is couched in language peculiar to a lease, and contains terms which leave no doubt that it was the intention of the parties that the service station operators should have exclusive possession of the land demised, subject to certain reservations and restrictions which, in the circumstances, are not extraordinary. There is nothing in the leases or the retail dealers' agreements which suggest that the lessors intended to retain possession of and control of the service station premises in a manner which would be inconsistent with the grant of a right of exclusive possession to the lessees. Not only do the agreements in question give exclusive possession to the respondents in clear and unmistakable terms, but the very nature of the acts to be done and the business to be carried on by them required that they should have exclusive possession. In plain and simple terms these agreements impose on the grantees, in substance, the rights and obligations of tenants, and on the grantors in substance the rights and obligations of a landlord. There is nothing in the surrounding circumstances which in any way modifies or qualifies that determination. I cannot avoid the conclusion that the appropriate effect to be given to the agreements under consideration is to hold that they created a tenancy rather than a mere licence.

Considerable argument was directed to the point that s. 75(1) of the *Landlord and Tenant Act* deals with cases where a "tenant after his lease or right of occupation ... has expired ... wrongfully refuses or neglects to go out of possession."

Reference was also made to s. 1(b) of the Act where "landlord" is defined as follows: "'landlord' includes lessor, owner, the person *giving or permitting the occupation of the premises in question*, and his and their heirs and assigns and legal representatives, and in Parts II and III also includes the person entitled to the possession of the premises."

In s. 1(d) "tenant" is defined as follows: "'tenant' includes lessee, occupant, sub-tenant, under-tenant, and his and their assigns and legal representatives."

It was therefore argued that Part III of the Act and the summary procedure thereby authorized could be invoked against the respondents, even if they were licensees entitled only to a right of occupancy under a personal licence. Since I have decided that the relationship between the parties is that of landlord and tenant, it becomes unnecessary to consider this alternative contention and I express no opinion upon the point involved.

It was not contended that the notice given by the landlord did not fully comply with the terms of the lease. I would therefore allow the appeals with costs, set aside the orders in appeal, and order that writs of possession do issue directed to the Sheriff of the County of York commanding him forthwith to place the appellants in possession of the service station premises now occupied by the respondents as tenants. The respondents should pay to the appellant the costs of the respective applicants to the County Court Judge.

Appeals allowed.

Discussion Notes

Factors Suggesting a Lease

List the factors that, according to the court, suggested that the agreement was a lease. What factors suggested a licence? What appeared to be the most legally significant facts that enabled the court to reach its conclusion that this agreement was a lease?

Shell-Mex and BP Ltd. v. Manchester Garages Ltd.

In *Shell-Mex and BP Ltd. v. Manchester Garages Ltd.*, [1971] 1 WLR 612 (CA), Manchester Garages signed a "licence" with Shell-Mex to occupy a filling station. The agreement provided that Manchester was to occupy the premises for one year and to sell only Shell-Mex products. The agreement also included a provision that allowed Shell-Mex's employees to visit the premises at their discretion.

Shell-Mex attempted to terminate the agreement pursuant to the terms of the "licence." However, Manchester argued that the "licence" was in fact a lease, and could be terminated only pursuant to the relevant provisions of the landlord and tenant legislation in effect at the time. How might such a position be in Manchester's interest? The court considered whether the agreement was a personal privilege given to a person (a licence), or whether it was an estate in land transferable to third parties (a lease). The court noted that the agreement was called a "licence," the provisions seemed personal in nature as the defendant was to deal only in Shell-Mex products, and, most important, the agreement included a provision permitting the employees of Shell-Mex to enter the premises at any time. The court found that these provisions were inconsistent with exclusive possession, thus creating a licence only. The court added that, whether an agreement were a licence or a tenancy, the court should not have regard only to the label or formal language of the document, but should instead examine the substance of the transaction and look at the agreement as a whole. Is *Shell-Mex* consistent with *Re British American Oil*?

In the following case, consider the extent to which the expressed intention of the parties is relevant. Does it matter whether the parties describe their agreement as a lease or a licence, or do the courts instead look to the substance of the agreement rather that the name given it by the parties?

Metro-Matic Services Ltd. v. Hulmann
(1973), 48 DLR (3d) 326 (Ont. CA)

BROOKE JA: This is an appeal by the plaintiff from the judgment of the Honourable Mr. Justice Houlden dated April 16, 1970, dismissing the plaintiff's action for loss of profit and damages for breach of a lease dated November 20, 1963, made between the appellant as tenant and 130 Jameson Apartments as the landlord, which lease was duly assigned to the defendant respondent on June 2, 1964.

The appellant carries on the business of leasing and operating coin-operated washing machines and in June of 1963, it installed a number of its machines in the apartment building located at 130 Jameson Ave. This building is a large 108-suite apartment building and was in 1963 owned by eight individuals as tenants in common, two of whom are S.J. Mendelson and Abraham Bleeman who were at all material times also officers of the appellant company.

On November 20, 1963, the document here in question being an agreement in writing entitled "Lease Agreement," was entered into between the appellant as the tenant and 130 Jameson Avenue as the landlord. By this agreement the landlord purported to "demise and lease" to the tenant the "laundry room or rooms located on the ground floor of the Landlord's premises." The document is now set out in full:

METRO-MATIC SERVICES LIMITED
Toronto, Ontario
LEASE AGREEMENT

THIS INDENTURE OF LEASE made the twentieth day of November, 1963, BETWEEN:
130 Jameson Apartments
hereinafter called "the Landlord"
—and—
METRO-MATIC SERVICES LIMITED
hereinafter called "the Tenant"

WHEREAS the Landlord is the owner of certain lands and apartment building(s), known as 130 Jameson Apartments located at 130 Jameson Avenue, in the City of Toronto, hereinafter called the "Landlord's premises."

NOW THIS INDENTURE WITNESSETH:

1. In consideration of the rents, covenants and agreements hereinafter reserved and contained on the part of the Tenant, the Landlord does demise and lease unto the Tenant the laundry room or rooms located on the ground floor(s) of the Landlord's premises.

2. To have and to hold the demised premises for and during the term of five (5) years to be computed from the 20 day of November, 1963; provided that this lease shall automatically renew itself for a further term of Five (5) years, unless either party, at least three months prior to the end of the term hereby granted or any renewal thereof, gives notice in writing to the other party of its intention to terminate this Lease.

3. Yielding and paying therefor during the term hereby granted, and any renewal thereof, unto the Landlord the sum of:
ONE DOLLAR AND TWENTY-FIVE CENTS ($1.25) per suite per month payable quarterly, the first of such payments to become due and payable on the 31st day of December 1963.

4. The Tenant covenants and agrees that the demised premises shall be used only for the purpose of carrying on the business of an automatic laundry.

5. The Landlord covenants with the Tenant for quiet enjoyment.

6. The Landlord further covenants and agrees as follows:
    (a) the Tenant shall have the sole and exclusive right to install and maintain as many automatic washing machines and dryers, coin changers and soap machines as the Tenant in its absolute discretion shall deem necessary to properly serve the tenants of the Landlord's premises, as well as installing

from time to time such other machines and equipment as the Tenant shall deem necessary.

(b) the authorized employees and agents of the Tenant shall have free access to the demised premises at all reasonable times to install, inspect, service, repair or remove the said machines and equipment and to collect the monies deposited therein;

(c) notwithstanding anything contained in the Landlord and Tenant Act, Revised Statutes of Ontario, 1960, Chapter 206, and amendments thereto (the benefit of which the Landlord hereby irrevocably waives) or any other Act of the Province of Ontario both present and future, the said machines and equipment referred to herein shall not be subject to distress or seizure by the Landlord or its agents by reason of any default whatever by the Tenant, its employees and agents; and the said machines and equipment shall not become fixtures of the Landlord, but shall remain the personal property of the Tenant;

(d) to pay all charges for water and electricity incurred as a result of the use of the said machines and equipment;

(e) to permit the tenants of the Landlord's premises to have free access to the demised premises and to have the use of the machines and equipment at all reasonable times;

(f) in the event the Landlord's premises shall be sold during the term hereby granted or any renewal thereof, then the Landlord shall, prior to the closing of any such purchase and sale, obtain from the purchaser and remit to the Tenant a written acknowledgment by the purchaser that he agrees to be bound by the terms, covenants and conditions set forth herein;

(g) the Landlord will pay all taxes, duties and assessments whatsoever whether municipal, parliamentary or otherwise which during the said term may be charged upon the demised premises or upon the Landlord or Tenant in respect hereof;

(h) no part of the Landlord's premises shall during the term hereby granted or any renewal thereof, be leased, licensed or in any other way granted to any other person or corporation other than the Tenant for any of the aforementioned purposes.

7. Provided that the Tenant may remove the said machines and equipment.

8. Provided that in the event the demised premises are damaged by reason of fire, lightning, tempest or any of the other elements, then rent shall cease until the demised premises are rebuilt.

9. Provided that in the event the Landlord's premises other than the demised premises are rendered wholly unfit for occupancy by the tenants thereof, by reason of fire, lightning, tempest or for any other reason whatever, then the rent provided for herein shall cease until such time as the Landlord's premises are restored to the condition they were in prior to being rendered unfit for occupancy and the said Landlord's premises are again reoccupied to the extent of the occupancy prior to such damage; provided further that in the event only part of the Landlord's premises normally occupied by tenants are rendered unfit for occupancy, then the rent provided for herein shall abate in the proportion that the part of the Landlord's

premises occupied by tenants after such damage bears to that part of the Landlord's premises ordinarily occupied by tenants.

10. Provided that if in the opinion of the Tenant, the Landlord has been in breach of any of the terms, covenants and agreements contained herein, the Tenant may terminate this Lease upon seven (7) days' written notice to the Landlord.

11. Any notice required or contemplated by any of the provisions of this Lease or which the Landlord or Tenant may desire to give to the other shall be sufficiently given to the Tenant by personal delivery or by registered letter, postage prepaid addressed to the Tenant at 153 Viewmount Avenue, Toronto 19, Ontario, and to the Landlord by registered mail postage prepaid and addressed to the said Landlord at 130 Jameson Avenue, Toronto, Ontario.

12. This Lease shall ensure to the benefit of and be binding upon the parties hereto, their heirs, executors, administrators, successors and assigns respectively.

IN WITNESS WHEREOF the parties hereto have executed these presents.

130 Jameson Apartments

SIGNED SEALED AND DELIVERED,

in the presence of

Per:

Landlord

(Seal)

METRO-MATIC SERVICES

Per:

(Seal)

On May 14, 1964, an offer was made by the respondent to S.J. Mendelson in trust for the eight tenants in common to purchase the building. It is clear from the evidence that before making this offer to purchase, the respondent had carried out an inspection of the building and was fully aware that the coin-operated laundry machines were in place on the premises and that they were not owned by the vendor, a fact which is set out in a schedule to the agreement of purchase and sale to the respondent's knowledge.

The offer to purchase provided in para. 12:

The Vendor will deliver to the Purchaser's solicitor at least one week before closing date, all existing leases with sufficient assignment of leases, together with appropriate direction to all the tenants with respect of payment of rent to the Purchaser.

The respondent's offer was accepted and prior to closing the transaction the respondent's solicitors availed themselves of the opportunity of examining the lease agreement and other relevant leases. On June 1, 1964, the transaction was closed and at that time the respondent's solicitors received an assignment of the "lease agreement." The respondent took possession on June 2, 1964, and thereafter, while he accepted two rent cheques dated June 30, and September 30, 1964, almost immediately after taking possession commenced to negotiate for the supply of laundry equipment with another company and requested the appellant to remove its equipment from the premises. In October of 1964, the appellant contends that the respondent disconnected its equipment which the appellant then removed from the premises claiming damages arising from a breach of the lease and for loss of profit.

Houlden J dismissed the plaintiff's action, finding that the "lease agreement" did not constitute a valid lease between the parties named therein and that it was no more than a mere licence, as it failed to create any estate in the appellant. The appeal to this Court is upon two grounds; first, that the trial Judge erred in finding that there was no valid lease and secondly, and in the alternative, that the appellant had an equitable interest in the premises and, in the circumstances here present, the respondent had actual notice of the appellant's interest.

Turning to the first question, what is the effect of the "Lease Agreement" dated November 20, 1963?

After considering the authorities, the learned trial Judge considered the "Lease Agreement" and it appears directing his attention to the meaning and interpretation arising from the covenants, particularly cl. 6, held that the tenant had no exclusive possession of the premises or right to exclusive possession. Indeed, he found the right of occupation was not in the tenant but rather in the landlord and that the appellant's right to enter was limited to a right to enter at reasonable times to service its machines as set out. His view of the document was really that it was no more than a concession agreement to make laundry services available to the tenants in the 108 suites of the building.

Perhaps the most recent authoritative statement on the subject of the requirements of a lease and the interpretation of such documents is that of Schroeder JA in *Re BA Oil Co. and Halpert*, [1960] OR 71, 21 DLR (2d) 110 *sub nom. Re BA Oil Co. Ltd. and dePass*. This was a case in which conditions attached to agreements entitled leases were said to prevent them from being in law a demise of land. At p. 77 OR, p. 115 DLR, Schroeder JA said:

Wherever the relationship of landlord and tenant exists there is present the element of permission or consent on the part of the landlord, and subordination to the landlord's title and rights on the part of the tenant. There must be a reversion in the landlord, the creation of an estate in the tenant, and a transfer of possession and control of the premises to the tenant. The reservation of rent to the landlord is usual but not in all cases essential, and whether the rent reserved is payable in money or through some other medium has no particular significance. It will be observed, therefore, that the transmission of an estate to the tenant is an essential characteristic of the relationship of landlord and tenant. No estate in the land passes to a licensee and this, on the authorities, is the principle distinguishing trait between the two relationships. An agreement which confers exclusive possession of the premises as against all the world, including the owner, is a lease, while if it merely confers a privilege to occupy under the owner, it is a licence. It is often difficult to determine whether a particular agreement is to be regarded as a lease or a licence. Broadly speaking, however, the general concept of a licence is that it is a mere permission to occupy the land of another for some particular purpose.

He went on to consider the question raised by a statement in the judgment of Denning LJ in *Errington v. Errington and Woods*, [1952] 1 KB 290 at p. 297, a case which required consideration of the distinction between contractual or equitable rights as opposed to the rights of a tenant to remain in possession of property so long as conditions under a long term agreement of purchase and sale were fulfilled. In this context he said: "The test of exclusive possession is by no means decisive."

After considering the explanation of this statement quoted in the judgment of Jenkins LJ in *Addiscombe Garden Estates Ltd. v. Crabbe*, [1958] 1 KB 513, and the speech of Lord Davey in *Glenwood Lumber Co. Ltd. v. Phillips*, [1904] AC 405 at p. 408, the learned Judge concluded that to create the relationship of landlord and tenant the tenant must have exclusive possession of the demised premises and proceeded to examine documents there in question to determine if it was the intention of the parties to confer such an estate on the tenant. See also E.K. Williams, *Canadian Law of Landlord and Tenant*, 3d ed. (1957), pp. 4, 9, 11.

Turning then to the document before the Court entitled "Lease Agreement," it is significant that the parties have been careful to employ numerous words customarily used in leases but, perhaps more important, words traditionally required to create an estate or interest in land. One cannot ignore the important effect of the words "demise" and "lease" and of the *habendum* and the covenant for quiet enjoyment which I should think, in the absence of a clear statement of the parties' intention to the contrary, are conclusive of the intention to grant a lease of the land in question with exclusive possession and control thereof.

However, the document contained a restriction that the premises shall only be used for the purpose of carrying on the business of an automatic laundry. Relying upon this and cl. 6 of the agreement, Mr. Hately firmly contends that the parties' intention was to create nothing more than a concession to provide a service for tenants in the building and at the same time that the landlord retain the right to possession and to control the use of the premises. He points out that the document provides for automatic machines with no reference to attendants being provided or needed and that provision is made to assure that all of the tenants in the building will have free access to the laundry premises and the appellant has not the freedom of access to the building of an ordinary tenant but is restricted rather to "reasonable times" and then only for specific purposes. In the result, he contends that there can be in these circumstances no exclusive possession or control in the appellant.

With deference to these arguments and to the judgment in appeal, I am persuaded that the appeal must succeed. While it is true that the appellant has by its own covenant restricted the use to which it will put the premises, such a covenant does not affect the demise any more than would be the case when a tenant covenants to use his apartment as a dwelling place only. This does not make his possession any the less exclusive. I do not think that cl. 6 of the landlord's covenant should now be interpreted at his suit to change or modify an intention otherwise expressed in the document by important words as above set out so that he or his assigns can escape liability as now contended for. When in consideration of the tenant's covenant to pay rent and do those things required of him, the landlord demised the premises to the tenant surely except in unusual circumstances only an express restriction as to possession and control should be regarded and restrictions should not be read into the document because of positive covenants on the part of the landlord as are found in cl. 6.

This "Lease Agreement" provided for the demise of the premises and for carrying on of a business there. In such circumstances I should think that it was really unnecessary to include covenants to provide for the tenant's occupancy of the premises or the installation of the machinery and equipment needed for the business contemplated by the parties and the access to the premises in a multiple occupancy building should be implied with the demise and in circumstances such as these it was really unnecessary to require a covenant to permit the installation, maintenance, replacement and removal of the automatic machines. Further, perhaps because the appellant was a limited company and carried on business by its employees and agents, it considered it better to obtain the covenant cl. 6(b) and it was no doubt prudent to obtain the covenant cl. 6(a) when at the same time obtaining from the landlord its covenant with respect to competition. As to cl. 6(c) the tenants of the building were to be the appellant's customers and if the demised premises were to be kept locked and used only for the purposes as the parties intended at any hour of the night or day, it was also prudent for the appellant to obtain the covenant in cl. 6(c).

None of these covenants make the appellant's possession any the less exclusive; none of these covenants relinquish any control by the appellant to the landlord; indeed to the contrary, they assure the appellant's exclusive possession and assure its control and occupancy.

In the circumstances, I hold that the document was intended to and did in fact confer upon the appellant exclusive possession and exclusive control of the demised premises. Under this agreement the landlord had no right to possession and no right to control of the demised premises. Conversely, the appellant alone had these rights and with them all of the obligations and liabilities of a tenant. The document is a valid lease and the defendant has breached it as alleged.

Counsel contended that the document was ineffective because the lessor lacked the status to enter into such a contract. This issue was not raised at the trial. Having regard to all of the circumstances and the evidence, I am of the conclusion that the document was properly entered into by persons duly authorized to do so.

In the result, then, the appeal is allowed. The finding as to damages made by the learned trial Judge is not disputed in this appeal. Accordingly, the judgment below will be set aside and judgment will go for the plaintiff in the sum of $2,043.75. The appellant should have its costs at the trial and in this Court.

Appeal allowed.

Discussion Notes

A Lease or a Licence?

If the agreement in *Metro-Matic Services Ltd.* were a "lease," why did the drafters of the agreement include clause 6(b), providing that the tenant shall have "free access to the demised premises at all reasonable times"?

If this agreement were a licence only, could the occupier Metro-Matic still successfully argue that the licence, notwithstanding the absence of privity of contract, nonetheless bound the new owner of the building? Is it relevant that the purchaser took the building with actual notice of the agreement with Metro-Matic, and further accepted two cheques from Metro-Matic after the sale was completed? What legal arguments might Metro-Matic raise?

Pacific Wash-A-Matic Ltd. v. R.O. Booth Holdings Ltd.

In *Pacific Wash-A-Matic Ltd. v. R.O. Booth Holdings Ltd.*, [1979] 6 WWR 458 (BC CA), the plaintiff laundry company entered into an agreement, called a "location agreement," with the owner of an apartment building. The agreement granted Pacific Wash-A-Matic the exclusive right to install and maintain coin-operated laundry machines in the apartment building. Clause 16 stated that the agreement was binding on the parties and that, should the owner sell or assign his interest in the premises, his successor would be fully bound by the terms of the agreement.

The building was sold to a third party, the entire "location agreement" was attached to the agreement for sale, and the sales agreement made specific mention of the location agreement. Seven months later, the new owner attempted to terminate the agreement, and eventually locked the laundry room and removed the machines to a storage area. At trial, the court found that the location agreement was a lease and consequently was binding on the new owner. On appeal, this decision was reversed, and the court held that there were no provisions in the present agreement such as those in *Metro-Matic*. In particular, the agreement did not provide for any demise of any portion of the apartment building. Instead, the court held that the agreement was merely a licence to place laundry machines in the building. The court thus concluded that the trial judge had been wrong and that the location agreement did not constitute a lease and was not binding on the new owner.

Why was clause 16 held to be of no effect by the court? Is it fair that the new owner should not be bound by this agreement?

The following case considers circumstances that include aspects of both a commercial and a residential agreement, raising the question whether a long-term resident in a hotel can evolve from a mere licensee to a tenant. Consider the legal consequences of determining that a hotel resident can be a tenant. Is it fair that a long-term resident in a hotel should be accorded no more than the same legal rights provided to a short-term resident? Should it matter how long a person has been resident in the hotel? Why?

Re Canadian Pacific Hotels Ltd. and Hodges
(1978), 23 OR (2d) 577 (Co. Ct.)

COO CCJ: Default judgment under the provisions of the *Landlord and Tenant Act*, RSO 1970, c. 236 having been set aside, this matter has come on again for formal and contested hearing.

The applicant, Canadian Pacific Hotels Limited, asks for judgment against the respondent, William E. Hodges, in the amount of $13,290 for rent owing for rooms nos. 11-297 and 11-299 at the Royal York Hotel in the City of Toronto.

The applicant claims that the relationship between the parties at all material times was that of landlord and tenant, there being a tenancy at will between the contracting parties.

The respondent takes the position that there was never in existence a landlord and tenant relationship, and that, in consequence, the applicant has no right to make use of the provisions of the *Landlord and Tenant Act* to attempt to recover rent owing.

There has been reserved for later disposition, if necessary, a defence upon which the respondent would seek to rely, if the landlord and tenant relationship is established, which defence, briefly set forth in Mr. Hodges' affidavit sworn September 19, 1978, is to the effect that the premises involved were dirty and unsafe, this presumably leading to a claim for abatement of rent. The alleged arrears of rent have not been paid into Court pursuant to the provisions of s. 106(6) [rep. & sub. 1975 (2d sess.), c. 13, s. 5(1)] of the *Landlord and Tenant Act*. Counsel for the respondent has argued that these proceedings ought never to reach the point where the strength and validity of the aforementioned defence of the respondent comes into issue, this in the light of the alleged inapplicability of all of the provisions of the *Landlord and Tenant Act* to the circumstances of this case. In addition, counsel for the respondent argues that the case of *Re Sam Richman Investments (London) Ltd. and Reidel et al.* (1974), 6 OR (2d) 335, 52 DLR (3d) 655, a decision of the Divisional Court, stands for the proposition that the only funds which in any event the respondent would be obliged to pay into Court under the provisions of s. 106(6), are those which might otherwise be said to be payable after notice of early termination was given by the applicant on June 26, 1978. In fact, Mr. Hodges and his family quit the two hotel rooms on July 22, 1978, which would mean, if counsel for the respondent is right, that the amount which ought to be paid into Court to permit the foregoing defence by his client to be presented would be at a daily rate of $54 for the period of time between the two above-mentioned dates.

The applicant of course takes the view that, assuming the landlord and tenant relationship to have existed, the amount of rent which would have to be paid into Court to permit the respondent to put forward the foregoing defence would involve the total amount allegedly owing, and not just the rent due for the approximate one-month period referred to by counsel for the respondent.

I have read the *Richman* case with some care and I do not accept that it stands for the proposition put forward by counsel for the respondent and, on this narrow issue, I would be prepared to rule that the respondent would be obliged, all other matters apart, to pay into Court the whole amount claimed as being arrears of rent, as a condition precedent to his being heard with respect to his other defences.

Counsel for the respondent also argued that the hotel rooms occupied over the years by the Hodges family were not "residential premises," to which kind of premises Part IV of the *Landlord and Tenant Act* applies. He referred to the definition section, s. 1(c) [rep. & sub. 1975 (2d Sess.), c. 13, s. 12] and argued that the evidence supported the proposition that the rooms constituted "premises occupied for business purposes with living accommodation attached, ..." and that by reason of s. 1(c)(iii) the rooms could not constitute "residential premises."

On all of the evidence I cannot agree. I am satisfied that the rooms constituted "residential premises" as they are defined in the Act, and that, although the respondent did indeed engage in some business activities in the rooms, they were indeed "premises used or intended for use for residential purposes" as that phrase is used in s. 1(c)(i).

That leaves for determination the major problem, which is whether there was in existence between the parties to these proceedings a landlord and tenant relationship.

Essentially the facts are that the respondent and his family, as it was constituted from time to time over the years, have lived in the two hotel rooms for well over 15 years. There was at no time any agreement in writing with regard to this occupancy.

The respondent decided, for reasons which at least satisfied him, that it made sense to live in a well-constructed, well-managed hotel. The hotel was willing to provide to Hodges the two rooms which he and his wife ultimately selected. Hodges was charged on a *per diem* basis a somewhat lower rate than would have been charged to a transient guest. He was apparently generally billed monthly, for a long time, not only for room charges but also for room service, meals, and other sorts of services generally provided to its guest by a hotel. It is to be emphasized that the claim in these proceedings is limited to the amount allegedly owing for the rooms themselves.

There is really very little evidence indeed on the basis of which any meaningful, sensible and firm conclusions can be reached as to what was intended by the parties.

What seems to me to be fairly clear is that what was furnished to Hodges and members of his family was really in no way different from that which any guest at the hotel could reasonably expect to have had furnished to him. Daily maid service was provided and was available, although Hodges himself indicated that he was reluctant to have maids in the rooms at certain times.

Hodges introduced into at least one, and probably both of the rooms, some of his own furniture, this at least mostly coming from a room in the same hotel occupied by Hodges' mother for some years prior to her death. No one told me how much decorating was done of the two rooms over the period of 15 years, who did the decorating, who paid for it, or who was responsible for choosing the form and nature of the decoration. From the little evidence that was given on this point I gathered that the hotel took the view that they were entitled to decorate these rooms as they would the others, and that perhaps Hodges took a slightly different view.

The hotel kept putting up what one might call the usual standard innkeeper's signs within the two rooms. This I suppose might, to a very minor degree, tend to lead one towards one conclusion as to the relationship between the parties. The difficulty about the signs is that Mr. Hodges took it upon himself to remove the signs as soon as they were put up by the hotel forces which in, and of itself, would tend to lead to another conclusion.

Little or no cooking of any kind was done in either of the two rooms by the Hodges family during all the years they occupied the premises.

I gather that save for the introduction into the premises of some pieces of privately-owned furniture and, at the request of Hodges, a well-worn piano which the hotel was willing to place in the premises, and subject to the question of decoration, the two rooms were like any others which might be found in a hotel containing something between one and two thousand rooms.

Mr. Hodges had introduced into one of the two rooms and at one stage in his stay an extension of a telephone line which was introduced into a store in the basement arcade of the hotel building, at a time when that store was occupied by a company in which Hodges had a major interest. It is not clear from the evidence whether that telephone continued in existence after vacation of the store premises by the company. In any event, the rooms were serviced in the ordinary way and in accordance with ordinary custom by hotel telephones connected to the hotel switchboard.

When the Hodges family ultimately came to vacate the premises they "checked out" in pretty much precisely the same sort of way that anyone else would check out, save and except of course for the fact that there allegedly was owing by Hodges at the time he checked out many, many thousands of dollars.

The sum and substance of the evidence is to indicate that the Hodges family acted and were treated by the hotel and its staff as though they were just four more guests in the hotel. The only difference of any moment was that Hodges remained in the hotel for over 15 years.

Very few cases were cited by counsel in argument touching upon the problem which is before me now for determination. I have read all of them, and a very large number in addition, including some of the basic cases which are found referred to again and again in cases dealing with whether a particular fact situation reflects a true landlord and tenant relationship, a licenser and licensee relationship, or some other. I include in this much shorter list of cases such decisions as *Cobb et al. v. Lane*, [1952] 1 All ER 1199, *Errington v. Errington et al.*, [1952] 1 All ER 149, and *Abbeyfield (Harpenden) Society Ltd. v. Woods*, [1968] 1 All ER 352.

I have gone through all the textbooks on the subject which I thought might be of any guidance and I have read a very large number of the cases therein referred to. I have frankly not found any number of cases of any direct and conclusive guidance or assistance.

It is relatively easy to state the principles. In determining whether an agreement between the parties constitutes a relationship of landlord and tenant or only that of licenser and licensee, the major consideration is the intention of the parties. If there is no formal agreement, in writing or otherwise, this intention must be gathered from all of the facts and circumstances and the conduct of the parties. The fact that the agreement grants a right of exclusive possession is, while important, by no manner or means conclusive.

Having reviewed again and again all of the factual circumstances of this case, including, but not to the exclusion of others, those elements to which I have made specific and direct reference, it has not been made out in this case that there existed at the material time a landlord and tenant relationship. It seems to me that essentially the only factual circumstance which points in this direction is the length of occupancy of the rooms by Hodges and his family. That is obviously of some importance but the difficulty is that whatever its length, the relationship between the parties was really no different than would have been that same relationship had Hodges' stay in the hotel lasted for a week. I do not and cannot accept that it was ever in the mind of either party to these proceedings that a legal estate of any kind had passed from the applicant to the respondent.

There was what might generally be described as exclusivity of possession but there remained a general, over-all control of the property by the applicant. While it is by no manner or means conclusive or even perhaps particularly important in this case, given the specific argument made on behalf of the applicant, I think, had the parties been asked before litigation became a possibility, both would have agreed that the occupant had absolutely nothing which he was entitled to assign or sublet to anyone else.

I have come to the conclusion on all of the evidence before me that the applicant has not made out its right to proceed under the provisions of Part IV of the *Landlord and Tenant Act*, and that it has not demonstrated that it was at the material time a "landlord" under the provisions of that statute. In this regard I should emphasize that counsel for the applicant specifically stated that he was not seeking to allege or argue that his client was a "person giving or permitting the occupation of the premises in question" thus qualifying to be considered as a landlord whether or not the applicant was a lessor. Similarly, counsel indicated that he did not wish to adopt the position that Mr. Hodges was an "occupant" and thus a tenant as that word is defined in the *Landlord and Tenant Act*. The whole case has proceeded and has been argued on both sides on the basis that the question for ultimate determination is whether there was a landlord and tenant relationship, that is, whether there was a lessor and lessee relationship involved between the parties during the period of time which is relevant to these proceedings and to the claim for arrears of rent now presented.

In the result, the applicant's claim must be dismissed with costs.

Claim dismissed.

Discussion Notes

In the above case, the court concluded that the parties never intended that the occupant in *Canadian Pacific Hotels Ltd.* acquire an estate in land assignable to third parties, and concluded that this indicated that the agreement was a licence only. It is not clear that either party ever put their minds to this question. Is it fair to base the decision on such speculation?

What are the most relevant facts identified by the court that led to the conclusion that the agreement in question was a licence only? How does this case differ from *British American Oil* and *Metro-Matic Ltd.*?

Principles of Property and Contract in Leaseholds: Termination Remedies

The lease is a very common arrangement in property law, whereby the owner of real property (the lessor) grants the right of exclusive possession of the land to another (the tenant) for a specified period of time, thereby creating a leasehold estate. It is a typical example of the division that can occur between title and lawful possession. As long as the lease continues, the lessor will retain a reversionary interest, and the lessor's right to actual possession of the land is suspended during the tenancy. As chapter 3 examines, a lease is a non-freehold interest in land because the period of the lease is either certain or can be rendered certain by the lessor. On the other hand, a freehold interest in land—for example, a life estate or an estate in fee simple—is an estate of uncertain duration. Because a lease is non-freehold, the lessor remains "seised" of the land for the duration of the lease.

The applicable legislation and common law governing leaseholds is complex and vast. This area of the law is now largely divided between commercial and residential leases, and significantly different regimes govern the two areas. On the whole, the legislation in this area has attempted to provide greater security of tenure to residential tenants, recognizing that, for most residential tenants, the lease represents their primary residence and accordingly they require an enhanced security of tenure. Moreover, in the context of residential tenancies, there may be a serious inequality of bargaining power between a large lessor and individual tenants; the legislation (both landlord and tenant law, and rent control legislation) in some measure attempts to address this problem. However, in the context of commercial leases, there is less reason to assume an inequality of bargaining power between the lessor and the tenant, and the law governing commercial tenancies tends to favour freedom of contract between the parties.

This section of the casebook does not provide a comprehensive introduction to landlord and tenant law—there are a variety of areas that are not covered, including the question of the right of the tenant to assign or sublet his or her leasehold estate, the lessor's obligation to permit the tenant "quiet enjoyment" of the premises, and the tenant's obligation to act in a "tenant-like" manner and keep the premises in reasonable repair. For a further discussion of these issues, see Ziff, 254-64.

Instead, this section focuses on one particular issue in landlord and tenant law—the termination of leasehold estates in relation to both commercial and residential leaseholds. It considers the variety of ways in which leasehold estates may be terminated, either by the tenant or the lessor, and some of the remedies available for wrongful termination or eviction.

The issue of termination is critical for a number of reasons. First, in the context of commercial leaseholds, there have been significant recent changes. The remedies available to the lessor, and the duties imposed on the lessor, on the wrongful termination by the tenant have been significantly enhanced and modified. As we examine below, the law in this area is once again returning to what might be described as a "contract" analysis in the context of commercial leasehold estates. Second, in the context of residential tenancies, wrongful termination by the lessor has serious and potentially devastating consequences for the residential tenant. As compared to the lessor, the residential tenant is frequently in a weaker bargaining position. As we will see below, recent amendments to residential landlord and tenant legislation in Ontario have attempted to provide increased protection for residential tenants, with the goal of enhancing their weaker bargaining position and providing them with greater security of tenure.

Termination of Leasehold Estates

A lease can be terminated in a number of ways—for example, a fixed-term lease will expire naturally at the end of the term in question. Alternatively, the tenant or the lessor can wrongfully terminate the lease before the end of its term. A tenant may wrongfully repudiate the lease, vacate the premises, and cease paying rent. On the other hand, the lessor may attempt wrongfully to evict the tenant before the end of the lease. These situations can arise in either a commercial or a residential context.

The following section examines the wrongful repudiation of a commercial lease by a commercial tenant, and considers the various remedies available to the lessor, both in contract law and property law. These remedies have evolved and changed over time, raising important issues regarding law reform in a commercial setting. In addition, these property law and contract law remedies may occasionally be in conflict, raising the question of how this conflict should be resolved.

The section then proceeds to consider the residential context, in particular the example where a lessor might wrongfully attempt to evict a residential tenant. The residential context raises an important question of social policy and the extent to which the law should enhance security of tenure in residential tenancies. This question has most recently arisen in the context of the "no pet" clauses in residential tenancies, and attempts of lessors to evict tenants who have violated such a clause.

Commercial Leaseholds

The following case examines the various remedies available to commercial lessors in the event that the tenant wrongfully repudiates a lease and ceases to pay rent. When reviewing this case, take careful note of the remedies available under property law for wrongful breach by the tenant, and compare this to the typical remedies available for breach of a contract—that is, the recovery of expectation damages. How do the three property law remedies differ from the recovery of expectation damages? Why did property law develop remedies so different from those developed at contract law? What rationale can be offered for this distinction? Do the various property law remedies result in the overcompensation or undercompensation of lessors? Do the property law remedies merely supplement the contact law remedies, or do the contract law remedies now effectively replace the property law remedies?

Highway Properties Ltd. v. Kelly, Douglas & Co.
[1971] SCR 562

LASKIN J: The issue in this appeal arises out of the repudiation of an unexpired lease by the major tenant in a shopping centre and the resumption of possession by the landlord with notice to the defaulting tenant that it would be held liable for damages suffered by the landlord as a result of the admittedly wrongful repudiation. This issue raises squarely the correctness of the decision of the Ontario Court of Appeal in *Goldhar v. Universal Sections and Mouldings Ltd.*, which was followed by the majority of the British Columbia Court of Appeal in the present case.

　　The substantial question emerging from the facts is the measure and range of damages which the landlord, the appellant before this Court, may claim by reason of the repudiation by the tenant, the respondent herein, of its lease of certain premises, and its consequent abandonment of those premises, where the landlord took possession with a contemporaneous assertion of its right to full damages according to the loss calculable over the unexpired term of the lease. It will be necessary, in dealing with this question, to consider the situations where, upon the tenant's repudiation and abandonment, the landlord does not resume possession but insists on enforcing the lease, or takes possession on his own or on the tenant's account. A common characterization of the problem in this appeal is whether it is to be resolved according to the law of property or according to the law of contract; but, in my opinion, this is an over-simplification.

　　The dispute between the parties stems from a lease of August 19, 1960, under which the landlord demised certain premises in its shopping centre to the tenant "to be used for grocery store and super market." A term of fifteen years from October 1, 1960, was specified at a prescribed annual rent, payable monthly in advance, plus an additional rent based on a certain formula which need not be reproduced here. The tenant covenanted, *inter alia*, to pay rent, certain taxes and maintenance costs; not to do or suffer anything to be done on the demised premises without the landlord's consent whereby insurance policies thereon might become void or voidable or the premiums increased; and to pay into a promotion fund to be used for the benefit of the shopping centre. There were covenants for repair and provisions for renewal but their terms are not germane to the disposition of this appeal. There was also a covenant by the landlord for quiet enjoyment. Clause 5(a), so far as relevant here, provided that if the rent or any part thereof be in arrears for 15 days or if any covenant by the tenant should be unfulfilled, and the failure to pay rent or fulfill the covenant should continue 15 days after notice thereof to the tenant, then the current month's rent and three months' additional rent should immediately become due and the landlord might forthwith re-enter and thereupon the demise should absolutely determine but without prejudice to any right of action in respect of any antecedent breach of the tenant's covenants.

Clause 9, which was central to the landlord's claim for damages, was as follows:

> The tenant further covenants and agrees that it will commence to carry on its business within thirty (30) days from the completion of the demised premises and will carry on its business on the said premises continuously. The demised premises shall not be used for any other purpose than as to conduct the Tenant's business in the said premises during such hours as the Landlord may from time to time require on all business days during the term hereby created and in such manner that the Landlord may at all times receive the maximum amount of income from the operation of such business in and upon the demised premises. The Tenant shall install and maintain at all times in the demised premises first class trade fixtures and furniture adequate and appropriate for the business of the Tenant thereon. The Tenant further agrees to conduct its business as aforesaid in the said premises during such evenings and for such hours thereof during the term hereby created as permitted by the By-laws of the Corporation of the District of North Vancouver, BC and consistent with the practices generally accepted by retail outlets in the area.

The shopping centre built by the appellant consisted of eleven stores, including the supermarket premises let to the respondent. Before buying the land on which the shopping centre was later built, the appellant obtained the commitment of the respondent to lease space therein for a food supermarket to be constructed according to its specifications. This commitment was evidenced by a lease dated blank day of May, 1960, whose terms were carried into the document of August 19, 1960. The respondent went into possession through a subtenant (with the appellant's consent) on or about October 20, 1960. By February 1961, only five other stores in the shopping centre had been let, and the venture did not prosper. The supermarket subtenant indicated its intention to close the business down on March 24, 1962, and did so. The appellant drew the respondent's attention to clause 9 of the lease and received an assurance in a letter from the respondent of March 26, 1962, that it was standing by the lease and was endeavouring to sublet its leasehold. Nothing came of its endeavours.

The closing down of the supermarket adversely affected the other tenants in the shopping centre, and by November 22, 1963 (a date whose relevance will appear later) three of those tenants had moved out. The shopping centre began to take on a "ghost-town" appearance and suffered from petty vandalism. On April 13, 1962, following the closing down of the supermarket, the appellant's solicitors wrote to the respondent, again drawing attention to clause 9 of the lease, complaining that the appellant was suffering damage and advising that they would seek compliance to have the business reopened or would claim damages. The appellant learned in July 1962 that the respondent was removing fixtures, and its solicitors wrote in objection on July 11, 1962, relying on clause 9 and on the covenant in clause 10(a) permitting removal if the tenant is not in default. The letter threatened resort to an injunction unless the removal was halted.

The action, out of which this appeal arises, was commenced on July 16, 1962, and an interlocutory injunction was sought but refused. Rent was paid by the respondent to June 1963. The statement of claim, which was delivered on May 31, 1963, asked for a declaration that the lease was binding upon the respondent, asked for a decree of specific performance and for a mandatory order and an injunction, and also sought damages. The respondent delivered a defence and counterclaim on September 12, 1963. Paragraph 8 of the counterclaim said flatly: "The Defendant hereby repudiates the said agreement dated August 19, 1960." As a result of this repudiation, the appellant's solicitors wrote to the respondent's solicitors on November 22, 1963 (a date mentioned earlier in these reasons) in these terms:

> Dear Sirs: Re: Highway Properties Limited and Kelly Douglas & Co. Ltd.
>   This is to advise you that in view of your pleadings, our client takes the position that your client has repudiated the lease in question.
>   Our client, therefore, intends to take possession of the premises and will attempt to lease these upon the same terms and conditions as set out in the lease of the 19th of August, 1960.
>   We would further advise you that our client intends to hold your client responsible for any damages suffered by them as a result of your client's breach and wrongful repudiation of the said lease.

Following this letter the appellant took possession of the supermarket premises and attempted, without success, to re-let them for the unexpired term of the lease of the respondent. Subsequently, the appellant subdivided the premises into three stores which were eventually rented, two under a lease of March 1, 1965, and the third under a lease of November 1, 1965. At the opening of trial on November 29, 1966, the appellant obtained leave to amend its statement of claim. The amendment referred to the respondent's repudiation of the lease and to the consequent rescission of the agreement thereunder in accordance with the letter of November 22, 1963, and claimed damages not only for loss suffered to the date of the so-called rescission but also, and mainly, for prospective loss resulting from the respondent's failure to carry on a supermarket business in the shopping centre for the full term of the lease.

The theory upon which the appellant claimed damages was rejected by the trial judge, Macdonald J, and by the majority of the Court of Appeal, Davey CJBC dissenting. The holding both at trial and on appeal was that there had been a surrender of the lease by reason of the repudiation and the taking of possession by the appellant; that the principles enunciated in the *Goldhar* case were applicable; that the lease and its covenants ceased to exist with the surrender; and that the appellant could recover only for breaches occurring to the date of surrender. The damages on this footing totalled

$14,256.38, composed of five months' rent; the decline in rental income in 1962 and in 1963 to the date of surrender by reason of the closing of other stores; a portion of the taxes payable for 1963; a sum for increased insurance premiums for 1963; and a portion of maintenance costs for 1963 to the date of surrender.

It is common ground, as appears from the reasons of Davey CJBC in the Court of Appeal, that if it should be determined that damages must be assessed on the basis claimed by the appellant, the assessment should be remitted to the trial judge to be made on the evidence adduced before him.

I approach the legal issue involved in this appeal by acknowledging the continuity of common law principle that a lease of land for a term of years under which possession is taken creates an estate in the land, and also the relation of landlord and tenant, to which the common law attaches various incidents despite the silence of the document thereon. For the purposes of the present case, no distinction need be drawn between a written lease and a written agreement for a lease. Although by covenants or by contractual terms, the parties may add to, or modify, or subtract from the common law incidents, and, indeed, may overwhelm them as well as the leasehold estate by commercial or business considerations which represent the dominant features of the transaction, the "estate" element has resisted displacement as the pivotal factor under the common law, at least as understood and administered in this country.

There has, however, been some questioning of this persistent ascendancy of a concept that antedated the development of the law of contracts in English law and has been transformed in its social and economic aspects by urban living conditions and by commercial practice. The judgments in the House of Lords in *Cricklewood Property and Investment Trust Ltd. v. Leighton's Investment Trust Ltd.* are illustrative. Changes in various states of the United States have been quite pronounced as is evident from 1 *American Law of Property*, 1952, #3.11.

In the various common law Provinces, standard contractual terms (reflected, for example, in Short Forms of Leases Acts) and, to a degree, legislation, have superseded the common law of landlord and tenant; for example, in prescribing for payment of rent in advance; in providing for re-entry for non-payment of rent or breaches of other covenants exacted from tenant; in modifying the absoluteness of convenants not to assign or sublet without leave; and in blunting peremptory rights of termination or forfeiture. The contractual emphasis, even when reinforced by commercial clauses testifying to the paramount business considerations in a lease of land, has hitherto stopped short of full recognition of its remedial concomitants, as, for example, the principle of anticipatory breach and the principle governing relief upon repudiation. I note that this Court had no hesitation in applying the doctrine of anticipatory breach to a contract for the sale of land, even to the point of allowing an immediate suit for specific performance (but, of course, at the time fixed for completion): see *Kloepfer Wholesale Hardware and Automotive Co. v. Roy.* I think it is equally open to consider its application to a contractual lease, although the lease is partly executed. Its anticipatory features lie, of course, in the fact that instalments of rent are payable for future periods, and repudiation of the lease raises the question whether an immediate remedy covering the loss of such rent and of other advantages extending over the unexpired term of the lease may be pursued notwithstanding that the estate in the land may have been terminated.

The developed case law has recognized three mutually exclusive courses that a landlord may take where a tenant is in fundamental breach of the lease or has repudiated it entirely, as was the case here. He may do nothing to alter the relationship of landlord and tenant, but simply insist on performance of the terms and sue for rent or damages on the footing that the lease remains in force. Second, he may elect to terminate the lease, retaining of course the right to sue for rent accrued due, or for damages to the date of termination for previous breaches of convenant. Third, he may advise the tenant that he proposes to re-let the property on the tenant's account and enter into possession on that basis. Counsel for the appellant, in effect, suggests a fourth alternative, namely, that the landlord may elect to terminate the lease but with notice to the defaulting tenant that damages will be claimed on the footing of a present recovery of damages for losing the benefit of the lease over its unexpired term. One element of such damages would be, of course, the present value of the unpaid future rent for the unexpired period of the lease less the actual rental value of the premises for that period. Another element would be the loss, so far as provable, resulting from the repudiation of clause 9. I say no more about the elements of damages here in view of what has been agreed to in that connection by the parties.

There is no need to discuss either the first or second of the alternatives mentioned above other than to say, in respect of the second, that it assumes a situation where no prospective damages could be proved to warrant any claim for them, or even to warrant taking the third alternative. I wish, however, to examine the underpinnings and implications of the third course because they have a decided bearing on whether the additional step proposed by counsel for the appellant should be taken in this case.

Where repudiation occurs in respect of a business contract (not involving any estate in land), the innocent party has an election to terminate the contract which, if exercised, results in its discharge *pro tanto* when the election is made and communicated to the wrongdoer. (I agree with the opinion of such text writers as Cheshire and Fifoot, *The Law of Contract*, 7th ed., 1969, at p. 535, that it is misleading to speak of the result as rescission when there is no retrospective cancellation *ab initio* involved.) Termination in such circumstances does not preclude a right to damages for prospective loss as well as for accrued loss.

A parallel situation of repudiation in the case of a lease has generally been considered in the language of and under the principles of surrender, specifically of surrender by operation of law or implied surrender. It is said to result when, upon the material breach or repudiation of a lease, the innocent party does an act inconsistent with the continued existence of that lease. The *Goldhar* case applied the doctrine where, upon a tenant's repudiation of a lease, the landlord re-let the premises. The further consequence of this was said to be not only the termination of the estate in the land but also the obliteration of all the terms in the document of lease, at least so far as it was sought to support a claim thereon for prospective loss.

The rule of surrender by operation of law, and the consequences of the rule for a claim of prospective loss, are said to rise above any intention of the party whose act results in the surrender, so long as the act unequivocally makes it inconsistent for the lease to survive. Even if this be a correct statement of the law, I do not think it would apply to a case where both parties evidenced their intention in the lease itself to recognize a right of action for prospective loss upon a repudiation of the lease, although it be followed by termination of the estate. There are cases in other jurisdictions which have recognized the validity of covenants to this effect: see 11 *Williston on Contracts* (Jaeger) 3d ed., 1968, #1403. One of the terms of the lease in *BelBoys Buildings Ltd. v. Clark* was in the nature of such a covenant applicable to a guarantor, and the dissenting judgment of Allen JA of the Alberta Appellate Division recognized the enforceability of the guarantee notwithstanding the termination of the obligation to pay rent. I should add that the reasons proceeded on the ground that the guarantee obligation arose before there had been an effective surrender.

English and Canadian case law has given standing to a limitation on the operation of surrender, although there is a repudiation and repossession, if the landlord, before repossessing, notifies the defaulting tenant that he is doing so with a view to re-letting on the tenant's account. No such notice was given in the *Goldhar* case; and although it was argued in the present case that the letter of November 22, 1963, asserted that position, neither the trial judge nor the Court of Appeal accepted the argument. I agree that the letter is not sufficiently explicit to that end, but I would think that the recognition of such a modifying principle would suggest a readiness to imply that a re-letting was on the repudiating tenant's behalf, thus protecting the landlord's rights under the lease and at the same time mitigating the liability for unpaid rent. Some of the views expressed in *Oastler v. Henderson* point to a disposition to such an implication; and there is authority in the United States to that effect: see 11 *Williston on Contracts, supra.* I know that under the present case law the landlord is not under a duty of mitigation, but mitigation is in fact involved where there is a re-letting on the tenant's account.

Since the limiting principle under discussion is based on a unilateral assertion of unauthorized agency, I find it difficult to reconcile with the dogmatic application of surrender irrespective of intention. One of the earliest of the cases in England which gave expression to this limiting principle was *Walls v. Atcheson.* I read it as indicating that a landlord upon an abandonment or repudiation of a lease by his tenant may qualify his re-entry to make it clear that he is not forgoing his right to insist on continuation of the tenant's obligation to pay rent. Since rent was regarded, at common law, as issuing out of the land, it would be logical to conclude that it ceased if the estate in the land ceased. But I do not think that it must follow that an election to terminate the estate as a result of the repudiation of a lease should inevitably mean an end to all covenants therein to the point of denying prospective remedial relief in damages.

I appreciate, however, that this principle of denial has been carried into modern doctrine from the older cases that were founded on the relation of surrender to a continuing claim for rent. *Woodfall on Landlord and Tenant*, 27th ed., 1968, vol 1, at p. 869 cites only the *Goldhar* case for the proposition, but it is evident from other English cases such as *Richmond v. Savill*, that the English law is to the same effect. I have the impression from a reading of the cases that the glide into this principle was assisted by translating repudiation or abandonment into an "offer" of surrender and by compounding this legal solecism by a further lapse into the language of rescission.

Nothing that was decided by this Court in *Attorney General of Saskatchewan v. Whiteshore Salt and Chemical Co. Ltd. and Midwest Chemicals Ltd.* bears on the issues now before it. That case was concerned with whether certain unexpired mining leases of Saskatchewan land, granted under federal authority before the 1930 transfer to Saskatchewan of its natural resources by Canada, must be taken to have been surrendered when in 1931 the leases were replaced by others granted by the Province, these being in turn replaced in 1937. On the answer to this question depended the liability of the lessees to increased royalties prescribed under provincial law. If there was no surrender, the lessees were protected by a provision of the National Resources Agreement of 1930. Kellock J, who spoke for the majority, was not addressing himself to any issue of damages such as is involved here when he referred generally to the proposition that on a surrender "the lease is gone and the rent is also gone" (a proposition which brooks no disagreement); or when he referred to *Richmond v. Savill*, *supra*, as standing for the principle that the lessee remains liable for rent accrued due or breaches of covenant committed prior to surrender. These observations were unnecessary for the determination of the question before him, and I do not regard them in any event as controlling for the present case.

As long ago as 1906, the High Court of Australia in *Buchanan v. Byrnes* held that upon an abandonment by a tenant, in breach of covenant, of the hotel property which he had leased, the landlord was entitled to claim damages over the unexpired term of the lease notwithstanding a surrender. It is coincidence that the lease in case was for fifteen years and that it also included a covenant by the tenant, similar to the covenant here, to carry on the business for which the lease was given, for the full term of the tenancy. I quote two passages from the various reasons for judgment, one from those of Griffith CJ and the second from those of Barton J, as follows (found, respectively, at pp. 714 and 719):

> In this case he covenanted to carry on [the business] for fifteen years, and on 30th June he not only left the place, but he did so under such circumstances that he could not carry it on, and he sold the furniture. That was as complete a breach of the covenant to carry on the business as it was possible for him to commit, and under these circumstances the plaintiff had at once a complete cause of action against him. He was entitled to bring an action forthwith for the breach of that covenant, and he was entitled to such damages as would properly flow from such a breach of covenant. The surrender, therefore, if accepted at all, took place after breach, and the defence is not proved. ...
>
> It must not be forgotten that a right of action had arisen on the termination of the correspondence on the 28th June, as the defendant had given distinct notice of his intention not to perform his covenant. There was at that time a renunciation which, at the plaintiff's option, amounted to a breach of the covenants that throughout the term he would carry on a licensed victualler's business upon the premises and keep them open and in use as an inn, & c., and of the covenant not to do anything which might entail forfeiture of the licence (*Licensing Act* 1885, sec. 101), as well as of the subsidiary covenants. The plaintiff was then entitled to claim in an immediate action, prospectively, such damages as would be caused by a breach at the appointed time, subject to any circumstances which might operate in mitigation of damages: *Leake on Contracts*, 4th ed., 617-618, and cases there cited, especially *Hochster v. Delatour*, 2 E & B, 678; 22 LJQB, 455, and *Johnstone v. Milling*, 16 QBD, 460. But it is said that the conduct of the plaintiff in resuming possession under the circumstances estops him from suing upon the covenants. I[t] must not be taken to hold that it has that effect as to the covenant to pay rent. But, however, that may be, can it estop him as to the other covenants which relate to the keeping [of] the premises as an inn throughout the term, and the doing of the other things necessary for that purpose? Conduct, to constitute an

estoppel, must have caused another to believe in the existence of a certain state of things, and have induced him to act on that belief so as to alter his own position. How can that be said to be the effect of the plaintiff's conduct, when the act of the defendant, so far from having been induced by it, has preceded it? In my judgment the doctrine of estoppel cannot be applied against the plaintiff, and I am driven to the conclusion that the learned Judge who tried the case, and who held that the plaintiff was bound by estoppel, has based his judgment on facts which do not entitle a Court to apply that doctrine.

I note that *Buchanan v. Byrnes* was applied a few years ago by the Supreme Court of Western Australia in *Hughes v. NLS Pty. Ltd.*

The approach of the High Court of Australia commends itself to me, cutting through, as it does, artificial barriers to relief that have resulted from overextension of the doctrine of surrender in its relation to rent. Although it is correct to say that repudiation by the tenant gives the landlord at that time a choice between holding the tenant to the lease or terminating it, yet at the same time a right of action for damages then arises; and the election to insist on the lease or to refuse further performance (and thus bring it to an end) goes simply to the measure and range of damages. I see no logic in a conclusion that, by electing to terminate, the landlord has limited the damages that he may then claim to the same scale that would result if he had elected to keep the lease alive.

What is apparently the majority American view is to the same effect as the view taken in Australia and that I would take: see 4 *Corbin on Contracts*, 1951, #986, at p. 955. The *American Law of Property*, 1952, vol 1, pp. 203-204, states that "If the lessee abandons the premises and refuses to pay rent, the cases quite generally hold, in accordance with the doctrine of anticipatory breach, that the lessor may sue for complete damages without waiting until the end of the term"; and I may add that, under the case law, this is so at least where the suit is for damages and not for rent as such.

There are some general considerations that support the view that I would take. It is no longer sensible to pretend that a commercial lease, such as the one before this Court, is simply a conveyance and not also a contract. It is equally untenable to persist in denying resort to the full armoury of remedies ordinarily available to redress repudiation of covenants, merely because the covenants may be associated with an estate in land. Finally, there is merit here as in other situations in avoiding multiplicity of actions that may otherwise be a concomitant of insistence that a landlord engage in instalment litigation against a repudiating tenant.

Lest there be any doubt on the point, clause 5(a) of the lease (previously referred to in these reasons) does not preclude the claim made herein for prospective damages. The landlord did not invoke the clause, and hence no question arises of an irrevocable election to rely on it.

I would, accordingly, allow his appeal, with costs to the appellant throughout, and remit the case to the trial judge for assessment of damages. It follows that I would overrule the *Goldhar* case.

Appeal allowed with costs.

Discussion Notes

Property Law Remedies for a Tenant's Repudiation of the Lease

Before the Supreme Court's decision in *Highway Properties*, there were three mutually exclusive options available to the lessor where a tenant vacated the premises and ceased paying rent before the end of term. These three options were developed in property law at a time when the lease was regard primarily as a *conveyance* rather than a *contract*. First, the lessor could refuse to accept the abandonment and treat the lease as subsisting, suing for rent as it came due. Second, the lessor could terminate the lease and sue for rent accrued to the date of termination. Under this second option, the lessor was not entitled to rent or damages for any period after the termination. Third, the lessor could inform the tenant that he proposed to relet the premises on the tenant's behalf, and at the end of the term, the lessor would claim any deficiency between the rent payable by the tenant and the rent obtained by reletting the premises.

Why did the construction of a lease as primarily a conveyance, rather than a contract, lead to these three remedies? Why did property law develop remedies—for example, the first property law remedy—that effectively relieve the lessor from any duty to mitigate in the face of the tenant's wrongful repudiation of the lease? Compare this with the duty to mitigate as it has developed under contract law. For further discussion, see B. Zarnett, "Damages for Breach of Lease" (1987), 8 *Advocates' Quarterly* 257.

Contract Law Remedies for a Tenant's Repudiation of the Lease

In *Highway Properties*, the Supreme Court added another option for a lessor faced with a tenant's wrongful repudiation of the lease, one modelled on contract law rather than on property law. The Supreme Court held (at 570 SCR) that a lessor is entitled "to terminate the lease but with notice to the defaulting tenant that damages will be claimed on the footing of present recovery of damages for losing the benefits of the lease over its unexpired term." The court determined that a lessor was entitled to terminate the lease and still recover damages for the period after the retaking of possession. Under property law principles, a lessor was not entitled to recover damages for any period after the lessor had accepted the tenant's repudiation and terminated the lease. The court held that the normal rules relating to the recovery of expectation damages for a breach of contract ought to be applied to commercial leases. Why did the court adopt this fourth remedy modelled on contract law? Why did the court determine that the three property law remedies were inadequate?

Lessor's Duty To Mitigate

Subsequent courts have held that where a lessor intends to rely on the fourth contract remedy in *Highway Properties*, the lessor is under an obligation to mitigate any loss, and his or her damages will be accordingly reduced if he or she fails to mitigate: *Adana Realty Ltd. v. Humpty's Egg Place Ltd.* (1991), 78 Alta. LR (2d) 383 (QB). In *Keneric Tractor Sales Ltd. v. Langille*, [1987] 2 SCR 440, where the court held that contract law remedies should be applied to a chattel lease (farm equipment in this case), the court also assumed that where the lessor seeks to obtain expectation damages pursuant to *Highway Properties*, the lessor must take reasonable steps to mitigate any damages. However, if the lessor seeks to rely on the first property law remedy, and elects to treat the lease as remaining in force and sues for rent as it comes due, it remains unclear at law whether the lessor is under a duty to mitigate. In *Almad Investments Ltd. v. Mister Leonard Holdings Ltd.* (March 13, 1996), Toronto 94-CQ-55718 (Ont. Gen. Div.), the court notes that this remains an unresolved issue. Is there any reason to relieve the lessor of a duty to mitigate? Should the lessor be permitted to shift to the defaulting tenant the costs of the lessor's failure to mitigate? Is this an efficient result?

In *Toronto Housing Co. Ltd. v. Postal Promotions Ltd.* (1981), 128 DLR (3d) 51; 34 OR (2d) 218 (HCJ), aff'd. 140 DLR (3d) 117; 39 OR (2d) 627 (CA), the lessor left the premises vacant for nine months after the tenant's wrongful repudiation of the lease. After nine months, the lessor terminated the lease and rented the premises at a much higher rent to a new tenant. Taking into account the income from the new much higher rent, the lessor would receive enough from the new tenant to cover any loss suffered during the nine months when the premises were vacant and no rent was paid. In short, the lessor effectively mitigated and avoided any loss by entering into the new lease. Nonetheless, seeking to rely on the first property law remedy, the lessor sued for the rent due during the nine-month period before the lease was terminated. The Court of Appeal determined that the lessor was not entitled to these damages because the lessor had successfully avoided any loss. The court did not expressly find that the lessor had a duty to mitigate in the face of the tenant's breach. But the case indicates that if the lessor does successfully avoid any loss, the lessor cannot then rely on the first property remedy that would otherwise entitle the landlord to treat the lease as subsisting until termination.

Given that courts are increasingly incorporating contract law remedies in situations where the tenant is in breach of a commercial lease, can a lessor still rely in confidence on the first property law remedy, which imposes no obligation on the lessor to mitigate his or her loss? Is there any reason why a lessor should be relieved of the duty to mitigate what would otherwise apply under contract law? Has the first property law remedy been effectively, if not expressly, repealed by *Highway Properties*?

Pacific Centre Ltd. v. Micro Base Development Corp.

There are a number of problems with the property law remedies for a tenant's wrongful repudiation of a lease. The first property law remedy identified by the court in *Highway Properties* effectively relieves the lessor from any duty to mitigate. The second and third property law remedies effectively prevent the lessor from recovering his or her entire prospective loss (expectation interest)—that is, the present value of the unpaid future rent for the remaining period of the lease, minus the actual rental value of the premises. For example, if the lessor seeks to rely on the third property remedy (to relet the premises on the tenant's behalf), the lessor must relet the premises on the same terms as the original lease, and cannot relet the premises for a period longer than the original lease. If the lessor relets for a longer term, the court may deem the lessor to have terminated the lease and the lessor will be able to recover only losses to the date of the termination (as in the second property remedy).

In *Pacific Centre Ltd. v. Micro Base Development Corp.* (1990), 43 BCLR (2d) 77 (SC), aff'd. on other grounds 49 BCLR (2d) 218 (CA), the lessor sought to rely on the third property law remedy, but (foolishly, as it turned out) relet the premises for a term that exceeded the original lease. The tenant argued that on reletting for a longer term, the lessor had effectively terminated the original lease and therefore could not recover any further prospective damages subsequent to the termination, consistent with the second property law remedy. The court accepted this argument. Although the lessor had relet the premises at a lower rent, and sustained an expectation loss of over $46,000 over the course of the original lease, the court held that the lessor was able to recover only those losses sustained until the premises had been relet, in this case only $1,400. In effect, because the lessor attempted to mitigate its loss under the third remedy but unwisely entered into a lease that exceeded the term of the original lease, the lessor could no longer recover its expectation loss. The court also found that the lessor had failed to provide the tenant with the required notice that it would rely on the fourth contract law remedy in *Highway Properties*, and accordingly the lessor was not able to recover its prospective loss under this fourth remedy either. Does this case effectively punish the lessor for having attempted to mitigate its loss? Does that result make any sense? What should the lessor have done to avoid this outcome? Given the problems associated with the property law remedies, do they remain practical or useful after *Highway Properties*?

Notice

In contract law, is the plaintiff required to provide the defendant with notice that the plaintiff intends to hold the defendant liable for any expectation loss arising from the defendant's breach? Why does the Supreme Court in *Highway Properties* suggest that such notice is required when the tenant is in breach of the lease and the lessor seeks to rely on the fourth remedy to recover his expectation loss? What function does such notice serve? Would it be unfair to hold the tenant liable for expectation loss in the absence of any such notice? Under the first of the property law remedies, the lessor could refuse to accept the abandonment of the lease, refuse to mitigate any loss by reletting the premises, and simply sue for rent as it comes due. Does it make sense that a lessor should be required to give the tenant notice if he or she seeks to recover expectation losses, and yet not be required to give notice if he or she chooses to refuse to accept the abandonment and sue for rent as it comes due? Under which remedy are the damages likely to be the highest?

Some courts continue to adhere to the view that some notice, even before the statement of claim, may be required if the lessor seeks to rely on the fourth remedy in *Highway Properties*. If the period of time between reletting the premises and the statement of claim is too long, the statement of claim may not be regarded as timely notice. In *Harvey v. Burger* (February 18, 1994), Picton 559/93 (Ont. Gen. Div.), the lessor had not provided any notice until the delivery of the statement of claim, over three years after the reletting of the premises by the lessor. The court distinguished *North Bay TV & Audio Ltd. v. Nova Electronics Ltd.* (1983), 44 OR (2d) 342 (HCJ), aff'd. (1984), 47 OR (2d) 588 (CA), where the statement of claim had been delivered approximately two months after the taking of possession by the lessor. In *North Bay*, the court found that this statement of claim itself was sufficient notice. In *Harvey*, the court held that the period of time between reletting the premises and the statement of claim was too great, and the notice requirement set out in *Highway Properties* had not been met. Accordingly, the lessor was not entitled to rely on the fourth remedy.

Privity of Contract

Problems can arise when the lessor and the tenant are no longer in privity of contract. For example, in *Wing Lee Holdings Ltd. v. Coleman* (August 25, 1995), Victoria 90/3289 (BC SC), the tenant had assigned his remaining leasehold interest to a third party. This third party was later in breach of the lease, and the lessor sought, pursuant to *Highway Properties*, to recover the present value of the unpaid future rent for the unexpired term of the lease, minus the rental value of the premises for that period. The court stated that "fundamental to the principle in *Highway Properties* is the existence of a contract between the parties." The court held that because there was no privity of contract between the parties in this case, the lessor could not rely on the fourth remedy in *Highway Properties*. How does this result illustrate the continuing interaction between contract law and property law remedies in this area of law? Does the result in *Wing Lee Holdings Ltd.* make any sense?

Residential Tenancies and the Duty To Mitigate

With regard to residential tenancies, the question of the lessor's duty to mitigate is usually addressed in the legislation governing residential tenancies. For example, s. 90 of Ontario's Landlord and Tenant Act, RSO 1990, c. L.7 provides, "Where a tenant abandons the premises in breach of the tenancy agreement, the lessor's right to damages is subject to the same obligation to mitigate damages as applies generally under the rule of law relating to breaches to contract." A similar provision is included in Bill 96, the Tenant Protection Act, 1996, 1st Sess., 36th Leg. Ont., 1997. Section 13 of Bill 96 provides that when "a landlord or a tenant becomes liable to pay any amount as a result of a breach of a tenancy agreement, the person entitled to claim the amount has a duty to take reasonable steps to minimize the person's losses." How does s. 13 of Bill 96 differ from s. 90 of the Landlord and Tenant Act? How might the situation arise where a tenant is under an obligation to mitigate loss in the face of the lessor's breach? Should a tenant in a residential tenancy be under such an obligation?

Similar provisions can be found in other provinces. For example, the New Brunswick Residential Tenancies Act, SNB 1975, c. R-10.2, s. 11(3) provides that where a tenant wrongfully terminates the lease, "the landlord shall mitigate any damages that are caused by such abandonment or termination to the extent that a party to a contract is required generally under the law relating to breaches of contract."

Where a duty to mitigate has been imposed on the lessor under the applicable residential tenancy legislation, a residential tenant is not liable for the entire amount of rental payments due for the remainder of the term of the residential lease, providing the premises have some market value. In effect, this legislation prevents residential lessors from relying on the first property law remedy, which otherwise permits a lessor to refuse to accept a tenant's repudiation of the lease and sue as rent comes due. Instead, pursuant to this legislation, the residential lessor will only be able to recover his or her expectation loss, after taking into account the market rate for the premises in question, and the loss that the lessor can reasonably avoid by mitigating appropriately. Should a similar rule govern commercial tenancies? Why should residential tenants be given preferential treatment over commercial tenants?

190 Lees Avenue Ltd. Partnership v. Dew, Tanguary and Whissell

In *190 Lees Avenue Ltd. Partnership v. Dew, Tanguary and Whissell* (1991), 2 OR (3d) 686 (Gen. Div.), the court considered the question whether a lessor who had served notice to terminate a residential tenancy, and the resident has vacated, can still sue for prospective loss of rent at common law. The court applied *Highway Properties* to the residential tenancy and held that the lessor could sue for prospective loss. The court noted, at 689, "Allowing the landlord to have a claim in contract makes good policy sense as, otherwise, a defaulting tenant would simply have to behave badly enough to push the landlord into early termination in order to avoid the financial consequences of breaking the lease." Should defaulting residential tenants be held liable for prospective loss? On this point, should residential tenancies be treated differently from commercial tenancies? Why?

Bailment and Prospective Loss

Under the law of bailment, is a bailor entitled to recover prospective losses after accepting a wrongful repudiation of the bailment? At one time, consistent with landlord and tenant law before *Highway Properties*, if a bailor accepted a bailee's repudiation, the bailment was brought to an end and the bailor had no right to sue for prospective loss. For example, if A leased a car from B for six months, and B accepted A's repudiation of the agreement after one month (by accepting the return of the car), B could not sue for prospective loss (B's expectation loss over the remaining five months in the agreement). As with the leasehold estate, consider the consequences of constructing a bailment primarily as a type of conveyance rather than a contract. Is there any reason why the law should prevent a bailor in this situation from recovering his expectation loss? As with *Highway Properties*, it is now clear that the bailor may sue for prospective loss even if the bailor accepts the repudiation: *Keneric Tractor Sales Ltd. v. Langille*, [1987] 2 SCR 440; 43 DLR (4th) 171.

Residential Leaseholds

Wrongful termination is also a subject of great importance in the context of residential leaseholds. According to Statistics Canada (*Canada Yearbook 1990*, at 7-16), almost 40 percent of all Canadians live in rental accommodation, and most lower-income families live in rental accommodation. Rental accommodation will likely become more, rather than less, common, as the dream of owning a home becomes increasingly remote for many Canadians. A generation ago, a person could easily purchase a home on a single middle-income wage with a mortgage at a fixed rate. However, with the increased speculation in housing prices, home ownership has become increasingly an option available to only upper-income Canadians.

Residential tenancies are distinct from commercial tenancies for at least two reasons. First, the residential tenancy is the tenant's home, and represents a considerable emotional investment. Wrongful or unfair eviction by the lessor can have a devastating impact on the tenant. Second, similar to other areas of consumer protection, there may be a disparity of bargaining power between the lessor and the tenant, and some measures to address this disparity are warranted. As a result, there has been considerable reform of residential tenancy law in Canada. In addition to measures that enhance security of tenure, reform has included:

• statutory guidelines governing the standard obligations of the lessor and the tenant (see s. 94 of the Ontario Landlord and Tenant Act, RSO 1990, c. L.7), and a prohibition of the bargaining away of these statutory rights (see s. 80);

• an increase in the tenant's remedies—for example, s. 89 provides the tenant with a right to sublet the premises and further provides that the consent of the lessor cannot be "unreasonably withheld," and s. 82 prohibits security deposits in excess of one month's rent;

• a curtailment of the lessor's remedies—for example, s. 84 abolishes the "right of distress" whereby a lessor may impound the tenant's goods until payment of the rent is received; and

• a general requirement of written 24 hours notice before the lessor may enter the tenant's premises (see s. 91).

Similar provisions are found in Bill 96, The Tenant Protection Act, 1996, 1st Sess., 36th Leg. Ont., 1997. On the publication of this text, Bill 96 has not yet been enacted into law; however, enactment is anticipated, and the relevant provisions of the Tenant Protection Act, 1996 are examined in this section. In Bill 96, the standard obligations of the lessor and tenant are found in ss. 24-28, and s. 16 provides that any provision in a tenancy agreement that is inconsistent with the Act is void. Section 17 provides the tenant with the right to sublet the premises and further provides that the lessor may not unreasonably withhold consent. Security deposits in excess of one month's rent are prohibited in ss. 110-11. The right of distress is abolished in s. 29, and ss. 20-21 provide that 24 hours notice is generally required before the landlord may enter the premises.

For similar provisions elsewhere in Canada, see the Nova Scotia Residential Tenancies Act, RSNS 1989, c. 410; the New Brunswick Residential Tenancies Act, SNB 1975, c. R-10.2; and the Alberta Residential Tenancies Act, RSA 1980, c. R-15.3.

The following materials focus on the termination provisions governing residential tenancies in the Ontario Landlord and Tenant Act, RSO 1990, c. L.7, as well as the anticipated amendments in Bill 96, the Tenant Protection Act, 1996, 1st Sess., 36th Leg. Ont., 1997. In general, the Landlord and Tenant Act regulates the relations of lessors and tenants in the context of both commercial and residential settings; however part IV of the Act provides a scheme for residential premises only. The Tenant Protection Act, 1996 will replace part IV of the Landlord and Tenant Act, thus creating a separate statute dealing specifically with residential tenancies.

Note the types of residences that are covered under part IV of the Landlord and Tenant Act, and the types that are not covered. For example, as discussed earlier, some residences that provide supportive care were added by amendment in 1994, although not all such residences are covered under the Act. The definition of "residential premises" is set out in s. 1:

> (a) any premises used or intended for use for residential purposes, including accommodation in a boarding house, rooming house or lodging house,
>
> (a.1) any premises occupied or intended to be occupied by a person for the purpose of receiving care services, whether or not receiving the services is the primary purpose of the occupancy,
>
> (b) land intended and used as a site for a mobile home or a land lease community home used for residential purposes, whether or not the landlord also supplies the mobile home or the land lease community home,

The definition of "residential premises" found in s. 1 expressly excludes premises where the occupants share a bathroom or kitchen with the owner, most school residences, hotels and camping grounds, correctional facilities, and short-term accommodation for the purposes of receiving rehabilitative or therapeutic services. Consider why such premises are excluded under the Act. Should some of these premises be governed by residential landlord and tenant legislation?

A similar definition of "residential units" is found in s. 1 of Bill 96, the Tenant Protection Act, 1996, 1st Sess., 36th Leg. Ont., 1997. The Bill defines a "residential unit" as "any living accommodation used or intended for use as residential premises," including "(a) a site for a mobile home or on which there is a land lease home used or intended for use as a residential premise, and (b) a room in a boarding house, rooming house or lodging house and a unit in a care home."

Section 80(1) of the Landlord and Tenant Act provides that Part IV "applies to tenancies of residential premises and tenancy agreements despite any other Act or Parts I, II or III of this Act and despite any agreement or waiver to the contrary except as specifically provided in this Part." This section prohibits the parties from contracting out of any of the rights or obligations contained in Part IV. As a result, even though a tenant may expressly agree to waive his or her rights under the Act, the agreement will be unenforceable. A similar provision is found in s. 16 of Bill 96.

Grounds for Early Termination of the Lease by the Lessor

Part IV of the Landlord and Tenant Act includes provisions for terminating leaseholds and generally constrains lessors from effecting termination except in compliance with the statutory requirements of notice (s. 96) *and* a court order for possession (s. 113). Moreover, a court will grant the order for possession *only* where the requirements of ss. 103-8 have been met. Of particular interest here is s. 107, which defines the circumstances in which a lessor may terminate the leasehold estate for breach of a term contained in the lease document. Because of the combined effect of s. 80 (which prohibits contracting out of the provisions of the Act) and s. 107 (which limits the circumstances in which a lessor may evict a tenant in breach of the lease), a lessor may be confined to damages for breach of contract, but may not be able to terminate the lease, even though the tenant has not complied with the terms of the lease.

The protections available to the tenant in landlord and tenant law do not, however, have any direct impact on those who are without shelter—the homeless. For those who are homeless, the law provides little redress. Some have argued that a right to shelter can be found in the Canadian Charter of Rights and Freedoms, part I of the Constitution Act, 1982, being schedule B of the Canada Act, 1982 (UK), 1982, c. 11 (hereafter the Charter). See Parkdale Community Legal Services, "Homelessness and the Right to Shelter: A View from Parkdale" (1988), 4 *Journal of Law and Social Policy* 35, and the related discussion in chapter 8.

Section 107 of the Ontario Landlord and Tenant Act specifies the grounds on which a lessor may terminate a residential tenant's lease. The landlord may serve on the tenant a notice of termination where:

(a) a tenant causes or permits undue damage to the rented premises or its environs and whether by the tenant's own wilful or negligent acts or by those of any person whom the tenant permits on the residential premises;

(b) a tenant at any time during the term of the tenancy exercises or carries on, or permits to be exercised or carried on, in or upon the residential premises or any part thereof, any illegal act, trade, business, occupation or calling;

(c) the conduct of the tenant or a person permitted in the residential premises by the tenant is such that it substantially interferes with the reasonable enjoyment of the premises for all usual purposes by the landlord or the other tenants;

(d) the safety or other lawful right, privilege or interest of any other tenant in the residential premises is or has been seriously impaired by an act or omission of the tenant or a person permitted in the residential premises by the tenant where such act or omission occurs in the residential premises or its environs;

(e) the number of persons occupying the residential premises on a continuing basis results in the contravention of health or safety standards including any housing standards required by law; or

(f) a tenant of residential premises administered for or on behalf of the Government of Canada or Ontario or a municipality or any agency thereof or forming part of a non-profit, limited dividend housing project financed under the National Housing Act (Canada) has knowingly and materially misrepresented the tenant's income or that of other members of the tenant's family occupying the residential premises.

Section 107 further provides that the notice must specify the act or acts complained of, and must require the tenant to correct the wrong in question within seven days. Where the tenant corrects the wrong within seven days, the notice of termination is null and void. If the tenant fails to comply within seven days, the lessor may then make an application for a court order of possession under s. 113. Section 107(5) provides that a judge hearing an application under s. 113 brought by a lessor "shall not direct the issue of a writ of possession unless the judge is satisfied that one or more of the causes of termination set out in subsection (1) exist." Section 107(8) provides that a notice of termination given by a lessor to a tenant is void and of no effect if the landlord fails to bring an application under s. 113. What is the legal distinction between a "notice of termination" and an "order for possession"? Why is this distinction important?

Bill 96, the Tenant Protection Act, 1996, 1st Sess., 36th Leg. Ont., 1997, also specifies the circumstances where a lessor may issue a notice of termination. Section 37(1) provides that a tenancy may only be terminated in accordance with part III of the Act. As with the Landlord and Tenant Act, Bill 96 provides that a lessor may only terminate the tenancy for certain specified breaches of the tenancy agreement. These grounds are similar to those contained in the Landlord and Tenant Act considered above. As regards a notice of termination before the end of the tenancy, Bill 96 provides that the lessor may only make such a notice if there has been a non-payment of rent (s. 58), an illegal act (s. 59(1)), a misrepresentation of income in publicly subsidized housing (s. 59(2)), undue damage (s. 60), acts that impair safety (s. 61(1)), or too many persons occupying the unit (s. 62). Section 61(1) also provides that a lessor may issue a notice of termination "if the conduct of the tenant is such that it substantially interferes with the reasonable enjoyment of the residential complex for all usual purposes by the landlord or any other tenant." Section 65(1) provides that a landlord may apply to the Ontario Rental Housing Tribunal for an order terminating a tenancy and evicting the tenant if the landlord has given notice to terminate under the Act.

"No Pets" Clauses

There has been considerable controversy regarding the enforceability of "no pets" clauses, commonly included in residential tenancy agreements. In some cases the violation of these clauses by the tenant resulted in the lessor obtaining a writ of possession against the tenant on the grounds that the tenant had substantially interfered with the reasonable enjoyment of the premises by the landlord or other tenants. A number of celebrated cases in Ontario eventually led to statutory reform, making it more difficult for lessors to obtain a writ of possession against tenants who violate "no pets" clauses. The "no pets" cases illustrate the operation of both ss. 107 and 121 of the Landlord and Tenant Act. The cases demonstrate the tension that can exist between the goal of providing enhanced security of tenure to residential tenants and the need to provide the lessor with effective remedies in the event that the tenant is in breach of the leasehold agreement.

In examining s. 107 and the following cases, consider the appropriateness of the statutory protection of the tenant's leasehold estate, and the relation between property and contract principles in this context.

Kay v. Parkway Forest Developments
(1982), 35 OR (2d) 329 (Div. Ct.)

LINDEN J: This is an appeal by a tenant, Fern Kay, from a judgment in favour of the landlord Parkway Forest Developments, delivered on December 12, 1980, declaring a tenancy agreement terminated and granting a writ of possession pursuant to s. 109 of the *Landlord and Tenant Act*, RSO 1980, c. 232 [now s. 107 of the Landlord and Tenant Act, RSO 1990, c. L.7].

The tenant has lived with her son Jeff at the landlord's residential complex, known as Bayview Mews, at 2911 Bayview Ave., in the City of North York, since 1970. In May of 1978, she moved into a townhouse unit, suite J-105, pursuant to a lease which contained the following term:

> 19. The Tenant further covenants
>
> • • •
>
> (g) That no animals or noisy birds will be kept or allowed on or about the rented premises.

All the other tenants executed a similar lease for their own and the landlord's protection.

In June of 1980, in clear breach of this term, Ms. Kay bought a dog, Buddy, which she described as being a "Heinz 57" breed, for her son and kept it in the townhouse. There are 13 or 14 other dogs in the complex, which has 340 units. Although Ms. Kay had agreed earlier in 1978 to get rid of a cat that she had kept for her son, seeing these other dogs in the area, she decided to get one for her son.

There were several complaints by tenants to the landlord, who then obtained a letter from the North York Board of Health dated October 24, 1980, which warned about the "public health nuisance" being caused by the dogs, though no specific evidence was directed against Buddy. Armed with that letter the landlord wrote to the tenants who owned dogs, requesting their removal.

When Ms. Kay did not comply, the landlord sent her a notice of early termination on October 15, 1980, charging that the harbouring of the dog was in violation of the tenancy agreement and her promise made in 1978 and it contributed to complaints from tenants. An application was brought on before His Honour Judge Greenwood on December 12, 1980, who, after a hearing, terminated the lease and granted a writ of possession. It is that decision which is challenged on this appeal.

Mr. Reinhardt, for the tenant, contends that even though Ms. Kay may be in violation of the tenancy agreement, the remedy of termination of the tenancy agreement is available only if her conduct comes within s. 109(1)(c), which reads:

> 109.
>
> • • •
>
> (c) the conduct of the tenant or a person permitted in the residential premises by him is such that it substantially interferes with the reasonable enjoyment of the premises for all usual purposes by the landlord or the other tenants.

He also cites s. 98, which forbids any termination except by notice in accordance with Part IV. He urges that these provisions cannot be contracted out of by the parties because of s. 82, which stipulates that Part IV applies "notwithstanding any agreement or waiver to the contrary." Hence, although other contractual remedies may be available to the landlord, the remedy of termination cannot be employed in this case unless there was a violation of s. 109(1)(c).

Mr. Greenblatt, for the landlord, contends that the trial judge was justified in holding that the tenancy should be terminated because the conduct of the tenant in the keeping of a dog by itself substantially interfered with the reasonable enjoyment of the landlord and the other tenants. The complaints, he says, demonstrated that other tenants were disturbed. This was given weight by the trial judge, he argues, who considered the "interest of the tenants" in coming to his conclusion, even though he found that Ms. Kay was a "competent person, careful in the handling of the dog."

It is now established law that every breach of a tenancy agreement does not necessarily permit a termination of that tenancy. The Landlord and Tenant Act sets out those circumstances that must be proven before a tenancy agreement can be terminated for cause. Thus, if the rent is not paid, the tenancy can be ended (s. 108). Further, if the provisions of s. 109 are violated, the tenancy can be terminated.

In *Re London Housing Authority and Appleton* (1978), 18 OR (2d) 345 at 350, 82 DLR (3d) 559, 5 RPR 324, Judge Killeen explained the purpose of Part IV as follows:

> It is clear, therefore, that Part IV of the Act sets up a new regime for landlords and tenants in this Province. Many of the old—even ancient—doctrines of feudal tenure have been swept away and replaced by statutory rules more consistent with some of the more benevolent aspects of modern contract law. Equally as clear is the fact that, by virtue of the recent amendments in 1975, the Legislature sought to achieve a more substantial measure of security of tenure for tenants than previously obtained. It is now clear that no grounds exist for recovery of possession from a tenant during the currency of the lease, save for non-payment of rent ... or the enumerated causes within [s. 109]. ...

See also *Re London Housing Authority and Coulson* (1978), 18 OR (2d) 353, 82 DLR (3d) 754, Street Co. Ct. J. As was stated by Professor Upans in his book *Ontario Residential Tenancies Manual* (1976), at p. 45

> ... breach of a lease covenant by a tenant will no longer *necessarily* constitute cause for the issue of a writ of possession.

(Emphasis added.)

Consequently, when a clause in a lease forbidding the keeping of a pet is breached, that, *by itself*, is not enough to permit a court to terminate a lease, unless it is also found that s. 109(1)(c) has been violated.

In *Re Oshawa Housing Authority and Maule* (March 12, 1979), Grange J set aside an order evicting a tenant because it was not shown that the dog "interfered with the reasonable enjoyment of the premises by the landlord or the other tenants." In that case, it was felt by the court that the fence that had been built to enclose the dog was being complained about, not the keeping of the dog, but this fact had not been made clear in the notice of termination. Further, the fence had been removed before the decision was rendered.

Professor Gorsky, in his article, "An Examination of Some of the Recent Amendments to the Ontario Landlord and Tenant Act," 3 Dalhousie LJ 663 at 677 (1976-77), explains it in this way:

> Because no grounds exist for regaining possession during the currency of the tenancy, other, than those listed in the amended Act, landlords will be limited to an action for damages or for an injunction, if the tenant commits a prohibited act which does not fall within the above-listed causes for termination of the tenancy and recovery of possession. For example, the not unusual clause prohibiting the keeping of animals in

the rented premises would not be grounds for ... an application unless the keeping of the particular animal resulted in a breach of one of the matters dealt with in section [109].

In our view, it is necessary in a case such as this for the landlord to prove on the balance of probabilities that "the conduct of the tenant substantially interferes with the reasonable enjoyment of the premises" by the landlord or the other tenants. This is a question of fact and must always depend on all the circumstances of the case. The Court will look at the nature of the conduct complained of, its duration, its extent, and its seriousness. The Court should examine also the nature of the premises in question. Moreover, complaints by tenants must be taken into account. Further, the reasonable expectations of the other tenants when they entered their leases cannot be ignored. The fact that all the tenants signed a similar lease, agreeing to forgo pets, would also be relevant. Another factor would be whether other pets were permitted to be kept in the complex. Additional factors might also be considered in arriving at a conclusion.

In this case, we cannot say that the learned trial judge applied the proper test. In failing to admit the further evidence, which was available, about whether there had been substantial interference, he erred. What was called for was a specific finding of fact in terms of the language in s. 109(1)(c) based on all the facts.

We will, therefore, set aside the judgment of December 12, 1980, and refer the matter back to a different judge for a new trial on all of the evidence for a decision in accordance with these views. In the circumstances, there will be no costs.

It should be pointed out that this decision in no way holds that the terms of leases need not be obeyed by tenants. Nor does it grant immunity to dog-owners who ignore the provisions of leases forbidding pets. All that is decided here is that the remedy of termination is not available to enforce those terms unless it is established that s. 109 has been violated. If this cannot be shown, landlords are not powerless because the ordinary remedies of damages and injunctive relief are still available to them.

Appeal allowed; new trial ordered.

Discussion Notes

Grounds To Terminate the Tenancy

As the above case demonstrates, even though a tenant may be in breach of the lease agreement, the lessor will not necessarily be able to terminate the tenancy. He or she may obtain a writ of possession only if (1) the lessor can establish a breach of the agreement, and (2) the breach in question falls within one of the enumerated grounds in s. 107. Historically, lessors had enjoyed broader powers to terminate the tenancy if the tenant had breached even comparatively minor terms of the lease, and this power represented a considerable threat to the tenant's security of tenure. In an effort to enhance this security of tenure, the lessor's ability to terminate the lease in the event of the tenant's breach has now been limited. Does the law strike a fair balance between the conflicting goals of freedom of contract, the protection of the lessor's reversionary interest in the land, and the security of tenure for the residential tenant?

As held in *Kay v. Parkway Forest*, if a tenant were in breach of a "no pets" clause, and the lessor could establish that this breach has substantially interfered with the reasonable enjoyment of the premises by the lessor or other tenants, a writ of possession could be obtained. As the following case illustrates, in some cases lessors were successful in establishing this substantial interference, and the courts would issue writs of possession against tenants with pets. These cases (the following being one of the more notorious) led to the law reform measures of 1990. Consider the type of evidence the court requires in order to establish substantial interference. Does there need to be evidence that the pet in question has caused substantial interference, or is it sufficient to establish merely that pets in general can cause substantial interference?

M and N Properties (Cassandra Towers) v. Ryll
(1989), 6 RPR (2d) 299 (Ont. Dist. Ct.)

[In this case, the lessor brought an application under then s. 109(1)(c), now s. 107(1)(c) of the Landlord and Tenant Act, for a declaration that the tenancy agreement was terminated and requested a writ of possession, on the grounds that the tenant had a cat. The tenants, Mr. and Mrs. Ryll, refused to vacate their apartment, and they refused to get rid of their cat, Fluffy. According to Judge Gotlib, Fluffy was "16 years of age, declawed, slightly blind in one eye, and admittedly not a troublesome cat." The tenants asked that the application be dismissed pursuant to s. 121(2)(a) of the Landlord and Tenant Act.

The tenancy agreement provided that "the tenant will not permit a dog, cat or other animal, noisy bird, insect or reptile to be kept or allowed on, in or about the rented premises or its environs." The Rylls had covenanted in writing in their annual renewal application that they would abide by this and other covenants. The court found on the evidence that there was no complaint about Mr. and Mrs. Ryll as tenants, and that there had been no complaints from other tenants about Fluffy. The lessor discovered Fluffy when workers were in the apartment doing some repairs and they spotted the cat. The lessor argued that he had strictly enforced the no-pets clause in the past, and he was concerned that the maintenance costs of the building would increase if pets were allowed. He submitted that this constituted sufficient "substantial interference" to issue a writ of possession. The lessor did not, however, provide any evidence before the court that Fluffy had caused any damage to the premises. The following evidence was given on behalf of the tenants.]

On behalf of the tenants, evidence was given by Barry Ryll, the adult son of these tenants. He is now age 30, and formerly lived with his wife in apartment 823. He left in September of 1985 and his parents took over the apartment after him and moved in with their cat Fluffy. His evidence was that he saw numerous cats in the apartment building and gave a number of 20 or more, give or take five either way. He was not exact in his evidence and he did not name names or number of apartments. He continues to visit with his parents in apartment 823, and says he still sees pets, and indicated that he never complained about others having pets. I accept the evidence of Mr. Barry Ryll, one of the tenants, that this particular cat has not created an odour nor is there any evidence in this hearing that this cat is a problem of any kind. Mr. Barry Ryll says he knew about the "no pet" clause in the lease, and he also knew his parents were in breach of that clause.

Mrs. Marian Ryll gave evidence and her husband Mr. Richard Ryll gave evidence. They were, in their evidence, extremely emotional. The Court takes judicial notice of their extreme attachment formed with this pet, which has been their pet for 16 years.

Mrs. Ryll, in her evidence, says she signed the agreement with this landlord knowing full well that no pets were allowed. She needed the apartment badly and it was very hard to get an apartment which they could afford. She justified the fact that she lied to the landlord in undertaking not to bring a cat in, by saying that she had to do it. She got this apartment because her son vacated it. She says her cat never leaves the apartment except to go to the vet. It sleeps six out of eight hours a day. The cat is declawed and spayed.

On behalf of the tenants, five letters were introduced, only one of which was signed by a Mrs. Bull in apartment 830, saying that she was a pet lover and did not want the cat disturbed and suggested that the landlord leave the Rylls in peace. I find the unsigned letters unacceptable evidence. They are no proof of anything.

Mrs. Ryll has my sympathy in that she is in poor health. She has had a hip replacement operation in 1985 and again in 1986. She is home a great deal because she finds it difficult to get around. She uses a wheelchair for travelling long distances. She stated that Mr. Liscoe, the then superintendent, knew about the cat and said to her that she was not to worry, because she was not the only one in the building with a pet. Mrs. Ryll knows she is risking her tenancy and steadfastly refuses to give up her cat. She thinks the landlord is being petty and silly. She made no efforts to strike out the covenant, taking the view that that was the landlord's obligation, even though it was clear from the beginning that she did not intend to comply with that covenant. She stated in her evidence that if you need an apartment badly enough, you would sign anything. She has indicated that she is willing to pay extra rent for the cat. She has also indicated that she has tried to get another apartment that she can afford and has been unsuccessful in that aspect. She intends to continue to breach the rule and will not give up her cat voluntarily.

Mr. Ryll is also not in the best of health. Mrs. Ryll receives disability pension and Mr. Ryll receives Worker's Compensation. He, too, states that Mr. Liscoe, the then superintendent, said it was okay to keep a pet as long as there was no smell and the place was kept clean. He said there were no complaints about Fluffy, and I find on the facts that that is so. Mr. Ryll was very upset that the landlord was not repairing some outstanding matters quickly enough, and that he had to pay for his own apartment painting. He was also of the view that both buildings have pets in at least half of the apartments, and that the tenants were afraid of speaking out because they fear the landlord will kick them out too. He too knew that he intended to bring in a cat when he signed the tenancy agreement, but he says that Mr. Liscoe knew about that and knew for three years. He is of the view that the landlord should not be so strict. He also indicated that he broke the rule and he intends to continue to break it.

Miss Elizabeth White is a co-ordinator of public relations for the Toronto Humane Society. While her evidence was interesting as a community matter, it really does not help us in this particular case. It was her evidence that 17% of pet euthanasia arises from "no pet" clauses in apartment leases, and indeed, the numbers could be higher. I accept her evidence, because there is no reason to believe that that is not so. She indicated that there is a large cost to the Toronto Humane Society to euthanise the excess of animals that are in the Toronto area, and not just because of "no pet" clauses, but also for stray animals, and I take judicial notice of the excessive birth rate among stray animals. She has seen Fluffy, an older cat, and she expressed the view that the cat could live to be 20 years old, and that kittens are the quickest to be adopted. She indicated that if Fluffy were to be taken by the Humane Society, that the inevitable result would be that she would have to be put down or euthanised.

On behalf of the tenant, Mr. Jeffery Freedman gave evidence. He is a freelance journalist for the Toronto Star, and he wrote about Mrs. Ryll and her predicament in his column of October 30, 1988. He is on a campaign to require the legislature to amend the *Landlord and Tenant Act* so that the "no pet" clause in apartment leases can be done away with. I am not certain why his evidence should be important to this case. I am neither a politician nor a legislator, and it is my duty to apply the law as it exists both by way of statute and decided cases. Mr. Freedman produced in evidence a book of letters that number about three hundred supporting his position. Those were written, I find, entirely in support of an article he wrote on September 11th, and had nothing to do with his publication of Mrs. Ryll's predicament. The book of letters is filed as Exhibit 30, but has no relevance at all in this matter.

I have considered all the evidence, including the exhibits, and I find, in addition to the Agreed Statement of Facts, the following:

1. These tenants, upon coming into the building, signed a "no pet" covenant in five different documents. Those documents are Exhibits one, two, three, four and fifteen.

2. All the tenants who come into that building sign "no pet" covenants, and all the new agreements have the same covenant.

3. Employees of the landlord are instructed to advise management if they become aware of pets, and the landlord has consistently enforced the "no pet" rule, when the existence of pets was brought to their attention. I have referred to apartments 130, 326 and 926. In the past, when infractions of the rule have come to the attention of the landlord, it has dealt with those tenants, and I find the rule was and is enforced without exception.

4. There has been no specific or special investigation of the building to determine which tenants have pets and which tenants do not have pets, as was the case in *Re LaSalle Towers Ltd. and Ivey*, a case which I will refer to later. ...

[Judge Gotlib considered a variety of precedents, including *Kay v. Parkway Developments*, and concluded:]

I am mindful of the public issues involved, but they are of little help in deciding this case. The role of this Court is to apply the law as it exists and interpret the will of the legislature as evidenced by the statutes, and the *Landlord and Tenant Act*, insofar as Part Four has been passed concerning residential tenancies. That legislation is very clear and direct in addressing the imbalance in power between an impecunious tenant and a wealthier landlord. It is apparent in some cases that the landlord, not particularly in this case, is equally impecunious. Not all landlords are powerful. If the legislature has a change of heart, then the legislation must be amended to reflect that. Much has been made of the fact that these tenants are disadvantaged members of our community. Mrs. Ryll is in poor health, and has memory problems. Mr. and Mrs. Ryll have limited income. They are certainly within the group most seriously affected by the serious lack of low-cost housing and reasonable accommodation in Metropolitan Toronto.

I question whether there really should be one set of rules for the poor and one set of rules for the rich. I think not. It is not acceptable for either class of persons to engage in lying. All persons, including corporate entities, must be equal before the law. Mr. and Mrs. Ryll both admit to the Court that they lied in executing the documents which created their tenancy agreement. Their credibility is therefore suspect, and I find that Mr. Liscoe, the then superintendent, knew nothing about the cat. It was open to the tenants to call Mr. Liscoe, if they wished, to prove otherwise. In any event, I am satisfied that Mr. Liscoe did not have any authority to make any concessions or make deals on behalf of the landlord. That was for the property managers to do and not the superintendent.

The arguments of counsel are fairly basic. On behalf of the landlord, Mr. Glass argues that these tenants signed five documents not to bring an animal into the premises. He argues that these covenants have been in all of the documents for the building since 1966. The tenants acknowledged knowing of the rule when they moved in, and were prepared to breach it immediately. The landlord has given these tenants much time to relocate their pet. It is the landlord's intention to evict the pet, not a good tenant, which the Rylls have been. The landlord does not always know when the rule is being broken, but once aware, the rule is enforced, and the landlord has never turned a blind eye. The landlord states that if one tenant is allowed to have pets, then other tenants will be encouraged to do the same; and accordingly, maintenance will be more expensive, the superintendent will have more work to do, and the ensuing problems would disturb the smooth management and administration of the apartment building. The landlord says further that the rules were not changed in mid-stream. A standard procedure has been followed, and the tenants are not prepared to honour their contractual obligations. The landlord is under an obligation to enforce the covenants, and this landlord is not discriminating against these tenants. The landlord may not know about every pet in the building, but when it knows, it enforces the rules for the benefit of all the tenants and to assist the landlord in managing the building in accordance with its standards. The landlord has indicated that the tenants are free to stay on without the cat, and that if these tenants undertook to remove the animal and undertake not to bring another, that they could stay, and also takes the position that it is unfair for the landlord and other tenants to permit this tenant to oppose the terms of the landlord, and to impose their terms on the landlord, and also require the other tenants to comply.

On behalf of the tenants, Mr. Jefferies argues for compassion due to the fact that the tenants are an older couple. I would say that their chief problem is their health. I would not say that persons aged 56 are over the hill. These tenants have knowingly signed a "no pets" clause. I am very sympathetic to their medical problems and their existing circumstances. The tenants have said that there are other pets in the building, but I really have no evidence on that point, because they have admitted that they have lied when they signed the tenancy agreement. Their arguments lack credibility, and there is a high degree of emotionality in their evidence. I find them simply not credible witnesses in many areas. It was open to the tenants to call the current and past superintendent, and they did not. It was also argued on behalf of the tenants that neither Mr. Steinhart nor Mrs. Cooney had worked in buildings where pets were allowed, and therefore, it is [neither] within their knowledge nor competence to speculate on the additional costs of maintenance in a building where pets are permitted. That is an argument that I cannot accept. They are experienced property managers, and have a very good idea of what is involved in maintaining an apartment building. I agree with counsel concerning Mr. Jones in apartment no. 326 where the damage was done, [with respect to] the cost of over one thousand dollars for repairs, that not all of that damage was caused by the pet.

I agree and recognize that Mr. and Mrs. Ryll are very attached to their pet. There was no indication in the unsigned letters, gathered by Mrs. Ryll, that the writers were pet owners. Those tenants could have come forward to give evidence, but nobody did. I agree with counsel for the tenants who argues that the tenants have little bargaining power in the Toronto apartment market.

Counsel invites me to find the lease an archaic form of document, which the tenant has no opportunity to amend and to overlook the kind of clauses that are contained therein, particularly the "no pets" clause. That is a suggestion that I am completely unable to accept. There would be complete commercial anarchy if I were to rule that contracts entered into freely and voluntarily by adults, who know what they are signing, have no effect and mean nothing. It is true that real estate and lease documents use language which is not necessarily understood by lay persons, but this lease document could easily have been interpreted to the tenants, if they did not understand it. There is all kinds of help available to all tenants, but on the evidence before me, they fully understood what they were signing, both in terms of the tenancy agreement and the lease, and all the renewal agreements.

Mr. Jeffries, on behalf of the tenant, points out that in the case of *Enterprising Developments Ltd. v. Elgar*, one of the reasons for the decision there involved the fact that 40 tenants had signed a petition. There is, of course, no evidence of any petition in this case.

The real question, he says, and I agree, is what is substantial interference? With respect to the landlord, it is said that substantial interference would be looked at in terms of profit. What is substantial interference vis-a-vis the tenants? Do the other tenants want strict enforcement of the covenant? There is no evidence before me as to what the other tenants want. The evidence before me is that all the other tenants have signed "no pets" covenants. My understanding of the procedure is that if a tenant complains, that tenant has no right of action directly against an offending tenant. It is for the landlord to enforce the covenants. The concept that a tenant should be permitted to keep a pet cockroach is, I find, appalling. I would not like to think that somebody could actually keep a cockroach as a pet, even though we must deal with each pet on an individual basis. A dog is very obviously a different pet than a cat, and a cat is a different pet than a fish, and a fish is a different pet than a bird. In each case, there are different issues involved and different circumstances to be considered. If I had a tenant who insisted on keeping a cockroach for a pet in a building managed by me, I would quickly get rid of both the tenant and the cockroach, given the degree at which they multiply, not to mention the fact that they are offensive. Public policy gives one the right to choose one's pets, but properties have been ruined by cockroaches, and I would not even entertain the notion that that is a possible pet.

On behalf of the tenant, it is suggested that the whole lease is filled with ways for the landlord to evict the tenants. I doubt that that is so. We are dealing with one issue. Many tenants live for many years in peace with their landlords in multiple dwelling buildings.

The fact that, in our community, people must live in close quarters with one another, particularly in highrise buildings, puts a duty on the landlord to have very strict rules so that the tenants do not get into each other's hair. Living in close quarters is a difficult enough problem, without suggesting that a lease is full of ways for a landlord to evict tenants. What is a landlord to do about a tenant who insists on playing loud stereo music at five o'clock in the morning? Most people like to sleep at night, but there are no doubt people who like loud stereo music at five o'clock in the morning.

On behalf of the tenant, it is said that it is unfair to evict them given all of the circumstances of the case.

In the end result, I rely on the decision in *Re LaSalle Towers Ltd. v. Ivey*, approved by the Divisional Court. Judge Quinlan, in making that decision, states as follows:

> It appears clear that the tenants not only agreed not to bring pets on the premises but are relying on the enforcement of that clause. I take judicial notice of the fact that there are a significant number of people who are allergic to animals and, in particular, cats. I also take judicial notice of the fact that there are a significant number of people who have an aversion to cats.

I also apply the rules set out in *Kay v. Parkway Forest Developments*, where it is stated the Court should examine the nature of the conduct complained of, its duration, extent and seriousness. I have examined the nature of the premises, considered whether complaints have been made, and considered what the reasonable expectations of the other tenants would be when they entered their leases. In *Kay v. Parkway Forest Developments*, the Court directed that it would be relevant to consider if all of the tenants signed a similar agreement to forgo pets, and whether, in fact, other pets were permitted in the complex.

In this case, all of the tenants signed the same agreement covenanting not to have pets, or went in on the expectation that there would be no animals on the premises. I am satisfied on the balance of probabilities that the conduct of these tenants substantially interferes with the reasonable enjoyment of the premises by other tenants and interferes with the reasonable operation of the building by the landlord. With respect to the latter finding, it is clear that the landlord cannot make an exception for one tenant, and has completely adopted the policy to enforce the "no pets" clause. I find, therefore, that the other tenants and the landlord are being substantially interfered with by the bringing of an animal on to the premises by these tenants.

In the result, the Tenancy Agreement is terminated, and based on the undertaking of the landlord throughout this proceeding, I am prepared to issue a writ of possession that is not to be acted upon until April 1st, and that it is understood that if these tenants relent and relocate their cat, then, of course, the judgment is stayed and the writ of possession is stayed.

I will endorse the record to say, "Order to go terminating Tenancy Agreement, writ of possession to issue, not to be acted on before April 1st. Oral reasons dictated."

Discussion Notes

Substantial Interference

On what grounds did the court find that Fluffy's presence substantially interfered with the reasonable enjoyment of the premises by other tenants, and interfered with the reasonable operation of the building by the lessor? What reasons does the court offer for reaching this conclusion, notwithstanding the fact that there was no evidence before the court that Fluffy had in any way caused damage to the premises, and there were no complaints by other tenants?

Freedom of Contract and Leases

The court worried that there might be "complete commercial anarchy" if it found that the agreement entered into by the parties, "freely and voluntarily," were of no effect. Consider s. 80 of the Landlord and Tenant Act, which provides that the residential tenancy provisions of the Act generally apply notwithstanding any agreement or waiver to the contrary. As a result, if a tenant, for example, "freely and voluntarily" agrees to pay a security deposit in excess of one month's rent, the agreement is nonetheless unenforceable (see s. 82). Does such a provision threaten "complete commercial anarchy"? Is there a difference between this provision and a no-pets clause? Would it make any difference if the tenant were aware of the provisions of the Landlord and Tenant Act, knew that the agreement to pay a security deposit in excess of one month's rent was unenforceable, and deliberately signed the agreement without any intention to comply with the agreement? Has the tenant in this case engaged in a "lie" when signing the agreement? Is intent relevant?

Judicial Discretion

The court found that its duty is to "apply the law as it exists and interpret the will of the legislature as evidenced by the statute." This suggests that the legislation leaves the courts very little room to manoeuvre. Do you agree? What other possible interpretations might the court have adopted? Consider how this case might be distinguished on its facts—for example, if a lessor had failed consistently to enforce a no-pets clause, and appeared to be enforcing it selectively against certain tenants. What if all of the tenants had not been required to sign a no-pets clause? Could M and N Properties be easily distinguished on those grounds?

Amendments to the Landlord and Tenant Act

Following the decision in M and N Properties in 1989, the Landlord and Tenant Act was amended in 1990—Landlord and Tenant Amendment (Animals) Act, SO 1990, c. 19. The amendments to s. 107 provide that where notice of termination is served on the grounds that a pet has substantially interfered with the reasonable enjoyment of the premises (s. 107(1)(c)) or threatened the safety of other tenants (s. 107(1)(d)), a judge hearing the application under s. 113 shall not issue a writ of possession unless the judge is satisfied that the tenant is keeping an animal and that:

107(6)(a) the past behaviour of an animal of that species has substantially interfered with the reasonable enjoyment of the premises for all usual purposes by the landlord or the other tenants;

(b) the presence of an animal of that species has caused the landlord or another tenant to suffer a serious allergic reaction; or

(c) the presence of an animal of that species or breed is inherently dangerous to the safety of the landlord or the other tenants.

Even if the judge is satisfied that s. 107(6)(a) or s. 107(6)(b) has been established, s. 107(7) further provides that the judge shall not issue a writ of possession if he or she is satisfied:

107(7)(a) in the case of a finding under clause (6)(a), that the animal kept by the tenant did not cause or contribute to the substantial interference;

(b) in the case of a finding under clause (6)(b), that the animal kept by the tenant did not cause or contribute to the allergic reaction.

Section 108(1) provides that "no injunction, mandatory order or other order" shall be granted against a tenant unless the court is satisfied that the tenant has violated the same provisions as outlined in ss. 107(6) and (7). As a result, the lessor can obtain neither a writ of possession nor an injunction unless the tenant has violated the provisions contained in ss. 107(6) and (7). What other remedies might be available to the lessor, if any? What if the animal has caused property damage, but not any injury sufficient to satisfy the requirements of ss. 107(6) and (7)? What remedy does the lessor have?

Finally, s. 109 generally restricts the relevance of any "no pets" clause in a tenancy agreement:

109(1) The provisions of an agreement to which the tenant is a party respecting the presence, control or behaviour of animals and the provisions of similar agreements to which other tenants are parties shall not be considered in determining,

(a) for the purposes of clauses 107(1)(c), 107(6)(a) and 108(1)(a), whether there has been substantial interference with the reasonable enjoyment of the premises for all usual purposes by the landlord or the other tenants; or

(b) for the purposes of clause 107(1)(d), whether the safety or other lawful right, privilege or interest of any other tenant in the residential premises has been seriously impaired.

Review the amendments included in ss. 107(6), 107(7), 108, and 109 above. How do the amendments change the law? In particular, consider how the amendments might alter the outcome in *M and N Properties*. Under these amendments, could a court simply take "judicial notice" of the fact that pets such as cats can cause serious allergic reactions, and conclude that this is sufficient grounds to find "substantial interference"? Similarly, under the amendments could a court simply take "judicial notice" that keeping a lion in a residential tenancy is inherently dangerous, and issue a writ of possession, even in the absence of any evidence that the lion in question posed any danger?

Section 109 provides that the provisions of a no-pets agreement shall not be considered when determining whether there has been substantial interference or a serious impairment of the rights of other tenants. In *M and N Properties*, the court held that the fact that all the tenants were required to sign a no-pets clause gave rise to a reasonable expectation on the part of the tenants that there would be no pets in the building. Failure to enforce this reasonable expectation amounted to "substantial interference." Does s. 109 change the law on this point? In *Dassios v. Budai* (May 16, 1996), Ontario no. 96-LT-113341 (Gen. Div.), the tenants had a dog and cat on the premises after falsely stipulating in their application to the lessor that they had no pets. The tenants decided not to disclose this information because they had been advised by a paralegal that the presence of pets was not a legitimate basis for the termination of a tenancy. The court found that the lessor had failed to provide any evidence that the pets in question were a significant source of noise or other disturbance. The court then considered the application of s. 109 of the Act:

> It appears that a landlord cannot, therefore, use the mere presence of pets as a basis for invoking s. 107(1)(c) of the Act. It is necessary to prove, even in the case of the presence of pets, that the conduct of the tenant or other persons permitted on the premises by the tenant is such that it substantially interferes with the reasonable enjoyment of the premises for all the usual purposes by the landlord and other tenants. The onus has not been met, and the application is therefore dismissed.
>
> The tenants' misrepresentation renders them undeserving of costs. Accordingly, there shall be no costs.

The amendments to the Landlord and Tenant Act were also considered in *Jordan & Geisel Management Ltd. v. Napham*, [1990] OJ no. 1600 (Dis. Ct.). The tenant had four dogs of a miniature breed known as Yorkies. The lessor argued that the presence of the four dogs was substantially detrimental to the enjoyment of the premises by the other tenants, such as to provide sufficient grounds for eviction under s. 107(1)(c). The tenant, a widow subsisting on a veteran's allowance, countered that the dogs were her whole life and without them her life would be meaningless. The court considered and rejected as unreliable the evidence presented by the lessor that the tenant's dogs had urinated and defecated in the elevator. The court made it clear that under the 1990 amendments, the lessor can no longer merely rely on the no-pets clause, but must also demonstrate substantial interference by the tenant's animals with the reasonable enjoyment of the premises by the lessor or other tenants.

No-Pets Clauses and Non-Profit Housing Cooperatives

No-pets clauses are commonly included in occupancy agreements issued by various housing cooperatives created pursuant to the Co-operative Corporations Act, RSO 1990, c. C.35. These housing projects are non-profit housing cooperatives and are managed by a board of directors. In *Ventura Park Housing Co-operative Inc. v. Conway* (September 1, 1994) Toronto 33,461/94 (Gen. Div.), the court considered an occupancy agreement that included a no-pet policy. The cooperative was seeking to evict a resident who had a one-year-old siamese cat. There was no evidence that the cat had caused any damage to the premises. The court noted that the provisions of the Landlord and Tenant Act do not apply to housing cooperatives: *McBride v. Comfort Housing Co-operatives Inc.* (1992), 7 OR (3d) 394 (CA), at 400-2. The court also held that the pet policy in question "if uniformly applied is a reasonable one and one which the Co-operative has the power to make and enforce with eviction if necessary." On the facts, however, the court did not order an eviction because the policy had not been uniformly applied.

No-Pets Clauses and Condominiums

No-pets clauses are also commonly included in condominium bylaws. The Condominium Act, RSO 1990, c. C.26, s. 3(3)(b) permits a condominium corporation to prohibit pets. The corporation may enforce this provision against any of the owners in the condominium, and the provisions of the Landlord and Tenant Act do not apply because there is no landlord and tenant relationship.

Owners of condominiums sometimes rent their units to tenants. In *Metropolitan Toronto Condominium Corporation No. 949 v. Irvine* (1992), 24 RPR (2d) 140 (Ont. Gen. Div.), aff'd. (1994), 42 RPR (2d) 319 (Ont. CA), the condominium bylaws prohibited pets. One of the owners had rented his condominium to a tenant who had a miniature poodle, 16-years-old, deaf, and almost blind. The condominium corporation sought the eviction of the tenant pursuant to the no-pets policy in the condominium bylaws. The tenant argued that the provisions of s. 108 of the Landlord and Tenant Act applied, and the corporation could not obtain his eviction because there was no evidence that the pet in question had caused any substantial interference. The court found that the rented unit fell within the definition of "residential premises" under the Landlord and Tenant Act. However, the court also held that s. 108 did not prohibit the corporation from enforcing the no-pets policy. The court noted that s. 108 prohibits an eviction on the basis of a no-pets agreement in the lease. In this case, the corporation sought its remedy not on the basis of a no-pets agreement in the lease, but on the basis of the corporation bylaws authorized under the Condominium Act. Accordingly, the court found that s. 108 did not prohibit the eviction of the tenant.

As a result of this decision, tenants in condominiums may find that they are not entitled to the protection of s. 108. Is this a fair result? On the other hand, would it be fair if the condominium owners were to remain bound by the no-pets agreement enforced under the Condominium Act, but the tenants of such premises were not so bound?

Animals and Bill 96

Bill 96, the Tenant Protection Act, 1996, 1st Sess., 36th Leg. Ont., 1997 provides for somewhat different provisions dealing with animals in residential tenancies. Section 15 provides that a "provision in a tenancy agreement prohibiting the presence of animals in or about a residential complex is void." The Landlord and Tenant Act contains no such provision. Instead, the Landlord and Tenant Act permits "no pets" clauses, but merely restricts the grounds on which the violation of such clauses can result in eviction. Which approach is preferable? Is there a difference?

Although Bill 96 declares that "no pets" clauses are void, under s. 61(2) it nonetheless provides that the lessor may issue a notice of termination if the tenant has committed an act or omission that "seriously impaired the safety of another tenant in the residential complex or another lawful right, privilege or interest of the other tenant."

This provision is similar to s. 107(1)(d) of the Landlord and Tenant Act considered above. Similarly, s. 61(1) of Bill 96 provides that a lessor may issue a notice of termination if the tenant's conduct "is such that it substantially interferes with the reasonable enjoyment of the residential complex for all usual purposes by the landlord or any other tenant." This provision is similar to s. 107(1)(c) of the Landlord and Tenant Act. Either ground might still be used by a lessor to issue a notice of termination if the pet in question seriously impaired the safety of other tenants or substantially interfered with their reasonable enjoyment of the premises. Anticipating this possibility, s. 70(2) limits the extent to which a lessor may issue a notice of termination on the grounds that the pet has substantially interfered with reasonable enjoyment:

> 70(2) If an application claiming substantial interference with the reasonable enjoyment of a residential complex is based on the presence, control or behaviour of an animal in or about the residential complex, the Tribunal shall not make an order terminating the tenancy and evicting the tenant without being satisfied that the tenant is keeping an animal and that,
>
> (a) subject to subsection (3), the past behaviour of an animal of that species has substantially interfered with the reasonable enjoyment of the residential complex for all usual purposes by the landlord or other tenants;
>
> (b) subject to subsection (4), the presence of an animal of that species has caused the landlord or another tenant to suffer a serious allergic reaction; or
>
> (c) the presence of an animal of that species or breed is inherently dangerous to the safety of the landlord or the other tenants.
>
> (3) The Tribunal shall not make an order terminating the tenancy and evicting the tenant relying on clause (2)(a) if it is satisfied that the animal kept by the tenant did not cause or contribute to the substantial interference.
>
> (4) The Tribunal shall not make an order terminating the tenancy and evicting the tenant relying on clause (2)(b) if it is satisfied that the animal kept by the tenant did not cause or contribute to the allergic reaction.

Does Bill 96 significantly change or alter the legislative provisions governing pets in residential tenancies? Would the outcome of any of the above cases differ if they were decided under Bill 96?

Judicial Discretion and the Termination of Residential Tenancies

The following case considers the application of s. 121 under the Landlord and Tenant Act, which provides the court with a general discretion to refuse to grant an application for a writ of possession, unless the court is of the view that it would be "unfair" to refuse to grant the application. Section 121 permits a judge to refuse to grant a writ of possession, even though the tenant is in breach of the lease agreement and the landlord has been able to establish grounds to issue a writ of possession pursuant to s. 107. Section 121(2)(a) requires a judge to consider "all the circumstances" when a landlord seeks a writ of possession:

> 121(2) Upon any application of a landlord for a writ of possession a judge may, despite any other provision of this Act or the tenancy agreement,

(a) refuse to grant the application unless he or she is satisfied, having regard to all the circumstances, that it would be unfair to do so; or

(b) order that the enforcement of the writ of possession be postponed for a period not exceeding one week.

(3) Without restricting the generality of subsection (2), the judge shall refuse to grant the application where he or she is satisfied that,

(a) the landlord is in breach of the landlord's responsibilities under this Act or of any material covenant in the tenancy agreement;

(b) a reason for the application being brought is that the tenant has complained to any governmental authority of the landlord's violation of any statute or municipal by-law dealing with health or safety standards including any housing standard or by-law;

(c) a reason for the application being brought is that the tenant has attempted to secure or enforce his or her legal rights;

(d) a reason for the application being brought is that the tenant is a member of an association, the primary purpose of which is to secure or enforce legal rights of tenants, or that the tenant is attempting to organize such an association; or

(e) a reason for the application being brought is that the premises are occupied by children, provided that the occupation by the children does not constitute overcrowding and the premises are suitable for children.

In the case that follows, the lessor was seeking the eviction of a tenant in a public housing development on the grounds that he had misrepresented his income, as provided for in s. 107(1)(f) of the Landlord and Tenant Act. The court considered whether it should exercise its discretion under s. 121.

Peel Non-Profit Housing Corporation v. McNamara and Cherry
(1990), 74 OR (2d) 450 (Dist. Ct.)

LANGDON DCJ: This is an application for an order declaring the tenancy agreement terminated and for a writ of possession. In 1984, the defendant Henry McNamara (Henry) and Debbie Cherry (Debbie) entered into a lease of the premises in question with the applicant. The relevant portions of the lease between the parties were as follows:

1.2 To furnish at the request of and in a form prescribed by the Management, a statement of income of the Tenant from all sources and a statement of assets of the Tenant and their value at such time or times as the Management may require and, in any event, not less frequently than once every twelve (12) months.

1.3 To furnish, at the request of the Management, such evidence of the authenticity of the statements referred to in paragraph 1.2 as the Management may reasonably require.

1.4 That any statement furnished or to be furnished by the Tenant pursuant to paragraph 1.2 is complete and accurate.

1.5 To notify the Management forthwith of any increase or decrease in income of the Tenant greater than $100.00 per month.

3.2 The Tenant shall be deemed to have ceased to meet the qualifications for occupancy of the premises if he fails to comply with paragraph[s] 1.2 [and] 1.3 of this Lease.

3.3 In the event that the Tenant furnishes any incorrect or misleading information as to his income or assets in his application for rental of the premises or in any subsequent statement furnished by him pursuant of this Lease, the rent shall be re-calculated based on the corrected information, and re-adjusted accordingly. In the event that such recalculation indicated that additional rent is owing, the Tenant shall, upon demand by the Management forthwith pay such additional rent.

3.4 In the event that the Tenant knowingly and materially misrepresents to the Management his income or his assets, this Lease may at the option of the Management, be terminated forthwith.

Background

Henry is a man of some 52 years of age, who suffers under the double yoke of ill health and poverty. In 1985, the Social Assistance Review Board of Ontario, in considering an appeal by Henry from a refusal of Family Benefits Allowance, reported as follows:

> I find as a fact that the Appellant is a permanently unemployable person as defined in the regulation made pursuant to the Family Benefits Act.

Some of the medical conditions which were referred to in the foregoing report and to which the accused alluded as still being present were severe bronchial asthma, congenital tremor, tumour in esophagus, speech difficulties.

Henry says, and I accept, that his health has, if anything, continued to deteriorate and, as he put it, each year another part of him seems to break down.

The co-tenant, Debbie, did not appear on the motion. The evidence is that she is a young woman, now in her twenties. She was in her teens when she executed the lease and moved in with Henry. In due course, she presented him with two children, who now live in the rented premises with Henry. They are, respectively, five and four years of age and were recently attending junior and senior kindergarten.

The trouble seems to have begun in November 1988, when Debbie got a job with Servio Limited as a gas station/car wash attendant. Between then and the commencement of these proceedings, she earned $30,400.

This newfound wealth was the beginning of the end. Henry says, and I accept, that Debbie devoted the vast majority of her revenues to the pursuit of her own pleasures, going out to bars and parties and running up large accounts for non-necessities on her several credit cards.

As a result of continuing quarrels and aggravations, Henry and Debbie split up. She left the premises in or about June of 1990. One might suspect the genuineness of the "breakup" in view of the timing with reference to this application, but it seems to be genuine. Henry was on his way to the Provincial Court (Family Division) following these proceedings.

Henry has kept *de facto* custody of the two children, to whom he is devoted and for whom he is clearly the primary care-giver.

Henry is especially concerned with these two children since, he says, he lost custody of the children of a previous marriage in earlier divorce proceedings and the results—in terms of the present status and prospects of those children—were disastrous. He does not want history to repeat itself.

Without in any way being pejorative, there is not much about Henry to commend itself to any woman, let alone a 20-year-old.

Conversely, one can appreciate the hold that such a young woman might have on Henry, who would quite naturally be reluctant to give up her consortium.

He says, and I accept, that when the inevitable annual review of their financial qualification to remain in non-profit housing came round and with it the awkward issue of disclosing any material change in income, Debbie threatened him that if he disclosed her revenues, she would leave him and that would be the last he would see of the children.

Thus was Exhibit 2 created, wherein Henry and Debbie signed admittedly false declarations stating that their only revenues were Henry's disability income from the province. Most recently, that has been about $1,241 a month, a sum said to be designed to provide for Henry, Debbie and the two children.

In consequence of these misrepresentations, the applicant lost over $8,000 in rents to which it would have been entitled if rents payable had been calculated on accurate revenue figures.

Henry, of course, has no prospect of repaying underpaid rent. The prospect of recovery from Debbie also seems remote.

Henry's social assistance payments were computed on the basis that he and Debbie were living together without other revenues. His evidence is to the effect that his social assistance or disability payments will be reduced to reflect her departure and perhaps some recovery of excess monies paid to him.

Mr. Latimer argues quite correctly that material non-disclosure and *a fortiori* material misrepresentation of income is adequate cause to terminate such a lease: *Re Nipissing and Parry Sound Districts Housing Authority and Tremblay* (1979), 23 OR (2d) 566, 96 DLR (3d) 571 (Dist. Ct.).

Mr. Edgar does not dispute this proposition. The only issue to be determined is whether, under s. 121(2)(a) of the *Landlord and Tenant Act*, RSO 1980, c. 232, I ought to refuse the application. That section provides:

> (2) Upon any application of a landlord for a writ of possession a judge may, notwithstanding any other provision of this Act or the tenancy agreement,
> (a) refuse to grant the application unless he is satisfied, having regard to all the circumstances, that it would be unfair to do so ...

As to this, Mr. Latimer refers to *Metropolitan Toronto Housing Co. v. Gabriel* (1988), 2 RPR (2d) 284 (Ont. Dist. Ct.), where, in a remarkably similar case, District Court Judge Hawkins held, in exercising the discretion conferred by that section [at 288 RPR]:

> I take that section to give the Court an *absolute discretion* on these matters as to whether or not to issue a writ of possession. As to *whether it would be unfair* not to do so, having regard to all the circumstances, that *can only be directed as to whether it would be*

unfair to the landlord since refusing to grant a writ of possession could never be unfair to the tenant. Is it or would it be unfair to the landlord?

In my view, it would be unfair to the landlord not to grant a writ of possession in these circumstances. *Subsidized housing is a very precious commodity* in this community, *and those who are lucky enough to get it,* in my view, *ought to follow the regulations and the rules and provisions of their lease strictly.*

(Emphasis added.)

There is much in those two paragraphs about which no issue can be taken but there are also some statements with which I respectfully disagree.

I question the use of the term "*absolute* discretion." While the section clearly confers a discretion, it seems to me that it is a discretion which ought to be based on a full review of all the equities between the parties and, as well, on consistent and judicial principles.

I dispute the notion of unfairness only as regards the landlord. The Legislature could have written s. 121(2)(a) in terms that the judge might refuse the application unless he were satisfied that it would be unfair *to the landlord* to do so. It did not. I do not think that the expression can be so limited. Indeed, the statute itself requires the court to have "regard to all the circumstances."

I also have serious difficulty with the last sentence quoted. Generally speaking, one recognizes that subsidized housing is available only to disadvantaged persons. Is the law to be interpreted so that disadvantaged people must abide by their leases more strictly than those of better means?

I suggest the better approach to considering the issue of unfairness to refuse to evict is to weigh the impact that refusal to evict would have (a) on the landlord, (b) on the tenant, and (c) to the extent that it is a relevant consideration, on the public interest and then to come to a conclusion based on weighing the results of all those considerations, whether to refuse to evict would be unfair.

Because the public has a substantial stake in subsidized housing, obviously, the weighing process in cases such as this becomes more difficult by the addition of public interest factors.

Mr. Latimer argues forcibly that there are two particular public interest factors that weigh against Henry. The first, I will call, for a lack of a better expression, "general deterrence." This argument recognizes that everyone would like to have subsidized accommodation. Those who get it are naturally reluctant to report an increase in their revenues because that will increase the rent they must pay. Thus, if the court fails to enforce disclosure requirements strictly, then of course disclosure requirements will become even more difficult to enforce.

The next argument is that, when occupants of subsidized housing cheat as Henry did, they cheat not only the housing authority, but as well, those more needy persons who are on the waiting list. Evidence at the hearing indicates that there are now in Peel approximately 3,800 people awaiting subsidized housing units.

These arguments are telling. I make this observation in respect of the principle of general deterrence: there is no empirical evidence that it works. There is empirical evidence that it fails. General deterrence has been a factor in criminal sentencing longer than living memory. We do not know how much crime, if any, is, in fact, deterred by the fear of punitive consequences. We do know that crime and criminals are still with us. Nevertheless, we proceed on the assumption (and it is probably a fair one) that law enforcement unquestionably gains from public realization that illegal conduct will be visited with consequences. These, however, are but some of the factors in the overall equation.

What will be the impact of refusal to evict on the landlord? Will it be able to shrink its waiting list by substituting a less undeserving tenant for Henry? The answer to this question is no, for, if it does so, Henry will go right back on the waiting list. (The applicant's representatives, however, made it abundantly clear at the hearing that hell would freeze over before Henry got readmitted; misrepresentation results in permanent disqualification.) There is only a minuscule chance that Henry might repay some of his arrears if he stays. There is no chance whatever if Henry is evicted and dumped on the open market to find housing. Whatever was the case when Debbie was working, the applicant's representatives acknowledge that Henry, but for his misrepresentation, in his present circumstances, abundantly qualifies for the housing he now has from the applicant.

What will be the impact of refusal to evict on Henry? From Henry's point of view, one cannot overlook that there are some mitigating factors concerning his misrepresentation. One must understand the power which Debbie had over him, his reluctance to lose his relationship with her and his children. After them, he had nothing else but his disability pension. He offended, it is true, but under considerable pressure.

I observe that it would unquestionably have been kinder for the applicant to have caused Henry to be prosecuted for fraud than to have taken these civil proceedings. On conviction for the former, Henry might, it is true, run the risk of a short period of imprisonment and probation, both of which he could well survive. If evicted in civil proceedings, however, Henry is permanently dispossessed. He may find alternate accommodation, but no one knows when that might occur and, when it does, it will surely only be with some form of public subsidy. In the meantime, he may be unable to house his children. Will they be turned over to the less responsible care giver—if she can put them up—or be given into foster care? I do not doubt that Henry is deserving of some punishment by jointly signing with Debbie two statements misrepresenting the family's income. I do not wish to fail to support the public housing authority in the enforcement of its leases. I do not wish that people who are waiting by the rules in the line for subsidized housing should in any way be cheated. On the other hand, I fail to see any net societal benefit in evicting Henry and his two children. I find it particularly distasteful to visit very real, immediate and possibly damaging consequences on innocent players.

From the applicant's point of view, refusal to evict hurts it only from the public interest aspect. With Henry in place as a disadvantaged and qualified applicant for public housing, the applicant is still carrying out its mandate.

I will be the first to agree that this is a subject on which reasonable men may disagree. Respondent's counsel has cited to me at least four decisions in similar cases where judicial discretion has been exercised in favour of the tenant: *Metropolitan Toronto Housing Authority v. Joudrey*, Ont. Co. Ct., Judicial District of York, April 19, 1984; *Ontario Housing Corporation v. Wade*, Ont. Co. Ct., November 30, 1978; *MacNeil v. Ontario Housing Corp.*, Ont. Co. Ct., Judicial District of York, December 15, 1976; *Ontario Housing Corp. v. Herrington*, Ont. Co. Ct., Judicial District of York, August 28, 1978.

Giving the matter the best consideration of which I am capable, I have concluded that eviction would be a disproportionate penalty to Henry and an altogether unjustified punishment to his two children. It would profit the applicant little or nothing and, in the final equation, would provide little or no societal benefit, largely because in some way, directly or indirectly, from another of its myriad pockets, the taxpayer would have to subsidize Henry.

Perhaps the damage to public interest principles which refusal to evict causes might be assuaged to some degree by granting this application only as against the respondent Debbie Cherry. There would be a certain perverse fairness about placating fairly theoretical considerations with a fairly theoretical order. However, my reading of s. 121(2)(a) makes it clear to me that the only discretion authorized by the section is to refuse the application or to grant it. It does not authorize refusal in part.

Application refused. No order as to costs.

Application dismissed.

Discussion Notes

In the above case, the court suggests that the law should not be interpreted "so that disadvantaged people must abide by their leases more strictly than those of better means." Does it matter that the tenant in question deliberately misrepresented his income? Does s. 107(1)(f) expressly require the courts to hold tenants in public housing to a more "strict" standard by making a misrepresentation of income grounds for a writ of possession? The court suggests that there is a larger public responsibility for tenants with disabilities. Does the court implicitly recognize some kind of legal right to social assistance and housing? Are you persuaded by the court's conclusion that s. 121(2)(a) should not be interpreted as addressing only the matter of fairness to lessors? Is this conclusion consistent with the language found in s. 121(2)(a)?

Proposed Amendments in Bill 96

Bill 96, the Tenant Protection Act, 1996, 1st Sess., 36th Leg. Ont., 1997, s. 79 provides the Ontario Rental Housing Tribunal with a similar type of extraordinary discretion to refuse to order the eviction of a tenant:

> 79.(1) Upon an application for an order evicting a tenant or subtenant, the Tribunal may, despite any other provision of this Act or the tenancy agreement,
> (a) refuse to grant the application unless satisfied, having regard to all the circumstances, that it would be unfair to refuse; or
> (b) order that the enforcement of the order of eviction be postponed for a period of time.

Note that the language employed in s. 79(1) is not identical to that contained in s. 121(2). What is the difference? How might this alter the reasoning or outcome in *Peel Non-Profit Housing Corporation*?

Section 79(2), reproduced below, also provides a variety of examples where the tribunal is required to refuse to order the eviction of a tenant. Note that these grounds are not identical to those contained in s. 121(3). How has the legislation been changed? How does this affect the level of discretion given to the Tribunal?

79(2) Without restricting the generality of subsection (1), the Tribunal shall refuse to grant the application where satisfied that,

(a) the landlord is in serious breach of the landlord's responsibilities under this Act or of any material covenant in the tenancy agreement;

(b) the reason for the application being brought is that the tenant has complained to a governmental authority of the landlord's violation of a law dealing with health, safety, housing or maintenance standards;

(c) the reason for the application being brought is that the tenant has attempted to secure or enforce his or her legal rights;

(d) the reason for the application being brought is that the tenant is a member of a tenants' association or is attempting to organize such an association; or

(e) the reason for the application being brought is that the rental unit is occupied by children and the occupation by the children does not constitute overcrowding.

PROBLEMS

1. Bob works for a large downtown insurance company, Insurco. The company provides Bob with a car and downtown parking facilities in a lot owned and operated by a local company, Park Inc. Insurco and Park Inc. entered into an agreement under which Insurco rents a number of underground parking spots from Park Inc. for a small monthly fee. The agreement states that Park Inc. may occasionally need to move one or more of Insurco's parked cars. For this reason, the agreement provides that Insurco employees are required to leave their keys in the ignitions of their cars whenever they park in the Park Inc. lot. The agreement also states that Park Inc. will provide certain security services in the parking lot. There will always be an attendant on duty, "no trespassing" signs will be posted, and members of the general public will be strictly excluded from the lot unless they have parked their cars in the lot.

The agreement also provides that, "Park Inc. is not responsible for theft or damage to Insurco's cars however caused."

Six months ago, Bob left work at approximately 7 pm and went to Park Inc. to pick up his company car. He discovered that his car was missing, and the Park Inc. attendant had no idea where it was. Bob's company car has never been found. Insurco wants to know if it has any claim against Park Inc. for the lost company car.

Advise Insurco.

2. Last week Ahmad decided to rent a car to drive to Ottawa. He went to "Rent-a-Lemon," a rather haphazard operation that rents lousy cars. Gail, the manager at "Rent-a-Lemon," handed Ahmad a standard-form contract to sign. A clever law student, Ahmad actually read the contract, which provided, among other things, that the lessee of

the car was "absolutely liable for any theft of the car." For an additional $10.00 a day, the lessee could purchase theft insurance.

Ahmad was not happy with the "liability for theft" clause, as he believed that cars are frequently stolen in Ottawa, and he did not want to pay for the additional insurance. He told Gail that he would not rent the car unless the "liability for theft" clause were removed. He asked Gail to agreed to the addition of the following clause to the agreement:

> Regardless of any negligence or gross carelessness on the part of the lessee, the lessee is hereby rendered free from any liability whatsoever for any theft of the rented vehicle.

Gail was on the verge of financial ruin and was desperate for business. The car was in poor shape and she could not imagine that anyone would steal it. She agreed to Ahmad's request. Ahmad struck out the liability clause and wrote in the additional clause as above. Both parties initialled the changes to the contract. Ahmad paid his money and drove off to Ottawa.

In Ottawa, Ahmad stayed with a friend. He had no use for the car there, so he left it with his sister, Sue, who also lives in Ottawa. Sue asked Ahmad to leave the keys in the glove compartment in case she needed to move the car, which was parked in her driveway. Of course the car was stolen, and it has never been recovered.

Gail has come to you for advice. She is devastated by the loss of this car, which was not insured for theft. If she cannot recover any money for the car, Gail is afraid she will have to close "Rent-a-Lemon." Gail leases the premises where she conducts her rent-a-car business. Gail's landlord, hearing of Gail's business troubles, has warned Gail that if she breaches the lease, he will sue her for the entire amount due under the remainder of the lease—another ten months at $2,000.00 per month.

Advise Gail.

CHAPTER FIVE

Transferring Property Interests by Gifts and Sale: The Role of Equity

The Legal Context

This chapter considers the transfer of interests in property and explores further the relationship between contract and property law, emphasizing the role of equity in shaping gift and sale transactions. The transfer of a property interest by contractual arrangement (sale) involves a mutual exchange of obligations that are enforced by way of legal and equitable remedies for breach. Such a transaction is regarded as a bargain promise. By contrast, transfer by way of gift involves a gratuitous, unilateral transaction, and is often referred to as a non-bargain promise. In general, non-bargain promises are unenforceable in the law of contract, although it may be possible to create a legally enforceable unilateral promise if the promise includes nominal consideration (the "peppercorn" requirement).

Bargain promises typically occur in a commercial context where there is a need to enforce the expectations of contracting parties, while non-bargain promises such as gifts among family members and friends seem less important matters for legal regulation. Yet, some critics have suggested that to consider transfers by way of sale and gift only in economic terms is to miss the point. For example, wedding presents "transfer material capability, but also cement relations between groups and mark important changes of status for the partners to the marriage." See W.T. Murphy and S. Roberts, *Understanding Property Law* (London: Fontana Press, 1987) (hereafter Murphy and Roberts), at 140. In any event, property interests transferred by way of gift may be legally enforced in some circumstances.

Principles of equity are important in the transfer of property interests. A number of modern equitable principles are relevant to an understanding of gift transactions. As well, equity is important in sale transactions, especially in the context of contracts for the sale of land and the doctrine of part performance, and in relation to the recognition of "equities" in family property arrangements. Equity is also important in the context of priorities among competing interests in land, a matter that is briefly considered along with registration schemes at the end of this chapter.

The legal regulation of transfers of property interests is a major focus of lawyers' work, although transfers of property interests do not always require lawyers. Most people, for example, give birthday presents without the help of a lawyer. However, even the giving of birthday presents may necessitate lawyers and, in some cases, even involve litigation. In *Michael Gruen v. Kemija Gruen*, 68 NY 2d 48; 496 NE 2d 869 (NY CA 1986), for example, a successful architect in New York named Victor Gruen wrote to his son, Michael, to tell him that he was giving him a painting by Gustav Klimt to mark Michael's 21st birthday. A short time later, Victor Gruen sent a second letter (replacing the first one) to his son to announce the gift, explaining that his lawyer had concluded that the wording of the first letter would have attracted tax liability. (The painting had been purchased in 1959 for $8,000, but was valued at the time of the litigation in 1986 at $2.5 million.) As has been suggested, therefore, the role of lawyers is often critical to the efficacy of such transactions, and is one of the reasons for the "complexity of land law" in particular. For an exploration of the role of lawyers in transferring interests in land, see Murphy and Roberts, at 141.

TRANSFERRING PROPERTY INTERESTS BY GIFT

Gift Relationships

As a non-bargain promise, a gift does not attract legal regulation in the same way as a contract. Yet, gifts may have great social significance:

> Lawyers look upon gift as at core a unilateral transaction, by contrast with the bilateral character of sale. Gift is not treated as a mode of exchange. In this respect the legal definition of gift differs sometimes quite sharply from the social meaning of gift in many cultures, including, perhaps, our own.
>
> In some societies, giving "buys" you prestige. As Mauss put it:
>
> > Between vassals and chiefs, ... the hierarchy is established by means of ... gifts. To give is to show one's superiority, to show that one is something more and higher, that one is magister. To accept without returning or repaying more is to face subordination, to become a client and subservient, to become minister (1925; tr. 1966, 1969:72).

(Murphy and Roberts, at 145.)

The social role of gifts and gift-giving may also attract legal regulation. In Canada, for example, T. Loo has analyzed amendments to the Indian Act, beginning in 1884, that made the "potlatch" an indictable criminal offence. "Potlatch" derives from the language of trade along the coast of British Columbia, a combination of English and a variety of Indian languages, and means "to give." In traditional native culture in British Columbia, it is a ceremony given by a family to display its hereditary possessions, including dances, songs, and carvings, and ends with the distribution of gifts to those attending. The traditional ceremony of potlatch changed with increasing contact between First Nations people and European settlers and traders, so that the quantity and commercial value of gifts being distributed increased substantially. Apparently, these changes attracted governmental attention and resulted in the enactment of a series of amendments to the Indian Act after 1884 in an effort to curtail potlatches. Although concerns were expressed about the wastefulness of the potlatch ceremonies, "the antithesis to the twin pillars of the Protestant work ethic: industry and sobriety," Loo identified anthropological interpretations of the potlatch that showed its similarity to European cultures:

> In [the anthropologists'] opinion, the law was flawed in part not because it was ethnocentric, but because its architects failed to appreciate the broad similarities between the potlatch and modern Western economic behaviour. If Indians were economic people just like whites and their potlatch was a central economic institution, then neither they nor their culture was in need of reform through the law ... . Harlan Smith was ... struck by the capitalist aspects of the potlatch. "It is said to be more blessed to give than to receive," he wrote. "Mr. Carnegie is honored for what he gives away." ...
>
> The problem with and the significance of the ceremony to white society lay in the distributive aspect of the ceremony. Accumulation was laudable, but the way Indians disposed of their goods stood as a radical counterpoint to the existing material order in white society ... . Working to consume and accumulate was intelligible behaviour, but when Indians gave away or destroyed all they had worked for they debased the very commodity—property—around which white society was constructed.

(T. Loo, "Dan Cranmer's Potlatch: Law as Coercion, Symbol, and Rhetoric in British Columbia, 1884-1951," in T. Loo and L. McLean, eds., *Historical Perspectives on Law and Society in Canada* (Toronto: Copp Clark Longman, 1994) (hereafter Loo and McLean), 219, at 231-32.) The prohibition against the potlatch was left out of the Indian Act in 1951 (Loo, at 222).

Legal prohibition of the potlatch ceremony was part of governmental efforts to encourage assimilation among First Nations in Canada. Yet, as was pointed out by some critics in 1904, the feasting, dancing, singing, and use of masks at a potlatch were not so different from some European celebrations, "[T]he white man calls his friends at Christmas time & feasts them & has Xmas trees & gives presents & he dresses up a man & calls him Father Xmas & says he brings presents, etc." See Loo and McLean, at 233-34, quoting correspondence. Others have suggested that one method of evading the law's prohibition of potlatches was to "[disguise them] as Christmas dinners and the gift giving as holiday presents." See D. Cole and I. Chaikin, "'A Worse Than Useless Custom': The Potlatch Law and Indian Resistance" (1992), 5:2 *Western Legal History* 187, at 209. For an overview of the policy of the Indian Act, see J. Tobias, "Protection, Civilization, Assimilation: An Outline History of Canada's Indian Policy," in Loo and McLean, 290. Why was the similarity between gift ceremonies among First Nations and European settlers not accepted? To what extent is the giving of presents at Christmas (or on other similar occasions) a matter that reflects status in the community? In the context of tax benefits for charitable and other donations, is it correct to characterize gifts as outside usual commercial transactions? Should the law encourage gift-giving *per se*, or affect the form that gifts may take? For an interesting analysis of the social relationships involved in donations of blood, see R. Titmuss, *The Gift Relationship: From Human Blood to Social Policy* (New York: Pantheon Books, 1971). You may wish to consider the relationship between legal and social conceptions of gifts as you examine the materials that follow.

Requirements for a Valid Gift Inter Vivos

A gift of real or personal property can be made by a deed of gift, a document in writing that is sealed and delivered and almost always signed by the donor. In practice, however, a deed of gift is not often used for gifts of personal property. In the absence of a deed, a gift of personal property is legally recognized if three requirements are met—the intention to make a gift on the part of the donor, acceptance of the gift by the donee, and a sufficient act of delivery. All three requirements are essential, as is reflected in one of the classic maxims of equity that "[e]quity will not perfect an imperfect gift"—that is, equity will not recognize a gift if any one of the requirements is absent. See *Milroy v. Lord* (1862), 45 ER 1185 (Ch.D).

A gift *inter vivos* is the most usual form of gift, but it needs to be distinguished from other kinds of gifts, including those made in contemplation of death such as testamentary gifts and the *donatio mortis causa*, both of which are considered later.

Delivery

A sufficient act of delivery is required for a valid gift. According to Ziff, "the gift must literally be *given* away, ... [with the] act of transfer ... providing tangible proof of a gift."

> The requirement of proper delivery is therefore the functional counterpart of the ancient ceremony of livery of seisin. Words alone are insufficient as proof of delivery because there is a "facility with which words may be distorted." The stress placed on the transfer of possession is a symptom of a cynical society which assumes bargains and not gifts, so much that when the trappings of a contract are missing, tangible proof of donative action is demanded.

(B. Ziff, *Principles of Property Law*, 2d ed. (Scarborough, ON: Carswell, 1996) (hereafter Ziff), at 135, quoting *Kingsmill v. Kingsmill* (1917), 41 OLR 238 (HC), at 241.)

The issue of delivery must be examined in the context of the subject matter of gifts. How would you define delivery in the context of a donor who wishes to make a gift of a part interest in a horse? Consider the reasoning in the following decision addressing this problem.

Cochrane v. Moore
(1890), 25 QBD 57 (CA)

FRY LJ: The judgment I am about to read is that of Lord Justice Bowen and myself.

The question in this interpleader issue arises in respect of a sum of money representing one-fourth of the proceeds of a horse called Kilworth, sold by Messrs. Tattersall. The plaintiff claims the money under a bill of sale executed by one Benzon, comprising this and other horses. The defendant claims it under an earlier gift of one-fourth of the horse to him by Benzon.

The relevant facts, as they appear in the judgment of Lopes LJ, and in that part of the evidence to which he attached credence, are shortly as follows:

The horse was in June, 1888, the property of Benzon, and was kept at the stables of a trainer named Yates, in or near Paris, and on the 8th of that month was ridden in a steeplechase by Moore, a gentleman rider. In consequence, as it appears, of some accident, the horse was not declared the winner, and on the same day, according to the view of the evidence taken by the learned judge, Benzon by words of present gift gave to Moore, and Moore accepted from Benzon, one undivided fourth part of this horse.

A few days subsequently Benzon wrote to Yates, in whose stables the horse was, and told him of the gift to Moore. But he did not inform Moore, nor did Moore know of any communication to Yates of the fact of the gift.

On July 9, 1888, Cochrane advanced 3000*l*. by way of loan to Benzon, and took from him a promissory note for 3500*l*., payable on August 9 following.

On July 16 of the same year, Cochrane advanced to Benzon a further sum of 4000*l*., and took a promissory note for 4800*l*., payable on September 16.

On July 26 Cochrane advanced to Benzon two sums of money: One, 1680*l*. 10*s*. 11*d*. (to be paid to one Sherard, a trainer), and 745*l*.; making together 2425*l*. 10*s*. 11*d*. And on the same day Benzon executed a bill of sale for 10,000*l*., under which Cochrane claims. Kilworth and other horses were included in the schedule to this instrument.

It is proved by the evidence of the witnesses, whom the learned judge believed, that, before the execution of the bill of sale, Benzon, with the assistance of a friend, Mr. Powell, was going through the list of horses to be included in the schedule, and that when Kilworth was mentioned Powell spoke of Moore's interest in the horse, and that thereupon a discussion arose as to what was to be done with it, and that Cochrane undertook that it should be "all right." After this the bill of sale was executed by Benzon.

On these facts, it was argued that there was no delivery and receipt of the one-fourth of the horse, and, consequently, that no property in it passed by the gift. The learned judge has, however, held that delivery is not indispensable to the validity of the gift.

The proposition on which the Lord Justice proceeded may perhaps be stated thus: that where a gift of a chattel capable of delivery is made per verba de praesenti by a donor to a donee, and is assented to by the donee, and that assent is communicated to the donor by the donee, there is a perfect gift, which passes the property without delivery of the chattel itself. This proposition is one of much importance, and has recently been the subject of some diversity of opinion. We therefore feel it incumbent upon us to examine it, even though it might be possible in the present case to avoid that examination.

The proposition adopted by the Lord Justice is in direct contradiction to the decision of the Court of King's Bench in the year 1819 in *Irons v. Smallpiece*. That case did not proceed upon the character of the words used, or upon the difference between verba de praesenti and verba de futuro, but upon the necessity of delivery to a gift otherwise sufficient. The case is a very strong one, because a Court consisting of Lord Tenterden CJ, and Best and Holroyd JJ, refused a rule nisi, and all held delivery to be necessary. The Chief Justice said: "I am of opinion that, by the law of England, in order to transfer property by gift there must either be a deed or instrument of gift, or there must be an actual delivery of the thing to the donee," and he went on to refer to the case of *Bunn v. Markham* as a strong authority.

These observations of the Chief Justice have created some difficulty. What did he mean by an instrument as contrasted with a deed? If he meant that an instrument in writing not under seal was different from parol in respect of a gift inter vivos, he was probably in error; but if in speaking of the transfer of property by gift, he included gifts by will as well as gifts inter vivos, then by instrument he meant testamentary instrument, and his language was correct.

Holroyd J was equally clear on the principal point: "In order to change the property by a gift of this description" (by which we understand him to mean, a gift inter vivos) "there must be a change of possession."

The correctness of the proposition thus laid down has been asserted in many subsequent cases of high authority. ...

[The court reviewed several decisions that supported the proposition, then several that seemed to negate it, and continued:]

There is thus some difference of judicial opinion as to the rule stated in *Irons v. Smallpiece*. We cannot think that the few recent decisions to which we have referred are enough to overrule the authority of that decision, and the cases which have followed it, but they make it desirable to inquire whether the law as declared before 1819 was in accordance with that decision, or with the judgment of Pollock B, in *Danby v. Tucker*.

This inquiry into the old law on the point is one of some difficulty, for it leads into rarely-trodden paths, where (as is very natural) we have not had the assistance of counsel, and where the materials for knowledge are for the most part undigested.

The law enunciated by Bracton in his book "de acquirendo rerum dominio," seems clear to the effect that no gift was complete without tradition of the subject of the gift. ...

In Bracton's day, seisin was a most important element of the law of property in general; and, however strange it may sound to jurists of our day and country, the lawyers of that day applied the term as freely to a pig's ham (Select Pleas in Manorial Courts, p. 142(2)); see also Professor Maitland's papers on the Seizin of Chattels, the Beatitude of Seizin, and the Mystery of Seizin: Law Quarterly Rev., i, 324; ii, 484; iv, 24, 286) as to a manor or a field. At that time the distinction between real and personal property had not yet grown up: the distinction then recognised was between things corporeal, and things incorporeal: no action could then be maintained on a contract for the sale of goods, even for valuable consideration, unless under seal: the distinction so familiar to us now between contracts and gifts had not fully developed itself. The law recognised seisin as the common incident of all property in corporeal things, and tradition or the delivery of that seisin from one man to another as essential to the transfer of the property in that thing, whether it were land or a horse, and whether by way of sale or of gift, and whether by word of mouth or by deed under seal. This necessity for delivery of seisin has disappeared from a large part of the transactions known to our law; but it has survived in the case of feoffments. Has it also survived in the case of gifts?

It has been suggested that Bracton, whilst purporting to enunciate the law of England, is really copying the law of Rome. But by the law of Rome, at least since the time of Justinian, gift had been a purely consensual transaction, and did not require delivery to make it perfect (Inst. ii, vii). ...

[The court reviewed a number of law writers from the early years of common law decisions, and then focused on the Tudor developments in contract and property doctrines:]

It was in the reigns of the early Tudors that the action on the case on indebitatus assumpsit obtained a firm foothold in our law; and the effect of it seems to have been to give a greatly increased importance to merely consensual contracts. It was probably a natural result of this that, in time, the question whether and when property passed by the contract came to depend, in cases in which there was a value consideration, upon the mind and consent of the parties, and that it was thus gradually established that in the case of bargain and sale of personal chattels, the property passed according to that mind and intention, and a new exception was thus made to the necessity of delivery.

This doctrine that property may pass by contract before delivery appears to be comparatively modern. It may, as has been suggested, owe its origin to a doctrine of the civil law that the property was at the risk of the purchaser before it passed from the vendor; but at any rate the point was thought open to argument as late as Elizabeth's reign (see Plowd. 11b, and see a learned note, 2 Man. & Ry. 566). ...

In 1818 the year before *Irons v. Smallpiece* was decided, the then Master of the Rolls, Sir Thomas Plumer, in *Hooper v. Goodwin* said: "A gift at law or in equity supposes some act to pass the property: in donations inter vivos ... if the subject is capable of delivery, delivery."

These are, so far as we can find, all the relevant authorities before the decision in *Irons v. Smallpiece*, though they are not all the authorities that have been cited as relevant. But several that have been relied upon appear to us to have no real bearing on the point at issue. Thus in *Wortes v. Clifton*, Coke ... uses as an illustration of the difference between the Civil law and ours—that in the Civil law a gift is not good without tradition—but that it is otherwise in our law. Here for aught that appears, the gift which the learned counsel referred to as good without delivery is a gift by deed.

In like manner several authorities which affirm that a gift of chattels may be good without deed and are silent as to delivery (Perkins' Profitable Book, Grant 57; 2 Shep. Touchs. 227; Comyn Digt. Biens D 2) have been cited as if they likewise asserted that a gift was good without delivery—a proposition which they do not affirm, or, as we think, imply.

This review of the authorities leads us to conclude that according to the old law no gift or grant of a chattel was effectual to pass it whether by parol or by deed, and whether with or without consideration unless accompanied by delivery: that on that law two exceptions have been grafted, one in the case of deeds, and the other in that of contracts of sale where the intention of the parties is that the property shall pass before delivery: but that as regards gifts by parol, the old law was in force when *Irons v. Smallpiece* was decided: that that case therefore correctly declared the existing law: and that it has not been overruled by the decision of Pollock B, in 1883, or the subsequent case before Cave J.

We are therefore unable in the present case to accept the law on this point as enunciated by Lopes LJ in deference to the two latest decisions.

But assuming delivery to be necessary in the case of the gift of an ordinary chattel, two questions would remain for consideration in the present case—the first, whether the undivided fourth part of the horse admits of delivery, or whether on the other hand it is to be regarded as incorporeal and incapable of tradition; the other, whether the letter written by Benzon to Yates was either a constructive delivery of this undivided fourth part of the horse, or an act perfecting the gift of this incorporeal part so far as the nature of the subject-matter of the gift admits. On these points we do not think it needful to express any decided opinion, because in our judgment what took place between Benzon and Cochrane before Benzon executed the bill of sale to Cochrane, constituted the latter a trustee for Moore of one-fourth of the horse Kilworth.

Another objection to Cochrane's title was based on the bill of sale, which bore date July 26, 1888, and stated the consideration as a sum of 7575*l.* then owing by Benzon to Cochrane, and of the further sum of 2425*l.*, then paid by Cochrane to Benzon, making together a sum of 10,000*l.*; whereas in fact at the date of the bill of sale Benzon was only indebted to Cochrane on two promissory notes then current and payable respectively in August and September, and for sums amounting together to 8300*l.* It is said that by an agreement arrived at at the time, this 8300*l.* due in futuro was to be taken as between the parties as represented by the sum of 7575*l.*; but if so, this agreement should in our opinion have been stated in the bill of sale, and we are therefore of opinion that the document was void as not truly stating the consideration for which it was given.

For these reasons we are of opinion that this appeal should be dismissed with costs.

LORD ESHER MR: In my opinion, it always was the law of England that an owner of a chattel could transfer his ownership thereof to another person by way of exchange or barter, or by way of bargain and sale for a consideration, or by way of and as a mere gift, or by will. Once conclude that such was always the law, and it follows that it is the common law. That law could not and cannot be altered by mere judicial decision, but only by Act of Parliament. The authority of any judicial decision to the contrary would be overruled at any time, however remote, by a competent Court. But each of the above propositions is a fundamental proposition of law, i.e., a proposition which is not evidence of some other proposition which has to be proved, but a proposition the existence of which—i.e., the facts necessary to constitute which—is to be proved by evidence. The moment those facts are proved the proposition of law is proved, to which the legal tribunal will give effect. Although no Court can properly alter such a fundamental proposition, the amount or nature of the evidence which will satisfy a Court of the existence of such a proposition, as applicable to a particular case, may vary, and has varied, at different epochs. I have no doubt that in every one of the propositions above enumerated, unless it be in the case of a gift by will, there was a time when, as part of the evidence of the existence of the proposition in a particular case, the Courts always required that there should have been an actual delivery of the chattel in question. Though there was proof of a contract for good consideration, in a form which would now pass the property in a chattel without delivery, proof of actual delivery was required. Though the transfer was contained in a deed, proof of actual delivery was required. Equally the statement that one had declared in mere writing or in words that he did then, at the moment, transfer, without consideration, his chattel to another, and that the other did at the same moment state in writing or in words that he accepted such transfer, was not acted upon by the Courts as proof of a gift executed, without proof also of an actual delivery. The evidence required in all cases was not complete without proof of an actual delivery. But in some of the cases the Courts undoubtedly do not now require proof of an actual delivery. They do not require that piece of evidence. They do not in the case of a transfer by deed, or in the case of a transfer by a contract for good consideration, shewing in its terms an intention that the ownership should pass at once before or without immediate delivery. If I thought that there was not a difference between those cases and the case of what has been called a gift in words by the donor, and an acceptance in words by the donee of a chattel, I should be strongly inclined to think that, even though the Courts would have required in such case proof of an actual delivery, up to and including the case of *Irons v. Smallpiece*, the Courts might now in such case, as former Courts did in the other cases, be satisfied by other evidence of the gift by the one and the acceptance of the gift by the other, which are the facts which constitute the proposition of a transfer of ownership of a chattel by way of and as a gift.

Up to the time of *Irons v. Smallpiece*, and afterwards, I have no doubt the Courts did require proof of an actual delivery in such a case. Upon long consideration, I have come to the conclusion that actual delivery in the case of a "gift" is more than evidence of the existence of the proposition of law which constitutes a gift, and I have come to the conclusion that it is a part of the proposition itself. It is one of the facts which constitute the proposition that a gift has been made. It is not a piece of evidence to prove the existence of the proposition; it is a necessary part of the proposition, and, as such, is one of the facts to be proved by evidence. The proposition is not—that the one party has agreed or promised to give, and that the other party has agreed or promised to accept. In that case, it is not doubted but that the ownership is not changed until a subsequent actual delivery. The proposition before the Court on a question of gift or not is—that the one gave and the other accepted. The transaction described in the proposition is a transaction begun and completed at once. It is a transaction consisting of two contemporaenous acts, which at once complete the transaction, so that there is nothing more to be done by either party. The act done by the one is that he gives; the act done by the other is that he accepts. These contemporaneous acts being done, neither party has anything more to do. The one cannot give, according to the ordinary meaning of the word, without giving; the other cannot accept then and there such a giving without then and there receiving the thing given. After these two things done, the donor could not get possession of the chattel without bringing an action to force the donee to give it back. Short of these things being done, the donee could not get possession without bringing an action against the donor to force him to give him the thing. But if we are to force him to give, it cannot be said that he has given. Suppose the proposing donor offers the thing saying, "I give you this thing—take it"; and the other says, "No, I will not take it now; I will take it tomorrow." I think the proposing donor could not in the meantime say correctly to a third person, "I gave this just now to my son or my friend." The answer of the third person would (I think rightly) be: "You cannot say you gave it him just now; you have it now in your hand." All you can say is: "That you are going to give it him tomorrow, if then he will take it." I have come to the conclusion that in <u>ordinary English language</u>, and in legal effect, there cannot be a "gift" without a giving and taking. The giving and taking are the two contemporaenous reciprocal acts which constitute a "gift." They are a necessary part of the proposition that there has been a "gift." They are not evidence to prove that there has been a gift, but facts to be proved to constitute the proposition that there has been a gift. That being so, the necessity of their existence cannot be altered unless by <u>Act of Parliament</u>. For these reasons, I think that the decision in *Irons v. Smallpiece* cannot be departed from, and I cannot agree with the decisions, which have been cited to us, of Pollock B and Cave J.

I think, therefore, that we cannot agree with the main reason given by Lopes LJ for his decision in the present case, which he gave because he thought that, sitting as a judge of the Queen's Bench Division, he ought to follow the later decisions. His own opinion was in favour of maintaining *Irons v. Smallpiece*. But I do entirely agree with what I understand was another ground on which he was prepared to decide this case, and which he found, as a fact, existed in this case, namely, that the deed on which the claimant's case rested was obtained by a fraudulent misrepresentation, and was repudiated by the giver of it as soon as he discovered the fraud.

For this reason, and the others mentioned by my brother Fry, I think the appeal must be dismissed. I wish to say that I am not prepared to differ in any respect from the judgment of my learned brothers; but I wish to add my own particular reason.

Appeal dismissed.

Discussion Notes

Historical Development of the Requirement of Delivery

As the reasoning in *Cochrane v. Moore* suggests, a transfer of *any* interest in land historically required "livery of seisin," the handing over of a clump of earth to the transferee. Similarly, a transfer of personal property required delivery of possession. These requirements illustrate the emphasis on possession as evidence of title in the early development of property law. With the later development of the law of contract, however, it became evident that proprietary rights could be transferred by contract without a transfer of physical possession. Moreover, as the sale of land came to be effected by deed, rather than livery of seisin, the concept of delivery also changed to reflect this new context. The court in *Cochrane v. Moore* had to decide whether physical delivery should remain an essential requirement for a valid oral gift, as had been declared in the earlier case of *Irons v. Smallpiece* (1819), 106 ER 467 (KB).

Moore argued that actual delivery should no longer be required, and that Benzon's stated intention to make a gift of a quarter of the horse (what the court referred to as Benzon's "words of present gift") were sufficient to effect a transfer of property rights. The court admitted that the requirement of delivery was now obsolete in other kinds of transactions, but confirmed that it was still essential to a valid oral gift of personal property. Why? What rationale is offered by the court for treating oral gifts of personal property differently from other kinds of transfers? Are there policy reasons for continuing to require delivery in relation to oral gifts of personal property? To what extent do you agree with the following assessment of *Cochrane v. Moore*:

> This reliance on historical precedent, resting as it does on now nearly obsolete doctrines of seisin, is hardly satisfactory to the modern mind. The survival of the dogma is doubtless due to the perfectly reasonable desire on the part of the courts to protect the property of the individual against ill-founded and fraudulent claims of gift, resting only

on the assertion of oral words of gift, concerning which the evidence may be doubtful and open to controversy.

(R. Brown, *The Law of Personal Property*, 3d ed., rev. W. Raushenbush (Chicago: Callaghan & Co., 1975) (hereafter Brown), at 78.) It has also been suggested that the requirement of delivery is based on sound public policy and should be retained in the modern law of gifts, because the requirement provides clear evidence of the donor's intent. See P. Mechem, "The Requirement of Delivery in Gifts of Chattels and Choses in Action Evidenced by Commercial Instruments" (1926), 21 *Illinois Law Review* 341.

Defining "Delivery" in Cochrane

Exactly what actions constitute delivery for a valid gift is a question that has received much attention. Was there sufficient delivery in *Cochrane v. Moore*? How could the donor have made effective delivery of a quarter of a horse? In *Hillebrant v. Brewer*, 6 Tex. 45; 55 Am. Dec. 757 (1851) (cited in Brown, at 94), for example, it was held that the branding of range cattle by the donor with the recorded brand of the donee constituted delivery.

Consider the situation of householders who place used newspapers at the curb in front of their homes so that they can be collected by the municipality for recycling. If an enterprising group of students collects the newspapers before the municipal employees are able to do so, and then sell them to a recycling depot, are the students guilty of theft from the municipality? Was there a valid gift of the newspapers by the householders to the municipality? Does the placement of newspapers at the curb for the purpose of municipal collection for recycling constitute delivery? See *State v. Weinstein*, 31 SE 2d 920 (NC SC 1944); *cert. den.* 324 US 849; 65 SC 689 (1945). For a tragic case where delivery was incomplete, see *Liebe v. Battman*, 54 P 179 (Ore. SC 1898). For further analysis, see W.L. Roberts, "The Necessity of Delivery in Making Gifts" (1926), 32 *West Virginia Law Quarterly* 313; P.J. Rohan, "The Continuing Question of Delivery in the Law of Gifts" (1962), 38:1 *Indiana Law Journal* 1; and Sir Frederick Pollock, "Gifts of Chattels Without Delivery" (1890), 6 *Law Quarterly Review* 446.

Gifts and Trusts

In *Cochrane v. Moore*, the court concluded that delivery was required for a valid oral gift, and that there was not sufficient delivery. Yet, the court nonetheless awarded Moore one quarter of the value of the horse, and ordered Cochrane to pay Moore the amount owing, even though Cochrane had never purported to give Moore anything. On what basis did the court reach these conclusions?

EXPRESS TRUSTS

Cochrane v. Moore is an example of a transfer of title without a change in possession. The court declared that "what took place between Benzon and Cochrane before Benzon executed the bill of sale to Cochrane, constituted [Cochrane] a trustee for Moore of one-fourth of the horse Kilworth." Cochrane, who had possession of the horse, became a trustee with respect to a one-quarter share for Moore, the beneficiary of the trust arrangement. As explained in chapter 3, a trustee has an equitable duty to the beneficiary and the duty is enforceable in equity against a subsequent purchaser—for example, Cochrane, here—who has notice of the equitable interest. Even though there was no valid gift because of the lack of delivery, the court held that there was a trust with respect to the interest in the horse. What is the relationship between gifts and trusts?

As chapter 3 explains, trusts were recognized in the 17th century, when courts of equity first provided protection for the grant of a "use upon a use." In the 20th century, the trust relationship is regarded as a remarkable and creative feature of modern property law. Since trusts can be created when a person transfers property to a trustee to hold it for named beneficiaries, there is an obvious similarity between the transfer of a gift and the creation of a trust. To create a trust, a person usually executes a deed of trust, defining the property that is to form the trust, identifying the trustee and the beneficiaries, and specifying the trustee's duties. For an express trust, three matters must be certain—the intention to create a trust, the subject matter of the trust, and the objects of the trust. However, there is no need for any physical delivery of trust property, and it is possible, although somewhat unusual, to create an express trust of personal property by means of an oral declaration, as appears to have happened in *Cochrane*. For a further analysis of trusts, see A.H. Oosterhof and E.E. Gillese, *A.H. Oosterhof: Text, Commentary and Cases on Trusts*, 4th ed. (Scarborough, ON: Carswell, 1992) (hereafter Oosterhof and Gillese) and Brown, at 145ff. The trust relationship is also an important concept in modern legal analyses of the relationship between the Crown and First Nations. See *Guerin v. The Queen*, [1984] 2 SCR 335, discussed in chapter 3.

In another case concerning gifts and trusts, the plaintiff was fond of boating and was a good friend of the owner of a marina. For more than 20 years, the plaintiff provided unpaid assistance in the running of the marina. Over a four-year period, the plaintiff's husband and the marina owner built a boat called "Thunderbird." The boat was registered in the name of the marina owner, although its log book showed the marina owner and the plaintiff as co-owners. The plaintiff and the marina owner both had keys to the boat, and the plaintiff and her family used the boat freely. Some time later, the marina owner, who was apparently concerned about "being sued by customers," wrote out a document declaring that "the boat commonly known as 'Thunderbird' is now owned jointly by" the marina owner and the plaintiff. He gave the document to the plaintiff. The marina owner subsequently died, and the boat was claimed by his estate. The plaintiff claimed entitlement to the boat as a gift from the marina owner.

Was there a valid gift *inter vivos* of "Thunderbird"? The analysis of the case at trial focused on the concept of concurrent ownership, discussed in chapter 7. However, the appeal court concluded that there was no valid gift because the delivery of the keys to "Thunderbird" did not constitute delivery of a gift, especially since the marina owner also retained a set of keys. The appellate court applied the reasoning of *Cochrane*, stating:

> It is clear that what [the marina owner] wrote, said, and did constituted an executed trust which made him and, subsequently, his estate a trustee of the one-half interest in "Thunderbird" on behalf of [the plaintiff] .... . The document signified the existence of trust and the right to a one-half interest in the boat.

(*Watt v. Watt Estate* (1987), 28 ETR 9 (Man. CA), at 13.) The court also considered the form of co-ownership, a matter examined more fully in chapter 7. You may want to reconsider *Watt* in relation to the requirement that transfers of land (by contrast with the horse in *Cochrane* and the boat in *Watt*) must be in writing, pursuant to the Statute of Frauds, an issue examined below.

Is *Watt* exactly the same as *Cochrane* in terms of how the trust was created? Is it appropriate for a court to hold that a trust exists when there is no valid gift? Is equity being used here to "perfect an imperfect gift," evading the requirement of delivery for a valid gift? There is a well-known exception to the equitable maxim that "equity will not perfect an imperfect gift," defined in *Strong v. Bird* (1874), LR 18 Eq. 315 (CA), where a donor expresses an intention to make a present gift during his or her lifetime, and then appoints the donee the executor by will. For another example, see *Re Stewart*, [1908] 2 Ch. 251 (Ch.D). How does the trust created in *Watt* differ from the principle in *Strong v. Bird*?

Note that the creation of a trust focuses on three certainties, including the certainty of intention to create a trust, but does not require physical delivery. By contrast, a valid gift requires both intention on the part of the donor as well as delivery. Is there a legal difference between the statements "I am giving you my car" and "I will hold my car (on trust) for you"? See Ziff, at 136-37. For a compelling critique of gifts and trusts, see M. Pickard, "The Goodness of Giving: The Justice of Gifts and Trusts" (1983), 33 *University of Toronto Law Journal* 381.

RESULTING AND CONSTRUCTIVE TRUSTS

In addition to express trusts, there are two other forms of trust relationships—the resulting trust and the constructive trust. Although both of these trusts are examined in more detail below, it is important to have a basic understanding of them in relation to gifts. A resulting trust arises when there is a transfer of property without an intention to create a gift—that is, there is delivery but no intention of gift. In a resulting trust, the recipient of the property holds it in trust for the transferor. A resulting trust may also arise when one person purchases property in the name of another without intending to make a gift. In a family context, there was a traditional presumption against a resulting trust when a husband or father transferred property to his wife or children; in this context, the legal presumption was that the husband/father intended to make a gift to family members, a situation known as the "presumption of advancement." The presumption of advancement operates in a family context to create a gift rather than a resulting trust because of "the absence of any reason for assuming that a [resulting] trust arose." See *Martin v. Martin* (1959), 110 CLR 297, at 303 and *Pettit v. Pettit*, [1970] AC 777 (HL). Modern family property statutes in Canada have sometimes repealed the presumption of resulting trust and the presumption of advancement—for example, see the Family Law Act, RSO 1990, c. F.3, s. 14; Marital Property Act, SNB 1980, c. M-1, s. 15; Matrimonial Property Act, SNS 1980, c. 9, s. 21; Matrimonial Property Act, SN 1979, c. 32, s. 29; and Family Law Reform Act, SPEI 1979, c. 6, s. 12.

In the 20th century, there have been different judicial responses to claims to treat transfers from wives and mothers as similarly subject to the presumption of advancement.

Some Canadian courts have concluded that women's participation in paid work means that the presumption should apply to gifts to their children—see *Radway v. Radway*, [1938] 2 DLR 578 (Ont. HC); *Rupar v. Rupar* (1964), 46 DLR (2d) 553 (BC SC); and *Re Dagle* (1990), 70 DLR (4th) 201 (PEI SC). However, other courts have taken somewhat different approaches—see *Edwards v. Bradley* (1957), 9 DLR (2d) 673 (SCC); *Lattimer v. Lattimer* (1978), 82 DLR (3d) 587 (Ont. HCJ); and *Mehta v. Canada Trust* (1993), 104 DLR (4th) 24 (Man. CA). For a further analysis and discussion of cases in other jurisdictions, see A. Dowling, "The Presumption of Advancement Between Mother and Child" (1996), 60 *The Conveyancer and Property Lawyer* 274.

By contrast with the emphasis on intention in the creation of a resulting trust, courts have recognized constructive trusts to ensure a just result in cases where a person without title to property has made a significant contribution to acquiring or maintaining it, thus preventing the "unjust enrichment" of the title holder. Canadian courts have frequently "constructed" such trust relationships in the context of cohabiting couples where the person without title has, usually over a period of time, made valuable contributions of money or labour to the property so that it would be unjust not to recognize an interest on the part of the non-title holder. In these cases, the court declares that the title holder is a constructive trustee and the person who made the contribution is a beneficiary of a defined interest that corresponds to the contribution he or she has made. The Supreme Court of Canada first enunciated these principles for cohabiting couples in *Pettkus v. Becker* (1980), 117 DLR (3d) 257 (SCC), a case examined in detail in chapter 7. The court held that Ms. Becker had not intended to make a gift of her money and labour over nearly 20 years to her cohabitee, Mr. Pettkus; and Mr. Pettkus denied that he had intended to hold the property for her benefit; thus the majority of judges concluded that there could not be a resulting trust.

Can you make an argument that the trust in *Cochrane* was a constructive trust, rather than an express trust? What about the trust in *Watt*?

Deed of Gift

There is no need for delivery if there is a deed of gift. As Ziff suggested:

> This is a sensible qualification since a deed will normally serve the probative and reflective functions performed by a transfer of possession, perhaps even more effectively than a mere delivery of the object. Documentary evidence can be less ambiguous than an act of delivery which, standing on its own, is as consistent with an intention to loan some item as to donate it.

(Ziff, at 138-39.) Do Ziff's arguments suggest that there is a need to reform the law of gifts to achieve greater certainty? Should it be necessary in all cases to have a deed of gift to ensure a valid transfer? What are the competing considerations that must be taken into account here? For further analysis, see T. Youdan, "The Formal Requirements of a Deed" (1979), 5 *Business Law Review* 71. It seems that the traditional requirement that a deed had to be delivered to be effective has been interpreted to mean that there must be evidence that the person executing the deed intended to be immediately and unconditionally bound by it. See *Re Sammon* (1979), 94 DLR (3d) 594 (Ont. CA).

Consider a situation where a donor executed a deed conveying a one-half interest in fee simple to the donee, and then a few years later, after a discussion of marriage between the donor and donee, the donor executed a second deed conveying the remaining one-half interest as well. The solicitor for the donee was expected to register it. Subsequently, the marriage plans fell through and the donor then sought to set aside the second deed of gift. How should the court determine whether there was a valid gift pursuant to the second deed? In *Schilthuis v. Arnold* (1991), OJ no. 2212 (Gen. Div.), the trial court concluded that there was a valid and irrevocable gift at the time when the donor executed the deed conveying the remainder of the property to the donee, and left it in the office of the donee's solicitor. On the facts, the donor was a successful entrepreneur and had made several gifts to the donee over the years, and the court concluded that the gift was wholly separate from the discussion of marriage plans. As the court stated (at 2), a gift "is not a kiss in the dark. Unlike the memory of a kiss which fades in time, the giving of a gift has lasting consequences." Do you agree with this analysis? Consider this problem in the context of the responsibilities of the donee's solicitor who drafted the deed of gift. If the donor did not intend his gift to be unconditional, how could this intention have been reflected in the document? On appeal, the Ontario Court of Appeal suggested that it would have been prudent for the donee's solicitor to have insisted that the donor execute the deed in his own solicitor's office. However, the court decided the appeal on the basis that the gift was conditional on marriage, and that there could be no gift if the condition remained unfulfilled. The Court of Appeal also noted that the half-interest was valued at about $100,000. See *Schilthuis v. Arnold* (1996), 95 OAC 196. Do you find the trial judgment or that of the appellate court more persuasive? Why? Is it relevant that the donor was 73 years old, while the donee was just 44? For further analysis of conditional gifts, see Oosterhof and Gillese, at 83ff. In some cases, note that it may also be necessary to consider registration requirements that affect the validity of a transfer—for example, see *Re Sammon* (1979), 94 DLR (3d) 594 (Ont. CA). The principles of registration are examined briefly at the end of this chapter.

In the United States, "the majority view today seems to recognize the validity of gifts by ordinary writings," whether or not the documents conform to technical requirements for a deed. For an overview of the historical developments and analysis of US cases, see Brown, at 106ff. According to *Jones v. Jones Estate* (1979), 5 Sask. R 27 (QB), a written document that does not qualify as a deed will not be sufficient to transfer personal property—that is, a chose in possession. Is the US or Canadian approach preferable in the light of policy goals for the law of gifts?

In re Cole
[1964] 1 Ch. 175 (CA)

[In this case, consider the issue of delivery of a gift in a family context. Are there different factors to be taken into account in the case of gifts to family members? How can delivery of gifts be proved when family members reside together?]

HARMAN LJ: This is an appeal from an order of Cross J made on March 22, 1963, on a motion by the trustee in the bankruptcy of Theodore Cole by which the court declared that certain articles of furniture specified in the schedule to the notice of motion were the property of the applicant who is the bankrupt's wife. The value of these articles is comparatively small but we are told that the decision will probably cover other articles of very much greater value in respect of which a like claim has been made. These particular articles have been sold by the applicant and the order affects the proceeds of sale.

We first hear of the bankrupt and his wife in 1937 when they were living in a modest rented house at Hendon which, as well as its furniture, were the bankrupt's property. In July, 1940, the bankrupt, being Australian by nationality, was apprehensive of internment as an enemy alien and he executed a deed of gift transferring the house to his wife and also gave her the furniture. The method of this latter gift is not known and is not in question. The family then moved to Clitheroe in Lancashire where they rented a house which was furnished largely from the Hendon house. The activities of the bankrupt during the war, apparently in the textile trade, resulted in his becoming before its end a very rich man indeed. In July, 1945, the war being over, he acquired a long lease of a large mansion at Hendon which he proceeded to furnish. A few articles were sent down from Clitheroe, three or four thousand pounds worth was bought from the vendor, and the rest to the tune of some £20,000 the bankrupt purchased himself and caused to be installed in the new house, to which he, together with two children and their nannie, removed in September, leaving the applicant and another child who was unwell at Clitheroe. In December, 1945, however, the wife came down to London with the other child and the bankrupt met her at the station and took her to the new home. He brought her into the house, took her into a room, put his hands over her eyes and then uncovered them saying "Look." He then accompanied her into other rooms on the ground floor where she handled certain of the articles—a silk carpet and an inlaid card table: next she went upstairs by herself and examined the rest of the house. When she came down again the husband said: "It's all yours." She now says that this was a gift to her of the furniture in the house, though apparently not of the house itself, and the judge accepted the evidence of the husband and wife that they had since believed that this was the position. We must accept the judge's finding in this respect, notwithstanding that the house and its contents and also £20,000 worth of furs and jewellery, said to have been other presents to the wife, remained insured in the bankrupt's name. Until the mid-'50s the bankrupt lived the life of a very rich man owning, among other things, a villa at Cannes and a fleet of cars, but the death of one of his associates, one Littman, was followed by a judgment against him by Littman's executors for a very large sum which remained unsatisfied; and in 1961 bankruptcy ensued and there is a very large deficiency. The trustee on behalf of the creditors resists the wife's claim to the furniture in the house, except the small items from Clitheroe, and that was the question tried on this motion: the judge acceded to the wife's claim: the trustee now appeals.

Mr. Megarry on behalf of the wife boldly put forward an entirely novel proposition to the effect that a perfect gift of chattels is constituted by showing them to the donee and speaking words of gift. It is enough, he says, that the donee should be brought to the chattels rather than the chattels to the donee and that she should be "near" the chattels (though what degree of proximity is needful remained vague) when the words of gift are spoken. This amounts to a change of possession, says Mr. Megarry, particularly if you are dealing with a collection of chattels, a fortiori if the chattels are or come under the physical control of the donee; and the case is strengthened if the donee handles some of the chattels in the donor's presence.

This remarkable submission is unsupported by authority and is in my judgment entirely heterodox. It is, I think, trite law that a gift of chattels is not complete unless accompanied by something which constitutes an act of delivery or a change of possession. The English law of the transfer of property, dominated as it has always been by the doctrine of consideration, has always been chary of the recognition of gifts. Witness the equitable doctrine of the resulting trust. In the early days when no clear distinction was made between what we now call real and personal property, transfer lay in livery and until a comparatively recent date the transfer of realty or chattels real lay in livery and not in grant. Indeed, until the Statute of Frauds no written instrument was required. I need not, I think, for the purposes of this judgment touch further on the question of the transfer of anything except chattels personal. Where consideration is given, possession of these is regulated by the Sale of Goods Act which, broadly speaking, causes possession to pass when the parties intend that it should; but in the absence of consideration, delivery is still necessary except in the cases of a gift by will or by deed, which latter itself imports both consideration and delivery. Attempts have been made to make use of the law of trusts to perfect gifts, particularly in the case of gifts mortis causa, but it has long been the doctrine of equity that it will not assist imperfect gifts by the introduction of the doctrine of trusts. In *Milroy v. Lord* Turner LJ thus stated the law:

> I take the law of this court to be well settled, that, in order to render a voluntary
> settlement valid and effectual, the settlor must have done everything which, according to
> the nature of the property comprised in the settlement, was necessary to be done in order
> to transfer the property and render the settlement binding upon him. He may of course
> do this by actually transferring the property to the persons for whom he intends to
> provide, and the provision will then be effectual, and it will be equally effectual if he
> transfers the property to a trustee for the purposes of the settlement, or declares that he
> himself holds it in trust for those purposes; and if the property be personal, the trust
> may, as I apprehend, be declared either in writing or by parol; but, in order to render the
> settlement binding, one or other of these modes must, as I understand the law of this
> court, be resorted to, for there is no equity in this court to perfect an imperfect gift. The
> cases I think go further to this extent, that if the settlement is intended to be effectuated
> by one of the modes to which I have referred, the court will not give effect to it by
> applying another of those modes. If it is intended to take effect by transfer, the court will
> not hold the intended transfer to operate as a declaration of trust, for then every
> imperfect instrument would be made effectual by being converted into a perfect trust.
> These are the principles by which, as I conceive, this case must be tried.

The leading case on delivery is *Irons v. Smallpiece*, an action of trover for two colts said to have been given to the plaintiff by his father under an oral gift. This was rejected by the court, Abbott CJ saying that:

> ... by the law of England, in order to transfer property by gift there must either be a
> deed or instrument of gift, or there must be an actual delivery of the thing to the donee.

Holroyd J said:

In order to change the property by a gift of this description, there must be a change of possession: here there has been no change of possession.

The delivery may be what has been called "constructive delivery," as in *Winter v. Winter*, which was a case about a barge which belonged to the plaintiff's father, a lighterman. It appeared that the plaintiff had been put into actual possession of the barge by his father and worked it as his father's agent or servant and was so doing when the father gave it him by word. It was held that this was sufficient, the delivery preceding the gift: and this it may do or it may accompany the gift or succeed it—see *Anderson v. Peel* and *In re Stoneham, Stoneham v. Stoneham*. In *Winter's* case Crompton J went so far as to cast doubt on *Irons v. Smallpiece* which had indeed been doubted in other cases about that time, but the leading case was fully re-established in the elaborate judgments in *Cochrane v. Moore*. This was a case about a quarter undivided share in a horse and the Court of Appeal held that the property did not pass by the gift because there had been no delivery. Fry LJ, in a judgment concurred in by Bowen LJ, reviewed the whole of the cases and came to this conclusion:

> This review of the authorities leads us to conclude that according to the old law no gift or grant of a chattel was effectual to pass it whether by parol or by deed, and whether with or without consideration unless accompanied by delivery: that on that law two exceptions have been grafted, one in the case of deeds, and the other in that of contracts of sale where the intention of the parties is that the property shall pass before delivery: but that as regards gifts by parol, the old law was in force when *Irons v. Smallpiece* was decided: that that case therefore correctly declared the existing law: and that it has not been overruled by the decision of Pollock B in 1883, or the subsequent case before Cave J.

Lord Esher concurred.

If the chattels be many or bulky there may be symbolical delivery, as, for instance, of a chair—*Lock v. Heath*, or the case about the gift of a church organ—*Rawlinson v. Mort*, where the donor put his hand upon it in the presence of the donee and accompanied his gesture with words of gift.

The question, therefore, for our decision is whether there has been anything here which amounts to an act of delivery or a change of possession either preceding or following or coincident with the words of gift so as to make it perfect. The judge dealt with this point very briefly. He assumed that there must be delivery and that words of gift alone are not enough, but he said he could not decide in the trustee's favour without deciding that a husband cannot give his wife the contents of the matrimonial home without executing a deed of gift. He said he did not see what more Mr. Cole could have done to put Mrs. Cole into the possession of the gift which he thought he was making. It seems to me that this was in fact a reliance on the word or words of gift which was the very thing which the judge said he could not do. Mr. Megarry, however, argued that when the question was of a gift to a wife of chattels in the matrimonial home, the introduction of the wife to the house was itself a putting of her into possession of its contents and that was a sufficient change of possession so that mere words of gift were enough. I reject this view. Mr. Megarry relied on two cases, *Ramsay v. Margrett* and *French v. Gething*. The former of these was a case under the Married Women's Property Act and decided that where the furniture is in the house where the husband and wife are living together, you cannot say in whose possession they are and, therefore, you must decide it by the title. In that case, however, the furniture had been bought by the wife from her husband and the property had passed to her for a good consideration. Similarly, in *French v. Gething* the furniture had been given to the wife by deed and that passed the possession to her and it was held that it was not in the apparent order and disposition of the husband. Those two cases, therefore, are no authority for Mr. Megarry's argument. *Bashall v. Bashall* shows that delivery is necessary to perfect a gift between spouses. This was an action by a wife for certain articles, notably a pony and trap, and Lord Esher MR said this:

> [I]t was clear law that in order to pass property in chattels by way of gift mere words were not sufficient, but there must be a delivery. And this requirement was as essential in a case of husband and wife as in a case of two strangers. But a difficulty arose when they came to consider how a husband was to deliver a chattel to his wife so as to pass the property in it. The difficulty arose, not from the legal relation between them, but from the fact of their living together. When a husband wished to make a present of jewellery to his wife, he generally gave it into her own hands, and then it was easy to see that there was a delivery. But in the case of a horse or a carriage, that would not be so. In such a case it was true the husband might wish to make an absolute gift to his wife, but, on the other hand, he might wish to keep the horse or carriage as his own property and merely to let his wife have the use of it. In an action by the wife it was necessary for her to show that the husband had done that which amounted to a delivery.

Similarly, in *Valier v. Wright and Bull Ltd.*, an action concerning a motor car said to be the subject-matter of a gift by a husband to a wife:

> **Held**, that after the gift no change had taken place in the custody of the car, and there had been no valid gift because there had been no actual or constructive delivery.

Mr. Megarry also relied on the old case of *Smith v. Smith*. This was a decision of Lord Hardwicke when Chief Justice and is merely an example of what amounted to a good delivery. There the donor had furniture and plate in the defendant's house where he lodged, which he was said to have given to the defendant's wife. I read this passage:

> And now in trover for the goods which were there at the intestate's death, it was ruled, that a parol gift, without some act of delivery, would not alter the property, and that such an act was necessary to establish a donatio causa mortis. Upon this opinion it came to the question, Whether there was any delivery? And to prove one, the defendant showed that the intestate, when he went out of town, used to leave the key of his rooms with the defendant: and that was insisted to be such a mixed possession that the law will adjudge the possession to be in him who has the right. And the Chief Justice ruled it so, and the jury found for the defendant.

This is merely a jury's view of what amounts to a sufficient delivery and is no authority here.

A stronger case is *In re Magnus, Ex parte Salaman*, where the husband settled furniture upon his wife by a marriage settlement and covenanted to add further furniture. He purchased a large amount of additional furniture which he installed in the house; he did not formally deliver it to the trustee of the settlement, but the trustee visited the house and saw the furniture there. It was held that this was a sufficient delivery to the trustee and that the wife was enjoying the furniture under the trusts of the settlement. This was enough to defeat the claim of the trustee in the husband's bankruptcy. It does not in my judgment cover the present case.

Perhaps the strongest case in the wife's favour is *Kilpin v. Ratley*. In that case furniture belonging to the husband and in the matrimonial home was purchased by his father-in-law who took an assignment of it by deed. Subsequently the father visited his daughter at the house and standing in one of the rooms orally gave her the furniture and then walked out of the house, leaving it behind him, and this was held to amount to a sufficient delivery to the wife. This furniture, until the time of the gift, was owned by the father and was in the possession of the son-in-law, but the father by pointing the furniture out to his daughter and then leaving the house put her and not her husband in possession of it and there was, therefore, a sufficient change of possession.

I cannot find that there was any change of possession here. It is argued that a wife living in her husband's house, and therefore having control to some extent of the furniture in it, is in possession of it, but this, I think, does not follow. In the ordinary case where a wife lives with her husband in a house owned and furnished by him, she has the use of the furniture by virtue of her position as wife, but that gives her no more possession of it than a servant has who uses the furniture. As to this, see Goddard LJ in *Youngs v. Youngs*. It is true that it may be doubtful who is in possession of the furniture and that you must look to the title, as in *Ramsay v. Margrett*, but in the absence of delivery there is no title in her, as was pointed out by Lord Evershed MR in *Hislop v. Hislop*.

I conclude, therefore, although I feel considerable sympathy with the wife who has believed this furniture to be hers, that it never became so because the gift was never perfected and that therefore she has no answer to the trustee's claim. I would allow the appeal.

PEARSON LJ: Although at one time there were conflicting opinions, it has been established that oral words of gift, or even written words of gift not embodied in a deed or will, are not sufficient to make an effective gift unless there has been or is delivery of possession to the donee. The basic idea is that there must be giving and taking, and if the donor retains possession he has not yet given and the donee has not yet taken: *Irons v. Smallpiece*; *Winter v. Winter* (conflicting opinions); *Cochrane v. Moore*; *Bashall v. Bashall*; and *Valier v. Wright and Bull Ltd.*

It is also established that the delivery of possession may be prior to or contemporaneous with or subsequent to the words of gift: *Cochrane v. Moore*; *In re Alderson, Alderson v. Peel*; and *In re Stoneham, Stoneham v. Stoneham*. In the case of prior delivery, it may not be necessary that the delivery should have been made by the donor: a pre-existing possession of the donee, however it arose, may be sufficient. In *Stoneham v. Stoneham* P.O. Lawrence J said:

> From a common-sense point of view it seems to me strange that articles already in the possession of an intended donee could not be effectually given by word of mouth without first removing them from the possession of the intended donee and then handing them back to him.

Later he said:

> The donor if he wanted to recover the chattels would have to bring an action against the donee whether he had delivered the chattels prior to the gift or the delivery had accompanied or followed the gift, and the donee in such an action could plead the gift as a defence whenever the chattels had been delivered to him and, in the case of a prior delivery, in whatever capacity he had originally received them.

Reference was made to Lord Esher's judgment in *Cochrane v. Moore.*

In the case of husband and wife living together or other persons having a common establishment, the possession, as it would otherwise be doubtful, is attached by law to the title: *Ramsay v. Margrett.* That was a case of goods bargained and sold, so that the ownership passed from husband to wife without delivery, and when she had become the owner she was considered in law to have the possession: *French v. Gething.* In that case the husband gave furniture in the home to the wife by deed, so that no delivery was required, and when she had become the owner she was considered in law to have the possession. *Youngs v. Youngs* refers to a common establishment.

As to what is necessary to constitute delivery from husband to wife, guidance is afforded by the judgment of Lord Esher in *Bashall v. Bashall.* The earlier part of that judgment has been read by Harman LJ, and so I need only read the concluding part of it:

> In an action by the wife it was necessary for her to show that the husband had done that which amounted to delivery. If the facts proved were equally consistent with the idea that he intended to deliver the thing to the wife so as to be her property, and with the idea that he intended to keep it as his own property, then the wife failed to make out her case. He thought there was no sufficient evidence of delivery here, and the appeal must therefore be allowed.

As I understand that passage, it is dealing with delivery, and the effect of it is that an act to constitute delivery must be one which in itself shows an intention of the donor to transfer the chattel to the donee. If the act in itself is equivocal—consistent equally with an intention of the husband to transfer the chattels to his wife or with an intention on his part to retain possession but give to her the use and enjoyment of the chattels as his wife—the act does not constitute delivery.

In the present case the intended gift was from husband to wife. Be it assumed that he spoke words of gift—words expressing an intention of transferring the chattels to her, and not merely an intention to give her the use and enjoyment of them as his wife—and that in the circumstances the chattels intended to be given were sufficiently identified by the words of gift. There was no pre-existing possession of the donee in this case. The husband was the owner of the chattels and therefore considered in law to be in possession of them. No act of delivery has been proved, because the acts relied upon are in themselves equivocal—consistent equally with an intention of the husband to transfer the chattels to his wife or with an intention on his part to retain possession but give to her the use and enjoyment of them as his wife.

Mr. Megarry's main proposition was that there is a perfect gift where the intending donor shows the chattel to the donee and utters words of present gift in the presence of the donee and the chattel. He also relied upon several special features of this case as adding strength to his main proposition. The special features mentioned were (a) that the husband brought the wife to the chattels; (b) that some of the chattels were bulky, so that handing over would not be a natural mode of transfer; (c) that the chattels were in a place where they would be under the wife's physical control, and she could touch and move them; and (d) the wife handled some of the chattels in the husband's presence.

The argument was clearly and cogently presented, but in the end the answer to it is simply that it fails to show any delivery of the chattels. Delivery was needed to perfect the gift of the chattels, of which the donee did not have pre-existing possession: *Hislop v. Hislop.*

In my judgment the applicant, Mrs. Cole, did not establish title to any of the chattels referred to in the motion, and accordingly the motion should have been wholly rejected, and therefore the appeal should be allowed.

PENNYCUICK J: I agree that this appeal should be allowed. It is established beyond question that in the absence of a written instrument a gift of chattels requires for its efficacy transfer of possession to the donee. Such transfer may be antecedent to or concurrent with or subsequent to the gift (*In re Stoneham,* per P.O. Lawrence J). Normally the transfer takes the form of physical delivery of the chattel, either actual or symbolical. But where the donee is already in possession of the chattel no further act of physical delivery is necessary. See, for example, *Winter v. Winter*; *Kilpin v. Ratley*; and *In re Stoneham.*

A special position arises in the case of a common establishment whether the relation of the parties is that of husband and wife or otherwise. In such a case possession of the chattels is in the party who has the title. (*French v. Gething, per* Scrutton LJ.) But the other party shares the physical enjoyment, i.e., sleeps in the bed, eats at the table, and the like. In such circumstances, apart from authority, it might have been argued with force that where the owner expresses himself as making a gift of the chattels to the other party, the words of gift operate without further physical delivery to transfer concurrently the possession which is requisite to title and the title which carries possession. Some support for this view is perhaps to be found in the old and very imperfectly reported case of *Smith v. Smith.* The learned author of Lush on Husband and Wife appears to treat *Smith v. Smith* as an authority to this effect.

It seems to me, however, that this contention is negatived by the decision of the Court of Appeal, in *Hislop v. Hislop*, a decision which was not, I understand, cited to the judge and apparently did not come to light until Mr. Arnold cited it in reply in this court. In that case a husband gave the lady who afterwards became his second wife a written document in respect of chattels in their joint establishment. The document was not registered as a bill of sale. His first wife subsequently sought to levy execution on the chattels and the county court judge held that they were still in the apparent possession of the husband. In the Court of Appeal Lord Evershed MR, with whom the two lords justices agreed, considered and rejected a contention on precisely the lines indicated above, describing it as a circular argument. The judgment is expressed by reference to apparent possession, but unequivocally indicates that the intended donee did not take such possession as is necessary in order to constitute a valid gift.

Mr. Megarry advanced the proposition that there is a perfect gift where the intending donor of a chattel shows it to the donee and utters words of present gift in the presence of the donee and of the chattel. This proposition appears to be entirely novel and is, I think, contrary to well-established principle.

Nor, in my opinion, is there any validity in the contention that the husband, by the mere act of bringing his wife for the first time into the house which was to constitute the matrimonial home, in some way gave her possession of the chattels. Again, I think it clear that the husband did not by standing by while his wife handled the carpet and the table make any constructive delivery to her of these articles or of the furniture generally.

Appeal allowed with costs in the Court of Appeal and below.

Leave to appeal to the House of Lords refused.

Discussion Notes

"Delivery" in the Context of Common Possession of the Donor and Donee

In *In re Cole*, the husband attempted to make a gift of the contents of the home to his wife, and they both then continued to reside together there. How can the test of delivery be met in such cases? Consider the problem in the context of another case where a father purchased a piano and had it delivered to his home. Subsequently, he gave the piano to his daughter who resided with him. Is this gift valid? The court in *Tellier v. Dujardin* (1906), 16 Man. LR 423 (CA) held that it was a valid gift, stating (at 425):

> Until the gift the legal possession was in the father, although the actual possession was common to both. By the gift he transferred the legal title to the plaintiff, and she being in actual possession, although then only as an agent, became the full legal owner. Being in actual possession and assenting to the gift as found by the trial judge, she became fully possessed in her own right.

Is this case consistent with the reasoning in *In re Cole*? Consider the following critique:

> [The rationale in *Tellier*] hardly satisfies, for it assumes the point in issue. If the court is to insist that delivery is essential to the transfer of title by gift, it is obvious that mere words of donation ... cannot be relied upon to produce a change in title, from which the legal possession of the donee can constructively be declared.

(Brown, at 104.) The author further suggested that it is undesirable to support gifts in circumstances where the chattel is in the possession of both the donor and donee because the "temptation to defraud creditors of the alleged donor by a simulated claim of gift would be great, and disputes between members of the family as to their respective rights to the household goods would be almost impossible of satisfactory determination." Does this comment help to explain the reasoning in *In re Cole*? In cases where there is a change in user after the alleged gift, even though it is in the household of the donor and donee, it has been held to be valid. See *Fletcher v. Fletcher*, 55 Vt. 325 (1883) and *Morgan v. Williams*, 200 SW 650 (Ky. CA 1918). For analysis of similar problems that may arise when a donor purports to make a gift of a chattel that is already, for other purposes, in the possession of the donee. See Brown, at 99-103.

In addition to the problem that the donor and donee lived in the same household, there was an additional element in *In re Cole* because the gift was one between members of the same family. In a BC case, *Langer v. McTavish Brothers Ltd.*, [1932] 4 DLR 90 (BC CA), a man brought his fiancee to a new home, showed her an array of furniture and declared, as the husband did in *In re Cole*, "It's all yours." The court held that there was a valid gift, taking into account the nature of the property and the circumstances of the parties. What is the difference, if any, between these two cases? Which approach accords with social reality? Could the court in *In re Cole* have found a declaration of trust in the absence of a valid gift, as occurred in *Cochrane v. Moore*? For further analysis, see Ziff, at 138; B. Hovius and T. Youdan, *The Law of Family Property* (Scarborough, ON: Carswell, 1991), at 23ff; and J.W.A. Thornley, "Transfer of Choses in Possession Between Members of a Common Household" (1953), 11:3 *Cambridge Law Journal* 355. See also *Re Waite and Waite*, [1953] 3 DLR 142 (BC SC), where a husband's declaration in the presence of witnesses of a wedding present (a car) to his wife did not result in a valid gift because there was no delivery.

Suppose that you live with your Uncle Robert who owns an important Steinway piano. After two years of sharing a house with him, he tells you that he no longer needs the piano and that you can have it. Both of you continue to play the piano; he plays Bach and you play mostly Sondheim. A year after the alleged gift to you, you decide to move to your own apartment and thus make arrangements for the piano to be moved there. At this point, Uncle Robert furiously declares that Sondheim is a fraud and refuses to allow you to take the piano. When you explain that he made a valid gift of the piano, Uncle Robert laughingly says that you were "no more in possession of the piano for the last year than the person who comes once a week to clean the house and who regularly dusts the piano." Was there a valid gift? Would it make a difference if, instead of the facts above, Uncle Robert agreed when you decided to move out that he would lend you the piano; then, a year later, after you have had the piano in your apartment, he says that you can have it. If he subsequently asks for the return of the piano, can you argue that there was a valid gift? What are the relevant differences in these fact situations? Define precisely what issue of delivery is raised in each of them.

Constructive (and Symbolic) Delivery

A valid gift does not require contemporaneous delivery of possession. An expression of intention that is preceded or followed by delivery may suffice. As well, courts have permitted constructive delivery where the chattel is too large or difficult to transfer easily—for example, a car. In such cases, delivery of the "means of control"—for example, the keys to the car—may be sufficient, although the factual context will be examined carefully to ensure that the donor has done everything possible to part with possession. If a donor gives his daughter a set of keys to a new car, saying, "This is for you," but retains a duplicate set of keys, is there a valid gift to the daughter? Recall the joint ownership of the boat in *Watt v. Watt Estate*, above. In a case where a donor placed a gift in his safety deposit box, and gave a duplicate key to the donee, the court concluded that there was no change in the donor's control over the subject matter of the alleged gift. See *Bauernschmidt v. Bauernschmidt*, 54 A 637 (Md. CA 1903). By contrast, when a donor handed over the only set of keys to a safety deposit box to a donee, while stating that the donee could have whatever was in the box, the court held that the donee was entitled to the securities valued at over $185,000 contained in the box. See *Thomas' Adm'r. v. Lewis*, 15 SE 389 (Va. CA 1892). The use of constructive delivery seems to be restricted to the transfer of possession of goods that would be difficult or inconvenient to transfer *per se*. However, this area of the law of gifts remains controversial; as Brown suggested, at 92, there is no part of the law of gifts with "greater uncertainty and confusion than … the matter of constructive delivery." For further analysis, see A.C.H. Barlow, "Gift *Inter Vivos* of a Chose in Possession by Delivery of a Key" (1956), 19 *Modern Law Review* 394 (hereafter Barlow).

By contrast with constructive delivery (delivery of the means of control), some cases have considered the idea of symbolic delivery. For example, if the donor delivers a photo of a new car, using words of gift, it may be argued that there has been symbolic delivery. According to Ziff, at 140, however, "[T]here is little authority on which to base the view that symbolic delivery is adequate to complete a gift." Similarly, Brown concluded, at 92, that "[the] surrender of power and dominion is, as has been seen, the heart of the delivery concept, and without it a mere symbolic delivery is customarily declared to be insufficient." If your Uncle Robert placed his hands on his piano and said to you, "This is now yours," and you enthusiastically thanked him for the wonderful gift, would there be a valid gift? How can a donor give "power and dominion" over a piano? Why was the husband's effort to transfer a gift to his wife in *In re Cole* ineffective because of a failure of delivery? Was he trying to make a constructive or symbolic delivery?

Delivery of a Chose in Action

As you will recall from chapter 1, personal property includes both *choses in possession* and *choses in action*. Arguably, the one-quarter interest in the horse in *Cochrane v. Moore* was in the nature of an intangible interest or *chose in action*—that is, the gift was *not* a gift of one quarter of a horse. Gifts of *choses in action* may require compliance with special rules (including statutory provisions) regarding the transfer of these interests. These principles are usually examined in more advanced courses, such as Commercial Law. The history of the right to assign a *chose in action* reveals, once again, the intervention of equity in the context of common law concerns about such assignments. For overviews of the history, see J.B. Ames, "The Disseisin of Chattels" (1889), 3 *Harvard Law Review* 23 and S. Williston, "Is the Right of an Assignee of a Chose in Action Legal or Equitable?" (1916), 30 *Harvard Law Review* 97. More generally, see O.S. Rundell, "Gifts of *Choses* in Action" (1918), 27 *Yale Law Journal* 643 and L.A. Sheridan, "Informal Gifts of Choses in Action" (1955), 33 *Canadian Bar Review* 284. For examples of judicial decisions, see *Midland Bank Executor and Trustee Co. Ltd. v. Rose*, [1949] 1 Ch. 78 (Ch.D) (shares in a private company); *Sanderson v. Halstead* (1968), 67 DLR (2d) 567 (Ont. HC) (proceeds of an insurance policy); and *Nesbitt v. Chester* (1969), 1 DLR (3d) 655 (Ont. HC) (securities).

Intention

A second requirement for a valid gift is the intention to make a donative transfer. The issue of intention was considered in the reasoning of *Cochrane v. Moore* and in *In re Cole*, examined above in relation to the issue of delivery. However, the issue of intention may also present difficulties. In reading the case that follows, note carefully which factors the court relied on to determine the donor's intent.

Thomas v. Times Book Co. Ltd.
[1966] 1 WLR 911 (Ch.D)

PLOWMAN J: This is an action by Mrs. Caitlin Thomas, who is the widow of the late Dylan Thomas and the sole administratrix of his estate, to recover from the defendants, the Times Book Company Ltd., the manuscript of Dylan Thomas's best-known work, "Under Milk Wood." The defendants claim that Dylan Thomas made a gift of this manuscript to Douglas Cleverdon, a British Broadcasting Corporation producer, and they claim title through him. It is also pleaded by way of defence that even if the plaintiff ever had a claim to the return of the manuscript it is a stale claim and barred by the Limitation Act, 1939.

The primary question with which I am concerned is, therefore, whether Dylan Thomas made a gift of this manuscript to Cleverdon. The manuscript in question consists of two parts. The first part, which is the earlier part of the play, is a fair copy in Dylan Thomas's own handwriting of some earlier draft, or drafts, or sketches. The latter part is a typescript, not made by Dylan Thomas, but made by a copyist of the later part of the play, and it contains emendations made by Dylan Thomas himself.

"Under Milk Wood" is a work which was commissioned by the BBC in, I think, 1943 or 1944. In 1946, when Cleverdon first enters this story, very little had been done by Dylan Thomas. About this time, that is to say, 1946, Cleverdon, who was on the staff of the BBC, inherited the "Under Milk Wood" project from another producer, one Burton, and Cleverdon, as he says, badgered and cajoled Dylan Thomas to get on with "Under Milk Wood."

The work proceeded slowly. There was a time, apparently, when Dylan Thomas got stuck with it, and there was an interval before it was restarted. But eventually, on Thursday, October 15, 1953, Dylan Thomas delivered the manuscript to Cleverdon at his office in the BBC. In that office there was also present Cleverdon's secretary, Miss Fox. Dylan Thomas was due to fly to America on the following Monday, October 19, and he was going there to try to raise some money by giving readings of "Under Milk Wood." He told Cleverdon that he wanted his manuscript back by Monday to take to the United States with him. Cleverdon told his secretary, Miss Fox, to cut a stencil of the manuscript as quickly as possible. She did so, and she gave Dylan Thomas his manuscript back on the morning of Saturday, October 17, and he lost it. He was perturbed about this loss; he had not any other copy of it, he was due to fly to America on the following Monday and he needed the manuscript for that trip.

Some time over the weekend Dylan Thomas telephoned Cleverdon at the latter's home and told him that he had lost the manuscript. Cleverdon told him not to worry about it because the BBC had had this script stencilled, and he, Cleverdon, would take three copies of it to the London air terminal at Victoria Station on Monday and hand them over before Dylan Thomas left for America. On the Monday Cleverdon told his secretary what had happened; he asked her to get three copies rushed off, and that was done. Cleverdon, in the early evening, took a taxi to the London air terminal and there he found Dylan Thomas in company with his wife and a Mr. and Mrs. Locke. Cleverdon handed over to him the three copies of the BBC script. I now quote the actual words of Cleverdon's evidence, which I read from a press cutting which is substantially the same, and is the same in all material respects as my own note. Cleverdon said that the poet was extremely grateful, and then I quote:

> The only words I can recall him actually saying were that I had saved his life. I said it seemed an awful pity that the original had been lost, and that it meant an awful lot to me. I had been working on it very closely over six or seven years, and it was the culmination of one of the most interesting things I had produced. He said if I could find it I could keep it. He told me the names of half a dozen pubs, and said if he had not left it there he might have left it in a taxi.

Either later that day or the next day—probably, I think, the next day—Cleverdon told his secretary, Miss Fox, what had happened. He told her that Dylan Thomas had given him the manuscript, which was still missing, and he told her that he was going to look for it. Within a day or two he found it, and he found it in one of the public-houses in Soho, the name of which he had been given by Dylan Thomas. He took possession of it and he retained it until 1961, when he sold it to one Cox, through whom it came to the defendants.

Two or three days after finding it, a friend of Cleverdon's, one Cranston, a reader in political science at the London School of Economics, and literary adviser to Messrs. Methuen's, the publishers, was having lunch with Cleverdon at his house. On this occasion Cleverdon told him the story of the loss of the manuscript; he told him how he had delivered copies of it to Dylan Thomas at the air terminal, that Dylan Thomas had said that if he could find the original which had been lost he could keep it, and he told him how he had found it.

To go back a little way, as I have already said, on Monday, October 19, Dylan Thomas flew to the United States. About three weeks later, namely, on November 9, 1953, he died in that country. On December 7, 1953, letters of administration were granted to the plaintiff in this action. On December 28, 1953, the plaintiff made a settlement of the copyrights in Dylan Thomas's works. There were three trustees of that settlement: namely, David Higham, who had been Dylan Thomas's literary agent; Dr. Daniel Jenkyn Jones, who was an old friend of Dylan Thomas's going back to school days, who wrote the music for "Under Milk Wood" and who edited the first published edition for Messrs. J.M. Dent & Sons Ltd., the publishers, and Stuart Thomas, a solicitor. The manuscript of "Under Milk Wood," as a chattel was not included in that settlement and, therefore, if there was no gift of it, and if the Limitation Act, 1939, is not a defence to this action, the plaintiff, as administratrix of the estate, is entitled to recover this manuscript.

The plaintiff submits that there was no gift of this manuscript to Cleverdon, but let me make it quite plain from the start that the onus is not on the plaintiff to disprove that it was a gift; the onus is on the defendants, and is accepted by their counsel as being on them, to prove affirmatively that a gift was made. But Mr. Sparrow, on behalf of the plaintiff, submits that there was no gift. He further submits, and I accept this submission, that in order to establish a gift the defendants have to prove two things, first of all, the relevant animus donandi, or the intention of making a gift, and secondly, a delivery of the subject-matter of the gift, this manuscript, to the donee. Mr. Sparrow submits that the gift claimed in this action fails on both scores: first, for the reason that there was no intention to give and, secondly, for the reason that there was no sufficient delivery of the subject-matter of the gift.

Let me first of all say something about the question whether the defendants have succeeded in establishing the necessary intention. It is said, first of all, and accepted by both sides, that in considering whether the defendants have discharged the onus of proof which is on them, I must approach the claim made by the defendants that there was a gift with suspicion. Reference was made in this connection to the decision of the Court of Appeal in *In re Garnett*, where Brett MR said this:

> Another point was taken. It was said that this release cannot be questioned because the person to whom it was given is dead, and also that it cannot be questioned unless those who object and state certain facts are corroborated, and it is said that that was a doctrine of the Court of Chancery. I do not assent to this argument; there is no such law. Are we to be told that a person whom everybody on earth would believe, who is produced as a witness before the judge, who gives his evidence in such a way that anybody would be perfectly senseless who did not believe him, whose evidence the judge, in fact, believes to be absolutely true, is, according to a doctrine of the court of equity, not to be believed by the judge because he is not corroborated? The proposition seems unreasonable the moment it is stated. There is no such law. The law is that when an attempt is made to charge a dead person in a matter, in which if he were alive he might have answered the charge, the evidence ought to be looked at with great care; the evidence ought to be thoroughly sifted, and the mind of any judge who hears it ought to be, first of all, in a state of suspicion; but if in the end the truthfulness of the witnesses is made perfectly clear and apparent, and the tribunal which has to act on their evidence believes them, the suggested doctrine becomes absurd. And what is ridiculous and absurd never is, to my mind, to be adopted either in law or in equity.

Therefore, not only in this case is the onus of proof on the defendants, but I am enjoined by authority to approach their story with suspicion having regard to the fact that the other actor in this story, the late Dylan Thomas, is dead and cannot therefore give his own version of what took place.

Then Mr. Sparrow submits that the story which is put forward on behalf of the defendants is so improbable as not to be credible. For example, it is said that the late Dylan Thomas was always hard up—and on the evidence it appears quite clearly that he was. It is said that he was setting off on this trip to the United States in order to try to raise some money, and that, no doubt, is equally true. It is said that this was the major work of a great poet; that he must have known that the manuscript was of considerable value; that he had had previous experience of using his manuscripts as a form, as it were, of currency; that he had sold manuscripts of poems previously for an odd pound or two; that the manuscript was a thing over which he had lavished great care and devotion over a number of years, and that in those circumstances it is really inconceivable that he should have made this present of it to Cleverdon.

In addition, it is said that when Dylan Thomas got to America he spent a good deal of time with a close friend of his, one Ruthven Todd—and Ruthven Todd has given evidence before me. His evidence was that Dylan Thomas used to come and see him at his house in Greenwich Village and that he remembers that Dylan Thomas told him on his arrival in the United States about the loss of the manuscript, and how upset he was; that he had said, "I have done it now"; that the manuscript contained material he wanted to refer to; that he hoped the manuscript was going to turn up, and that he would hear about it; that he had said that "Douglas"–that is to say, Cleverdon—had given him the scripts he had; that "Douglas" was looking for the other manuscript and that that was all that he said about it.

It is submitted by Mr. Sparrow that there, in effect, is Dylan Thomas giving evidence in this court, and that on that evidence, as it were, given by Dylan Thomas, I am bound to deduce that he had not made a gift of the manuscript to Cleverdon, because if he had done so he could not have said what he did to Ruthven Todd. Against that, of course, I have to remember this: while I have no doubt that Ruthven Todd was telling what he remembered to the best of his ability, what he was deposing to were conversations which took place over twelve years ago. It is hard enough to remember a conversation one had a week ago, let alone twelve years ago; and while those matters are no doubt matters which have remained in Ruthven Todd's recollection, the fact that these conversations were so long ago is a matter which I am bound to take into account in evaluating the evidence which he gave.

There is no contemporaneous record of the conversations that Dylan Thomas had with Ruthven Todd in the way in which there is an almost contemporaneous record by Cleverdon of the conversation which he had with Dylan Thomas, and on which the defendants base their claim that there was a gift.

I agree with Mr. Sparrow that it is right to weigh probabilities in assessing the weight of the affirmative evidence which is given. But I am bound to say that I think Mr. Balcombe was perfectly justified in saying that a great many of these matters which are now being put forward as establishing the inherent improbability of a gift are pure matters of hindsight.

At the time the alleged gift was made, that is to say, in October, 1953, Dylan Thomas was a comparatively young man; he was 39 years old, and he was still alive. "Under Milk Wood" had not then been performed in England. It had its first performance on the BBC in January, 1954. It had not been published in England. It is quite true, as Mr. Sparrow said, that Dylan Thomas was recognised as a considerable poet, but he was recognised as such by a comparatively small number of people. It was only after the BBC performance of "Under Milk Wood" that Dylan Thomas's name became known to the public at large. Although I do not think the question of the value of the manuscript has really very much to do with this case, it was only after the death of Dylan Thomas that this manuscript, with which I am concerned, became really valuable.

Another thing that I have to bear in mind in weighing the probabilities of the matter is this. When he made the alleged gift, he had not got the manuscript—it had been lost. Nobody knew whether it would ever turn up again. The character of Dylan Thomas, so far as it is delineated by the evidence that I have heard in this court, shows that he was generous, impulsive and capable of spontaneous gestures. It seems to me quite in keeping with that character—in so far as that has emerged in the course of this hearing—that he should have made the gesture of telling Cleverdon that if he found this manuscript he could keep it.

Let me just say a word about the word "keep," because a good many semantic points have been made about the actual words used, whether they were "keep it," or "have it," or "welcome to keep it," or "keep it for yourself." I shall not attempt to draw any distinction between them. They all seem to me to come to exactly the same thing, if Cleverdon is to be believed, because he was quite clear, and always has been quite clear, that the words used were not words by which Dylan Thomas was enjoining him to do something, but were words of gift.

There is another matter which seems to me to be relevant. Obviously, Dylan Thomas was very relieved to have these BBC manuscripts. He had even hinted that having lost his own manuscript there might not be any point in his going to America and now it was all right. He was clearly relieved. Cleverdon was not a stranger to him who had suddenly come on the scene. They had been working together for the past six or seven years, and for myself I see no inherent improbability at all in the story which the defendants put forward in this case through the mouth of Cleverdon.

Any question of probability or improbability fades into the background and disappears once I find myself forced to the conclusion that Cleverdon was telling the truth and that I ought to accept his evidence. Having seen him and listened carefully, and having approached this matter in, I hope, a proper state of suspicion, I find myself, in the end, forced to the conclusion that Cleverdon was speaking the truth, and I accept his evidence.

One of the reasons which certainly assists me very much in coming to that conclusion is this. I cannot believe that Cleverdon would have told Miss Fox and Cranston that Dylan Thomas had given him the manuscript if it were not true, because Dylan Thomas, at the time when he told both those persons, was still alive, and everybody was expecting him to come back from America within a short time. It would have been absolutely stupid to have invented a lie in those circumstances, and Cleverdon certainly is not a stupid person.

I think perhaps I ought to say a word about the evidence of Dr. Jones. As I have already said, it was he who edited the first published text of "Under Milk Wood" in this country. As an editor, he would naturally be interested in any manuscript material which was available. As I understand it, the object of introducing his evidence into this case was to support the suggestion that from the death of Dylan Thomas until the year 1961, when the manuscript was sold, Cleverdon was concealing the existence of this manuscript from Dr. Jones. That does not seem to me to make sense. As early as January, 1954, Cleverdon was writing to one of Dr. Jones' co-trustees of the Dylan Thomas copyrights, telling him the story of the gift of the manuscript to him, just as it was told to me. And, incidentally, Higham, who was the trustee in question, had no hesitation in accepting that story. From that time on Cleverdon told the story of the recovery of the manuscript both in broadcasts and in press interviews, and I have been shown the reports of three press interviews in the year 1956 in which Cleverdon was telling the story of the gift, and how Dylan Thomas told him that if he could find the manuscript he could keep it, and how he found it. I am unable to find any foundation for the suggestion that Cleverdon was concealing this manuscript from anyone.

So much for the question of intention. It is then said on behalf of the plaintiff that even if Dylan Thomas intended to give this manuscript to Cleverdon, he did not succeed in giving effect to that intention because there was no delivery of the subject-matter of it to Cleverdon by Dylan Thomas. I feel bound to reject that argument. The fact is that Cleverdon got possession of this manuscript from the Soho public-house in which it had been left by Dylan Thomas and that he got that possession with the consent of Dylan Thomas. That, in my judgment, is sufficient delivery to perfect a gift in Cleverdon's favour. I can see nothing in *In re Cole, A Bankrupt* which was relied upon by Mr. Sparrow, which precludes me from taking what appears to me to be the common-sense view of the matter, and concluding that when Cleverdon got possession of the manuscript with the consent of Dylan Thomas, the gift was perfected.

In those circumstances, my conclusion is that the defendants have succeeded in establishing that Dylan Thomas made a gift of this manuscript to Cleverdon, and in those circumstances the plaintiff's action must fail.

Action dismissed with costs.

Discussion Notes

Evidence, Presumptions, and Onus

A determination of the donor's intention to make an *inter vivos* gift in *Thomas* was rendered especially difficult because the donor was not available to give evidence. Examine carefully the court's analysis of the question of onus in establishing a valid gift. Why was the onus in this case on the defendant rather than the plaintiff? On what does the court rely in terms of evidence and presumptions to reach the conclusion that a valid gift was made in this case? Is the court defining Thomas's actual intention, or deciding what intent it is reasonable to conclude was present at the time of the gift? According to Brown, the issue of intention requires a court to consider "the circumstances of the donor, the relationship between the parties, and the size of the gift and its relation to the total amount of the donor's property, in order to discover the reasonableness of the claim that the donor really intended to make the donation claimed." See Brown, at 114. To what extent is the court's general knowledge of Dylan Thomas as a public figure a factor in the court's assessment of Cleverdon's claim that there was a valid gift? See comments on *Thomas* at (1967), 53 *Iowa Law Review* 243 and (1966), 82 *Law Quarterly Review* 304. For other cases involving judicial assessment of intention in relation to gifts between family members, see *Surette v. Surette* (1980), 40 NSR (2d) 482 (SCTD) and *Kooner v. Kooner* (1979), 100 DLR (3d) 76 (BC SC).

The general problem of claims involving a deceased person is addressed in some jurisdictions by statutory provisions concerning the need for corroborating evidence. For example, s. 13 of the Evidence Act, RSO 1990, c. E.23 provides:

> In an action by or against the heirs, next of kin, executors, administrators or assigns of a deceased person, an opposite or interested party shall not obtain a verdict, judgment or decision on his or her own evidence in respect of any matter occurring before the death of the deceased person, unless such evidence is corroborated by some other material evidence.

What is the purpose of this section? Would the outcome in *Thomas* be the same, taking into account this statutory provision? In *Brown v. Rotenburg*, [1946] 4 DLR 139 (Ont. CA), the court held (at 148) that it is sufficient to meet the test of s. 13 if "the evidence relied upon as corroborative is evidence of some material fact or facts support-ing the testimony to be corroborated." See also *Sands Estate v. Sonnwald* (1986), 22 ETR 282 (Ont. HCJ) and similar statutory provisions in the evidence acts of other jurisdictions—RSNS 1989, c. 154, s. 45; RSPEI 1988, c. E.11, s. 11; and RSN 1990, c. E-16, s. 16.

Capacity (Fraud, Undue Influence, and Duress): Csada v. Csada

The requirement of intention for a valid gift means that the donor must have the capacity to form the intention to make a gift to the donee. In *Csada v. Csada*, [1985] 2 WWR 265 (Sask. CA), the plaintiff brought an application to set aside two gifts to his brother, including a transfer of two quarter sections of land (valued at $150,000 to $200,000) and a cheque for $10,300. The plaintiff, who was 58 years old at the time, had requested that his older brother, aged 66, return to Canada from New Zealand (where he had made his home for some years), so that the two brothers could live together. Both were twice married but now divorced. The plaintiff paid for his brother's airfare, and then the expenses for both of them to move from the plaintiff's apartment to a house he had purchased for them. During a nine-month period, the plaintiff transferred large sums of money and land to the defendant and executed a power of attorney in his favour, in addition to the two gifts of land and money noted above. When the plaintiff applied to set aside these two transactions, the trial judge considered evidence from several medi-cal experts regarding the plaintiff's depression and their views that he was dominated by his brother. The court held that the plaintiff had the requisite intention to make these gifts to the defendant, that he had sufficient capacity, and that there was no undue influence. Thus the gifts were valid. The plaintiff appealed, arguing that the gifts should be set aside on the basis of undue influence.

After reviewing the evidence and the decision of the trial judge, the appellate court considered the applicable legal principles, quoting (at 273) from the judgment of Lindley LJ in the English Court of Appeal decision in *Allcard v. Skinner* (1887), 36 Ch.D 145 (Ch.D):

> What then is the principle? Is it that it is right and expedient to save persons from the consequences of their own folly? Or is it that it is right and expedient to save them from being victimized by other people? In my opinion the doctrine of undue influence is founded upon the second of these two principles. Courts of Equity have never set aside gifts on the ground of the folly, imprudence, or want of foresight on the part of donors. The Courts have always repudiated any such jurisdiction. *Huguenin v. Baseley* is itself a clear authority to this effect. It would obviously be to encourage folly, recklnessness, extravagance and vice if persons could get back property which they foolishly made away with, whether by giving it to charitable institutions or by bestowing it on less worthy objects. On the other hand, to protect people from being forced, tricked or misled in any way by others into parting with their property is one of the most legitimate objects of all laws; and the equitable

doctrine of undue influence has grown out of and been developed by the necessity of grappling with insidious forms of spiritual tyranny and with the infinite varieties of fraud.

As no Court has ever attempted to define fraud so no Court has ever attempted to define undue influence, which includes one of its many varieties. The undue influence which Courts of Equity endeavour to defeat is the undue influence of one person over another; not the influence of enthusiasm on the enthusiast who is carried away by it, unless indeed such enthusiasm is itself the result of external undue influence. But the influence of one mind over another is very subtle, and of all influences religious influence is the most dangerous and the most powerful, and to counteract it Courts of Equity have gone very far. They have not shrunk from setting aside gifts made to persons in a position to exercise undue influence over the donors, although there has been no proof of the actual exercise of such influence; and the Courts have done this on the avowed ground of the necessity of going this length in order to protect persons from the exercise of such influence under circumstances which render proof of it impossible. The Courts have required proof of its non-exercise, and, failing that proof, have set aside gifts otherwise unimpeachable.

Cotton LJ in the same case at p. 171 categorized the cases that fall under this doctrine, thus:

These decisions [by the Court of Chancery in setting aside voluntary gifts on the ground of undue influence] may be divided into two classes—first, where the Court has been satisfied that the gift was the result of influence expressly used by the donee for the purpose; second, where the relations between the donor and donee have at or shortly before the execution of the gift been such as to raise a presumption that the donee had influence over the donor. In such a case the Court sets aside the voluntary gift, unless it is proved that in fact the gift was the spontaneous act of the donor acting under circumstances which enabled him to exercise an independent will and which justifies the Court in holding that the gift was the result of a free exercise of the donor's will. The first class of cases may be considered as depending on the principle that no one shall be allowed to retain any benefit arising from his own fraud or wrongful act. In the second class of cases the Court interferes, not on the ground that any wrongful act has in fact been committed by the donee, but on the ground of public policy, and to prevent the relations which existed between the parties and the influence arising therefrom being abused.

These same principles have been variously expressed by Canadian courts. Mulock CJ of the Ontario Divisional Court in *Finn v. St. Vincent de Paul Hosp., Brockville* (1910), 22 OLR 381 at 392-93 (CA), discussed some of the authorities in these terms:

... in *Hoghton v. Hoghton*, 15 Beav. 278, it is stated (pp. 298, 299) "that wherever one person obtains, by voluntary donation, a large pecuniary benefit from another, the burthen of proving that the transaction is righteous, to use the expression of Lord Eldon, in *Gibson v. Jeyes* (1801), 6 Ves. 266, falls on the person taking the benefit. But this proof is given, if it be shewn that the donor knew and understood what it was that he was doing. If, however, besides obtaining the benefit of this voluntary gift from the donor, the donor and donee were so situated towards each other, that undue influence might have been exercised by the donee over the donor, then a new consideration is added, and the question is not, to use the words of Lord Eldon, in *Hugeurenin v. Baseley*, 14 Ves. 273, 300, 'whether the donor knew what he was doing, but how the intention was produced'; and though the donor was well aware of what he did, yet if his disposition to do it was produced by undue influence, the transaction would be set aside. In many cases, the Court, from the relations existing between the parties to the transaction, infers the probability of such undue influence having been exerted. These are cases of guardian and ward, of solicitor and client, spiritual instructor and pupil, medical adviser and patient, and the like; and, in such cases, the Court watches the whole transaction with great jealousy, not merely for the purpose of ascertaining that the person likely to be so influenced fully understood the act he was performing, but also for the purpose of ascertaining that his consent to perform that act was not obtained by reason of the influence possessed by the person receiving the benefit."

In *Wannamaker v. Livingston* (1917), 43 OLR 243, Ferguson JA, on behalf of the Appellate Division of the Supreme Court of Ontario, said (at pp. 258-59):

... these transactions fall within the rule that if such a transaction takes place when the grantee or donee is in a position of confidence or in a position to exercise influence over the grantor, it is not necessary to the setting aside of such a gift, on the ground of undue influence, that there should be proof of the exercise of undue influence. Undue influence is presumed, and it rests upon the grantee or donee to rebut that presumption by proving that the transaction was righteous and was fairly conducted as between strangers; that the grantor was not unduly impressed by the influence of the grantee; and by satisfying the Court that the grantor, knowing and appreciating the effect of the transaction, acted voluntarily and deliberately, free from the influence of the grantee: Halsbury's Laws of England, vol. 15, p. 420; *Delong v. Mumford*, 25 Gr. 586; *Vanzant v. Coates* (1917), 39 OLR 556, 37 DLR 471, 40 OLR 556, 39 DLR 485.

The defendants have not only failed to rebut the presumption and to satisfy the other requirements of the rule, but the learned trial Judge has, after seeing witnesses and weighing their evidence, and passing upon their credibility, come to the conclusion that undue influence was in fact exercised, and that these gifts were all the result of the exercise of such influence. Keeping in mind that in an action to set aside a gift *inter vivos*, where confidence and dependence are shewn on one side and advice and persuasion on the other, such advice and persuasion, although not wrongful or improper, may in such a transaction amount to undue influence—I have, on that branch of the case, no doubt as to the correctness of the judgment appealed from.

The Supreme Court of Canada in *Krys v. Krys*, [1929] SCR 153, [1929] 1 DLR 289, speaking through Newcombe J, approved (at p. 162) the following excerpt from the judgment of Lord Chelmsford LC in *Tate v. Williamson* (1866), LR 2 Ch. App. 55 at 61:

Wherever two persons stand in such a relation that, while it continues, confidence is necessarily reposed by one, and the influence which naturally grows out of that confidence is possessed by the other, and this confidence is abused, or the influence is exerted to obtain an advantage at the expense of the confiding party, the party so availing himself of his position will not be permitted to retain the advantage, although the transaction could not have been impeached if no such confidential relation had existed.

The manner in which the presumption referred to in the second of the two classes delineated by Cotton LJ in *Allcard v. Skinner* may be rebutted is dealt with in the Privy Council case of *Inche Noriah v. Shaik Allie Bin Omar*, [1929] AC 127, 45 TLR 1, as follows (p. 3):

> ... their Lordships are not prepared to accept the view that independent legal advice is the only way in which the presumption can be rebutted; nor are they prepared to affirm that independent legal advice, when given, does not rebut the presumption, unless it be shown that the advice was taken. It is necessary for the donee to prove that the gift was the result of the free exercise of independent will. The most obvious way to prove this is by establishing that the gift was made after the nature and effect of the transaction had been fully explained to the donor by some independent and qualified person so completely as to satisfy the Court that the donor was acting independently of any influence from the donee and with the full appreciation of what he was doing; and in cases where there are no other circumstances this may be the only means by which the donee can rebut the presumption. But the fact to be established is that stated in the judgment already cited of Lord Justice Cotton, and if evidence is given of circumstances sufficient to establish this fact, their Lordships see no reason for disregarding them merely because they do not include independent advice from a lawyer. Nor are their Lordships prepared to lay down what advice must be received in order to satisfy the rule in cases where independent legal advice is relied upon, further than to say that it must be given with a knowledge of all relevant circumstances and must be such as a competent and honest advisor would give if acting solely in the interests of the donor.

The Supreme Court of Canada in *Krys* followed the *Inche* decision.

There is no express reference in the reasons for judgment of the trial judge in the present case to the principles of the equitable doctrine of undue influence as elucidated in the foregoing authorities, and specially, to the two-fold classification of cases by Cotton LJ, to the presumptions governing each class of case and to the relevant onus provisions. Nor is it implicit in the reasons for judgment that the judge directed himself in the manner prescribed by these authorities.

He resolved the issue of undue influence in these words:

> I am satisfied notwithstanding certain medical and other evidence called by the plaintiff (and which I will comment on later) that the plaintiff knew he was transferring the N½ 2-12-7-W3d to the defendant on 9th April 1980, that he intended to make a gift of the half section of land to his brother and that he carried out this conveyance free of any mental impediment and undue influence. The

factors that influenced the plaintiff were his belief that the defendant should have received land from the father's estate, his desire to satisfy the defendant's complaints about his present circumstances and the plaintiff's wish to ingratiate himself with his brother. When differences later arose between the parties and the defendant threatened to sell the $N\frac{1}{2}$ 2-12-7-W3d and to leave the plaintiff, the plaintiff's distress was related, not to the fact that the defendant had title to the land, but that such action would prevent the parties from farming as the plaintiff understood they would with each other.

The judge appears to have examined the evidence from the standpoint of only the first of Cotton LJ's two classes of cases. Having found nothing in the evidence that he assessed as *express* influence used by the defendant for the purpose of acquiring the gifts, he reached the conclusion there was no undue influence. In other words, he found an intention on the part of the plaintiff to make a gift to the defendant, an intention not brought about through wrongful or improper acts of coercion by the defendant, and in consequence concluded there was no undue influence. It is a conclusion with which I respectfully agree. He failed, however, to examine the evidence from the standpoint of the second of the two classes of cases. Having determined that the plaintiff knew what he was doing, the judge failed to determine how the plaintiff's intention was produced. He failed to consider whether the circumstances presented a situation of confidence and dependence on one side and advice and persuasion on the other, and whether such advice and persuasion, although not wrong or improper, amounted to undue influence. The evidence clearly warranted an examination of those questions and the judge should have conducted such examination.

The provisions of s. 8 of the Court of Appeal Act, RSS 1978, c. C-42, empower this court to do what the trial judge should have done. The section reads:

> 8. Upon appeal from, or motion against, the order, decision, verdict or decree of a trial judge, or on the rehearing of any cause, application or matter, it shall not be obligatory on the court to grant a new trial, or to adopt the view of the evidence taken by the trial judge, but the court shall act upon its own view of what the evidence in its judgment proves, and the court may draw inferences of fact and pronounce the verdict, decision or order that, in its judgment, the judge who tried the case ought to have pronounced.

In doing what the trial judge omitted to do, it is important for this court not to disturb his findings of primary facts. No similar constraint, however, is imposed upon this court respecting the findings of inferential or evaluative facts. I proceed now to do what the trial judge should have done.

Did the defendant on 9th or 10th April 1980, the dates of the impugned gifts, occupy a position of natural influence in relation to the plaintiff? The evidence established beyond peradventure that although the plaintiff was not mentally incompetent on these dates, he was mentally weak, vulnerable and highly susceptible to influence from a domineering person. The evidence established with equal force that the defendant, the plaintiff's older brother, was just such a domineering person. As noted, the most potent evidence on these two questions was given by the defendant himself. That evidence is strongly reinforced by the testimony of the doctors, Mr. Stringer and the plaintiff. That the facts of this case present a situation of confidence and dependence on the side of the plaintiff and advice and persuasion on the side of the defendant is, in my respectful view, clear. This case, in other words, falls into the second of the two classes delineated by Cotton LJ. It follows then that the presumption of undue influence was engaged. It rested upon the defendant to rebut that presumption. Has he met the onus?

As stated in the *Inche* case, the best way to meet the onus is [to] furnish proof of independent legal advice having the quality described by the Privy Council. The defendant adduced no evidence of such legal advice. A careful perusal of Mr. Stringer's testimony discloses nothing that would meet the test prescribed by the Privy Council in this respect.

Does, nevertheless, the evidence establish that "in fact the gift was the spontaneous act of the donor acting under circumstances which enabled him to exercise an independent will and which justifies the Court in holding that the gift was the result of a free exercise of the donor's will?" It does nothing of the sort in my respectful view. Indeed, the trial judge expressly found the contrary. He found that the defendant's persistent complaints about his present circumstances and about not having received any land from his father's estate played a dominant role in the plaintiff's acting as he did. As already noted, he found:

> The factors that influenced the plaintiff were his belief that the defendant should have received land from the father's estate, his desire to satisfy the defendant's complaints about his present circumstances and the plaintiff's wish to ingratiate himself with his brother.

To paraphrase, the plaintiff at the time of the impugned transactions was well ensconced within the defendant's orbit of influence. The plaintiff's act does not have the quality of spontaneity and the circumstances under which he acted do not bear the mark of independence which would justify this court in holding that the gifts were the result of a free exercise of the donor's will. As noted, the question here is not one of wrongful acts committed by the defendant but whether the intention by the plaintiff was produced entirely free of the defendant's dominance. Exercising the "great jealousy" that a court must in these cases, I find that the defendant did not discharge the heavy onus placed upon him.

In the result, the appeal is allowed. The judgment of the trial judge insofar as it relates to the gift of lands and the gift of $10,300 made on 10th April 1980 is set aside.

The plaintiff will have judgment setting aside the transfer of the lands in question. The defendant is ordered to retransfer these lands at his own expense. Upon his failure to do so within 30 days, title to the lands will vest in the plaintiff subject to such encumbrances as are now registered against the lands. The registrar of the appropriate land titles office is directed accordingly. The plaintiff will have leave to apply to have removed such encumbrances as he is advised should be removed. There will be a further order entitling the plaintiff to judgment for $10,300 in addition to the sums awarded by the trial judge.

The appellant will have his costs here and below.

Appeal allowed.

Is the court's reasoning about intention to make a valid gift different in *Csada* by contrast with *Thomas*? What are the elements required to establish undue influence? Should there be a presumption of undue influence for gifts between family members? In general, courts have not recognized such a presumption except in some cases involving gifts made by children—see *Re Pauling's Settlement Trusts*, [1964] Ch. 303 (CA). Similarly, there is no presumption that an elderly person is necessarily under the influence of others, although there are frequent examples of actions to set aside transactions entered into by elderly persons on the basis of undue influence—for example, see *Slovchenko v. Toronto Dominion Bank* (1963), 42 DLR (2d) 484 (Ont. HC). Consider the responsibilities of the solicitor in *Csada*—what should have been done to ensure that the plaintiff understood the nature of the transaction? What precautions should be taken in such cases? For another example, see *Stoppel v. Loesner* (1974), 47 DLR (3d) 317 (Man. QB).

Consider a case in which an elderly woman executed a deed of gift of her house to one of her three daughters, at a time when the woman was in an advanced state of senile dementia. It was explained to her that she was making a gift of the house (her only major asset), but she was not told of the effect of the gift on her other daughters. Is this sufficient for a valid gift? See *Re Beaney*, [1978] 1 WLR 770 (Ch.D), where the court declared that the purported transfer was void because the deceased was unable to understand that she was depriving her other children of a share in her estate. See also J.P. Dawson, "Economic Duress—An Essay in Perspective" (1947), 45 *Michigan Law Review* 253.

Intention and Future Enjoyment: Inter Vivos and Testamentary Gifts

It is a clear principle that a donor must have the intention to make a present gift, not an intention or promise to make a gift at some point in future. However, a donor may make a present gift, the enjoyment of which is postponed to the future. In such a case, the title passes at the moment of the gift, but the donee's enjoyment may not occur until some time in the future. In one well-known case, for example, Gabriel Pascal, a theatrical producer who held 98 percent of the stock of a company that had exclusive world rights to produce a musical play based on G.B. Shaw's "Pygmalion," made a gift in writing to Marianne Kingman, his executive secretary, of a portion of the profits for a stage version in England and in the United States and of the profits worldwide for the film version. At the time of the gift, the right to produce a musical version of "Pygmalion" remained unexercised, so there were no profits to distribute. However, the court concluded that there was a valid, completed gift to Kingman, making an analogy between the expectancy of royalties in this case with contingent remainders in land. Subsequently, there was a highly successful production of "My Fair Lady." See *Speelman v. Pascal*, 178 NE 2d 723 (NY CA 1961).

This case is an example of an *inter vivos* gift in which there is a present gift, with enjoyment postponed to the future. It is important to distinguish *inter vivos* gifts of this kind from testamentary gifts—that is gifts that are not intended to take effect at all until the donor's death. Testamentary gifts must meet the requirements for succession of property interests at death, usually including a written document signed by the testator in the presence of two witnesses who sign the will in the presence of the testator and of each other—for example, see Ontario's Succession Law Reform Act, RSO 1990, c. S.26. See also Wills Act, RSNS 1989, c. 505 and RSNB 1973, c. W-9. A testator does not relinquish any rights to such property interests until the moment of death. However, it is sometimes difficult to distinguish cases such as *Speelman* from testamentary gifts, particularly when (as happened in *Speelman*) the donor died before his estate exercised the right to produce "My Fair Lady." For an analysis of some of these issues, see A.G. Gulliver and C.J. Tilson, "Classification of Gratuitous Transfers" (1941), 51 *Yale Law Journal* 1.

Reconsider *Thomas v. Times Book Co. Ltd.*—was the gift correctly characterized as an *inter vivos* gift? For an interesting analysis of the issues where a donor makes a gift to a donee, without immediate delivery, see Sir Frederick Pollack, "Gifts of Chattels without Delivery" (1890), 6 *Law Quarterly Review* 446, at 446. Is *Thomas* essentially a case about the problem of delivery, the problem of intention, or both?

The relationship between *inter vivos* gifts in which enjoyment is postponed and testamentary gifts must also take account of a special form of gift made in contemplation of death, the *donatio mortis causa*, discussed below.

Acceptance

A valid gift also requires the donee to accept it. Thus, in *Gottstein v. Hedges*, 228 NW 93 (Ia. SC 1929), where a father of the alleged donee transferred property to trustees to pay an annual sum to his daughter for life, she refused to accept the gift. She was insolvent and refused the gift to thwart her creditors, but the court clearly held that, as donee, she was entitled to refuse the gift. In a well-known English decision, *Standing v. Bowring* (1883), 31 Ch.D 282 (CA), the plaintiff wished to make a gift to the defendant and thus transferred certain stock into a joint account in the names of herself and the defendant. However, the plaintiff kept her gift a secret from the defendant. Some time later, when the plaintiff had married, she disclosed the gift to the defendant and asked him to retransfer the stock to her. The defendant refused and the plaintiff sought to compel the retransfer. The court held, however, that a gift vests immediately, subject to the donee's right, on learning about the gift, to decide whether or not to accept it. That is, the donee has the right to repudiate it, but until doing so, the gift belongs to the donee. A similar US decision arose in connection with assets in the United States that were transferred from a brother in Germany to the plaintiff in the United States just before the entry of the United States into World War I. See *Miller v. Herzfeld*, 4 F2d 355 (3d Cir. 1925) and "Note" (1926), 3 *Wisconsin Law Review* 492. In general, however, courts have tended to expect donees to decide whether to accept a gift within a reasonable time of discovery of the gift. For an example where the donee delayed too long, see *Mahoney v. Martin*, 83 P 982 (Kan. SC 1905). This issue is relevant to the donee of a *donatio mortis causa* as well.

Donatio Mortis Causa

A *donatio mortis causa* is a gift made in contemplation of death; the gift is subject to revocation if the donor recovers and does not die. The intention for a *donatio mortis causa* is different from that in a gift *inter vivos* because the donor of a *donatio mortis causa* has an automatic right to revoke the gift on recovery. There is also a requirement of delivery, and there is some difference of opinion as to whether the test for delivery for a *donatio mortis causa* is similar to that for a gift *inter vivos* or whether it is less stringent. As well as the requirements of intention and delivery, there is also a need for acceptance of a *donatio mortis causa*.

To understand the *donatio mortis causa*, it is important to place it in a historical context. Brown has suggested that these gifts are of Roman origin and probably existed alongside testamentary dispositions in English law for some time in the feudal period. However, after the enactment of the Statute of Frauds in the 17th century, most transfers of interests in land were required to be in writing, thus placing severe restraints on the making of oral wills (sometimes called non-cupative wills). The Statute thus created problems for the beneficiaries of gifts made by deceased persons on their deathbeds (apparently a frequent practice), and these beneficiaries turned to the Court of Chancery for relief. After a number of years, the decision in *Ward v. Turner* (1752), 2 Ves. Sr. 431; 28 ER 275 (Ch.) held that such gifts could be sustained only when accompanied by an actual delivery of the subject matter of the gift. According to Brown:

> In this case [*Ward v. Turner*] emerge gifts causa mortis as known to the common law. Like gifts inter vivos a delivery, or its equivalent, is required. The difference is in their conditional or revocable character. Like the testamentary disposition they do not take effect finally and irrevocably until the death of the donor. Until such time a power of revocation is reserved to him. Indeed if the donor survives the anticipated peril, the gift is automatically by operation of law revoked.

(Brown, at 131.)

It is also possible for a person who may be dying to make a valid gift *inter vivos*: it is thus a question of intention whether the donor intended a present and irrevocable gift *inter vivos* or a *donatio mortis cause* revocable on recovery. As noted in *Ward v. Turner*, delivery is required for a valid *donatio mortis causa*. Consider these issues in the case that follows. Is the test for delivery used here sufficient to meet the requirement of delivery for an *inter vivos* gift? If you conclude that it is a different test, identify the rationale for using a different test for delivery for a *donatio mortis causa* by contrast with a gift *inter vivos*.

Re Zachariuc; Chevrier v. Public Trustee
(1984), 16 ETR 152 (Ont. Dist. Ct.)

WARREN DCJ: At the outset of trial, counsel for the plaintiff advised the Court there would be a preliminary objection by counsel for the Public Trustee. Counsel for the Public Trustee argued that a District Court Judge did not have jurisdiction to hear a claim to property as having been the subject of a donatio mortis causa under the Surrogate Courts Act, RSO 1970, c. 451, s. 68, now RSO 1980, c. 491, s. 69, and referred to the case *Re Graham* (1911), 25 OLR 5, to support this contention.

The plaintiff, who was advised by counsel for the Public Trustee prior to trial of this objection, simultaneously, to expedite the disposition of this action, instituted an action in the District Court for the District of Algoma, no. 9393, 1983, styled *Re Zachariuc (a.k.a. Zachariuc and Macharuk)*; *Chevrier v. The Public Trustee* (the deceased hereinafter referred to as Zachariuc).

The Court reserved decision on the objection by counsel for the Public Trustee with regard to s. 69 of the Surrogate Courts Act and requested the plaintiff to proceed with the District Court action.

This is an action that arises as a result of the death of Zachariuc, who died sometime between the hours of 9:30 p.m. November 17, 1982, and 7:00 a.m. November 18, 1982, in his home in Wawa, Ontario. It is the contention of the plaintiff that he was given an inter vivos gift by the deceased, referred to in law as a donatio mortis causa.

The Facts

Counsel are in agreement as to the facts. Zachariuc and John Chevrier (hereinafter referred to as Chevrier) lived in Wawa as friends and neighbours for 33 years. They had worked together collecting scrap, had built three homes together, and Chevrier was constantly available to help Zachariuc at his request. They visited back and forth frequently on a daily basis.

The deceased at the time of his demise was in his 81st year and had no living relatives. He lived a very quiet, conservative existence, and associated socially with no one other than Chevrier.

Chevrier testified that he attended on Zachariuc on November 17, 1982, when he finished work, as he had done on many occasions. Zachariuc complained to Chevrier that he felt sick, was holding his head and thought he was poisoned. Chevrier suggested he should take him to a doctor, but Zachariuc stated he had no desire to see a doctor, and be confined to hospital. Mr. Chevrier testified that Zachariuc fashioned himself to be his own medicine man.

Mr. Chevrier testified while he was in attendance at Zachariuc's home that the paper-boy arrived, and Zachariuc, in the process of paying for the paper fell on the floor. With effort he got up and sat on a chair. In the opinion of Chevrier, Zachariuc seemed very strange and ill.

Chevrier suggested to Zachariuc that he was getting very old and asked Zachariuc if he had a will. Zachariuc replied to Chevrier, "No, I give what I have to you; you are my only friend." Chevrier further testified that Zachariuc commenced to reminisce and tell him things about the past that Chevrier had never heard before during their long acquaintance. In particular, he talked of things and locations that had happened years before while Zachariuc was a resident of Rouyn and Val d'Or in Quebec. Chevrier was about to leave for home at 8:30 p.m. when Zachariuc suggested they have a drink. They both had a drink and Zachariuc did a little jig and announced he was "not going to die tonight."

He then reiterated that Chevrier was his best and only friend, and that he had some money hidden which he was giving to Chevrier. He then explained in detail that the money was located in the crawl space under the two-room house. Chevrier was to look for barrels and underneath them, buried in the earth [were] jars full of money. He then gave Mr. Chevrier his house key and told Chevrier to check on him in the morning, and to bring a friend to witness a paper (presumably to act as a will), leaving his assets to Chevrier. Chevrier left for home at 9:30 p.m., had his supper and went to bed.

On the morning of the 18th of November, at 7:00 a.m., Mr. Chevrier went to Zachariuc's house as requested. He knocked on the door, went into the house, and saw a motionless body on the bed. I think it is essential to state that the witness Chevrier broke down in the witness box and cried when he gave this evidence, obviously very sad and emotional at the recall of finding his dear friend dead.

Chevrier immediately called the police station, and Constable Kennedy arrived shortly. Mr. Chevrier testified, "Officer Kennedy came over and found George dead. The old sun of a gun died and no paper." Subsequently, he was officially pronounced dead by the doctor.

Later on that day Chevrier was made aware that the deceased's house would be torn down, then contacted Mr. Frank Macdonald, the Justice of the Peace, and told him about the money given to him by Zachariuc. Mr. MacDonald told Chevrier to contact Mr. Quino who was appointed an agent for the Public Trustee.

If I may digress, Mr. Aquino gave evidence that he was appointed an agent for the Public Trustee on November 19, 1983. Aquino attended at the house of the deceased, did a thorough search of the house and contents. He testified the building and contents were of no value on November 20, 1982. Aquino secured the house and disposed of the contents of the home at the dump. He did however find four $100 bills in a cupboard, and $2,770 in a bag in the freezer.

Subsequently, on Saturday, around 5:00 p.m. he received a phone call from Mr. Chevrier who advised him that there was money in the house. They decided to attend with the police chief after church. They all attended, and on the instructions of Chevrier they found the jars which contained the sum of $16,280. I wish to add that Police Chief Egan testified and gave the same evidence as Mr. Aquino. They both stated that if it had not been for Mr. Chevrier they would not have found the money.

Counsel for the Public Trustee referred the Court to the *Ontario Evidence Act*, c. 145, s. 13, which states:

> In an action by or against the heirs, next of kin, executors, administrators or assigns of a deceased person, an opposite or interested party shall not obtain a verdict, judgment or decision on his own evidence in respect of any matter occurring before the death of the deceased person, unless such evidence is corroborated by some other material evidence.

In *Brown v. Rotenberg*, [1946] OR 363, [1946] 4 DLR 139 (CA), Laidlaw JA at pp. 375-76 stated:

> It has been held that "it is sufficient if the evidence relied upon as corroborative is evidence of some material facts or facts supporting the testimony to be corroborated": *Ollson v. Fraser, Barned and Powell*, [1945] OR 69, [1945] 1 DLR 481. The evidence tendered in corroboration need not be in respect of the vital and essential portion of the respondent's evidence. "All that the statute requires is that the evidence to be corroborated shall be strengthened by some evidence which appreciably helps the judicial mind to believe one or more of the material statements or facts deposed to": *George McKean and Company Limited et al. v. Black et al.*, 62 SCR 290 at 308, 68 DLR 34; *Bayley v. Trusts and Guarantee Co. Ltd.* [66 OLR 254, at 258; 1 DLR 500].

In my view, the evidence of Chief Egan and Mr. Aquino corroborates the evidence of Mr. Chevrier, who was advised by the deceased the night before his death of the location of the money. In knowing the whereabouts of the money I am satisfied on a balance of probabilities that Zachariuc advised Chevrier the money was his.

There is no question in the Court's mind on the evidence, submissions by both counsel, and the witnesses that Mr. Chevrier is an honest, reliable witness. Someone lesser could easily have removed the money under the same circumstances, upon finding Zachariuc dead in his home on the morning of November 17, [sic] 1982, but not Mr. Chevrier.

The question to be answered: is this a donatio mortis causa, in other words a gift in contemplation of death? It is conceded by counsel that the case law appears to take the view that keeping in mind certain tests each case is settled on its own facts.

In 13 CED (Ont. 3d), Title 68 "Gifts," p. 68-8, para. 3, a donatio mortis causa is described as:

> ... a gift made in contemplation of death intended to take effect only upon the death of the donor. There must be delivery of the subject of the gift. It is not necessary that the donor expressly state that the gift is effective only in the event of death since the condition may be implied from the circumstances. It is sufficient that the gift be made in contemplation of and not in expectation of death. ...

In the case of *Brown v. Rotenberg, supra*, Laidlaw JA said at p. 368:

> It has been said that "for an effectual donatio mortis causa three things must combine: first, the gift or donation must have been made in contemplation, though not necessarily in expectation, of death; secondly, there must have been delivery to the donee of the subject-matter of the gift; and thirdly, the gift must be made under such circumstances as shew that the thing is to revert to the donor in case he should recover": per Lord Russell of Killowen CJ in *Cain v. Moon*, [1896] 2 QB 283 at 286.

Chevrier testified he had known the deceased for over 30 years and during this period of time the deceased showed no interest in the services of a doctor. The deceased was in his 81st year and in failing health, probably due to his age and was reluctant to see a doctor. On the night of November 17, 1982, when Chevrier visited Zachariuc, after he realized that Zachariuc was not well he asked him if he had a will, and Zachariuc replied, "No, what I have I give to you." Chevrier testified further that Zachariuc fell on the floor of his home and complained of being poisoned, and in his opinion Zachariuc looked very ill. Chevrier suggested Zachariuc should see a doctor immediately, but he refused.

Zachariuc advised Chevrier that he was his only friend and confidant, and reminisced at some length about his past, which Chevrier thought was unusual for his friend who was a very private person, but on the same evening he became specific as to the gift he intended his friend to have. At one point, Zachariuc remarked he "would not die tonight."

It is my view that taking into consideration the total conversation, the physical appearance of the deceased, and the fact that he made reference to his not dying tonight is indicative that he was contemplating the possibility of death. I am satisfied that the first rule for a valid donatio mortis causa has been established in that the gift was given in contemplation of death, though not necessarily in expectation of death.

Mr. Chevrier testified further that, before he had left on the evening of November 17, 1982 to go home, the deceased returned to the subject of his possessions and suggested Mr. Chevrier should return the following day with a witness, presumably to make a will leaving his estate to his friend Chevrier. However, this was not to be in that Zachariuc died in the interim.

During this conversation, Zachariuc became very specific as to the location of some of his personalty. In particular, he described to Mr. Chevrier in detail the location of a hidden cache of money that was buried in the ground in the crawl space under his two-room home.

It is my view he revealed this information because he realized if the location [were] not made known, upon his death the secret money cache would probably go undetected, and therefore Chevrier would not have received this gift.

Subsequent events bore out the deceased's thinking in that the agent for the Public Trustee, the day following Zachariuc's death, found money in the house which was put in an estate account. He arranged to have the remaining house contents taken to the dump. He advised Mr. Chevrier that the house would be razed, and it was at this jucture Chevrier spoke to Mr. MacDonald, the Justice of the Peace, regarding the alleged hidden cache of money.

It is significant to the Court that just prior to Mr. Chevrier's departure on the 17th of November 1982, the deceased for the first time in his life gave his house key to Chevrier and asked him if he would check on him in the morning. It is my view that the giving of the house key is similar to the line of cases that have established where the safety-deposit box key has been given to the donee this has been found to constitute delivery of the gift.

In the case of *Kooner v. Kooner* (1979), 100 DLR (3d) 76 (BC CA), Locke J said at p. 80:

> However, the second prerequisite of delivery has been relaxed by an anomalous doctrine peculiar to these gifts but established by the House of Lords in *Duffield v. Elwes* (1827), 1 Bligh NS 497, 4 ER 959. Choses in action may pass by gifts mortis causa in circumstances ineffective to constitute a valid transfer inter vivos: i.e., equity will in this case complete an imperfect gift: *Vaines, op. cit.* 318; *Re Dillon* (1890), 44 Ch.D 76; *Re Wasserberg*, [1915] 1 Ch. 195.

> *Brown v. Rotenberg* was a case where the key to a safety-deposit box was given to the donee. Laidlaw JA at p. 370 asked the question:

> Was there delivery to the donee of the subject matter of the gift? It is to be noted at once that an inchoate or imperfect delivery of chattels may be sufficient for effectuating a donatio mortis causa: In *Re Wasserberg; Union of London and Smith's Bank, Limited v. Wasserberg*, [1915] 1 Ch. 195; "... a transfer of the means of, or part of the means of, getting at the property" is sufficient.

It is my view when the deceased Zachariuc gave the location and description of the jars that contained the money and the key to his home, and advised Chevrier this money was his, that he gave up control and dominion of the cache of money and therefore Chevrier acquired title to the gift. Thus, the second essential has been satisfied in that there was a valid delivery of the cache of money.

The third essential to a valid donatio mortis causa is "... the gift must be made under such circumstances as shew that the thing is to revert to the donor in case he should recover: ... *Chain v. Moon, supra.*" In *Brown v. Rotenberg, supra,* Laidlaw JA said at p. 374:

> Was the gift to the respondent made in such circumstances as to show that the property was to revert to the donor in case he should recover? This question may be put in other

language as follows: Was it intended that the gift should be effective only in the event of the death of the donor? It is not necessary that the donor should expressly state that term or condition at the time the gift is made. The inference may be drawn that the gift was intended to be absolute but only in case of death: *Gardner v. Parker et al.* (1818), 3 Madd. 184, 56 ER 478, cited in *In re Beaumont, supra*, and *Kendrick v. Dominion Bank and Bownas* (1920), 48 OLR 539 at 542, 58 DLR 309.

I am of the view that this inference can be made in this case in that the deceased, although ill, remained in the premises and did indicate that Chevrier could return the next day with a friend to witness the paper. The testimony of Mr. Chevrier was quite clear that he would only have considered the cache of money his on the death of Zachariuc. Thus, the last essential for an effectual donatio mortis causa is, in my opinion, satisfied.

I want to take this opportunity to express my thanks for the assistance which counsel have given the Court in their research and presentation of the law in argument.

There will be judgment for the plaintiff in the sum of $16,280, plus accrued interest from the time the Public Trustee deposited this sum to the estate account. The estate of Zachariuc will bear the costs of the plaintiff's solicitor and the solicitor for the Public Trustee on a party-and-party basis.

Judgment for plaintiff.

Discussion Notes

Delivery

What factors were relied on by the court in concluding that there was delivery of a gift to Chevrier in this case? If Zachariuc had told his friend about the secret cache, but had not provided a key to his home, would the court have held that there was sufficient delivery of a *donatio mortis causa*? Did Zachariuc give his friend a key to his home to enable him to obtain the cache of money, or for some other purpose?

Does the court's reasoning represent a different approach to the issue of delivery here, by contrast with *inter vivos* gifts? Do you agree that there was a "relaxation of the requirements for delivery ... as a dispensation in favour of the dying"? See R. Brazier, "Death-Bed Gifts of Land" (1992), 43 *Northern Ireland Legal Quarterly* 35, at 48; S. Stoljar, "The Delivery of Chattels" (1958), 21 *Modern Law Review* 27; and W.H.D. Winder, "Requisites for Transference as *Donation Mortis Causa*" (1940), 4 *The Conveyancer and Property Lawyer (NS)* 382. Most commentators agree that there was no requirement for delivery in the original *donatio mortis causa* of Roman law, and that this requirement was not introduced until Lord Hardwicke's decision in *Ward v. Turner* (1752), 2 Ves. Sen. 431; 28 ER 275 (Ch.). Is this history of *donationes mortis causa* important in understanding the standards applied to delivery in relation to such gifts?

In the light of the reasoning in *Zachariuc*, consider a situation where a donor purports to make a *donatio mortis causa*, in relation to money in a bank account, by handing to the donee the passbook to the account. Does this action constitute sufficient delivery? Is this constructive delivery? For some examples, see *McMillan v. Brown* (1957), 12 DLR

(2d) 306 (NS SC) and *Re Smith Estate* (1995), 9 ETR (2d) 127 (Nfld. TD). Consider also a purported *donatio mortis causa* where the donor handed to the donee the key to a safety deposit box, as a way of making a gift of the jewellery contained in it. However, the donor did not provide the donee with the password or any written authorization, both required to open the box. Does this action constitute sufficient delivery? Is it relevant that the donor no longer has any control over the safety deposit box because there is only one key? See *Re Lillingston*, [1952] 2 All ER 184 (Ch.D).

In *Zachariuc*, the court considered s. 13 of the Evidence Act (now RSO 1990, c. E.23), discussed above, following *Thomas v. Times Book Co. Ltd.* Why was this section relevant in *Zachariuc*? Is such a statutory provision adequate protection against fraud? Since the donor is not available to give evidence of a *donatio mortis causa*, is it appropriate to use a different standard of delivery, or is this a matter that should be addressed in relation to the donor's intention? For one analysis, see R.G. Murray, "Note" (1953), 31 *Canadian Bar Review* 935.

Intention

The intention required for a *donatio mortis causa* reveals its historical roots as a "compromise" between an *inter vivos* gift and a testamentary disposition. It is both a present gift and one that nonetheless becomes irrevocable only on death. Its characterization is often stated to be *sui generis*. Consider, for example, the following descripion:

> [It] is not correct to characterize a *donatio* as a declaration of trust *inter vivos* immediately effective although conditioned in operation by reference to the death of the settlor. In truth the institution of the *donation mortis causa* is peculiar and not to be understood by attempts to rationalize it within traditional ideas of trust, gift or legacy [testamentary gifts]; for while it has some attributes of each of these it has all of none.

(R.P. Meagher, W.M.C. Gummow, and J.R. Lehane, *Equity: Doctrines and Remedies*, 3d ed. (Sydney: Butterworths, 1992), at 742.) The authors also explore in detail the rights of the donee after the gift of a *donatio mortis causa* and before the death of the donor—see 741-50. See also D. Waters, *Law of Trusts in Canada*, 2d ed. (Scarborough, ON: Carswell, 1984) (hereafter Waters 1984), at 176.

Consider a situation where a donor, in immediate apprehension of death, gave a valuable ring to a long-time friend. However, the donor survived the peril and recovered, whereupon his friend urged him to take back the ring. The donor did so reluctantly, and only after summoning witnesses to hear his declaration that the ring still belonged to the donee. The donor wore the ring until his death some years later, when the donee sought the ring from the donor's executor. The executor refused to give it to the donee. Was there a valid *donatio mortis causa*? Was there a valid gift *inter vivos*? What was the donor's intention? See *Newell v. National Bank of Norwich*, 212 NYS 158 (CA 1925), where the court held that the donor's attempt to grant a *donatio mortis causa* was revoked automatically on his recovery. To give effect to the donor's obvious intent, the court characterized the original gift as a gift *inter vivos*. Is this reasoning satisfactory? According to Brown, this case might have been considered as one in which the donor made an *inter vivos* gift by means of his declaration while the ring was still in the possession of the donee, with a bailment to the donor until his death. See Brown, at 141-43, and note 9.

As was evident in *Zachariuc*, a *donatio mortis causa* must be made in the contemplation (although not necessarily expectation) of death—the contemplation of a death more likely than that which all mortals expect. For some examples, see *Thompson v. Mechan*, [1958] OR 357 (CA) and *Canada Trust Co. v. Labadie*, [1962] OR 151 (CA). See also commentary by R.E. Megarry, "Note" (1965), 81 *Law Quarterly Review* 21 and Ziff, at 140-41. If death is certain, should it be possible for a donor to make a *donatio mortis causa*, or should the donor be required to make a will with its formal requirements? How should a court deal with a *donatio mortis causa* that was made in contemplation of death from one peril, but where the donor died as a result of another? See *Rosenberger v. Volz* (1945), 12 ILR 34 (Ont. HC), where the donor died in a railway accident in 1942, having "put his affairs in order" because of his enlistment in the armed forces. The purported *donatio mortis causa* was held to be valid..

To some extent, these questions reveal the need to consider whether there is a continuing need for legal recognition of the *donatio mortis causa*. While it is possible that such "deathbed gifts" were essential when many people lived in rural communities (without easy access to lawyers) and where the level of literacy was low, it is arguably less fruitful to devote legal resources to such gifts in the late 20th century. According to this argument, it is preferable to encourage people to make proper testamentary gifts, so that the scope of *donationes mortis causa* should be more and more narrowly interpreted. Do you agree? What goals are achieved by preserving a wide scope for the *donatio mortis causa*? In considering these questions, examine the issues below concerning recent developments about *donationes mortis causa* of land. For further analysis, see J. Schouler, "Oral Wills and Death-Bed Gifts" (1886), 2 *Law Quarterly Review* 444 and Brown, at 130-45.

The Donatio Mortis Causa and Land: Sen v. Headley

Traditionally, the scope of the *donatio mortis causa* was limited so that it was not possible to make a deathbed gift of land by the delivery of title deeds. In *Sen v. Headley*, [1991] 2 All ER 636 (CA), however, the court held that the exclusion of land from *donationes mortis causa* was anomalous. In that case, the plaintiff, Mrs. Sen, claimed to have received a *donatio mortis causa* of a house in Ealing worth £450,000 from the donor, Mr. Hewett. She gave evidence that she and the donor were extremely close friends, and that when she had visited him in hospital shortly before his death and inquired about what was to be done with his house if he died, he replied:

> The house is yours, Margaret. You have the keys. They are in your bag. The deeds are in the steel box.

In this way, Mr. Hewett gave Mrs. Sen the only key to the steel box containing the title deeds to the house. She also had one of two keys to the house; Mr. Hewett had the other. The court held that there was a sufficient parting with dominion in this case, although it did not resolve whether the case might have been decided differently if there had been two keys to the steel box and Mr. Hewett had retained one. However, the central issue in

Sen v. Headley was whether English law recognized a *donatio mortis causa* of land, and the Court of Appeal held that there was no reason to distinguish land and other objects in relation to gifts.

The decision in *Sen v. Headley* has been critiqued extensively, both in terms of the court's reasoning about earlier decisions and in relation to underlying policy issues. According to P. Sparkes, the decision represents "a revolutionary extension ... with a wide and uncertain ambit":

> The Court of Appeal has validated a death-bed gift of a house, reportedly worth
> £450,000 made by the key to a deed box being slipped into the donee's handbag. There
> was no evidence apart from that of the donee, which [the trial judge] expressly found to
> be reliable and truthful. A door pushed open by an honest plaintiff, like Mrs. Sen, can be
> pushed further ajar by later dishonest claims. Land was not transmissable simply by
> delivery of title deeds, and should not be.

(P. Sparkes, "Death-Bed Gifts of Land" (1992), 43:1 *Northern Ireland Legal Quarterly* 35, at 52.) Since a full analysis of the issues in this case requires considerable knowledge about the principles of equity and the Statute of Frauds, you may need to reconsider this case in relation to these principles, discussed below. The case has prompted recommendations for the abolition of all *donationes mortis causa* on the basis that there is no need for them any longer. For example, C.E.F. Rickett, in "No *Donatio Mortis Causa* of Real Property—A Rule in Search of a Justification?" (1989), *The Conveyancer and Property Lawyer* 184, supporting the assessment of Waters 1984, argued:

> What has particularly concerned both courts and administrators, however, is that, while
> the whole object of the Wills Act is to eliminate fraud by requiring witnessed and signed
> wills or wills in the deceased's own handwriting ["holograph wills," permitted by statute
> in some provincial jurisdictions], the doctrine of gifts *mortis causa* reintroduces all the
> difficulties of oral and informal written evidence. ...
>
> There can be little doubt that the law of gifts *mortis causa* ought to be critically
> reviewed. The present law on the subject results in the drawing of lines between the
> valid and the invalid gift which is too often indefensible, and it is equally difficult to
> justify the position that a gift conditional on the donor's death is not testamentary. The
> truth is that the present law is largely a clutter of rules which have accrued over the
> centuries ... . The preferable course may well be for those Canadian jurisdictions
> without the holograph will to introduce it, and for all Canadian common law
> jurisdictions to abolish the gift *mortis causa*.

(Waters 1984, at 176-79.)

Do you agree with this assessment? Note that it is not usual to keep deeds in a steel box in Canadian jurisdictions, a matter that is considered below in relation to registration systems. For statutory provisions concerning holograph wills, see Succession Law Reform Act, RSO 1990, c. S.26, s. 6 and RSS 1978, c. W-14, s. 7, as am. 1989, c. 66, ss. 4 and 5. Ziff has identified a Canadian decision concerning a *donatio mortis causa* of land—see *Cooper v. Severson* (1955), 1 DLR (2d) 161 (BC SC). He recommends abolition of any distinction between land and other gifts of *donationes mortis causa*, but not their abolition altogether. See Ziff, at 140-41. In *Naylor v. Naylor* (1990: OJ no. 287), the court dismissed an application for a declaration of a *donatio mortis causa* but with little analysis of the fact that the subject matter of the alleged gift was real property. The appeal to the Ontario Court of Appeal was dismissed—(1993), 1 ETR (2d) 308; leave to appeal to the Supreme Court of Canada was denied—(1994) 4 ETR (2d) 193n.

You may want to consider these issues concerning gifts of real and personal property, as well as the relationship between gifts *inter vivos*, *donationes mortis causa*, and testamentary gifts, after examining the remainder of this chapter.

TRANSFERRING INTERESTS IN LAND: LEGAL AND EQUITABLE INTERESTS

Conveyances and Contracts for Sale

Transfers of interests in land by sale are common legal transactions. Although they often involve multimillion dollar developments and large corporations, many individuals are familiar with such transactions as a result of purchasing a home. Typically, the vendor and purchaser first negotiate a contractual agreement, usually with the help of their real estate agents. The vendor and purchaser sign an agreement of purchase and sale that defines the terms of the sale, including the purchase price. In most respects, the negotiation of these contracts is similar to other kinds of contract bargaining. However, the validity and enforceability of contracts for the sale of land are subject to some special requirements, reflecting the historical role of land as a unique form of proprietary interest. This section focuses on basic principles of law and equity reflected in modern real estate transactions concerning the sale of land. For a more specialized analysis of real estate transactions, see A.H. Oosterhof and W.B. Rayner, *Anger and Honsberger Law of Real Property*, 2d ed. (Aurora, ON: Canada Law Book, 1985) and B.J. Reiter, B.J. McLellan, and P.M. Perell, *Real Estate Law* (Toronto: Emond Montgomery, 1992).

The history of conveyancing reveals a complex web of legal practices from the medieval period to the present, all designed to accomplish specified purposes of vendors and purchasers of land in the context of changing laws and policies. In addition to feoffment by *livery of seisin* (see earlier chapters) and grant by deed, conveyancers developed practices such as "bargain and sale" after the enactment of the Statute of Uses in 1535 and, later, a refined "lease and release" procedure that was used for conveying estates in possession in England from the 17th until the 19th century. Property reform legislation in England, the Law of Property Act, 1925, 15 & 16 Geo. V, c. 21 made conveyance by deed of grant virtually the only permissible means of conveyance.

Although ss. 2 and 3 of the Conveyancing and Law of Property Act, RSO 1990, c. C.34 use different (and perhaps less than felicitous) language concerning the use of feoffments by livery as well as by deed, it has been held that the effect of these sections and others in the Registry Act, RSO 1970, c. 409 (see now RSO 1990, c. R.20 as am.) require a deed and registration to transfer interests in land so as to be enforceable against third parties—see *Bea v. Robinson* (1977), 81 DLR (3d) 423 (Ont. HC). See also *Re Bouris and Button* (1975), 60 DLR (3d) 233 (Ont. HC), suggesting that feoffment by livery may continue to be valid; a useful discussion of these issues is contained in Mendes da Costa, Balfour, and Gillese, *Property Law: Cases, Text and Materials*, 2d ed. (Toronto: Emond Montgomery,

1990), at 9:1-5. For further detail about methods of conveyancing, see R. Megarry and H.W.R. Wade, *The Law of Real Property*, 5th ed. (London: Stevens & Sons, 1984); S.F.C. Milsom, *Pollack and Maitland: The History of English Law* (Cambridge: Cambridge University Press, 1968); D.C. Hoath, "The Sealing of Documents—Fact or Fiction?" (1980), 43 *Modern Law Review* 415; and T. Youdan, "The Formal Requirements of a Deed" (1979), 5 *Business Law Review* 71. See also Property Act, RSNB 1973, c. P-19, ss. 10(2) and 11 and Real Property Act, RSPEI 1974, c. R-4, ss. 7, 8, and 9. For a comment on the "indenture," a traditional form of deed used in conveyancing, see B. Bucknall, "What the Indenture Witnessed" (1985), 19 *Gazette* 169.

The modern process of real estate transactions in Canada usually involves two steps. After the vendor and purchaser have agreed on the basic terms for the sale, they sign an agreement of purchase and sale and the purchaser tenders a "deposit," a sum of money that represents consideration for the contractual agreement. Pursuant to the terms of this contract, and on a date fixed for "closing" the transaction, the vendor agrees to execute a deed conveying the vendor's proprietary interest to the purchaser, and the purchaser agrees to pay the balance of the purchase price. The closing date is usually scheduled a few weeks after the signing of the agreement of purchase and sale. If all goes as planned, the vendor and purchaser agree that the vendor's title is satisfactory (perhaps after the purchaser has submitted a number of "requisitions on title"), the purchaser arranges details of financing, and on the closing date, the vendor hands over the deed and the keys to the property in return for the balance of the purchase price. In some jurisdictions, it may be essential to register the purchaser's deed to ensure the transfer of title to the purchaser, a matter discussed briefly at the end of this chapter.

Not all real estate transactions go entirely smoothly, however. For example, the purchaser may not be able to pay the purchase price at closing, the vendor may die after signing the contract and before closing, or buildings erected on the land may burn to the ground between the date of the contract and the date set for closing. Thus, it is necessary to define exactly what interests are created for the vendor and purchaser at the time of the agreement of purchase and sale, and what remedies are available to a vendor or purchaser in the event that the other party to the agreement fails to perform the terms of the contract at closing. These issues form a substantial part of the law of real estate transactions, a subject that you may want to pursue in detail in more specialized courses. The material that follows provides an introduction to these issues in terms of the role of law and equity in defining conveyances and contracts for the sale of land, and offers some comparisons and contrasts with legal and equitable principles concerning gifts of chattels and land.

Conveying the Legal Estate: Requirements of the Statute of Frauds

The transfer of the legal estate occurs at closing, so long as the statutory requirements of transfer (and registration, if required) have been met. In addition to the statutory provisions identified above, the Statute of Frauds, 1677, 29 Charles II, c. 3 was enacted to ensure written evidence of transfers of interests in land. As Megarry and Wade have explained, the Statute of Frauds was intended to "prevent fraud and perjury, and to make it impossible for certain contracts to be alleged upon purely oral testimony by witnesses who might be perjuring themselves." See R. Megarry and H.W.R. Wade, *The Law of Real Property*, 3d ed. (London: Stevens & Sons, 1966) (hereafter Megarry and Wade, 3d ed.), at 554.

The Statute of Frauds required in s. 1(1) that the creation of a freehold estate must be in writing and signed by the parties, and that failure to meet these requirements would result in an estate at will only. Similarly, s. 1(2) required that leases "are void unless made by deed." Section 2 provided that no estate of freehold or leasehold could be "assigned, granted or surrendered" unless by deed or note in writing signed by the transferor. Leases (or agreements for leases) for a term not exceeding three years (with a rent that amounted to two-thirds of the value of the land) were excluded from the operation of these provisions by s. 3. Other sections extended these requirements to the creation of trusts and other kinds of transactions relating to land.

The Statute of Frauds remains current law in most provincial jurisdictions in Canada— for example, see Statute of Frauds, RSO 1990, c. S.19; RSNB 1973, c. S-14; RSNS 1989, c. 422; and RSPEI 1974, c. S-6. The Statute of Frauds, 1677 "forms part of the law of Newfoundland by virtue of the reception of English law doctrine." See *Hollett v. Hollett* (1993), 31 RPR (2d) 251, at 261 (Nfld. SCTD). There is lingering debate about whether a deed under seal (but not signed) meets the requirements of the Statute of Frauds, a matter discussed but not resolved in *Town of Eastview v. Roman Catholic Episcopal Corporation of Ottawa* (1918), 44 OLR 284 (CA). For an analysis of the need for a seal in England as part of "the social anthropology of land law," see Gray and Symes, *Real Property and Real People* (London: Butterworths, 1981) (hereafter Gray and Symes), at 89.

Thus, in a modern real estate transaction, it is only when the vendor delivers a deed to the purchaser at closing (along with registration, if required) that the legal estate in land is transferred to the purchaser. This conclusion may suggest that the purchaser has no recognizable interest in land between the signing of the agreement of purchase and sale and the time fixed for closing. Yet, although the purchaser may not have a legal estate, equitable principles have developed to provide protection for both the vendor and the purchaser in relation to their agreement. These principles reflect the historical importance of land as the object of proprietary interests and the availability of the remedy of specific performance in relation to contracts for the sale of land.

Equitable Interests in Agreements for Purchase and Sale

The classic description of the interests of a vendor and purchaser at the time of a contract for the sale of land is found in *Lysaght v. Edwards* (1876), 2 Ch.D 499 (Ch.D). The decision in *Lysaght v. Edwards* was given shortly after the "fusion" of the courts of law and equity in England, described in chapter 3, and in a context where courts were only beginning to decide some of the effects of a unified court of law and equity. In reading the decision, identify the nature of the interests acquired by the vendor and the purchaser at the time of their contract.

Lysaght v. Edwards
(1876), 2 Ch.D 499 (Ch.D)

[The vendor, Edwards, entered into an agreement dated December 23, 1874 to sell his interests in certain land to the purchaser, Lysaght, at a price of £59,750. The purchaser paid a deposit and the parties agreed on October 11, 1875 as the closing date. There was an investigation of the vendor's title and the parties agreed on all the issues of title, etc., before the date set for closing, and before the vendor's death on May 1, 1875. After the vendor's death, the purchaser brought an appplication for specific performance of the contract; the defendants were several heirs specified in Edwards's will. Much of the decision was concerned with the proper interpretation of provisions concerning the disposition of real and personal property under the will, but Jessel MR also considered (at 505) the effect of the contract for the sale of land entered into by the deceased and the plaintiff in December 1874.]

[T]he next point I have to consider is [w]hat is the effect of the contract? It appears to me that the effect of a contract for sale has been settled for more than two centuries; certainly it was completely settled before the time of Lord Hardwicke, who speaks of the settled doctrine of the Court as to it. What is that doctrine? It is that the moment you have a valid contract for sale the vendor becomes in equity a trustee for the purchaser of the estate sold, and the beneficial ownership passes to the purchaser, the vendor having a right to the purchase-money, a charge or lien on the estate for the security of that purchase-money, and a right to retain possession of the estate until the purchase-money is paid, in the absence of express contract as to the time of delivering possession. In other words, the position of the vendor is something between what has been called a naked or bare trustee, or a mere trustee (that is, a person without beneficial interest), and a mortgagee who is not, in equity (any more than a vendor), the owner of the estate, but is, in certain events, entitled to what the unpaid vendor is, viz., possession of the estate and a charge upon the estate for his purchase-money. Their positions are analogous in another way. The unpaid mortgagee has a right to foreclose, that is to say, he has a right to say to the mortgagor, "Either pay me within a limited time, or you lose your estate," and in default of payment he becomes absolute owner of it. So, although there has been a valid contract of sale, the vendor has a similar right in a Court of Equity; he has a right to say to the purchaser, "Either pay me the purchase-money, or lose the estate." Such a decree has sometimes been called a decree for cancellation of the contract; time is given by a decree of the Court of Equity, or now by a judgment of the High Court of Justice; and if the time expires without the money being paid, the contract is cancelled by the decree or judgment of the Court, and the vendor becomes again the owner of the estate. But that, as it appears to me, is a totally different thing from the contract being cancelled because there was some equitable ground for setting it aside. If a valid contract is cancelled for non-payment of the purchase-money after the death of the vendor, the property will still in equity be treated as having been converted into personalty, because the contract was valid at his death; while in the other case there will not be conversion, because there never was in equity a valid contract. Now, what is the meaning of the term "valid contract"? "Valid contract" means in every case a contract sufficient in form and in substance, so that there is no ground whatever for setting it aside as between the vendor and purchaser—a contract binding on both parties. As regards real estate, however, another element of validity is required. The vendor must be in a position to make a title according to the contract, and the contract will not be a valid contract unless he has either made out his title according to the contract or the purchaser has accepted the title, for however bad the title may be the purchaser has a right to accept it, and the moment he has accepted the title, the contract is fully binding upon the vendor. Consequently, if the title is accepted in the lifetime of the vendor, and there is no reason for setting aside the contract, then, although the purchase-money is unpaid, the contract is valid and binding; and being a valid contract, it has this remarkable effect, that it converts the estate, so to say, in equity; it makes the purchase-money a part of the personal estate of the vendor, and it makes the land a part of the real estate of the vendee; and therefore all those cases on the doctrine of constructive conversion are founded simply on this, that a valid contract actually changes the ownership of the estate in equity. That being so, is the vendor less a trustee because he has the rights which I have mentioned? I do not see how it is possible to say so. If anything happens to the estate between the time of sale and the time of completion of the purchase it is at the risk of the purchaser. If it is a house that is sold, and the house is burnt down, the purchaser loses the house. He must insure it himself if he wants to provide against such an accident. If it is a garden, and a river overflows its banks without any fault of the vendor, the garden will be ruined, but the loss will be the purchaser's. In the same way there is a correlative liability on the part of the vendor in possession. He is not entitled to treat the estate as his own. If he wilfully damages or injures it, he is liable to the purchaser; and more than that, he is liable if he does not take reasonable care of it. So far he is treated in all respects as a trustee, subject of course to his right to being paid the purchase-money and his right to enforce his security against the estate. With those exceptions, and his right to rents till the day for completion, he appears to me to have no other rights.

Discussion Notes

Equitable Interests and the Remedy of Specific Performance:
Semelhago v. Paramadevan

As Jessel MR explained, an enforceable contract for the sale of land results in the creation of a trust relationship between the vendor and the purchaser. With respect to the interest in land, the vendor holds the legal estate and the purchaser acquires the beneficial or equitable interest. Similarly, the vendor acquires a charge or lien on the purchase money, and (unless the contract alters the arrangement) the right to remain in possession of the land until closing. In doing so, however, the vendor, as trustee for the purchaser, has an obligation to take reasonable care of the property. See *Clarke v. Ramuz*, [1891] 2 QB 456 (CA) and *Earl of Egmont v. Smith* (1877), 6 Ch.D 469 (Ch.D). Note also that any risk of loss also passes to the purchaser in equity at the time of the contract for sale, although this result is sometimes expressly altered by the parties in their agreement for purchase and sale.

As the court declared, "a valid contract actually changes the ownership of the estate in equity." According to Gray and Symes, the explanation for this result is the availability of the remedy of specific performance to a purchaser in the event that the vendor fails to convey the legal estate in accordance with the terms of the contract for sale.

> The end result is that once a contract for the sale of a legal estate in land has been concluded, the eventual conveyance of that estate is virtually inevitable. Either the vendor will duly convey according to his contract or the purchaser will enlist the aid of

equity towards this end by means of a decree of specific performance. The assistance of equity will normally be forthcoming in each case unless the purchaser has forfeited such help by reason of some unconscionable act or default or [unless] specific performance would prejudice the rights of third parties.

(Gray and Symes, at 84-85.) The remedy of specific performance for such a contract also reflects the equitable maxim that equity deems as done that which ought to be done, so that it is appropriate to award equitable remedies to enforce the agreement for sale. Gray and Symes described (at 85) the interests of the vendor and purchaser under a contract for sale, using a diagram similar to the one below:

	Before contract	*Contract*	*Conveyance*
Law	Vendor (fee simple)	Vendor (fee simple)	Purchaser (fee simple)
Equity	Vendor (fee simple)	Purchaser (fee simple)	Purchaser (fee simple)

Note too that the decree of specific performance is one that "compels the defendant personally to do what he promised to do." See *Lubben v. Veltri & Sons Corp.* (1997), 32 OR (3d) 65 (CA), where the court decided that a decree of specific performance required a purchaser personally to close a transaction and that the purchaser could not avoid this obligation by assigning the purchaser's rights under the agreement to an impecunious numbered company. See generally G. Jones and W. Goodhart, *Specific Performance*, 2d ed. (London: Butterworths, 1996).

The purchaser's equitable interest in relation to an agreement for purchase and sale derives from the availability of the remedy of specific performance. Historically, the remedy of specific performance has almost always been available in relation to a contract concerning land, because land was regarded as having a unique character so that damages would not be appropriate—for example, see *Wroth v. Tyler*, [1974] 1 Ch. 30 (Ch.D). This principle was examined recently in the Supreme Court of Canada in *Semelhago v. Paramadevan*, [1996] 2 SCR 415, a case where a vendor reneged on an agreement for sale of a home in the context of rising prices in the residential house market. In effect, the vendor's failure to complete the transaction meant that the purchaser was unable to complete the purchase of a home, which was worth $325,000 at the date of trial, and for which he had agreed to pay $205,000 in the contract for sale. Thus, the value of the purchaser's loss was $120,000, and the purchaser sued the vendor successfully for $120,000 as damages in lieu of specific performance. At the same time, however, the purchaser's own home (which he had intended to sell to finance the purchase of the new home) had increased in value from $190,000 at the time of the agreement of purchase and sale to $300,000 by the time of the trial. The trial judge characterized the result as a "windfall" for the plaintiff. The vendor appealed to the Ontario Court of Appeal which made some adjustments but substantially confirmed the claim of damages as properly based on the value of a decree of specific performance to the plaintiff. On appeal to the Supreme Court of Canada, the appeal was dismissed. Sopinka J reviewed the principles concerning damages at common law, by contrast with damages as a substitute for specific performance and concluded that it was appropriate to use the date of trial to assess the purchaser's loss in this case.

However, Sopinka J also suggested (in arguably *obiter* comments at 428) that "it is no longer appropriate ... to maintain a distinction in the approach to specific perform-ance as between realty and personalty." As was suggested by the Newfoundland Court of Appeal in *Chaulk v. Fairview Construction Ltd.* (1977), 14 Nfld. and PEIR 13 (Nfld. CA), at 21:

> The question here is whether damages would have afforded [the plaintiff] an adequate remedy, and I have no doubt that they could, and would, have. There was nothing whatever unique or irreplaceable about the houses and lots bargained for. They were merely subdivision lots with houses, all of the same general design, built on them, which the respondent was purchasing for investment or re-sale purposes only ... . It would be quite different if we were dealing with a house or houses which were of a particular architectural design, or were situated in a particularly desirable location.

Do you agree with Sopinka J's conclusion that there is no longer any need to treat real property as almost always unique, by contrast with personal property, in terms of the availability of the remedy of specific performance? Should there be an obligation to mitigate in such circumstances? Note that, so long as a plaintiff is entitled to either specific performance or damages in lieu of specific performance, there is no impact on equitable interests arising out of a contract for sale. For an overview of these issues (before *Semelhago v. Paramadevan*), see J.J. Chapman, "A Stacked Deck: Specific Per-formance and the Real Estate Transaction" (1994), 16:3 *Advocates' Quarterly* 240. For an analysis of *Semelhago v. Paramadevan* and an earlier Ontario Court of Appeal decision, *306793 Ontario Ltd. in Trust v. Rimes* (1979), 100 DLR (4th) 350 (Ont. CA), see P.M. Perell, "Damages and Fluctuating Land Values" (1996), 18:4 *Advocates' Quarterly* 401.

As Gray and Symes explained, the creation of an equitable interest in land as a result of an enforceable contract for sale means that "the purchaser of land acquires not merely a *contractual* right but also a *proprietary* right." See Gray and Symes, at 86. What consequences flow from characterizing the purchaser's interest as an equitable propri-etary interest as of the date of the contract for sale? Consider a situation in which a vendor (V) and purchaser (P) sign an agreement of purchase and sale (valid and enforce-able in all respects). After signing the agreement of purchase and sale, but before closing, V executes and delivers a deed in favour of a third party (T) in relation to the same land that V agreed to sell to P in the above agreement of purchase and sale. Ignoring for the moment any special remedies that may be available to a purchaser in such a situation, what are the proprietary relationships among these parties? If P acquired an equitable interest at the time of the agreement of purchase and sale, and T subsequently acquired a legal estate, will P's equitable interest be enforceable against T's subsequent legal estate? Recall the discussion in chapter 3 about the enforceability of equitable interests against everyone except a *bona fide* purchaser for value of the legal estate without notice. How should the purchaser with an agreement of purchase and sale ensure that there is notice of this interest to any subsequent third party dealing with the land? If the purchaser's interest under the agreement of purchase and sale were contractual, rather than propri-etary, could the purchaser bring an action against the third party directly?

A Valid Contract

As *Lysaght v. Edwards* indicated, an agreement of purchase and sale creates an equitable interest in the purchaser if there is a "valid contract" that is capable of specific performance. Thus, it is necessary for the contract for sale to meet the usual requirements for a valid contract, including offer, acceptance, and consideration. Moreover, since the equitable relationship depends on the availability of the remedy of specific performance, there is a need for the contract to specify the basic matters of agreement, including a description of the property, identification of the parties to the contract, and definition of the purchase price so that the decree of specific performance results in a contract with defined terms.

The requirement of defined terms concerning the property, the parties, and the price was one of the issues in *Walsh v. Lonsdale*, [1882] 21 Ch.D 9 (CA). In that case, the court considered an agreement for a lease of a weaving shed known as Providence Mill, and whether it was sufficiently detailed to permit the court to consider the remedy of specific performance. The agreement for a lease, like a contract for the sale of land, evidenced the parties' agreement to execute a leasehold conveyance sometime later. Their agreement for a lease set out a number of matters on which the parties were agreed, including the lessee's undertaking that after the first year of the lease, the lessee would run not less than 540 looms a year, and that the rent would be £1 10s per loom. The agreement also stated that the lease itself would be prepared by the solicitor for the lessor and would contain other covenants "as are usually inserted in leases of a similar nature, and particularly those inserted in a lease of the Newfield Mills, Darwen." The Newfield Mills lease included a clause that the rent was payable in advance on May 1, each year.

In litigation to define the parties' obligations, one issue facing the court was whether it was possible to characterize the agreement for a lease as a valid and enforceable agreement on the basis that there was sufficient certainty of its terms. Clearly, there was no doubt as to the identity of the parties or the property subject to the lease. The issue was whether it was possible to define the rent precisely enough to grant specific performance. Since the Newfield Mills lease required payment of rent in advance, while the agreement for a lease stated that the amount of rent payable was dependent on the number of looms in use each year (an amount that could not be determined until the end of each year), this issue might well have been regarded as an insuperable problem for purposes of the remedy of specific performance. Can you suggest how the amount of rent might be defined in this situation so that the agreement is "a valid contract" as defined in *Lysaght v. Edwards*?

On appeal, Jessel MR (at 16) held that it was necessary for the lessee to have a minimum of 540 looms, and thus "the stipulation as to paying rent beforehand can apply to that £810 a year (540 looms at £1 10s), and the covenants and provisions in the lease of the Newfield Mills, Darwen, could be made applicable to this minimum rent." In *Walsh v. Lonsdale*, the court was considering an appeal from an order that the lessee pay money into court in relation to an order for an injunction, so the case did not involve a final determination on the issue of the rent payable. Nonetheless, it is a good illustration of the extent to which the court may be prepared to exercise discretion to find the existence of "a valid contract."

The Statute of Frauds and Contracts for Sale

In addition to the requirements for a valid contract noted by Jessel MR in *Lysaght v. Edwards*, a contract to transfer an interest in land must meet the requirements of s. 4 of the Statute of Frauds, 1677. As noted above, the Statute of Frauds defines the requirements for the creation and transfer of freehold and leasehold estates. In addition, the Statute of Frauds includes provisions for contractual agreements about land. Section 4 states:

> No action shall be brought whereby to charge any executor or administrator upon any special promise to answer damages out of his own estate, or whereby to charge any person upon any special promise to answer for the debt, default or miscarriage of any other person, or to charge any person upon any contract or sale of lands, tenements or hereditaments, or any interest in or concerning them, or upon any agreement that is not to be performed within the space of one year from the making thereof, unless the agreement upon which the action is brought, or some memorandum or note thereof is in writing and signed by the party to be charged therewith or some person thereunto by him lawfully authorized.

(RSO 1990, c. S.19; RSNB 1973, c. S-14; RSNS 1989, c. 442; RSPEI 1988, c. S-6; and 29 Car II, c. 3 (Nfld.).)

Section 4 of the Statute of Frauds thus requires a contract for the sale of land, or any interest in or concerning it, to be evidenced by "a memorandum or note ... in writing" that is "signed by the party to be charged" with contractual responsibility. Both these requirements have been the subject of litigation, particularly in a context of rising land prices. For example, consider the situation of a vendor who orally accepts an offer from a purchaser, and then before this purchaser can deliver an offer in writing, the vendor "signs back" a written offer with a higher purchase price from a second purchaser. Why does the Statute of Frauds protect the vendor from liability to the first purchaser in this situation? Would the position of the first purchaser be improved if he or she had written out and signed an offer on a piece of paper and delivered it to the vendor, pending the formal written offer of purchase? Whose signature is needed in this example to make the agreement enforceable pursuant to the Statute of Frauds? Consider also situations where a purchaser may be able to avoid a conveyance if the vendor has signed a contract for sale and the purchaser has not yet done so. How might such a situation occur?

The problem of vendors negotiating with multiple purchasers at the same time to obtain the highest sale price, and using the Statute of Frauds to avoid the consequences of their oral agreements, has been referred to in England as "gazumping." Partly in an effort to prevent the Statute of Frauds from being used for these somewhat shady dealings, the English Court of Appeal construed a solicitor's letter as meeting the requirements of the Statute when the letter contained the terms of the proposed agreement, but also expressed the view that the letter was "subject to contract"—*Law v. Jones*, [1974] Ch. 112 (CA). However, this decision substantially altered usual conveyancing practices to such an extent that the same court (differently constituted) decided in *Tiverton Estates Ltd. v. Wearwell Ltd.*, [1975] Ch. 146 (CA) that the insertion of the phrase "subject to contract" prevented a written agreement from meeting the requirements of s. 4 of the Statute. In *Tiverton*, Lord Denning stated (at 154) that the analysis in *Law v. Jones* "virtually repealed the Statute of

Frauds." The English Law Commission approved the approach in *Tiverton*. See Law Commission, "Report on 'Subject to Contract' Agreements" (Law Comm. no. 65, January 1975). To what extent do you agree with Lord Denning's assessment of the impact of *Law v. Jones*? Does Lord Denning's approach focus on the protection of consumers or the preservation of lawyers' conveyancing practices?

Consider a situation in which a corporation entered into an agreement of purchase and sale for land in Peterborough, and, as part of the purchase price, agreed to give back a second mortgage of $70,000. The agreement of purchase and sale, which provided that the mortgage would be guaranteed by W and T, was signed on behalf of the corporation by W. T did not sign the agreement of purchase and sale. The transaction was completed and the corporation obtained legal title. The corporation also gave back the mortgage, and it was executed by both W and T as officers of the corporation. In addition, both W and T signed as guarantors of the mortgage. A subsequent agreement to extend the mortgage was also signed by W and T as officers of the corporation and as guarantors. The mortgage went into default, and there were a number of financial problems. When T was sued on the guarantee, he pleaded the Statute of Frauds because he had not signed the agreement of purchase and sale, and because (as he argued) his signature on the mortgage above the word "guarantor" did not meet the requirements of s. 4 of the Statute. How should T's claim be resolved? Can the court look at the two documents (the agreement of purchase and sale, and the mortgage) together? If the court focuses solely on the mortgage, is T's signature above the word "guarantor" sufficient to invoke the Statute of Frauds? See *Connelly v. 904 Water Street Ontario Ltd.* (1994), 42 RPR (2d) 267 (Ont. CJ), where the court held that the agreement of purchase and sale and the mortgage document could be looked at together to satisfy s. 4 of the Statute of Frauds. As well, the mortgage document (and the use of the word "guarantor" on it) was held to be sufficient to satisfy the statutory requirements. See also *Grime v. Bartholomew*, [1972] 2 NSWLR 827 (SC Eq. Div.), where an incomplete receipt signed by the vendor and the deposit cheque of the purchaser were read together to constitute the necessary memorandum of the agreement of purchase and sale. For a case in which the court concluded that the property was sufficiently defined in a condominium development, see *Ryan v. Cam-Valley Developments Ltd.* (1993), 15 OR (3d) 24 (Gen. Div.).

Note that equity has permitted the enforcement of oral contracts concerning land on the basis of the equitable doctrine of part performance, even though there has been no compliance with the Statute of Frauds. Part performance is addressed in more detail below.

The "Fusion" of Law and Equity: Walsh v. Lonsdale

The impact of an agreement to lease on the parties' remedies *inter se* is well illustrated by *Walsh v. Lonsdale*, discussed above. Like *Lysaght v. Edwards*, this case was also decided shortly after the fusion of the courts of law and equity in England. As a result, it provides a good illustration of the procedural efficiency of a single court administering principles of both law and equity in interpreting an agreement to lease. As explained above, the lessor agreed in writing to lease a mill to the tenant at a rent based on the number of looms run annually. In addition to specifying some terms in their agreement for a lease, the parties also agreed to incorporate clauses contained in another lease, the Newfield Mills lease. According to the Newfield Mills lease, the tenant was obliged to pay rent in advance. Although the parties never executed a deed of lease, the tenant went into possession and paid rent. As a tenant with an oral lease who paid rent that was accepted by the lessor, the common law regarded the tenant as holding a periodic tenancy—that is, a tenancy defined by the period of the rental payment, annual in this case. The tenant was thus a yearly tenant at law.

When the lessor subsequently demanded rent in advance (presumably as a result of the clause in the Newfield Mills lease that was to be incorporated in the deed of lease), the tenant refused. Accordingly, the lessor exercised the remedy of distress, a remedy still available (mainly to commercial tenants) in Canada that permits a lessor to seize goods belonging to a tenant and to sell them to satisy rent payments in arrears. The tenant claimed that he had no obligation to pay rent in advance, since he was in possession under an oral lease only, and the formal lease, which included the requirement to pay rent in advance, had never been executed. By contrast, the lessor relied on the agreement to lease as an agreement capable of specific performance, so that the parties had equitable interests as if the deed of lease containing the requirement to pay rent in advance had been executed. At trial, Fry J ordered the tenant to pay into court the whole sum claimed as rent (including rent in advance and rent owing to date) in return for the lessor's cessation of his distress against the tenant. On appeal, Jessel MR stated (at 14):

> It is not necessary on the present occasion to decide finally what the rights of the parties are. If the Court sees that there is a fair question to be decided it will take security so that the party who ultimately succeeds may be in the right position. The question is one of some nicety. There is an agreement for a lease under which possession has been given. Now since the *Judicature Act* the possession is held under the agreement. There are not two estates as there were formerly, one estate at common law by reason of the payment of the rent from year to year, and an estate in equity under the agreement. There is only one Court, and the equity rules prevail in it. The tenant holds under an agreement for a lease. He holds, therefore, under the same terms in equity as if a lease had been granted, it being a case in which both parties admit that relief is capable of being given by specific performance. That being so, he cannot complain of the exercise by the landlord of the same rights as the landlord would have had if a lease had been granted. On the other hand, he is protected in the same way as if a lease had been granted; he cannot be turned out by six months' notice as a tenant from year to year. He has a right to say, "I have a lease in equity, and you can only re-enter if I have committed such a breach of covenant as would if a lease had been granted have entitled you to re-enter according to the terms of a proper proviso for re-entry." That being so, it appears to me that being a lessee in equity he cannot complain of the exercise of the right of distress merely because the actual parchment has not been signed and sealed.
>
> The next question is, how ought the lease to be drawn? And that is a question of some nicety. I do not wish now finally to decide it, and on an application of this kind it is not necessary to do so, but I think the Court is bound to say what its present opinion is, because that is material on the question of what ought to be done until the trial. The whole difficulty arises from a single clause. Instead of taking the trouble to state in detail what covenants the lease was to contain they have adopted this short form. ...
>
> When we look at the lease of the Newfield Mills we find that it is a lease at a rent certain payable beforehand, and the question is how far that provision can be made

applicable to the present very peculiar agreement. That agreement provides that the lessor at his own expense is to find steam power for driving and running the machinery, and that the rent is to be £2 10s. for every loom run, but for the first year the lessee is not to run less than 300, and afterwards not less than 540 looms. Then there is a proviso that the lessee is to have the right, whenever he shall think fit, to find the steam power for himself, and in that case his rent is to be 30s. [£1 10s] per loom. There is a further proviso that until the lessee shall find the steam power the engine-house, boiler-house, mechanics' shop, stables, and yard adjoining thereto shall be excluded from the demise. As I read that it means that when the lessee once elects to provide his own steam power, the excepted particulars are included in the demise, and then the lessor is no longer bound to find the steam power because he has demised the very thing that produces the steam power, and the lessee is now the lessee of the engine-house, and the rest, and has to find steam power for himself. The lessee has exercised the option to find his own steam power, and the result is that now he is only liable to pay 30s. per loom.

Now the lessee agrees to run not less than 540 looms, and the next question is, whether in drawing the lease a dead or minimum rent ought to be reserved for 540 looms, or is it to be left on covenant. My present opinion is that there ought to be a dead rent. There is no longer any obligation on the lessor to find the steam power; and it appears to me, therefore, that it would be a right thing to reserve in the lease a dead rent of £810, being at the rate of 30s. a loom for 540 looms. If that is so, the stipulation as to paying rent beforehand can apply to that £810 a year, and the covenants and provisions in the lease of the Newfield Mills, Darwen, could be made applicable to this minimum rent. Therefore it is my present opinion, though I do not give it as a final opinion, that the rent is payable beforehand to the extent of £810.

The result, therefore, will be to vary the order of the Court below by making the sum to be paid into Court £810 instead of £1005 14s. The plaintiff will pay the costs of the appeal.

COTTON LJ: I am of the same opinion. The question as to whether the defendant was right in putting in this distress must depend upon questions which have to be decided at the hearing of the cause, and the only question we have now to consider is what is right to be done between the parties for the purpose of keeping things *in statu quo*, and preserving their rights until the questions between them can be decided.

This landlord has put in a distress. He is right if the lease under which the tenant must be taken to be holding this land or premises would give him rent beforehand. This is not the time for finally deciding whether he is entitled to any and to what rent payable beforehand, but the question before us is whether we are now at once to deprive the landlord of any security which he has in his hands for the payment of his rent? In my opinion we ought not. Of course, before allowing the landlord to retain the security given by the distress we must be satisfied that there is a *prima facie* case in his favour, and in my opinion there is. It would be wrong for us absolutely to decide now how this lease should be framed, for there are many matters which would require consideration, one clause may depend on another, and the question how one clause is to be dealt with may affect the other provisions in the lease. But it is my present opinion that there ought to be reserved as dead-rent a rent which will correspond to the minimum number of looms which the Plaintiff is to run in any particular year, and after the first year it is to be always 540.

If, then, there is to be a dead-rent, the provision in the lease of the 1st of May that the rent thereby reserved shall be beforehand rent can be made applicable to the present tenancy by making it apply to the dead or fixed rent of £810 a year, leaving the payment of the remaining sum, if any, which is to be paid by the tenant to be enforced by the landlord under the covenants when it is ascertained how many looms the tenant has run.

The court concluded that the parties' rights should be determined *as if* there had been specific performance of the agreement to lease. Why did this conclusion result in the tenant owing rent in advance? Did the tenant also benefit from the court's characterization of the agreement to lease as one that created rights in equity for the lessor and the tenant? What advantage did the tenant gain from characterizing the agreement *as if* a lease had been executed? In thinking about this question, it is important to note that, as a yearly tenant with an oral lease, the tenant could have been evicted by the lessor on six months' notice. Was the tenant's position under the agreement preferable? Why? For a comprehensive analysis of the principles in *Walsh v. Lonsdale*, see S. Gardner, "Equity, Estate Contracts and the Judicature Acts: *Walsh v. Lonsdale* Revisited" (1987), 7 *Oxford Journal of Legal Studies* 60.

In *Walsh v. Lonsdale*, the court treated the tenant and the lessor *as if* they had executed the lease. Does this mean that an agreement for a lease is always as good as a lease? Recall that an agreement will create equitable proprietary interests only if it is a valid contract with terms that are sufficiently certain so that specific performance is available. In addition, in some cases, an equitable remedy may be denied if the plaintiff is guilty of conduct that makes an equitable remedy inappropriate. For example, in *Cornish v. Brook Green Laundry Ltd.*, [1959] 1 QB 394 (CA), the English Court of Appeal refused to recognize an equitable interest where the tenant had failed to carry out repairs that were required, pursuant to the agreement, to be completed before the formal lease was executed. Finally, as illustrated above, recall that an equitable interest may be defeated by a *bona fide* purchaser for value without notice.

Equity and Part Performance: Beyond the Statute of Frauds

The equitable doctrine of part performance may make enforceable a contract for the sale of land even if the contract does not meet the requirements of s. 4 of the Statute of Frauds. As explained by Megarry and Wade, the possibility that the Statute of Frauds might itself be used to foster inequity resulted in the development of enforceability based on part performance of an oral contract:

> The contract will be unenforceable by action unless there is either a sufficient memorandum in writing or a sufficient act of part performance. This branch of the law dates from the Statute of Frauds, 1677, the object of which was to prevent fraud and perjury, and to make it impossible for certain contracts to be alleged upon purely oral testimony by witnesses who might be perjuring themselves. The design of the statutory provision was to prevent any legal action unless the defendant had signed some paper containing the terms of the contract. The doctrine of part performance, on the other hand, was an invention of equity which created in effect an important exception to the statute.

(Megarry and Wade, 3d ed., at 553-54.) What kinds of situations might require the intervention of equity? Consider, for example, a situation in which a vendor makes an oral agreement with a purchaser to sell a parcel of land and, before the execution of the deed, the purchaser pays for improvements to the parcel. In doing so, the purchaser has relied on the vendor's oral promise and has enriched the vendor. If the vendor subsequently refuses to execute a deed, relying on the Statute of Frauds, on what basis can the purchaser claim that equity should intervene?

The principles of part performance were fully defined in a 19th-century case, *Maddison v. Alderson* (1883), 8 App. Cas. 467 (CA). A later case referred to *Maddison v. Alderson* as having stated the principle that

> in a suit founded on part performance of a parol contract relating to land the defendant
> is really charged "upon the equities resulting from the acts done in execution of the
> contract, and not (within the meaning of the Statute) upon the contract itself." It is clear
> from what the learned Lord Chancellor says [in *Maddison*] that in such a case the Court
> is not asked to give a better remedy in aid of a legal right, based on the contract, but is
> called upon to enforce an equity (independent of the Statute ...) which has arisen by
> force of circumstances subsequent to the contract itself, namely by acts of part
> performance sufficient to attract the equitable jurisdiction of the Court. ... [The] proper
> course in such a proceeding is that of "seeking to establish primarily such a performance
> as must necessarily imply the existence of the contract, and then proceeding to ascertain
> its terms." ... No harm can arise from reversing that order as a matter of convenience in
> taking evidence, ... [b]ut if the terms of the oral bargain are first ascertained and then
> the alleged acts of part performance are judged of merely by their consistency with and
> applicability to that bargain, grievous error may result.

(*McBride v. Sandland* (1918), 25 CLR 69, at 77.) Note that the principle of part performance is primarily based on the inequity arising out of the plaintiff's reliance on an oral promise, and that it is necessary, as a matter of evidence, to show the reliance first and then the existence of the terms of the promise that resulted in the plaintiff's actions.

The Supreme Court of Canada considered the elements of part performance in *Deglman v. Guaranty Trust Co. of Canada*, [1954] SCR 725 (indexed as *Deglman v. Brunet Estate*). Quoting from *Maddison v. Alderson*, Cartwright J stated (at 734) that "the part performance relied upon must be unequivocally referable to the contract asserted. The acts performed must speak for themselves, and must point unmistakeably to a contract affecting the ownership or the tenure of the land and to nothing else." These principles were reconsidered in *Taylor v. Rawana* (1990), 74 OR (2d) 357 (HCJ). In *Taylor*, a 33-year-old married man applied for a declaration of an interest in land owned by the defendants, stating that the defendant had agreed to sell the land to the plaintiff for $56,000 with a downpayment of 10 percent payable over two years. The plaintiff moved in and undertook repairs to the building and surrounding land. Although the plaintiff claimed that the defendant had signed an agreement incorporating these terms, he said that the defendant had retained the only copy of the agreement. The defendant stated that the plaintiff was only a tenant and that, while there had been some discussions about a sale, the price was higher and the time-frame for submitting the downpayment was only six months. The defendant was a friend of the parents of the plaintiff.

In examining the evidence, the court found (at 359-60) that the plaintiff was more credible than the defendant. The judge also found that an agreement existed and that there were numerous actions on the part of the plaintiff that constituted "performance" of the agreement. The court held (at 362-64) that the situation in *Taylor* clearly satisfied the principles established in *Deglman*: (1) the performance must be "referable to the contract"; (2) the acts relied on to establish part performance must have been performed by the plaintiff, not the defendant; (3) the contract must be "one which, if it were properly evidenced by writing, would have been specifically enforceable"; and (4) there must be "clear and proper evidence, either oral or written, of the existence of a contract." As a result, the court in *Taylor* ordered a sale to the plaintiff at the price of $56,000.

In examining the case that follows, consider how the evidence of part performance was presented by the plaintiff and the extent to which the emphasis in the reasoning focuses on evidence of an agreement or on the inequity resulting from the plaintiff's reliance. Which approach is more consistent with the principles of part performance?

Starlite Variety Stores Ltd. v. Cloverlawn Investments Ltd.
(1979), 92 DLR (3d) 270 (Ont. HCJ), aff'd. 106 DLR (3d) 384 (Ont. CA)

STARK J: This is an action for specific performance of a contract, or in the alternative for damages for breach of an agreement, brought by the plaintiff, called herein Starlite, against the defendant, referred to herein as Cloverlawn. The action against Mac's Convenience Stores Limited was discontinued.

Starlite is the operator of a chain of small variety stores, chiefly in Windsor and London, Ontario. It selects sites which are commercially suitable, leases the location, and then sublets the property on a franchise basis, to a tenant who uses the name and the goodwill, and the buying power of Starlite, in return paying to Starlite a royalty on gross sales, usually 2%. The tenants are known as franchisees.

The defendant Cloverlawn is a private company, which buys commercial land, builds shopping plazas, rents the stores in the plazas, and if required provides financing.

Among the plazas owned and operated by Cloverlawn was one situated at the corner of Grand Marais and Longfellow, in the City of Windsor. About 6,000 sq. ft. of this property was available for expansion and Cloverlawn decided to use this space if suitable franchisees could be obtained. Cloverlawn had frequently used the services of James Morrow, a well-known real estate salesman in Windsor, who had found commercial locations and franchisees for them, from time to time. Morrow was entrusted with a master key to all the plazas, checked on stores, sometimes collected rents, and investigated complaints. It was Morrow who in 1974 acted on the purchase by Cloverlawn of the land used by this plaza. Three years later, Morrow suggested that Cloverlawn build an addition to their plaza. Morrow found that a free-standing building of some 6,000 sq. ft. could be erected. The area was considered desirable, since it is surrounded by an upper middle class population and available commercial property was extremely limited.

Cloverlawn decided to proceed with the expansion. However, Cloverlawn told Morrow they would not commence construction until a certain 1,800-sq. ft. area adjacent to a sporting goods store in the new section had been leased.

These events occurred in the spring of 1977. In April of that year, Morrow approached Ray Myers, brother of Don Myers, who was the sole owner of Starlite. Ray Myers was the operation manager of his brother's company, and his duties consisted of general store supervision, promotion, office management and similar functions. Ray expressed great interest in the proposed location and told Morrow a suitable franchisee would have to be found. While the search for the franchisee was being conducted by Ray, Morrow suggested that his own wife would be qualified. Mrs. Morrow had at one time operated a Mac's variety store. The proposal was accepted.

In view of Morrow's close relationship with Cloverlawn, and in view of his own personal involvement through his wife, it was agreed that Morrow would do the negotiating with Cloverlawn's representative, Frank D'Amico as to rent and terms. According to the evidence of Ray Myers and Morrow, which appears to have been grudgingly accepted by D'Amico in his evidence, a draft agreement on Cloverlawn's standard agreement to lease forms was drawn up, embodying the verbal terms they had discussed and presented to Morrow by D'Amico. The two men then went to Ray Myers' office. It was at this meeting that, according to Morrow, "Frank shook hands with Ray and said 'you've got a deal.' Then we had a liquid lunch." The agreement was then forwarded to Don Myers, for execution by Starlite, and was returned to the defendant with a deposit cheque as required by the agreement. The offer to lease agreement, ex. 1, was retained but was never executed by Cloverlawn.

During the course of the trial, considerable criticism was directed to Morrow, on the ground that his dealings constituted a conflict of interests. But I consider this criticism unjustified. His personal interest in the deal, through his wife, was well known to all concerned. He wanted to obtain the best arrangements he could for Starlite and for his wife, and since he would not be entitled to a real estate agent's fee, he asked for an equivalent amount by way of reduction from the rent, and this was accepted. It was evident that Cloverlawn was anxious to retain Morrow's goodwill, in view of the many services he had rendered in the past.

Construction on the addition to the plaza was now commenced. A well-known builder, one John Drazic, was asked to tender and in due course his bid was accepted. Construction began early in June of 1977. The store to be occupied by Starlite was designated on the plans as store no. 3. On August 16th, Ray Myers produced a sketch, known as a vellum drawing, which in effect provided for changes in the store front and in the location of certain electric conduits. These changes were made. Other changes were later requested. Drazic contacted Bairstow, an employee of Cloverlawn's who was supervising construction, and he gave verbal approval of the changes, and this approval was later confirmed in writing by Drazic, although Bairstow's letter of acceptance did not arrive until September 27th. The witness Drazic, whose records were very complete, testified that at all times he was given the impression from Bairstow and from other Cloverlawn employees that the tenant of store no. 3 was to be Starlite. The cost of the last-mentioned changes was $851.50. Certain additional changes had been requested but were refused by Cloverlawn.

Throughout the construction period, Starlite was busily engaged in preparing for the occupancy of the new store. They attended at the site and selected their colours. Ray Myers was at the location constantly, observing and pressing for progress. On June 16th,

Starlite ordered their new advertising signs for the store, at a price of $1,540.80. On August 15th, Starlite ordered shelving for the new store at a cost of $3,697.74.

Viewing the evidence as a whole, it seems clear that the various managers of departments at Cloverlawn, acted on the understanding that a deal had been completed, with the single exception of Cloverlawn's president, Kenneth McGowen. Thus, Bairstow, the property manager, authorized structural changes. D'Amico was Cloverlawn's representative who negotiated the deal, just as he had previously negotiated deals on behalf of his company. I accept the evidence of Morrow and Myers that no suggestion was ever made to either of them that the deal as negotiated with D'Amico was conditional upon formal execution by the company.

The president of Cloverlawn, McGowen, admitted that on August 25th he accepted a better rental offer which he received from Mac's Convenience Stores Limited. He contended that his delay in formal acceptance of the Starlite deal was because of his dissatisfaction with Don Myers' handling of certain rental arrears on another property, leased by another company owned by Myers. McGowen said that he instructed D'Amico to get that settled and then he would consider the proposed lease. He also wanted Myers to take over a certain vacant store in another plaza. Nevertheless, he admitted that he authorized Bairstow to make the specific changes requested by Starlite which I have earlier described. He had also approved of the inclusion of air conditioning for store no. 3, a feature not ordinarily provided for tenants except when specially negotiated. Moreover, it also appeared from the evidence that one of McGowen's senior officers had already approved of a settlement of the rental arrears which had loomed large in persuading McGowen to delay his acceptance of the disputed deal. McGowen admitted his knowledge of the franchise deal with Mrs. Morrow. He said he felt sorry for Morrow but had no regrets for Starlite.

Two defences are raised by Cloverlawn. The first is that no agreement was ever reached between the parties, because the offer to lease was never formally accepted. The second defence is reliance on the *Statute of Frauds*, RSO 1970, c. 444.

In my view, a verbal agreement was in fact reached between the three men, Morrow, D'Amico and Ray Myers, subsequently accepted by Don Myers. The draft memorandum on Cloverlawn's standard forms, embodied certainly the principal points of agreement; and D'Amico's acting as representative of the defendant company never suggested that any formal or different kind of acceptance would be required. The conduct of all parties throughout was consistent with the completion of the deal and inconsistent with an unaccepted unilateral offer. I therefore reject that defence.

I turn now to the alleged failure to comply with the *Statute of Frauds*. Section 4 reads as follows:

> 4. No action shall be brought whereby to charge any executor or administrator upon any special promise to answer damages out of his own estate, or whereby to charge any person upon any special promise to answer for the debt, default or miscarriage of any other person, or to charge any person upon any agreement made upon consideration of marriage, or upon any contract or sale of lands, tenements or hereditaments, or any interest in or concerning them, or upon any agreement that is not to be performed within the space of one year from the making thereof, unless the agreement upon which the

action is brought, or some memorandum or note thereof is in writing and signed by the party to be charged therewith or some person thereunto by him lawfully authorized.

To the defendants' reliance on this section, the plaintiff contends that in the case at bar, there is an oral agreement, that ex. 1 contains the terms of the oral agreement, and that the document does not require an actual signature. It is argued that the word "signature" in the statute has been very loosely interpreted. Thus, in 1862, Blackburn J, in *Durrell v. Evans* (1862), 1 H & C 174 at p. 191, 158 ER 848, said:

> If the matter were *res integra*, I should doubt whether a name printed or written at the head of a bill of parcels was such a signature as the statute contemplated; but it is now too late to discuss that question. If the name of the party to be charged is printed or written on a document, intended to be a memorandum of the contract, either by himself or his authorized agent, it is his signature, whether it is at the beginning, or middle, or foot of the document.

Again, in the English case of *Leeman v. Stocks*, [1951] 1 Ch. 941, there is provided a more modern example of flexible interpretation. In that case the defendant had in- structed an auctioneer to offer his house for sale. Before the sale the auctioneer partially filled in a printed form or agreement of sale by inserting the tenant's name as vendor, and the date fixed for completion. The plaintiff was the highest bidder, and after the sale the auctioneer inserted in the form the plaintiff's name as purchaser, the price and a description of the premises. The plaintiff signed the form. The defendant then refused to carry out the contract and the plaintiff sued for specific performance. The defendant pleaded failure to satisfy s. 40(1) of the *Law of Property Act, 1925* [the equivalent of s. 4 of the Statute of Frauds] and in particular that he had never signed any document. It was held that there was a sufficient memorandum to satisfy the statute and that the defendant was liable. It was true that he had not "signed" it in the ordinary sense of the word. But his agent, acting with his authority, had inserted his name as vendor into the printed form, and this form was clearly designed to constitute the final written record of the contract made between the parties. However, I am not satisfied that the law in Ontario has gone this far. I therefore do not choose to base my decision on this argument.

The plaintiff contends further, that whether there was a verbal acceptance of the deal or not, there was an acceptance by conduct, by the alterations of the plans to suit the plaintiff's needs, by a continuing series of acts and of acquiescences to such an extent that any reasonable man would consider the deal accepted. The plaintiff points to the decision of the Manitoba Court of Appeal in *Greenberg v. Manitoba Hudson-Essex Ltd.*, [1934] 1 WWR 790, where it was held that if a person to whom an offer is made so conducts himself that a reasonable man would believe that he is accepting that offer, and the offeror acts upon that belief, the offeree will be held to have accepted the offer and therefore to have contracted on the terms proposed. However, that case dealt with the sale of an automobile, and does not in my view afford a sufficient answer to the defence raised by the *Statute of Frauds*, where the selling or leasing of real estate is concerned.

Finally, there is the doctrine of part performance. The essential elements required to establish the part performance which will exclude the statute are listed in 8 Hals., 3d ed., p. 110, para. 190, as follows:

... (1) the acts of part performance must be such as not only to be referable to a contract such as that alleged, but to be referable to no other title; (2) they must be such as to render it a fraud in the defendant to take advantage of the contract not being in writing; (3) the contract to which they refer must be such as in its own nature is enforceable by the court; (4) there must be proper parol evidence of the contract which is let in by the acts of part performance.

The part performance, in order to take the case out of the operation of the statute, must be by the person seeking to enforce the parol agreement.

The leading Canadian authority is the decision of the Supreme Court of Canada in *Deglman v. Guaranty Trust Co. of Canada et al.*, [1954] SCR 725, [1954] 3 DLR 785, where the above principles are followed. That case made it clear that the mere payment of money, as occurred in the case at bar in the payment of the two deposit cheques, will not qualify as part performance. In view of the recent English decision in *Steadman v. Steadman*, [1974] 2 All ER 977, a case which reached the House of Lords, that may no longer be the fixed rule in England; and it seems logical that money clearly referable to the specific contract should no longer be treated as equivocal. However, I am bound by the *Deglman* decision.

As I have indicated there are acts of part performance on the part of Starlite which, in my view, meet the requirements of the common law so as to relieve the burden imposed by the *Statute of Frauds*. The preparation by the plaintiff of the plans to meet its peculiar requirements, the conduct of the plaintiff throughout the whole period of construction, the actions by the plaintiff in the preparation of its advertising signs and the shelving for its products, and the payment of various expenses concerned with these matters, all these are acts of part performance which meet the law's requirements. Accordingly, I hold that the agreement to lease is enforceable, and that the defendant breached the agreement, and that the plaintiff is entitled to damages in lieu of specific performance, which latter remedy is no longer available.

The matter of damages in a case of this kind is one which raises great difficulties. The plaintiff produced figures to show the revenue it receives from various other franchised stores in Windsor. This revenue in each case is based on 2% of the gross sales. The figures filed vary in amount from an annual volume of $576,000 to a low of $240,000. Thus, even if the low figure of $240,000 were accepted an annual income of about $5,000 continuing for the lease term of 10 years, would result in a claim for lost income of some $50,000. But there are many important contingencies before such a figure could be accepted. It was admitted that not all franchise stores succeed. Some fail in their attempts. The success of any new store is unpredictable. Much depends on the initiative and capabilities of the franchisee. Much depends on population changes and traffic conditions. Allowance must be made for expenses incurred by Starlite in the collection of its royalties and in the supervision of its franchises. It would be unrealistic not to discount any suggested figures by at least 50%.

One possible measure of the value to Starlite of the loss of the deal, is provided by the higher rental figures which Mac's Convenience Stores Limited undertook in their lease to pay. Exhibit 1 indicates that the total rent to be paid by Starlite for the 10-year period is $110,700. But the rent called for in Mac's Convenience Stores Limited lease, ex. 20, for the 10-year period is fixed at $126,000. Thus, it might be argued that Starlite, by the loss of its contract, has forfeited a property which was worth $16,000 more, over the 10-year period than they were required to pay under their agreement.

Under the above circumstances, and since in my view the plaintiff is clearly entitled to some relief by way of damages, even though those damages are ephemeral and difficult to determine, I would fix the amount to which the plaintiff is entitled for breach of contract at $20,000, as being a not unreasonable estimate of the damages he has suffered. The deposit payments of $790 should be returned to the plaintiff. I do not allow interest on that amount. Judgment for the plaintiff therefore should issue in the sum of $20,790 plus the costs of this action.

Judgment for plaintiff.

Discussion Notes

The Principles of Part Performance

In *Starlite*, the court concluded that all the elements were present for the application of part performance. Note that the first requirement is that the performance must be referable to the alleged contract. This requirement means that the court must be satisfied that the basic terms of the agreement can be determined with sufficient precision to enforce the parties' agreement. Evidence of reliance alone is not sufficient; there must be an agreement with identifiable terms to which the acts of reliance are referable. In *Britain v. Rossiter*, [1879] 11 QBD 123 (CA), it was held that the doctrine of part performance applies only to contracts in respect of which specific performance can be ordered. Similarly, in *Taylor v. Rawana* (1990), 74 OR (2d) 357 (HCJ), discussed above (just before *Starlite*), the court noted (at 362) that it is necessary to find "acts done in performance" of a contract, and that "acts done in preparation" are not sufficient. The court suggested that "acts done in preparation" might include instructing a surveyor to prepare a valuation, or a solicitor to prepare a conveyance. What acts on the part of Starlite were relied on by the court to conclude that there were acts of part performance? Examine these actions carefully—were all of them "acts of part performance"? Are there any acts that might better be characterized as "acts of preparation"?

In *Starlite*, the court considered a number of arguments submitted by the plaintiff in response to the defendant's reliance on the Statute of Frauds—for example, that the requirements of the Statute had been met by the signature of the defendant company. Why was this argument rejected? Are there reasons of policy for accepting the approach of cases such as *Leeman v. Stocks*, [1951] 1 Ch. 941 (Ch.D) in relation to corporate "signatures" in order to comply with the Statute of Frauds in England, now contained in the Law of Property Act, 1925, s. 40(1)? Would it have been preferable to adopt this approach in *Starlite*?

Why did the court reject the approach in *Greenberg v. Manitoba Hudson-Essex Ltd.*, [1934] 1 WWR 790 (CA)? For a case in which the principles of the Statute of Frauds and of part performance were reviewed, see *Sansalone v. Sansalone* (1997), 34 OR (3d) 102 (Gen. Div.)

Acts of Part Performance, the Contract, and the Payment of Money:
Deglman v. Guaranty Trust Co. of Canada

As the court explained in *Starlite*, the Supreme Court of Canada held in *Deglman v. Guaranty Trust Co. of Canada*, [1954] SCR 725 that the mere payment of money does not qualify as part performance. As well, quoting again from *Maddison v. Alderson*, the court stated (at 733) that the acts of part performance must be "unequivocally, and in their own nature, referable to some such agreement as that alleged." By contrast, the decision of the English House of Lords in *Steadman v. Steadman*, [1974] 2 All ER 977 (HL) suggested (at 982) that it is sufficient for the acts of part performance to point, on a balance of probabilities, to *some* contract that is consistent with the alleged contract. The *Steadman* decision also indicated that, taking into account all the circumstances of a case, the payment of money might in itself amount to part performance under the doctrine. In *Starlite*, the court stated that it was bound by the *Deglman* decision. Can you identify the acts that were "unequivocally referable" to the agreement alleged by the plaintiff? What actions, in addition to the payment of money by the plaintiff, were relied on as sufficient acts of part performance?

The different approaches of *Deglman* and *Steadman* were considered in *Alvi v. Lal* (1990), 13 RPR (2d) 302 (Ont. HCJ). The plaintiff brought an application for summary judgment in relation to an alleged oral trust arrangement in respect of land, relying on the payment of a deposit as part performance. In dismissing the application for summary judgment, the court reviewed the principles for establishing part performance, noting (at 312) that "the narrower view ... has won repeated support of the Supreme Court of Canada," and citing *Deglman*; *McNeil v. Corbett* (1907), 39 SCR 608; *Brownscombe v. Public Trustee (Administrator of Vercamert Estate)*, [1969] SCR 658; and *Thompson v. Guaranty Trust Co.*, [1974] SCR 1023 (indexed as *Thompson v. Copithorne Estate*). However, the court in *Alvi v. Lal* also stated (at 313) that there were no known Canadian cases "specifically disapproving the more liberal English decision," and identified some cases (including *Starlite*) that favoured the approach in *Steadman*, including *Severin v. Vroom* (1977), 15 OR 636 (CA), which referred to *Steadman* without expressing either concurrence or disapproval. The court concluded (at 313), however, that "[w]hatever may be the current judicial trend, it seems clear that until the Supreme Court of Canada accepts *Steadman*, the payment of money cannot constitute part performance of a contract involving land."

What concerns are reflected in the court's approach in *Deglman*, as applied in *Alvi v. Lal*? Are these concerns the same as those that resulted in the enactment of the Statute of Frauds? Does the approach in *Deglman* reflect a need to limit equitable intervention in the context of legislative action? Can the approach in *Steadman* also be justified as a balance between equitable intervention and legislative action? How? Which of these approaches is preferable? For another case in which the court followed *Deglman* rather than *Steadman*, see *Mid Park Construction Ltd. v. Cleland* (1992), 27 RPR (2d) 68 (Ont. CJ).

The Principles in Context: Hollett v. Hollett

Consider the following situation. The defendant purchased several acres of land in 1965. He subsequently agreed verbally with the plaintiff, his brother, that the plaintiff could have one

half of this land in order to construct a home; in return, the plaintiff would pay the defendant one half of the 1965 purchase price. The plaintiff made the payments by four instalments throughout 1965 and 1966, and, for each of these payments, the defendant provided
the plaintiff with a written receipt that stated, "For payment on land." The defendant,
however, refused to issue a bill of sale to the plaintiff, contending that the plaintiff was not
entitled to it until he built the home that had been agreed on. The plaintiff had started
construction of the home, but had abandoned it, stating that he was concerned about not
having proper title to the land. There was also evidence that the plaintiff's wife preferred to
live closer to her family, in another community. Twenty years later, in 1986, when the
defendant planned to sell the land, the plaintiff brought an application for a declaration that
he was entitled to a one-half interest in the land. Should the plaintiff succeed? Was there
compliance with the Statute of Frauds in this case? In the alternative, can the plaintiff
succeed on the basis of the principles of part performance in *Deglman*? Does it matter
whether the court adopts the principles of *Deglman* or of *Steadman*? Why?

In *Hollett v. Hollett* (1993), 31 RPR (2d) 251 (Nfld. SCTD), the court concluded (at
282) that there was compliance with the writing requirement pursuant to the Statute of
Frauds, noting that the four receipts

> establish the parties to the contract, the total consideration and the subject matter of the
> contract. All that is required is an identification of the material terms of parties, price
> and property. The only question here is whether or not the phrase "for payment on land"
> adequately describes the subject matter. In my view, the phrase implies a purchase; if
> the payment was for rental or usage, it is likely that in common parlance, a word such as
> rent would be used.

The court also considered the plaintiff's alternative argument that there were sufficient acts
of part performance, stating (at 263) that "[it] is an open question as to whether the
Steadman approach is the law in Canada," and citing the decisions of the Supreme Court of
Canada, all of which were decided before the House of Lords decision in *Steadman*. The
court also referred to Robertson, *Discussion Paper on the Statute of Frauds, 1677* (St.
John's: Newfoundland Law Reform Commission, 1991), which (at 22) suggested that the
Supreme Court of Canada's decision in *Thompson v. Guaranty Trust Co. of Canada*, [1974]
SCR 1023 actually "applied a more liberal test while enunciating the stricter one." Noting
that the *Steadman* approach had been adopted by a number of decisions in Newfoundland
(including *Jenkins v. Strickland* (1990), 10 RPR (2d) 17 (Nfld. SC TD), the court concluded
that it was appropriate to apply *Steadman* in the absence of any post-*Steadman* decision of
the Supreme Court of Canada. The court continued (at 280 and 283):

> This case in many ways typifies the informal arrangements which frequently are
> involved in land holding in rural Newfoundland. It seems to me that a court ought to be
> sensitive to the fact that land holding, from a practical point of view, is often based upon
> arrangements which do not fit neatly into formal legal categories. If courts take too
> formalistic an approach to the application of property law concepts in such
> circumstances, the result may be the frustration of normal social expectations. ...
>
>   Here, we have the acts of the payment of the purchase price which was
> acknowledged by the Defendant "for payment of land," and we also have the acts of the

Plaintiff in entering on the property and commencing, with the concurrence and assistance of the Defendant, the excavation of a house basement. Neither of these acts would, in my opinion, satisfy the "unequivocally referable" test of *Maddison v. Alderson* [(1883), 8 App. Cas. 467 (CA), adopted by the Supreme Court of Canada in *Deglman*]. Even the construction of a basement on the property would not be unequivocally referable to the purchase of property because, in rural Newfoundland, it is common for family members to allow other members to build houses on their property without necessarily adverting to the question of whether this amounts to a gift or transfer of property. However, on the "equally consistent" test of *Steadman*, these two acts, taken together, in my view satisfy the test.

Consider the court's comments in the light of the principles in *Deglman* and *Steadman*. Is it arguable that the acts of part performance in *Hollett* were in fact sufficient to meet the *Deglman* test? To what extent are the "common practices" of the community relevant in the application of the test. Imagine that the decisions in *Hollett* (a Newfoundland decision) and in *Taylor v. Rawana* (an Ontario decision), discussed above, were both on appeal to the Supreme Court of Canada—what principles should the court adopt in relation to part performance principles? Do you think that the plaintiffs should succeed in both cases or neither? To what extent does the decision in *Taylor* depend on unexpressed "common practices" in the community?

Part Performance, Specific Performance, and Damages in Lieu of Specific Performance

Reconsider *Walsh v. Lonsdale*, [1882] 21 Ch.D 9 (CA) in relation to the principles of part performance. Why did the tenant in that case not plead part performance? Recall that the lessor and tenant had signed a written agreement to lease and thus, even though they never executed a deed of lease, the agreement to lease satisfied the requirements of the Statute of Frauds. As a result, there was no need for the lessor and tenant to rely on their actions to establish part performance in order to obtain a decree of specific performance. Consider a situation in which the facts are similar to *Walsh v. Lonsdale*, except that the parties have entered into their lease agreement orally. Can the lessor and tenant be held to be in a relationship *as if* they had a deed of lease?

In *South Shore Venture Capital Ltd. v. Haas*, [1994] NSJ no. 110 (SC), the tenant took possession under an oral lease for five years. No lease was ever executed, and the lessor subsequently tried to evict the tenant, arguing that (in the absence of a written lease) the tenant was merely a periodic (monthly) tenant. Thus, the tenant had no right to remain in the premises for five years. The tenant claimed, however, that he could rely on part performance to establish an equitable leasehold and that, applying *Walsh v. Lonsdale*, he was in the same position in relation to the lessor *as if* he had a deed of lease for five years. What is the appropriate result here? The court accepted the tenant's argument, in part relying on an unexecuted draft lease prepared by the solicitor for the lessor, as well as the acts of the tenant. Is this result consistent with the principles of part performance required by *Deglman* or by *Steadman*?

In *Starlite*, the court concluded that there were sufficient acts of part performance to permit a decree of specific performance. Yet, the court decided to order damages in lieu of specific performance because the latter remedy was no longer available. Why was specific performance precluded? Does this conclusion suggest that there are limits on the enforceability of Starlite's equitable interest? Can you explain why Starlite's interest was not enforceable against Mac's Convenience Stores Limited?

The issues concerning assessment of damages in lieu of specific performance in this case are similar to those addressed above in the Supreme Court of Canada's decision in *Semelhago v. Paramadevan*, [1996] 2 SCR 415. In *Starlite*, the plaintiff had expended funds in anticipation of its occupancy of the space in the mall, amounting to approximately $5,000 or $6,000. Should this amount be recoverable? Why? How did the court actually calculate the damages to be paid by Cloverlawn? Is it appropriate to assess damages in lieu of specific performance according to the value of the proprietary interest at issue? Recall that equity granted specific performance for contracts for the sale of land on the basis that land was unique and an award of damages was therefore inadequate. To what extent is a commercial leasehold interest in a shopping mall sufficiently unique to justify this approach? Is your view different from that expressed by Sopinka J in *Semelhago* in relation to residential subdivision property? Recall the discussion in chapter 4 in relation to *Highway Properties Ltd. v. Kelly Douglas & Co. Ltd.*, [1971] SCR 562, and whether a commercial lease should be characterized primarily as a proprietary or contractual interest for purposes of termination remedies. Are these arguments equally relevant in relation to the assessment of damages in lieu of specific performance?

Note that part performance is relevant to oral contracts relating to interests in land. Thus, even though the contract is not in writing, it must nonetheless be a contract—that is, an agreement that includes offer, acceptance, and consideration. In other words, the principles of part performance do not apply to non-bargain promises. However, even in the case of non-bargain promises, there are some situations in which equitable property interests can be created, some of which are illustrated below.

Equities: At the Boundaries of Gift, Trust, Contract, and Sale?

Our analysis of transfers of proprietary interests by gift and sale in this chapter reveals the extensive role of equitable principles in the achievement of goals apparently intended by the parties to these transactions. This section focuses on selected examples of "equities"—interests relating to land that are recognized and enforced even though they do not satisfy the requirements of traditional equitable interests. In most of these cases, family members have made informal arrangements for the occupation of residential premises, and subsequent difficulties have arisen because the title holder has died or become bankrupt, because the parties fail to remain on good terms and can no longer live together, or because someone who has no proprietary interest has contributed money or labour to land owned by someone else, and wishes to be compensated for that "investment." In these cases, courts have sometimes recognized "equities" associated with land in order to carry out the parties' intentions in a way that seems to accord with fundamental fairness, in spite of the absence of any contract or effective effort by the parties to satisfy traditional legal or equitable requirements concerning the transfer of interests in land.

Lord Denning was particularly visible in many, but not all, of these cases involving "equities," and many of the decisions reflect his views about the remedial role of law, perhaps expressed most directly in *Hill v. C.A. Parsons Ltd.*, [1972] Ch. 305 (CA), at 316:

> [It is a] fundamental principle that, whenever a man [sic] has a right, the law should give a remedy. The Latin maxim is ubi jus ibe remedium. This principle enables us to step over the trip-wires of previous cases and to bring the law into accord with the needs of today.

It may be helpful to consider this comment as you examine the cases and commentary in this section. The concept of "equities" has developed significantly in recent decades, expanding beyond its origins in 19th-century cases. In this way, it is an example of the continuing evolution of proprietary concepts, although its current evolutionary character also presents conceptual and practical difficulties within traditional principles of property law. As Gray and Symes have suggested, "[D]evelopments in this area are occurring apace, and serve to demonstrate yet again the shifting nature of the concept of 'property.'" See Gray and Symes, at 505.

The focus of this section is on informal, non-bargain family arrangements concerning land. Of course, family members often make formal arrangements concerning property—for example, a mother executes a valid will devising property interests to her children, or a brother executes a deed and sells his interest in a cottage to his sister. However, family members also make less formal arrangements in a variety of circumstances. As was evident in *In re Cole*, [1964] 1 Ch.D 175 (CA), a husband may tell his wife, standing in the entry to a new home, "It's all yours and everything in it." Or, as was the case in *Deglman v. Guaranty Trust Co. of Canada*, [1954] SCR 725, an aunt may offer to leave her home to her nephew if he takes care of her in her old age. Neither of these latter transactions was effective to transfer the property interests. Why? Note that neither involved a contract. Recall the need for intention and delivery, and the need for a deed in relation to real property, in order to make an effective gift.

Provincial legislation in Canada now regulates many proprietary relationships among family members—for example, dividing property interests, or the value of these interests, when married couples separate or divorce. Moreover, even though provincial statutes do not regulate property relationships among cohabiting couples, courts have increasingly used constructive trusts to reorganize proprietary interests for both opposite-sex and same-sex couples, in order to achieve fairness for them at family breakdown. These "family property" relationships are examined in more detail in chapter 7.

In this section, we examine the concept of "equities" arising out of family arrangements, most of which involve family members other than those who are in married or cohabiting couple relationships. Thus, in *Inwards v. Baker*, [1965] 2 QB 29 (CA), a father encouraged his son to build a home on land that the father owned, and the son subsequently sought to enforce some proprietary claim against his father's widow and her children after his father's death. Similarly, in *Hussey v. Palmer*, [1972] 3 All ER 744 (CA) a mother transferred her life savings to her son-in-law and daughter, and they built an extension on their home for her. However, after she moved in, she had a falling out with her children and wanted to be compensated for her financial contribution so that she could move elsewhere.

As is evident, these kinds of relationships usually result from generous efforts to accommodate family needs, and as long as everyone continues to "get along," they present no major legal problems. When the relationships are no longer cordial, however, it becomes necessary to decide whether there was a valid gift, whether the court should "construct" a trust relationship in relation to the property interest, or whether there was a contractual licence or other recognized interest. In relation to these cases, Gray and Symes have suggested that the courts' increasing willingness in recent decades to recognize "equities" as proprietary interests may be resulting in "a new order of 'property' (at least in the residential sphere) in which the distinction between personal rights and proprietary rights is completely eliminated." See Gray and Symes, at 504-5. At the same time, concerns have been expressed about the uncertainty created in the context of so much judicial creativity. For one example, see *Re Sharpe (A Bankrupt)*, [1980] 1 WLR 219 (Ch.D), and an analysis of the "conflicting social interests" in such cases in G. Woodman, "Note: Social Interests in the Development of Constructive Trusts" (1980), 96 *Law Quarterly Review* 336.

A NOTE ON UNJUST ENRICHMENT, TRUSTS, AND QUANTUM MERUIT

Equitable intervention in family arrangements concerning property falls into a number of different but related categories. For example, some kinds of arrangements may constitute contractual licences "coupled with an equity." Such an analysis is reflected in *Errington v. Errington*, [1952] 1 KB 290 (CA), a case often studied in contract law, which concerned a daughter-in-law's right to enforce an informal arrangement for the "purchase" of a home from her father-in-law. Other arrangements may involve significant contributions from a family member (who has no title to the subject land) to another family member (who does have title), usually relying on the family relationship as protection for such an "investment." In some cases, a court may decide that the family members intended that the title holder would hold the property interest on trust for the family member who made the contribution—that is, as a resulting trust. The resulting trust was discussed briefly, above, in relation to gifts (and the presumption of advancement among family members), and is explored again in relation to couples in chapter 7.

In other cases, where the court is unable to find evidence of the parties' intention to create a resulting trust, and where the non-title holder suffers a detriment as a result of the contribution and reliance, a court may hold that it is unjust for the title holder to retain the benefit, thus establishing a claim based on unjust enrichment. In such cases, a court may impose a constructive trust, again construing the title holder as trustee in relation to a beneficial interest for the non-title-holding family member. In some cases, however, a court may determine that a constructive trust (a proprietary interest) is not required to satisfy a claim of unjust enrichment, and may therefore order a monetary award pursuant to *quantum meruit* (based on restitution law). For example, the court in *Deglman v. Guaranty Trust Co. of Canada*, [1954] SCR 725 granted an award in *quantum meruit* to the nephew who had performed services for his aunt, even though the court held that there was no part performance according to the narrow test there adopted (as discussed above).

The constructive trust has been used extensively in Canada in response to claims of unjust enrichment when relationships between opposite-sex or same-sex couples end, thus providing a means of distributing property at family breakdown for those excluded from provincial statutory schemes that are available only to married couples. The constructive trust is examined in relation to couples in more detail in chapter 7, but it is also important to assess its usefulness in informal arrangements involving other family members. The case that follows presented considerable difficulty for the court, both in terms of characterizing the arrangement and in designing an appropriate solution. In reading the case, consider whether it is preferable to characterize it as a resulting trust or as a constructive trust. Is it arguable that an award of *quantum meruit* would have been preferable? What are the consequences of the court's choice of a trust?

Hussey v. Palmer
[1972] 3 All ER 744 (CA)

LORD DENNING MR: This case is of very considerable interest. Mrs. Emily Hussey, the plaintiff, is getting on in years. She is well over 70 and an old age pensioner. In 1967 she had a little house which was in a very dilapidated condition. It was condemned. She sold it for the sum of £1,100. She had a daughter who was married to a Mr. Palmer, the defendant. Mr. and Mrs. Palmer had two children and lived at no. 9 Stanley Road, Wokingham. It belonged to Mr. Palmer. When the mother sold her little house, the young couple invited her to go and live with them. That often happens. But there was not much room for them all. So they built on a bedroom as an extension for the old lady. She paid for it. She paid £607 for it in June and September 1967. She paid it direct to the builder, Mr. May. Nobody said anything about repayment. No doubt they all thought that the old lady would go and live there, using the bedroom, for the rest of her days. For a few months all went well. The old lady used to make payments to the daughter if she was short of money. But then differences arose. I am afraid that mothers and daughters do not always get on when they are living in the same house. After about 15 months they could not live in harmony any more in the house. So in March 1968, Mrs. Hussey went and lived elsewhere, leaving the Palmers there in their house. After a year or so, Mrs. Hussey wrote to her son-in-law and said she was very hard up. She asked if he could manage £1 or £1 10s. a week to help her out. He did not do it. He did not even reply. So she asked for the money back, the £607 which she had paid for the extension. They did not pay. She got legal aid.

In April 1970, she took out a default summons in the county court against Mr. Palmer. She claimed £607 for money lent. Mr. Palmer wrote a defence in his own hand. He said:

> The payments, made to a builder, were not a loan, but were paid by the plaintiff for her own benefit and at the time the question of repayment was not raised. I assumed that the payments were in effect a gift.

Later on, Mr. Palmer got legal aid too, and, with the help of legal advisers, he put in an amended defence in which he denied liability. He said that

> the moneys were only to be repaid in the event of the defendants' house, 9 Stanley Road, Wokingham, being sold within a short period of building works having been

completed by the said Mr. May. The said building works were mainly in respect of an extension to the said house, which extension was for occupation by the plaintiff.

He also said that "the said agreement was merely a family arrangement and was not intended to have legal consequences."

On February 10, 1971, the case came before the county court. The judge was fully occupied with another case. So it went before the registrar by consent. The registrar heard the evidence of Mrs. Hussey and also Mr. Palmer. He intimated a strong view that this was not a loan at all: but that it was a family arrangement. Mrs. Hussey's advisers were so impressed that they submitted to a non-suit and started a fresh action. This time they issued a plaint claiming £607 on a resulting trust. They said that, as she had contributed this £607 towards the extension of the building, at all events Mr. Palmer held the house on trust to repay it at some time or other to her: and that she would have an interest in the house to that extent in proportion to the amount she had contributed.

In July 1971, the fresh action came on for hearing before the county court judge himself. Mrs. Hussey went into the witness box and gave her story again. She said of Mr. Palmer: "... [H]e said he would build a bedroom on for me. He asked me if I would lend him the money. I agreed to lend it to him." In cross-examination she said: "They would give me a home for life, if I wanted it."

The defendant, Mr. Palmer, elected to call no evidence. The judge felt that, on Mrs. Hussey's own evidence, there was a loan, and not a resulting trust. After some discussion, Mrs. Hussey's counsel sought leave to amend the claim by adding an alternative claim for money lent. The defendant opposed the amendment. So the judge did not grant it. He made a note, saying: "The plaintiff's advisers decided to drop the claim for loan before the registrar and have in this action elected not to claim on a loan." So the claim remained on a resulting trust only.

On April 4, 1971, the judge decided in favour of the defendant. He said in his note for this court:

> I thought that the plaintiff was an honest witness, and at the end of her evidence I was satisfied that I ought to find that the money had been lent by the plaintiff and that there was no case for a resulting trust ... I ... reserved judgment to see if I could find for the plaintiff on the case pleaded. I could not.

So Mrs. Hussey went away a second time taking nothing. Now she appeals to this court.

Mr. Owen, on her behalf, rests her case on a resulting trust. He says that, despite Mrs. Hussey's own evidence, there was no loan. I agree that Mrs. Hussey did not lend the £607 to Mr. Palmer. Test it this way: suppose that, a week or two later, Mrs. Hussey had demanded from Mr. Palmer repayment of the £607, and he had refused. Could she recover it as money lent, and have the house sold up to regain it? Clearly not. The courts would undoubtedly have said—as the registrar said here—that it was a family arrangement. There was no intention that it should be repaid on demand. Again, if she had stayed on in the house, making use of the bedroom, could she have sued Mr. Palmer for money lent? Clearly not. There was no intention that it should be repaid whilst she had the benefit of the bedroom. Suppose that she had stayed there until she died, could her executors have sued Mr. Palmer for money lent? Clearly not. There was no intention that it should be repaid after her death.

If there was no loan, was there a resulting trust, and, if so, what were the terms of the trust?

Although the plaintiff alleged that there was a resulting trust, I should have thought that the trust in this case, if there was one, was more in the nature of a constructive trust: but this is more a matter of words than anything else. The two run together. By whatever name it is described, it is a trust imposed by law whenever justice and good conscience require it. It is a liberal process, founded upon large principles of equity, to be applied in cases where the legal owner cannot conscientiously keep the property for himself alone, but ought to allow another to have the property or the benefit of it or a share in it. The trust may arise at the outset when the property is acquired, or later on, as the circumstances may require. It is an equitable remedy by which the court can enable an aggrieved party to obtain restitution. It is comparable to the legal remedy of money had and received which, as Lord Mansfield said, is "very beneficial and therefore, much encouraged" [*Moses v. MacFarlan* (1760), 2 Burr. 1005, at 1012]. Thus we have repeatedly held that, when one person contributes towards the purchase price of a house, the owner holds it on a constructive trust for him, proportionate to his contribution, even though there is no agreement between them, and no declaration of trust to be found, and no evidence of any intention to create a trust. Instances are numerous where a wife has contributed money to the initial purchase of a house or property; or later on to the payment of mortgage instalments; or has helped in a business: see *Falconer v. Falconer*, [1970] 1 WLR 1333; *Heseltine v. Heseltine*, [1971] 1 WLR 342; and *In re Cummins, decd.*, [1972] Ch. 62. Similarly, when a mistress has contributed money, or money's worth, to the building of a house: *Cooke v. Head*, [1972] 1 WLR 518. Very recently we held that a purchaser, who bought a cottage subject to the rights of an occupier, held it on trust for her benefit: *Binions v. Evans*, [1972] Ch. 359. In all those cases it would have been quite inequitable for the legal owner to take the property for himself and exclude the other from it. So the law imputed or imposed a trust for his or her benefit.

The present case is well within the principles of those cases. Just as a person, who pays part of the purchase price, acquires an equitable interest in the house, so also he does when he pays for an extension to be added to it. Mr. Owen has done a lot of research and has found a case in 1858 to that very effect. It is *Unity Joint Stock Mutual Banking Association v. King* (1858), 25 Beav. 72. A father had land on which he built a granary. His two sons built two other granaries on it at a cost of £1,200. Sir John Romilly MR held that the two sons had a lien or charge on the property as against the father, and any person claiming through him. The father had never promised to pay the sons £1,200. He was not indebted to them in that sum. He had never engaged or promised to make over the land to them or to give them a charge on it. Yet they had a lien or charge on the land. That case was approved by the Privy Council in *Chalmers v. Pardoe*, [1963] 1 WLR 677, 681-682, where it was said to be based on the "general equitable principle that ... it would be against conscience" for the owner to take the land without repaying the sums expended on the buildings. To this I would add *Inwards v. Baker*, [1965] 2 QB 29, when a son built a bungalow on his father's land in the expectation that he would be allowed to stay there as his home, though there was no promise to that effect. After the father's death, his trustees sought to turn the son out. It was held that he had an equitable interest which was good against the trustees. In those cases it was emphasised that the court must look at the circumstances of each case to decide in what way the equity can be satisfied. In some by an equitable lien. In others by a constructive trust. But in either case it is because justice and good conscience so require.

In the present case Mrs. Hussey paid £607 to a builder for the erection of this extension. It may well be, as the defendant says, that there was no contract to repay it at all. It was not a loan to the son-in-law. She could not sue him for repayment. He could not have turned her out. If she had stayed there until she died, the extension would undoubtedly have belonged beneficially to the son-in-law. If, during her lifetime, he had sold the house, together with the extension, she would be entitled to be repaid the £607 out of the proceeds. He admits this himself. But he has not sold the house. She has left, and the son-in-law has the extension for his own benefit and could sell the whole if he so desired. It seems to me to be entirely against conscience that he should retain the whole house and not allow Mrs. Hussey any interest in it, or any charge upon it. The court should, and will, impose or impute a trust by which Mr. Palmer is to hold the property on terms under which, in the circumstances that have happened, she has an interest in the property proportionate to the £607 which she put into it. She is quite content if he repays her the £607. If he does not repay the £607, she can apply for an order for sale, so that the sum can be paid to her. But the simplest way for him would be to raise the £607 on mortgage and pay it to her. But, on the legal point raised, I have no doubt there was a resulting trust, or, more accurately, a constructive trust, for her, and I would so declare. I would allow the appeal, accordingly.

PHILLIMORE LJ: I agree. It is common ground that Mrs. Hussey paid £607 to enable her son-in-law to have an extension made to his house in which she was going to live. It is quite clear that she did not intend to make him a gift of the money. She herself said she regarded it as a loan. It is true that the son-in-law in his defence said that he assumed the money was paid by her as a gift to him; but in a later amended defence he said that she was to be repaid if the house was sold at an early date. That clearly does not fit with a gift: it goes a long way to confirm her case that it was not a gift. Here is an example of what so often happens. This mother-in-law advanced money to improve the property of her son-in-law. She did not intend to make a gift of the money. She could not afford to do that. No terms of repayment were agreed except perhaps in the event of the house being sold at an early date. She has described it as a loan, and that might be true. I do not for myself think that it would be inconsistent with the transaction also being or involving a resulting trust. In all the circumstances here, in the absence of clear arrangements for repayment and in circumstances where repayment on demand might be very difficult for the son-in-law, I should have thought it was more appropriate to regard it as an example of a resulting trust; and I would accordingly entirely agree with Lord Denning MR that she has an interest in this house proportionate to the £607 which she paid. It follows that this appeal should be allowed.

CAIRNS LJ: I am afraid I differ from my Lords in this case; and, but for the fact that they have both taken the view that the plaintiff was entitled to succeed, I should have regarded this as a plain case where she had failed to establish the cause of action which she set up.

Having in an earlier action alleged that this money was lent by her to the defendant, having elected to be non-suited in that action, she then starts this fresh action in which her case is based solely upon the claim of a resulting trust. She then gives her evidence and in the course of it she says:

> When I sold my house my son-in-law suggested that I should live with him as long as I liked to stay there. My daughter agreed. I went to see him one night and he said he would build a bedroom on for me. He asked me if I would lend him the money. I agreed to lend it to him.

Later she referred to going to the bank manager with her son-in-law, and said:

> My son-in-law told the bank manager that he would like me to lend him the money. As I lent the money, I expected to receive it back. As it was a loan I expected it back … . While living with my son-in-law he said he was going to Cornwall and would sell his Wokingham house, and try and buy a house and repay me what he owed me.

And in cross-examination: "I did not give my son-in-law the money—I lent it to him." In my view it is going a very long way to say that, all that evidence having been given by this lady, there was some misunderstanding by her of the legal position and that she was describing as a loan something which was not a loan at all. It is to my mind nothing to the point that in all probability no express terms as to repayment were ever agreed. It must be a common thing indeed for a parent or a parent-in-law to make a loan of money to a son or daughter or a son-in-law which both of them know is a loan, as to which it is obvious that there is no immediate prospect of repayment, but which in law is a loan repayable on demand. In my view that is the position here. As it was a loan, I think it is quite inconsistent with that to say that it could create a resulting trust at the same time. I accept as a correct statement of law the short passage in *Underhill's Law of Trusts and Trustees*, 12th ed. (1970), p. 210, in these words:

> Where the purchase money is provided by a third party at the request of and by way of loan to the person to whom the property is conveyed there is no resulting trust in favour of the third party, for the lender did not advance the purchase-money as purchaser … but merely as lender.

And it seems to me that that proposition is equally applicable where it is not a matter of the property being purchased, but a matter of a builder being paid for an extension to a property which already belongs to the borrower of the money. For these reasons I consider that the plaintiff was certainly not entitled to succeed on the evidence which she had given. As the particulars of claim stood, the only doubt that I could have had about the matter, if my judgment had been decisive, would be as to whether she should simply have the appeal dismissed or whether at this late stage she should have been given an opportunity of amending her particulars of claim and having a re-trial. I should have been anxious that she should have that opportunity, because I think the strong probability is that one way or another she ought to have got this money back. So far as concerns the inconvenience of having a third hearing, I do not think that is owing to anything done or omitted on the defendant's side. However, in the circumstances it is unnecessary for me to arrive at any final opinion as to which would have been the right course.

Appeal allowed.

Declaration that defendant held 9 Stanley Road, Wokingham, upon a resulting trust for plaintiff and that the plaintiff was entitled to a beneficial interest in the property of the value of £607.

Legal aid taxation of both parties' costs.

Discussion Notes

Characterizing the Nature of a Family Arrangement

In *Hussey v. Palmer*, the court considered whether the arrangement between Mrs. Hussey and her son-in-law represented a loan, or whether it represented a contribution that should be reflected in a declaration of resulting or constructive trust. Why was it so difficult for the court to characterize the parties' arrangement? Are the judges in agreement about what arrangement was intended by the parties? To what extent does the plaintiff's evidence compound the difficulty of characterizing the arrangement? Is the result more dependent on concerns about the son-in-law's unjust enrichment, or the intention of the parties? Do you agree with Gray and Symes when they suggest that "[i]t is extremely difficult to analyse the legal effect of informal family arrangements within the traditional categories of property and contract."? See Gray and Symes, at 473.

What was Mrs. Hussey entitled to as a result of this decision? Lord Denning MR, suggested that "[the plaintiff] has an interest in the property proportionate to the £607 which she put into it," but he then went on to suggest that the son-in-law can extinguish the trust by a repayment of £607. Are these statements consistent? It has been suggested, for example, that the case resulted in Mrs. Hussey having a proportionate share in the increasing value of the house (due to inflation) rather than a mere right to have the amount of her contribution repaid—see T.C. Ridley, "A Family Affair" (1973), 36 *Modern Law Review* 436. To what extent do the judgments of Phillimore LJ and Cairns LJ support this view? For another analysis, see R.E. Poole, "Equities in the Making" (1968), 32 *The Conveyancer and Property Lawyer* 96.

Consider a situation in which the owner of land permitted a woman, the widow of a former employee of the owner, to live in a cottage rent-free for the rest of her life. The woman continued to live in the cottage, which had been her home for over 50 years. Subsequently, the owner conveyed the property, expressly subject to the widow's right to live in the cottage, to a purchaser who obtained the land at a reduced price as a result of the widow's occupation of the cottage. In spite of the reduced price, the purchaser initiated an action for possession against the widow. At the time of the action, the widow was 79 years old. How should this case be resolved? See *Binion v. Evans*, [1972] Ch. 359 (CA), where the court of appeal confirmed a trial court decision declaring that the purchaser held the cottage on trust for the widow for life or "as long as she desired." See also commentaries on this decision—J. Martin "Contractual Licensee or Tenant for Life?" (1972), 36 *The Conveyancer and Property Lawyer (NS)* 266; R.J. Smith, "Licences and Constructive Trusts: 'The Law Is What It Ought To Be' " (1973), 32 *Cambridge Law Journal* 123; and A.J. Oakley, "The Licensee's Interest" (1972), 35 *Modern*

Law Review 551. See also M.A. Neave, "The Constructive Trust as a Remedial Device" (1977-78), 11 *Melbourne University Law Review* 343.

In spite of ambiguity about the precise nature of her proprietary interest, it is apparent that the court did not consider remedies that would have enforced Mrs. Hussey's right to remain in the house itself. Lord Denning MR referred to *Inwards v. Baker*, [1965] 2 QB 29 (CA), in which the court resolved a family-arrangement problem by making an order that permitted a non-title-holding family member to remain in possession for life or for as long as he wanted it as a home. Why was such an order inappropriate in *Hussey v. Palmer*? As you consider *Inwards v. Baker* below, reflect on the extent to which the parties' wishes may influence the scope of the court's remedial action.

Proprietary Estoppel: Estoppel by Acquiescence

In addition to the legal categories discussed above, there are cases where courts have recognized "equities" because the actions of the parties result in estoppel. A full analysis of these cases is beyond the scope of this chapter, but it is important to recognize this alternative approach to problems arising out of family arrangements. The context for these cases usually involves a request or encouragement by a title holder to another family member, and subsequent action by the other family member in reliance on the request or encouragement—for example, a promise by an aunt that, if her nephew builds a home on land owned by her, she will transfer the property interest to him. If the nephew subsequently expends money to build the home in reliance on her promise, she may be estopped from evicting her nephew as a trespasser. The principles of proprietary estoppel are complicated, especially in their application to diverse factual situations and in relation to the variety of remedies granted by courts to enforce them. According to Gray and Symes, at 493-94, "the jurisprudence of proprietary estoppel provides an extremely flexible means by which the courts can so fashion discretionary relief as to do justice in the light of the interaction and expectation of the litigants." Proprietary estoppel is also similar to promissory estoppel, originally highlighted in *Central London Property Trust Ltd. v. High Trees House Ltd.*, [1947] KB 130 (CA), another decision of Lord Denning. However, proprietary estoppel may result in an interest binding on third-party purchasers with notice of the equity—see *E.R. Ives Investment Ltd. v. High*, [1967] 2 QB 379 (CA).

Recent decisions about "equities" are based on some 19th-century decisions involving informal family relationships. In one of these, *Dillwyn v. Llewelyn* (1862), 45 ER 1285 (Ch.D), a father made a will devising his real property in trust for his widow for life, remainder in trust for the plaintiff for life, and remainder in certain other trusts. After making the will (which would not take effect until the father's death), the father offered his son a farm property on which the son could build a home. Unlike many family arrangements, the father actually signed a memorandum stating that he was presenting the farm to his son for the purpose of building a home. The son (the plaintiff) built a valuable house on the property, but no deed was executed by the father to transfer the property interest to his son. After his father's death, the son brought an application for a conveyance of the fee simple estate. The court granted the son's application, stating (at 1286):

[I]f A puts B in possession of a piece of land, and tells him: "I give it to you that B may build a house on it," and B on the strength of that promise, with the knowledge of A, expends a large sum of money in building a house accordingly, I cannot doubt that the donee acquires a right from the subsequent transaction to call on the donor to perform that contract and complete the imperfect donation which was made. The case is somewhat analogous to that of verbal agreement not binding originally for the want of the memorandum signed by the party to be charged, but which becomes binding by virtue of the subsequent part performance.

What exactly was the basis for the court's decision to grant the son's application in *Dillwyn v. Llewelyn*? Consider this approach in relation to *Inwards v. Baker*, which follows, a case in which the court relied on the precedent of *Dillwyn v. Llewelyn*. Is the reasoning the same in both these cases?

Inwards v. Baker
[1965] 2 QB 29 (CA)

LORD DENNING MR: In this case old Mr. Baker, if I may so describe the father, in 1931 was the owner of a little over six acres of land at Dunsmore in Buckinghamshire. His son, Jack Baker, was living in those parts and was thinking of erecting a bungalow. He had his eye on a piece of land but the price was rather too much for him. So the father said to him: "Why not put the bungalow on my land and make the bungalow a little bigger." That is what the son did. He did put the bungalow on his father's land. He built it with his own labour with the help of one or two men, and he got the materials. He bore a good deal of the expense himself, but his father helped him with it, and he paid his father back some of it. Roughly he spent himself the sum of £150 out of a total of £300 expended. When it was finished, he went into the bungalow; and he has lived there ever since from 1931 down to date. His father visited him there from time to time.

In 1951 the father died. The only will he left was one he made as far back as 1922 before this land was bought or the bungalow was built. He appointed as executrix Miss Inwards, who had been living with him for many many years as his wife and by whom he had two children. He left nearly all his property to her and her two children by him. He left his son, Jack Baker, £400. Miss Inwards appointed her two children as trustees of the will with her. The trustees under the will did not take any steps to get Jack Baker out of the bungalow. In fact they visited him there from time to time. They all seem to have been quite friendly. But in the year 1963 they took proceedings to get Jack Baker out. Miss Inwards died during these proceedings. Her two children continue the proceedings as the trustees of the father's will.

The trustees say that at the most Jack Baker had a licence to be in the bungalow but that it had been revoked and he had no right to stay. The judge has held in their favour. He was referred to *Errington v. Errington and Woods*, but the judge held that that decision only protected a contractual licensee. He thought that, in order to be protected, the licensee must have a contract or promise by which he is entitled to be there. The judge said:

I can find no promise made by the father to the son that he should remain in the property at all—no contractual arrangement between them. True the father said that the son could live in the property, expressly or impliedly, but there is no evidence that this was arrived at as the result of a contract or promise—merely an arrangement made casually because of the relationship which existed and knowledge that the son wished to erect a bungalow for residence.

Thereupon, the judge, with much reluctance, thought the case was not within *Errington's* case, and said the son must go.

The son appeals to this court. We have had the advantage of cases which were not cited to the county court judge—cases in the last century, notably *Dillwyn v. Llewelyn* and *Plimmer v. Wellington Corporation*. This latter was a decision of the Privy Council which expressly affirmed and approved the statement of the law made by Lord Kingsdown in *Ramsden v. Dyson*. It is quite plain from those authorities that if the owner of land requests another, or indeed allows another, to expend money on the land under an expectation created or encouraged by the landlord that he will be able to remain there, that raises an equity in the licensee such as to entitle him to stay. He has a licence coupled with an equity. Mr. Goodhart urged before us that the licensee could not stay indefinitely. The principle only applied, he said, when there was an expectation of some precise legal term. But it seems to me, from *Plimmer's* case in particular, that the equity arising from the expenditure on land need not fail "merely on the ground that the interest to be secured has not been expressly indicated ... the court must look at the circumstances in each case to decide in what way the equity can be satisfied."

So in this case, even though there is no binding contract to grant any particular interest to the licensee, nevertheless the court can look at the circumstances and see whether there is an equity arising out of the expenditure of money. All that is necessary is that the licensee should, at the request or with the encouragement of the landlord, have spent the money in the expectation of being allowed to stay there. If so, the court will not allow that expectation to be defeated where it would be inequitable so to do. In this case it is quite plain that the father allowed an expectation to be created in the son's mind that this bungalow was to be his home. It was to be his home for his life or, at all events, his home as long as he wished it to remain his home. It seems to me, in the light of that equity, that the father could not in 1932 have turned to his son and said: "You are to go. It is my land and my house." Nor could he at any time thereafter so long as the son wanted it as his home.

Mr. Goodhart put the case of a purchaser. He suggested that the father could sell the land to a purchaser who could get the son out. But I think that any purchaser who took with notice would clearly be bound by the equity. So here, too, the present plaintiffs, the successors in title of the father, are clearly themselves bound by this equity. It is an equity well recognised in law. It arises from the expenditure of money by a person in actual occupation of land when he is led to believe that, as the result of that expenditure, he will be allowed to remain there. It is for the court to say in what way the equity can be satisfied. I am quite clear in this case it can be satisfied by holding that the defendant can remain there as long as he desires to as his home.

I would allow the appeal accordingly and enter judgment for the defendant.

DANCKWERTS LJ: I agree and I will add only a few words. It seems to me the claim of the defendant in respect of this property is amply covered by *Errington v. Errington and Woods, Dillwyn v. Llewelyn* and *Plimmer v. Wellington Corporation*. Further, it seems to me to be supported by the observations of Lord Kingsdown in *Ramsden v. Dyson*. It is true that in that case Lord Kingsdown reached a result on the facts of the case which differed from that reached by the other members of the House of Lords, but Lord Kingsdown's observations which are relevant in the present case have received support since that case was decided; and, in particular, I would like to refer to the observations in the judgment of the Privy Council in *Plimmer v. Wellington Corporation*. It is said there:

> Their Lordships consider that this case falls within the principle stated by Lord
> Kingsdown as to expectations created or encouraged by the landlord, with the addition
> that in this case the landlord did more than encourage the expenditure, for he took the
> initiative in requesting it.

There are similar circumstances in the present case. The defendant was induced to give up his project of building a bungalow on land belonging to somebody else other than his father, in which case he would have become the owner or tenant of the land in question and thus have his own home. His father induced him to build on his, the father's, land and expenditure was made by the defendant for the purpose of the erection of the bungalow.

In my view the case comes plainly within the proposition stated in the cases. It is not necessary, I think, to imply a promise. It seems to me that this is one of the cases of an equity created by estoppel, or equitable estoppel, as it is sometimes called, by which the person who has made the expenditure is induced by the expectation of obtaining protection, and equity protects him so that an injustice may not be perpetrated.

I am clearly of opinion that the appeal should be allowed and judgment should be entered for the defendant.

SALMON LJ: I agree.

Appeal allowed.

Discussion Notes

Characterizing the Arrangement

How did the court characterize the family arrangement in *Inwards v. Baker*? Did the father make a promise to his son? What is the evidence before the court in relation to this family arrangement? Is it appropriate for the court to rely only on Jack Baker's evidence after his father's death? Is the court's reasoning based on the parties' intentions or on Jack Baker's detrimental reliance? Are these facts different from the facts in *Dillwyn v. Llewelyn*? How?

What is the test used by the court to establish the equity? Does the test require "a request or permission" or merely "acquiescence"? Based on the reasoning in *Inwards v.*

Baker, what difference would it make if the evidence showed that Jack Baker's father had said: "If you build your bungalow on my land, I will give the land to you."? What if Jack Baker's father had simply said, "I give you this land."?

"A Licence Coupled with an Equity"

Lord Denning MR concluded that Jack Baker could "remain there as long as he desires to as his home." What kind of property interest was thereby created? If the interest were simply a licence, rather than a licence coupled with an equity, what difference would it make? Recall that a licence is a contractual agreement—is it enforceable against third parties?

Why was Jack Baker's interest in *Inwards v. Baker* enforceable against his father's widow and her children? Recall that an equitable interest is enforceable against everyone except a *bona fide* purchaser for value without notice. Is the sphere of enforceability of an equity the same as that of an equitable interest?

Can Jack Baker sell or transfer his property interest? It has been suggested that the decision in this case failed to meet societal goals for alienability of land because the decision both rendered the land unsalable and discouraged Jack Baker from ever moving—see F.R. Crane, "Estoppel Interests in Land" (1967), 31 *The Conveyancer and Property Lawyer (NS)* 332. Do you agree? See also R.H. Maudsley, "Note" (1965), 81 *Law Quarterly Review* 183. The principle of *Inwards v. Baker* has been applied in *Stiles v. Tod Mountain Development Ltd.* (1992), 22 RPR (2d) 143 (BC SC), and in *Blatnick v. Walklin Investments Ltd.* (1990), 13 RPR (2d) 268 (Ont. CJ).

What other options were available to the court in this case? The decision in *Inwards v. Baker* was criticized in *Dodsworth v. Dodsworth* (1973), 228 *Estates Gazette* 1115 (cited in Gray and Symes, at 490), where the plaintiff invited her younger brother and his wife to live with her. They did so, and spent about £700 on improvements to the plaintiff's house in the expectation, encouraged by the plaintiff, that they could remain there as long as they desired. Nine months later, the plaintiff repented her invitation and brought an application for possession. The Court of Appeal ordered that the equity would be satisfied by securing the occupation of the defendants until the expenditure had been reimbursed. Is this a more satisfactory result than *Inwards v. Baker*? Are there differences in the extent of the expenditures that may justify the differing outcomes?

In *Pascoe v. Turner*, [1979] 1 WLR 431 (CA), which follows, the court again considered proprietary estoppel. The plaintiff and defendant had cohabited in a home owned by the plaintiff for some years, but their relationship eventually ended when the plaintiff became involved with another woman. There was conflicting evidence about what the plaintiff said to the defendant about the home where they had lived together, but the defendant expended considerable money on improving it and maintaining it, assuming that it was to be "a roof over her head." In due course, the plaintiff brought an application for possession. In reading the case that follows, note the evidentiary problems presented as well as the court's reasoning about the nature of the defendant's interest and the order granted. What are the differences between this case and *Inwards v. Baker*, or *Dillwyn v. Llewelyn*?

Pascoe v. Turner
[1979] 1 WLR 431 (CA)

CUMMING-BRUCE LJ read the following judgment of the court: This is an appeal from the orders made on April 21, 1978, by Mr. McKintosh, sitting as a deputy circuit judge in the Camborne and Redruth County Court, whereby he dismissed the plaintiff's claim for possession of a house at 2 Tolgarrick Road, Tuckingmill, Camborne in Cornwall, and granted the defendant declarations upon her counterclaim that the plaintiff held the house on trust for the defendant, her heirs and assigns absolutely and that the contents of the house belonged to her. The plaintiff asks for an order of possession, and that the counterclaim be dismissed.

The Issues

The appeal raises three issues about the house: (a) Did the defendant prove the trust found by the judge? (b) Did she prove such facts as prevented the plaintiff by estoppel from asserting his legal title? (c) If the answer to that question is yes, what is the equitable relief to which she is entitled? In respect of the contents of the house, did the defendant prove that they were given to her by the plaintiff's voluntary gift?

The Facts

The plaintiff was a business man in a relatively small way and at all material times was and had been building up some capital assets which he invested in purchases of private and commercial property. In 1961 or 1962 he met the defendant, a widow recovering from the distressing circumstances of her husband's death. She had invested about £4,500 capital and had some income from this and from an invalidity pension. They made friends. She was happy to help him in small ways in business activities. The relationship deepened and she took the plaintiff's young son under her wing, and helped to guide him through his problems. In 1963 she moved into the plaintiff's home, at first as his housekeeper. In 1964 the boy went away to his own mother, and shortly afterwards the plaintiff and the defendant began to share a bedroom and live in every sense as man and wife. The plaintiff's business was expanding, and she worked in the business as well as doing the housekeeping. She did all that a wife would have done. He offered marriage, but she declined. In 1965 they moved. He took her to see 2 Tolgarrick Road, and asked her if she liked it. He bought it. They moved in and continued living there as man and wife. He paid for the house and contents. He gave her £3 a week housekeeping. She used her own money to buy her clothes. She only bought small things for the house. Then she began to collect some rents for him and was allowed to keep part of them, bringing her housekeeping allowance up to £6 per week. He bought a place in Spain which they visited on holidays. At some stage there was some mention of the position with regard to the plaintiff's property, including the house, and the defendant. There was what the judge describes as a sort of will on which there was mention of the defendant having the house if anything happened to the plaintiff. In 1973 Cupid aimed his arrow. It struck the plaintiff, who began an affair with a Mrs. Pritchard. All unknowing, the defendant went for a few days with her daughter to Capri. In her absence the plaintiff moved in for two days to the house with Mrs. Pritchard, but they removed themselves before her return. Immediately the defendant got back, he visited her. There was a conflict of evidence on what was then said. His version was that all he told her was that he would never see her without a roof over her head. The account given by the defendant and the witnesses called on her behalf was that he declared to her and later to them that she had nothing to worry about as the house was hers and everything in it. The judge rejected the plaintiff's evidence and accepted the evidence of the defendant and her witnesses. The plaintiff declared to the defendant not once but on a number of occasions after he had left her, "The house is yours and everything in it." He told a Mrs. Smejhal and a Mrs. Green the same thing. To Mrs. Smejhal he said that he'd put it in a solicitor's hands. Mrs. Green asked him at the end of 1973 if he'd given the defendant the deeds, and he replied that he hadn't yet but was going to see to it. In fact he never did. There was no deed of conveyance, nothing in writing at all. The defendant stayed on in the house. She thought it was hers and everything in it. In reliance upon the plaintiff's declarations that he had given her the house and its contents, she spent money and herself did work on redecoration, improvements and repairs. The judge found that the plaintiff as donor stood by knowingly while she improved the property thinking it was hers. In 1973 when he left and told her that the house was hers she had about £1,000 of her own capital left. She spent some £230 on repairs and improvements and redecoration to the house, and also paid a man an unspecified sum in cash for working on the house. She bought carpets for the lounge, stairs and hall and fitted carpets to the bedrooms. She bought curtains. Though the house was full of furniture, she got rid of a good deal and replaced it by purchases made out of savings. The work which she carried out in 1974 and 1975 was pleaded in a list given in further particulars of defence and counterclaim as follows. (1) Partly replumbing house, providing hot water from immersion system to kitchen and installing new sink unit and other fitments. Installing gas into the kitchen. (2) Joining outside toilet to rear door of premises by blockwork covered way. (3) Installing gas conduits and installing a gas fire into the lounge. (4) Repairing and retiling the roof where necessary and repairing lead valleys. (5) Repairing and redecorating interior. So she stayed on. He lived nearby and sometimes visited her. She continued to collect some rents for him. Then there was a quarrel. He decided to throw her out of the house if he could. On April 9, 1976, his solicitors wrote to her giving her two months notice "to determine her licence to occupy," and demanded possession on June 10, 1976. She refused to go.

On August 25 he filed his plaint in the county court, claiming possession and mesne profits at £10 per week from June 10, 1976, until possession. On February 14, 1977, she filed her defence and counterclaim. She pleaded his declarations that the house and contents were hers and that in reliance on his statements she carried out extensive works on the house with the plaintiff's full knowledge and encouragement. By her counterclaim she sought a declaration that the house and its contents were hers, and that the plaintiff held the realty on trust for her, her heirs and assigns. Alternatively she sought a declaration that the plaintiff had given her a licence to occupy the house for her lifetime. She claimed that the plaintiff was estopped from denying the trust or the licence. By his reply and defence to counterclaim the plaintiff joined issue on the extent of the works alleged to have been done since 1973, denied that they had been done in reliance upon his promises, or that they were of sufficient substance to give rise to the estoppel alleged. The judge decided the issue of estoppel against him. It is implicit in his conclusion that he accepted the defendant's evidence about what was done to the house after 1973, and how the plaintiff knew all about it and advised and encouraged her.

The judge found that the plaintiff had made a gift to her of the contents of the house. I have no doubt that he was right about that. She was already in possession of them as a bailee when he declared the gift. Counsel for the plaintiff submitted that there was no gift because it was uncertain what he was giving her. He pointed to a safe and to the defendant's evidence that she had sent round an orange bedroom suite to the plaintiff so that he should have a bed to sleep on. The answer is that he gave her everything in the house, but later, recognising his need, she gave back some bits and pieces to him. So much for the contents.

Her rights in the realty are not quite so simply disposed of because of section 53 and section 54 of the Law of Property Act, 1925. There was nothing in writing. The judge considered the plaintiff's declarations, and decided that they were not enough to found an express trust. We agree. But he went on to hold that the beneficial interest in the house had passed under a constructive trust inferred from words and conduct of the parties. He relied on the passage in *Snell's Principles of Equity*, 27th ed. (1973), p. 185, in which the editors suggest a possible definition of a constructive trust. But there are difficulties in the way. The long and short of events in 1973 is that the plaintiff made an imperfect gift of the house. There is nothing in the facts from which an inference of a constructive trust can be drawn. If it had not been for section 53 of the Law of Property Act, 1925 the gift of the house would have been a perfect gift, just as the gift of the contents was a perfect gift. In the event it remained an imperfect gift and, as Turner LJ said in *Milroy v. Lord* (1862), 4 De FG & J 264, 274: "[T]here is no equity in this court to perfect an imperfect gift." So matters stood in 1973, and if the facts had stopped there the defendant would have remained a licensee at will of the plaintiff.

But the facts did not stop there. On the judge's findings the defendant, having been told that the house was hers, set about improving it within and without. Outside she did not do much: a little work on the roof and an improvement which covered the way from the outside toilet to the rest of the house, putting in a new door there, and Snowcem to protect the toilet. Inside, she did a good deal more. She installed gas in the kitchen with a cooker, improved the plumbing in the kitchen and put in a new sink. She got new gas fires, putting a gas fire in the lounge. She redecorated four rooms. The fitted carpets she put in the bedrooms, the carpeting, and the curtains and the furniture that she bought are not part of the realty, and it is not clear how much she spent on those items. But they are part of the whole circumstances. There she was, on her own after he left her in 1973. She had £1,000 left of her capital, and a pension of some kind. Having as she thought been given the house, she set about it as described. On the repairs and improvement to the realty and the fixtures she spent about £230. She had £300 of her capital left by the date of the trial, but she did not establish in evidence how much had been expended on refurbishing the house with carpets, curtains and furniture. We would describe the work done in and about the house as substantial in the sense that that adjective is used in the context of estoppel. All the while the plaintiff not only stood by and watched but encouraged and advised, without a word to suggest that she was putting her money and her personal labour into his house. What is the effect in equity?

The cases relied upon by the plaintiff are relevant for the purpose of showing that the judge fell into error in deciding that on the facts a constructive trust could be inferred. They are the cases which deal with the intention of the parties when a house is acquired. But of those cases only *Inwards v. Baker*, [1965] 2 QB 29 is in point here. For this is a case of estoppel arising from the encouragement and acquiescence of the plaintiff between 1973 and 1976 when, in reliance upon his declaration, that he was giving and, later, that he had given the house to her, she spent a substantial part of her small capital upon repairs and improvements to the house. The relevant principle is expounded in *Snell's Principles of Equity*, 27th ed., p. 565 in the passage under the heading "Proprietary Estoppel," and is elaborated in *Spencer Bower and Turner, Estoppel by Representation*, 3d ed. (1977), chapter 12 entitled "Encouragment and Acquiescence."

The cases in point illustrating that principle in relation to real property are *Dillwyn v. Llewelyn* (1862), 4 De FG & J 517; *Ramsden v. Dyson* (1866), LR 1 HL 129 and *Plimmer v. Wellington Corporation* (1884), 9 App. Cas. 699. One distinction between this class of case and the doctrine which has come to be known as "promissory estoppel" is that where estoppel by encouragement or acquiescence is found on the facts, those facts give rise to a cause of action. They may be relied upon as a sword, not merely as a shield. In *Ramsden v. Dyson* the plaintiff failed on the facts, and the dissent of Lord Kingsdown was upon the inferences to be drawn from the facts. On the principle, however, the House was agreed, and it is stated by Lord Cranworth LC and by Lord Wensleydale as well as by Lord Kingsdown. Likewise in *Plimmer's* case the plaintiff was granted a declaration that he had a perpetual right to occupation.

The final question that arises is: to what relief is the defendant entitled upon her counterclaim? In *Dillwyn v. Llewelyn*, 4 De GF & J 517 there was an imperfect gift of land by a father who encouraged his son to build a house on it for £14,000. Lord Westbury LC said at p. 521:

> About the rules of the court there can be no controversy. A voluntary agreement will not be completed or assisted by a court of equity, in cases of mere gift. If anything be wanting to complete the title of the donee, a court of equity will not assist him in obtaining it; for a mere donee can have no right to claim more than he has received. But the subsequent acts of the donor may give the donee that right or ground of claim which he did not acquire from the original gift. Thus, if A gives a house to B, but makes no formal conveyance, and the house is afterwards, on the marriage of B, included, with the knowledge of A, in the marriage settlement of B, A would be bound to complete the title of the parties claiming under that settlement. So if A puts B in possession of a piece of land, and tells him, "I give it to you that you may build a house on it," and B on the strength of that promise, with the knowledge of A, expends a large sum of money in building a house accordingly, I cannot doubt that the donee acquires a right from the subsequent transaction to call on the donor to perform that contract and complete the imperfect donation which was made.

In *Plimmer's* case, 9 App. Cas. 699 the Privy Council pose the question, how should the equity be satisfied? (See pp. 713, 714.) And the Board declare that on the facts a

licence revocable at will became irrevocable as a consequence of the subsequent transactions. So in *Thomas v. Thomas*, [1956] NZLR 785 the Supreme Court of New Zealand
ordered the defendant to execute a proper transfer of the property.

In *Crabb v. Arun District Council*, [1976] Ch. 179 this court had to consider the
principles upon which the court should give effect to the equity: see Lord Denning MR at
p. 189. Lawton and Scarman LJJ agreed with the remedy proposed by Lord Denning MR.
On the facts of that case Scarman LJ expressed himself thus at pp. 198-199:

> I turn now to the other two questions—the extent of the equity and the relief needed to
> satisfy it. There being no grant, no enforceable contract, no licence, I would analyse the
> minimum equity to do justice to the plaintiff as a right either to an easement or to a
> licence upon terms to be agreed. I do not think it is necessary to go further than that. Of
> course, going that far would support the equitable remedy of injunction which is sought
> in this action. If there is no agreement as to terms, if agreement fails to be obtained, the
> court can, in my judgment, and must, determine in these proceedings upon what terms
> the plaintiff should be put to enable him to have the benefit of the equitable right which
> he is held to have. It is interesting that there has been some doubt amongst distinguished
> lawyers in the past as to whether the court can so proceed. Lord Kingsdown refers in
> fact to those doubts in a passage, which I need not quote, in *Ramsden v. Dyson*, LR 1 HL
> 129, 171. Lord Thurlow clearly thought that the court did have this power. Other
> lawyers of that time did not. But there can be no doubt that since *Ramsden v. Dyson* the
> courts have acted upon the basis that they have to determine not only the extent of the
> equity, but also the conditions necessary to satisfy it, and they have done so in a great
> number and variety of cases. I need refer only to the interesting collection of cases
> enumerated in *Snell's Principles of Equity*, 27th ed., pp. 567-568, para. 2(b). In the
> present case the court does have to consider what is necessary now in order to satisfy
> the plaintiff's equity.

So the principle to be applied is that the court should consider all the circumstances, and
the counterclaimant having at law no perfected gift or licence other than a licence
revocable at will, the court must decide what is the minimum equity to do justice to her
having regard to the way in which she changed her position for the worse by reason of
the acquiescence and encouragement of the legal owner. The defendant submits that the
only appropriate way in which the equity can here be satisfied is by perfecting the
imperfect gift as was done in *Dillwyn v. Llewelyn*.

Counsel for the plaintiff on instructions has throughout submitted that the plaintiff
is entitled to possession. The only concession that he made was that the period of notice
given in the letter of April 9, 1976 was too short. He made no submission upon the way
the equity, if there was an equity, should be satisfied save to submit that the court should
not in any view grant a remedy more beneficial to the defendant than a licence to occupy
the house for her lifetime.

We are satisfied that the problem of remedy on the facts resolves itself into a choice
between two alternatives: should the equity be satisfied by a licence to the defendant to
occupy the house for her lifetime, or should there be a transfer to her of the fee simple?

The main consideration pointing to a licence for her lifetime is that she did not by
her case at the hearing seek to establish that she had spent more money or done more

work on the house than she would have done had she believed that she had only a licence to live there for her lifetime. But the court must be cautious about drawing any inference from what she did not give in evidence as the hypothesis put is one that manifestly never occurred to her. Then it may reasonably be held that her expenditure and effort can hardly be regarded as comparable to the change of position of those who have constructed buildings on land over which they had no legal rights.

This court appreciates that the moneys laid out by the defendant were much less than in some of the cases in the books. But the court has to look at all the circumstances. When the plaintiff left her she was, we were told, a widow in her middle fifties. During the period that she lived with the plaintiff her capital was reduced from £4,500 to £1,000. Save for her invalidity pension that was all that she had in the world. In reliance upon the plaintiff's declaration of gift, encouragement and acquiescence she arranged her affairs on the basis that the house and contents belonged to her. So relying, she devoted a quarter of her remaining capital and her personal effort upon the house and its fixtures. In addition she bought carpets, curtains and furniture for it, with the result that by the date of the trial she had only £300 left. Compared to her, on the evidence the plaintiff is a rich man. He might not regard an expenditure of a few hundred pounds as a very grave loss. But the court has to regard her change of position over the years 1973 to 1976.

We take the view that the equity cannot here be satisfied without granting a remedy which assures to the defendant security of tenure, quiet enjoyment, and freedom of action in respect of repairs and improvements without interference from the plaintiff. The history of the conduct of the plaintiff since April 9, 1976, in relation to these proceedings leads to an irresistible inference that he is determined to pursue his purpose of evicting her from the house by any legal means at his disposal with a ruthless disregard of the obligations binding upon conscience. The court must grant a remedy effective to protect her against the future manifestations of his ruthlessness. It was conceded that if she is granted a licence, such a licence cannot be registered as a land charge, so that she may find herself ousted by a purchaser for value without notice. If she has in the future to do further and more expensive repairs she may not be able to finance them by a loan, but as a licensee she cannot charge the house. The plaintiff as legal owner may well find excuses for entry in order to do what he may plausibly represent as necessary works and so contrive to derogate from her enjoyment of the licence in ways that make it difficult or impossible for the court to give her effective protection.

Weighing such considerations this court concludes that the equity to which the facts in this case give rise can only be satisfied by compelling the plaintiff to give effect to his promise and her expectations. He has so acted that he must now perfect the gift.

Appeal dismissed.

[The court further declared that the estate in fee simple in the house was vested in the defendant. The plaintiff was ordered to execute a conveyance at his expense within 28 days, and in default, the registrar of the county court was authorized to execute it. Leave to appeal was refused.]

Discussion Notes

Characterizing the Arrangement

The court had no difficulty concluding that the plaintiff made a valid gift of the contents of the house to the defendant. Why? Why was this reasoning not available to support a gift of the realty? Recall the discussion of gifts of personal and real property and the principle of *Milroy v. Lord* (1862), 45 ER 1185 that "equity will not perfect an imperfect gift." How does this principle relate to the court's reasoning about the real and personal property in *Pascoe v. Turner*?

Proprietary Estoppel

Why did the the court conclude that the defendant should succeed on the basis of proprietary estoppel rather than resulting or constructive trust? Would it have been possible to order a transfer of the fee simple if the court had concluded that there was a trust? Is the court considering what remedy is appropriate in the process of characterizing the nature of the family arrangement?

Consider a situation in which a young woman and a man began to cohabit, each of them having separated from their former spouses. They had a daughter. They then bought a home; the man took title in his name alone because, he said, the woman was not yet 21-years old. He later explained that he said this as an excuse for not putting the house in their joint names. The house was somewhat dilapidated, and the young woman did a lot of work to the house and garden. They had a second child in 1970. Although their respective marriages had been dissolved by this time, they did not marry. Eventually the man left the relationship and married someone else. The young woman brought an application for a share in the house. The trial judge dismissed the application and the plaintiff appealed. How should this case be resolved? Is this case similar to *Pascoe v. Turner*, or *Hussey v. Palmer*? See *Eves v. Eves*, [1975] 1 WLR 1338 (CA). For a feminist critique of *Eves* and similar cases, see A. Bottomley, "Self and Subjectivities: Languages of Claim in Property Law," in A. Bottomley and J. Conaghan, eds., *Feminist Theory and Legal Strategy* (Oxford, UK: Basil Blackwell, 1993), 56.

Was the defendant's expenditure in *Pascoe v. Turner* as substantial as that of Jack Baker in *Inwards v. Baker*. Recall *Dodsworth v. Dodsworth* (1973), 228 Estates Gazette 1115, above, where the court merely required the repayment of the amount of the expenditure rather than creating a substantial property interest. Is *Pascoe v. Turner* a case in which the amount of the expenditure is so small that it is not appropriate to grant an interest in land? Why?

Some cases have suggested that promissory estoppel, by contrast with proprietary estoppel, can be used only as a shield, not a sword. It seems to be well established, however, that proprietary estoppel may be used as either shield or sword. For further analysis, see E.H.T. Snell, *Snell's Principles of Equity*, 28th ed., rev. P.V. Baker and P. St.J. Langan (London: Sweet and Maxwell, 1982) and J. Manwaring, "Promissory Estoppel in the Supreme Court of Canada" (1986), 10 *Dalhousie Law Journal* 43. Related issues are explored in J. Beatson, "Proprietary Claims in the Law of Restitution" (1995), 25 *Canadian Business Law Journal* 66; P.T. Evans, "Choosing the Right

Estoppel" (1988), *The Conveyancer and Property Lawyer* 346; and D. Waters, "Proprietary Relief: Two Privy Council Decisions—A Canadian Perspective" (1995), 25 *Canadian Business Law Journal* 90.

Pascoe v. Turner can be distinguished from *Hussey v. Palmer* and *Inwards v. Baker*
on its facts—the parties in *Pascoe v. Turner* were a cohabiting couple, unlike the parties
in the other two cases. *Pascoe v. Turner* also needs to be considered in relation to cases
involving the allocation of property interests at family breakdown, issues considered in
more detail in chapter 7. Gray and Symes have characterized the decision in *Pascoe v.
Turner* as "remarkable" because

> the equitable jurisdiction of the court was effectively invoked to bring about a
> redistribution of assets on the breakdown of a de facto marriage relationship. The
> manner and extent of the redistribution lay entirely within the discretion of the court,
> and the common law wife was thereby enabled to circumvent the rule that a de facto
> spouse cannot claim property adjustment or financial provision from her partner on the
> demise of their relationship.

(Gray and Symes, at 493.) After examining such cases as *Pettkus v. Becker*, [1980] 2
SCR 834 and *Peter v. Beblow*, [1993] 1 SCR 980 in chapter 7, assess whether *Pascoe v.
Turner* would be regarded as "remarkable" in the Canadian context. Consider the differ-
ences in the remedies provided in these cases—which outcome is preferable? For a
further comparison of arrangements for cohabiting partners in different jurisdictions, see
M.A. Neave, "Three Approaches to Family Property Disputes—Intention/Belief, Unjust
Enrichment, and Unconscionability," in T.G. Youdan, *Equity, Fiduciaries and Trusts*
(Scarborough, ON: Carswell, 1989), 252.

Judicial recognition of "equities" in these cases is an example of recent reform of
property law principles. Some commentators have compared this judicial reform activity
to 19th-century developments concerning the enforcement of negative or restrictive
covenants. As chapter 6 explains, contractual agreements between landowners may
sometimes be enforceable in equity against third parties with notice. However, the broad
nature of enforceability, established in *Tulk v. Moxhay* (1848), 47 ER 1345 (CA), was
gradually constrained by subsequent judicial decision making—see H.W.R. Wade, "Licences and Third Parties" (1952), 68 *Law Quarterly Review* 337. After considering the
materials in chapter 6, reflect on the need for similar constraints in relation to equities.

A NOTE ON PRIORITIES AND REGISTRATION

As this and other chapters have demonstrated, there will often be a number of different
proprietary interests in relation to chattels or land in existence at the same time. Principles for establishing priority are necessary as a way of determining relative priority
among a number of competing interests. Recall how priority was determined among a
number of claimants of chattels in chapter 2, using the concept of prior possession.
Principles of priority were similarly developed by courts for documentary and equitable
interests, usually based on the order of their creation. These principles have been successively modified by statutes that create systems for the registration of property interests
and that accord priority based on the order in which documents are registered. Principles

of priorities form a substantial part of the law of real estate transactions and also affect legal relationships in commercial, securities, and bankruptcy law. Thus, this note provides only a short introduction to issues that you may wish to examine in greater depth in more advanced courses.

Priorities at Common Law

The basic common law principle, *nemo dat quod non habet,* or one cannot give what one does not have, means that (with a few special exceptions) a transferor cannot confer on a transferee a title that is greater than that held by the transferor. In property law, the transferee thus needs to ensure that the title being conveyed is the same as that which the transferor purports to be able to convey. One reason for the development of systems of registration was the need to facilitate the process of determining the validity of a transferor's title. As will be explained, however, there are some registration systems that, in fact, confer title by registration.

Initially, in the absence of systems of registration, courts developed principles for determining priority among competing legal and equitable interests; these principles continue to be important in determining the priority among unregistered interests in some situations. Essentially, where two claimants both hold legal interests, or where two claimants both hold equitable interests, the rule is that priority is determined in accordance with the order of creation of the interests. For example, if A conveyed a legal estate to B, and then purported to convey the same legal estate to C, B's interest took priority. This result follows from the rule that the first of two legal interests takes priority. Can the result be explained in another way as well? Consider the application of the *nemo dat* rule here, for example. Note also that C's problem, at least in theory, could have been avoided if C had properly investigated A's title, a process infinitely easier where there is a system for registering property interests. As is obvious, moreover, A has been either negligent or fraudulent in conveying the same interest to two transferees, a situation that might permit recovery by C against A, but which may not affect B's priority. For an example where a prior interest was "postponed" in favour of a later one, however, see *Northern Counties of England Fire Insurance Company v. Whipp* (1884), 26 Ch.D 482 (CA).

Where there are two equitable claims, the principle is somewhat modified—the rule is that the prior claim prevails, but only if the equities are otherwise equal: *Rice v. Rice* (1854), 61 ER 646 (Ch.D). Thus, in a contest between two equitable claims, a court examines all the equities between the parties before permitting the first-created equitable claim to prevail. Where a legal claim is prior to an equitable claim, the legal claim generally takes priority—that is, where the equities are equal, the law will prevail, but there may be postponement of such a legal claim if the prior claimant has engaged in inequitable conduct. See, for example, *Tyrell v. Mills,* [1924] 3 WWR 387 (BC Co. Ct.).

The position of a prior equitable claim and a subsequent legal claim has already been considered above and in earlier chapters. The prior equitable interest is enforceable against everyone except the *bona fide* purchaser for value without notice. This formulation includes the idea that a claimant in equity must come with clean hands (the *bona fide* requirement). As well, since equity will not assist "a volunteer," the holder of the subsequent interest must be a "purchaser for value," not a donee. Some commentators have questioned whether transactions in which land is conveyed for "$1.00 and other good and valuble consideration" will be sufficient to establish that the transferee is a purchaser for value—see, for example, G.V. La Forest, "The History and Place of the Registry Act in New Brunswick Land Law" (1970), 20 *University of New Brunswick Law Journal* 1.

The necessity to show that the transferee is "without notice" is also significant. A transferee who inspects land before purchasing it may discover the existence of other inconsistent claims if, for example, someone other than the purchaser is in possession and the resident provides clear evidence of an inconsistent interest. Such notice is characterized as actual notice of inconsistent claims. However, in addition to actual notice, a transferee may be affected by imputed or constructive notice of inconsistent claims. In general, imputed notice means notice to any agent of the transferee. More significantly, constructive notice means that a transferee will be bound by anything that should have come to his or her attention. Thus, if a transferee fails to inspect premises, or fails to make full inquiries with respect to the interests of any person in possession, the transferee will be subject to any interests that would have come to his or her attention in a proper inspection. For example, if a transferee inspects the premises and discovers someone other than the transferor in possession, the transferee will be bound by a claim asserted by such a person in possession, on the basis that there was an obligation to make full inquiries—see *Hunt v. Luck*, [1902] 1 Ch. 428 (CA). Even though the transferee may not have received actual notice, a court may find that the transferee had constructive notice.

The issue of constructive notice shows the extent to which purchasers bear the risk of ensuring that the transferor has title to convey. Consider a situation in which an elderly woman initially transferred title to her home to her male boarder, apparently so that he could take care of it for her. Pursuant to this understanding, they agreed orally that the boarder would hold the property as trustee for her benefit. Subsequently, the male boarder transferred legal title to a purchaser. When the elderly woman discovered the conveyance to the purchaser, she brought an application to enforce her equitable interest under the oral trust agreement against the purchaser of the legal estate. The purchaser had inspected the premises prior to the transfer, and had noticed that the elderly woman was present as well as the male boarder, but the purchaser had assumed (without asking) that she was the wife of the male boarder. Did the purchaser have constructive notice of the woman's interest under the trust agreement? See *Hodgson v. Marks*, [1971] Ch. 892 (CA), where the court held that the woman's equitable interest was enforceable against the purchaser because the transferee, although a *bona fide* purchaser for value, was not without notice of the prior interest.

Does this case mean that a prospective purchaser must question everyone on the premises in case there are "hidden" interests? Should a person in the position of the woman in *Hodgson v. Marks* be permitted to enforce an interest when she remained silent during the purchaser's inspection (apparently because she did not understand the situation and was unaware of her boarder's fraudulent activity)? Does this case suggest a need to require registration of equitable interests as a condition of their enforceability?

As was evident in *Inwards v. Baker*, [1965] 2 QB 29 (CA), above, an "equity" may also be enforceable against the transferee of the legal estate if the transferee is not a purchaser for value. Recall that the widow and her children acquired the legal estate under the will of Jack Baker's father. As a result, the court concluded that, since they were not purchasers for value, Jack Baker's prior "equity" was enforceable against them. Thus, it is clear that there are some cases in which an equity will be enforced as if it were an equitable interest. However, the nature of an equity, by contrast with an equitable interest, means that an equity may not always be so enforceable. For further analysis, see D. Jackson, *Principles of Property Law* (Sydney: Law Book Co., 1967), 72-77, and a discussion of the apparently different views on this issue in *National Provincial Bank v. Ainsworth*, [1965] AC 1175 (CA) in England and *Latec Investment Ltd. v. Hotel Terrigal Pty. Ltd.* (1965), 113 CLR 265 in Australia. In terms of principle, Jackson concluded (at 77):

> [I]t makes more theoretical and practical sense to admit the existence of a category of proprietary interest, in the sense of an interest enforceable against a person other than the grantor, which is neither an equitable nor a legal interest. It consists of situations where equity intervenes to protect, and therefore create, the interest because of the particular circumstances. In time the category may consist of a list of interests as does that of legal and equitable interest. At the present it represents a still developing concept of a proprietary interest.

Recall the concerns expressed above in the discussion of equities in relation to the uncertainty created by judicial recognition of these interests and the difficulties created for purchasers who may be bound by them even if they fail to discover them before receiving a transfer of the legal estate. Do you agree with Jackson? You may want to reconsider these issues in relation to the discussion of registration systems that follows, since some interests may be rendered unenforceable unless they are registered. For a further analysis of priorities at common law, see Ziff, at 399-407 and A.R. Everton, "Equitable Interests and 'Equities': In Search of a Pattern" (1976), 40 *The Conveyancer and Property Lawyer* 209.

Registration

The history of registration systems in England began with the Statute of Enrolments of 1535, enacted in conjunction with the Statute of Uses. There were subsequent efforts to establish systems for registering title to land, but many of them applied only to designated counties or to London. Registration reforms were introduced by the Law of Property Act, 1925, 15 & 16 Geo. V, c. 21, but the reform process remains ongoing. See R.R.A. Walker, "The Genesis of Land Registration in England" (1939), 55 *Law Quarterly Review* 547 and H.W. Wilkinson, "I Have a Dream" (1993), *The Conveyancer and Property Lawyer* 101.

Registration systems for land title were introduced into Canada from an early period. According to Ziff, the earliest statute was introduced in Nova Scotia by imperial ordinace in 1752, and an early statute was enacted by the Nova Scotia legislature in 1759. Ontario enacted legislation concerning land registration in the Registry Act, 35 Geo. III, c. 5. For an account of the evolution of registration in Ontario, see T. Youdan, "The Length of a Title Search in Ontario" (1986), 64 *Canadian Bar Review* 507 and Ziff, at 407ff.

In general, these early registration statutes created systems of deeds registration. A deeds-registration system creates a public record and place of deposit for documents relating to the title to all parcels of land. However, the deposit of title documents in a public register does not confer any additional validity on these documents; their validity and effect on the vendor's title must be satisfied by the purchaser's careful examination. In some situations, the failure to register may diminish the enforceability of an interest against another registered interest. Thus, although registration may not affect the inherent validity of a document, failure to register it may limit its enforceability, especially against a registered interest. Deeds-registration statutes define how priority will be accorded to competing documents. For examples in relation to Ontario's Registry Act, see M.A. Neave, "Conveyancing Under the Ontario Registry Act: An Analysis of the Priority Provisions and Some Suggestions for Reform" (1977), 55 *Canadian Bar Review* 500 and J. Chapman, "A Stacked Deck: Specific Performance and the Real Estate Transaction" (1994), 16:3 *Advocates' Quarterly* 273. As a result of amendments to Ontario's Registry Act introduced in 1981, there was some uncertainty for a period of time about the precise obligations of purchasers in searching titles, particularly in relation to the length of search required. In *Fire v. Longtin* (1995), 46 RPR (2d) 1 (SCC), the Supreme Court of Canada affirmed the interpretation of these provisions set out in the earlier Court of Appeal decision—(1994), 38 RPR (2d) 1 (Ont. CA). For a full discussion (and a consensus opinion on the part of several real estate lawyers), see B. Bucknall et al., "Title Searching Under the Ontario Registry Act After *Fire v. Longtin*: A Consensus Opinion" (1996), 1 RPR (3d) 173.

Deeds-resistration systems were introduced in Ontario and in the four Atlantic provinces. By contrast, the western provinces legislated statutory registration systems that were based on a scheme developed by Robert Torrens and introduced in the state of South Australia in 1858. (The Land Titles Act system in Ontario has also been characterized as a "modified" Torrens system, operating in relation to some parts of the province with other parts subject to the Registry Act.) In general, a Torrens registration system provides greater simplicity and cost-effectiveness, and it is distinguished from deeds-registration systems because the registration of an interest in Torrens registration confers validity. Thus, as Ziff explained:

> Under Torrens the register is supposed to be everything. This means that one should (in theory anyway) be able to examine an abstract of title for a specific parcel of land and see listed there all of the interests in land that pertain to that parcel. The register is said to be a *mirror* of all rights in relation to that land. As a result, the failure to register a property interest alters the priorities that would otherwise govern that entitlement. A person registering without proper notice of a prior interest can claim priority over it.

(Ziff, at 412.) The idea that the register is a mirror is the basis for the concept of "indefeasibility" of title in Torrens registration systems, although both statutory provisions and judicial interpretation have somewhat qualified indefeasibility of title in most jurisdictions that have adopted Torrens registration schemes. A Torrens system of registration also includes a compensation fund, available to persons whose interests are compromised as a result of errors produced by the system. As is evident, therefore, a Torrens system of registration represents significantly more public or state involvement in defining the validity of titles to land, by contrast with the private process of land transfers reflected in a deeds-registration system.

The lack of uniformity with respect to land-registration systems among provincial jurisdictions in Canada makes the process of transferring interests in land complex and sometimes difficult. In recent years, there have been a number of efforts to reform registration processes. For example, representatives of the Council of Maritime Premiers and other provincial jurisdictions published a draft Model Land Recording and Registration Act for real property in 1990. See Joint Land Titles Committee, *Renovating the Foundation: Proposals for a Model Land Recording and Registration Act for the Provinces and Territories of Canada* (Edmonton: Alberta Law Reform Institute, 1990). In Ontario, the Province of Ontario Land Registration and Information System (POLARIS) introduced a computerized system for organizing and managing data related to land holdings; it is anticipated that an electronic registration process will be in place very soon. Accompanying computerization, land holdings are being converted from Registry Act lands to "qualified" Land Titles registration, and there are plans to introduce a title insurance scheme, as well as changes to lawyers' traditional errors and omissions insurance accordingly—see (1996), 6:1 *The Adviser* 1 (The Law Society of Upper Canada); and (1997), 18:4 *Briefly Speaking* (Canadian Bar Association-Ontario). In Alberta, the Model Land Recording and Registration Act has been used in establishing a Métis land-registry system—see C. Bell, *Alberta's Métis Settlements Legislation: An Overview of Ownership and Management of Settlement Lands* (Regina: Canadian Plains Research Centre, 1994).

In spite of this reform activity, however, it remains important to understand the basic concepts examined in this chapter that concern the transfer of interests by gift and sale. As Ziff stated, "[S]ystems of registration ... [provide] a thin procedural veneer that covers the substantive law of property. ... [The rules concerning registration] presuppose existing entitlements and seek to determine only how these stand in relation to each other." See Ziff, at 399. Although a full assessment of this statement requires a more sophisticated knowledge of real estate transactions, Ziff's statement reinforces the need to understand the fundamental principles concerning creation and transfer of property interests as the basis for more sophisticated work in advanced courses.

PROBLEMS

1. Aunt Mary lived alone in her large home after the death of her husband, a concert pianist of some note. She found it distressing and sad to see her deceased husband's piano in the living-room each day. When her nephew Timothy came for his weekly visit on Saturday morning, she told him of her feelings about the piano, and quite spontaneously said, "I want to give you the piano. Right this minute! Take it with you." Timothy expressed his delight and appreciation for such a wonderful gift, especially because it would provide such fond memories of his uncle. He looked in the telephone book for a piano mover, and then called and made arrangements to have the piano moved as soon as possible, which turned out to be the following Monday afternoon. Timothy left his aunt's home very happy, and spent the rest of the weekend rearranging the furniture in his home to make room for the piano.

On Monday afternoon, Timothy and the piano movers arrived at Aunt Mary's to find the piano gone. Aunt Mary explained that she changed her mind on Sunday after talking to the minister at her church, who expressed great enthusiasm about providing a suitable "public" place for her husband's piano in the church. Thus, with her consent, church movers came and took the piano on Monday morning.

Can Timothy claim the piano from the church? Consider the legal principles applicable here—are they congruent with social conventions or moral expectations? What concerns underlie legal principles about gifts? Is this a case involving undue influence, in the light of Aunt Mary's grief?

This situation may also require an analysis of contract remedies. For example, if Timothy had paid for the piano movers in advance, using his credit card, has he suffered detrimental reliance? Should his remedy be related to the cost he incurred for the removal of the piano, or to his expectation loss—the value of the piano itself? Note that these issues show the relationship between principles in property concerning gifts and those relating to remedies in contract law.

2. An elderly man, originally from France but now living in Nova Scotia, became ill with severe stomach pains. Convinced that he might die, he decided to return to France for treatment and, if treatment were unsuccessful, to die in his native land. Before leaving for France, he purchased a deposit certificate in his grandson's name. He apparently told his grandson that he was ill, and that he planned to return to France. He also said that, if he were he to die in France, his grandson could keep the money, but if he were to return to Nova Scotia, his grandson would have to return the money. The deposit certificate was not negotiable; the grandfather retained it and the passbook in his possession. Interest cheques were sent to the grandfather's address.

The grandfather went to France, recovered, and returned to Nova Scotia. The bank would not return the money to the grandfather without the signature of his grandson, and the grandson refused to sign a release. Eventually, the grandfather brought an action against his grandson for the return of the money.

Was there a valid gift to the grandson? Who has the onus to prove a valid gift? Were the requisite elements present for a gift *inter vivos*, or for a *donatio mortis causa*? How would you characterize the plaintiff's intention? Was there sufficient delivery? For a case similar to these facts, see *Kooner v. Kooner* (1979), 100 DLR (3d) 76 (BC SC).

3. Pam Cohen signed a document, entitled "Agreement to Lease," that was dated February 20, 1997. Immediately after signing the document, she made arrangements to do substantial renovations to the leased property and paid nearly $20,000 to the contractor who undertook the work for her. Since March 1, 1977, Pam has been using the premises as a trendy hair cutting salon for men and women. However, the lessor has recently advised her that she must move out because he wants to lease the premises to another tenant. Pam Cohen is therefore seeking advice about her legal position, having regard to the renovations she completed and in the light of the document she signed. The document is very short. It simply states:

Pam Cohen hereby agrees to enter into a lease with the usual covenants with Dominion Investments Ltd. The parties agree that Pam Cohen will pay rent in the amount of

$2,000 per month in respect of a lease of the premises at 2019 Bath Road (Suite 2), Kingston, commencing March 1, 1997, for a period of five years.

(Signed)
Pam Cohen

If the lessor had indicated an interest in leasing the premises to another tenant after Pam had signed the agreement to lease and completed the renovations, but before she had commenced her business, what would be her legal position? Would it make any difference if the lessor had granted possession to a subsequent tenant?

4. Gisela Cicero is a recently graduated lawyer living in Toronto. She works hard and enjoys her law practice, but because many of her clients are poor, her annual income is not large. Recently, however, her uncle in Italy died and left her a small inheritance of approximately $15,000. Gisela would like to use this money to invest in a house.

She has investigated the possibility of using the money as a downpayment on a house, but the sum is really too small. She is also concerned about monthly mortgage payments, since her earnings are somewhat uneven and precarious. Her good friend, Sam Simmons, has suggested that she could use the money effectively by moving into a house that he has inherited (mortgage-free). With her inheritance, she could afford to do necessary renovations to the kitchen and bathroom. Even though he does not have to pay a mortgage, Sam has no money to do these renovations because he is still a student and his funds are only sufficient to pay the taxes and monthly expenses on the house. Thus, Sam thinks that the arrangement would suit both of them very well.

Sam has assured Gisela that they will marry when he completes his Ph.D in three years, and that he will pay back her $15,000 when he obtains a university teaching job. In the meantime, he says that she will have a good home and that she will have made an excellent investment with her uncle's inheritance.

Advise Gisela about her legal rights in relation to Sam's proposal, and explain how she can protect her potential investment.

CHAPTER SIX

Non-Possessory Interests in Land: "Private" Planning and the Use of Land

This chapter provides an introduction to non-possessory property interests—that is, proprietary interests that do not include a right to possession. As we explored in earlier chapters, possession is often fundamental to the creation of property interests, as in finders' cases or adverse possession of land, and it is possible to divide property interests on the basis of holders of possession and title, as in bailment and leases. In this chapter, we examine property interests that exist without a right to possession, a somewhat abstract but very common and important set of proprietary interests in land.

Specifically, this chapter examines three kinds of non-possessory interests—*profits à prendre*, easements, and covenants. Conceptually, these non-possessory interests are often linked to a larger group of interests that "limit" the rights of landowners in their use of land—for example, rights of occupation in a licence or lease (chapter 4), or other limits on landowners set out in fee simples that are determinable or subject to condition (chapter 3). Similarly, the Supreme Court of Canada has recognized a right of the public in the nature of an implied licence in relation to government property, pursuant to the Charter's guarantee of freedom of expression—a right that constrains the rights of the landowner. See *Committee for the Commonwealth of Canada v. Canada*, [1991] 1 SCR 139 (and chapter 1).

Yet even though some aspects of *profits à prendre*, easements, and covenants share functional similarities with these other arrangements limiting a landowner's use of land, legal principles about these three interests have been regarded as conceptually distinct because they do not include rights to possession. In the United States, there have been lively debates about the appropriateness of maintaining easements and covenants as separate doctrinal categories and some persuasive arguments about adopting a redefined "law of servitudes" (including both easements and covenants) in their places. See, for example, U. Reichman, "Toward a Unified Concept of Servitudes" (1982), 55 *Southern California Law Review* 1177 (hereafter Reichman (1982)) and the work of the American Law Institute, *Restatement of the Law, Property (Servitudes)* (Philadelphia, PA: American Law Institute, 1989), discussed at the end of this chapter.

Easements and covenants have also been characterized as mechanisms of "private" land-use planning. Prior to more widespread enactment of local planning statutes and zoning regulations, easements and covenants were used to achieve neighbourhood planning objectives. As will become clear, however, such private planning devices could also be used to prohibit access to certain neighbourhoods on the basis of race and class, a result of the lack of public scrutiny inherent in "private" planning activities. Since most private planning occurs in the context of privately negotiated contracts, non-possessory interests raise, once again, the intersection of property and contract law principles and the relationship between law and equity. As will be explained below, non-possessory interests are also concerned with the public/private dichotomy in law, an issue reflected in chapters 7 and 8 as well.

In this chapter, the balancing of private rights of landowners to "do as they like" with their land and the concomitant rights of others (including non-owners of land) to constrain landowners' choices is evidenced in the tension within some of the legal principles and their application in practice. As you consider the issues in this chapter, think about the following comment concerning US landowners, and assess the degree to which it applies in Canada as a description of the balancing of these interests:

> The property owner is the primary planner of land use. This statement may appear to conflict with the conventional notion that planning and resource management are public functions, to be exercised by government officials, boards, and professional staff. But the public role in the United States is essentially reactive to the decisions of the property owner. It is the owner who determines *how* to utilize his or her land in light of geographic, economic, legal and personal circumstances. It is also the owner who determines *when* a change in existing land use should occur. It is the owner's decision to change the use of land that triggers the public reactive role.

(R. Platt, *Land Use and Society: Geography, Law, and Public Policy* (Washington, DC: Island Press, 1996), at 93.)

THE PROFIT À PRENDRE

According to Megarry and Wade, *The Law of Real Property*, 5th ed. (London: Stevens & Sons, 1984), at 850, a *profit à prendre* is "a right to take something off another's land," including such things as timber, minerals, or wildlife. Bruce Ziff described a *profit à prendre* as entitling the holder of this non-possessory interest "to enter onto the land of another to extract some part of the natural produce, such as timber, crops, turf, soil, grass or animals." It may also entitle one "to extract oil and natural gas: this is the type of grant sometimes used in modern drilling and extraction operations." See Bruce Ziff, *Principles of Property Law*, 2d ed. (Scarborough, ON: Carswell, 1996) (hereafter Ziff (1996)), at 333-34.

The idea of a *profit à prendre* was illustrated in a well-known decision about the doctrine of part performance (discussed in chapter 5), *Mason v. Clarke*, [1955] 1 All ER 914 (HL). Mr. Mason paid £100 for the right to kill and take rabbits on the Holthorpe Estate for a year from October 11, 1950. When he tried to exercise this right, however, he was prevented from doing so by the respondent. In the suit that followed, Lord Morton of Henryton stated (at 923): "A profit à prendre is an interest in land." The court found for Mr. Mason on the basis that he had an equitable interest arising from the doctrine of part performance. Thus, he had an equitable *profit à prendre*.

The *profit à prendre* exhibits some similarities to a licence, since both permit the use of another's land for defined purposes. According to Mendes da Costa, Balfour, and Gillese, *Property Law: Cases, Text and Materials*, 2d ed. (Toronto: Emond-Montgomery, 1990), at 19:14, however, "a profit à prendre is not revocable in the sense of a licence, which is generally terminable at any time upon reasonable notice." As well, the nature of a *profit à prendre* is the right to remove something from land.

The Supreme Court of Canada considered the nature of the *profit à prendre* in *R in Right of British Columbia v. Tener*, [1985] 1 SCR 533. In this case, the plaintiffs sought compensation in respect of mining rights that were adversely affected by the enactment of provincial legislation establishing the subject lands in British Columbia as a provincial park. The judges in the court were not entirely in agreement about how to characterize the mining rights, but Madam Justice Wilson (with the concurrence of Chief Justice Dickson) concluded (at 540) that the claim should be characterized as a *profit à prendre*:

> I think that the learned Chambers judge may have been in error in treating the respondents as having two separate and distinct interests in the land—the mineral claims and a right to go on the surface for the purpose of developing them ... . I believe that what the respondents had was one integral interest in land in the nature of a profit à prendre comprising both the mineral claims and the surface rights necessary for their enjoyment.

This case focused on the basis for compensation to be awarded, and is interesting as an example of the intersection of private property interests and public regulatory issues. For further discussion of the case and these issues, see M.J. Mossman, "Developments in Property Law: The 1984-85 Term" (1986), 8 *Supreme Court Law Review* 319, at 321-30.

There are numerous cases where aboriginal claims to hunt or fish on lands might also be categorized as *profits à prendre*, although jurisprudence in Canada has tended to recognize these claims on the basis of special principles applicable to aboriginal rights. For example, in *R v. Sparrow*, [1990] 1 SCR 1075, the Supreme Court of Canada recognized that the Musqueam band held an aboriginal right to fish for food, going beyond mere subsistence and extending to fish consumed for social and ceremonial purposes. In its analysis, the court referred (at 1094) to *Guerin v. The Queen*, [1984] 2 SCR 335 and the need to ensure the recognition of such aboriginal claims as "*sui generis*" interests:

The Aboriginal Right

We turn now to the aboriginal right at stake in this appeal. The Musqueam Indian Reserve is located on the north shore of the Fraser River close to the mouth of that river and within the limits of the city of Vancouver. There has been a Musqueam village there for hundreds of years. This appeal does not directly concern the reserve or the adjacent waters, but arises out of the band's right to fish in another area of the Fraser River estuary known as Canoe Passage in the south arm of the river, some 16 kilometres (about 10 miles) from the reserve. The reserve and those waters are separated by the Vancouver International Airport and the Municipality of Richmond.

The evidence reveals that the Musqueam have lived in the area as an organized society long before the coming of European settlers, and that the taking of salmon was an integral part of their lives and remains so to this day. Much of the evidence of an aboriginal right to fish was given by Dr. Suttles, an anthropologist, supported by that of Mr. Grant, the band administrator. The Court of Appeal thus summarized Dr. Suttles' evidence, at pp. 307-308:

> Dr. Suttles was qualified as having particular qualifications in respect of the ethnography of the Coast Salish Indian people of which the Musqueams were one of several tribes. He thought that the Musqueam had lived in their historic territory, which includes the Fraser River estuary, for at least 1,500 years. That historic territory extended from the north short of Burrard Inlet to the south shore of the main channel of the Fraser River, including the waters of the three channels by which that river reaches the ocean. As part of the Salish people, the Musqueam were part of a regional social network covering a much larger area but, as a tribe, were themselves an organized social group with their own name, territory and resources. Between the tribes there was a flow of people, wealth and food. No tribe was wholly self-sufficient or occupied its territory to the complete exclusion of others.
>
> Dr. Suttles described the special position occupied by the salmon fishery in that society. The salmon was not only an important source of food but played an important part in the system of beliefs of the Salish people, and in their ceremonies. The salmon were held to be a race of beings that had, in "myth times," established a bond with human beings requiring the salmon to come each year to give their bodies to the humans who, in turn, treated them with respect shown by performance of the proper ritual. Toward the salmon, as toward other creatures, there was an attitude of caution and respect which resulted in effective conservation of the various species.

While the trial for a violation of a penal prohibition may not be the most appropriate setting in which to determine the existence of an aboriginal right, and the evidence was not extensive, the correctness of the finding of fact of the trial judge "that Mr. Sparrow was fishing in ancient tribal territory where his ancestors had fished from time immemorial in that part of the mouth of the Fraser River for salmon" is supported by the evidence and was not contested. The existence of the right, the Court of Appeal tells us, "was not the subject of serious dispute." It is not surprising, then, that, taken with other circumstances, that court should find that "the judgment appealed from was wrong in … failing to hold that Sparrow at the relevant time was exercising an existing aboriginal right." …

Our earlier observations regarding the scope of the aboriginal right to fish are relevant here. Fishing rights are not traditional property rights. They are held by a collective and are in keeping with the culture and existence of that group. Courts must be careful, then, to avoid the application of traditional common law concepts of property as they develop their understanding of what the reasons for judgment in *Guerin*, supra, at p. 382, referred to as the "sui generis" nature of aboriginal rights. (See also Little Bear, "A Concept of Native Title," [1982] 5 Can. Legal Aid. Bul. 99.)

While it is impossible to give an easy definition of fishing rights, it is possible, and, indeed, crucial, to be sensitive to the aboriginal perspective itself on the meaning of the rights at stake. For example, it would be artificial to try to create a hard distinction between the right to fish and the particular manner in which that right is exercised.

Discussion Notes

R v. Sparrow: Sui Generis Aboriginal Rights

Consider the nature of the aboriginal claim asserted in *R v. Sparrow*. Is it possible to characterize it as a *profit à prendre*? If it could be characterized in this way, what are the reasons for finding the right to be *"sui generis"*? For further discussion of these issues, see *R v. Jack*, [1980] 1 SCR 294. See also B. Slattery, "Understanding Aboriginal Rights" (1987), 66 *Canadian Bar Review* 726; K. McNeil, "The Constitutional Rights of the Aboriginal People of Canada" (1982), 4 *Supreme Court Law Review* 255; N. Lyon, "An Essay on Constitutional Interpretation" (1988), 26 *Osgoode Hall Law Journal* 95; and W. Pentney, "The Rights of the Aboriginal Peoples of Canada in the *Constitution Act, 1982*, Part II, Section 35: The Substantive Guarantee" (1988), 22 *University of British Columbia Law Review* 207.

Licence or Profit à Prendre?

In 1989, a landowner granted to R Ltd. "the sole and exclusive licence to remove all gravel" from his property for the economical lifetime of the gravel pit. Before R Ltd. registered its interest, the bank registered a charge (mortgage) relating to a loan to the landowner. The bank subsequently brought an application for a declaration that its mortgage had priority over R Ltd.'s licence agreement. The bank's application required the court to decide whether the agreement was an "instrument" as defined by s. 1 of the Registry Act, RSO 1990, c. R.20, and the court concluded that the agreement met the Registry Act requirements. Did the agreement create a *profit à prendre*? What is the difference between a licence and a *profit à prendre*? The issue was discussed briefly in *Canadian Imperial Bank of Commerce v. Rockway Holdings Ltd.* (1996), 29 OR (3d) 350, at 352-53.

EASEMENTS

Characterizing Easements: Gypsum Carrier Inc. v. The Queen

On July 2, 1968, the *Harry Lundeberg*, an ocean going freighter (owned by Gypsum Carrier Inc., and carrying gypsum from Mexico to New Westminster, BC), collided with the New Westminster Railway Bridge, which spanned the Fraser River near New Westminster. The bridge, owned by the federal government, was constructed in the early part of the 20th century for railway, vehicular, and passenger traffic. However, after the construction of the Pattullo Bridge upstream in the late 1930s, the New Westminster Railway Bridge was used only by railway companies, including the Canadian National Railway.

In the ensuing litigation after the collision, Gypsum Carrier Inc. was held liable for damages to the federal Crown in respect of the cost of repairs and loss of profits. In addition, three railway companies made claims for their expenses in rerouting their trains during the bridge closure, but Gypsum Carrier Inc. resisted these claims on the basis that "no damage or injury was caused to any property owned by the railway companies, or to any property in which they had a proprietary interest."

In evaluating the validity of the argument made by Gypsum Carrier Inc., the court reviewed the contractual agreements between each of the companies and the federal government. The railway companies argued that, pursuant to the contracts, they each had an easement. In reviewing the contracts, the federal court in *Gypsum Carrier Inc. v. The Queen*, 78 DLR (3d) 175 (FC TD) held that the railways were given the right to construct and maintain connections between their own tracks and those on the bridge and its approaches, and to run their trains over the bridge and its approaches, during the term of each agreement. The federal government, however, was given "full control over the maintenance and betterment of the property covered by this agreement," and had responsibility for repairing the bridge and its approaches at its own expense. Pursuant to the contracts, the railway companies agreed to pay $.53 per car passing over the bridge.

In rejecting the claim that the contracts created easements for the railway companies, Collier J stated (at 180):

> An easement has been defined as
>
>> a right annexed to land to utilise other land of different ownership in a particular manner (not involving the taking of any part of the natural produce of that land or of any part of its soil) or to prevent the owner of the other land from utilising his land in a particular manner. [*Halsbury's Laws of England*, 4th ed., vol. 14, at 4.]
>
> The railway companies contend that all the essential characteristics of an easement are here present. ...
>
> In my opinion, the agreements between the Crown and the railway companies did not create easements in favour of the railway companies. The documents, superficially, appear to contain the so-called essentials of an easement. But I think one must ascertain the intention of the parties. To my mind, when the agreements are read as a whole, there was no intention to create easements. The purpose was to create certain contractual rights whereby the railways, in return for stipulated fees, were permitted to run their trains over the bridge and approaches. There was no intention to create any rights annexed to land, or any interest in land.

Discussion Notes

The *Gypsum Carrier* case is an interesting illustration of property analysis about easements. Note, for example, that the court reviewed the substantive requirements for the creation of an easement and held that they were all present in these contracts. Nonetheless, the court declined to find that easements were created. Why? Compare Collier J's emphasis on the overall "intention of the parties" in *Gypsum Carrier* and cases examined later in this chapter. What is the significance of "intention" in the characterization of easements? Why does the court characterize the relationships as merely contractual rather than proprietary as well? What form of agreement might have satisfied the court that the parties intended to create easements in their respective contracts? Does the decision reflect a concern for "form over substance"? Was *Gypsum Carrier* wrongly decided?

In exploring these questions, note also that claims about easements often raise the *"numerus clausus"* principle of real property law—that is, the general hesitancy to admit new forms of proprietary interests. This reluctance to create new interests has been especially evident in the law of easements:

> English law is notorious for its reluctance to recognize new interests in land. Within the particular confines of the law of easements this reluctance has been illustrated by the fluctuation of opinion over the years on the question of whether or not new rights may be admitted to the company of the old and well recognized easements.

(A.J. McClean, "The Nature of an Easement" (1966), 5 *Western Law Review* 32 (hereafter McClean), at 32.)

To what extent did this general reluctance to create new easements appear to influence the decision in *Gypsum Carrier*? What options are available to assist a client who wishes to create an easement in such a situation? In *Gypsum Carrier* the railway companies also submitted arguments that they had "some lesser proprietary interest," although the exact nature of that interest was not specified. The court concluded (at 181) that "at best, they may have had some kind of licence in respect of land (the bridge and approaches)," but concluded that any such interest would not create liability here. What other possible kinds of property interests might have been created by these agreements? How should an easement be distinguished from a licence, for example?

The Four Requirements for Creating an Easement

Ziff stated the four requirements for the creation of an easement as follows:

1. There must be a dominant tenement (that enjoys the benefit of the easement) and a servient tenement (that is burdened).
2. The easement must accommodate the dominant tenement.
3. The dominant and servient tenements cannot be both owned and occupied by the same person.
4. The easement must be capable of forming the subject matter of a grant.

(Ziff (1996), at 329-31.)

Requirement of a Dominant and Servient Tenement

The requirement that there must be a "dominant" and a "servient" tenement means that an easement must be linked with two parcels of land, one over which the easement is exercised (the servient tenement) and one in favour of which the easement is created (the dominant tenement). Although this requirement is well-accepted in Canada and the United Kingdom, it does not apply in the United States, where it is possible for someone who does not hold an interest in adjoining land to hold an easement over a servient tenement. Such an easement is called an easement "in gross."

Traditionally, the authority relied upon for the requirement of a dominant and servient tenement in English and Canadian law is *Ackroyd v. Smith* (1850), 138 ER 68 (Common Pleas). In that case, the plaintiff's predecessor in title had entered into an agreement to permit the defendant's predecessor in title to use a road to cross the plaintiff's land. Subsequently, there was a dispute about whether this arrangement constituted merely a licence between the two original parties, or whether it was an easement and thus binding on the plaintiff (whose land would have been the servient tenement). The right had been granted to "owners and occupiers" of the defendant's land and "to all persons having occasion to resort thereto." The court held (at 77) that the right of way was a licence, not an easement, because the words of the grant were too broad and might have conferred rights on those other than the owner of the dominant tenement. The court thus confirmed that an easement cannot be granted in gross: "No one can have such a way but he who has the land to which it is appendant." (This case is also cited to support another requirement for an easement: that it must accommodate the dominant tenement. In *Ackroyd* the court held that the interest granted was a right unconnected with the enjoyment or occupation of the land. This requirement is further examined below.)

Even though the requirement of a dominant and servient tenement is well-accepted in English and Canadian law, both the authority for this requirement and its underlying policy rationale have been criticized. For example, McClean has argued that neither *Ackroyd v. Smith* nor other cases relied on in the texts as authority for the requirement are determinative, suggesting that *Ackroyd* is better cited for the proposition that an easement must accommodate the dominant tenement, not for the requirement that there must be both a dominant and servient tenement. McClean was critical of Canadian judges who accepted the English decisions on this issue as if the principle were "self-evident," sometimes even without referring to any authority at all (citing *Pitman v. Nickerson* (1891), 40 NSR 20; *Adamson v. Bell Telephone Co.* (1920), 48 OLR 24; and *Re Toscano and Dorien* (1965), 51 DLR (2d) 298). He suggested a need to re-examine the underlying policy rationale for such a requirement. See McClean, at 38-39.

In *Ackroyd*, the court justified the approach it adopted, suggesting (at 68) that it was appropriate to limit the powers of vendors to annex rights to their interests in land, especially if the rights would render the land subject to "a new species of burthen, so as to bind it in the hands of an assignee." (This concern will also be evident in the discussion of covenants later in this chapter, and in relation to *Keppell v. Bailey* (1834), 2 My. & K 517, a leading case in the history of the law of covenants, used to support the conclusion adopted in *Ackroyd*.) By contrast with these arguments, McClean suggested (at 40) that there is no continued justification for such a limit on easements, especially in the light of the recognition of easements in gross in the United States:

> The argument in favour of the recognition of easements in gross is an extremely simple one. If to give effect to what is a socially desirable use of property it is necessary to have easements in gross, why should such easements not exist? If, to take Gale's example, A wants to grant to B a right, enforceable to the extent an easement is today, to land helicopters on A's property why should this be impossible if there is no dominant tenement? Similarly, if a long distance trucker wishes to acquire easements of parking along his routes, why should this not be possible?

According to McClean, concerns about the alienability of such interests can be satisfactorily resolved with modern registration systems, and there is no reason why easements, like *profits à prendre*, should not exist in gross. Which of these policy approaches do you find most satisfactory in relation to property principles? For further analysis of these issues, see M.F. Sturley, "Easements in Gross" (1980), 96 *Law Quarterly*

Review 557. In the United States, the existence of the easement in gross has required some limiting principles to prevent "overburdening" of the servient tenement: see A.D. Hegi, "The Easement in Gross Revisited: Transferability and Divisibility Since 1945" (1986), 39 *Vanderbilt Law Review* 109.

Although McClean concluded that there was no real basis in legal authority or public policy for the principle that the existence of an easement requires both a dominant and servient tenement, he suggested that the principle was so well settled that it probably could not be changed without legislation. In practice, there are numerous examples of legislatively created easements where there is no dominant tenement. Most of these easements relate to public utilities such as water, sewage and electricity, etc. See, for example, Ontario Water Resources Act, RSO 1990, c. 0.40, s. 13. Another approach was evident in *Vannini v. Public Utilities Commission of Sault Ste. Marie*, [1973] 2 OR 11 (Ont. HC), where the court held that the commission's ownership of the waterworks system (even though the commission owned no contiguous land) constituted a "dominant tenement." How do these statutory provisions and cases affect your view about the desirability of permitting "easements in gross" in Canada? For a comparable approach in the United States, where easements in gross are recognized, see *Henley v. Continental Cablevision of St. Louis County, Inc.*, 692 SW 2d 825 (Missouri CA 1985).

For an "exceptional" and rather macabre context concerning easements in gross, see *Hubbs v. Black* (1918), 46 DLR 583, where the defendant responded to an action for trespass against a cemetery plot by claiming that he had a right of easement. According to Riddell J (at 589), "[W]hile the right of burial is still called an easement, it is an exception to the general rule that an easement cannot be in gross." (This case also provides an interesting discussion of part performance and the equitable jurisdiction of the county court in Ontario.)

Requirement That the Easement Accommodate the Dominant Tenement

No right may qualify as an easement unless it can be shown that the right confers benefit upon the dominant tenement and not merely some purely personal advantage upon the dominant owner. The criterion of benefit rests ultimately upon whether the right in question makes the dominant tenement "a better and more convenient property." In other words, an easement must accommodate not persons but land.

(Gray and Symes, *Real Property and Real People* (London: Butterworths, 1981) (hereafter Gray and Symes), at 582.) The requirement that an easement must accommodate the dominant tenement was carefully considered in a decision of the English Court of Appeal: *In re Ellenborough Park*, [1956] 1 Ch.D 131 (CA). In that case, there were a number of houses in a square in Weston-super-Mare with a garden or park in the centre (Ellenborough Park) enclosed by the houses. Title to the garden was vested in trustees and each of the owners of the houses around the garden paid a proportionate cost of maintaining the garden. Only those who resided in the houses were entitled to use the garden or park. A question arose as to whether the owners of the houses surrounding the park had an enforceable right in respect of the use and enjoyment of Ellenborough Park. To validate such an enforceable right, it was necessary to find that they had an easement.

The court considered all four requirements for an easement in reviewing the arguments in this case. In relation to this second requirement (that an easement must accommodate the dominant tenement), the court concluded that the right to use the garden or park conferred "a benefit on the dominant tenement" and not merely "a personal advantage upon the dominant owner." In examining the court's reasoning on this issue, try to distinguish the factors considered relevant in relation to *Re Ellenborough Park* by contrast with those in *Hill v. Tupper* (1863), 2 H & C 121 (Ex. Chamber), discussed in the court's reasoning. Are the distinctions drawn by the English Court of Appeal compelling?

In re Ellenborough Park
[1956] 1 Ch.D 131, at 173 (CA)

EVERSHED MR: As appears from the map, the houses, which were built upon the plots around and near to Ellenborough Park, varied in size, some being large detached houses and others smaller and either semi-detached or in a row. We have already stated that the purchasers of all the plots, which actually abutted on the park, were granted the right to enjoy the use of it, as were also the purchasers of some of the plots which, although not fronting upon the park, were only a short distance away from it. As to the nature of the right granted, the conveyance of 1864 shows that the park was to be kept and maintained as a pleasure ground or ornamental garden, and that it was contemplated that it should at all times be kept in good order and condition and well stocked with plants and shrubs; and the vendors covenanted that they would not at any time thereafter erect or permit to be erected any dwelling-house or other building (except a grotto, bower, summer-house, flower-stand, fountain, music-stand or other ornamental erection) within or on any part of the pleasure ground. On these facts Mr. Cross submitted that the requisite connexion between the right to use the park and the normal enjoyment of the houses which were built around it or near it had not been established. He likened the position to a right granted to the purchaser of a house to use the Zoological Gardens free of charge or to attend Lord's Cricket Ground without payment. Such a right would undoubtedly, he said, increase the value of the property conveyed but could not run with it at law as an easement, because there was no sufficient nexus between the enjoyment of the right and the use of the house. It is probably true, we think, that in neither of Mr. Cross's illustrations would the supposed right constitute an easement, for it would be wholly extraneous to, and independent of, the use of a house as a house, namely, as a place in which the householder and his family live and make their home; and it is for this reason that the analogy which Mr. Cross sought to establish between his illustrations and the present case cannot, in our opinion, be supported. A much closer analogy, as it seems to us, is the case of a man selling the freehold of part of his house and granting to the purchaser, his heirs and assigns, the right, appurtenant to such part, to use the garden in common with the vendor and his assigns. In such a case, the test of connexion, or accommodation, would be amply satisfied; for just as the use of a garden undoubtedly enhances, and is connected with, the normal enjoyment of the house to which it belongs, so also would the right granted, in the case supposed, be closely connected with the use and enjoyment of the part of the premises sold. Such, we think, is in substance the position in the present case. The park became a communal garden for the benefit and enjoyment of those whose houses adjoined it or were in its close proximity. Its flower beds, lawns and walks were calculated to afford all the amenities which it is the purpose of the garden of a house to provide; and, apart from the fact that these amenities extended to a number of householders, instead of being confined to one (which on this aspect of the case is immaterial), we can see no difference in principle between Ellenborough Park and a garden in the ordinary significations of that word. It is the collective garden of the neighbouring houses, to whose use it was dedicated by the owners of the estate and as such amply satisfied, in our judgment, the requirement of connexion with the dominant tenements to which it is appurtenant. The result is not affected by the circumstance that the right to the park is in this case enjoyed by some few houses which are not immediately fronting on the park. The test for present purposes, no doubt, is that the park should constitute in a real and intelligible sense the garden (albeit the communal garden) of the houses to which its enjoyment is annexed. But we think that the test is satisfied as regards these few neighbouring, though not adjacent, houses. We think that the extension of the right of enjoyment to these few houses does not negative the presence of the necessary "nexus" between the subject-matter enjoyed and the premises to which the enjoyment is expressed to belong.

Mr. Cross referred us to, and to some extent relied upon, *Hill v. Tupper*, but in our opinion there is nothing in that case contrary to the view which we have expressed. In that case, the owner of land adjoining a canal was granted the exclusive right to let boats out for hire on the canal. He did so and then sought to restrain a similar activity by a neighbouring landowner. He sought to establish that his grant constituted an easement but failed. Pollock CB said in his judgment:

> It is not competent to create rights unconnected with the use and enjoyment of land, and annex them to it so as to constitute a property in the grantee.

It is clear that what the plaintiff was trying to do was to set up, under the guise of an easement, a monopoly which had no normal connexion with the ordinary use of his land, but which was merely an independent business enterprise. So far from the right claimed sub-serving or accommodating the land, the land was but a convenient incident to the exercise of the right.

For the reasons which we have stated, we are unable to accept the contention that the right to the full enjoyment of Ellenborough Park fails in limine to qualify as a legal easement for want of the necessary connexion between its enjoyment and the use of the properties comprised in the conveyance of 1864, and in the other relevant conveyances.

Discussion Notes

Defining the Nature of "Accommodation"

In a note about this decision, A.L. Goodhart and R.E. Megarry stated, "Plainly a right appurtenant to houses to use a garden for normal domestic purposes was beneficial to those houses, and so accommodated the dominant tenement." See Goodhart and Megarry, "Jus Spatiandi in a Pleasure Ground" (1956), 72 *Law Quarterly Review* 16, at 17. By contrast, other authors have criticized the distinctions created by *Re Ellenborough Park* and *Hill v. Tupper*. For example, Ziff has identified several possible ways of looking at the decision in *Hill v. Tupper*:

> In that case, it was decided that an exclusive right to place boats on a lake did not accommodate the dominant tenement, because this monopoly was unconnected with the normal use and enjoyment of the land. The case is an important one in the development of the law of easements, but the general principle it establishes is not obvious. If this ruling means that an easement does not meet the second requirement if it serves only to enhance business activity, then it seems both illogical and inconsistent with other authority [citing *Moody v. Steggles* (1879), 12 Ch.D 261]. In *Hill* the dominant land was used in connection with the boating operations, and the monopoly obviously made that enterprise more viable, so the ruling might be too restrictive, even wrong. Another approach to this issue, one that would support the holding in the case, is to regard easements as serving to supply an attribute of ownership normally or frequently associated with land. Viewed in this way, the law of easements is designed to allow such deficiencies to be remedied. Because the bundle of rights over land does not include monopolies of the type found in *Hill v. Tupper* the court in that case was correct in denying the easement claim.

(Ziff (1996), at 330.) Ziff's criticism suggested that the English Court of Appeal might have seized the opportunity to clarify *Hill v. Tupper* in the context of deciding *Re Ellenborough Park*. Note that Ziff's critique does not suggest that *Re Ellenborough Park* was itself wrongly decided, only that the basis for distinguishing it from *Hill v. Tupper* may not withstand careful scrutiny. Do you agree? In a similar critique, Gray and Symes suggested that the issue of whether a right accommodates the dominant tenement (and therefore constitutes an easement) may reflect a value judgment about the interest claimed:

> Throughout our consideration of the law relating to easements, we shall have cause to observe that the definition of the rights which are capable of constituting an easement is heavily coloured by value judgments. These value judgments concern not only the sorts of activity claimed as amounting to an easement, but also the relative degree of merit which is thought to attach to the party making the claim. In *Re Ellenborough Park* the Court of Appeal had little difficulty in applying the terminology of easements to the civilised user by civilised people of a communal garden situated in an excessively bourgeois location.

(Gray and Symes, at 584.)

Is there a difference in the activity of the claimants in *Re Ellenborough Park* and *Hill v. Tupper* that justifies this assertion on the part of Gray and Symes? Do you agree with their critique? For another discussion of this problem, see McClean, at 44-45. For a recent discussion of the distinction between personal and proprietary interests in the context of condominiums, see *Re Metropolitan Toronto Condominium Corp. No. 979 v. Camrost York Development Corp.* (1995), 26 OR (3d) 238 (Ont. Gen. Div.).

Jengle v. Keetch

Three cottage properties existed side-by-side. The lot that A owned was subject to an easement or right of way in favour of the adjoining lot, which B owned. B used the easement to gain access to his lot. C, who owned the lot adjoining B's lot, had no easement over either A's or B's land, and thus had to approach his own lot by water. After some years of living with the inconvenience of water access, and unsuccessful negotiations with A for an easement over A's lot, C leased a triangular portion of B's lot as "a parking area," for which C agreed to pay B $500 per year. As B's tenant, C began to use the easement across A's land, and A commenced an action for an injunction and damages for nuisance and trespass. Should A succeed?

In *Jengle v. Keetch* (1992), 22 RPR (2d) 53 (Ont. CA), the Ontario Court of Appeal reversed the trial decision and allowed A's appeal. Although the appellate court did not decide whether C's right was an easement or merely a licence, the court stated (at 58) that

> [in any event C's] right of way over the appellants' servient tenement would be restricted to a means of access to and egress from their leased portion of the dominant tenement *for some purpose connected with the enjoyment of their portion of the dominant tenement ... .* If therefore, [C's] object and purpose in entering into the lease was to park vehicles on [B's] property in order to reach his own property, it would constitute an unlawful user of the right of way.

Is this conclusion too restrictive as an application of the principle that an easement must accommodate the dominant tenement? For another example, see *Gordon v. Regan* (1989), 71 OR (2d) 736 (Ont. CA).

The Dominant and Servient Tenements Cannot Be Owned or Occupied by the Same Persons

This requirement appears to be common sense since there would usually be more extensive rights available to an owner of land than could be granted by an easement to himself or herself. However, this issue may arise in a context where two parcels of land have been owned by different persons (with an easement in place) and the owner of the dominant tenement subsequently acquires by sale the servient tenement as well. What happens if the owner then sells the servient tenement to a third party? Similarly, issues may arise in the context of land development where there are good reasons for creating easements in relation to lots for sale, prior to the lots being transferred to individual owners. The problem has also arisen in the context of a tenant's easement where the landlord retains title to the property overall. For further discussion of these issues, see S.G. Maurice, *Gale on Easements*, 15th ed. (London: Sweet & Maxwell, 1986), at 343-44.

The Easement Must Be Capable of Forming the Subject Matter of a Grant

Since an easement is a non-possessory interest, it cannot be created by a transfer of possession. Thus there is a need for a grant. However, as a number of commentators have suggested, this requirement presents some difficulty. According to McClean (at 61), for example, this fourth requirement for the creation of an easement is "both obscure and unhelpful." In *Re Ellenborough Park*, [1956] 1 Ch.D 131 (CA), the English Court of Appeal identified three grounds for determining whether the rights in question met this fourth requirement and thus constituted an easement:

• the rights claimed were too vague;
• the rights claimed amounted to a claim to joint occupation of the park or would have substantially deprived the owners of proprietorship or legal possession; and
• the rights claimed were ones of mere recreation and amusement and were not of utility and benefit.

In *Re Ellenborough Park*, court held that the rights claimed were not too vague, that they did not amount to claims to joint occupation, and that they represented claims beyond mere recreation and amusement and were of real utility and benefit. These factors have been important in recent litigation in Canada as well. In examining the following decision, consider how the fourth requirement (and particularly its relationship to an easement's "non-possessory" nature) was defined by the court.

Shelf Holdings Ltd. v. Husky Oil Operations Ltd.
(1989), 56 DLR (4th) 193, at 195 (Alta. CA)

[One issue in this case concerned a grant of easement in favour of the appellant, Husky Oil, to permit construction of a pipeline under lands owned by the respondent. The grant permitted the respondent, owner of the servient tenement, to continue farming the surface of the land. The issue whether the interest was an easement or a possessory interest was relevant to the enforceability of the interest in the light of the registration provisions of the Land Titles Act, RSA 1980, c. L-5, ss. 64 and 65(1)(g). The interest would be enforceable if it were an easement, but probably not if it were another kind of property interest. At trial, the court concluded that the interest conveyed, in spite of the language used in the grant, represented an interest in land rather than an easement because it conveyed a right to possession. The appellant appealed from this decision.]

HADDAD JA:

The Issue

With due respect to the considered reasons delivered by the learned trial judge, I am of the opinion that the interest conveyed in the grant of easement is a right of way in the form of an easement and not a grant of an interest in land yielding exclusive rights consistent with ownership. I construe the grant of easement as merely conferring upon Husky certain rights of occupation of a corridor for the purposes of a pipeline without divesting the owner of the servient tenement of its proprietary rights. Moreover, the easement attaches to the land by implication and without endorsement on the title by virtue of the provisions of the *Land Titles Act*, s. 65(1)(g).

The grant of easement must be recognized as a contract reflecting the terms of the agreement made by the contracting parties. It is elementary that any contract is the primary source of reference to determine a dispute involving the rights and obligations of those parties. Where a dispute arises over rights involving the acquisition of lands those rights are also subjected to and governed by legislative enactments regulating land titles.

The grant of easement provides that in consideration of the payment of a sum of money by the grantee (Husky) to the grantor (Peregrym) "and the grantee hereby covenanting to perform and observe all of the terms and conditions hereinafter mentioned on the part of the grantee to be performed and observed," the grantor does

GRANT, TRANSFER and CONVEY unto and to the Grantee, for itself, its servants, agents and contractors, the right, license, liberty, privilege and easement to use so much of the said lands as may be necessary for a right-of-way for the laying down, construction, operation, maintenance, inspection, removal, replacement, reconstruction and repair of a pipeline together with all such stations, drips, valves, fittings, meters and other equipment and appurtenances as may be necessary or convenient in connection therewith, for the carriage, conveyance, transportation and handling of petroleum or petroleum products, water and/or gas through or by means of the same, and the right of ingress and egress for all purposes incidental to this grant as and from the date hereof and for so long hereafter as the Grantee may desire to exercise the rights and privileges hereby given, on the following terms and conditions: ...

SECOND: The Grantor shall not without the prior written consent of the Grantee, excavate, drill, install, erect or permit to be excavated, drilled, installed or erected on or under the said right-of-way any pit, well, foundation, pavement, or other structure or installation, but otherwise the Grantor shall have the right fully to use and enjoy the said right-of-way except as the same may be necessary for the purposes herein granted to the Grantee.

THIRD: The Grantee shall have the right to do whatever may be requisite for the enjoyment of the rights herein granted, including the right of clearing the said right-of-way of timber.

FOURTH: The Grantee shall compensate the Grantor and/or other interested parties, as their respective interests for the time being may appear, for damage done to any crops, pasture, fences or livestock on the said lands by reason of the exercise of the rights hereinbefore granted, and the Grantee will not at any time fence the said right-of-way, except as is hereinafter provided. ...

SIXTH: The Grantee shall, as soon as weather and soil conditions permit, bury and maintain all pipelines so as not to interfere with the drainage or ordinary cultivation of the said lands.

SEVENTH: Upon the abandonment of the said right-of-way and release of all of the rights hereby granted, the Grantee shall and will restore the surface of the said lands to the same condition, so far as may be practicable so to do, as the same were in prior to the entry thereon and the use thereof by the Grantee. ...

NINTH: The Grantee, performing and observing the terms and conditions on its part to be performed and observed, shall and may peaceably hold and enjoy the rights, license, liberty, privileges and easement hereby granted without hindrance, molestation or interruption on the part of the Grantor or of any person, firm or corporation claiming by, through or under the Grantor. ...

Although "easement" is a term to be found in various statutes, the trial judge quite rightly made the observation that neither the word "easement" or the expression "right of way" is given a statutory definition. A right of way is a form of easement. A definition of "right of way" is to be found in Halsbury's Laws of England, 4th ed., vol. 14, para. 144, p. 68:

... a right to utilise the servient tenement as a means of access to or egress from the dominant tenement for some purpose connected with the enjoyment of the dominant tenement, according to the nature of that tenement.

Gale in his text, *Gale on Easements*, 15th ed., at p. 6, is cautious about fixing a precise definition:

An easement was defined by Lord Esher MR in *Metropolitan Railway v. Fowler* as "some right which a person has over land which is not his own," but this definition lacks precision, as not every right which one has over another's land is necessarily an easement, and perhaps no precise definition is possible.

The Court of Appeal of England in *Re Ellenborough Park; Re Davies; Powell v. Maddison*, [1956] 1 Ch. 131 at p. 163, [1955] 3 All ER 667 at p. 673, approved the following characteristics proposed in Dr. Cheshire's *Modern Real Property*, 7th ed., p. 456, to properly identify an easement. He said:

... (1) there must be a dominant and a servient tenement: (2) an easement must "accommodate" the dominant tenement: (3) dominant and servient owners must be different persons, and (4) the easement must be capable of forming the subject-matter of a grant.

The first three characteristics present no problem in this case. The issue at hand concerns the fourth characteristic as the trial judge concluded that this requirement had not been satisfied. Evershed MR in *Re Ellenborough Park* dissected the fourth characteristic into the following three questions:

1. Is the right too wide and vague?
2. Is the grant inconsistent with the proprietorship or possession of the alleged servient owner?
3. Is it a mere right of recreation without utility or benefit?

The issue in this case can be narrowed to resolution of the second question.

The following statement by Lopes LJ in *Reilly v. Booth* (1890), 44 Ch.D 12 at p. 26, provides the premise upon which the learned trial judge proceeded: "[T]here is no easement known to law which gives exclusive and unrestricted use of a piece of land."

This statement was quoted with approval in *Metropolitan R Co. v. Fowler*, [1893] AC 416 (HL), to which I will refer in due course. For the reader to better apprehend the statement of Lopes LJ, I will elucidate upon the context in which it was made. The report of that case reveals that certain land which embraced a large yard was conveyed absolutely to one W. A gateway gave access to the yard from a street known as Oxford Street. The conveyance to W was accompanied by the words "Together with the exclusive use of the said gateway into *Oxford Street*." ... The court examined the agreement to ascertain the intention of the parties and found the words "exclusive use" to be explicit and clear. The conveyance was therefore construed as saying that the right of W to the gateway was to be exclusive and consistent with ownership. The comments of Lord Justice Lopes contained in this passage from which the foregoing extract as to exclusivity was lifted [(at 26) follow]:

> I think ownership passed. The exclusive use of the said gateway was given. The exclusive or unrestricted use of a piece of land, I take it, beyond all question passes the property or ownership in that land, and there is no easement known to law which gives exclusive and unrestricted use of a piece of land. It is not an easement in such a case, it is property that passes. Again, a mere easement can be conveyed, or may be conveyed, by words other than these, and would pass under general words.

In *Re Ellenborough Park* characteristic number 4 provided the issue. Unlike *Reilly v. Booth* no express intention could be found in the *Ellenborough* grant. At pp. 175-6 Ch., p. 681 All ER, of the *Re Ellenborough Park* report, Sir Raymond Evershed MR discussed the elements required to satisfy Dr. Cheshire's fourth condition. He said:

> We turn next to Dr. Cheshire's fourth condition for an easement—that the right must be capable of forming the subject-matter of a grant. As we have earlier stated, satisfaction of the condition in the present case depends on the consideration of the questions, whether the right conferred is too wide and vague, whether it is inconsistent with proprietorship or possession of the alleged servient owners, and whether it is a mere right of recreation without utility or benefit.

In reaching his decision in this action the learned trial judge was persuaded by the decision of the Saskatchewan Court of Appeal in *Re Interprovincial Pipeline Co.*, [1951] 2 DLR 187, 1 WWR (NS) 479, 67 CRTC 128, where the document before the court was similar to that under consideration in this appeal. The court there construed the terms of the document to mean that the rights conveyed went beyond the grant of an easement by giving the grantee exclusive use of a portion of the substratum in which the pipeline was buried—thereby conveying an interest in land sufficient to vest title.

The judgment in *Re Interprovincial Pipeline* relied on the decision handed down by the House of Lords in *Metropolitan R Co. v. Fowler, supra*, which adopted the principle expressed by Lopes LJ in *Reilly v. Booth, supra*. The learned trial judge also cited Canadian authorities which applied the same principle. In my opinion *Metropolitan R Co.* and other cases cited by the learned trial judge to support his conclusions are not applicable as they deal with absolute rights to land authorized by statute and can be distinguished.

The *Metropolitan R Co.* litigation was taken to determine the validity of a land tax assessed against the railway in respect of a tunnel it constructed under a highway for an underground rail line. The railway resisted the assessment contending that it merely acquired an easement. The House of Lords held that the railway was vested with more than an easement. It acquired a hereditament for its exclusive use and on that account it was liable for the tax assessed. To be precise, I distinguish this case from *Metropolitan* on the ground that Husky acquired its grant by private agreement which defines the rights of the parties whereas Metropolitan R Co. acquired land for its railway by appropriation pursuant to a statute authorizing the construction of the railway. The "appropriation" vested the land in the railway company for its exclusive use. Lord Herschell LC defines the railway's position in this way, at p. 423:

> Now, my Lords, the language used is this, that "the two companies may appropriate and use the subsoil and undersurface of any such roadway or footway." The word "appropriate" is one which seems to me clearly to point to a right of property becoming vested in the companies; they were to "appropriate and use"; and it seems to me that when they have thus made their appropriation and constructed the tunnel, that tunnel is as much their property as if it had been constructed upon land which they had purchased and paid for, and being their property held by them to the exclusion of any other person, it is as much a hereditament as if it had been constructed on land which they had purchased in the ordinary way.

And at p. 426 Lord Watson expressed the same view. He said:

> To appropriate, according to its natural meaning, is to take and keep a thing by exclusive right; and, as I construed their Act, the authority which it confers upon the company is to take and exclusively possess as much of the subsoil below highways as may be required for the purposes of the undertaking. There is no substantial distinction between the interest which they get by appropriation, and that which they acquire by purchasing in terms of the Lands Clauses Act.

Consumer Gas Co. of Toronto v. City of Toronto (1897), 27 SCR 453 at p. 457, is another tax assessment case. The validity of an assessment for taxes of the mains and pipes to supply gas laid under a highway was challenged and taken to the Supreme Court of Canada. The gas company was given the authority by statute to lay the gas pipes. Citing the *Metropolitan R Co.* case, Chief Justice Strong interpreted the governing statute at p. 457:

> I am of the opinion that the gas pipes of the appellants laid under the streets of the city were under this Act real property belonging to them, and as such liable to assessment. I regard the case of *The Metropolitan Railway Company v. Fowler* as conclusively showing that these pipes are not to be considered chattels placed beneath the public streets and highways, in the exercise of a mere easement, but being affixed to the land, as actual real property within the meaning of the interpretation clause.

Jarvis v. City of Toronto (1894), 21 OAR 395 at p. 400 is also a case of a compulsory acquisition by statute. Osler JA delivering the judgment of the Ontario Court of Appeal again cited the *Metropolitan R Co.* case for the principle that exclusive use of land cannot be equated with an easement. In that case a provincial statute empowered the municipal corporation to pass a by-law authorizing it to take land by compulsion for a sewer. A predecessor in title to the owner of the land through which the sewer was constructed gave his permission to the municipal corporation to acquire the land without the passing of a by-law. The court in these circumstances concluded that the corporation had acquired exclusive use of the land. Osler JA said at p. 400:

> What may thus be compulsorily taken from the owner by means of a by-law duly passed, may, of course, be acquired by agreement of the parties, and may be granted and assigned to the corporation by an appropriate conveyance.
>
> Property thus acquired for the permanent and exclusive use of the municipality for the construction thereon of a sewer is not properly described as an easement. ...

It is worthy of note that six months after the release of the judgment in this action MacPherson J gave judgment in the Court of Queen's Bench in the case of *Card v. TransAlta Utilities Corp.* (1987), 57 Alta. LR (2d) 155, where a similar issue arose. Mr. Justice MacPherson described [at 156] the issue there as "... whether an unregistered easement can be enforced and if so is there a proper easement in this case." The defendant TransAlta, pursuant to an agreement with a landowner, constructed a power line across the owner's land. The plaintiff subsequently purchased the land and acquired title free and clear of an endorsement for an easement. The plaintiffs contended, firstly, that the agreement did not create an easement and, secondly, that in any event it was ineffectual for lack of registration.

Mr. Justice MacPherson, rejecting the plaintiff's stand, held that the agreement did provide for an easement as it met the criteria set out in *Ellenborough Park, supra.* At the same time he also rejected the proposition that the right granted to TransAlta involved exclusive and permanent occupation to create a proprietary interest in the land. Moreover, he said that notwithstanding lack of registration the title was subject to the easement by implication pursuant to the exception provided by s. 65(1)(*g*).

Belanger v. CP Ltd. (1978), 93 DLR (3d) 734, [1979] 1 WWR 734; reversing 65 DLR (3d) 726, [1976] 3 WWR 235 (QB), like *Interprovincial*, is a decision of the Saskatchewan Court of Appeal and in that instance gave recognition to the implied exception to indefeasibility according to s. 71(*c*) of the *Land Titles Act* of that province, the provisions of which are similar to s. 65(1).

I have had the opportunity of perusing two articles from which I have derived assistance in the preparation of these reasons. I allude firstly to an article entitled "The Nature of An Easement," 5 Western L Rev. 32, by Albert J. McClean. The second article, "The Road Not Taken: Some Important Questions About the Nature of Easements," 57 Alta. LR (2d) 326 (1988), authored by M.M. Litman and B.H. Ziff, is a commentary on the judgment subject of this appeal. The influence of these articles will be reflected to some extent in the remarks which follow.

The key to resolving the issue at hand is to look at the grant of easement to assess the extent of the rights relinquished by Peregrym as opposed to the rights it reserved.

The simple test applied by Lindley LJ in *Reilly v. Booth, supra,* at p. 25, is this: "Now if we look at the matter we must see what has been granted and what has been reserved."

The author Gale in his book, *supra,* at p. 139, describes the modern interpretive approach:

> The modern tendency, as has been seen, is to rest the right to an easement on the supposed intention of the parties to the contract, or, if there was no contract, on the

intention of the testator or grantor, irrespectively of the presence of general words in the conveyance.

In his article "The Nature of an Easement," Mr. McClean, at p. 51, puts into perspective the quality and extent of the limitations a grant will impose upon the servient tenement and the balancing process to be engaged to ascertain whether the grant is an easement or something more. I adopt these general observations:

> As was pointed out earlier, it follows from the general nature of the recognized interests in property that an easement cannot amount to a claim quite at variance with the proprietary rights of the servient owner. On the other hand, it is also quite obvious that an easement does to some extent detract from those rights. A right of way cuts down the servient owner's right to exclude people from his property or to develop it as he pleases; and a negative easement such as light, also hinders development. The issue in fact is the perennial one of drawing the line, of deciding when the point has been reached that the right in question detracts so substantially from the rights of the servient owner that it must be something other than an easement.
>
> Where this problem has been the most canvassed is in relation to the degree of occupation or possession of the servient tenement that is compatible with the existence of an easement.

The degree of occupation or possession will be governed by the document conceding the grant. I mention this simply to point out that Mr. McClean's approach, in effect, falls within the test adopted by Lindley LJ.

By the very nature of an easement it is inevitable that some measure of occupation by the easement taker is present in all cases—and that the dominant tenement will to some extent, at least, interfere with the servient tenement. Moreover, because of the rights it carries, an easement, for its limited purpose, is an interest in land.

By the character of its utility the purpose of an easement is to confer a benefit on the dominant tenement. At p. 17 of his text Gale reminds us that "An easement must accommodate the dominant tenement." This easement accomplishes that aim.

Examination of the grant in this case discloses, in my view, that the privileges granted to Husky do not detract from the servient owner's rights of ownership.

The tenor of the grant is such that it reflects the intention of the parties that the grantee Husky acquire a benefit subject to its compliance with certain terms and conditions. The right of Shelf as the servient owner to use the land free from interference has been curtailed to the extent only of prohibiting it from interfering with the subsoil or to erect works on the strip comprising the right of way "but otherwise the Grantor shall have the right fully to use and enjoy the said right-of-way except as the same may be necessary for the purposes herein granted to the Grantee."

I infer from the material filed and the comments of counsel that the lands are farm lands. It is apparent from the literal construction of the second term that curtailment of the appellant's use of its land does not deprive it completely of use of the surface of the right of way. All conventional rights of way will, to some degree, impair the use of the land.

The fourth term requires Husky to compensate the grantor (Shelf) for damages to crops, pasture, fences and livestock occasioned by the exercise of its rights and prohibits

Husky from fencing the right of way thereby leaving Shelf free to cultivate and run cattle over the surface. This in effect allows Shelf full use of the entire parcel subject only to those limitations prescribed in the second term. Moreover, Husky in burying and maintaining its pipeline is prohibited from interfering with the drainage or ordinary cultivation of the lands.

The seventh term obliges Husky upon abandonment of the right of way to restore the lands to the same condition as they were prior to its use and entry thereon. This contemplates that the right of way will revert to Shelf after it has served Husky's purposes. I read this as confirmation that the parties intended the grant to create nothing more than an easement.

The ninth term is not consistent with the conveyance of an interest in land to Husky. It recognizes the mutual undertakings of the parties and it is explicit in providing that Husky is entitled to enjoy the rights it received under the grant subject to it "performing and observing the terms and conditions on its part to be performed and observed." I construe this paragraph to say that the rights conferred on Husky under the grant will be subject to termination in the event of its failure to perform and observe.

Husky acquired from Peregrym the privilege of using a corridor across a parcel consisting of 150 acres, and nothing more. The document reserves to the servient tenement a high degree of possession and control with only a low level of interference from the dominant tenement. The rights granted to Husky do not detract from the rights of the servient owner with the force required to raise the grant above the status of an easement. The grant is free of the words "appropriate" and "exclusive use" or words of that connotation. I view the document as having been devised to ensure that [the] servient owner's property rights in the corridor are preserved.

It is common knowledge that grants of easements for pipelines have been widely used in the development of the petroleum industry and accepted and operate as easements.

Accordingly in my judgment the grant to Husky is an easement valid and enforceable within the scope of s. 65(1)(*g*).

I would allow the appeal with costs to Husky here and at trial.

Appeal allowed.

Discussion Notes

"Exclusive" Possession and Intention

Do you agree with the analysis of the Court of Appeal? For a critique of the trial decision, see M. Litman and B. Ziff, "The Road Not Taken: Some Important Questions About the Nature of Easements" (1988), 57 *Alberta Law Reports* (2d) 326. According to Gray and Symes, the issue whether an interest is an easement, using the test of "non-exclusive possession," has not been applied consistently in the cases. For example, see *Copeland v. Greenhalf*, [1952] Ch. 488 (Ch.D), where the court held that the defendant's use for over 50 years of a strip of land owned by the plaintiff for storing vehicles being repaired was a claim of "joint user of the land," not an easement. See also *Ward v. Kirkland*, [1967] 1

Ch. 194 (Ch.D); *Grigsby v. Melville*, [1972] 1 WLR 1355; *Wright v. Macadam*, [1949] 2 KB 744; and *Miller v. Emcer Products*, [1956] 1 Ch. 304 (Ch.D). As Gray and Symes suggest (at 588-89), it may be difficult to reconcile all these cases:

> It may be that the courts have in fact used the supposed requirement of non-exclusive user as a smokescreen for judicial discretion, invoking the requirement in order to strike down claims felt to be unmeritorious while suppressing the requirement in cases where it has been felt that a remedy should be given.

Does this comment apply to the decision in *Husky Oil*? Why might the court have "felt that a remedy should be given" in this case? Are there other bases for reaching the same conclusion? Although the federal court decision in *Gypsum Carrier*, discussed earlier, did not analyze in detail the four requirements for the existence of an easement, consider whether you are in agreement with the court that all four requirements were met in that case. If you conclude that the four requirements were met, why did the court in that case conclude that the interest of the railway companies was not an easement? To what extent did the court in *Husky Oil* rely on the parties' intentions in defining the interest created as an easement?

The "Jus Spatiandi": Sufficiently Definite?

The requirement that an interest must be capable of forming the subject matter of a grant to be recognized as an easement has also been interpreted as a requirement that the nature of the interest granted must be sufficiently definite. This requirement was considered extensively in *Re Ellenborough Park* because the nature of the interest there permitted the owners of the surrounding houses to walk in the garden or park. Thus, there was a question as to whether the interest created was merely a "*jus spatiandi*," a right to wander at will, which could be regarded as indefinite in scope. The decision of the court (at 179) was that the right granted was "a right to use the park as a garden, and that it was well defined and differed from the 'indefinite and unregulated' privilege encompassed in the term 'jus spatiandi' " (although the court also seemed to approve of the *jus spatiandi* as capable of being an easement in some cases as well: see 179-87). According to McClean, this conclusion shows "a willingness to look at the actual terms of the grant and a disposition not to judge certainty 'in the air' nor to assume that because the rights are wide in their scope they must 'ipso facto' be uncertain." See McClean, at 51.

For an example of a case in which this issue was considered by the Supreme Court of Canada, see *Dukart v. District of Surrey*, [1978] 2 SCR 1039. In that case, the court examined in detail the wording of a document used by a development company in British Columbia, providing that the Foreshore Reserves (beside Boundary Bay) were to be held "for the purpose of giving free access to the waters of the Bay" to persons who owned houses in the surrounding subdivision. Prior to his examination of the documents to determine whether they created an easement, Estey J stated (at 1050):

> At one time there may have been some doubt as to whether a right to cross over or move generally about on another's land was a right known in the common law as an easement, but this matter was put to rest [in] *Re Ellenborough Park*.

For a somewhat different view of the extent to which a right to wander over another's land meets the requirement of definiteness in the United States, see the American Law Institute, *Restatement of the Law of Property* (1944), vol. 5 (hereafter the American Law Institute), at s. 450(e): Commentary.

The Creation of Easements: General Principles

In general, easements are expressly created by way of grant or by way of reservation. In the case of a grant, a vendor sells part of a larger parcel of land to a purchaser, granting the purchaser a right of way—for example, over the land retained by the vendor. In this example, the purchaser holds the dominant tenement and the vendor holds the servient tenement. By contrast, if the vendor sells the parcel to the purchaser, with a reservation of a right of way over the purchaser's land in favour of the vendor, the purchaser's land is the servient tenement while the vendor holds the dominant tenement. (A detailed analysis of the concept of "reservation" is beyond the scope of this chapter, even though it often raises important issues in relation to easements and related interests in land. For a good overview, see Ziff (1996), at 341-42. The issue whether a Crown patent had included a "reservation," by contrast with an "exception," was canvassed at great length in a dispute about the public's continued right to use a beach at Grand Bend on Lake Huron: see *Gibbs v. Grand Bend (Village)* (1995), 26 OR (3d) 644 (CA), (1989), 71 OR (2d) 70; 64 DLR (4th) 28 (HCJ).

Express Grant or Reservation: Hill v. Attorney General of Nova Scotia

Many easements are created by express grant or express reservation and included as part of a deed transferring a fee simple estate to a purchaser. Such a grant or reservation must comply with requirements for the transfer of an interest in land, such as the Statute of Frauds (see chapter 5). In addition, easements may be created in equity by an agreement to grant or reserve that is enforceable by specific performance, in accordance with the doctrine of *Walsh v. Lonsdale* (1882), 21 Ch.D 9 (CA). Although it may not technically appear to be an "express" grant or reservation, it is also possible to create an equitable easement pursuant to the doctrine of part performance. See Ziff (1996), at 338. Easements may also be created expressly by statute, especially in relation to public utilities.

In *Hill v. Attorney General of Nova Scotia* (1997), 142 DLR (4th) 230 (SCC), the appellants claimed entitlement to compensation as a result of provincial expropriation of an easement. In 1966, the province had expropriated farm land, then owned by the appellant's father, in order to construct a section of the Trans-Canada Highway in Nova Scotia. In carrying out the expropriation, the province severed the farm with one parcel north of the highway and the other to the south. In constructing the Trans-Canada Highway, the Nova Scotia Department of Highways created two ramps from the north and south parcels to the highway, fences on both sides of the highway, and gateways across the ramps. Subsequently, in 1992, when the highway was expanded by the construction of two additional lanes (for which no additional land was required to be expropriated), the access ramps were removed, and the appellants were advised that access to the highway from these ramps was prohibited. The appellants claimed compensation on the basis of an expropriation of an easement as a result of the 1992 construction. Assuming that the documents relating to the expropriation in 1966 did not expressly refer to a grant of an easement, on what basis could the appellants succeed in claiming that there was a grant of an easement?

The appellants initially succeeded before Scanlan J in chambers, on the basis of affidavits describing the 1966 negotiations relating to the expropriation. The chambers judge held that the province had granted an equitable easement across the highway in 1966. This decision was reversed by the Nova Scotia Court of Appeal, but the Supreme Court of Canada allowed the appeal, citing (at 236) *Steadman v. Steadman*, [1976] AC 536 (HL) in relation to the doctrine of part performance:

> In summary, there was then a representation made by authorized representatives of the Crown that Hill would have an interest orally and by letters ... permitting him to cross the highway with cattle and equipment. There was the compliance by the Crown with its representations by means of both construction and maintenance. It was contemplated that Hill would, as he did, rely upon them. He did so to his detriment. The words and actions of the Crown created an equitable interest in the land in the form of a right of way over the highway. The Crown intended it to be used and it was for over 27 years. It would be unjust not to recognize the representations and actions of the Crown which created the equitable interest in land when they were relied upon by Hill.

Accordingly, the Supreme Court of Canada concluded that the appellants were entitled to compensation in relation to the 1992 expropriation of their equitable interest in land. For another example where the Supreme Court of Canada found an easement created by reservation, see *Abell v. Corporation of The County of York* (1920), 61 SCR 345.

Implied Grant or Reservation: Necessity, Common Intention, and Non-Derogation: Hirtle v. Ernst

There are a number of different principles for implying the existence of an easement when none has been expressly created. For example, an easement of necessity has been recognized where a parcel of land has been transferred and is completely landlocked and without access, so long as there is adjoining land retained by the vendor over which an easement can be created. This principle may, however, be difficult to apply in practice—must the land be completely inaccessible, inaccessible by land but accessible by water, or inaccessible only with great difficulty or expense? In *Dobson v. Tulloch* (1994), 17 OR (3d) 533 (Gen. Div.), the court concluded that the defendants were entitled to an easement in relation to their cottage property, which was completely landlocked except for a small portion that abutted the Mississagi River. They were thus entitled to an easement over land owned by a neighbouring owner who had initially brought an action for trespass against the defendants when she (the neighbouring owner) "became irritated with the increased traffic resulting from construction ... and visits from family members" (at 538). In this case, the court declined to hold that access by way of the river made the defendants' lot accessible, distinguishing other authorities such as *Fitchett v. Mellow* (1897), 29 OR 6 (HCJ). An appeal from this decision was dismissed: (1997), 33 OR (3d) 800. (In *Dobson*, the trial court also held that there was an implied easement of "apparent accommodations" in addition to an implied easement of necessity, and that the defendants were entitled to succeed on the basis of s. 15 of the Conveyancing and Law of Property Act, RSO 1990, c. C.34. For a similar provision, see Property Act, RSNB 1973, c. P-19, s. 22.)

Principles about the creation of an easement of necessity were reviewed in a Nova Scotia decision, *Hirtle v. Ernst* (1991), 21 RPR (2d) 95 (NS SC). The applicant was seeking a certificate under the Quieting Titles Act, RSNS 1989, c. 382 in relation to his parcel of land, as well as a declaration of a right of way of necessity. The applicant had purchased a parcel of land bounded on three sides by Big Mushamush Lake and on the fourth side by a neighbouring parcel of land, without access to a roadway. The applicant purchased his lot knowing that it was landlocked and after making some unsuccessful attempts to purchase a right of way. He wished to build a home on the parcel and there was evidence that it would be difficult to transport all the needed materials by water because of a lack of docking facilities on the lake.

Nathanson J reviewed the principles concerning easements of necessity and held that when a larger parcel had been divided between two brothers in 1857, one brother (a predecessor in title to the applicant) received a landlocked parcel, and that an easement of necessity had consequently been created at that time. He considered *Fitchett v. Mellow*, where an Ontario court had concluded that an inconvenient means of access by water meant that a lot could not be characterized as inaccessible. He also referred to two decisions in New Brunswick concerning landlocked cottage lots bordering on water, in which courts had recognized easements of necessity: see *Harris v. Jervis* (1980), 31 NBR (2d) 264, 75 APR 264 (QB) and *Michalak v. Patterson* (1986), 72 NBR (2d) 421, 183 APR 421 (QB), and a number of US decisions recognizing easements of necessity. Suggesting that the doctrine of easements of necessity had continued to evolve over the years, he formulated the following principles in reaching a conclusion (at 107) that the applicant was entitled to an easement of necessity in *Hirtle v. Ernst*:

1. The doctrine of right of way of necessity is based on public policy—that land should be able to be used and not rendered useless (see Goddard, *A Treatise on the Law of Easements*, supra, pp. 359-361; *Feoffees of Grammar School in Ipswich v. Proprietors of Jeffreys' Neck Passage*, supra; and *Hancock v. Henderson*, supra).

2. Although there can be no right of way of necessity where there is an alternative inconvenient means of access, the requirement of an absolute necessity or a strict necessity has developed into a rule of practical necessity (see *Redman v. Kidwell*, supra, and *Littlefield v. Hubbard*, supra).

3. Water access is not considered to be the same as access over adjacent land (see *Harris v. Jervis*, supra; *Michalak v. Patterson*, supra; *Hancock v. Henderson*, supra; and *William Dahm Realty v. Cardel*, supra). That is especially so in cases where the water access is not as of right, or would be contrary to law (see Megarry and Wade, *The Law of Real Property*, supra, at p. 831), where access is not available for transportation of things needed for reasonable use of the land to be accessed (see *Feoffees of Grammar School in Ipswich v. Proprietors of Jeffreys' Neck Passage*, supra), where the water access does not have transportation facilities for carrying on the ordinary and necessary activities of life to and from the land (see *Cookston v. Box*, supra), or where the water is not navigable or usable as a highway for commerce and travel (see *Peasley v. New York (State)*, supra).

In the present case, I find: that without a right of way of necessity, the lot in question will not be able to be used and will be useless; that this is not a case where there exists an alternative, though inconvenient, means of access; and that water access over Big Mushamush Lake to the lot in question is not by right and, indeed, would probably be contrary to law pursuant to ss. 2(*j*) and 3 of the *Water Act*, RSNS 1989, c. 500. ...

I also find no evidence that Big Mushamush Lake can be used for transportation of things needed for reasonable use of the plaintiff's land, that Big Mushamush Lake has transportation facilities for carrying on the ordinary and necessary activities of life to and from the land, and that Big Mushamush Lake has been used or is usable as a highway of commerce and travel.

Conclusion

As previously indicated, the applicant's claim for a certificate of title pursuant to the *Quieting Titles Act* is granted.

The plaintiff has satisfied the court that, in the present circumstances, he is entitled to a right of way of necessity in order that he should have access to his land. An order will issue recognizing and granting a right of way over and along the so-called cottage road, in common with all other persons having use of the same road, with the plaintiff being required to pay the full cost of construction of any extension of the roadway as it presently exists, and a proportionate share of any cost of maintaining the roadway and keeping it in good repair and condition.

I consider it unnecessary to consider the plaintiff's alternative claim to a prescriptive right of way.

I consider the plaintiff's claim for damages to be inappropriate in the circumstances. Moreover, the plaintiff has not proved any general or special damages.

A claimant under the *Quieting Titles Act* usually bears the costs of the application, but where the application is contested unsuccessfully, such costs should be shared. Therefore, the plaintiff will have 50 per cent of his costs of the action to be taxed in accordance with Tariff A (the amount involved being $35,000 under Scale 3) and Tariff D.

Action allowed in part.

Discussion Notes

Judicial or Legislative Evolution of Easements of Necessity

What is the basis of the court's willingness to acknowledge the "evolution" of principles concerning easements of necessity? In the light of the decision in *Hirtle v. Ernst* how would you formulate the test of "necessity" in this context? In reflecting on these issues, consider this proposal:

> [All] jurisdictions should develop a body of laws designed to ensure that its courts have the power to prevent land from remaining landlocked. The possibility of land remaining landlocked, as can occur in common law jurisdictions in the absence of legislation as a consequence of the limitations on the scope of the easement of necessity, is contrary to the basic tenet of real property law that land should be freely alienable ... . It would also

seem to be clearly in the public interest that land should not lie unused and that its potential for development should be fully realized.

(A.J. Bradbrook, "Access to Landlocked Land: A Comparative Study of Legal Solutions" (1983), 10 *Sydney Law Review* 39.)

Is there any need for legislation in the light of *Hirtle v. Ernst*? Why or why not? Are there other competing policy considerations that should be taken into account in formulating solutions to problems similar to those in *Hirtle*? Is it relevant that the market value of landlocked land may be less than it would be with access? Who should bear the cost of ensuring access? If there is a public policy interest in land development, should the cost of access be borne only by the owners of adjoining land? Is this issue one that can be resolved by common law principles, or is a legislative solution required?

Bradbrook's analysis examined different kinds of solutions to the problem of landlocked land in several jurisdictions in Australia, Europe, and the United States. For examples of legislative solutions, see Property Law Act, 1974-1978, s. 180 (Queensland) and Conveyancing and Law of Property Act 1884, s. 84j, an amendment added in 1978 (Tasmania). These statutes apply "where it is reasonably necessary in the interests of effective use in any reasonable manner of land" (Queensland), and generally provide for a court to order an easement where it is consistent with the public interest and where the owner of a servient tenement has unreasonably refused to accept the obligation but can be adequately compensated for doing so. See also H. Tarlo, "Forcing the Creation of Easements—A Novel Law" (1979), 53 *Australian Law Journal* 254.

Intention: Wong v. Beaumont

In addition to easements of necessity, implied easements may be created by the common intention of the parties, taking into account the purpose for which land has been granted. It has been suggested that *Wong v. Beaumont*, [1965] 1 QB 173, [1964] 2 All ER 119 (CA) is a good example of such an easement. In that case, Lord Denning held that an implied easement existed with respect to the construction of a ventilation duct in a restaurant because it was required by public health regulations. Even though the landlord objected to the tenant's need for the ventilation duct, the court held that the tenant was entitled to have it constructed since the landlord knew of the tenant's intended use of the premises as a restaurant when the lease was signed.

What is the difference, if any, between the basis for an implied easement of necessity and an implied easement based on the common intention of the parties? According to Gray and Symes (at 593), there may not be a difference, since "a common intention to grant a particular easement will normally be found only in cases of necessity." By contrast, Ziff (1996) (at 339) has suggested that *Wong* is not a case of necessity since the premises could have been used for purposes other than a restaurant, in which case the ventilation duct would not have been needed. He has suggested that the rationale for an implied easement based on common intention is the vendor's obligation of non-derogation—that is, "it would have amounted to a derogation from the grant not to recognize the easement over part of the property retained." Which view is preferable? In the *Wong* case, Lord Denning used the language of an easement of necessity. Is the language determinative here? For other examples, see *Duchman v. Oakland Dairy Co. Ltd.*, [1929] 1 DLR 9 (Ont. SC AD) and *Aircraft Maintenance Enterprises Inc. v. Aerospace Realties (1986) Ltd.* (1992), 94 Nfld. and PEIR 271 (Nfld. SC TD).

The Principle of Wheeldon v. Burrows: Its Application in Baton v. Raine

Easements may also be implied under the principle of *Wheeldon v. Burrows* (1872), 12 Ch.D 31 (CA). According to this principle, a vendor who holds a parcel of land, and who uses a path across one section to gain access to another, may create an implied easement at the time of a transfer of one section to a purchaser. Even though there was no easement so long as the whole parcel belonged to the vendor (remember that one requirement for an easement is that the dominant and servient tenements be held by different persons), the division of the parcel and its transfer to a purchaser "creates" an implied easement. The situation prior to the division of the parcel may sometimes be referred to as one of a "quasi-easement." According to Ziff (1996) (at 339):

> *Wheeldon* is a pronounced application of the principle of non-derogation. It serves as a form of consumer protection, allowing a purchaser to acquire amenities (in the form of easements) that the purchased land *appears* to enjoy. As such, it is a minor deviation from the principle of *caveat emptor* (let the buyer beware).

See also A.W.B. Simpson, "The Rule in *Wheeldon v. Burrows* and the Code Civile" (1967), 83 *Law Quarterly Review* 240.

In *Barton v. Raine* (1980), 114 DLR (3d) 702 (Ont. CA), for example, such an implied easement was created when a vendor (who owned two adjoining city lots with a mutual driveway between them) conveyed one lot to his son and daughter-in-law. The son and his family had been living in the adjoining home for over a decade before the transfer of title, and thus the use of the mutual driveway had been established before the father's conveyance. After this transfer, both families continued to use the mutual driveway. The property line between the two houses meant that the owner of one house did not have sufficient room to drive a car to the garage at the back of the property without access to the mutual driveway. Some years later when both lots had been transferred to new purchasers, a dispute arose about the right to use the driveway.

According to Thorson JA (at 709), the trial judge had concluded that there was an implied easement in the deed transferring the adjoining lot to the son and daughter-in-law, suggesting that it could be supported either on the basis of the "mutual or reciprocal easement exception" in *Wheeldon v. Burrows* or on the basis of the "broader, umbrella-like 'common intention' principle." After reviewing the authorities carefully, Thorson JA agreed, stating (at 709):

> In my opinion, the learned trial Judge was correct in the conclusion which he drew from the authorities referred to above, namely, that the development of the case-law since *Wheeldon v. Burrows* has softened the rigour of the general rule set out in that case or has enlarged the scope of the exceptions to the rule. On the facts of the case at bar, I am satisfied that, although the 1952 conveyance made no mention of a right of way over the driveway between the two properties, there was, by necessary inference from the

circumstances in which the conveyance was made, a common intention on the part of both the father on the one hand and the son and daughter-in-law on the other hand that, after the conveyance, each of them would continue to use the driveway in the same manner as, in fact, it had been used without interruption since the late 1920s.

In 1952 when the property next door was conveyed to them, the son and daughter-in-law of the grantor had been occupying the property for over a decade. The use of the driveway as a common passageway to and from the two garages was an accepted reality of their lives throughout the whole of their occupancy of the property, just as it had been an accepted reality for the owners of the two properties for many years before their occupancy of the property began. Were it not for the fact that the plaintiff's father became the owner of both properties in 1941, it is almost certain that the plaintiff's father would have acquired a right of way by prescription over the driveway well before the 1952 conveyance, since its use by him had been uninterrupted and had gone unchallenged throughout most of his lifetime as the owner of the originally-acquired property.

Throughout the whole of this period the driveway was a tangible physical fact, there to be seen by all who chose to see it, and the manner of its use would have been obvious to even the most casual observer of the physical features of the two properties. There could be no doubt that it was there to provide access to and from both garages near the rear of the two properties.

In my view, furthermore, it is not credible that when the son and daughter-in-law purchased the property which they had been occupying for over a decade with the father's permission, there could have been any misunderstanding by them about the basis on which the driveway was to be used thereafter by each of the parties to the conveyance, including of course, the father, with whom they had so long been sharing its use. That there was in fact no such misunderstanding seems evident. For example, it must be assumed that at the time they purchased the property next door, the son and daughter-in-law knew or were made aware of the location of the property line dividing the two properties, yet it is apparent from the known facts that at no time did they see it to be or treat it as being a consequence of their purchase of the property next door, any more than did the father, that thereafter the father would be obliged to have their permission to use the driveway in order to get to and from his own garage. In my opinion, the only reasonable inference to be drawn from all of the facts and circumstances surrounding the 1952 conveyance is that each of the parties had a common intention that the father would continue to have the right to use the driveway after the 1952 conveyance as he had before.

Quite possibly if, in 1952, the property next door had been purchased by some hypothetical third party who was a stranger to the father, the inference as to the intention of the parties would have been considerably less compelling, inasmuch as the property was then being severed from other property owned by the father, but in this case it is not necessary to indulge in speculation of this kind. Here the purchase was by the son and his wife from the father who, on all the evidence, borne out by the subsequent history of events, intended to and in fact continued to remain as owner and occupier of the retained property and to use it as he had used it before.

It follows that I agree with Killeen Co. Ct. J that an easement in the nature of a right of way over the driveway in question, in favour of the grantor of the property next door, was acquired by implied reservation from the 1952 grant. I also agree that the interruption in its use which occurred following the father's stroke did not impair that easement, which, once acquired, could only be lost by [a] non-user on evidence clearly establishing an intention to abandon it. As pointed out by the trial Judge, the circumstances of the non-user in this case were not consistent in any way with an intention to abandon the right.

In the result the defendants who purchased the property next door from the son and daughter-in-law in 1971 are, in my opinion, bound by the easement. It is well established (see, for example, *Israel v. Leith* (1890), 20 OR 361 (QB)) that the *Registry Act* does not interfere with legal rights, such as an implied grant of an easement, arising other than by a written instrument, and does not alter the priority of the grantee of the easement over a subsequent purchaser. In my view, there is no rational basis for distinguishing in this regard between an easement arising by implied grant and one arising by implied reservation. See, in support of this position, *Gale on Easements*, *supra*, at p. 113, and 9 CED (Ont. 3d), title 51, p. 51-38, §74, and the authorities referred to therein.

Counsel for the appellants, the defendants in this case, argued forcefully that this Court in the case at the bar should feel bound to reach a decision consistent with what he termed the "definitive decision" circumscribing the exceptions to the general rule set out in *Wheeldon v. Burrows*, namely, *Re Webb; Sandom v. Webb*, *supra*, in which the Court is said to have declined to find in favour of an easement based on common intent in the absence of "affirmative evidence admitting of no alternative possibilities." He also argued that for this Court to adopt the reasoning of Killeen Co. Ct. J in this case would be to throw the practice of conveyancing in this Province into wild confusion.

With great respect to counsel for the appellants and in spite of the very able presentation made to this Court by him, I am unable to agree with either proposition. With regard to the absence in this case of the kind of affirmative evidence argued on the basis of *Re Webb* to be needed, it seems to me that in the very nature of cases such as this, where the conveyance itself is silent on the question of the right sought to be established, the passage of time that not infrequently occurs between the making of the conveyance and the event giving rise to the dispute about the right necessarily militates against the likelihood of any such "affirmative evidence" being available, at least in the form of oral testimony by persons who might be expected to have some personal knowledge or recollection of the intention of the original parties. In my view, the existence of this kind of evidence ought not to be an absolute requirement when it is open to the Court, on a reconstruction of the surrounding facts and circumstances involving a particular grant, to conclude that a reservation from the grant has been established by necessary inference from those facts and circumstances.

Nor am I persuaded that to adopt the reasoning of the learned trial Judge in this case would lead to "wild confusion" among the ranks of conveyancers. It is trite to repeat that every case is to be decided on its own facts, yet the facts of this case surely bear little resemblance to the facts that can be expected to be encountered in most cases involving adjoining property owners who share facilities such as driveways with their neighbours.

Furthermore, on the facts of this case, this is not a case in which the defendants came to the position in which they now find themselves, without any notice of a user of their property contrary to what they now assert to be their right, title and interest in it. At the time they purchased the property, the driveway was no less a physical fact than it had been in 1952, and the manner of its use could have been no less apparent to them than to any other person who chose to observe the physical features of the two properties. If it were necessary to do so, I would conclude that the defendants in this case in fact had actual notice of the very user they later chose to dispute when they erected the fence which blocked through access to the plaintiff's garage. In this case the defendants, before they concluded the purchase of their property, had clear cause to suspect an adverse possessory interest, and could readily have called for a declaration of possession by the vendor. Yet there is no evidence that they did so; on the contrary, the evidence is that they accepted the situation as they came to it and continued to do so until the time of the incident, involving the parking of the defendant's car in the driveway, which seems to have triggered the dispute now before this Court.

Do you agree that there was a "common intention" in *Barton*? What evidence was relied upon to reach this conclusion? If the adjoining lot had been transferred by the father to an unrelated party instead of to his son and daughter-in-law, what difference would it have made, if any? Could this concept of common intention in relation to an implied easement have been considered in *Gypsum Carrier*, described earlier in this chapter? What would have been the result? Remember that the court concluded that there had been no intention to create an easement in that case. What was the evidence relied on to support the court's conclusion?

The Scope of Easements

Intention may also be important in determining the scope of easements. In *Giecewicz v. Alexander* (1989), 3 RPR (2d) 324 (HCJ), for example, an express easement had been granted across the defendants' land in relation to land owned by the plaintiffs. The plaintiffs had no other access to a public highway. As a result of development some years later, however, the plaintiffs gained access to a new public highway, so long as they built a suitable driveway, and the defendants thereupon blocked the former access route by building on their land. The court dismissed the plaintiffs' application for a declaration of easement, holding that the extent of an express easement depends on the wording of the instrument, ascertainable by circumstances existing at the time of the grant and known to the parties or within their reasonable contemplation at the time (citing *Laurie v. Winch*, [1953] 1 SCR 49; [1952] 4 DLR 449). In addition, the court in *Giecewicz* held (at 335) that

> subsequent changes in circumstances may alter the justifications for the use of the easement. A grant may be made for a limited purpose and when that purpose is accomplished, the right of way shall cease.

Accordingly, the court concluded that the right of way terminated when the plaintiffs acquired suitable access to a public highway. For further discussion of the termination of an implied easement of necessity, see *Holmes v. Goring* (1824), 130 ER 233 (CP) and *BOJ Properties v. Allen's Mobile Home Park Ltd.* (1979), 108 DLR (3d) 305 (NS SC).

There may also be important issues about the scope or extent of an easement—that is, assuming that an easement has been created, there may be disputes about the extent of the rights of the holder of the dominant tenement. For examples, see *Pearsall v. Power Supermarkets Ltd.* (1957), 8 DLR (2d) 270 (Ont. HC); *Malden Farms Ltd. v. Nicholson*, [1956] OR 415 (CA); and *Jengle v. Keetch* (1989), 68 OR (2d) 238 (HCJ). See also P. Huff, "Overburdening the Right of Way: Where the Right of Way Ends" (1991), 4:5 *National Real Property Law Review* 49, and American Law Institute.

Easements by Prescription

In addition to creating easements by express grant or by implication, easements may be created by prescription. Basically, an easement by prescription is created as a result of "length of user" of servient land on the part of the owner of the dominant tenement. In this respect, the principles of prescription appear similar to ideas about the acquisition of title by possession (especially because possession may also be proved by acts of use). However, there are important distinctions, both in theory and in practice, between principles of prescription and those of possessory title.

First of all, prescription applies to non-possessory interests and thus usually requires acts that are less controlling than would be required to show a possessory title. Second, the acquisition of a possessory title extinguishes the right of the owner against whom possession has been established, and the new owner becomes solely entitled to use and possession of the land. By contrast, prescription provides for the encumbrance of the servient tenement by the owner of the dominant tenement, so that one landowner's options for using land may be constrained by the rights of the other. As well, the owner of the servient land obtains no compensation for the rights acquired by a neighbour in the servient land. On this basis, underlying concerns about the need to promote, not punish, neighbourly behaviour may influence judicial decisions concerning claims of prescriptive easements. Where one person permits another to use his or her land for a particular purpose, without compensaton, it may not be appropriate to conclude that an easement has been created. For this reason, it may often be difficult to establish an easement by prescription. See, for example, *Tupper v. Campbell* (1876), 11 NSR 68 (SC). See also S. Anderson, "Easement and Prescription—Changing Perspectives in Classification" (1975), 38 *Modern Law Review* 641. It is also useful to consider *Keefer v. Arillotta* (1976), 13 OR (2d) 680 (CA), discussed in chapter 2, in relation to prescription.

At common law, there were two methods of acquiring an interest by prescription. The first method involved proof of usage extending back to time immemorial (established by statute in England as the date of the beginning of the reign of Richard I, the year 1189). However, since any such claim could be rebutted by showing any period of adverse use since 1189, this method of acquiring prescriptive easements is of no use in Canada, except perhaps for First Nations. In *Abell v. Village of Woodbridge* (1917), 39 OLR 382 (SCC), at 388, the court took judicial notice of the discovery of America as of 1492, thus denying the availability of this common law method of prescription to anyone except First Nations claimants.

The second method at common law, called the doctrine of the "lost modern grant," assumed the existence of a grant that had disappeared. According to this approach, continuous use for a period of 20 years raises a presumption of a lost modern grant. This common law approach continues to exist in Canada, along with statutory provisions (a third method for the creation of prescriptive easements). According to the Ontario Law Reform Commission's report in 1969, the purpose of the Prescription Act (an English statute of 1832 made applicable to Upper Canada in 1847; see now Limitations Act, RSO 1990, c. L.15, ss. 30-35) was "to reduce uncertainties of establishing prescriptive easements at common law." However, the provisions of the statute are widely regarded as "ill-drafted," and the Law Reform Commission conceded that the prescription provisions of the Ontario limitations statute "remain a mystery to many a practising lawyer." For details about the operation of prescription in the Ontario legislation, see *Report of the Ontario Law Reform Commission on the Limitation of Actions* (Toronto: Department of the Attorney-General, 1969), at 143-48. See also the Limitations of Actions Act, RSNS 1989, c. 258, ss. 32-37 and the Easements Act, RSNB 1973, c. E-1.

Discussion Notes

Review the arguments about the need for principles recognizing the creation of title by possession in chapter 2. To what extent do these arguments apply in the context of prescriptive easements? What are the consequences of recognizing prescriptive rights in terms of goals of neighbourly cooperation? Should courts interpret prescriptive claims broadly or narrowly? For different approaches, see *Temma Realty Co. Ltd. v. Ress Enterprises Ltd.* (1968), 69 DLR (2d) 195 (Ont. CA) and *Brass Rail Tavern (Toronto) Ltd. v. DiNunzio* (1979), 12 RPR 188 (Ont. HC). Should prescription be part of the modern law of property in Canada? Note that it has been abolished in Alberta: see Limitation of Actions Act, RSA 1980, c. L-15, s. 50. In *Monaghan v. Moore* (1966), 31 OR (3d) 232 (CA), the court concluded that the claimants could not acquire an easement by prescription in relation to a road allowance because they were entitled by law to use public highways. Thus, when the road allowance was closed and sold to a purchaser, the claimants could not continue to use it to gain access to a beach on Lake Muskoka. Does this case reveal some limits in relation to prescriptive easements?

If it is possible to obtain rights by prescription, should the opposite also be possible—that is, the extinguishment of rights through non-use? In the United States, for example, easements may be extinguished by prescription: see American Law Institute, at s. 506. In thinking about these issues, consider the legislative law reform process. Why might reform on these issues be comparatively slow?

Negative Easements: The Relationship Between Easements and Covenants

Phipps v. Pears
[1965] 1 QB 76 (CA)

LORD DENNING MR: In the 1920s there were two old houses in Warwick, standing side by side, Nos. 14 and 16, Market Street. They were both owned by Ralph Spencer Field. About 1930, he pulled down No. 16 but left the old No. 14 standing. He erected a new house at No. 16, Market Street, with its flank wall flat up against the old wall of No. 14. He did not bond the two walls together, but the new wall was built up touching the old wall of No. 14.

On July 17, 1931, Ralph Spencer Field conveyed the new No. 16, Market Street to Helena Field, but remained himself owner of the old No. 14. Helena Field disposed of No. 16 and eventually in 1951, the plaintiff bought it, as it was, standing then alongside the old No. 14. Ralph Spencer Field died and his personal representative in 1957 conveyed No. 14, Market Street to the governors of the Lord Leycester Hospital.

So there were the two houses—new No. 16 and old No. 14—standing side by side. In 1962, the Warwick Corporation made an order for the demolition of old No. 14, Market Street because it was below the required standard. It was, I suppose, unfit for human habitation. In consequence, in September, 1962, the governors of the Lord Leycester Hospital demolished it. And when they did so, there was left exposed the flank wall of new No. 16. This was in a very rough state. It had never been pointed. Indeed, it could not have been because of the way it was built, flat up against the old No. 14. It had never been rendered or plastered. So it was not weatherproof. The result was that the rain got in and during the winter it froze and caused cracks in the wall. The plaintiff seeks to recover for the damage done.

In his particulars of claim the plaintiff alleged that No. 16 had a right of support from No. 14 and that the defendant had withdrawn that support. But he failed on this point because the judge found that No. 16 did not depend on No. 14 for its support. "There was, in fact, no support the one for the other. They were independent walls, untied one to the other."

Then the plaintiff said—or rather it was said on his behalf—that at any rate his house No. 16 was entitled to protection from the weather. So long as No. 14 was there, it afforded excellent protection for No. 16 from rain and frost. By pulling down No. 14, the defendant, he said, had infringed his right of protection from the weather. This right, he said, was analogous to the right of support. It is settled law, of course, that a man who has his house next to another for many years, so that it is dependent on it for support, is entitled to have that support maintained. His neighbour is not entitled to pull down his house without providing substitute support in the form of buttresses or something of the kind, see *Dalton v. Angus*. Similarly, it was said, with a right to protection from the weather. If the man next door pulls down his own house and exposes his neighbour's wall naked to the weather whereby damage is done to him, he is, it is said, liable in damages.

The case, so put, raises the question whether there is a right known to the law to be protected—by your neighbour's house—from the weather. Is there an easement of protection?

There are two kinds of easements known to the law: positive easements, such as a right of way, which give the owner of land *a right himself to do something* on or to his neighbour's land: and negative easements, such as a right of light, which gives him *a right to stop his neighbour doing something* on his (the neighbour's) own land. The right of support does not fall neatly into either category. It seems in some way to partake of the nature of a positive easement rather than a negative easement. The one building, by its weight, exerts a thrust, not only downwards, but also sideways on to the adjoining building or the adjoining land, and is thus doing something to the neighbour's land, exerting a thrust on it, see *Dalton v. Angus*, *per* Lord Selborne LC. But a right to protection from the weather (if it exists) is entirely negative. It is a right to stop your neighbour pulling down his own house. Seeing that it is a negative easement, it must be looked at with caution. Because the law has been very chary of creating any new negative easements.

Take this simple instance: Suppose you have a fine view from your house. You have enjoyed the view for many years. It adds greatly to the value of your house. But if your neighbour chooses to despoil it, by building up and blocking it, you have no redress. There is no such right known to the law as a right to a prospect or view, see *Bland v. Moseley* cited by Lord Coke in *Aldred's* case. The only way in which you can keep the view from your house is to get your neighbour to make a covenant with you that he will not build so as to block your view. Such a covenant is binding on him by virtue of the contract. It is also binding in equity on anyone who buys the land from him with notice of the covenant. But it is not binding on a purchaser who has no notice of it, see *Leech v. Schweder.*

Take next this instance from the last century. A man built a windmill. The winds blew freely on the sails for thirty years working the mill. Then his neighbour built a schoolhouse only 25 yards away which cut off the winds. It was held that the miller had no remedy: for the right to wind and air, coming in an undefined channel, is not a right known to the law, see *Webb v. Bird.* The only way in which the miller could protect himself was by getting his neighbour to enter into a covenant.

The reason underlying these instances is that if such an easement were to be permitted, it would unduly restrict your neighbour in his enjoyment of his own land. It would hamper legitimate development, see *Dalton v. Angus*, *per* Lord Blackburn. Likewise here, if we were to stop a man pulling down his house, we would put a brake on desirable improvement. Every man is entitled to pull down his house if he likes. If it exposes your house to the weather, that is your misfortune. It is no wrong on his part. Likewise every man is entitled to cut down his trees if he likes, even if it leaves you without shelter from the wind or shade from the sun; see the decision of the Master of the Rolls in Ireland in *Cochrane v. Verner.* There is no such easement known to the law as an easement to be protected from the weather. The only way for an owner to protect himself is by getting a covenant from his neighbour that he will not pull down his house or cut down his trees. Such a covenant would be binding on him in contract: and it would be enforceable on any successor who took with notice of it. But it would not be binding on one who took without notice.

There is a further point. It was said that when the owner, Ralph Spencer Field, conveyed No. 16 to Helena Field, the plaintiff's predecessor, there was implied in the conveyance all the general words of section 62 of the *Law of Property Act, 1925.* The conveyance included all "easements, rights and advantages whatsoever appertaining or reputed to appertain to the land." On the conveyance of No. 16, Market Street, to the plaintiff's predecessor, there passed to him all these "advantages" appertaining to No. 16. One of these advantages, it was said, was the benefit of having the old No. 14 there as a protection from the weather. I do not think this argument avails the plaintiff for the simple reason that, in order for section 62 to apply, the right or advantage must be one which is known to the law, in this sense, that it is capable of being granted at law so as to be binding on all successors in title, even those who take without notice, see *Wright v. Macadam.* A fine view, or an expanse open to the winds, may be an "advantage" to a house but it would not pass under section 62. Whereas a right to use a coal shed or to go along a passage would pass under section 62. The reason being that these last are rights known to the law, whereas the others are not. A right to protection from the weather is not a right known to the law. It does not therefore pass under section 62.

In my opinion, therefore, the plaintiff has not made out any right to the protection he seeks. I find myself in agreement with the county court judge: and I would dismiss the appeal.

PEARSON LJ: I agree and cannot add anything.

SALMON LJ: I also agree.

Appeal dismissed with costs. Leave to appeal refused.

Discussion Notes

Negative Easements: The Policy Context

In *Phipps*, Lord Denning stated that the law has been "very chary of creating any new negative easements." What justification did he offer for the law's concern about negative easements? It is important to understand the nature of these concerns in relation to *Phipps* and in the context of covenants, discussed later in the chapter. Are these concerns applicable only to negative easements? Consider, for example, the positive easements recognized by courts in cases discussed earlier in this chapter—would any of these easements have tended to restrict the owner of the servient tenement "in his enjoyment of his own land" or "hamper legitimate development"? If so, why should there be a distinction between positive and negative covenants? In thinking about these issues, consider the definitions of positive and negative easements in the American Law Institute:

451: Affirmative Easement

An affirmative easement entitles the owner thereof to use the land subject to the easement by doing acts which, were it not for the easement, he would not be privileged to do.

452: Negative Easement

A negative easement assures to the owner thereof a particular use or enjoyment of the land subject to the easement by enabling him to prevent the possessor of the land from doing acts upon it which, were it not for the easement, he would be privileged to do.

Do these definitions suggest that negative easements may interfere more substantially than positive easements with the activities of the owner of the servient land? Why or why not? Is it always perfectly clear that an easement is negative or positive? Should the enforceability of an easement depend entirely on the way it is drafted or characterized by a court? You may want to re-examine these questions in the context of the enforceability of positive and negative covenants, discussed later in the chapter.

Lord Denning's restrictive approach to the recognition of negative easements illustrated in *Phipps* may have resulted from his view that, if the owner of no. 16 Market Street had wished to protect the wall of the house from damage from the weather, an easy method was available to accomplish such a purpose—an agreement between the two householders, referred to by Lord Denning as a covenant binding on the parties in contract, and binding on subsequent purchasers with notice. If the owner of no. 16 Market Street had wished to enter into such a contract with the owner of no. 14, it is possible that it would have been necessary to provide some consideration for the assumption of this obligation on the part of the owner of no. 14. Is Lord Denning's real concern not to create an interest without compensation for the owner of no. 14? Or are there other considerations as well? For example, how would a subsequent purchaser know of the existence of such an easement? Is Lord Denning's concern really about problems of notice? Are there other ways of dealing with these concerns?

By contrast with English law, US law in the 19th century embraced negative easements as a method of enforcing subdivision controls, and it has been suggested that negative easements were generally more useful than covenants for achieving these purposes:

> The negative easement was reluctantly acknowledged by English law, which recognized only four negative easements: the rights to air, light, support, and water in an artificial stream. But negative easements came to be used expansively in the United States, not only for protecting light and air, but also for enforcing setback lines and limiting noxious uses. The easement was superior to the covenant as a restrictive tool because it was not subject to a requirement of privity. ...
>
> As actions for injunctions to enforce subdivision deed restrictions became more common, it became increasingly clear that courts were not particularly concerned with the legal classification of restrictions, only with whether the restrictions ought to be enforced at equity. Thus, [another] kind of restriction enforceable at equity, variously called an equitable servitude, equitable easement, or sometimes an (equitable) negative easement, came to the fore as the primary tool the courts recognized for enforcing subdivision restrictions.

(R. Chused, *Cases, Materials and Problems in Property* (New York: Matthew Bender, 1988) (hereafter Chused), at 971.) This analysis suggests that the underlying rationale for the enforcement of such obligations (including those in negative easements) in the United States was an equitable one. As will be seen in the next section, negative or restrictive covenants were also enforced in England on the basis of equity, although separate principles concerning the enforceability of easements and covenants have been largely maintained in England and Canada, by contrast with the United States. Indeed, as suggested earlier in this chapter, some commentators in the United States support the recognition of just one form of servitudes. In spite of these apparent differences among common law jurisdictions, it has been argued that recent English decisions (like decisions in the United States) have tended to emphasize equitable considerations in injunction actions initiated to preserve a view—for example, of the sea. See P. Polden, "Views in Perspective" (1984), 48 *The Conveyancer and Property Lawyer* 429 (hereafter Polden). Moreover, in spite of Lord Denning's concerns to limit the range of negative easements recognized in law, courts have nonetheless enforced a wide range of positive easements. For a useful catalogue, see D. Mendes da Costa, R. Balfour, and E. Gillese *Property Law*, 2d ed. (Toronto: Emond Montgomery, 1990), at 19:36-37. See also K. Scott, "Comment" (1964), 22 *Cambridge Law Journal* 203.

The Issue of Prescriptive Rights to Light and Air

The appropriateness of recognizing easements in relation to air, light and unobstructed views may need to be assessed in the context of prescriptive rights. For a case in which a US court rejected a claim to prescriptive rights of access to air and light, see *Fontainebleau*

Hotel Corp. v. Forty-Five Twenty-Five, Inc., 114 So. 2d 357 (Fla. CA 1959). In that case, a luxury hotel owner brought an injunction application to prevent a rival luxury hotel next door from building a 14-storey addition, on the ground that the new addition would create a shadow after 2 pm every day in the winter over the area of the plaintiff's cabana, swimming pool, and sunbathing areas. Although the trial court had issued a temporary injunction based on nuisance principles, the appellate court reversed this decision. There was no suggestion at trial or on appeal that the plaintiff had any prescriptive rights to light or air or an unobstructed view of the Atlantic Ocean in this case.

The issue of prescriptive rights to light and air has also been considered frequently in the context of solar energy facilities. For example, see *Prah v. Maretti*, 108 Wis. 2d 223; 321 NW 2d 182 (Wis. SC 1982). While this case was pending, the Wisconsin legislature adopted a statute permitting local communities to create a land use permit system for those installing solar energy systems. See J.O. Grunow, "Comment: Wisconsin Recognizes the Power of the Sun: *Prah v. Maretti* and the Solar Access Act" (1983), *Wisconsin Law Review* 1263. For a good review of the principles in Canada, see M.A. Bowden, "Protecting Solar Access in Canada: The Common Law Approach" (1985), 9 *Dalhousie Law Journal* 261. According to Bowden, current interpretation of nuisance principles may present some difficulties in preventing subsequent interference with a householder's solar energy facility, and she has recommended legislative action. In addition, while suggesting that restrictive covenants may be the most useful device, she has also commented on the usefulness of a solar easement (at 286):

> An individual solar user should attempt to negotiate a solar easement with his neighbour to secure the long-term viability of his home heating alternative. Once again the enforceability of such an easement demands a liberal attitude in the courts. However, if the easement is carefully drafted to meet the technical requirements of this tool, if the acceptability of solar easements in other jurisdictions can be outlined, and the perceived social need highlighted, the hesitancy of the courts to accept new easements should be overcome.

Do you agree with this advice? You may want to reconsider it after examining the material concerning covenants in the following section of this chapter.

COVENANTS AND THE USE OF LAND

Most home owners in Ontario would likely be surprised to learn that, if they agree with their neighbour, for example, that the neighbour and her successors in title will maintain a common boundary fence, or a common driveway, the obligation will not bind subsequent owners of the neighbour's property ... . [This is an example] of the generally unsatisfactory state of the law of covenants related to land.

(Ontario Law Reform Commission (OLRC), *Report on Covenants Affecting Freehold Land* (Toronto: Ministry of the Attorney General, 1989) (hereafter OLRC), at 1.) Why are the subsequent owners not bound by the promise made by the homeowner and his or her neighbour? What are the consequences for the homeowner and his or her neighbour, for subsequent purchasers of their land, and for other homeowners in the same neighbourhood?

To what extent should the law permit the enforceability of such promises beyond the sphere of privity of contract and on what basis?

These questions are fundamental to understanding why some covenants have been recognized as proprietary interests. Although, as the quotation from the commission's report, above, illustrates, such covenants may not always bind successors in title, they may be effectively enforced as proprietary interests in other cases. For example, consider again the adjoining landowners at nos. 14 and 16 Market Street, discussed above in *Phipps v. Pears*. In that case, the owner of no. 16 Market Street claimed a right of protection from the weather from the adjoining building, no. 14 Market Street. Lord Denning concluded that there was no easement of protection from the weather because any such easement would be a negative easement and, for the reasons discussed there, the law would not recognize any new negative easements. At the same time, Lord Denning suggested that the owner of no. 16 could have accomplished the same objective by entering into a covenant with the neighbour at no. 14. According to Lord Denning, the covenant would have been enforceable in contract between the parties. In addition, Lord Denning asserted that it would have been binding in equity on subsequent purchasers with notice. In this way, the contractual agreement relating to land entered into by the owners of nos. 14 and 16 would bind their successors in title, at least with notice in equity, even though the successors in title to nos. 14 and 16 were not involved in the original contract, nor in any contract with each other. This means that privately negotiated promises about land, "operating outside the realm of contract, may effectively impose controls over the use of land which bind all parties into whose hands the land may come at any future time." (Gray and Symes, at 605.)

Covenants in relation to land, like easements and profits, create non-possessory interests in land. Like easements, covenants affect the rights of owners of neighbouring, although not always contiguous, parcels of land; covenants may also limit the scope of activities on servient land, similar to the impact of other non-possessory property interests and licences. In addition, the principles of covenants relating to land reflect the historical development of property law and contract, principles of law and equity, and social changes in land use and development over the past two centuries. Since many of the principles were fashioned by courts on a case-by-case basis, they may appear highly technical and, according to OLRC (at 1) "unnecessarily complex and occasionally illogical." Indeed, Lawrence Berger suggested some years ago that they were "so complex that only a very few specialists understand them," and he recommended that, rather than just relying on legal precedents, the principles should be re-examined in relation to underlying policies. See L. Berger, "A Policy Analysis of Promises Respecting the Use of Land" (1970), 55 *Minnesota Law Review* 167 for an overview of principles and policies concerning covenants relating to land in the United States. The OLRC's review of the law of covenants also resulted in recommendations to simplify and rationalize the principles but, to date, there has been no legislative response to the commission's recommendations.

This introduction to the law of covenants provides an overview of legal and equitable principles in the context of public policies concerning the use and development of land. In the 19th century, covenants provided an important means of private land-use planning in common law jurisdictions. For example, Timothy Jost examined early US legal techniques for controlling land use, particularly the defeasible fee simple estate, and the reasons why it was eventually rejected in favour of covenants (and other kinds of servitudes) and, in the 20th century, zoning legislation: see Timothy Jost, "The Defeasible Fee and the Birth of the Modern Residential Subdivision" (1984), 49 *Missouri Law Review* 695. For further examination of the development of these legal policies, see O.L. Browder, "Running Covenants and Public Policy" (1978), 77 *Michigan Law Review* 12 and U. Reichman, "Residential Private Governments: An Introductory Survey" (1976), 43 *University of Chicago Law Review* 253. Significantly, covenants have continued to be important as private planning techniques in the 20th century in spite of legislation enacting municipal zoning and other kinds of public regulation of land use. Indeed, in response to suggestions that modern statutory controls on land use make continued reliance on private covenants unnecessary, OLRC concurred (at 99) with recommendations of the English Law Commission that

> it would not be realistic to extend the ambit of planning law to take the place of private restrictions. Planning law paints with an extremely broad brush, and it is therefore unsuited to the task of resolving the finer details. The planning authorities do not have the wherewithal to regulate the interests of adjoining landowners, and it would be unreasonable to expect them to do so.

Accordingly, it is important to consider the law of covenants in relation to the enactment, especially after World War II, of significant statutory changes concerning the use of land, developments that have attempted to balance landowners' freedom of contract with broader interests of public policy. Some of these policy debates are reviewed in Gregory S. Alexander, "Freedom, Coercion, and the Law of Servitudes" (1988), 73 *Cornell Law Review* 883, specifically assessing competing approaches in U. Reichman, "Toward a Unified Concept of Servitudes" (1982), 55 *Southern California Law Review* 1177 and R. Epstein, "Notice and Freedom of Contract in the Law of Servitudes" (1982), 55 *Southern California Law Review* 1353 (hereafter Epstein). See also S. Sterk, "Neighbors in American Land Law" (1987), 87 *Columbia Law Review* 55.

The tension between landowners' freedom of contract and broader interests of public policy has frequently occurred in relation to discriminatory covenants, an issue addressed in more detail below. These concerns also require an assessment of the extent to which rationales of encouraging land use and productive development, so apparent during the industrial revolution in the 19th century, remain relevant in the late 20th century in the context of ideas about the need for conservation and environmental protection. Indeed, the law of covenants has provided the model for statutes in several Canadian provinces, permitting the creation of "conservation easements" as part of a strategy for protecting the natural environment. It is important to consider the principles and policies of covenants relating to land, not only as technical aspects of the law, but also in terms of their impact on social and economic policies about land use. For an overview of some of these issues, see B. Rudden, "Economic Theory v. Property Law: The 'Numerus Clausus' Problem," in J. Eekelaar and J. Bell, eds., *Oxford Essays in Jurisprudence*, 3d series (Oxford: Clarendon Press, 1987), 239 and The Law Commission, England, *Transfer of Land: The Law of Positive and Restrictive Covenants* (Law Com. no. 127: 1984).

General Principles: Privity of Contract and Estate

Ontario Law Reform Commission, Report on Covenants Affecting Freehold Land
(Toronto: Ministry of the Attorney General, 1989), at 6-8

Historically, a covenant bound only the parties to it. At a relatively early date, however, it was determined that an action for breach of the contract (then an action in *assumpsit*) could be transmitted to the personal representatives of the parties upon their deaths. The right of action could also be released, but it was not generally assignable at common law, because that was thought to encourage maintenance. Although choses in action did later become assignable, in part, in equity, and although they are now generally assignable by statute, it does not follow that covenants are capable of running with land when it is transferred. In this context, the law has developed peculiar and complex rules.

Since covenants relating to land involve both contract law and land law, the principles of both must be considered throughout our discussion of covenants. The two leading principles emerging from these areas are privity of contract and privity of estate. Privity of contract means simply that the parties stand in direct contractual relation to each other and may enforce their rights under the law of contract. Privity of estate, on the other hand, connotes a relationship of tenure between the parties. In modern law, disregarding the relationship between the Crown and subject, a tenurial relationship exists only between lessor and lessee.

Functionally, three basic situations may be identified in connection with these principles. The first is a situation in which privity of contract exists between the parties. The second is one in which privity of estate, but not privity of contract, exists between the parties. The third is a situation in which neither privity of contract nor privity of estate exists between the parties. The fundamental rules, applicable in each of these circumstances, will be discussed in turn.

Privity of contract exists between a lessor and a lessee, the original parties to the lease, and between a vendor and a purchaser upon a transfer of freehold land. If privity of contract exists, the parties to the contract and, as we have indicated, their personal representatives, can bring action against each other to enforce the contract. An action lies either at law for damages for breach of the contract, or sometimes in equity for an injunction or specific performance. It should be noted that the benefit of the contract, that is, the right to sue upon it, is assignable, but the burden, that is, the liability under it, is not.

Privity of estate (as well as privity of contract) exists between a lessor and a lessee, because their relationship is based on tenure. Moreover, if the lessor assigns the reversion, or the lessee assigns the term of the lease, privity of estate will exist between the following: (1) an assignee of the lessor and the original lessee; (2) an assignee of the lessee and the original lessor; and (3) an assignee of the lessor and an assignee of the lessee. As we noted above, privity of estate exists only between lessor and lessee (and their respective assignees). Privity of estate does not exist, therefore, between the lessor and a sublessee, since no direct lessor–lessee relationship exists between them. Nor does privity of estate exist in the context of freehold land.

If privity of estate exists, but privity of contract does not, an assignee of the term or of the reversion may enforce only those covenants that "touch and concern," or relate to the subject-matter of, the lease. As we discuss below, these are covenants that concern the relationship of lessor and lessee. Covenants that do not touch and concern the land are not enforceable by the assignees of the original parties. It must be remembered, however, that such covenants would be enforceable by the original parties themselves.

Since privity of contract continues notwithstanding an assignment of the lease or the reversion, the original parties remain liable to each other for breaches of covenant during the entire term of the lease. On the other hand, since privity of estate continues only so long as the relationship of tenure exists, an assignee of the term or of the reversion is liable only for breaches of covenants that occur while she holds the estate in the land.

Neither privity of estate nor privity of contract exists, in the leasehold context, between a lessor and a sublessee, that is, a person to whom the lessee has sublet part of the term, rather than one to whom he has assigned the remainder of the term. In the freehold context, where the vendor of freehold land has retained adjoining or other land, there is neither privity of contract nor privity of estate between the following: (1) the vendor and the purchaser's assignee; (2) the vendor's assignee and the purchaser; or (3) the vendor's assignee and the purchaser's assignee.

If there is neither privity of contract nor privity of estate between the parties, a covenant is not enforceable, subject to two exceptions. First, in equity, the benefit and the burden of a restrictive covenant, that is, a covenant that is negative in substance, can run with the land. Secondly, at law, the benefit, although not the burden, of a positive or restrictive covenant that touches and concerns the land can run with an estate in the land. Moreover, the benefit of any convenant, whether or not it touches or concerns the land, can be assigned in equity or, more recently, at law by virtue of statute. By contrast, in Ontario, the burden of a covenant cannot be assigned, either at law, in equity or by statute.

Discussion Notes

Covenants and Priority of Contract

There is now general agreement that a "covenant" is simply a contractual promise. As Ziff explained, a covenant was formerly a "promise under seal," but the requirement for a seal in land transactions has now been discarded in many Canadian jurisdictions—for example, see Ontario's Land Registration Reform Act, 1984, RSO 1990, c. L.32, s. 13(1). See also Ziff (1996), at 348-51, and A.H. Oosterhoff and W.B. Rayner, *Anger and Honsberger Law of Real Property* (Aurora, ON: Canada Law Book, 1985) (hereafter Oosterhoff and Rayner), at 899ff. However, because a covenant represents only a contractual promise, it is generally enforceable only where there is privity of contract between the maker of the promise (the covenantor) and the person who benefits from it (the covenantee).

The idea of privity of contract is fundamental to common law analysis. V. Palmer, *The Paths to Privity: A History of Third Party Beneficiary Contracts at English Law* (San Francisco: Austin & Winfield, 1992), explored the development of the concept of privity in contract, noting some differences in ideas about this concept between England and the United States and suggesting (at 10):

> The American position stands at one extreme from the English position, but it
> demonstrates that the scope and purpose of the term has changed in the course of history

and in the geographical dispersal of the common law. To postulate a fixed constant definition, even within one tradition, can only lead to false conclusions. Indeed, the contrary is the case: we can only understand its meaning in relation to period, context and function.

Consider this statement about the fluidity of the concept of privity of contract in the context of legal and equitable principles of the law of covenants. Does Palmer's assessment accurately describe the concept in this context? For other critical perspectives that suggest that the idea of privity of contract is not "a fixed constant definition," see J. Feinman and P. Gabel, "Contract Law as Ideology," in D. Kairys, ed., *The Politics of Law* (New York: Pantheon Books, 1982), 373 and M. Tigar and M. Levy, *Law and the Rise of Capitalism* (New York: Monthly Review Press, 1977). What is the difference between privity of contract and privity of estate? Why is there no privity of estate between a vendor and purchaser, by contrast with a lessor and lessee?

Terminology of Covenants: "Benefit" and "Burden"

Before proceeding to analyze the principles of covenants, it is important to become familiar with the terminology. Consider *Phipps v. Pears* again. In relation to Lord Denning's suggestion that the owners of nos. 14 and 16 Market Street might have negotiated a promise, no. 16 would have received the "benefit" of such a covenant, while no. 14 would have had the "burden" of it. If the owner of no. 16 had transferred his estate to a subsequent purchaser, the issue would have been whether the "benefit of the covenant had passed" to the subsequent purchaser (the "assignee of the benefit") along with the fee simple estate. Similarly, if the corporate owner of no. 14 had transferred its estate to a subsequent purchaser, the issue would have been whether the "burden of the covenant had passed" to the subsequent purchaser (the "assignee of the burden" of the covenant) along with the fee simple estate. As is apparent, it is necessary to determine in what circumstances the benefit of a covenant will run, and similarly in what circumstances the burden of a covenant will run with the estate in land that is being transferred.

For example, consider a vendor who wishes to sell a portion of a block of land, retaining the remainder. The vendor may negotiate with the purchaser that, in relation to the parcel being transferred, the purchaser may not "build any structure on the land except a single-family dwelling." Who has the benefit of the covenant in this case? Who has the burden? If both the vendor and the purchaser subsequently convey their respective blocks to assignees, will the covenant be enforceable? Note that the assignee of the vendor and the assignee of the purchaser have no privity of contract. Why do they not have privity of estate? If the purchaser's assignee decides to build a 40-storey apartment building, what can the vendor's assignee do to prevent this action?

This legal problem is complicated by the fact that the principles concerning the running of the benefit of a covenant are different from those concerning the running of the burden. Moreover, the legal principles for the running of benefits and burdens are somewhat different from the equitable principles, especially in relation to the running of the burden of a covenant. Thus it may be necessary to define, as a matter of technical application of the principles, whether the legal or equitable principles should be used.

Moreover, since it is possible for landowners to enter into "mutual covenants," so that each of them has both benefit and burden when the original promise is made, it may also be necessary to determine whether both the benefit and the burden have passed, or not. Since the principles concerning the running of the benefit and the burden may differ, the position of subsequent purchasers in such cases may not be exactly the same as those of the original contracting parties. Thus it is important to any analysis of covenants to determine at the outset which land is benefitted and which is burdened (just as it was necessary to decide, in the context of easements, which land was the dominant tenement and which was the servient land).

The principles concerning covenants also require an analysis of the nature of the covenant, and whether it "touches and concerns the land" or is merely a personal covenant. In some cases, the benefit or burden of a covenant will bind a successor only if the covenant touches and concerns the land. The question when a covenant touches and concerns the land is explored in more detail in the following sections.

Leasehold Covenants: An Overview

A lessor and lessee have privity of contract, so they are usually entitled to enforce all the covenants in a lease for the duration of the leasehold estate. Even if the lessee transfers the leasehold estate to an assignee, the original lessee generally remains liable for the covenants, although the lessee may be able to seek indemnification from the assignee. Similarly, the original lessor generally remains liable on the covenants for the duration of the leasehold estate even if the reversion is assigned. For further analysis, see Oosterhoff and Rayner, at 902-3.

If either the lessor or lessee makes an assignment, the parties may have privity of estate. For example, if the lessor assigns the reversion, the assignee of the reversion and the lessee will have privity of estate. Similarly, if the lessee assigns the leasehold, the assignee of the leasehold and the lessor will have privity of estate. As explained above, the benefit and burden of some covenants may be enforceable between parties who do not have privity of contract, if they have privity of estate.

The principles concerning the enforceability of the benefit and burden of a covenant in relation to the assignment of the leasehold estate were established in *Spencer's Case* (1583), 77 ER 72 (KB). According to *Spencer's Case*, both the benefit and burden of covenants that "touched and concerned" the land passed to the assignee. The legal test to determine whether a covenant touches and concerns the land is whether the covenant affects the lessor as lessor, or the tenant as tenant. However, the application of this definition in practice is sometimes perplexing. For example, in *Regent Oil Co. v. J.A. Gregory (Hatch End) Ltd.*, [1966] Ch. 402 (CA), a clause in a lease providing that the tenant in a commercial establishment would purchase products from the landlord was held to touch and concern the land. By contrast, a covenant by a lessor to repay a security deposit provided by the tenant was held not to be enforceable against the assignee of the lessor, as "the covenant did not touch and concern the land in the sense of affecting the landlord and tenant relationship." See *Re Dollar Land Corp. Ltd. and Solomon*, [1963] 2 OR 269 (HCJ). For further analysis, see Oosterhoff and Rayner, at 903-4, and other cases cited there.

The principles concerning the enforceability of the benefit and burden of a covenant in relation to the assignment of the reversion were established by the Grantees of Reversion Act in 1540, thus predating *Spencer's Case*. According to this legislation, the benefit and burden of covenants "having reference to the subject matter of the lease" run with the reversion. This legislation is now contained in the Landlord and Tenant Act, RSO 1990, c. L.7, ss. 4-8; see also Landlord and Tenant Act, RSNB 1973, c. L.1, ss. 2-3. According to *Davis v. Town Properties Investment Corporation Ltd.*, [1903] 1 Ch. 797 (CA), the phrase "having reference to the subject matter of the lease" has the same meaning as covenants that "touch and concern" the lease. For further analysis of the effect of an assignment of the leasehold and the reversion, and recommendations for reform, see OLRC, at 9-11.

These principles apply in relation to assignments of the reversion and the leasehold estate. As OLRC, excerpted above, explained, they do not apply in relation to a sublease by the lessee. In a sublease arrangement, the lessee transfers only part of his or her leasehold estate, creating a new lessor/lessee relationship between the lessee and the sublessee. By contrast, when the lessee assigns the leasehold estate, the new assignee takes on the entire interest of the lessee. Thus, when a lessee assigns the leasehold estate, there is privity of estate between the lessor and the assignee of the leasehold. However, when the lessee creates a sublease, there is no privity of estate between the lessor and the sublessee. As a result, the lessor cannot directly enforce covenants in the original lease against the sublessee, although the lessor can do so indirectly by enforcing them against the lessee (with whom there remains both privity of contract and privity of estate). In addition, as in the context of freehold covenants discussed in the next section, it may be possible for the lessor to enforce the benefit and burden of negative covenants against the sublessee if they touch and concern the land and meet the other requirements established in equity.

Discussion Notes

Leasehold Covenants: Tichborne v. Weir

Consider the position of a squatter who takes possession against a lessee, eventually barring the lessee's right to recover possession. Can the lessor enforce covenants that touch and concern the leasehold against the squatter? As will be apparent, there is no privity of contract between the lessor and the squatter, and so this question requires a determination as to whether there is privity of estate between the lessor and the squatter. In *Tichborne v. Weir* (1892), 67 LT 735 (CA), the court held that the squatter was not the assignee of the lessee, and thus there was no privity of estate between the lessor and the squatter. As a result, the lessor could not enforce covenants against the squatter. Recall the discussion of this problem in the context of possessory title to land in chapter 2.

Freehold Covenants: Enforcement at Law

Freehold covenants are sometimes created by contractual agreements between two adjoining landowners to achieve particular objectives (as Lord Denning suggested in

Phipps v. Pears discussed above). However, they are more often created when a vendor (or developer) transfers one or more lots to purchasers and, as part of a transaction, creates a burden on a purchaser's land in favour of the land retained by the vendor. If the purchaser subsequently breaches the agreement, the vendor may sue for damages for the breach and, in some cases, obtain an injunction in equity preventing a breach from occurring or continuing to occur. As is apparent, the vendor's entitlement in such cases is based on privity of contract between the vendor and purchaser. There are also common law principles and statutory provisions in some provinces that provide that personal representatives and others may be bound by such covenants according to contract principles. For a summary, see OLRC, at 15. See also Department of Education, *Easements and Restrictive Covenants* (Toronto: Law Society of Upper Canada, 1989).

The legal principles concerning the enforcement of covenants by or against assignees of freehold interests are more straightforward than those in equity. In general, according to the legal principles, the benefit of a covenant may pass in defined circumstances, but the burden of a covenant cannot pass with the assignment of a freehold interest under any circumstances. The reasons for these principles, as well as underlying policy considerations, are explained in the material that follows.

The Benefit of the Covenant

In relation to legal principles for the passing of the benefit of a covenant with the assignment of the freehold, two requirements are relatively clear. First, the covenantee (the landowner for whom the covenant provided a benefit) must have a legal interest in land. Second, it has been suggested traditionally that the covenantee and the assignee of the covenantee must have the same legal estate in the land, although this requirement may have been altered by s. 24(1) of Ontario's Conveyancing and Law of Property Act, RSO 1990, c. C.34 and by s. 78 of the English Law of Property Act, 1925 (15 & 16 Geo. 5), c. 20.

More complex is the principle that the benefit of a covenant can pass at law only if it touches and concerns the land. As Gray and Symes suggested (at 609), this requirement means that "it must be shown that the covenant was entered into for the benefit of the land owned by the covenantee and not merely for his personal benefit." In *Smith and Snipes Hall Farm Ltd. v. River Douglas Catchment Board*, [1949] 2 KB 500 (CA), at 506, the court stated that a covenant that touched and concerned the land "must either affect the land as regards the mode of occupation, or it must be such as *per se*, and not merely from collateral circumstances, affects the value of the land." Thus, where the board had covenanted to keep the banks of a river in good repair, an assignee of the covenantee was able to require the board to undertake needed repairs because the covenant "touched and concerned the land."

By contrast with equitable principles, it is important to note that the legal principles for the running of the benefit of the covenant set out above make no distinction between positive covenants (requiring the covenantor to take some action) and negative covenants (requiring the covenantor to refrain from defined activities). As is evident, the covenant that was held to be enforceable by an assignee of the covenantee in *Smith*, above, was a positive covenant, requiring the board to undertake action to repair the banks of the river to prevent flooding. As well, the running of the benefit of the covenant at law may occur even if the covenant does not concern the covenantor's land. The classic illustration cited for this principle is *Pakenham's Case* (1368), YB 42 Edw. 3, Co. Litt. 385a. In that case, the covenantee entered into an agreement with a prior who undertook to celebrate divine service each week in the covenantee's chapel. Some years later, the covenantee's great-grandson, as assignee of the covenant, sued to enforce the covenant successfully. As in *Smith*, the covenantor did not have to own land to make the covenant enforceable.

The Burden of the Covenant

As stated above, the burden of a covenant relating to land cannot pass at law. Although this principle is simple, it is also important to understand the rationale for this approach. Although the principle has existed for centuries, the justification for the common law's approach is usually explained by reference to a 19th-century case, *Keppell v. Bailey* (1834), 39 ER 1042 (Ch.). In *Keppell v. Bailey*, the occupiers of an ironworks covenanted for themselves and their assigns to transport all limestone along a specific railroad, and then the original covenantors assigned their interest to the defendant. When the plaintiffs sought to enforce the covenant, it was held that the burden of a covenant did not run with the land at law. In stating this conclusion, Lord Brougham explained the policy underlying the legal principle (at 1049):

> [It] must not ... be supposed that incidents of a novel kind can be devised and attached to property at the fancy or caprice of any owner. It is clearly inconvenient both to the science of the law and to the public weal that such a latitude should be given ... . [Great] detriment would arise and much confusion of rights if parties were allowed to invent new modes of holding and enjoying real property, and to impress upon their lands and tenements a peculiar character, which should follow them into all hands, however remote.

As OLRC stated (at 20-21), the burden of such covenants was not permitted to run with freehold land "because property titles would become heavily encumbered, and, consequently, the assignability of the land would be impeded." In addition to rendering land less alienable, persons subsequently dealing with the land "would have great difficulty in ascertaining the existence of such covenants because they do not normally have a physical manifestation." Interestingly, the legal principle was adopted in Canada even though the existence of land registration systems in most provinces has never presented an obstacle to determining whether there was a covenant affecting land, by contrast with the situation in England at the time that *Keppell v. Bailey* was decided. Moreover, in relation to Lord Brougham's concern about covenants making land less alienable, there may be other arguments suggesting that land that is subject to restrictions may, in some cases, become more valuable and thus more alienable.

Discussion Notes

Applying the Principle: Parkinson v. Reid

OLRC described (at 21) the consequences of the legal principle concerning the running of the burden of a covenant in *Parkinson v. Reid*, [1966] SCR 162:

[The] owners of adjoining lots entered into an agreement under which the defendant's predecessor in title covenanted for himself, his heirs, executors, administrators and assigns (1) to construct a stairway on his lot to serve as a common entrance for the buildings on both lots; (2) to repair and replace the stairway as needed; and (3) to permit the plaintiff's predecessor in title free and uninterrupted access via the stairway. The lots subsequently having passed into the hands of the plaintiff and the defendant and the stairway having been destroyed, the plaintiff brought action to require the defendant to replace the stairway. The Supreme Court of Canada refused to grant a mandatory injunction.

Why did the court conclude that the plaintiff was not entitled to an injunction in the context of the legal principles concerning the running of the burden of covenants? What effect would the court's conclusion have on the value of the plaintiff's land? Would it be more or less alienable? What effect would the decision have on the defendant's land? Is this covenant negative or positive? You may want to reconsider this case again after examining the principles for the running of the burden of covenants in equity later in this section. For further details, see OLRC, at 21-22.

Austerberry v. Corporation of Oldham

In 1837, John Elliott conveyed a part of his land to trustees who undertook to make a toll road and to keep it in good repair. The trustees made the road and maintained it until it was taken over by the Corporation of Oldham. In 1881, the corporation sought to recover the costs of repairing this road from the landowners, including the plaintiff Austerberry, the assignee of John Elliott. Both Austerberry and the Corporation of Oldham had taken their conveyances with notice of the covenant. The plaintiff initiated an action to determine his rights pursuant to the covenant, requesting an injunction to restrain the Oldham Corporation. When the court found in favour of the defendant corporation, the plaintiff Austerberry appealed to the Court of Appeal.

Consider these facts in relation to the running of the benefit and burden of covenants at law. Is the plaintiff entitled to succeed? Note that it is necessary to decide whether the burden of the covenant passed and also whether the benefit passed. In *Austerberry v. Corporation of Oldham* (1885), 29 Ch.D 750 (CA), Lindley LJ concluded (at 780) that neither the benefit nor the burden of the covenant to repair could run with the land:

First it seems to have been thought that that covenant was so worded as to cover everything which the corporation had done—I mean by "everything" the metalling, and paving, and sewering; but when the covenant is looked at it is seen that it is not extensive enough to cover that; and, therefore, whatever may be the merits of the case, the corporation must be right as to a great portion of the charges made against the Plaintiff. But then there is the covenant which extends (to use a short word) to repairing and the Plaintiff says that at all events to the extent to which you, the corporation, have incurred expense in repairing the road, to that extent you are bound to exonerate me by virtue of that covenant. That gives rise to one or two questions of law.

The first question which I will consider is whether that covenant runs with the land, as it is called—whether the benefit of it runs with the land held by the Plaintiff, and whether the burden of it runs with the land held by the Defendants; because, if the covenant does run at law, then the Plaintiff, so far as I can see, would be right as to this portion of his claim. Now, as regards the benefit running with the Plaintiff's land, the covenant is, so far as the road goes, a covenant to repair the road; what I mean by that is, there is nothing in the deed which points particularly to that portion of the road which abuts upon or fronts the Plaintiff's land—it is a covenant to repair the whole of the road, no distinction being made between the portion of that road which joins or abuts upon his land and the rest of the road; in other words, it is a covenant simply to make and maintain this road as a public highway; there is no covenant to do anything whatever on the Plaintiff's land, and there is nothing pointing to the Plaintiff's land in particular. Now it appears to me to be going a long way to say that the benefit of that covenant runs with the Plaintiff's land. I do not overlook the fact that the Plaintiff as a frontage has certain rights of getting on to the road; and if this covenant had been so worded as to shew that there had been an intention to grant him some particular benefit in respect of that particular part of his land, possibly we might have said that the benefit of the covenant did run with this land; but when you look at the covenant it is a mere covenant with him, as with all adjoining owners, to make this road, a small portion of which only abuts on his land, and there is nothing specially relating to his land at all. I cannot see myself how any benefit of this covenant runs with his land.

But it strikes me, I confess, that there is a still more formidable objection as regards the burden. Does the burden of this covenant run with the land so as to bind the Defendants? The Defendants have acquired the road under the trustees, and they are bound by such covenant as runs with the land. Now we come to face the difficulty; does a covenant to repair all this road run with the land—that is, does the burden of it descend upon those to whom the road may be assigned in future? We are not dealing here with a case of landlord and tenant. The authorities which refer to that class of cases have little, if any, bearing upon the case which we have to consider, and I am not prepared to say that any covenant which imposes a burden upon land does run with the land, unless the covenant does, upon the true construction of the deed containing the covenant, amount to either a grant of an easement, or a rent-charge, or some estate or interest in the land. A mere covenant to repair, or to do something of that kind, does not seem to me, I confess, to run with the land in such a way as to bind those who may acquire it.

It is remarkable that the authorities upon this point, when they are examined, are very few, and it is also remarkable that in no case that I know of, except one which I shall refer to presently, is there anything like authority to say that a burden of this kind will run with the land. That point has often been discussed, and I rather think the conclusion at which the editors of the last edition of *Smith's* Leading Cases have come to is right, that no case has been decided which does establish that such a burden can run with the land in the sense in which I am now using that expression ... . There is no other authority that I am aware of that such a covenant as this runs with the land, unless it is *Western v. Madermott* (4), where the Court of Appeal did not sanction the notion that the covenant in that case ran with the land, although the covenant was a purely restrictive covenant. I am not aware of any other case which either shews, or appears to shew, that a burden such as this can be annexed to land by a mere covenant, such as we have got here; and in the absence of authority it appears to me that we shall be perfectly warranted in saying that the burden of this covenant does not run with the land. After all it is a mere personal covenant. If the parties had intended to charge this land for ever, into whatsoever hands it came, with the burden of repairing the road, there are ways and means known to conveyancers by which it could be done with comparative ease; all that would have been necessary would have been to create a rent-charge and charge it on the tolls, and the thing would have been done. They have not done anything of the sort, and, therefore, it seems to me to shew that they did not intend to have a covenant which should run with the land. That disposes of the part of the case which is perhaps the most difficult.

The last point was this—that even if it did not run with the land at law, still, upon the authority of *Tulk v. Moxhay* (1), the Defendants, having bought the land with notice of this covenant, take the land subject to it. Mr. Collins very properly did not press that upon us, because after the two recent decisions in the Court of Appeal in *Haywood v. Brunswick Permanent Benefit Building Society* (2) and *London and South Western Railway Company v. Gomm* (3) that argument is untenable. *Tulk v. Moxhay* cannot be extended to covenants of this description. It appears to me, therefore, that upon all points the Plaintiff has failed, and that the appeal ought to be dismissed with costs.

The other judges agreed that the appeal should be dismissed.

Does the reasoning of Lindley LJ reflect underlying policy concerns about the enforcement of freehold covenants, or a more technical application of the principles without much regard to policy concerns? To what extent are the same concerns identified in *Keppell v. Bailey*, discussed above, reflected in this case 50 years later? You may want to reconsider the court's concluding paragraph after examining the section in this chapter concerning the running of the burden of a covenant in equity.

Overcoming the Common Law Principle About the Burden of Covenants

As the court's decision in *Parkinson v. Reid*, above, demonstrates, there are some circumstances in which plaintiffs may wish to enforce covenants relating to land, even though the legal principles do not permit them to be enforced directly. Not surprisingly, a number of methods were developed to achieve the result that could not be achieved because of the common law's intransigence with respect to the running of the burden of covenants. As described in OLRC (at 22-24):

The inconvenience of the rule that the burden of a covenant cannot run with the land at law, particularly as it applies to positive covenants, has resulted in the development of a number of methods by which the effect of the rule may be circumvented.

One such method of avoiding the rule is to rely on a chain of personal covenants, and thereby maintain privity of contract. For example, if a vendor exacts a covenant from a purchaser to maintain a watercourse running across the land sold and the land retained by the vendor, the purchaser can require a similar covenant from the person to whom he subsequently sells. The purchaser will do so because he will remain liable to the vendor for any breach of covenant, even after the subsequent resale, by reason of privity of contract. Although the vendor may not sue the transferee, he may sue the original purchaser who, in turn, can sue the transferee. The longer such a chain grows, however, the less likely it is to remain effective. It can be broken by the death, insolvency, or disappearance of one of the parties, or by the failure of one of them to take a covenant from his assignee. Moreover, the only remedy available in these cases is damages, whereas injunctive relief might be preferable in certain circumstances.

In England, a variety of other devices has been employed to avoid the problem. The first involves the use of a rentcharge, which is a periodic payment charged on land. The device is useful in the enforcement of positive covenants because it is possible both to annex a right of entry, and impose a positive covenant, under a rentcharge. Indeed, it is common for the payment to be a nominal amount only, the purpose of the rentcharge being simply to enable the enforcement of the positive covenants. Such covenants are then enforceable in perpetuity. It would appear that such a right of entry would also be exempt from perpetuities in Ontario.

A third method of avoiding the rule is to rely upon the doctrine in *Halsall v. Brizell*. This doctrine is based upon the old rule, relating to deeds, that a person who claims the benefit of a deed must also take it subject to the burdens. In the *Halsall* case, the purchasers of lots in a subdivision were entitled, under a trust deed, to use private roads and other amenities. Each purchaser convenated to pay a share of the cost to maintain the amenities. The court held that their successors were liable to pay their share of the cost. The usefulness of the doctrine, however, is somewhat limited. It will operate only if there is a benefit to be claimed under the deed, and further, it will operate only so long as the assignee of the covenantor continues to claim that benefit.

In addition to the devices discussed above, the burden of certain positive covenants made in favour of public bodies can be made to run by statute. For example, provisions to this effect are contained in the *Planning Act, 1983*. Under this Act, a person who purchases or otherwise acquires land in a community improvement area from a municipality must covenant to maintain the land and buildings and the use thereof in conformity with the plan until a zoning bylaw is passed for the area. Similarly, an owner of land may be required to enter into an agreement with a municipality respecting the provision of facilities, services or matters in return for an increase in the height or density of a development.

Either of the above agreements may be registered on title to the land, and the municipality is entitled to enforce the agreement against the other party or, subject to the provisions of the *Registry Act* and the *Land Titles Act*, against subsequent owners of the land. ...

The rule prohibiting the running of the burden of positive covenants with freehold land presents a particular difficulty in the context of condominiums. Accordingly, legislation has been enacted to permit the enforcement of such covenants for condominiums governed by the legislation. Under the *Condominium Act*, each unit owner is bound by the Act, the declaration establishing the condominium and the condominium corporation's bylaws and rules, and each has a right to the compliance thereof by the other owners. Thus, for example, the unit owners are required to contribute to common expenses in the proportions specified in the declaration, which obligation is enforceable by lien. Furthermore, a unit owner has a duty to maintain, and may have a duty to repair, his unit.

Discussion Notes

Applying the Principles: Re Metropolitan Toronto Condominium Corp. No. 979

Two adjoining landowners entered into an agreement that the lands to be purchased by CYD Corp. would be subject to an easement in favour of CH Ltd. The purpose of the easement was to permit loading and garbage removal on adjoining lands. Since it would cost CYD Corp. about $250,000 to construct the easement, it was agreed that CH Ltd. would pay $25,000 annually to CYD Corp. as a fee for the use of the easement. CYD Corp. constructed the easement and then transferred its interest, subject to the easement, to MTCC No. 979. CYD Corp. also transferred its right to the annual fee to QQ Inc., a related company. MTCC No. 979 brought an application to determine its entitlement to the annual fee, contending that the fee ran with the land as payment for the easement. The respondents CYD Corp. and QQ Inc. argued that the fee was a personal right of CYD Corp.

What are the legal issues here? Does this covenant touch and concern the land so that the benefit of the covenant runs with the land? Can the burden of the covenant run with the land, and if so, how? To what extent are the documents in the transactions relevant to deciding these questions? Assuming that the burden cannot pass at law, how could the documents have been worded so that the result desired by the applicants could have been achieved? In *Re Metropolitan Toronto Condominium Corp. No. 979 v. Camrost York Development Corp.* (1995), 26 OR (3d) 238 (Gen. Div.), Sharpe J reviewed the principles set out in Ziff (1996) and in *Parkinson v. Reid*, above, and concluded (at 249) that the covenant in question did not run with the land:

> I conclude, therefore, that ... an interest of the kind at issue in this case is not capable of running with the land and that, absent a specific assignment of the right from an original party to the covenant, the applicants have no claim to the fee.

Do you agree with this analysis? For a comprehensive review of the authorities, see *Grant v. Edmondson*, [1931] 1 Ch. 1 (CA).

The Principle of Halsall v. Brizell: Tito v. Waddell

The principle of *Halsall v. Brizell*, [1957] Ch. 169 (Ch.D), referred to in OLRC, excerpted above, represented an important development, challenging the legal principle that prevented the running of the burden of a covenant. As Ziff pointed out, however, the case had limited value as a precedent since the judgment in the case was obiter on this point and the benefit/burden issue had not been fully argued by counsel. In spite of these limitations, however, *Halsall v. Brizell* was subsequently used to support the judgment in *ER Ives Investment Ltd. v. High*, [1967] 2 QB 379 (CA), another English case involving estoppel by acquiescence in relation to the benefit and burden of covenants.

The most significant application of the principle of *Halsall v. Brizell* however, occurred in *Tito v. Waddell (Ocean Island)*, [1977] Ch. 106 (Ch.D). In that case, the discovery of large deposits of high grade phosphate on the British South Pacific colony of Ocean Island (Banaba) resulted in an exclusive mining licence being granted to a British company. The company then set up arrangements to obtain the right to remove phosphate and trees in the late 19th century. By the time of World War I, the existing arrangements had fallen into disfavour and after 1913 they were replaced by a new set of agreements with landowners on Ocean Island that, among other matters, required the company to replant the lands subject to mining operations with coconut and other food-bearing trees at the conclusion of the mining operations. After the war, the original company was bought out by other interests, and in 1971, a number of Banabans (including Rotan Tito) filed suit, successfully seeking performance of the replanting obligations that were then due. As Ziff explained:

> The liability of [the assignees of the covenantor] could not be founded on contract *simpliciter*; they were not parties to the original contracts or deeds ... . Moreover, under orthodox views the benefit but not the burden of a contractual promise may be assigned, and equally, the burden of positive covenants cannot run with land at law or in equity. Therefore, the liability of the defendants ... had to rest on some other footing: enter [the principle in *Halsall v. Brizell*].

(Bruce Ziff, "Positive Covenants Running with Land: A Castaway on Ocean Island?" (1989), 27 *Alberta Law Review* 354, at 356.)

The decision in *Tito v. Waddell* was expressly rejected in *Government Insurance Office v. K.A. Reed Services Pty. Ltd.*, [1988] VR 829 (SC Full Ct.) in Australia. In that case, A proposed to construct a multi-storey office tower in Melbourne in a way that would have infringed local planning regulations by including windows in its north wall, close to the neighbouring property owned by B. A obtained an exemption from the strict application of the planning regulations, subject to a number of conditions including A's undertaking that if the height of the building on B's land were ever extended, A would seal up its windows at A's expense. A and B entered into an agreement to this effect, and then A constructed its office tower. Subsequently, A sold this property to C and B sold its property to D, purporting to assign the benefit of the agreement with A. When D then built its building to a height requiring C to seal up the windows, and C refused to do so, D sued for enforcement on the basis of *Halsall v. Brizell*. Although there were a number of bases for the unsuccessful outcome of the plaintiff's suit, the court also attacked the principle of *Halsall v. Brizell* directly, suggesting that it was based on an illusory foundation. Do you agree with this analysis? How important are traditional concerns about the problems of the running of the burden of covenants, as established in cases such as *Keppell v. Bailey*? To what extent is there is a need for more flexibility and creativity in the principles?

According to Ziff, the current controversy illustrated in the different outcomes in *Tito v. Waddell* on the one hand and *Reed Services* on the other suggests a need for legislative reform concerning covenants relating to land. Ziff compared these cases to the situation in the early 19th century when there was a need for parliamentary reform of the law of covenants in England, but no such reform occurred. As a result, there was a dramatic new development in equitable principles concerning the running of the burden of covenants in the case of *Tulk v. Moxhay* (1848), 41 ER 1143 (Ch.):

> In 1832, the Real Property Commissioners recommended that legislation be introduced to make it clear that affirmative and restrictive covenants could be effectively annexed to land. Parliament did not act but the mantle of reform was taken up in 1848 in the landmark case of *Tulk v. Moxhay*. In the years which followed, the scope of the new

doctrine was refashioned and constricted. In a curious way, history may be repeating itself. Calls for reform of the law pertaining to the running of positive burdens have so far fallen on deaf ears, but there has been movement in this area nonetheless, through *Tito v. Waddell*. Even if that judgment is deficient—and *Reed Services* points to some of its vagaries and flaws—*Tito* as with *Tulk* may yet prove to be a valuable first step in the reform process.

(Ziff, "Positive Covenants Running with Land: A Castaway on Ocean Island?" (1989), 23 *Alberta Law Review* 354, at 372.) For other comments on these cases, and the idea of enforcing positive covenants, see A. Prichard, "Making Positive Covenants Run" (1973), 37 *Conveyancer and Property Lawyer (NS)* 194; R.E. Megarry, "Note" (1957), 73 *Law Quarterly Review* 154; R.J. Smith, "The Running of Covenants in Equitable Leases and Equitable Assignments of Legal Leases" (1978), *Cambridge Law Journal* 98; W.H. Lloyd, "Enforcement of Affirmative Agreements Respecting the Use of Land" (1928), 14 *Virginia Law Review* 419; and S.F. French, "Servitudes Reform and the New Restatement of Property: Creation Doctrines and Structural Simplification" (1988), 73 *Cornell Law Review* 928.

Freehold Covenants: Enforcement in Equity

The Burden of the Covenant

The legal arrangements adopted to overcome the common law principle that the burden of a covenant does not run with the land occurred in a changing social and economic context in 19th-century England. As Gray and Symes, at 614, explained:

> The mid-19th century was a period of significant expansion, when the tension was greatest between the desire to keep land unfettered by private covenant (and therefore profitable for industrial development) and the conflicting desire to curb the effects of commercial and urban growth (by preserving residential amenity for the private householder). These conflicting policies were reflected in the case law of the period [including *Keppell v. Bailey*, discussed above].

In the absence of public regulation of land use and development, the inability of private landowners to make enforceable arrangements to preserve the character and amenities around them resulted in considerable pressure for reform. As S.I. George noted, real property commissioners were appointed in the 1930s to examine English law on real property, and their third report in 1832 considered the state of leasehold and freehold covenants. In relation to freehold covenants, the report of the commissioners recommended that they should be enforceable in equity. In this context, the decision in *Tulk v. Moxhay* represented a judicial response to a problem in the absence of any legislative action, although there continued to be disagreements among members of the judiciary after *Tulk v. Moxhay* as to the scope of the decision. For an account of the legal context in which *Tulk v. Moxhay* was decided, see S.I. George, *"Tulk v. Moxhay* Restored—To Its Historical Context" (1990), 12:2 *Liverpool Law Review* 173 (hereafter George), and cases cited there.

In examining the decision in *Tulk v. Moxhay*, consider the extent to which the case represents a departure from previous authority about the running of the burden of covenants.

Tulk v. Moxhay
(1848), 41 ER 1143 (Ch.)

[Tulk was seised in fee simple of the enclosed gardens and several houses in Leicester Square. In 1808, he conveyed in fee simple the enclosed garden called Leicester Square to Elms and his heirs and assigns. A covenant in this deed stated that Elms, and his heirs and assigns would at their own expense maintain in sufficient and proper repair the square garden with the equestrian statue in the centre in an open state and uncovered with any buildings. For the payment of a reasonable rent, Tulk's tenants (the inhabitants of Leicester Square) and their heirs and assigns would have keys and the privilege of admission into the garden. Many years later, the gardens were conveyed to Moxhay and his heirs, but this conveyance did not include the covenant in the 1808 deed. Nonetheless, Moxhay admitted that he had had notice of the covenant in the deed of 1808 at the time of the conveyance to him. Moxhay intended to cut down the trees and shrubs in the garden, remove the equestrian statue and the iron railing around the garden, and erect a building on the square. According to Moxhay, the square had totally altered in character since the original covenant and was in a neglected and ruinous condition at the time of his conveyance. Tulk brought an application for an injunction preventing Moxhay from carrying out his plans. The master of the rolls granted the application to restrain Moxhay from converting or using the garden, and the iron railing around it, for any purpose other than as a square garden in an open state and uncovered with buildings. See *Tulk v. Moxhay* (1848), 18 LJ Ch. 83 (Ch.D). Moxhay then brought a motion to discharge that order.]

The Lord Chancellor [Cottenham]: ... That this Court has jurisdiction to enforce a contract between the owner of land and his neighbour purchasing a part of it, that the latter shall either use or abstain from using the land purchased in a particular way, is what I never knew disputed. Here there is no question about the contract: the owner of certain houses in the square sells the land adjoining, with a covenant from the purchaser not to use it for any other purpose than as a square garden. And it is now contended, not that the vendee could violate that contract, but that he might sell the piece of land, and that the purchaser from him may violate it without this Court having any power to interfere. If that were so, it would be impossible for an owner of land to sell part of it without incurring the risk of rendering what he retains worthless. It is said that, the covenant being one which does not run with the land, this Court cannot enforce it; but the question is, not whether the covenant runs with the land, but whether a party shall be permitted to use the land in a manner inconsistent with the contract entered into by his vendor, and with notice of which he purchased. Of course, the price would be affected by the covenant, and nothing could be more inequitable than that the original purchaser should be able to sell the property the next day for a greater price, in consideration of the assignee being allowed to escape from the liability which he had himself undertaken.

That the question does not depend upon whether the covenant runs with the land is evident from this, that if there was a mere agreement and no covenant, this Court would enforce it against a party purchasing with notice of it; for if an equity is attached to the property by the owner, no one purchasing with notice of that equity can stand in a different situation from the party from whom he purchased. There are not only cases before the Vice-Chancellor of England, in which he considered that doctrine as not in dispute; but looking at the ground on which Lord Eldon disposed of the case of *The Duke of Bedford v. The Trustees of the British Museum* (2 My. & K 552), it is impossible to suppose that he entertained any doubt of it. ...

With respect to the observations of Lord Brougham in *Keppell v. Bailey*, he never could have meant to lay down that this Court would not enforce an equity attached to land by the owner, unless under such circumstances as would maintain an action at law. If that be the result of his observations, I can only say that I cannot coincide with it.

I think the cases cited before the Vice-Chancellor and this decision of the Master of the Rolls perfectly right, and, therefore, that this motion must be refused, with costs.

Discussion Notes

Covenants and the Creation of Property Interests

Tulk v. Moxhay is regarded as a significant departure from previous authority:

> The doctrine of *Tulk v. Moxhay* ... had a dramatic effect upon both the law of contract and the law of property. The covenantee was widely regarded as having not merely a contractual interest in the performance of the covenant made with him, but also a *proprietary* interest in the land of the covenantor. Moreover, the covenantee's proprietary interest could run with the land of the covenantor, so as to bind all those into whose hands that land came, until eventually the covenantor's land was conveyed to a bona fide purchaser of a legal estate for value without notice of the covenant. The covenantee was thus given a contractual right to control activities on the land of the covenantor, and, by virtue of the equitable doctrine, that contractual right enlarged into—and arrogated to itself the status of—*a proprietary right in land*.

(Gray and Symes, at 615-16.) The decision in *Tulk v. Moxhay* thus extended the enforceability of the burden of covenants in equity, beyond privity of contract and privity of estate. How would you formulate the principle for the running of the burden of covenants in equity, pursuant to *Tulk v. Moxhay*? You may want to reconsider your formulation of the principle in the light of subsequent developments in later cases, explained below.

Policy Rationales for Enforcing Covenants

As S.I. George noted, there were other cases similar to *Tulk v. Moxhay* before the courts in the early years of the 19th century. An interesting case concerned an application by the Duke of Bedford to restrain the British Museum from building an extension to house the Elgin Marbles. The Duke's application for an injunction to restrain the museum was based on an alleged breach of a covenant entered into in 1675 by predecessors in title of the Duke and the museum: *The Duke of Bedford v. The Trustees of the British Museum* (1822), 39 ER 1055 (Ch.D). The Duke's application was unsuccessful because "the character of the adjoining lands had been so altered with reference to the land conveyed, that the restriction in the covenant had ceased to be applicable according to the intent and spirit of the contract." See George, at 176, quoting S. Atkinson, *The Theory and Practice of Conveyancing*, 2d ed. (London: Sweet, 1839), vol. I, at 447. In *Tulk v. Moxhay*, the master of the rolls distinguished the Duke of Bedford's case as follows (see (1848), 18 LJ Ch. 83 (Ch.D), at 85-86):

> First of all, that there is such a change of circumstances that performance of the covenant ought not to be required. It was likened to the case of *The Duke of Bedford v. The Trustees of the British Museum* (3). I think Mr. Palmer, with the ability and sense with which he has conducted the whole of this business, did not press that strongly in his reply: and he was perfectly right in doing so, because there is a manifest and plain difference between the two cases. In the case of *The Duke of Bedford v. The Trustees of the British Museum* the party who was seeking against the other the performance of the covenant, had himself, by his own acts, placed the property under such different circumstances that it was perfectly manifest there was no reciprocity; the parties were not in any way in the same situation.

Do you agree with this analysis? In reviewing *Tulk v. Moxhay* in the context of these early cases, George concluded (at 183):

> It is submitted that, while there may have been some legal foundation for the rules which developed, they were essentially formulated as a matter of public policy to give "business efficacy" to long-standing arrangements. It matters not what the foundation is thought to be: if the result is desirable the injunctions will be awarded.

Do you agree with this assertion? Why would the courts have wished to respond to public policy in these cases? As George also suggested, the breadth of the principle enunciated in *Tulk v. Moxhay* resulted in subsequent disagreements among judges about the basis for the decision, and in some judicial efforts to narrow the scope of the ruling in *Tulk v. Moxhay*. Thus, it is evident that while courts established a new principle for the running of the burden of covenants in equity in *Tulk v. Moxhay*, they then continued to develop the principle in subsequent cases. As a result, these principles provide a good illustration of judicial law reform activity in relation to private planning by landowners.

The Requirement of Notice

Tulk v. Moxhay firmly established the requirement of notice to an assignee of the covenantor in order for the burden of the covenant to run in equity. As it has developed, this requirement means that the covenant will not be enforceable if the assignee of the covenantor is a *bona fide* purchaser for value without notice. Consider the position of a squatter who takes possession of a covenantor's land. Will the covenant be enforceable against the squatter? It was held in *Re Nisbet and Potts' Contract*, [1905] 1 Ch. 391 (Ch.D) that even though the squatter may not have notice, the squatter does not qualify as a *bona fide* purchaser for value, and thus the covenant will be enforceable. The concept of

notice must also take account of the requirements of provincial registration statutes, and
the extent to which they may define the process for establishing effective notice. For an
example, see *White v. Lauder Developments Ltd.* (1975), 60 DLR (3d) 419 (Ont. CA).

The Requirement That the Covenant Be Negative

As the principles developed in later cases, additional requirements for the running of the
burden of covenants were established. For example, in *Haywood v. The Brunswick
Permanent Benefit Building Society* (1881), 8 QBD 403 (CA), the court held that it had
no jurisdiction to enforce a positive covenant to build and repair, but only those that
restricted the use of land. Thus, the court distinguished positive covenants, unenforceable against an assignee of the covenantor in equity, from those that were negative or
restrictive that could bind successors in title of the covenantor. The test for deciding
whether a covenant is positive or negative is substantive, so that a covenant may be
phrased positively and yet be negative in substance—for example, a covenant "to use
the property for residential purposes only."

Recall the covenant in *Tulk v. Moxhay*—was it positive or negative? According to
George (at 188) it was a "hybrid" one in that the covenantor undertook not to build on the
land and also to maintain it "in neat and ornamental order." OLRC agreed, stating (at 26)
that the covenant in *Tulk v. Moxhay* was "positive in form, insofar as the covenantor
agreed to maintain Leicester Square in an open state uncovered by any buildings, but it
was negative in essence, since it was designed to prevent the covenantor from building in
the square." Whether the covenant is positive or negative in substance may create problems of interpretation for courts since only negative covenants are enforceable against the
assignee of the covenantor in equity. As OLRC explained, it may be possible for covenants to be severed to be enforced in some cases. For other examples and analysis, see
Ziff (1996), at 355-58; Gray and Symes, at 616-17; OLRC; and George.

Is there any justification for limiting the enforceability of covenants against assignees on the basis of whether or not they are negative in substance? Recall that the court in
Keppell v. Bailey, discussed above, seemed concerned about the enforceability of the
burden of all covenants on the basis that it would render land less valuable and affect
alienability, and also that it would be difficult for subsequent purchasers to obtain clear
notice of such covenants. According to OLRC (at 100-1), however, the existence of
covenants may enhance alienability since "they operate to protect the amenities of
neighbourhoods and the competitiveness of businesses." Moreover, the system of land
registration in Canada means that there should be no problem ascertaining what covenants may bind successors in title to the covenantor. Accordingly, OLRC considered
the utility of positive covenants in subdivision developments, the fact that the burden of
positive covenants has always run in leaseholds, and the enactment of legislation in
some provinces permitting the running of positive covenants in condominiums. OLRC
concluded (at 101-2):

> We have reached the conclusion that the present law, which prohibits the running of the
> burden of positive covenants upon a transfer of freehold land, operates to defeat the
> legitimate expectations of the parties. In our view, there can be no principled rationale

for a rule that would preclude neighbours from agreeing, for example, to maintain a boundary fence, or, to keep certain drains clear, such that the covenant would run with the land ... . In addition, to the extent that a variety of methods have been developed to circumvent the undesirable effect of the present law, it has been productive of much uncertainty and confusion. For the foregoing reasons, the Commission recommends that the law should be reformed to permit the burden of affirmative obligations to run upon a transfer of freehold land.

OLRC defined legislative changes required to effect its recommendations for reform of the law of covenants (see 104ff). Do you agree that it would be appropriate to permit the running of the burden of positive covenants? Note that OLRC declined to recommend the creation of a single unified law of servitudes—comprising profits, easements, and covenants—concluding (at 103) that such an approach was "overly ambitious." Do you agree? What would be the advantage of a single law of servitudes? To date, there has been no legislative response to the OLRC's recommendations.

The Requirement That the Covenantee Retain Land Benefited by the Covenant

In addition to requirements that the assignee of the covenantor have notice and that the covenant be negative in substance, the enforceability of the burden of a covenant in equity requires that the covenantee retain land benefited by the covenant. For example, in *Re British United Automobiles Ltd. and Volvo Canada Ltd.* (1980), 29 OR (2d) 725 (HCJ), a homeowners' association was unable to enforce a restrictive covenant since it owned no land capable of benefiting from the covenant. This requirement distinguishes covenants "personal" to the covenantee from those that relate to the land owned by the covenantee and successors in title, and is reminiscent of the requirement of a dominant and servient tenement for a valid easement in English and Canadian law. Thus, just as there is no recognition of an "easement in gross" in these jurisdictions, the burden of a negative covenant is not enforceable against an assignee of the covenantor's land unless the covenantee retains land benefited by the covenant. For other examples of the application of this requirement, see *Re Sekretov and City of Toronto*, [1973] 2 OR 161 (CA) and *Galbraith v. The Madawaska Club Ltd.*, [1961] SCR 639. In *Galbraith*, the original covenantee brought the application, demonstrating clearly the requirement that the enforceability of the covenant against an assignee of the covenantor depends on the existence of land benefited by the covenant. As Ziff argued, it is important for the covenantor and assigns of the covenantor to be able to identify precisely which lands are benefited by a covenant for purposes of both litigation and the negotiation of discharges of covenants. See Ziff (1996), at 355-58.

This requirement has sometimes created difficult problems for municipal authorities. In *London County Council v. Allen*, [1914] 3 KB 642, for example, the English Court of Appeal held that the LCC could not enforce a restrictive covenant against the covenantor's successor in title because the LCC held no land for the benefit of which the covenant had been taken. Similarly, in *One Twenty-Five Varsity Road Ltd. v. Township of York* (1960), 23 DLR (2d) 465 (Ont. CA), the court considered a covenant entered into by a municipality and a developer and held that it was not enforceable against the assignees of the developer because the municipality (the covenantee) did not retain lands capable of being benefited by the covenant. Counsel for the municipality argued that the case should be decided by reference to the basic principle in *Tulk v. Moxhay*—that is, notice to assignees—without taking account of later developments, including the requirement that the covenantee retain land benefited by the covenant. Morden JA declined to accept this argument, stating (at 470):

> [T]he plaintiff in *Tulk v. Moxhay* had lands capable of being benefited by the covenant at the time he exacted it and when he sought to enforce it. Altogether apart from this consideration and assuming that the result in that case was based solely upon notice, it is, not only undesirable but in my opinion, too late now for this Court to return to the position as it was in 1849 and give countenance to a development of the doctrine along such substantially different lines; we ought, I think, to adhere to the greatly restricted scope of the doctrine in *Tulk v. Moxhay* as evidenced by the numerous decisions subsequent to that case. A restrictive covenant enforceable between persons other than the original parties is, in effect, an equitable interest in property. It is well recognized that decisions affecting real property upon the basis of which titles are passed and accepted should not lightly be disturbed; this is one branch of law which requires stability.

Is this reasoning consistent with the approach in *Tulk v. Moxhay*? What are the underlying concerns of the court in *One Twenty-Five Varsity Road*? What options exist for a municipal authority that wishes to exert continuing control over development within its boundaries? Compare the approach in *One Twenty-Five Varsity Road* with *Re Daly and City of Vancouver* (1956), 5 DLR (2d) 474 (BC SC), where the court held that the municipality's proprietary interest in its streets was sufficient as a "dominant tenement" to support a restrictive covenant. Is this approach consistent with *Tulk v. Moxhay*? This problem has been overcome in some cases by precise legislative amendments permitting the burden of covenants to run on behalf of a municipal authority in the absence of land retained by the municipality—see, for example, Ontario Water Resources Act, RSO 1990, c. O.40, s. 27(1):

> A right or interest in ... any land or any covenant or condition relating thereto, in respect of water or sewage works, in favour of the Crown or any municipality ... is valid and enforceable ... notwithstanding that the right or interest ... is not appurtenant or annexed to or for the benefit of any land of the Crown or the municipality.

This requirement has also created problems in circumstances where the land to be benefited by a covenant is not clearly identified in the documents, so that there is a need for the court to interpret, perhaps through oral evidence, what land is benefited. In *Canadian Construction Co. v. Beaver (Alberta) Lumber Ltd.*, [1955] SCR 682, the court held that the burden of a covenant in an agreement did not run because the land to be benefited was not identified in the agreement. There was some difference among the judges as to whether oral evidence could be admitted, but the majority stated that, even if the oral evidence were admitted, the agreement was personal to the covenantee and not intended to benefit land. For other examples, see *Guaranty Trust Co. Canada v. Campbelltown Shopping Centre Ltd.* (1986), 44 *Alta. LR* (2d) 270 (CA); *Sawlor v. Naugle* (1990), 101 NSR (2d) 160 (NS SC TD); and *Canada Mortgage and Housing*

Corp. v. Hong Kong Bank of Canada (1990), 75 DLR (4th) 307 (Alta. CA), reversed on other grounds (1993), 100 DLR (4th) 40 (SCC).

In England, a related issue was considered in *Re Ballard's Conveyance*, [1937] Ch. 473 (Ch.D), where the court held that the burden of a covenant could not run because the covenantee had retained 1,700 acres of land and it was not reasonable that the covenant could benefit such a large dominant tenement. More recently, however, in *Wrotham Park Estate Co. Ltd. v. Parkside Homes Ltd.*, [1974] 1 WLR 798, the court held that it would generally accept that a covenant benefited the covenantee's land unless there was evidence that it would be unreasonable to do so. What is the difference between the approaches of these two cases? Which is more likely to result in enforceable covenants? What explanation is there for these differences? To what extent are both these cases consistent with the approach of *Tulk v. Moxhay*?

The Need to Reassess Developments After Tulk v. Moxhay

Related to the requirement that the covenantee retain land benefited by the covenant is a requirement that the covenant must touch and concern the land, and not be merely a personal covenant. The covenant must also be intended by the original parties to bind the heirs and assigns of the covenantor, not just the covenantor personally. Thus, the principles for the running of the burden of a covenant in equity now require:

1. notice on the part of the assignee of the covenantor;
2. a negative or restrictive covenant, in substance;
3. land benefited by the covenant retained by the covenantee;
4. a covenant that touches and concerns the land and not merely a personal covenant; and
5. intention on the part of the covenantor to bind successors and not just the covenantor personally.

Reconsider *Tulk v. Moxhay* in relation to these principles. To what extent is the case consistent with these principles, some of which were developed after *Tulk v. Moxhay* was decided? To what extent are these principles appropriate in the late 20th century? Some experts have argued that if there is inconsistency in the application of the principles, it is because courts have become frustrated by a lack of legislative initiative, just as may have occurred at the time when *Tulk v. Moxhay* was decided. In this context, how should we assess *Tito v. Waddell*, discussed above? In thinking about these questions, consider the following comment:

> The anxiety of judges in the 19th century to limit the kinds of incumbrance which might be imposed upon the freehold estate is not particularly apposite under the vastly changed conditions of modern life where most people live in large cities. The property law of the 19th century was highly individualistic and made little provision for "freeholders living like battery hens in urban developments" where much of the land may consist of amenities which belong to none personally but which are socially necessary for all.

(Gray and Symes, at 611-12.) See also H.W.R. Wade, "Covenants—A Broad and Reasonable View" (1972B), 31 *Cambridge Law Journal* 157.

The Benefit of the Covenant

In some situations, the assignee of a covenantee is unable to rely upon the legal principles for the running of the benefit of a covenant. For example, if the assignee has only an equitable interest in the land, the legal principles will not be available. In addition, where the assignee wishes to enforce a covenant against the assignee of the covenantor—that is, where both the covenantee and the covenantor have assigned their interests—so that enforcement depends on equitable principles for the running of the burden of a covenant, the assignee of the covenantee must satisfy the equitable rules for the running of the benefit. As D.A.L. Smout once suggested, these principles illustrate equity's "unnatural and uncharacteristic interest in sheer technicalities," requiring great accuracy in the drafting process. See D.A.L. Smout, "Easements and Restrictive Covenants," in *Special Lectures of the Law Society of Upper Canada 1951: Conveyancing and Real Property* (Toronto: Richard DeBoo, 1951), 105, at 113.

In order for the benefit of a covenant to pass to an assignee in equity, it must touch and concern the land, a requirement that is similar to the legal principles. The assignee must, in addition, demonstrate entitlement to the benefit. To do so, the assignee must show either that the covenant was annexed to the land—either expressly or, in some cases, by implication—and thus passed with the conveyance of the interest in land, that the covenant was assigned in addition to the conveyance, or that the covenant was between owners whose parcels of land comprise a building scheme.

Annexation of a covenant occurs when a deed expressly provides that a covenant is for the benefit of an identified parcel of land, or for the benefit of the present and subsequent owners of the benefited land. In *Galbraith v. The Madawaska Club Ltd.*, [1961] SCR 639, for example, a covenant entered into by purchasers of land from the club was held to be unenforceable, because the deeds failed to refer to any land to be benefited, and the covenant did not touch and concern the land but was merely a personal covenant. As well, the court held that there had been no express annexation of the benefit of the covenant to any lands of the club. Similarly, in *Re Sekretov and City of Toronto*, [1973] 2 OR 161 (CA), a covenant was held to be unenforceable because the dominant tenement could not be ascertained from the deed. Although there have been cases in England that have recognized implied annexation, where the parties' intentions have been clear, these principles have tended to be less accepted in Canada as a result of requirements of detailed descriptions in provincial registration statutes. There is also some continuing debate about statutory provisions in Canada and England that may affect issues of implied annexation—for example, see Law of Property Act, 1925 (15 & 16 Geo. 5), c. 20, s. 78; Conveyancing and Law of Property Act, RSO 1990, c. C.34, s. 24; *Federated Homes Ltd. v. Mill Lodge Properties Ltd.*, [1980] 1 WLR 594 (CA); and D. Hayton, "Revolution in Restrictive Covenants Law?" (1980), 43 *Modern Law Review* 445. Annexation also requires that a deed must specify whether the covenant is annexed to all, or only part, of the covenantee's land, although the *Federated Homes* decision seems to create a presumption that a covenant is annexed to all parts of the land unless a contrary intention appears. For further analysis, see OLRC, at 34-37.

An assignee of the benefit of the covenant may also be able to enforce it against an assignee of the burden, in the absence of annexation, if the covenant has been expressly assigned. Generally, it is necessary for an assignment of the benefit of the covenant to occur at the same time as the conveyance of the freehold estate from the covenantee to the assignee. Only covenants that benefit the dominant land, and not personal covenants, are enforceable. As well, the assignment must identify the benefited land clearly in Canada (although there is some relaxation of this requirement in England). For a more detailed analysis of the relationship between assignment and annexation, see OLRC, at 38-39, and the cases cited there.

The benefit of a covenant may also be enforced in equity through the creation of a development scheme. Traditionally, these were "building schemes" in which a developer imposed mutual covenants on the purchasers of all the lots in a defined area for the benefit of the development as a whole. The creation of such a community of interest among the purchasers of the lots in the development was held in equity to require reciprocity of obligation among the vendor and all the purchasers. Equity established clear requirements for recognizing a building scheme, including a common vendor who had clearly defined the land subject to the building scheme, made all the lots subject to similar covenants, and then sold lots with the intention that the covenants should be for the benefit of all the lots in the scheme. In addition, all the purchasers must have purchased their lots in expectation that the covenants applied to all the lots and were intended to benefit all of them. These traditional requirements were enunciated in *Elliston v. Reacher*, [1908] 2 Ch. 374 (Ch.D), although they have been somewhat relaxed in English cases, such as *Re Dolphin's Conveyance*, [1970] Ch. 654 (Ch.D) and in Prince Edward Island in *Re Spike and Rocca Group Ltd.* (1979), 107 DLR (3d) 62 (PEI SC). This more flexible approach was rejected in Ontario in *Re Lakhani and Weinstein* (1980), 31 OR (2d) 65 (HCJ), where there was no common owner. However, see *Dorrell v. Mueller* (1977), 16 OR (2d) 795 (Dt. Ct.), where the court held that a common vendor may not be required where land is registered under the Land Titles Act, RSO 1990 c. L.5. The recognition of a building scheme requires a clear description of the land subject to the scheme and clear notice to purchasers of its existence: see *McGregor v. Boyd Builders Ltd.*, [1966] 1 OR 424 (HCJ) and *Kirk v. Distacom Ventures Inc.* (1996), 4 RPR (3d) 240 (BC CA). For further details about building schemes, see OLRC, at 41ff.

A Case Study: Restrictive Covenants and Business Competition

In considering the appropriate role of covenants in the 20th century, examine the reasoning in the following case, and especially the discussion about the requirement that the covenant must touch and concern the land.

Canada Safeway Ltd. v. Thompson (City)
[1997] 5 RPR (3d) 1, at 8 (Man. QB)

[The lessor (Woolworth) owned land on which there was a shopping mall, and also held an option to buy certain adjacent lands. In 1971, Woolworth agreed to a long-term lease with Safeway, a major tenant in the shopping mall. Among other clauses in the lease, clause 12.04 provided that, if Woolworth acquired the adjacent lands, it would refrain from leasing any individual store exceeding fifteen hundred (1500) square feet ... in the Shopping Centre and Phase II thereof for the purposes of carrying on all or any of the following businesses ... :

  (a) a retail food store;
  (b) a butcher shop;
  (c) a produce (green grocery) store;
  (d) a fish market;
  (e) a grocery store;
  (f) a frozen food store;
  (g) a delicatessen; [and]
  (h) a cheese shop.

The lease also constrained the lessor (Woolworth) from developing the adjacent lands except in accordance with the above clause. The parties agreed that the lease would benefit and be binding on successors and assigns. There were also clauses creating packing rights in the Phase II lands (clause 12.05) and requiring (clause 10.01) an interpretation of clause 12.04 prohibiting the listed uses.

In 1975, Woolworth exercised its option and acquired the adjacent lands (the Phase II lands), and these were later transferred to the city in 1995. Safeway initiated an action for a declaration of its equitable interest in the Phase II lands. Although the case also required an analysis of issues of registration, the analysis of the covenant issue was its primary focus.]

CLEARWATER J:

The Issues

The law dealing with covenants that may or may not "run with the land" and be binding on subsequent owners of the land is complex. An application such as this brings many issues and sub-issues into play. The central question or issue to be determined may be summarized as follows:

Do any of the covenants contained in Safeway's lease of a portion of the shopping centre lands "run with" the Phase II lands thereby creating an interest in the Phase II lands now owned by the City? Alternatively (and as submitted by the City), are the covenants in question in the lease mere personal undertakings binding only on the parties to the lease and (or) merely a restriction on alienation as opposed to a restriction on use such that the City, as a successor or assign of Woolworth to title to the Phase II lands, does not bear the burden of the covenants?

Just as Safeway covenanted not to compete with certain other businesses leased by Woolworth to other tenants in the shopping centre, Woolworth granted reciprocating rights (covenants) to Safeway. It is these covenants that are the subject matter of this Application. ...

There is no doubt that the City had, or should have had, notice of the contents of the Safeway caveat when it elected to purchase the Phase II lands from Woolworth and take title. Neither notice nor the adequacy of notice are issues in this proceeding.

Safeway's Position

Safeway submits that the covenants contained in the lease (most specifically, those covenants contained in Articles 10 and 12, supra) are properly described as "restrictive covenants" and that these covenants "run with" the Phase II lands, thereby giving Safeway an equitable interest in those lands.

The City's Position

The City maintains two positions against Safeway. These positions are not necessarily "alternate" but perhaps may best be described as "complimentary" [sic]. The City submits that the covenants in question, and in particular Article 12.04 are merely covenants obliging Woolworth to "refrain from leasing" the Phase II of Shopping Centre lands. The City describes these covenants as being mere "restrictions on alienation" as opposed to "restrictions on use." The City says these covenants, in the form and content as found in this lease, do not run with the land; at best they are personal covenants enforceable only as between Safeway and Woolworth. The City points out that nowhere in the lease document did the parties provide expressly that the covenants in question would "run with the land." Further, if Woolworth had not exercised its option and purchased the Phase II lands, then neither Woolworth (nor Safeway) could ever have had any control over what happened on the Phase II lands. This fact, the City submits, supports its position that the parties never intended (and never expressed any such intention) that the covenants would run with the Phase II lands.

Secondly, the City submits that even if the court were to disagree with its interpretation and find that the covenants in question do run with the land, and are not merely personal in nature, nevertheless the covenants ceased to be in effect upon the sale of the lands by Woolworth in 1982 to the numbered Ontario Corporation (subsequently renamed "Thompson Mall Inc."). The City points to clause 9.06 of the lease ... which relieves Woolworth, as landlord, from any and all liability under the lease when it sold the shopping centre and assigned its leases to Thompson Mall Inc. in April 1982. This, the City says, means that Safeway no longer has any rights which could be enforced against any successor in title to the landlord.

Decision

The preparation of an enforceable restrictive covenant, particularly one which purports to limit competition in the market place, is a difficult task for a lawyer. To read even a significant portion of what has been written and published on the topic, going back to at least the 16th century, is an almost impossible task. The late Chief Justice of Canada, Bora Laskin, in his 1958 text (Revised Edition, 1964), *Cases and Notes on Land Law*, quoted at p. 475 from *Spencer's Case* (1583), 5 Co. Rep. 16a, 77 ER 72 (KB), where the English judge commented on some of the problems which continue to beset practitioners today:

> And many differences taken and agreed concerning express covenants, and covenants in law, and which of them run with the land, and which of them are collateral, and do not

go with the land, and where the assignee shall be bound without naming him, and where not; and where he shall not be bound although he be expressly named, and where not.

In this case, Safeway must turn to and rely on equity for the relief sought. There is no privity of contract between Safeway and the City. Although Safeway and the City each derive their respective interests in the lands in question from a common owner/vendor (Woolworth), this is not a situation where there is privity of estate between the parties. Safeway has a *leasehold interest* in the Shopping Centre lands and the City is *the owner* of the Phase II lands. Although the parties derived their respective interests from the same owner/vendor (Woolworth), the City does not stand in the shoes of the original parties to the lease; at least not in all respects. Woolworth's lease to Safeway was assigned by it (ultimately to the current owner of the Shopping Centre lands, Thompson Mall Inc.). Woolworth itself has no further responsibility to Safeway under the terms of the lease. ...

To a large extent Safeway relies upon the decision in *Tulk v. Moxhay* (1848), 2 Ph. 774, 41 ER 1143 (Ch.), and the law on the enforceability of restrictive covenants as it developed both before and after the *Tulk* decision. In *Tulk*, Lord Cottenham said (pp. 777-78):

> It is said that, the covenant being one which does not run with the land, this court cannot enforce it; but the question is, not whether the covenant runs with the land, but whether a party shall be permitted to use the land in a manner inconsistent with the contract entered into by his vendor, and with notice of which he purchased.

Mr. Justice Morse, in *Lorne Ritchie Enterprises Ltd. v. Canada Life Assurance Co.*, [1976] 5 WWR 130 (Man. QB), referred to (at p. 136) and relied on the majority judgment of the Ontario Court of Appeal in *White v. Lauder Developments Ltd.* (1975), 60 DLR (3d) 419 (Ont. CA), where Kelly JA, for the majority of the Ontario Court of Appeal, stated at p. 427:

> For the creation of such a negative easement certain qualifying conditions must be present:
>
> 1. The covenant or agreement must be negative in essence.
> 2. It must affect, and to have been intended by the original parties to affect, the land itself by controlling its use.
> 3. Two plots of land must be concerned, one bearing the burden and one receiving the benefit, in a sense a servient and a dominant tenement.
>
> Where any of these conditions is absent the covenant will be personal or collateral and will not impose a burden on the servient tenement nor confer a benefit on the dominant tenement.

In their brief, counsel for Safeway referred to and relied upon DiCastri, in his text, *Registration of Title to Land*, ([Scarborough, ON:] Carswell, 1987), where he summarizes the conditions which must be fulfilled in order to create a restrictive covenant enforceable against the covenantor and his successors in title (pp. 10-3 to 10-5):

> (a) The covenant must be negative in substance and constitute a burden on the covenantor's land analogous to an easement. No personal or affirmative covenant,

requiring the expenditure of money or the doing of some act, can, apart from statute, be made to run with the land.

(b) The covenant must be one that touches and concerns the land; i.e., it must be imposed for the benefit, or to enhance the value of the benefited land. Further, that land must be capable of being benefited by the covenant at the time it is imposed. ...

(c) The benefitted as well as the burdened land must be defined with precision in the instrument creating the restrictive covenant. ...

(d) The conveyance or agreement should state the covenant is imposed on the covenantor's land for the protection of specified land of the covenantee. ...

(e) Unless the contrary is authorized by statute, the titles to both the benefited land and the burdened land are required to be registered. ...

(f) Apart from statute the covenantee must be a person other than the covenantor. ...

Counsel for the City submits that on the true construction of the lease in question, the covenants are merely personal to Safeway and Woolworth, do not run with the Phase II lands which it purchased from Woolworth, and are not, therefore, enforceable against the City. The determination as to whether or not the lease and covenants in question meet any or all of the foregoing criteria depends upon the true construction of the lease agreement of May 10, 1971. The City relies upon the dicta of Mr. Justice Cartwright of the Supreme Court of Canada in *Canadian Construction Co. v. Beaver (Alberta) Lumber Ltd.*, [1955] SCR 682. As Cartwright J observed at p. 687:

> ... [I]t may first be observed that it is a formal and carefully prepared instrument obviously intended to be a complete statement of the whole bargain between the parties. ...

The lease before me must be considered in the same light. In discussing the numerous cases dealing with the enforceability of covenants such as these, Cartwright J observed, at p. 688:

> ... The question is whether, on the true construction of the agreement, the respondent and Henderson intended the restrictive covenant therein contained to be (a) for the vendor's own benefit and personal to it, or (b) for the protection or benefit of the vendor's land, Parcel B. ...

He went on to refer to some of the numerous cases on this issue and stated:

> ... In these cases and in the text books dealing with them the importance of the difference between covenants intended to be for purpose (a) and those intended to be for purpose (b) is repeatedly stressed, and can hardly be supposed to have been absent from the mind of the draftsman of the agreement under consideration when he made no mention of any lands retained by the vendor and inserted in paragaraph 2 the words "the said restriction and condition shall be binding upon each of the lots hereby conveyed for the benefit of the vendor." ...

Simply put, it is the function of this court to ascertain the true intention of the parties from the words used in the lease agreement.

I will deal with the six criteria or conditions which Safeway must satisfy to succeed. ...

Firstly, are the covenants negative in substance? On a plain reading of the covenants contained in Articles 10 and 12 of the lease, I am satisfied that the covenants are negative in substance, if not expressly negative. The last sentence in Article 10.01, with reference to the opening provisions of that Article, requires a reader of the document (and any successor or assign of Woolworth) to construe the document and the provisions of Article 12.04 in a manner such that certain uses of the Phase II lands are prohibited. These Articles are, in my opinion, clearly intended to restrict or limit the use of the Phase II lands for certain specific purposes during the currency of the Safeway lease.

Article 12.04 uses the words "refrain from leasing" with reference to future use of either the Shopping Centre lands or the Phase II lands. This can only be reasonably interpreted to be negative in substance; that is, Woolworth and its successors and assigns will not lease any individual stores on either of the lands except as permitted by the balance of this clause as it must be construed with reference to Article 10.

Secondly, do the covenants in question touch and concern the land? Whether or not the lease in question satisfies this criteria, having regard to the wording used, or not used, as the case may be, is perhaps the most difficult issue to determine in this fact situation.

The law as to whether or not any particular covenant "touches and concerns the land" is concisely summarized in DiCastri's text, *Registration of Title to Land* ([Scarborough, ON:] Carswell, 1987), pp. 10-3, para. 332(b) and somewhat more fully discussed by one of the editors of this text, Albert H. Oosterhoff, in his recent article entitled "The Law of Covenants: Background and Basic Principles" (1993), vol. 2, National Real Property Law Review, p. 166, at p. 173:

> A covenant touches and concerns the land or, as it is sometimes said, has reference to the subject-matter of the lease, if it "affects either the landlord qua landlord or the tenant qua tenant." This means that the covenant must be intimately involved in the lessor–lessee relationship and must directly concern or benefit the land. In other words, it must affect the nature, quality or value of the demised land or its mode of use.

When one considers the covenants in question (Articles 10 and 12, supra) in the context of the entire lease document, including the recital which clearly expresses the intention of the parties for "planning" and "merchandising unity," I am satisfied that the covenants in Articles 12.04 and 12.05, with the proviso contained in the last sentence of Article 10.01, do in fact touch and concern the demised land. The ability to restrict competition on the Phase II lands and to maintain parking rights for its customers on the Phase II lands clearly has a value to Safeway and adds value to its leasehold interest. It should be noted that pursuant to Article 4.03 of the lease, Safeway is generally prohibited from transferring or assigning its lease without the consent of Woolworth. However, Woolworth is obliged to consent to any assignment of the lease or a sublease of the whole of Safeway's leased premises to *another grocery supermarket*; that is, at any time during the currency of its lease Safeway has the right to sell its premises and its interest in the lease to another grocery supermarket. The value of this right is clearly enhanced if Safeway can restrict competition on the adjacent lands and maintain parking rights over the adjacent land.

In *Pacific International Equities Corp. v. Royal Trust Co.* (1994), 42 RPR (2d) 66, the Ontario Court of Justice (General Division) held that a restrictive covenant regarding parking "touched and concerned" the neighbouring leasehold estate because it would benefit a successor tenant of that leasehold estate. In *Merger Restaurants v. DME Foods Ltd.* (1990), 66 Man. R (2d) 22, Justice Philp for the Manitoba Court of Appeal stated, at p. 27:

> There can be no doubt that the extent and availability of parking spaces in a shopping plaza will directly affect the nature and value of the land. ...

Clearly it would have been preferable if the parties would have used more precise or specific language to express their intention that the benefit and burden of these covenants have attached themselves to the lands, the benefit to the dominant land (Safeway's leasehold interest) and the burden to the Phase II lands (now owned by the City). However, on reading the lease in its entirety and with particular reference to the fact that both parties expressly agreed that the lease would enure to the benefit of and be binding upon Woolworth, its successors and assigns and upon the heirs, executors, administrators and other personal legal representatives, successors and assigns of the tenant (Article 9.04, supra), I am satisfied that the requisite intention to so annex the benefits (and the burden) of the covenants to the respective interests in the lands is found in the lease document itself.

The City relies heavily on the British Columbia Court of Appeal decision in *Nylar Foods Ltd. v. Roman Catholic Episcopal Corp. of Prince Rupert* (1988), 48 DLR (4th) 175 (BC CA). In the *Nylar* case one party leased certain lands to another party and covenanted not to lease other adjoining lands to competitive businesses. The covenant was termed a restrictive covenant and was registered against the adjoining lands. The adjoining lands were then subdivided and the applicant purchased lots in the subdivision, subject to the restrictive covenant. The applicant then brought an application for an order striking out the covenant. The British Columbia Court of Appeal found in favour of the applicant and struck out the covenant. McLachlin JA (as she then was) recited the wording of the covenants in question at p. 176 of the *Nylar* decision as follows:

> The Landlord shall not during the term hereof without the prior consent in writing of the tenant entered [sic] into or be a party to any Lease [of] its Lands or any part thereof described as Lot A, except Plans 26624, 29151, and 30349, District Lot 753, Cariboo District, Plan 24027 under the terms of which the same would be used for a purpose competitive in nature with that set forth in Article XX hereof.
>
> Article XX provides:
>
> > The tenant shall use the Demised Premises for a combination convenience store and retail gas bar outlet.

She goes on to refer to authorities which support what she describes as "the policy of the courts to favour competition and alienability" leading "to a strict construction of restrictive covenants." Notwithstanding the apparent presumed intention of the parties to these covenants, she concludes that the covenant in question in *Nylar* did not create a charge on land but was confined to restricting the ability of the Episcopal Corporation to lease the land. She states (pp. 176-7):

... The only prohibition found in these words is against entering a lease in the forbidden terms. The land can be sold, assigned or otherwise dealt with free of such restriction. In fact this is what happened when the land was subdivided and ultimately purchased by the appellants.

This analysis of the covenant leads me to the conclusion that it is a personal covenant between the parties who made it and not a restrictive covenant running with the land. In order to create a valid restrictive covenant, clear language is required showing unambiguously that the parties intended to create an interest in land in favour of one of them. If it is not entirely clear from the language that the parties intended to create an equity and correlative burden on the land, the restrictive covenant will be treated merely as a personal covenant between the parties who made it.

It has repeatedly and consistently been held that clauses restricting the right to alienate or deal with the land do not evince the necessary intention to create a charge on the land. In so concluding, the courts distinguish between restrictions on "use," which may be taken as running with the land, and restrictions on alienation or other incidental matters, which are viewed as collateral to the land itself. ...

The covenants in question in the Safeway lease do not "simply control a party to the agreement" as McLachlin JA opined in her analysis of *White v. Lauder*, found at p. 179 of *Nylar*. It is clear from the decision in *Nylar* and the authorities referred to in *Nylar* that a covenant which is only a restriction on alienation (in *Nylar* it was a restriction on leasing) will not run with the land. That type of covenant will not control the land itself or the use of the land. If one were considering Article 12.04 only, *Nylar* would apply. However, when one considers the proviso in the last sentence of Article 10.01 combined with the prohibition "from leasing" in Article 12.04 and combined with the parking rights created in the Phase II lands if and when Woolworth acquired ownership of the Phase II lands (as it did—Article 12.05, supra), I find there is sufficient intention expressed to restrict the use of the Phase II lands and to prevent these covenants from being interpreted strictly as being a restriction on alienation. Here, the proviso in the last sentence of Article 10.01 *combined with* the prohibition "from leasing" in Article 12.04 *and combined with* the parking rights created (Article 12.05) in the Phase II lands if and when Woolworth acquired ownership of the Phase II lands (as it did) is, in my view, a sufficient expression of intention that these covenants are more than just a restriction on alienation or a simple restriction on leasing.

In a recent Article entitled "Covenants," vol. 1, CCH Ontario Real Estate Law Guide, 8589 (paras. 52,142 to 52,164) published in March 1966, C.S. Goldfarb, an editor of the report in question, makes an accurate observation at p. 8589:

> This area is highly technical and the cases are not easily reconcilable. How a particular set of facts is characterized may produce different results in similar situations. ...

The theme of "strict construction" to be applied to covenants such as this in support of a policy of the courts to favour competition and alienability is a theme which runs throughout the decision of the British Columbia Court of Appeal in *Nylar*. While recognizing and accepting this principle, the court should not, in my opinion, impose such a "strict construction" that the obvious and apparent commercial reasons for the existence of the covenants in a lease such as this are obviated. The decision of the British Columbia Court of Appeal does not specifically consider the commercial realities of the ownership, development, leasing and operation of shopping centres and malls in urban centres in Canada. Mr. Justice Spence, writing for a majority of the Supreme Court of Canada in *Russo v. Field*, [1973] SCR 466 at 477, in upholding a restrictive covenant that both affected competition and alienability in a somewhat similar situation (a small shopping centre serving a suburban residential area) considered the principle as follows (at p. 486):

> It has been said that covenants such as those under consideration in this action are covenants in the restraint of trade and therefore must be construed restrictively. I am quite ready to recognize that as a general proposition [of] law and yet I am of the opinion that it must be considered in the light of each circumstance in each individual case. The mercantile device of a small shopping centre in a residential suburban area can only be successful [if it] ... is planned on the basis that the various shops therein must not be competitive. Since the shopping centre is a local one and not a regional shopping centre, the prospective purchasers at the various shops which it is planned to attract are residents in the neighbourhood. They are, of necessity, limited in number and therefore the business which they bring to the shopping centre is limited in extent. The prospective purchaser attracted to shop A in the plaza may well turn from shop A to shop B to purchase some other kind of his or her needed goods or service but if the limited number of prospective purchasers are faced in the same small shopping centre with several prospective suppliers of the same kind of goods or service then there may not be enough business to support several suppliers. They will suffer and the operator of the shopping plaza will suffer.
>
> I am therefore of the opinion that the disposition as a matter of public policy to restrictively construe covenants which may be said to be in restraint of trade has but little importance in the consideration of the covenants in the particular case.

In my opinion, the same analysis can and should be applied to covenants which may also be a restraint or restriction on alienation in the context of a shopping centre developed in an urban community, as is the case before me. When one is required to ascertain the intention of the parties by the wording that they used in their written contract, the court should look at the entire factual situation as evidenced by the entire contract. To accept and apply *Nylar*, as the City urges, in the context of this shopping centre and this lease is to, in effect, find that both Safeway and Woolworth intended (although Safeway had committed itself, as a major tenant in this shopping centre for a minimum period of 20 years, paid or agreed to pay a minimum base rent in the area of $100,000 per year plus a percentage rent based on sales on top of the base rent, together with other expenses, and paid $50,000 on the execution of the lease and an additional $100,000 on the date the leased premises were certified by Woolworth's architect as ready for occupancy) that Woolworth could, on May 11, 1971 or any date thereafter, *if it acquired the Phase II lands as it did*, assign its interests in the Phase II lands to a major competitor of Safeway who in turn could immediately develop and operate a grocery supermarket in direct competition with Safeway. This analysis of the document simply ignores commercial reality and commercial reasonableness. It is true that Woolworth gave no undertaking whatsoever to either exercise its option and acquire the Phase II lands or, if it did, to develop them in any particular way. However, it did agree that if it acquired the Phase II lands neither it nor any of its successors and assigns (which include the City) would construe the lease (Article 10) to permit the operation of specified restrictive uses on these lands during the currency of the Safeway lease.

Provided the "exclusive rights" clauses or "non-competition" clauses are properly drafted and do not otherwise offend public policy as being "too restrictive" or "too broad as to distance or time" (and in my opinion that is not the case with the clauses in question in this lease; they are, *prima facie*, reasonable as to scope and time, although a finding or decision in that regard must be left to be dealt with upon any trial of such an issue with appropriate evidence), experienced and well-qualified solicitors have been negotiating and using similar clauses in commercial shopping centre leases since at least the 1970s in Canada. Specifically, in an article entitled, "Exclusive Rights and Non-Competition Clauses," written by Harvey M. Haber and Stephen J. Messinger, and found in the text entitled, *Shopping Centre Leases—A collection of articles and precedents*, edited by Harvey M. Haber, Canada Law Book (1976), these practitioners give numerous examples of similar clauses which they recommend for inclusion in shopping centre leases. At p. 418, the writers state:

> An example of a clause which would be the tenant's "ideal" type of clause might be worded as follows:
>
> > To the intent that this covenant shall run with and burden the lands comprising the Shopping Centre as described in Schedule "A" attached hereto and *any enlargement thereof or addition thereto or any lands within a radius of one (1) mile from the Shopping Centre which now or may hereafter be owned or controlled by the Landlord.* ... (italics supplied)

Prima facie, parties in the position of Woolworth and Safeway as they were in 1971 ought to be permitted, within reasonable parameters, to build and develop shopping centres to serve the citizens of a community and ought to be permitted, again within reasonable parameters, to control the use and the competition to be permitted on those lands. Moreover, and again within reasonable parameters, when the parties clearly contemplate a possible expansion on adjoining or adjacent lands, the parties ought to be able to contract to control uses and competition on these lands.

Authorities referred to by the City such as *Noble v. Alley* (1950), [1951] SCR 64, and *Canadian Construction* (supra), are distinguishable on their facts and in principle. In *Noble* the covenant in question was an attempt to prevent the sale of lands to persons of Jewish or Negro race. In *Canadian Construction*, there was no reference in the covenant to any specific land retained by the vendor (the dominant tenement in that situation) such that the covenant could run with the land; the mere fact that the vendor owned other lands which were capable of being regarded as a "dominant tenement" was not sufficient.

Here, Safeway's land (their leasehold interest in the shopping centre lands adjacent to the Phase II lands) is clearly identified and set out in the caveat and in the lease.

The City's submission to the effect that because Woolworth sold the Shopping Centre lands in 1982 and thus obtained a release from Safeway in terms of Safeway being able to enforce the covenant against Woolworth is, in my opinion, premised on the assumption or belief that there is no longer any "dominant tenement" in existence from and after that date to enjoy the benefit of the restrictive covenant. Applying the clear and concise analysis of H.M. Haber, QC in his most recent text, *The Commercial Lease, A Practical Guide*, (2d ed., 1994) at p. 332, and acknowledging the principle stated by Kelly JA in *White v. Lauder Developments Ltd.* (supra) to the effect that two plots or parcels of land must be involved, one bearing the burden and one receiving the benefit, I find that Safeway's "leasehold interest" is an equitable, if not a legal, interest in a portion of the Shopping Centre lands which are clearly identified in the caveat and the lease. The Phase II lands are clearly identified. Safeway's leasehold interest, being an interest in land, receives the benefit of the covenants (and is the dominant tenement) and the City's lands (the Phase II lands) bear the burden of the covenants and are the servient tenement.

On the question of whether or not the fact that Safeway did not own the Shopping Centre lands (it only has a "leasehold interest") affects Safeway's ability to create an interest in the adjoining lands, the decision of the Ontario Supreme Court, Appellate Division, in *Besinnett v. White* (1925), [1926] 1 DLR 95 (Ont. CA), is instructive and, in my opinion, applicable to this situation. In *Besinnett* the party attempting to uphold or enforce a restrictive covenant in a deed of land had, at the time the covenant was taken, only a right under a verbal agreement to later acquire an interest in the land. Middleton JA, writing for the appellate division, analyzed the authority and the fact situation as follows (p. 98):

> From this I conclude that the question is in each case one of intention—was the covenant taken to protect or benefit land in which the covenantee had an interest, using this term in its widest sense, or was it merely personal and collateral to the conveyance? If the former, then so long as the interest intended to be protected remains, or is augmented as in the case in hand, there is no reason why the Court should not compel the covenantor, or those who claim under him, with notice of the covenant, to regard the terms of the covenant. The question in each case is one of substance and reality and not of technicality.
>
> Here there is no question that the plaintiff at the time the covenant was taken had a real and actual interest in the land, an interest that might have been defeated if the sister had chosen to repudiate her verbal contract, but it was nevertheless a real interest, and the covenant was taken unquestionably for the protection of that interest, and not as a collateral and personal covenant.

Middleton JA goes on to analyze an earlier leading English decision in *Millbourn v. Lyons*, [1914] 1 Ch.D 34, which stands for the principle that in order for a covenantor (in this case Woolworth) to bind lands by a covenant, the covenantor must own the lands. *Millbourn* is authority for the proposition that the equitable interest of a purchaser under an agreement for sale is not "ownership" so as to make the covenant run with the land. However, Middleton JA goes on to state in *Besinnett*, at p. 98, that:

> ... The obligation must depend upon the actual conveyance and the state of affairs at the date of the conveyance.

In the case before me, Woolworth did not purport to burden the Phase II lands, or create any interest in the Phase II lands, on the date that it entered into the lease with Safeway (May 10, 1971). However, it did intend to burden the Phase II lands *if* it ever exercised its option and acquired title to them. This occurred in 1975 and the lease agreement, as it affects the Phase II lands, comes into effect at that time. There is nothing inherently wrong or unenforceable about a contract between two competent parties to create an interest in land at a defined point in time in the future, upon the happening of a defined event; that is, if and when one acquires the land, the interest or right comes into being.

On this issue as to whether or not the covenants in question touch and concern the land and are, by the terms of the lease agreement, annexed to the land, the City referred to and relied on the decision of Danis J of the Ontario High Court in *Coast-to-Coast Industrial Developments Ltd. v. Gorhim Holdings Ltd.* (1960), 22 DLR (2d) 695 (Ont. HC). In that case, one parcel of the land in question (Lot 8) was not acquired by the covenantor until after the tenant (covenantee) had gone into possession. At p. 698, Danis J refers to that fact and goes on to add:

> The grammatical and ordinary meaning of the language of the covenant is not such as to include after-acquired lands (11 Hals., 3d ed., p. 385).

I do not understand this decision to mean that in no circumstances can a covenantor (in this case Woolworth) create an interest in lands that it acquires at a later date, by virtue of an option to purchase or otherwise. Rather, it depends on the language of the agreement. In this case the lease expressly and clearly contemplates the later acquisition by Woolworth of the Phase II lands. Any ancient or technical rules which might suggest that the parties cannot agree to create an interest in land if and when one or other of them acquires the land is not, in my view, reasonable in today's market place. ...

In my opinion, the City's position that Article 9.06 of the lease, which releases Woolworth from any obligation to Safeway when it sold the Shopping Centre lands in 1982, should be construed to mean (or be evidence of the fact) that the covenants could not or should not run with the Phase II lands, at least after 1982, misses the point. If these covenants touch and concern the Phase II lands, then whether or not Woolworth may be personally liable on the covenants to Safeway is irrelevant. If these covenants touch and concern the land and are annexed to the land, as I have found, they run with the land and they bind the successors and assigns of Woolworth if those successors and assigns acquired title or notice, actual or constructive, of the existence of the covenants.

In conclusion, I find and declare that Safeway has an equitable interest in the Phase II lands by virtue of its lease dated May 10, 1971 and the covenants contained therein. Accordingly, Safeway is entitled to maintain the registration of its caveat against the titles to the Phase II lands. Safeway will have its costs, on a Class III basis, to be taxed or spoken to if the parties cannot agree on the amount.

Application allowed.

Discussion Notes

"Non-Competition" Covenants and the "Touch and Concern" Requirement

Does the covenant in clause 12.04 meet the test of touching and concerning the land? Is the reasoning in *Canada Safeway* more persuasive than that in *Nylar Foods Ltd. v.*

Roman Catholic Episcopal Corp. of Prince Rupert (1988), 48 DLR (4th) 175 (BC CA), discussed in this case? In an Annotation to the decision in *Canada Safeway*, Jeffrey Lem stated ((1996), 5 RPR (3d) 1, at 4):

> With utmost respect, this annotator finds it difficult to distinguish the two cases on their facts and would invite those further interested in the issue (and not bound by stare decisis) to critically compare the decisions and decide for themselves why the restriction in *Nylar* is really any different than the restrictive covenant in *Canada Safeway*. Even if one finds no material factual distinctions between the two competing cases, this annotator would nonetheless still lean towards *Canada Safeway* as the better view, and *Nylar* as the heretic.

Do you agree that *Canada Safeway* is preferable? Is Lem's view based on legal principles or policy concerns? Is it possible that the context of the modern shopping centre is so different from *Tulk v. Moxhay* that new principles are required? For an analysis of some of these issues in the United States, see P. Franzese, " 'Out of Touch': The Diminished Viability of the Touch and Concern Requirement in the Law of Servitudes" (1991), 21 *Seton Hall Law Review* 235. In relation to non-competition covenants, Franzese argued (at 243) that:

> [The touch and concern requirement] suggests that one's fiscal interests exist wholly separate and apart from one's ownership interests, use and enjoyment of ... land. Most fundamentally, it [is used as] a means to avoid covenants thought to restrain trade. At bottom, thinly disguised public policy concerns (and not some failure of the covenant to touch and concern the burdened parcel), oftentimes precluded the burden of an anticompetition covenant from running.

Why should non-competition covenants be permitted in shopping centres as a matter of policy? Whose interests are fostered by such covenants? What limits, if any, should be imposed? Consider these questions again after reviewing the next section and the cases about discriminatory covenants.

Covenants and Discrimination

The law of covenants provides an opportunity to consider the relationship between private contractual rights of landowners and public policies of non-discrimination. This issue is similar to the problems considered in chapter 3 with respect to limits imposed by law on the freedom of grantors and testators to impose conditions in grants and devises. Recall, for example, the principles invalidating grants and devises as restraints on alienation or marriage, or because they were uncertain, or contrary to public policy. These principles are related to covenants because it is arguable that the form in which a limitation is drafted may affect its validity. For example, it may be important to decide whether a particular document contains a restrictive covenant or a determinable fee simple. Even if a restrictive covenant is merely personal, and does not touch and concern the land, it will still be enforceable between the covenantor and covenantee because of their relationship of privity of contract. In this way, the issue of characterization remains an important one.

In addition, issues about freedom of contract and public policy also require an examination of the public/private dichotomy in law. Increasingly in the 20th century, public policies of non-discrimination have been legislated and enforced by courts, restricting the scope of private choice on the part of landowners and others. Some of the historical context is required to understand the cases concerning discriminatory covenants. Early on, for example, the Innkeepers' Act (now RSO 1990, c. I.7) required innkeepers to receive all travellers willing to pay for accommodation. A. Borovoy described the rationale for this statutory requirement on the basis that the lack of communication systems in earlier times made advance bookings for travellers impossible so that "travellers who were denied accommodation endured great inconvenience, often hardship," and the legal principles were therefore designed "for the greater convenience and safety of travellers and wayfarers." Borovoy suggested a need in post-World-War-II Canada to redefine the rationale for these principles in terms of public policies of non-discrimination, and examined in particular the extension of innkeepers' duties to restaurant proprietors. See A. Borovoy, "The Fair Accommodation Practices Act: the 'Dresden' Affair" (1956), 14:1 *University of Toronto Faculty of Law Review* 13, and the cases reviewed there, including *Christie v. York Corporation*, [1940] 1 DLR 81 (SCC); *R v. Emerson* (1955), 113 CCC 69 (Ont. Cty. Ct.); and *R v. McKay* (1955), 113 CCC 56 (Ont. Cty. Ct.). For a comment on *Christie*, see B. Laskin "Comment" (1940), 18 *Canadian Bar Review* 314. See also C. Backhouse, "Racial Segregation in Canadian Legal History: Viola Desmond's Challenge, Nova Scotia, 1946" (1994), 17 *Dalhousie Law Journal* 299. For a historical analysis of the public/private dichotomy in contractual relations in the United States, see M. Horowitz, "The History of the Public/Private Distinction" (1982), 130 *University of Pennsylvania Law Review* 1423. See also J.W. Singer, "No Right to Exclude: Public Accommodations and Private Property" (1995-96), 90 *Northwestern University Law Review* 1283.

In reading the two cases that follow, note the differences in characterization, and the extent to which each case illustrates the tension between "private" and "public" law issues.

Re Drummond Wren
[1945] 4 DLR 674 (Ont. HC)

MacKAY J: This is an application brought by Drummond Wren, owner of certain lands registered in the Registry Office for the County of York, to have declared invalid a restrictive covenant assumed by him when he purchased these lands and which he agreed to exact from his assigns, namely,—"Land not to be sold to Jews or persons of objectionable nationality."

The application is made by way of special leave and pursuant to s. 60 of the *Conveyancing and Law of Property Act*, RSO 1937, c. 152, and Rules 603 and 604 of the Rules of Practice and Procedure.

Under s. 60 of the *Conveyancing and Law of Property Act*, a wide discretion is given to a Judge to modify or discharge any condition or covenant "where there is annexed to any land any condition or covenant that such land or any specified portion thereof is not to be built on or is to be or not to be used in a particular manner, or any other condition or covenant running with or capable of being legally annexed to land."

Rules 603 and 604 provide respectively that:

603(1) Where any person claims to be the owner of land, but does not desire to have his title thereto quieted under *The Quieting Titles Act*, he may have any particular question which would arise upon an application to have his title quieted determined upon an originating notice.

(2) Notice shall be given to all persons to whom notice would be given under *The Quieting Titles Act*, and the Court shall have the same power finally to dispose of and determine such particular question as it would have under the said Act, but this shall not render it necessary to give the notice required by Rule 705.

604. Where the rights of any person depend upon the construction of any deed, will or other instrument, he may apply by originating notice, upon notice to all persons concerned, to have his rights declared and determined.

While, pursuant to an order made by me, notice of this application was served upon various persons interested in this and in adjacent lands subject to the same or a similar restrictive covenant, no one appeared in Court upon the return of this motion to oppose it.

The restrictive covenant which is the subject of this proceeding and which by the deed aforesaid the grantee assumes and agrees to exact from his assigns, reads as follows: "Land not to be sold to Jews, or to persons of objectionable nationality." Counsel for the applicant seeks the discharge and removal of this covenant on these alternative grounds: first, that it is void as against public policy; secondly, that it is invalid as a restraint on alienation; thirdly, that it is void for uncertainty; and fourthly, that it contravenes the provisions of the *Racial Discrimination Act*, 1944 (Ont.), c. 51. The matter before me, so defined, appears to raise issues of first impression because a search of the case law of Great Britain and of Canada does not reveal any reported decision which would be of direct assistance in this proceeding.

Counsel for the applicant did refer me to three Ontario cases dealing with restrictive covenants similar to that here involved, but, in my view, he rightly took the position that in none of those cases was the Court called upon to pass on the validity of the particular restriction in the way in which I am obliged to do in this case. Garrow J in *Essex Real Estate Co. v. Holmes* (1930), 37 OWN 392, did not have to determine the validity of the restriction in that case because he found that the purchaser of the land was not within its terms. Again, in *Re Bryers and Morris* (1931), 40 OWN 572, which was a vendor's and purchaser's motion, Hodgins JA refrained from passing on the validity of the restrictive covenant there in question. The third case mentioned by counsel for the applicant is a recent decision of Chevrier J, *Re McDougall and Waddell*, [1945] 2 DLR 244, OWN 272, which arose out of a vendor's and purchaser's motion for an order that the particular restrictive covenant there objected to offended against the terms of the *Racial Discrimination Act*, 1944 (Ont.), c. 51. The issue raised in that case was a narrow one and I shall return to a discussion of it later in my judgment.

In this short canvass of the authorities directly applicable, it may not be amiss to point out that, according to an affidavit filed on behalf of the applicant, the present Master of Titles at Toronto has not knowingly permitted anyone to register deeds containing restrictive covenants of a character similar to that in question here, and has on several occasions refused to accept for registration documents containing such covenants, and in no case has an appeal been taken from such refusal.

The applicant's argument is founded on the legal principle, briefly stated in 7 Hals. (2d ed.), pp. 153-4: "Any agreement which tends to be injurious to the public or against the public good is void as being contrary to public policy." Public policy, in the words of Halsbury, "varies from time to time."

In "The Growth of Law," Mr. Justice Cardozo says: "Existing rules and principles can give us our present location, our bearings, our latitude and longitude. The inn that shelters for the night if not the journey's end. The law, like the traveller, must be ready for the morrow. It must have a principle of growth."

And Mr. Justice Oliver Wendell Holmes, in "The Common Law" says: "The very considerations which judges most rarely mention and always with an apology are the secret root from which the law draws all the juices of life. I mean, of course, what is expedient for the community concerned."

The matter of not creating new heads of public policy has been discussed at some length by Mr. Justice McCardie in *Naylor, Benzon & Co. v. Krainische Industrie Gesellschaft*, [1918] 1 KB 331, later affirmed by the Court of Appeal, [1918] 2 KB 486.

There he points out [at 342-43] that "the Courts have not hesitated in the past to apply the doctrine (of public policy) whenever the facts demanded its application." "The truth of the matter," he says, "seems to be that public policy is a variable thing. It must fluctuate with the circumstances of the time. This view is exemplified by the decisions which were discussed by the House of Lords in *Nordenfelt v. Maxim Nordenfelt Guns and Ammunition Co.*, [1894] AC 535 .... The principles of public policy remain the same, though the application of them may be applied in novel ways. The ground does not vary. As it was put by Tindal CJ in *Horner v. Graves* (1831), 7 Bing. 735, 743 [131 ER 284], 'Whatever is injurious to the interests of the public is void, on the ground of public policy.' "

It is a well-recognized rule that Courts may look at various Dominion and Provincial Acts and public law as an aid in determining principles relative to public policy: see *Walkerville Brewing Co. v. Mayrand*, [1929] 2 DLR 945, 63 OLR 573.

First and of profound significance is the recent San Francisco Charter, to which Canada was a signatory, and which the Dominion Parliament has now ratified. The preamble to this Charter reads in part as follows:

We the peoples of the United Nations determined to save succeeding generations from the scourge of war, which twice in our lifetime has brought untold sorrow to mankind, and to reaffirm faith in fundamental human rights, in the dignity and worth of the human person, in the equal rights of men and women and of nations large and small ... and for these ends to practice tolerance and live together in peace with one another as good neighbours. ...

Under Articles 1 and 55 of this Charter, Canada is pledged to promote "universal respect for, and observance of, human rights and fundamental freedoms for all without distinction as to race, sex, language, or religion."

In the Atlantic Charter to which Canada has subscribed, the principles of freedom from fear and freedom of worship are recognized.

Section 1 of the *Racial Discrimination Act* provides:

> 1. No person shall,
>   (a) publish or display or cause to be published or displayed; or
>   (b) permit to be published or displayed on lands or premises or in a
> newspaper, through a radio broadcasting station or by means of any other medium
> which he owns or controls,
> any notice, sign, symbol, emblem or other representation indicating discrimination
> or an intention to discriminate against any person or any class of persons for any
> purpose because of the race or creed of such person or class of persons.

The Provincial Legislature further has expressed itself in the *Insurance Act*, RSO 1937, c. 256, s. 99, as follows:

> Any licensed insurer which discriminates unfairly between risks within Ontario because
> of the race or religion of the insured shall be guilty of an offence.

Moreover, under s. 6 of the Regulations passed pursuant to the *Community Halls Act*, now RSO 1937, c. 284, it is provided that

> Every hall erected under this Act shall be available for any public gathering of an
> educational, fraternal, religious or social nature or for the discussion of any public
> question, and no organization shall be denied the use of the hall for religious, fraternal
> or political reasons.

Proceeding from the general to the particular, the argument of the applicant is that the impugned covenant is void because it is injurious to the public good. This deduction is grounded on the fact that the covenant against sale to Jews or to persons of objectionable nationality prevents the particular piece of land from ever being acquired by the persons against whom the covenant is aimed, and that this prohibition is without regard to whether the land is put to residential, commercial, industrial or other use. How far this is obnoxious to public policy can only be ascertained by projecting the coverage of the covenant with respect to both the classes of persons whom it may adversely affect, and to the lots or subdivisions of land to which it may be attached. So considered, the consequences of judicial approbation of such a covenant are portentous. If sale of a piece of land can be prohibited to Jews, it can equally be prohibited to Protestants, Catholics or other groups or denominations. If the sale of one piece of land can be so prohibited, the sale of other pieces of land can likewise be prohibited. In my opinion, nothing could be more calculated to create or deepen divisions between existing religious and ethnic groups in this Province, or in this country, than the sanction of a method of land transfer which would permit the segregation and confinement of particular groups to particular business or residential areas, or conversely, would exclude particular groups from particular business or residential areas. The unlikelihood of such a policy as a legislative measure is evident from the contrary intention of the recently enacted *Racial Discrimination Act*, and the judicial branch of government must take full cognizance of such factors.

Ontario, and Canada too, may well be termed a Province, and a country, of minorities in regard to the religious and ethnic groups which live therein. It appears to me to be a moral duty, at least, to lend aid to all forces of cohesion, and similarly to repel all fissiparous tendencies which would imperil national unity. The common law Courts have, by their actions over the years, obviated the need for rigid constitutional guarantees in our polity by their wise use of the doctrine of public policy as an active agent in the promotion of the public weal. While Courts and eminent Judges have, in view of the powers of our Legislatures, warned against inventing new heads of public policy, I do not conceive that I would be breaking new ground were I to hold the restrictive covenant impugned in this proceeding to be void as against public policy. Rather would I be applying well-recognized principles of public policy to a set of facts requiring their invocation in the interest of the public good.

That the restrictive covenant in this case is directed in the first place against Jews lends poignancy to the matter when one considers that anti-semitism has been a weapon in the hands of our recently-defeated enemies and the scourge of the world. But this feature of the case does not require innovation in legal principle to strike down the covenant; it merely makes it more appropriate to apply existing principles. If the common law of treason encompasses the stirring up of hatred between different classes of His Majesty's subjects, the common law of public policy is surely adequate to void the restrictive covenant which is here attacked.

My conclusion therefore is that the covenant is void because [it is] offensive to the public policy of this jurisdiction. This conclusion is reinforced, if reinforcement is necessary, by the wide official acceptance of international policies and declarations frowning on the type of discrimination which the covenant would seem to perpetuate.

It may not be inexpedient or improper to refer to a few declarations made by outstanding leaders under circumstances that arrest the attention and demand consideration of mankind [sic]. I first quote the late President Roosevelt:

> Citizens, regardless of religious allegiance, will share in the sorrow of our Jewish fellow-citizens over the savagery of the Nazis against their helpless victims. The Nazis will not succeed in exterminating their victims any more than they will succeed in enslaving mankind. The American people not only sympathize with all victims of Nazi crimes but will hold the perpetrators of these crimes to strict accountability in a day of reckoning which will surely come.
>
> I express the confident hope that the Atlantic Charter and the just World Order to be made possible by the triumph of the United Nations will bring the Jews and oppressed people in all lands to four freedoms which Christian and Jewish teachings have largely inspired.

And of the Right Honourable Winston Churchill:

> In the day of victory the Jew's sufferings and his part in the struggle will not be forgotten. Once again, at the appointed time, he will see vindicated those principles of righteousness which it was the glory of his fathers to proclaim to the world. Once again it will be shown that, though the mills of God grind slowly, yet they grind exceeding small.

And of General Charles de Gaulle:

> Be assured that since we have repudiated everything that has falsely been done in the name of France after June 23d, the cruel decrees directed against French Jews can and will have no validity in Free France. These measures are not less a blow against the honour of France than they are an injustice against her Jewish citizens.

When we shall have achieved victory, not only will the wrongs done in France itself be righted, but France will once again resume her traditional place as a protagonist of freedom and justice for all men, irrespective of race or religion, in a new Europe.

Also, the resolution passed by the representatives of over 60,000,000 organized workers at the World Trade Union Congress recently held at London that "every form of political, economic or social discrimination based on race, creed or sex, shall be eliminated.

The resolution against discrimination adopted unanimously by the Latin American nations and the United States in Mexico City on March 6, 1945, at the time of the Act of Chapultepec, is that the governments of these nations "prevent with all the means in their power all that may provoke discrimination among individuals because of racial and religious reasons."

It is provided in Article 123 of The Constitution of the Union of Soviet Socialistic Republics, that:

Equality of rights of citizens of the USSR, irrespective of their nationality or race, in all spheres of economic, state, cultural, social and political life, is an indefeasible law.

Any direct or indirect restriction of the rights of, or, conversely, any establishment of direct or indirect privileges for, citizens on account of their race or nationality, as well as any advocacy of racial or national exclusiveness or hatred and contempt, is punishable by law.

The second point raised by counsel for the applicant is that the covenant is invalid as a restraint on alienation. It is unnecessary to quote authorities in support of the long-established principle of the common law that land should be freely alienable. True, a limited class of exceptions to this general principle has from time to time been recognized, as in *Re Macleay* (1875), LR 20 Eq. 186, though it may be pointed out that this decision runs counter to the earlier case of *Attwater v. Attwater* (1853), 18 Beav. 330, 52 ER 131. Moreover, in *Re Rosher, Rosher v. Rosher* (1884), 26 Ch.D 801, Pearson J stated that he failed to appreciate how the exception recognized in *Re Macleay* arose. It is not necessary to challenge the doctrine of *Re Macleay*, which has been followed in some Canadian cases, in order to find that the covenant with which I am concerned is invalid as a restraint on alienation. The particular covenant in the case before me is not limited either in time or to the life of the immediate grantee (see Sweet, Restraints on Alienation, 33 LQ Rev., 236, 342, particularly at p. 354), which would seem to be characteristic of the partial restraints which were enforced in the decided cases that I have been able to find. The principle of freedom of alienation has been too long and too well established in the jurisprudence of English and Canadian Courts to warrant me at this late stage in recognizing a limitation upon it of a character not hitherto the subject of any reported case, especially in view of my conclusions as to public policy.

Counsel for the applicant contended before me that the restrictive covenant here in question is void for uncertainty. So far as the words "persons of objectionable nationality" are concerned, the contention admits of no contradiction. The conveyancer who used these words surely must have realized, if he had given the matter any thought, that no Court could conceivably find legal meaning in such vagueness. So far as the first branch of the covenant is concerned, that prohibiting the sale of the land to "Jews," I am bound by the recent decision of the House of Lords in *Clayton v. Ramsden*, [1943] 1 All

ER 16; to hold that the covenant is in this respect also void for uncertainty; and I may add, that I would so hold even if the matter were *res integra*. The Law Lords in *Clayton v. Ramsden* were unanimous in holding that the phrase "of Jewish parentage" was uncertain, and Lord Romer was of the same opinion in regard to the phrase "of Jewish faith." I do not see that the bare term "Jews" admits of any more certainty.

I should like, in conclusion, to refer to the judgment of Chevrier J in *Re McDougall and Waddell*, [1945] 2 DLR 244. The learned Judge there decided that the registration of a deed containing a covenant restricting the sale or user of land to "gentiles (non-semitic) of European or British or Irish or Scottish racial origin" did not constitute an infringement of the *Racial Discrimination Act*. He came to this conclusion by holding that registration of a deed was not among the proscribed means of publishing or display-ing enumerated in s. 1 of the Act. Counsel for the applicant herein contended that those proscribed means related only to the terms of cl. (b) of s. 1, and that they did not qualify cl. (a) of s. 1 which reads as follows:

> 1. No person shall,
>   (a) publish or display or cause to be published or displayed; ...
> any notice, sign, symbol, emblem or other representation indicating discrimination or an intention to discriminate against any person or any class of persons for any purpose because of the race or creed of such person or class of persons.

Mr. Cartwright further submitted that if this section had been read by the learned Judge without this limitation, that registration in the Registry Office constituted publica-tion of a notice or other representation as aforesaid, and that following Halsbury (2d ed.), vol. 29, p. 444, "registration constitutes actual notice to all the world," therefore he should have found that the particular clause was in breach of the said Act.

I do not deem it necessary for the purpose of this case to deal with this argument, except to say that it appears to me to have considerable merit. My opinion as to the public policy applicable to this case in no way depends on the terms of the *Racial Discrimination Act*, save to the extent that such Act constitutes a legislative recognition of the policy which I have applied; in fact my brother Chevrier, as I read his judgment in *Re McDougall and Waddell*, is in accord with me in this respect.

An order will therefore go declaring that the restrictive covenant attacked by the applicant is void and of no effect.

Order declaring covenant void.

Noble and Wolf v. Alley
[1951] SCR 64

The judgment of Kerwin and Taschereau JJ was delivered by

KERWIN J: This is an appeal against a judgment of the Court of Appeal for Ontario [[1949] 4 DLR 375; OR 503] affirming the judgment of Schroeder J [[1948] 4 DLR 123; OR 579] on a motion under s. 3 of the *Vendors and Purchasers Act*, RSO 1937, c. 168.

That section, so far as relevant, provides that a vendor of real estate may apply in a summary way to the Supreme Court in respect of any requisition or objection arising out of, or connected with, a contract for the sale or purchase of land. The motion was made by the present appellant, Mrs. Noble, as the vendor under a contract for the sale by her to the purchaser, her co-appellant Bernard Wolf, of land forming part of a summer resort development known as the Beach O'Pines.

This land had been purchased in 1933 by Mrs. Noble from the Frank S. Salter Co. Ltd., and in the deed from it to her appeared the following covenant:

> AND the Grantee for himself, his heirs, executors, administrators and assigns, covenants and agrees with the Grantor that he will carry out, comply with and observe, with the intent that they shall run with the lands and shall be binding upon himself, his heirs, executors, administrators and assigns, and shall be for the benefit of and enforcible by the Grantor and/or any other person or persons seized or possessed of any part or parts of the land included in Beach O'Pines Development, the restrictions herein following, which said restrictions shall remain in full force and effect until the first day of August, 1962, and the Grantee for himself, his heirs, executors, administrators and assigns further covenants and agrees with the Grantor that he will exact the same covenants with respect to the said restrictions from any and all persons to whom he may in any manner whatsoever dispose of the said lands. ...
>
> "(f) The lands and premises herein described shall never be sold, assigned, transferred, leased, rented, or in any manner whatsoever alienated to, and shall never be occupied or used in any manner whatsoever by any person of the Jewish, Hebrew, Semitic, Negro or coloured race or blood, it being the intention and purpose of the Grantor, to restrict the ownership, use, occupation and enjoyment of the said recreational development, including the lands and premises herein described, to persons of the white or Caucasian race not excluded by this clause."

Although the deed was not signed by Mrs. Noble, I assume that she is bound to the same extent as if she had executed it.

Each conveyance by the company to a purchaser of land in the development contained a covenant in the same form. The present respondents, being owners of other parcels of land in the development, were served with notice of the application either before Schroeder J or the Court of Appeal, and they and their counsel affirmed the validity of the covenant, its binding effect upon Mrs. Noble, and that any of the respondents are able to take advantage of the covenant so as to prevent by injunction its breach. While before the Judge of first instance the vendor and purchaser apparently took opposite sides, each of them appealed to the Court of Appeal and, there, as well as before this Court, attacked the contentions put forward on behalf of the respondents.

In the Courts below emphasis was laid upon the decision of MacKay J, in *Re Drummond Wren*, [1945], 4 DLR 674, OR 778, and it was considered that the motion was confined to the consideration of whether that case, if rightly decided, covered the situation. The motion was for an order declaring that the objection to the covenant made on behalf of the purchaser had been fully answered by the vendor and that the same did not constitute a valid objection to the title or for such further and other order as might seem just. The objection was: "REQUIRED in view of the fact that the purchaser herein might be considered as being of the Jewish race or blood, we require a release from the restrictions imposed in the said clause (f) and an order declaring that the restrictive covenant set out in the said clause (f) is void and of no effect."

The answer by the vendor was that the decision in *Re Drummond Wren* applied to the facts of the present sale with the result that cl. (f) was invalid and the vendor and purchaser were not bound to observe it. In view of the wide terms of the notice of motion, the application is not restricted and it may be determined by a point taken before the Court of Appeal and this Court, if not before Schroeder J.

That point depends upon the meaning of the rule laid down in *Tulk v. Moxhay* (1848), 2 Ph. 774, 41 ER 1143. This was a decision of Lord Cottenham LC affirming a decision of the Master of the Rolls. The judgment of the Master of the Rolls appears in 18 LJ Ch. 83, and the judgment of the Lord Chancellor is more fully reported there than in Phillips' Reports. In the latter, the Lord Chancellor is reported as saying, p. 777: "That this Court has jurisdiction to enforce a contract between the owner of land and his neighbour purchasing a part of it, that the latter shall either use or abstain from using the land purchased in a particular way, is what I never knew disputed."

In the Law Journal, the following appears at pp. 87-8: "I have no doubt whatever upon the subject; in short, I cannot have a doubt upon it, without impeaching what I have considered as the settled rule of this Court ever since I have known it. That this Court has authority to enforce a contract, which the owner of one piece of land may have entered into with his neighbour, founded, of course, upon good consideration, and valuable consideration, that he will either use or abstain from using his land in any manner that the other party by the contract stipulates shall be followed by the party who enters into the covenant, appears to me the very foundation of the whole of this jurisdiction. It has never, that I know of, been disputed."

At p. 88 of the Law Journal the Lord Chancellor states that the jurisdiction of the Court was not fettered by the question whether the covenant ran with the land or not but that the question was whether a party taking property, the vendor having stipulated in a manner, binding by the law and principles of the Court of Chancery to use it in a particular way will be permitted to use it in a way diametrically opposite to that which the party has covenanted for. To the same effect is pp. 777-8 of Phillips's.

In view of these statements I am unable to gain any elucidation of the extent of the equitable doctrine from decisions at law such as *Congleton v. Pattison* (1808), 10 East 130, 103 ER 725, and *Rogers v. Hosegood*, [1900] 2 Ch. 388. It is true that in the Court of Appeal, Collins LJ, after referring to extracts from the judgment of Sir George Jessel MR in *London & South Western R Co. v. Gomm* (1882), 20 Ch.D 562 at p. 583, said at pp. 405-6: "These observations, which are just as applicable to the benefit reserved as to the burden imposed, shew that in equity, just as at law, the first point to be determined is whether the covenant or contract in its inception binds the land. If it does, it is then capable of passing with the land to subsequent assignees; if it does not, it is incapable of passing by mere assignment of the land."

This, however, leaves untouched the problem as to when a covenant binds the land.

Whatever the precise delimitation in the rule in *Tulk v. Moxhay* may be, counsel were unable to refer us to any case where it was applied to a covenant restricting the alienation of land to persons other than those of a certain race. Mr. Denison did refer to three decisions in Ontario: *Essex Real Estate Co. v. Holmes* (1930), 37 OWN 392 [aff'd. 38 OWN 69]; *Re Bryers & Morris* (1931), 40 OWN 572; *Re McDougall & Waddell*, [1945] 2 DLR 244, OWN 272; but he was quite correct in stating that they were of no assistance. The holding in the first was merely that the purchaser of the land there in question did not fall within a certain prohibition. In the second an inquiry was directed, without more. In the third, all that was decided was that the provisions of s. 1 of the *Racial Discrimination Act*, 1944 (Ont.), c. 51, would not be violated by a deed containing a covenant on the part of the purchaser that certain lands or any buildings erected thereon should not at any time be sold to, let to or occupied by any person or persons other than Gentiles (non-semitic (*sic*)) of European or British or Irish or Scottish racial origin.

It was a forward step that the rigour of the common law should be softened by the doctrine expounded in *Tulk v. Moxhay* but it would be an unwarrantable extension of that doctrine to hold, from anything that was said in that case or in subsequent cases, that the covenant here in question has any reference to the use, or abstension from use, of land. Even if decisions upon the common law could be prayed in aid, there are none that go to the extent claimed in the present case.

The appeal should be allowed with costs here and in the Court of Appeal. There should be no costs of the original motions in the Supreme Court of Ontario.

The judgment of RAND, KELLOCK and FAUTEUX JJ was delivered by

RAND J: Covenants enforceable under the rule of *Tulk v. Moxhay*, 11 Beav. 571, 50 ER 937, are properly conceived as running with the land in equity and, by reason of their enforceability, as constituting an equitable servitude or burden on the servient land. The essence of such an incident is that it should touch or concern the land as contradistinguished from a collateral effect. In that sense, it is a relation between parcels, annexed to them and, subject to the equitable rule of notice, passing with them both as to benefit and burden in transmissions by operation of law as well as by act of the parties.

But by its language, the covenant here is directed not to the land or to some mode of its use, but to transfer by act of the purchaser; its scope does not purport to extend to a transmission by law to a person within the banned class. If, for instance, the grantee married a member of that class, it is not suggested that the ordinary inheritance by a child of the union would be affected. Not only, then, is it not a covenant touching or concerning the land, but by its own terms it fails in annexation to the land. The respondent owners are, therefore, without any right against the proposed vendor.

On its true interpretation, the covenant is a restraint on alienation. The grantor company which has disposed of all its holdings in the subdivision has admittedly ceased to carry on business and by force of the provisions of the *Companies Act*, RSO 1937, c. 251, s. 28, its powers have become forfeited; but by s-s. (4) they may, on such conditions as may be exacted, be revived by the Lieutenant-Governor in Council. Assuming the grantor would otherwise be entitled to enforce the covenant in equity against the original covenantor—and if he would not the point falls—it becomes necessary to deal with the question whether for the purposes of specific performance the covenant is unenforceable for uncertainty.

It is in these words: "The lands and premises herein described shall never be sold, assigned, transferred, leased, rented or in any manner whatsoever alienated to and shall never be occupied or used in any manner whatsoever by any person of the Jewish, Hebrew, Semitic, Negro or coloured race or blood, it being the intention and purpose of the Grantor, to restrict the ownership, use, occupation and enjoyment of the said recreational development including the lands and premises herein described, to persons of white or Caucasian race not excluded by this clause."

If this language were in the form of a condition, the holding in *Clayton v. Ramsden*, [1943] AC 320, would be conclusive against its sufficiency. In that case the House of Lords dealt with a condition in a devise by which the donee became divested if she should marry a person "not of Jewish parentage and of the Jewish faith" and held it void for uncertainty. I am unable to distinguish the defect in that language from what we have here: it is impossible to set such limits to the lines of race or blood as would enable a Court to say in all cases whether a proposed purchaser is or is not within the ban. As put by Lord Cranworth in *Clavering v. Ellison* (1859), 7 HLC 707 at p. 725, 11 ER 282, the condition "must be such that the Court can see from the beginning, precisely and distinctly, upon the happening of what event it was that the preceding vested estate was to determine."

The effect of the covenant, if enforceable, would be to annex a partial inalienability as an equitable incident of the ownership, to nullify an area of proprietary powers. In both cases there is the removal of part of the power to alienate; and I can see no ground of distinction between the certainty required in the one case and that of the other. The uncertainty is, then, fatal to the validity of the covenant before us as a defect of or objection to the title.

I would, therefore, allow the appeal and direct judgment to the effect that the covenant is not an objection to the title of the proposed vendor, with costs to the appellants in this Court and in the Court of Appeal.

[Estey J agreed that the appeal should be allowed, while Locke J dissented on the basis that it was not appropriate to decide the case on a point not raised in the original motion. As Locke J pointed out, the covenant had been attacked before Schroeder J on the basis that it contravened public policy, that it was void for uncertainty, and that it represented an unlawful attempt to restrain alienation. However, the appeal was allowed, Locke J dissenting.]

Discussion Notes

The Litigation Context

In *Noble and Wolf*, the vendor and purchaser had entered into an agreement for the sale of Annie Noble's cottage property in the Beach O'Pines Development. As part of the real estate transaction, the purchaser's solicitor forwarded a requisition in respect of title to the vendor's solicitor, as follows:

> Required, in view of the fact that the purchaser herein might be considered as being of the Jewish race or blood, we require a release from the restrictions imposed in the said cl. (f) and an order declaring that the restrictive covenant set out in the said cl. (f) is void and of no effect.

The vendor's solicitor responded to this request, stating:

> In our opinion the decision rendered in the case of *Re Drummond Wren* ... applies to the facts of the present sale, with the result that the clause (f) objected to is invalid and the vendor and purchaser are not bound to observe it.

When the purchaser's solicitor insisted on a declaratory order, the vendor initiated an application to determine the matter. The vendor claimed that the covenant was unenforceable because it was contrary to public policy, void for uncertainty and a restraint on alienation. The motion was heard by Schroeder J who decided that the restrictive covenant in cl. (f) was a valid and enforceable covenant, rejecting all the vendor's arguments, and that the vendor had thus not answered the purchaser's objection satisfactorily. The vendor and purchaser then appealed to the Court of Appeal, together arguing that the covenant was invalid as contrary to public policy, void for uncertainty and a restraint on alienation, and "unenforceable as a restraint upon the alienation, occupancy and user of land because of race or blood, such being a novel restraint unknown to and unrecognized by the Common Law." See [1949] 4 DLR 375, at 378-79. The respondents were most of the other owners of cottage properties at Beach O'Pines Development, and the Court of Appeal unanimously dismissed the appeal and confirmed the decision of Schroeder J. From this decision, the appellants appealed to the Supreme Court of Canada.

As is evident in the judgment of Kerwin J in the Supreme Court of Canada, the court concluded that the covenant in question did not touch and concern the land, and thus could not bind successors in title of the covenantor. Relying on the "wide terms of the notice of motion," Kerwin decided that the Supreme Court of Canada could decide *Noble and Wolf* on a point that had not been raised or argued before Schroeder J, and which the Court of Appeal had apparently declined to consider; only Hogg JA in the Court of Appeal briefly mentioned the issue whether the covenant touched and concerned the land (see [1949] 4 DLR 375, at 394-95) and he concluded that the appellate court could not consider it since it had not been raised or argued previously nor included as one of the grounds of appeal. In these circumstances, reliance on this issue in the Supreme Court of Canada is interesting. To what extent does this procedural issue suggest that the Supreme Court was seeking a "technical" basis for holding the covenant void, by contrast with the "policy" basis in *Re Drummond Wren*? In considering this question, note a contemporaneous comment about the two cases:

> [*Re Drummond Wren*] was of general interest to all lawyers because of the bold manner in which Mackay J sought out public policy without regard to previous judicial opinion on the subject. It was refreshing to find a judge trying to recapture some of the spirit that enabled the greatest of his judicial forebears to systematize the common law and yet leave it the elasticity necessary to keep it in harmony with changing social needs. On the other hand, in *Re Noble and Wolf*, the judges of the Ontario courts took a cautious approach and refused to take notice of any change in the public policy of Canada or Ontario.

(C.B. Bourne, "Comment" (1951), 29 *Canadian Bar Review* 969, at 974.)

To what extent are there factual differences in the two cases that may justify differing approaches?

Approaches to Interpreting Racially Restrictive Covenants

Although the two cases illustrate different approaches to reasoning about racially restrictive covenants in Ontario just after World War II, the covenants in both cases were held to be void and unenforceable. How different were the covenants in substance? In *Drummond Wren*, for example, the covenant prohibited sales to "Jews or persons of objectionable nationality," while in *Noble and Wolf*, the clause prohibited sale, assignment, transfer, leasing, renting, use or occupation "in any manner whatsoever by any person of the Jewish, Hebrew, Semitic, Negro or coloured race or blood." Are the same groups excluded by both these covenants? Are they equally broad or narrow in the activities proscribed? Did the language of the covenants affect the reasoning in the two cases?

What were the grounds for concluding that the restrictive covenant in *Re Drummond Wren* was invalid? In technical terms, which part of the judgment of Mackay J was ratio, and which parts obiter? Why did Mackay J make voidness for reasons of public policy such a prominent part of his decision? Was the covenant clearly void as a restraint on alienation or on the ground of uncertainty? To what extent did the existence of the Racial Discrimination Act, SO 1944, c. 51 influence the reasoning of Mackay J? To what extent did Mackay J focus on principles of law and equity concerning the enforceability of covenants on successors in title? Is this case about the running of the benefit or burden of a covenant? Is the covenant in *Re Drummond Wren* one that touches and concerns the land, or is it merely a personal covenant as the covenant in *Noble and Wolf*?

The decision in *Re Drummond Wren* was clearly argued before Schroeder J in *Noble and Wolf*, and Schroeder J expressly decided to disagree with the reasoning of Mackay J. Schroeder J pointed out that Mackay J reached his conclusions in *Re Drummond Wren* without the benefit of opposing argument, while in *Noble and Wolf*, the other cottagers were notified and joined the litigation. In addition, however, Schroeder distinguished *Re Drummond Wren* as follows (at 133):

> Let it also be stated that in the case before my brother Mackay he was not concerned with a summer colony as in the case under consideration, but with a residential subdivision on O'Connor Drive in the City of Toronto, where the residents sought shelter rather than recreation. Also, the restriction in that case was unlimited in point of duration.

What is the difference between a racially restrictive covenant in an urban area and in a summer colony? Significantly, this point was also addressed in the reasons of Robertson CJO in the Court of Appeal in *Noble and Wolf* (at 386):

> It is common knowledge that, in the life usually led [in a summer community], there is much intermingling in an informal and social way, of the residents and their guests, especially at the beach. That the summer colony should be congenial is of the essence of a pleasant holiday in such circumstances. The purpose of cl. (f) here in question is obviously to assure, in some degree, that the residents are of a class who will get along well together. To magnify this innocent and modest effort to establish and maintain a place suitable for a pleasant summer residence into an enterprise that offends against some public policy, requires a stronger imagination that I possess ... . There is nothing

criminal or immoral involved; the public interest is in no way concerned. These people have simply agreed among themselves upon a matter of their own personal concern that affects property of their own in which no one else has an interest. If the law sanctions [this action], then I know of no principle of public policy against which this is an offence.

To what extent does this reasoning depend on the existence of a dichotomy between private property and public policy? How should courts decide issues of public policy? To what extent does the Court of Appeal's reasoning result from an approach of non-intervention? In thinking about this question, consider the reasoning of Schroeder J in concluding (at 139) that it was not appropriate for him to adopt *Re Drummond Wren* as a precedent:

It is trite law that common law rights are not to be deemed to be abrogated by statute unless the legislative intent to do so is expressed in very clear language. It follows logically, it seems to me, that for a Court to invent new heads of public policy and found thereon nullification of established rights or obligations—in a sense embarking upon a course of judicial legislation—is a mode of procedure not to be encouraged or approved.

To what extent do these views reflect typical concerns in the law of property? For an interesting assessment of *Noble and Wolf* in relation to international norms of public interest and private property rights, see Edward Morgan and Ofer Attias, "Rabbi Kahane, International Law, and the Courts: Democracy Stands on its Head" (1990), 4 *Temple International and Comparative Law Journal* 185, at 194-96. See also Karen Pearlston, "A Restricted Country?: The Racist Legacy of Restrictive Covenants" (Unpublished: Osgoode Hall Law School, 1996); W. Tarnopolsky, "Discrimination and the Law in Canada" (1992), 41 *University of New Brunswick Law Journal* 215, at 224; and J. Walker, *"Race," Rights, and the Law in the Supreme Court of Canada: Historical Case Studies* (Toronto: Osgoode Society, 1997). For another case involving covenants and a recreation club, see *Galbraith v. The Madawaska Club*, [1961] SCR 639.

Restrictive Covenants and Restraints on Alienation

Both the excerpted cases addressed at length the issue of the validity of restraints on alienation, a problem that may occur in numerous situations other than those of covenants that run with the land. Interestingly, Mackay J held that the covenant in *Re Drummond Wren* was a restraint on alienation, and therefore void. By contrast, Schroeder J and the members of the Ontario Court of Appeal concluded that the covenant in *Noble and Wolf* was not a restraint on alienation. In both cases, the judges referred to *Re Macleay*, a case that considered a devise of land to the deceased's brother on condition that the brother should not sell out of the family. The family was a large one, and the court held that the condition was valid, apparently because there was a "large enough class of potential purchasers" to make the condition only a partial restraint on alienation. As D.A.L. Smout commented further:

The situation does not lack irony, for the first Jew to hold judicial office in England [Sir George Jessel, the judge who decided *Re Macleay*] thus provided the basis for the subsequent contention that, if such a condition conforms to the principles of common law, then a restraint forbidding alienation outside the racial or religious group approved by the testator or vendor must also necessarily be valid.

(D.A.L. Smout, "An Inquiry Into the Law on Racial and Religious Restraints on Aliena-tion" (1952), 30 *Canadian Bar Review* 863, at 866.) Smout provided an analysis of *Re Drummond Wren* and *Noble and Wolf*, suggesting (at 872) that even if "it is readily conceded that one cannot legislate intolerance, ... surely there is nothing worthless in legislating against certain intolerant practices ... . There would seem to be no reason why the courts should wait for the intolerant to become tolerant before holding the discrimination covenant to be also unenforceable."

After the decision in the Ontario Court of Appeal, and prior to the hearing in the Supreme Court of Canada, the Ontario legislature enacted an amendment to the Convey-ancing and Law of Property Act (now RSO 1990, c. C.34, s. 22) as follows:

> Every covenant made after the 24th day of March, 1950, that but for this section would be annexed to and run with land and that restricts the sale, ownership, occupation or use of land because of the race, creed, colour, nationality, ancestry or place of origin of any person is void and of no effect.

Consider the wording of this section in the context of the decision of the Supreme Court of Canada. To the extent that the court concluded that the covenant in *Noble and Wolf* was a personal covenant only and not one that touched and concerned the land, what impact would s. 22 above have on similar covenants involving racial restrictions? As Smout concluded (at 880), the legislative provision is very limited in its application:

> The choice of words ... is curious. The sections are expressly limited to covenants and thus have no effect upon any testamentary stipulation; a restraint set out in a will ... will be effective if expressed with certainty. In further emphasizing that the covenant must be one that but for the sections would be annexed to and run with the land, the amendments clearly do not affect the personal covenant ... . The language used by the legislature in these amendments is the language usually used to describe restrictive covenants. It may be wondered whether it does anything to prejudice a restraint on alienation or a determinable fee.

Is further legislative action necessary here? How would you draft an amendment to the Conveyancing and Law of Property Act that would be effective to invalidate racially restrictive covenants? To what extent is the reasoning in *Re Drummond Wren* or *Noble and Wolf* useful in the drafting process? Is it more effective to adopt a "technical" or a "policy" approach here? Why?

Restrictive Covenants: Beyond Racial Restrictions

The problems of racially restrictive covenants are not confined to Canada, of course. In the United States, at about the same time as *Re Drummond Wren* and *Noble and Wolf* were being decided, the US Supreme Court considered similar issues in *Shelley v. Kraemer*, 334 US 1 (1948). The court held that enforcement by state courts of restrictive agreements denied the equal protection of the laws pursuant to the 14th amendment of the US Constitution. For further analysis of US developments, see Chused, at 161-250;

Editors, Harvard Law Review, "The Antidiscrimination Principle in the Common Law" (1989), 102 *Harvard Law Review* 1993; Patricia Williams, "Spirit-Murdering the Messenger: The Discourse of Fingerpointing as the Law's Response to Racism" (1987), 42 *University of Miami Law Review* 127; and C. Harris, "Whiteness as Property" (1993), 106 *Harvard Law Review* 1709.

In relation to these issues, how would you respond to a request to draft a covenant restricting parcels of land in a community to single-family use? In the United States, courts have held that single-family-use covenants prohibit occupancy of property by an extended family; a foster home for disabled children; a group of elderly citizens; two single men jointly owning a home; a group home for the mentally and developmentally disabled; a number of college students, boarders, and tenants; and religious groups. See G. Korngold, "Single Family Use Covenants: For Achieving a Balance Between Traditional Family Life and Individual Autonomy" (1989), 22 *University of California, Davis* 951, at 953, and cases cited there. Korngold concluded (at 977-78) that part of the solution in these situations could be provided by the "touch and concern" test:

> Personal choices within the homes could not be regulated, while objective, disturbing actions outside the home that affect the neighbourhood could be prevented ... . To be sure, the touch and concern test has its flaws. Most notably, it is only a rough vehicle for addressing the contracts/antirestrictions conflict and does not straightforwardly examine the issues. Rather, it forces the problem into an arcane framework replete with jargon. The touch and concern test needs to be reformulated or replaced in a modern law of servitudes. However, it is better than nothing when it comes to single family use covenants.

For another analysis, see Dirk Hubbard, "Group Homes and Restrictive Covenants" (1988), 57:1 *University of Missouri Kansas City Law Review* 135. For an analysis of the need for special recognition of private homes in the context of servitudes, see J. Winokur, "The Mixed Blessings of Promissory Servitudes: Toward Optimizing Economic Utility, Individual Liberty, and Personal Identity" (1989), 1 *Wisconsin Law Review* 1.

A Note on Breach of Covenant, Extinguishment, and Discharge

In general, the remedy for breach of covenant is an injunction, restraining the continuing breach. In some cases in the 19th century in England, it was suggested that the court of equity had no discretion to exercise in granting an injunction—for example, see *Doherty v. Allman*, [1878] 3 AC 709 (HL). However, in *Shepherd Homes Ltd. v. Sandham*, [1971], Ch. 340 (Ch.D), Megarry J concluded that judicial discretion was required to avoid unfairness, and this approach was subsequently adopted in *Wrotham Park Estate v. Parkside Homes*, [1974] 1 WLR 798 (Ch.D). In *Wrotham Park*, developers began work on the construction of houses, in violation of a covenant prohibiting such development without the plaintiff's approval of the plans. The plaintiff brought action against the developers for a prohibitory injunction restraining building, and, more controversially, for a mandatory injunction to demolish the houses already built in violation of the covenant. The plaintiff did not seek an interlocutory injunction, however, so the developers continued to work pending the hearing in the matter. By the time of the hearing,

14 houses had been constructed and sold to purchasers, and the purchasers were added as defendants.

Brightman J concluded that there had been no financial damage to the plaintiff as a result of the breach and noted that the homes were already occupied and that there was a shortage of housing. As a result, he refused a mandatory injunction and instead ordered damages, assessed on the basis of an estimate of the sum that the plaintiff would have demanded to release the covenant. This approach was followed in a British Columbia case, *Arbutus Park Estates Ltd. v. Fuller* (1976), 74 DLR (3d) 257 (BC SC). More recently, see *Federated Homes Ltd. v. Mill Lodge*, [1980] 1 WLR 594 (CA) and *Wakeham v. Wood* (1981), 125 SJ 608. For an analysis of these and other cases, see Polden, "Views in Perspective" (1984), *The Conveyancer and Property Lawyer* 429.

The parties to a covenant may release it expressly, and it is possible to provide for modification or discharge in the document creating a covenant as well. In some cases, an application to a court may be submitted pursuant to statutory provisions such as the Conveyancing and Law of Property Act, RSO 1990, c. C.34, s. 61. For a more detailed analysis, see OLRC, at 49-57.

Discussion Note

The West Edmonton Mall leased space in the mall to McDonald's Restaurants. The lease contained a covenant by which the mall undertook not to permit another "fast food restaurant" to operate in that phase of the mall property. The terminology of the covenant was further defined in the lease to preclude a restaurant primarily engaged in the sale of hamburgers and/or chicken products. The mall later leased space to another restaurant that, on the evidence of its menu, company brochures, and sales volumes, was primarily engaged in the sale of hamburgers, and the court concluded that the mall was in breach of the restrictive covenant. What remedy is appropriate in these circumstances—an injunction or damages? What factors should be considered by a court in determining what remedy to grant to McDonald's? See *McDonald's Restaurants of Canada Limited v. West Edmonton Mall Ltd.* (1994), 42 RPR (2d) 215 (Alta. QB), where the court concluded that it was appropriate to grant the plaintiff's application for a permanent injunction.

Reforming the Law of Covenants

The rigid and highly technical character of the law of covenants has resulted in law reform proposals in a number of common law jurisdictions, including the United Kingdom and Canada as well as the United States. In Ontario, OLRC addressed both current issues and recommended reforms. After reviewing legal principles about covenants in a number of other jurisdictions, OLRC focused on the problem of positive covenants and recommended (at 102) that "the law should be reformed to permit the burden of affirmative obligations to run upon a transfer of freehold land." To implement this recommendation, OLRC recognized that a choice is required—either to reform the law of covenants only, or to "consolidate, to the extent possible, not only positive and restrictive covenants, but also easements and *profits à prendre*, into a single unified law of servitudes." After examining these alternative approaches, OLRC concluded (at 103) that reform of all the non-possessory interests as part of the law of servitudes generally would be "overly ambitious within the limited context of the ... *Report*." Thus, OLRC's recommendations focused more specifically on the principles of covenants.

OLRC recommended (at 105) the creation of a new interest in land called a "land obligation," and argued that it should "comprehend both positive and restrictive obligations, and should permit both the benefit and the burden of such obligations to run upon a transfer of freehold land." The benefit of land obligations would be permitted to exist either as appurtenant to land or in gross. For further analysis, see OLRC, at 105ff.

By contrast with the approach of OLRC, a more general reform process has been undertaken in the United States in relation to the American Law Institute's servitudes project. As S. French has described the US project:

> The American Law Institute's current servitudes project began with a lofty mission—to simplify, clarify, and modernize the law—and a bold and sweeping design—to unify the heretofore separate bodies of law governing easements, profits, irrevocable licenses, equitable servitudes, and real covenants under the single conceptual heading of servitudes ... . The new Restatement ... continues long traditions of coupling private rearrangement of property rights with active judicial scrutiny of those arrangements. It creates a new conceptual framework for thinking about servitudes and achieves substantial simplification of the law by eliminating several overlapping servitude categories ... . Traditional at the core, the new Restatement should provide substantial material for innovative evolution of the common law.

(S. French, "Tradition and Innovation in the New Restatement of Servitudes: A Report From Midpoint" (1994), 27 *Connecticut Law Review* 119, at 119 and 129.) For other comments on the Restatement project, see J. Winokur, "Ancient Strands Rewoven, or Fashioned out of Whole Cloth?: First Impressions of the Emerging Restatement of Servitudes" (1994), 27 *Connecticut Law Review* 131 and S. Sterk, "Publicly Held Servitudes in the New Restatement" (1994), 27 *Connecticut Law Review* 157. For another view, see R. Epstein, "Notice and Freedom of Contract in the Law of Servitudes" (1982), *Southern California Law Review* 1353.

What are the advantages of the American approach to covenant reform? What are the limitations of such an approach? Do you agree that it was preferable for OLRC to make recommendations about covenants without taking a more comprehensive approach to the reform of non-possessory interests and other limits on the use of land? You may want to reconsider these questions in relation to the discussion of conservation easements and covenants in the next section.

NON-POSSESSORY INTERESTS: "PRIVATE" PLANNING, "PUBLIC" PLANNING, AND CONSERVATION

Although landowners have often used non-possessory interests, particularly covenants, as a means of accomplishing private planning goals within defined communities, the rigidity of common law requirements for their creation and enforcement has sometimes resulted in uncertainty and disappointment. Accordingly, as public regulation increased with the enactment of provincial planning statutes and municipal zoning and bylaws in the 20th century, the role of non-possessory interests as tools for planning became secondary. Thus, planning legislation and governmental agencies created and enforced a scheme of public regulation with respect to land use, leaving landowners less scope to engage in private planning by means of non-possessory interests, especially covenants. For a recent example, see Ontario Planning and Development Act, 1994, SO 1994, c. 23. In the United States, although there were a number of constitutional challenges to zoning bylaws, with arguments about whether these statutes constituted an "unlawful taking" of private property, the priority of governmental regulation of community planning was confirmed in *Village of Euclid v. Ambler Realty Company*, 272 US 365 (1926). For a full examintion of the background to this case, see Chused, at 1156ff. In the Australian context, see J. Tooher, "Restrictive Covenants and Public Planning Legislation—Should the Landowner Feel 'Touched and Concerned'? (1992), 9 *Environmental and Planning Law Journal* 63.

Two developments in recent decades have, however, created new interest in the use of covenants, as well as easements and *profits à prendre*, as planning tools. First, there has been increasingly widespread recognition of a need for individual and group action, in addition to governmental efforts, to foster protection of the environment, both in urban areas and in natural settings. In this context, for example, L. Caldwell identified the problems of current land law reform as the result of tension between the traditional concept of "land ownership" and a more recent concept of "land stewardship":

> The absence of an ingrained ethic of stewardship has been a major deterrent to the shift toward responsible land management ... . Legal and economic circumstances place the power to decide land use policies in those people who have the greatest incentive to regard land as a commodity and to discount noneconomic and long-range considerations. People committed to an ethic of stewardship and ecological sustainability continue to collide with those who make land use decisions upon a very different ethic, an ethic that regards economic development and monetary return as evidence of the land's highest and best use.

(L. Caldwell, "Land and the Law: Problems in Legal Philosophy" (1986), *University of Illinois Law Review* 319, at 329.) Caldwell noted that ideas about the relationship between natural objects and human beings are reflected in current legal debates about environmental protection. For example, see C. Stone, " 'Should Trees Have Standing?' Revisited: How Far Will Law and Morals Reach? A Pluralist Perspective" (1985), 59 *Southern California Law Review* 1. Similarly, E. Freyfogle suggested a need to change land ownership norms so as to encourage land use that is respectful, not only of other land owners, but also of the land itself. See E. Freyfogle, "The Construction of Ownership" (1996), *University of Illinois Law Review* 173. These views express attitudes to property relationships that are reflected in traditional aboriginal property concepts.

In addition to a growing sense of concern about the environment, a renewed interest in the use of non-possessory interests as planning tools has resulted from political changes in Canada and elsewhere that emphasize private, rather than public, methods of regulation. After noting the former priority enjoyed by governmental planning arrangements, a report of the North American Wetlands Conservation Council in 1995 stated bluntly:

But the 1990s have changed all that. Now, there is a general malaise and disillusionment with government, significant financial constraints on once pervasive agencies, ongoing degradation of resources and loss of biodiversity, and a recognition that not all land of conservation could—or should—be owned by a public entity. In fact, many private landowners and their families have demonstrated good stewardship over the years, in contrast to some poor management examples on public lands.

(T. Silver, I. Attridge, M. MacRae, and K. Cox, *Canadian Legislation for Conservation Covenants, Easements and Servitudes: The Current Situation*, Report no. 95-1 (Ottawa: North American Wetlands Conservation Council (Canada), 1995), at i (hereafter Silver, Attridge, MacRae, and Cox).) As the authors explained, one response to these changed circumstances is "private stewardship programs." For example, a landowner who wanted to preserve a woodlot could grant a *profit à prendre* to a conservation organization, entitling the organization to cut the trees. This grant would prevent any future group from harvesting the trees because the right to do so had been transferred. However, such an arrangement creates a situation of non-exercise of the right and is not really well-designed for widespread use. A more viable solution is the creation by legislation of statutory conservation covenants, easements, or servitudes.

Historically, conservation "easements" were used to protect parkways around Boston in the 1880s, and they have been used by the federal government in the United States for habitat preservation since the 1930s. However, in 1981, the United States adopted the Uniform Conservation Easement Act, and many states have enacted complementary legislation. See W.J. Andrews and D. Loukidelis, *Leaving a Living Legacy: Using Conservation Covenants in BC* (Vancouver: West Coast Environmental Law Research Foundation, 1996), at 2. For an earlier assessment of conservation easements in Canada, see S. Silverstone, "Open Space Preservation Through Conservation Easements" (1974), 12 *Osgoode Hall Law Journal* 105.

In Canada, a conservation covenant is a written agreement negotiated between a "qualified holder" (often an environmental organization or a governmental agency) and a landowner, pursuant to which the landowner agrees to protect the land in defined ways. The conservation covenant is registered and binds successive owners. Legislation enabling the creation and enforcement of conservation covenants generally permits departures from the common law requirements for enforceable covenants—for example, the covenants may be either positive or negative, there is no requirement for the covenantee to hold land, and the principles concerning the "touch and concern" requirement are relaxed. For examples, see Ontario's Conservation Land Act, RSO 1990, c. C.28, as amended by SO 1994, c. 27 and Nova Scotia's Conservation Easements Act, SNS 1992, c. 2. There are also statutes concerning heritage preservation that have similar provisions—see Ontario Heritage Act, RSO 1990, c. O.18; Historic Sites Protection Act, RSNB 1973, c. H-6; Heritage Property Act, RSNS 1989, c. 199; Museum Act, RSPEI 1988, c. M-14; and Historic Resources Act, RSN 1990, c. H-4. For a full account of provincial and territorial statutes and efforts to achieve beneficial tax arrangements for landowners who enter these agreements, see Silver, Attridge, MacRae, and Cox.

The authors argue that private efforts to protect the environment using conservation covenants can succeed only if there is complementary public restructuring of institutional arrangements, including (at 42) "legal reforms to ensure effective, inexpensive and stream-lined use of these legal tools." They also suggest a need for immediate action (at ii):

> But for now, we—conservationists, land professionals, and especially landowners—need to become more familiar with conservation covenants, easements and servitudes, understand their supporting legislation, and push for reforms where necessary. Then we need to get out there and make these tools work on the landscape. Time is short. Older landowners will be transferring much of their holdings over the next decade, creating a golden opportunity for land securement; and the wealth of biodiversity, especially in southern settled landscapes, is increasingly "losing ground." Conservation covenants, easements and servitudes provide a key new means for seizing this opportunity and stemming these losses.

Are conservation covenants private or public property? Are such covenants an appropriate tool for fostering environmental concerns? Compare the advantages and disadvantages of private and public, or private–public arrangements. For further analysis, see the collection of essays in A. Kwasniak, ed., *Private Conservancy: The Path to Law Reform* (Edmonton: Environmental Law Centre, 1994).

PROBLEMS

1. In 1985, Arthur Adams inherited 60 acres of land in the Niagara Peninsula. As an ardent conservationist, he was determined to preserve the land for farming purposes in spite of all the problems inherent in so doing. In 1986, he leased a 20-acre parcel for 30 years to his neighbour Ben Brooks who wanted to increase his acreage for growing grapes for the production of Niagara wine. In 1987, Adams sold a 10-acre parcel to another local farmer, Cathy Clayton, who also wanted to extend her grape production for the wineries. In both transactions, Arthur Adams required the insertion of a special clause in the documents requiring that the land be used productively for purposes of agriculture. By 1988, however, as a result of the North American Free Trade Agreement (NAFTA), the market for Niagara grapes had collapsed and both Brooks and Clayton advised Adams that they intended to transfer their interests to Toronto residents who wanted to purchase holiday property in the Niagara area. Adams wants advice about the enforceability of his special clause.

Advise Adams whether he can enforce the clause against:

    a. the assignee of the parcel leased to Brooks, and

    b. the assignee of the parcel sold to Clayton.

2. In a September 16, 1958 conveyance of a 2-acre lot, part of a large piece of land owned by the vendor, the following clauses appear:

>   a. The purchaser hereby covenants that the purchaser and her assigns will not build any structure that is more than two storeys in height on the said lot.
>
>   b. The purchaser further covenants that the purchaser and her assigns will not transfer or convey the said lot to any person or persons of the Catholic faith.

Explain *with reasons* whether these two covenants are enforceable against a subsequent purchaser of the lot in 1997.

3. In *Phipps v. Pears*, Denning MR stated:

A right to protection from the weather (if it exists) is entirely negative. It is a right to stop your neighbour pulling down his own house. Seeing that it is a negative easement, it must be looked at with caution. Because the law has been very chary of creating any new negative easements.

Explain the legal context in which Lord Denning's statement was intended to define the limits of easement and covenants, and the resolution of this problem in *Phipps v. Pears*. Assess the extent to which the law of property demonstrates "caution"; in doing so, provide an additional example to explain how property law does (or does not) reflect the approach expressed by Lord Denning.

4. In *Bruce and Bruce v. Dixon*, [1957] OWN 489 (CA), Laidlaw JA stated:

Mr. Jones was the owner of the east half of Lot 27 in the 10th Concession in the Township of Otonabee in the County of Peterborough. The defendant Dixon owned an adjoining lot. There was no well on either lot. Both Jones and Dixon agreed that they would search for a well and if they found a supply of water that they would construct a well. They employed the method of "witching" for a well. They were successful in finding water at or near the boundary line between the two lots. They intended to build the well as near as possible to the boundary line. They entered on the joint undertaking of finding and constructing a well with the certain and mutual intention that the well was to be for the benefit of the owners of both lots and their successors in title. The location of the boundary line was not known precisely and it happened that the well as constructed was located wholly on the lands owned by Dixon. After construction of the well, Jones made use of the water from the well for a period of time and, in so doing, used a portion of the lands owned by Dixon as a right of way. Subsequently, Jones sold the land owned by him to the plaintiffs. The plaintiffs and the defendant became involved in a dispute as to the right of the plaintiffs to use any part of the defendant's land by way of an easement for the purpose of getting water from the well. The defendant denied the plaintiffs any right to such user, or to any easement over his land.

Explain the arguments that counsel for the plaintiffs can make to demonstrate that:

a. the right of way is an easement; and
b. the plaintiffs can enforce the easement against the defendants.

5. Merry and Pippin live on adjoining lots in the salubrious suburb of Downsview. They are very good neighbours. There is a driveway between their lots that belongs to Merry. However, ever since Pippin moved into his house in 1945, he had used this driveway to get to the laneway at the rear of his lot. Merry had expressly agreed that Pippin could use the driveway anytime, so long as he did not block Merry's access to his garage at the far end of the driveway.

For some years, this amicable arrangement continued. However, in 1960, Merry was persuaded by energy conservationists to give up using an automobile and to ride a bicycle. Thus, in 1960, Merry told Pippin that he could use the driveway from that time forward without worrying about blocking Merry's access to his garage. Thereafter, Pippin parked his car in the driveway quite regularly.

In 1966, Pippin became interested in vintage cars, and he began to park these cars in the driveway. From that time, he generally parked his own car on the street, and there were usually three or four vintage cars parked in the driveway. Since Merry was interested in Pippin's hobby, he never objected. In 1977, however, Merry decided to move to Rosedale and Gandalf now wants to buy his house. Merry has told Gandalf that the driveway will also available to Gandalf.

Gandalf wants advice about his right to use the driveway. (You may want to reconsider *Keefer v. Arillotta*, chapter 2.)

CHAPTER SEVEN

Concurrent Interests and "Family" Property

The Concept of Concurrent Interests

The idea of shared or concurrently held interests in property—that is, more than one person having a property interest in the same object at the same time—occurs in a number of different contexts. Historically, the idea of shared ownership was a common feature of feudal property relationships. For example, you may recall the use of "joint tenants" in early grants to uses (explained in chapter 3) that enabled the grantor to achieve the objective of transferring beneficial ownership to the grantee. The grant to "joint tenants" to the use of the grantee represented shared or concurrently held property interests among the feoffees to uses, and was designed to meet particular needs in feudal society. Although the 20th century context is quite different, grants to "joint tenants" continue to offer one way of creating shared or concurrent property interests for two or more grantees. Thus, several decades ago, it was not unusual for farm property to be devised to surviving children of a testator "in common." In *Re O'Reilly (No. 2)* (1980), 111 DLR (3d) 238 (HCJ), for example, James O'Reilly's will devised the remainder interest in a dairy farm near Hawkesbury (including livestock, tools, and a milk quota) to his nine children as a shared or concurrent interest. The subsequent litigation, discussed in chapter 2, occurred when disputes arose among the children in relation to their respective interests.

The idea of shared or concurrent interests in property also represents an important challenge to dominant concepts of individual ownership and "private" property. In relation to environmental protection efforts, for example, it may be argued that interests in air or water are held "in common" by everyone. Moreover, as was explained in chapter 1, the basic concept of property for First Nations people in Canada is one of communal rather than individual "ownership," and property interests are shared not only among those currently living but also with members of past and future generations. According to this conception of shared interests in land, entitlement "in common" depends on membership in the community, and these entitlements cannot be alienated as "private" property.

Bruce Ziff has drawn comparisons between this conception of shared property interests in First Nations communities in Canada and some kinds of shared "customary" rights traditionally recognized at common law. In *Wyld v. Silver*, [1963] 1 Ch. 243 (CA), for example, the English Court of Appeal recognized a shared, customary right of the residents of Wraysbury to hold an annual fair. As well, Lord Denning MR noted the relationship between these customary rights and the concept of shared property interests among First Nations people in *R v. Secretary of State for Foreign and Commonwealth Affairs, ex parte Indian Association of Alberta*, [1982] 1 QB 892 (CA). Indeed, as Ziff explained:

> Communal sharing systems are found all over the world. Within Canada, some groups have established communal arrangements within the strictures of the common law. In Hutterite communities, for example, all property is vested in the congregation. ... Moreover, there was a time, not that long ago, when vast expanses of land on the prairies were regarded as being used and enjoyed, effectively, as commons [citing I.M. Spry, "The Tragedy of the Loss of the Commons in Western Canada," in Getty and Lussier, eds., *As Long as the Sun Shines and Water Flows* (Vancouver: University of British Columbia Press, 1983), at 203].

(Bruce Ziff, *Principles of Property Law*, 2d ed. (Scarborough, ON: Carswell, 1996), at 323-24 (hereafter Ziff).) Communal land-holding arrangements among the Hutterites in western Canada also raised questions about the scope of federal and provincial constitutional authority when provincial legislators attempted to restrict them: see *Walter v. Alberta (Attorney-General)*, [1969] SCR 383.

This chapter focuses on forms of concurrent interests as they have developed at common law, and now frequently modified by statutory reforms. At the outset, it is important to distinguish the concept of concurrent interests (sometimes called "co-ownership") from other kinds of shared property interests. For example, recall the arrangements for "successive" interests (explained in chapter 3) such as a grant to A for life with a fee simple remainder to B. Even though both A and B receive vested interests in this example, their rights to enjoyment of an *estate in possession* are successive, not concurrent. That is, B's right to possession is postponed until the termination of A's life estate. Shared interests in property are also created, of course, in bailment and leasehold arrangements and in the relationship of a trustee and beneficiary of trust property. In the leasehold context, for example, the tenant is entitled to exclusive possession for the duration of the leasehold estate. In all of these examples, the right to possession belongs to one party to the arrangement at a time. It is not shared. By contrast with these shared interests in property, concurrent interests identify a situation in which two or more people hold property interests entitling (and requiring) them to share possession.

Since concurrent property interests require grantees to share possession, they more often have been created among family members than among strangers. In this way, a study of concurrent interests requires some examination of family property relationships, both historically and in relation to 20th-century developments. Indeed, as this chapter illustrates, statutory reforms concerning property interests held by married couples, and judicial extension of the remedy of constructive trust to unmarried couples (including same-sex couples) have significantly transformed the nature of concurrent interests for these family members. Therefore, as we will explain, traditional common law principles concerning concurrent interests are now less often applied to married couples or cohaitees. However, they remain relevant for concurrent interests held by other family members—for example, James O'Reilly's children—and by unrelated co-owners. This chapter also examines constitutional law principles that have prevented application of statutory reforms concerning family property to First Nations peoples on reserve lands.

The concept of concurrent interests in property thus demonstrates connections between common law historical roots in feudal society and modern challenges—both legislative and judicial—in relation to their roles in family property. This chapter explores the ways that social and political ideas in the 20th century have shaped legal principles about concurrent interests, just as feudal ideas influenced traditional common law principles. In the United States, a similar assessment of the culture of legal reforms concerning women and property is found in Richard Chused, *Cases, Materials and Problems in Property* (New York: Matthew Bender, 1988), at 251. See also Richard Chused, "Married Women's Property Law: 1800-1850" (1983), 71 *Georgetown Law Journal* 1359.

TRADITIONAL CONCURRENT INTERESTS

Four forms of concurrent interests were traditionally recognized at common law:

1. joint tenancy;
2. tenancy in common;
3. tenancy by the entireties; and
4. co-parcenary.

Joint tenancies and tenancies in common continue today as the usual forms for holding concurrent interests, although there are significant differences between them—differences in the rights and responsibilities of grantees of concurrent interests, differences in how they are defined conceptually, and differences in the language used to create them. (Note that the use of the word "tenant" here is completely unrelated to a leasehold estate.)

Joint Tenancies and Tenancies in Common

Several decades ago, Finlay McEwen died, devising a life estate to his wife Helen in relation to lots 5 and 18 in the town of Carleton Place, Ontario. According to his will, he devised the fee simple remainder interest in lot 5 after his wife's death to his son Robert. His will also made provision for the remainder interest in lot 18 after his wife's death, as follows:

> [T]he said lot 18, that is the property fronting on Beckwith Street is to become the property of my daughters Bertha V. McEwen and Janet I. McEwen jointly and should they decide to sell the said property each of them is to have an equal share of the proceeds of the said sale.

It was clear that the testator intended to create concurrent interests in lot 18 for his two daughters, but after Bertha's subsequent death (when she devised her one-half interest in lot 18 to her brother, Robert), a dispute arose within the family about exactly what form of concurrent interests had been devised to the two sisters by Finlay McEwen's will. Did they hold their concurrent interests as joint tenants or as tenants in common?

In this fact situation, the difference between holding a concurrent interest as joint tenant or as tenant in common is highly significant. According to traditional common law principles, one important feature of a joint tenancy is an inherent "right of survivorship." However, a tenancy in common did not include such a "right of survivorship." What consequences flowed from this distinction for Bertha and Janet? In reading the case, examine the court's approach to the language used in the will, and how the words affect the judge's interpretation of the concurrent interest at issue.

McEwen v. Ewers and Ferguson
[1946] 3 DLR 494 (Ont. HCJ)

BARLOW J: The plaintiff's claim is for a declaration that by the will of his father Finlay McEwen, lot 18 in section D of the Town of Carleton Place, in the County of Lanark, was devised to Janet I. Ewers and Bertha V. McEwen as tenants in common and that by a devise in the last will and testament of Bertha V. McEwen he became entitled to a one-half interest in said lot 18. In the alternative the plaintiff claims that if it is found that lot 18 was left to Janet I. Ewers and Bertha V. McEwen, as joint tenants, then the defendant Janet I. Ewers is put to her election because upon the death of Bertha V. McEwen she, (Janet I. Ewers) became the sole owner of lot 18, and Bertha V. McEwen having made certain bequests to Janet I. Ewers and also having bequeathed to the plaintiff one-half of lot 18, which belonged to Janet I. Ewers, the latter must elect which she must take under the will of the late Bertha V. McEwen.

The property in question, lot 18, has been sold. Exhibit 3 is an undertaking given by the defendant Janet I. Ewers, which provides that in the event of the Court finding that there was a tenancy in common, she will pay to the plaintiff one-half of the proceeds, namely $1,456.45.

The plaintiff is a son and Janet I. Ewers (formerly Janet I. McEwen) and Bertha V. McEwen were daughters of the late Finlay McEwen.

The paragraph in question in the will of Finlay McEwen (ex. 1) is as follows:

I give devise and bequeath all my real estate to my wife Helen F. McEwen during the time of her life, said property consisting of the west half of lots No. 5 and 18 in Section D of the Town of Carleton Place in the County of Lanark. After her death the said lot 5 is to become the property of my son Robert L. McEwen and the said lot 18, that is the property fronting on Beckwith Street is to become the property of my daughters Bertha V. McEwen and Janet I. McEwen jointly and should they decide to sell the said property each of them is to have an equal share of the proceeds of the said sale.

After the death of the life tenant, Helen F. McEwen, Bertha V. McEwen the surviving executrix of the will of Finlay McEwen, purported to convey lot 18, being the property in question, to herself and Janet I. Ewers as joint tenants. This was merely purporting to carry out what was thought to be the terms of the will.

Bertha V. McEwen by her will (ex. 2) provides as follows:

2. I give and bequeath to my sister Janet Isobel Ewers, one thousand dollars and to my niece Helen Ruth Ewers three hundred dollars and my piano, to my brother Robert Latimer McEwen I direct that half of the lot no. 18, that is the property fronting on Beckwith Street to be given to him or the price of the same when sold in cash.

Does the bequest of part of lot 18 in the above-quoted paragraph from the will of Finlay McEwen create a joint tenancy or a tenancy in common? The specific words that fall for interpretation are as follows: "to become the property of my daughters Bertha V. McEwen and Janet I. McEwen jointly and should they decide to sell the said property each of them is to have an equal share of the proceeds of the said sale."

Under the common law it would probably be interpreted as the creation of a joint tenancy. However, under the *Conveyancing and Law of Property Act*, RSO 1937, c. 152, s. 12, unless an intention sufficiently appears on the face of the will, it must be interpreted that Bertha V. McEwen and Janet I. Ewers took as tenants in common and not as joint tenants.

Counsel for the defendant Janet I. Ewers cites *Re Campbell* (1912), 7 DLR 452, 4 OWN 221, and *Re Quebec* (1929), 37 OWN 271, where the word "jointly" was held to create a joint tenancy. In the case at bar the word "jointly" does not stand alone. The testator, in my opinion, shows his intention by the words following the word "jointly," *viz.*, "should they decide to sell the said property each of them is to have an equal share of the proceeds."

It appears to me that not only does the testator not show an intention to create a joint tenancy, but in the use of the words "equal share" he shows clearly an intention to create a tenancy in common. See Theobald on Wills, 9th ed., pp. 352-3, where cases are cited to show that where the words "jointly" and "equally" have been used the Courts have held the gift a tenancy in common. Also, that where there are words of division or distribution such as "to be divided" or "equally" it creates a tenancy in common. Further, that the use of the word "share" or similar words also imports a tenancy in common.

The Court undoubtedly leans towards a tenancy in common and will prefer it where there is a doubt. See also Jarman on Wills, 7th ed., vol. 3, pp. 1768-9, to the same effect as Theobald. Jarman says: "Anything which in the slightest degree indicates an intention to divide the property must be held to abrogate the idea of a joint tenancy, and to create a tenancy in common." I am, therefore, of opinion that the words in question must be held to have created a tenancy in common. This is sufficient for the disposition of this action.

The plaintiff's alternative claim alleging that by virtue of the terms of the will of Bertha V. McEwen the defendant Janet I. Ewers is put to her election, does not require to be dealt with. If, however, the action did fall to be determined upon the ground that the words of the will created a joint tenancy, then I am of opinion that the plaintiff would be entitled to succeed on the ground that the defendant Janet I. Ewers is put to her election, under the will of Bertha V. McEwen, for the reason that if a joint tenancy existed Janet I. Ewers became the sole owner of lot 18 upon the death of Bertha V. McEwen, whereas the latter in her will, after making certain bequests to Janet I. Ewers, purported to give to the plaintiff half of lot 18, which, on the basis of a joint tenancy did not form part of her estate. See Theobald on Wills, 9th ed., p. 83; 11 CED (Ont.), p. 209.

Counsel for the estate of Bertha V. McEwen merely submitted his rights to the Court. As Bertha V. McEwen in her lifetime was partially responsible for causing the situation which resulted in this litigation, I am of opinion that I should make no order as to costs in so far as she is concerned.

Judgment will go for the plaintiff for $1,456.45 and costs as against the defendant Janet I. Ewers.

Judgment for plaintiff.

Consequential Differences: The Right of Survivorship

The right of survivorship means that when one joint tenant dies, the interest of the deceased joint tenant is extinguished. In *Wright v. Gibbons* (1949), 78 CLR 313, the court reviewed the status of a joint tenancy held by three sisters, Olinda Gibbons, Ethel Rose Gibbons, and Bessie Melba Gibbons. Latham CJ described the right of survivorship for a joint tenancy as follows (at 323):

> If one joint tenant dies his interest is extinguished. He falls out, and the interest of the surviving joint tenant or joint tenants is correspondingly enlarged.

The conceptual impact of the right of survivorship was also described in Mendes da Costa, "Co-Ownership Under Victorian Land Law" (1961), 3 *Melbourne University Law Review* 137 (hereafter Mendes da Costa), at 153:

> It seems ... inaccurate to speak of the interest of one joint tenant "passing" on his death to the other. Although as a practical consequence of the death, considerable benefits do accrue to the survivor in that he alone is now exclusively entitled, it appears that the interest of a joint tenant lacks the capacity to devolve upon that joint tenant's death, and so is thereupon exhausted, neither adding to nor subtracting from the seisin of the surviving joint tenants.

According to these principles, if Finlay McEwen's will created a joint tenancy (with a right of survivorship), then at Bertha's death, her interest was extinguished and Janet's interest was correspondingly enlarged—that is, her interest became an exclusive one. (Note that it is not technically appropriate to say that Bertha's interest "passed" to Janet.) The major consequence of the right of survivorship here, however, is that Bertha's death terminated her interest in lot 18 and thus she had no interest in lot 18 that could be devised by her will. If Finlay McEwen's will created a joint tenancy for Bertha and Janet, the right of survivorship required that Janet be recognized as holding an exclusive interest upon Bertha's death, the position asserted by Janet in the litigation that took place in this case.

By contrast, if Finlay McEwen's will created a tenancy in common instead of a joint tenancy, then there was no right of survivorship. If Bertha and Janet were tenants in common, each had a devisable one-half share (as co-owners) in lot 18, and thus Robert was entitled to half the proceeds of sale of lot 18 in accordance with Bertha's will. This was the position asserted by Robert in the litigation in 1949 after Bertha's death.

Discussion Notes

Joint Tenancy or Tenancy in Common

Since a joint tenancy includes a right of survivorship and a tenancy in common does not, a grantor of concurrent interests must choose which form of concurrent interests to create for grantees. In what kinds of circumstances would it be preferable to create a joint tenancy rather than a tenancy in common? When might a tenancy in common be preferable?

Since the effect over time of a joint tenancy will be to reduce a number of co-owners to one remaining title-holder, a joint tenancy will be preferred in situations where there are advantages to (eventually) having only one owner. Historically, there was a preference for joint tenancy because the right of survivorship worked so as to reduce the number of persons from whom feudal dues had to be collected (a position reflecting a greater interest in easily identifying the payee responsible rather than in "spreading the risk" of non-payment among several persons). More recently, joint tenancies have sometimes been preferred because they make title searching less complicated. By contrast with the shares of tenants in common (each of which can be devised), the interest of each joint tenant ceases at death, so that the title ultimately is consolidated in the last surviving joint tenant prior to being devised. Such objectives led to the 1925 legislative reforms in the United Kingdom that require that any legal concurrent interests must be held in joint tenancy: see Law of Property Act, 1925, c. 20 s. 1(6). Tenancies in common continue to exist only as equitable or beneficial estates. (See Gray and Symes, *Real Property and Real People* (London: Butterworths, 1981) (hereafter Gray and Symes), at 240-41.)

According to Gray and Symes (at 241), the common law's preference for joint tenancy was motivated by concerns of efficiency and convenience, especially in the context of title-searching. By contrast, they suggested that equity preferred tenancies in common:

> Tenancy in common represents certainty and fairness in the property relations of co-owners. Each tenant in common holds a fixed beneficial interest immune from the caprice of survivorship. Each share constitutes a tangible quantum of wealth which can serve as the subject matter of family endowment. Thus, whereas the law leaned in favour of joint tenancy largely for reasons of convenience, equity has leaned towards tenancy in common for reasons of fairness.

Do these arguments suggest a need for reforms in Canada? Is the context the same? Is there a similar need for joint tenancies to ensure "convenience" in determining legal title in Canada? What is the balance of convenience and fairness here?

Joint Tenancies: Family Property Arrangements

In the light of the impact of the right of survivorship, it is not surprising that joint tenancies are most often used in family property arrangements. Indeed, it has been suggested that many common law developments (perhaps including the concept of joint tenancy) were motivated originally by the needs of families rather than those of commerce: "Historically, the demands of the family preceded the demands of commerce, and the manner in which they were met left an indelible and permanent mark upon the framework of the law." (See G.C. Cheshire, *The Modern Law of Real Property*, 7th ed. (London: Butterworths, 1954), at v.) In any event, joint tenancy in Canada in the 20th century has frequently been used by a husband and wife in their arrangements for holding interests in the matrimonial home. Such an arrangement seemed logical to couples who expected to remain married for their whole lives, so that the survivor would become sole owner by right of survivorship, and then devise the interest to surviving children or others. However, in the context of rising divorce rates in recent decades, the right of survivorship in a joint tenancy may be more ephemeral. Moreover, there may be complicated problems where the husband and wife jointly own a farm or business, rather than just a matrimonial home: see M. McCall, "Economic Security for Farm Women: A Discussion Paper" (Ottawa: National Association of Women and the Law, 1995). The relationship between the right of survivorship in joint tenancy and recent statutory reforms concerning family property will be considered later in this chapter.

Although joint tenancy is the form of concurrent interest often used by married couples, it is also available for use by cohabiting couples (same-sex or opposite sex). What factors would need to be taken into account by a cohabiting couple in relation to concurrent interests in property in choosing a joint tenancy or a tenancy in common?

Simultaneous Death of Joint Tenants

In the *McEwen* case discussed above, if Bertha and Janet were joint tenants and Bertha died, Janet would become sole owner as a result of the right of survivorship. What if Bertha and Janet had died together in an accident, so that it was not possible to determine which of them died first? How would the right of survivorship operate in such a case? This possibility is now regulated by statute. For example, in Ontario, the Succession Law Reform Act, RSO 1990, c. S.26, s. 55(2) provides that "unless a contrary intention appears," where two or more joint tenants die at the same time or in circumstances rendering it uncertain as to the order of death, each person is "deemed to have held as tenants in common." See also RSNB 1973, c. S-19, s. 1; RSNS 1967, c. 299, s. 1; RSN 1970, c. 366, s. 2 (as am. SN 1971, no. 5, s. 2); and RSPEI 1974, c. C-13.

Joint Tenancies: Corporations

Logically, one would expect that interests as joint tenants with consequent rights of survivorship could be held only by human beings, and not by corporations that have no natural life span although they may be subject to dissolution in other ways. At common law, therefore, it was not possible for a corporation and an individual to hold interests as joint tenants, but this principle has been revised by statute in Ontario. Section 43 of the Conveyancing and Law of Property Act, RSO 1990, c. C.34 provides that two or more corporations, or a corporation and an individual, "are and have been" capable of holding property as joint tenants in the same manner as individuals (subject to the usual conditions for the acquisition and holding of property by a corporation in severalty). Subsection 2 provides that when a corporation that holds property as a joint tenant subsequently dissolves, "the property devolves on the other joint tenant."

Severance of Joint Tenancy

In the context of the right of survivorship in a joint tenancy, there may be situations where one or more of the joint tenants decides that it would be preferable for them to be tenants in common. The process for changing a joint tenancy into a tenancy in common can be accomplished by the "severance" of the joint tenancy, an issue discussed later in this chapter.

Conceptual Distinctions: The Four Unities

In addition to the right of survivorship that applies ony to a joint tenancy, there are conceptual differences between joint tenancies and tenancies in common. A joint tenancy has four unities—unity of possession, interest, title, and time. By contrast, a tenancy in common has just one—unity of possession. While holders of concurrent interests in joint tenancies and tenancies in common all have undivided rights to possession of the whole of the relevant property, they are conceptually different in other respects. In particular, the interest of a joint tenant is a unified interest in the whole, while that of a tenant in common is a fractional share—for example, one-half or one-third—of the whole. A tenant in common holds an "undivided" share. For example, a tenant in common who holds a one-third share in land cannot identify any particular part of the land as the one-third share, because of the unity of possession enjoyed by all the tenants in common.

By contrast, a joint tenant holds an interest in the whole. According to Gray and Symes, at 234:

> Indeed, the essence of joint tenancy consists in the dogma that each and every joint tenant is "wholly entitled to the whole" of the land. No joint tenant holds any specific share in the property himself, but each is (together with the other joint tenant or tenants) invested with the absolute interest in the land. In Bracton's expressive language, each joint tenant "totum tenet et nihil tenet": each holds everything and yet holds nothing. Joint tenancy is thus an amorphous kind of co-ownership in which the entire estate or interest in property—rather than any defined proportion or share in that property—is vested simultaneously in each and all of the co-owners.

Conceptually, therefore, the interest of a joint tenant is an interest in the whole estate, by contrast with the interest of a tenant in common, which is described as an undivided share in the whole.

The joint tenancy's unity of interest, title, and time means that joint tenants must have interests of the same quality and duration; they must derive them through the same title documents; and their interests must commence at the same time. The concepts were identified in the *Working Paper on Co-Ownership of Land* (Vancouver: Law Reform Commission of British Columbia, 1987) (hereafter BCLRC), at 2:

> Co-owners acquiring their title by separate instruments are not joint tenants. There is no unity of title. Similarly, where their interests are acquired at different times, there is no unity of time. If they have differing interests in property, there is no unity of interest. The absence of any of these unities means that co-ownership is by tenancy in common, not joint tenancy.

Discussion Notes

Unities of Possession, Interest, Title, and Time

In relation to Finlay McEwen's will devising concurrent interests in lot 18 to Bertha and Janet, were there unities of possession, interest, title, and time?

1. Were the sisters' interests the same in terms of size and duration (unity of interest)?
2. Were the sisters' titles derived from the same document (unity of title)?
3. Were the sisters' interests expected to commence at the same time (unity of time)?

Compare the concurrent interests in the *McEwen* case with the following:

- grant to A for life and to B in fee simple;
- grant to A for life, remainder to B and C when B and C graduate from law school;
- grant to A and B in fee simple; and then grant from A to C.

Note that there are some complex difficulties of interpretation in such grants. For an informed discussion of some of the cases, see Mendes da Costa.

In *Re Speck* (1983), 51 BCLR 143 (SC), two persons applied to register their interests in land as joint tenants with one party having an undivided $71/_{100}$ interest and the other an undivided $29/_{100}$ interest. The court denied their claim, stating that by trying to register a joint tenancy without a unity of interest, the applicants were trying to create "a monster unknown to the law." By contrast with the court's view in *Speck*, BCLRC has suggested that there may be cases where joint tenancies with undivided shares should be recognized. For example, the commission explained (at 26-27) that

> a husband and wife may purchase a matrimonial home with the wife putting up 80% of the money. They find the notion of a joint tenancy attractive for its right of survivorship, but fear that if the husband's business activities should lead to his bankruptcy, the trustee [in bankruptcy] would be entitled to half the property. A form of joint tenancy which recognized unequal interests would seem to satisfy their needs.

The Law Reform Commission's report reviewed several options for achieving the needs of joint tenants in such cases, including the use of contractual agreements or trust arrangements. (As well, the report pointed out (at 27) that there are some cases recognizing tenancies in common with rights of survivorship, although there are uncertainties in these cases because such interests can also be devised.) Having regard to the needs of joint tenants, however, the report recommended legislation providing that "unity of interest is unnecessary to create a joint tenancy"—that is, that joint tenants could hold interests that differ in extent. Is this recommendation appropriate for consideration by other provincial legislatures in Canada?

Mutual Rights and Responsibilities Among Co-Owners

The unity of possession that applies to both joint tenancies and tenancies in common required the development of quite complex rules about mutual rights and responsibilities among co-owners, a topic considered later in this chapter in relation to rights of accounting, partition, and sale.

Language: Identifying Forms of Concurrent Interests

In *McEwen*, above, it is clear that there are important consequences that follow if the interests of Finlay McEwen's daughters Bertha and Janet are characterized as those of joint tenants rather than tenants in common. Moreover, although it seems that Finlay McEwen's will met the requirements of the four unities for a joint tenancy (and not just the unity of possession required for a tenancy in common), these principles alone do not help to determine which form of concurrent interests was created. As with other aspects of property law, it is necessary to take account of the language adopted by the testator in creating the interests for Bertha and Janet. Re-examine the language considered in the case in deciding which form of concurrent interests was created.

Discussion Notes

Statutory Presumption in Favour of Tenancies in Common

As the *McEwen* case demonstrates, the words used to create concurrent interests are important. The common law's traditional preference for joint tenancies meant that ambiguity in language would be resolved in favour of the creation of a joint tenancy. This presumption was reversed by statute in the 19th century. For example, s. 13 of the Conveyancing and Law of Property Act, RSO 1990, c. C.34 now provides:

> Where by any letters patent, assurance or will, made and executed after the 1st day of
> July, 1834, land has been or is granted, conveyed or devised to two or more persons,
> other than executors or trustees, in fee simple or for any less estate, it shall be
> considered that such persons took or take as tenants in common and not as joint tenants,
> unless an intention sufficiently appears on the face of the letters patent, assurance or
> will, that they are to take as joint tenants.

Note that this section was s. 12 at the time of the *McEwen* case. See also Property Act, RSNB 1973, c. P-19, s. 20 and Real Property Act, RSNS 1967, c. 261, s. 4.

As is apparent, the statutory provision (where it is applicable) resolves ambiguity in language in favour of tenancies in common. Aa a result, the creation of a joint tenancy now requires clear words—for example, a grant to A and B in fee simple "as joint tenants and not as tenants in common." Is it appropriate to have such a statutory presumption in favour of tenancies in common so that those who wish to create a joint tenancy must take care to ensure that they use appropriate language to achieve their objective? What are the assumptions on which such a policy is based? Is this statutory presumption consistent with the Law Reform Commission's recommendation in British Columbia that would permit the creation of a joint tenancy without a unity of interest? How would such a reform proposal affect the statutory presumption in favour of tenancies in common?

The Interpretation of Section 13

Like many statutory reforms of property law, s. 13 has been strictly interpreted. It does not apply to grants other than "after 1 July 1834." Nor does it apply to grants to executors or trustees, as was demonstrated in relation to comparable legislation in Australia in *Mitchell v. Arblaster*, [1964-65] NSWR 119 (SC). In that case, a will devised interests to co-owners (Harry Mitchell and Nellie Mitchell) as executors and trustees of the will, and also to them as residuary beneficiaries. The statutory presumption did not apply to the grant to executors and trustees, but was applicable to the grant to Harry and Nellie Mitchell as beneficiaries. Thus, the same wording resulted in a grant to the executors and trustees as joint tenants (the legal interest as trustees) and to them as beneficiaries as tenants in common (the equitable or beneficial interest). See also *Robertson v. Fraser* (1871), 7 Ch. App. 696 (CA), where the court interpreted words of sharing in a codicil to a will so as to conclude that the will devised a tenancy in common.

Similarly, it was held in *Campbell v. Sovereign Securities and Holdings Co. Ltd.* (1958), 16 DLR (2d) 606 (Ont. CA) that s. 13 was not applicable where the language creating concurrent interests was in an agreement for purchase and sale, on the basis that such an agreement is not an "assurance" pursuant to the wording in the section. For a case where the court was required to interpret an oral agreement concerning co-owner-ship of a horse, see *Dennis v. Dennis* (1971), 45 ALJR 605 (HC).

Note that the court in *McEwen* interpreted the testator's intention according to the language chosen to define the interests devised to Bertha and Janet. Having regard to Finlay McEwen's will as a whole, what arguments might be made in support of Janet's position that the will created interests for Janet and Bertha as joint tenants? Is there inconsistency in Bertha's actions in conveying lot 18 to herself and Janet as joint ten-ants, and then subsequently devising a one-half interest to her brother? How can this apparent inconsistency be explained?

It is unclear from the case report whether Janet and her brother were engaged in amicable litigation just to confirm the title to lot 18, or whether this was a bitterly contested family dispute involving other matters as well. The issue of family property disputes will be addressed in more detail later in this chapter.

A Note on Tenancies by the Entireties and Co-Parcenary

These forms of concurrent interests are uncommon, and there is some controversy about their continuing existence in practice. Both involve concurrent interests arising out of particular kinds of familial relationships, so that they too raise issues about the relation-ship between traditional common law principles and statutory reforms.

Tenancy by the Entireties

J.M. Glenn has described tenancies by the entireties as follows:

> At common law, when property was conveyed to a husband and wife in any estate in such a way that had they been strangers they would have taken as joint tenants, they took rather as tenants by the entireties. This was so because of the doctrine of unity of legal personality, according to which husband and wife were considered in law as one: to the four unities of time, title, interest and possession was added a fifth unity, unity of the person. This unity was so complete that neither spouse was regarded as having even a potential share in the property; both were seised together as one individual of the whole, that is, of the entirety. They were, in other words, together tenants of the entirety.

From this flows one of the most important features of a tenancy by the entireties: its unseverability. And it follows from this unseverability that the right of survivorship is indestructible.

(Glenn, "Tenancy by the Entireties: A Matrimonial Regime Ignored" (1980), 58 *Canadian Bar Review* 711, at 715.)

As is apparent, this form of concurrent interests is based on the traditional common law conception of a husband and wife as one person, with the wife's legal status "suspended" during coverture. Obviously, many legal reforms in the 20th century have been intended to promote more equality for women in marriage, but there is some uncertainty about whether statutory reforms have repealed tenancies by the entireties in all Canadian provinces. Some provinces (including Prince Edward Island and Newfoundland) have expressly repealed such tenancies, while others (including Ontario) may arguably have done so by the combined effect of married women's property acts and family property statutes. In *Campbell v. Sovereign Securities and Holdings Co. Ltd.* (1958), 16 DLR (2d) 606 (Ont. CA), (1958), 13 DLR (2d) 195 (Ont. HCJ) it was suggested that tenancies by the entireties continued to exist in Ontario, although this view was distinguished later in *Demaiter v. Link*, [1973] 3 OR 140 (Co. Ct.). Glenn provides a persuasive argument for the continuing utility of such tenancies in spite of substantial reform of family property arrangements in Canada.

Co-Parcenary

This form of concurrent ownership occurred at common law when there was an intestacy and the land would then devolve to the common law heir. If, however, no male heir existed, female heirs together were deemed to be the heir, and were together entitled as co-parceners. The right of survivorship did not apply and each co-parcener was entitled to a distinct undivided share. According to Gray and Symes (at 233), it can arise now "only in certain highly anomalous situations." In Canada, however, it has been suggested that "co-parcenary may still arise upon the death of a tenant in tail who dies, without barring the entail, leaving no male heir and more than one female descendant in the same degree." See Mendes da Costa, Balfour, and Gillese, eds., *Property Law: Cases, Text and Materials*, 2d ed. (Toronto: Emond Montgomery, 1990), at 18:10.

Discussion Note

These forms of concurrent ownership clearly derive from traditional common law principles fashioned in a quite different context. Do you agree with Dixon J in the High Court of Australia in *Wright v. Gibbons* (1949), 78 CLR 313 when he said (at 329), referring to the joint tenancy in particular, that it was "a form of ownership bearing many traces of the scholasticism of the times in which its principles were developed"? If different kinds of concurrent interests were to be created now, what principles would be appropriate? Should there be different principles for family situations by contrast with commercial arrangements? Is it easier to adapt traditional principles or to fashion entirely new ones?

Severance of a Joint Tenancy

Since a joint tenancy requires that the four unities be present, acts that destroy these unities result in a severance of the joint tenancy and creation of a tenancy in common. In this way, severance of a joint tenancy eliminates the right of survivorship so that the co-owners, now tenants in common, hold undivided shares that are devisable. Where a joint tenancy exists among three persons, all three may join in a deed to sever the joint tenancy so that they become tenants in common instead. In the absence of agreement among all the joint tenants, common law principles have identified circumstances by which one joint tenant acting alone may effect severance of a joint tenancy, sometimes without notice to other joint tenants. Some commentators have suggested that there are good reasons for insisting that requirements for unilateral severance should be strictly interpreted since joint tenancies can be created only where express words are used to do so—that is, words sufficient to overcome the statutory presumption of tenancy in common. At the same time, the fairness inherent in a tenancy in common seems to continue to be influential in judicial interpretation in some circumstances—see, for example, *Burgess v. Rawnsley*, [1975] 3 All ER 142 (CA). Reconsider the balance between "convenience" and "fairness" in these forms of concurrent ownership in reviewing the general principles of severance in the following excerpt.

General Principles of Severance

A.J. McClean, "Severance of Joint Tenancies"
(1979), 57 *Canadian Bar Review* 1, at 1-4 (footnotes omitted)

A joint tenancy may be ended by severance, that is, by any act or conduct which, occurring during the lifetime of a joint tenant, has the effect of turning the joint tenancy into a tenancy in common. The same principles apply to interests in both realty and personalty, but most of the decisions deal with the application of those principles to realty, and that will be the emphasis of this article.

Despite the fact that joint tenancies have long been with us, there are still doubts about the operation of the common law rules on severance. In England and Canada these rules have been affected by legislation. The 1925 [UK] legislation made changes to the law of joint tenancy generally, and in one instance to severance in particular. Post 1925 English cases are therefore relevant in Canada, and will be considered here, only to the extent that they throw light on the common law principles. In Canada the common law has been modified by legislation, either expressly, or sometimes clearly, sometimes arguably, impliedly, and in some respects there is still uncertainty about the blending of common law and statute.

The starting point for any discussion of the modern law is the well-known passage in the judgment of Sir W. Page Wood VC in *Williams v. Hensman* [(1861), 70 ER 862 (Ch.D), at 867]:

A joint-tenancy may be severed in three ways: in the first place, an act of any one of the persons interested operating upon his own share may create a severance as to that share.

The right of each joint-tenant is a right by survivorship only in the event of no severance having taken place of the share which is claimed under the *jus accrescendi*. Each one is at liberty to dispose of his own interest in such a manner as to sever it from the joint fund—losing, of course, at the same time, his own right of survivorship. Secondly, a joint-tenancy may be severed by mutual agreement. And, in the third place, there may be a severance by any course of dealing sufficient to intimate that the interests of all were mutually treated as constituting a tenancy in common. When the severance depends on an inference of this kind without any express act of severance, it will not suffice to rely on an intention, with respect to the particular share, declared only behind the backs of the persons interested.

In *Burgess v. Rawnsley* Sir John Pennycuick called the three propositions in this passage the three "rules" and, with the proviso that too much should not be read into the word rule, this is a convenient way of referring to them.

The reasons why these rules are effective to sever are clear. The first is based on the fact that generally a joint tenant, without the consent of or even notice to the other joint tenants, is as free to deal with his interest as any other owner, and may deal with it in such a way as to destroy one of the unities. If that happens it follows that the joint tenancy is severed. The second and third turn on the common intention of the joint tenants. And, if some recent English decisions are to be believed, rules one and three may also operate on the basis of the unilateral intention, express or implied, of a single joint tenant. In theory if one of the unities is destroyed, or if the common or unilateral intentions are shown to exist, there is a severance, and nothing else need be considered. This is generally the attitude taken by the Canadian courts, and in some cases the law is so well settled on this basis that it would be futile to debate the issues further. But there are two other factors which may be thought to be relevant, particularly where there is doubt about the destruction of the unities or the existence of the requisite intentions.

The first, and more general, consideration is the well-established judicial preference for the tenancy in common. This means that it can be expected that the courts will lean in favour of severance. It is arguable that in Canada, with respect to realty, there is no longer any justification for this attitude. Equity developed a preference for tenancies in common in light of the common law rule that, in the absence of a contrary intention, a conveyance or devise to two or more persons automatically created a joint tenancy. Thus, often without the parties realizing it, the right of survivorship, which runs contrary to equity's sense of equality, arose by implication. In Canada most jurisdictions have legislation reversing the common law rule; a conveyance or devise to two or more persons will create a tenancy in common, unless it is provided in the instrument that a joint tenancy is intended. Joint tenancies, therefore, need to be deliberately created, and it is doubtful if there should be any special preference for severance. This is particularly true in what is today probably the most common example of a joint tenancy—the conveyance of the matrimonial home to a husband and wife. We will have occasion to look at this argument at various places in the article.

The second, and more specific, consideration arises where a joint tenant and a third party engage in some type of dealing which in itself would not destroy any of the unities. In many such cases it is argued that in fairness to the third party there nonetheless ought to be a severance if the transaction is to be fully effective. Sometimes the argument is also put in terms of the presumed intention of the joint tenant himself to give full and faithful effect to the transaction. Therefore, although the point can arise in relation to other modes of severance, this consideration will be dealt with primarily in that part of the article where severance based upon the presumed intention of a joint tenant is discussed.

Discussion Notes

Severance of Joint Tenancies: Intention, Negotiation, and Completed Acts

Although the principles in *Williams v. Hensman*, above, are often used as the starting point for judicial analysis concerning severance of a joint tenancy, application of the principles in practice may be more difficult. For example, although it is clear that a conveyance of an estate by one joint tenant to a third party (the first method set out in *Williams v. Hensman*) will result in severance, the grant of a mere "encumbrance" such as an easement or a leasehold may not. The principles regarding one joint tenant's creation of a mortgage may depend on the applicable principles concerning mortgages as well as on the principles of severance. See, for example, *Re McKee and National Trust Co. Ltd.* (1975), 56 DLR (3d) 190 (Ont. CA); *Frieze v. Unger*, [1960] VR 230 (SC); and *Re Sorensen and Sorensen* (1977), 90 DLR (3d) 26 (Alta. SCAD).

The second method, mutual agreement, contemplates an agreement among joint tenants to sever the joint tenancy, and the cases have shown that even agreements not reduced to a registrable deed may suffice to sever a joint tenancy in equity. In *Robichaud v. Watson* (1983), 147 DLR (3d) 626 (Ont. HCJ), a cohabiting couple (who held property as joint tenants) separated, and their lawyers conducted "without prejudice" negotiations to settle June Watson's claim for her share of the value of a house, some household furnishings, and a car. Although an offer of settlement was made by Raymond Robichaud, it was rejected, and sometime later he was murdered. His mother applied for a declaration that the joint tenancy had been severed and that a one-half interest passed to Robichaud's estate. The Ontario High Court concluded (at 636) that "the negotiations carried on between the parties through their solicitors in this case clearly indicated that each regarded themselves as tenants in common, that their interests had been severed and what was at issue in the negotiations was the value only of their respective interests." See also *Re Walters and Walters* (1977), 16 OR (2d) 702 (HCJ) and *Ginn v. Armstrong* (1969), 3 DLR (3d) 285 (BC SC). By contrast, see *Rodrigue v. Dufton* (1976), 13 OR (2d) 613 (HCJ), also discussed in *Robichaud v. Watson* (above) but distinguished on the facts. In *Morgan v. Davis* (1984), 42 RFL (2d) 435 (NB QB (Fam. Div.)), the court concluded that negotiations between a husband and wife in the context of their divorce did not effect a severance of their joint tenancy (the divorce decree was silent with respect to any property settlement). When the former husband died, the court held (at 440) that the right of survivorship operated in favour of his former wife (subject to the interpretation of sections of the relevant family property legislation in New Brunswick regarding the former husband's more extensive financial and other contributions to the maintenance of the property):

I am satisfied that the divorce by itself did not sever the joint tenancy even though the relationship between Donald and Doreen Morgan was terminated. Nor could the devise of the property in the will of Donald Morgan have this effect. The only basis upon which severance might be found is the negotiations between the parties and, having regard to my comments on the quotes made earlier, it is my view that it is not possible to infer from the particular facts of this case a common intention to sever. There was simply an offer and an unreasonable counter offer, but no agreement. There was a presentation of documents for conveyance, which were never acknowledged. It seems clear the parties intended to return to the status quo and the matter was "to be held in abeyance and resolved at some later date." Having regard to their attitude and course of conduct, it is not difficult to infer that the parties, following the incomplete negotiations and the divorce, accepted the situation with respect to the joint tenancy as it was prior to the negotiations. I am satisfied they knew and understood the meaning and significance of the title being registered in their joint names and neither did anything to change that situation. Consequently, I find there was no severance and, by virtue of the joint tenancy, title to the property in question passed to Doreen Davis at the moment of Donald Morgan's death.

For a discussion as to the admissibility of "without prejudice" solicitors' letters written in the course of divorce negotiations, see *Kish v. Tompkins* (1992), 86 DLR (4th) 759 (BC SC).

The decision in *Robichaud v. Watson* (above) may also be viewed as "a course of conduct," the third means of achieving severance set out in *Williams v. Hensman*. Another example is found in the obiter comments in *Murdoch v. Barry* (1975), 10 OR (2d) 626 (HCJ) where Patricia Murdoch (a joint tenant with her husband of some cottage property) conveyed her estate to herself and then devised her interest in the cottage property to her sister just prior to her death. One question in this case was the effect of a conveyance by a joint tenant to herself (an issue addressed in relation to *Knowlton v. Bartlett, post*). However, the court in *Murdoch* also considered the test for "a course of conduct," as set out in *Re Wilks; Child v. Bulmer*, [1891] 3 Ch. 59 (Ch.D), requiring an act that precludes a joint tenant from claiming by survivorship any interest in the subject matter of the tenancy. In *Murdoch*, Patricia Murdoch executed a deed, declaring her intention to sever the joint tenancy in her affidavit of marital status on the deed, and then arranged for the deed to be registered. According to the court (at 633):

> That constituted an irrevocable act on her part, the purpose of which was to sever the joint tenancy and it was an act which, in my opinion, constituted more than a mere declaration of intention but, rather, an endeavour on her part to carry out by her act the intention expressed in her affidavit ... . [These acts] effectively estopped her from claiming by survivorship any interest in the subject-matter of the joint tenancy in the event she had survived the applicant.

Accordingly, the court held that she had effectively severed the joint tenancy. Do you agree with this analysis? Is it consistent with *Morgan v. Davis*, above?

Severance of a Joint Tenancy by Murder

Severance of a joint tenancy has also been confirmed in circumstances where one joint tenant has murdered the other (although this result is usually characterized as a legal result outside the terms of *Williams v. Hensman*). In *Schobelt v. Barber* (1966), 60 DLR (2d) 519 (Ont. HC), the court rejected arguments that any modification of the usual rules concerning the right of survivorship would constitute an unacceptable "further penalty" for the murderer, a return of the principle of forfeiture abolished by the Criminal Code. Relying on a case comment of *Re Pupkowski* (1956), 6 DLR (2d) 427 (BC SC) written by R. St. J. MacDonald (in (1957), 35 *Canadian Bar Review* 966), the court considered four options:

1. Permit the estate of the deceased to accrue to the survivor by right of survivorship (rejected because a person should not benefit from his own wrongful act).
2. Deprive the survivor of the right of survivorship (rejected because it is an inherent characteristic of a joint tenancy).
3. Vest the estate in the survivor, but the victim should be deemed to have died after the wrongdoer (rejected because it requires substantial change to property law and thus should be accomplished only by legislation).
4. Apply the normal rule so that the estate accrues to the survivor, subject to a constructive trust of an undivided one-half interest for the victim's estate.

The court adopted the fourth option, approved also by *Scott on Trusts*, and quoted from a statement by John W. Wade in "Acquisition of Property by Wilfully Killing Another—A Statutory Solution" (1936), 49 *Harvard Law Review* 715, at 720:

> [T]he court is not taking away from the slayer an estate which he has already acquired, but "is simply preventing him from acquiring property in an unauthorized and unlawful way, ie, by murder."

Do you agree that the court's choice is the best way to resolve this problem?

Unintentional Severance of a Joint Tenancy

Severance of a joint tenancy may also occur without an intentional act in the context of bankruptcy and in the execution of a judgment. See, for example, *Re Ali (No. 1)* (1987), 62 CBR 61 (Ont. HCJ) and *Sirois v. Breton* (1967), 62 DLR (2d) 366 (Ont. Co. Ct.). A joint tenancy at law may also be held as a tenancy in common in equity in the context of partnership property or where the purchase price of property is advanced by joint tenants in unequal proportions. For example, if A and B are grantees as joint tenants and A has paid $30,000 while B has paid $10,000 of the total purchase price, A and B will be joint tenants in law and tenants in common in equity (with A having a ¾ undivided share and B a ¼ undivided share). What will be the result if A dies?

Severance and Conveyance by One or More Joint Tenants

Suppose that A, B, and C are joint tenants in fee simple. A conveys A's interest to D. This means that B and C are now joint tenants in relation to a two-thirds share, which they hold together as tenants in common with D in respect to D's one-third share. Explain why D takes as a tenant in common, and why B and C remain joint tenants. What happens when D dies? When B dies?

In relation to the above problem, assume that A conveys to B (another of the joint tenants) instead of to D (a stranger). What is the result? Similarly, assume that A conveys to B and B conveys to A, C taking no part in these transactions. It seems that A, B, and C are now tenants in common, each with an undivided one-third share. See *Wright v. Gibbons* (1949), 78 CLR 313.

Severance in a "Family" Context

Knowlton v. Bartlett
(1984), 35 RPR 182 (NB QB Fam. Div.)

JONES J: This comes before me on a notice of application wherein the applicant seeks an order for partition or sale of property.

The property in question is in the parish of St. Stephen, Charlotte County, and consists of a residence as well as approximately 47 acres of ground. It was formerly owned by the parents of the respondent. The respondent's parents deeded a substantial part of the property to the respondent in 1951 and in December of 1953 the respondent deeded that portion of the property to himself and his wife as joint tenants. A further lot of land abutting the original property was deeded by the respondent's mother to the respondent and his wife as joint tenants in December of 1965. The latter two deeds were recorded in the Charlotte County registry office in 1966.

The respondent and his late wife were married in the late 1940s and lived in the home on the premises until as a result of marital differences Mrs. Bartlett apparently left about 1971. On February 3, 1977, a decree absolute was granted with respect to this marriage in which the respondent was the petitioner and the late Mrs. Bartlett filed a counter-petition. One of the provisions of the decree absolute provided as follows:

> 2. AND THIS COURT DOTH ORDER AND ADJUDGE that Everett Eugene Bartlett shall pay to the said Laura Martha Bartlett a lump sum of $3,000.00 providing that Laura Martha Bartlett conveys to him all her interest in the property at RR #4, St. Stephen, NB, assessment code F1201019-2000.

It is common ground that the aforesaid sum of $3,000 was not paid and Mrs. Bartlett did not convey to her husband her interest in this property. It is further agreed that the property referred to in the decree absolute is the property in question in this matter. Mr. Bartlett stated that subsequent to the decree absolute he offered to his late wife the sum of money but that she "did refuse to accept such sums on the basis that she did not want to be bothered."

It further appears that the late Mrs. Bartlett became terminally ill sometime in 1979 and passed away December 22, 1982.

On October 6, 1981, Mrs. Bartlett executed a deed from herself to herself with respect to the aforementioned lands. This deed was recorded in the Charlotte County registry office on the 9th of October 1981. On the 15th of September 1982, Martha Laura Bartlett signed a last will and testament wherein she appointed her brother Kenneth Leon Knowlton to be her executor and also her sole beneficiary. Mr. Knowlton, the applicant in the within matter, makes this application asserting that he holds this property as a tenant in common with the respondent and seeking an order either for partition or sale. The respondent Mr. Bartlett opposes this application and raises several issues.

Joint Tenancy

It is common ground between the parties that certainly until Mrs. Bartlett executed the deed referred to, she and her husband owned this property as joint tenants and not as tenants in common. Had this interest continued it is the contention of the respondent that he as the survivor would be seised of full title in the property.

Joint tenancy consists of four unities, being that of title, interest, possession and time. The unity of time refers to the time of vesting but should any of the remaining unities cease to exist the joint tenancy and right of survivorship would cease. If the parties otherwise remain entitled to the property, it would be as tenants in common.

Joint tenancy can be severed by mutual consent or by conduct of the parties from which an intention to sever would be inferred. A joint tenancy may also be severed by the act of one of the joint tenants: see *Williams v. Hensman* (1861), 1 J & H 546, 70 ER 862 at 867, per Wood VC:

> A joint tenancy may be severed in three ways: in the first place, an act of any one of the persons interested operating upon his own share may create a severance as to that share.

At common law a party could not deed property to oneself but could employ the Statute of Uses, 1535 (Eng., 27 Hen. 8), c. 10, and thus a joint tenant could in this manner create a tenancy in common. The Law of Real Property, Megarry and Wade (2d ed., 1959), p. 423:

> The common law mitigated the uncertainty of the jus accrescendi by enabling a joint tenant to destroy the joint tenancy by severance, which had the result of turning it into a tenancy in common. "The duration of all lives being uncertain, if either party has an ill opinion of his own life, he may sever the joint tenancy by a deed granting over a moiety [that is, conveying one-half] in trust for himself; so that survivorship can be no hardship, where either side may at pleasure prevent it." (*Cray v. Willis* (1729), 2 P. Wms. 529) "Severance" strictly includes partition, but the word is normally used to describe the process whereby a joint tenancy is converted into a tenancy in common, and it is used in this sense here.

Mrs. Bartlett of course did not deed to another for use of herself but rather conveyed directly to herself. Section 23 of the Property Act, RSNB 1973, c. P-19, provides as follows:

> 23(1) Freehold land may be conveyed by a person to himself jointly with another person by the like means by which it might be conveyed by him to another person.
>
> 23(2) Freehold land may, in like manner, be conveyed by a husband to his wife, or by a wife to her husband, alone or jointly with another person.
>
> 23(3) A person may convey land to or vest land in himself.

In the case of [*Murdoch v. Barry*] (1975), 10 OR (2d) 626, 64 DLR (3d) 222, the Ontario High Court had to consider a circumstance somewhat similar to that in the present case. In that case a husband and wife owned property as joint tenants. The wife became ill in July of 1973. On July 20 of that year, she executed a deed to herself which was duly recorded. She died shortly thereafter, having made a will leaving her assets to her sister. The question before the Court was whether or not the execution of the deed constituted her termination of the unity of title so as to mean that the beneficiary of her will held a half interest in the property as tenant in common. The Court in that case reviewed the authorities and held that such conveyance did constitute a severance of the joint tenancy. In fact the provisions of the Conveyancing and Law of Property Act of the Province of Ontario are slightly different than those of New Brunswick on this particular point. The following is an excerpt of the pertinent portions of the Conveyancing and Law of Property Act, RSO 1970, c. 85 [now RSO 1990, c. C.34, ss. 40 and 41]:

> 41. Any property may be conveyed by a person to himself jointly with another person by the like means by which it might be conveyed by him to another person, and may in like manner be conveyed or assigned by a husband to his wife, or by a wife to her husband, alone or jointly with another person.
>
> 42. A person may convey property to or vest property in himself in like manner as he could have conveyed the property to or vested the property in another person.

Counsel on behalf of the respondent makes the point that in the decision of [*Murdoch v. Barry*] the trial Judge referred to a history of cases showing that a person may sever a joint tenancy by a conveyance to a third party which in fact the trial Judge in that case did do. Counsel then makes the point that in the Ontario statute, s. 42 provides that a person may convey property to or vest property in himself in like manner as he would have conveyed it or vested property in another person. For some reason s. 23(3) of the Property Act in this province does not make such a provision. In other words s. 23(1) provides that freehold land may be conveyed to the grantor jointly with another by the like means that it might be conveyed to another person. Section 23(2) indicates that conveyances described there may be done in like manner, i.e. in like manner to 23(1), but there is no such tie-in with respect to 23(3). I do not know nor can I interpret from the wording the reason for this particular variation on the face of the statute. Nevertheless it is clear that s. 23(3) provides that a person may convey land to or vest land in himself.

It was not necessary for the Court in [*Murdoch v. Barry*] to consider this point as they had the Ontario statute available indicating that such conveyance would be in like manner as a conveyance to another person. As previously indicated in my reference to Megarry and Wade on the Law of Real Property, even at common law, if one proceeded by way of the Statute of Uses, one could sever a joint tenancy with a conveyance in effect to oneself and I see no reason why the same result would not obtain by simply conveying the property as authorised by s. 23(3) of the Property Act of this province.

In [*Murdoch v. Barry*], the Court went a step further and found that in that case Mrs. Murdoch had made an affidavit with respect to her married status in which she had expressly indicated her purpose, "[T]his deed is given to sever the joint tenancy which existed with grantor's husband Alexander Murdoch." In that case, the Court found that even if the execution of the deed did not constitute a severance of title, that this affidavit was sufficient to constitute an irrevocable act on her part sufficient to sever the joint tenancy in that it would preclude her from claiming by survivorship the interest in the subject matter of the joint tenancy had she survived her husband.

In the present case, there is no documentation beyond the execution of the deed, and I find that this constituted a severance of the unity of title, and that following the execution and registration of the deed Mr. and Mrs. Bartlett held this property as tenants in common.

Divorce Decree

The provision in the decree absolute of the divorce action does not vest any title in Mr. Bartlett. Subject to any question as to the jurisdiction of the Court to deal with the title of land in the decree absolute, which question I do not need to address in this circumstance, the provision simply directs that Mr. Bartlett shall pay to his wife the sum of $3,000 and makes it a condition of his obligation that she convey him her interest in the property in question. He did not pay her the money, make any advance of the money, nor pay the money into Court which would have been a precondition of any right which he had to call upon her for a conveyance of her interest.

At the time of Mrs. Bartlett's demise, she was entitled to a half interest in the property as a tenant in common and her interest passed under the provisions of her will to the applicant Kenneth Knowlton.

[The court then considered the appropriate remedy in these circumstances—see the discussion below.]

Discussion Notes

Severance: Principles of Interpretation and Notice

In *Knowlton*, the court compared the relevant New Brunswick statutory provisions to those in Ontario and concluded that there was no necessary distinction between them. Are there other arguments that might have been made in such a comparison? For similar legislation, see RSPEI 1974, c. R-4, s. 16(2). There appears to be no such legislative provision in Nova Scotia. How would the fact situation in *Knowlton* be resolved in Nova Scotia? Are the policy considerations in *Knowlton* the same as those in *Murdoch v. Barry*? What aspects of the facts of these two cases are significant in relation to these policy issues? Is it relevant at all that the joint tenants are husband and wife?

The issue whether a joint tenant should be able to sever the joint tenancy without notice to other joint tenants remains a matter of debate. A.J. McClean ("Severance of Joint Tenancies" (1979), 57 *Canadian Bar Review* 1, at 38-39) has suggested that joint consent to any severance should be required when the joint tenancy involves a husband and wife and the matrimonial home, having regard to "the expectation of the spouses that the consent of both is needed to change the nature of their interests, and that, without that mutual consent, on the death of one the property will pass to the survivor." McClean suggests that this rule should apply to spouses who are joint tenants, leaving the traditional rules to apply to other joint tenants. On the other hand, if this proposal is regarded as too drastic, McClean has proposed that severance should not occur until other joint tenants have been notified of the proposed transaction, arguing (at 39) that:

Severance may now take place without his [sic] even being informed. This element of secrecy is at the minimum unfair, and may also lead to a suspicion of fraudulent dealing. To require notice would achieve a fair balance between the competing interests of all the joint tenants.

See also *Stonehouse v. AG of British Columbia*, [1962] SCR 103. Assess the merits of these differing proposals. Which is preferable? Why? Note that Saskatchewan is currently the only common law province in Canada with legislation requiring the consent of other joint tenants before a transfer can sever a joint tenancy: see Land Titles Act, RSS 1978, c. L-5, s. 240. Should such a provision be enacted in other common law provinces?

This issue has also been considered by law reform commissions. In Australia, the New South Wales (NSW) Law Reform Commission recommended legislation providing for unilateral severance of a joint tenancy by the registration of a declaration of severance. See NSW Law Reform Commission, *Discussion Paper: Unilateral Severance of a Joint Tenancy* (1991). In British Columbia, BCLRC also reviewed the issue of "secret severance" and proposed new legislation (at 48), providing in part:

> 41(1) Where ownership of land is registered as a joint tenancy, a co-owner's interest may be severed from the joint tenancy only by
>
>   a) registration of a disposition of all of a co-owner's interest to himself or to a third party, that is
>
>   (i) presented for registration before the co-owner's death, or
>
>   (ii) recorded in an instrument [executed in accordance with the Evidence Act] and presented for registration within 5 days of the execution, ...
>
>   b) serving notice to all other co-owners of the land of the joint tenant's decision to sever, whether or not he has entered into a transaction relating to his interest,
>
>   c) the agreement of all co-owners of the land, or
>
>   d) a court order.

Does this proposal meet the needs of joint tenants? The commission considered as well the possibility of a contract among co-owners not to sever the joint tenancy. For a case interpreting s. 240 of the Saskatchewan Land Titles Act, see *R in right of Canada v. Peters*, [1983] 1 WWR 471 (Sask. QB).

Severance and Family Property Statutes

The *Knowlton* case illustrates one aspect of the relationship between traditional principles about severance of joint tenancies and family property statutes. Many of these statutes contain provisions prohibiting "dispositions" of "family" property (especially the matrimonial home) without the consent of the other spouse. Where the matrimonial home is held in joint tenancy, such statutory provisions might thus preclude severance by one spouse without consent of the other. Although this issue has been resolved in different ways, the court in *Horne v. Horne Estate* (1987), 45 RPR 223 (Ont. CA) held that a conveyance by a joint tenant to himself or herself for the purpose of severing a joint tenancy did not constitute a "disposition" for the purposes of the Family Law Reform Act, RSO 1980, c. 152 (FLRA) (now Family Law Act, RSO 1990, c. F.3 (FLA)) provisions. Confirming the earlier decision of the Ontario High Court in *Re Lamanna and Lamanna* (1983), 145 DLR (3d) 117 (Ont. CA), the court stated (at 231-32):

> In light of the scheme of these Acts and their very restricted and carefully defined effect on spousal rights to the matrimonial home after death, I cannot accept that the Legislature intended to include a joint tenant's "right of survivorship" in the class of "interests" in the matrimonial home to which the restrictions against alienation imposed by s. 42 of the FLRA and s. 21 of the FLA are applicable. These Acts do not purport to dictate the manner in which spouses may hold title to their matrimonial home. A severance of a joint tenancy neither interferes with nor affects the existing balance between spouses with respect to the ownership or occupation of their matrimonial home during their marriage. In practical terms, its only consequence is that the spouses' undivided one-half interests thereafter form part of their individual estates thereby permitting them to devise their respective interests as they wish. ...
>
> The right of a joint tenant to sever a joint tenancy unilaterally is a long-recognized common law right. In my opinion, the family law legislation in question ought not be construed as restricting that right in the absence of express language to that effect. As the Acts are now framed, a severance is not inconsistent with the general scheme of the legislation or incompatible with the provisions respecting matrimonial homes. No policy considerations have been advanced which compel the conclusion that a party to a marriage, without the consent of the other party or a court order, should be barred so long as the marriage subsists (and regardless of the state of the marriage) from taking the steps necessary to ensure that this property interest form part of his or her estate and that the survivor, whichever party that might be, does not acquire sole ownership by operation of law. In my view, no matter how the "right of survivorship" may be characterized in law, a deed from a joint tenant to himself or herself designed to remove that right does not constitute the "disposition" of an "interest" covered by s. 42 of the FLRA or s. 21 of the FLA. In sum, I agree with the result reached by Walsh J in *Re Lamanna and Lamanna* in this factual situation.

The Court of Appeal thus disapproved *Re Van Dorp and Van Dorp* (1981), 30 OR (2d) 623, where the court held that the act of severance constituted a "disposition" prohibited by the statute without the other spouse's consent. Do you agree with the result and the reasoning of the Ontario Court of Appeal? What are the policy reasons for treating joint tenants who are spouses the same as other joint tenants, contrary to McClean's recommendations, above? For similar provisions in other provinces, see Marital Property Act SNB 1980, c. M-1.1, s. 19; Family Law Act, RS Nfld. 1990, CF.2, SN 1979, c. 32, ss. 8-9; Matrimonial Property Act, SNS 1980, c. 9, s. 8; and Family Law Reform Act, RSPEI 1988, c. F-3, s. 36.

Rights and Obligations of Co-Owners: General Principles

Whether co-owners are joint tenants or tenants in common, their interests are characterized by unity of possession, the only unity common to both kinds of co-ownership. Unity of possession means that each co-owner is entitled, along with all other co-owners, to possession of the whole of the land. Such a possessory right among all co-owners raises numerous questions about the respective co-owners' rights:

1. What happens if one co-owner remains in possession of a farm, for example, while others leave to work elsewhere?

2. What if one co-owner wrongly excludes others from possession?

3. When are co-owners out of possession entitled to share in profits from the land? What about setoffs for expenses paid by the co-owner in possession?

4. If some co-owners are out of possession voluntarily, are they liable to contribute to the cost of improvements, or entitled to share in the increased value effected by improvements undertaken by the co-owner in possession?

Common law principles provided that a co-owner in possession was required to pay "occupation rent" to co-owners out of possession in three situations:

1. where the co-owner in possession has excluded the other ("ouster")—this concept was extended to "constructive exclusion" in a case where a wife left home because of her husband's continued violence in *Dennis v. McDonald*, [1981] 1 WLR 810 (Fam. Div.);

2. where the co-owners have made an agreement respecting occupation and occupation rent; and

3. where the circumstances require that the co-owner in possession be regarded as agent for the other co-owners.

In addition, the Statute of Anne (1705) 4 Anne c. 16, s. 27 provided that a co-owner was required to account for benefits received as co-owner from third parties but not for benefits that a co-owner achieved through the co-owner's own efforts. The effect of the Statute of Anne is found in Ontario in the Courts of Justice Act, RSO 1990, c. C.43, s. 122(2):

An action for accounting may be brought by a joint tenant or tenant in common ... against a co-tenant for receiving more than the co-tenant's just share.

In *Henderson v. Eason* (1851), 17 QB 701, a former co-owner was not required to share farm profits with absent co-owners who had not been excluded. What should be the result where one co-owner uses the premises as a boarding house, collecting rent from boarders? Should the rent moneys be shared with absent co-owners? See *Spelman v. Spelman*, [1944] 2 DLR 74 (BC CA).

For a case reviewing many of the authorities in the application of these principles, see *Osachuk v. Osachuk* (1971), 18 DLR (3d) 413 (Man. CA), where the court concluded (at 432):

The law, as I have found it, respecting the rights of joint tenants, where one of them is in sole possession of the joint property, appears in some cases to operate unfairly, and some amendment, with proper safeguards, may be desirable. This would be a matter for the Legislature.

In Alberta, the principles for accounting among co-owners have been codified in the Law of Property Act, RSA 1980, c. L-8, s. 17. In a context where many co-owners are husband and wife, there may also be a need to reconsider these traditional principles, having regard to "family" property regimes. Once again, it may be important to decide whether it is appropriate to have the same principles applicable to co-owners who are husband and wife or cohabitees and to those who are not. For example, issues about occupation rent and compensation for improvements were considered in the context of a divorce application in *McColl v. McColl*

(1995), 13 RFL (4th) 449 (Ont. CJ), a three-day trial in which the matrimonial home was the only issue in dispute other than child support. To what extent would legislative principles (such as those in Alberta) help to resolve such disputes?

Termination of Concurrent Interests by Partition and Sale

When co-owners no longer wish to hold concurrent interests as joint tenants or as tenants in common, they may invoke the provisions of the Partition Act, RSO 1990, c. P.4, s. 2, which provides that co-owners "may be compelled to make or suffer partition." This statutory provision permits a court to order the destruction of the co-owners' unity of possession by defining boundaries for entitlement to individual parcels. The former concurrent interest is divided into separate units held as sole proprietary interests. See also Partition Act, RSNS 1989, c. 333. Some provisions concerning partition are also found in the Judicature Act, RSNB 1973, c. J.2 and the Judicature Act, RS Nfld. 1970, c. 187.

One issue in such cases is how a court should choose between ordering partition on one hand or ordering judicial sale and division of the proceeds of sale. Such a problem was addressed in the case that follows, an appeal from an order for partition rather than sale.

Cook v. Johnston
[1970] 2 OR 1 (HCJ)

GRANT J: In this appeal from the Senior Master's report dealing with partition of property jointly owned by the parties, the appellant's contention is that the remedy ought to have been by way of sale rather than partition. Section 3(1) of the *Partition Act*, RSO 1960, c. 287, reads as follows:

> 3(1) Any person interested in land in Ontario, or the guardian appointed by a surrogate court of an infant entitled to the immediate possession of an estate therein, may take proceedings for the partition of such land or for the sale thereof under the directions of the court if such sale is considered by the court to be more advantageous to the parties interested.

In *Morris v. Morris* (1917), 12 OWN 80, Middleton J, in dealing with a similar matter, stated at p. 81: "Sale as an alternative for partition is quite appropriate when a partition cannot be made."

In *Gilbert v. Smith* (1879), 11 Ch.D 78, Jessel MR, at p. 81 stated:

> The meaning of the Legislature was that when you see that the property is of such a character that it cannot be reasonably partitioned, then you are to take it as more beneficial to sell it and divide the money amongst the parties.

In *Lalor v. Lalor* (1883), 9 PR (Ont.) 455, Proudfoot J, who was deciding whether partition or sale should be ordered, stated:

> I do not think any party has a right to insist on a sale; and it will not necessarily be ordered, unless the Court thinks it more advantageous for the parties interested.

In *Ontario Power Co. v. Whattler* (1904), 7 OLR 198, Meredith CJ reviewed the legislation in the Province giving jurisdiction to the Court to order a sale instead of partition. In reference to the form for such remedies then adopted by the Consolidated Rules, he stated at p. 203:

> That form must be read in the light of the legislation by which jurisdiction has been conferred on the Court to order a sale instead of a partition; and the provision as to proceedings being taken for partition or sale is, I think, a compendious mode of saying that proceedings are to be taken to partition unless it appears "that partition cannot be made without prejudice to the owners of, or parties interested in, the estate," but that if that is made to appear proceedings are then to be taken for the sale of the lands.

The evidence taken before the learned Master in this case reveals that there are very few similar islands in the area that are now available. The appellant urged that the island was not of such an area as permitted two families to enjoy the same in separate cottages. The last survey, however, indicates the island is slightly over two acres in area. It is between 500 and 600 ft. in length and probably 150 ft. in width. The Master was quite justified on the evidence in coming to the conclusion, as I think he did, that it was actually more advantageous to the parties to partition the property than take the chances as to what might develop if it was sold. Even if the parties received more than the actual value of the property from a stranger, neither of them could readily find another suitable summer island home in that district. If one of them was successful in buying the property at a sale, the other would be deprived entirely of his right to spend vacations in the area where he had enjoyed summer vacations for some 30 years. As it stands under the Master's report, each of the parties will have the privilege of enjoying one-half for the whole summer of what they formerly enjoyed for only one-half of the summer. Under the report Cook is getting the portion of the island on which the cottage and dock are built. It was never contemplated that Johnston should contribute anything towards the erection of these. He lived in a tent while enjoying his vacation. The area adjoining the suitable swimming portion of the bay is equally divided between the parties. There may have to be some slight alterations made in the path that leads from the dock to the cottage but I cannot think this will be costly.

On the whole, it is my opinion that the division was more advantageous to Cook than to Johnston. I believe the Master has exercised his discretion properly. In any event it should not be interfered with lightly.

The motion by way of appeal will therefore be dismissed with costs, if demanded.

Appeal dismissed.

Where co-owners are or have been husband and wife, the considerations may be more complicated. For several years, there was uncertainty about how judges should respond to an application for partition in such cases: for an analysis, see J.M. Glenn, "Comment" (1976), 54 *Canadian Bar Review* 149.

Some of these concerns were addressed in *Knowlton v. Bartlett*, reviewed above, in which Mrs. Bartlett secretly executed a deed to herself severing the joint tenancy with her husband. She died, leaving her one-half undivided interest as tenant in common to her brother, Kenneth Knowlton. The court then considered Knowlton's application for partition.

Knowlton v. Bartlett
(1984), 35 RPR 182 (NB QB Fam. Div.)

In the present case, the evidence before me indicates that this property as in most cases does not lend itself to partition. There is a residence on the property and some 47 acres of land. Therefore if an order is to be made in this matter, it would only be an order for sale of the property and an apportionment of the proceeds from such sale.

It is argued on behalf of the respondent that I have a discretion as to whether or not to order a sale at this time. Counsel for the respondent cites to me various authorities to this effect. In the case of *Davis v. Davis*, [1954] OR 23, [1954] 1 DLR 827, the Ontario Court of Appeal held that under the legislation then existing in their province there was a right to a partition or sale and that a Court should compel a partition or sale if no sufficient reason appears as to why an order should not be made. Laidlaw JA speaking for the Court at p. 830 [DLR] said:

> I do not attempt to enumerate or describe what reasons would be sufficient to justify refusal of an order for partition or sale. I am content to say that each case must be considered in the light of the particular facts and circumstances and the Court must then exercise the discretion vested in it in a judicial manner having due regard to those particular facts and circumstances as well as to the matters which I have said are, in my opinion, fundamental.

In that particular case, a wife was claiming partition or sale of a dwelling owned by her and her husband as joint tenants. The husband had been awarded custody of the infant children, and was residing in the house. The argument was made on behalf of the husband that this created a ground for hardship and that in any event the wife had a moral and legal duty to support the children and an order for partition or sale should be refused at that time. On the facts in that case the Ontario Court of Appeal held that there was not sufficient reason for refusal of an order for partition or sale.

There are other judgments subsequent to that where Courts applying this principle have found sufficient reasons or grounds to refuse an order at the time of application. In the case of *Re Yale and MacMaster* (1974), 3 OR (2d) 547, 18 CBR (NS) 225 (sub nom. *Yale v. MacMaster*), 18 RFL 27, 46 DLR (3d) 167 at 182 (Ont. HC), Galligan J held that

> ... a consideration of relative hardship is a relevant consideration in determining how a Court ought to exercise the discretion conferred upon it by the Partition Act. ...

In that case the trustee in bankruptcy of the husband was endeavouring to obtain an order for partition or sale of the property in which the wife and minor children were living. The Court in this case dismissed the application at that time, but a subsequent application when the circumstances had changed, i.e. the children were no longer dependent upon the home for shelter, might well have been successful.

This matter came before the Court of Appeal in New Brunswick in the case of *Melvin v. Melvin* (1975), 11 NBR (2d) 351, 23 RFL 17, 58 DLR (3d) 98 (NB CA). In that case the applicant was the former wife of a divorced man. She had deserted her husband and taken the three youngest children to British Columbia where she was living with and being supported by another man. The husband remained at the marital home along with the two older children. The trial Judge found that the plaintiff was not acting in good faith and was endeavouring to deprive her husband of use of the matrimonial home.

The Court of Appeal, in dismissing an appeal from the refusal of the trial Judge to exercise his discretion in ordering a partition or sale, approved the consideration of the relative hardships of the parties involved and held that real hardship would obtain to Mr. Melvin and his children if an order were made. The Court of Appeal judgment was based on the fact that no real hardship would obtain to the mother if this matter were delayed for such time as there remained minor children and observed at that time that in any event the value of interest in real estate was appreciating.

In the case of *Bruce v. Bruce* (1976), 14 NBR (2d) 422, 28 RFL 190, the New Brunswick Court of Appeal postponed the partition and sale of the home which was owned in joint tenancy by a husband and wife until such time as a minor son completed his education or until further order.

In the present case a property is involved which does not lend itself to partition. If the owners cannot agree as to disposition of the property then it can only be done by an order for sale. Prima facie either party to the ownership of property as in this case as tenants in common is entitled ultimately to have the property disposed of and the proceeds realized. The Court has a discretion to postpone the sale of property in these circumstances where it would result in hardship to one particular party.

In the present case, the house and property involved is the home of Mr. Bartlett. The property was originally that of his parents. He has lived in the property since 1946 and continued living there after his wife left in 1971. He still lives on the property and is now 63 years of age. I am satisfied that he planned to live in this property in the foreseeable future and probably the rest of his days.

Mr. Bartlett was apparently not aware of the fact that his wife had severed the joint tenancy in the property. His testimony is that in recent years he had made improvements to the home. These had included replacing the furnace, putting a cement floor in the basement, replacing some floors in the house, shingling of the roof, installing some insulation on one side of the house and rebuilding a rear porch. If I were to order a sale in this matter I would consider the amounts expended by Mr. Bartlett in considering the disposition of the proceeds of such sale: *Mastron v. Cotton*, 58 OLR 251, [1926] 1 DLR 767 (Ont. CA).

Mr. Bartlett has had of course the use and occupation of the premises since his wife left in 1971. On the other hand he has paid the charges against it including taxes and insurance and is taking care of ongoing maintenance. These would be offsetting. Tax bills filed in this matter indicate for example an assessed value of $9,450 in 1974 and an assessed value of $35,200 in 1984. A portion of this increase would be the result of inflation of values, but I feel I am justified in inferring from this increase in assessed value confirmation that the property has been maintained and in fact improved in value during this period of time.

There is no question that if I order a sale of this property at this time a very real hardship will be sustained by Mr. Bartlett at a relatively late stage in his life. No evidence was given by Mr. Knowlton. He resides out of the province. It is not suggested that he would have any particular use for the property but rather that he wishes to realize the value of his legal interest in the property. This is a legitimate desire.

It is open to a Court to exercise discretion with respect to granting or refusing an order for partition or sale. The cases to which I have referred have stated that a Court in exercising this discretion should consider the relative hardship to the parties.

I have considered these matters in the present circumstances. I am satisfied that at this time I should exercise my discretion and decline to order the sale of the property. Should circumstances change, a further application can be made to the Court and quite possibly a sale could be ordered at that time. Without predetermining or indicating what the decision of a Court might be on a future application, matters which might be considered are any failure of Mr. Bartlett to maintain the property at its present standard, or Mr. Bartlett no longer residing on the property or requiring it as his residence. It may well be that circumstances in the future would be such that Mr. Knowlton could satisfy a Court that failure to order the sale of this property is forcing a hardship on him.

This decision is simply that at the present time and in the present circumstances I find that an order for the sale of this property would constitute a very real hardship upon Mr. Bartlett and that I should exercise my discretion in these circumstances and decline to order a partition or sale of the property.

Under the circumstances each party will bear their own costs in this matter.

Application refused.

Courts have also considered the appropriate approach to an application for partition where the application is presented in the course of divorce proceedings that require the resolution of property issues between a husband and wife, now pursuant to "family" property statutes. The Ontario Court of Appeal decided in *Silva v. Silva* (1990), 1 OR (3d) 436 (CA) that the Family Law Act, 1986, RSO 1990, c. F.3 did not oust the jurisdiction of the Partition Act. However, the court concluded that an application under the Partition Act should be deferred where there is evidence that an order for partition would prejudice the rights of either spouse in relation to proceedings under the Family Law Act, 1986. In the circumstances of the *Silva* case, the court found no such prejudice, but the case also confirmed the existence of judicial discretion in such cases. As is evident, therefore, traditional principles regarding concurrent interests may be substantially revised in the "family" property context.

"FAMILY" PROPERTY: A STUDY IN LEGISLATIVE AND JUDICIAL REFORMS

There is a sense in which the law of matrimonial property is concerned, not with property at all, but with human relations and ideologies in respect of property … . [The] law of matrimonial property "comprises a substantial portion of the secular definition of the institution of marriage." The law regulating the spouses' property relations is fundamentally an index of social relations between the sexes, and, for this reason, affords a peculiar wealth of commentary on such matters as the prevailing ideology of marriage, the cultural definition of the marital roles, the social status of the married woman, and the role of the state *vis-à-vis* the family.

(K. Gray, *Reallocation of Property on Divorce* (Abingdon, UK: Professional Books, 1977), at 1, quoting Ontario Law Reform Commission [OLRC], *Report on Family Law, Part IV: Family Property Law* (Toronto: Ministry of the Attorney-General, 1974) (hereafter OLRC, *Family Property Law*), at 2.)

As Gray has explained, the idea of family property offers useful insights about gender relations and property in a social and economic context. Moreover, as was evident in the first part of this chapter on concurrent interests, the traditional principles have been abridged from time to time where the co-owners were husband and wife. Since for practical purposes, many co-owners are spouses or in relationships "tantamount to spousal," it is appropriate to examine the special principles applicable to property relationships in the family context. In looking at "family" property, we focus on selected aspects of spousal entitlement to property at marriage breakdown, most of which now require interpretation of legislative schemes specifically enacted for these purposes. In addition, we also examine judicial principles extending similar kinds of property entitlements to those in "marriage-like" relationships—both opposite-sex and same-sex couples. Finally, the materials examine the situation of First Nations spouses on reserves, and the issues arising from the limited application of provincial legislative schemes to their circumstances.

By contrast with many other areas of property law, the issues of family property illustrate considerable legal change and reform, particularly in the last century or so. Thus, this area is one that has attracted the interest of legal historians and those interested in examining progressive social change movements. More specifically, because reform of family property has tended to coincide with greater equality for wives and other women in spouse-like relationships, this area of law offers an important opportunity to reflect on gender and property, as well as the relationships between private family arrangements and the organization and structure of public life, including paid work. For an interesting analysis, see Wallace Clement and John Myles, "Linking Domestic and Paid Labour: Career Disruptions and Household Obligations," in *Relations of Ruling: Class and Gender in Postindustrial Societies* (Montreal: McGill-Queen's University Press, 1994), at 175:

> People experience class not only as individuals but through households, both *within* the household and *between* the household and the labour market. We say "people" but in fact the experience is specifically gendered. Men tend to be empowered by their households, while women have their powers diminished because of domestic responsibilities.

As you examine the materials that follow, assess the relationships between property and gender in households and in the labour market.

The Historical Background

The classic formulation concerning marriage and property is found in Blackstone's *Commentaries* (vol. I), at 442:

By marriage, the husband and wife are one person in law: that is, the very being or legal existence of the woman is suspended during the marriage, or at least is incorporated and consolidated into that of the husband: under whose wing, protection, and *cover*, she performs everything; and is therefore called in our law-french a *femme-covert* ... and her condition during her marriage is called her *coverture*.

The legal status of a married woman pursuant to the doctrine of coverture was a complex matter relating to many areas of law in addition to property. For an overview in the Canadian context, see M. McCaughan, *The Legal Status of Married Women in Canada* (Scarborough, ON: Carswell, 1977) (hereafter McCaughan); in relation to restrictions on women's personal freedom, see M. Doggett, *Marriage, Wife-Beating and the Law in Victorian England* (London: Weidenfeld and Nicolson, 1992). In relation to property, J. Johnston Jr. has succinctly explained the historical differences between single women and married wives as follows:

[A] *sui juris* single woman, like her male counterpart, was free to own, manage and transfer property; to sue and be sued; and to enjoy the income attributable to her property and personal labor. At the instant she was married, however, her status changed radically:

(1) Her tangible personalty, subject to minor exceptions, instantly became her husband's property [as did personalty acquired by her after the date of the marriage].

(2) She did not lose title to real property formerly held by her solely in fee, but her husband acquired an interest known as *jure uxoris*, entitling him to sole possession and control during the marriage. A fortiori, all income from this realty belonged to the husband, with no duty to account to the wife. His interest was alienable at his discretion and was subject to attachment by his creditors. [After-acquired property was treated in the same way.]

(3) [The husband had a right to an estate, if a child was born, called "curtesy," an arrangement explained later in this chapter.]

(4) After their marriage, all real property transferred to the spouses jointly was held in tenancy by the entirety; while the marriage lasted, the husband was entitled to sole control and enjoyment of this property. At the death of either party, the survivor assumed sole ownership.

(5) During the marriage, the wife could not contract, sue or be sued on her own behalf.

(6) Her husband was entitled to all of her earnings.

(J. Johnston, Jr., "Sex and Property: The Common Law Tradition, the Law School Curriculum, and Developments Toward Equality" (1972), 47 *New York University Law Review* 1033, at 1045-46 (footnotes omitted).)

As Johnston stated, "In short, marriage converted the wife into a legal cipher, or nonperson." He examined in detail a number of differing theoretical explanations for this legal treatment of women and men at marriage. Some commentators have concluded that the legal principle of coverture reflected the biblical teaching that husband and wife become "one flesh," while others have suggested that the principle represented a version of guardianship within marriage. After examining and rejecting these and other explanations, however, Johnston stated (at 1051):

Unfortunately ... a general theory that will fully account for the common law system—and for female acquiescence in it over the years—has not yet been formulated.

In considering the materials that follow, note the kinds of explanations proffered for the treatment of married women in law and the assumptions underlying legislative and judicial reforms.

Dower and Curtesy: Common Law Entitlements

In addition to coverture, the rights of married spouses included dower and curtesy. Although these rights were not the same, they both provided life interests in some of the other spouse's property for a surviving spouse—that is, after the other spouse's death. Both dower and curtesy rights were available in most provinces until quite recently.

A wife's right to dower (not to be confused with "dowry") was technically described by B. Laskin, in *Cases and Notes on Land Law* (Toronto: University of Toronto Press, 1958), at 72:

At common law, whenever a husband became seised (otherwise than as a joint tenant) of an estate of inheritance during coverture[,] which issue of the marriage, if any, could inherit, the wife obtained an inchoate right of dower therein which became consummate on the husband's death survived by his wife. The dower right was a life interest in one-third of such freeholds of inheritance and constituted a clog on the husband's title even in his lifetime.

In practice, the wife's right to dower created problems for conveyancing. Unless the wife joined in barring her right to dower when her husband transferred his interest by deed, a subsequent purchaser's interest would be subject to the wife's dower right. Since the dower right did not attach to an equitable interest, however, conveyances frequently utilized deeds to uses to avoid dower rights (and the inconvenience of having to arrange for a wife to bar her dower), although these arrangements sometimes were fraught with conceptual problems. See, for example, *Freedman v. Mason*, [1956] OR 849 (HCJ), (1957), 9 DLR (2d) 262 (CA) and (1958), 14 DLR (2d) 529 (SCC) and *Re Hazell*, [1925] 3 DLR 661 (Ont. CA). For further details, see G.L. Haskins, "The Development of Common Law Dower" (1948-49), 62 *Harvard Law Review* 42 and OLRC, *Family Property Law*, at 105-49. In most provinces, the wife's right to dower at common law was augmented by statute—for example, see The Dower Act, RSO 1970, c. 135. See also Dower Act, RSNB 1973, c. D-13, repealed by Matrimonial Property Act 1980, c. M-1.1; Dower Act, RSNS 1967, c. 79 and Dower Procedure Act, RSNS 1967, c. 80, both repealed by Matrimonial Property Act, SNS 1989, c. 19; and Dower Act, RSPEI 1974, c. D-17, repealed by Family Law Reform Act, SPEI 1978, c. 6. Dower was abolished in the United Kingdom by the Administration of Estates Act, 1925, c. 23.

There are important historical differences[,] between provinces in eastern Canada (which received English common law, including dower, prior to the 1833 English legislation) and some in western Canada. For an account of the political movement to enact "dower" rights on the prairies in the early 20th century, see M. McCaughan, "Prairie Women and the Struggle for a Dower Law, 1905-1920," in T. Loo and R. McLean, eds., *Historical Perspectives on Law and Society in Canada* (Toronto: Copp Clark Longman, 1994), 306. For an account of modern "homestead" legislation that "replaced" dower in the western provinces, see Ziff, at 167ff.

The husband's right of curtesy was similar to but also different from a wife's dower right. McCaughan has described curtesy as follows:

> Tenancy by the curtesy arose when a man married a woman seised of inheritable estates, that is of lands and tenements in fee-simple or fee-tail, and had by her issue born alive and capable of inheriting such estate: in such a case the husband, on his wife's death, held the lands for his life as tenant by the curtesy of England.

For further details, see McCaughan, at 7.

Equitable Settlements and Statutory Reforms

The common law rights of dower and curtesy, as well as the doctrine of coverture, have existed for many centuries. Dower, for example, was the subject of one article of the Magna Carta in 1215. By the 17th and 18th centuries, the common law doctrine of coverture had been ameliorated to some extent by the use of family trusts or settlements. Prior to marriage, a woman's father could set up a trust, in which the father or the woman's brother would be trustee, so that she could be the beneficial owner of her "separate estate"—that is, the trust property would not pass to her husband on marriage. Although such an arrangement successfully avoided the problems of the common law doctrine of coverture, it was not generally available to women in England unless their families were wealthy and had access to expert advice in drafting such settlements. In Canadian provinces in the 19th century, there was even less access to these equitable arrangements.

By contrast with these equitable responses to the common law doctrine of coverture, there was a significant movement for statutory reform of the law of married women's property in the 19th century both in England and in North America. A number of US states enacted married women's property legislation in the first half of the 19th century, and the first of these statutes in Canada was enacted in New Brunswick in 1851: see An Act To Secure to Married Women Real and Personal Property held in their own Right, SNB 1851, c. 24. Similar legislation was enacted in Ontario in 1859—An Act Respecting Certain Separate Rights of Property of Married Women (1859), 22 Vict., c. 73 (Ontario)—and in Nova Scotia in 1866—An Act for the Protection of Married Women in Certain Cases, SNS 1866, c. 33.

There has been considerable debate recently about the rationale for these statutory reforms. Some historians have argued that the reform statutes frequently resulted from the needs of men involved in commercial activities to "preserve" their homes and other assets from being subject to bankruptcy or other debt-collecting processes. By ensuring that a wife held title to personal holdings (which the reform statutes enabled a husband to do), he could carry on commercial activities without fear of losing everything if these activities proved unsuccessful. In this way, the reform statutes were less the result of a desire to recognize equality for women and more frequently a means of enhancing men's burgeoning commercial activity. For some analyses of the purposes of such statutes in the United States, see N. Basch, *In the Eyes of the Law: Women, Marriage and Property in Nineteenth-Century New York* (Ithaca, NY: Cornell University Press, 1982); P. Rabkin, *Fathers to Daughters: The Legal Foundations of Female Emancipation* (Westport, CT: Greenwood Press, 1980); and Marylynn Salmon, "The Legal Status of Women in Early America: A Reappraisal" (1983), 1 *Law and History Review* 129. In relation to the United Kingdom, see L. Holcombe, *Wives and Property* (Toronto: University of Toronto Press, 1983). See also A. Sachs and J. Hoff Wilson, *Sexism and the Law* (Oxford: M. Robertson, 1978).

The reform statutes in Canada have also been subjected to assessment. According to C. Backhouse, in "Married Women's Property Law in Nineteenth-Century Canada" (1988), 6 *Law and History Review* 211, Canadian statutes fall into three categories. In the first and earliest group of statutes, the objective was to provide emergency relief for wives whose husbands had deserted them and whose well-being depended on their being able to (re)control their assets. Such statutes represented very little encroachment on traditional common law principles. In relation to later legislation, however, Backhouse suggested (at 212) that

> [t]he second wave of legislation can more clearly be characterized as an encroachment on common-law principles. These statutes established "separate estates" on the part of all women, which insulated a married woman's property from her husband and his creditors, but failed to bestow broader dispositive powers. The acts were essentially protective measures, designed to function as a form of debtor-relief in a harsh economic climate.
>
> The legislative leadership that Canada exhibited during the first two-thirds of the nineteenth century had considerably dissipated by the later decades. England passed a statute in 1870 setting the tone for a belated set of Canadian enactments that slowly began to introduce truly egalitarian measures. Ironically in 1868 English legislators had called upon the example of earlier Canadian legislation to assist them with married women's property reform, and then Canadian legislators slavishly copied the resulting 1870 Married Women's Property Act. This third wave of statutes attempted to grant married women control of their earnings, as well as dispositive powers over their separate property. Ambiguous wording and restrictive judicial interpretation necessitated extensive additional enactments to accomplish significant reform, but substantial progress was eventually achieved. By the close of the century, most Canadian wives would be entitled to property rights markedly greater than those held by their sisters in the early nineteenth century.

According to Backhouse, the legislative purposes of these reform statutes were not always implemented in their interpretation by courts, and they may not have served the interests of women in Canada who were active in the process of trying to achieve substantive reform in relation to married women and property. Writing about the Ontario legislation of 1859, and providing an overall assessment of the reform statutes, Backhouse concluded (at 223):

> Feminist initiative seems to have played at least some role here. It is generally assumed that the organized women's movement did not appear in Canada until 1876, but Mary Jane Mossman, examining the genesis for the 1859 act, uncovered [unpublished] records of a series of petitions presented by Elizabeth Dunlop and other women to the Legislative Assembly between 1852 and 1857. The *Globe* published portions of one of

the petitions on 9 January 1857. [For further information, see A. Prentice et al., *Canadian Women: A History* (Toronto: Harcourt, Brace, Jovanovich, 1988), at 174.] The female lobbyists were claiming that by the act of marriage, "a woman ... is instantly deprived of all civil rights." Placing women's property and earnings in the "absolute power" of their husbands "occasion[ed] manifold evils becoming daily more apparent." Although the women argued that the suffering extended "over all classes of society," the lower classes were at particular risk: "[M]uch more unequivocal is the injury sustained by women of the lower classes for whom no [marriage settlements] can be made ... . The law in depriving the mother of all pecuniary resources ... obliges her in short to leave [her children] to the temptations of the street, so fruitful in juvenile crime." The reasoning here combines an interesting blend of women's rights and children's welfare concerns. ...

III. Conclusion

The nineteenth century witnessed a dramatic transformation in the property rights of married women in Canada. From a position of virtual powerlessness in 1800, married women gradually amassed significant control over their real and personal property, wages, and business profits by 1900. The change was initiated by the provincial legislators, who accomplished this reform through three successive waves of married women's property enactments. These statutes seem to have been generated by distinctive and sometimes conflicting goals. Some were motivated by a paternalistic desire to provide women with a limited form of income as an emergency measure when the marriage was no longer functioning. Others expressed protective impulses, in which legislators sought to preserve married women's property from seizure for their husbands' debts. Some were also meant as egalitarian measures, to increase the status of married women with respect to their property. The later legislation seems to have been enacted largely as a form of self-imposed genuflexion on the part of an imitative subservient colony to an imperial power. To the extent that the last wave was viewed as a substantive reform, the goal seems to have been to regularize creditors' rights, by subjecting married women to the same property laws that governed everyone else.

It fell to the judges to determine how to apply these waves of statutory reform. Seemingly in agreement with the motivation of the first statutes, Canadian judges enthusiastically enforced their provisions in a broad and general manner. The second and third waves of legislation met with quite a different fate. Scornful of the legislative goals and palpably concerned about the dangers such reform measures posed for the Canadian family, the majority of judges deliberately embarked upon a campaign of statutory nullification. They consistently refused to grant women the *jus disponendi* over their property. They restricted a married woman's right to contract. They refused to recognize domestic labor as work done for separate wages. They narrowly construed what constituted "separate" property, and what constituted a "separate" business undertaking, giving married men control over the vast bulk of family assets and business ventures.

These rulings were issued within a frame of reference that the judges believed was critical for the maintenance of peaceful and harmonious marital relations. The nineteenth-century Canadian family was never to be viewed as a partnership of equals, where both spouses were permitted to contribute independently to the well-being of the domestic unit. To the contrary, the hierarchical family the judges idealized required that married women be rigorously restricted from exercising control over their property. The autonomy that full married women's property rights would have given Canadian wives was an appalling prospect to nineteenth-century judges. Their beliefs and prejudices about women, property, and the nature of marriage prompted an archly conservative approach. Not until the end of the century would their rulings be supplanted by successive legislative amendments that ultimately put an end to the judicial foot-dragging and catapulted Canadian married women into the modern era.

Formally entitling married women to the same rights over property as men, the law would now appear to be egalitarian and even-handed. Actual access to resources and wealth, of course, would remain markedly skewed in favor of men. Property allocation would continue to be gender-imbalanced despite theoretically equal entitlements. It leaves one to wonder whether the battle to obtain formal property rights for married women, a struggle that engaged so many for so long, was the best choice that feminists of the nineteenth century could make. One is left speculating whether the petitioning women, like Elizabeth Dunlop, would have been satisfied with the outcome of their activism.

In their study of married women's property reforms in Nova Scotia, P. Girard and R. Veinott have suggested that men and women may have generally accepted the common law principles, and that the statutory reforms were necessary only for purposes of the "exceptional" cases when husbands were delinquent in their duties to their families. In "Married Women's Property Law in Nova Scotia, 1850-1910," in J. Guildord and S. Morton, eds., *Separate Spheres: Women's Worlds in the 19th-Century Maritimes* (Fredericton: Acadiensis Press, 1994), 67, Girard and Veinott suggested a different conception of the reform statutes:

> The Nova Scotia experience is worthy of study because of the extent to which reform was propelled for much of the 19th century by conservative rather than liberal conceptions of the family. That this development occurred with the apparent support of Nova Scotia women sits uneasily with much of the existing literature, which tends to assume that a "harsh" common law was distrusted by women yearning for the adoption of separate property. The Nova Scotia experience makes us aware that in some jurisdictions at least, the application of liberal economic principles to family life possessed little appeal for much of the 19th century. Simultaneously, it reveals a perception by contemporaries that the conservative idea of the family, based on familial responsibility rather than individual independence, was capable of being transformed to serve the interests of women and children. Finally, it urges us to reconsider whether an explanatory paradigm based upon a movement from separate spheres to sexual equality adequately captures the dynamic of law reform in this instance.

For another analysis of the legislation in Nova Scotia, see P. Girard, "Married Women's Property, Chancery Abolition, and Insolvency Law: Law Reform in Nova Scotia, 1820-1867," in P. Girard and J. Phillips, eds., *Essays in the History of Canadian Law*, vol. III:

Nova Scotia (Toronto: University of Toronto Press, 1990), 80. As you read the recent cases later in these materials, examine the assumptions they make about the role of statutory reform of married women's property—and the impact of differing approaches on judicial interpretation of modern statutory language.

Property and the Impact of Divorce Reforms

Regardless of the motives for the 19th-century reform statutes, they were generally enacted in Canadian provinces according to the models adopted in England in 1870 and again in 1882. More recently, it has become clear that the right to separate property was not in itself a means of transforming women's access to wealth. In spite of women's rights to hold interests in property, the pattern of husbands being title-holders of family property remained substantially intact. Indeed, women's rights to hold "separate property" conferred a right that relatively few women implemented.

This situation was not really addressed in the legal system until the enactment (for the first time) of federal divorce legislation in Canada in 1968. Thereafter, both federal and provincial law reform commissions began to examine the impact of divorce (rather than death) on married spouses, and in relation to those in similar kinds of relationships. They made recommendations for changes in both property and financial support entitlements. Beginning with Ontario's Family Law Reform Act, now RSO 1980 c. 152, first enacted in 1978, all the common law provinces outside Quebec reformed provincial laws regarding spousal entitlements to property on marriage breakdown. Moreover, Ontario significantly altered its approach only eight years later in 1986 in adopting the Family Law Act, now RSO 1990, c. F.3.

The issue of property entitlement is a complex one as a result of the process of reform over the past two decades and because of differing views about the rationale for these statutory reforms. It is also complex because of the socioeconomic implications of the creation of two economic units after divorce in place of one, with the inevitable need to stretch (sometimes limited or even non-existent) resources among former family members. Throughout the cases in this area, there is also an ongoing debate about the appropriate role for judges and the extent to which they must apply statutory provisions rigidly (to achieve consistency, predictability and uniformity) on the one hand, or to exercise discretion in each case (because "each marriage is different") on the other.

The recent reform developments were significantly influenced by the decision of the Supreme Court of Canada in *Murdoch v. Murdoch*, [1975] 1 SCR 423. The Murdochs married in 1943; Mrs. Murdoch separated from her husband in 1968. At separation, she filed claims for (among other things) financial support, and a declaration that her husband was trustee for her of an undivided one-half interest in property owned by him and in relation to which she claimed that they were "equal partners." At trial, the judge concluded that there was no evidence of partnership and denied her claim to share in the property; he awarded her $200 per month by way of support. The Court of Appeal of Alberta dismissed her appeal.

In the Supreme Court of Canada, Mrs. Murdoch's claim to share in the property was based, not on the idea of partnership, but rather on the doctrine of resulting trust, a doctrine then subject to numerous and sometimes conflicting judgments both in Canada and in the United Kingdom. In an earlier case before the Supreme Court of Canada in 1960 (*Thompson v. Thompson*, [1961] 1 SCR 3), the court had stated its conclusion on the property issue (at 13-14) succinctly:

> [N]o case has yet held that, in the absence of some financial contribution, the wife is entitled to a proprietary interest from the mere fact of marriage and cohabitation and the fact the property in question is the matrimonial home.

On the facts of the *Murdoch* case, therefore, the court concluded that there had been no financial contribution by Mrs. Murdoch that would sustain a declaration of resulting trust. Moreover, the court distinguished the cases in which a non-financial, but nonetheless valuable, contribution had been made by spouses to the acquisition of property because the claims of the non-titled spouses in all of those cases were directed to property interests in matrimonial homes.

In discussing the previous cases, however, Mr. Justice Martland for the majority also reiterated the trial judge's conclusion that the work done by Mrs. Murdoch during the twenty-five years of her marriage was merely "work done by any ranch wife," thereby distinguishing *Murdoch* from earlier cases. It was this characterization of Mrs. Murdoch's contribution that provided the catalyst for reassessing the contribution of women at marriage breakdown, particularly because the majority judgment stood in stark contrast to the dissenting judgment of Mr. Justice Laskin. The latter held that the facts justified a declaration of constructive trust, and also recognized the significant "contribution of physical labour beyond ordinary housekeeping duties" made by Mrs. Murdoch.

Ironically, it was the majority judgment that provided the catalyst for reform, particularly the judicial comment negating her contribution to the farm labour. Most commentators on this case began suggesting the need for immediate legislative action. An editorial in the *Toronto Star*, for example, suggested that the decision was both "a warning to women and a cue to legislators." The article cited the recommendation of the 1970 Royal Commission on the Status of Women in Canada that the law should be amended to recognize "the concept of equal partnership in marriage" and supported law reform efforts to prevent other " 'Irene Murdochs' [from being] left out in the cold with less than $60 a week to show for a quarter-century of labour."

The law reform process at both the federal and provincial levels also reflected public reaction to the outcome of the *Murdoch* decision. The federal Law Reform Commission (LRC) report, issued in 1975, stated pointedly:

> The need for some fundamental reorganization of the existing property laws ... regulating the rights and obligations of family members was underlined in the recent decision of the Supreme Court of Canada in *Murdoch v. Murdoch*. The public reaction to that decision clearly indicates that the existing laws discriminate to the prejudice of the married woman and are no longer acceptable in contemporary society. A property regime must be devised that will promote equality of the sexes before the law.

(Law Reform Commission of Canada, *Studies on Family Property Law* (Ottawa: Information Canada, 1975) (hereafter LRC), at 3.) See also the recommendations in the *Report of the Royal Commission on the Status of Women in Canada* (Ottawa: Information Canada, 1975).

Thus, both public opinion and law reformers were in agreement about the need for reform after *Murdoch*. Turning away from the courts which seemed to hold so little promise for appropriate decision making in this area, they focused attention on legislative reform. As a result, a number of statutes reforming family law were enacted in the common law provinces in the years after the *Murdoch* decision. In the face of widespread enthusiasm for these new statutory reforms, the decision of the Supreme Court of Canada in *Rathwell v. Rathwell*, [1978] 2 SCR 436 was not initially regarded as very significant for divorcing couples, even though it recognized the appropriateness of constructive trusts in this context.

On the other hand, since the statutory reform applied only to married couples at divorce and not to cohabiting couples at separation, the constructive trust doctrine remained useful to cohabiting couples and was adopted by the Supreme Court of Canada in *Pettkus v. Becker*, [1980] 2 SCR 834.

These recent statutory reforms seem to ensure property sharing at divorce as a matter of entitlement based on the existence of the marriage relationship (subject to a few exceptions, including short marriages). By contrast with the right to ongoing spousal support, property entitlement is based on status, rather than need or compensation. In considering the cases that follow, try to identify the relationships between marital status, need, and compensation in relation to the claims of married spouses and cohabitees.

It is also important to note the extent to which recent statutory reforms in common law provinces in Canada have borrowed the traditional civil law concept of "community property" from Quebec. Community property regimes generally create some joint ownership of family assets during marriage. In this context, it is interesting that the LRC's study of family property in 1975 commenced with a long analysis of matrimonial regimes in Canada—see LRC. The influence of the idea of "deferred sharing" (recognition that partners have separate property entitlements during marriage, but a form of community property at divorce) is also evident in the 1989 statute in Quebec: see An Act to amend the Civil Code of Quebec and other legislation in order to favour economic equality between spouses, 1989, SQ, c. 55.

Legislating "Family" Property Reform for Married Spouses After 1968

Provincial legislatures in Canada have enacted reform statutes redefining entitlement to share in family property on the part of married spouses. Some statutes, such as the Nova Scotia Matrimonial Property Act, SNS 1980, c. 9 require the division of property at marriage breakdown, while others, such as Ontario's Family Law Act, 1986, RSO 1990, c. F.3 require that the value of all property held by the spouses be shared at marriage breakdown. In both cases, of course, it is necessary to define what is "property" for purposes of division or for sharing. For example, the Ontario statute defines "property" in general terms in s. 4 as follows:

"[P]roperty" means any interest, present or future, vested or contingent, in real or personal property and includes,
    (a) property over which a spouse has, alone or in conjunction with another person, a power of appointment exercisable in favour of himself or herself,

(b) property disposed of by a spouse but over which the spouse has, alone or in conjunction with another person, a power to revoke the disposition or a power to consume or dispose of the property, and

(c) in the case of a spouse's rights under a pension plan that have vested under clause 20(1)(a) of the *Pension Benefits Act*, the employer's contributions to the spouse's pension.

The statute then provides for the valuation of property interests, the exclusion of some interests (such as gifts from third parties), and the calculation of each spouse's "net family property" after the deduction of debts and liabilities and property (other than a matrimonial home) owned prior to marriage. After calculating each spouse's net family property in this way, it is possible to determine equal shares of the total value of "property" owned by the spouses, and the court can order the payment of a sum of money to "equalize" the spouses' entitlements. As noted above, provincial schemes across Canada all illustrate some form of equal sharing of property at family breakdown. For example, see Matrimonial Property Act, SNS 1980, c. 9; Marital Property Act, SNB 1980, c. M-1.1; Family Law Reform Act, RSPEI 1988, c. F-3; and Family Law Act, RS Nfld. 1990, c. F-2.

All these legislative arrangements require courts to interpret what constitutes "property." One important issue that has been addressed is the question of whether a professional degree held by one spouse constitutes "property" so that it must be valued for purposes of equalization between the spouses. Such claims were made in several cases, especially where a spouse had contributed through financial and other support to the acquisition of the other spouse's degree.

Thus, for example, in *Corless v. Corless* (1987), 5 RFL (3d) 256 (Ont. UFC), a wife claimed that her husband's LLB degree should be valued as "property" at the time of divorce. The couple had met as students and married when the husband had completed his second year of the LLB program at the University of Western Ontario (the wife had just completed her BA). The wife worked as a clerk in a printing company in London to support them while the husband completed his third year. He also worked part time as a carpet seller and then worked for the summer as a research assistant for a professor. When, the husband got an articling position in Brantford, the couple moved there, and the wife quit her job in London to take up a job in the customer relations department of a sporting goods company in Brantford. At the end of the year, the couple moved to Toronto so that the husband could attend the bar admission course. The wife quit her Brantford job and began to work in an employment agency in Toronto. On being called to the bar, the couple moved to Troy (near Brantford), rented (and later purchased) a home, and the husband went to work at the same firm at which he had articled, eventually becoming a partner there. The wife worked selling real estate, and as a bookkeeper, and looked after the three children of the marriage. In 1981, the wife began a company called Canadian Living Accents, which had not shown any profits at the date of separation (after 12 years of marriage) in 1985.

In *Corless*, the court held that the husband's professional degree was property within s. 4 of the FLA, but that it had no value and thus was not included in the calculation of the net family property. (The value of the husband's share in the law partnership was, however, included.) This outcome was different from that in *Keast v.*

Keast (1986), 1 RFL (3d) 401 (Ont. Dist. Ct.), where a wife had put her "mature student" husband through medical school. In *Keast*, the court awarded her extra "compensatory" support, but did not include the medical degree as property. Similarly, in *Linton v. Linton*, 11 RFL (3d) 444 (Ont. HCJ), a Ph.D degree was not included as part of the net family property of the husband even though his wife had supported him financially to enable him to acquire it. In this case, also, the wife was instead awarded substantial and ongoing financial support to recognize her contribution.

By contrast with all these cases, in *Caratun v. Caratun* (1987), 9 RFL (3d) 337 (Ont. HCJ), Madame Justice Van Camp decided that a wife who had supported her husband's acquisition of a degree in dentistry was entitled to a beneficial interest, thereby recognizing a constructive trust. Both *Linton* and then *Caratun* went to the Court of Appeal, where the court held that there was no property in a professional degree. The Court of Appeal's review of the property claim in *Caratun* follows.

Caratun v. Caratun
(1992), 42 RFL (3d) 113 (Ont. CA)

Contribution Towards the Obtaining of Appellant's Dental Licence

The reasons of the trial judge make it quite clear that Dr. Caratun's primary objective in marrying Mrs. Caratun and fathering their child was to assist him in immigrating to North America to practise dentistry. Mrs. Caratun worked extremely hard over a number of years in Israel and in Canada to assist Dr. Caratun in attaining his ultimate objective. Two days after attaining that objective, he rejected Mrs. Caratun as his wife, at a time when family assets were next to non-existent but his future income-earning ability was substantial.

Facts such as these raise difficult legal questions, given the purpose of the FLA, on the one hand, and its specific provisions, on the other. The combining of spousal efforts over a number of years to provide for the education and professional qualification of one spouse is not unusual in our society. The inevitable result, if there is a separation on attaining the joint objective, is that one family member is left with no assets and often very little in the way of educational or professional qualifications with which to sustain herself or himself in the future. The extreme unfairness of the situation is patent, but the possibility of a legal remedy is far from settled law.

Dental Licence as "Property"

Mrs. Caratun's position at trial, which was accepted by the trial judge, was that Dr. Caratun's dental licence is property within the meaning of that word as defined in s. 4(1) of the FLA, of which the relevant portion reads:

> "property" means any interest, present or future, vested or contingent, in real or personal property.

That definition is broadly framed, and includes all conceivable types of property in the traditional common law sense. However, it does not, by its terms, extend the meaning of property beyond those limits. The contrary argument is that in construing that definition one must keep in mind the FLA policy of marriage partnership, which requires, on final separation, the equal division of wealth accumulated during the marriage; and that a licence to practise a particular profession constitutes wealth in the matrimonial context.

Two important cases at the trial level have reached opposite conclusions on this issue—the trial decision in this case and the decision of Killeen LJSC in *Linton v. Linton* (1988), 11 RFL (3d) 444, 29 ETR 14, 64 OR (2d) 18, 49 DLR (4th) 278 (HC). Both decisions include detailed and thoughtful analyses of this issue, and substantial reference to authorities, both Canadian and American. The American decisions are so varied as to be of little assistance. Although all purport to be based on the wording of the particular statute involved, they reach varying results based on statutes with very similar wording.

In determining the issue of whether a professional licence constitutes "property," the cases and the numerous articles written on the subject concentrate primarily on two aspects of the problem: first, the nature or characterization of a licence, and, second, the difficulty of valuing a licence in the family property context.

(i) Characterization of Licence

The broad definition of property in the FLA clearly encompasses many forms of intangibles—a classification into which a licence must fall if it is to be considered property. The common law has never had any difficulty in dealing with property evidenced by pieces of paper representing bundles of rights—such as a share certificate with its attendant rights to dividends, voting privileges, and distribution of assets on corporate dissolution. If a licence to practise a profession is property, what are its attendant rights? Apart from possible benefits, such as the right to join professional groups and clubs—which are not relevant in this context—the only real right conferred on the holder of the licence is a right to work in a particular profession. That right, assuming it is held at the time of separation, is a present right to work in the future, and it will continue for as long as the holder of the right is professionally and personally able to perform the activity involved. It is the nature of the right given by the licence which, in my view, causes insurmountable difficulties in treating such a licence as property for matrimonial purposes. Those difficulties arise, first, because it is not a right which is transferable; second, because it requires the personal efforts of the holder in order to be of any value in the future; and, third, because the only difference between such a licence and any other right to work is in its exclusivity.

(a) Non-Transferability

One of the traditional indicia of property is its inherent transferability. That transferability may, of course, be precluded either by law or by contract. In contrast, the right or licence to practise a particular profession is, by its very nature, a right personal to the holder, incapable of transfer. It is very different in nature from the professional practice which may be built up by the licensee after attaining the licence. The practice itself is clearly capable of transfer for value, although the market is limited to other licensees. Where spouses separate before a practice has been built up, there is nothing available for transfer.

In *Brinkos v. Brinkos* (1989), 20 RFL (3d) 445, 69 OR (2d) 225, 60 DLR (4th) 556, 33 OAC 295, 34 ETR 55 (CA), Carthy JA speaking for this court, discussed the distinction between rights which are inherently inalienable and those which are rendered inalienable either by law or by agreement. At p. 451 he quoted the definition of "property" in *Jowitt's Dictionary of English Law*, 2d ed. by John Burke (London: Sweet & Maxwell, 1977), at p. 1447:

> In its largest sense property signifies things and rights considered as having a money value, especially with reference to transfer or succession, and to their capacity of being injured. Property includes not only ownership, estates, and interests in corporeal things, but also rights such as trade marks, copyrights, patents, and rights *in personam* capable of transfer or transmission, such as debts.

It is clear that many rights or things which are restrained from transfer by law are, by agreement or otherwise, inherently transferable and are of value to their owners. Such rights or things fall within the normal legal definition of property, and would clearly fall within the statutory definition of property in the FLA. However, rights or things which are inherently non-transferable, such as the right to practise a profession, clearly do not constitute property in any traditional sense.

(b) Requirement of Personal Efforts of the Licensee

Under the FLA the types of property included in the statutory definition are very broad-ranging. The definition is in the FLA for the purpose of determining the value of the property to be included in arriving at "net family property" to be equalized under s. 5. I see no way in which that definition can be interpreted to include work to be performed by either spouse in the future. It goes without saying that without the personal efforts of the licensee, the licence will produce nothing. The only provisions in the FLA that allow one spouse to share in the fruits of the other spouse's future labours are the support provisions, which do not form a part of the equalization payment under s. 5.

The policy of the FLA emphasizes principles of partnership during marriage, and self-sufficiency following its termination. When the marriage ends, the partnership ends. Placing a value on future labours of either spouse for purposes of the equalization payment would frustrate those policy objectives.

(c) Right To Work in General

The only difference between a professional licence and the ability and right of any individual to perform a particular type of work is in the exclusive nature of a professional licence. Only those who have successfully survived the rigours of professional training have the right to practise their profession. Nonetheless, the difference between the right to practise a profession and the right to work at any job which requires special skill or knowledge is a right which differs only in scope, but not in substance. A plumber, carpenter, or an electrician spends a substantial period of time in apprenticeship before becoming proficient at his trade; a salesman spends a substantial period of time developing a clientele in order to enhance his income; a business executive may spend a substantial period of time in university and then working his way up the corporate ladder to attain his level of income. Should the law consider all of these attainments as property for the purposes of determining the equalization payment under the FLA? Clearly not. I see no interpretation of the FLA, either specifically under s. 4, or generally, which would allow the court to treat such attainments as property

(ii) Valuation of Licence

It is clear from the considerations referred to above that there are substantial difficulties, both practical and conceptual, in treating licences as "property." In addition, the valuation of such a right would be unfairly speculative in the matrimonial context. A myriad of contingencies, including inclination, probability of success in practice of the profession, length of physical and mental capability to perform the duties of the profession, competition within the profession, and many others, all render a fair valuation of the licence unusually difficult. But a further potential inequity arises: support orders may be varied if circumstances change, but no amendment of an equalization payment is possible regardless of changed circumstances.

The valuation approach approved by the trial judge in this case was to compare the appellant's actual professional income since attaining his dental licence up to September 1986 with the average earnings of an honours university graduate of the same age during the same period. His future professional income from 1986 until his expected retirement age of 65 was determined, based on his actual income level adjusted by the rate of growth of income for dentists according to the American Dental Association. The difference between his projected future earnings and those of honours graduates was valued at an annual discount rate of 2.5 per cent according to the *Rules of Civil Procedure*. Based on this approach, a valuation of the dental licence as of valuation date, July 18, 1981, was found to be $379,965. This valuation did not take into account any of the contingencies of the type referred to above. Another method of valuation, which resulted in the figure of $219,346, was to compare the expected career earnings of the average dentist obtaining his licence in July 1981 and retiring in November 2012, to the average earnings of honours university graduates for the same period.

Either valuation approach is logical, if the licence is "property." However, it would be equally logical to treat a university degree as property, and then value that degree by comparing incomes of university graduates with those of high school graduates. In the matrimonial context, the fallacy lies in treating a licence as property on valuation date, when most of its value depends on the personal labour of the licensed spouse after the termination of the relationship. That future labour does not constitute anything earned or existing at the valuation date.

For all of the above reasons, it is my view that a professional licence does not constitute property within the meaning of s. 4 of the FLA.

Constructive Trust

The trial judge decided that the appellant's dental licence was property within the meaning of s. 4 of the FLA. However, she did not include the value of the licence in the appellant's net family property, but rather decided that the licence would be held by the appellant subject to a constructive trust in favour of the respondent in the amount of $30,000—that amount representing the value of the respondent's contribution to the acquisition of the licence. Given a finding that the licence constituted property, it is my view that the court had no discretion as to whether or not to include its value in net family property under s. 5(1) of the Act.

The finding of constructive trust was based on cases involving circumstances substantially different than those in this case. The two decisions of the Supreme Court of Canada in *Rathwell v. Rathwell*, [1978] 2 SCR 436, 1 RFL (2d) 1, [1978] 2 WWR 101, 1 ETR 307, 83 DLR (3d) 289, and *Becker v. Pettkus*, [1980] 2 SCR 834, 19 RFL (2d) 165, 8 ETR 143, 117 DLR (3d) 257, 34 NR 384, were decided at a time when the relevant statutes of Saskatchewan and of Ontario would not have permitted appropriate recovery to the spouses. Both cases involved real property and other tangible assets which would clearly come within the definition of "property" under the Ontario FLA. Since the enactment of the FLA, cases have applied the constructive trust doctrine for the purpose of allowing a spouse, in appropriate circumstances, to share in the increased value of property from the valuation date until the time of trial. But, again, those cases involve tangible physical assets. The three British Columbia decisions referred to by the trial judge—*Piters v. Piters* (1980), 19 RFL (2d) 217, [1981] 1 WWR 285, 3 Fam. L Rev. 123, 20 BCLR 393 (SC); *Underhill v. Underhill*, 34 RFL (2d) 419, [1983] 5 WWR 481, 45 BCLR 244 (CA); and *Jackh v. Jackh* (1980), 18 RFL (2d) 310, [1981] 1 WWR 481, 22 BCLR 182, 113 DLR (3d) 267 (SC), are all cases dealing with the issue of a proprietary interest in a *professional practice*, as contrasted with the claimed proprietary interest in a *licence to practise*.

The trial judge stated that she did not see "any reason in principle why a professional licence cannot be subject to a similar proprietary interest in the form of a constructive trust" [at 355 RFL]. I agree that if the licence constituted "property," then there is no reason why, in a proper case, that property could not be subject to a constructive trust. However, if the licence does not constitute property, then there is nothing to which the constructive trust could attach. None of the cases relied on by the trial judge in this case assist in establishing that a licence is property to which a constructive trust can attach.

Discussion Notes

Property and Professional Degrees

In examining the reasoning of the Court of Appeal from a property perspective, consider how it resembles the reasoning about "property" in the analysis of Latham CJ in *Victoria Park*, chapter 1. Identify similarities and differences in the approaches of the two courts. What other analysis might have been used in *Caratun*?

This issue whether a degree is "property" has been addressed by a number of courts in Canada and in the United States. In a 1983 decision of the Michigan Court of Appeals, *Woodworth v. Woodworth*, 337 NW 2d 332 (1983), for example, the court envisioned the husband's law degree as a "family asset" to which the wife had contributed. Thus, the court decided (at 337) that she was entitled to realize "her expectation of economic benefit from the career for which the education laid the foundation." As the court stated (at 335):

> [W]hether or not an advanced degree can physically or metaphysically be defined as "property" is beside the point. Courts must instead focus on the most equitable solution in dividing among the respective parties what they have.

The approach of the Michigan court was adopted by courts in other US states and was also reflected in some legislative provisions. In other states, however, courts refused to recognize a professional degree as marital property. For example, see *In re Marriage of Goldstein*, 423 NE 2d 1201 (Ill. App. Ct. 1981). In reviewing the US decisions, Lenore Weitzman concluded that courts there had used three basic approaches:

• a reimbursement of costs (usually including direct out-of-pocket expenses such as tuition, loans, and living expenses, and sometimes such indirect costs as forgone opportunities);

• a sharing in enhanced earning capacity or benefits gained as a result of the professional education (sometimes calculated by subtracting the present value of "pre-education earning capacity and the present value of the costs of education" from the present value of "post-education earning capacity"—the difference is the return on investment to be shared by both spouses); or

• an equivalent opportunity—in a 1975 decision in New York, *Morgan v. Morgan*, 366 NYS 2d 977 (1975), 383 NYS 2d 343 (1976), the trial court ordered a husband (who had been fully supported through college and law school by his wife) to support her attendance at medical school. The Court of Appeal, however, overturned this decision.

See Weitzman, *The Divorce Revolution: The Unexpected Social and Economic Consequences for Women and Children in America* (New York: The Free Press, 1985), at 131-35. To what extent are these three approaches reflected, if at all, in the reasoning of the Court of Appeal in *Caratun*?

Critical Perspectives on Property and Professional Degrees

In addition to fulfilling the expectations of spouses, matrimonial property rules may also reflect invisible economic relationships within households. For example, J. Knetsch has argued that households are organized so as to maximize the overall economic well-being of the family *as a unit*, but without necessarily ensuring that the economic capacity *of each individual* is also maximized. Thus, if and when the unit disappears, some individual family members will benefit more than others, an inequity which matrimonial property rules should redress. More significantly, Knetsch has also suggested that the broader social and economic context constrains the kinds of real choices available to household units in maximizing the unit's well-being, suggesting a role for matrimonial property rules in adjusting inequities between men and women beyond an individual family context.

In examining Knetsch's argument, consider how such an approach would be reflected in a statutory definition of family property.

J. Knetsch, "Some Economic Implications of Matrimonial Property Rules"
(1984), 34 *University of Toronto Law Journal* 263, at 271-75 (footnotes omitted)

Most systems of matrimonial property settlement imply assumptions about how families organize their sharing of opportunities and responsibilities within a household—the division of labour. The current trend, for example, reflects an acknowledgment that household production is clearly valuable and that wives typically have fewer opportunities to acquire assets or, as it has been put: "The cock can feather the nest because he does not have to spend most of his time sitting on it." ...

A major rationale for the traditional organization of families and for various preferences for systems of matrimonial property rules is that the welfare of a family is likely to be maximized through a division of labour that allows for the advantages of specialization. As Posner suggests: "By specializing in production for the market the husband maximizes his money income and thus the market commodities that the family can buy. By specializing in household production the wife maximizes the value of her time as an input into the production of the household's output. The division of labour—the husband working in the job market, the wife in the household—operates to maximize the total real income of the household by enabling husband and wife to specialize in complementary activities."

To the extent that this view of the organization of households is descriptive of the behaviour of families, it suggests a role of individual contributions that is, at least at first blush, compatible with moves towards equality in the allocation of marital assets. It is one that calls attention not only to the economic value of household production but also to the sacrifice that is made by the spouse contributing such services, in the form of forgoing both income opportunities and the maintenance and enhancement of marketable skills. In order to encourage such investment on the part of one spouse some provision is needed to ensure a return in the event of marriage breakdown. The settlement system that recognizes this is then akin to one offering severance pay for the market labour opportunities forgone and the market skill depreciation.

While the specialization rationale may partly explain the organization of households, it may not be fully adequate for the purpose. Institutional and other constraints may seriously distort incentives so that families are encouraged to allocate their efforts in ways that without such restraints would not be optimal for either the individuals or the wider community.

The traditional family organization—a wife producing household inputs and a husband producing money income—may be described as optimum, although there is surely some circularity or tautology in this. Do families organize themselves this way because it is optimal, or is it deemed to be optimal because this is, or has been until recently, the way they organize themselves? In any event, it may well be too easy a presumption to say that this is better than alternative ways of sharing market and household tasks; the benefits of specialization are very easily exaggerated.

Apart from the obvious instance of birth and the less obvious one of infant care, there would seem to be little reason why household production could not be carried out as productively by differing proportional contributions of the husband and wife, or by differing proportions involving purchased services. The fact that the traditional roles are so frequently observed may well have more to do with the biases in the system than to any natural ordering that prescribes this as more efficient.

An important variable that is to some extent, but certainly not wholly, beyond the control of individuals is the socialization process that encourages and discourages given interests and activities on the basis of sex. Men are clearly able to cook and women are equally capable of repairing cars, but on average neither is as likely to do these things as they are the opposite ones. The fact that girls are discouraged from taking physical risks probably has a carry-over effect that results in women being less inclined to take on responsibilities for which they are qualified.

A related bias is that women generally make smaller investments in human capital, particularly in forms useful for wage employment, than do men. Given the other biases and forms of discrimination, such decisions may not be entirely irrational from the point of view of the individual, but these choices may not be allocatively efficient for the community. Further, such decisions provide additional incentives for more families to choose traditional forms of organization.

Tax laws also bias choices. Here, the major incentive comes from the fact that household production is not taxed, thereby increasing the attractiveness to families of producing such services themselves rather than paying for substitutes out of after-tax earnings. The usual provision that if one spouse chooses to participate in the labour force, the other spouse loses the exemption for the "dependent" is a further bias.

The lack of flexibility in the labour market, especially with respect to time, imposes another important constraint on family choices. A couple may well prefer to divide responsibilities so that they share the household chores equally and each works, say, twenty or thirty hours for market wages. Because of the nature of most job offerings, the couple is, as a practical matter, forced to choose between one full-time job of thirty-five to forty hours, and a zero/one split of the household production, or two outside jobs totalling seventy to eighty hours and whatever arrangements they can make on domestic chores.

Another related market deficiency is the generally poor availability of market substitutes for household production. Quite clearly, preferred labour allocation decisions are often frustrated by the lack of satisfactory services, including dependable child care facilities. In part this may be a deficiency in supply response and is probably partially explained by resistance to large-scale provision of, for example, franchised day-care centres. In perhaps larger part, however, it may well be due to a reluctance on the part of potential consumers to pay very much for these services—evidence that many household services may not be worth such sacrifice.

A further and important bias is caused by discrimination against women in a labour market that decreases their wage returns and leads to a greater emphasis on household production than would have been preferred if this restraint did not exist. While such discrimination is, at least in its most overt forms, diminishing, there seems to be little doubt that it has been an influence on decisions—including ones of human capital formation—and that it continues. The extent of discrimination against women in the work force is not easily demonstrated. Comparisons of wage levels between men and women, for example, probably overstate at least some aspects of discrimination, because such figures usually fail to take account of the larger proportion of women in or near entry level as a result of the recent large increase in the participation of women in the labour force.

It also seems likely that there is another form of discrimination that is to some degree self-imposed. Women are more likely to choose lower paying jobs that are located in familiar and secure settings such as offices, stores, schools, and so forth, rather than ones offering higher wages but involving exposure to possible harassment or even physical abuse. There may well be a threshold problem, as no disincentive to choose such situations would be present if large numbers of other women were also around, but as they often are not, there may be a reluctance on the part of individual women to expose themselves to such real or perceived risks. The high drop-out rates of women enrolled in apprenticeship programs in various non-traditional trades are frequently ascribed to harassment from male colleagues rather than discrimination on the part of superiors or in employment opportunities and, again, lead women back to more secure if less monetarily rewarding employment.

The distortions in the incentives facing individual family members most likely result in choices in the division of labour that do not necessarily square with their evaluation of all the relevant values, including the erosion in the money income earning capacity of the spouse who provides household services. Given the biases they might choose a mix that not only gives them less current satisfaction but encourages a non-economic deterioration of skills. One consequence or question that this poses for a system of matrimonial property settlement is which party should bear this cost in the case of divorce. A second, related question is the extent to which a settlement system should reinforce, rather than counter, these distortions by the incentives it provides.

In this context, consider also the criticism of the property analysis in *Caratun* offered by M. McCallum, in "*Caratun v. Caratun*: It Seems That We Are Not All Realists Yet" (1994), 7 *Canadian Journal of Women and the Law* 197, at 205-7 (footnotes omitted):

> The definition of property in the Act is of little help in determining whether a career asset is property, since it suffers from the "horrible circularity" of most definitions of property. Mr. Justice Killeen, when faced with a similar problem in *Linton v. Linton*, said that the court cannot "torture basic personal property concepts" or jettison out of hand the "so-called 'traditional' forms of real and personal property, as established in the common law decisions and earlier statutes" in order to permit a spouse to claim a share in the value of a career asset of the other spouse. Mr. Justice Killeen noted that the definition of property in the *Family Law Act* is indeed broad, but argued that the specific examples of what was included in this definition showed the legislature's intention to "keep manageable and particularized limits on the concept of property. If the legislature had wished to go into terra incognita, or invited the courts to go there, surely the language could and would have been different."
>
> In coming to this conclusion, Mr. Justice Killeen accepted the direction in the *Interpretation Act* to read the *Family Law Act* purposively and with the large and liberal construction necessary to give effect to its obvious remedial purpose. But in his view, a limited reading of the meaning of the word property was appropriate given that the

Family Law Act did not create a full economic partnership, but only a form of partnership, in which the equalization payment permitted "a narrow and deferred sharing of accretions in value to defined spousal properties." Thus, the argument based on statutory interpretation is itself circular.

An alternative approach would recognize that the meaning of property cannot be found in lists of the resources, tangible or intangible, that have been recognized as property in the past. Property is not things or rights, but relationships. Saying "this is my book" is meaningless if there is no one else in the world. "This is my book" describes my relationship not to the book but to other people who might want to use the book, and who will be able to do so only with my permission. So the court, in deciding whether Mr. Caratun's career asset is property, could inquire about the appropriate relationship envisioned by the *Family Law Act* between him and his former wife with respect to sharing in the benefits of his right to practise dentistry, a right that he acquired with her help, although only he could exercise it.

Analogy to Business Partnerships

Could the court in *Caratun* have found any guidance in the handling of similar problems when a business partnership ends? The *Partnerships Act* defines partnership property as "all property and rights and interests in property originally brought into the partnership stock or acquired, whether by purchase or otherwise, on account of the firm, or for the purposes and in the course of the partnership business." On dissolution of a business partnership, the Act provides for distribution of the partnership property, after payment of the firm's debts, in accordance with each partner's share in the partnership. In addition, where one partner pays a premium to another on entering the partnership and the partnership is dissolved before the expiration of its term, the court may order repayment of all or some of the premium, unless, *inter alia* the dissolution is wholly or chiefly due to the misconduct of the partner who paid the premium. If a partnership agreement is rescinded on the ground of fraud or misrepresentation, the party entitled to rescind may claim a lien on or retain the surplus of the partnership assets to recover any sum paid to purchase a share in the partnership and any capital contributed, and may also claim indemnification for all the debts and liabilities of the firm.

It does not require much imagination to put Mrs. Caratun in the place of the wronged partner, who paid a premium to join the partnership, expecting to share in the future profits, but finds out that she has been the victim of fraud and misrepresentation. The *Partnership Act* remedies, however, do not provide for a situation where the premium paid has been in kind rather than in money, and the assets are future profits. Yet courts could interpret the Act as giving one partner a lien on future profits of the other, given that its purpose is to provide a remedy for individuals whose investment plans go awry because they have chosen an untrustworthy partner.

Business partnerships raise similar issues to those in *Caratun* in another context, too: courts have to determine the value of the firm's goodwill in determining who has to pay whom when a partner withdraws or is expelled from the partnership. Goodwill as an asset on a firm's balance sheet is intangible property, and is usually of value only while the firm is an ongoing concern. Often in professional firms, the goodwill comes from the reputations of individual firm members, not from that of the firm itself. A recent article reviewing American case law on the value of professional partnership goodwill concludes that courts value goodwill differently for different purposes. Recognizing that goodwill is really the human capital owned by the partners individually, courts will value it highly if the spouse of a partner, in an action for property division on marriage breakdown, is claiming part of the value of his or her spouse's share in the professional partnership. If the partnership owns few assets, placing a high value on goodwill may be the only way to ensure that the partner's spouse is compensated for a contribution to the partner's ability to earn a good living. If courts can thus adopt a purposive approach to valuing goodwill, why not adopt a similar purposive approach to defining property? Surely such flexibility is within the means of a legal system that accepted a fee simple estate in time-shared condominium resorts, giving absolute ownership of a freehold estate but only for certain weeks every year.

Conclusion

Among the many meanings that one can draw from the result in *Caratun*, one stands out: a woman who sacrifices her own career opportunities in order to improve those of her husband is making a bad investment, unless she is able to obtain the benefits of her husband's career during the marriage. The wave of family law reform following the decision of the Supreme Court of Canada in *Murdoch v. Murdoch* profoundly altered the rights and obligations of spouses within marriage, and enhanced women's property and support rights on marriage breakdown. But the legislation works best for women who least need it, those who have resisted the idea that marriage is a partnership and have provided for themselves.

In the light of McCallum's critique, how could "property" be defined so as to lead to a different outcome in a case like *Caratun*? To what extent would a revised definition in the statute respond to McCallum's concerns? Are these concerns the same as those identified by Knetsch?

In *Caratun*, the Court of Appeal ordered a lump-sum payment of support for Mrs. Caratun of $30,000, having concluded that the husband's degree was not "property." By contrast with the court's unwillingness in Ontario to recognize a professional degree as "property" in *Caratun*, however, the Supreme Court of Canada decided that a spouse's pension constituted "property" under s. 4 of the Nova Scotia Matrimonial Property Act, SNS 1980, c. 9. Unlike s. 4 of the Family Law Act, 1986 in Ontario, the Nova Scotia statute did not expressly include pensions in the definition of sharable property. Even so, the trial court included future pension payments as property for purposes of the Act. The Nova Scotia Court of Appeal overturned the trial court's decision, and the Supreme Court of Canada then allowed the appeal unanimously. Justice Wilson's decision in *Clarke v. Clarke*, [1990] 2 SCR 795 expressly noted (at 811) the importance of pensions as family assets—sometimes the only significant assets—and the inadequacy of support payments in relation to such an asset:

> Discretionary support payments are a wholly inadequate and unacceptable substitute for an entitlement to share in the assets accumulated during the marriage as a result of the combined efforts of the spouses.

Wilson J specifically noted that the problems of valuation should not preclude the characterization of a pension as a matrimonial asset. How should these comments in the Supreme Court of Canada be interpreted in relation to *Caratun*? For further analysis of pensions as family assets, see A. Bissett-Johnson, "Three Problems of Pensions—An Overview" (1990), 6 *Canadian Family Law Quarterly* 137; B. Hovius and T. Youdan, *The Law of Family Property* (Scarborough, ON: Carswell, 1991); and the OLRC, *Report on Pensions as Family Property: Valuation and Division* (Toronto: Ministry of the Attorney-General, 1995).

In relation to these arguments, the American Law Institute has proposed that occupational licences and educational degrees be excluded from division, consistent with its general exclusion as "property" of "spousal earning capacity, spousal skills, and post-dissolution spousal labor." See American Law Institute, *Principles of the Law of Family Dissolution: Analysis and Recommendations* (Tentative Draft no. 1: 1995), at 83ff. The Institute's report also stated (at 84):

> Some cases rejecting property claims on degrees rely entirely on the fact that degrees are not marketable. That explanation sweeps too broadly, however, for nonmarketable assets are routinely and properly treated as marital property. Pension rights, which are typically nontransferable, perhaps provide the most common example. The principle [relied on here] is not marketability and therefore does not exclude property claims on spousal pensions. Pensions differ from degrees because even though pensions are not saleable, market data can establish a value for them that does not include the value of "spousal earning capacity, spousal skills" [etc.].

Do you agree with this analysis? How would such an approach affect the reasoning in *Caratun*, and in *Clarke*?

The Context of Claims to Property in Degrees

As was evident in McCallum's critique of *Caratun*, the outcome of the decision left Mrs. Caratun in a precarious economic situation by contrast with her husband. Part of the pressure to include "new property" in the family law statutory definitions derives from increasing concern about post-divorce rates of poverty, especially for women and children. For example, T. Lemprière, in "A New Look at Poverty" (1992), 16 *Perceptions* 18, quoted the following statistics:

> [T]he end of a marriage or common-law relationship increased the likelihood of poverty substantially. For those who were married and had children, the risk of poverty rose from 3.1 per cent to 37.6 per cent after divorce or separation ... . In 1982-86, the family income of women (adjusted for changes in family size) dropped by an average of about 30 percent in the year after their marriage ended. In contrast, the family income of divorced or separated men rose by an average of 12 per cent.

Are these concerns relevant to the definition and/or interpretation of "property" interests in cases such as *Caratun*? How should they be addressed? See also M.J. Mossman, " 'Running Hard to Stand Still': The Paradox of Family Law Reform" (1994), 17 *Dalhousie Law Journal* 5. For an interesting analysis of the relative wealth of men and women and differences in their respective approaches to the acquisition of property, see C. Rose, "Women and Property: Gaining and Losing Ground" (1992), 78 *Virginia Law Review* 421. Issues about property and poverty are also examined in chapter 8.

Equity and "Family" Property Reform for Cohabitees

Provincial family property statutes focus on the entitlements of married spouses at separation or divorce. The statutory provisions concerning "property" have not applied to cohabiting couples, even though there may be practical circumstances when cohabiting couples make similar kinds of family decisions that may disadvantage individual family members. In these circumstances, principles of equity have been used by courts to achieve goals of equality for cohabitees. In considering these issues, note the court's assumptions abut the acquisition of property in these familial relationships.

Pettkus v. Becker
[1980] 2 SCR 834

DICKSON J (Laskin CJC, Estey, McIntyre, Chouinard, and Lamer JJ concurring): The appellant Lother Pettkus, through toil and thrift, developed over the years a successful bee-keeping business. He now owns two rural Ontario properties, where the business is conducted, and he has the proceeds from the sale, in 1974, of a third property located in the province of Quebec. It is not to his efforts alone, however, that success can be attributed. The respondent Rosa Becker, through her labour and earnings, contributed substantially to the good fortune of the common enterprise. She lived with Mr. Pettkus from 1955 to 1974, save for a separation in 1972. They were never married. When the relationship sundered in late 1974 Miss Becker commenced this action, in which she sought a declaration of entitlement to a one-half interest in the lands and a share in the bee-keeping business.

The Facts

Mr. Pettkus and Miss Becker came to Canada from central Europe separately, as immigrants, in 1954. He had $17 upon arrival. They met in Montreal in 1955. Shortly thereafter, Mr. Pettkus moved in with Miss Becker, on her invitation. She was 30 years old and he was 25. He was earning $75 per week; she was earning $25-$28 per week, later increased to $67 per week.

A short time after they began living together, Miss Becker expressed the desire that they be married. Mr. Pettkus replied that he might consider marriage after they knew each other better. Thereafter, the question of marriage was not raised, though within a few years Mr. Pettkus began to introduce Miss Becker as his wife and to claim her as such for income tax purposes.

From 1955 to 1960 both parties worked for others. Mr. Pettkus supplemented his income by repairing and restoring motor vehicles. Throughout the period Miss Becker paid the rent. She bought the food and clothing and looked after other living expenses.

This enabled Mr. Pettkus to save his entire income, which he regularly deposited in a bank in his name. There was no agreement at any time to share either moneys or property placed in his name. The parties lived frugally. Due to their husbandry and parsimonious life-style, $12,000 had been saved by 1960 and deposited in Mr. Pettkus' bank account.

The two travelled to western Canada in June 1960. Expenses were shared. One of the reasons for the trip was to locate a suitable farm at which to start a bee-keeping business. They spent some time working at a bee-keeper's farm.

They returned to Montreal, however, in the early autumn of 1960. Miss Becker continued to pay the apartment rent out of her income until October 1960. From then until May 1961 Mr. Pettkus paid rent and household expenses, Miss Becker being jobless. In April 1961 she fell sick and required hospitalization.

In April 1961 they decided to buy a farm at Franklin Centre, Quebec, for $5,000. The purchase money came out of the bank account of Mr. Pettkus. Title was taken in his name. The floor and roof of the farmhouse were in need of repair. Miss Becker used her money to purchase flooring materials and she assisted in laying the floor and installing a bathroom.

For about six months during 1961 Miss Becker received unemployment insurance cheques, the proceeds of which were used to defray household expenses. Through two successive winters she lived in Montreal and earned approximately $100 per month as a baby-sitter. These earnings also went toward household expenses.

After purchasing the farm at Franklin Centre the parties established a bee-keeping business. Both worked in the business, making frames for the hives, moving the bees to the orchards of neighbouring farmers in the spring, checking the hives during the summer, bringing in the frames for honey extraction during July and August and the bees for winter storage in autumn. Receipts from sales of honey were handled by Mr. Pettkus; payments for purchases of beehives and equipment were made from his bank account.

The physical participation by Miss Becker in the bee operation continued over a period of about 14 years. She ran the extracting process. She also, for a time, raised a few chickens, pheasants and geese. In 1968, and later, the parties hired others to assist in moving the bees and bringing in the honey. Most of the honey was sold to wholesalers, though Miss Becker sold some door to door.

In August 1971, with a view to expanding the business, a vacant property was purchased in East Hawkesbury, Ontario at a price of $1,300. The purchase moneys were derived from the Franklin Centre honey operation. Funds to complete the purchases were withdrawn from the bank account of Mr. Pettkus. Title to the newly acquired property was taken in his name.

In 1973 a further property was purchased, in West Hawkesbury, Ontario, in the name of Mr. Pettkus. The price was $5,500. The purchase moneys came from the Franklin Centre operation, together with a $1,900 contribution made by Miss Becker, to which I will again later refer. 1973 was a prosperous year, yielding some 65,000 pounds of honey, producing net revenue in excess of $30,000.

In the early 1970s the relationship between the parties began to deteriorate. In 1972 Miss Becker left Mr. Pettkus, allegedly because of mistreatment. She was away for three months. At her departure Mr. Pettkus threw $3,000 on the floor; he told her to take the money, a 1966 Volkswagen, 40 beehives containing bees, and "get lost." The beehives represented less than ten per cent of the total number of hives then in the business.

Soon thereafter Mr. Pettkus asked Miss Becker to return. In January 1973 she agreed, on condition he see a marriage counsellor, make a will in her favour and provide her with $500 per year so long as she stayed with him. It was also agreed that Mr. Pettkus would establish a joint bank account for household expenses, in which receipts from retail sales of honey would be deposited. Miss Becker returned; she brought back the car and $1,900 remaining out of the $3,000 she had earlier received. The $1,900 was deposited in Mr. Pettkus' account. She also brought the 40 beehives, but the bees had died in the interim.

In February 1974 the parties moved into a house on the West Hawkesbury property, built in part by them and in part by contractors. The money needed for construction came from the honey business, with minimal purchases of materials by Miss Becker.

The relationship continued to deteriorate and on 4th October 1974 Miss Becker again left, this time permanently, after an incident in which she alleged that she had been beaten and otherwise abused. She took the car and approximately $2,600 in cash, from honey sales. Shortly thereafter the present action was launched.

At trial Miss Becker was awarded 400 beehives, without bees, together with $1,500, representing earnings from those hives for 1973 and 1974.

The Ontario Court of Appeal varied the judgment at trial by awarding Miss Becker a one-half interest in the lands owned by Mr. Pettkus and in the bee-keeping business. ...

[Chief Justice Dickson first considered the doctrine of resulting trust, suggesting that this case offered "an opportunity to clarify the equivocal state in which the law of matrimonial property was left following [the SCC decision in] Rathwell."

To establish a resulting trust, it is necessary to show that there was a "common intention" on the part of the title holder as well as the claimant that the property would be shared. After reviewing the cases and some of the academic literature which showed the artificiality of such a concept in the family context, Dickson CJ noted that the trial judge had found, as a fact, at trial that there was no common intention in this case on the basis of Mr. Pettkus' testimony.

He continued:]

In the view of the Ontario Court of Appeal, speaking through Wilson JA, the trial judge vastly underrated the contribution made by Miss Becker over the years. She had made possible the acquisition of the Franklin Centre property and she had worked side by side with him for 14 years, building up the bee-keeping operation.

The trial judge held there was no common intention, either express or implied. It is important to note that the Ontario Court of Appeal did not overrule that finding.

I am not prepared to infer, or presume, common intention when the trial judge has made an explicit finding to the contrary and the appellate court has not disturbed the finding. Accordingly, I am of the view that Miss Becker's claim grounded upon resulting trust must fail. If she is to succeed at all, constructive trust emerges as the sole juridical foundation for her claim.

III

Constructive Trust

The principle of unjust enrichment lies at the heart of the constructive trust. "Unjust enrichment" has played a role in Anglo-American legal writing for centuries. Lord Mansfield, in the case of *Moses v. MacFerlan* (1760), 2 Burr. 1005, 97 ER 676, put the matter in these words: "[T]he gist of this kind of action is that the defendant, upon the circumstances of the case, is obliged by the ties of natural justice and equity to refund the money." It would be undesirable, and indeed impossible, to attempt to define all the circumstances in which an unjust enrichment might arise. (See A.W. Scott, "Constructive Trusts" (1955), 71 LQR 39; Leonard Pollock, "Matrimonial Property and Trusts: The Situation from Murdoch to Rathwell" (1978), 16 Alta. Law Rev. 357.) The great advantage of ancient principles of equity is their flexibility: the judiciary is thus able to shape these malleable principles so as to accommodate the changing needs and mores of society, in order to achieve justice. The constructive trust has proven to be a useful tool in the judicial armoury. See *Babrociak v. Babrociak* (1978), 52 DLR (3d) 146 (NS CA); *Douglas v. Guar. Trust Co.* (1978), 8 RFL (2d) 98 (Ont. HC); [and] *Armstrong v. Armstrong* (1978), 22 OR (2d) 223, 93 DLR (3d) 128 (Ont. HC).

How then does one approach the question of unjust enrichment in matrimonial causes? In *Rathwell* I ventured to suggest there are three requirements to be satisfied before an unjust enrichment can be said to exist: an enrichment, a corresponding deprivation and absence of any juristic reason for the enrichment. This approach, it seems to me, is supported by general principles of equity that have been fashioned by the courts for centuries, though, admittedly, not in the context of matrimonial property controversies.

The common law has never been willing to compensate a plaintiff on the sole basis that his actions have benefited another. Lord Halsbury scotched this heresy in the case of *Ruabon SS. Co. Ltd. v. London Assce.*, [1900] AC 6 (HL) with these words, at p. 10: "I cannot understand how it can be asserted that it is part of the common law that where one person gets some advantage from the act of another a right of contribution towards the expense from that act arises on behalf of the person who has done it." Lord Macnaughten, in the same case, put it this way, at p. 15: "There is no principle of law that a person should contribute to an outlay merely because he has derived a benefit from it." It is not enough for the court simply to determine that one spouse has benefited at the hands of another and then to require restitution. It must, in addition, be evident that the retention of the benefit would be "unjust" in the circumstances of the case.

Miss Becker supported Mr. Pettkus for five years. She then worked on the farm for about 14 years. The compelling inference from the facts is that she believed she had some interest in the farm and that that expectation was reasonable in the circumstances. Mr. Pettkus would seem to have recognized in Miss Becker some property interest, through the payment to her of compensation, however modest. There is no evidence to indicate that he ever informed her that all her work performed over the 19 years was being performed on a gratuitous basis. He freely accepted the benefits conferred upon him through her financial support and her labour.

On these facts, the first two requirements laid down in *Rathwell* have clearly been satisfied: Mr. Pettkus has had the benefit of 19 years of unpaid labour, while Miss

Becker has received little or nothing in return. As for the third requirement, I hold that where one person in a relationship tantamount to spousal prejudices herself in the reasonable expectation of receiving an interest in property and the other person in the relationship freely accepts benefits conferred by the first person in circumstances where he knows or ought to have known of that reasonable expectation, it would be unjust to allow the recipient of the benefit to retain it.

I conclude, consonant with the judgment of the Court of Appeal, that this is a case for the application of constructive trust. As Wilson JA noted [at RFL 348]: "The parties lived together as husband and wife although unmarried, for almost 20 years, during which period she not only made possible the acquisition of their first property in Franklin Centre by supporting them both exclusively from her income during 'the lean years,' but worked side by side with him for 14 years building up the bee-keeping operation which was their main source of livelihood."

Wilson JA had no difficulty in finding that a constructive trust arose in favour of the respondent by virtue of "joint effort" and "team work," as a result of which Mr. Pettkus was able to acquire the Franklin Centre property, and subsequently the East Hawkesbury and West Hawkesbury properties. The Ontario Court of Appeal imposed the constructive trust in the interests of justice and, with respect, I would do the same.

IV

The "Common Law" Relationship

One question which must be addressed is whether a constructive trust can be established having regard to what is frequently, and euphemistically, referred to as a "common law" relationship. The purpose of constructive trust is to redress situations which would otherwise denote unjust enrichment. In principle, there is no reason not to apply the doctrine to common law relationships. It is worth noting that counsel for Mr. Pettkus, and I think correctly, did not, in this court, raise the common law relationship in defence of the claim of Miss Becker, otherwise than by reference to the *Family Law Reform Act,* 1978 (Ont.), c. 2.

Courts in other jurisdictions have not regarded the absence of a marital bond as any problem. See *Cooke v. Head*, [1972] 1 WLR 518, [1972] 2 All ER 38; *Eves v. Eves*, [1975] 1 WLR 1338, [1975] 3 All ER 768; *Re Spears, supra*; and, in the United States, *Marvin v. Marvin* (1976), 557 P (2d) 106 and a comment thereon, (1977) 90 Harv. LR 1708. In *Marvin* the Supreme Court of California stated that constructive trust was available to give effect to the reasonable expectations of the parties, and to the notion that unmarried cohabitants intend to deal fairly with each other.

I see no basis for any distinction, in dividing property and assets, between marital relationships and those more informal relationships which subsist for a lengthy period. This was not an economic partnership, nor a mere business relationship, nor a casual encounter. Mr. Pettkus and Miss Becker lived as man and wife for almost 20 years. Their lives and their economic well-being were fully integrated. The equitable principle on which the remedy of constructive trust rests is broad and general; its purpose is to prevent unjust enrichment in whatever circumstances it occurs.

In recent years, there has been much statutory reform in the area of family law and matrimonial property. Counsel for Mr. Pettkus correctly points out that the *Family Law Reform Act* of Ontario, enacted after the present litigation was initiated, does not extend the presumption of equal sharing, which now applies between married persons, to common law spouses. The argument is made that the courts should not develop equitable remedies that are "contrary to current legislative intent." The rejoinder is that legislation was unnecessary to cover these facts, for a remedy was always available in equity for property division between unmarried individuals contributing to the acquisition of assets. The effect of the legislation is to divide "family assets" equally, regardless of contribution, as a matter of course. The court is not here creating a presumption of equal shares. There is a great difference between directing that there be equal shares for common law spouses and awarding Miss Becker a share equivalent to the money or money's worth she contributed over some 19 years. ...

VI

Causal Connection

The matter of "causal connection" was also raised in defence of Miss Becker's claim, but does not present any great difficulty. There is a clear link between the contribution and the disputed assets. The contribution of Miss Becker was such as enabled, or assisted in enabling, Mr. Pettkus to acquire the assets in contention. For the unjust enrichment principle to apply it is obvious that some connection must be shown between the acquisition of property and corresponding deprivation. On the facts of this case, that test was met. The indirect contribution of money and the direct contribution of labour is clearly linked to the acquisition of property, the beneficial ownership of which is in dispute. Miss Becker indirectly contributed to the acquisition of the Franklin Centre farm by making possible an accelerated rate of saving by Mr. Pettkus. The question is really an issue of fact: Was her contribution sufficiently substantial and direct as to entitle her to a portion of the profits realized upon sale of the Franklin Centre property and to an interest in the Hawkesbury properties and the bee-keeping business? The Ontario Court of Appeal answered this question in the affirmative, and I would agree.

VII

Respective Proportions

Although equity is said to favour equality, as stated in *Rathwell*, it is not every contribution which will entitle a spouse to a one-half interest in the property. The extent of the interest must be proportionate to the contribution, direct or indirect, of the claimant. Where the contributions are unequal, the shares will be unequal.

It could be argued that Mr. Pettkus contributed somewhat more to the material fortunes of the joint enterprise than Miss Becker but it must be recognized that each started with nothing; each worked continuously, unremittingly and sedulously in the joint effort. Physically, Miss Becker pulled her fair share of the load: weighing only 87 pounds, she assisted in moving hives weighing 80 pounds. Any difference in quality or quantum of contribution was small. The Ontario Court of Appeal in its discretion favoured an even division and I would not alter that disposition, other than to note that in any accounting regard should be had to the $2,600 and the car, which Miss Becker received on separation in 1974.

Appeal dismissed

[Ritchie, Martland, and Beetz JJ agreed with the conclusion of Dickson J, but for "substantially different" reasons. Ritchie J reviewed the cases concerning resulting trusts and the reasons of the Court of Appeal and decided (at 860) that

> the advances made by [Becker] throughout the period of the relationship between the parties [were] such as to support the existence of a resulting trust which is governed by the legal principles adopted by the majority of this court in [*Murdoch* and *Rathwell*].

Ritchie J expressly held that Becker had made a financial contribution and that there was a common intention that it be used for the benefit of both parties.

Martland J (Beetz J concurring) similarly concluded that the case could be resolved using the doctrine of resulting trust. After reviewing the idea of constructive trust in Anglo-Canadian law, he concluded (at 859) that

> the adoption of this concept [of constructive trust] involves an extension of the law as so far determined in this court. Such an extension is, in my view, undesirable. It would clothe judges with a very wide power to apply what has been described as "palm tree justice" without the benefit of any guidelines. By what test is a judge to determine what constitutes unjust enrichment? The only test would be his individual perception of what he considered to be unjust.]

Discussion Notes

Defining Contribution: Household Work

As this case demonstrates, the Supreme Court of Canada applied the reasoning of its earlier decision in *Rathwell v. Rathwell*, [1978] 2 SCR 436 (a case concerning property entitlement at divorce for married spouses) to the situation of a cohabiting couple. Even though the provincial legislature had excluded cohabitees from the application of its family property regime, the court decided that there was "no bar to the availability of an equitable remedy in the present circumstances." What is the fundamental basis for the remedy provided in *Pettkus v. Becker*? How significant to the court's reasoning is the relationship between the parties, a relationship described in the judgment in the lower courts as "tantamount to spousal"? What factors are relevant to the conclusion in the Supreme Court of Canada that "Mr. Pettkus and Miss Becker lived as man and wife for almost 20 years"?

In some later cases, there were suggestions that a constructive trust would be awarded only where the non-titled spouse had performed exceptional work, especially work outside the home. In *Georg v. Hassanali* (1989), 18 RFL (3d) 225 (Ont. HCJ), the woman cohabitee did most of the work of running a 183-suite apartment building in

Scarborough for 10 years, including responding to service requests for tenants (plumbing and electrical problems, broken windows, etc.). The apartment was owned by the male cohabitee who eventually ended this cohabiting relationship when he married someone else. In this case, the court concluded that the test for unjust enrichment in *Pettkus v. Becker* had been met. By contrast, in *Stanish v. Parasz* (1989) 23 RFL (3d) 207 (Man. QB [Fam. Div.]), where the woman cohabitee provided only household labour and child care, while the male cohabitee worked at paid employment and provided for the couple's financial needs, the court concluded that each of the parties had received some compensation for their efforts, and there was no "unjust" enrichment.

This issue was addressed again in the Supreme Court of Canada in *Peter v. Beblow*, [1993] 1 SCR 980. In this case, Ms. Peter sought an order declaring a constructive trust in relation to "family" assets at the end of a 12-year "common law" relationship with Mr. Beblow in British Columbia. She had done all of the domestic work, looked after the children, worked part time and paid some of the costs of groceries and household supplies.

The trial court in British Columbia allowed the action, concluding that there was an enrichment, a corresponding deprivation, and the lack of any juristic reason for the enrichment. The BC Court of Appeal allowed an appeal, concluding that there was an unjust enrichment, but no corresponding deprivation and no causal link to the property. On appeal to the Supreme Court of Canada, a unanimous court allowed the appeal, with judgments by Madam Justice McLachlin (for La Forest, Sopinka, and Iacobucci JJ) and by Mr. Justice Cory (for L'Heureux-Dubé and Gonthier JJ). In part of her judgment (at 992), Madam Justice McLachlin addressed the argument that

> some types of services in some types of relationships should not be recognized as supporting legal claims for policy reasons. More particularly, [the argument is that] homemaking and childcare services should not, in a marital or quasi-marital relationship, be viewed as giving rise to equitable claims against the other spouse.

After reviewing legal principles and academic literature, she concluded (at 993) that "this argument is no longer tenable in Canada, either from the point of view of logic or authority ... . The notion, moreover, is a pernicious one that systematically devalues the contributions which women tend to make to the family economy."

Is it appropriate to conclude after *Peter v. Beblow* that household labour performed in a cohabiting relationship will result in the award of a constructive trust? For further analysis of this issue, see *Nowell v. Town Estate* (1994), 5 RFL (4th) 353 (Ont. CJ); *Pelican v. Karpiel* (1994), 20 OR (3d) 659 (CA) (leave to appeal to the SCC denied); and *Mariano v. Manchisi* (1994), 8 RFL (4th) 7 (Ont. CJ).

Subsequent Refinements of the Constructive Trust

The award of a constructive trust in these cases also raised other issues. In *Sorochan v. Sorochan*, [1986] 2 SCR 38, for example, the Supreme Court of Canada held that a trust could be awarded where the non-titled cohabitee had contributed to the maintenance of property already owned by the other cohabitee (thus, not requiring a contribution to the "acquisition" of property). There have also been different approaches to the "causal

connection" between the contribution of the non-titled cohabitee and the property interests to be made subject to an award of a constructive trust, an issue addressed at some
length in *Peter v. Beblow*. As well, this case focused on the issue of whether a constructive trust is required once there is a finding of unjust enrichment, or whether money
damages must first be shown to be an inadequate remedy. On this question, McLachlin J
and Cory J expressed somewhat different views even though they concurred in the outcome. These differing views were discussed in an earlier case in relation to the appropriateness of a constructive trust being awarded to married spouses in the process of
defining shares under the statutory "family" property regime: see *Rawluk v. Rawluk*,
[1990] 1 SCR 70. See also R. Scane, "Relationships 'Tantamount to Spousal,' Unjust
Enrichment, and Constructive Trusts" (1991), 70 *Canadian Bar Review* 260.

Same-Sex Cohabitees and Constructive Trusts

The constructive trust has also been used in the context of cohabiting relationships
involving same-sex couples. In *Anderson v. Luoma* (1986), 50 RFL (2d) 127 (BS SC), a
lesbian couple separated after 10 years. One partner had borne two children by means of
artificial insemination and had provided the bulk of the work in the home, including
childcare, while the partner with title to the property had engaged in paid work outside
the home. The court provided an exhaustive analysis of the legal principles, concluding
that the couple were not entitled to statutory remedies under the "family" property
regime because they were a same-sex couple. However, the court awarded a constructive
trust in relation to some property owned by the titled spouse.

In a recent report, the OLRC has recommended the extension of the "family" property regime of the Family Law Act, 1986 to all heterosexual cohabitees and to same-sex
cohabitees if they are registered as "registered domestic partners," an arrangement proposed by the report. This recommendation means that heterosexual cohabitees, and same-
sex cohabitees who are registered domestic partners, would have the same entitlement to
family property arrangements now available to married spouses under the statute. What
are the advantages and disadvantages of such a proposal? In a companion report, the
OLRC has also recommended the elimination of constructive trusts for those entitled to
the statutory regime. See OLRC, *Report on Family Property Law* (Toronto: Ministry of
the Attorney-General, 1993) and *Report on the Rights and Responsibilities of Cohabitants
under the Family Law Act* (Toronto: Ministry of the Attorney-General, 1993).

Problems of Enforcement in Pettkus v. Becker

Although the decision in *Pettkus v. Becker* appeared to provide Rosa Becker with a
beneficial interest in one-half of the property held by her partner, subsequent newspaper
reports indicated that there were problems in the enforcement of the judgment. On
November 13, 1986, the *Globe and Mail* reported that:

> After fighting in vain for six years to gain the fruits of a landmark 1980 court case—
> which awarded her a half-interest in her former common-law husband's bee farm—Rosa
> Becker shot herself in the forehead. She had been working in Franklin Centre, Quebec
> as a $60-a-week housekeeper. At her bedside, Miss Becker left several letters, written in

German, in which she described her death as a protest against a legal system that prevented her from seeing a penny of a Supreme Court of Canada award worth about $150,000.

The report further explained that a part of Pettkus's property was ordered to be sold in 1984 to comply with the decision of the Supreme Court of Canada, but the total amount ($68,000) went to pay the legal fees of Becker's lawyer. In a further report on May 26, 1989, the *Globe and Mail* indicated that the sum of $13,000 was paid to the trustees of Becker's estate, an amount agreed to by them and Pettkus as a financial settlement of her claims. These reports illustrate the need, perhaps especially in the family property context, to appreciate that a court's decision may sometimes be difficult to enforce in practice. Thus, even though *Pettkus v. Becker* may have established important principles about the use of the constructive trust, the "successful" litigant did not benefit from the decision in any material way. Although this problem is one that has ramifications far beyond the instant case, it is salutary to remember the "hidden" limits of judicial decision making, reported cases, and law school casebooks.

In September 1996, the *Lawyers Weekly* reported on a successful appeal by an artist living in Van Kleek Hill, Ontario, in relation to an action for libel initiated by L. Pettkus, as a result of a letter to a newspaper written by the artist, along with a painting he advertised as "Homage to Rosa Becker." Rey J, in the Divisional Court, held that the artist's statements did not constitute a libel. See *Cartwright v. Pettkus* (unreported: July 10, 1996).

The Limits of "Family" Property Reform: First Nations Communities

In 1986, the Supreme Court of Canada considered two cases on appeal from British Columbia concerning the legal interests of aboriginal women in matrimonial property on an "Indian reserve"—*Derrickson v. Derrickson*, [1986] 1 SCR 285 and *Paul v. Paul*, [1986] 1 SCR 306. In both cases, the court concluded that the statutory family property regime in British Columbia was not applicable because of the constitutional division of powers in Canada—that is, because of the federal Indian Act, which comprehensively regulates the lives of "Indian" peoples. In *Derrickson*, Rose Derrickson had petitioned for divorce and a division of family assets, including the matrimonial home located on the Westbank Reserve, for which her husband held a certificate of possession. In *Paul*, Pauline Paul had requested an order for exclusive occupancy of the matrimonial home, also on reserve land, under the BC Family Relations Act so as to avoid continuing violence on the part of her spouse, who held the certificate of possession.

M.E. Turpel criticized these decisions, because they represent the imposition of an alien political and legal culture on indigenous practices and institutions. In examining her arguments, consider the need to take account of the context in defining "family" property rights.

M.E. Turpel, "Home/Land"
(1991), 10 *Canadian Journal of Family Law* 17, at 21

I want to explore the colonial character of Canadian law and its capacity to silence aboriginal peoples through an analysis of two Supreme Court of Canada decisions,

Derrickson v. Derrickson and *Paul v. Paul*. Both considered the legal interests of aboriginal women in matrimonial property on an "Indian reserve." I chose these cases for two reasons. First, they illustrate the formalist stream of discourse in the colonial legal framework as it affects aboriginal peoples. As such, they make interesting study of the hegemonic character of Canadian law over aboriginal peoples. Secondly, these two cases invite analysis because they bring to light the violence inflicted upon aboriginal peoples in a colonial legal (and political) regime where there is little scope for the construction of an aboriginal vision of social and political relationships. The intermingling of several key factors in *Derrickson* and *Paul*—women, property and violence—facilitates an appreciation not only of the law's (in)capacity to situate aboriginal disputes in a social, political or cultural context, but also the price aboriginal people (in this case, aboriginal women) pay as a consequence of their subjugation to a colonial regime. ...

A brief explanation of the system of land holding for Indians pursuant to the federal *Indian Act* is required to provide the colonial history to the conflicts which arose in *Derrickson* and *Paul*. The *Indian Act* provides for a system of assignment of reserve lands to members of the reserves by band councils, municipal-style institutions also created by the *Act*. Final authorization for any assignment of land rests with the Minister of Indian Affairs. A band council allots a parcel of reserve land to an individual band member and this allotment is then approved by the Minister of Indian Affairs, at which time a "certificate of possession" for the land may be issued as proof of the band member's right to possession. For nearly a century before the 1951 amendments to the *Indian Act*, land holding on reserves was regulated by location tickets which were converted to certificates of possession. Alongside the issuance of certificates of possession are "certificates of occupation." These are issued for a period of two years in cases where ministerial approval for possession was denied. The Department of Indian Affairs maintains a "Reserve Land Register" on which the particulars of every certificate of possession or land allotment are recorded.

The system regulating Indian land allotments is not uniform across Canada. Some bands retained customary systems of land allotment and, while these are not expressly contemplated in the *Indian Act*, they have been recognized and continue to be followed. Under these systems, certificates are not issued and land holding is based on kinship and genealogy consonant with tribal practice. The provisions of the *Act* govern nearly all of the 633 bands in Canada. The system of land holding it decrees is a colonialist scheme designed for the complete regulation of Indian life in order to facilitate "orderly" Canadian settlement and the "protection" of the Indians. It was not devised in consultation with aboriginal peoples, nor does it coincide with any traditional practices. No tribe issued papers to its members to confirm possessory title: in close-knit tribal communities, everybody knows where each family lives, hunts or gathers food.

Alongside massive dispossession of aboriginal homelands, both through outright confiscation and breach of treaty, these colonial bureaucratic structures were imposed on a large number of aboriginal peoples (not the Métis or Inuit). In addition, elections, land surveys and allotments, criteria for membership and other administrative structures were established by the *Act* while traditional practices such as potlatches, longhouses and customary law were outlawed as offensive and anti-Christian. The certificate of possession system is part of the colonial effort to displace tribal structures, to confiscate tribal lands and to integrate Indians into Canadian society.

No Indian individual can own reserve lands in fee simple as reserve lands are set aside for the benefit of the band as a whole under the *Indian Act*. To some extent this might seem laudable as it fortuitously coincides with aboriginal beliefs regarding the land. Although varied by tribe, an all-sustaining relationship with the land is the foundation of a spiritual conception of social life for aboriginal peoples. This is based upon a non-exploitative protectorship or trusteeship of the earth in which land is not "owned," but shared and protected. Canadian law has yet to categorize this relation, or fully recognize its legitimacy as a distinct cultural conception, different but no less legally-significant than Anglo-European conceptions of property which have been imposed upon aboriginal peoples. The possessory nature of individual interests in reserve lands and the registration system is, of course, a convenient component of bureaucratic regulation as it ensures that the Department of Indian Affairs can keep tabs on every allotment in nearly every Indian community, while retaining final say on all of it.

The legal question framed in *Derrickson* (and *Paul*) was whether a partition of reserve lands under provincial family legislation would be an encroachment on the federal authority granted in the *Constitution Act, 1867*. This is a classic question of who does what in a colonial administration. In other words, is it up to the federal or provincial government to control Indians? The framing of the question focuses the issue into a division of powers conflict and erases the social and political context for the dispute. The basic issue of why the dispute is one of division of colonial powers over Indian lands and not a matter of aboriginal custom regarding family breakdown and land consequences upon breakdown is lost on all courts. The fact that it is never raised attests to the inability of colonial Canadian law to be anything but self-perpetuating. ...

C. The Supreme Court of Canada Judgments

In 1986 the Supreme Court of Canada released its judgments in the *Derrickson* and *Paul* appeals. They were both relatively brief decisions dismissing the appeals. The *Paul* judgment is particularly curt, applying the reasoning in *Derrickson*, with no reference to the violent conflict at the base of that particular dispute. Mr. Justice Chouinard wrote the unanimous judgment for the Supreme Court of Canada in the two appeals. Both reasons are adroitly evasive in confronting the underlying conflict in the cases and together provide a classic illustration of the colonialist approach to aboriginal conflicts utilizing formalist division of powers rhetoric.

In *Derrickson*, Mr. Justice Chouinard confirms that the reasoning of the British Columbia Court of Appeal that the provincial *Family Relations Act* is inapplicable, either on its own or as a law of general application which would extend to Indians by virtue of section 88 of the *Indian Act*. He accepts that "[t]itle to reserve lands is vested in the Crown ... . So long as they remain as such, reserve lands are administered by the Federal Government and Parliament has exclusive legislative authority over them." The "very essence" of the exclusive federal jurisdiction over Indians, Mr. Justice Chouinard opines, is the right to possession of lands on an Indian reserve, consequently provincial legislation cannot apply. The *Family Relations Act* of British Columbia must, therefore, be "read down and given the limited meaning which will confine it within the limits of the provincial jurisdiction."

The issue of the extension of provisions of the British Columbia *Family Relations Act* to Indians in the province by virtue of section 88 of the *Indian Act* was one in which Mr. Justice Chouinard took a particular interest. He viewed the provincial family legislation as a law of general application eligible for extension according to section 88 of the [Indian Act]. Furthermore, he found that even if a court granted an order conditional upon ministerial approval under the *Indian Act*, this would not change the constitutional status of the provincial legislation as subordinate to the *Indian Act*.

Nevertheless, Mr. Justice Chouinard upheld the findings of the Court of Appeal on the issue of compensation in lieu of division of matrimonial property. The provisions of the *Family Relations Act* on compensation could be extended to Indians, he accepted, as these were not inconsistent with the property aspect of the *Indian Act*, particularly when awarded for the purposes of "adjusting the division of family assets between the spouses."

At no point in his decision does Mr. Justice Chouinard explore the consequences of his decision for aboriginal women, who are now without recourse for a just share of matrimonial property upon family breakdown. In passing he mentioned that he was "not unmindful of the ensuing consequences for spouses." He justified his disinterest in the consequences by borrowing a phrase from a noted constitutional publicist:

> Whether such laws are wise or unwise is of course a much-controverted question, but it is not relevant to their constitutional validity.

Mr. Justice Chouinard's reasons for judgment in *Paul* are similar. Following a brief statement of facts, he finds that

> ... this case is indistinguishable from *Derrickson*. To hold otherwise would mean that the husband by virtue of his Certificate of Possession would be entitled to possession and consequently to occupation of the family residence while the wife ... would be entitled to interim exclusive occupancy of the same residence.

He rejected the distinction between occupation and possession as too fine a legal argument to justify the extension of provincial family law to include Indian lands. Moreover, Mr. Justice Chouinard made no comment on the violent nature of the conflict which lead to the appeal.

III. Situating the Cases in Their Colonial Legal Context

The decisions in *Derrickson* and *Paul*, particularly at the Supreme Court of Canada level, project an image of a perfunctory division of powers conflict resolved by application of the constitutional doctrine of exclusivity of federal jurisdiction over Indians and lands reserved for the Indians. This style of reasoning masks the political complexity of the conflict(s) which were at the basis of *Derrickson* and *Paul*. The complexity stems from what can be called the "aboriginal dimension" of the legal dispute. This refers to the fact that the disputes that have arisen in these cases stem directly from the legacy of a colonial regime that continues to be imposed on aboriginal people by decontextualizing these conflicts and ignoring the impact of the law on aboriginal peoples' lives. To do otherwise would demand critical reflection on the inadequacy and oppressive nature of the colonial regime established by the *Constitution Act, 1867* and the *Indian Act*.

The chosen legal issue in *Derrickson* and *Paul* is which branch of the state should control which aspects of aboriginal life, not the very matter of state control itself. The state control of aboriginal life is the central political issue in these cases. Framing the issue in constitutional division of powers doctrine is an effective strategy for depoliticizing the cases and silencing any questioning of the overwhelming state control of (jurisdiction over) aboriginal peoples. The court, as an emanation of the colonial political regime for aboriginal peoples, is blinded to its role and to the political nature of the law it applies in this context.

A. Insensitivity to Aboriginal Conceptions of Property

The consequence of the *Derrickson* and *Paul* decisions is that an aboriginal woman who resides in a home on a reserve with her spouse cannot make an application under provincial family legislation for occupation or possession of the home upon marriage breakdown or in the event of physical and emotional abuse from her spouse. There is no federal family legislation to govern these conflicts. In the *Paul* case, for Pauline Paul, this meant she was denied legal access to the matrimonial home of sixteen years which she herself helped to build. With the sanction of constitutional law, she was, effectively, left out in the cold.

Even if an aboriginal woman holds a certificate of possession jointly with her spouse under the *Indian Act*, she will have no recourse under provincial family law (the only family law) for access to her home. Moreover, the situation on Indian reserves is such that the certificates of possession are invariably issued to male band members so an appeal to the Department of Indian Affairs or the band council would be equally futile in most, if not all, cases. The practice of issuing certificates to men is a carry-over from the late nineteenth century practice of issuing location tickets to males, an extension of Anglo-European patriarchal notions of land holding and succession. It was this same philosophy that infused the gender discrimination provisions in relation to Indian status.

The *Indian Act* requirement of ministerial approval for any transfer of reserve land likely forecloses the possibility of successfully pursuing a remedy for the situation at common law, although trust doctrines may have limited application. Applications pursuant to the *Canadian Charter of Rights and Freedoms* are possible, but fraught with another set of difficulties. Essentially, an aboriginal woman has no legally recognizable interest in her matrimonial home, unless she solely holds the certificate of possession. Even if this is the case, gaining an interim order for exclusive possession will be impossible as there is no legislation which will apply in this context. While this is an obvious injustice, there is another layer here which makes the injustice particularly cruel and oppressive: that is the cultural significance of property from an aboriginal perspective.

For aboriginal women, it is not the commodity character of property which is vital to her survival. The progressive literature on matrimonial property in Canada espouses the concept of the equality of the spouses and the notion of marriage as an economic partnership. The matrimonial home has been viewed in this light as the single most important unit of property in the relationship, of significance economically and perhaps even emotionally. The fair division of the matrimonial home upon marriage breakdown is seen to save women and children from financial breakdown and impoverishment.

While this is undoubtedly the case for non-aboriginal people, when the context of aboriginal marriages is considered, especially when the spouses are living on the reserve, the situation must be appreciated as being different because of a combination of economic, cultural and linguistic factors.

Access to matrimonial property does not save aboriginal women from impoverishment because the value of a possessory interest in reserve land is circumscribed by restrictions on alienation and the limited interest (mortgagability [sic]) in the property. Moreover, aboriginal peoples on reserves already live far below the poverty line in Canada. Consequently, theories of economic partnerships and a woman's access to the home as an important commodity do not apply to aboriginal peoples as they would in a non-aboriginal context. Indeed these theories arguably devalue the significance of the matrimonial home for aboriginal women.

The significance of matrimonial property for aboriginal women must be understood in the context of what the reserve represents: it is the home of a distinct cultural and linguistic people. It is a community of extended families, tightly connected by history, language and culture. It is often the place where children can be educated in their language and with culturally-appropriate pedagogies. The reserve home is generally not that of a nuclear family—parents, grandparents, brothers, sisters and others in need will all share the home. The home may be the only access a woman and her children have to their culture, language and family. The economic value of the land is secondary to its value as shelter within a larger homeland—the homeland of her people, her family.

The second aspect of matrimonial property theory that infuses this area, the notion of equality of the spouses, is, similarly, not entirely applicable in the aboriginal matrimonial context. In most aboriginal communities, the belief is that women, children and elders come before men and the responsibility of the men is to live life as a good helper toward women, children and elders. Traditional tribal control of property did not lead to the victimization of aboriginal women. As one Mohawk lawyer suggests of property customs in the Iroquois Confederacy:

> The Iroquois woman's rights to the family property was based on political influence via the control over the economic wealth of the family ... she had real property rights even superior to those of her husband ... . The property situation of the modern day Iroquois woman is vastly different from her historical sister prior to European contact. Traditionally she had the control of the family assets and family life. There has been a complete demotion. If she is not the legal owner of the family asset situated on an Indian reserve, then upon marriage dissolution she has no possibility of real property rights ... . She is truly the forgotten victim in a matrimonial dissolution. Her situation is equivalent to that under the "separate as to property regime" which was remedied by provincial matrimonial legislation in the common law provinces. She has recourse only under common law trust doctrines and provincial compensation schemes. She no longer has her traditional real property rights over family assets.

The decisions in *Derrickson* and *Paul* sanction a situation which is completely opposite to that of the customs of many tribes. There are no obligations on aboriginal men now recognized at law to provide shelter for women, children or elders. Indeed, customary law has no place in matrimonial property disputes as Canadian law will not recognize it—it is the federal or provincial government which exercises jurisdiction over Indians upon marriage breakdown. The impact of this oppression of aboriginal custom on communities cannot be underestimated. When men no longer have to fulfil their responsibilities to women, children and elders, the social control network of the community disintegrates and respect for social responsibilities is lost.

B. Disregard for the Violence Aboriginal Women Endure

The cultural and spiritual conceptions of property held by aboriginal peoples find no recognition in the cases on matrimonial property. The social reality for aboriginal peoples also does not enter into the discourse of division of powers which has been seized upon by all levels of courts in these cases. The appellants had to structure their arguments into claims based upon alien property notions and legal doctrines foreign to the customs of their communities. Could a claim have been made on the basis of customary (that is, the aboriginal) practice of the community? Undoubtedly, this was the farthest thing in the minds of lawyers advising the appellants in *Derrickson* and *Paul*, or the court in examining the legitimacy of their claims under Canadian (i.e. federal or provincial) law. Moreover, it would be difficult, if not impossible, according to Canadian constitutional law.

The Canadian legal system is revealed, once again, as a thoroughly colonial regime. It is too busy trying to categorize jurisdictional matters between federal and provincial governments to step back and realize the oppressive and presumptuous nature of its exercise. To expect it to do so is to expect too much given that this branch of the state is an emanation and expression of a colonial state. In fact, the role of the judicial branch of the state is going to be, in such a regime, to justify the colonial mentality using legal doctrine. It is little wonder that the legal system enjoys a low level of respect from aboriginal peoples who see this exercise. The actors within the system and, even most academic commentators, often fail to see the violence this situation foists on aboriginal peoples. Aboriginal peoples have nowhere to turn to voice their grievances—taking them to court means accepting an alien system. Doing nothing has only meant continued oppression and an implosion of violence and social upheaval in communities. The violence of silence is difficult to ensure, and *it is violence*. The decisions in *Derrickson* and *Paul* mean that brutal victimization of aboriginal women and children will continue because of a "gap" in the colonial regime. The extent of this brutalization can only be fully appreciated if we reflect upon the situation in which Pauline Paul found herself and which a disproportionately high number of aboriginal women confront—family violence.

Pauline Paul wanted to stay in her home on the Tsarslip Reserve with her children and she sought protection from her abusive spouse. The law offered her no such protection because she is an Indian. Pauline Paul had to find shelter elsewhere, she had to leave the reserve because there was no mechanism to allow her to stay. She had to endure violence and banishment from the community in order to be safe.

This issue of protection was never addressed in *Derrickson* or *Paul*. The court was silent. The (in)appropriateness of the *Indian Act* in its provisions for dissolution of matrimonial property upon family breakdown or during violence was left unexamined. As noted earlier, the *Indian Act* does not provide for marriage breakdown, property division, or for situations of family violence and protecting the property rights of the abused in such situations. There is some scope for argument that the provisions of the *Act* empowering bands to enact by-laws would include jurisdiction over property. However, this is unlikely given the restrictive interpretation of band council by-law jurisdiction and the common practice of disallowance of by-laws by the Minister of Indian Affairs when they come before the Minister for review.

The Supreme Court of Canada offered no analysis of the (in)adequacy of the present legislative scheme. Indeed, in reviewing the fact situations in *Derrickson* and *Paul*, one may wonder why the *Indian Act*, which is supposedly the comprehensive legislative enactment for Indians, does not regulate property division and access to the home in violent situations or during marriage breakdowns. However, this type of questioning further illustrates how the aboriginal dimension of *Derrickson* and *Paul* can be lost in a colonial legal framework. The *Indian Act* is not simply inadequate given its lack of comprehensiveness. Colonial gaps are not there just to be filled. The regime is problematic as a whole because it is a system which seeks to bureaucratically administer Indian people according to Anglo-European standards. Aboriginal peoples do not support the reform or tinkering amendments to the *Indian Act*. Aboriginal peoples do not want to continue as wards of the federal government with bureaucratic custodians. The problems of violence are connected with this model. Aboriginal peoples would like their inherent rights of self-government recognized by the Canadian state and their authority to deal with conflicts in their communities according to their customs recognized and respected.

Yet, the situation aboriginal women are left with after *Derrickson* and *Paul*, especially *Paul*, is one in which no law protects them. Given the magnitude of the problem of family violence in aboriginal communities, this is barbaric. The failure of the court to explicitly recognize the violence in the *Paul* case reveals a callous and wilful blindness. Recent empirical studies have suggested that the incidence of physical family violence perpetrated against aboriginal women is approximately 70% or seven times the national average. In a study, released in 1990 by the Ontario Native Women's Association, of the situation for aboriginal women in Ontario, 91% of respondents indicated that family violence occurs in their communities; 71% indicated they had personally experienced it. These are shocking findings. The reasons behind the figures are complex, as the Ontario Native Women's Association suggests:

> Living under bureaucratic control, with no real self-government or self-determination, means that we do not control our everyday affairs, including our family life, and as a result, the level of social problems in our communities is frequently severe. Alcoholism, drug and solvent abuse, family violence, and other crimes are uniform tragedies in aboriginal communities. The first and foremost place where the impact of these social problems is felt is in the family. The treatment of the members of the family is a reflection of the treatment of the community on a broader basis. This is especially true for us because we have an important cultural value in our communities which is the notion of the extended family.

As a consequence of *Derrickson* and *Paul*, aboriginal women who are abused will have to seek shelter off the reserve, usually in non-aboriginal run shelters for battered women, frequently at considerable distances away from the reserve. More likely, an aboriginal woman's economic situation would prohibit a move to a shelter and she may simply be trapped in an abusive situation with dim hopes for improvement. In situations where the marriage breaks down, the inability of a spouse (most frequently woman) to gain access to the matrimonial home is an aggreviously unjust one. An order for compensation is no redress. Indian reserves do not have cash economies and compensation awards would be nominal, if even enforceable. Moreover, where compensation was awarded in lieu of division, the task of obtaining another house on the reserve is a cumbersome endeavour. Housing lists on all Indian reserves are heavily backlogged and women will be forced to live in the already crowded homes of relatives, or more likely off the reserve, until housing can be obtained.

As noted above, the lack of recourse for protection of an aboriginal woman's interest in the matrimonial home may mean the loss of an entitlement to live in the community. When aboriginal women and children are forced to leave the reserve, with the hopes of returning only if and when housing becomes available, or violence subsides, they leave behind more than simply shelter or an asset. They leave behind their culture, language and family. Life in an urban centre is not the same as living on a reserve. It is difficult to maintain your language, educate your children, not to mention battle racism in attempts to secure housing and employment. The reserve represents the home of your people. It is a distinct cultural and linguistic community which cannot be found elsewhere.

In many ways, it seems that history is repeating itself for aboriginal women. In the 1970s and early 1980s, aboriginal people were engaged in a bitter struggle over section 12(1)(b) of the *Indian Act*; a section which provided that an Indian woman who married a non-Indian man was disenfranchised of her Indian status and lost, among other things, her privileges of residing on the reserve, her rights to education and to be buried on the reserve. Two well known cases came before the Supreme Court of Canada challenging this provision of the *Indian Act* as contrary to the *Canadian Bill of Rights*. *Lavell* and *Bedard* were turning points in constitutional legal history because they revealed the limitations of the *Canadian Bill of Rights*. In these cases, the Supreme Court of Canada failed to directly address the issue of sexual inequality or the predicament of aboriginal women as a result of section 12(1)(b) of the *Indian Act*. Their decision to uphold section 12(1)(b) in the face of challenge under the *Canadian Bill of Rights* rested upon a procedural ruling that the *Bill* could not be used to strike down federal legislation. In the course of their decision, some members of the court, particularly Mr. Justice Ritchie, articulated a concept of equality as equal application of the law to all persons similarly situated which was later vigorously criticized as misguided.

The predicament in which Indian women found themselves after *Lavell*, with the discriminatory section 12(1)(b) of the *Indian Act* intact for over a decade, led to outrage throughout Indian communities. It was not until international attention was drawn to the situation that changes were made. Sandra Lovelace, a Maliseet woman of the Tobique Reserve in New Brunswick, petitioned the United Nations Human Rights Committee alleging numerous violations on the part of Canada of international commitments under the *International Covenant on Civil and Political Rights*. Lovelace argued that section 12(1)(b) of the *Indian Act* denied her the right to live in her community and be with her people, a right she said was protected under the *Covenant*. Several years after filing the petition, and decades after suffering unjustly as a result of section 12(1)(b), the Human

Rights Committee expressed its views on the petition. In finding Canada in violation of its international human rights obligations, they stated that:

> It has been considered whether Sandra Lovelace, because she is denied the legal right to reside in the Tobique Reserve, has by that fact been denied of the right guaranteed by article 27 to persons belonging to minorities, to enjoy their own culture and to use their own language in community with other members of their group.
>
> 15. ... in the opinion of the Committee the right of Sandra Lovelace to access her native culture and language "in the community with other members" of her group, has in fact been, and continues to be interfered with, because there is no place outside the Tobique Reserve where such a community exists. ...
>
> 16. In this respect, the Committee is of the view that statutory restrictions affecting the right to residence in a reserve of a person belonging to the majority concerned, must have both a reasonable and objective justification and be consistent with the other provisions of the Covenant, read as a whole. ...

There are several interesting parallels between the Lovelace complaint regarding section 12(1)(b) of the *Indian Act* and the matrimonial property situation. Both situations affect aboriginal women by taking them and their children away from their communities. It is the loss of access to the aboriginal community, the place where aboriginal language and culture are vital, that reveals the discriminatory impact of these two situations. In the matrimonial property context, the absence of any law under which to claim protection is the problem which forces women off the reserve whereas with section 12(1)(b) of the *Indian Act*, the section disenfranchised women of their Indian status and forced them out of their homes and communities. The impact on women is uniform: they have to leave their homes and communities. The Supreme Court of Canada's decisions in *Derrickson* and *Paul* must be understood in this light.

IV. Conclusion

The complete silencing of aboriginal women's experiences and indeed of the aboriginal dimension of *Derrickson* and *Paul*, exposes the deleterious colonial character of Canadian constitutional law. The reasoning employed in the two decisions demonstrates the role played by the Canadian legal system in camouflaging the social and political aspects of aboriginal peoples' conflicts. Courts have been unable to grasp the impact of aboriginal peoples' treatment by a colonial legal system because this would require its dismantling and a critical examination of the function of the court and law in perpetuating the oppression. Dismantling it would require recognizing aboriginal peoples' presence as political communities in Canada with distinct cultural linguistic and social systems. It would require ending bureaucratic regulation of Indian life through the *Indian Act*. No court has been honest or reflective enough to acknowledge the colonial character of the regulation of aboriginal life in Canada. Meanwhile, aboriginal peoples have had to endure the violence of a colonial regime which silences aboriginal reality and displays disregard for aboriginal peoples' suffering. One cannot help wondering whether the courts and legislature would be as blind to the violence if it was endured by non-aboriginal women? Of course they would not be so blind because non-aboriginal women are "their" women and part of their cultural and imaginative world. Hence, doctrines of fairness and constructive trust could be stretched to soften gender bias.

There have been no initiatives taken since these decisions in 1986 to remedy the violence aboriginal women endure. How can this be explained? Has the colonial mentality become so engrained that non-aboriginal people in Canada are hardened to aboriginal peoples' suffering?

The decisions in *Derrickson* and *Paul* illustrate the need for highly contextualized readings of cases. Very little of the story in *Derrickson* and *Paul* can be found in the text of the decisions because the constitutional discourse which enveloped the cases silenced the colonial nature of those disputes. The system of white patriarchy is deeply embedded in Canadian legal thought, doctrine and jurisprudence. These two cases are clear and revealing examples of that system at work: a system which needs to be dismantled. The central question is whether we can expect the courts to accomplish this.

Discussion Notes

In *Wynn v. Wynn* (1989), 14 ACWS (3d) 107 (Ont. Dist. Ct.), the court distinguished *Paul*. In *Wynn*, the plaintiff wife sought interim exclusive possession of the matrimonial home, which was located on reserve land. Wright DCJ acknowledged that the court could not grant an order under the provincial Family Law Act for exclusive possession of a matrimonial home that is located on an Indian reserve. Instead, he made an "*in personam*" order, without reference to the property, restraining the plaintiff's husband from interfering with her possession of the home. Does *Wynn* offer a solution to the problems identified by Turpel? For a different solution to this problem in the United States, see *Lonewolf v. Lonewolf*, 657 P2d 627 (NM Sup. Ct. 1982) and a brief discussion of these issues in M.J. Mossman, "Developments in Property Law: The 1985-86 Term" (1987), 9 *Supreme Court Law Review* 419, at 430ff. See also *George v. George*, [1997] 2 CNLR 62 (BC CA), where the court dismissed an appeal from an order for compensation, rather than division of assets, under the BC Family Relations Act, thereby distinguishing *Derrickson*.

Indian Self-Government and Family Property

Issues about land-holding arrangements on reserve lands create problems in relation to family breakdown. However, the issue may need to be addressed in the larger context of self-government.

In "Indian Self-Government, the Equality of the Sexes, and the Application of Provincial Matrimonial Property Laws" (1986), 5 *Canadian Journal of Family Law* 188, Richard Bartlett argued (at 194-95) that this problem can be resolved best in the context of a broader self-government process for native peoples.

> The decisions of the Supreme Court of Canada have affirmed the wide ambit of the grant of federal jurisdiction under section 91(24). They recognize the continued inability of the provinces, as the representatives of local interests, to seek to legislate with respect to the management and government of Indian lands. The Court affirmed the power of

Parliament to provide for assimilation, as section 88 suggests, or to provide for self-government as the federal government claims that it contemplates.

Whether section 88 applies provincial laws to Indian reserves in the absence of conflicting federal legislation remains unresolved. The Court determined that a conflict existed and refused to interweave the provincial and federal legislation to attempt to give effect to both.

The reaction of Joe Mathias, Chief of the Squamish Band of British Columbia, and spokesperson for Union of British Columbia Indians on constitutional issues, to the decisions in *Derrickson* and *Paul* was mixed. He expressed sympathy for divorced Indian spouses who are denied a share of the matrimonial home as a result of the decision, but emphasized that the decisions indicated the need for Indian self-government.

Indian self-government assumes the need for different rules and the possession of different values than those in the larger society. In the context of the division of matrimonial property it may be necessary inter alia to consider the extended Indian family rather than the Western nuclear family, the lands as the property of the band and not of any individual, the customs of the band with respect to cohabitation, marriage, custody and adoption, the support of children, and the disadvantaged circumstances of Indians on reserves. Such factors may suggest a different result than the iconoclastic application of provincial laws. The application of Euro-Canadian rules and values relating to the family and property may be inappropriate.

In 1985 Indian women who lost their status on marriage to non-Indians were restored to status under the *Indian Act*. The amendment was a legal recognition of the separate and special nature of Indian people which the loss of status had denied to such women. It was an acknowledgement that such women should not be considered "assimilated" merely because they married non-Indians. It would have been a significant step in the *other* direction if the provincial laws respecting division of matrimonial property had been applied to reserve lands. It would have indicated that the special rights and character of Indian people were to be wiped out. The restoration of Indian status would have meant nothing. The decisions in *Derrickson* and *Paul* indicate that the Court continues to recognize that the Constitution of Canada contemplates a special status for Indian people, to be enjoyed by both Indian men and women. The equality of the sexes must be considered in that context. The decisions keep alive the potential of Indian self-government to meet the circumstances and aspirations of Indians of both sexes.

The oppression of women in Canadian society is widely acknowledged. Perhaps a greater appreciation of the degree of subjugation of Indians in Canada is demanded. Non-Indian women were granted the vote by Parliament in 1920. Indian men and women were not granted the vote until 1960. It is not a sufficient response, as appears favoured by the National Action Committee on the Status of Women, to merely suggest that Indians, men or women, should be treated just like everybody else.

See also M. Montour, "Iroquois Women's Rights with Respect to Matrimonial Property on Indian Reserves" (1987), 4 *Canadian Native Law Reporter* 1. Montour provides a description of women in traditional Iroquois family life and the ways in which the imposition of colonial culture transformed traditional roles. In addition to concluding that "the only recourse for spouses is under the trusts doctrine," she suggested (at 6-8) the possibility of constitutional or international human rights challenges, as well as political action.

The political route is for the woman to regain her former place in Iroquois society. But this requires that she have the same economic clout as in the past. This may be unrealistic as Iroquois women are generally dependent homemakers with no income of their own. This is the present day reality. The unemployment rate is high on most Indian reserves. Husbands will continue to be issued certificates of possession and to accumulate assets on the reserve in their name only.

One could try to challenge the landholding scheme under the *Indian Act* as discriminatory under section 15 of the *Canadian Charter of Rights and Freedoms* .... . As a result of this federal scheme, Indian spouses have no equality before and under provincial matrimonial property law because of their ethnic origin. It could also be argued that the land scheme's most negative effect is on dependent spouses who are most likely to be women. Therefore, it discriminates on the basis of sex. If one could convince the courts of a contravention of section 15, then maybe one could apply for a remedy under section 24. This remedy could be to order the federal government to rectify the lack of matrimonial property legislation for Indian reserves. But this would be a remedy that the courts would be most reluctant to order.

The most realistic solution is for the tribes to enact matrimonial property regimes as part of their right of self-government. If the federal government were to legislate on the matter under section 91(24) of the *Constitution Act, 1867*, it could possibly be challenged as a colourable attempt to legislate in the provincial jurisdiction over property and civil rights between spouses. But the regime could be upheld as being valid because it is essential to the use of reserve lands by Indian spouses whether enacted under Indian self-government or under the exclusive federal power of section 91(24).

Another remedy is based on international law. In the *International Covenant on Civil and Political Rights*, Article 23 states, in part:

> 4. States Parties to the present Covenant shall take appropriate steps to ensure equality of rights and responsibilities of spouses as to marriage, during marriage and at its dissolution. In the case of dissolution, provision shall be made for the necessary protection of any children.

If neither the courts nor the government bodies rectify the inequity Iroquois women could appeal to the international arena. Spouses upon marriage dissolution have equal rights according to the Covenant. This should include an equal right to family property. Although this is not binding on Canadian courts, it can be politically embarrassing for Canada as a signatory to the Covenant. They are obliged to take the necessary steps to remedy any inequality of rights upon marriage dissolution. This may result in appropriate legislative action by the federal government or Indian governments. This was the result when Sandra Lovelace appealed to the international court because she had lost her rights as an Indian woman upon marriage to a non-Indian spouse. Her appeal was received and the federal government passed legislative amendments to the *Indian Act* ending sexual discrimination. (See "Selected Documents in the Matter of Lovelace versus Canada Pursuant to the International Covenant, 08/81.")

If the legislative avenue is chosen it will be an opportunity to achieve an ideal matrimonial property regime. One could aim at restoring the influential position of the Iroquois women in the social and economic life of their tribes by vesting real matrimonial property rights in them. However, this will only happen if women become politically and economically strong as they were in the past when they selected the political representatives and produced the necessities of life. Otherwise, they may have limited access to real property rights depending on the classification of divisible family property under any future regime for matrimonial reserve lands.

Reconsider the quotation at the beginning of this section concerning "family" property. Assuming self-government is achieved, what processes are appropriate to create "ideal" matrimonial property regimes for First Nations communities?

PROBLEMS

1. Jane Turner, a widow, died in 1970. She left a will with somewhat complicated provisions about her extensive land holdings in Perth County—for example, in relation to a farm property of about 200 acres, her will stated:

I hereby devise the old farm fronting on the Roberts sideroad (about 200 acres in all and including the farmhouse built by my grandfather in 1850) to two of my children—Esther and George in fee simple jointly; and if they should decide to sell the farm, they are entitled to share in the proceeds, share and share alike, equally.

Esther and George lived together after their mother's death in the old farmhouse. George farmed the property, continuing to raise some sheep on the pastureland and growing soybeans on the fertile acreage. He also started a modest Christmas tree business by careful management and replanting of the woodlot on the 200 acres. Esther managed the household for her brother, but she also went to work every day at a shop in Perth where she had been employed at the time of her mother's death. Esther and George generally contributed equally to their household expenses, and George used the proceeds of the farming operation to pay for seed, to transport the Christmas trees to the market in Ottawa, and to repair the farm buildings. By agreement between them, Esther kept her earnings from the shop separate from George and he kept the proceeds of the sale of Christmas trees.

Recently, George decided to get married. As part of the wedding arrangements, he wants to make a will; in particular, he wants to ensure that his interest in the farm will pass to his wife, should he predecease her. At the same time, Esther has decided that she should move to Perth. Accordingly, she and George want to know how to arrange their financial matters.

2. In a search of the title to property in Chatham, the following documents were found:

a. *June 14, 1899.* A deed from Arthur Andrews to his sons Brian and Charles in fee simple "as joint tenants and not as tenants in common."

b. *May 18, 1900.* A deed from Brian Andrews to Mary Stephens in fee simple.

c. *April 26, 1922.* A deed from Charles Andrews to the local Presbyterian Church in fee simple, reciting that his conveyance was that of a surviving joint tenant, Brian having been absent at the Great War from 1914 to 1918 when Charles had been solely in possession; and that Brian had died in France in 1918.

Explain what interest (if any) was received by the Presbyterian church. You may also wish to consider the church's position, assuming it has been in possession of the land since 1922.

3. Dorothy Dixon and Henry Chong met five years ago and began to live together a year later. Both are lawyers. Dorothy is an associate lawyer in a thriving practice in London, Ontario. She was recently advised that she is very likely to be invited to join the partnership next year. Henry has a sole practice, in a small community south of London, from which he receives a steady but not large income. He is very content with his work and his life with Dorothy, and would like to marry her.

Dorothy is seeking advice about the implications of marriage for the couple's property arrangements. At present, Dorothy owns the house in which they live, but Henry has contributed to some major renovations, both financially and by means of work he has done on weekends. Henry has also done most of the household chores since his hours are generally more regular than Dorothy's, and he likes to cook and prepare meals more than she does.

What principles are applicable to assessing Henry's entitlement at present to an interest in the home owned by Dorothy? To what extent would his entitlement change if Dorothy and Henry were married? Note that the couple could also make a marriage contract and define property entitlement as they see fit. What arrangement would you recommend to Dorothy; to Henry? Why? To what extent would your advice be different if Dorothy's partner were female? Do you think that these principles should be applicable to reserve lands? Why or why not? If you think that they are not appropriate, what principles would you recommend?

CHAPTER EIGHT

Current Challenges in Property Law: The "Public" Nature of Private Property

This chapter focuses on contemporary challenges in property law—issues concerning native title; constitutional entrenchment of property rights, including "new property" claims; and property law reform. Significantly, each of these challenges raises questions about the nature of property law in Canada in the late 20th century and whether it remains a matter of exclusively "private" law. Some political analysts, for example, have observed significant changes in the nature of property:

> [In the context of] the limitless power, wealth and capacity of the state and of major social and capitalist institutions ... modern man [sic] is having increasing difficulty in thinking of property as private, as the concretisation of an individual will reifying itself in land or objects, as a walled-in area into which others may not enter. There is, in other words, a shift of attention from the property whose paradigm is the household, the walled-in or marked-off piece of land, the specific bales that make up a cargo or consignment, to the corporation, the hospital, the defence establishment, the transport or power utility whose "property" spreads throughout the society and whose existence is dependent upon subsidies, state protection, public provision of facilities, etc. ... .
> Property becomes social in the sense that its base and its effects can no longer be contained within the framework of the traditional picture ... . This explains one of the most striking of modern phenomena—the decline in respect for private property, the popularity of the sit-in, of the demand for *access* as independent of ownership and as something that ought to be maintainable against it.

(E. Kamenka and A. Erh-Soon Tay, "Beyond Bourgeois Individualism: The Contemporary Crisis in Law and Legal Ideology," in E. Kamenka and R.S. Neale, eds., *Feudalism, Capitalism and Beyond* (London: Edward Arnold, 1975), 127, at 132-33.)

The argument that property is becoming more "public" than "private" law is reflected in decisions about native title. Some recent Australian cases, for example, rely on norms of international law such as duties of non-discrimination in analyzing entitlement to interests in land. As B. Slattery suggested, "[T]he question of Aboriginal land rights is not a narrow matter of private right but a subject of far-reaching constitutional significance." See B. Slattery, "First Nations and the Constitution: A Question of Trust"

(1992), 71 *Canadian Bar Review* 261, at 289. The "public" nature of private property is also evident in the work of academic scholars who see property concepts as a mechanism for defining collective relationships rather than individual rights. In an analysis of the constitutional protection for property in the decisions of the Supreme Court of the United States, for example, L. Underkuffler-Freund argued that there are two separate ideas about property, one of which is the well-accepted concept of an "individual's protected interests." By contrast, she suggested that there is a second, quite different conception of property:

> Under this understanding, individual interests are part of the concept of property, but there is no assumption of the primacy of individual interests over collective ones. Property *describes the tension* between individual and collective, rather than a particular outcome of that tension. It does not represent the autonomous sphere of the individual, to be asserted against the collective; rather, the tension between the individual and collective *is a part of the concept of property* itself.

(L. Underkuffler-Freund, "Takings and the Nature of Property" (1996), 9 *Canadian Journal of Law and Jurisprudence* 161, at 168.) A need to redefine private property was similarly evident in the work of C.B. Macpherson, discussed in chapter 1, and is reflected in Gray's suggestion that individual property rights must now be seen as subject to the values of human dignity and the "sense of the reciprocal responsibility which each citizen owes to his or her community." See K. Gray, "Equitable Property" (1994), 47 *Current Legal Problems* 157, at 209 and C.B. Macpherson, *Property: Mainstream and Critical Positions* (Toronto: University of Toronto Press, 1978) (hereafter Macpherson).

This chapter provides a short introduction to ideas about changing conceptions of property, including its increasingly "public" law character. Included are property issues concerning native land claims, the Canadian Charter of Rights and Freedoms, part I of the Constitution Act, 1982, being schedule B of the Canada Act, 1982 (UK), 1982, c. 11 (hereafter the Charter), and "new property," all of which present important and continuing challenges for the law of property. You may want to examine some of these issues more fully in advanced courses and seminars after this introduction to property law. The chapter concludes with some comments and questions about the nature and process of law reform in property law.

PROPERTY CLAIMS AND FIRST NATIONS

For First Nations, issues about property reveal the connections between land claims and aspirations of self-government. As George Erasmus, former National Chief of the Assembly of First Nations, explained, it is difficult to separate negotiations about land rights from political issues about self-government and control of resources:

> Land, and jurisdiction over land, go hand in hand. We have been pressing for fair land settlement to provide the basis for an economically viable life for our people, but we have also insisted on our right to aboriginal self-government over that land. By this we mean our right to exercise jurisdiction over our traditional lands, resources, and people. We must share in the benefits that come from the resources of the land, and we must make decisions in the best interests of our people, the land, and its resources.

(G. Erasmus, "Twenty Years of Disappointed Hopes," in B. Richardson, ed., *Drumbeat: Anger and Renewal in Indian Country* (Toronto: University of Toronto Press, 1989), 3, at 13.) The link between self-government and land claims for First Nations was also noted in the report of the Royal Commission on Aboriginal Peoples, *Bridging the Cultural Divide: A Report on Aboriginal People and Criminal Justice in Canada* (Ottawa: Minister of Supply and Services Canada, 1996), at 11:

> [A] larger vision of justice, one that is linked to recognition of the Aboriginal right of self-government and to the resolution of treaty and Aboriginal rights based on claims to lands and resources, is one that our Commission shares and endorses, and it is one that forms the backbone of our recommendations in this report.

These two issues—native title to land and the right to self-government—were addressed in British Columbia in *Delgamuukw v. The Queen* (discussed below), a decision of the BC Supreme Court that was appealed to the Court of Appeal and then to the Supreme Court of Canada. In the following comment, Bruce Ryder examines the judicial reasoning about these two related issues. In reviewing his comments, consider the extent to which it is possible and/or desirable to separate issues of title to land and issues about self-government.

B. Ryder, "Aboriginal Rights and Delgamuukw v. The Queen"
(1994), 5 *Constitutional Forum* 43 (footnotes omitted)

[The relationship between self-government and land claims was addressed in British Columbia in *Delgamuukw v. British Columbia* (1991), 79 DLR (4th) 185 (BC SC), (1993), 104 DLR (4th) 470 (BC CA). In *Delgamuukw*, hereditary chiefs of the Gitsan and Wet'suwet'en peoples asserted claims to ownership of and jurisdiction over 58,000 square kilometres of territory in central British Columbia. The trial decision dismissed both claims, stating that the claim to self-government was extinguished by the exercise of British sovereignty over the mainland colony of British Columbia. As well, the trial decision concluded that the underlying assertion of Crown title in the land in colonial enactments prior to British Columbia's entry into Canada in 1871 extinguished aboriginal title over all unceded territory in British Columbia. Thus, there were no "existing rights" under s. 35 of the Charter for the Gitsan and Wet'suwet'en peoples to assert. On appeal to the BC Court of Appeal, however, the newly elected provincial government abandoned the argument that there had been a complete extinguishment of aboriginal title by colonial enactments prior to 1871, and the Court of Appeal unanimously held in favour of the claimants, issuing a declaration that the plaintiffs held existing aboriginal rights of occupation and use over much of the territory claimed, to be defined more precisely by negotiation between the parties. However, the trial judge's conclusion with respect to the self-government issue was affirmed by a majority of 3-2. The Supreme Court granted leave to appeal and the appeal was argued in July 1997.]

On the long and tortuous path to justice for the First Nations of Canada, the case of *Delgamuukw v. The Queen* is likely to become one of the most important landmarks.

Whether the outcome of this ongoing litigation will represent a step towards, or a sidetrack from, the achievement of a just settlement for Aboriginal Peoples is now in the hands of the Supreme Court. The case raises a number of issues of immense consequence that were not addressed in the Supreme Court's decision in *Sparrow* (1990) or that have been left unresolved by the failure of attempts to amend the constitution to explicitly recognize an inherent Aboriginal right of self-government. Is Aboriginal title an "existing aboriginal right" protected by section 35 of the *Constitution Act, 1982* in those parts of the country where Aboriginal lands have not been ceded by treaty? Does the concept of Aboriginal rights entail a right of self-government, and if so, was that right extinguished prior to 1982? ...

Aboriginal Title and Self-Government as Common Law Aboriginal Rights

The Supreme Court in *Sparrow* defined Aboriginal rights as including customs or practices that constitute "an integral part" of a "distinctive" Aboriginal culture. This test was applied by the judges of the BC CA in *Delgamuukw*. While Aboriginal title is a well-established component of the common law doctrine of Aboriginal rights, the Supreme Court has yet to rule on the question of whether the doctrine of Aboriginal rights entails a right of self-government. The majority judges in *Delgamuukw* seemed to presume that it does, although they did not find it necessary to directly address the point given their conclusions on extinguishment, to be discussed below. The dissenting judges did address the point. Lambert JA found that "the aboriginal rights of self-government and self-regulation," to the extent that they "formed an integral part" of a "distinctive culture," are recognized as part of the common law doctrine of Aboriginal rights. Hutcheon JA reached a similar conclusion regarding a more narrowly conceived "aboriginal right of self-regulation." Indeed, once one accepts, as Macfarlane JA did, that the Gitksan and Wet'suwet'en peoples had an "organized society" at the time that British sovereignty was asserted, the conclusion seems inescapable that a right of self-government was an "integral part of their distinctive culture," and thus was incorporated in the common law doctrine of Aboriginal rights.

The Test for Extinguishment

The Supreme Court decision in *Sparrow* held that any common law Aboriginal rights that were not extinguished prior to 1982 are "existing" and thus "recognized and affirmed" in a contemporary fashion by section 35 of the *Constitution Act, 1982*. The Court made clear that extensive and detailed regulation or impairment of a right does not amount to extinguishment. Adopting the test put forward by Hall JA in *Calder* (1973), the Court held that a right is extinguished only when it is completely abrogated by a "clear and plain" intention of the sovereign. The Crown has the burden of establishing these elements of extinguishment.

Neither the Aboriginal title nor the Aboriginal right of self-government of the Gitksan and Wet'suwet'en peoples have ever been explicitly extinguished. A question that arises, therefore, is whether sovereign intent can ever be "clear and plain" if not explicitly stated in legislation. All members of the BC CA in *Delgamuukw* held that implicit legislative extinguishment is possible. For example, Macfarlane JA noted that the Supreme Court had not stated in *Sparrow* that intent to extinguish must be expressly stated in legislation. It followed, in his view, that a clear and plain sovereign intention "may be declared expressly or manifested by unavoidable implication." Extinguishment by necessary implication is possible only in those rare cases where "the interpretation of the statute permits no other result."

This conclusion, allowing the possibility of extinguishment by necessary legislative implication, is faithful to the word of the *Sparrow* decision but, arguably, not to its spirit. The strict test for extinguishment is an important limitation on the orthodox and draconian view that prior to 1982 Aboriginal rights existed at "the pleasure of the Crown." The unilateral expropriation of Aboriginal rights was an extraordinary possibility that was apparently available to the colony of British Columbia prior to 1871 and to the government of Canada from 1871 to 1982.

The legal basis for untrammelled British, and later Canadian, sovereign authority over Aboriginal nations has never been adequately explained. Ultimately it rests on the common law doctrine of discovery, or the notion that sovereignty over an uninhabited territory vests in the discovering or settling power. In applying this principle to British North America, judges have managed to skirt the fact that Aboriginal Peoples did indeed inhabit the territory. The *Delgamuukw* decision continues a tradition that has woven this ugly fiction into the fabric of our law. Wallace JA, for example, relied on decisions that limited the application of the doctrine of discovery to "uninhabited" or "unoccupied" territories, yet he did not find it necessary to explain how the principle could possibly be relevant to territories occupied by the Gitksan and Wet'suwet'en.

If Canadian courts are unwilling to question the validity of the assertion of British or Canadian sovereignty over Aboriginal societies, as it appears they are, then the principle of extinguishment has an especially crucial role to play in limiting the ability of contemporary Canadian governments to argue that the actions of their predecessors amounted to effective unilateral expropriation of Aboriginal interests. One important role that the "clear and plain intention" test could fulfil is the prevention of expropriation without at least some notice to the persons most affected, namely, the holders of the Aboriginal rights. Expropriation without notice is especially offensive, because those persons detrimentally affected are not informed of the change in their legal position and thus are deprived of an opportunity to object to the taking without consent.

The "clear and plain intention" test is closely related to the "honour of the Crown": if the Crown has not explicitly conveyed its intention to Aboriginal Peoples, how can it be said that its intention is either honourable or "clear and plain"? Clear and plain to whom? Surely it is not just the subjective intention of non-Aboriginal authorities that ought to be relevant. There ought to be a requirement that the intention be made clear and plain in an objective or public sense, particularly to Aboriginal persons whose knowledge and awareness of the significance of European legal practices cannot be presumed. These considerations suggest that a stricter understanding of the requirement of "clear and plain intention" than that adopted by the BC CA would be more consistent with the twin goals of upholding the honour of the Crown and promoting a just settlement for Aboriginal Peoples that the Supreme Court has said should guide the interpretation of section 35.

Extinguishment of Aboriginal Title

The BC CA held unanimously that thirteen colonial instruments passed between 1858 and 1870 did not manifest a clear and plain sovereign intention to extinguish Aboriginal title by necessary implication. These enactments asserted Crown title over all lands in BC and empowered the Governor to sell Crown lands in the colony. They made no mention of Aboriginal interests in land. Macfarlane JA stated that the purpose of these enactments was to facilitate settlement, not to disregard Aboriginal interests nor to foreclose the treaty process. The other judges all agreed that the taking of underlying title by the Crown was not inconsistent with a recognition of the burden constituted by Aboriginal title.

All of the judges agreed that after BC joined Confederation in 1871, section 91(24) of the *Constitution Act, 1867* placed the extinguishment of Aboriginal title beyond provincial legislative competence. Nor had the federal government passed any legislation extinguishing Aboriginal title between 1871 and 1982. After 1982, extinguishment is constitutionally prohibited because it would not meet the justificatory standard set out by the Supreme Court in *Sparrow*. The judges noted that the ways in which Aboriginal title and grants of fee simple and other property rights will co-exist "cannot be decided in this case, and are ripe for negotiation."

It followed, then, that Aboriginal title is an existing Aboriginal right in British Columbia, now afforded constitutional protection by section 35 of the *Constitution Act, 1982*. The question of extinguishment that had divided the Supreme Court 3-3 in the *Calder* case twenty years earlier has finally been resolved. It seems highly unlikely that the present Supreme Court will disagree with the persuasive reasoning of the BC CA on this point, especially in light of the BC (and federal) government's demonstrated willingness to begin negotiations on settling the land claims covering most of the province. ...

Conclusion

Together with the change in provincial government policy signalled by the establishment of the BC Treaty Commission, the Court of Appeal judgment in *Delgamuukw* brings an end to the era of official denial of the existence of Aboriginal title in BC. Nevertheless, in other respects, the majority decisions are open to many of the same objections that critics have levelled at the McEachern [trial] judgment. I have focussed here on the failure of the majority to apply the same rigour to the question of extinguishment of Aboriginal self-government as they did to their analysis of the extinguishment of Aboriginal title.

Given the position taken by the majority judges, their statements wishing the parties success in resolving their differences through negotiation ring rather hollow in so far as self-government is concerned. To understate the obvious, blanket extinguishment places Aboriginal Peoples in an unenviable bargaining position. In their defence, the judges insisted that the role of the court was to state the law rather than to facilitate a just settlement through negotiations. Yet this insistence on marking clear boundaries between law and politics is futile and compromises the ability of section 35 jurisprudence to achieve its remedial promise of a just settlement for Aboriginal Peoples. A glance at the history of relations between Aboriginal Peoples and the Canadian state reveals that the content of legal doctrine and the outcome of negotiations have moved together in a close dialectical relationship. Legal decisions have played and will continue to play a crucial role in setting the parameters of negotiations and shaping the realm of the possible for Aboriginal Peoples.

Discussion Notes

Aboriginal Title to Land and the Charter

It is difficult to characterize the property claims in *Delgamuukw* as matters of (merely) private law. In previous chapters, we examined the nature of aboriginal concepts of property and the impact of common law doctrines such as possessory title and the reception of English law on some aspects of native land claims in Canada. As the material in these earlier chapters demonstrated, the characterization of property interests in land for indigenous peoples has continued to evolve in Canadian law. The early concept of a "usufructuary" interest on the part of indigenous peoples was reflected in 19th-century cases such as *St. Catherines Milling and Lumber Co. v. The Queen* (1888), 14 AC 46 (PC) in Canada, and *Johnson and Graham's Lessee v. M'Intosh*, 8 Wheaton 543; 21 US 543 (1823) in the United States. More recently, courts seemed divided on the issue of whether aboriginal title had been extinguished—see *Calder v. Attorney General of British Columbia* (1973), 34 DLR (3d) 145 (SCC). The Supreme Court of Canada defined *"sui generis"* fiduciary responsibilities on the part of the Crown in its dealings with First Nations in *Guerin v. The Queen*, [1984] 2 SCR 335, discussed in chapter 3. For an overview of different legal approaches, see B. Slattery, *Ancestral Lands, Alien Laws: Judicial Perspectives on Aboriginal Title, Studies in Aboriginal Rights No. 2* (Saskatoon: University of Saskatchewan Native Law Centre, 1983). See also R. Ross, *Dancing With a Ghost: Exploring Indian Reality* (Markham, ON: Octopus Book, 1992); M. Boldt and J.A. Long, eds., *The Quest for Justice: Aboriginal Peoples and Aboriginal Rights* (Toronto: University of Toronto Press, 1985); and B. Morse, ed., *Aboriginal Peoples and the Law: Indian, Métis and Inuit Rights in Canada* (Ottawa: Carleton University Press, 1991).

The "public" law character of aboriginal property rights has been reinforced by s. 35 of the Charter. Section 35(1) recognizes and affirms "existing aboriginal and treaty rights of the aboriginal peoples" (defined by s. 35(2) to include "Indian, Inuit and Métis peoples of Canada"). For other assessments of *Delgamuukw*, see B.D. Cox, "The Gitksan–Wet'suwet'en as 'Primitive' Peoples Incapable of Holding Proprietary Interests: Chief Justice McEachern's Underlying Premise in *Delgamuukw*" (1992), 1 *Dalhousie Journal of Legal Studies* 141; M. Walters, "British Imperial Constitutional Law and Aboriginal Rights: A Comment on *Delgamuukw v. British Columbia* (1992), 17 *Queen's Law Journal* 350; and J. Fortune, "Construing *Delgamuukw*: Legal Arguments, Historical Argumentation, and the Philosophy of History" (1993), 51 *University of Toronto Faculty of Law Review* 80.

In *R v. Sparrow*, [1990] 1 SCR 1075 (briefly examined in chapter 6), the Supreme Court of Canada held that s. 35 of the Charter provides constitutional protection to aboriginal rights (including rights to fish in *Sparrow*) that were not extinguished prior to the enactment of the Charter in 1982. After *Sparrow*, a number of other claims have been litigated in relation to hunting and fishing rights pursuant to s. 35—for example, see *R v. Nikal* (1996), 133 DLR (4th) 658 (SCC); *R v. Van der Peet*, [1996] 4 CNLR 177 (SCC); and *R v. Côté*, [1996] 4 CNLR 26 (SCC). See also *Perry v. Ontario* (1997), 33 OR (3d) 705 (CA). In *R v. Pamajewon*, [1995] 2 CNLR 188 (Ont. CA), it was held that lottery activities that infringed sections of the Criminal Code were not protected by s. 35, since the First Nations accused failed to demonstrate that the regulation of gambling was an integral part of their distinctive cultures according to the test set out in *Van der Peet*. For an overview of s. 35 and *Sparrow* in relation to self-government, see K. McNeil, "Envisaging Constitutional Space for Aboriginal Governments" (1993-94), 19 *Queen's Law Journal* 95. See also P. Macklem, "First Nations Self-Government and the Borders of the Canadian Legal Imagination" (1991), 36 *McGill Law Journal* 382; and J. Borrows, "Constitutional Law from a First Nations Perspective: Self-Government and the Royal Proclamation" (1994), 28 *University of British Columbia Law Review* 1.

Section 35 was also considered in *Ontario Sawridge Band v. Canada*, [1995] 4 CNLR 121. The plaintiffs sought a declaration that amendments to the Indian Act (the Bill C-31 amendments enacted in 1985) were inconsistent with s. 35, because they infringed the right of Indian bands to determine their own membership. The plaintiffs claimed protection for their marital custom that permits an Indian husband, but not a wife, to bring a non-Indian spouse into residence on a reserve. The Bill C-31 amendments had created a system to permit equality for Indian men and women. The court focused on s. 35(4), in addition to s. 35(1). Section 35(4) states that "[n]otwithstanding any other provision of this Act, the aboriginal and treaty rights referred to in subsection (1) are guaranteed equally to male and female persons." Muldoon J dismissed the plaintiffs application, stating (at 141):

> The plaintiffs are firmly caught by the provisions of s. 35 of the *Constitution Act* which they themselves invoke. The more firmly the plaintiffs bring themselves into and under s.-s. 35(1) the more surely s.-s. 35(4) acts upon their alleged rights pursuant to s.-s. 35(1) which, therefore, are modified so as to be guaranteed equally to the whole collectivity of Indian men and Indian women.

How does this interpretation of s. 35 affect native title? As Turpel explained in the excerpt in chapter 7, the resolution of these issues must take account of both historical developments and the contemporary context. An appeal from the decision of Muldoon J was granted by the Federal Court of Appeal in June 1997, when the appellate court concluded that there was a reasonable apprehension of bias (but no actual bias) on the part of the trial judge. A new trial was ordered, on the ground that if a reasonable apprehension of bias is found to exist in a tribunal, its decision is void (citing *Newfoundland Telephone Co. Ltd. v. Board of Commissioners of Public Utilities*, [1992] 1 SCR 623, at 645). For another examination of the provisions concerning Bill C-31 and gender equality in the Indian Act, see *Barry v. Garden River Band of Ojibway* (1997), 33 OR (3d) 782.

The Context of Land Claims and Self-Government

In *Delgamuukw*, the claim did not involve an interpretation of s. 35 in relation to treaty rights. By contrast, there have been a number of cases concerned with aboriginal rights and treaties. For some examples, see *Simon v. The Queen* (1985), 24 DLR (4th) 390 (SCC) concerning treaty rights in Nova Scotia. In Ontario, see *Bear Island Foundation v. Attorney General of Ontario* (1991), 83 DLR (4th) 381 (SCC) and *Chippewas of Kettle and Stony Point v. Attorney General of Canada* (1996), 31 OR (3d) 97 (CA), leave granted to appeal to the SCC, May 29, 1997. See also K. Coates, ed., *Aboriginal Land Claims in Canada: A Regional Perspective* (Toronto: Copp Clark Pitman Ltd., 1992). In the context of treaties, consider the claim to self-government described by D. Johnston in "The Quest of the Six Nations Confederacy for Self-Determination" (1986), 44 *University of Toronto Faculty of Law Review* 1, at 10-12, 16-19, and 23-24 (footnotes omitted):

Of Ancient Covenants and Friendships

When the Europeans first arrived in northeastern North America, the Iroquois confederacy enjoyed a position of dominance over other Indian nations. In the ensuing competition between the French and the British for control of the continent, the confederacy was recognized as holding the balance of power. The British, convinced that an alliance with the Iroquois was essential to limiting French expansion, endeavoured to establish diplomatic relations. ...

In light of the dominant status of the confederacy at the time, it was incumbent upon the British envoys to adopt Iroquois council procedure and treaty protocol. The context in which Iroquois diplomatic convention was adopted has to be recognized in order to understand the nature of the political relationships that subsequently developed.

The Iroquois perception of the nature of the alliance formed with the British is captured by the Gus-Wen-Qah, the Two-Row Wampum Belt. The first of these belts was delivered and explained at the Treaty of Fort Albany, in 1664, marking the commencement of formal relations between the British and the confederacy. It has remained an integral feature of Iroquois negotiations into the twentieth century. The Special Committee on Indian Self-Government received an explanation of the import of Gus-Wen-Qah by an authorized representative of the confederacy at a hearing in May 1983:

> when your ancestors came to our shores, after living with them for a few years, observing them, our ancestors came to the conclusion that we could not live together in the same way inside the circle ... . So our leaders at that time, along with your leaders, sat down for many years to try to work out a solution. This is what they came up with. We call it Gus-Wen-Qah, or the two row wampum belt. It is on a bed of white wampum, which symbolizes the purity of the agreement. There are two rows of purple, and those two rows have the spirit of our ancestors; those two rows never come together in that belt, and it is easy to see what that means. it means that we have two different paths, two different people.
>
> The agreement was made that your road will have your vessel, your people, your politics, your government, your way of life, your religion, your beliefs—they are all in there. The same goes for ours ... . They said there will be three beads of wampum separating the two, and they will symbolize peace, friendship, and respect.

The vessel metaphor was used to characterize the distinct jurisdictions: the British vessel and confederacy canoe. The two were to co-exist as independent entities, each respecting the autonomy of the other. The two rows of purple wampum, representing the two governments, ran parallel, never crossing. The two vessels travel together, as allies, but neither nation tries to steer the other's vessel. In the relationship envisioned by the Two-Row Wampum, neither government has the authority to legislate for the other. The vessels are always separated by the three white beads symbolizing peace, friendship, and respect. The principles captured by the Two-Row Wampum formed the basis of the alliance between the British and the confederacy. Perhaps the most striking feature of the Iroquois vision of diplomatic relations with the British is its consistency. For over three centuries, the confederacy has abided steadfastly in its "canoe" and has reminded the British nation of its obligation to do the same.

The commitment of the confederacy to its alliance with the British was demonstrated by its participation in the Seven Years' War.

The author explained the Royal Proclamation of 1763, and then governmental policies over the next century which resulted in the enactment of the federal Indian Act in 1876. In the annual report of the Department of Indian Affairs in 1870, the Deputy Superintendent justified increasing interference in internal Indian government as follows:

The Acts framed in the years 1868 and 1869, relating to Indian Affairs, were designed to lead the Indian people by degrees to mingle with the white race in the ordinary facilities for electing, for a limited period, members of bands to manage as a Council, local matters—that intelligent and educated men, recognized as chiefs, should carry out the wishes of the male members of mature years in each band, who should be fairly respresented in the conduct of their internal affairs.

Thus establishing a responsible, for an irresponsible system, this provision, by law, was designed to pave the way to the establishment of simple municipal institutions.

These justifications would carry little weight in the case of the Six Nations Confederacy.

In order to acquaint the various tribes with the new elective system and to obtain their formal acquiescence, a council was held at Sarnia in June 1871. When the Six Nations delegates discovered that the council was being held to gain their approval for the enactment of the 1868-69 legislation, they immediately withdrew. The presumption of the Dominion of Canada to attempt to govern the internal affairs of the Six Nations people was a great affront to them. The ethnocentric assumption that Indian nations could progress only by imitating the dominion's parliamentary system was particularly galling to a government as firmly democratic as the Six Nations Confederacy. The federal legislation was acutely inconsistent with the nature of Iroquois authority and government, especially with respect to the roles of the women and the chiefs. The confederacy's insistence on full consultation and consensus in decision-making could hardly be more "responsible." Apart from the many contradictions between the federal legislation and the laws of the confederacy, the singular concept that such legislation would govern the internal affairs of the Six Nations was inimical to their national integrity and sovereignty.

In 1876, the Canadian parliament passed *The Indian Act*, consolidating and revising all previous legislation dealing with Indians in all existing provinces and territories. It was, in effect, a code to govern virtually every aspect of Indian Life. As "the baggage of assumed powers continued to accumulate," the Six Nations Confederacy was constant in its refrain: "we have laws of our own, which are proper to govern us." Meanwhile, the fifty chiefs continued to sit and guard the council fire of the confederacy.

"We Are Not Part of Canada"

In the last century, the Six Nations Confederacy has produced a series of formal protests and defiant assertions of independence and sovereignty. It must be understood that its persistence is not merely a jealous defence of political autonomy. In the Great Law of Peace, the constitution of the confederacy, the political principles are intimately connected with the spiritual and the social. For the Iroquois, the Great Law constitutes a way of life, going far beyond a formula for division of powers. This concept has been captured (as noted earlier) in the symbolism of the Covenant Circle Wampum. To choose to submit to the law of a foreign nation is to forsake the confederacy, to go outside the circle. As the wampum depicts: "inside the Circle is our language and culture, our clans and the ways we organize ourselves socially, our laws and the way we organize ourselves politically, and our ceremonies which reflect our spirituality and our cycle of life." Those who leave the circle are alienated from all that it contains. Hence the resistance of the Six Nations to the Canadian government's assertion of jurisdiction assumes the proportion of a people struggling for their very existence.

The claims to special status and relations with the Crown did not fall on sympathetic ears. Sir John A. Macdonald, writing in 1887 while he was both prime minister and superintendent general of indian affairs, dismissed the Six Nations' claim to exceptional status in the following manner:

> It is extremely inexpedient to deal with Indian Bands in the Dominion ... as being in any way separate nations. They are governed by Canadian statutes, and for any wrongs and grievances have the right of recourse to the legal tribunals of the country as fully and readily as their white fellow subjects ... . It would be difficult, if not impossible, to make another tribe understand why it should not receive the same consideration as the Six Nations, and great consequent heart-burnings and jealousies ensue. ...

This denial of the confederacy's sovereignty—based on expediency rather than on the legal and historical merits, as justice would require—set the tone for subsequent considerations of the issue. Especially disturbing is the *non sequitur* that the Six Nations are subject to Canadian statutes because Canadian courts are prepared to redress their grievances. "In a way," writes one commentator, "it is like saying that, because a door is open to you, you must be inside the house."

In keeping with their laws and with the history of their relations with the Crown, the Six Nations directed their claims to the Governor-General of Canada. In 1890, a formal petition, maintaining that the *Indian Act, per se*, constituted a violation of ancient treaties and covenants, was delivered to the governor-general. Because this petition captures the essence of the confederacy's continuing claim to sovereignty, it warrants quotation at length:

> We will address your Excellency according to our ancient Treaties as Brothers.

Brother, We will now let you know our way of thoughts. You are the Governor of Canada sent by the Queen our Mother to whom we the allies of to keep the Treaty the same as of whom our forefathers and Your forefathers made in the ancient time. The treaty made whenever we see anything wrong to tell once. And now we will tell you that we are disappointed because there never was yet any treaty made between you and Us, the Five Nations Indians, that You would force any kind your laws that we did not like. And now in some cases we see you are doing so.

Brother, We have kept patience for a long time, because, knowing the Treaty of which our forefathers and your forefathers made in the year 1758 being durable to us. But in the way you have treated us thinking for to ask you if the sun and moon has gone out of your sight. But we see the sun and moon as when our forefathers and your forefathers made the agreement. The treaty whenever you or us the Indians see anything wrong or dissatisfaction, we are to renew brighten and strengthen the ancient Covenant. And we want to be always free and satisfied to be governed by our own laws and customs, for we have laws of our own. And those that are in favour of your laws and customs we have nothing to do with suppose they are to be governed by it. But we cannot help them in no way, for they broken our word rules and customs. Here is law of our forefathers laid down for us.

The dark blue wampum twenty five courses mixed with white represents the figures of men, and Chiefs of the Five Nations Indians hands joined together, and Union of the Five Nations. And if any man or child were to go through outside where these men stands in form of a circumference. Then the emblem of this Chiefship strikes on their arms and falls from him, thus it remains inside the circumference ... . So he is nothing but a man no more Chief and longer but *how does he goes through well that is if he receives the laws of other Nations to be governed by it accordingly.*

Wampum belt treaty having two white rows, parallel and represents the two Governments, namely the Five Nations and the British Government will exist and shall not interfere with each other. Of which the British made an illustration that the British will remain in their vessel, that is their government. While the Five Nations will also abide in their birch bark canoe, meaning their Government. The British will never make compulsory, and *door way laws for the Five Nations to enter in so that should become a British subject.* [Emphasis added.]

Although the English is halting and much of the construction awkward, the petition conveys the central concepts underlying the confederacy's understanding of its historical relationship with the Crown: the Covenant Circle Wampum and the Two-Row Wampum. The introductory paragraphs refer to the ancient tradition of renewing the alliance. Then, the theme of alienation through submission to foreign laws—anathema to the confederacy—is developed. In asking whether the sun and moon have gone from the governor's sight, the chiefs are referring to the understanding that the alliance would last as long as the sun and moon endure and implying that, in legislating "door way laws," the Crown has broken its covenant with the Six Nations Confederacy.

The author explained subsequent developments, including legal challenges in Ontario and before international tribunals, and concluded:

These unsuccessful attempts have not daunted the confederacy's intention to voice its grievances within the international forum. Rather, the confederacy has been encouraged by the dramatic evolution of self-determination from an abstract, idealistic theory to an articulate and forceful international right. Although the right to self-determination has achieved international recognition, the task of identifying the appropriate unit of self-determination has been highly problematical. An equally troublesome problem has been the interplay between the right of peoples to self-determination and the right of existing states to territorial integrity. These two obstacles must be addressed in order for the Six Nations Confederacy to establish the legitimacy of its claim to exercise the right of self-determination.

Reconsider the relationship between land claims and rights to self-government. To what extent can they exist separately? How should assertions of traditional sovereignty, such as those described by Johnston in relation to the Six Nations Confederacy, be recognized?

Aboriginal Land Rights: Mabo v. Queensland

Claims based on aboriginal land rights have been initiated in other common law jurisdictions, including the United States, Australia, and New Zealand. One of the most significant was the Australian decision, *Mabo v. Queensland*, [1992] 66 ALJR 408 (HC). In *Mabo*, the Australian High Court overturned the doctrine of "*terra nullius*" in so far as it applied to Australia. This doctrine permitted the British Crown to assert ownership of unoccupied land, but the common law doctrine had been extended to include inhabited lands if there were no recognizable laws or social organization, so that they were too "barbaric" for English law to recognize: see *Cooper v. Stuart*, [1889] 14 AC 286 (PC) and *Milirrpum v. Nabalco Pty. Ltd.* (1971), 17 FLR 141 (N Terr. SC). In *Mabo*, the Australian High Court rejected this approach and (at 422) confirmed legal recognition of land rights of the Meriam people, residents of the Murray Islands in Torres Strait:

> The fiction by which the rights and interests of indigenous inhabitants in land were treated as non-existent was justified by a policy which has no place in the contemporary law of this country ... . Whatever the justification advanced in earlier days for refusing to recognise the rights and interests in land of the indigenous inhabitants of settled colonies, an unjust and discriminatory doctrine of that kind can no longer be accepted. The expectations of the international community accord in this respect with the contemporary values of the Australian people.

The court analyzed the relationship between the acquisition of territorial sovereignty in international law and the acquisition of property according to common law principles. According to Brennan J (at 425), "The Crown was invested with the character of Paramount Lord in the colonies by attributing to the Crown a title, adapted from feudal theory, that was called a radical, ultimate or final title," and this radical title permitted the Crown to grant lands in accordance with tenurial requirements. Yet, as Brennan J stated emphatically (at 425-26):

> [It] is not a corollary of the Crown's acquisition of a radical title to land in an occupied territory that the Crown acquired absolute beneficial ownership of that land to the

exclusion of the indigenous inhabitants. If the land were desert and uninhabited, truly a terra nullius, the Crown would take an absolute beneficial title (an allodial title) to the land ... : there would be no *other* proprietor. But if the land were occupied by the indigenous inhabitants and their rights and interests in the land are recognised by the common law, the radical title which is acquired with the acquisition of sovereignty cannot itself be taken to confer an absolute beneficial title to the occupied land ... . Whether or not land is owned by individual members of a community, a community which asserts and asserts effectively that none but its members has any right to occupy or use the land has an interest in the land that must be proprietary in nature: there is no other proprietor ... . Where a proprietary title capable of recognition by the common law is found to have been possessed by a community in occupation of a territory, there is no reason why that title should not be recognised as a burden on the Crown's radical title when the Crown acquires sovereignty over that territory.

Thus, the court concluded that the Crown's radical title could be subjected to a beneficial title on the part of the indigenous people of the Murray Islands. In reaching this conclusion, the court acknowledged that earlier precedent cases were being overruled, and Brennan J stated (at 429):

To maintain the authority of those cases would destroy the equality of all Australian citizens before the law. The common law of this country would perpetuate injustice if it were to continue to embrace the enlarged notion of terra nullius and to persist in characterising the indigenous inhabitants of the Australian colonies as people too low in the scale of social organisation to be acknowledged as possessing rights and interests in land.

The decision in *Mabo* was "greeted by enthusiasm in many quarters committed to Aboriginal land rights," even though a close inspection of the reasoning in the case suggested that it raised a number of issues for subsequent claimants. See S.B. Phillips, "A Note: *Eddie Mabo v. The State of Queensland*" (1993), 15 *Sydney Law Review* 121 (hereafter Phillips), at 141. For other assessments, see additional comments in the same volume; P. Butt, "Native Land Rights in Australia: The *Mabo* Case" (1995), *The Conveyancer and Property Lawyer* 33 (hereafter Butt); and G. Nettheim, "The *Mabo* Response: Reconciliation or Continuing Conquest" (1993), 3 *University of New South Wales Law School Bulletin* 19. Note also that there were concurring judgments in the case—a joint judgment by Deane and Gaudron JJ and another by Toohey J. Dawson J dissented, concluding that native title was extinguished upon acquisition by the British Crown. The political significance of *Mabo* was underlined by efforts on the part of the Queensland government to defeat the claim of the Meriam people. In 1985, the Queensland legislature had passed the Queensland Coast Islands Declaratory Act 1985 (Qld.), but the High Court subsequently held the statute inconsistent with valid federal legislation, the Racial Discrimination Act 1975 (Cth.). This earlier High Court decision is referred to as *Mabo (No. 1)*, (1989), 166 CLR 186, while the 1992 decision is referred to as *Mabo (No. 2)* (1992), 175 CLR 1; 66 ALJR 408. The main claimant in the case, Eddie Mabo, died before the High Court decision in *Mabo (No. 2)*, and his claim was denied because he had lived for too long away from the Murray Islands. See Phillips.

The *Mabo* case is important for its recognition of native title to occupied land. According to Butt, the decision provided a number of important propositions concerning the nature and content of native land title:

1. Native title (or "traditional" title, or "customary" title) reflects the indigenous inhabitants' entitlement to their traditional lands, in accordance with their laws and customs. So its nature and extent is essentially a question of fact. It may possess characteristics unknown in the common law. To prove the existence of native title, there must be an established entitlement to occupy or use particular land—an entitlement of sufficient significance to demonstrate a locally recognised special relationship between the users and the land.

2. There can be no native title without native "presence" on the land—presence amounting to occupancy, but not necessarily possession at common law. The presence on the land must be an established fact at least from the time the Crown asserted sovereignty over the land. ...

3. Native title is usually communal, although in rare cases it may be individual.

4. Native title cannot be alienated outside the clan or group, although it can be voluntarily surrendered to the Crown.

5. Is native title "personal" or "proprietary"? Brennan J thought that in some circumstances it may be "proprietary," and that where this is so it nevertheless can accommodate personal usufructuary rights that are enjoyed under that proprietary title. ...

6. Where a clan or group has continued to observe its traditions and customs, maintaining its connection with the land, the native title remains in existence. ...

7. Since native title is recognised by the common law, it can be protected by any legal or equitable remedies appropriate to the particular rights and interests established by the evidence.

(Butt, at 35-37.) For an account of the relationship between the spiritual and economic connections in *Mabo*, see N. Sharp, "No Ordinary Case: Reflections Upon *Mabo (No. 2)*" (1993), 15 *Sydney Law Review* 143. For a discussion of the importance of clarifying the fiduciary principles, see P. O'Connor, "Aboriginal Land Rights after *Mabo*" (1992), *Law Institute Journal* 1105. The issues in *Mabo* were addressed again in subsequent cases—for example, see *Pareroultja v. Tickner* (1993), 117 ALR 206 (FC) and *Coe v. Commonwealth* (1993), 118 ALR 192 (HC).

The *Mabo* case resulted in a significant reappraisal of issues of native land claims in a variety of contexts. For some examples, see F. Merlan, "The Regimentation of Customary Practice: From Northern Territory Land Claims to *Mabo*" (1995), 6:1-2 *Australian Journal of Anthropology* 64; H. Amankwah, "*Mabo* and International Law" (1994), 35:4 *Race and Class* 57; R.P. Hill, "Blackfellas and Whitefellas: Aboriginal Land Rights, the *Mabo* Decision, and the Meaning of Land" (1995), 17:2 *Human Rights Quarterly* 303; J. Webber, "The Jurisprudence of Regret: The Search for Standards of Justice in *Mabo*" (1995), 17 *Sydney Law Review* 5; B.A. Keon-Cohen, "*Mabo*, Native Title and Compensation: Or How to Enjoy Your Porridge" (1995), 21:1 *Monash University Law Review* 84; and K. Puri, "Cultural Ownership and Intellectual Property Rights Post-*Mabo*: Putting Ideas into Action" (1995), 9 *Intellectual Property Journal* 293. See also F. Brennan, *One Land, One Nation: Mabo—Towards 2001* (St. Lucia, Qld.: Queensland University Press, 1995). One commentator has contrasted the approach of the BC courts in *Delgamuukw* with the High Court judges in *Mabo*, suggesting that:

> The *Mabo* decision lends credence to the idea that in contrast to the trial and Court of Appeal decisions in *Delgamuukw*, a "reverse weight of history" argument may be used to say that self-government is in existence today. This argument would say the following: the recognition in legislation and case law of continued aboriginal powers to govern themselves in certain spheres implies the contemporary existence of the aboriginal right of self-government.

(B. Freedman, "The Space for Aboriginal Self-Government in British Columbia: The Effect of the Decision of the British Columbia Court of Appeal in *Delgamuukw v. British Columbia* (1994), *University of British Columbia Law Review* 49, at 72-73.) Do you agree with this assessment? On what basis?

The federal government in Australia responded to *Mabo* by enacting the Native Title Act 1993 (Cth.). The statute permitted "validation" by government of pre-existing grants of freehold and of residential, pastoral and tourist leasehold, and permanent public works. Validation extinguishes native title, but compensation on "just terms" is payable. No grant over native land can be made after December 31, 1993 unless the government could do the same over freehold land (subject to limited provisions for mining and other leases). Native title is inalienable except for surrender to the relevant government, and the Federal Court can determine the existence of native title and compensation for its extinguishment. As well a federal native title tribunal can determine whether grants should be made over land subject to native title, and judges of the Federal Court are assisted by appropriately qualified mediators or assessors who are intended to be aboriginal people.

The federal legislation was generally endorsed by all states in Australia, sometimes with reservations, except the state of Western Australia. Western Australia introduced state legislation extinguishing native title and providing statutory rights of use and occupancy (not property rights), but the High Court held the legislation unconstitutional in *Western Australia v. The Commonwealth* (1995), 128 ALR 1 (HC), reaffirming the principles outlined in *Mabo*:

> The *Mabo No 2* and the *Western Australia* decisions established that native title originates from a connection with the land by indigenous peoples in accordance with their own customary systems of law prior to British colonization. The effect of colonization was to give the British Crown sovereignty and radical title to the land, but that did not affect the rights of possession and use of the indigenous peoples under their own laws. The indigenous peoples became British subjects and their land rights continued and are enforceable today as common law legal entitlements, in the absence of valid acts of extinguishment or loss of connection with the land by the indigenous titleholders.

(K. McNeil, "Racial Discrimination and Unilateral Extinguishment of Native Title" (1996), *Australian Indigenous Law Reporter* 181, at 181-82.) See also R. Bartlett, "Racism and Constitutional Protection of Native Title in Western Australia: The 1995 High Court Decision" (1995), 25 *The University of Western Australia Law Review* 127; "Post-*Mabo*: The Hard Road to Settlement in Australia" (1993), 4 *Canadian Native Law Reporter* 1; and

"The National Native Title Tribunal in Australia: Dispossession Not Settlement?" (1996), 2 *Canadian Native Law Reporter* 1. See also the collection of essays in R. Bartlett and G. Meyers, eds., *Native Title Legislation in Australia* (The Centre for Commercial and Resources Law, University of Western Australia and Murdoch University, 1994). A Native Title Act (Amendment) Bill was introduced in 1995, but it lapsed when a federal election was called in 1996, and a new discussion paper with draft amending legislation was then released in mid-1997. The amendments clarify issues that became important after the High Court's decision in *The Wik Peoples v. Queensland* (1996), 141 ALR 129 (HC), in which the court held (at 4:3) that the grant of pastoral leases pursuant to state legislation (the Land Act 1910 (Qld.) and the Land Act 1962-74 (Qld.)) did not necessarily extinguish native title. The test was whether such grants were "inconsistent" with the continued existence of native title. There was some difference of opinion in the judgments about whether it was the grant, or the exercise of rights, that would result in extinguishment. For judicial opinions concerning the work of the National Native Title Tribunal, see *Re Waanyi People's Native Title Application* (1995), 129 ALR 100 (NNTT), (1995), 129 ALR 118 (NNTT), (1996), 135 ALR 225 (HC). In September 1997, the Native Title Amendment Bill 1997 was introduced in the Australian Parliament. For further analysis of these issues, see K. Hazlehurst, *Legal Pluralism and the Colonial Legacy: Indigenous Experiences of Justice in Canada, Australia and New Zealand* (Aldershot: Avebury, 1995).

"OLD" PROPERTY, "NEW" PROPERTY: CONSTITUTIONAL PROTECTION?

Property and the Charter of Rights and Freedoms

J. McBean, "The Implications of Entrenching Property Rights in Section 7 of the Charter of Rights"
(1988), 26 *Alberta Law Review* 548 (footnotes omitted)

I. Introduction

In April of 1982 Canada entrenched into its Constitution the Charter of Rights and Freedoms. Section 7 of the Charter reads as follows:

> Everyone has the right to life, liberty, and security of the person and the right not to be deprived thereof except in accordance with the principles of fundamental justice.

The predecessor to this section is s. (1)(a) of the Canadian Bill of rights which provides:

> It is hereby recognized and declared that in Canada there have existed and shall continue to exist without discrimination by reason of race, national origin, colour, religion or sex, the following human rights and fundamental freedoms, namely, (a) the right of the individual to life, liberty, security of the person and *enjoyment of property*, and the right not to be deprived thereof except by due process of law. [Emphasis added.]

Although the federal Liberal government originally proposed that s. 7 also include the enjoyment of property as a protected right, provincial opposition convinced it to remove that phrase, and the present wording is identical to that which was proposed by the federal government in the Constitutional Resolution proposed in October 1980. Since that Resolution was introduced there have been legislative attempts, both before and after the enactment of the Charter, to amend s. 7 to add property as a protected category. Moreover, there have been attempts by various litigants to attain in effect a "judicial amendment" to the section by importing a wide meaning to the terms "liberty" and "security of the person" to encompass economic rights. The potential effects of adding property to s. 7 are the concern of this article.

Depending on the definition of property that is adopted, the entrenchment of property rights in s. 7 can have two possible consequences. In the first instance, if the traditional definition of property is utilized by the courts, it might simply act as a protection against the unfair deprivation of property in its traditional sense from property owners. In this case, the section would have positive effects for property owners, but would be generally irrelevant to the propertyless class of Canadians, although in some cases it might actually have a negative impact. An example of such a negative effect would be if an amended s. 7 were the means of preventing a propertyless individual from successfully asserting some right, such as a wife claiming a share of matrimonial property under one of the provincial matrimonial property laws. Moreover, as is surmised in the final part of this article, the entrenchment of property could affect negatively environmental, land utilization, social welfare, labour and other socially useful laws of general benefit. For example, courts might strike down a labour law which prevented the firing of workers who join a union if it was found that such a law was a deprivation of the property of the employer. Only if the law could be upheld under s. 1 of the Charter as justifiable in a democratic society would it remain valid.

Alternatively, if the courts were to use a less traditional definition of property, the entrenchment of property rights could have very positive effects for both propertied and propertyless Canadians. This would result from an interpretation of the term "property" that included the "new" property of government benefits. This issue will be explored in the last part of the article.

To date there has been little public debate on this important and complex question of entrenching property rights in the Charter, a proposal which to some extent has been treated as a "motherhood issue," designed only to protect the corner grocery store and the family home. It has been suggested that the fact that the supporters of the amendment are largely big landowners, pit and quarry owners, and banks who wish protection from government interference with their enjoyment of property, to some extent belies this characterization. Certainly a major supporter is the National Citizens Coalition which in a large advertisement in the Globe and Mail in May 1983 not only advocated the introduction of property to the Charter, but also demanded that the s. 33 override provision would not be applicable to property rights. Other groups which have passed resolutions in favour of entrenching property rights include the Canadian Chamber of Commerce, the Canadian Real Estate Association, the Ontario Real Estate Association, the Canadian Institute of Planners, and the Canadian Bar Association. Opposition has been voiced by such womens' groups as the Canadian Advisory Council on the Status of Women, and some environmental groups.

Whether this is an innocuous amendment, designed only to placate Canadian free enterprisers, or is indeed the dangerous vehicle which some perceive will take away the hard won rights of Canadian workers to occupational health and safety laws, of Canadian wives to the benefit of matrimonial property laws, and of Canadian citizens in general to the benefits of environmental laws, rent control legislation and numerous other acts of government which benefit Canadians while encroaching on the property rights of those affected by the law, turns on the issue of what notions of fairness the courts will consider as inherent in the "principles of fundamental justice." To answer that question this article will review Canadian litigation to date by examining relevant judicial decisions both on s. 7 of the Charter and of its predecessor provisions in the Canadian Bill of Rights, and compare and contrast our law on this matter with the law of other countries, particularly, the United States.

A. The Legislative History of Section 7

As stated above, the present wording of s. 7 is identical to that which was originally proposed by the federal government in October, 1980. During the Committee hearings on the Constitution, and later in the House of Commons, the Progressive Conservative opposition proposed that s. 7 be amended to include as a protected right the "enjoyment of property." Although the Liberal government indicated initially in the Committee hearings that it would support that amendment, it subsequently changed its position, and the amendment was defeated in both the Committee and later in the House. Throughout, Justice Minister Chretien indicated that on principle the Liberal government supported the concept of entrenching property rights, but in view of the opposition from many of the provinces, who feared for their zoning legislation and foreign ownership of land regulations, he indicated that the government would have to withdraw its support for the amendment, promising to keep the proposal as an item for the next round of discussions on the Constitution. In addition to the opposition directly from the provinces, opposition came from the New Democratic party which opposed the amendment on the grounds that the provision would adversely affect the right of both the provincial and federal governments to engage in public ownership of resource-based and other industries, and would generally render the provinces incapable of effectively legislating with respect to land utilization. At one point it appears that the leader of the New Democratic party, Ed Broadbent, threatened to withdraw support for the various constitutional measures which had been discussed and agreed on to date if the government continued to support adding property to the Charter. Wherever the definitive opposition came from, the net result was that s. 7 was enacted without reference to property.

However, the idea of adding property to s. 7 did not die. Since 1982 the Legislative Assemblies of both British Columbia and New Brunswick have passed resolutions asking that s. 7 be amended to include property. More recently, on November 27, 1986, the Ontario Legislature during private members' hour, by a vote of 44 to 20, passed a similar resolution, although that resolution is not binding on the government of Ontario as it did not receive the required majority of the Legislature. Members of the federal Progressive Conservative party, both while in opposition and in government, have introduced bills to the same effect on four different occasions. On several occasions members of the government, including Prime Minister Mulroney, have indicated that the matter will again be placed on the agenda for future constitutional discussions with the provinces. As a result, the meeting of Attorneys General of the provinces and the Attorney General of Canada in February 1986 established a working group to look at the implications of entrenchment. The method and likelihood of achieving this legislative amendment will be the next consideration.

B. The Proposed Amendment: Political Status, Terms, and Procedure for Enactment

The proposed amendment would add the phrase "and enjoyment of property" after the phrase "security of the person." Property would not be defined, and, therefore, might include all types of property, including not only tangible assets, such as land or chattels, but also enforceable rights. A discussion on the effects of a wide definition of property which might include the so called "new" property is found in part III(H) of this article.

What are the reasons for putting forward the amendment? No doubt they vary. Professor Hogg stated the rationale to be as follows:

> The omission of property rights from s. 7 greatly reduces its scope. It means that s. 7 affords no guarantee of compensation or even of a fair procedure for the taking of property by government. It means that s. 7 affords no guarantee of fair treatment by courts, tribunals or officials with power over the purely economic interests of individuals or corporations.

It should be noted that in order for s. 7 to grant the protection claimed for it by adherents of an amendment depends on whether there is substantive review of legislation as in the United States, for if there is not, even adding property rights to s. 7 will not offer a great deal more protection to those who are being unfairly deprived of their property. Moreover, in considering the necessity of such an amendment, as Professor Hogg admits, even in the absence of the Charter, the courts will imply that a fair procedure must be employed in taking property, at least unless there is an express provision to the contrary in the law. Moreover, at least on the federal level, there is the Canadian Bill of Rights which guarantees the right to the enjoyment of property. At the provincial level the equivalent legislation to the Bill of Rights only exists in the Yukon, Alberta, Saskatchewan and Quebec, and of these only Alberta and the Yukon have a due process clause.

The statements made by politicians to support the proposal are that throughout the history of civilization democracy has been based on four basic rights: life, liberty, security of the person and the enjoyment of private property. Others feel that the fundamental right to enjoyment of property dates back to the reference to property in the Magna Carta.

How historically accurate these statements are as to the fundamental nature of property rights to democracy is questionable, and how compatible the amendment would be to the principles of the modern welfare state and modern society where the "new" property far outstrips the value of land and other traditional forms of property referred to by the politicians in their speeches is even more questionable. However, proponents of the amendment also argue that the inclusion of property as a protected right in the American Constitution prevented the sale of the seized property of the Japanese Americans during World War II, and might have better protected the seized property of Japanese Canadians during that same period, albeit it would not have protected against the actual seizure. Moreover, it is pointed out that Canada signed the Universal Declaration of Human Rights in 1948 which includes in Article 17 a right not to be arbitrarily deprived of one's property, and it is argued that the inclusion of property in s. 7 would be a way of giving effect to this right. ...

[The author reviewed the stated positions of federal and provincial governments concerning a constitutional amendment to include protection of property in s. 7 of the Charter—for example:]

[T]he Prince Edward Island opposition was expressed as being based on both psychological and economic reasons arising out of the history of the struggle of peasant farmers against the oppression and neglect of absentee landlords which had led the government to impose restrictions on the acquisition of land by aliens and non-resident persons or corporations. Newfoundland, in confirming its opposition at this time, gave as some of its concerns the implications such an amendment would have with respect to provincial jurisdiction over property rights, the inherent problems associated with the meaning of the phrase "enjoyment of property" and what that phrase would include. It was the concern for provincial jurisdiction over property rights that was emphasized by Mr. Horsman, the Minister of Intergovernmental Affairs for Alberta, who also relied on the fact that property rights were already included in the Alberta Bill of Rights. Both he and Mr. Moore, who had prepared the Prince Edward Island position paper, felt that provincial laws related to property should be dealt with in the Legislature, which could deal most sensitively to the particular needs of a province, not in the courts. Prince Edward Island suggested that if property rights were to be included in the Charter it should be in a separate section of its own, not in s. 7. ...

C. The Possibility of Entrenching Property by "Judicial Amendment"

It has been argued by a number of legal commentators that even without a legislative amendment to incorporate the phrase "the enjoyment of property," some, or all, forms of property rights are already protected under the terms "liberty" or "security of the person." The argument that this is the case is based largely on American jurisprudence wherein the term "liberty" appears to have received an expansive interpretation, particularly with regards to cases involving the Fourteenth amendment, as the American courts sought to selectively incorporate into matters of state jurisdiction most of the important rights and freedoms already applicable in areas of federal jurisdiction by virtue of the first eight amendments of the American Constitution. The result in the United States has been to interpret "liberty" not merely as providing freedom from bodily restraint, but to incorporate into one or the other of these terms, the property related concepts of freedom to contract, freedom to take up any livelihood or lawful occupation, and freedom from state action that deprives a person of all or a substantial portion of his or her capacity to earn a living.

"Security of the person" is not a term used in the American Bill of Rights, but it too has been interpreted to go beyond physical integrity and include the necessaries for life, although jurisprudence under the European Convention on Human Rights has given the term a more restrictive meaning.

The argument put forward in Canada is that the words used in s. 7 override both its contextual connotation and its legislative history. It is true that the debate in the Special Joint Committee of the Senate and House of Commons and later in the Commons centred on the traditional concept of property, that is, the family home or the corner grocery store. Thus, there may be room to interpret "liberty" or "security of the person" as including protection for the "new property" (a concept which is more fully discussed below in part III(H), but one that includes economic interests such as rights to welfare, public housing and other forms of government aid) without offering such protection to the "old property." However, many of the cases in which some form of protection from the deprivation of property has been claimed concerned traditional forms of property, and some of the legal commentators have argued that s. 7 can be interpreted to protect all types of property. Others argue that at least any state action which deprives a person of all (or a substantial portion) of his or her capacity to produce an income could be seen as a threat to the security of the person. To date, there has been no attempt by the courts in s. 7 litigation to draw distinctions between the two types of property. ...

The earliest judgment wherein it was suggested that the enjoyment of property might be included within the scope of s. 7 was the decision of *The Queen in the Right of New Brunswick v. Fisherman's Wharf Ltd.*, wherein Dickson J found, without hearing argument from counsel on the point, that the term "security of the person" must extend to the right not to be deprived of property rights which relate to the security of the person. He, therefore, gave this as a "corollary ground" for finding that no lien attached to certain goods seized pursuant to the New Brunswick law under review. No reference was made to any authority for this proposition, nor was there any comment on the legislative history of s. 7. The decision was upheld by the New Brunswick Court of Appeal on non-Charter grounds, with the comment by LaForest JA (as he then was), that "security of property" was not expressly protected by the Charter, in order not to frustrate "regulatory schemes ... obviously intended to reallocate rights and resources" which of necessity affect vested rights. ...

[The author reviewed a number of other decisions, concluding:]

Clearly the question of whether economic rights are protected under s. 7 is at present unanswered. In view of the very limited weight given by the Supreme Court to the debates surrounding the enactment of the Charter, it is an open question what its interpretation will be. It is possible that the "new property" economic interests such as welfare rights and licences will be included in s. 7, even if more traditional types of property interests remain excluded. However, until the Supreme Court gives some definitive statement, there will likely continue to be contradictory decisions made by lower courts on this issue. ...

[The author reviewed a number of areas of law that might be challenged if property were constitutionally protected: legislation concerning rent control, environmental protection, labour law, nationalization of industries, taxation, and matrimonial property. In relation to some of these areas, the author suggested:]

A. *Landlord and Tenant*

In 1981 the Irish Supreme Court, relying on the constitutional guarantee of property that existed in Article 40 of the Constitution of Ireland, 1937, struck down rent control legislation that had been in existence in various statutory forms since 1915. At the same time provisions which were regarded as integral to the rent control scheme such as limits on the ability of landlords to obtain possession of rent controlled premises were also struck out, despite the voiced concern of the Court of the effect this would potentially have on tens of thousands of tenants. The main provision regarding the entrenchment of property rights in the Irish Constitution, Article 43, contained explicit recognition that the exercise of the rights to property must be regulated by "the principles of social justice," and accordingly "the State may on occasion delimit by law the exercise of the said rights with a view to reconciling their exercise with the exigencies of the common good." However, the Court acted under Article 40 which was headed "personal rights," and which had a requirement that the State shall in the case of "injustice done ... vindicate the property rights of every citizen." The Court refused to accept arguments that all references to property rights elsewhere in the Constitution were subject to the limitations found in Article 43.

Would that happen to Canadian landlord and tenant laws? Even those landlord and tenant laws without an aspect of rent control clearly encroach on the enjoyment of property rights, and so there is a deprivation under s. 7. Whether that deprivation is in violation of any fundamental principle of justice awaits a fuller exposition of the substantive content of these principles, whether for example, the presumption of the common law suggested by Professor Tremblay as to the sacredness of private property, will be considered to be a fundamental principle of justice. Definitive answers also await further indications from the Court as to the criteria to be used in assessing whether a deprivation in violation of fundamental justice will be allowed to stand under s. 1, as a justifiable measure in a free and democratic society. ...

C. Labour Law

It was in the field of labour legislation that the US Supreme Court, in the heyday of substantive due process applied to social and distributive legislation, made such an indelible mark on the memories of progressive legislators both in the United States and Canada. The Canadian labour laws of today are more far reaching than the American maximum hours and minimum wage laws which were then overturned. Some laws which clearly would encroach on the enjoyment of property and/or the freedom to contract would be legislation forbidding the use of strike-breakers during a strike, legislation requiring companies to justify plant closures, occupational health laws, and equal pay laws, particularly those incorporating the idea of equal pay for work of equal value. While it may be thought that these laws are all easily justifiable in a democratic society, and that we should ignore what happened in the United States, in another era when less far reaching laws were declared invalid as irrelevant to the constitution and culture, we should remember, that even though the same strict scrutiny is not applied to American economic laws as was once applied, as late as 1978, routine factory inspections were held to be unconstitutional in the United States.

Again what will happen in Canada will depend on the content that is inserted into the principles of fundamental justice and the attitudes of the courts. ...

F. Matrimonial Property Laws

In all provinces except Quebec there are provisions for a distribution of marital property on separation or divorce, and in all provinces, including Quebec, provisions to allow a court to grant exclusive possession of the matrimonial home to one spouse on separation. These provisions clearly result in a deprivation of property to the spouse who owns the most property. It was the fear that matrimonial property laws would be subject to attack under s. 7 that led the Canadian Advisory Council on the Status of Women to take a position in opposition to the entrenchment of property rights in the Charter. These fears have been communicated successfully to the politicians, and the majority of speeches by elected politicians on this subject, in and out of the legislature, now refer to this potential problem, and contain assurances that if property rights are to be entrenched, they will be done so in such a way as to protect these hard won rights.

For there to be a successful challenge to a law under the Charter there must be some state action. In the American context it is quite clear that government enforcement of private claims to property by one person against another is a deprivation of property which invokes the application of the due process clause. In Canada the Supreme Court has ruled that a court order by itself does not constitute state action. However, where that court order is based on a statutory instrument (as opposed to the common law), even in litigation between two private individuals where no government agency is directly involved, the Charter can be invoked. Thus, a spouse who is ordered to turn over half of his farm or half of his pension should be able to use a Charter argument to challenge the validity of the legislation under s. 7.

But how successful would such a challenge be? In the United States, despite the existence of the due process clauses, it has generally been considered that matrimonial support laws and matrimonial property laws providing for the division of matrimonial assets, while they may amount to a deprivation of property, are valid exercises of the governmental interest in maintaining social institutions as part of the larger governmental concern for the protection of its citizens. Since our courts to date have in general been very supportive of these types of laws, and in particular, have interpreted them in a remedial way, for the most part giving effect to the principles of sharing, equality and equity in such laws, it appears likely that in this area at least, even an entrenched property right in s. 7 would be unable to invalidate these laws. The public interest in such laws would no doubt be given effect in any application by reference to s. 1, if resort was needed to that section because such laws were found to violate some principle of fundamental justice.

This is not to say that the inclusion of property in s. 7 will have no effect on Canadian spouses. It is quite likely that there will be challenges until there have been some definitive decisions on s. 7 and matrimonial support and property division legislation. While the remote possibility exists of a tremendous change in judicial attitudes in this area, which would result in a change in successful Charter challenges to matrimonial property laws, this is very unlikely in the writer's view. Accordingly it is predicted that such litigation will be fruitless to all except the lawyers involved, and will simply have the effect of depriving both spouses of more of their property as a result of the costs of litigation. ...

[The author also reviewed "new property" claims, a subject explored later in this chapter, and then proposed a "compromise" solution.]

IV. A Possible Compromise

In view of the fact that property and civil rights is a matter of strictly provincial concern under s. 92(13) of the BNA Act, it is difficult to justify any reference to property in the Charter. As indicated above, this is one of the major reasons why some provinces, in particular

Alberta, oppose the addition of property rights to the Charter. If despite this, the provinces and federal government in the future make some kind of compromise, and decide to entrench property rights in the Charter, then in view of the potential minefield of problems associated with including property rights in s. 7, some other placement should be considered.

My proposal would be to place property rights into a new section in the Charter which would make it clear that these property rights were only to be protected by principles of procedural fairness. This would be accomplished by using the term of art, "procedural fairness." It is understood that this does not prevent review of the substance of any challenged legislation, but it does limit the ambit of that review to procedural matters only.

It is interesting to note that this was the original plan of the federal government. In the Constitutional Amendment Bill introduced into Parliament in June 1978, clause 6 included, *inter alia*, "the right of the individual to life, liberty and security of his or her person and the right not to be deprived thereof except by due process of law," but "the right of the individual to the use and enjoyment of property, and the *right not to be deprived thereof except in accordance with law*." [Emphasis in original.] Thus two different tests were established, one including substantive protection, and the other limited to procedural protection. It also appears from the position paper of the government of Prince Edward Island to be a solution which they might endorse.

It is quite possible that if property interests are judicially or legislatively incorporated into s. 7, the courts, as in the United States, might on their own develop a different standard of fairness where a deprivation of an economic interest is alleged. Thus certain rights would be considered more fundamental than others, and economic rights would be protected from deprivation only by procedural safeguards such as a right to a hearing. But if that is what is desired, and particularly if a legislative amendment is going to be made anyway, it appears best to establish the two tests clearly in the legislation.

Such an amendment would have the effect of satisfying those people who feel a need to give property rights constitutional protection. Moreover, if property rights are kept out of s. 7, the courts are more likely to give a broad interpretation to the principles of fundamental justice which will then have the effect of enhancing the protection granted to life, liberty and security of the person, for the more rights which are protected, the more likely there would be a watering down of the protection granted them. Finally, in view of the provisions of s. 33, if some provinces still remained opposed to such an amendment, they could take advantage of the right to opt out of the operation of the new clause.

As it has often been said: "Compromise is the Canadian way of life."

J. Whyte, "Fundamental Justice: The Scope and Application of Section 7 of the Charter"
(1983), 13 *Manitoba Law Journal* 455, at 455-56 and 472-75 (footnotes omitted)

I Introduction

It is an inevitable feature of constitutional documents which protect human rights against encroaching state action, that the perplexities and ambiguities presented by their language are such that the interpretive enterprise is marked with uncertainty. Furthermore, the passing months and years of interpretive experience do not significantly lessen the extent to which clear ideas of the meaning of the text remain elusive. Rights are constitutionally entrenched by reference to political activities (speech, exercise of religious belief and voting) and political values (equality, justice and fairness), both of which are identified in bold, even resounding, language. The reality of the difficult reconciliation between these values and activities and the needs of the activist state often goes unmentioned in the constitutional text, as in the amendments to the *United States Constitution*, or is represented in the text by words which offer virtually no guide, as in section 1 of the *Canadian Charter of Rights and Freedoms*.

At the time of entrenchment it is, of course, clearly understood that some large and indeterminate part of our public life has been delegated to the judicial branch. That branch has been entrusted with giving proper content to the rights which have been recognized in gross, and allowing that degree of limitation on rights which properly permits governmental programs to go forward unhampered by individual claims. It is hoped that the contours of rights and limitations will become clearer as decisions flow forth. But, in fact, little ever becomes clearer; the closing off of one conception of right or limitation by the recognition of another merely deflects attention to elaborating the meaning or boundary of the chosen conception. In any event, even if some day we can come to understand more clearly what our *Charter* means, or even if some day we have a more definite sense of what meanings Canadian courts will stipulate for the various sections, the first eighteen months decidedly have not been the time frame within which that understanding and that sense have been developed. ...

III Security of the Person

The second issue to be dealt with in this paper is the meaning of "security of the person," the interpretative problem being to identify the sorts of interests which fall within that phrase. There is no reason to believe that "security of the person" is restricted to those invasions of personal integrity traditionally inflicted by the criminal justice system. The appearance of section 7 in the "Legal Rights" portion of the *Charter* might suggest that it be directed only to criminal and penal processes, but the words of the section clearly override any such contextual connotation. The rights referred to in section 7 arise in respect of any invasions of personal security (however defined) regardless of whether the process causing it is criminal or civil, judicial or administrative. In the absence of structural limitations the question posed by "security of the person" is whether the phrase includes such things as livelihood, property, family and other relationships, patterns of daily life, and generally matters which are essential to a person's capacity to act as an autonomous being.

"Security of the person" was considered in *The Queen v. Fisherman's Wharf* a remarkably early use of the *Charter* by Dickson J of the New Brunswick Court of Queen's Bench. The question was whether the collection provisions of the provincial retail sales tax legislation permitted the formation of a lien on all property used in the business of a taxpayer, including that property which was owned by third parties. The defaulting taxpayer was a restaurant and its cooking appliances, (and other equipment), were owned by others and held under lease, loan, conditional sales contract and licence. The claim of the various owners of the equipment was that the legislation did not allow a lien to be established on their property. Dickson J agreed. He gave ten reasons for this conclusion. One, (the ninth), was that to interpret the legislation otherwise would violate section 7's protection of "security of the person" which he said "must be construed as comprising the right to enjoyment of the ownership of property which extends to 'security of the person.'" Unfortunately, Dickson J did not elaborate on the sort of property which relates to personal security. Nor, on the particular facts of the case before him, did he show how the property belonging to the propane distributor, the dairy, the bottling company and the cigarette distributor related to their "security of the person." It can be assumed, of course, that this was property from which these companies produced their income and the loss of the property would negatively affect their earning capacity. From this it might be inferred that any property loss which causes a decrease in income is property which relates to security of the person. This view seems extravagant. A more plausible view of the outer edge of section 7 is that state action which deprives a person of all (or a substantial portion) of his or her capacity to produce an income could be seen as invading security of the person. Such action would include the removal of a person from the welfare scheme, the confiscation of property (tools, equipment, etc.) essential to a person's work, or the cancellation of a licence which is essential to the pursuit of one's occupation (taxi driver, lawyer or stationary engineer).

The *Fisherman's Wharf* decision is, however, correct in opening up section 7 to protect economic rights. One of the reasons this would seem to be a correct reading is that "security of the person" may be presumed to include rights not comprised in the ideas of "life" and "liberty." It must include some of the conditions of living beyond liberty. Assuming that the *Charter* is dedicated to granting rights over matters of fundamental importance, "security of the person" will include conditions necessary for life, such as food and shelter. Hence governmental actions which take away shelter and food, (or the capacity to obtain shelter and food), would be subject to court review under section 7. Since any substantial income loss affects the capacity to meet bodily needs, it would seem likely that economic interests, such as property and jobs, are protected against deprivation except, of course, when imposed in accordance with principles of fundamental justice.

It could be argued that section 7 should be given a more limited meaning—a meaning which does not include interests derived from property. It could relate only to interests of social interaction such as bodily integrity, privacy, association and equality. While the latter two are covered elsewhere in the Charter, the former two are clearly aspects of security of the person. However, there seems to be no compelling reason to view security of the person as being exhaustively defined by reference to privacy and bodily integrity and not as encompassing economic aspects of personhood. The concept of person includes such things as autonomy, self-direction and social activism (in the sense of being one who interacts). This means that not only bodies, and physical and social choices, should be protected from "unjust" interference, but one's ability to function with a degree of self-direction should be as well. A pre-condition of that self-direction is the ownership of (or at least the power to control) property.

A further argument for reading section 7 as providing constitutional protection for persons' livelihoods has been advanced by Professor Bryan Schwartz.

> ... the ability to carry on the economic activity of one's choice may be essential to a person's conception of how to live "the good life." It may be vital to a person that he be able to work as a farmer, a lawyer or a musician. It may be no less important to one person that he be permitted to practise his vocation as a tailor than to another that he be

allowed to publish his poetry. Few doubt that it is unacceptable that a person not be able to work at his profession because that person be black or Jewish or a woman. I see no reason to protect economic opportunity only from discriminatory attacks and not from tyrannical restrictions which affect everyone equally.

To the argument that the democratic process can be trusted in matters of economic regulation (even though not trusted to sustain free speech and freedom of religion or to refrain from discriminating against racial minorities) Schwartz argues that legislative "ganging up" is not confined to ideological, cultural, religious or racial minorities. He observes that money has a lot of power in a democratic system, and that power is quite capable of being directed to creating laws which are unjustifiably oppressive to groups on simple economic grounds. A legislative or regulatory arrangement which precludes entry to professional or economic activity based not on factors of competence, but in order to avoid a harmful effect to those already certified, is one example.

Perhaps the most compelling argument for viewing "security of the person" as a protection of vital economic interests is the simplest argument. Since the idea of section 7 is primarily to protect minorities against the imposition of an unjust burden or cost flowing from a public welfare scheme it makes no real sense to exclude economic interests from the list of values to be protected. Admittedly the framers of the *Charter* did not include "enjoyment of property" in section 7, which would have placed economic burdens clearly under the protection of the Charter. But the phrase "security of the person" connotes the notion of interests central to personal integrity. Economic interests can, in many circumstances, be seen as indispensable to the dignity and integrity of individuals and the capacity of individuals to pursue their own ideas of the good life.

In other words, once we have accepted, through the inclusion of section 7 in the Charter, that personal interests cannot be put aside for the public good in ways which are substantively unjust, then it is hard to make the case that economic interests are less weighty or less the object of majority oppression against the central attributes of personhood than are other interests. In fact, to consider economic interests as less vital, less central to a person's conception of himself or his idea of the good life is exactly the sort of state determination of value which the *Charter* is designed to place beyond state power. The idea of the liberal state is to put questions of ultimate value, and debate over those questions, outside state prescription—to leave them forever the subject of political dialogue. Discounting economic interests as interests to be protected against intrusions amounting to fundamental injustice is the perfect expression of the illiberalism which the *Charter* is designed to forestall.

Discussion Notes

Property and the Charter

Examine the arguments in the preceding comments. Do the authors agree about the interpretation of s. 7 of the Charter, or about the usefulness of an amendment to provide protection for property? Recall the categories of property identified in chapter 1— private, common, and state. Which are the subject of concern in relation to s. 7? You might consider this question again after examining the concepts of "old" and "new" property explored later in this chapter.

As McBean explained, the Canadian Bill of Rights provides protection for property. Section 1(a) states:

1. It is hereby recognized and declared that in Canada there have existed and shall continue to exist without discrimination ...
(a) the right of the individual to life, liberty, security of the person and enjoyment of property, and the right not to be deprived thereof except by due process of law.

In the light of this protection, what is the role for s. 7 of the Charter in relation to property? For an overview, see P. Hogg, *Constitutional Law of Canada*, 3d ed. (Scarborough, ON: Carswell, 1992), at §28.5(d). As Hogg explained, the US constitutional concept of substantive (as opposed to procedural) "due process" has been rejected in Canada—see *R v. Appleby* (1976), 76 DLR (3d) 110 (NB AD). Nonetheless, the omission of "property" in s. 7 of the Charter provides a continuing role for the Canadian Bill of Rights, as was explained at the beginning of McBean's comment.

The Charter amendment issue is not closed, however. As part of its constitutional package in September 1991, the federal government proposed that the Charter be amended to guarantee property rights. In the same year, a committee of the Legislative Assembly of Prince Edward Island recommended that property rights not be included under the Charter. For an overview of the issues, see D. Johansen, *Background Paper: Property Rights and the Constitution* (Ottawa: Library of Parliament, Research Branch, 1991).

The Queen v. Fisherman's Wharf Ltd. (1982), 135 DLR (3d) 307 was considered in several subsequent cases—for example, see *Vanguard Coatings & Chemicals Ltd. v. Minister of National Revenue*, [1988] 3 FC 560; 88 NR 241 (FCA); *Nova Scotia (Workers/Workmen's) Comp. Bd. v. Coastal Rentals Sales and Service Ltd.* (1983), 12 DLR (4th) 564 (NS SC); and *Bank of Nova Scotia v. Paradise Motor Inn (Guelph) Ltd.* (1982), 30 CPC 183 (Ont. HCJ).

Economic Rights and Section 7

Does a statute limiting the extent of corporate land holdings in a province infringe rights to liberty and security of the person? In *Reference re Lands Protection Act (PEI)* (1987), 64 Nfld. and PEIR 249 (PEI SC), the court considered a constitutional reference on this issue. Section 2 of the provincial statute limited corporate land holdings to 3,000 acres. However, the Irving Pulp and Paper Ltd., doing business as "Cavendish Farms" and processing french fried potatoes, argued that it was necessary to hold significantly more than 3,000 acres (either in freehold or leasehold) to ensure proper crop rotation. At the outset, the court had to determine whether the corporation's interests as lessor of leased farmland was within the statutory definition of "land holding," concluding that they were not. In relation to the Charter issue, the court held (at 259) that "economic rights, including the right to the enjoyment of property, do not fall within the protective arm of s. 7." The judgment cited *Reference Re s. 94(2) of the Motor Vehicle Act (BC)*, [1985] 2 SCR 486 and *Singh v. Minister of Employment and Immigration*, [1985] 1 SCR 177 to support this conclusion. For another case involving the issue of economic rights and s. 7 of the Charter, see *Wilson v. Medical Services Commission of British Columbia* (1988), 53 DLR (4th) 171 (BC CA).

The Charter's impact on municipal land-use controls was examined in R.G. Doumani and J. Matthews Glenn, "Property, Planning and the Charter" (1989), 34 *McGill Law Journal* 1036. The authors concluded (at 1061-62) that the Charter's impact is minimal:

> Its effect is limited, firstly and most obviously, because the *Charter* does not specifically recognize a right to property, so that whatever protection it does afford is indirect. At present, it guarantees a right to property only to the extent necessary to ensure the protection of the right to life, liberty and security of the person under section 7, for example; or it affords property owners some additional protection against discriminatory treatment under section 15. Its effect is limited, secondly, because a municipality's powers are already restricted by the traditional rules of judicial review based in the notion of *ultra vires* and, where invoked, in the strict construction approach to statutes and other provisions interfering with property rights.

The authors also concluded that entrenchment of property rights in the Charter would not have a significant impact because of the "legislative override" provision in s. 33 and the balancing of interests required pursuant to s. 1. As well, they argued (at 1062) that the Charter has enhanced "the status of other human rights instruments" that recognize rights including a right to property so that "the right to property is thus afforded a quasi-constitutional protection." For an excellent overview of the impact of entrenching economic rights in the Charter, see R. Bauman, "Business, Economic Rights and the Charter," in D. Schneiderman and K. Sutherland, eds., *Charting the Consequences: The Impact of Charter Rights on Canadian Law and Policies* (Toronto: University of Toronto Press, 1997), 58. After reviewing some of the decided cases in the context of public choice theory, Bauman concluded (at 96-97) that "on balance, justice requires that economic rights continue to be left out of the Charter, and, further, that the Supreme Court of Canada re-examine how its doctrines so far have distributed economic rights unequally."

Manitoba Fisheries Ltd. v. The Queen

The plaintiffs owned and operated a fish exporting business, and did so quite successfully until the federal government enacted legislation giving the exclusive rights to carry on such a business to a statutory corporation. The plaintiffs claimed compensation for their property interests against the Crown. Should the plaintiffs succeed? On what basis? Would the plaintiffs' claim be more successful if protection for property rights were entrenched in the Charter?

In *Manitoba Fisheries Ltd. v. The Queen* (1978), 88 DLR (3d) 462 (SCC), the court concluded that the plaintiffs were entitled to compensation for the governmental "taking" of the goodwill of their business. Ritchie J stated (at 465) that he had great difficulty in following the reasoning of the Court of Appeal which suggested that "implementation of the legislation had the effect of putting the appellant out of business but that result did not occur due to any deprivation of property of the appellant." (See Urie JA (1978), 78 DLR (3d) 393, at 400-1 (FCA).) By contrast, Ritchie J concluded (at 473) that:

> It will be seen that in my opinion the *Freshwater Fish Marketing Act* and the Corporation created thereunder had the effect of depriving the appellant of its goodwill as a going concern and consequently rendering its physical assets virtually useless and that the

goodwill so taken away constitutes property of the appellant for the loss of which no compensation whatever has been paid. There is nothing in the Act providing for the taking of such property by the Government without compensation and as I find that there was such a taking, it follows, in my view, that it was unauthorized having regard to the recognized rule that "unless the words of the statute clearly so demand, a statute is not to be construed so as to take away the property of a subject without compensation": *per* Lord Atkinson in *Attorney-General v. De Keyser's Royal Hotel* [[1920] AC 508].

To what extent does this analysis depend on construing goodwill as a proprietary interest? How should it be valued? In awarding compensation, Ritchie J stated (at 473) that it should be valued as "the fair market value of [the plaintiff's business] as a going concern ... , minus the residual value of its remaining assets."

In the light of the outcome of *Manitoba Fisheries*, decided prior to the enactment of the Charter, what would be the advantage of amending s. 7 to include express protection for property? In the absence of express inclusion, how might *Manitoba Fisheries* be used in interpreting the current wording of s. 7? Does the outcome in this case require a reassessment of the comments made by McBean and Whyte?

Property Rights and Liberty

The "liberty" interest in s. 7 is important in relation to property. For a discussion of property rights and liberty in Canada, see "Discussion: Property Rights and Liberty" (1988), 1:2 *Canadian Journal of Law and Jurisprudence* 217. For an overview of some of the US literature, see M.J. Radin, "The Liberal Conception of Property: Cross Currents in the Jurisprudence of Takings" (1988), 88 *Columbia Law Review* 1667.

There are a number of situations in which constitutional protection for liberty and property has been connected to issues of privacy. In *Davis v. Davis*, 842 SW 2d 588 (Tenn. Sup. Ct. 1992), the court considered the rights of former spouses to custody in relation to "preembryos." In deciding to award custody to the former husband, the court held that there was a right to privacy (including procreational autonomy) under the liberty clauses of the Tennessee Declaration of Rights. As between the parties, the court concluded that the husband's desire not to use the preembryos after the marriage ended was of greater concern than the wife's wish to donate the preembryos to another couple. Is this decision concerned with both liberty and property? In *Canadian AIDS Society v. Ontario* (1995), 25 OR (3d) 388 (Gen. Div.), the court held that testing of blood samples for the AIDS virus without the knowledge or consent of blood donors violated the donors' rights to life, liberty, and security of the person pursuant to s. 7 of the Charter, but that the deprivation was not contrary to the principles of fundamental justice. In any event, the violation under s. 7 was justified under s. 1 of the Charter. Is this decision concerned with both liberty and property? Recall the discussion in chapter 1 about property and bodily tissues.

Wartime Confiscation of Property: The Need for Charter Protection?

In the earlier comment, McBean suggested that entrenchment of protection for property in s. 7 of the Charter might be useful in preventing future confiscation of property, as happened to citizens and residents of Japanese origin on the west coast of Canada during World War II. According to a Price Waterhouse study in the mid-1980s, "the Japanese Canadian community suffered a total economic loss after 1941 of not less than $443 million [1986 dollars]," not including some kinds of economic loss that could not be quantified, such as disruption of education. In 1948 dollars, the total loss was over $48 million. For a detailed account of the confiscation of property, see K. Adachi, *The Enemy That Never Was: A History of the Japanese Canadians* (Toronto: McClelland and Stewart, 1991) (hereafter Adachi), at 375 and table 2. Adachi described (at 319-34) legal challenges and petitions during and immediately after the war, as well as the work of the Bird commission, established in 1947 to provide compensation in cases where negligence could be proved on the part of government officers involved in the process of confiscation. Although the terms of reference were later broadened, Adachi concluded (at 331-32):

> The awards came too late and were too little—despite Bird's claim that "rough justice" had been achieved. An old Issei in 1950 could stare at his cheque for $140.50 awarded as his recovery on a house in Vancouver for which he paid $3000 in 1930 and which was sold by the [governmental officer] for $1200 in 1943. He could stare and stare and wonder what remote connection it had with the destruction of his life's work and security.

In 1988, the government of Canada issued an acknowledgement of the injustice of governmental actions in relation to Canadians of Japanese ancestry during the war, and entered into an agreement with the National Association of Japanese Canadians for "symbolic" redress payments—see Adachi, appendices XIV and XV. See also W.P. Ward, *White Canada Forever: Popular Attitudes and Public Policy Toward Orientals in British Columbia*, 2d ed. (Montreal and Kingston: McGill-Queen's University Press, 1990). For a haunting "fictional" account, see J. Kogawa, *Obasan* (Toronto: Lester and Orpen Dennys, 1981). In the United States, similar issues concerning Japanese-Americans were explored in J. tenBroek, *Prejudice, War and the Constitution* (Berkeley: University of California Press, 1954) and L. and R. Reiner, *Removal and Return: The Socio-Economic Effects of War on Japanese Americans* (Berkeley: University of California Press, 1949).

International Protection for Property

A right to property is recognized in other constitutions and in international covenants. In relation to constitutional guarantees, see the American Bill of Rights, amendments 5 and 14; and the Quebec Charter of Human Rights and Freedoms, RSQ 1977, c. C-12, s. 6. Among international covenants and agreements, see the Universal Declaration of Human Rights (1948), art. 17; the International Convention on the Elimination of all Forms of Racial Discrimination (1965), art. 5(d)v; the European Convention on Human Rights (1950), art. 1 of the First Protocol; and the African Charter on Human and Peoples' Rights (1981), art. 14. For an examination of the provisions of the new South African Constitution in relation to protection for property, see A.J. van der Walt, "Property Rights, Land Rights and Environmental Rights," in D. van Wyk, J. Dugard, B. de Villiers, and D. Davis, *Rights and Constitutionalism: The New South African Legal Order* (Kenwyn, SA: Juta & Co., 1994), 455. In relation to the European Community, see J.

Kingston, "Rich People Have Rights Too? The Status of Property as a Fundamental Human Right," in L. Heffernan, ed., *Human Rights: A European Perspective* (Dublin and Portland, OR: Roundhill Press in association with Irish Centre for European Law, 1994).

"New Property" Challenges

M.A. Glendon, The New Family and the New Property
(Toronto: Butterworths, 1981), at 185-99 (footnotes omitted)

The classic, but not the first, formulation of the individual's increasing dependence on new forms of wealth was made by Charles Reich in his 1964 article, "The New Property":

> [T]oday more and more of our wealth takes the form of rights or status rather than of tangible goods. An individual's profession or occupation is a prime example. To many others, a job with a particular employer is the principal form of wealth. A profession or a job is frequently far more valuable than a house or bank account, for a new house can be bought, and a new bank account created, once a profession or job is secure. For the jobless, their status as governmentally assisted or insured persons may be the main source of subsistence. ...
>
> The kinds of wealth dispensed by government consist almost entirely of those forms which are in the ascendancy today. To the individual, these new forms, such as a profession, job, or right to receive income, are the basis of his various statuses in society, and may therefore be the most meaningful and distinctive wealth he possesses.

He particularly emphasized the role of government as a major source of wealth:

> Government is a gigantic syphon. It draws in revenue and power, and pours forth wealth: money, benefits, services, contracts, franchises, and licenses. Government has always had this function. But while in early times it was minor, today's distribution of largess is on a vast, imperial scale.
>
> The valuables dispensed by government take many forms, but they all share one characteristic. They are steadily taking the place of traditional forms of wealth—forms which are held as private property. Social insurance substitutes for savings; a government contract replaces a businessman's customers and goodwill. The wealth of more and more Americans depends upon a relationship to government. Increasingly, Americans live on government largess—allocated by government on its own terms, and held by recipients subject to conditions which express "the public interest."

Reich's purpose in calling attention to the increasing importance of work and government as bases of standing and security was to illustrate the precariousness of claims based on them unless legal protection, analogous to that traditionally accorded to property rights, was extended to new statuses: "[I]t must be recognized that we are becoming a society based on relationships and status—status deriving primarily from source of livelihood. Status is so closely linked to personality that destruction of one may well destroy the other. Status must therefore be surrounded with the kind of safeguards once reserved for personality."

Fifteen years later, as perception of the importance of "new property" for economic security has widened, its legal protection has been increased. We have already seen the legal protection crystallizing around the job itself, both in the public and in the private sector. In Europe, retirement income has long been assured through various public funding devices. In the United States, the Employee Retirement Income Security Act of 1974 (ERISA) was an important beginning step toward protection of the form of new property represented by private pensions. *Sniadach v. Family Finance Corp.* has accorded heightened protection to wages in garnishment proceedings.

With regard to governmental benefits, the Supreme Court, starting with *Goldberg v. Kelly*, began to award the most important of them the status of "property" for purposes of due process. Justice Brennan, writing for the majority, adopted the term "entitlement" that Reich had used to refer to such sources of security as franchises, professional licenses, union membership, employment contracts, pensions, stock options and welfare benefits. What these "entitlements" have in common, according to Reich, is that "all are devices to aid security and independence." (We may note in passing that all are also devices which are tailored primarily to the individual.) Reich had argued that the entitlements of the poor especially needed legal recognition. Justice Brennan seemed to agree, holding that welfare "benefits are a matter of statutory entitlement for persons qualified to receive them," and that New York could not terminate them without prior notice and hearing. He emphasized that what was at stake was "the means to obtain essential food, clothing, housing, and medical care"—"the basic demands of subsistence"—and he took notice of the difficulties an individual can have in dealing with the "welfare bureaucracy" that controls the dispensation of vital necessities. In a footnote Justice Brennan said: "It may be realistic today to regard welfare entitlements as more like 'property' than a 'gratuity.' Much of the existing wealth in this country takes the form of rights that do not fall within traditional common-law concepts of property."

Later cases made clear that the Court was not prepared to redefine as "property" for due process purposes the whole spectrum of "entitlements" nor to require full hearings before any government action. The Court has, however, reinforced the pervasive legislative and administrative schemes through which government increasingly becomes the insurer of health, employment and retirement, as well as the provider of a minimum level of subsistence for those in need. Recent Supreme Court cases do provide heightened protection to education (which in turn provides access to work-related new property), and they also promote the right of an individual to follow his chosen occupation. Protection of the individual's interest in a particular job, however, is coming primarily, not through the Supreme Court, but through the developments traced above in the ties that bind the job to the employee.

Not only is the individual acquiring more legal rights with respect to his particular job, he is seen as having a *right* to have work. Government is increasingly seen as having the obligation to provide work to everyone who wants it. In his dissenting opinion in *Board of Regents v. Roth*, Mr. Justice Marshall was prepared to say that any citizen who wants a government job should get one or be given a reason for its denial. He characterized this right not only as a liberty, but a constitutionally protected property interest:

> In my view, every citizen who applies for a government job is entitled to it unless the government can establish some reason for denying the employment. This is the

"property" right that I believe is protected by the Fourteenth Amendment and that cannot be denied "without due process of law." And it is also liberty—liberty to work— which is the "very essence of the personal freedom and opportunity" secured by the Fourteenth Amendment.

This version of a right to work has not become accepted constitutional doctrine, but it has increasingly become official policy, as exemplified, for instance, in the preamble of the Full Employment and Balanced Growth Act of 1978 which states the purpose of the Act as: "To translate into practical reality the right of all Americans who are able, willing, and seeking to work the full opportunity for useful paid employment at fair rates of compensation; to assert the responsibility of the Federal Government to use all practicable programs and policies to promote full employment. ..."

The changing law has been a sensitive indicator of the fact that, for the majority of Americans, the most important relationship in their lives, so far as economic security is concerned, is their own actual or potential employment relationship, with government and the family serving as back-up systems. This is true even of spouses and children who may be dependent for periods of time on the employment of a family provider. This is not to speak of "economic security" in the sense of the day-to-day pooling of contributions by members of a functioning family, but in the sense of an economic haven for the situations of old age, illness, disability, unemployment, death of a family provider— the ills which all fear and to which all are susceptible. There has been a shift, though not a complete transfer, of responsibility for the aged, the ill or disabled, and surviving dependents away from the family in two directions. Maintenance is increasingly linked to employment, particularly through pensions, insurance, and social security; and it is increasingly becoming the concern of the social welfare state.

The relationships among the strengthening of claims against government and changes in the structure of the family and the world of work are complex. What can be said at this point is that for most Americans the situation Alva Myrdal prescribed in her report to the Swedish Social Democratic party in 1971 has become a reality: "Income from one's own job and the modern social insurance system are the two foundation stones upon which the security of the individual will rest in the future." Myrdal's emphasis on the individual rather than the family is increasingly echoed by realistic American critics of those government policies that continue to treat welfare, poverty, income, health insurance and other social questions as family rather than individual issues.

The trend that has been traced in this and the foregoing chapters toward the attenuation of legal family ties as legal work ties tighten has accompanied changes in the family and the world of work. In its day, the unilateral dismissal rule reflected and interacted with the growth of industry just as strict legal limits on divorce at that time "fitted" the prevailing model of marriage as a support institution. The current law reflects and interacts with newer social trends, well-developed in the late 20th century, toward grounding the individual's social standing and economic security in work or employment-related benefits backed up by government, rather than in family relationships. But this law, too, is subject to change. How accessible, durable and beneficial to the individual is security grounded in new property? As the following discussion indicates, the answer depends in part on who is asking the question.

D. The Job as Property: Access, Instability and Ambiguity

The discussion in this chapter has concentrated primarily on the situation of those persons who depend for their economic security on work and work-related benefits and on the ways in which they are both supported and constrained by work relationships. This is the great middle range of the population. But not all persons and groups in society are affected in the same way or to the same degree by the processes identified and discussed here. In particular, women and members of certain racial and ethnic minority groups have limited access to the preferred forms of new property (good jobs and fringe benefits) that at present are the important sources of economic security in our society. For some, this means that their relationship to government and government benefits, a less desirable form of new property, assumes paramount importance. For others, it means that they depend on family relationships which seem to be becoming increasingly fragile.

Thus, while "locking-in" to the job is a major constraint on one large segment of the work force, mere access to a niche in the occupational structure is difficult for a large minority, especially non-whites and many women. They may be bound to a different kind of status, locked into welfare dependency and public housing. As the Carnegie Council put it: "Although a slight majority (55 percent) of white males move up the economic ladder during the course of a lifetime, the most common trends for women and blacks are no movement at all or movement downward." On the persistence of difficulties experienced by non-whites in gaining access to and mobility within the forms of new property represented by work and work-related benefits, a 1976 Labor Department monograph stated:

> Controlling for all other factors that we have been able to measure, the occupations taken at the beginning of their careers by blacks now in their thirties and forties were lower in the status hierarchy than those taken by whites with comparable characteristics. Moreover, the relative disparity in this respect widened over their careers—even during the half decade between 1967 and 1972. This is an additional reminder that the rather impressive effort in recent years in combatting racial discrimination in the labor market still leaves something to be desired.

Discussion Notes

"New" Property in Welfare Benefits and Jobs?

As Glendon explained, the decision of the US Supreme Court in *Goldberg v. Kelly*, 397 US 254 (1970) adopted the idea of "new property" in governmental entitlements that had been proposed by Charles Reich in "The New Property" (1964), 73 *Yale Law Journal* 733. As a result of the court's conclusion that the welfare benefits in *Goldberg* constituted property, the court held that a "due process" hearing was required before welfare benefits could be terminated. In later cases, however, American courts restricted the application of *Goldberg*. Nonetheless, Reich remained convinced of a need to recognize forms of new property, asserting that "it makes a vital difference whether or not the individual owns and has sovereignty over the economic means of survival."

If we allow these benefits [such as entitlement to welfare] to be the property of government, the result is to give power to government that ought to belong to the individual. There is a world of difference between allowing government to hold in its hands the individual's survival, and vesting this power in the individual. The former is tyranny, even if administered by the most reasonable bureaucrats. The latter is what this country is supposed to be all about.

(C. Reich, "Beyond the New Property: An Ecological View of Due Process" (1990), 56 *Brooklyn Law Review* 731, at 736.) According to Reich, much of the poverty in late 20th-century North America results from changes in the social environment. Making an analogy between poverty and homelessness in modern times and the enclosure system of the 16th century that forced people off common lands, Reich asserted (at 741) that "the whole history of industrialization tells us that we are seeing forced loss of habitat, not a refusal to contribute to society." He also argued (at 743) that poverty should be compared to "internal exile."

Suppose that the dispossessed of our society had been sentenced to internal exile because of their political beliefs, because of their religion, or because of their race. If children in foster care, or families in rural poverty, or the people camped out over heating grates were all political dissenters, or Jews, or persons thought dangerous to the regime, we would react very differently to the suffering in our midst ... . [If] we would never tolerate internal exile for political or religious dissent ... , why do we tolerate it for the innocent people, including children, the aged, and the mentally ill?

How would you characterize Reich's arguments in relation to property? Is it necessary to characterize governmental benefits as property to achieve his goals? What are the advantages and disadvantages of doing so? In the context of s. 7 of the Charter, how would Reich's arguments affect the scope of protection for new property? Consider again the arguments about amending s. 7 to include protection for property—would such an amendment further the goal of protecting governmental benefits? Is the concept of "internal exile" useful in interpreting the scope of s. 7?

Richard Epstein criticized the majority judgment in *Goldberg* (agreeing with Justice Black's dissenting opinion in the case) from the perspective of both property analysis and constitutional doctrine, concluding that the majority judgment failed to take account of the negative impact of a due process requirement for such hearings on the overall welfare budget. That is, since the overall funds available could be spent either on direct payments to recipients or on procedural safeguards for them, the court's decision effectively reallocated governmental priorities in relation to the welfare budget. See R. Epstein, "No New Property" (1990), 56 *Brooklyn Law Review* 747 (hereafter Epstein), at 767-75. In articulating his criticism of *Goldberg*, Epstein assumed that such benefits could be characterized as property, thus attracting the protection of constitutional due process. However, he also argued (at 760-61) that welfare benefits should be distinguished from other forms of new property such as patents, copyright, and broadcast frequencies.

Public benefits have a pedigree different from that of any of the other forms of new property with which they are sometimes confused ... . [By contrast with these other intangible property rights,] welfare rights are not designed to allow the exploitation of

new forms of wealth, nor to facilitate the aggregation and efficient use of capital ... .
Welfare benefits are transfer payments that rely on the taxes imposed upon some in
order to provide the benefits that are received by others.

What are the underlying assumptions about the fundamental nature of proprietary
interests, as expressed in the differing views of Reich and Epstein? Recall the definition
of property explored in chapter 1—to what extent are the two authors' views consistent
with this definition? Is the debate about whether welfare benefits constitute property
important *per se*, or is it more important as the basis for achieving procedural protection
for recipients in relation to governmental decision-making? Is it possible to achieve
procedural protections for welfare recipients without characterizing their interests as
property?

These issues remain highly contested in constitutional litigation in the United States
and Canada. For further analysis of the US context, see S. Loffredo, "Poverty, Democracy and Constitutional Law" (1993), 141 *University of Pennsylvania Law Review* 1277,
at 1305-13; H. Hershkoff, "Rights and Freedoms Under the State Constitution: A New
Deal for Welfare Rights" (1996-97), 13 *Touro Law Review* 631; G. Binion, "The Disadvantaged Before the Burger Court" (1982), 4 *Law and Policy Quarterly* 37; and L.
Tribe, "Unraveling *National League of Cities*: The New Federalism and Affirmative
Rights to Essential Government Services" (1977), 90 *Harvard Law Review* 1065.

There have also been cases about the scope of s. 7 in relation to governmental benefits
in Canada. For example, in *Masse v. Minister of Community and Social Services* (1996),
134 DLR (4th) 20 (Ont. Gen. Div.); leave to appeal denied [1996] OJ no. 1526 (CA); leave
to appeal denied [1996] SCCA no. 373, the applicants argued (among other arguments) that
a 20 percent reduction in the level of welfare benefits in Ontario infringed recipients' "life,
liberty and security of the person" contrary to s. 7 of the Charter, but the court held that it
was within the government's competence to determine the level of such benefits. See also
Falkiner v. Ontario (Ministry of Community and Social Services) (1996), 140 DLR (4th)
115 (Ont. Gen. Div.). Similarly, a Nova Scotia court held that the security of tenure of a
public housing tenant was an economic interest and thus not protected by s. 7—see *Bernard
v. Dartmouth Housing Authority* (1989), 88 NSR (2d) 190 (SCAD). If s. 7 were amended to
include protection for property, would these cases be decided differently? For some analyses of the potential of s. 7 in relation to governmental benefits in Canada, see M. Jackman,
"The Protection of Welfare Rights Under the Charter" (1988), 20 *Ottawa Law Review* 257;
M. Jackman, "Poor Rights: Using the Charter To Support Social Welfare Claims" (1993),
19 *Queen's Law Journal* 65; and I. Morrison, "Security of the Person and the Person in
Need: Section 7 of the Charter and the Right to Welfare" (1988), 4 *Journal of Law and
Social Policy* 1. For a critical view, especially in relation to women's interests, see J. Fudge,
"The Public/Private Distinction: The Possibilities of and Limitations to the Use of Charter
Litigation To Further Feminist Struggles" (1987), 25 *Osgoode Hall Law Journal* 485. The
role of federal legislation was reviewed by M. Jackman, in "Women and the Canada Health
and Social Transfer: Ensuring Gender Equality in Federal Welfare Reform" (1995), 8 *Canadian Journal of Women and the Law* 371.

The arguments about whether governmental benefits constitute new property are
similar to some approaches to issues about job security for workers. Just as differences

in underlying assumptions about property may lead to divergent views of the correctness of *Goldberg v. Kelly*, they may also lead to different outcomes in relation to issues of job security. For example, Beermann and Singer suggested that there is a "social vision" embodied in the common law of contract and property, and that "conceptualization of the worker–management relationship in terms of the prevailing social vision leads to common law categories that resolve conflicting claims between workers and management in favor of management." See J.M. Beermann and J.W. Singer, "Baseline Questions in Legal Reasoning: The Example of Property in Jobs" (1988-89), 23 *Georgia Law Review* 911, at 916. See also J.W. Singer, "The Reliance Interest in Property" (1988), 40 *Stanford Law Review* 614, arguing for legal recognition of workers' rights arising out of long-term employment relationships, especially in the context of corporate reorganization or restructuring. For a Canadian critique, see W. Clement, *The Challenge of Class Analysis* (Ottawa: Carleton University Press, 1988), especially chapter 10.

Protection of "New" Property Interests in Intangible Objects

Proprietary interests such as copyright, patents, and trademarks have been traditionally recognized as intellectual property and are now usually regulated by statute. See, for example, Copyright Act, RSC 1985, c. C-42. For an overview of intellectual property interests in Canada, see D. Vaver, *The Law of Intellectual Property: Copyright, Patents, Trademarks* (Concord, ON: Irwin Law, 1996). According to R. Epstein, however, these forms of proprietary interests should be categorized as "old new property," because they are distinguishable from new property claims to governmental benefits. By contrast with governmental benefits, Epstein argued that intellectual property interests create incentives to productive labour that is enhanced by legal protection. See Epstein, at 756. What are the underlying assumptions in such a distinction? Recall the examination of the labour theory of property in chapter 1—what arguments can be made in response to Epstein's assertions?

There are other kinds of intangible property that are characterized as new property in some cases. In chapter 1, we examined *Victoria Park Racing and Recreation Grounds Co. Ltd. v. Taylor* (1937), 58 CLR 479, and the absence of protection for the plaintiff's property interest in a "spectacle." The case also involved an early situation of broadcasting, another intangible property interest now regulated by statute—see Canadian Radio-Television and Telecommunications Commission Act, RSC 1985, c. C-22. Pursuant to this legislation, radio frequencies are to be regarded as public property. If a community cable company videotapes television programs produced by another company and then broadcasts them on its own cable network, can the television producer claim infringement of copyright? Can the cable company argue that it simply recorded on video the electrical impulses that were being broadcast (since broadcast frequencies are public property), and thus that there was no infringement of the television program's copyright because the copyright lapsed when the programs were converted into television signals? See *Warner Bros-Seven Arts Inc. v. CESM-TV Ltd.* (1971), 65 CPR 215 (Ex. Ct.), where the cable company was held to have infringed the television producer's copyright. Identify the property interest protected in this case. For another situation involving broadcast frequencies, see *Canadian Admiral Corporation Ltd. v. Rediffusion Inc.*, [1954] Ex. Ch. 382.

Claims about intangible property interests have also been litigated in relation to the appropriation of personality—that is, a claim that an individual's name, image, or personality has been used without permission. Such claims are related to the tort of defamation, but they have also been recognized in Canada as a more broadly based common law tort—see, for example, *Krouse v. Chrysler Canada Ltd.*, [1974] 1 OR (2d) 225 (CA) and *Athans v. Canadian Adventure Camps Ltd.* (1977), 80 DLR (3d) 583 (Ont. HCJ). In *Burnett v. The Queen in Right of Canada* (1979), 23 OR (2d) 109 (HC), a film of the plaintiff's home formed part of the image in a CBC documentary, and the plaintiff brought an action alleging an invasion of his privacy. Should the plaintiff succeed? Does the plaintiff have a property interest in the image of his home that is distinct from his home itself? What are the consequences of finding that such a proprietary interest exists in relation to news and documentary programs?

The issue of new property has also been important in the context of developments in technology, especially computers. For example, in *R v. Stewart* (1988), 41 CCC (3d) 481 (SCC), (1983) 149 DLR (3d) 583 (Ont. CA), (1982) 138 DLR (3d) 73 (Ont. HCJ), the accused was charged pursuant to the Criminal Code in relation to his efforts to obtain computerized employee records without authorization. The accused was requested by someone whom he assumed was associated with a union to act as an agent to obtain a list of employees of a hotel, in the context of a union organizing drive. The accused approached an employee of the hotel and offered to pay for access to the computerized records. The accused was charged with counselling the offences of mischief, theft, and fraud, all of which required some interference with "property." Assuming that the accused intended to make a copy of the computerized records, but otherwise to leave the records intact, was the accused guilty of these offences? In relation to the charge of counselling theft, for example, s. 283 (now s. 322) of the Criminal Code defined theft in terms of taking "anything" with intent to deprive the owner "of the thing or of his property or interest in it." Did the accused commit theft? What "property" did he intend to take?

R v. Stewart raised the issue whether confidential information constitutes property, especially in the context of the Criminal Code. At trial, Krever J acquitted the accused, holding that confidential information is not property for purposes of the law of theft. On appeal, the accused was convicted of theft. Houlden JA concluded that, although the hotel's computerized employee information would have remained intact, its confidential character would have been lost. Cory JA agreed, suggesting that lists compiled for business purposes should be characterized as "literary works" and recognized as property protected by copyright legislation. Lacourcière JA dissented. In the Supreme Court of Canada, an appeal was allowed and the acquittals restored. The Supreme Court expressed caution about criminalizing the unauthorized appropriation of confidential information, and suggested that such action should be taken only by Parliament, not by the courts. Since confidential information was not property, there was no *actus reus* in relation to the charge of theft.

What concepts of property are reflected in these judicial opinions? Why was the Supreme Court of Canada concerned about the consequences of criminalizing the appropriation of confidential information? If a student gained access to an examination before the examination date and copied it, would the student be liable for the tort of conversion? What difference would it make whether the student copied an examination paper or a computer file containing the examination questions? Should confidential information constitute property in the context of civil (rather than criminal) liability? See *Oxford v. Moss* (1979), 68 Cr. App. R 183 (Div. Ct.); and *R v. Offley* (1986), 28 CCC (3d) 1 (Alta. CA). For an overview of some of these issues, see A.S. Weinrib, "Information and Property" (1988), 38 *University of Toronto Law Journal* 117. For a critique in a different context, see S. Wright, "A Feminist Exploration of the Legal Protection of Art" (1994), 7 *Canadian Journal of Women and the Law* 59.

"New" Property, "New" Poverty, and Homelessness

Is it appropriate to try to categorize all of these kinds of claims as "new property"? Particularly in relation to rights to welfare or to jobs, are there disadvantages to using the idea of property to achieve certainty, fairness, and security? In a review of Glendon's work, for example, Pamela Symes suggested that recognition of welfare entitlements and jobs as forms of new property offers no guarantee that everyone will have access to them, just as access to traditional property is not available to all. As well, the existence of jobs and the value of governmental benefits may be just as subject to economic fluctuations as traditional property interests. Yet, in additon to these problems, she has asserted that there is a more troubling aspect.

> [T]he ties that bind the employee to the job, the job to the employee, the welfare recipient to the state, may be simply weaving a tighter and tighter web of dependence. There may be protection but is there freedom? Once "locked in" to this particular type of economic security, this particular property, how easy is it to withdraw, change job, move to another area … ? There is more than a hint that the "new property" could be a new tyranny. …
>
> Traditional property, traditional forms of wealth, brought with them a kind of personal power, power to effect change, power to exercise choice, to be a self-determining individual; traditional property brought independence. Does this power accompany the new property? On the contrary, so-called new property very often reveals a new dependence. And so I am suggesting that the real measure of property is the degree of freedom from dependence, freedom of self-determination, the ability to effect change and to exercise choice. Real property, then, is real choice—and the key issue to be explored is that which eliminates choice: dependence.

(P. Symes, "Property, Power and Dependence: Critical Family Law" (1987), 14 *Journal of Law and Society* 199, at 201-2.) Do you agree with the dichotomy between traditional and new concepts of property, as described by Symes? Are all those who hold traditional property interests able to exercise personal power, effect change, exercise choice? Does dependence always mean the absence of choice and lack of self-determination? In *Goldberg v. Kelly*, what difference did it make to the welfare recipient to have the right to a hearing prior to the termination of benefits? Does such a right affect the applicant's dignity, choice, or control over her life? Is such an applicant more vulnerable, dependent, or poor without new property?

New property claims have also been asserted in relation to individuals' rights to shelter, especially in the context of the problem of homelessness. In a comprehensive review of these issues a few years ago, Parkdale Community Legal Services in Toronto identified the reasons for increasing numbers of homeless people in Ontario—policies of deinstitutionalization in relation to mental health care, lack of security of tenure for some roomers and boarders, unemployment, a shortage of affordable housing, the uncertainties of refugee status, and the feminization of poverty. The clinic cited data showing that in 1986, 86.9 percent of single tenants and 96.4 percent of single parents in public housing and non-profit and co-operative housing programs were women. See Parkdale Community Legal Services, "Homelessness and the Right to Shelter: A View from Parkdale" (1988), 4 *Journal of Law and Social Policy* 35, at 38-54. The authors reviewed the arguments in international, US, and Canadian law for recognizing shelter as a legal right, including s. 7, and also s. 15, the equality rights section of the Charter. In relation to s. 15 and homelessness, the authors argued (at 67) (footnotes omitted):

D. The Canadian Charter of Rights and Freedoms

By means of its protection of equality rights and the right to life, liberty and the security of the person, the *Charter* may be a means to construct a right to shelter for the homeless. While no right to shelter has been found within the Constitution of United States, significant differences between the *Charter* and the American *Bill of Rights* and the judicial history of the two countries means that the *Charter's* potential to assert rights for the homeless may not be limited to the American experience. ...

2. *Section 15*

> s. 15(1) Every individual is equal before and under the law and has the right to the equal protection and benefit of the law without discrimination and, in particular, discrimination based on race, national or ethnic origin, colour, religion, sex, age or mental or physical disability.

The main issues in the interpretation of this section in the context of equality rights for the homeless ... are: whether s. 15 guarantees a basic level of economic equality; the requirements s. 15 imposes regarding the distribution of government benefits; and how the "equal protection" component may assist the homeless.

(a) Section 15 and Economic Equality

Whether the equality provisions in the *Charter* should extend to provide everyone with a level of basic economic security has been a question of considerable debate. The language of s. 15 is broad and malleable enough to support a number of interpretations. The traditional approach would require only procedural equality, ensuring everyone "equality of opportunity" and political rights rather than economic substantive rights. The American Fourteenth Amendment has been interpreted in this way so that systemic economic inequalities do not abridge the right to equal protection.

One key factor in s. 15 litigation to date has been the definition of equality adopted by the courts: treating likes alike. To benefit from s. 15's protection the affected person must establish that she or he is similarly situated to the group receiving the benefit. The benefit may be a monetary benefit such as a veteran's allowance, the right to practice a profession, or the grounds for discharge of a criminal offence. Lawyers litigating on behalf of the homeless should meet with success in cases involving equality between homeless persons (for example homeless women and homeless men, homeless youths and homeless adults) especially where the difference between the two groups is one of the enumerated grounds under s. 15.

Difficulties will arise, however, where the success of the case depends on the acceptance of a homeless person as being similarly situated to a person with accommodation. Not only is homelessness not a protected ground under s. 15, but the fact of homelessness itself may be sufficient to distinguish the two groups in the minds of the courts, notwithstanding the fact that it is the disputed issue. Further, equality in itself does not necessarily imply a specific standard of services or treatment. For example, treating homeless men and women equally may be achieved both by opening more shelters for women and by closing some of the shelters for men.

In a discussion of s. 15 in terms of its impact on social assistance, Sandra Wain states:

> The equality guaranteed by section 15 (and by the *Human Rights Code*) appears to be a modified form of equality of opportunity. Although it does permit some check on prevailing values, its main purpose is to permit individuals to compete on a more equal basis within existing value structures. The government is authorized to do more in the name of equality under s. 15(2) but is not required to do so.

A potential test case regarding the right to shelter might therefore focus on the denial of equality of opportunity to those who are homeless. Health problems, lack of employment opportunities and children's learning difficulties are directly related to homelessness and thus deny homeless people the equality of opportunity protected by s. 15 of the *Charter*. Although such litigation, if successful, would not necessarily establish a right to shelter *per se*, it could have that indirect result because the provision of shelter would remedy the problem noted above.

In Canada it has been argued that analysis of equality under the *Charter* requires a purposive or equality-promoting approach to ensure substantive equality, or equality of outcome, for "the powerless, excluded and disadvantaged." In the poverty law context this might be characterized as an ironclad government assurance that everyone is entitled to a subsistence level of economic security or the right to adequate shelter.

A number of arguments can be put forward in support of the view that s. 15 does establish a right to some degree of economic equality. The *Charter* guarantees equality before the law, equality under the law and equal benefit of the law in addition to equal protection which is the sole guarantee under the Fourteenth Amendment. Our courts thus need not be constrained by American precedent. It has also been asserted that "a more progressive interpretation of the equality rights provision would be in line with the international tendency to define the principle of nondiscrimination in both political and economic terms." The assumption underlying the substantive view is that political rights such as free speech are meaningless to a person without any economic security who is struggling for basic survival.

Will this "post-liberal" vision of equality be embraced by Canadian courts? Although economic rights have been discussed under s. 7, it appears that no court has yet grappled with the profound issue of economic equality under s. 15. There are many reasons to doubt that courts will recognize such rights. The implications of finding such a right are both far-reaching and threatening to those who benefit most from current socio-economic arrangements. The Ontario government has already indicated that it would argue stridently against a constitutional right to demand government benefits if the government does not offer them. Furthermore, even if a court was willing to recognize the right to economic subsistence, s. 1 may well be used to justify a government's failure to provide for basic needs. As one commentator notes, "[I]t may logically be argued that a right to economic equality is fundamentally inconsistent with the values of a free and democratic society."

While the "post-liberal" interpretation of s. 15 is at least conceptually possible, perhaps these practical obstacles have discouraged poverty lawyers from raising it. However, at a time when courts are still considering equality theories, it is important for advocates to persistently urge courts to accept the concept of a *Charter* guarantee of economic equality. Two proponents of this approach both conclude that if advocates insist on substantive interpretations of equality provisions, the courts will be forced to confront fundamental socio-economic structures. Also, by repudiating classic liberal notions of equality, advocates will sensitize and educate others, particularly judges, about the root causes of inequality.

Advocates for the homeless should be encouraged, then, to consider framing the question in an action on behalf of the homeless both as one of equality of opportunity and as one of economic equality, given that homelessness is arguably the most dramatic evidence that our conventional views of equality are increasingly and literally leaving people in the cold.

The relationship between constitutional rights of equality pursuant to s. 15 of the Charter and governmental discretion in the allocation of benefits remains highly contested. For example, see *Egan v. Canada*, [1995] 2 SCR 513 and *M v. H* (1996), 142 DLR (4th) (Ont. CA), leave to appeal to SCC granted: *M v. H*, [1997] SC CA no. 101. For a recent analysis of s. 15 in Ontario welfare cases, see *Masse v. Minister of Community and Social Services* (1996), 134 DLR (4th) 20 (Ont. Gen. Div.); leave to appeal denied [1996] OJ no. 1526 (CA); leave to appeal denied [1996] SCCA no. 373 and *Falkiner v. Ontario (Ministry of Community and Social Services)* (1996), 140 DLR (4th) 115 (Ont. Gen. Div.). See also J. Keene, "Discrimination in the Provision of Government Services and S[ection] 15 of the Charter: Making the Best of the Judgements in *Egan, Thibaudeau*, and *Miron*" (1995), 11 *Journal of Legal and Social Policy* 107. For an earlier analysis, see L. Gehrke, "The Charter and Publicly Assisted Housing" (1985), 1 *Journal of Law and Social Policy* 17.

The issue of homelessness and the related question whether there is a right to shelter have received considerable attention. For example, see R. Sweeney, *Out of Place: Homelessness in America* (New York: Harper Collins, 1993); A. Bennett, ed., *Shelter, Housing and Homes: A Social Right* (Montreal: Black Rose Books, 1997); M.-O. Herman, "Fighting Homelessness: Can International Human Rights Law Make a Difference?" (1994), 2:1 *Georgetown Journal on Fighting Poverty* 59; Symposium, "Homelessness and the Law" (1994), 23 *Stetson Law Review* 331; and Minister's Advisory Committee on the International Year of Shelter for the Homeless, *More Than Just a*

Roof: Action To End Homelessness in Ontario (Toronto: Ontario Ministry of Housing, 1988). In relation to litigation on behalf of the homeless in the United States, see F.R. Trinity, "Shutting the Shelter Doors: Homeless Families in the Nation's Capital" (1994), 23 *Stetson Law Review* 401, especially the discussion (at 412ff) of class action suits filed by the Washington Legal Clinic for the Homeless.

Do issues such as homelessness suggest that property and equality are irreconcilable opposites? In considering this question examine the critique of conceptions of property identified by C.B. Macpherson in "Liberal-Democracy and Property," in Macpherson, 199 (footnotes omitted):

> The central problem of liberal-democratic theory may be stated as the difficulty of reconciling the liberal property right with that equal effective right of all individuals to use and develop their capacities which is the essential ethical principle of liberal democracy. The difficulty is great. For when the liberal property right is written into law as an individual right to the exclusive use and disposal of parcels of the resources provided by nature and of parcels of the capital created by past work on them, and when it is combined with the liberal system of market incentives and rights of free contract, it leads to and supports a concentration of ownership and a system of power relations between individuals and classes which negates the ethical goal of free and independent individual development. There thus appears to be an insoluble difficulty within the liberal-democratic theory. If, as liberal theory asserts, an individual property right is required by the very necessities of man's nature and condition, it ought not to be infringed or denied. But unless it is seriously infringed or denied, it leads to an effective denial of the equal possibility of individual human fulfilment.
>
> The difficulty was inherent in the liberal theory at least as soon as it had any concern about equality. One way out was proposed by Rousseau, who argued that the property right that is required to permit the realization of the human essence is not the right of unlimited individual appropriation, but a limited right to as much as a man needs to work on. The essentially human property right, being thus limited, would not contradict the equal right: everyone could have it. But Rousseau's (and Jefferson's) way out was no way out. For the capitalist market society, to operate by free contract, required a right of individual appropriation in amounts beyond that limit. And by the nineteenth century the possibility of a society consisting entirely of worker–owners could no longer be seriously entertained. A proletariat existed, as Mill and Green saw. It was the fact that it did exist, and that its condition of life was a denial of humanity, that made sensitive liberals, beginning with Mill and Green, seek some other way out. They did not find one, nor could they have done so from their postulates. For they assumed the need for an unlimited exclusive individual property right, and equated it with the property right which is essential to the very nature and condition of man. So they were back with the basic contradiction.
>
> Liberal-democratic theory has not yet found a way out of this difficulty. I have argued elsewhere that the difficulty could be traced to the deep-rootedness of what I called the possessive individualism of the liberal theory, a set of assumptions about man and society which proved incompatible with democratic aspirations but which could not be given up as long as society was to rely on market incentives and institutions.

Alternatively, I have suggested that the difficulty could be stated as an incompatibility between two concepts of the human essence both of which are present within liberal-democratic theory—a concept of man as consumer, desirer, maximizer of utilities, and a concept of man as doer, as exerter and developer of his uniquely human attributes. I do not wish to retract or abandon either of these analyses, but I want now to propose a theoretically simpler statement of the central difficulty, which may point the way to a simpler resolution of it.

The difficulty, I suggest, is not that a liberal-democratic society, in order to have any prospect of achieving its ethical goals, must infringe and thus narrow an individual property right which is derived from the very nature of man. On the contrary, the difficulty is that the individual property right which liberal theory has inferred from the nature of man is already too narrow. What is needed is to broaden it. When this is seen, the old difficulty disappears. I shall argue that we have all been misled by accepting an unnecessarily narrow concept of property, a concept within which it is impossible to resolve the difficulties of any liberal theory. We have treated as the very paradigm of property what is really only a special case. It is time for a new paradigm, within which we may hope to resolve difficulties that could not be resolved within the old.

As I have already shown, property, although it must always be an individual right, need not be confined, as liberal theory has confined it, to a right to exclude others from the use or benefit of some thing, but may equally be an individual right not to be excluded by others from the use or benefit of some thing. When property is so understood, the problem of liberal-democratic theory is no longer a problem of putting limits on the property right, but of supplementing the individual right to exclude others by the individual right not to be excluded by others. The latter right may be held to be the one that is most required by the liberal-democratic ethic, and most implied in a liberal concept of the human essence. The right not to be excluded by others may provisionally be stated as the individual right to equal access to the means of labour and/ or the means of life. ...

Property is a right, not a thing. It is an individual right. It is an enforceable claim created by the state.

What I would now point out is that none of these propositions, nor all of them together, require that property be only an individual right to exclude others from the use or benefit of something. Property as an individual right not to be excluded from the use or benefit of something meets these stipulations equally well. Exclusiveness is not logically entailed in the concept of property as an individual right needed to enable men to realize their human essence as moral or rational beings: a right not to be excluded from something is as much an individual right as is the right to exclude others. Both kinds may be created by society or the state, and neither can be created otherwise. Both meet the essential requisites of property, in that both are enforceable claims of individuals to some use or benefit of something. An individual right not to be excluded from something held in common is as much an individual property as is the right to exclude.

How, then, did the idea that property is an exclusive right get so firmly embedded as it has done in the very concept of property? It goes back a long way, although it was not so firmly established in pre-liberal theory as it was from Locke on. From Plato to Bodin, theorists could talk about common property as well as private. But most of the concern was about property as an individual exclusive right. Whether the theorist opposed it, as Plato did for his guardian class, or supported it, as Aristotle and the medieval theorists did within limits, it was property as *meum* and *tuum*, my right to exclude you, that they were mainly concerned with.

Why should these early theorists, who were familiar enough with common property not to think it a contradiction in terms, nevertheless generally have taken property to mean an exclusive right? When we recall that they were deriving property from human needs and the human condition it is not difficult to see a reason for their treating property as an exclusive right. Given their postulate about human inequality they needed to do so. Slaves and serfs they regarded as not fully human, not naturally capable of a fully moral or rational life. These lower ranks therefore did not need, and were not entitled to, a property right, exclusive or otherwise. But citizens, freemen, those above the level of slave or serf, those who were capable of a fully human life, did need a property right which would exclude those others. They had to have an exclusive right. And since they were the only ones who needed a property right at all, the property right as such was taken to be the exclusive right. Strictly, of course, the exclusion of the lower orders did not require that property be taken as the right of each individual to exclude every other individual within as well as beyond the propertied upper orders. But it did require that property be a right to exclude, and this was very easily generalized into an individual right to exclude all others.

This derivation of an exclusive right from the nature of rational man obviously ceases to be valid when all men are asserted to be naturally equally capable of a fully human rational life. And this is the assertion made by liberal theory, from at least Locke on (though Locke was ambiguous about this, as about much else). How, then, could the liberal theorists still see property as only an exclusive right? They could, of course, assert intelligibly enough that each individual needed an exclusive right to a flow of consumable things which would enable him to live. But it had never been merely a property in consumable things that theorists of property had sought to justify by derivation from human needs. The theory of property had always been a theory of rights in land and capital.

Once the natural equal humanity of all men was asserted, the derivation, from human needs, of an exclusive right in land and capital required another postulate. The additional postulate was found by the first generation of liberal theorists, in the seventeenth century: it was the postulate that a man's labour is his own. On this postulate the labour justification of property was built, and it had the effect of reinforcing the concept of exclusiveness. The labour of a man's body, the work of his hands, was seen as peculiarly, exclusively, his. So the right to that with which he has mixed his labour is an exclusive right. This was the principle which Locke made central to the liberal concept of property.

The labour justification of individual property was carried down unquestioned in the liberal theory. Even Bentham, scorning natural rights and claiming to have replaced them by utility, rested the property right on labour. Security of enjoyment of the fruits of one's labour was the reason for property: without a property in the fruits and in the means of labour no one would have an incentive to labour, and utility could not be maximized. Mill and Green also held to the labour justification. "The institution of property," Mill wrote, "when limited to its essential elements, consists in the recognition, in each person, of a right to the exclusive disposal of what he or she ha[s] produced by their own exertions, or received either by gift or by fair agreement, without force or fraud, from those who produced it. The foundation of the whole is the right of producers to what they themselves have produced." Similarly Green: "The rationale of property, in short, requires that everyone who will conform to the positive condition of possessing it, viz. labour, and the negative condition, viz. respect for it as possessed by others, should, so far as social arrangements can make him so, be a possesser of property himself, and of such property as will at least enable him to develop a sense of responsibility, as distinct from mere property in the immediate necessaries of life." So the derivation of property in things from the property in one's labour stamped property as an exclusive right from the beginning of the liberal tradition.

Our question—how could liberal theorists regard property as only an exclusive right?—is now answered: they did so by deducing property in things from the property in one's labour. In doing so, they created a new difficulty. For the derivation of the property right from labour was added to, it did not replace, the derivation from the needs of man. It was still, for Locke, the individual right to life that made property necessary; the labour expended merely justified particular appropriations. And for Green it was man's essence as a moral being that required that each should have the property without which he could not fulfil his moral vocation: labour expended was simply an additional requirement. Unfortunately, the added derivation of property from labour conflicted with the more basic and continuing derivation from the human essence.

The derivation from labour, as we have seen, was only needed when, and because, the liberal postulate of natural equality displaced the pre-liberal postulate of natural inequality. But we have also to notice that it was only needed when and because a moral case had to be made for putting every individual on his own in a market society, for letting the allocation of incomes and wealth be done by the market rather than by a political authority. If the market was to do the job of inducing people to work and of allocating the whole product, men had to be given the right to alienate the use of their labour. A man's labour, his own exclusive property, had to be made an alienable property: the right to its exclusive use had to be made something he could sell. And whenever there was not enough free land for everyone, the man who had none had to sell the use of his labour. Those who had no land lost the right to the product of their labour. They lost also the possibility of their labour entitling them to a property in what they had mixed their labour with. They lost, therefore, the effective right to that which they needed in order to be fully human.

In short, in the circumstances in which the labour derivation of the property right was developed, the exclusive property right derived from labour became a denial, for many, of the property right derived from their essential human needs. As soon as a property in things is derived from an exclusive right which is at the same time an alienable right, i.e., the right to or property in one's labour, the damage is done: property as a right needed by all to enable them to express their human essence is denied to many. ...

I have argued that the narrow concept of property as an individual right to exclude others from the use or benefit of something became the paradigm of property for historical rather than logical reasons: in the pre-liberal era it was the postulate of natural human inequality that required exclusiveness; in the liberal era it has been the postulate that a man's labour is his own. Each postulate was, in its time, needed to justify and support the prevailing or desired system of productive relations—slavery or serfdom in the earlier period, the free competitive market system in the later. But, by whichever postulate the narrow paradigm was reached, it led to a denial of property as a right to what is needed to be human.

What are the prospects that liberal-democratic theory may now move beyond the narrow paradigm? The market system is no longer freely competitive, and it is acknowledged not to be an adequate *system*, as witness the myriad government interferences with it and partial take-overs of it that all liberal-democratic societies have deemed necessary. But the monopolistic corporate structure, with government patchwork, which has become the twentieth century version of the market system, is still supported by the supposed sacredness of the exclusive individual property right. And its sacredness rests on no firmer basis than the acceptance of the narrow paradigm of property, that is, on the equation of individual property with exclusive property, an equation which never had any logical standing (except as applied to consumables).

It is surely now time to recognize that the concept of property as the right to exclude others is unnecessarily narrow; that its acceptance as the paradigm of property stands in the way of any rethinking of liberal-democratic problems; and that the assertion of the need for the exclusive right now works against the realization of liberal-democratic goals. If liberal-democratic societies are to be the guarantors of rights essential to the equal possibility of individual members using and developing their human capacities, the individual property right that is needed is not the exclusive right but the right not to be excluded from the use or benefit of those things (including society's productive powers) which are the achievements of the whole society. And the latter right does not contradict, but includes part of, the former, as will be shown in a moment.

Property, as the individual right not to be excluded from the use or benefit of the achievements of the whole society, may take either or both of two forms: (a) an equal right of access to the accumulated means of labour, i.e., the accumulated capital of society and its natural resources (with a consequent right to an income from one's work on them); or (b) a right to an income from the whole produce of the society, an income related not to work but to what is needed for a fully human life.

Some questions arise when this new paradigm of property, as the individual right not to be excluded, is proposed.

First, is such a new concept of property legitimate, or is it so contradictory of everything property has always meant as to be an improper forcing of the very concept of property? I suggest that it is legitimate, on two grounds. (i) As already noticed, from Plato to Bodin "property" was not confined to an exclusive individual right: that confinement is a modern phenomenon—an invention of the liberal seventeenth century. (ii) The new paradigm of property, now proposed, is not wholly contrary to the confined liberal concept of property as an exclusive individual right. It does not contradict, but subsumes, as much of that exclusive right as is consistent with the liberal-democratic ethic. For it does include an individual exclusive right to consumables (though not an individual exclusive right to accumulated social capital and parcels of natural resources). This is evident from the definition of property as the right not to be excluded. For that right consists, as we have seen, in either or both a right of access to the means of labour (and consequently a right to an income from work on those), or a right to an income unrelated to work. In either case there is a right to an income, that is, a right to a flow of consumables, and it is assumed that this includes consumables which can be enjoyed only as exclusive property.

A second question arises: is the acceptance of this new paradigm of property consistent with twentieth century liberal-democracy? There are already some indications that it is: that liberal-democratic societies are moving away from the concept of property as exclusion. Practice is moving faster than theory. The theorist may not have seen it yet, but the businessman is perfectly accustomed to looking at property as the right to an income not necessarily related to work, i.e., not derived from one's own exclusive labour. And the politician is coming to see that the right to an income has to be regarded as a right to a share in the annual produce which is increasingly the creation of technology rather than of current labour.

Does Macpherson's argument suggest that it would be useful to entrench property rights in the Charter? In the context of property law, as reflected in these course materials, do you agree that Canadian society is "moving away from the concept of property as exclusion"? Is is possible to consider this question in general, or is it necessary to take account of different forms of property? Keep these questions in mind as you examine issues of property law reform in the next section.

THE NEED FOR REFORM OF PROPERTY LAW?

M.J. Mossman, "Toward 'New Property' and 'New Scholarship' "
(1985), 23 *Osgoode Hall Law Journal* 633 (footnotes omitted)

I. Approaching the Task: Problems and Pitfalls

Twenty years ago, in the preface to his casebook, *Cases and Notes on Land Law*, Professor Laskin (as he then was) quoted and agreed with a statement of Professor Hargreaves, written in 1956, assessing the state of property scholarship; Hargreaves had asserted:

Not since Littleton has there been a serious attempt to isolate [the principles of English land law] from their historic origin, to examine them as living contributions to contemporary thought, and to apply them in the construction of a systematic analysis of the whole field which would satisfy the demands of scientific jurisprudence and prove worthy of the greatest system of property law that the world has ever known.

Hargreaves' assertion was an assessment of property scholarship in England, and Laskin was even less enthusiastic about the state of property scholarship in Canada at that time:

There has been nothing in Canada comparable to the English texts, let alone those in the United States (where there is a proliferation of general casebooks and specialized treatises as well). We have to go back to Armour's second edition of Real Property, 1916, to find any general treatment of the subject, and this is a work which, basically, is founded on Blackstone. We will get no farther than Armour unless it be by the efforts of the law teachers, to whom Professor Hargreaves feels England too will have to look for any systematic study of basic land law problems.

Twenty years after Laskin so stated the challenge to the law teachers, the question is whether the state of property scholarship in Canada has fundamentally changed, or even changed at all.

The answer to this question requires an assessment of property scholarship in Canada. This task is a daunting one for a number of reasons. First, "property and civil rights" are [matters] within provincial jurisdiction under the Canadian *Constitution*; any assessment of property scholarship should therefore take account of published work in several different provincial jurisdictions. Moreover, unlike some other areas of law that also fall within provincial legislative jurisdiction, property laws, especially those in relation to land law, often differ greatly from one province to another depending on the time of reception of English law; the Torrens registration systems of the four western provinces make land law and procedure very different from those in the east, while the civil law system in Quebec is based on concepts very different in theory from those of the common law provinces. The provincial nature of property law thus complicates an assessment of property scholarship, to a greater extent perhaps than some other areas of law.

A second difficulty in the task of assessing property scholarship is that property law is more dependent upon statutes than upon common law principles. However, unlike some other areas of law that are essentially statute-based, the framework of property law depends upon statutes often enacted several centuries ago; the task of interpreting and applying statutes may thus depend upon both an understanding of the context in which the legislation was originally enacted, as well as creativity in its use in a modern context. This process is further complicated by the need to take account of common law principles that have developed interstitially when outdated legislation has not been repealed, despite wholly failing to meet modern needs.

This difficulty is compounded by the absence, at least until recently, of any constitutional principles overtly protecting property interests. Unlike the United States, Canada has had no constitutionally entrenched rights to property that override enacted legislation. The advent of constitutionally entrenched rights and freedoms in the Charter created demands for extending such protection to property. Although property protection has been expressly omitted to date from the Charter, it has been suggested that this does not prevent full protection, either pursuant to section 7 of the Charter or by reason of a "common law" right.

Thus property scholarship must take account of statutes, both ancient and modern, which are interwoven with common-law principles; as well, it must accommodate a background of ideas, often only implicit, about the constitutional protection of property interests. The tasks of enunciating the law and demonstrating the efficacy of its application in a particular context may be overwhelming in themselves; and these difficulties may provide at least a partial explanation for the absence of property scholarship that advances beyond explication of this sort. Moreover, the combination of provincial jurisdiction over property and the nature of property law analysis—an amalgam of statutes, common law, and constitutional principles—makes the task a daunting one indeed.

However, there is also a third and even more telling reason why the task of assessing property scholarship is so difficult. This reason is the scope of "property analysis." From the perspective of legal philosophy, "property" is a concept, not a thing, and moreover it is a concept that evolves and changes according to the societal context:

> The meaning of property is not constant. The actual institution, and the way people see it, and hence the meaning they give to the word, all change over time ... . The changes are related to changes in the purposes which society or the dominant classes in society expect the institution of property to serve [Macpherson, at 1].

Using this approach, the scope of property analysis includes not only the traditional categories of property interests—land, chattels, non-possessory interests, leaseholds, and so forth—but also other categories of "new property," including government benefits and jobs; such an approach might also include an assessment of categories of interests in which proprietary interests are no longer recognized, such as slaves, children, or wives. Clearly, the adoption of the concept of property used in legal philosophy makes an assessment of property scholarship a difficult if not impossible task.

An alternative and more pragmatic approach to defining the scope of property analysis may be the use of "property" subject headings in the *Index to Canadian Legal Periodical Literature*. However, even this approach evidences the great breadth of scope for property analysis. Although the subject headings have changed to some extent over the period 1960-1984, a very large number have remained generally in use throughout the period: adverse possession; chattel mortgages; city planning; community property, condominium, and cooperative housing; conveyancing; copyright; dower; easements; estate planning; expropriation; family law; forfeiture; fraudulent conveyances; future interests; homesteads; housing; husband and wife; immovables; implied trusts; inheritance and succession; inheritance, estate and gift taxes; intellectual property; joint tenancy; landlord and tenant; leases; marriage; property; mortgages; movables; perpetuities; personal property; lost goods; pledges; possessions; property (civil law); property taxes; public lands; pollution; natural resources; real estate agents; real property covenants; regional planning; restraints on alienation; secured transactions; title to land; Torrens system; trusts and trustees; vendors and purchasers; water pollution; wills; and zoning. The breadth of "property" topics, even using the more pragmatic approach of the *Index*, is still overwhelming and makes any attempt to assess "property" scholarship a challenging one indeed.

These same problems, which make an assessment of property scholarship so difficult, also operate to make it difficult to undertake property scholarship *per se* in Canada. A legal scholar who works in the property area is much more likely to be a specialist in municipal zoning, or charitable trusts, or matrimonial property; he or she is much less likely to be interested in drawing connections and pointing out similar themes among these categories, assuming such connections and similar themes even exist any longer. Indeed, the startling conclusion may be that what is property is now so diverse that the concept is no longer useful, except as a starting point for analyses that are completely divergent depending on the special context. If this is so, the usefulness of the property concept as a means of extending legal protection to "new property" interests may also be in doubt. For both these reasons, it seems important to assess the potential for property scholarship more generally.

Bearing in mind the difficulties that have been identified, and particularly the breadth of scope, which defies complete mastery by any single scholar, it seems none-theless important to try to identify some of the trends in Canadian legal scholarship in property since Laskin's casebook was published in 1964. In doing so, it may be possible to identify some of the strengths as well as the weaknesses of the work to date, and to suggest directions for scholarly inquiry for the future.

II. Property Scholarship: A Preliminary Appraisal

A. Overview

The task of appraising legal scholarship in the property context seems to require, first, an overview of the scholarly work produced by lawyers and legal academics and then, some comparison of this work to that produced by scholars of property in Canada, or by legal and other scholars elsewhere. In drawing comparisons, it may be useful to consider whether the work is essentially doctrinal (explaining the law and its application in the legal context); normative (assessing implicit or underlying values according to expressly stated policy or criteria); comparative (comparing the law and its functions in different contexts or jurisdictions); or interdisciplinary (examining the law in its social, political, or economic context). It may also be of use to consider whether the intended audience for scholarly work on property includes persons other than law students, academic colleagues, practising lawyers, or judges.

In this framework, the legal scholarly work on property topics listed in the *Index to Canadian Legal Periodical Literature* for the years 1960-1984 might be assessed as follows. First, the total number of entries is very substantial due to the scope of the property concept; however, the number of entries for any single subject heading is usually not excessive. Second, the entries are specialized by topic rather than general in focus, and authors' names seem to recur in relation to specialized topic headings rather than appearing in relation to more than one property topic. Third, the entries seem to be essentially doctrinal; they explain a particular legal development in terms of earlier cases or statutory provisions, and sometimes present a new decision in the context of overall doctrinal development. Finally, the intended audience for most of the writing seems to be lawyers, whether students, academics, practitioners, or judges; there is no pervasive sense of a framework for analysis outside the legal system itself.

At the same time, the list of entries in the *Index* discloses some interesting develop-ments. Beginning in the early 1970s, the *Index* included two new titles: "environmental control" and "industrial property." At this time, there was also a noticeable increase in the number of entries for some topic headings including "copyright," "landlord and tenant," "marriage: property," "pollution," and "regional planning"; at the same time, there was, for example, a decrease in the number of entries for "personal property." Although it would be inappropriate to form any significant conclusions from such a quantitative analysis alone, it is perhaps noteworthy that the legal periodical literature seems to reflect, at least in quantitative terms, attentiveness by legal scholars to some of the controversial property issues of the past two decades.

Beyond quantitative analysis, however, how should property scholarship be ap-praised? What are the critical elements and how should we determine when the standard has been met? This question is both necessary and interesting, driving us to the heart of scholarly inquiry: how to ask the right question. Inevitably, the act of assessing scholarly writing requires a determination of criteria for assessment. Yet the process of defining appropriate criteria itself provokes critical questions about how all the possible factors can be assembled, how a selection of factors can be identified, and how these factors can be applied fairly to the literature in order to reach a conclusion about the state of property scholarship in Canada. Indeed, the really significant point about a Symposium on Canadian Scholarship is not the debate about the relative merits of different kinds of scholarly writing in Canada, but the underlying methodological inquiry: *how* do we decide the relative merits?

This question is a provocative one in the context of legal writing. It is generally accepted that legal writing as a form of writing is reasoned, logical, and precise. Notwithstanding this perception however, many lawyers both in practice and in academe recognize that judicial decisions are usually affected by judges' values, beliefs, and assumptions; thus, the reasoned argument of judges' decisions is best understood in light of such unstated factors in their legal writing. What is then surprising is the apparent lack of awareness in scholarly legal writing of the significance of the writers' perspectives. If asking the right question is important to the scholarly method, then it must be important as well to know why a legal writer has concluded that the question posed is the right one.

The point of this discussion is to suggest that most Canadian legal writing in property law reflects little interest in the methodology of its inquiry; it is a "closed" system in which persons with legal training first read the reasoned arguments of other persons who are legally trained and then critique the reasoning or the logic or the precision of the writing:

> Legal scholarship is in fact a sophisticated and elaborated form of legal brief. Doctrinal analysis, the chief method for legal scholarship, is undertaken to establish a particular interpretation of case law on the basis of arguments and authority which would be acceptable to an appellate judge. As a method of inquiry, conventional legal scholarship serves the narrow professional function of supporting lawyers' advocacy.

Of course, such writing may be defended on the basis that it is useful and that legal writers may provide assistance through such efforts. The question here, however, is whether such writing can be regarded as scholarly in terms of its method of inquiry.

This question is fuelled by the critiques of legal method expressed most recently both by the critical legal studies movement and by feminists. In both cases, the critiques have centred on the liberal bias inherent in the law's rationality and logic. Moreover, feminism has focused very systematically on methodology and has developed a compelling critique of the law's "point-of-view-lessness" and, arguably, also of its use by legal scholars. In this context, it seems desirable to face up to the question of method in scholarly inquiry: "How can one do critical scholarship without considering one's role as a scholar engaged in a social enterprise?" And we can add: How can one assess scholarship on property without addressing these same questions?

These questions do not have easy answers. At the very least, they seem to require a statement about perspective from an assessor of legal scholarship. Since I am interested in law as a central element in social relations among people, I am primarily interested in whether scholarly writing about law addresses such process questions as follow about the creation, interpretation, and application of the law:

- How were legal principles adopted, or why are they appropriate, having regard to the "outside world" as well as the "closed system" of the law?
- How can we explain the cases "at the margin" as well as those in the mainstream; are legal decisions useful as legitimating forces for the mainstream?
- Why are some problems beyond law or outside the boundaries of legal decision making and what factors make them so?

In choosing to adopt these kinds of questions for an assessment, I will find doctrinal explication less meritorious than legal writing that pursues these broader issues. The critical issue remains: what is fundamental to scholarly inquiry is the how and why for the choice of questions, and not the answers.

B. The Development of Property Analysis

As a starting point for my inquiry, I have chosen to examine three topics in property law:

1. the doctrine of estates in land;
2. landlord and tenant; and
3. matrimonial property.

These three areas represent different stages in the development of property analysis. The first is a topic with ancient origins and few modern developments; the second is a topic with medieval beginnings but dramatic changes in the twentieth century, and the last is a topic that has emerged in its modern form within the last decade or so. What follows is a preliminary assessment of some of the scholarship in light of the questions posed.

1. The Doctrine of Estates in Land

This topic has not been one of significant controversy in the past two decades, even though it is obviously what both Hargreaves and Laskin had in mind when, in the quotations at the beginning of this essay, they directed the attention of law reformers and legal scholars to further efforts. In fact, most of the legal scholarship about the doctrine of estates in land appears in casebooks or texts for use by law students. For example, Laskin's casebook of 1964 includes a brief introduction to the nature of feudalism and the doctrine of estates, as well as legal and equitable interests in land. The material includes excerpts from treatises, statutory provisions, and cases. Some of the material places the legal concepts in a broader socio-political context, but the main focus is the enunciation of legal doctrine. By comparison, a more recent student casebook, *Property Law* [Mendes da Costa and Balfour, 1st ed. (Toronto: Emond Montgomery, 1982)], contains a greater amount of descriptive material, along with statutory and case excerpts; however, it is not much more successful than Laskin's casebook was in placing the legal concepts in a socio-political context.

There are three criticisms that can be directed at these casebooks and texts. The first is that they misrepresent the variety of legal ideas that flourished in the medieval period, when the basic concepts of modern land law were being established. The history is usually presented as an inexorable drive to universal fee simple estates held in free and common socage tenure. The work of medievalists is ignored in this process, even though some of them have clearly demonstrated the diversity and creativity within feudalism and its legal concepts; for example, widows, who were systematically excluded from land ownership by the doctrines of tenure and primogeniture, nonetheless, often succeeded in their objectives of keeping the family and the land intact. The legal scholarship, by contrast, analyses the history of developing legal concepts in terms of modern ideas, particularly those that have been successful or become dominant, and ignores the variety of concepts or ideas, some of which were quite flourishing at the relevant time.

If the only result were inaccuracy in legal history, that might alone prompt a reassessment of the scholarship. In addition, however, the approach of the casebooks generally presents five centuries of development of land law concepts as if change occurred in a legal vacuum. Although there are usually references to the problems created for Henry VIII by the widespread existence of conveyances to uses, there is usually little acknowledgment of the impact of the power struggle between King and Parliament, or the efforts of Sir Thomas More and others to establish the Lord Chancellor's role as subject to the rule of law. In the result, the vision of legal change, and especially its relation to political, economic, and social factors, is incomplete and often misleading.

Finally, given the treatment of legal reform during the late medieval period, when basic legal concepts about land were being developed, it is hardly surprising that this legal writing virtually ignores the possibility of land law reform. With a few exceptions, the legal writing evidences no interest in modern reform of the principles developed under feudalism in England. Since other possible concepts exist, and since conditions of modern society in Canada differ markedly from those in England under feudalism, a conscious perception of change and reform in the legal scholarship of the medieval period would likely result in a conscious re-examination of the need for legal change in the principles of land law in modern Canada. However, since such legal changes would affect not just those holding interests in land, but also those who "manage" the existing system of land law—the lawyers—it has been suggested [A. Watson, "Legal Change: Sources of Law and Legal Change" (1983), 131 *University of Pennsylvania Law Review* 1121, at 1153] that:

> A change that made the law simpler or less ambiguous ... could have an adverse effect on their [lawyers'] income. In addition, the stock-in-trade of a practising attorney is his or her knowledge of the *existing* law. A drastic change could reduce the most experienced practitioner almost to the level of a beginner.

Is Laskin's challenge, therefore, to go unheeded, even by law teachers?

2. Landlord and Tenant

In contrast to the problem of estates in land, the legal concepts of landlord and tenant have been under careful scrutiny during much of the past two decades. Laskin stated the essential question in his casebook in 1964:

> The pertinent question is to what extent is the transaction regarded as the transfer of an interest in land (and hence governed by rules and doctrines developed as part of the law of estates) and to what extent is it regarded as a business dealing (and hence governed by rules and doctrines developed later as part of the law of contracts).

Shortly after stating the issue in this way, Laskin noted without further comment that "the effect of the domination of property conceptions was to subordinate the tenant to the landlord." Virtually nothing in Laskin's 1964 treatment of the subject departed from a basic doctrinal approach to the subject matter.

By the end of the 1960s, however, law reform proposals regarding residential leases were significantly altering the legal rights and obligations of tenants. Nonetheless, except for the law reform documents, there is little in the scholarly legal writing of the period that examines the impetus for the law reform initiatives. Nor is there much in the legal writing after 1970 that assesses the effect or significance of the legal changes introduced by amendments to residential leasehold law across Canada. As the authors of *Property Law* laconically state:

> The legal system's treatment of the lease as a conveyance was no doubt sensible and adequate in a largely agrarian society ... . Subsequent economic and social developments, however, have rendered inadequate the conception of the lease as solely a conveyance.

There is no real exploration of the nature of the "economic and social developments" that formed the basis for so fundamental a shift in legal doctrine.

By contrast, much of the analysis conducted by Ontario's recent Commission of Inquiry into Residential Tenancies was not legal but economic. It included assessments of the legislative and political background to the *Residential Tenancies Act*, a statistical description of the Ontario housing market, a survey of other jurisdictions and of alternative systems of rent regulation, and computerized simulation models of financial performance of hypothetical buildings. The thrust of the Commission's inquiry is in stark contrast to most of the legal scholarship in the landlord–tenant context.

Is the lack of attention in scholarly legal writing to the underlying economic issues of landlord and tenant law significant? Arguably, the legal principles may operate without regard to economic consequences, but it is unlikely that they do so. Ignoring the underlying economic principles is likely to distort the analysis of the law of landlord and tenant, just as ignoring medieval history is likely to result in a distorted understanding of basic doctrines of land law.

Yet once again, it is not only accuracy that is at stake. The broader perspective is also needed here to understand the legal change that has occurred within a few decades in the landlord–tenant context and to appreciate the possible relationship between legal and social change. Landlord and tenant law is, perhaps, a microcosm of the usefulness of law in the twentieth century as a means of economic regulation, on the one hand, and redistributive justice on the other. An English study of the criminalization of landlord harassment of tenants has been said to:

> ... sow further doubts as to the capacity of law to correct the effects of inequalities in economic resources to the extent which "progressive" lawyers had hoped. There is increasing recognition that law is not a neutral tool that can be employed at will in the service of Fabian projects of piecemeal social engineering but that it partakes of and is subject to internal and external constraint in its ability to achieve social change.

The challenge for Canadian legal scholarship in landlord–tenant [law] is to assess, in the broader context, the neutrality of the law and its inherent limits.

3. Matrimonial Property

If the legal scholarship on land tenures generally ignores the socio-political context, and the legal scholarship on landlord and tenant law seems to discount the impact of economic forces, the legal scholarship on matrimonial property appears imprisoned in both outmoded historical conceptions and larger economic forces. In some respects, the principles of matrimonial property present an illustration of property law at the brink: do the principles really have enough inherent dynamism to be useful in a radically different context, and if the principles are apt, can they be applied systematically notwithstanding a hostile economic context?

The tension is evident once again in the casebooks. Professor Laskin considered property relations in marriage in the context of life estates, which were often created by operation of law through the doctrines of dower or curtesy for a surviving widow or widower. At the time he was writing, there was a prevailing sense that legal equality had been substantially achieved for husbands and wives:

> The "property" relations of husband and wife at common law exhibited the disabilities of the married woman found in other branches of the law, most of which have now been remedied by legislation and to some extent also by judicial decision.

Two comments can be made. First, there is a sense in Laskin's treatment that there are no problems remaining in the law's treatment of married women in relation to property; with all the benefit of hindsight, of course, it is easy to suggest how inadequate this assessment would prove in the *Murdoch* case, in the *Rathwell* case, and in the drive to reform "family property" regimes in every province of Canada by the late 1970s. Second, matrimonial property seems to sit somewhat uncomfortably in the midst of life estates; it is as if matrimonial property does not deserve treatment on its own, but must be "fitted in" somewhere in the traditional scheme of things.

The treatment of matrimonial property by Mendes da Costa and Balfour twenty years later demonstrates an awareness of all the intervening legal developments that have occurred. Yet, despite the existence of a unique statutory framework in Ontario after 1978, the subject of matrimonial property still receives no separate treatment; instead, it is "fitted in" interstitially under the subject of co-ownership. Even though many husbands and wives are co-owners prior to marriage breakdown, it is the statutory framework of the *Family Law Reform Act*, and not the common law principles, that governs property distribution. In this sense, the *Family Law Reform Act* probably offers the main principles for division of property between co-owners, with the common-law principles applying only in relatively less frequent circumstances. However, the material is presented in the casebook with the new statutory framework being "fitted in" among older legal principles.

Perhaps because of this choice about the method of presentation, the underlying values of the reform legislation and the microcosm of its social and economic context are scarcely addressed. These issues were, however, generally evident in the reports of federal and provincial law reform commissions throughout the decade of the seventies. Additionally, a number of articles in the periodical literature, particularly in recent years, have focused on the inadequacies of the law in achieving equity in the division of property upon marriage breakdown. Yet there has been no substantial and fundamental re-thinking in Canadian property scholarship of the role of law in allocating wealth between husbands and wives when marriage ends in divorce. The economic analysis of the male-breadwinner and female-housewife model of marriage has only infrequently been considered in terms of the legal system's goals and values. It is interesting to speculate whether the creation of entitlement to family property under the reform legislation has failed to attract the legal deference usually granted to "property" (and the legal scholarly inquiries it deserves) because the idea of family property has made it available to the many rather than the preserve of the lucky few. If everyone is "a man [sic] of property," the value of such property diminishes accordingly:

> In a time of transition, both in family behaviour and in the nature and forms of wealth, the law is reflecting and interacting with social trends which affect the majority of persons, primarily those who are at neither the highest nor the lowest economic levels.

Is scholarly inquiry less appropriate when the "property" is "family property"?

III. Toward Blackacre's New Horizons ...

This review of three areas of scholarly interest within property law demonstrates a range of different types of analytical problems. In the context of title to land, the scholarship evidences a lack of contextual understanding; this results in a rigidity of thinking about basic concepts in modern property analysis and an institutional disinterestedness in legal reform. The legal scholarship too often seems to view law in a vacuum, a practice that results in masking the underlying forces and values that shape the development of legal principles. This approach is, however, consistent with the interests of the legal profession in maintaining a system, which because of its intricacy, reinforces dependence upon lawyers' services in property transactions.

In the landlord–tenant context, the scholarship evidences an institutional will to continue to regard law and the legal process as essentially neutral and impartial in the resolution of disputes; there is also a desire to eschew the underlying economic forces within which legal rules have been negotiated or adopted, and according to which disputes are resolved. There seems little awareness in the legal scholarship of the extraordinary rise in the numbers of Canadians who look to residential leaseholds as their life-long shelter and the impact of this branch of law upon the actual relations between landlords and tenants. The possibility that the law of landlord and tenant needs to be examined, taking account of governmental housing policies generally and the private investment market, seems as obvious as is the absence of such examination from legal scholarship.

Finally, the matrimonial property context confronts the limits of traditional property analysis. In implementing a statutory scheme for dividing property upon marriage breakdown, judges truly perform the role of redistributive justice when they transfer title on the basis of equity arising out of the marriage relationship. In this respect, the legal principles declare that the traditional principles of property, which presumably are rationally based, are to be superseded by principles based on equity between a husband and a wife. The major effect of such statutes is to confer property rights on those with the status of wives, a status that barely one hundred years ago deprived its holder of any property interest whatsoever. To the extent that the scholarship generally fails to take account of the radical nature of matrimonial property principles, it is not difficult to understand why it is not confronted more successfully.

Thus, it seems that much of the scholarship on property is essentially doctrinal rather than normative, comparative, or interdisciplinary. It is also fragmented and specialized rather than synthesized and theoretical. And it is mainly directed to those who are legally trained rather than to others. What conclusions should we draw from these observations?

The conclusions should not necessarily be negative. In terms of the training and experience of most legal writers, their writing reflects what they are best able to do: analyse and explicate abstract and rational principles about a process for decision making that is insulated from social, economic, and political forces, and in which disputes are resolved by neutral rules applied with fairness and objectivity. That this process is mythical does not necessarily detract from its *internal* coherence. And its internal coherence must offer some solace to even the most jaded philosopher.

Yet there is a crisis: a demand that property law demonstrate coherence to the external (non-legal) world and that principles of property law be adapted to provide protection for new interests, including those of tenants, and wives on marriage breakdown. On one hand, a rational, logical analysis leads inevitably to the conclusion that "new property" claims can be sustained just as easily as more traditional ones. Because "property" is simply a conceptual construct of law, there is no logical reason to deny "new property" claims. However, the structure of our society cannot admit new claims without (inevitably) modifying older ones because the concept of property is essentially a distributive mechanism for society's benefits. The extension of the property concept to benefit all individuals stretches classic J.S. Mill liberalism to an Orwellian egalitarian checkmate:

> [T]he crisis is a crisis in the individualistic view of society, in a legal model attuned to the needs of the individual house- or property-holder, the entrepreneur, the settled citizen living on terms of equality with those around him, secure and confident as an individual in his bearing *vis-à-vis* the state and the rest of society. Against this, the new demands elevate the interests or "requirements" of the comparatively poor and/or underprivileged as contrasted with those who are "at home" with law; they pit the interests of "society" or of "humanity" against "excessive" respect for abstract individual rights and powers, especially proprietorial rights and powers. ...

Yet any suggestion that the "new property" claims should be rejected in order to preserve the integrity of the concept sounds suspiciously like an argument in favour of the *status quo*, in other words, the protection of existing property interests.

What does seem necessary, however, is a recognition that societal changes external to the legal system now make the property concept less and less a matter of only "private law":

> There is ... a shift of attention from the property whose paradigm is the household, the walled-in or marked-off piece of land ... to the corporation, the hospital, the defence establishment ... whose "property" spreads throughout the society and whose existence is dependent upon subsidies, state protection, public provision of facilities, etc. ... .

Property becomes social in the sense that its base and its effects can no longer be contained within the framework of the traditional picture.

Thus, property has become public rather than private and so pervasive that the fragmentation and specialization of scholarship are not only inevitable but perhaps a necessity. Yet the need to take the measure of the individual parts to the whole remains. The task is unenviable, since it must by nature be concerned not just with internal consistency but also must meet the demands of ideas external to the law itself.

The complexity of the demands means that it is unlikely that any one scholar, or type of scholar, can perform the whole task. Both those who are legally trained and those trained in other disciplines may participate; scholars with experience of "law in action" and those without it may all offer useful insights. What also seems essential is that legal scholars develop self-awareness of the perspective from which they write, of the underlying values and assumptions they bring to the task, and of the limits of rational argument in legal discourse. To argue that the law's internal coherence is alone sufficient no longer seems persuasive; yet to prefer other frameworks for analysis, without critical inquiry into their underlying rationales, seems equally inappropriate to scholarly inquiry. The real task is the critical assessment of why choices among ideas are made and advanced by scholars.

In the context of this assessment of property scholarship in Canada, it is clearly evident that my experience and understanding of law as it impacts on those at the margins of society inform my critique of the scholarly writing and my assessment of appropriate directions for future change. What is interesting to me is that perceptions of law differ so greatly among legal scholars, nearly all of whom were trained in a country where legal education has been remarkably homogeneous for several decades; does this not itself suggest the mythical nature of the idea of the law's neutrality? My experience is that law is seldom neutral and that it may even be humane rather than objective on occasion. Surely legal scholarship, as well as law, should be informed by experience as well as logic.

What seems most critical for the future of property scholarship is to focus attention on these issues in the classroom, and to help students to appreciate the experiential nature of legal ideas and not just their content. On this basis, it still seems necessary to "look to the law teachers," not to codify the traditional principles, as Professor Laskin suggested twenty years ago, but rather to construct Blackacre's new horizons for the twenty-first century.

Discussion Notes

Why is property law reform difficult to achieve? Why are some areas of property law more amenable to reform than others? Consider the reforms achieved in relation to family property, conservation covenants and easements, and "no-pet" clauses in tenant law—why have these reforms been successfully legislated, by contrast with the rule in *Shelley*'s case, or the principles of possessory title or of the *donatio mortis causa*? To what extent is the following comment about law reform as valid today as when it was originally presented in 1885:

Those who have acquainted themselves with [the law's] provisions have generally neither the time nor the inclination to undertake any other tasks than that of administering [the law] as an existing system. Besides, when a man [sic] has mastered an intricate and difficult system, he takes a positive pleasure not only in the superiority which his knowledge gives him, but in that knowledge itself.

(J.F. Stephen and F. Pollock, "Section Seventeen of the Statute of Frauds" (1885), 1 *Law Quarterly Review* 1.) For a discussion of law reform and critical thinking in teaching property law in order to encourage lawyers to attempt property law reform, see R. Warrington, "Land Law and Legal Education: Is There Any Justice or Morality in Blackacre?" (1984), 18 *The Law Teacher* 77, at 90. For one response to Warrington, see K. Green, "'There Once Was an Ugly Duckling': Land Law in 1985" (1985), 19 *The Law Teacher* 65. For a critique of legal reform efforts in family property cases, see A. Bottomley, "Self and Subjectivities: Languages of Claim in Property Law" (1993), 20 *Journal of Law and Society* 56.

PROBLEMS

1. A well-known US case involved a claim by the widow and son of Bela Lugosi, who had played the title role in *Dracula*. After Lugosi's death, his widow and son claimed a right to share in profits acquired by Universal Pictures, who were displaying Lugosi's likeness in their marketing program. Should the plaintiffs succeed? What is the nature of their proprietary interest?

The majority of the court held that the property interest in this case was personal to Lugosi and could not be inherited, but Bird CJ dissented, emphasizing the proprietary nature of the interest and its presumptive capacity to be inherited. Which view is preferable? What are the concerns underlying the decision of the majority? Is it a response to these concerns to suggest, as Bird CJ did in his dissenting opinion, that this property interest should be treated as other intangible property interests such as copyright, and that rights should be limited to the lifetime of the originator and 50 years from his or her death? See *Lugosi v. Universal Pictures*, 603 P2d 425 (Cal. SC 1979).

2. In short, the concept of property never has been, is not, and never can be of definite content ... . Changing culture causes the law to speak with new imperatives, invigorates some concepts, devitalizes and brings to obsolescence others.

> —F. Philbrick
> "Changing Conceptions of Property in Law"
> (1938), 86 *University of Pennsylvania Law Review* 691, at 696

Assess the validity of the above statement by comparing recent approaches to the idea of property interests in relation to aboriginal land claims, confidential information, and welfare entitlements. To what extent is Philbrick's statement an accurate reflection of legal approaches to these issues? What is the explanation for similarities and differences in legal approaches to them?

3. The meaning of property is not constant. The actual institution, and the way people see it, and hence the meaning they give to the word, all change over time. We shall see that they are changing now. The changes are related to changes in the purposes which society or the dominant classes in society expect the institution of property to serve.

—C.B. Macpherson
Property: Mainstream and Critical Positions
(Toronto: University of Toronto Press, 1978), at 1

Consider the extent to which you agree or disagree with this statement (in whole or in part). In doing so, assess its appropriateness by reference to materials about property in this chapter.

4. You should see the development of English property law largely as the consequence of an ongoing struggle between those who owned land and wanted to assure control of it for themselves and their successors, and those who wished to curtail the privileges of the landed gentry.

—J.W. Bruce, J.W. Ely, Jr., and C.D. Bostick
Cases, Materials on Modern Property Law
(St. Paul, Minn.: West Publishing Company,
1989), at 253

This statement was made in the context of the authors' discussion of the nature of real property principles and the ways in which they developed in the feudal period. However, it may also be useful in exploring themes about more recent property reforms, and the role of law in promoting and/or resisting changes in property principles in the context of changes in society.

Assess the applicability of the above statement in relation to the following topics concerning the development of property principles, taken from the casebook as a whole. Assess the nature of the law reform process and the roles of courts and legislatures in such a process:

Topic 1   The rise of principles of equity in relation to
property interests in the feudal period, *and*
the continued usefulness of equity in the context of cases like *Tulk v. Moxhay.*

Topic 2   The challenges to traditional ideas of property presented by
ideas of native title in cases like *Mabo, and*
in arguments about the need for entrenched property rights in the Canadian constitution.

Topic 3   The creation of property rights in family relationships
in the context of legislative schemes *and*
in principles developed by courts in such cases as *Inwards v. Baker.*

Topic 4   The interpretation of language about property interests
in wills in cases like *Re Rynard, and*
in *inter vivos* documents concerning leases and licences.

Which areas seem most amenable to reform? Why?